MW00784298

Culturally Diverse Counseling

I wish to dedicate this book to Eli John Jones, my older brother, and to my son, Travis Smith. Both of you have helped make my life worth living. I treasure the moments that we have spent together. In quiet times, I watch cherished reruns in the cinematography of my mind and heart of the times we spent talking with, being with, and just loving each other. I am so grateful that God placed you in my life.

Sara Miller McCune founded SAGE Publishing in 1965 to support the dissemination of usable knowledge and educate a global community. SAGE publishes more than 1000 journals and over 800 new books each year, spanning a wide range of subject areas. Our growing selection of library products includes archives, data, case studies and video. SAGE remains majority owned by our founder and after her lifetime will become owned by a charitable trust that secures the company's continued independence.

Los Angeles | London | New Delhi | Singapore | Washington DC | Melbourne

Culturally Diverse Counseling

Theory and Practice

Elsie Jones-Smith

Diplomate in Counseling Psychology
American Board of Professional Psychology

Los Angeles | London | New Delhi
Singapore | Washington DC | Melbourne

FOR INFORMATION:

SAGE Publications, Inc.
2455 Teller Road
Thousand Oaks, California 91320
E-mail: order@sagepub.com

SAGE Publications Ltd.
1 Oliver's Yard
55 City Road
London EC1Y 1SP
United Kingdom

SAGE Publications India Pvt. Ltd.
B 1/I 1 Mohan Cooperative Industrial Area
Mathura Road, New Delhi 110 044
India

SAGE Publications Asia-Pacific Pte. Ltd.
3 Church Street
#10-04 Samsung Hub
Singapore 049483

Copyright © 2019 by SAGE Publications, Inc.

All rights reserved. No part of this book may be reproduced or utilized in any form or by any means, electronic or mechanical, including photocopying, recording, or by any information storage and retrieval system, without permission in writing from the publisher.

Printed in the United States of America

ISBN: 9781483388267

Acquisitions Editor: Abbie Rickard
Editorial Assistant: Elizabeth Cruz
Content Development Editor: Emma Newsom
Production Editor: Bennie Clark Allen
Copy Editor: Melinda Masson
Typesetter: C&M Digitals (P) Ltd.
Proofreader: Sue Schon
Indexer: Jeanne Busemeyer
Cover Designer: Alexa Turner
Marketing Manager: Kara Kindstrom

This book is printed on acid-free paper.

18 19 20 21 22 10 9 8 7 6 5 4 3 2 1

BRIEF CONTENTS

Preface   **xxvii**

Acknowledgments   **xxxiv**

About the Author   **xxxviii**

Chapter 1 • Culturally Responsive Strengths-Based Therapy: The Journey   1

Chapter 2 • Cultural Meaning Systems, Cultural Trust, and Cultural Humility   35

Chapter 3 • Neuroscience, Multiple Cultural Identities, and Cultural Strengths   71

Chapter 4 • Strengths-Based Development, Culture, and Clinical Practice   104

Chapter 5 • The Strengths-Based Therapy Model and Culturally Responsive Counseling   131

Chapter 6 • Culturally Responsive Assessment and the Cultural Formulation Interview   163

Chapter 7 • Culturally Responsive Case Conceptualization and Treatment Planning   199

Chapter 8 • Culturally Responsive Strengths-Based Therapy for African Americans   231

Chapter 9 • Culturally Responsive Strengths-Based Therapy for American Indians and Alaska Natives   262

Chapter 10 • Culturally Responsive Strengths-Based Therapy for Asian Americans, Native Hawaiians, and Pacific Islanders   289

Chapter 11 • Culturally Responsive Strengths-Based Therapy for Hispanic and Latino/a Americans   317

Chapter 12 • Culturally Responsive Strengths-Based Therapy for Arab and Muslim Americans   341

Chapter 13 • Culturally Responsive Strengths-Based Therapy for White Americans of European Ancestry   366

Chapter 14 • Culturally Responsive Strengths-Based Therapy for Women   401

Chapter 15 • Culturally Responsive Strengths-Based Therapy for LGBTQ Individuals 425

Chapter 16 • Culturally Responsive Strengths-Based Therapy for Individuals With Disabilities 452

Chapter 17 • Culturally Responsive Strengths-Based Therapy for Older Adults 478

Chapter 18 • Culturally Responsive Strengths-Based Therapy for Immigrants and Refugees 512

Chapter 19 • Culturally Responsive Strengths-Based Therapy for Multiracial People 541

Chapter 20 • Social Class, Social Justice, Intersectionality, and Privilege 569

Index **604**

DETAILED CONTENTS

Preface   xxvii

Acknowledgments   xxxiv

About the Author   xxxviii

**Chapter 1 • Culturally Responsive Strengths-Based Therapy:
The Journey**   1

   Chapter Objectives   1

   Introduction: The Journey to Becoming a Culturally Responsive
     Strengths-Based Therapist   1

   The Profound Influence of Culture   2

   Our Brains Are Culturally Connected   3

   Affirming Each Person's Importance   3

   The Integration of Culturally Responsive and Strengths-Based Therapy 4
     Culturally Responsive Therapy: A Beginning Definition   4
     Organization of Chapter 1   4

   Brief History and Overview of the Multicultural Movement   4

   Mastering the Multicultural Counseling Competencies   6

   Ethical Issues and Multiculturalism   8

   **Box: Multicultural counseling competencies: counselors' awareness of their
   assumptions, values, attitudes, and biases**   8
   • **Case Vignette 1.1** Jim Huang: An Unintended Ethical Violation   10

   The Evidence-Based Movement in Multicultural Counseling   11

   Beginning the Cultural Competency Journey   11

   Levels of Counselor Competency Development   12

   Clinical Skill Development: Cultural Awareness and Knowledge   13
     Cultural Congruence and Cultural Incongruence   13
     Culturally Competent Awareness Checklist for Mental Health Workers 16

   Major Barriers to Culturally Competent Counseling   17
     The Inappropriate Use of Eurocentric Psychotherapy Theories 17
   • **Case Vignette 1.2** Erica and Therapist Cultural Encapsulation   **18**
     Cultural Encapsulation: Barrier to Cultural Competence   18
     Monocultural Clinical Orientation   19
     The Cultural Barriers of Race and Ethnocentrism   19
     Race: A Social Construction   19
   • **Case Vignette 1.3** Race as a Social Construction   **20**
     Ethnic Group   20
     Ethnocentrism and Cultural Relativism   21

   Neuroscience, the Brain, and the Invisible Neural Barrier of Ethnic/Racial Bias 22
     Neural Prejudice Networks in the Human Brain   22
     Implicit and Explicit Bias: A New Paradigm for Cultural Diversity 23

Key Points About Implicit Biases	24
Reducing Your Implicit Biases	25
Implicit Bias: Prejudice Against Immigrants and Refugees	25
Summary of Key Points	25
Discussion Questions	26
Key Terms	27
References and Suggested Reading	29

Chapter 2 • Cultural Meaning Systems, Cultural Trust, and Cultural Humility — **35**

Chapter Objectives	**35**
Introduction	35
Organization of Chapter 2	36
Cultural Principles	36
The Iceberg Concept of Culture	37
Emic and Etic Perspectives on Culture	37
Culture and Neuroscience	38
Neuroscience and Cultural Differences	38
The Globalization of Culture	39
Culture and the Process of Identity Development: The Tripartite Model	41
Cultural Introjection and Cultural Attachment	42
Cultural Countertransference	43
Cultural Intelligence and Cultural Identity Development	43
Summary of Factors That Influence Cultural, Ethnic, and Racial Identity	46
The Ethnic Self: Ethnicity as a Schema	46
Research on the Positive Benefits of a Cultural Identity	47
Does One Have to Be of the Same Cultural/Ethnic/Racial Background to Counsel Clients Effectively?	47
The Cultural Compatibility Hypothesis for Counseling Culturally Diverse Clients	48
The Universalistic Hypothesis for Counseling Culturally Diverse Clients	49
Assimilation, Marginalization, Acculturation, and Acculturative Stress	49
Assimilation	49
Marginalization and Marginal Individuals	49
Acculturation	50
The Berry Model of Acculturation	50
Acculturative Stress: Its Definition and Meaning	51
Culturally Responsive Counseling: Reaching Across Barriers	51
Understanding Clients' Cultural Stories	52
Culturally Competent Clinical Knowledge	52
Culturally Responsive Knowledge Skills for the Initial Interview	52
Cultural Trust: A Critical Issue in Culturally Diverse Counseling	53
Cultural Empathy and Cultural Competence	54
Levels of Culturally Competent Clinical Responding	55

The Culturally Competent Skill of Counselor Cultural Humility 56
- **Case Vignette 2.1** A Service Provider: Cultural Competence Versus Cultural Humility 58

Toward a Model for Evaluating Culturally Competent Clinical Skill
  Development of Counselors 58
- **Case Vignette 2.2** Absame, A Somali Immigrant: Cultural Humility and
  Cultural Empathy 59

Summary of Key Points 63

Discussion Questions 64

Key Terms 65

References and Suggested Reading 66

Chapter 3 • Neuroscience, Multiple Cultural Identities, and Cultural Strengths 71

Chapter Objectives 71

Introduction 71

Neuroscience, CACREP Standards, and Major Counseling Associations 72

Foundational Concepts in Neuroscience for Counselors 72

The Brain 72
  The Brain Is a Social Organ 73
  Neurons 73
  Neurotransmitters 74
  Neuroplasticity 74
  The Mind 75

Mapping the Cultural Architecture of the Brain 75

Cultural Identity Formation and Neuroscience 76
- **Case Vignette 3.1** Rachel Dolezal: A White Woman Who Says She Is Black 77

Brain Regions and Cultural Identity 78

Some Important Findings in Cultural Neuroscience 79

Cultural Identity and the Cultural Formulation Interview for the *DSM-5* 79

The Negativity Bias of the Brain: Findings in Neuroscience 81

Is the Brain Hardwired to See the Glass Half Empty or Half Full? 82

Mental Health From a Neuroscientific Perspective 84

Neuroimaging Techniques and the Brain 84

Neuroscience: Psychotherapy Changes Your Brain 85

The Therapeutic Relationship From a Neuroscientific Perspective 85
- **Case Vignette 3.2** Brad: A Case of Stress 87

Neuroscience and the Culturally Responsive Counselor 87

Mirror Neurons and Counselors 88
- **Case Vignette 3.3** The Case of Justin From a Neuropsychotherapy Perspective 89

What Happens When a Counselor Focuses on a Client's Negative Life Events? 90

Neuroscience and Multiple Cultural Identities 91

What Is a Multicultural Identity? 93

The Need for Clinicians to Adopt a Multicultural Identity 93

Summary of Key Points 96

Discussion Questions 97

Key Terms 97

References and Suggested Reading 98

Chapter 4 • Strengths-Based Development, Culture, and Clinical Practice 104

Chapter Objectives 104

Introduction 104

Culture, the Brain, and Strengths Development 105
   Definition of Strength 105
   Characteristics of Strengths 105
   Culturally Bound Strengths 105

The Neurobiology of Human Strengths Development 106
   The Brain and Strengths Development 106

Strengths and the Brain's Pruning Process 107

Relational Components of Strengths Development 108

Attachment Theory and Strengths Development 108

Bowlby's Theory of Attachment: The Foundation for Understanding
   Individual Strengths Development 109

Significance of Attachment Relationships and Strengths Development 109

Strengths Development and the Importance of a Trusted Relationship 110

Strengths Development and Attention 111

Attachment Patterns Across Cultures 111

Significance of Cultural Attachment, Migration, and Acculturation 112

Strengths Development, the Narrative Process, and the Mind 113

Strengths as Dialogic Conversations With the Self 113

Western and Eastern Views on Human Strengths: The Chinese Perspective 114
   Strengths as Possessions of the Collective Group Rather Than of the
     Individual 114
   The Chinese Authority Orientation and Permission to Demonstrate
     Strengths 115
   Chinese Relational Orientation and Strengths 115
   Chinese Other Orientation and Strengths 116
   Some Considerations for Cultural Strengths 116

How Do I Make Culturally Responsive Counseling Strengths-Based? 116

The Philosophy of Strengths-Based Therapy 117

Cultural Mindsets 118
   Strengths Mindset 119
   Deficit Mindset 120

Culturally Responsive Strengths-Based Practice 120
   Helping Clients Manage Weaknesses and Negative Self-Limiting Thoughts 120
   Creating a Culturally Responsive Strengths-Building Therapy Environment 120
   • **Case Vignette 4.1** Marissa: From Noticing What's Missing to Noticing What's There 121
   The Initial Culturally Responsive Interview 123

Box: The culturally responsive therapy physical environment: social justice quotations for posters in therapists' office 123

Summary of Key Points   125

Discussion Questions   126

Key Terms   126

References and Suggested Reading   126

Chapter 5 • The Strengths-Based Therapy Model and Culturally Responsive Counseling   131

Chapter Objectives   131

Introduction   131
    Neurocultural Dynamics: Cultural Consonance and
       Cultural Dissonance   131
    Strengths-Based Therapy and the Law of Neuroplasticity   133
    The Neuroscience of Belief   135
    The Power of Cultural Beliefs and Dying: A Comparison of Chinese
       Americans and White Americans   136
    Self-Limiting Beliefs   136
       Self-limiting beliefs create anxiety.   137
       Negative thinking causes pain.   137

The Revised Strengths-Based Therapy Model   138
    New Concepts and Clinical Strategies   138
    Basic Assumptions of Strengths-Based Therapy   139
    The Role of the Client in Strengths-Based Therapy   139
    The Role of the Strengths-Based Therapist   140
    The Strengths-Based Therapy Model: Overview of Phases   141
       Acknowledge the client's pain.   142
       Let go and surrender.   142
       Let go of fear.   142
       Let go of self-limiting beliefs.   143

Strengths-Based Therapy Techniques   144
    Culturally Responsive Strengths-Based Therapist Communication   144
    Compassionate Strengths-Based Communication in Therapy   144
    Creating a Culturally Responsive Therapeutic Alliance   145
    Building Trust: Ways to Enhance the Therapeutic Alliance   146
    Strengths Discovery: Using SWOB Analysis   147
    SWOB and Strengths Analysis   148
    Strengths-Based Therapy and Opportunity Awareness   149
       Opportunities exist because adversity strengthens individuals.   150
       Opportunities exist because clients become aware of other positives in the environment.   150
    Eliciting Clients' Hopes and Dreams   151
    Strengths Talk   152
       Culturally Responsive Strengths Talk   153
    Surrendering: Contributions From Chinese Culture and Mindfulness   153
       Therapist "Surrender" Intervention Procedures   155
       The Surrender Process and Culturally Responsive Counseling   156
    Setting a Strengths-Based Intention: Contributions From India   156
       Culturally Responsive Strengths-Based Intention Setting   158

Summary of Key Points   159

Discussion Questions   159

Key Terms   160

References and Suggested Reading   160

Chapter 6 • Culturally Responsive Assessment and the Cultural Formulation Interview 163

Chapter Objectives 163

Introduction 163

General Assessment Principles in Counseling and Psychotherapy 163
    Cultural Bias in Assessment 164
• **Case Vignette 6.1** Culturally Responsive Skill Development: Assessment, Equivalence, and Bias in Assessment Instruments 166
    Models of Assessment for Culturally Responsive Counseling 166
    Neuropsychology and Cross-Cultural Assessment: Barriers to Client Change 167
        Fear, the Human Brain, and Clinical Assessment 167
        The Role of Culture in Quieting the Brain 168
    Assessment, Cultural Resonance, and Empathy 168
    Assessment and Cultural Knowledge About Clients 169

Clinical Issues in Conducting a Qualitative, Culturally Responsive Assessment 169
    Learning How to Listen for Culture in the Client's Story 170
    Assessment: Cultural Communication in High- and Low-Context Cultures 171
    Honoring the Client's Communication Style for Feelings, Space, and Contact 172
    Culturally Responsive Counseling and the Intake Process 172

The DSM-5 and the Cultural Formulation Interview 175
    Brief History of the Cultural Formulation Interview 178
    Usefulness and Effectiveness of the Cultural Formulation Interview 178
    Description and Overview of the Cultural Formulation Interview 178

The Four Domains of the Cultural Formulation Interview 179
    Domain 1: Cultural Definition of the Problem 179
        Clinician Questions for Domain 1 of the CFI 179
    Domain 2: Cultural Perceptions of Cause, Context, and Support 179
        Clinician Questions for Domain 2 of the CFI 179
    Domain 3: Cultural Factors Affecting Self-Coping and Past Help Seeking 179
        Clinician Questions for Domain 3 of the CFI 180
    Domain 4: Cultural Factors Affecting Current Help Seeking 180
        Clinician Questions for Domain 4 of the CFI 180
    Cultural Formulation Interview Summary Statements 180
    Supplementary Modules to the Core Cultural Formulation Interview 181
    Criticisms and Limitations of the Cultural Formulation Interview 181
    Culturally Relevant V Codes in the DSM-5 182
    Culture-Bound Syndromes and Assessment 182
• **Case Vignette 6.2** Culturally Responsive Clinical Skill Intervention: Using the Cultural Formulation Interview With a Chinese American Client 183

Cultural Genogram: An Assessment Tool 186

The Strengths-Based Therapy Model's Assessment Process 188
Box: Strengths discovery topics 189
    Assessment of Clients' Internal Strengths 189
    A Word About Models of Strengths-Based Measurement 189
        Strengths Assessment and the Treatment Process 191
    Adversity Assessment: Coping Skills Strengths 191
    Assessment of Clients' External Strengths 191
    Relational Strengths: Friends' Strengths 192

Creating a Strengths Genogram   193

Assess the Client's Potential for Self-Harm and Risk to Others   193

Summary of Key Points   193

Discussion Questions   194

Key Terms   194

References and Suggested Reading   195

**Chapter 7 • Culturally Responsive Case Conceptualization and
Treatment Planning**   **199**

Chapter Objectives   **199**

Introduction   199

    White Clinicians and Culturally Diverse Clients   200

    Cultural Bias and Disparities in Mental Health Service

        Delivery Systems   201

    What Happens When Clinicians Are Biased Against Their Clients?   202

    Overdiagnosis of People of Color: Seeing Greater Pathology

        Than There Is in a Client   203

    Counseling Attrition Rate for Members of Ethnic/Racial Minorities   203

Case Conceptualization: Some General Elements   204

    The Five *P*s of Case Conceptualization   205

Culturally Responsive Case Conceptualization   205

• **Case Vignette 7.1** Emily: A Young White American Woman of German Descent   206

    Case Conceptualization, Diagnosis, and the Revisions in the DSM-5   208

    Important Revisions in the DSM-5   209

Case Conceptualization and the Cultural Formulation Interview   210

    Advantages of Using the CFI in Case Conceptualization   210

    Advantages of Using the CFI to Assess Clients' Cultural Identity   212

    Using the CFI to Reveal Clients' Immigration History   212

    Using the CFI to Help Clients Deal With Acculturation Issues   214

    Cultural Explanations of the Individual's Illness   214

    Cultural Factors Related to the Psychosocial Environment   216

• **Case Vignette 7.2** Astrid: A Haitian Woman Experiencing Cultural
Psychosocial Issues   217

    Cultural Issues in the Counseling Relationship: Ethnocultural

        Transference and Countertransference   217

    Overall Cultural Assessment for Diagnosis and Treatment   218

Strengths-Based Case Conceptualization   218

Strengths-Based Treatment Plans   219

Culturally Responsive Strengths-Based Therapy Techniques   219

    Strengths Journal   219

    "What Is the Truth?" Question   221

• **Case Vignette 7.3** Mario: A Puerto Rican Male and Strengths-Based Therapy   222

    The Oracle: Conversations About Life Purpose   224

    The Gratitude Diary   224

    Strengths Memories   224

    Strengths Cards   224

    Strengths Charts   225

Summary of Key Points   226

Discussion Questions   227

Key Terms   227

References and Suggested Reading   228

**Chapter 8 • Culturally Responsive Strengths-Based Therapy
for African Americans**   **231**

   Chapter Objectives   **231**

   Introduction   231

   The African American Population: Some Basic Demographics   232

      The Overall Socioeconomic Status of African Americans   232

      The Black Underclass   233

      Black Poverty: Implications for Counseling   234

      The White Underclass   234

      The African American Middle Class   235

      Counseling Implications for Middle-Class African Americans   236

      Is There an African American Upper Class?   236

   Historical and Psychosocial Issues for Blacks: Oppression, Discrimination,
     and the Legacy of Slavery   236

      The African American Response to Slavery   236

      Microaggressions and Prejudice Against African Americans   238

      African American Population Mixed With Other Ethnic/Racial Groups:
        Microaggressions   238

   • **Case Vignette 8.1** Tiger Woods and Multiracial Identity   **239**

   African Americans and Cultural Values   239

      The African American Worldview   239

      African American Ethnocultural Identity   240

      Acculturation and African Americans   242

   • **Case Vignette 8.2** Natasha: A Young Black Girl Who Found Her Black Identity   244

      Structure of the African American Family   244

      The Extended African American Family   245

   Cultural Strengths of African Americans   245

      African American Resiliency: The Greatest and Most Formidable Strength   246

        Religion and Spirituality   247

      Counseling and Psychotherapy Approaches for Working With African
        American Clients   248

      Role of the Therapist in Working With African American Clients   249

      Clinical Issues in Counseling African Americans: Trust and Cultural Mistrust   250

      How Therapists Drive Away African American Clients: Microaggressions   251

      Clinician, "Do No Harm"   252

      Clinician's Acknowledgment of Racism and Oppression   252

   NTU: An Afrocentric Model for Counseling African Americans   252

      Cultural Issues in Strengths-Based Therapy With "At-Promise Youth"   253

   • **Case Vignette 8.3** Morris: An African American Adolescent "At Promise"
   Instead of "At Risk"   253

   Summary of Key Points   256

   Discussion Questions   257

   Key Terms   257

   References and Suggested Reading   258

Chapter 9 • Culturally Responsive Strengths-Based Therapy for American Indians and Alaska Natives — **262**

    Chapter Objectives — **262**

    Introduction — 262

    Defining Group Membership — 262

    Demographic and Population Statistics — 263

    Who Is an "Authentic" or "Real Indian"? — 264

    Socioeconomic Status — 265

    Theory of Historical Trauma Among American Indians — 265

    Ethnic/Racial Stereotypes, Racism, and Microaggressions — 266

    Worldview — 266

    Family Structure: The Tribe as Family — 268

    Cultural Identity — 268

    Cultural Values — 269

        Sharing and Generosity — 270

        Time Orientation — 270

        Spirituality — 270

        Cooperation and Harmony — 271

        Noninterference — 271

        Communication Style and Silence — 271

    Cultural Strengths — 272

    Healing: The Circle and Medicine Wheel in Indian Life — 273

    Counseling Applications of the Circle and Medicine Wheel — 274

    Mental Health Challenges — 276

        Traditional Healing — 276

        Acculturation Conflicts — 276

        Alcohol Abuse — 277

        Suicide Rates for American Indians and Alaska Natives — 277

    Counseling Approaches for American Indians and Alaska Natives — 278

    • **Case Vignette 9.1** Johnathan: An American Indian Man Caught Between Two Cultures — 280

    Summary of Key Points — 283

    Discussion Questions — 284

    Key Terms — 284

    References and Suggested Reading — 285

Chapter 10 • Culturally Responsive Strengths-Based Therapy for Asian Americans, Native Hawaiians, and Pacific Islanders — **289**

    Chapter Objectives — **289**

    Introduction — 289

    Demographic and Population Statistics — 290

        Who Are Asian Americans and Pacific Islanders? A Census Definition — 290

        Multiple-Race Reporting for Asian Americans — 291

        Subgroup Representation of Asian American Groups — 291

Historical Changes in the Asian American Profile 292
    Intermarriage and the Asian American Population 292

Socioeconomic Status of Asian Americans and Pacific Islanders: 2013 293
    Native Hawaiians and Other Pacific Islanders: Socioeconomic Issues 293

Asian Americans as the "Model Ethnic Minority": Myth or Reality? 293

Ethnic/Racial Stereotypes, Racism, and Microaggressions 294

Cultural Issues of Asian Americans and Pacific Islanders 295
    Worldviews of Asian Americans and Pacific Islanders 295
    Collectivistic Versus Individualistic Orientation 295
    Cultural Values of Asian Americans and Pacific Islanders 296
    High Value on Education and Hard Work 296
    Family Hierarchical Structure, Family Values, and Parenting Styles 296
    Five Types of Asian American Families 297
    The Suppression of Family Problems: Self-Control, Emotional
        Restraint, and Shaming 298
        Gender Issues in Asian American Families 299
        Children and Adolescents in Asian American Families 299
        Young Adult Asian Americans 299
        The Elderly Asian American Community 300

Asian American and Pacific Islander Communication: High-Context Culture 300

Cultural Identity of Asian Americans: No One Identity Model for All 301

Cultural Strengths and Contributions of Asian Americans 301

Acculturation and Cultural Issues Affecting Mental Health 302
    Acculturation Conflicts 302
    Acculturation Level and Counseling 303
    Help-Seeking Attitudes of Asian Americans 303
        Mental Health and Asian Americans 303
    Mental Health of Native Hawaiians and Other Pacific Islanders 304
        Mental Illness and Substance Use Among Asian Americans and Pacific Islanders 305
    Asian Americans' Expectations About Counseling 305
    Cultural Healing and Indigenous Practices 306

Cultural Factors in Counseling Asian Americans 306
    Eliciting Clients' Views About Their Presenting Problem 307
    Focus on Clients' Cultural and Group Strengths 307
    Native Hawaiian Values and Cultural Healing Practices 308
        The Ho'oponopono: A Native Hawaiian Culturally Based Intervention for Resolving Conflict 309

• **Case Vignette 10.1** Eve Zhang: Multicultural Issues in Strengths-Based Recovery 310

Summary of Key Points 312

Discussion Questions 313

Key Terms 313

References and Suggested Reading 314

**Chapter 11 • Culturally Responsive Strengths-Based Therapy for
Hispanic and Latino/a Americans 317**

    Chapter Objectives 317

    Introduction 317
        Overall Hispanic/Latino American Population 318
        Historical Changes in the Hispanic/Latino Demographic Profile 318

Hispanic/Latino Subgroup Percentages 319

The "Other Hispanics" 319

Geographical Location of Hispanics and Latinos in
the United States 320

Racial Identification(s) for the Hispanic/Latino Population 320

Subgroup Migration History of Some Major Hispanic/Latino Groups 320

Mexican Americans 321

Puerto Ricans 321

Cubans 321

Central Americans 321

Immigration Status, Naturalization, and Pathways to Citizenship 322

Socioeconomic Status of Hispanic/Latino Americans 323

Ethnic/Racial Stereotypes, Racism, and Microaggressions 324

Hispanic and Latino/a Americans' Worldviews 324

Communication Style of Hispanics and Latinos 325

Hispanic/Latino American Cultural Values 326

The Hispanic/Latino Family and the Cultural Value of *Familismo* 326

Family Structure of Hispanic/Latino Americans: *Machismo*,
Respeto, and *Marianismo* 326

The Cultural Value of *Personalismo* 328

The Cultural Value of *Fatalismo* 328

Spiritual and Religious Values 328

Acculturation Conflicts for Hispanic/Latino Americans 329

Cultural Identity of Hispanics and Latinos 330

Hispanic/Latino Cultural Strengths 331

Hispanic/Latino Physical and Mental Health Issues 332

Counseling Approaches for Working With Hispanic/Latino Clients 333

Making a Culturally Responsive Strengths-Based Diagnosis for
Hispanic/Latino Clients 333

• **Case Vignette 11.1** Enrique: Strengths-Based Therapy and the Juvenile
Justice System 335

Summary of Key Points 336

Discussion Questions 337

Key Terms 337

References and Suggested Reading 337

**Chapter 12 • Culturally Responsive Strengths-Based Therapy
for Arab and Muslim Americans** 341

Chapter Objectives 341

Introduction 341

Who Are Arab and Muslim Americans? 342

Distinguishing Between the Terms *Arab* and *Muslim* 342

Three Waves of Arab Migration to the United States 343

Demographic Data on Arab Americans 344

Socioeconomic Status of Arab Americans 345

American Muslims: Some Demographics 345

Muslims, African Americans, and Jews 345

Socioeconomic Status of Muslim Americans 346

Muslims and Immigration 346

Microaggressions Against Arab and Muslim Americans 346

Arab and Muslim Americans and "Passing" 347

Cultural Values and Worldview of Arabs and Muslims 348

The Religion of Islam 348

Islam Prayer Rituals: Wudhu 348

Collectivist Worldview of Arabs and Muslims 349

The Arab and Muslim Family 349

The Extended Patriarchal Family Structure and the Eldest Son 350

Community 351

Communication Patterns and Arab and Muslim Americans 351

Time and Space 352

The Cultural and Racial Identity of Arab/Muslim Americans: White? 352

Acculturation: Patterns and Conflicts 353

Cultural Strengths of Arab and Muslim Americans 354

Mental Health Issues for Arab and Muslim Americans 354

Mental Health, Religiosity, Arab Elders, and Posttraumatic Stress Disorder 355

Counseling Arab and Muslim Americans 355

Role of Family, Friends, and Religious Leaders With Mental Health Concerns 356

Counseling Arab and Muslim Americans: Some Recommendations 356

• **Case Vignette 12.1** Nadia: Strengths-Based Therapy for Arabs and Muslims 357

Summary of Key Points 359

Discussion Questions 360

Key Terms 360

References and Suggested Reading 361

Chapter 13 • Culturally Responsive Strengths-Based Therapy for White Americans of European Ancestry **366**

Chapter Objectives **366**

Introduction 366

Historical Perspectives and Immigration of White Europeans
to the United States 367

Demographics and Population Statistics 367

German Americans 368

Irish Americans 368

English Americans 368

American Ancestry 368

Italian Americans 368

Scandinavian Americans 369

Polish Americans 369

French Americans 369

Scottish Americans 369

Scotch-Irish 369

Jewish Americans 369

Dutch Americans 370

Russian Americans 370

Slovak Americans 370

Greek Americans 370

Socioeconomic Status of White Americans 370

The White Population, Intermarriage, and Multiple-Race Identification 370

Ethnic Group Saliency for White Americans 371
    Racial Stereotyping of White European Americans 372
    Is an American Identity Synonymous With a White Identity? 373
    Cultural Description of White American Ethnic Groups 374
    Cultural Description of Anglo or English Americans 374
        Microaggressions, English American Culture, and the Designation of "WASP" Culture 375
        Cultural Strengths of English Americans 375
        Communication Style and Attitudes Toward Talk and Psychotherapy 376
        Counseling English Americans 376
    Cultural Description of Italian Americans 377
        Microaggressions and Italians 378
        Communication Style and Attitudes Toward Talk and Psychotherapy 378
        Cultural Strengths of Italian Americans 378
        Counseling Italian Americans 378
    Cultural Description of American Jews 379
        Jewish Americans: Cultural Values and Counseling Issues 379
        Microaggressions and American Jews 380
        Cultural Strengths of American Jews 380
        Communication Style and Attitudes Toward Talk and Psychotherapy 381
        Counseling American Jews 381

The White American Worldview 381
    Whiteness and White Privilege 382

Box: Decentering whiteness **383**

Models of White Racial Identity Development 383
    Brief Historical Overview of White Racial Identity Models 383

The Hardiman White Racial Identity Model 384
    Stage 1: Naivité or Lack of Social Consciousness 385
    Stage 2: Acceptance 385
    Stage 3: Resistance 386
    Stage 4: Redefinition 386
    Stage 5: Internalization 387

The Helms Model of White Identity Development 387
    Phase 1: Abandonment of Racism 388
        1. Contact Status 388
        2. Disintegration Status 388
        3. Reintegration Status 388
    Phase 2: Defining a Nonracist Identity 389
        4. Pseudo-Independent Status 389
        5. Immersion/Emersion Status 389
        6. Autonomy Status 389
    Criticism of the Helms Model of White Racial Identity 390
    Significance of the White Identity Models 390
    Research Findings and White Identity Development Models 390
    White Dialectics: The Promising Research of White Multicultural
        Scholars on White Identity Development 391
    White Americans of European Ancestry and Mental Health Issues 391

Counseling White Americans of European Ancestry 392
• **Case Vignette 13.1** Jessie and a Strengths-Based Therapy Approach **393**

Summary of Key Points 396

Discussion Questions 396

Key Terms   397

References and Suggested Reading   397

Chapter 14 • Culturally Responsive Strengths-Based Therapy for Women   401

Chapter Objectives   401

Introduction   401

Demographics of American Women   402

Socioeconomic Status of U.S. Women   402

    Women in Poverty   402

Microaggressions Against Women and Gender Inequality   403

The Mental Health Issues of Women   404

    Biological Factors Related to Mental Illness in Women   405

    Sex Roles and Sexualization   405

    Intimate Partner Violence and Sexual Abuse   405

    Women's Strengths   406

Counseling Approaches for Women: Feminist Therapy   406

    Four Main Philosophies of Feminists   407

    Rationale for a Specialization in Therapy for Women   408

Dissatisfaction With Existing Psychological Theories   408

Dissatisfaction With Diagnostic Categories and Mother Blaming   408

Traditional Theories Versus Feminist Therapies: Six Characteristics   409

Key Concepts of Feminist Therapy   409

    View of Human Nature   409

    Sex Role Stereotypes and Androgyny   409

    Gender Schema Therapy   410

Gender Role Stereotyping Across Cultures   410

The Social Construction of Gender   410

Gender and Power Differentials   411

Box: Core feminist beliefs   411

Feminist Therapy Approaches   412

    Consciousness Raising   412

    Social and Gender Role Analysis   412

    Social Activism   412

    The Therapeutic Relationship   412

Goals of Feminist Therapy   412

The Role of Men in Feminist Therapy   413

Techniques of Feminist Therapy   414

    Gender Role Analysis   414

    Gender Role Intervention   414

    Assertiveness Training   414

    Power Analysis   415

    Bibliotherapy   415

    Relational-Cultural Theory: The New Feminist Psychotherapeutic Approach   415

Feminist Therapy and Multicultural Therapy   416

     Contributions and Criticisms of Feminist Therapy   417

Integration of Feminist Therapy With Other Approaches   417

• **Case Vignette 14.1** Case Analysis Using the Strengths-Based
Therapy Model: McIntosh Family   418

Summary of Key Points   420

Discussion Questions   421

Key Terms   421

References and Suggested Reading   421

**Chapter 15 • Culturally Responsive Strengths-Based Therapy
for LGBTQ Individuals**   **425**

     Chapter Objectives   **425**

Introduction   425

Demographic and LGBTQ Population Data   426

Socioeconomic Status   427

Discrimination and the Gay Rights Movement   428

     Homophobia Persists   429

     Heterosexism   430

     Microaggressions Against LGBTQ People   430

LGBTQ Identity Development   431

     Defining Sex, Sexual Orientation, and Gender Identity   431

     Gender Dysphoria in Children and Adolescents   432

Transgender Identity Development   433

Coming Out and Gender Identity Development for Gays,
Lesbians, and Bisexuals   434

Coming Out for People of Color: A "Tricultural Experience"   435

LGBTQ Youth and Schools   436

LGBTQ Families: Some Facts   437

Mental Health Issues and the LGBTQ Community   438

Top 10 Physical and Mental Health Concerns of LGBTQ College Students   439

Strengths of LGBTQ Populations   439

Counseling Members of the LGBTQ Community   440

The Therapeutic Process in Gay and Lesbian Psychotherapy   441

Role of the Therapist in Working With LGBTQ Clients   441

Gay Affirmative Psychotherapy   442

     Barriers to Assessment of LGBTQ Clients   443

     Positive Clinical Assessment of LGBTQ Clients   443

     Reparative Therapy and Sexual Orientation Conversion Therapy   443

• **Case Vignette 15.1** Sal and the Strengths-Based Therapy Model   **444**

Summary of Key Points   445

Discussion Questions   446

Key Terms   447

References and Suggested Reading   448

Chapter 16 • Culturally Responsive Strengths-Based Therapy for Individuals With Disabilities 452

Chapter Objectives 452

Introduction 452

Definition of Disability and the Americans With Disabilities Act 453

Demographics of People With Disabilities 453

Socioeconomic Status 454

Major Categories of Disabilities 455
Some Invisible Disabilities 456
Some Facts About People With Disabilities 457

Models of Disability 457

Disability as a Multicultural Issue 458
Ableism 459

Privilege and People With Disabilities 459

Microaggressions Toward People With Disabilities 459

Spread: A Form of Ableism 460

Interaction Strain and People With Disabilities 460

Identity Development and People With Disabilities 461

Experiencing a Disability Identity After Trauma 461

Strengths of People With Disabilities 463

Counseling Approaches for Individuals With Disabilities 464
Counseling Issues and the Effects of Disability 465

People With Disabilities and Risk for Abuse 465

Empowerment 466

Family Counseling and People With Disabilities 467

Disability Affirmative Therapy and Disability Orientation 467

Olkin's Model of Disability and Counseling Approach 469
APA's Guidelines for Assessment of and Intervention With Persons
With Disabilities 470
Guidelines for Disability Awareness, Accessibility, and Diversity (1–10) 470
Guidelines Related to Assessment and Testing of Individuals With
Disabilities (11–16) 470
Guidelines That Cover Interventions (17–22) 470
• **Case Vignette 16.1** Elizabeth: Strengths-Based Therapy and a
Young Teenager Suffering Trauma From a Car Accident 471

Summary of Key Points 472

Discussion Questions 473

Key Terms 474

References and Suggested Reading 475

Chapter 17 • Culturally Responsive Strengths-Based Therapy for Older Adults 478

Chapter Objectives 478

Introduction 478

Demographics for Older Adults   479
    Numbers of Older American Adults   479
    Racial Composition of Older Adults   480
    Labor Force Participation and Socioeconomic Conditions   480
    Marital Status   481
    Health Status of Older Adults   481

Western and Eastern Cultural Views on Aging   482

Ageism   483

Microaggressions and the Older Adult   483
    Prevention of Chronic Physiological Disease   484

Mental Health Issues of the Older Adult   484

Depression and Older Adults   485
    Treatment for Depression Among Older Adults   485
    Depression and Physical Illness in Older Adults   485
    Suicide and Depression in Older Adults   486
    Elder Abuse   486

Alzheimer's Disease and Other Cognitive Impairments   487

Substance Abuse and Older Adults   488
    Alcohol and Pain Medications   488

Sexuality and the Older Adult   489
    The LGBTQ Older Adult   491
    Intimate Partner Abuse of Older LGBTQ Adults   492

The Strengths-Based Therapy Model and the Older Adult   492
    Strengths-Based Therapy's Philosophy About Older Adults   492
    Role of the Strengths-Based Therapist and Older Adults   493
• **Case Vignette 17.1** Rebecca Gervase   **494**

Phases of Strengths-Based Therapy for Older Adults   494
    Phase 1: Establishing a Therapeutic Alliance   494
    Phase 2: Strengths Discovery   495
        12-Component Model of Strengths Assessment for Aging Well 496
    Phase 3: Letting Go, Harvesting the Good, Eliciting Clients'
        Hopes and Dreams, and Letting In the Good/Change   498
    Phase 4: Framing Solutions and Strengths-Based Treatment Plans 500
    Phase 5: Building New Competencies   501
    Phase 6: Building a Healthy New Identity   502
    Phase 7: Moving Forward and Terminating Treatment   502

Additional Strengths Assessment Issues   502

A Final Note on Clinical Intervention and Treatment Issues   502
• **Case Vignette 17.2** Using the Strengths-Based Therapy Model With Sarah   **503**

Summary of Key Points   506

Discussion Questions   506

Key Terms   507

References and Suggested Reading   507

**Chapter 18 • Culturally Responsive Strengths-Based Therapy
for Immigrants and Refugees**   **512**

Chapter Objectives   **512**

Introduction   512

Refugee, *Asylee*, and *Immigrant*: Some Working Definitions ... 513

    Demographics and Population Statistics: Some Key Facts About the
      World's Refugees ... 515

    Foreign-Born in the United States ... 515

    Undocumented Immigrants ... 515

    DACA: Deferred Action for Childhood Arrivals ... 516

    The Forces of Migration ... 517

    Educational Levels and Socioeconomic Status of Immigrants ... 517

    Immigrants as Contributing Members of American Society ... 517

Microaggressions, Hate Crimes, and Discrimination Against
    Immigrants and Refugees ... 518

Mental Health Issues of Immigrants and Refugees ... 519

    Cultural Bereavement: Migrants and Refugees ... 519

    Cultural Identity and Stress for Immigrants and Refugees ... 519

Mental Health Issues and Pre- and Postmigration ... 520

    Acculturative Stress: A Postmigration Mental Health Issue ... 520

    Postmigration: Helping Clients With Basic Resettlement Needs ... 522

    Torture Experiences: A Key Mental Health Issue for Refugees,
      Immigrants, and Asylees ... 522

    The Refugee/Asylee Experience: The Triple Paradigm ... 523

    Core Counseling Competencies for Working With Torture Survivors ... 524

    Cultural Humility and Clinical Practice With Refugees and Immigrants ... 525

    Use of Interpreters With Immigrants and Refugees ... 526

    Secondary Trauma for Mental Health Therapists and Counselors ... 528

Competency Assessment for Practitioners Working With
    Refugees and Immigrants ... 528

Counseling and Therapy Models for Working With Refugees With PTSD ... 528

    The Psychoeducational Counseling Model for Refugees and Immigrants ... 530

    Narrative Exposure Therapy and PTSD ... 531

    Counseling Refugees and Immigrants Using a Strengths-Based Approach ... 531

      Strengths of Migrants and Refugees ... 531

Culturally Responsive Strengths-Based Therapy ... 532

• **Case Vignette 18.1** Using a Culturally Responsive Strengths-Based Approach
  With Mohammed ... **533**

Summary of Key Points ... 534

Discussion Questions ... 536

Key Terms ... 536

References and Suggested Reading ... 537

**Chapter 19 • Culturally Responsive Strengths-Based
Therapy for Multiracial People** ... **541**

Chapter Objectives ... **541**

Introduction ... 541

    Race: A Social Construction ... 542

    Definition of *Multiracial* ... 542

    Demographic and Population Data on the Multiracial Population in
      the United States ... 543

    Age of Multiracial Population ... 544

    Interracial Marriage in the United States ... 545

The "One-Drop Rule" 545

Microaggressions Directed Toward Multiracial Individuals 546

Forcing an Ascribed Identity on Multiracial Individuals 547

Racism, Skin Color, and Multiracial Backgrounds 547

The "What Are You?" Question 548

Marginality and Mixed Heritage 548

- **Case Vignette 19.1** Multiple-Heritage Case Example: Norwegian Father, African American Mother 549

The Sense of Not Quite Belonging, of Being Different 549

- **Case Vignette 19.2** Where Do I Belong? **550**

Models of Multiethnic/Multiracial Identity Development 550

"Passing" for Black 552

Commonalities Across Multiracial Identity Development Models 554

Multiracial Individuals' Views on Race 554

Racial Self-Identification Is Situational for Some Multiracial Individuals 555

Strengths of a Multiethnic/Multiracial Identity 555

Intersectionality and Multiracial Identity Development 556

- **Case Vignette 19.3** A Multiracial Woman: The Intersection of Race, Gender, Sexual Orientation, and Class 557

Multiracial Identity Development and Mental Health 557

Multiracial Bill of Rights 557

Competencies for Counseling Multiracial Individuals 558

Psychotherapy With Multiethnic/Multiracial People 559

Counseling Multiracial Children 559

Counselor's Role in Working With Multiracial Individuals 560

Psychoeducational Approach with Multiracial Individuals 560

Assist Clients With Knowledge About Racial Identity Formation 561

Multiracial Children and Divorce 561

Develop Supportive Interracial Relationships 561

Find an Acceptable Name to Reflect One's Racial Identity 561

Develop Cultural Genograms for Multiracial/Multicultural Family 561

Encourage Parental Discussion of Race and Racial Experiences 562

- **Case Vignette 19.4** A Multiracial Teenage Girl: Simone 562

Summary of Key Points 563

Discussion Questions 564

Key Terms 565

References and Suggested Reading 565

Chapter 20 • Social Class, Social Justice, Intersectionality, and Privilege **569**

Chapter Objectives **569**

Introduction 569

Social Class and Culturally Responsive Counseling 569

Definition of Terms: *Social Class* and *Classism* 569

Demographic Data on Social Class and Poverty 571

The Neuroscience of Poverty and Social Class 573

Poverty Among Children in the United States 574

Parental Education and Family Structure 575

Effects of Poverty on a Child's Brain 575
Small Amounts of Money Can Reverse the Negative Effects of Poverty 577
Neurogenesis: Healing the Brain With Long-Term Exposure to Poverty 577
Poverty and Mental Health 578
Social Class, Trauma, and Counseling 579
Liu's Social Class Worldview Model 580

Neuroscience, Social Class, and Empathy 582

The Social Justice Movement in Counseling 583
Social Justice and Oppression 585

Intersectionality, Social Class, and Social Justice 585
Social Class Identity Development and Intersectionality 586
The Counseling Profession and Class Elitism 586

Internalized Oppression: Social Class and Ethnicity/Race 587
Microaggressions and Social Class 588
Neuroscience and Social Justice 588
Neuroscience, Counselor Training, and Social Justice 589

Privilege, Race, and Social Class 589
White Privilege and Dominant Group Identities 589
Consequences of White Privilege 590
White Privilege: The Other Side of the Coin: White Empathy, White Guilt 591
Social Class Privilege 592

Summary of Multidimensional Privileges in a Society 592

Social Class and Cultural Strengths: Antidote for Internalized Oppression and
Stereotype Threat 593
Search for the Strengths in the Client's Culture 593
Culturally Responsive Strengths-Based Client Empowerment 595
• **Case Vignette 20.1** Rebecca: A White Woman Who Says She's "White Trash" 596

Summary of Key Points 597

Discussion Questions 598

Key Terms 598

References and Suggested Reading 599

Index **604**

PREFACE

Life is all about change and learning how to respond appropriately to unfolding change not only in our individual lives, but also in the professions for which we have trained—for example, psychology, counseling, and the helping professions in general. Change comes whether we like it or not, and trying to stop change is like trying to stop the rain from falling. In many respects, this book, *Culturally Diverse Counseling: Theory and Practice*, is about the change that has taken place, about how we conceptualize diversity, and about how we go about counseling individuals who are culturally different from and similar to us.

Since its early inception during the late 1960s and early 1970s, multicultural counseling has changed. The field has evolved from simply exhorting people to become aware of the influence of culture on a person's views about mental health and problems to the relatively new branch called cultural neuroscience and cultural genetics. For example, research studies on cultural neuroscience have revealed that there are cultural connections in the neural pathways of our brains. Culture is locked into our very brains (Azar, 2010; Cheung, van de Vijver, & Leong, 2011; Chiao & Blizinsky, 2010; Chiao et al., 2008; Lu & Gilmour, 2004).

Researchers have begun to find hard scientific evidence that one's culture interacts with one's brain to form what have been labeled "culture" genes (Boyd & Richerson, 1983, 2005; Davies, 2013). Human behavior is the product of two different and interacting evolutionary processes (culture and biology/genes). Human genes and culture interact in a feedback loop such that changes in culture can lead to changes in one's genes and vice versa (Boyd & Richerson, 2005). As Goldman (2014) has asserted, "It no longer makes sense to think of genetics and culture as two separate uninteracting monoliths. The difficulty is identifying how and if one is influencing the other."

GUIDING PRINCIPLES OF THIS BOOK

Culturally Diverse Counseling emphasizes consolidating what is already known about culturally diverse counseling and then moving forward with the new developments in neuroscience and "culture" genes as well as in the areas of implicit and explicit bias, microaggressions, and the Cultural Formulation Interview. Moreover, this book highlights the relatively recent developments in positive psychology and strengths-based counseling, especially as these areas relate to counseling culturally diverse individuals. It is a book about adapting to change in the field of multicultural counseling—change in our knowledge base about cultures, the human brain, and our mental health.

GOALS OF THE BOOK

Counseling, psychology, and social work have all called for culturally responsive ways of working with people from diverse cultural backgrounds (Hoshmand, 2006; Pedersen, Lonner, Draguns, Trimble, & Scharrón del Rio, 2016; Ponterotto, Casas, Suzuki, & Alexander, 2010; Ridley, 2005; Saleebey, 2002). This book integrates two approaches to psychotherapy: (1) culturally responsive therapy and (2) strengths-based therapy. Culturally responsive strengths-based therapy traces its historical roots to the multicultural movement, the positive psychology movement in psychology, the strengths perspective in social work (Saleebey, 2002), and the author's own theory of strengths-based therapy (Jones-Smith, 2014).

Culturally responsive counseling may be defined as therapy that understands the interaction of a client's presenting problem/issue and his or her culture; it refers to a therapist's ability to recognize the cultural influences not only on a client's presenting problems, but also on the counseling relationship.

The strengths-based therapy model is based on the premise that people have a basic need to find some kind of strength within themselves. Finding one's strengths can be compared to finding one's purpose in life; it is self-affirming and gives a person some measure of self-esteem. Strengths are inevitably defined and developed within a cultural context. Each culture establishes a cultural valence for the value of specific behaviors and strengths. Therefore, different ethnic and cultural groups will have their own worldview on what their group's cultural strengths are and how to use such strengths in their interactions with the world. One benefit of strengths-based therapy (Jones-Smith, 2014) is that it contains definitive phases and therapeutic interventions.

Promoting human strengths has been an important part of multicultural literature, especially in counseling psychology and social work (Gelso & Woodhouse, 2003; Georges & Tomlinson-Clarke, 2015; Owens, Magyar-Moe, & Lopez, 2015). This author predicts that as new studies confirm and reveal what happens in the brain of a person when one emphasizes deficits as opposed to strengths, more counseling theories will adopt a strengths-based focus.

Discussing a client's strengths can be a curative factor in and of itself. A person's strengths have been found to be a crucial component of reducing mental distress (Lampropoulous, 2001). Fredrickson's (1998) research has shown that the positive emotions often associated with strengths can function to undo negative emotions. Other studies have reported that focusing on clients' strengths can improve individuals' quality of life and can prevent or serve as a buffer to mental illness—especially acting as a buffer to depression (Seligman, 2002; Seligman & Csikszentmihalyi, 2000; Seligman, Schulman, DeRubeis, & Hollon, 1999). A therapist's focus on clients' strengths rather than on their deficits has been found to increase their resilience (Scales, Benson, Leffert, & Blyth, 2000). Human strengths have been portrayed as the building blocks of positive human functioning (Harbin, Gelso, & Perez Rojas, 2013; Owens et al., 2015).

This book, *Culturally Diverse Counseling*, highlights accomplishing six major goals.

Goal 1: Focus on culturally responsive therapy skill development. For the most part, books on multicultural or cross-cultural counseling have not stressed cultural skill development, the third building block in the American Psychological Association's multicultural competencies. Instead, they have tended to stress development of cultural awareness and cultural knowledge. In contrast, this book emphasizes the three components of multicultural competencies—cultural awareness, cultural knowledge, and cultural skill development. As Toporek (2012) has pointed out, most counseling training programs rely on one course to provide the bulk of multicultural training and struggle with a patchwork of multicultural training, which focuses primarily on increasing students' cultural awareness. Cultural awareness is at best a starting point, and not an end destination, in therapy. The emphasis on increasing students' cultural awareness has resulted in giving minimal attention to clinical skill building in multicultural counseling (Priester et al., 2008; Tomlinson-Clarke & Georges, 2014). This book contains more than 25 culturally responsive clinical skill development exercises. After receiving instruction in using this book, students will be able to counsel individuals who are culturally different from themselves.

Goal 2: Focus on clients' strengths. Another major goal of this book is to focus on clients' strengths, especially their individual and cultural strengths. The basic strength of any group of people stems from their shared experiences of historical and cultural continuity. That is, the strengths of African Americans, Germans, Asians, Italians, and so forth are to be found in their participation as members of a distinct cultural group. This book maintains that clients' strengths—rather than their weaknesses—will form the primary reservoir to combat the challenges they face. As Weick and Chamberlain (2002) once said, "Strengths are all we have to work with" in therapy (p. 95). Culturally responsive strengths-based therapy is based on the premise that *what we focus on in life and in therapy materializes in our lives. Emphasizing a person's strengths provides a positive source of motivation to deal with his or her life issues.*

Goal 3: Focus on the interaction between culture, neuroscience, and the brain. A third major goal of this book is to focus on current developments in the field involving studies of culture, neuroscience, and the brain. Culture pervades all aspects of a person's function. An individual constructs himself or herself within the backdrop of culture. As Llorente (2010) has stated,

> Most recently, it appears that our brains and culture are interwoven by biological mechanisms, and humans may actually possess "culture" genes that mediate a complex interaction between biology and the environment, providing an interactive mechanism capable of allowing human brains to assimilate cultural characteristics. (p. xi)

Studies in functional magnetic resonance imaging (fMRI) have helped researchers to understand just how deep culture penetrates a person's entire being (Chiao & Blizinsky, 2010; Chiao et al., 2008; Freeman, Rule, Adams, & Ambady, 2009; Goh et al., 2010; Hedden, Aron, Markus, & Gabrieli, 2008).

Researchers conducting brain research have found that culture can influence how people experience the world at the most basic levels, such as what they see when they look at a city street or how they perceive a simple line in a square (Hedden et al., 2008). For instance, it has been found that Western culture conditions people to think of themselves as highly independent entities. Hence, when looking at scenes in their environment, they tend to focus on central objects more than on their surroundings. Quite the opposite is true for people from East Asian cultures that stress interdependence. Hedden and his colleagues (2008) conducted an experiment that involved two tasks. In the first task, participants looked at a line simply to estimate its length—a task that emphasizes American strengths. In the second task, participants were asked to estimate the line's length relative to the size of a square—an easier task for Asians whose culture emphasizes contextual clues.

Hedden et al. (2008) showed that deeply ingrained ways of thinking affect the brains of East Asians and Americans, even as they perform simple tasks that involve estimating the length of a line. In each group, activation in frontal and parietal brain regions known to be associated with attentional control was greater when participants engaged in culturally preferred judgments (e.g., American cultural strength—judging the length of a line; East Asian strength—judging the length of a line against context, a square). The authors concluded that "the cultural background of an individual and the degree to which the individual endorses cultural values moderate activation in brain networks engaged during even simple visual and attentional tasks" (p. 12). Brain findings may help people to become more aware of deep cultural differences that are so basic that people don't even see them.

Moreover, culture affects what a therapist and client give attention to during therapy. Culturally responsive counseling helps clients to make connections in their brains and to engage in, where necessary, the modification of old neural pathways and the creation of new ones. A therapist's knowledge of neuroscience provides the potentiality of promoting a therapeutic alliance and increasing therapy engagement as a therapist takes into consideration the creation of therapist–client mirror neurons developed during therapy (Jones-Smith, 2014). A therapist's belief in clients' ability to change unproductive and self-defeating behaviors is buttressed by his or her knowledge of the role that neuroplasticity plays in helping clients recover from trauma and other challenges in life.

Goal 4: The Cultural Formulation Interview and culturally responsive case conceptualization. A fourth goal of this book is to present the Cultural Formulation Interview from the fifth edition of the *Diagnostic and Statistical Manual of Mental Disorders* (*DSM-5*; American Psychiatric Association, 2013b) and to demonstrate how it might be used in working with culturally diverse clients. To this end, I expand upon the 16 questions provided in the Cultural Formulation Interview. For instance, I present culturally responsive clinical skill development exercises to help the counselor understand his or her client's acculturation and migration as well as clinical skill exercises regarding how to organize a cultural genogram and a family's strength genogram.

Chapter 7 presents a case conceptualization format for conducting culturally responsive counseling. Culturally responsive strengths-based case conceptualization refers to the extent to which therapists identify and integrate cultural factors into their conceptualization regarding the etiology and treatment of a client's presenting concerns (Constantine, 2001; Constantine & Ladany, 2000; Lee, Sheridan, Rosen, & Jones, 2013; Owens et al., 2015). In this section of the book, I develop an outline for culturally responsive interviewing and case conceptualization. Diagnosis alone of a mental disorder is insufficient. This section offers clinical questions therapists can use in both case conceptualization and the therapeutic interview. A brief section is included on cultural syndromes and case conceptualization.

Goal 5: Cultural strengths of major cultural and ethnic groups. All cultures have strengths. This book presents cases involving members of minority cultural groups within American society (i.e., African Americans, Asian Americans, Latino Americans, the LGBTQ population, and those experiencing disabilities). Over 30 case vignettes are presented throughout this book. Each chapter on a specific ethnocultural group examines the strengths of that particular group.

Goal 6: Focus on resiliency and social justice. A sixth goal of *Culturally Diverse Counseling* is that it emphasizes counselors working toward the goal of social justice. The book does not concentrate on the issue of oppression. While it acknowledges racism, ethnocentrism, and other methods of social injustice, this book adopts the view that people are not their circumstances and that they are resilient. Racism, ethnocentrism, and oppression are conceptualized as roadblocks over which clients are helped to jump. Moreover, in the United States, the focus on race and ethnicity, whether intended or not, has sometimes resulted in finger pointing and blaming of the dominant White majority group. This book is not about finger pointing and placing blame on various ethnic groups, even though history itself may provide sufficient ground for such finger pointing. Each chapter on a specific ethnocultural group deals with the issue of microaggressions toward that group.

OUTLINE/ORGANIZATION OF THE BOOK

This book is organized into four distinct parts. Part I provides foundational knowledge, and it includes Chapters 1 through 3. *Chapter 1 is foundational* in that it provides a general blueprint of what is involved in becoming a culturally competent helping professional. The chapter highlights key multicultural issues and concepts. Subsequent chapters describe in more detail the concepts under consideration. Chapter 1 maintains that becoming a culturally competent practitioner involves (1) learning the history of the multicultural movement—what issues sparked its development and continue to sustain its development, as well as the global impact of migration and shifting cultural populations; (2) learning the language, key terms, and concepts of multiculturalism—therefore, a rather substantial section of Chapter 1 defines and explains these terms and concepts; (3) understanding the various helping professions' guidelines for culturally appropriate planning and treatment—therefore, brief sections are presented on the multicultural competencies and ethical multicultural issues; and (4) acquiring the clinical skills of cultural awareness, cultural humility, and cultural empathy, as well as other skills.

In Chapter 1, I examine basic concepts in traditional multicultural psychotherapy, such as worldview, cultural awareness, Eurocentric psychology, cultural encapsulation, race as a social construction, ethnic group, and ethnocentrism. Information on neuroscience (Losin, Dapretto, & Iacoboni, 2010), the brain, and the invisible neural barrier of ethnic/racial bias is also presented (Amodio, 2014; Amodio et al., 2004; Amodio & Ratner, 2011; Baron & Banaji, 2006; Greenwald & Krieger, 2006; Greenwald, Poehlman, Uhlmann, & Banaji, 2009). Chapter 1 raises the question: Do the concepts of implicit and explicit bias form the new paradigm for examining racial and cultural prejudice? Chapter 1 contains six culturally responsive skill development exercises focusing on cultural awareness, understanding the impact of one's culture, and understanding one's worldview. A culturally competent awareness checklist for mental health workers is also presented. In addition, Chapter 1 contains three case vignettes with discussion questions.

Similar to Chapter 1, both Chapter 2 and Chapter 3 are foundational. Chapter 2 addresses cultural meaning systems, cultural trust, and cultural humility. The author's tripartite model of ethnic identity is presented. Some of the topics included in Chapter 2 are cultural countertransference, cultural intelligence, cultural identity development, and ethnicity as schema. Consideration is also given to the positive effects of an ethnic/cultural identity (Lu & Gilmour, 2004). Discussion is presented on the topics of assimilation, marginalization, acculturation, and acculturative stress. Several culturally responsive clinical skill developments are provided in the areas of cultural humility and cultural empathy, and levels of culturally competent therapist response.

Chapter 3 examines neuroscience, multiple cultural identities, and cultural strengths. The chapter begins with the Council for Accreditation of Counseling and Related Educational Programs (CACREP) Standards and their endorsement of neuroscience as a major area of study and expertise for counselors. Basic foundational concepts in neuroscience are presented, such as a review of the brain as a social organ, neurons, neurotransmitters, neuroplasticity, and mind.

Cultural identity is reviewed, and the cultural identity questions contained in the Cultural Formulation Interview (American Psychiatric Association, 2013a) are discussed. Information is presented on the negativity bias of the brain, and the question is raised: Is the brain hardwired to see the glass half empty or half full? Both mental health and counseling are viewed from a neuroscience perspective. The chapter presents research evidence that psychotherapy can change a person's brain. The importance of mirror neurons firing during counseling is addressed. An important theme of Chapter 3 is that each one of us has multiple cultural identities—for instance, as Asian American or White American, male or female, gay or straight, young or old, and so forth. Three case vignettes are presented to illustrate how concepts from neuroscience might be used in counseling.

Part II of this book deals with culturally responsive strengths-based clinical practice, and it includes Chapters 4 and 5. Chapter 4 deals with strengths development and culture. It begins with a definition of strength, and then it proceeds to consider the characteristics of strengths and the nature of culturally bound strengths. A brief section is presented on the neurobiology of human strengths development. In part, strengths are defined as well-traveled pathways in the brain.

Chapter 4 also considers the relational components of strengths development. It makes the point that a person's development of recognized strengths is based on the existence of a trusting human relationship, usually but not always begun early in life. The people who are close to us nourish and help us to develop our strengths. Chapter 4 traces the development of human strengths to a person's early attachment relationships; therefore, a brief section is presented on Bowlby's (1988) theory of attachment as the foundation for understanding individual strengths development. Strengths development is also characterized as dialogic conversations with the self. A section compares Western and Eastern views on human strengths, with an emphasis on

American and Chinese outlooks on strengths. A brief case vignette is analyzed for a woman who may be experiencing the brain's negativity bias in that she has a tendency to notice what's missing rather than what is in front of her. Four culturally responsive clinical skill development exercises are presented.

Chapter 5 begins with a discussion of the neurocultural dynamics of cultural consonance and cultural dissonance. The bulk of this chapter deals with a summary of the revised strengths-based therapy model. Emphasis is placed on examining strengths-based therapy and the law of neuroplasticity. The power of cultural beliefs is discussed. In addition, Chapter 5 discusses strengths-based counseling and clients' self-limiting beliefs. A strengths-based client bill of rights for treatment is proffered. Phases of culturally responsive strengths-based counseling are reviewed, and the chapter deals with strengths-based concepts found in Chinese culture (mindfulness and the concept of surrendering) and in Hindu culture (setting a strengths-based intention).

Chapter 5 presents SWOB (strengths, weaknesses, opportunities, and barriers) analysis, and clinical skill development exercises are offered on strengths talk counselors can use with their client, as well as helping counselors to set counselor intentions for counseling. Chapter 5 also examines strengths-based culturally responsive competencies for therapists. It deals with such issues as strengths assessment for therapists.

Part III of *Culturally Diverse Counseling* involves Chapters 6 and 7. Chapter 6 addresses culturally responsive assessment and the Cultural Formulation Interview in detail. It begins with a general discussion of assessment principles in counseling and psychotherapy. It deals with topics such as cultural bias in assessment, models of assessment for culturally responsive counseling, and fear, the human brain, and clinical assessment. A number of culturally responsive clinical exercises and tables are presented in Chapter 6, including assessing differences in client/clinician communication styles, using the Culturally Responsive Intake Checklist, and learning how to listen for culture in a client's story.

A dominant theme in Chapter 6 is that culture is, as Llorente (2010) has stated, "not something to be sprinkled upon our diagnostic considerations, theoretical formulations, clinical impressions or neuropsychological inferences, as if it were of secondary importance or an afterthought, as realism might have been to the impressionistic movement. Culture should not be an afterthought because culture is in our brains. . . . Culture is to brain what color is to light on the canvas, of the impressionists" (p. xi).

Chapter 6 contains an examination of the *DSM-5* and culturally relevant V codes, as well as a discussion of the criticisms and limitations of the Cultural Formulation Interview. Culture-bound syndromes are reviewed, and additional assessment tools are discussed, such as cultural genograms. Clinical exercises are offered on ways to ask strength questions about overcoming adversities, ways to ask questions about family strengths, and ways to ask questions about the strengths of friends.

Chapter 7 highlights culturally responsive case conceptualization and treatment planning. It examines what happens when clinicians are biased against their clients, the overdiagnosing of people of color—that is, seeing greater pathology than there is in a client. In addition, this chapter reviews basic principles of case conceptualization, diagnosis, and revisions in the *DSM-5*. This chapter contains seven culturally responsive clinical skill development exercises that expand on the Cultural Formulation Interview. Three case vignettes are provided in this chapter, including the cases of a woman of German descent, a Haitian woman experiencing psychosocial issues, and Mario, a Puerto Rican male who needs strengths-based counseling. Chapter 7 also contains seven strengths-based therapy techniques such as the strengths journal, the "What is the truth?" question, the Oracle, the gratitude journal, and so forth.

Part IV of *Culturally Diverse Counseling* consists of 12 chapters on various ethnocultural groups—African Americans (Chapter 8); American Indians and Alaska Natives (Chapter 9); Asian Americans, Native Hawaiians, and Pacific Islanders (Chapter 10); Hispanic and Latino/a

Americans (Chapter 11); Arab and Muslim Americans (Chapter 12); White Americans of European ancestry (Chapter 13); women (Chapter 14); LGBTQ individuals (Chapter 15); individuals with disabilities (Chapter 16); older adults (Chapter 17); immigrants and refugees (Chapter 18); and multiracial/multiethnic individuals (Chapter 19)—as well as one on social class, social justice, and privilege (Chapter 20).

Although the above chapters vary based on the unique historical situations of the ethnocultural groups involved, they also share certain similarities. Each chapter begins with an introduction to the ethnocultural group, followed by a basic demographic description that emphasizes the group's population numbers and its present socioeconomic status. Chapters 8–19 also provide information about the group's worldviews, cultural values, and family dynamics; microaggressions against the group; and the group's strengths, mental health, and counseling issues.

INSTRUCTOR RESOURCE SITE

Visit **study.sagepub.com/jonessmithcdc** to access the password-protected instructor resources that accompany this text.

A **test bank** provides a broad range of options as well as the opportunity to edit any question and/or insert personalized questions to effectively assess students' progress and understanding.

Editable, chapter-specific **PowerPoint® slides** offer complete flexibility for creating a multimedia presentation.

ACKNOWLEDGMENTS

In making my acknowledgments to SAGE Publications and to the people who have supported my efforts in writing this book, it is fitting to point out the symbolism of the three feathers on the cover of this book. Throughout different cultures within the world, feathers have traditionally been used to represent symbolically achievement, courage, and spiritual ascension. Beginning in Greek mythology, Icarus tried to escape prison by attaching feathered wings to his shoulders with wax, which was melted by the sun. The Egyptians believed that feathers were a symbol of the gods.

In American Indian culture, a feather symbolizes trust, honor, strength, wisdom, power, and freedom. For an American Indian to be given a feather denotes that one has been chosen from the rest of the people in the tribe. The most prized feather is that of an eagle because eagles fly so very high in the sky. The American Indian cultural belief is that feathers are meant to be displayed. Once an American Indian is given a feather, he must take care of it and display it in his home, rather than hide it away in a drawer or a closet.

It is noteworthy that the *Culturally Diverse Counseling* book has three feathers of different colors, not only symbolizing the diversity of the world, but also denoting the movement forward of multicultural counseling and theory to a higher and broader plan—one that includes connecting the field with developments in cultural neuroscience, the brain, and culture genes.

On a personal level, the feathers on the *Culturally Diverse Counseling* book represent my years of conducting research on culturally diverse populations. Like the Indian warrior who gets a feather because of some brave deed he has done, this book brings everything that I wanted to do in the field of multicultural counseling full circle for me. When I first began writing about culturally responsive counseling, I mainly wanted to create an awareness of the importance of culture in counseling. I am now in a position to assess where the field of multicultural counseling began with its early scholars and where it is now headed.

My views on multicultural counseling have changed. Culture is not just something that we sprinkle onto our theories of counseling and assessment as if it is some sort of condiment; nor can we tack it onto theories that were not designed to take into account other individuals' culture. What I have learned about culture over the years is that it has a much more profound and meaningful influence than I originally thought. Culture is located in the neural pathways of our brains. Culture is similar to biology in that both engage a coevolutionary process. That is, culture evolves, much in the same way that human beings have evolved in their gene development. When we work with clients, we need to take into consideration how their cultures have evolved and what impact their cultural evolutionary process has had on their clients' thinking and behavior.

Just as American Indian culture maintains that feathers should be displayed rather than tucked away in a drawer, I am hoping that students will prominently display the *Culturally Diverse Counseling* book in their personal libraries, use it to prepare for the licensing examinations, and take it out every now and then for consultation when they are faced with questions about multicultural counseling. If there are any feathers to be gained for writing this book, I hope they will stand for my having moved the field of multicultural counseling forward conceptually into the realm of cultural neuroscience and clinical skill development.

Very few accomplishments in life are ever accomplished through the efforts of one person alone, and such is the case in writing this book. My deepest gratitude goes to Abbie Rickard for her tireless editing of the chapters and her suggestions for improving the book. Thanks also is extended to Nathan Davidson, who worked on the middle drafts of this book, and to Kassie Graves, the acquisition editor who signed me to write this book. Additional thanks are extended to Jennifer Cline, Alissa Nance, Elizabeth Cruz, Emma Newsom, Bennie Clark Allen, and Alexa Turner. I also want to thank my reviewers who made helpful suggestions for each chapter.

Dr. Mary Olufunmilayo Adekson, St. Bonaventure University

Jessica Reno Burkholder, Monmouth University

Tomasina L. Cook, Niagara University

Teah L. Moore, Fort Valley State University

Julie K. West Russo, Trinity International University

John C. Wade, Emporia State University

Dr. Nicole S. Warren, University of Pennsylvania

Cirecie A. West-Olatunji, Xavier University of Louisiana

In addition, I am grateful for the continued encouragement and support of my cousin, Willie Ella Hones-Ladner who throughout the years has shown that she believes in me and in my ability, and my two close friends, Carolyn Phillips and Barbara Hughes, who have stood lovingly by my side. In addition, I wish to thank Mary Joyce Jones-Lawrence, who opened her home to me during my travels and who also supported my books. I deeply appreciate the loving encouragement of my son, Travis Smith, for me to continue writing.

Finally, I thank my God and the Holy Spirit for helping me to write the 20 chapters contained in this book. Without the continual presence of God in my life, this book may have never been written. I know on a personal level that He never leaves me, that I can do all things with His strength, and that whatever happens in my life, He always finds a way to make it turn out for my good.

REFERENCES AND SUGGESTED READING

American Psychiatric Association. (2013a). Cultural Formulation Interview. In *Diagnostic and statistical manual of mental disorders* (5th ed.). Arlington, VA: Author.

American Psychiatric Association. (2013b). *Diagnostic and statistical manual of mental disorders* (5th ed.). Arlington, VA: Author.

American Psychological Association. (2003). Guidelines on multicultural education, training, research, practice, and organization change for psychologists. *American Psychologist, 58*, 377–404.

Amodio, D. M. (2014). A neuroscience of prejudice and stereotyping. *Nature Reviews Neuroscience, 15*(10), 670–682.

Amodio, D. M., Harmon-Jones, E., Devine, P. G., Curtin, J. J., Hartley, S. L., & Covert, A. E. (2004). Neural signals for the detection of unintentional race bias. *Psychological Science, 15*, 88–93.

Amodio, D. M., & Ratner, K. G. (2011). A memory systems model of implicit social cognition. *Current Directions in Psychological Science, 20*, 143–148.

Azar, B. (2010). Your brain on culture. *Monitor on Psychology, 41*(10), 44.

Baron, A. S., & Banaji, M. R. (2006). The development of implicit attitudes: Evidence of race evaluations from ages 6 and 10 and adulthood. *Psychological Science, 17*(1), 54–58.

Bowlby, J. (1988). *A secure base: Parent-child attachment and healthy human development.* New York, NY: Basic Books.

Boyd, R., & Richerson, P. (1983). The cultural transmission of acquired variations: Effects of genetic fitness. *Journal of Theoretical Biology, 100*, 567–596.

Boyd, R., & Richerson, P. (2005). *The origin and evolution of cultures.* New York, NY: Oxford University Press.

Cheung, F. M., van de Vijver, F. J. R., & Leong, F. T. L. (2011). Toward a new approach to the study of personality in culture. *The American Psychologist, 66*(7), 593–603.

Chiao, J. Y., & Blizinsky, K. D. (2010). Culture gene coevolution of individualism-collectivism and the serotonin transporter gene. *Proceedings of the Royal Society of Biological Sciences, 277*(1681), 529–537.

Chiao, J. Y., Harada, T., Komeda, H., Li, Z., Mano, Y., Saito, D., . . . Iidaka, T. (2008). Neural basis of individualistic and collectivistic views of self. *Human Brain Mapping, 30*(9), 2813–2820.

Constantine, M. G. (2001). Multicultural training, theoretical orientation, empathy, and multicultural case conceptualization ability in counselors. *Journal of Mental Health Counseling, 23*(4), 357–372.

Constantine, M. G., & Ladany, N. (2000). Self-report multicultural counseling competence scales: Their relation to social desirability attitudes and multicultural case conceptualization ability. *Journal of Counseling Psychology, 47*(2), 155–164.

Davies, J. (2013). Genes affect culture; culture affects genes. *Psychology Today.* Retrieved from https://www.psychologytoday.com/blog/the-science-imagination/201305/genes-affect-culture-culture-affects-genes

Fredrickson, B. (1998). What good are positive emotions? *Review of General Psychology, 2*, 300–319.

Freeman, J. B., Rule, N. O., Adams, R. B., & Ambady, N. (2009). Culture shapes a mesolimbic response to signals of dominance and subordination that associates with behavior. *NeuroImage, 47*(1), 353–359.

Gelso, C. J., & Woodhouse, S. (2003). Toward a positive psychotherapy: Focus on human strength. In W. B. Walsh (Ed.), *Counseling psychology and human strength* (pp. 171–97). New York, NY: Erlbaum.

Georges, C. M., & Tomlinson-Clarke, S. M. (2015). Integrating positive psychology into counseling psychology doctoral education. *The Counseling Psychologist, 43*(5), 752–788.

Goh, J. O. S., Leshikar, E. D., Sutton, B. P., Tan, C. J., Sim, S. K. Y., Hebrank, A. C., & Park, D. (2010). Culture differences in neural processing of faces and houses in the ventral visual cortex. *Social Cognitive and Affective Neuroscience, 5*(2–3), 227–235.

Goldman, J. G. (2014). How human culture influences our genetics. *BBC Future.* Retrieved from http://www.bbc.com/future/story/20140410-can-we-drive-our-own-evolution

Greenwald, A. G., & Krieger, L. H. (2006). Implicit bias: Scientific foundations. *California Law Review, 94*(4), 945–967.

Greenwald, A. G., Poehlman, T. A., Uhlmann, E. L., & Banaji, M. R. (2009). Understanding and using the implicit association test: III. Meta-Analysis of Predictive Validity. *Journal of Personality and Social Psychology, 97*(1), 17–41.

Harbin, J. M., Gelso, C. J., & Perez Rojas, A. E. (2013). Therapist work with strengths: Development and validation of a measure. *The Counseling Psychologist, 42*, 345–373.

Hedden, S. K., Aron, A., Markus, H. R., & Gabrieli, J. D. E. (2008). Cultural influences on neural substrates of attentional control. *Psychological Science, 19*(1), 12–17.

Hoshmand, L. T. (Ed.). (2006). *Culture, psychotherapy, and counseling: Critical and integrative perspectives.* Thousand Oaks, CA: Sage.

Jones-Smith, E. (2014). *Strengths-based therapy: Connecting theory, practice, and skills.* Thousand Oaks, CA: Sage.

Lampropoulos, G. K. (2001). Integrating psychopathology, positive psychology, and psychotherapy. *American Psychologist, 56*, 87–88.

Lee, D. L., Sheridan, J. J., Rosen, A. D., & Jones, I. (2013). Psychotherapy trainees' multicultural case conceptualization content: Thematic differences across three cases. *Psychotherapy, 50*(2), 206–212.

Llorente, A. M. (Ed.). (2010). *Principles of neuropsychological assessment with Hispanics.* New York, NY: Springer.

Losin, E. R., Dapretto, M., & Iacoboni, M. (2010). Culture and neuroscience: Additive or synergistic? *Social Cognitive and Affective Neuroscience, 5*(2–3), 148–158.

Lu, L., & Gilmour, R. (2004). Culture and conceptions of happiness: Individual oriented and social oriented. *Journal of Happiness Studies, 5*, 269–291.

Owens, R. L., Magyar-Moe, J. L., & Lopez, S. J. (2015). Finding balance via positive psychological assessment and conceptualization: Recommendations for practice. *The Counseling Psychologist, 43*(5), 634–670.

Pedersen, P. B., Lonner, W. J., Draguns, J. G., Trimble, J. E., & Scharrón del Rio, M. R. (Eds.). (2016). *Counseling across cultures* (7th ed.). Thousand Oaks, CA: Sage.

Ponterotto, J. G., Casas, J. M., Suzuki, L. A., & Alexander, C. M. (Eds.). (2010). *Handbook of multicultural counseling* (3rd ed.). Thousand Oaks, CA: Sage.

Priester, P., Jones, J., Jackson-Bailey, C., Jana-Masri, A., Jordan, E., & Metz, A. (2008). An analysis of content and instructional strategies in multicultural counseling courses. *Journal of Multicultural Counseling and Development, 36*(1), 29–39.

Ridley, C. R. (2005). *Overcoming unintentional racism in counseling and therapy* (2nd ed.). Thousand Oaks, CA: Sage.

Saleebey, D. (2002). *The strengths perspective in social work practice.* New York, NY: Longman.

Scales, P. C., Benson, P. L., Leffert, N., & Blyth, D. A. (2000). Contribution of developmental assets to the prediction of thriving among adolescents. *Applied Developmental Science*, *4*, 27–46.

Seligman, M. (2002). *Authentic happiness: New positive psychology to realize your potential for lasting fulfillment.* New York, NY: Free Press.

Seligman, M. E. P., & Csikszentmihalyi, M. (2000). Positive psychology: An introduction. *American Psychologist*, *19*, 5–14.

Seligman, M. E. P., Schulman, P., DeRubeis, R., & Hollon, S. (1999). The prevention of depression and anxiety. *Prevention and Treatment*, *2*. Retrieved from http://journals .apa.org/prevention

Tomlinson-Clarke, S. M., & Georges, C. M. (2014). A commentary on integrating multicultural and strength-based considerations into counseling training and practice. *The Professional Counselor*, *4*, 272–281.

Toporek, R. L. (2012). So what should I actually do? Developing skills for greater multicultural competence. In M. E. Gallardo, C. J. Yeh, J. E. Trimble, & T. Parham (Eds.), *Culturally adaptive counseling skills: Demonstrations of evidence-based practices* (pp. 267–286). Thousand Oaks, CA: Sage.

Weick, A., & Chamberlain, R. (2002). Putting problems in their place: Further explorations in the strengths perspective. In D. Saleebey (Ed.), *The strengths perspective in social work practice* (3rd ed., pp. 95–105). Boston, MA: Allyn & Bacon.

ABOUT THE AUTHOR

Elsie Jones-Smith is a clinical psychologist, a licensed psychologist, a counselor educator, and the president of the Strengths-Based Institute, which provides consultation to schools and organizations dealing with youth experiencing challenges with violence, lack of a sense of purpose, and drug addiction. She is the developer of two theories in psychology: strengths-based therapy (SBT) and ethnic identity development; an article about this theory was featured as a major contribution to psychological research by *The Counseling Psychologist* in 1985. She is a member of the American Academy of Counseling Psychology, and a fellow in two divisions of the American Psychological Association, including Division 17 Counseling Psychology. She holds dual PhDs in clinical psychology and counselor education. She is the author of *Strengths-Based Therapy: Connecting Theory, Practice, and Skills*; *Spotlighting the Strengths of Every Single Student*; and *Nurturing Nonviolent Children*. Previously a professor at Temple University, Michigan State University, and Boston University, she has served on numerous editorial boards.

1 CULTURALLY RESPONSIVE STRENGTHS-BASED THERAPY
The Journey

- *"What lies behind us and what lies before us are tiny matters compared to what lies within us."* —Henry S. Haskins and Nock, 1940.

- *"We developed a multi-faceted prejudice habit-breaking intervention to produce long-term reductions in implicit race bias. The intervention is based on the premise that implicit bias is like a habit that can be reduced through a combination of awareness of implicit bias, concern about the effects of that bias, and the application of strategies to reduce bias."* —Patricia Devine, Devine, et al, 2012.

- *"It's not what you look at that matters, it's what you see."* —Henry David Thoreau, 2012.

CHAPTER OBJECTIVES

1. Contextualize the multicultural movement in the helping professions.

2. List and define several key concepts in cultural counseling.

3. Explain the role of neuroscience in understanding the cognitive processes that lead to conscious and unconscious racial, ethnic, cultural, and gender bias.

4. Evaluate whether there is a new paradigm of implicit and explicit racial bias that will influence multicultural competence and training.

5. Describe the relationship among neuroscience, racial bias, and cultural strengths as an emerging framework for culturally responsive counseling/psychotherapy.

6. Utilize the clinical skills of cultural awareness, cultural humility, and cultural empathy.

7. Understand how your own cultural background and family experiences have influenced your cultural worldview and outlook.

INTRODUCTION: THE JOURNEY TO BECOMING A CULTURALLY RESPONSIVE STRENGTHS-BASED THERAPIST

All life is a journey. From the day we're born, we each embark on a journey called life. There are over 7.3 billion people in the world, yet no two journeys are exactly alike. Our life journeys are fueled by our families, friends, beliefs, values, struggles, challenges, injustices, and dreams. This book is designed to take you, the reader, on a journey where you will encounter yourself as a cultural human being, and where you will come face-to-face with who you are culturally. By taking this journey, you will better position yourself to counsel or provide therapy to those who are culturally different from you. Once you begin, you will realize that cultural competence in counseling others is a lifelong journey.

The journey toward gaining cultural competence begins with our awareness of culture and the impact it has on our own lives as well as the lives of others. Centuries ago, Socrates said that the unexamined life is not worth living. One of the critical factors we must examine is our culture and the effect it has had, not only on our own lives but also on the lives of those whom we seek to counsel. For instance, I have become a richer person as I have considered my many influences and the varied tapestry that constitutes my life. I am who I am because I was dipped in different cultural waters, with different people having various skin colors, hair textures, languages, values, and geographic places of origin. Each day I live out my tripartite level of being—that is, I know on a deep level three facts: I am like all other people (universal level of experience), I am like some other people (cultural and ethnic level of being), and I am like no other person in the world (unique individual level of experience). This book places an emphasis upon culture, cultural strengths, and human strengths. Culture encompasses virtually all that we believe, value, and do. We are first and foremost cultural beings.

THE PROFOUND INFLUENCE OF CULTURE

Culture is the force that humanizes each one of us; it plays a key role in determining who we are; what we think; what we eat; the music that we listen to; what we believe about men, women, and the family; and how we respond to our environment. Culture is probably one of the most powerful forces in the world—far more powerful than guns or airplanes carrying bombs. In fact, culture is what exists long after the bombing is over. Each person is born into a culture that shapes and influences how he or she views the world—what researchers have called a **worldview** (Cheung, van de Vijver, & Leong, 2011; Jones-Smith, 2014; McAuliffe & Associates, 2013; Sue & Sue, 2013). Culture has assumed a pivotal role in making me who I am and in making you who you are.

The influence of culture is so profound that it affects us even before our actual birth. From the time of one's birth (and possibly even during stages of development in the womb), the brain is organized to prefer or to lean toward the culture of the mother. A mother's womb is a child's first cultural experience. In the womb, a baby is exposed to cultural food; sounds of living, including music; and the ebb and flow of culture as the mother experiences it. Even the birth process is influenced by the culture of the people who attend to the mother. Certain cultural responses are made to signal the birth of a child (Rosenberg & Trevathan, 2003).

Culture may be defined as the sum of intergenerationally transmitted lifestyles, behavior patterns, and products of a people that involve their language, music, art, artifacts, beliefs, values, history, eating preferences, customs, and social rules (Harper & McFadden, 2003). People learn their cultures through a process of enculturation; that is, they learn skills needed to function in a particular society. The family and the community are the major transmitters of culture.

The cultural rules each ethnic group adopts are not universally or consistently obeyed; yet, all members recognize them, and individuals usually live by limiting the range within patterns of communication, beliefs, and social behavior found in cultures. Each culture produces (a) shared ways of behaving among group members, (b) a basic motivational structure for behavior, and (c) psychological needs within its members. Culture is an inevitable silent partner in counseling. Counseling is a culture-specific human invention. Each form of counseling reflects the culture that produces it. Culture guides our behavior and provides the framework for observing and identifying problems. Culture also teaches people problem-solving behaviors.

Cultural Reflections

What is the cultural relevance of your name?

What values, beliefs, and attitudes do you subscribe to that are consistent with the dominant culture?

Studies have revealed that culture influences the meaning that individuals give to their symptoms and to the cause and implications of the personal difficulties they experience in life (Andrade, 2017; Gopalakrishnan & Babacan, 2015; Huang & Zane, 2016). For example, in Italian and Jewish families, members may use emotional expressiveness to share personal suffering, while those from Scandinavian, Asian, and American Indian backgrounds may be inclined to withdraw and not discuss their feelings. The Euro American worldview that dominates counseling subscribes to the values of rugged individualism, competition, and individuals' mastery over nature (Katz, 1985).

OUR BRAINS ARE CULTURALLY CONNECTED

Culture's profound influence has been shown in recent studies that demonstrate that culture affects one's biology in that it organizes one's brain rather than the other way around. For instance, a study by Zhu, Zhang, Fan, and Han (2007) found that American brains function differently when they consider traits of themselves versus traits of others, while Chinese brains function the same whether considering their own traits or the traits of others. This study supports behavioral studies that have reported that people from collectivist cultures, such as China, think of themselves as being connected to others in the community, while Americans adhere to a strong sense of individuality.

Culture shapes a person's biology, including his or her perceptual field and reward system. For instance, one study used functional magnetic resonance imaging (fMRI) to measure brain activity in American and Japanese study participants while viewing silhouettes of people in both dominant and submissive poses (Freeman, Rule, Adams, & Ambady, 2009). The researchers theorized that they would be able to see the cultural distinction between American and Japanese participants in the manner the brain responds to visual input. When Americans viewed dominant silhouettes, the reward circuitry fired in the brain's limbic system; however, there was no such firing when they viewed submissive silhouettes. The opposite effect was observed among Japanese participants. The researchers concluded that the brain's response reflects the values of the **dominant culture**, even when viewing the same stimulus. Counselors and therapists need to become aware that culture affects the reward systems in our brains.

How we learn is another brain activity, and, it too, is based on a person's cultural frame of reference. When the brain encounters information during therapy, it is searching for and making connections to what is personally relevant and meaningful. As such, culture affects what one gives attention to during therapy. Culturally relevant therapy helps clients to make connections in the brain, and it promotes the process of therapeutic alliance, therapy engagement, and neuroplasticity (Jones-Smith, 2014).

AFFIRMING EACH PERSON'S IMPORTANCE

This book affirms the importance of each person and every ethnic and cultural background— White Americans, African Americans, Asian Americans, Latino Americans, and members of other ethnic minority groups—as well as males and females, members of the LGBTQ community, the disabled, the young, and the old. Each person is important because together we form the one and only race in this world, and that is the human race. We are all part of our individual families, as well as the family of human beings.

Some students find it difficult to untangle the various strands of their cultural identity. They say, "I have different cultural groups in my family, and I'm not really attached to any specific cultural group. On my mother's side, I'm Italian and Irish, and on my father's side, there is a German background. We don't celebrate any of these cultures at home. I guess I am just an American. I have an American culture—whatever that means." This book helps students to untangle their cultural history and to come to terms with what it means to say, "I have an American culture." What does it really mean to be a White American, an African American, a Latino/Hispanic American, an Asian American, an American Indian, a Muslim or Arab American, a member of the LGBTQ community, a person with a disability, a new immigrant or a refugee, an older person, and so forth? Can we really walk in another person's shoes? Or, are we predisposed not to want to walk in another person's shoes because doing so is uncomfortable? For counselors and therapists, it is important to bring such thoughts to the surface and deal constructively with them so that we can sincerely focus on the client's strengths within the context of cultural and other characteristics that make a person who he or she is.

THE INTEGRATION OF CULTURALLY RESPONSIVE AND STRENGTHS-BASED THERAPY

Most members of the helping professions—counseling, psychology, and social work—have called for culturally responsive ways of working with people from diverse cultural backgrounds (Hoshmand, 2006; Pedersen, Lonner, Draguns, Trimble, & Scharrón del Rio, 2016; Ponterotto, Casas, Suzuki, & Alexander, 2010; Ridley, 2005; Saleebey, 2002). This book integrates two approaches to psychotherapy: (1) culturally responsive therapy and (2) strengths-based therapy (Saleebey, 2008; Seligman, 1998; Smith, 2006). **Culturally responsive therapy** traces its roots to the multicultural movement during the early 1970s, whereas **strengths-based therapy** is founded on concepts from the strengths perspective in social work, as well as from positive psychology (Jones-Smith, 2014).

Culturally Responsive Therapy: A Beginning Definition

Culturally responsive therapy refers to a counseling relationship in which a client and a therapist are of different ethnicities, cultures, races, and backgrounds and the therapist (1) evidences awareness of the significance of both his and the client's cultural stories, (2) has specific knowledge of the client's culture, and (3) uses culturally appropriate clinical skills in working with the client. The culturally responsive therapist sees clients' descriptions of their life stories as different ways of constructing meaning out of their life experiences. Culturally responsive therapy can be conducted using a variety of theoretical approaches, such as cognitive behavior therapy, person-centered therapy, or psychodynamic therapy. In contrast, culturally responsive strengths-based therapy (CR-SBT) uses a human strengths framework to conduct therapy, and it is the major theoretical framework presented in this book. CR-SBT should be designed to help people answer the question: How can I use my strengths to achieve my goals, to find happiness in life, and to feel a sense of purpose? This theoretical approach is based on the premise that what we focus on in life and in therapy materializes in our lives. Emphasizing a person's strengths provides a positive source of motivation to deal with his or her life issues. An important theme is that therapy should create a strengths-building environment for clients. Case studies using CR-SBT are provided in each of the chapters that discuss specific culturally diverse groups.

Organization of Chapter 1

Chapter 1 is organized in three basic parts. Part 1 provides a brief history and overview of the multicultural movement in counseling and psychology. It examines multicultural competencies, ethics and multiculturalism, evidence-based multicultural research, and the social justice movement. Part 2 explores cultural competence and the cultural competence continuum. It contains several awareness skill development exercises. Part 3 deals with barriers to a counselor's cultural competence. Included in this part of the chapter are discussions of implicit and explicit racial and gender/sexual orientation bias.

BRIEF HISTORY AND OVERVIEW OF THE MULTICULTURAL MOVEMENT

Multiculturalism can be defined as a school of thought or philosophy that recognizes and values the various contributions of multiple cultures to a nation's life (Anderson & Middleton, 2018). The prevailing view is that because all cultures make valuable contributions to the society, there is no one standard cultural norm. In the context of counseling and therapy, multiculturalism refers to clinicians' efforts to integrate and embrace the cultural differences of their clients, while also acknowledging the influence of their own culture on how they perceive and respond to clients (Ratts & Pedersen, 2015). More specifically, multiculturalism is defined as the recognition and inclusion of relevant cultural factors, such as client and counselor worldviews, ethnicity/race, gender, **sexual orientation**, religion, and **social justice**, during the process of providing counseling services, and it has become a global movement. The doctrine of multiculturalism is built on **cultural relativism**, the perspective that behavior in one culture should not be judged by the standards of another. Cultural relativism posits that all cultures have equal intrinsic value, are equally entitled to respect, and should be appreciated for their differences.

The **multicultural counseling** movement can be traced to several factors, including the global trend in which large numbers of people of color migrate from their native lands to Europe and the United States (Gallardo, 2012; Ridley, Mollen, & Shannon, 2011). As a consequence of many civil wars within countries, as well as wars between countries—World War II, the Korean War, the Vietnam War, and much later the Gulf Coast, Iraq, and Afghanistan Wars—most countries in the world are multicultural in terms of religion, culture, and/or color/race. For instance, Iceland has an African and an Asian population. Most of what was previously predominantly White Christian Europe now has significant African, Asian, and Middle Eastern populations and many adherents of religions other than Christianity. At the same time, many countries in the developing world have multiple traditional cultures. India, for example, has 23 official languages and more than 1,000 other languages spoken by various ethnic groups within the country. According to some researchers, this worldwide multicultural phenomenon is leading to a paradigm shift across many different academic disciplines (Gallardo, 2012; Ridley et al., 2011).

This is no less true in the fields of counseling and psychology. Both clients and therapists have come to recognize that culture is often a "silent intruder" in the therapeutic relationship. Clients' cultural beliefs about the causes and solutions for their mental health issues affect what they believe to constitute appropriate treatment for the issues they bring to therapy (Anderson & Middleton, 2018). Traditional therapeutic approaches to assessment might be inappropriate and even harmful when applied to culturally diverse clients. Counselors and therapists can no longer ethically treat clients without understanding the cultural influences in the therapeutic relationship. Multicultural counseling is considered socially constructive because it acknowledges each culture's perspective within the therapeutic process (Anderson & Middleton, 2018).

The multicultural counseling movement has experienced three phases. Phase 1 focused primarily on ethnic/racial minority groups. Phase 2 broadened the scope of multiculturalism to include other groups, such as gays, lesbians, women, individuals with disabilities, and so forth. This broadening of the field of multiculturalism prompted Paul Pedersen (1991) to describe multiculturalism as a fourth force in counseling. Phase 3, which is the current phase, has focused on multicultural counseling competencies and on providing evidence-based multicultural research (Harris, 2012). The three phases of the multicultural movement are described in more detail below.

Phase 1 can in some respects be traced to the civil rights movement of the 1960s and the women's movement of the 1970s. Harper (2003) has labeled the 1960s as the pioneering years of the multicultural movement in counseling. The first phase of the multicultural movement was inspired primarily by researchers of color who asserted that the theories of counseling and psychotherapy were Eurocentric and lacked consideration of their ethnocultural groups' life circumstances and cultural values (Helms, 1989, 1990; Smith, 1985, 1991; Sue, 1972).

The 1970s brought about a number of new courses on counseling ethnic minorities, as well as an increase in the number of published articles on ethnicity and culture. This era also marked the beginning of research on ethnic/racial identity development with William Cross's (1971) model of Black identity development. During the 1970s, the dominant terminology used to describe members of ethnic minority groups was "culturally different"; counseling culturally different clients was referred to as "cross-cultural counseling."

Phase 2 took place during the 1980s. It was characterized by a push for inclusiveness for other cultural groups, including women, LGBTQ individuals, people with disabilities, and others. In his authoritative account of the multicultural movement, Frederick Harper (2003) wrote:

The early 1980s marked an increasing use of culture-characterizing terms as an attempt to be more inclusive of special populations, gender, and various identity groups in addition to non-White ethnic minorities. The interest in cross-cultural counseling got a push from Pedersen and colleagues' revised edition of *Counseling Across Cultures* (Pedersen, Draguns, Lonner, & Trimble, 1981) and a special issue of *The Counseling Psychologist* on "Cross-Cultural Counseling" (Elsie Jones-Smith & Melba Vasquez, 1985). (p. 8)

Phase 3, the current phase, began in the 1990s. It emphasizes multicultural competencies together with evidenced-based research. The Association for Multicultural Counseling and Development (AMCD) approved 31 multicultural competencies in 1991. In addition to these multicultural competencies, researchers began to focus on the development and testing of cultural assessment inventories and multicultural competence instruments (Ibrahim & Owen, 1994; Ponterotto, Casas, Suzuki, & Alexander, 2010). The 1990s also witnessed a burgeoning of textbooks on culture and diversity. According to Harper (2003),

> This increasing interest in and prevalence of books on the topic of "culture and diversity" was apparently influenced by (1) the increasing number of required "culture and diversity" courses in counselor preparation programs throughout the country, (2) multicultural counseling requirements of credentialing groups for counseling program accreditation and counselor certification, and (3) the developing professional demands for multicultural competence, including AMCD's 31 competencies for multicultural counselors that were approved in 1991 (Sue, Arredondo, & McDavis, 1992). (p. 9)

In addition, the third phase of the multicultural movement has involved efforts to respond to evidence-based studies. Initially, discussions of evidence-based practice focused on providing evidence for the treatment efficacy for specific disorders. The essential question being asked was: What kind of psychological treatment works best for specific mental disorders? The multicultural movement has continued to develop and change, suggesting in some respects that all theories of psychotherapy should be examined for multicultural contributions and limitations (Helms & Richardson, 1997).

MASTERING THE MULTICULTURAL COUNSELING COMPETENCIES

In April 1991, the AMCD approved a paper outlining the need and rationale for a multicultural perspective in counseling. Subsequently, this professional association proposed 31 **multicultural competencies**. These competencies were outlined in three broad categories: (1) counselor awareness of his or her own cultural values and beliefs, (2) counselor awareness of clients' worldviews, and (3) counselor learning of appropriate intervention strategies. Within each of these three categories, the AMCD further delineated attitudes and beliefs, knowledge, and skills (Arredondo et al., 1996).

Moreover, the American Counseling Association took an early stance on endorsing multicultural competencies (Arredondo et al., 1996; Sue et al., 1992). This professional organization has also adopted social justice advocacy competencies (Lewis, Arnold, House, & Toporek, 2003). Both of these professional organizations continue to have a profound influence on the way mental health professionals conceptualize their roles with regard to clients from diverse backgrounds. They challenge therapists to analyze carefully how best to respond to clients from cultural backgrounds that differ from their backgrounds.

Since the 1990s, a number of professional organizations and accrediting bodies have published or endorsed what they consider culturally responsive clinical practice. In 2003, the American Psychological Association (APA) published the *Guidelines on Multicultural Education,*

Training, Research, Practice, and Organizational Change for Psychologists as a policy statement. The policy contained six guidelines:

> ***Guideline 1:*** "Psychologists are encouraged to recognize that, as cultural beings, they may hold attitudes and beliefs that can detrimentally influence their perceptions of and interactions with individuals who are ethnically and racially different from themselves" (p. 382).

> ***Guideline 2:*** "Psychologists are encouraged to recognize the importance of multicultural sensitivity/responsiveness to, knowledge of, and understanding about ethnically and racially different individuals" (p. 385).

> ***Guideline 3:*** As educators, psychologists are encouraged to employ the constructs of multiculturalism and diversity in psychological education" (p. 386).

> ***Guideline 4:*** Culturally sensitive psychological researchers are encouraged to recognize the importance of conducting culture-centered and ethical psychological research among persons from ethnic, linguistic, and racial minority backgrounds" (p. 388).

> ***Guideline 5:*** "Psychologists are encouraged to apply culturally appropriate skills in clinical and other applied psychological practices" (p. 390).

> ***Guideline 6:*** "Psychologists are encouraged to use organizational change processes to support culturally informed organization (policy) development and practices" (p. 393).

Also in 2003, the AMCD published an updated version of its Multicultural Counseling Competencies (Roysircar, Arredondo, Fuertes, Ponterotto, & Toporek, 2003). In 2016, the Council for Accreditation of Counseling and Related Educational Programs (CACREP) included the centrality of "social and cultural diversity" in its curriculum standards for counseling programs.

Not all counseling or mental health professionals are in favor of the multicultural competencies. Weinrach and Thomas (2004) and Thomas and Weinrach (2004) criticized the multicultural competencies on the grounds that they focused primarily on four ethnic groups: African, Asian, Hispanic, and American Indian. They expressed concern that definitions of *multiculturalism* and *diversity*, as well as other terms used throughout the competencies, were imprecise and contradictory. In addition, these researchers maintained that the competencies seemed to stereotype clients by suggesting that those who were members of a given group should be treated as examples of that group rather than as individuals.

For the most part, however, objections to the multicultural guidelines have gone by the wayside. The APA has made it clear that one must abide by the guidelines to provide good clinical practice and that failure to do so might result in ethical actions being taken against a psychologist.

The basic competencies for culturally responsive counseling can be grouped into three broad categories: (1) awareness, (2) attitudes, and (3) skills (Sue et al., 1992). Culturally responsive counselors have:

- ***Awareness of their own cultural values and biases.*** They must be aware of the impact of their culture on their values, choices, manners, and privileges. They should understand the processes involving discrimination and stereotyping and exhibit a desire to seek additional training where diversity issues are concerned. They are aware of how their own cultural background, experiences, values, and biases affect the counseling relationship and service delivery. They are comfortable with the cultural and other differences that exist between themselves and their clients.

Cultural Reflections

How valuable do you think the multicultural competencies and standards are for your own practice and for the clinical practice of others?

Should counselor trainees be evaluated on their ability to enact the multicultural guidelines?

- *Knowledge of their clients' worldviews.* They must demonstrate a reasonable level of multicultural literacy or knowledge of different ethnic and cultural groups' worldviews involving such areas as race, ethnicity, class, gender, sexual orientation, disability, and religion. They have specific knowledge about their clients' cultural membership group.

- *Competence in implementing clinical intervention strategies that are culturally appropriate for their clients.* They are capable of using both individual and system intervention techniques for the benefit of their clients.

ETHICAL ISSUES AND MULTICULTURALISM

Counselors face a number of ethical issues when working with culturally different clients. Increasingly, multicultural counseling standards, ethical codes, guidelines, and competencies now pervade the counseling and helping profession. Currently, CACREP requires that counseling programs include "social and cultural issues" in their curricula. To meet CACREP's

---

MULTICULTURAL COUNSELING COMPETENCIES: COUNSELORS' AWARENESS OF THEIR ASSUMPTIONS, VALUES, ATTITUDES, AND BIASES

Awareness Competencies

Culturally competent counselors:

1. Move from being culturally unaware to being aware of and sensitive to their cultural heritage, and to being respectful of the cultural differences of their clients.

2. Are aware of their own cultural values and how such values may enter the counseling relationship with culturally diverse clients.

3. Are comfortable with race, gender, sexual orientation, beliefs, and other cultural differences that exist between themselves and their clients.

4. Are aware of cultural issues that may suggest referral of clients to members of their own cultural group or other counselors in general.

5. Are aware of their own racist, sexist, heterosexist, and other intolerant attitudes and how these may intrude in the counseling relationship.

Knowledge Competencies

Culturally competent counselors:

1. Are knowledgeable and informed about a variety of culturally diverse groups, especially those groups with which they work.

2. Are knowledgeable about the sociopolitical system in their country, and understand how oppression, racism, discrimination, and stereotyping affect their clients' psychological, political, and economic functioning.

3. Possess specific knowledge related to the generic characteristics of counseling and psychotherapy.

4. Are knowledgeable about how institutional barriers may hinder or thwart culturally diverse clients from using mental health services.

Cultural Competence Skills

Culturally competent counselors:

1. Are comfortable using a wide variety of verbal and nonverbal counseling responses.

2. Communicate accurately and appropriately with their clients.

3. Use institutional intervention skills to help their clients become more effective.

4. Understand and anticipate the effect of their counseling styles and limitations on culturally diverse clients.

5. Are not restricted by conventional counseling methods in that they use helping roles that are characterized by an active systemic and social justice focus.

Source: Adapted from Sue, D. W., Arredondo, P., & McDavis, R. J. (1992). Multicultural competencies/standards: A call to the profession. *Journal of Counseling and Development, 70*(4), 477–486.

requirement, counselor training programs disperse multicultural perspectives throughout their counseling program and offer separate coursework in multicultural counseling.

Professional associations have also played significant roles in the movement toward multiculturalism. The American Counseling Association (2005) presents diversity as a central issue in the Preamble to its *Code of Ethics*: "Association members recognize diversity and embrace a cross-cultural approach in support of the worth, dignity, potential, and uniqueness of people within their social and cultural contexts" (p. 3). The ACA *Code of Ethics* also states that mental health counselors "will actively attempt to understand the diverse cultural backgrounds of the clients with whom they work" (p. 4).

The American Psychological Association has recently updated its multicultural guidelines to "Multicultural Guidelines: An Ecological Approach to Context, Identity, and Intersectionality" (2017). APA's 2017 multicultural guidelines differ from the earlier ones cited in this chapter in that they emphasize intersectionality, lifelong development of an **ethnic identity**, and strengths-based therapy for culturally diverse clients. These guidelines will expire as APA policy in 10 years (2027). The following paraphrases APA's 10 new multicultural guidelines:

Guideline 1: Psychologists understand the fluid nature of cultural, racial, ethnic, and individual identity of people and that one's identity undergoes a process of intersectionality, meaning that it is affected by a multiplicity of social, political, and ecological environments.

Guideline 2: Psychologists recognize that people are cultural beings and that their cultural backgrounds influence their perceptions and interactions with clients. They endeavor to move beyond their own stereotypes and prejudices of individuals from different cultures.

Guideline 3: Psychologists understand the significance of language and communication and how their own language affects their relationships with clients and others.

Guideline 4: Psychologists take an ecological perspective when working with clients in that they take into consideration the impact of social and physical environments on the lives of their clients and students.

Guideline 5: Psychologists understand the historical and current implications of power, privilege, and oppression on the lives of their clients and on the communities from which they come. They address as best they can institutional barriers, disproportionalities, and disparities of law enforcement and mental health delivery systems, as well as other systems to promote human justice and access to equitable mental health services.

Guideline 6: Psychologists endeavor to promote culturally responsive interventions within and across systems in the areas of prevention, early intervention, and recovery.

Guideline 7: Psychologists examine and explore the profession's assumptions about human behavior and mental health on both a national and an international level to assess cultural bias and misconceptions about individuals from different cultures.

Guideline 8: Psychologists understand that cultural, racial, or ethnic identity is a lifelong process that evolves as people age and interact with others and their environment.

Guideline 9: Psychologists endeavor to conduct culturally responsive research, teaching, assessment, diagnosis, and consultation and they respond to the first four levels of the multicultural guidelines.

Guideline 10: Psychologists seek to take a strengths-based approach when working with clients, families, groups, communities, and organizations that endeavor to build resilience and to mitigate or decrease trauma within the sociocultural context.

CASE VIGNETTE 1.1

JIM HUANG: AN UNINTENDED ETHICAL VIOLATION

Dr. Becker was surprised to hear that one of his students, Jim Huang, had filed a complaint against him with the dean of arts and sciences. Dr. Becker had received several outstanding teaching awards within the university, and the complaint now facing him threatened his very academic reputation, as well as his chairman position in the counseling psychology department. The student complaint alleged that Dr. Becker had lowered Jim Huang's grade in the counseling seminar because he refused to share personal information about his upbringing and his family. Jim said he felt pressured to self-disclose in order to get along with the other students in his class, who were all White. The students complained that they had revealed personal information about themselves while Jim sat silently listening. They did not feel as if he wanted to be in the class, and they challenged whether he should even be in the master's level counseling psychology program. The class was a required one that Dr. Becker had taught for the past seven years, and it was required for completion of the master's level counseling psychology degree.

The student said he had indicated to Dr. Becker that his cultural background made him hesitant about revealing personal information about himself, his upbringing, and his family. He indicated that his clients would not require him to reveal such information and that he intended to work in a Veterans Administration hospital with elderly clients who suffered from depression, dementia, and/or the late stages of alcoholism. He filed the complaint because Dr. Becker said that it would be disruptive to the class if he did not self-disclose as did the other students.

The complaint was forwarded to an ethics committee within the school of arts and sciences. The committee ruled in favor of the student, but noted that the ethical infraction was not intentional. The ethics committee held that there was insufficient notice or warning to the student that a high degree of self-disclosure would be required in the course. The description of the seminar in the course catalog and the professor's own course syllabus did not mention that students would be required to disclose personal information about themselves in front of the class. If the requirement of high student self-disclosure had been mentioned in either of these documents, the committee would have ruled in favor of Dr. Becker.

The ethics committee held that Jim Huang be required to write a paper or provide evidence of his mastery of the subject matter for the course. The committee also held that the counseling psychology department had a heavy emphasis on multiculturalism and that it should have been sensitive to the student's cultural background. The course was heavily directed toward White American students instead of students from culturally diverse backgrounds.

Discussion Questions

1. To what extent should all students within a counseling psychology program be required to self-disclose as part of the course requirement?

2. Do you find it contradictory that the counseling program emphasized multiculturalism, all the while requiring students to respond in a manner that reflected White American response patterns?

3. To what extent should the professor modify his course so that it is responsive to the needs of different cultures?

4. Do many counseling courses reflect the value orientations of White American culture?

5. If you were on the ethics committee, how would you have voted, and why?

6. Do you think that Jim should have filed the complaint against Dr. Becker? Explain.

APA maintains that psychologists have an ethical obligation to develop cross-cultural competencies when working with clients who are culturally different from themselves. The counselor's role is to help clients to deal with life challenges that are consistent with the clients' worldviews.

It is unethical for clinicians to provide therapeutic services to culturally diverse clients when they are not competent to work with such clients (Fouad et al., 2009; Gallardo, Johnson, Parham, & Carter, 2009; Herlihy & Corey, 2015).

Ethical practice requires that clinicians develop multicultural competencies in testing and assessment. Diagnosis using the *DSM-5* (American Psychiatric Association, 2013) may present major ethical problems when working with some culturally diverse clients if clinicians do not have the requisite multicultural competencies. Corey, Corey, and Callahan (2011) maintain that a comprehensive code of ethics needs to respect the values of all cultures. They point out that "when counselors are overly self-conscious about their ability to work with diverse client populations, they may become too analytical about what they say and do during counseling. Counselors who are afraid to face the differences between themselves and their clients, who refuse to accept the reality of these differences, who perceive such differences as problematic or are uncomfortable with working out these differences are likely to fail" (p. 136).

THE EVIDENCE-BASED MOVEMENT IN MULTICULTURAL COUNSELING

A major criticism of multicultural counseling approaches is that they are not evidence-based. Gradually, however, evidence-based practice (EBP) has been broadened to include "understanding the influence of individual and cultural differences on treatment" and the need to take into account client "characteristics, culture, and preferences in assessment, treatment plans and therapeutic outcome" (American Psychological Association, Presidential Task Force on Evidence-Based Practice, 2006). In an article asserting that EBPs with ethnic minorities had come of age, Morales and Norcross (2010) stated, "Multiculturalism without strong research risks becoming an empty political value, and EBT [evidence-based training] without cultural sensitivity risks irrelevancy" (p. 283).

Despite these concerns, studies of mental health treatment efficacy with members of ethnic minority groups have provided evidence that EBPs may be successful within diverse populations (National Alliance on Mental Illness [NAMI], 2008). A study by Miranda et al. (2005) reported that evidence-based care may translate to both African American and Latino populations as effectively as it does to White American populations. Kohn, Oden, Munoz, Robinson, and Leavitt (2002) found that EBPs that used culture-specific issues and concerns during the delivery of cognitive behavioral therapy for African American women with depression showed greater decreases in symptoms than did similar women who were treated with the culturally unadapted cognitive behavioral therapy. Significant data are not yet available for the effect of EBPs with Asian American or American Indian populations.

A critical challenge in EBP studies is the adequate sampling of ethnic/racial populations; however, this situation appears to be improving. Higa and Chorpita (2007) gathered information from 26 efficacy trials of cognitive behavioral therapy, and deemed this EBP to be a "best support" treatment of anxious or avoidant behavior problems among Asian, African American, Caucasian, Hindu, Latino, Indonesian Dutch, and multiethnic youth populations (NAMI, 2008).

This book adopts the view that multicultural counseling will continue to change over the years, that it will become more evidence-based, and that it will combine its emphasis with other theoretical approaches, such as cognitive behavioral theory (Comas-Díaz, 2006; Garrett et al., 2011; Geva & Weiner, 2015).

BEGINNING THE CULTURAL COMPETENCY JOURNEY

Cultural competence refers to a clinician's ability to demonstrate cultural awareness, knowledge, and skills in working therapeutically, effectively, with a client (Sue, Zane, Nagayama, Hall, & Berger, 2009). Culturally competent clinicians are aware of their own cultural identities, assumptions, and biases toward other cultural groups. To achieve cultural competence in clinical practice, clinicians should begin by exploring their own cultural heritage, and examining how it influences their perceptions of normality, abnormality, mental health, and the therapy process (Kirmayer, 2012).

What is the significance of a counselor's cultural competence for working with clients? Therapists who are aware of their own cultural heritage are more inclined to explore how culture affects their client–counselor relationship (Sue et al., 2009). Lack of cultural awareness may lead to therapists' discounting or underestimating the influence of their own cultural beliefs, values, and attitudes on their diagnostic impressions of clients (Tseng & Streltzer, 2004). When counselors lack cultural awareness, they are inclined to use their own cultural experiences as a template to judge clients and to evaluate their presenting problems. In addition, they may be oblivious to the cultural uniqueness of their clients, as well as how their clients' cultural background interacts with their presenting problem (Anderson & Middleton, 2018; Geva & Weiner, 2015).

Culturally competent counselors and therapists identify culturally specific and universal domains of helping. They do not view the Eurocentric healing standards as normative in evaluating their culturally diverse clients, and they do not use inappropriately the Eurocentric approach to therapy on their culturally diverse clients because such actions may result in the cultural oppression of their clients (Kirmayer, 2012). They understand that different cultures may have different standards for what constitutes mental health and healing practices. While some clients might respond best to culturally specific strategies, others do better when the emphasis is on universal issues of human functioning (Velez, Moradi, & DeBlaere, 2015). Moreover, culturally competent counselors and therapists familiarize themselves with the multicultural competencies that have been developed for their respective profession.

LEVELS OF COUNSELOR COMPETENCY DEVELOPMENT

Assuming that a clinician's cultural identity and cultural competence develop over a period of time, what might be some common stages through which individuals pass? T. Cross, Bazron, Dennis, and Isaacs (1989) have identified six stages that a person experiences as he or she moves toward gaining cultural competence. Although their model was originally designed for organizations, it has also been used for clinicians who work with individual clients.

1. **Cultural Destructiveness:** This is the lowest level of cultural competency, and is characterized by policies and practices that are destructive to cultures and individuals. One extreme example of the cultural destructiveness continuum is cultural genocide, or the purposeful destruction of a culture.

2. **Cultural Incapacity:** Although a therapist might not purposely act to be culturally destructive, he or she may lack the ability to help culturally diverse clients. The therapist delivers counseling service from an extremely biased perspective. He or she may believe in the racial superiority of the dominant group in society and may assume a paternal attitude toward "lesser races." The therapist operates within a biased therapy system, with a paternal attitude toward other groups. He or she may fear other groups and cultures or participate in discriminatory practices, thereby lowering expectations or devaluing such groups.

3. **Cultural Blindness:** Therapists and agencies operate with the express purpose of being unbiased; they may even post on their doors a philosophy of such. Culturally blind therapists and agencies are characterized by the belief that counseling approaches used by the dominant culture are universal and without bias. Although the cultural blindness philosophy appears to be a well-intentioned philosophy, in actuality it represents a Eurocentric and ethnocentric approach.

4. **Cultural Pre-competence:** This approach is characterized by acceptance and respect for cultural difference, and by continual self-assessment regarding culture. The therapist

might make a variety of cultural adaptations to therapy models in order to better serve the needs of culturally diverse clients. The agency makes a deliberate attempt to hire unbiased employees, and agencies may actively seek advice and consultation from the culturally diverse communities representing the clients their agency serves. The therapist understands his or her own weaknesses in working with people from other cultures, and may engage in culturally responsive training.

5. **Cultural Competence:** The therapist and agency accepts and respects cultural differences. The therapist has acquired culturally relevant intervention skills and adopts a policy of being open and sensitive to other cultures. The therapist actively engages in expanding his or her cultural knowledge.

6. **Cultural Proficiency:** The therapist holds a wide range of cultures in high esteem. He or she obtains training of new counseling approaches for working with culturally diverse clients. He or she becomes an advocate for cultural competency at the individual and agency level.

CLINICAL SKILL DEVELOPMENT: CULTURAL AWARENESS AND KNOWLEDGE

To achieve cultural competence, a counselor should have reached a level of proficiency with regard to (1) cultural awareness and (2) cultural knowledge. The clinical skill of cultural awareness is examined, and a chart is provided for this skill (Table 1.1).

Therapist **cultural awareness** is crucial for effective counseling. Counselors who are aware of their own cultural backgrounds tend to acknowledge and explore how culture affects their client–counselor relationships. A counselor who is culturally aware does not ignore effects of obvious issues involving race, gender, and culture on the therapeutic relationship. Cultural awareness works to prevent clinicians from using their own culture as the template from which they view clients' culture. With cultural awareness, clinicians are more in tune with how their own beliefs, experiences, and biases affect their definitions of what constitutes normal and abnormal behavior. Because of its critical role during therapy, cultural awareness is the first step toward becoming a culturally competent counselor.

> ### Cultural Reflections
>
> *Cultural awareness means understanding what you feel about members of cultural groups who are different from you.*
>
> *What are the values of the cultural group that has had the most influence on your life?*
>
> *How does your family view itself as similar to or different from other cultural groups?*

Cultural Congruence and Cultural Incongruence

The culturally responsive therapist is aware of the client's degree of cultural congruence, cultural knowledge, and self-knowledge. **Cultural congruence** is defined as a positive relationship between an individual's cultural identity and his or her behavior and lifestyle. Conversely, **cultural incongruence** refers to the inconsistencies between how a person lives and his or her cultural identification. Individuals who display a high degree of cultural incongruence may be predisposed to or vulnerable to mild, moderate, or severe mental disturbance (Parham, 2012). For instance, Julio is a second-generation Mexican American who feels a sense of cultural incongruence because he does not subscribe to the Latino cultural value of machismo. A middle- or upper-class African American might feel a sense of cultural incongruence if he or she does not subscribe to the values of African American culture or if he or she "speaks like a White person." A White American who grew up in a predominantly Black or Latino neighborhood and feels close associations with one of those cultures might also feel a lack of cultural congruence.

Table 1.1 lists the components of the clinical skill of cultural awareness in greater detail.

TABLE 1.1 ■ Components of the Clinical Skill of Cultural Awareness

Component 1: The clinician has taken steps to learn about his or her own culture. Before entering into a counseling relationship, the clinician must become aware of his or her cultural and historical background. A person who recognizes the different influences on his or her cultural background is better able to recognize the different influences in a client's background.

Component 2: The clinician understands his or her own personal worldview and is aware of how his or her cultural background might affect the clinical relationship.

Component 3: The clinician appreciates his or her multiple identities and comprehends his or her cultural identity and the stage of cultural identity he or she is in. Most people have identities related to gender, age, religion, ethnicity, socioeconomic status, professional status, and so forth.

Component 4: The clinician has cognitive and emotional knowledge about his or her implicit and explicit biases toward members of a group that is culturally different from his or her own.

Component 5: The clinician understands, appreciates, and is respectful of the culture and worldviews of his or her clients and understands the cultural identity stage that his or her client is in.

Component 6: The clinician recognizes the limits of his or her cultural competency in working with culturally diverse clients. Cultural awareness requires a lifelong commitment to self-evaluation.

Tables 1.2 and 1.3 provide class exercises that can be used to examine Component 1 (understanding the influence of our culture) and Component 2 (comprehending our worldviews). Other class discussion questions and exercises are provided at the end of this chapter.

TABLE 1.2 ■ Culturally Responsive Clinical Skill Development, Component 1: Understanding the Impact of Your Own Culture

This exercise is designed to get students and participants thinking about the influence of their own cultural, ethnic/racial, gender/sexual orientation, and religious background on their lives. Participants are asked to respond to the following questions (15–20 minutes) and to then discuss their answers or responses in groups of four or five. The group can decide to choose a person to serve as a recorder for the group so that a record can be made of the similarities and differences noted among the participants.

1. Where were you born, and during what year were you born?

2. Where did you grow up?

3. Where did your parents, grandparents, and great grandparents grow up?

4. In your family, what cultural events did you celebrate?

5. What is your earliest memory of being a member of a cultural group?

6. Is that a pleasant or an unhappy memory?

7. Do you eat any foods associated with your cultural group? What influence has your cultural group had on the type of music you listen to or the way that you dress?

8. Is there one cultural, ethnic/racial, gender/sexual orientation, or religious group toward which you feel bias? What is the source of your bias—family, cultural group, mainline society, or another factor?

9. Do you feel you were a member of a privileged group within the society or country in which you grew up?

10. What factors made you a member of a privileged group? Was it your race/ethnicity, gender/sexual orientation, religion, and so forth?

11. What impact has your cultural group, ethnic/racial group, gender/sexual orientation group, or socioeconomic group had on your life?

12. If a magic wand could be waved and you could change your cultural or racial group, of what group would you choose to be a member? Explain your answer.

13. If you had to select one major influence that your dominant cultural, ethnic/racial, religious, or gender/sexual orientation group had on your present life, what would that influence be?

14. How comfortable are you working with people who are culturally different from you?

TABLE 1.3 ■ Culturally Responsive Clinical Skill Development, Component 2: Understanding Your Worldview

Our perceptions of our clients are shaped by our own individual worldviews. We learn our worldviews through the process of socialization from childhood to adulthood. Culture has a major influence on our worldviews, and most of the time, our worldviews are perceived as "the way things are" or "the way that things should be." Our worldviews oftentimes go unquestioned because they are "silent intruders" into our relationships with others. To get at our worldviews, we have to examine the beliefs and social values that sustain them. For instance, in Western society (including Europe and the United States), one commonly accepted worldview is that the individual should be the captain of his or her soul, which is in direct contrast to the view that the group is the most important. People who are blind to their own worldviews will not be able to discern the differences in values between various cultures.

There are different aspects of worldview. For instance, worldview may deal with time, space, territoriality, relationships, and spirituality. For instance, in the United States and Europe in general, time is viewed as something that has to be mastered; it is a commodity, and people must adhere to strict time, especially being on time. The following is a short exercise to help you become clearer about your worldview.

Class Activity 1

In small groups of three to five people, answer individually on a blank sheet of paper the following questions. Then discuss the individual group members' responses to the following questions or situations:

• How do you view time? To what extent do you agree with the statement, "Time is money"? Or do you tend to believe that time is a process and that the needs of people may interfere with keeping to a set time?

• To what degree do you tend to form relationships quickly and end them quickly? Are there many people located inside your circle or just a few people?

• Do you believe that how things get done depends on relationships with people and attention to the group process, or do you adhere to the belief that things get done by following procedures and paying attention to detail?

• To what extent is your identity rooted in yourself and your accomplishments? Or is it rooted in various groups, such as your family or your work group?

Class Activity 2

Take a few minutes to write down five important beliefs you have about yourself, people, and the world in general. Next, rank order your beliefs from most to least important to you. Which beliefs are most important to you? How do your beliefs shape your view of yourself and others? In small groups of three to five people, discuss and compare your core beliefs about life and people.

According to Tervalon and Murray-Garcia (1998) cultural self-awareness requires a lifelong commitment to self-evaluation and assessment. How committed do you feel to taking a lifelong journey of cultural self-awareness? As it stands right now, how aware are you of your own cultural background? Before beginning a client–counselor relationship, a counselor must become aware of his or her cultural background. As a counselor recognizes the different influences on his or her cultural background, he or she will be more capable of responding sensitively to the client.

Culturally Competent Awareness Checklist for Mental Health Workers

Before working with a culturally diverse client, the mental health worker completes the Culturally Competent Awareness Checklist (Table 1.4). The checklist is not exhaustive, but it does outline important areas to take into consideration when working with culturally diverse clients.

TABLE 1.4 ■ Culturally Competent Awareness Checklist for Mental Health Workers

1. _____I am aware of the impact of culture on my client's presenting counseling problem.

2. _____I am aware of the *family roles* that are dominant in my client's culture, and I understand how those family roles may differ both within his or her culture and across cultures.

3. I am aware that my client's culture can affect his or her *child-rearing practices*, including:

    A. _____Discipline

    B. _____Relationships with parents, siblings, and other family members

    C. _____Expectations for academic achievement and job success

    D. _____Communication style with parents, siblings, and other family members

    E. _____Educational decisions

    F. _____Career choices

    G. _____Dating others

4. I am aware of the impact of culture on my client's *life activities*, involving:

    A. _____Attitudes toward mental health and mental health services

    B. _____Religious-faith-based practices

    C. _____Views on gender roles

    D. _____Outlook on alternative medicine

    E. _____Marriage, divorce, etc.

    F. _____Customs or superstitions

    G. _____Jobs and employment

    H. _____Perception of time

    I. _____Views on wellness

    J. _____Views on disabilities

5. I am aware of how my client's cultural norms may influence *communication* with me and others, including:

    A. _____Eye contact

    B. _____Interpersonal space relationships

    C. _____Comfort with silence

    D. _____Asking and responding to questions

    E. _____Considerations for appropriate topics of conversation

    F. _____Greeting others

    G. _____Alternative communication methods for sharing information (i.e., storytelling)

    H. _____Interruptions

    I. _____Use of gestures

    J. _____Use of humor

Source: © Jones-Smith, 2015.

MAJOR BARRIERS TO CULTURALLY COMPETENT COUNSELING

This section reviews barriers to a counselor's development of cultural competence. Five major barriers to cultural competence include (1) inappropriate use of Eurocentric theories of psychotherapy and Western cultural values, (2) cultural encapsulation of the counselor, (3) monoculturalism, (4) cultural oppression with regard to lack of consideration of a client's worldview, and (5) implicit and explicit counselor and client ethnic/racial, gender, sexual orientation, and disability and age biases. Let's examine these barriers.

The Inappropriate Use of Eurocentric Psychotherapy Theories

Because theories of psychotherapy are usually influenced by the cultural background of the theorist, most current theories need to be expanded in terms of multicultural issues. A major issue is: Do we need to separate multicultural theories for psychotherapy, or can the current major theoretical schools simply be modified to include multicultural perspectives? Multicultural counseling will continue to change over the years, and it will combine its emphasis with other theoretical approaches, such as cognitive behavioral theory and relational theory.

Historically, psychologists and other mental health professionals have used **Eurocentric counseling theories** to formulate their thinking about client issues. Yet, each of the Western theoretical formulations is value laden. How could they be otherwise? Whatever theory a person constructs is influenced by his or her cultural framework. Multiculturalists contend that traditional counseling theories fail to consider the ways in which culturally diverse persons construct their own meanings of mental health, psychological stress, and appropriate coping strategies (Ponterotto et al., 2010). They argue that no theory, however objective it appears on the surface, is value free. In evaluating each theoretical approach for psychotherapy, it is important to know something about the zeitgeist that was prevalent during the theorist's lifetime.

Despite the criticism against Eurocentric counseling theories, many of these theories have made good contributions to psychotherapy. For instance, the behavioral contributions of B. F. Skinner and the cognitive behavioral school of Albert Ellis and Aaron Beck have relevance to most cultures (Jones-Smith, 2014). Every ethnic and cultural group establishes culturally relevant cognitions or thoughts that influence individuals' behavior. Likewise, most cultures use the principle of reinforcement to ensure that individuals' behavior will conform to that group's norms or values. Counselors and therapists must become aware of the dominant cultural cognitions within each ethnic group.

Even though there are benefits to adopting a cognitive behavioral framework, mental health professionals must examine how a Western perspective may hold certain cultural biases. For instance, most Western counseling theories assume that people are capable of change and that they should pick themselves up by their own bootstraps. Such theories maintain that the self is more important than the community, that an individual should have an internal locus of control rather than an external (group) locus of control, and that an individual's spirituality should be de-emphasized in therapy. People who come from cultures that emphasize the importance of the group over the individual may find it offensive to stress the importance of the self. They may not value self-disclosure, especially when such disclosure deals with revealing family secrets.

Moreover, the therapeutic process is laden with certain beliefs, such as the value of talk therapy—the belief that establishing a relationship with another person skilled in psychological principles and intervention strategies can help that person deal with deep-seated personal issues. Counseling students frequently value client characteristics and behaviors that involve clients making their own choices rather than those of their parents, being open and self-revealing, and gaining independence from their families and other groups.

Eurocentric counseling interventions may not work with clients from Eastern, Asian, and African cultures. Does this mean that only Asians should counsel other Asians, or only African Americans should treat other members of their ethnic group? Research shows that one does not have to be a member of the client's ethnic group to counsel a client. However,

CASE VIGNETTE 1.2

ERICA AND THERAPIST CULTURAL ENCAPSULATION

Erica sat in her office reflecting on her morning counseling session with Latisha. She was frustrated because she never seemed to get anywhere with her. She realized that deep down inside she felt a sense of anger toward Latisha, an African American woman in her late twenties. Latisha was poor, barely getting by financially, and she had two kids from two different relationships. Neither father was supporting the kids. Latisha had been forced off welfare by her caseworker because she had been on welfare too long. She shared a home with her mother, and the two of them struggled to pay the rent and utility bills. Sometimes the water, lights, and gas were turned off, even in the dead of winter.

Latisha's financial and housing problems seemed to exacerbate her struggle with depression, and vice versa. Depression had left her feeling so drained that she was unable to seek new employment. Her kids were having behavior problems in school, and she lacked the energy to address this with their teachers. Nothing was working for her; everything was working against her.

As a therapist, Erica felt overwhelmed by Latisha's problems. And if she were honest with herself, she felt angry at Latisha for not doing something more positive with her life. Latisha fit so many negative stereotypes.

Then, for a brief moment, Erica thought about her own life growing up in a middle-class White suburb. She could not imagine herself being in the same situation as Latisha, and found herself thinking that she probably would not have been able to survive half of what Latisha had survived. But still, a part of her blamed Latisha. She wished she could give her a magic pill that would end her depression so that she would not have to be confronted with a seemingly hopeless counseling situation. "I'm just glad that I'm White," Erica said to herself, "because I don't think I could make it as a Black person."

Discussion Questions

1. Have you ever worked with a client whose financial and personal circumstances seemed overwhelming to you and the client? How should a therapist deal with his or her own feelings of being glad not to be in the position of a troubled client?

2. Do you believe that Erica had established a therapeutic alliance with Latisha? Explain your answer.

3. What might be a beginning point that would establish a more productive therapeutic relationship between Erica and Latisha? The theme that the therapist seemed to embrace is "I'm glad that your life is not my life."

4. There are many aspects of Latisha's situation that might benefit from strengths-based therapy. Instead of focusing on the overwhelming negatives in Latisha's life, the therapist might consider Latisha's strengths. After all, Latisha did exhibit some measure of strength in getting up and coming to therapy.

5. What other strengths do you see in Latisha's life that might serve as a source of motivation for her? Latisha deserves credit for taking care of her children, however limited that might be. She was employed previously, so she has to have an employable skill.

6. One aspect of strengths-based therapy is helping clients to let go of past failed relationships and past financial and economic failures and to focus on changing just one thing—however small that might be.

7. How might the therapist help Latisha to set meaningful goals for her life and a reasonable plan to change her situation?

8. What steps could be useful in helping Latisha to deal more constructively with her depression? Medication? Exercise?

client-perceived similarity does have an influence on the rapidity with which one can establish a therapeutic alliance (Sue & Sue, 2013).

Cultural Encapsulation: Barrier to Cultural Competence

The journey toward becoming a culturally competent counselor can be thwarted if the clinician is culturally isolated and lacks knowledge of other ethnic groups. *Cultural encapsulation* is a term Gilbert Wrenn (1962) used to describe a culturally unaware counselor. The term suggests that a counselor has a lack of understanding of a client's culture and the influence of both the client's and counselor's culture on the therapeutic relationship. The culturally encapsulated counselor sees a client primarily through his or her own cultural lenses instead of those of the client. Each one of us is culturally encapsulated. Learning to see the world of another person through his or her cultural lenses is a process.

Monocultural Clinical Orientation

The term *monocultural* means having familiarity with only one culture or sharing a common culture to the exclusion of others. Sometimes therapists/counselors who are monocultural may apply their culture's values and norms to all clients, regardless of their cultural backgrounds.

Therapists/counselors who use a monocultural approach when working with a client from a different culture may encounter problems with diagnosis (over- or underdiagnosing disorders), assessment, interpretation of symptoms, and chosen treatment methods (Gallardo, Yeh, Trimble, & Parham, 2012). A monocultural orientation may function as a barrier to culturally competent counseling.

The Cultural Barriers of Race and Ethnocentrism

In order to build culturally competent therapeutic relationships, a counselor needs to recognize, confront, and overcome the biases that he or she holds, whether conscious or unconscious. These include biases related to race and ethnicity, gender, and sexual orientation, among others. The first issue involves how people in general feel about the topic of race. What is race? Are there really five races in the world, or is there only one race—the human race?

It is important that therapists/counselors understand what may potentially constitute barriers to counseling an individual who is culturally diverse from the counselor. Although there are a number of factors that may impact a culturally diverse counseling relationship, this section identifies differences in race, ethnic group membership, ethnocentrism, cultural encapsulation, and monocultural clinical orientation as major factors that have the potentiality of affecting a counseling relationship adversely.

Race: A Social Construction

Throughout history and the world, **race** has assumed a prominent role in people's minds. This book takes the perspective that race is primarily a social construction created by the Western world (Helms, Jernigan, & Mascher, 2005; Monk, Winslade, & Sinclair, 2008).

How did the concept of race develop? During the 15th and 16th centuries, British and European colonizers proposed that because people in the countries they colonized looked different from them and lacked some of the technological developments they possessed, these people were inferior to them and, therefore, not of the same race as them (Huntington, 2004). They promoted the idea that there are biological differences among groups of people that can be used to put them into various racial categories (Monk et al., 2008; Smedley & Smedley, 2005). Skin color has been the primary biological marker to place people into "racial" groups.

The term *race* was first used in the English language about 300 years ago (Smedley & Smedley, 2005). Meaning "breed" or "lineage," the term *race* can be traced to the French language. Race was associated with observable physical markers such as skin color, facial and bodily features, and hair type. The early colonizers placed meaning into these physical markers. Tracing the history of the social construction of race in the world, Smedley and Smedley (2005) stated:

> While colonists were creating the folk idea of race, naturalists in Europe were engaged in efforts to establish classifications of human groups in the 18th century. They had to rely on colonists' descriptions of indigenous peoples for the most part, and their categories were replete with subjective comments about their appearances and behaviors. Ethnic chauvinism and a well-developed notion of the "savage" or "primitives" dictated that they classify native peoples as inferior forms of humans. Although there were earlier attempts to categorize all human groups, then known, Linnaeus and Blumenbach introduced classifications of the varieties of humankind that later became the established names for the races of the world (Smedley, 2005). (p. 21)

CASE VIGNETTE 1.3
RACE AS A SOCIAL CONSTRUCTION

Dr. Hunt was an associate professor consulting in the area of multicultural counseling. As one of the panelists at a forum at a major university, he presented the idea of *race as a social construction* and that there were not five distinct races—Whites, Blacks, Asians, American Indians, and Latinos. One of the doctoral students attending the panel discussion stood up and angrily challenged Dr. Hunt's assertion that there were not five major races in this country. "How could you make such a stupid statement that there are not five different races, that there is only one race, and then that there are ethnic groups with various physical features? The U.S. Census categorizes people into different races! Is the Census wrong and you're right?"

Dr. Hunt responded, "I can understand your feelings. All your life, you have been taught that there are five races, and now here I come telling you that what you have been taught is just not true. Can you tell me what the biological differences are that form the basis of each of the five races? What is the race of a person whose mother is American Indian and White and whose father is Asian American and African American? Does this person have four races within her, and does the existence of four different races within her function to form a new race?"

The student shot back, "I don't believe you. I'm out of here!" He grabbed his backpack and left.

Discussion Questions

1. Most psychological research divides people into different racial groups. Should this practice be stopped, or should it continue?

2. As a participant in a forum, what might Dr. Hunt have done to better prepare the forum's moderator, the other panelists, and the audience for the assertion he was going to make?

3. Class Exercise: Discussions about race in the United States can evoke strong feelings. Form two groups in your class, one arguing in favor of five races and the other arguing in favor of there being only one race, the human race. Each group is asked to support its arguments with scientific facts gathered from current periodicals and books.

4. Reading/Discussion Exercise: Read the article by Helms, Jernigan, and Mascher (2005), "The Meaning of Race in Psychology and How to Change It: A Methodological Perspective," in *American Psychologist*, *60*(1), 27–36. Discuss the relative merits of the methodology advocated in this article. In the years since 2005, to what extent have you seen this methodology implemented?

This notion, referred to by today's scholars as **racialized science**, is based on an imprecise and distorted understanding of human differences and an agenda to empower White colonizers (Allen, 1994, 1997; Smedley & Smedley, 2005). Race is neither a biological nor an anthropological reality (see the American Anthropological Association's "AAA Statement on Race," 1998). There is no scientific evidence to support the view that there are sufficient different biological markers to form different races. As Shih, Pittinsky, and Trahan (2007) stated, "Racial categories are arbitrary, subjective, and ultimately meaningless in any biological sense. In other words, multiracial individuals come to the realization that race is a social construction" (p. 125).

There is only one race, and that is the human race—with people who have different variations in physical appearances, but all having the same biological features such as a heart, head, and so forth. Yet, the concept of race persists today and is used to stereotype people into artificial categories, often classifying people into inferior and superior groups.

Ethnic Group

Whereas the concept of race lacks a valid scientific basis, an ethnic group is based on two factors: genetic antecedents and cultural traditions. An **ethnic group** is a group of people who share a common history and culture, can be identified by similar physical features and values, and identify themselves as members of that group through social interactions (Smith, 1991). Further, a person becomes related to the ethnic group through emotional and symbolic ties. An ethnic group can be defined in terms of self-identification (Smith, 1991). From this viewpoint, an ethnic group may be described as a process of self and other ascription (Smith, 1991).

Ethnocentrism and Cultural Relativism

Ethnocentrism may be defined as the belief that one's worldview is correct and is inherently superior to the worldviews of others. William G. Sumner coined the term after observing people's tendency to differentiate between their own in-group and others. Sumner (1906) defined ethnocentrism as "the technical name for the view of things in which one's own group is at the center of everything, and all others are scaled and rated with reference to it" (p. 16). According to him, ethnocentrism leads to beliefs about one's own group's superiority and contempt for non–group members. For instance, in U.S. history, the European colonization involved enculturating indigenous people (American Indians) with the ethnocentric view that European cultures were superior.

Ethnocentrism is the inclination of people to use their own cultural standards to judge the behavior and beliefs of people from different cultures. The ethnocentric perspective judges one's own cultural beliefs as morally correct, and the beliefs of others as morally questionable. Most people are ethnocentric to some degree, in part because it is human nature to believe that our cultural beliefs are the correct ones. Despite this observation, ethnocentrism prevents us from becoming culturally competent and responsive to those who have different cultural beliefs, traditions, and social practices. (See Table 1.5.)

Cultural relativism is the opposite of ethnocentrism and follows the idea that behavior in one culture should not be judged by the standards of another culture. According to Kottak and Kozaitis (2002), cultural relativism seeks to be objective and sensitive to different cultures without ignoring basic stands of human justice and morality. To eliminate ethnocentrism, one must first acknowledge that he or she is ethnocentric.

Currently, in the United States, White middle-class values and worldviews are often presented as socially desirable, and these worldviews are used to judge other cultural and ethnic groups. As Neil Altman (2012) stated: "One aspect of Whiteness in the American context is that the culture associated with being a White American is considered the standard or the baseline from which other people diverge, as opposed to being one culture among many" (p. 183). Ethnocentrism provides an invisible barrier to those who are not members of the dominant group (Ponterotto, Utsey, & Pedersen, 2006). When it comes to counseling and therapy, from the ethnocentric Euro American perspective, pathology is usually viewed as located within the

---

TABLE 1.5 ■ Culturally Responsive Clinical Skill Development: Are You Ethnocentric?

Ethnocentric thinking goes beyond having pride in one's country. Ethnocentric thinking takes place when a person believes that his or her country does everything right, while the rest of the world does things the wrong way. One can have pride in one's own country while still believing that other countries also do things well, even though they may do things differently. Ethnocentric thinking is characterized by an unwillingness to consider different cultural points of view or by a reluctance to acknowledge the strengths of other cultures.

Some American examples of ethnocentrism are:

- People who speak differently from me have an accent, but I don't have an accent.
- People from such-and-such a place tend to always be . . .
- I was brought up with certain manners, and people who do not act with these manners are rude.
- Being proud of my heritage means I must not tolerate criticism of any aspect of my heritage.
- My religion is the one true religion; all others are erroneous.

individual rather than within the environment or the sociopolitical system in which the individual lives (Harper & McFadden, 2003).

NEUROSCIENCE, THE BRAIN, AND THE INVISIBLE NEURAL BARRIER OF ETHNIC/RACIAL BIAS

Racial and ethnic prejudices constitute a major barrier to culturally responsive counseling and psychotherapy. A major goal in this section is to acknowledge that all of us have **prejudices**—some of which we recognize because they are in our immediate awareness and still others that are not known or unconscious. Hopefully, this section will provide the foundation for honest discussion of prejudices, where they come from, and how they operate in each one of our lives. Are we more alike or different—deep down inside? What do we really share with each other as human beings?

Recent developments in neuroscience are beginning to provide critical information about how ethnic/racial bias is formed in the brain. Such research has even begun to locate the brain network that supports prejudice. This book maintains we must begin to look toward neuroscience for answers for dealing with ethnic/racial bias. The section begins with a brief description of the neural basis for ethnic/racial bias followed by what some researchers are labeling as the new paradigm for cultural diversity—the **paradigm of implicit and explicit racial bias** (Olson & Fazio, 2004; Phelps et al., 2000).

Neural Prejudice Networks in the Human Brain

Research on the neural basis of prejudice has emphasized neural brain structures that mediate emotion and motivation, such as the amygdala, insula, striatum, and regions of orbital and ventromedial frontal cortices. These structures can be conceptualized as the core neural brain network for the experience and expression of prejudice (Amodio, 2014; Amodio, Harmon-Jones, & Devine, 2003; Olson & Fazio, 2004; Phelps et al., 2000).

Neuroscientist David Amodio (Amodio, 2008, 2014; Amodio & Devine, 2006; Amodio & Ratner, 2011) has conducted critical research on neural functioning and the neural basis of prejudice. The neuroscience of prejudice investigates how our brains function to create and maintain human bias and prejudice against those who are different from us. Racial and ethnic prejudice is not just located in our thoughts and attitudes. Racism lives deep inside the very neural substrates of our brains (Amodio, 2014; Olson & Fazio, 2004; Phelps et al., 2000). According to Amodio (2014), prejudice "stems from a mechanism of survival, built on cognitive systems that 'structure' the physical world" (p. 670). The human brain has evolved to sustain survival and prosperity, and our brains respond to those who are different from us as threats to our survival and prosperity. A survival belief might be "We don't want immigrants coming to the United States because they threaten our jobs and well-being."

Racial prejudice is all about our views of what is necessary for our survival. The American Civil War was fought, in part, because Southern White male farmers saw the ending of slavery as a threat to their financial and economic survival. The Confederate flag has been used as a symbol of White superiority and as a reminder to African Americans about a war for slavery that Southern Whites lost. The Confederate flag produces neural reactions in the amygdala for both Whites and African Americans. Like the Confederate flag, the symbols of racism in each culture and country are deeply embedded in several neural substrates of the human brain. The **amygdala** processes social category cues, including racial groups in terms of their potential threat or reward. The primary role of the amygdala is to signal threat. Amygdala activation reflects an immediate or an implied threat response to racial out-group members. The amygdala is able to respond very rapidly to immediate threats because it receives direct (or nearly direct) afferents from all sensory organs into its lateral nucleus (Amodio, 2014; Amodio et al., 2003;

Phelps et al., 2000). Researchers interested in the neural substrate of implicit prejudice first looked to this brain structure when measuring prejudice.

Contained within the amygdala is the central nucleus (CeA), which has been implicated in Pavlovian (classical) fear conditioning in both rats and humans. Signals coming from the CeA activate hypothalamic and brain stem structures to bring about arousal, attention, freezing, and preparation for fight or flight—a fear response (Arkes & Tetlock, 2004; Banaji & Greenwald, 2013).

The **striatum** mediates approach-related instrumental responses. The insula conducts visceral and subjective emotional responses toward social in-groups or out-groups. The **orbitofrontal cortex (OFC)** mediates affect-driven judgments of social out-group members and may be characterized by reduced activity in the ventral **medial prefrontal cortex (mPFC)**, a region of the brain involved in empathy and mentalizing (Amodio, 2014).

Chapter 3 of this book provides more details about the neuroscience of bias and cultural competency.

Implicit and Explicit Bias: A New Paradigm for Cultural Diversity

Most people do not perceive themselves as prejudiced or racist. Typically, Americans say they think it is wrong to be prejudiced against members of other cultural groups. However, when people participate in psychological experiments designed to reveal unconscious attitudes, many of them are found to hold racial biases. For instance, Amodio and colleagues (2003) found that White participants would indicate on a questionnaire that they were positive in their attitudes toward Black people, but when given a behavioral measure of how they responded to pictures of Black people compared with White people, the results indicated otherwise. Amodio was basing his work on the earlier work of Anthony Greenwald and colleagues, who invented Project Implicit (see https://implicit.harvard.edu/implicit/).

Greenwald and colleagues (Banaji & Greenwald, 2013) designed a test that required the participant to sort categories of pictures and words. In the Black–White race attitude test, participants are asked to sort pictures of White and Black people's faces, and positive and negative words, by pressing one of two keys on a computer keyboard. The difference in time a participant needs to respond is the measure of implicit bias.

Explicit bias might be defined as bias of which one is aware—your conscious cognitions about your prejudices (Amodio & Devine, 2006). You know that you dislike members of a particular racial, religious, or gender-related group. You might even hurl racial or gender epithets at the targeted group—especially when you feel safe around others who share your prejudice.

Implicit bias is activated involuntarily. Implicit bias lives deep in a person's subconscious—that is, it usually lies outside a person's conscious awareness, thereby making it very difficult to change. Implicit bias differs from known or explicit biases in that individuals may choose to conceal explicit biases for the purpose of social or political correctness. We are all probably a little bit racist, even when we feel that we are not. A person says, "I am not a racist. I have some Asian or Black or Latino friends." Implicit bias takes place when, despite our best nonprejudiced intentions and without our awareness, racial stereotypes and negative racial assumptions seep silently and unobtrusively into our minds, thereby affecting our behaviors, decisions, and evaluations.

Implicit bias stems from the "messages, attitudes, and stereotypes we pick up from the world we live in," and research over time and from different countries shows that it tends to line up with general social hierarchies (Desmond-Harris, 2016).

More than 30 years of neurology and cognitive psychology studies have shown that implicit bias influences the way we see and treat others, even when we believe we are being fair to the other person (Banaji, Hardin, & Rothman, 1993; Devine, 1989; Dovidio & Gaertner, 1986). This may occur when prejudiced and stereotyped impressions of others are activated into memory and made part of judgment and activity by the brain structures involved in the neural prejudiced network (Amodio, 2014; Amodio & Devine, 2006). A form of racial prejudice focuses on clearly defined social categories associated with identifiable physical characteristics. Americans have deep historical roots, such that Whites may view African Americans as threatening, thereby requiring vigilant attention (e.g., being watched when they go shopping). Studies have found that participants with strong implicit bias against African Americans were anxious about appearing biased (Ofan, Rubin, & Amodio, 2014).

Studies have found that implicit racial bias takes place at the medical doctor's office when White medical doctors treat African American medical patients. In a study by Alexander R. Green and colleagues (2007), 220 medical resident doctors took an implicit association test to detect unconscious racial bias, and they also read a medical history of a patient (either Black or White) experiencing chest pains, with clinical details suggesting a possible heart attack. The results showed that implicit bias affected their medical decision making regarding Black patients. Specifically, White medical residents were less likely to prescribe thrombolysis, a drug treatment to reduce blood clots and prevent heart attacks, for Black patients than for White patients. Put succinctly, White medical resident doctors were less likely to administer a potentially life-saving treatment to Black patients.

The negative effects of implicit bias of White medical doctors can be even more far-reaching. Reviews of a substantial body of research have found that, at the same time as racial and ethnic minority patients often do not receive appropriate and necessary care, doctors are also more likely to recommend and perform unnecessary surgeries on racial and ethnic minority patients than on their White counterparts (Dovidio & Fiske, 2012; Kressin & Groeneveld, 2015). Implicit biases have been found to influence judges' decisions in criminal cases. According to the Kirwan Institute for the Study of Race and Ethnicity at The Ohio State University (2015), "Researchers found that when controlling for numerous factors (e.g., seriousness of the primary offense, number of prior offenses, etc.), individuals with the most prominent Afrocentric features received longer sentences than" those with less prominent African features.

> **Cultural Reflections**
>
> *To what extent are you aware of your implicit racial, ethnic, religious, or gender biases?*

Key Points About Implicit Biases

- Implicit bias research is critical in understanding why some counselor trainees might feel angry, defensive, or reluctant to take a multicultural counseling course.
  - Implicit bias of students can affect a number of factors and situations, including the negative or positive evaluation of teachers and college instructors, misdiagnosing of mental illness by therapists/counselors, and clinicians' use of inappropriate psychological treatment procedures. Everyone has implicit biases, even those people who think they do not have them. Even people who take oaths that mandate impartiality, such as judges, have implicit biases. Implicit associations that we maintain are not necessarily in alignment with our declared beliefs. For example, a person may say that he is not prejudiced against African Americans, but he may participate in a rally or march with known members of groups like the Ku Klux Klan or other White nationalist organizations.

- We usually are inclined to hold implicit biases that favor our own in-group; however, research has shown that we can also hold implicit biases against our in-group. Many ethnic or racial groups have derogatory words that they use to describe themselves or members of their own group.

- Implicit biases can change. However, a person just can't sit down and engage in introspection about his or her biases, or simply decide not to let implicit biases affect his or her attitudes and actions (Kirwan Institute, 2015).

- We can unlearn implicit biases through a variety of de-biasing techniques (Kirwan Institute, 2015).

Reducing Your Implicit Biases

As a counselor or therapist, it is important to employ constructive techniques to reduce your implicit biases. When assessing the behavior or performance of a person from a stigmatized group, you should make an effort to focus on concrete positive and negative factors and your memory of what actually happened, instead of relying on overall gut feelings. Pay attention when you have uneasy feelings that your responses, decisions, or behaviors might have been caused by bias or stereotypes, and make an intention to think positive thoughts when encountering members of stigmatized groups.

Another approach is to make a deliberate effort to think about members of stereotyped groups as individuals rather than as members of a specific racial, ethnic, or cultural group. Helping professionals should pay special attention to their physical feelings when they encounter members of a stigmatized group and determine if their clients' group membership has anything to do with the treatment plans used during therapy. Studies on implicit bias make it imperative that counseling programs introduce students to cultural neuroscience and the brain.

Implicit Bias: Prejudice Against Immigrants and Refugees

Helping professionals, like other people in various situations, may exhibit implicit bias toward immigrants and refugees who have migrated to their country. According to research findings by Efren Perez (2010), many Americans have a negative bias against Latino immigrants, and such bias deeply influences their outlook on policy proposals for immigration reform. In an original survey experiment, he used the implicit association test to assess people's implicit attitudes toward Latino immigrants and discovered that participants had a negative impression of Latino immigrants that influenced their immigration policy judgments, even when they were explicitly directed to focus on non-Hispanic immigrants.

Perez's research findings also showed that many White Americans make little distinction between Latino immigrants and Latinos born in the United States. In addition to highlighting the implicit bias many have against Latino immigrants, Perez's findings give insight into why there is such intense opposition among many voters in the United States to enacting any type of immigration reform. Implicit bias affects virtually all immigrants to the United States and to other countries because they are inclined to be met with resistance from members of the host country.

SUMMARY OF KEY POINTS

Within the past three decades, the field of multicultural counseling and psychotherapy has grown by leaps and bounds. Part of this phenomenal growth can be attributed to the fact that technology has helped to produce a global society that has within it the capacity to put individuals in contact with each other from diverse parts of the world within seconds. The world has begun to take note of the significance of culture on human lives. Counselors and therapists need to become aware of the impact of culture not only on their own lives but also on the lives of their clients. All counseling takes place within a multicultural and sociopolitical context. Counselors can function to liberate or to oppress their clients.

All counseling should be culturally responsive, regardless of whether one is using a psychodynamic, cognitive behavioral, humanistic-existential, or social constructivist theoretical framework. Culturally responsive strengths-based therapy (CR-SBT) maintains that in conducting counseling or therapy, the emphasis should be on clients' strengths and not on their weaknesses or problems, for only the clients' strengths can be used to solve their presenting problems.

It is clinical malpractice to be unaware of the cultural influences on our lives and the lives of our clients. Successful treatment of a client takes place when counselors and therapists consider the cultural variables that impact the client's presenting problem. It is unethical for psychologists to work with clients for whom they lack the cultural training to provide adequate services.

Current counseling reflects a Eurocentric perspective that espouses an individualistic and egocentric worldview. For the most part, the Eurocentric perspective fails to consider the role of social and cultural contexts of diverse clients; therefore, without a culturally diverse focus, Eurocentric-oriented counseling can do harm to people of culture and to LGBTQ clients.

The paradigm of implicit and explicit bias holds great promise for multicultural education and culturally responsive counseling. Understanding how bias is formed in the brain and how it is sustained should become part of each clinician's cultural competence journey. Clinicians should become aware of their own implicit biases so that they do not interfere with culturally responsive treatment. Implicit bias refers to the attitudes or stereotypes that affect our understanding, actions, and decisions in an unconscious manner. The following is a summary of some key findings on implicit bias that might be helpful to the practitioner:

- Implicit biases are activated in the brain (usually in the amygdala) involuntarily, unconsciously, and without one's awareness or intentional control (see, e.g., Greenwald & Krieger, 2006; Faigman et al., 2012; Nier, 2005; Rudman, 2004).

- Implicit biases are pervasive among all people, regardless of their gender, ethnicity, race, or culture (Kang & Lane, 2010; Nosek et al., 2007). Everyone is susceptible to them, even people who believe themselves to be impartial or objective, such as judges. Implicit biases have even been documented in children (Baron & Banaji, 2006; Newheiser & Olson, 2012; Rutland, Cameron, Bennett, & Ferrell, 2005).

- Because implicit associations arise outside of conscious awareness, these associations do not necessarily align with individuals' openly held beliefs or even reflect stances one would explicitly endorse (Graham & Lowery, 2004; Nosek, Banaji, & Greenwald, 2002a, 2002b).

- Studies have found that most Americans, regardless of race, display a pro-White/anti-Black bias on the implicit association test (Dovidio, Kawakami, & Gaertner, 2002; Greenwald, Poehlman, Uhlmann, & Banaji, 2009; McConnell & Liebold, 2009; Nosek et al., 2002a, 2002b).

- Once an implicit association is activated in the brain, it is difficult to inhibit the association (Dasgupta, 2013). Attempts to repress and to suppress automatic implicit associations are ineffective, and such attempts may actually amplify them by making them hyper-accessible (Galinsky & Moskowitz, 2000, 2007).

- An important way to engage in implicit bias cleansing is to openly acknowledge biases and then directly challenge or refute them.

- Our implicit biases can be changed by intentionally developing new cognitive and people associations (Blair, 2002; Dasgupta, 2013).

DISCUSSION QUESTIONS

Questions for Discussion: Cultural Assumptions

1. Identify an example of a culturally biased assumption in the counseling or psychotherapy literature.

2. Is the assumption you identified relevant for your membership in an ethnic, racial, or cultural group?

Culturally Responsive Exercise 1: Significant Events in One's Life and Culture

Each person experiences and interprets the events in his or her life differently. This exercise helps to identify if there are global events that are significant to everyone in the group or if different cultures have different significant life events.

Procedure

- Divide the students into groups of four or five.

- Each group should have participants of different ethnicities, races, or cultures.

- Give each student a blank sheet of paper.

- The participants are to indicate on the paper a timeline (past, present, or future), marking in each time period three events that are very significant to them.

- Among the three significant events they list, there should be at least one event that is not personal (i.e., fall of the Berlin Wall).

Group Presentation

- Each group should spend time comparing the similarities and differences within and between the people representing different cultures, ethnicities, or races.

- One person in each group is selected to report to the other groups what similarities and differences they found in their timeline of significant events.

Culturally Responsive Exercise 2: Cultural Life History

Students are asked to examine their lives primarily in terms of their cultural life history. The goal of this exercise is to help them delineate the dominant themes in their cultural life story.

Procedures

- Divide students into groups of three to five people.

- Ask them to write on a sheet of paper the dominant themes in their cultural life histories.

- Discuss in the groups the different cultural themes students identified.

- Do different students in the class come up with different or similar themes based on their cultural life histories?

- Discuss the similarities and differences in the dominant cultural themes students listed.

KEY TERMS

Amygdala: Part of the brain's limbic system that is responsible for memory and emotions, especially fear. It is often referred to as the seat of the "fight or flight" response. It controls the way people respond to others, especially those who are ethnically or culturally different or similar from them.

Cultural awareness: Being conscious of one's own cultural background and worldview, especially in relationship to other cultures and group identities.

Cultural competence: A clinician or therapist's ability to provide services to clients that take into consideration the client's cultural beliefs, cultural worldviews, and behaviors. The culturally competent counselor values diversity, has undergone cultural self-assessment, and knows how to adapt clinical services to reflect an understanding and appreciation of a client's culture.

Cultural congruence: A positive relationship between an individual's cultural identity and his or her behavior and lifestyle.

Cultural encapsulation: A term developed by Gilbert Wrenn to reflect the idea that therapists/counselors live in cultural cocoons in which they are unaware of the culture of others. The term is used to describe a person with a limited or myopic worldview.

Cultural incongruence: A dissonant relationship between a person's cultural identity and his or her behavior and lifestyle.

Cultural relativism: The perspective that holds that behavior in one culture should not be judged by the standards of another. This doctrine maintains that all cultures are equal, have intrinsic value, are equally entitled to respect, and should be appreciated for their differences.

Culturally responsive therapy: A counseling relationship in which a client and a therapist are of different ethnicities, cultures, races, and backgrounds and the therapist (1) evidences awareness of the significance of both his and the client's cultural stories, (2) has specific knowledge of the client's culture, and (3) uses culturally appropriate clinical skills in working with the client.

Culture: An ethnic group's organized body of beliefs and rules about the ways in which persons should communicate with one another, think about themselves, and behave toward each other and objects in their environment.

Dominant culture: The values and customs of the major group in a society that sets the standard for cultural correctness.

Ethnic group: A group of people who share a common history and culture, can be identified by similar physical features and values, and identify themselves as being a member of that group through social interactions.

Ethnic identity: Awareness of one's membership in a particular cultural or ethnic group.

Ethnocentrism: An ethnic group or a person's belief that an ethnic group's ways are right or superior in terms of cultural beliefs compared to other ethnic or cultural groups. An individual displays a strong preference for his or her ethnic group and strong dislike and devaluing of other ethnic groups.

Eurocentric counseling theories: Refers to White American culture or White, Western, European cultural values and ways of conceptualizing reality. The term is often used in reference to counseling theories because they were created primarily by White males of Euro American backgrounds. In general, the term means that which is oriented toward White Western culture. Most counseling theories are Eurocentric in that they are built on the value system of White Western Hemisphere culture.

Explicit bias: Those biases and prejudices of which people are aware and may even acknowledge.

Implicit bias: Biases that are activated involuntarily and without a person's awareness or intentional control. Implicit bias lives deep in a person's subconscious—that is, it usually lies outside a person's conscious awareness, thereby making it very difficult to change.

Medial prefrontal cortex (mPFC): The human brain consists of a network of specific brain areas called the social brain. The medial prefrontal cortex is part of the adult social brain, which is responsible for social recognition and moral judgment. The prefrontal cortex can be divided into two sections: the medial prefrontal cortex (mPFC) and the lateral PFC. The mPFC has connections with the amygdala, which is important in emotional processing. Individuals with mPFC lesions have severely impaired social behavior.

Monocultural: Focus on one ethnic or cultural group, especially viewing the world through the lenses of one cultural perspective, without taking into consideration other cultural views.

Multicultural competencies: A set of culturally appropriate guidelines (promulgated by the American Psychological Association and the American Counseling Association) or competencies for individuals working with culturally diverse groups.

Multicultural counseling: Counseling in which the therapist and client come from different cultural, ethnic, and gender backgrounds. Because no two people come from the exact same background (due to differences in their experiences), all counseling is, in some respects, multicultural.

Multiculturalism: A school of thought or a philosophy that recognizes and values the various contributions of multiple cultures to a nation's life. It is a philosophy and doctrine that holds that several different cultures (rather than one national culture) can coexist peacefully and equitably in a single country.

Orbitofrontal cortex (OFC): The orbitofrontal cortex is part of the prefrontal cortex that sits just about the eye sockets, sometimes referred to as the orbits. It is located in the front of the brain and has extensive connections with the limbic system structures that deal with emotion and memory. The orbitofrontal cortex plays a role in higher-order cognition such as decision making. Areas of the brain involving the prefrontal cortex are believed to be critical in thought and human reasoning. Both impulse control and response inhibition are commonly associated with the OFC.

Paradigm of implicit and explicit racial bias: The principle that we all have biases, both explicit and implicit.

Prejudice: A preconceived devaluing of a group because of its assumed behaviors, capabilities, or attributes.

Race: A term frequently used to refer to major subdivisions of the human family characterized by hair texture, color of skin and eyes, stature, and other bodily proportions and physical characteristics.

Race as a social construction: The understanding that there is only one race within the world: the human race; that the concept of race lacks a biological or genetic basis.

Racialized science: The notion, promulgated by 18th- and 19th-century British and European scientists, that observable physical markers such as skin color, facial and bodily features, and hair type were a valid means of categorizing humans into separate races.

Sexual orientation: The way in which a person views and expresses the sexual component of his or her being; a person's habitual sexual attraction to and sexual activities with a person of the same sex, the opposite sex, or some combination thereof.

Social justice: A goal of democratic societies that commits to equitable access to societal institutions, resources, opportunities, and services. Social justice counseling is counseling designed to foster social justice and equal opportunities for all.

Strengths-based therapy (SBT): A psychotherapeutic approach that uses clients' strengths as an integral part of the therapeutic process. The therapist assesses clients' strengths and uses the focus on strengths to motivate and instill hope in them. Therapist emphasis on clients' strengths in therapy increases client cooperation and acceptance of therapy, while preventing and mitigating the presenting problem that brought them to therapy and promoting and maximizing human growth potential. Strengths-based therapy was developed by Elsie Jones-Smith during the late 1990s and the early part of 2000 (see *Strengths-Based Therapy: Connecting Theory, Practice, and Skills*, 2014).

Striatum: Involved in voluntary motor control. It is important in movement planning and in understanding rewards in social situations.

Worldview: A frame of reference and beliefs that an individual holds about life. It includes the individual's assumptions, understandings, interpretations, and beliefs about his or her relationship to the people, institutions, and phenomena within his or her environment.

REFERENCES AND SUGGESTED READING

Allen, T. W. (1994). *The invention of the White race* (Vol. *1*). London, England: Verso.

Allen, T. W. (1997). *The invention of the White race* (Vol. *2*). London, England: Verso.

Altman, N. (2012). Whiteness. In L. Aron & A. Harris (Eds.), *Relational psychoanalysis* (Vol. *4*, pp. 177–98). New York, NY: Routledge.

American Anthropological Association. (1998). *AAA statement on race*. Retrieved from http://www.americananthro.org/ ConnectWithAAA/Content.aspx?ItemNumber=2583

American Counseling Association. (2005). *Code of ethics.* Alexandria, VA: Author.

American Mental Health Counselors Association. (2016). *AMHCA standards for the practice of clinical mental health counseling.* Retrieved from http://connections.amhca .org/HigherLogic/System/DownloadDocumentFile .ashx?DocumentFileKey=e6b635b0-654c-be8d-e18c-dbf75de23b8f

American Psychiatric Association. (2013). *Diagnostic and statistical manual of mental disorders* (5th ed.). Arlington, VA: Author.

American Psychological Association. (2003). *Guidelines on multicultural education, training, research, practice, and organizational change for psychologists.* Washington, DC: Author.

American Psychological Association. (2017). *Multicultural guidelines: An ecological approach to context, identity, and intersectionality.* Retrieved from http://www.apa.org/about/ policy/multicultural-guidelines.pdf

American Psychological Association, Presidential Task Force on Evidence-Based Practice. (2006). Evidence-based practice in psychology. *American Psychologist, 61*(4), 271–285. Retrieved from http://www.apa.org/pubs/journals/features/ evidence-based-statement.pdf

Amodio, D. M. (2008). The social neuroscience of intergroup relations. *European Review of Social Psychology, 19,* 1–54.

Amodio, D. M. (2014). A neuroscience of prejudice and stereotyping. *Nature Reviews Neuroscience, 15*(10), 670–682.

Amodio, D. M., & Devine, P. G. (2006). Stereotyping and evaluation in implicit race bias: Evidence for independent constructs and unique effects on behavior. *Journal of Personality and Social Psychology, 91,* 652–661.

Amodio, D. M., Harmon-Jones, E., & Devine, P. G. (2003). Individual differences in the activation and control of affective race bias as assessed by startle eyeblink responses and self-report. *Journal of Personality and Social Psychology, 84,* 738–753.

Amodio, D. M., Harmon-Jones, E., Devine, P. G., Curtin, J. J., Hartley, S. L., & Covert, A. E. (2004). Neural signals for the detection of unintentional race bias. *Psychological Science, 15,* 88–93.

Amodio, D. M., & Ratner, K. G. (2011). A memory systems model of implicit social cognition. *Current Directions in Psychological Science, 20,* 143–148.

Amodio, D. M., Shah, J. Y., Sigelman, J., Brazy, P. C., & Harmon-Jones, E. (2004). Implicit regulatory focus associated with resting frontal cortical asymmetry. *Journal of Experimental Social Psychology, 40,* 225–232.

Anderson, S. K., and Middleton, V. A. (2018). *Explorations in diversity: Examining the complexities of privilege, discrimination, and oppression.* New York, NY: Oxford University Press.

Andrade, S. (2017, April 16). Cultural influences on mental health. *The Public Health Advocate.* Retrieved from https://pha.berkeley.edu/2017/04/16/cultural-influences-on-mental-health

Arkes, H. R., & Tetlock, P. E. (2004). Attributions of implicit prejudice, or "Would Jesse Jackson 'fail' the implicit association test?" *Psychological Inquiry, 15*(4), 257–278.

Arredondo, P., Toporek, R., Brown, S. P., Jones, J., Locke, D. C., Sanchez, J., . . . Stadler, H. (1996). Operationalization of the multicultural counseling competencies. *Journal of Multicultural Counseling and Development, 24,* 42–78.

Ayres, I. (2015, February 24). When whites get a free pass. *The New York Times, Opinion.* Retrieved from https://www .nytimes.com/2015/02/24/opinion/research-shows-white-privilege-is-real.html

Azar, B. (2010). Your brain on culture. *Monitor on Psychology, 41*(10), 44.

Banaji, M. R., Bazerman, M. H., & Chugh, D. (2003, December). How (un)ethical are you? *Harvard Business Review, 81,* 56–64.

Banaji, M. R., & Greenwald, A. G. (2013). *Blindspot: Hidden biases of good people.* New York, NY: Delacorte Press.

Banaji, M. R., Hardin, C., & Rothman, A. (1993). Implicit stereotyping in person judgment. *Journal of Personality and Social Psychology, 65*(2), 272.

Baron, A. S., & Banaji, M. R. (2006). The development of implicit attitudes: Evidence of race evaluations from ages 6 and 10 and adulthood. *Psychological Science, 17*(1), 54–58.

Blair, I. V. (2002). The malleability of automatic stereotypes and prejudice. *Personality and Social Psychology Review, 6*(3), 242–261.

Blair, I. V., Ma, J. E., & Lenton, A. P. (2001). Imaging stereotypes away: The moderation of implicit stereotypes through mental imagery. *Journal of Personality and Social Psychology, 81*(5), 828–841.

Bryant, F. B., & Veroff, J. (2006). *Savoring: A new model of positive experience.* New York, NY: Taylor Francis.

Cheung, F. M., van de Vijver, F. J. R., & Leong, F. T. L. (2011). Toward a new approach to the study of personality in culture. *The American Psychologist, 66*(7), 593–603.

Chiao, J. Y., & Blizinsky, K. D. (2010). Culture gene coevolution of individualism-collectivism and the serotonin transporter gene. *Proceedings of the Royal Society of Biological Sciences, 277*(1681), 529–537.

Chiao, J. Y., Harada, T., Komeda, H., Li, Z., Mano, Y., Saito, D., Parrish, T. D., Sadato, N., & Iidaka, T. (2008). Neural basis of individualistic and collectivistic views of self. *Human Brain Mapping, 30*(9), 2813–2820.

Comas-Díaz L. (2006). Latino healing: The integration of ethnic psychology into psychotherapy. *Psychotherapy, Theory, Research, Practice, Training, 43*(4), 453–463.

Constantine, M. G. (2001). Multicultural training, theoretical orientation, empathy, and multicultural case conceptualization ability in counselors. *Journal of Mental Health Counseling, 23*(4), 357–372.

Constantine, M. G., & Ladany, N. (2000). Self-report multicultural counseling competence scales: Their relation to social desirability attitudes and multicultural case conceptualization ability. *Journal of Counseling Psychology, 47*(2), 155–164.

Corey, G., Corey, M. S., & Callahan, P. (2011). *Issues and ethics in the helping professions* (8th ed.). Belmont, CA: Brooks/Cole, Cengage.

Cross, T. L., Bazron, B. J., Dennis, K. W., & Isaacs, M. R. (1989). *Towards a culturally competent system of care: A monograph on effective services for minority children who are severely emotionally disturbed.* Retrieved from https://www.ncjrs.gov/App/Publications/abstract.aspx?ID=124939

Cross, W. E., Jr. (1971). The Negro-to-Black conversion experience: Toward a psychology of Black liberation. *Black World, 20,* 13–27.

Dasgupta, P. (2013). National wealth. *Population and Development Review, 38,* 243–264.

Desmond-Harris, J. (2016, August 15). Implicit bias means we're all probably at least a little bit racist. *Vox Media.* Retrieved from https://www.vox.com/2014/12/26/7443979/racism-implicit-racial-bias

Devine, P. G. (1989). Stereotypes and prejudice: Their automatic and controlled components. *Journal of Personality and Social Psychology, 56,* 5–18.

Devine, P. G., Plant, E. A., Amodio, D. M., Harmon-Jones, E., & Vance, S. L. (2002). The regulation of explicit and implicit race bias: The role of motivations to respond without prejudice. *Journal of Personality and Social Psychology, 82,* 835–848.

Dovidio, J. F., & Fiske, S. T. (2012). Under the radar: How unexamined biases in decision-making processes in clinical interactions can contribute to health care disparities. *American Journal of Public Health, 102*(5), 945–952.

Dovidio, J. F., & Gaertner, S. (1986). *Prejudice, discrimination, and racism: Historical trends and contemporary approaches.* Cambridge, MA: Academic Press.

Dovidio, J. F., Kawakami, K., & Gaertner, S. L. (2002). Implicit and explicit prejudice and interracial interaction. *Journal of Personality and Social Psychology, 82*(1), 62–68.

Faigman, D., Kang, J., Bennett, M. W., Carbado, D. W., Casey, P., Dasgupta, N., . . . Mnookin, J. (2012). Implicit bias in the courtroom. *UCLA Law Review, 59*(5), 1124–1186.

Fouad, N., Grus, C., Hatcher, R., Kaslow, N., Hutchings, P., Madison, M., . . . Crossman, R. E. (2009). Competency benchmarks: A model for understanding and measuring competence in professional psychology across training levels. *Training and Education in Professional Psychology, 3*(4), S5–S26.

Fredrickson, B. (1998). What good are positive emotions? *Review of General Psychology, 2,* 300–319.

Freeman, J. B., Rule, N. O., Adams, R. B., & Ambady, N. (2009). Culture shapes a mesolimbic response to signals of dominance and subordination that associates with behavior. *NeuroImage, 47*(1), 353–359.

Galinsky, A. D., & Moskowitz, G. B. (2000). Perspective-taking: Decreasing stereotype expression, stereotype accessibility, and in-group favoritism. *Journal of Personality and Social Psychology, 78*(4), 708–724.

Galinsky, A. D., & Moskowitz, G. B. (2007). Further ironies of suppression: Stereotype and counterstereotype accessibility. *Journal of Experimental Social Psychology, 43*(5), 833–841.

Gallardo, M. E. (2012). Therapists as cultural architects and systemic advocates: Latina/o skills identification stage model. In M. E. Gallardo, C. J. Yeh, J. E. Trimble, & T. A. Parham (Eds.), *Culturally adaptive counseling skills: Demonstrations of evidence-based practices* (pp. 77–112). Thousand Oaks, CA: Sage.

Gallardo, M. E., Johnson, J., Parham, T. A., & Carter, J. A. (2009). Ethics and multiculturalism: Advancing cultural and clinical responsiveness. *Professional Psychology: Theory, Research, Practice, Training, 40*(5), 425–435.

Gallardo, M. E., Yeh, C. J., Trimble, J. E., & Parham, T. (Eds.). (2012). *Culturally adaptive counseling skills: Demonstrations of evidence-based practices.* Thousand Oaks, CA: Sage.

Garrett, M. T., Torres-Rivera, E., Brubaker, M., Portman, T. A., Brotherton, D., West-Olatunji, C., . . . Grayshield, L. (2011). Crying for a vision. The Native American sweat lodge ceremony as therapeutic intervention. *Journal of Counseling and Development, 89*(3), 318–325.

Gelso, C. J., & Woodhouse, S. (2003). Toward a positive psychotherapy: Focus on human strength. In W. B. Walsh (Ed.), *Counseling psychology and human strength* (pp. 171–197). New York, NY: Erlbaum.

Georges, C. M., & Tomlinson-Clarke, S. M. (2015). Integrating positive psychology into counseling psychology doctoral education. *The Counseling Psychologist, 43*(5), 752–788.

Geva, E., & Weiner, J. (2015). *Psychological assessment of culturally and linguistically diverse children and adolescents*. New York, NY: Springer.

Goh, J. O. S., Leshikar, E. D., Sutton, B. P., Tan, C. J., Sim, S. K. Y., Hebrank, A. C., & Park, D. (2010). Culture differences in neural processing of faces and houses in the ventral visual cortex. *Social Cognitive and Affective Neuroscience, 5*(2–3), 227–235.

Gopalakrishnan, N., & Babacan, H. (2015). Cultural diversity and mental health. *Australasian Psychiatry, 23*(6, suppl.), 6–8.

Graham, S., & Lowery, B. S. (2004). Priming unconscious racial stereotypes about adolescent offenders. *Law and Human Behavior, 28*(5), 483–504.

Green, A. R., Carney, D. R., Pallin, D. J., Ngo, L. H., Raymond, K. L., Iezzoni, L. I., & Banaji, M. R. (2007). Implicit bias among physicians and its prediction of thrombolysis decisions for black and white patients. *Journal of General Internal Medicine, 22*(9), 1231–1238. DOI: http://doi.org/10.1007/s11606-007-0258-5.

Greenwald, A. G., & Krieger, L. H. (2006). Implicit bias: Scientific foundations. *California Law Review, 94*(4), 945–967.

Greenwald, A. G., McGhee, D. E., & Schwartz, J. L. K. (1998). Measuring individual differences in implicit cognition: The implicit association test. *Journal of Personality and Social Psychology, 74*(6), 1464–1480.

Greenwald, A. G., Nosek, B. A., & Banaji, M. R. (2003). Understanding and using the implicit association test: I. An improved scoring algorithm. *Journal of Personality and Social Psychology, 85*, 197–216

Greenwald, A. G., Poehlman, T. A., Uhlmann, E. L., & Banaji, M. R. (2009). Understanding and using the implicit association test: III. Meta-analysis of predictive validity. *Journal of Personality and Social Psychology, 97*(1), 17–41.

Hanson, R., & Mendius, R. (2009). *Buddha's brain: The practical neuroscience of happiness, love, and wisdom*. Oakland, CA: New Harbinger.

Harbin, J. M., Gelso, C. J., & Perez Rojas, A. E. (2013). Therapist work with strengths: Development and validation of a measure. *The Counseling Psychologist, 42*, 345–373.

Harper, F. D. (2003). Background: Concepts and history. In F. D. Harper & J. McFadden (Eds.), *Culture and counseling: New approaches* (pp. 1–19). Boston, MA: Allyn & Bacon.

Harper, F. D., & McFadden, J. (Eds.). (2003). *Culture and counseling: New approaches*. Boston, MA: Allyn & Bacon.

Harris, J. E. (2012). Multicultural counseling in a multitheoretical context: New applications for practice. In M. E. Gallardo, C. J. Yeh, J. E. Trimble, & T. A. Parham (Eds.), *Culturally adaptive counseling skills: Demonstrations of evidence-based practices* (pp. 287–312). Thousand Oaks, CA: Sage.

Hedden, S. K., Aron, A., Markus, H. R., & Gabrieli, J. D. E. (2008). Cultural influences on neural substrates of attentional control. *Psychological Science, 19*(1), 12–17.

Helms, J. E. (1989). Considering some methodological issues in racial identity counseling research. *The Counseling Psychologist, 17*, 227–252.

Helms, J. E. (1990). *Black and white racial identity attitudes: Theory, research, and practice*. Westport, CT: Greenwood Press.

Helms, J. E., Jernigan, M., & Mascher, J. (2005). The meaning of race in psychology and how to change it: A methodological perspective. *American Psychologist, 60*(1), 27–36.

Helms, J. E., & Richardson, T. Q. (1997). How "multiculturalism" obscures race and culture as differential aspects of counseling competency. In D. Pope-Davis & H. Coleman (Eds.), *Multicultural counseling competencies: Assessment, education, and training and supervision* (pp. 60–79). Thousand Oaks, CA: Sage.

Herlihy, B., & Corey, G. (2015). *ACA ethical standards casebook* (7th ed.). Alexandria, VA: American Counseling Association.

Higa, C. K., & Chorpita, B. F. (2007). Evidence-based therapies: Translating research into practice. In R. G. Steele, T. D. Elkin, & M. C. Roberts (Eds.), *Handbook of evidence-based therapies for children and adolescents: Bridging science and practice* (pp. 45–61). New York, NY: Springer-Verlag.

Hofstede, G. (1984). *Culture's consequences: International differences in work-related values* (2nd ed.). Beverly Hills, CA: Sage.

Hoshmand, L. T. (Ed.) (2006). *Culture, psychotherapy, and counseling: Critical and integrative perspectives*. Thousand Oaks, CA: Sage.

Huang, C., & Zane, N. (2016). Cultural influences in mental health treatment. *Current Opinion in Psychology, 8*, 131–136.

Huntington, S. P. (2004). *Who are we? The challenges to America's national identity.* New York, NY: Simon & Schuster.

Ibrahim, F. A., & Owen, S. V. (1994). Factor analytic structure of the Scale to Assess Worldview. *Current Psychology, 13,* 201–209.

Jones-Smith, E. (2014). *Strengths-based therapy: Connecting theory, practice, and skills.* Thousand Oaks, CA: Sage.

Jones-Smith, E. (2015). *Culturally responsive strengths-based therapy: Some interventions.* Paper written for a presentation, Philadelphia, PA.

Kang, J., & Lane, K. (2010). Seeing through colorblindness: Implicit bias and the law. *UCLA Law Review, 58*(2), 465–520.

Katz, J. N. (1985). The sociopolitical nature of counseling. *The Counseling Psychologist, 13,* 615–624.

Kirmayer, L. (2012). Rethinking cultural competence. *Transcultural Psychiatry, 49*(2), 149–164.

Kirwan Institute for the Study of Race and Ethnicity. (2015). Understanding implicit bias. *The Ohio State University.* Retrieved from http://kirwaninstitute.osu.edu/research/understanding-implicit-bias/

Kohn, L. P., Oden, T., Munoz, R. F., Robinson, A., & Leavitt, D. (2002). Adapted cognitive behavioral group therapy for depressed low-income African American women. *Community Mental Health Journal, 38*(6), 497–504.

Kottak, C., & Kozaitis, K. A. (2002). *On being different: Diversity and multiculturalism in the North American mainstream.* Boston, MA: McGraw-Hill.

Kressin, N. R., & Groeneveld, P. W. (2015). Race/ethnicity and overuse of care: A systematic review. *Milbank Quarterly, 93*(1), 112–138.

Lampropoulos, G. K. (2001). Integrating psychopathology, positive psychology, and psychotherapy. *American Psychologist, 56,* 87–88.

Lee, D. L., Sheridan, J. J., Rosen, A. D., & Jones, I. (2013). Psychotherapy trainees' multicultural case conceptualization content: Thematic differences across three cases. *Psychotherapy, 50*(2), 206–212.

Leu, J., Wang, J., & Koo, K. (2011). Are positive emotions just as "positive" across cultures? *Cognition and Emotion, 11,* 994–999. DOI: 10.1037/a0021332.

Lewis, J., Arnold, M., House, R., & Toporek, R. (2003). *Advocacy competencies.* Retrieved from http://www.counseling.org/Resources

Lopez, S. J., Edwards, L. M., Magyar-Moe, J. L., Pedrotti, J. T., & Ryder, J. A. (2003). Fulfilling its promise: Counseling psychology's efforts to understand and promote optimal human functioning. In W. B. Walsh (Ed.), *Counseling psychology and human strength* (pp. 297–308). New York, NY: Erlbaum.

Lopez, S. J., Floyd, R. K., Ulven, J. C., & Snyder, C. R. (Eds.). (2000). *Hope therapy: Helping clients build a house of hope.* New York, NY: Academic Press.

Lopez, S. J., Prosser, E. C., Edwards, L. M., Magyar-Moe, J. L., Neufeld, J. E., & Rasmussen, H. N. (2002). Putting positive psychology in a multicultural context. In C. R. Snyder & S. J. Lopez (Eds.), *Handbook of positive psychology* (pp. 700–714). New York, NY: Oxford.

Lopez, S. J., & Snyder, C. R. (2003a). The future of positive psychological assessment: Making a difference. In S. J. Lopez & C. R. Snyder (Eds.), *Positive psychology assessment: A handbook of models and measures* (pp. 461–468). Washington, DC: American Psychological Association.

Lopez, S. J., & Snyder, C. R. (Eds.). (2003b). *Positive psychology assessment: A handbook of models and measures.* Washington, DC: American Psychological Association.

Losin, E. R., Dapretto, M., & Iacoboni, M. (2010). Culture and neuroscience: Additive or synergistic? *Social Cognitive and Affective Neuroscience, 5*(2–3), 148–158.

Lu, L., & Gilmour, R. (2004). Culture and conceptions of happiness: Individual oriented and social oriented. *Journal of Happiness Studies, 5,* 269–291.

McAuliffe, G., & Associates. (2013). *Culturally alert counseling: A comprehensive introduction.* (2nd ed.). Thousand Oaks, CA: Sage.

McConnell, A. R., & Liebold, J. M. (2009). Weak criticisms and selective evidence: Reply to Blanton et al. *Journal of Applied Psychology, 94*(3), 583–589.

McIntosh, P. (1989). *White privilege: Unpacking the invisible knapsack.* Retrieved from https://nationalseedproject.org/white-privilege-unpacking-the-invisible-knapsack

Minkov, M. (with contributions by G. Hofstede). (2013). *Cross-cultural analysis: The science and art of comparing the world's modern societies and their cultures.* Thousand Oaks, CA: Sage.

Miranda, J., Bernal, G., Lau, A., Kohn, L., Hwang, W. C., & Lafromboise, T. (2005). State of the science on psychosocial interventions for ethnic minorities. *Annual Review of Clinical Psychology, 1,* 113–142.

Monk, G. D., Winslade, J. M., & Sinclair, S. L. (2008). *New horizons in multicultural counseling.* Thousand Oaks, CA: Sage.

Morales, E., & Norcross, J. C. (2010), Evidence-based practices with ethnic minorities: Strange bedfellows no more. *Journal of Clinical Psychology, 66*(8), 1–9.

National Alliance on Mental Illness. (2008). *Evidence-based practices and multicultural mental health.* Retrieved from http://www.healthalt.org/uploads/2/3/7/5/23750643/ebps_and_multicultural_mental_health.pdf

Newheiser, A., & Dovidio, J. F. (2012). Individual differences and intergroup bias: Divergent dynamics associated with prejudice and stereotyping. *Personality and Individual Differences, 53,* 70–74.

Newheiser, A., & Olson, K. R. (2012). White and Black American children's implicit intergroup bias. *Journal of Experimental Social Psychology, 48*, 264–270.

Nier, J. (2005). How disassociated are implicit and explicit racial attitudes? A bogus pipeline approach. *Group Processes and Intergroup Relations, 8*(1), 39–52.

Nosek, B. A., & Banaji, M. R. (2001). The go/no-go association task. *Social Cognition, 19*, 625–666.

Nosek, B. A., Banaji, M. R., & Greenwald, A. G. (2002a). Harvesting implicit group attitudes and beliefs from a demonstration web site. *Group Dynamics: Theory, Research, and Practice, 6*, 101–115.

Nosek, B. A., Banaji, M. R., & Greenwald, A. G. (2002b). Math = male, me = female, therefore math is not equal to me. *Journal of Personality and Social Psychology, 83*, 44–59.

Nosek, B. A., Smyth, F. L., Hansen, J. J., Devos, T., Linder, N. M., Ranganath, K. A., . . . Banaji, M. R. (2007). Pervasiveness and correlates of implicit attitudes and stereotypes. *European Review of Social Psychology, 18*, 36–88.

Ofan, R. H., Rubin, N., & Amodio, D. M. (2011). Seeing race: N170 responses to race and their relation to automatic racial attitudes and controlled processing. *Journal of Cognitive Neuroscience, 23*, 3152–3161.

Ofan, R. H., Rubin, N., & Amodio, D. M. (2014). Situation-based social anxiety enhances the neural processing of faces: Evidence from an intergroup context. *Social Cognitive and Affective Neuroscience, 9*(8), 1055–1061.

Olson, M. A., & Fazio, R. H. (2004). Trait inferences as a function of automatically activated racial attitudes and motivation to control prejudiced reactions. *Basic and Applied Social Psychology, 26*, 1–12.

Owens, R. L., Magyar-Moe, J. L., & Lopez, S. J. (2015). Finding balance via positive psychological assessment and conceptualization: Recommendations for practice. *The Counseling Psychologist, 43*(5), 634–670.

Parham, T. A. (2012). Delivering culturally competent therapeutic services to African American clients: The skills that distinguish between clinical intention and successful outcomes. In M. E. Gallardo, C. J. Yeh, J. E. Trimble, & T. A. Parham (Eds.), *Culturally adaptive counseling skills: Demonstrations of evidence-based practices* (pp. 23–41). Thousand Oaks, CA: Sage.

Pedersen, P. B. (1991, September–October). Introduction to the special issue on multiculturalism as a fourth force in counseling. *Journal of Counseling and Development*. Retrieved from https://onlinelibrary.wiley.com/doi/abs/10.1002/j.1556-6676.1991.tb01553.x

Pedersen, P. B., Lonner, W. J., Draguns, J. G., Trimble, J. E., & Scharrón del Rio, M. R. (Eds). (2016). *Counseling across cultures* (7th ed.). Thousand Oaks, CA: Sage.

Perez, E. (2010). *Implicit bias against Latinos affects all immigrants, Vanderbilt research shows*. Retrieved from https://news.vanderbilt.edu/2010/07/01/implicit-bias-against-latinos/

Phelps, E. A., O'Connor, K. J., Cunningham, W. A., Funayama, E. S., Gatenby, J. C., Gore, J. C., & Banaji, M. R. (2000). Performance on indirect measures of race evaluation predicts amygdala activation. *Journal of Cognitive Neuroscience, 12*, 729–738.

Plant, E. A., & Devine, P. G. (1998). Internal and external motivation to respond without prejudice. *Journal of Personality and Social Psychology, 75*(3), 811–832.

Ponterotto, J. G., Casas, J. M., Suzuki, L. A., & Alexander, C. M. (Eds.). (2010). *Handbook of multicultural counseling* (3rd ed.). Thousand Oaks, CA: Sage.

Ponterotto, J. G., Utsey, S., & Pedersen, P. B. (2006). *Preventing prejudice: A guide for counselors, educators, and parents.* Thousand Oaks, CA: Sage.

Priester, P., Jones, J., Jackson-Bailey, C., Jana-Masri, A., Jordan, E., & Metz, A. (2008). An analysis of content and instructional strategies in multicultural counseling courses. *Journal of Multicultural Counseling and Development, 36*(1), 29–39.

Ratts, M. J., & Pedersen, P. B. (2015). *Counseling for multiculturalism and social justice.* Alexandria, VA: American Counseling Association.

Ridley, C. R. (2005). *Overcoming unintentional racism in counseling and therapy* (2nd ed.). Thousand Oaks, CA: Sage.

Ridley, C. R., Mollen, D., & Shannon, M. K. (2011). Counseling competence: Application and implications of a model. *The Counseling Psychologist, 39*(6), 865–886.

Rogers, C. R. (1956). *Client-centered therapy: Its current practice, implications and theory* (3rd ed.). Boston, MA: Houghton Mifflin.

Rosenberg, K. R., & Trevathan, W. R. (2003, May). The evolution of human birth. *Scientific American*, Vol. 80–85.

Roysircar, G., Arredondo, P., Fuertes, J. N., Ponterotto, J. G., & Toporek, R. L. (2003). *Multicultural counseling competencies, 2003: Association for Multicultural Counseling and Development.* Alexandria, VA: American Counseling Association.

Rudman, L. A. (2004). Social justice in our minds, homes, and society: The nature, causes, and consequences of implicit bias. *Social Justice Research, 17*(2), 129–142.

Rutland, A., Cameron, L., Bennett, L., & Ferrell, J. (2005). Interracial contact and racial constancy: A multi-site study of racial intergroup bias in 3–5 year old Anglo-British children. *Applied Developmental Psychology, 26*, 699–713.

Saleebey, D. (2002). *The strengths perspective in social work practice.* New York, NY: Longman.

Saleebey, D. (2008). *The strengths perspective in social work* (5th ed.). Upper Saddle River, NJ: Pearson.

Scales, P. C., Benson, P. L., Leffert, N., & Blyth, D. A. (2000). Contribution of developmental assets to the prediction of thriving among adolescents. *Applied Developmental Science, 4*, 27–46.

Seligman, M. E. (1998). The president's address. *American Psychologist, 54*, 559–562.

Seligman, M. (2002a). *Authentic happiness: New positive psychology to realize your potential for lasting fulfillment.* New York, NY: Free Press.

Seligman, M. E. P. (2002b). Positive psychology, positive prevention, and positive therapy. In C. R. Snyder & S. J. Lopez (Eds.), *Handbook of positive psychology* (pp. 3–12). New York, NY: Oxford.

Seligman, M. E. P., & Csikszentmihalyi, M. (2000). Positive psychology: An introduction. *American Psychologist, 19*, 5–14.

Seligman, M. E. P., & Peterson, C. (2003). Positive clinical psychology. In L. G. Aspinwall & U. M. Staudinger (Eds.), *A psychology of human strengths: Fundamental questions and future research directions for a positive psychology* (pp. 305–318). Washington, DC: American Psychological Association.

Seligman, M. E. P., Schulman, P., DeRubeis, R., & Hollon, S. (1999). The prevention of depression and anxiety. *Prevention and Treatment, 2.*

Shih, M., Bonam, C., Sanchez, D., & Peck, C. (2007). The social construction of race: Biracial identity and susceptibility to stereotypes. *Cultural Diversity and Ethnic Minority Psychology, 13*, 125–133.

Slotkin, J. S. (Ed.). (1965). *Readings in early anthropology.* London, England: Methuen.

Smedley, A., & Smedley, B. D. (2005). Race as biology is fiction, racism as a social problem is real: Anthropological and historical perspectives on the social construction of race. *American Psychologist, 60*(1), 16–26.

Smith, E. J. (1985). Ethnic minorities: Life stress, social support, and mental health issues (Major contribution). *The Counseling Psychologist, 13*, 537–579.

Smith, E. J. (1991). Ethnic identity development: Toward the development of a theory within the context of majority/minority status. *Journal of Counseling & Development, 70*, 181–188.

Smith, E. J. (2006). The strengths-based counseling model (Major contribution). *The Counseling Psychologist, 34*, 13–79.

Smith, E. J., & Vasquez, M. J. T. (Eds.). (1985). Cross-cultural counseling [Special issue]. *The Counseling Psychologist, 13*(4).

Sue, D. W. (1972). Counseling Chinese Americans. *Personnel and Guidance Journal, 50*, 637–644.

Sue, D. W., Arredondo, P., & McDavis, R. J. (1992). Multicultural competencies/standards: A call to the profession. *Journal of Counseling and Development, 70*(4), 477–486.

Sue, D. W., & Sue, D. (2013). *Counseling the culturally diverse: Theory and practice* (6th ed.). Hoboken, NJ: Wiley.

Sumner, W. G. (1906). *Folkways: A study of the sociological importance of usages, manners, customs, mores, and morals.* Boston, MA: Ginn.

Tervalon, M., & Murray-Garcia, J. (1998). Cultural humility versus cultural competence: A critical distinction in defining physician training outcomes in multicultural education. *Journal Health Care for the Poor and Underserved, 9*(2), 117–125.

Thomas, K. R., & Weinrach, S. G. (2004). Mental health counseling and the AMCD Multicultural Counseling Competencies: A civil debate. *Journal of Mental Health Counseling, 26*(1), 41–43.

Tomlinson-Clarke, S. M., & Georges, C. M. (2014). A commentary on integrating multicultural and strength-based considerations into counseling training and practice. *The Professional Counselor, 4*, 272–281.

Toporek, R. L. (2012). So what should I actually do? Developing skills for greater multicultural competence. In M. E. Gallardo, C. J. Yeh, J. E. Trimble, & T. Parham (Eds.), *Culturally adaptive counseling skills: Demonstrations of evidence-based practices* (pp. 267–286). Thousand Oaks, CA: Sage.

Tseng, W., & Streltzer, J. (2004). *Cultural competence in clinical psychiatry.* Washington, DC: American Psychiatric Association.

Uchida, Y., Norasakkunkit, V., & Kitayama, S. (2004). Cultural constructions of happiness: Theory and empirical evidence. *Journal of Happiness Studies, 5*, 223–239. DOI: http://dx.doi.org/10.1007/s10902-004-8785-9.

Velez, B. L., & Moradi, B., & DeBlaere, C. (2015). Multiple oppressions and the mental health of sexual minority Latina/o individuals. *The Counseling Psychologist, 43*, 7–38. doi:10.1177/0011000014542836

Weick, A., & Chamberlain, R. (2002). Putting problems in their place: Further explorations in the strengths perspective. In D. Saleebey (Ed.), *The strengths perspective in social work practice* (3rd ed., pp. 95–105). Boston, MA: Allyn & Bacon.

Weinrach, S. G., & Thomas, K. R. (2004). The AMCD Multicultural Counseling Competencies: A critically flawed initiative. *Journal of Mental Health Counseling, 26*(1), 81–93.

Wrenn, C. G. (1962). The culturally encapsulated counselor. *Harvard Educational Review, 32*, 444–449.

Zhu, Y., Zhang, L., Fan, J., & Han, S. (2007). Neural basis of cultural influence on self representation. *NeuroImage, 34*(3), 1310–1316.

2 CULTURAL MEANING SYSTEMS, CULTURAL TRUST, AND CULTURAL HUMILITY

- *"The Chinese use two brush strokes to write the word 'crisis.' One brush stroke stands for danger; the other for opportunity. In a crisis, be aware of the danger—but recognize the opportunity."* —John F. Kennedy, 1959.

- *"The rapprochement of peoples is only possible when differences of culture and outlook are respected and appreciated rather than feared and condemned, when the common bond of human dignity is recognized as the essential bond for a peaceful world."* —J. William Fulbright

CHAPTER OBJECTIVES

- Identify cultural principles that affect clients' lives and their mental health issues.

- Discuss how culture influences the hemispheres of the brain.

- Describe how individuals' cultural attachments lay the groundwork for developing a cultural identity.

- Recognize that cultural attitudes, beliefs, and values are well-traveled neural pathways in the brain that allow individuals to develop their own "personal culture" that reflects their views on what should be the role of culture in their life.

- Explain the role of neuroscience in counselor education programs in helping students to develop an understanding of the neurobiology of behavior.

- Recognize and counsel clients effectively who are experiencing acculturative stress.

- Explain how to establish cultural trust, cultural empathy, and cultural humility in a ***culturally diverse counseling*** relationship.

INTRODUCTION

All counseling is inevitably multicultural counseling, if one takes into account the broad factors in which people differ, such as race, socioeconomic status, sexual orientation, age, physical disability, and so on. Each person has different life experiences, even when he or she comes from the same ethnic or cultural group and even when he or she comes from the same family. For each person, **culture** is an internalized object that becomes introjected, or taken inward, into one's being (Comas-Díaz & Jacobsen, 1991). We all make decisions about which aspect of culture we value and want to include as a part of our lives and heritage. All counseling is multicultural because no two people have the exact same cultural experiences in life (Anderson & Carter, 2003).

Culturally responsive counseling is not just something that can be tacked on to so-called regular therapy. Culture has both conscious and unconscious components that might have a bearing on the presenting issue that the client brings to counseling, or it might have an influence on how the client copes with or responds behaviorally and emotionally to the presenting issue (Jones-Smith, 2014). Counselors must comprehend how their cultural values and theoretical orientations provide a counseling worldview that determines how they observe, assess, define, and approach client problems (Bäärnhielm & Rosso, 2009; Groen, 2009; Jones-Smith, 2014).

This chapter presents a framework for understanding the importance of culture in a person's life.

Organization of Chapter 2

The chapter is divided into several parts. Part 1 examines generic principles regarding the nature of culture. It reviews Hall's (1976) iceberg conception of culture—that is, culture is more than what is visible to the eye. To understand a person's culture, one has to go beneath the visible surface to connect with its deeper meaning systems. Part 1 also provides important definitions for emic and etic culture. It provides a brief overview of Western and Eastern cultural differences, and it offers an exercise professors can use with counselor trainees to sensitize them to another person's culture.

Part 2 analyzes the globalization of culture. The world is becoming more similar than different as large corporations are located in most major countries in the world. Cultural globalization produces common worldwide habits and methods of communicating within one's country, as well as with other nations. Increasingly, the world is experiencing a type of cultural leveling and cultural diffusion (Lim, 2008). Moreover, this section presents information on culture and neuroscience, as well as the impact of the new Council for Accreditation of Counseling and Related Educational Programs (CACREP) Standards on neuroscience and counseling.

Part 3 deals with culture and the process of identity development, including a person's development of a cultural and ethnic self. The tripartite conception of culture and identity is presented as a way to address how culture fits into a person's overall identity (Jones-Smith, 2014; Smith, 1985). A model for understanding the cultural and racial identity for counselors and therapists is provided. The positive benefits of a cultural identity are considered.

Part 4 deals with culturally responsive clinical skill development. The clinical skills of cultural awareness, cultural empathy, and cultural humility are discussed, and a case example is provided.

The chapter begins by discussing principles of culture.

CULTURAL PRINCIPLES

Understanding the nature and influence of culture is a major goal for counselors and therapists. Table 2.1 lists general principles that researchers have written about the nature of culture (Hall, 1976; Ratts & Pedersen, 2014).

TABLE 2.1 ■ Cultural Principles
• It is easier to observe the culture of others than it is to recognize the beliefs, attitudes, and values of our own culture.
• All culture is learned. We learn our first culture by the age of five. Our cultural learning includes how to dress, what to eat, whom to talk with and how, what should be avoided, language, table manners, how to interact with those of different ages, and acceptable emotional responses.
• Culture is a shared programming of the mind that allows members of a group to distinguish themselves from other groups.
• Although culture is resistant to change, it nevertheless does change. At one time, for instance, women did not work outside the home in large numbers in American society.
• The family is the primary interpreter and reinforcer of culture to children.
• As a result of having been reared in our first culture, we are predisposed to make errors in interpreting a second culture.
• Culture consists of explicit and implicit patterns of behavior that have been learned and shared through symbols and artifacts. Culture involves symbolic communication of the traditional values of a people that are transmitted from one generation to another.
• We tend to behave as we have been culturally conditioned to respond. When we work cross-culturally with clients in counseling, we are inclined to use our learned cultural perspective to conceptualize clients' issues and interpret our clients' behavior.
• Within-group cultural differences may be as great as between-group cultural differences. For instance, there may be as many differences among Italian Americans as there are between Italian Americans and Germans.

TABLE 2.2 ■ The Iceberg Model of Culture	
Visible Culture	**Invisible Culture**
External	Internal
Conscious	Largely unconscious
Learned explicitly	Learned implicitly
Observable behaviors such as dance, music, clothing, flags, food, performance and visual arts, holidays, and festivals	Hidden, deeply held beliefs and values about interpersonal relationships, assumptions, and expectations about gender, time, age, and social status

Source: Jones-Smith, 2014.

THE ICEBERG CONCEPT OF CULTURE

Edward Hall (1976), a famous anthropologist, created what has become known as the iceberg theory of culture. According to him, a culture of any society could be compared to an iceberg. There are some visible aspects of a culture above the water, but there is a larger portion of culture that is hidden beneath the surface. In addition, culture is both external and internal. The external or conscious features of culture are those things that we can see, and these aspects form the tip of the iceberg. The visible, external parts of the culture that we can see plainly consist of a group's preferences for food, clothing, music, visual arts, language, flags, dance, and performing arts. A significant proportion of visible culture is behavioral. The visible parts of culture are typically explicitly learned and conscious, and may be changed more easily than the invisible parts (see Table 2.2).

In contrast, the invisible parts of culture are largely unconscious, learned implicitly, and difficult to change. Invisible parts of a person's culture consist of that culture's deeply held beliefs, values, and thought patterns. It is difficult for outsiders to understand easily the invisible parts of another culture. Those cultural features are known primarily by those who were born into the culture or by those who actively participated in the culture. We cannot judge another person's culture based only on what we see—that is, the visible part of his or her culture. Instead, we must take time to get to know other people and interact with them on an interpersonal basis. The best way to learn the internal culture of others is to participate actively in their culture.

EMIC AND ETIC PERSPECTIVES ON CULTURE

The terms *emic* and *etic* were coined by the linguistic anthropologist Kenneth Pike in 1954 and later expanded upon in his book, *Language in Relation to a Unified Theory of the Structure of Human Behavior* (1967). An **emic perspective** is culturally specific. Those who hold an emic perspective believe that cultural differences should be considered in the assessment and treatment of individuals from culturally diverse groups. An **etic perspective** is defined as culturally universal, and it is governed by the belief that people share far more commonalities than differences; consequently, mental disorders are similar across all cultures and societies (Locke & Bailey, 2014).

A counselor who functions from an etic perspective maintains that mental disorders such as depression, schizophrenia, and anxiety occur in all cultures and societies, and that the counselor must make only small or minor changes in treating these disorders from one culture to another (Arnett, 2009). The etic perspective says that depression is the same regardless of one's culture.

In contrast, the emic or culturally specific perspective maintains that there are cultural concepts of distress. For instance, people from a Hispanic or Latino/a cultural background may report feeling the culture-bound syndrome of *ataque de nervios* to describe what some etic-oriented clinicians define as a panic attack. Subsequent chapters of this book deal with culture-bound mental health syndromes (Locke & Bailey, 2014).

CULTURE AND NEUROSCIENCE

The discipline of neuroscience examines the neurobiological bases of human behaviors, thoughts, and feelings. Cultural neuroscience emphasizes the interaction of nature and nurture to understand how cultural and biological factors interact to have an impact on individuals. Neuroscience is helping researchers learn how values and beliefs affect the ways in which our brains function, as well as the way we see and then perceive objects and people. Counselors can use neuroscience in a number of ways. For instance, neuroscience can be used for the diagnosis and treatment of mental disorders.

Advocates of incorporating concepts from neuroscience in counseling maintain that counselors must know what is taking place in a client's brain in order to give a thorough diagnosis and treatment plan. The 2016 CACREP Standards recognize the importance of neuroscience in counselor education by requiring coursework that develops an understanding of the neurobiology of behavior: "the relationship among brain anatomy, function, biochemistry, and learning and behavior" (Myers & Young, 2012, p. 60). Myers and Young (2012) have suggested that the purpose of CACREP was to require counselors to get the training necessary to integrate neuroscience into their clinical work.

Montes (2013) has highlighted the importance of obtaining training in the neuroscience perspective because a number of newer theoretical approaches (e.g., cognitive enhancement therapy and eye movement desensitization and reprocessing therapy) use principles from neuroscience. Moreover, researchers are beginning to examine the efficacy of neurobiologically based counseling—such as neurofeedback.

Makinson and Young (2012) have described the neurobiological factors associated with posttraumatic stress disorder (e.g., the role of the prefrontal cortex and amygdala in processing traumatic events and in emotional self-regulation). These researchers have described how reprocessing therapy can be used to treat posttraumatic stress disorder from a neuroscience perspective. The neuroscience perspective has also been used to treat attention deficit disorder.

Our **cultural competence** is influenced by the neural pathways we have created in our brains as a result of cultural interactions or the lack thereof. We can only become as culturally competent as our brains will permit. The neural pathways that we have created in response to ourselves and other cultures and ethnic groups will create a fear or a comfort response in our brains. If there are deep neural pathways that have been created and sustained by negative cultural experiences with those who are different from us, our brains will put limits on us by sending danger signals to the amygdala. We have to retrain our brains to move beyond our implicit biases.

NEUROSCIENCE AND CULTURAL DIFFERENCES

The human brain and culture. Do the hemispheres of the brain influence culture, and vice versa, one might ask, and do cultures favor either the right or left brain? According to Iain McGilchrist's book, *The Master and His Emissary: The Divided Brain and the Making of the Western World* (2009), cultures do appear to prefer using either the right or left hemisphere of the brain. McGilchrist posits that what makes people happy is not wealth, but rather the relationships they establish between themselves and others, between themselves and the rest of the outer world. It is the right-brain hemisphere that understands the importance of relationships because it is that hemisphere that controls empathy and interconnectedness of people. In contrast, the left-brain hemisphere tends to view the world more in terms of separateness, or discrete parts rather than wholes.

According to McGilchrist (2009), culture can change the brain. The brain is primarily an information-processing structure. Culture reflects what a group of people living in a given environment have directed their attention to, as well as the attention of their children. Almost every culture contains some features of left-brain and right-brain activities and artifacts. McGilchrist proposes that cultures that emphasize a collectivist orientation toward life or an orientation that stresses the importance of the group over the individual are inclined to view life primarily from the right hemisphere. Hence, Eastern cultures tend to place a higher value on right-brain information processing and knowing based on right-brain perceptions.

In contrast, European cultures tend to value left-brain information processing. For instance, European cultures stress the scientific method as being the primary means by which something can become known or understood. The American Psychological Association's demand for "evidence-based" therapy reflects the high priority that European culture places on left-brain information processing.

Even approaches to therapy or counseling tend to favor right-hemisphere or left-hemisphere ways to interact with clients. For instance, mindfulness therapy (a Chinese therapeutic approach) is largely oriented toward right-brain information processing. In contrast, cognitive behavioral therapy (an American therapeutic approach) is oriented more toward left-brain information processing. The attraction of mindfulness therapy for many Westerners resides in its different way of knowing and viewing the world—its right-brain way of understanding self and others. Psychoanalytic therapy is largely a left-brain therapy. When working with clients, counselors need to take into account how culture has influenced or had an impact on a client's brain.

Table 2.3 compares and contrasts Western and Eastern philosophies. Nisbett's (2003) and Santee's (2007) books provide the basis for the following comparisons and contrasts between Eastern and Western philosophies.

THE GLOBALIZATION OF CULTURE

The cultural globalization of the world has arrived, and with it comes significant changes in our views about culture, its importance, and the nature of cultural and ethnic groups (Lim, 2008). Cultural globalization produces common worldwide habits, shared cultural norms, and common knowledge systems across diverse cultural populations. The forces that have created these emerging global trends can be conceptualized as (1) transnational media, (2) mass travel, (3) migration, and (4) technological change. According to Lim (2008), the globalization of culture has been spearheaded by large powerful corporations that place McDonald's, Apple, Walmart, and other American companies in cities throughout the world. Lim has stated, the "new global culture certainly seems to privilege Western consumerism, the spread of uncontrolled capitalism and the free market, and deregulated commercialism and to most benefit those in the most privileged positions in American and European societies" (p. 229). All over the world, people are having daily contact with those who come from a broad spectrum of cultural identities. Our identities are produced through having experienced complex processes. Because within-group differences are so great for people who classify themselves into a specific cultural or ethnic group, we must be cautious about identifying specific therapeutic practices that might best be appropriate for all members of an ethnic/racial group, cultural group, or gender/sexual orientation group.

TABLE 2.3 ■ Western and Eastern Philosophical and Cultural Differences		
Issue	Western Culture/Philosophy	Eastern Culture/Philosophy
Search for Truth and the Nature of Knowledge and Knowing	Truth is an absolute. The truth needs to be proved. Westerners search for truth outside of themselves—in the procedures that they establish or in the instruments that they use. Westerners developed mathematical procedures to discover absolute truth. The demand for "empirical verification" or "evidence-based studies" is part of the Western cultural value system. Behavioral therapy searches for the "right" reinforcement, considers extinction, and uses punishment—all Western values. Reason, logic, and science are the final arbiters for determining knowledge and truth occurrences about the world. There is a search for certainty. Western therapy is based on the scientific method, which is supposed to be objective, independent, and universal in understanding the underlying truth or reality. Western science is viewed as the source for truth. If something cannot be defined, operationalized, and measured, then its value is reduced.	Truth is relative. The truth is given and does not need to be proved. Truth can be discovered by searching within oneself—through meditation and right living. The true key is inside a person. What is valuable is the inner world of people and their natural ability to control and develop their emotional life. Morita therapy, Naikan therapy, and mindfulness all developed out of the tradition that maintains that it is the inner search that is most important. For Buddhism and Taoism, direct experience is the final arbiter of truth and knowledge. Confucius says, "The superior man understands what is right; the inferior man understands what will sell."
Individual vs. Group/ Collective; the Self	The sense of self is independent from others and from the physical world. An individual's sense of self must be strengthened. Western theorists focus on the process of separation and individuation and an independent self. A person has allegiance to the self first and to others second.	A person is an integral part of the universe and the society in which he or she finds himself or herself. There is no separate, independent, individual sense of self. There is no feeling of self-entitlement or self-centeredness. Who you are is always viewed from the context of a relationship. A person's sense of self as an independent, separate self is eliminated. The self must be experienced as relative (ever changing), interdependent, and part of the changing physical environment. A person's allegiance is first to the group.
Achievement and Winning	"Winning is the only thing." —Vince Lombardi High achievers and winners are admired and emulated. For the most part, achievement and winning are outside of yourself.	Winning is inside of yourself. "Though he should conquer a thousand men in the battlefield a thousand times, yet he, indeed, who would conquer himself is the noblest victor." —Buddha "He who conquers others is strong; he who conquers himself is mighty." —Lao Tzu
Goals and Keys to Success	Goals are materialistically oriented. Success is measured by the material wealth and objects one has accumulated.	Goals are more spiritual in nature. Lao Tzu says that "if you really want everything, then give up everything." "Be satisfied with whatever you have and enjoy the same. When you come to know that you have everything, and you are not short of anything, then the whole world will be yours." —Lao Tzu
Establishing Control Over Your Emotions	A person establishes control over his or her emotions by analyzing them.	A man can separate his mind from emotions and control them (Taoism). Meditation (mindfulness) helps a person to assume control over his or her emotions.

Issue	Western Culture/Philosophy	Eastern Culture/Philosophy
Independence of Life vs. Interrelatedness	The individual is separate from and independent of the physical world.	All life is interrelated and interdependent. Death is an ongoing part of the ongoing process of change and should be accepted rather than feared. The individual is not separate from the physical world.
Harmony vs. Conquering the External World	People seek to control and possess objects in the physical world.	People seek to be in harmony with the world because they realize that they cannot control and possess the continually changing world.

Source: Jones-Smith, 2014.

CULTURE AND THE PROCESS OF IDENTITY DEVELOPMENT: THE TRIPARTITE MODEL

The psychological pull of one's cultural group runs deep within a person. During the mid-1980s, I proposed a tripartite level of a person's cultural and ethnic identity (Smith, 1985). There are three levels of a person's identity development, as shown in Figure 2.1: (1) an individual level, which focuses on what psychologists label one's personality or idiosyncratic ways of responding to one's environment (individual learning styles, talents); (2) a group level, which contains a person's cultural and ethnic identifications (cultural styles of communicating, structure of social and families, gender roles for males and females, etc.), as well as other group-oriented identities (professional identity, wife, father, etc.); and (3) a universal level, which contains a person's identifications with the human race—"identifications that go beyond national and cultural borders" (Smith, 1991, p. 182). Some universal human qualities involve the common emotions of love, sadness, joy, courage, transcendence, and wisdom. Our universal level of identity is elicited when we donate money to those in another country who are suffering from famine, natural disasters, and so forth. We respond to such crises because we identify with the human race (Jones-Smith, 2014; Smith, 1985).

For the most part, psychologists have focused on a person's individual level of identity; however, a person's group-level identity may be just as powerful or even more powerful than one's

FIGURE 2.1 ■ The Tripartite Model of Identity

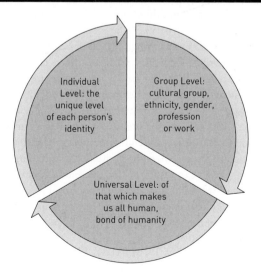

individual level of identity—one's personality. Culture takes on psychological characteristics when it becomes part of our group-level identity. The individual's identification with his or her culture takes place so very early and unconsciously in life that it forms part of the ethnic or cultural self. As a result of this process of identification and internalization, culture becomes part of who we are and prescribes the way in which we feel comfortable interacting with one another.

Cultural Introjection and Cultural Attachment

Ethnic identity development is a lifelong process that is begun in early childhood and that continues throughout one's life. During the early stages of ethnic identity development, the child first introjects the culture of his or her parents. Culture is introjected into one's psychological framework in a fashion similar to the manner in which children incorporate the views of their parents (Hong, Fang, Yang, & Phua, 2013). The parents' views, beliefs, and values very often become the views of their children. That is, the child accepts unquestionably the cultural values and attitudes of his or her parents, and these values form part of the ethnic self.

A child's introjection of his or her parents' cultural beliefs, values, and customs most often leads to the formation of a cultural attachment relationship. Each person forms an attachment relationship with his or her culture. While for some, the cultural attachment relationship is satisfying and strong, for others, the cultural attachment relationship is weak and inconsistent. These situations take place because sometimes parents demand that their children adhere to the cultural meaning system within their particular group, and at other times they ignore, discard, or minimize its importance to the family. People who claim that they have little or no cultural attachment are usually raised by parents or family members who engaged in few cultural traditions within their families.

What is the function of cultural attachment? Cultural attachment is very similar to a child's or individual's attachment to a caregiver or a parent (Harwood, Miller, & Irizarry, 1995). The child or individual feels safe around the symbols and artifacts of his or her culture. Remove the familiar symbols of an individual's culture, and he or she may become anxious or stressed out, as some immigrants feel when they move to a new host country. The loss of familiar cultural artifacts and symbols can be likened to the stranger situation involved in attachment studies. The child who is attached to his mother may experience emotional distress when she leaves the room; and analogously, the child who is suddenly thrust into a new country with new cultural values and symbols may feel anxiety about the loss of what was once familiar and comforting to him.

Moreover, young children engage in a number of cultural transactions within and outside of the family and community. As a result of these cultural transactions, the young child begins to form a sense of ethnocultural bonding between the group members. When a person says, "I'm an Italian," it may mean that he is simply stating the facts of his ethnocultural heritage, or it may mean something more: "I identify with being an Italian. I have the values, the beliefs, and the communication style of an Italian." The stronger a person's attachment to his or her culture, the stronger his or her ethnocultural bond with other members of the cultural group.

A child's cultural attachment forms his or her *cultural meaning system*, which can provide a source of comfort as he or she ages. A person's meaning system is warmed by memories of one's mother cooking certain cultural meals, of spending holiday celebrations with family members and friends, and of participating in certain cultural rituals and ceremonies.

The cultural meaning system can also provide a sense of discomfort if the individual has not attached to the culture or if he or she wishes to separate and individuate from that culture. Cultural separation and individuation are part of the growing-up process—part of the reason that culture changes from one generation to another (Ratts & Pedersen, 2014).

Culture and transference. Hall (1959, 1976) has described an individual's transactions with his or her communal culture as a type of cultural transference relationship. Cultural transference can take place both within members of a given group and between groups. We transfer onto other members of our group our cultural expectations. For instance, women in a given culture may transfer cultural expectations and views onto most men within that culture. Clients transfer their expectations onto their counselors and therapists also engage in cultural countertransference in the cross-cultural counseling relationship. As Foster (1998) has stated, "the cultural countertransference is viewed as a matrix of intersecting cognitive and affect-laden beliefs/experiences that exist within the therapist at varying levels of consciousness. Within this matrix lie: the clinician's American life value system; theoretical beliefs and practice orientation; subject biases about ethnic groups; and subjective biases about their own ethnicity. The author proposes that these countertransference attitudes are often disavowed by the clinician; exert a powerful influence on the course of treatment; and though unspoken, are frequently perceived by the client" (p. 253).

Cultural Countertransference

Counselors and therapists may experience cultural countertransference when they work with clients (Comas-Díaz & Jacobsen, 1991). The clinician's cultural countertransference can be thought of as a matrix of intersecting beliefs and experiences that take place within the counselor both consciously and unconsciously. The matrix consists of clinicians' American life value system, their theoretical beliefs and practice orientation, their subjective biases about ethnic groups, and their subjective biases about their own ethnicity. These countertransference attitudes may be disavowed by the clinician even when perceived by the client. Nevertheless, the clinician's cultural transference attitudes greatly influence the course of psychological treatment. How can therapists avoid cultural countertransference? First, they must have deep knowledge about their own cultural identity and an awareness regarding how their culture affects their interactions with others. Second, they must have a general attitude of respect for the cultures of their clients. Third, they must engage in the process of cultural empathy during which they try to see life through their clients' eyes and worldviews. Clinicians can mitigate their cultural countertransference by engaging in cultural awareness exercises (Foster, 1998). If counselors and therapists have unresolved issues about race, ethnicity, and culture, most likely the therapeutic relationship will be contaminated by their cultural countertransference. Table 2.4 provides a class exercise to teach counselor trainees how to conduct a clinical interview to help a counselor learn about a client's culture. Students might interview each other or a person within/outside their community.

Cultural Intelligence and Cultural Identity Development

Cultural identity development is also related to what researchers have recently begun to label as cultural intelligence, a construct Early and Ang (2003) have defined as an individual's capability to function and manage effectively in culturally diverse settings. Early and Ang have identified four factors of cultural intelligence (CQ):

- **CQ-Strategy** is how a person makes sense of intercultural experiences. It deals with the processes people use to acquire and understand cultural knowledge. CQ strategies include strategizing before an intercultural encounter, checking assumptions, and adjusting mental maps when actual experiences differ from expectations (Chiu, Lonner, Matsumoto, & Ward, 2013).

- **CQ-Knowledge** refers to a person's understanding of how cultures are similar and how they are different.

- **CQ-Motivation** indicates a person's interest in experiencing other cultures and interacting with those from different cultures. It measures the intrinsic value people place on culturally diverse interactions, as well as their confidence that they can function effectively in settings characterized by cultural diversity (Adair, Hideg, & Spence, 2013; van der Zee & van Oudenhoven, 2013).

- **CQ-Behavior** is a person's capability to adapt his or her verbal and nonverbal behavior so that it is compatible with different cultures. It includes having a flexible repertoire of behavioral responses appropriate for different settings (Adair et al., 2013).

Although researchers have described cultural intelligence in terms of one's cross-cultural understanding of another person (Wilson, Ward, & Fischer, 2013), I maintain that cultural intelligence should not just be limited to understanding a culturally different person's culture. It is *also* a process that relates to understanding and interpreting our own membership culture. In fact, it is very difficult to understand another person's culture without first understanding our own membership culture. The reference point for understanding another person's culture is inevitably our own membership culture. We compare and contrast another person's culture with our own. Viewed from this perspective, cultural intelligence has two major components: (1) attitudes, knowledge, skills, and expertise *in one's own cultural membership group*; and (2) attitudes, knowledge, skills, and expertise related to *a nonmembership cultural group*. The current global world demands knowledge of other cultures because of global economic and military interdependence (Chiu et al., 2013). I recommend that cultural intelligence should be added to Gardner's (1983) multiple intelligences because the seeds for its growth are sown very early in life and because of the importance of culture to human life.

TABLE 2.4 ■ Culturally Responsive Clinical Skill Development: Learning About Your Client's Culture

Directions: Identify a person who comes from a culture that is different from yours. Research that person's culture using the internet and library to acquire knowledge about the person's culture. Summarize important findings from your research.

Develop a set of questions you would like to ask the person in an interview.

The following are some questions you might ask during your interview:

1. What is your home or origin country?

2. What led your family to settle in _____?

3. What are some of your family customs and roles of family members? What is your role in the family?

4. How much do you identify with and affiliate with your culture? How assimilated into mainstream American culture are members of your family?

5. What religious or spiritual beliefs are important in your culture and within your family?

6. In your culture, who has the power in a family? Who has the power in your family?

7. What is considered appropriate touch with others in your culture? When you speak with a person, how close (spatially speaking) do you desire to be in relationship to the person?

8. How do people greet each other when they are first introduced, when they greet friends, and when they greet relatives?

9. How do members of your culture communicate with each other? How much eye contact is comfortable between two non–family members?

10. What customs, beliefs, and practices in your culture might be misinterpreted by established institutions within your community (schools, law enforcement, social services, health care providers, etc.)?

11. Thinking about your own culture, what does cultural difference mean to you in terms of American culture?

12. Have there been any events in your life wherein you have felt culturally misunderstood or disrespected by a member of the dominant American culture?

Source: Adapted from Lynch & Hanson (1998).

During the process of constructing an ethnic identity, every person develops a measure of cultural intelligence. That is, most people in a society are able to acquire cultural thought patterns, cultural behaviors, and language, as well as a host of preferences that distinguish their culture from the culture of others. They recognize, for example, that this dress is used by our people or this is the music or language of my cultural group. Cultural intelligence continues throughout a person's development. For instance, one learns the appropriate gender roles for males and females during one stage of development. There are cultural roles to be learned for each stage of life development.

In a culturally diverse society, it is extremely important for each person to increase his or her intra- and intercultural intelligence. In a global society, the demand for increased intercultural intelligence is paramount for many different sectors of our lives. I propose that each person has an overall cultural intelligence quotient that contains two major dimensions: (1) intercultural intelligence, which is cultural intelligence regarding nonmembership cultural groups; and (2) intracultural intelligence, which refers to cultural intelligence related to one's own cultural membership group (Jones-Smith, 2011). These two types of cultural intelligences interact with each other. Increasing one type of cultural intelligence may lead to increasing the other. For instance, the more people engage in self-cultural study, the more likely they will increase their understanding of both their own cultural group and that of others. Learning about other cultural groups can help you to understand your membership group.

The process of developing an ethnocultural identity is presented in Figure 2.2. Essentially, each family transmits an ethnocultural identity to each family member. The family interprets and defines for the individual what it means to be an Italian American, African American, Jewish American, or Asian American. The child comes into contact with his or her ethnic group's language, music, food, cultural artifacts, customs, and values. As a result of the child's cultural participation and learning, he or she develops a sense of "us and them" or "we and they."

FIGURE 2.2 ■ A Model of the Process of Ethnocultural Development

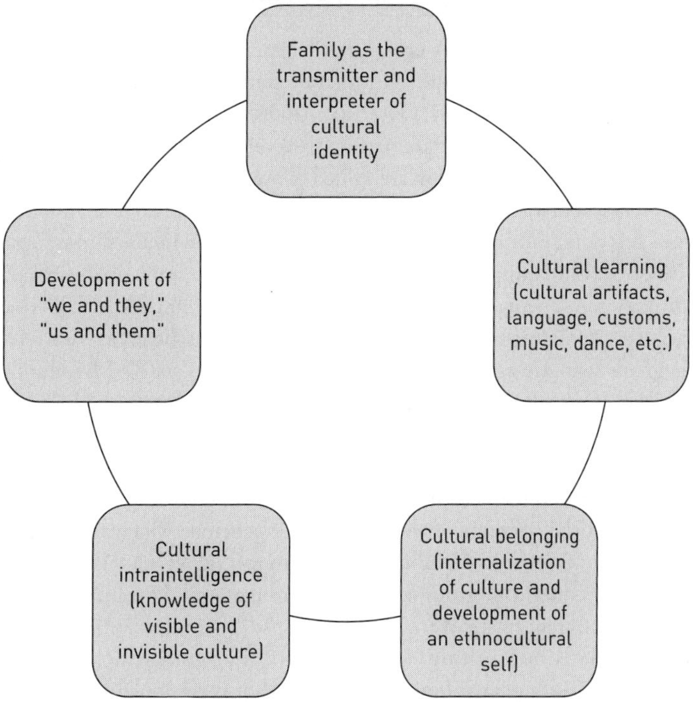

Summary of Factors That
Influence Cultural, Ethnic, and Racial Identity

Cultural, racial, and ethnic identity consists of (1) self-identification of the label an individual gives to himself or herself; (2) knowledge about one's culture, including its customs, values, beliefs, and traits; and (3) adoption of the feelings and attitudes of the group in question. A person's cultural identity is a group-level identity that is influenced by such factors as acculturation, assimilation, and migration. These three levels of identity are ever changing, depending upon a person's unique life circumstances. For instance, at one time, one's cultural identity may become more salient than one's ethnic or racial identity; at another time, one's gender identity may surge to the forefront. Traditional counseling tends to focus primarily on the individual level of identity and to minimize or ignore the client's multicultural reference group identities. The effective multicultural helping professional makes an effort to relate to all levels of a client's identity.

Ethnic identity is a powerful identity, perhaps in the final analysis much more powerful than an individual identity or what we call personality. It is often the source of interethnic conflict both within and between nations. Despite the power of ethnic identity on individuals' actions, psychology has focused primarily on the study of the individual level of identity—personality.

Individuals socially and personally construct ethnic identity as they interact with the environment (Yakushko, Mack, & Iwamoto, 2015). Ethnic identity development begins in childhood and continues through old age. It involves a process of differentiation and integration that helps one to move from a state of unawareness of ethnic differences to ethnic awareness, from nonethnic self-identification to ethnic self-identification, and from partial ethnic identifications to ethnic identity formation and integration. Individual differences in ethnic identity development occur within an ethnic group because individuals absorb culture differentially along a scale of acceptance to rejection (Smith, 1991). Different life experiences may cause one to recycle or to repeat parts of phases he or she has previously gone through.

THE ETHNIC SELF: ETHNICITY AS A SCHEMA

The ethnic self is part of an individual's overall self-schema (Smith, 2001; Yakushko et al., 2015). *Self-schemas* are organized views about the self, and they contain personally defining and important attributes (Montepare & Clements, 2001; Oyserman, 2008). Individuals are not schematic for all of the characteristics, traits, and skills that are true or observable about them (Yakushko et al., 2015). Rather, self-schemas indicate domains that are valued in one's social life (Oyserman, 2008). When a domain becomes self-schematic, it becomes important for the individual to maintain a specific view of the self within this domain (Oyserman, 2008). People are more inclined to refute, challenge, or dispute negative or disconfirming schema feedback. While some individuals organize themselves along their ethnicity self-schemas, others do not (Oyserman, Kemmelmeier, Fryberg, Brosh, & Hart-Johnson, 2003). Some members of ethnic groups may be aschematic with reference to their ethnicity. Individuals who are ethnic self-schematic are likely to state, "My ethnicity means the world to me; I'm glad of my ethnicity and would not want to be anything else." In contrast, individuals who are aschematic for ethnicity tend to state, "Really, my race does not matter to me. Ethnicity means nothing to me." Individuals who are schematic for their ethnicity make sense of who they are in terms of their ethnicity and their ethnic culture. Their ethnic culture is important to them.

Individuals vary in the contents of their ethnic self-schema. Whereas the content for some individuals contains only ethnic membership (in-group) values and issues, the ethnic self-schema for others may contain in-group and out-group material. Bicultural individuals' ethnic self-schema may have content from several ethnic groups (Oyserman, 2008).

Ethnic self-schema is not a thing, but the fulcrum around which one organizes one's entire ethnic identity. It is a psychological structure that is responsible for the maintenance of one's ethnic identification, ethnic self-esteem, and affiliative behaviors. During the early phases of development, the ethnic self is more unconscious than conscious. Ethnic self-schemas undergo a continual process of differentiation, integration, and reintegration of old and new partial identifications based on one's contact experiences (Oyserman, 2008; Oyserman et al., 2008).

RESEARCH ON THE POSITIVE BENEFITS OF A CULTURAL IDENTITY

Culture is a strength because it increases ethnocultural bonding, which, in turn, increases our resiliency. Utsey, Hook, Fischer, and Belvet (2008) investigated the roles of optimism, cultural orientation, and ego resilience in predicting levels of subjective well-being in African American populations. The researchers found that adherence to a traditional African American worldview (e.g., valuing religion) and pride in racial heritage predicted higher well-being and positive psychological functioning. Participants who demonstrated high levels of racial pride also had higher levels of resilience.

> **Cultural Reflections**
>
> *Describe your cultural or ethnic self.*
>
> *Has your ethnic self changed over the years?*
>
> *How has it changed?*

Studies have found that individuals who are embedded in their culture tend to be more "ethnically hardy" and resilient in their ethnic identity development than are those who are more marginal with respect to their culture. Culture provides a type of covering, a way of perceiving life's ups and downs and one's treatment within a given society so as to strengthen rather than to weaken the person. Studies have found a positive relationship between ethnic identity and self-esteem (Phinney, 1995; Phinney & Chavira, 1992). In a sample of 417 high school and 136 college students, ethnic identity development was positively correlated with high self-esteem in minority participants; White students only experienced this same correlation when they were in the minority.

Beale-Spencer, Noll, Stoltzfus, and Harpalani (2001) investigated the relationship of ethnic identity and academic achievement among a sample of 562 African American middle school students, 80% to 90% of whom were on the free lunch program. Building on Phinney's work, the proposed stages of ethnic identity development included Eurocentrism (unexamined acceptance of the majority culture), transition, reactive Afrocentrism (an early exploration of an Afrocentric identity, considered "superficial" identifying), and proactive Afrocentrism (the achieved, secure sense of racial identity; Beale-Spencer et al., 2001, p. 26). The investigators reported that the Eurocentrism and reactive Afrocentrism phases were associated with significantly lower levels of academic achievement, while the proactive Afrocentrism phase of racial identity development was positively associated with academic achievement. Wong, Eccles, and Sameroff (2003) found the following results:

> **Cultural Reflections**
>
> *Can you think of ways that your cultural group has brought a sense of healing and peace to your life?*
>
> *Please explain.*

> A strong, positive connection to one's ethnic group (our measure of ethnic identity) reduced the magnitude of the association of racial discrimination experiences with declines in academic self-concepts, school achievement, and perception of friends' positive characteristics, as well as the association of the racial discrimination experiences with increases in problem behaviors. (p. 1197)

DOES ONE HAVE TO BE OF THE SAME CULTURAL/ETHNIC/ RACIAL BACKGROUND TO COUNSEL CLIENTS EFFECTIVELY?

Counselors have raised the question: Should I be concerned about counseling a client from a different cultural/ethnic/racial background than my own background? Can a White counselor work effectively with an African American or Asian client, or would it be better for the counselor to refer these clients to a counselor matching their backgrounds? The counseling research has investigated same or different cultural backgrounds of clients in terms of two hypotheses: (1) the culture compatibility hypothesis and (2) the universality hypothesis.

The Cultural Compatibility Hypothesis for Counseling Culturally Diverse Clients

The **cultural compatibility hypothesis** maintains that the assessment and treatment of culturally diverse individuals are improved when the ethnic and cultural differences between the client and the counselor are low. This hypothesis suggests that the assessment and treatment of Asian American clients, for instance, are enhanced when the counselor is also an Asian American (Paniagua, 2014). Despite this hypothesis, studies have found that cultural compatibility between the counselor and the client may not necessarily improve the therapeutic relationship. In a study involving African Americans, Asian Americans, and Whites, Sue, Fujino, Hu, Takeuchi, and Zane (1991) found that racial "match failed to be a significant predictor of treatment outcome, except for Mexican Americans" (p. 539).

Similarly, Cabral and Smith (2011) reported no benefit in treatment outcomes from matching clients and clinicians on ethnicity and race. In their study of 16 therapists and 235 clients, Suarez-Morales et al. (2010) found that their results "did not support the hypothesized effects of matching client and therapist on cultural characteristics to produce positive treatment effects" (p. 203). In her review of the literature on counselor–client racial ethnicity matching, Comas-Díaz (2012) found that clinicians' "cultural competence, compassion, and sharing their client's worldview were more important than ethnic [and racial] matching between client and clinician" (p. 173).

The studies cited above provide hope that one does not have to be of the same ethnic or racial group to be effective in counseling or therapy. Counseling and therapy relationship variables, including cultural humility, are more powerful forces that permit the counselor and client to cross cultural lines and to relate to each other as human beings on a journey. I once taught a multicultural counseling class where one of the White female students complained that her African American male clients said that they did not want to work with her because coming from "her University of Pennsylvania background," she could never understand what it meant to be homeless or to be discriminated against at almost every juncture in life. When I asked the student how she responded, she said that she just sat there embarrassed and angry—all at the same time. After all, the student retorted, "What the hell did he know about what my life was all about? He was making assumptions that were all wrong for my life. He had put me in the White category that could not understand a Black male's life."

Cultural barriers are very real, and sometimes when therapists and clients see a person of another culture, they take the posture of assumed dissimilarity. "You could not possibly understand what my life is like." The client in the above example had taken the perspective of **assumed cultural dissimilarity** and adopted the perspective that such dissimilarities prevented him from working with a White female counselor. The concept of **assumed cultural similarity** is put into action when counselors and clients assume that they can work together because they share a similar cultural background or socioeconomic status.

What is an effective response that the student clinician might have made to her client who assumed that because of cultural differences they could not relate to each other on the universal level—that is, on the level of both being human beings? The counselor might have engaged in cultural humility—that is, acknowledged that she is not an African American male, that she wanted to learn more about his life, and that she respected his comments and his anger toward her, but that if he were willing to give her a chance to work with him, she would stretch her hand out to learn what it feels like to be him.

The Universalistic Hypothesis for Counseling Culturally Diverse Clients

The **universalistic hypothesis** with regard to cross-cultural counseling has led to cultural competency training because this hypothesis is based on the view that variables other than similar client–counselor race, ethnicity, or culture have a greater impact on the counseling relationship. Clarifying the universalistic position with regard to culturally responsive counseling, Paniagua (2014) has stated, "According to the universalistic hypothesis, White therapists are as effective as African American, American Indian, Asian, and Hispanic therapists in assessing and treating clients from these culturally diverse groups as long as the therapists maintain cultural sensitivity and competence in their clinical practice" (p. 12).

ASSIMILATION, MARGINALIZATION, ACCULTURATION, AND ACCULTURATIVE STRESS

Researchers have pointed out that it is important to understand both the concepts and the impact of assimilation, acculturation, and acculturative stress when counseling culturally diverse individuals (Padilla & Perez, 2003). These factors may influence an individual's responsiveness to counseling, even those who have been raised in their own country. For instance, there may be two families, one Asian American and the other Latino American, each of which may have assimilated or acculturated differently to mainstream American culture. Paniagua (2014) has suggested that the acculturation concept may be applied to American-born individuals. According to him, differences observed between African American middle-class individuals and the Black underclass are essentially variations in their degree of acculturation into the general American culture. Counselors should understand the differences among the terms *assimilation, marginalization, enculturation*, and *acculturation* and how the factors associated with each concept may influence the counseling relationship.

J. M. Herskovits (1948) coined the term ***enculturation*** to represent the process by which a person learns the culture that he or she is surrounded by or lives in. The process of enculturation can be either conscious or unconscious, and it refers to learning one's native or home culture. In contrast, acculturation refers to the process a person uses to adopt a foreign culture.

Assimilation

Assimilation is a term that describes a process in which an individual consciously decides to identify with the mainstream culture because he or she desires to be viewed as one who has adopted and accepted the culture of the general society. Individuals who choose the assimilation route relinquish their prior cultural identities in favor of the dominant mainstream culture because of a number of reasons: (1) They may consider the **dominant culture** as more valuable than their own culture, (2) they may believe that they will get significant benefits from the general culture as a result of their actions, and (3) they may believe that their original cultures have, for all practical purposes, been lost or subverted (Berry, 2006).

Marginalization and Marginal Individuals

People who are not assimilated into a given society or culture often become **marginalized**. *Marginalization* is a term used to describe the dynamic interplay between mainstream and bordering, or marginalized, social categories. The mainstream category of a society is traditionally associated with dominance, privilege, and power. In contrast, the margins of a society are associated with relative powerlessness and fewer, if any, privileges. A number of factors may be used to marginalize individuals or groups, including gender, culture, language, race, sexual orientation, religion, or socioeconomic position or class. Both individuals and entire populations of people can become marginalized, with different groups having varying distances from the center of society—from those who are privileged (Wallace & Wallace, 1997).

Marginalization is a process that allows individuals, especially those in power, to maintain boundaries between themselves and others deemed to possess different physical and social characteristics. Through the process of marginalization, social relations become codified and institutionalized so that it becomes extremely difficult for individuals to move beyond the barriers created to prevent them from moving toward the center. Marginalization has a psychological component in that it influences how individuals and groups feel about themselves and their place in the social order of a society. People who are marginalized tend to have feelings of anger, low self-worth, oppression, and alienation from the mainstream society (Wallace & Wallace, 1997). Marginalized people may be put "at risk" for both their physical and psychological health and well-being. Some strategies used to prevent or terminate marginalization include empowering people individually and collectively to secure control over their environment by improving their education and personal skills, strengthening communities, and developing socially just political and economic policies.

Acculturation

In contrast with assimilation, **acculturation** is not always a conscious process. Acculturation tends to occur over a period of time; it may be described as a process of accepting and adapting to the cultural values of the general or larger society. Acculturation is a concept that refers to how people change when individuals from different cultural groups come into contact with each other and subsequently undergo a process of change (Berry, 2006; Meghani & Harvey, 2016). The term *acculturation* has also been used to describe how ethnic and cultural groups relate to each other and undergo a process of change in a multicultural or multiethnic society. Individuals tend to experience emotional and psychological stress as they become acculturated within a given culture.

The Berry Model of Acculturation

Berry (2006) has pointed out that individuals and ethnic groups acculturate in different ways. He outlined four acculturation strategies:

- The assimilation strategy exists when individuals adopt the melting pot strategy. Individuals using this strategy seek to adapt completely to the identity, culture, and norms of the dominant culture and work to shed their original identity and culture.

- The separation strategy takes place when members of an ethnic or cultural group refuse to learn the language of the dominant culture and establish close relationships only with people of their own ethnic group; they reject the values and behaviors of the dominant culture.

- Integration is the acculturation strategy in which people and ethnic groups maintain some features of their cultural identity and heritage but also seek interaction and contact with the dominant culture.

- Marginalization takes place when individuals and ethnic groups display a lack of interest in maintaining their cultural heritage and lack interest in interacting with others.

Issues of acculturation almost invariably involve cultural awareness and ethnic loyalty (Rasmi, Chuang, & Hennig, 2015).

Acculturative Stress: Its Definition and Meaning

Acculturative stress may be defined as a "reduction in health status" of people who have to struggle to adapt to a new culture—both psychologically and socially (Meghani & Harvey, 2016; Torres, Driscoll, & Voell, 2012). Acculturative stress comes from an individual experiencing differences in social customs, norms, and values, as well as standards in education, politics, and so forth, between the new host culture and the person's native culture (Berry, 2006). This type of stress becomes more pronounced when there are few similarities between a person's native culture and his or her new host culture (Rasmi et al., 2015). The term *acculturative stress* can be conceptualized as an alternative for *culture shock*, which was first described by the Institute of International Education in Chicago in 1951 on the occasion of the arrival of the first Indian student in Germany to study (Alamilla, Kim, & Lam, 2010; Meghani & Harvey, 2016).

Acculturative stress occurs as individuals adapt to the values of a different culture (Meghani & Harvey, 2016). It may be conceptualized as the cultural adjustment stress that members of ethnic/racial minorities sometimes experience in a new or host country. Acculturative stress may take the form of feelings of powerlessness, inferiority, hostility, and discrimination. *Intergenerational acculturation stress* takes place when families are pulled in two different directions by the acculturative process. For instance, an adolescent may embrace the new culture, while older family members pull him or her to their culture of origin. Counselors need to take clients' levels of acculturation into consideration in therapy because it is closely related to the client's psychological functioning (Rasmi et al., 2015).

> ### Cultural Reflections
>
> *Acculturative stress is usually associated with people who have migrated from one country to another. However, some people have reported acculturative stress when they have moved from being in one social class to another.*
>
> *For instance, an African American who used to be in the "Black underclass" obtains a medical degree. When he returns to his old neighborhood, he is given the cold shoulder. Yet, on the other hand, he is rejected by some members of his new upper middle class.*
>
> *Can the term acculturative stress be applied to one who changes his or her social class membership and discovers that his or her new social class culture is vastly different from the one in which he or she grew up?*

CULTURALLY RESPONSIVE COUNSELING: REACHING ACROSS BARRIERS

Cross-cultural counseling essentially involves reaching across the barriers that each of us builds around ourselves. How does an Asian American counselor let an African American male know that he or she understands what he has been going through? What can a White American female counselor do in counseling to let a Latina feel that she feels her pain—her conflicting dilemma in being a Puerto Rican? Culturally responsive counseling involves tearing down walls between people and then going through the process of mending them again so that the light shines through to the benefit of both counselor and client. As Robert Frost once wrote in his poem "Mending Wall," "Something there is that doesn't love a wall, That wants it down."

Tearing down walls in counseling is not an easy process. Human feelings—sometimes rather fragile feelings—lie both within and behind those walls. One of the first skills a counselor must have in reaching across the cultural divide that separates people is to learn how to listen to our clients' cultural stories. Counselors are used to listening to their client stories on a noncultural level, especially listening to those stories that are filled with pain, regret, and pathology. After all, there is an entire counseling theoretical approach called narrative counseling whose foundation is based on helping clients to understand the stories they bring to counseling. We all have our stories. Yet, many counselors do not know how to listen for their clients' cultural stories. Hence, the counselor's first step in reaching across the human cultural divide is to learn how to listen for and discern clients' cultural stories—stories about what their families taught them about their cultural group, the customs and rituals that were important to them while growing up, what they learned about men and women and their cultural and sexual relationships. The following are some points for counselors to consider in listening to their clients' cultural stories.

UNDERSTANDING CLIENTS' CULTURAL STORIES

An important part of case conceptualization involves listening to and understanding a client's cultural story. Every client has his or her own cultural story, even when there are multiple strands of one's cultural identity (Smith, 2006a, 2006b). Every person has a cultural identity, however disjointed and unclear it may appear at first sight. Culture organizes our experiences, and it provides the lens through which we view our own lives, as well as the lives of others (Minkov, 2013).

In culturally responsive strengths-based therapy/counseling, the helping professional understands eight different types of cultural stories: (1) the therapist's own cultural story; (2) the cultural story that underlies the counseling theory to which the therapist subscribes; (3) the client's own cultural story that is specific to him or her; (4) the normative cultural story within a culture or society and how the client's cultural story differs from or is similar to that of the norm; (5) the client's family cultural story(ies); (6) the cultural heroes within a given society; (7) the cultural stories revolving around group experiences of oppression, discrimination, and socially unjust treatment; and (8) the stories about cultural strengths (McAuliffe, 2008).

If counselors ask clients to tell their cultural stories, they may look at them with a blank stare. Most clients don't go around with a conscious outline of their cultural history in their heads. Instead, the counselor must be skillful in helping clients to unravel their cultural stories.

How might a counselor help a client share his or her cultural story? The counselor might say, "Tell me, what are the things you remember most about your culture when you were growing up?" "What cultural values did your parents communicate to you?" "Did you have opportunities to participate in different cultural ceremonies?" "What kinds of cultural rituals did you most like participating in?" "Can you help me understand the things that you liked most and least about the culture in which you were raised?" "How were the experiences you had growing up in your culture similar to or different from those of your friends?" "What is the one thing that you hold most dear to your heart related to your culture?" "If you could change one thing about your culture, what would that be?" "What impact, if any, has your cultural background had on the problem that brought you to counseling?" "On a scale of 1 to 10, with 1 being not important at all and 10 being very important, how important are the cultural experiences you had in your community?" "Who are your cultural heroes?" "Is there anything you would like for me to know about your culture?"

CULTURALLY COMPETENT CLINICAL KNOWLEDGE

A major area of the multicultural competencies involves the clinician's mastery of cultural knowledge. What does a counselor have to know about clients' cultural background in order to work effectively with them? Counselors and therapists should continually be expanding their cultural knowledge so that they will be competent to work with a broad range of culturally diverse clients. The counselor acquires basic knowledge about the client's cultural background, daily living activities, hopes, aspirations, fears, and doubts. The Culturally Competent Awareness Checklist for Mental Health Workers (Table 1.4 in Chapter 1; Jones-Smith, 2014) contains an entire section on cultural knowledge skills.

CULTURALLY RESPONSIVE KNOWLEDGE SKILLS FOR THE INITIAL INTERVIEW

Clinicians must learn proper ways to greet/address clients and correctly pronounce names. Ask questions in a respectful manner. You can say, "I've observed other people call you _____" or "I'm wondering, what would you like for me to call you?"

Table 2.5 is presented to help counselors develop a general cultural knowledge base for working with their clients.

TABLE 2.5 ■ Culturally Responsive Clinical Skill Development: Counselors' Knowledge About Clients' Culture
• What is the client's history and home of origin?
• What religious or spiritual beliefs are at the center of the client's culture and/or family?
• What are the client's family customs and roles for parenting? What practices are considered good versus bad parenting in this culture?
• What are the gender roles within this culture?
• What is the client's understanding of mental health? What are his or her chosen mental health practices and beliefs?
• What is the cultural group's attitude toward work?
• What are the visible and invisible power structures in the client's culture? How are decisions made in the family? What is your client's role within the family?
• How can you communicate effectively in this culture? What constitutes direct and indirect communication? What nonverbal techniques are used to convey meaning?
• How does the client's concept of time compare to yours?
• What does the client consider to be appropriate touching between people of different relationships? What are his or her thoughts on personal space?
• How closely does your client identify with his or her culture? What is his or her family's impression of this?
• What are the client's customs, beliefs, and practices, especially ones that might be contrary to Western culture or beliefs?
• Ask the client, "As your therapist, what would you like me to know about your culture and your experience in it? How is your culture related to your present concerns?"

CULTURAL TRUST: A CRITICAL ISSUE IN CULTURALLY DIVERSE COUNSELING

Trust is a critical issue in working with members of ethnic minority groups. It is important that therapists discuss the client's preference or reaction to a therapist of a different ethnic/racial or cultural background. African American clients tend to show a preference for working with same-race practitioners, although studies also indicate that what is most important for them is to have a culturally competent counselor (Jones-Smith, 2014). During the first session or early sessions, a practitioner might ask, "Sometimes clients prefer working with a therapist of the same race or ethnic group. How do you feel about working with me?"

The clinician examines the worldviews of the client and explores his or her feelings about counseling. What does the client's culture say about mental health counseling? The clinician explores issues around ethnic/racial identity. Investigate whether external factors might be related to the client's presenting problem. What cultural values does the client maintain? What is the client's cultural identity? The extent to which a client places importance on an African American, American Indian, or Asian American identity should be explored. Does the client have feelings about oppression of his or her ethnic group?

Is the client experiencing acculturation conflicts with his or her parents or members of the extended family? For instance, youth of Asian descent may experience psychological stress over the difference in their values and those of their parents. Recent immigrants may experience a type of cultural grief. *Cultural grief* refers to bereavement caused by an individual's forced adaptation to a new culture. When immigrants come to a country, they experience many losses, such as loss of identity, loss of loved ones, and loss of culture. *Cultural grief* also refers to the loss that immigrants encounter due to loss of social structures, cultural values, and self-identity. To work with such individuals, counselors need to understand the meaning that clients give to their multiple losses.

Cultural Reflections

How do you feel about being White or a person of color in American society?

If you could choose the color of your skin or your ethnicity, what color or ethnicity would you choose? Why? Explain.

To people of color, how do you think White people feel about their color identity? Explain.

To White people, how do you think people of color feel about their color identity? Explain.

CULTURAL EMPATHY AND CULTURAL COMPETENCE

Carl Rogers (1961) was the first therapist to emphasize the value and function of an empathic response. Empathic responses promote or facilitate a client's exploration of himself or herself and the presenting problem. Rogers (1983) defined empathy as the "sensitive ability and willingness to understand the client's thoughts, feelings, and struggles from the client's point of view . . . . It means entering the private conceptual world of the other." A number of studies have been conducted on Rogers's core conditions for a helping relationship. A meta-analysis found a statistically and clinically significant relationship between empathy and positive therapeutic outcomes. The clinical factor most related to positive therapeutic outcomes was the client's feeling of being understood.

Empathy has several positive effects. It helps clients to trust the counselor, and it also helps clients understand their own feelings more clearly. Moreover, an empathic response facilitates the clients' own problem-solving ability because they begin to feel more in control when they are helped to understand their feelings.

The term *cultural empathy*, also known as intercultural or cross-cultural empathy, is central to culturally responsive therapy (Gallardo, 2014). Cultural empathy is a clinician's capacity to identify with the feelings, thoughts, and behaviors of people from different cultural backgrounds. **Cultural empathy** may be defined as a clinician's ability to understand and respond sensitively and appropriately to a client's cultural story and the cultural context of his or her presenting problem.

Another component of cultural empathy involves the clinician's ability to accurately understand the self-experience of clients from other cultures (Gallardo, 2014). Cultural empathic responsiveness is the process through which counselors communicate to clients their understanding of the impact of culture on their lives. It is used to explore the cultural messages to which the client is responding (Ridley, Ethington, & Heppner, 2008). Cultural empathy takes place when a counselor or therapist sees another person's culture through the eyes of those within that culture, instead of through the eyes of an outsider who sees and judges things based on his or her own cultural perspectives and prejudices. Cultural empathy is inhibited when the clinician stereotypes and depersonalizes a client. A therapist may show cultural empathy nonverbally by head nods and encouragements to talk and by a tone of voice that you are trying to understand the person's feelings. The best way to gain cultural empathy is to live in another culture (Pedersen & Pope, 2016).

Cultural empathy is governed by cultural trust, cultural openness to other cultures, and shared worldviews between the client and the therapist (Pedersen & Pope, 2016). The ultimate purpose of the cultural empathic response is for the counselor to communicate to the client a deep understanding of the complexities of his or her interlocking cultural identities in such a manner that the client arrives at a better understanding of himself or herself and the presenting issues in counseling (Pedersen, Crethar, & Carlson, 2008). The guidelines for cultural empathy involve counselors compassionately listening in a nonjudgmental manner and putting themselves in an "as if" position in the shoes of the client.

Pedersen and Pope (2016) have distinguished between empathy from an individualistic, Western cultural perspective and empathy from a collectivist or Eastern perspective. These researchers reframed empathy into what they call "inclusive cultural empathy"—that is, empathy based on a more relationship-centered perspective—as an alternative interpretation of the empathic process (see Table 2.6). Pedersen and Pope have stated,

Cultural Reflections

Let's assume that your agency allows you the right to choose the ethnicity (or race) of your clients.

With what race or ethnicity would you be most comfortable working? Why?

Is there a cultural, sexual orientation, or ethnic/racial group with which you would not choose to work? What group would that be? Explain.

Is there a group with which you feel you could not extend or enter into a state of cultural empathy? If so, what group would that be, and how would you go about handling the counseling or clinical situation?

TABLE 2.6 ■ The Culturally Competent Skill of Cultural Empathy
Component 1: Cultural empathy is a clinician's capacity to identify with the feelings, thoughts, and behavior of people from different cultural backgrounds. The counselor identifies and understands the client's cultural cognitions and cultural schema. The counselor can identify at least three cognitions prevalent in a client's culture. The counselor first checks to get an accurate sense of the client's world before assuming that he or she is "walking in the client's shoes."
Component 2: Cultural empathy takes place when counselors see and experience another person's culture through the eyes of those within that culture (emic), instead of through the eyes of an outsider who sees and judges things (etic) based on his or her own cultural perspectives and prejudices. Counselors move toward adopting an emic cultural perspective, and they suspend judgment, especially negative value-laden judgments regarding the client's culture.
Component 3: Cultural empathy is a counselor's ability to understand and respond sensitively and appropriately to a client's cultural story, cultural messages, and the cultural context of his or her presenting problem.
Component 4: The counselor communicates both verbally and nonverbally positive regard and respect for the client and his or her culture.
Component 5: Counselors communicate to a client their understanding of the impact of culture on his or her life situation or presenting problem in a culturally appropriate manner.

Empathy is reported in the research literature as a necessary factor in counseling and psychotherapy, but psychologists have historically interpreted empathy through an exclusively individual focus. Most of the research on empathy has been predicated on a definition of empathy as occurring when one person vicariously experiences the feelings, perceptions, and thoughts of another. In Western cultures, the study of empathy focuses exclusively on the individual, whereas in traditional non-Western cultures, empathy more typically involves an inclusive perspective focusing on the individual and significant others in the societal context. (p. 841)

LEVELS OF CULTURALLY COMPETENT CLINICAL RESPONDING

During the late 1960s and early 1970s, Robert Carkhuff (2009) identified seven major characteristics he maintained a counselor, therapist, or facilitator should have to promote empathy. The guidelines for empathy are:

1. The counselor focuses on understanding the client's communication and expression.

2. The counselor aims to respond in a compatible way to the client.

3. The counselor makes responses in language similar to the client.

4. The counselor responds in a tone similar to that of the client.

5. The counselor is most effective in communicating empathic understanding when he or she is most responsive.

6. The counselor moves tentatively toward expanding and clarifying the client's experiences at higher levels.

7. The counselor concentrates on nonverbal communication (Pedersen et al., 2008).

TABLE 2.7 ■ Levels of Culturally Competent Counselor Clinical Responding

Level 1: Subtractive. In a Level 1 response, the counselor's statement actually detracts from what the client has expressed either verbally or nonverbally about his or her culture. The counselor might have expressed an outsider's (etic) view of the client's cultural issue or situation, and his or her expression may show some evidence of cultural stereotyping or disrespect for the client's culture. Level 1 responses sometimes result in premature termination from therapy.

Level 2: Slightly subtractive. In a Level 2 response, the therapist's statement(s) captures part of what the client has stated. In a Level 2 response, the therapist demonstrates an understanding for most of what the client has been expressing culturally.

Level 3: Interchangeable. In a Level 3 response, the counselor's statement is almost interchangeable with the client's cultural statement. This is a basic cultural reflective statement. The counselor reflects back to the client what he or she has stated about his or her culture and the cultural issues involved in the presenting issue.

Level 4: Slightly additive. In a Level 4 response, the counselor's statement adds to what the client has stated so that the client gets a slightly better understanding of the cultural issue(s) under consideration. In the slightly additive response, the client might respond, "Yes, you're right. I never thought of it exactly that way."

Level 5: Additive. In Level 5 responses, the counselor's statement significantly adds to the client's understanding of the cultural issue or problem under consideration. A client might respond to a Level 5 response with just one word: "*Exactly—that's exactly what I meant to say.*" The client might have been struggling with finding the right words or feelings that he or she wanted to express.

This book has adapted Carkhuff's (2009) five levels of responding for teaching culturally responsive skill development (see Table 2.7). Counselor trainees can be rated on each of the five levels in evaluating their skill development of cultural empathy. The goal is to have the beginning counselor make at least a Level 3 response in terms of cultural empathy. A Level 3 response is essentially an interchangeable or reflecting response. The first two levels (Level 1 and Level 2) of responding detract from what the client has stated, while the last two responses (Level 4 and Level 5) actually add to the client's statements such that the client gains a deeper understanding of what he or she is feeling and experiencing.

THE CULTURALLY COMPETENT SKILL OF COUNSELOR CULTURAL HUMILITY

The term *humility* has been used to connote a kind of meekness and humbleness; however, it can also suggest a willingness to accurately assess oneself and one's limitations and an acknowledgment of gaps in one's knowledge about others and their cultures (Gallardo, 2014). I define **cultural humility** as a lifelong process of (1) seeking to understand oneself as a cultural human with several overlapping cultural identities; (2) being committed to understanding people from their own deep cultural perspective rather than from superficial, stereotypical views of them; (3) assessing the power imbalances that those who are culturally different from oneself experience in their daily living; and (4) working to develop mutually respectful relationships and partnerships (Gallardo, 2014).

The term *cultural humility* is an acknowledgment of a person's own cultural limitations and barriers to true intercultural understanding (Gallardo, 2014). Cultural humility represents the difference between intellectually knowing another person's culture and being able to truly understand and relate to it at a deep cultural level. It is the recognition that one's own perspective is limited by one's prejudices and assumptions and that such might affect one's interactions with people from different cultures. Along such lines, Hook, Davis, Owen, Worthington, and Utsey (2013) have described cultural humility as the "ability to maintain an interpersonal stance that is other-oriented (or open to the other) in relation to aspects of cultural identity that are most important to the [person]" (p. 2).

Cultural humility means not pigeon-holing all people of a given culture into the same square slot (Gallardo, 2014). To practice cultural humility, counselors must be willing to suspend what they think they know about clients based on generalizations about their culture. Instead, counselors learn about their clients' culture from being open to what they themselves have determined is their personal expression of their heritage and culture—what might be called their personal culture. Counselors must be humble enough to understand that their knowledge of different cultures and their assumptions, although important, can only go so deep, so far. Instead of assuming that all people of a culture conform to a certain stereotype, culturally competent counselors and therapists understand that while cultural differences will affect their counseling, each client still remains an individual and should be treated as such.

According to Tervalon and Murray-Garcia (1998), three factors make up cultural humility. The first factor is the knowledge that we are never finished learning about culture, both our culture and that of others. Therefore, counselors and therapists must become humble and be bold enough to examine themselves critically and desire to keep learning. The second component of cultural humility is to fix power imbalances where none should exist. Each person brings something to the counseling table. Both the counselor and the client can learn from each other.

> **Cultural Reflections**
>
> *When you are in the presence of someone culturally, ethnically, or racially different from you, how do you find common ground to talk, to establish a relationship, or even to avoid cultural conflict?*
>
> *Can you describe an experience in which you were proud of the way that you handled yourself when working with a person who is culturally different from you?*
>
> *Now, consider the opposite situation. Have you ever regretted how you handled yourself around a person from a different sexual orientation or a member of a different ethnic, racial, or cultural group? Describe what happened.*
>
> *How would you handle the situation differently if you could have a "do-over" in life?*

The third component of cultural humility involves working to develop partnerships with people and groups who advocate for others. Counselors and clinicians must advocate for cultural humility within the systems clients must operate in. This third part of cultural humility has become a cornerstone of the social justice movement.

Why is cultural humility important in the counseling relationship? Cultural humility in the counseling relationship is important in at least three different ways.

First, cultural humility helps to redress the imbalance of power in a counselor–client relationship. Culturally competent counselors and therapists understand that extensive knowledge of a culture is not the same as having been raised and enculturated in a given culture. When counselors and therapists approach each counseling relationship with the knowledge that their own perspectives are likely to be full of assumptions and prejudices, they are more likely to remain respectful of their clients, and therefore, the imbalance of power stands a greater chance of being corrected in therapy.

Second, cultural humility is important for counseling and therapy because it helps develop trust in the therapeutic relationship. When clients understand that a counselor is truly interested in learning about and respecting their culture, they are more inclined to trust him or her. Third, cultural humility may provide a source of motivation for the client to stay in counseling or therapy, as clients believe that the therapist will not judge them from a cultural perspective different from their own.

Cultural empathy and cultural humility are interrelated. Recently, researchers have begun to distinguish between cultural competency and cultural humility. According to Levi (2009), the concept of cultural humility goes beyond that of cultural competence:

> The approach of cultural humility goes beyond the concept of cultural competence to encourage individuals to identify their own biases and to acknowledge that those biases must be recognized. Cultural competency implies that one can function with a thorough knowledge of the mores and beliefs of another culture; cultural humility acknowledges that it is impossible to be adequately knowledgeable about cultures other than one's own . . . . Cultural humility requires us to take responsibility for our interactions with others beyond acknowledging or being sensitive to our differences. (p. 96)

CASE VIGNETTE 2.1

A SERVICE PROVIDER: CULTURAL COMPETENCE VERSUS CULTURAL HUMILITY

A White American female counselor was caring for a middle-aged Latino woman who had surgery a few days ago. The counselor was called in because the woman was crying and moaning, and the hospital staff was concerned that she might be depressed. When a Latino physician came in for a consultation, he commented to the counselor that the client seemed to be in a great deal of postoperative pain. The counselor dismissed his perception, stating that she had taken a course on multicultural counseling while earning her master's degree, and she knew that Latino/a clients often overexpress the pain that they are feeling. The Latino physician had a hard time changing the counselor's cultural analysis of the client. In fact, the counselor seemed pleased with her self-proclaimed cultural expertise on Latino/a people. Because of her cross-cultural competency training, the counselor believed that she was culturally competent to work with people from a Hispanic or Latino background.

The counselor failed to see her client as a unique individual, but rather saw her only as a Latino or a Hispanic client. She felt confident that her training in cultural competency had provided her with all she needed to know to make an assessment about her client's well-being.

Being trained or educated in cultural competence is but a beginning point in the development of a caring, compassionate, and culturally effective counselor. What the counselor had claimed was true for "Hispanics" was simply not true for her client. The counselor had failed to see her client as an individual, and she had overgeneralized such that her assessment was inaccurate for her client. Counselors should remember that every person has a *personal culture*—that is, a cultural identity that is deeply personal and unique based on his or her life and cultural experiences.

Discussion Questions

1. How might a course in multicultural counseling avoid promoting mistaken assumptions like the inaccurate assessment made by the counselor in this vignette?

2. How would you describe the different power dynamics at play in the hospital situation portrayed in the vignette?

3. Imagine a parallel scenario in which the hospital patient is of some other race or ethnicity. How might a White American counselor with the background as described provide a better or worse counseling experience for such a hypothetical client?

Cultural humility requires that counselors and therapists take responsibility for their interactions with others beyond simply acknowledging or being sensitive to their differences (Gallardo, 2014). It also suggests that therapists view clients as equals in spite of differences in beliefs or behaviors. Using cultural humility engenders an atmosphere of respect in the therapeutic relationship and fosters a positive therapeutic alliance (Hook et al., 2013). During the process of training students to exemplify cultural humility, it is very important that students are given an opportunity to reflect on their own cultural biases and to learn about cultures different from their own in a safe and nonthreatening environment. A counselor who has mastered the art of cultural humility is respectful of his or her clients and their culture and expresses an interest and asks about the client's worldviews or cultural outlooks on life (Gallardo, 2014). He or she has mastered the skill that exemplifies the five components of cultural humility described in Table 2.8.

TOWARD A MODEL FOR EVALUATING CULTURALLY COMPETENT CLINICAL SKILL DEVELOPMENT OF COUNSELORS

Culturally responsive counseling has been criticized repeatedly because few articles and books provide information on skill development (Toporek, 2012). The primary emphasis has been on training counselors, social workers, and clinicians in cultural awareness and cultural knowledge (Harris, 2012). The area of clinical skills has been largely neglected in the field of multicultural counseling (Toporek, 2012). In the past, the American Psychological Association has discussed

TABLE 2.8   ■   Components of the Cultural Humility Skill
Component 1: Clinicians understand themselves as cultural human beings with several overlapping cultural identities. They have developed the skill of cultural self-reflection and humility, to assess themselves as cultural beings. Counselors'/therapists' attitude of humility helps to create a strong working alliance with a client who is culturally different.
Component 2: Clinicians understand clients and other people from their own deep cultural perspective rather than from superficial, stereotypical views of them. They partner with clients to explore their cultural background and its impact on counseling. Counselors evidence cultural openness. They are open to explore the client's cultural background.
Component 3: Clinicians promote cultural trust between themselves and the client. They reflect back to the client a deep cultural understanding of him or her. Clinicians engender trust when they broach the issue of culture differences, ethnicity, and race with clients.
Component 4: Clinicians assess social injustice and power imbalances for clients who are culturally different from them. They investigate how the social, economic, or political situation may have contributed to a client's presenting problems. They know how to negotiate the system or help the client negotiate whatever system is relevant for a desired successful outcome.
Component 5: Clinicians demonstrate mutually respectful cultural relationships and partnerships with a client and his or her cultural community. They convey deep respect about the client's cultural background.

CASE VIGNETTE 2.2

ABSAME, A SOMALI IMMIGRANT: CULTURAL HUMILITY AND CULTURAL EMPATHY

Steve pulled up his chair to his desk and took a deep breath. For the first time, he was working with a Somali refugee who had asked for asylum in the United States. Steve had spent the last several days reading about Somalia, the people, and its culture. Steve wondered if his cultural knowledge about Somalia was sufficient to work effectively with his client, Absame. He had learned quite a bit about Somalia. The country was known to the ancient Egyptians, and it had been in a war with Ethiopia. Somalia is located on the outer edge of the Somali Peninsula, also called the Horn of Africa. Somalia is about the size of Texas. Somali is the official language of the Somali people. Most Somalis have adopted the religion of Islam. The camel is the most widely recognized symbol because it provides food, transportation, and income. Other symbols of Somalia include the five-pointed white star on the Somali flag and the crescent, which represents the new moon and is a universal symbol of the Islamic faith.

Absame walked into Steve's office somewhat hesitatingly, as if he were not sure he wanted to come in for therapy. People in his Somali culture did not go for counseling outside their family.

As Absame sat down, his eyes were fixed on a picture of flags that the counselor had put on his wall to represent the people of the world. "Oh, I see . . . I mean, I am surprised to see that your picture includes a picture of the Somali flag. Most Americans don't even know where Somalia is located, but you—you have our flag on your wall. Why? Why did you do this?"

The counselor came around from his desk and outstretched his hand to Absame and greeted him with the Islamic "As-Salaam-Alaikum," the Arabic greeting that roughly translates to "May peace be with you," and said, "I'm Steve, and I put the flag on my wall because I wanted to show that all people are welcome in my office. We are all part of the human race. I'm glad you noticed."

In response to the Islamic greeting, Absame smiled and said, "Wa-Alaikum-Salaam," meaning "And unto you peace."

"How do you know the Islamic greeting, you a White American man?" Absame asked. "What else do you know about my country and me?"

(Continued)

(Continued)

"I have learned to have deep respect for the Somali people and your struggles. You have a beautiful culture, and your people are also beautiful in looks and stature."

Steve continued, feeling he had made meaningful psychological contact with Absame. "I don't mean to suggest that I am an expert on Somalia, but I know a few things. I looked up the meaning of your name on the internet, and it said that the name Absame means 'the great one.' I also know that names are very important in Somalia and that if your mother and father named you 'the great one,' they had great hopes for you when you were born, and looking at you, I can see why."

Absame sat back, startled that his counselor would take the time to learn about the meaning of his name in Somali. "What manner of man is this?" he mused to himself. "He has my country's flag on his wall. He knows the meaning of my name in Somali." Absame began to relax and to think that maybe he could gain something out of this meeting.

"Tell me what brought you here today," Steve asked.

"I haven't been able to sleep for the past month. I wake up in a deep sweat shaking, as if someone is chasing me. I stop, turn around, and there's no one there. So I go back to sleep if I can. I've been able to get a job stocking things at night at Walmart, and maybe it's my new schedule that has me upset."

Steve responded, "It's rough when you can't get a good night's sleep and when you have dreams that are upsetting."

"Yes," Absame responded, "very upsetting."

Nodding his head empathically, Steve asked, "What do you believe is the reason for your sleepless nights and frightening dreams? How would you deal with this issue in Somalia?"

"Well, in Somalia, my family would pray for me. They would pray to remove the 'evil eye' from my life. But my family isn't here. My sister, brother, and mother are still in Somalia, and I am not even sure exactly where they are in my country."

Steve paused and looked at Absame with compassion, and asked, "What you are feeling now—in a strange land, with no family members—you're struggling to turn your life around. It's not easy, but you are strong enough to want to do something about those dreams. I want to compliment you in making a decision to do something about your situation."

The counseling continued with a more thorough assessment of Absame's mental health. The tentative diagnosis was depression caused by the separation from family members and quite possibly even the "evil eye."

Steve also took out the list he had made for Somali community support agencies, and he asked Absame if it would be possible for him to set up an appointment for him at the Somali Community Center, a place that Absame did not know. Absame seemed eager to meet with other Somalis who spoke his same language. The appointment was made. Steve also asked Absame to answer his medical and social support questionnaire to see if the two could gain additional insights.

Discussion Questions

1. Do you believe that the counselor established a positive therapeutic relationship with his client? If so, how did he go about doing this?

2. How did the counselor show cultural humility in this brief scenario?

3. Do you believe that he evidenced cultural empathy for Absame? Was it proper for the counselor to greet his client with the Islamic greeting?

4. How would you go about manifesting cultural empathy and cultural humility with your clients?

the importance of culture-centered skills. The ultimate goal is to identify culturally responsive skills that can be used across cultural groups. The APA (2017) multicultural guidelines describe what constitutes culture-centered practices:

> We use the term culture-centered throughout the guidelines to encourage psychologists to use a "cultural lens" as a central focus of professional behavior. In culture-centered practices, psychologists recognize that all individuals, including themselves, are influenced by different contexts, including the historical, economic, sociopolitical, and disciplinary. (p. 380)

This section presents RAKACBIAS, a conceptual model for culturally competent clinical skills that takes into consideration nine factors, including (1) culturally responsive *therapeutic relationship* skills (R = relationship skills); (2) *cultural awareness skills* (A = awareness skills); (3) culturally competent knowledge skills (K = knowledge skills); (4) *assessment and diagnosis* clinical skills (A = assessment skills); (5) understanding of clients' *culturally related cognitions* (C = cultural cognitions); (6) understanding of *clients' cultural behaviors* (B = cultural behaviors); (7) skills related to understanding and dealing effectively with issues related to *clients' cultural identity* (I = cultural identity); (8) clinical skills related to clients' *acculturation issues* (A = acculturation issues); and (9) skills related to *social justice and client in context* (S = social justice skills).

These culturally competent skill domains are presented in Table 2.9 for the beginning clinician, as well as the seasoned practitioner.

The clinical skills delineated in Table 2.9 can be used for training therapists at the graduate and professional level. Counseling and psychology departments could decide which clinical skills they would like trainees to master at the master's level and doctoral level. The trainees would then be evaluated on their competency using the five-level clinical scale for evaluating cultural competency.

TABLE 2.9 ■ Checklist of Culturally Responsive Strengths-Based Clinical Skills

This checklist deals with culture-centered skills that have been identified in the multicultural counseling literature. These culturally responsive skills can be used across cultural groups to help clinicians understand the impact of culture on their clients and their clients' presenting issues in counseling.

Instructors can evaluate the clinical skills listed below in terms of the following scale:

Level 1: The counselor makes a subtractive statement that detracts from what the client has expressed verbally or nonverbally.

Level 2: The counselor makes a slightly subtractive statement that captures part of what the client has been expressing culturally.

Level 3: The counselor provides a culturally interchangeable statement—a basic cultural reflective statement.

Level 4: The counselor's statement slightly adds to what the client has stated so that the client gets a better understanding of the cultural issue under consideration.

Level 5: The counselor's statement significantly adds to the client's understanding of the cultural issue or cultural problem under consideration.

Source: Jones-Smith (2014).

Culturally Responsive Clinical Skill Domains

1. **Culturally Responsive Therapeutic Relationship Skills Domain**
    The counselor demonstrates competency in the following *therapeutic relationship* clinical skill areas:

    Acronym = THEMACA (Building trust, humility, and empathy reduces cultural mistrust. Creating cultural ambiance increases counselor credibility and a strong therapeutic alliance.)

    _____A. Clinical skills to build cultural *trust*

    _____B. Clinical skills to demonstrate cultural *humility*

    _____C. Clinical skills to reflect cultural *empathy*

    _____D. Clinical skills to reduce cultural *mistrust*

    _____E. Clinical skills to create appropriate cultural *ambiance* for counseling environment

    _____F. Clinical skills to increase and sustain counselor *credibility*

    _____G. Clinical skills to build and maintain a *therapeutic alliance* with culturally diverse clients

(Continued)

TABLE 2.9 ■ (Continued)

2. **Clinical Cultural Awareness Skills Domain**

_____A. The clinician recognizes the therapeutic relationship as a cultural encounter.

_____B. The clinician understands his or her own worldviews.

_____C. The clinician assists the client in understanding his or her worldviews.

_____D. The clinician promotes the client's comprehension of his or her multiple identities.

_____E. The clinician recognizes cultural transference when it occurs during therapy.

_____F. The clinician comprehends cultural countertransference during therapy.

_____G. The clinician honors cultural resistance during therapy.

_____H. The clinician promotes culturally appropriate goals for the client.

3. **Clinical Culturally Competent Knowledge Skills Domain**

_____A. The clinician knows the client's cultural history related to his or her home of origin.

_____B. The clinician knows the religious or spiritual beliefs embedded in a client's culture.

_____C. The clinician has knowledge related to a client's concept of mental health and the client's chosen mental health practices and beliefs.

_____D. The clinician has knowledge of the visible and invisible power structures in the client's culture.

_____E. The clinician has knowledge of the power structures related to a client's family and interpersonal relationships with others.

_____F. The clinician has knowledge of how to communicate effectively within a client's culture and is aware of what constitutes direct and indirect communication.

_____G. The clinician has knowledge of the customs, beliefs, and practices in a client's culture, especially those customs that might be contrary to Western culture or beliefs.

4. **Clinical Assessment and Diagnosis Domain**

_____A. The clinician recognizes and understands the client's cultural terms for mental distress.

_____B. The clinician has knowledge of culture-bound syndromes and can identify them in the client.

_____C. The clinician has knowledge of the client's cultural attitudes toward mental health.

_____D. The clinician understands what constitutes healing in the client's culture.

_____E. The clinician evidences the skill of cultural adaptions, which involves including culture-specific variables and factors into specific treatment strategies, to more fully address the issues that a culturally diverse client brings to counseling.

_____F. The clinician understands and identifies the client's individual and cultural strengths.

_____G. The clinician assesses *cultural impasses* (i.e., cultural conflicts that take place during counseling). Culture may be used inappropriately, and problems may occur because of cultural similarity or dissimilarity between therapist and client.

_____H. The clinician assesses for trauma, especially as related to the immigration process.

_____I. The clinician assesses for shame, saving face, and who's involved in the decision-making process.

_____J. The clinician understands the importance of multiple sources of data, cultural bias in testing, cultural equivalence in assessment, and strengths assessment.

5. **Client's Cultural Cognitions—Cognitive Domain**

_____A. The clinician demonstrates clinical skills and interventions for understanding the client's cultural cognitions.

_____B. The clinician evidences skills for exploring cognitive and affective cultural schemas impacting the client's life.

_____C. The clinician identifies culturally sensitive cognitive variables related to the client's presenting problems or issues.

_____D. The clinician helps the client to identify alternative cultural cognitions.

6. **Client's Cultural Behavior—Behavior Domain**

   _____A. Clinical skills and interventions for understanding the client's cultural behavior

   _____B. Clinical skills and interventions for understanding the client's cultural emotions

   _____C. Assessing what constitutes cultural reinforcement for the client

7. **Client's Cultural Identity—Identity Domain**

   _____A. The clinician helps the client to articulate and understand his or her cultural identity.

   _____B. The clinician helps the client to understand his or her tripartite levels of identity (individual level, group or cultural level, and universal or panhuman level).

   _____C. The clinician assists the client in labeling cultural identity conflicts.

   _____D. The clinician develops strategies for helping the client to resolve cultural identity conflicts.

   _____E. The clinician helps the client to identify his or her stage of cultural identity development.

8. **Acculturation—Acculturation Domain**

   _____A. The clinician understands the *client's acculturation stage* of development.

   _____B. The clinician recognizes and identifies where appropriate a client's acculturative stress.

   _____C. The clinician helps the client identify acculturative conflicts and acculturative stress.

   _____D. The clinician assesses generation status/ethnocultural identification.

   _____E. The clinician helps the client to identify and deal with acculturation conflicts.

   _____F. The clinician helps the client to adapt to cultural change.

9. **Culturally Responsive Clinical Skills Related to Social Justice and Client in Context Domain**

   _____A. The clinician examines for social, economic, and political oppression.

   _____B. The clinician helps the client process encounters with cultural, racial, and gender oppression.

   _____C. The clinician advocates for positive social justice change and can describe the common needs of the culturally diverse clients within his or her therapy or agency service area.

   _____D. The clinician understands the impact of the environment on the client, including conflicts within and between culturally diverse groups in the therapy service area.

   _____E. The clinician knows the within- and between-group differences regarding the cultural group served.

   _____F. The clinician can describe the demographics within the culturally diverse communities in his or her service area, including the group's unemployment rate, income differentials, educational attainment, birth/death rates, and crime rates.

   _____G. The clinician is familiar with the formal social service agencies, formal leaders, informal leaders, and clergy or spiritualists.

   _____H. The clinician can describe the cultural or community strengths of the culturally diverse groups in his or her service area.

   _____I. The clinician is familiar with the social protocol within the culturally diverse community that he or she serves.

   _____J. The clinician understands the conceptual distinctions between the terms *marginalized, immigrant*, and *refugee*.

SUMMARY OF KEY POINTS

Within the past three decades, the field of multicultural counseling and psychotherapy has grown by leaps and bounds. Part of this phenomenal growth can be attributed to the fact that technology has helped to produce a global society that has within it the capacity to put individuals in contact with each other from diverse parts of the world within seconds. The world has begun to take note of the significance of culture on human lives. Counselors and therapists need to become aware of the impact of culture not only on their own lives but also on the lives of their clients. All counseling takes place within a multicultural and sociopolitical context. Counselors can function to liberate or to oppress their clients.

Cultural identity is a social and historical concept that helps people to answer the question, "Who am I?" We construct our own identities through interactions with family, peers, organizations, institutions, media, and other connections we make in our everyday life. Oftentimes, when we focus on our identity, we emphasize what we can see—the external characteristics or markers of our identity, such as our race/ethnicity or where we were born. Yet, our identities are also composed of ideas, ideologies, and ways of seeing the world around us.

Important aspects of our cultural, racial, or ethnic identity include our gender, social class, sexual orientation, race, and ethnicity. These features have significant roles in determining how we understand and experience the world, as well as shaping the kinds of opportunities and challenges we encounter. Our understanding of our identities means determining how we fit in (or don't) with other groups of people. Our cultural values influence our cultural identity because they help us to create meaning and define who we are. Cultural values have power because we internalize them as part of our identity. Cultural identities shape our life experience, determining how we are treated, whom we meet and become friends with, what kind of education and jobs we get, where we live, what opportunities we are given, and what kinds of inequities or social injustice we may encounter.

The counselor or therapist must take into account a person's cultural identity because it forms the filter through which the person sees life and his or her life circumstances. Clinicians should understand that within any given person, various layers of identity exist, sometimes in harmony with each other and sometimes in conflict. It is important for clinicians to test for the significance of a person's cultural or racial identity and to understand that within any given cultural group, there are wide variations in cultural identity. Clinicians should also recognize that they are not immune from being affected by the impact of culture during therapy. Whereas clients may experience cultural transference, clinicians may undergo a process of countertransference wherein they transfer unto clients their cultural views and ethnic or racial or cultural identity. Some of the key skills for counselors working with culturally diverse clients are listed below.

Self-awareness. You become culturally competent by increasing your self-awareness of your own culture. Counselors and therapists should ask themselves: Who are my ancestors? Where do I come from? What are the visible and the invisible signs of my culture? What values do I have, and what cultures do they come from?

Cultural knowledge. To become a multicultural counselor, you need to increase your knowledge of other cultures by intentionally choosing to interact with those who are culturally different from you. You can attend celebrations of their holidays, attend their worship services, or work on community projects with them.

Cultural attitudes. Examine your cultural attitudes. Do you have a tendency to stereotype those who are culturally different from you? How would you describe your desired social distance from such major ethnic groups as African Americans, Asian Americans, Latino/a Americans, American Indians, and Arab/Muslim Americans?

DISCUSSION QUESTIONS

Discussion Question Set 1

In small groups of three to five people, discuss the following:

1. What culturally learned assumptions shape your counseling interviews with clients?

2. Identify a client with whom you have had a clinical relationship and interpret that client's behavior within his or her cultural background.

3. How would you rate your culture-centered skill development for working with clients? For instance, to what degree do you feel competent in demonstrating the clinical skill of cultural empathy or cultural humility?

4. Name the dominant themes in your client's cultural life story.

5. Based on the cultural themes in your client's life, develop potential clinical intervention and assessment questions.

Discussion Question Set 2

It is important for a counselor to understand his or her own cultural identity and background. In small groups of three to five people, discuss the following questions:

1. What knowledge do you have about your own ethnic/racial/cultural/religious group?

2. What is the history of your ethnic/racial/cultural/religious group?

3. How does your ethnic/racial/cultural/religious group influence how you relate to and communicate with members of other ethnic/racial/cultural/religious groups?

4. What does it mean to be a member of your ethnic/racial/cultural/religious group?

5. Tell a brief story that symbolizes the meaning that your ethnic/racial/cultural/religious group has had on your life.

6. What is your comfort level in working with people from different ethnic/racial/cultural/religious groups?

KEY TERMS

Acculturation: A process whereby people change aspects of their lives based on their contact with people from other cultures. It can be conceptualized as a multidimensional and multidirectional process of immigrant groups in adopting both overt and covert cultural characteristics of the dominant culture. Some overt characteristics include adopting the host country's dress, language usage, eating habits, and celebrations. Some covert examples of acculturation include identifying as a member of the host culture. *all cultures are equal*

Acculturative stress: Stress directly emanating from the acculturation process and including such activities as learning a new language, dealing with confusing cultural rules and expectations, struggling to negotiate the new host country's cultural values with those of the country of origin, coping with prejudice and discrimination, and struggling to negotiate differences across the old and cultural boundaries. A higher level of stress takes place in the first generation of migrants than in the second generation.

Assimilation: A process through which a person or a minority group comes to adopt or accept the beliefs, values, attitudes, and behaviors of the majority or dominant culture, such that the person/group no longer retains the specific characteristics of the native culture or culture of origin. *Assumption other culture is better*

Assumed cultural dissimilarity: The assumption or belief that two people are different because they come from different ethnic, racial, or cultural groups.

Assumed cultural similarity: The assumption or belief that two people are similar because they come from the same ethnocultural group.

Cultural compatibility hypothesis: The hypothesis that the assessment and treatment of culturally diverse people are improved when ethnic and cultural differences between client and therapist are low. Most successful treatment takes place when both client and counselor are from the same ethnocultural group.

Cultural competence: A clinician or counselor's ability to provide services to clients that take into consideration the client's cultural beliefs, cultural worldviews, and behaviors. The culturally competent counselor values diversity, has undergone cultural self-assessment, and knows how to adapt clinical services to reflect an understanding and appreciation of a client's culture.

Cultural empathy: A clinician's ability to understand and respond sensitively and appropriately to a client's cultural story and the cultural context of his or her presenting problem.

Cultural humility: An acknowledgment of one's own limitation to true intercultural understanding. It involves understanding that one's own cultural perspective is necessarily limited. Cultural humility involves an accurate view of the self. Cultural humility tends to strengthen the bonds between client and counselor.

Cultural impasse: A cultural conflict that takes place during counseling.

Culturally diverse counseling: Counseling in which the counselor and client come from different cultural, ethnic, and gender backgrounds. Because no two people come from the exact same background (due to differences in their experiences), all counseling is, in some respects, multicultural.

Culture: An ethnic group's organized body of beliefs and rules about the ways in which persons should communicate with one another, think about themselves, and behave toward each other and objects in their environment.

Culture shock: Anxiety, stress, and psychological confusion precipitated by sudden immersion into a new and different culture; also refers to a rapidly changing American culture where very few things are stable and constant.

Dominant culture: The values and customs of the major group in a society that sets the standard for cultural correctness.

Emic perspective: (culturally specific)—A viewpoint from a particular culture. In counseling, emic is the viewpoint that cultural differences must be included in the cultural treatment planning for culturally diverse groups.

Enculturation: Immersion in one's own culture to the extent that a person assumes that his or her life is "natural" or "normal."

Ethnic identity: Awareness of one's membership in a particular cultural or ethnic group.

Etic perspective: (culturally universal)—The view that people share more commonalities than differences and that mental disorders manifest essentially the same across all cultures.

Marginalization: The dynamic interplay between two social categories: the "center" (or mainstream) and the outer part of the center area called the "margins." The center of a society is traditionally associated with dominance, privilege, and power. Those who are located in the margins

of a society are associated with relative powerlessness—with inadequate housing, racism, unemployment, and lack of education.

Marginalized: An individual placed in the margins of a society—on the fringes—and therefore excluded from the privilege and power located at the center.

Personal culture: A cultural identity that is deeply personal and unique based on one's life and cultural experiences.

Universalistic hypothesis: Proposes that what is important in assessment and treatment of culturally diverse clients is evidence that the clinician can demonstrate awareness of (1) cultural variables that might affect assessment and treatment and (2) cultural competence. According to this hypothesis, White clinicians are as effective as African American and Latino/a clinicians (and other ethnic groups) in treating nonmembership ethnic groups. Clients' and clinicians' sharing of the same ethnicity and gender does guarantee good treatment or positive treatment outcomes—cultural competence is the key.

REFERENCES AND SUGGESTED READING

Adair, W. L., Hideg, I., & Spence, J. R. (2013). The culturally intelligent team: The impact of team cultural intelligence and cultural heterogeneity on team shared values. *The Journal of Cross-Cultural Psychology, 44*(6), 941–962.

Alamilla, S. G., Kim, B. S. K., & Lam, N. A. (2010). Acculturation, enculturation, perceived racism, minority status stressors, and psychological symptomatology among Latino/as. *Hispanic Journal of Behavioral Sciences, 32*, 55–76.

American Psychiatric Association. (2013). *Diagnostic and statistical manual of mental disorders* (5th ed.). Arlington, VA: Author.

American Psychological Association. (2017). *Multicultural guidelines: An ecological approach to context, identity, and intersectionality, 2017.* Retrieved from http://www.apa.org/about/policy/multicultural-guidelines.aspx

Anderson, J., & Carter, R. W. (2003). *Diversity perspectives for social work practice.* Boston, MA: Allyn & Bacon.

Arnett, J. J. (2009). The neglected 95%, a challenge to psychology's philosophy of science. *American Psychologist, 64*(6), 571–574.

Atkinson, D. R., Morten, G., & Sue, D. W. (1998). *Counseling American minorities* (5th ed.). Boston, MA: McGraw-Hill.

Bäärnhielm, S., & Rosso, M. S. (2009). The cultural formulation: A model to combine nosology and patients' live

context in psychiatric diagnostic practice. *Transcultural Psychiatry, 46*(3), 406–428.

Beale-Spencer, M., Noll, E., Stoltzfus, J., & Harpalani, V. (2001). Identity and school adjustment: Revising the "acting white" assumption. *Educational Psychologist, 36*, 21–30.

Bernal, M. E., & Knight, G. P. (1993). *Ethnic identity: Formulation and transmission among Hispanics and other minorities.* Albany: State University of New York Press.

Berry, J. W. (2006). Acculturative stress. In P. T. P. Wong & L. C. S. Wong (Eds.), *Handbook of multicultural perspectives on stress and coping* (pp. 287–298). Langley, BC: Springer.

Brummett, B. R., Wade, J. C., Ponterotto, J. G., Thombs, B., & Lewis, C. (2007). Psycho-social well-being and a multicultural personality disposition. *Journal of Counseling and Development, 85*, 73–81.

Burntheaxis. (2011, March 8). Acculturative stress *[Blog post]*. Retrieved from https://barbielunus.wordpress.com/2011/03/08/5/

Cabral, R. R., & Smith, T. B. (2011). Racial/ethnic matching of clients and therapists in mental health services: A meta-analytic review of preferences, perceptions, and outcomes. *Journal of Counseling Psychology, 58*(4), 537–554.

Casas, M., & Pytluk, S. D. (1995). Hispanic identity development: Implications for research and practice. In J. Ponterotto, M. Casas, I. Suzuki, & C. Alexander (Eds.),

Handbook of multicultural counseling (pp. 155–180). Thousand Oaks, CA: Sage.

Chiu, C., Lonner, W. J., Matsumoto, D., & Ward, C. (2013). Cross-cultural competence. *Journal of Cross-Cultural Psychology, 44*(6), 843–848.

Comas-Díaz, L. (2012). *Multicultural care: A clinician's guide to cultural competence.* Washington, DC: American Psychological Association.

Comas-Díaz, L., & Jacobsen, F. (1991). Ethnocultural transference and countertransference in the therapeutic dyad. *American Journal of Orthopsychiatry, 61*(3), 392–402.

Cosaro, W. A., & Fingerson, L. (2003). Development and socialization in childhood. In J. Delamater (Ed.), *Handbook of social psychology* (pp. 125–155). New York, NY: Kluwer.

Cross, W. (1971). The Negro to Black conversion experience. *Black World, 20*, 13–25.

Cross, W. (1991). *Shades of Black.* Philadelphia, PA: Temple University Press.

Cuellar, J., & Weeks, J. (1980). *Minority elderly Americans: A prototype for area agencies on aging. Executive summary.* San Diego, CA: Allied Health Association.

Dahlsgaard, K., Peterson, C., & Seligman, M. E. P. (2005). Shared virtue: The convergence of valued human strengths across culture and history. *Review of General Psychology, 9*, 203–213.

Early, P. C., & Ang, S. (2003). *Cultural intelligence: Individual interactions across cultures.* Palo Alto, CA: Stanford University Press.

Erikson, E. (1950). *Childhood and society.* New York, NY: Norton.

Foster, P. R. F. (1998). The clinician's cultural countertransference: The psychodynamics of culturally competent practice. *Clinical Social Work Journal, 26*(3), 253–270.

Gallardo, M. E. (Ed.). (2014). *Developing cultural humility: Embracing race, privilege, and power.* Thousand Oaks, CA: Sage.

Gardner, H. E. (1983). *Frames of mind: Multiple intelligences for the twenty-first century.* New York, NY: Basic Books.

Gatignon, H., Eliashberg, J., & Robertson, T. S. (1989). Modeling multinational diffusion patterns: An efficient methodology. *Marketing Science, 8*(3), 231–247.

Groen, S. (2009). Recognizing cultural identity in mental health care: Rethinking the cultural formulation of a Somali patient. *Transcultural Psychiatry, 46*(3), 451–462.

Hall, E. T. (1959). *The silent language.* Greenwich, CT: Premier Books.

Hall, E. T. (1976). *Beyond culture.* New York, NY: Doubleday.

Harris, J. E. (2012). Multicultural counseling in a multitheoretical context: New applications for practice. In M. E. Gallardo, C. J. Yeh, J. E. Trimble, & T. A. Parham (Eds.), *Culturally adaptive counseling skills: Demonstrations of evidence-based practices* (pp. 287–312). Thousand Oaks, CA: Sage.

Harwood, R. L., Miller, J. G., & Irizarry, N. L. (1995). *Culture and attachment: Perceptions of the child in context.* New York, NY: Guilford Press.

Helms, J. E. (1990). *Black and White racial identity.* Westport, CT: Greenwood.

Helms, J. E. (1995). An update of Helms's White and people of color racial identity models. In J. G. Ponterotto, J. M. Casas, L. A. Suzuki, & C. M. Alexander (Eds.), *Handbook of multicultural counseling* (pp. 181–191). Thousand Oaks, CA: Sage.

Henslin, J. M. (2004). *Essentials of sociology: A down to earth approach* (5th ed.). Boston, MA: Allyn & Bacon.

Herskovitz, J. M. (1948). *Man and his works: The science of cultural anthropology.* New York, NY: Knopf.

Hitlin, S., Scott Brown, J., & Elder, G. H., Jr. (2007). Measuring Latinos: Racial classification and self-understandings. *Social Forces, 86*(2), 587–611.

Hodge, D. R., & Nadir, A. (2006). Moving toward culturally competent practice with Muslims: Modifying cognitive therapy with Islamic tenets. *Social Work, 53*(1), 31–41.

Hofstede, G. (1980). *Culture's consequences.* Beverly Hills, CA: Sage.

Hong, Y., Fang, Y., Yang, Y., & Phua, D. Y. (2013). Cultural attachment: A new theory and method to understand cross-cultural competence. *Journal of Cross Cultural Psychology, 44*(6), 1024–1044.

Hook, J. N., Davis, D. E., Owen, J., Worthington, E. L., & Utsey, S. O. (2013). Cultural humility: Measuring openness to culturally diverse clients. *Journal of Counseling Psychology, 60*, 353–366.

Hughes, D., Rodriguez, J., Smith, E. P., Johnson, D. L., Stevenson, H. C., & Spicer, P. (2006). Parents' ethnic-racial socialization practices: A review of research and directions for future study. *Developmental Psychology, 42*, 747–770.

Hunter, S., & Hickerson, J. C. (2003). *Affirmative practice: Understanding and working with lesbian, gay, bisexual, and transgender persons.* Washington, DC: NASW Press.

Jandt, F. E. (2017). Focus on Culture 1.1: Personalizing the concept. In *An introduction to intercultural communication*

(Chapter 1, p. 7). Thousand Oaks CA: Sage. Retrieved from http://www.sagepub.com/sites/default/files/upm-binaries/45974_Chapter_1.pdf

Jones-Smith, E. (2011). *Culture and intelligence.* Unpublished paper, Philadelphia, PA.

Jones-Smith, E. (2014). *Strengths-based therapy: Connecting theory, practice, and skills.* Thousand Oaks CA: Sage.

Jones-Smith, E. (2016). *Theories of counseling and psychotherapy: An integrative approach.* Thousand Oaks, CA: Sage.

Kerwin, C., & Ponterotto, J. (1995). Biracial identity development. In J. Ponterotto, M. Casas, I. Suzuki, & C. Alexander (Eds.), *Handbook of multicultural counseling* (pp. 199–212). Thousand Oaks, CA: Sage.

Kim, J. (1981). *The process of Asian-American identity development: A study of Japanese American women's perceptions of their struggles to achieve positive identities.* Doctoral dissertation, University of Massachusetts Amherst.

Kim-Ju, G. M., & Liem, R. (2003). Ethnic self-awareness as a function of ethnic group status, group composition and ethnic identity orientation. *Cultural Diversity and Ethnic Minority Psychology, 9*(3), 289–302.

Kwan, K. L. K. (2001). Counseling applications of racial and ethnic identity models: An introduction to the special issue. *Journal of Mental Health Counseling, 23*(23), 185–191.

Leung, A. K., Lee, S., & Chiu, C. (2013). Meta-knowledge of culture promotes cultural competence. *Journal of Cross-Cultural Psychology, 44*(6), 992–1006.

Levi, A. (2009). The ethics of nursing student international clinical experiences. *Journal of Obstetric, Gynecologic, and Neonatal Nursing, 38*(1), 94–99.

Lim, S.-L. (2008). The globalization of identity. In G. Monk, J. Winslade, & S. Sinclair (Eds.), *New horizons in multicultural counseling* (pp. 261–277). Thousand Oaks, CA: Sage.

Locke, D. C., & Bailey, D. F. (2014). *Increasing multicultural understanding.* Thousand Oaks, CA: Sage.

Lynch, E. W., & Hanson, M. J. (Eds.). (1998). *Developing cross-cultural competence: A guide for working with young children and their families.* Baltimore, MD: Paul H. Brookes.

Makinson, R. A., & Young, J. S. (2012). Cognitive behavioral therapy and the treatment of posttraumatic stress disorder: Where counseling and neuroscience meet. *Journal of Counseling and Development, 90*, 131–140.

Maslow, A. (1954). *Motivation and personality.* New York, NY: Harper & Row.

McAuliffe, G. (2008). What is culturally alert counseling? In G. McAuliffe & Associates (Eds.), *Culturally alert counseling: A comprehensive introduction* (pp. 2–44). Thousand Oaks, CA: Sage.

McCormack, J. (2007). Recovery and strengths-based practice. *Scottish Recovery Network Discussion Paper Series,* Report No. 6. Glasgow: Scottish Recovery Network.

McDermott, M., & Samson, F. L. (2005). White racial and ethnic identity in the United States. *Annual Review of Sociology, 31*, 246–261.

McGilchrist, I. (2009). *The master and his emissary: The divided brain and the making of the Western world.* New Haven, CT: Yale University Press.

Meghani, D. T., & Harvey, E. A. (2016). Asian Indian international students' trajectories of depression, acculturation, and enculturation. *Asian American Journal of Psychology, 7*(1), 1–14.

Minkov, M. (2013). *Cross-cultural analysis: The science and art of comparing the world's modern societies and their cultures.* Thousand Oaks, CA: Sage.

Monk, G., Winslade, J., & Sinclair, S. (2008). *New horizons in multicultural counseling.* Thousand Oaks, CA: Sage.

Montepare, J. M., & Clements, A. E. (2001). Age schemas: Guides to processing information about the self. *Journal of Adult Development, 8*, 99–108.

Montes, S. (2013). The birth of the neuro-counselor? *Counseling Today, 56*(6), 32–40.

Myers, J. E., & Young, J. S. (2012). Brain-wave feedback: Benefits in integrating neurofeedback in counseling. *Journal of Counseling and Development, 70*(1), 20–28.

Nisbett, R. E. (2003). *The geography of thought: How Asians and Westerners think differently and why.* New York, NY: Free Press.

Oyserman, D. (2008). Racial/ethnic self-schemas: Multidimensional identity-based. *Journal of Research in Personality, 42*(5), 1186–1199.

Oyserman, D., Kemmelmeier, M., Fryberg, S., Brosh, H., & Hart-Johnson, T. (2003). Racial-ethnic self-schemas. *Social Psychology Quarterly, 66*, 333–347.

Padilla, A. (2006). Bicultural social development. *Hispanic Journal of Behavioral Sciences, 28*, 467–495.

Padilla, A., & Perez, W. (2003). Acculturation, social identity, and social cognition: A new perspective. *Hispanic Journal of Behavioral Sciences, 25*(1), 35–55.

Paniagua, F. (2014). *Assessing and treating culturally diverse clients.* Thousand Oaks, CA: Sage.

Pedersen, P., Crethar, H., & Carlson, J. (2008). *Inclusive cultural empathy: Making relationships central in counseling and psychotherapy.* Washington, DC: American Psychological Association.

Pedersen, P. B., & Pope, M. (2016). Toward effectiveness through empathy. In P. B. Pedersen, W. J. Lonner, J. G. Draguns, J. E. Trimble, & M. Scharron-Delrio

(Eds.), *Counseling across cultures* (pp. 13–30). Thousand Oaks, CA: Sage.

Peterson, C., & Seligman, M. E. P. (2003). *Values in Action (VIA) classification of strengths manual.* Retrieved from https://www.researchgate.net/publication/255646903_Values_in_Action_VIA_Classification_of_Strengths_Manual

Phinney, J. S. (1990). Ethnic identity in adolescents and adults: Review of research. *Psychological Bulletin, 108,* 449–514.

Phinney, J. (1995). Ethnic identity and self-esteem: A review and integration. In A. Padilla (Ed.), *Hispanic psychology: Critical issues in theory and research* (pp. 57–70). Thousand Oaks, CA: Sage.

Phinney, J. S., & Chavira, V. (1992). Ethnic identity and self-esteem: An exploration longitudinal study. *Journal of Adolescence, 15,* 271–281.

Phinney, J. S., & Chavira, V. (1995). Parental ethnic socialization and adolescent coping with problems related to ethnicity. *Journal of Research on Adolescence, 5,* 31–53.

Pike, K. (1954). *Language in relation to a unified theory of the structure of human behavior.* Glendale, CA: Summer Institute of Linguistics.

Pike, K. (1967). *Language in relation to a unified theory of the structure of human behavior* (2nd ed.). The Hague, Netherlands: Mouton.

Ponterotto, J. G., Costa-Wofford, C., Brobst, K., Spelliscy, D., Kancanski, J., Scheinholtz, J., & Martines, D. (2007). Multicultural personality dispositions and psychological well-being. *Journal of Social Psychology, 147,* 119–135.

Ponterotto, J. G., Mendelowitz, D., & Collabolletta, E. (2008). Promoting multicultural personality development: A strengths-based, positive psychology worldview for schools. *Professional School Counseling, 12,* 93–99.

Ponterotto, J. G., & Pedersen, P. B. (1993). *Preventing prejudice: A guide for counselors and educators.* Thousand Oaks, CA: Sage.

Ponterotto, J. G., Utsey, S. G., & Pedersen, P. B. (2006). *Preventing prejudice: A guide for counselors, educators and parents* (2nd ed.). Thousand Oaks, CA: Sage.

Rasmi, S., Chuang, S. S., & Hennig, K. (2015). The acculturation gap-distress model: Extensions and application to Arab Canadian families. *Cultural Diversity and Ethnic Minority Psychology, 21*(4), 630–642.

Ratts, M. J., & Pedersen, P. B. (2014). *Counseling for multiculturalism and social justice.* Alexandria, VA: American Counseling Association.

Ridley, C. R., Ethington, L. L., & Heppner, P. P. (2008). Cultural confrontation: A skill of advanced cultural empathy. In P. B. Pedersen, J. G. Draguns, W. J. Loner, &

J. E. Trimble (Eds.), *Counseling across cultures* (6th ed., pp. 377–393). Thousand Oaks, CA: Sage.

Roberts, R. E., Phinney, J. S., Masses, L. C., Chen, Y. R., Roberts, C. R., & Romero, A. (1999). The structure of ethnic identity of young adolescents from diverse ethnocultural groups. *Journal of Early Adolescence, 19,* 301–322.

Rogers, C. (1961). *On becoming a person.* Boston, MA: Houghton Mifflin.

Rogers, C. (1983). *Freedom to learn for the 1980s.* Columbus, OH: Merrill.

Romanucci-Ross, L., & Devos, G. (Eds.). (1995). *Ethnic identity, creation, conflict and accommodation.* Walnut Creek, CA: Altamira.

Santee, R. G. (2007). *An integrative approach to counseling: Bridging Chinese thought, evolution theory, and stress management.* Thousand Oaks, CA: Sage.

Searle, J. R. (1995). *The construction of social reality.* New York, NY: Free Press.

Smith, E. J. (1985). Ethnic minorities: Life stress, social support, and mental health issues. *The Counseling Psychologist, 13,* 537–579.

Smith, E. J. (1989). Black racial identity development: Issues and concerns. *The Counseling Psychologist, 17,* 277–289.

Smith, E. J. (1991). Ethnic identity development: Toward the development of a theory within the context of majority/minority status. *Journal of Counseling and Development, 70,* 181–189.

Smith, E. J. (2001). *Ethnic self-schemas and ethnic identity development.* Unpublished manuscript.

Smith, E. J. (2002). *Ethnic identity development: Proposal for a theory.* Unpublished manuscript.

Smith, E. J. (2006a). The strengths-based counseling model [Major contribution]. *The Counseling Psychologist, 34,* 13–79.

Smith, E. J. (2006b). The strength-based counseling model: A paradigm shift in psychology. *The Counseling Psychologist, 34,* 134–144.

Smith, E. P., Walker, K., Fields, L., Brookins, C. C., & Seay, R. C. (1999). Ethnic identity and its relationship to self-esteem, perceived self-efficacy, and prosocial attitudes in early adolescence. *Journal of Adolescence, 22,* 867–880.

Sokolovsky, J. (1995). Ethnicity, culture and aging: Do differences really make a difference? *Journal of Orthopsychiatry, 8*(3), 763–781.

Suarez-Morales, L., Martino, S., Bedregal, L., McCabe, B. E., Cuzma, I. Y., Paris, M., . . . Szapocznik, J. (2010). Do therapist cultural characteristics influence the outcome of substance abuse treatment for Spanish-speaking adults? *Cultural Diversity and Ethnic Minority Psychology, 16*(2), 199–205.

Sue, S., Fujno, D. C., Hu, L. T., Takeuchi, D. T., & Zane, N. W. (1991). Community mental health services for ethnic minority groups: A test of the cultural responsiveness hypothesis. *Journal of Consulting Clinical Psychology, 59*(6), 533–540.

Tervalon, M., & Murray-Garcia, J. (1998). Cultural humility versus cultural competence: A critical distinction in defining physician training outcomes in multicultural education. *Journal of Health Care for the Poor and Underserved, 9*(2), 117–125.

Tomasello, M. (1999). *The cultural origins of human cognition.* Cambridge, MA: Harvard University Press.

Tomasello, M., Carpenter, M., Call, J., Behne, T., & Moll, H. (2005). Understanding and sharing intentions: The ontogeny and phylogeny of cultural cognition. *Behavioral and Brain Sciences, 28,* 675–735.

Toporek, R. L. (2012). So what should I actually do? Developing skills for greater multicultural competence. In M. E. Gallardo, C. J. Yeh, J. E. Trimble, & T. Parham (Eds.), *Culturally adaptive counseling skills: Demonstrations of evidence-based practices* (pp. 267–286). Thousand Oaks, CA: Sage

Torres, L., Driscoll, M. W., & Voell, M. (2012). Discrimination, acculturation, acculturative stress, and Latino psychological distress: A moderated mediational model. *Cultural Diversity & Ethnic Minority Psychology, 18*(1), 17–25.

Utsey, S., Hook, J., Fischer, N., & Belvet, B. (2008). Cultural orientation, ego resilience, and optimism as predictors of subjective well-being in African Americans. *Journal of Positive Psychology, 3,* 202–210.

van der Zee, K. I., & van Oudenhoven, J. R. (2013). Culture shock or challenge? The role of personality as a determinant of intercultural competence. *Journal of Cross-Cultural Psychology, 44*(6), 900–927.

Wallace, R., & Wallace, D. (1997). Community marginalization and diffusion of disease and disorder in the United States. *British Medical Journal, 314,* 1341–1345.

Wilson, J., Ward, C., & Fischer, R. (2013). Beyond culture learning theory. What can personality tell us about cultural competence? *Journal of Cross-Cultural Psychology, 44*(6), 900–927.

Wong, C., Eccles, J. S., & Sameroff, A. (2003). The influence of ethnic discrimination and ethnic identification on African American adolescents' school achievement and socioemotional adjustment. *Journal of Personality, 71*(6), 1197–1232.

Yakushko, O., Mack, T., & Iwamoto, D. (2015). Minority identity development model. *Encyclopedia of Cross-Cultural School Psychology,* 627–629.

3

NEUROSCIENCE, MULTIPLE CULTURAL IDENTITIES, AND CULTURAL STRENGTHS

- *"Experiences, thoughts, actions and emotions actually change the structure of our brains . . . . Indeed, once we understand how the brain develops, we can train our brains for health, vibrancy and longevity."* —John J. Ratey

- *"Culture is, after all, stored in people's brains. Moreover, human brains are biologically prepared to acquire culture."* —Daniel L. Ames and Susan T. Fiske

CHAPTER OBJECTIVES

1. Identify the roles neurons, neurotransmitters, mirror neurons, and neural pathways have in the brain.

2. Discuss how culture impacts the brain and how people may differ in basic ways because of culture's socialization of the brain.

3. Explain how cultural identity formation is a critical biological and social process necessary for each person's survival and adaptation.

4. Describe the negativity bias and how it affects each person's responses to his or her life events and to counseling.

5. Discuss how people develop both individual and cultural strengths.

6. Explain the role of new brain networks governed partly by the process of mirror neurons.

7. Demonstrate the benefits of counseling that focuses on individuals' strengths rather than negative qualities or weaknesses.

INTRODUCTION

Mental health clinicians are beginning to take notice of the neuroscientific revolution that is having an impact on the fields of counseling, education, psychology, social work, and psychiatry (Jones-Smith, 2016). Despite the fact that the field of neuroscience is gaining in prominence in the mental health professions, many clinicians lack the necessary training to benefit from many of the new developments in this field. What is neuroscience? A broad definition of **neuroscience** is that it is the scientific study of the nervous system (Luke, 2016). Although initially neuroscience was conceptualized as a branch of biology, it is now viewed as an interdisciplinary science that integrates knowledge from psychology, computer science, mathematics, physics, philosophy, and medicine (Luke, 2016).

This chapter focuses on three relatively new developments in multicultural counseling: (1) neuroscience and cultural identity, (2) multicultural identity theory, and (3) strengths-based therapy. The first goal of the chapter is to explore the field of neuroscience and its relationship to cultural and racial identity. The second goal is to investigate the concept that each one of us has a multicultural identity. The chapter concludes by examining the field of cultural strengths (Jones-Smith, 2016).

NEUROSCIENCE, CACREP STANDARDS, AND MAJOR COUNSELING ASSOCIATIONS

Having training in neuroscience has not always been a priority in counseling, psychology, and social work (Hansen, 2009, 2012, 2014). As noted in Chapter 2, the 2009 Council for Accreditation of Counseling and Related Educational Programs (CACREP) Standards acknowledged the importance of neuroscience in counselor education programs by requiring coursework that promotes an understanding of the neurobiology of behavior: "the relationship among brain anatomy, function, biochemistry, and learning and behavior" (p. 61). Building on the CACREP requirement, the American Mental Health Counselors Association's (AMHCA, 2016) Standards for the Practice of Clinical Mental Health Counseling recommended that clinical counselors have training in the biological bases of behavior. Various other mental health professions have likewise integrated neurobiological concepts within counseling practice, including social work (Applegate & Shapiro, 2005; Farmer, 2009) and psychology.

Mental health fields have embraced neuroscience in various ways. In social work, Applegate and Shapiro (2005) informed clinical social workers and social work educators about new research on the neurobiology of attachment and its implications for knowledge building and clinical practice. Farmer (2009) asserted that advances in neuroscience continue to be a missing link in social work given its strong emphasis on the biopsychosocial model. Lambert (2005) suggested that psychology should require a clinical neuroscience course for undergraduates interested in the mental health field. In the counseling literature, Ivey and Zalaquett (2011) have emphasized the relationship between neuroscience and social justice.

Moreover, major journals of the American Counseling Association (i.e., *Counselor Education and Supervision* and *Journal of Counseling and Development*) and of the AMHCA (i.e., *Journal of Mental Health Counseling*) have published articles that deal with neurobiological constructs (e.g., Kindsvatter & Geroski, 2014; Makinson & Young, 2012; Myers & Young, 2012) within the context of psychopharmacology (e.g., Ingersoll & Rak, 2016; Kaut, 2011). McHenry, Sikorski, and McHenry (2013) published the first text on introducing counselors to neuroscience.

FOUNDATIONAL CONCEPTS IN NEUROSCIENCE FOR COUNSELORS

The field of neuroscience has a number of basic concepts that counselors must come to understand in order to better work with their clients. These include (1) neurotransmitters, (2) neuroplasticity, (3) neurogenesis, (4) mirror neurons, (5) the importance of attention and focus, and (6) an emphasis on the positive in life and on wellness (Ivey, Ivey, Zalaquett, & Quirk, 2009).

THE BRAIN

The **brain** consists of a complex interwoven structure of billions of neurons that are described as the central nervous system (Siegel, 2012). Each neuron is an elongated cell that has the ability to reach out to other neurons. Moreover, each neuron contains synapses and dendrites at its ends.

Neurons send out electrical impulses that release chemical neurotransmitters. Synaptic connections produce a system of communication between the synapses and dendrites of neurons.

The brain is the receiver of information from both inside and outside a person. Neuroscience conceptualizes the brain as a dynamic structure that shapes and can be shaped, that changes and can be changed, that gets mired down in neural firing patterns, and that can heal or repair itself to become unstuck.

The Brain Is a Social Organ

Our human interpersonal interactions basically shape the construction of our brains (Cozolino, 2010). A person's brain is fundamentally shaped during the attachment process with a primary caregiver. Cozolino (2010) maintains that "there are no single brains" (p. 6), and in making this assertion, he puts attachment constructs and relationships at the heart of the development of both adaptive and maladaptive behaviors in children and adults. The brain is also an organ of adaptation, and its structures are built in interaction with other people and with the environment. Recent advances in brain imaging have found that the brain is an organ that continually builds and rebuilds itself by one's life experiences.

Some characteristics of the brain. A neuroscientific view of the brain is that people are emotional beings who think, rather than thinking beings who have emotions (LeDoux, 2003). The brain carries out many functions automatically, below the level of conscious control. These automatic functions that occur within the brain are located primarily in the occipital, parietal, and temporal lobes—the back, top, and sides of the brain. In contrast, consciously controlled actions primarily take place in the cerebral cortex (also called the forebrain)—the front of the brain (Restak, 2006). The brain is plastic; the brain changes due to influences from the environment. Even though the human brain is basically similar from one person to another, no two people are identical in the neural "wiring" of the brain because—among other reasons—we are each exposed to a unique combination of environmental conditions and influences. Tancredi (2005) has pointed out the neurobiology of notable differences between female and male brains (e.g., females evidence greater empathy on average than males). Research has found that the way the brain constructs meaning is very different from the way it processes information. According to Modell (2003), the brain's primary way of understanding and remembering the world is through metaphor.

Neurons

The brain functions as a complex system of circuits of neurons. **Neurons** may be defined as the electrically excitable cells that process and transmit information within the brain by electrical-chemical signaling. Neurons do not touch each other, but rather are connected by **synapses**, the structural space that allows for signaling from one neuron to another (Warnick & Landis, 2016). The word *synapse* comes from the Greek and means "point of contact." Neurons communicate with each other within the brain and down the spinal cord. Neurons are interconnected into networks that have chemical and electrical communication systems.

Three primary types of specialized neurons exist within the nervous system. These are (1) sensory neurons, which respond to touch, light, sound, and other stimuli; (2) motor neurons, which receive signals from the brain and the spinal cord, enabling them to cause muscle contractions and influence glands within the body; and (3) interneurons, which connect neurons in the same region of the brain or spinal cord (Luke, 2016).

Interpersonal relationships produce sensory information that can stimulate or inhibit neural functioning in the brain (Luke, 2016). Neuroscientists have found that there are certain time periods in the development of the brain when specific neurons fire and yield specific patterns of representations or understandings (Warnick & Landis, 2016). For instance, during infancy and early childhood, young people's brains are especially sensitive to experiences in the environment, and these experiences influence neuron firing. The time periods during which particular types of neuron development take place are called sensitive periods. For example, during infancy we learn to trust adult caregivers to love us and provide for our needs. Children who experience stress during these sensitive periods may become vulnerable to later stress and have difficulties managing their responses to stress at a later stage in their lives (Kindsvatter & Geroski, 2014). This is not to say that people cannot develop trust or resilience later on in life, but the early sensitive period is like a window of opportunity when the development of these capabilities is particularly likely.

Neurotransmitters

A **neurotransmitter** is a chemical that is released from a nerve cell, which transmits an impulse from one nerve cell to another nerve cell or to a muscle, organ, or other tissue. It is essentially a messenger of neurologic information from one cell to another (Warnick & Landis, 2016). Neurotransmitters contribute to a person's cognitive, emotional, psychological, and behavioral responses or patterns in life. A person's production of neurotransmitters has been linked to environmental stressors and his or her lifestyle (including diet, coping strategies, and leisure time). Many of the problems that clients mention during therapy and counseling can be traced to their brain chemistry and either the over- or underproduction of specific neurotransmitters (Warnick & Landis, 2016).

The brain's sensory stems respond to external input in the form of sensations that are received through the five senses. When individuals receive sensory material, they experience a pattern of neurotransmitter flow between the synapses of the neurons. The pattern of neurotransmitter flow between the neurons sets up "mental symbols" or representations of information that is transmitted. Repeated patterns of neurotransmission lead to the rise of meaning, which may be personal meaning or cultural meaning. Patterns of neurons that fire together form what has been called a **neural net profile** (Siegel, 2012).

The neural net profiles form what is called a concept representation—the application of a concept to a particular example of that concept. For instance, suppose an individual holds a cultural stereotype of a given ethnic group—for instance, that African Americans or Latinos are potentially dangerous. Then, if that individual sees a member of either of these two ethnic groups, it might set off a series of neurotransmitter firings that come together in a neural net profile to form the concept of a dangerous person. This concept is stimulated by the visual input of seeing the African American or Latino person, and the visual representation leads to an electrochemical meaning-making process between neurons within the complicated web of the central nervous system. A key point to remember is that there is a necessary link between the neural activity within the brain and the environmental input (i.e., the approaching person) that first stimulated the synaptic firings.

Although there are more than 100 neurotransmitters, 4 are directly connected to problem behaviors that often bring people to therapy. These are (1) acetylcholine, a neurotransmitter that is critical for learning, optimal cognitive functioning, emotional balance, and control (deficiency causes deterioration of memory, increased forgetfulness, lack of emotional control, and increased aggression); (2) serotonin, a person's natural mood stabilizer and sleep promoter (deficiency causes depression, difficulty sleeping, feeling disconnected, and lack of joy); (3) dopamine, a person's natural energizer; and (4) GABA (gamma-aminobutyric acid), which helps reduce anxiety and induce sleep (deficiency causes the feeling that it is hard to relax) (Farmer, 2009).

Therapy and counseling strategies that tend to release acetylcholine include exercising and using meditation on a consistent basis. Because serotonin deficiencies are associated with depression, therapists and counselors can help clients by assisting them to develop action-based strategies that produce new meaning in their lives. Dopamine production may be increased within a person via massages. Studies have reported that when patients with cancer and other medical disorders receive massage therapy, they experience increased levels of dopamine, serotonin, oxytocin, endorphins, and natural killer cells (Warnick & Landis, 2016).

Neuroplasticity

Neuroplasticity refers to the brain's ability to change and adapt as a result of life experiences (Butz, Worgotter, & van Ooyen, 2009; Holtmaat & Svoboda, 2009). During infancy and childhood, the brain produces new neurons in the person in a process called ***neurogenesis***. Many more neurons are produced than needed, and those that are not useful to the individual die off in a process called pruning. Giedd and colleagues (Giedd, Blumenthal, et al., 1999; Giedd, Clasen, et al., 2006) have maintained that neurogenesis has a "second peak" during puberty, the time during which children develop into adolescents and their bodies become biologically ready for sexual reproduction. There is a second wave of gray matter creation during puberty, and this leads to new neural connections and branches, followed by pruning (Schwartz, 2002). However, neurogenesis does not stop when we reach adulthood. Research has demonstrated that the brain continues to generate new nerve cells in adulthood and that new neurons can be generated in the learning process—even for older adults. In response to new experiences in the environment throughout the life span, the brain continues to create new neural pathways, and it modifies existing neural pathways in order to adapt to new experiences, learn new information, and create new memories (Siegel, 1999, 2010).

Neuroplasticity is moderated by genetic factors and by dynamic epigenetic changes that influence the expression of genes without changing the DNA sequence. Psychologists and other helping professionals are interested in epigenetic processes because their external triggers (e.g., parental care, attachment, diet, drug abuse, and stress) can influence people's vulnerability to many diseases, including mental or psychiatric disorders (Warnick & Landis, 2016). In future decades, researchers will gain additional insights about what forms the basis of neuroplasticity.

The Mind

The **mind** emerges from the brain, and it is shaped by interpersonal relationships. The mind can be defined as a process that regulates the flow of energy and information. Human relationships shape the neural connections from which the mind emerges. According to Siegel (1999), "1. The human mind emerges from patterns in the flow of energy and information within the brain and between brains. 2. The mind is created within the interaction of internal neuro-physiological processes and interpersonal experiences" (p. 2).

MAPPING THE CULTURAL ARCHITECTURE OF THE BRAIN

Cultural neuroscience may be defined as an interdisciplinary field of study that investigates interrelations among culture, mind, and the brain (Kitayama & Park, 2010). It investigates the relationship of culture, biology, brain functioning, psychology, and other social sciences. Early investigations involving cultural neuroscience sought to conduct a neuroscientific study of aging and culture (Park & Gutchess, 2006). Investigators studied aging and the compensatory mechanism for the decline in cognitive abilities due to neural changes in cellular and structural organization of the brain (Chiao, Cheon, Pornpattananangkul, Mrazek, & Blizinsky, 2013). The primary goal of a cultural neuroscience of aging was to promote an understanding of environmental and biological influences on cognitive development in late adulthood (Chiao et al., 2013).

Studies involving cultural influences on cognitive brain function led to the development of transcultural imaging (Han & Northoff, 2008). From there, researchers conducted studies investigating cultural influences on neural representations of self and identity (Kitayama & Park, 2010). Researchers also began examining **cultural mapping** or studying the kinds of cognitive processes that differ across cultures at the neural level, as well as where cultural universals and differences emerge. According to Ambady and Bharucha (2009), two fundamental objectives drive the neuroscience of culture:

The first is to map the cultural architecture of the brain. We call this culture mapping. The second is source analysis, the attempt to tease apart the sources of cultural mappings.

> Cultural mapping is a research strategy that involves mapping cognitive or neural differences across cultures. It involves determining which cognitive or neural processes vary across cultures without determining whether the differences are learned or innate. (p. 342)

Cultural mapping can show how the environments of different cultures are processed differently by people from different cultures. For instance, researchers at Tufts University's Music Cognition Lab have found that Americans process Western and Indian music differently (Curtis & Bharucha, 2009). Tang et al. (2006) examined the brain activity of native English and Chinese speakers as they performed various tasks and found that native English speakers showed more activation in the language processing part of the brain, whereas native Chinese speakers showed more activation in the visual–spatial processing part of the brain. Based on these findings, Tang and colleagues hypothesized that culture affects how individuals speak and process information.

Cultural neuroscience can make significant contributions by demonstrating how "deep" culture can go into the human brain. Because the human brain reflects the influence of culture, brain activation patterns can give important information about the characteristics of cultures. Our cultural habits and behaviors help shape brain neuropathways that influence our personal and cultural identity. In essence, our life experiences are patterned by our cultural experiences, and such cultural patterning "gets under the skin" during the human developmental process to influence the brain and behavior.

A number of questions can be raised about cultural mapping. For instance, what is the role of critical periods in the acquisition of culture-specific neural patterns? How malleable is the brain when it is exposed to new cultures and environments? How is neural processing affected by one's status as an immigrant, as a bicultural person, or as a multicultural person? Neuroscience provides an opportunity to investigate the interaction of culture and biology on the brain and its neural processes (Ambady & Bharucha, 2009).

CULTURAL IDENTITY FORMATION AND NEUROSCIENCE

Cultural identity formation is an important process from both a biological and a psychological standpoint—one that is necessary for a person's survival and adaptation to the world. **Cultural identity development** is an aspect of identity formation that takes place through a person's repeated participation in completing culturally related tasks and in interacting with various cultural artifacts. Cultural identity is facilitated by observing other people as they interact with each other within a given culture. The cultural or ethnic self does not develop optimally in isolation, but rather develops within the safety and security of a cultural community of relationships that affirm and soothe a person so that he or she can learn information and various cultural roles. Cultural attachment facilitates the process of cultural identity. As individuals develop, they experience a maturation of cultural attachment patterns that they formed and modified during their development from infancy through adulthood.

Cultural identity is formed in neural pathways of the brain. According to Siegel (1999), "human connections shape neural connections" (p. 48) such that people are influenced by human connections that make them feel safe and nourished, and neural connections are formed in response to these experiences. This also means that individuals' life experiences may make them identify with a culture different from the one into which they were born.

People from different cultures have been reported to have divergent perceptions of self. According to Ambady and Bharucha (2009), in the social domain, people from different cultures may have divergent perceptions of the self. Individuals from Western cultures tend to value uniqueness and freedom and view the self as independent from others, whereas individuals from cultures like Japan tend to value social harmony and adherence to group norms and view the self as interconnected and interdependent with others. Cultural variation in these self-representations has been found to affect both cognitive and emotional processes. (p. 343)

An important issue in the neuroscience of cultural identity is: Can one identify with an ethnic group of which one is not a member? Does living in a culture create neural pathways and culture attachment for that culture, even though one might not have been born into that culture? What if you are a White woman who has spent years living in and participating in African American culture as an African American woman and not as a White woman?

CASE VIGNETTE 3.1
RACHEL DOLEZAL: A WHITE WOMAN WHO SAYS SHE IS BLACK

In June 2015, Rachel Dolezal's life as an African American woman came to a screeching halt when information surfaced that her biological parents were White Americans. Both African Americans and White Americans called Dolezal, 39, a fraud, and she was removed from her position as head of the National Association for the Advancement of Colored People (NAACP) in Spokane, Washington.

For years, Dolezal, a professor in African studies, had represented herself as African American, styling her hair with a weave or with dreadlock extensions to resemble natural Black hair. After her parents appeared on national television asserting that Dolezal was White, she continued to say that she was not White. In an interview, she stated,

> I think that since the white parents did their TV tour on every national network, some people will forever see me as my birth category, as a white woman. But people who see me as that don't see me really for who I am and probably are not seeing me as a white woman in some kind of a privileged sense. (Oluo, 2017)

Can one change one's racial identity based on how one feels as a person? Dolezal's racial identity as an African American may not be as puzzling as one might think. According to Carolyn Yoon, a cognitive psychologist at the University of Michigan's Institute for Social Research, people are making too much of Dolezal's self-proclaimed racial identity. Yoon has stated that "identity is highly malleable and is a function of what she comes into contact with, what she spends her time doing, is interested in and motivated by. Over time that will change your brain" (quoted in Nutt, 2015).

How people respond to racial and cultural identity varies, even though the vast majority of people tend to identify with their biological race. Yet, the idea of "passing" has existed throughout American history, with African Americans and members of other ethnic minority groups presenting themselves as White in order to assume the privileged status of being White in America. Dolezal's assumption of an African American identity was puzzling to many people because she was doing just the opposite—denying her privileged White status in American society.

Is the case of Rachel Dolezal similar to that of Caitlyn Jenner, a person who changed her biological identity as a male to that of a female? Are there reasons why it is acceptable to secure a transgender identity but not to have a transracial identity? When interviewed by *The Guardian*, Dolezal said, "I feel like the idea of being trans-black would be much more accurate than 'I'm white.' Because you know, I'm not white . . . . Calling myself black feels more accurate than saying I'm white" (Aitkenhead, 2017).

The case of Rachel Dolezal presents some important questions, such as how does one acquire a racial identity? Where is racial identity formed in the brain? Can we have a birth racial identity and a socialized racial identity? Can our cultural and racial experiences change our brains so that we identify with a racial identity based on our lived, daily experiences?

BRAIN REGIONS AND CULTURAL IDENTITY

Neuroscientists have reported that cultural identity and even racial identity do not emanate from any single place in the brain, but certain brain regions are associated with these identities. Research has found, for example, that the medial prefrontal cortex, the part of the brain located just behind the forehead, is activated whenever we think about ourselves (Chiao & Ambady, 2007; Han & Northoff, 2008). Kitayama and Park (2010) have asserted that repeated performance in the same routines can lead to systematic differences in the brain pathways that are engaged. Cultural routines and one's repeated interactions with cultural artifacts and tools can change the brain. As Kitayama and Park have pointed out,

> Brain pathways can change as long as they are fired in certain scripted ways over an extended period of time. When fired together, the brain neurons begin to be wired together. (p. 114)

Different cultural tools, practices, and cultural tasks promote certain brain changes.

> Different cultural regions have been characterized in terms of different sets of cultural tools, practices, and tasks. Importantly, the cultural tools, practices, and tasks are not randomly assembled or distributed. To the contrary, they are organized by certain themes or values, including (but not limited to) independence or individualism and interdependence or collectivism (Markus and Kitayama, 1991; Nisbett et al., 2001; Triandis, 1995; Kitayama et al., 2007). Effects of culture, therefore, are likely to go beyond the effects that are attributable to each individual tool, practice, or task. Instead, culture is organized by meanings, folk beliefs, and values that tie together the relevant tools, practices, and tasks. Cultural influences are likely to be reinforced and determined by the layers of specific tools, practices, and tasks that are integrated into a more or less coherent, interconnected network. (Kitayama & Park, 2010, p. 114)

Participation in cultural practices and institutions can promote very different notions of the self and well-being. In the case of Rachel Dolezal, one might propose that her 10- to 15-year participation in African American culture led her to identify as an African American. She had created neural pathways in the brain consistent with self-identity as an African American woman.

Neuroscience measures, such as functional magnetic resonance imaging (fMRI), have provided important information about identity and the brain. Research by Zhu, Zhang, Fan, and Han (2007) has shown that the structure of the self varies systematically across cultures at the level of brain representations. Brain processes are, then, highly malleable, and they are shaped by the cultural tools and practices by any given society. The primary values of a culture, such as independence (Western culture, individualism) and interdependence (Eastern culture, collectivism), are reflected in individuals' daily routines and cultural tasks. The brain contains culturally patterned neural activities based on individuals' years of participation in completing cultural tasks and ceremonial activities. When two or more vastly different cultures are compared, one will find highly systematic differences in brain responses (Kitayama & Park, 2010; Zhu et al., 2007).

Neuroplasticity or brain plasticity is involved in learning and adapting to a given culture. Repeated engagement in cultural behavior and practices produces highly systematic changes in relevant brain responses. Culture produces neural pathways by providing individuals with cultural tasks designed to achieve the culture's values. On a daily and routine basis, individuals engage in such tasks in their effort to achieve cultural adaptation. As Kitayama and Park (2010) have stated, "through this repeated engagement in cultural tasks, new neural activities are induced, reinforced, and established. These culturally patterned neural activities enable the

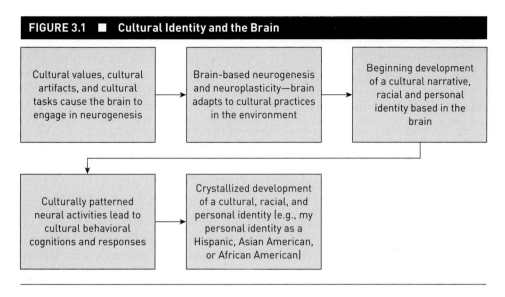

FIGURE 3.1 ■ Cultural Identity and the Brain

person to seamlessly perform his or her own significant cultural tasks, thereby solidly anchoring the self and identity in the cultural world" (p. 121).

SOME IMPORTANT FINDINGS IN CULTURAL NEUROSCIENCE

There are a number of findings in cultural neuroscience that have significance for counselors and therapists. Much of the current research might on the face of things appear to be difficult to understand because it deals with brain imaging. This section summarizes only a few key findings in cultural neuroscience that may have an important impact on counseling in schools and in mental health therapy. For current research on neuroscience, the reader is referred to the journal *Culture and Brain*, published by Springer.

A key finding in cultural neuroscience is that repeating certain routines can result in systematic differences in brain pathways engaged by those routines. Brain pathways can change as long as they are fired in certain scripted ways over a long period of time.

Moreover, there is some evidence for a culture–gene coevolutionary theory of human behavior. Research has identified at least three different cultural dimensions that moderate neural bases of social and emotional behavior: (1) individualism–collectivism, (2) power distance or preference for social hierarchy, and (3) racial identification (Chiao et al., 2009; Chiao et al., 2010; Harada, Li, & Chiao, 2010). For instance, Matsumoto et al. (2008) have posited that people living in cultures that prefer hierarchy, such as Korea, may not show their emotions in social situations due to strong display rules that emphasize low emotional expressivity.

These findings suggest that a counselor or therapist must carefully examine the degree to which a client identifies with a given culture.

CULTURAL IDENTITY AND THE CULTURAL FORMULATION INTERVIEW FOR THE *DSM-5*

Cultural, racial, or ethnic identity is so important for a person that the American Psychiatric Association (2013) has included a major section on cultural identity in its revised **Cultural Formulation Interview (CFI)** for the *Diagnostic and Statistical Manual of Mental Disorders*

(*DSM-5*) (discussed further in Chapter 7 of this book). The revised Outline for Cultural Formulation in the *DSM-5* calls for the systematic assessment of five categories dealing with a person's cultural background:

- Cultural identity of the individual
- Cultural conceptualization of distress (see the section on cultural meaning)
- Psychosocial stressors and cultural features of vulnerability and resilience
- Cultural features of the relationship between the individual and the clinician
- Overall cultural assessment

Cultural identity of the individual involves describing the client's racial, ethnic, or cultural reference groups, cultural resources, and current cultural conflicts or predicaments. Table 3.1 provides interview questions that a clinician might use to uncover or discover the importance of a client's cultural identity. The clinician examines the client's language preferences and his or her participation within a culture. Cultural identity refers to how people identify themselves in relation to others. Table 3.1 contains questions and items developed by the author of this book to reflect general themes of the CFI.

TABLE 3.1 ■ Clinical Skill: Cultural Identity Questions and the Cultural Formulation Interview

Language

- When you were growing up, what language did you primarily speak? Did you speak any other languages?
- What language is spoken in your home? With your friends? At work?
- How well do you speak English?
- Do you feel that you are able to express what you feel when you are speaking English?

Ethnic Belonging and Attachment

- Is there any group or groups that are important to you? You might want to consider national, ethnic, cultural, religious, or social groups.
- How important is your ethnic/racial/cultural membership to you?
- How do you think of yourself in terms of your cultural group membership? Do you see yourself primarily as a White American, African American, Asian American, Latino, or American Indian?
- What do you like most about your cultural group?
- Do you have a sense of belonging or attachment to your cultural group?
- Do you think of yourself as American?
- How important is it for you to belong to your cultural group?
- Do you have much contact with people from your cultural group? If so, would you like to have more contact with them? If not, could you clarify your feelings about your cultural group?
- To what extent do you think your culture differs from the American customs and culture?
- Do you think you fit in well in the United States? Do you have any American friends or acquaintances?
- Has your experience of belonging to your cultural group changed over time? What has this meant for you?
- How would you describe yourself? What is the most important thing about you?
- Would you marry outside your cultural group?

THE NEGATIVITY BIAS OF
THE BRAIN: FINDINGS IN NEUROSCIENCE

Let's assume that one accepts the findings that culture influences both the brain and an individual's identity. What are some characteristics of the brain that might influence how we respond to others who are different from us? Similarly, what are some of the characteristics of the brain that might affect how a client views life and himself or herself? This book maintains that the brain has a built-in **negativity bias**, meaning that negative experiences, or the fear of bad events, have a far greater impact than do neutral or positive experiences and that this bias will influence how a client responds to therapy. The brain's negativity bias is believed to cut across different cultures. It is important to deal with the negativity bias of the brain as part of how an understanding of neuroscience can make individuals better counselors and therapists.

Psychologists Roy Baumeister, Ellen Bratslavsky, Catrin Finkenauer, and Kathleen Vohs (2001) conducted a landmark study in which they noted a negativity bias of the brain. In their article titled "Bad Is Stronger Than Good," the authors argued that individuals are more affected by negative experiences or the fear of negative experiences than by neutral or even positive experiences. Human beings are biased toward behaving in a manner that will avoid negative experiences. People are more likely to recall and be influenced by past negative experiences. Baumeister and colleagues (2001) stated, "Bad emotions, bad parents, and bad feedback have more impact than good ones and bad information is processed more thoroughly than good. The self is more motivated to avoid bad self-definitions than to pursue good ones" (p. 323). The brain detects negative information more quickly than it does positive information. For instance, studies have found that fearful faces are perceived much more quickly than happy or neutral ones (Yang, Zald, & Blake, 2007). When the brain sees an event as negative, it stores it in memory for future reference.

The negativity bias carries with it low or negative expectations for success, and it exaggerates future obstacles. Seligman (2002) found that it was easy to develop feelings of learned helplessness from a few failures but hard to undo those feelings, even with positive successes. Accident victims tend to take longer to return to their original baseline of happiness than do lottery winners (Brickman, Coates, & Janoff-Bulman, 1978). It usually takes five positive interactions to overcome the effects of a single negative one (Gottman, 1995). The negativity bias affects the therapy assessment process.

Rashid and Ostermann (2009) point out that so entrenched are psychologists and clinicians in the belief that symptoms are authentic, central ingredients to be assessed that the former diagnostic and statistic manual (*DSM-IV*; American Psychiatric Association, 2006) designates affiliation, anticipation, altruism, and humor as "defense mechanisms." This conceptualization suggests that positive behaviors such as altruism are considered to be mere coping mechanisms in response to guilt instead of positive characteristics to be explored, understood, and encouraged because they promote a person's sense of well-being. The authors cited empirical research in which the participants, assuming the role of the clinician, were asked what information they would like to know about a client. When clients were initially presented in a negative light (e.g., having just been released from a psychiatric facility), clinicians asked for significantly more negative information (e.g., "Is the client cruel?" instead of "Is the client intelligent?") than when the client was initially presented in a positive light (e.g., having just completed undergraduate studies).

Clinicians typically seek to confirm negative evaluations with more negative questions, but they typically do not follow up positive evaluations or circumstances with more questions designed to ferret out a client's positive attributes. Rashid and Ostermann (2009) argue that this "deficit approach" in psychotherapy creates a power differential in favor of clinicians because they have the expertise to diagnose the client's presenting problem and recommend treatment. Clients who resist a therapist's negative diagnosis are labeled as noncompliant or being in denial.

Hecht (2013) conducted a review of the literature on the neurophysiology of optimism and pessimism and found that they are differentially associated with the two cerebral hemispheres of the brain. High self-esteem and an attitude inclined to look at the positive aspects of a given situation, including an optimistic belief in a bright future, are associated with physiological activity in the left hemisphere. In contrast, a melancholy or gloomy perspective, a tendency to focus on the negative and to exaggerate its significance, low self-esteem, and a pessimistic view of what the future holds are linked with the neurophysiological processes in the right hemisphere.

Sometimes mental health practitioners intentionally and unintentionally promote changes in different parts of the brain when providing counseling. Counseling and therapy should help clients to shift their attention from a negative issue or situation (e.g., the problems that are causing emotional distress) to a positive, strengths-based perspective (e.g., therapeutic goals and positive strengths-based outcomes). From a neurological perspective, when counselors help clients to shift their attention from negative thoughts and feelings to positive, strengths-based cognitions, emotion, and behavior, their brain changes, and clients begin to focus on solutions to their problems. Hence, there is a direct positive payoff when clients focus their attention on the positives in their lives. Using a neuroscience framework, clients can learn how to regulate and direct their attention in positive ways, and this positive focus can enable them to control their distress. When clients become upset, they can say, "I am causing my right hemisphere to respond, and consequently, I am experiencing distress signals in my body and mind."

IS THE BRAIN HARDWIRED TO SEE THE GLASS HALF EMPTY OR HALF FULL?

Counselors might find it difficult to use strengths-based therapy if either they or their clients have a tendency to see the proverbial "glass half empty." Conflicts or clinical impasses might occur in psychotherapy if the therapist has a tendency to see the glass as half empty while the client sees the glass as half full. Whether a client sees a situation as negative or positive might be related to his or her genes. Scientists have discovered that the ability to remain positive when times get tough may be innate in the brain (Nauert, 2013). A study by Rebecca Todd et al. (2013) suggests that some people are genetically predisposed to have a gloomy instead of a positive view of the world. According to these researchers, a previously unknown gene variant can cause individuals to perceive emotional events more vividly than positive ones. The gene, the ADRA2B deletion variant, affects norepinephrine, a neurotransmitter.

These findings by Todd et al. (2013) have shown ways that genetics interact with external factors such as education, culture, and mood to affect individual differences in emotional perception. The researchers reported ethnic and cultural differences for the participants in their study, finding that more than half of Caucasians are believed to have the ADRA2B gene variant, while it is found with much less frequency in other ethnic groups. For instance, a recent study (Omer, 2013) reported that only 10% of Rwandans had the ADRA2B gene variant. More studies need to be conducted to determine the percentage or extent to which members of a specific culture have the ADRA2B gene variant. It might be helpful for counselors/therapists conducting culturally responsive counseling/therapy to ask their clients, "To what extent do people from your culture tend to see the glass as half empty or half full?"

Jason Moser and colleagues (2014) found that a person's ability to stay positive during challenging times may be hardwired in the brain. The study examined the neurophysiological markers of positive reappraisal using event-related potentials (ERPs), which are brain signals that reflect the time course of neural mechanisms that underlie the way people process information. The study involved 71 female participants who were shown graphic images and asked to put a positive spin on them while their brain activity was recorded. The study used women participants because they are twice as likely as men to suffer from anxiety-related problems. Participants were shown a masked man holding a knife to a woman's throat, and they were informed that one potential outcome was that the woman breaks free and escapes. Prior to the beginning of the study, the participants were surveyed to establish who tended to think positively and who thought negatively or worried.

Moser and his colleagues (2014) found that positive thinkers' brain activity was much more quiet than that of worriers when they were asked to think positively. The worriers reflected a very different result:

Cultural Reflections

To what extent has your ethnic, cultural, or gender identity influenced you to see the glass half empty or half full?

> The worriers actually showed a paradoxical backfiring effect in their brains when asked to decrease their negative emotions. Such individuals have a hard time putting a positive spin on difficult situations and may actually make their negative emotions worse when they are asked to think positively . . . . You can't just tell your friend to think positively or to not worry—that's probably not going to help them . . . . So you need to take another tack and perhaps ask them to think about the problem in a different way to use different strategies. (p. 103)

Although Moser et al. (2014) suggested that negative thinkers could also practice thinking positively, they added that it would take a lot of time and effort to even start to make a difference. Therapists and counselors should take note of Moser et al.'s findings in that they must do more than just encourage clients to think positively in order to change their negative thinking. They must help clients to practice developing new neural pathways by focusing on the positives in their lives (see Figure 3.2).

Think about your own life and examine it to see if you have a negativity bias. For instance, try to remember a compliment you received in high school. Then try to remember an insult that

FIGURE 3.2 ■ The Negativity Bias: A Challenge for Strengths-Based Therapists and Counselors

Negativity Bias	
Brain detects negative information more readily than positive information.	Negative information about a person trumps positive information about him or her.

Negative Evaluation of Self	
Fear of bad events is stronger than promise of positive ones. Negativity bias leads to fear, avoidance, and learned helplessness.	Person has negative expectations of success and exaggrates present and future obstacles. Fear and avoidance are dominant emotions and strategies.

Negative Evaluation of Others	
People remember more negative than positive information about a person.	Negative relationships with others can develop out of one negative event. People don't forget how they have been treated.

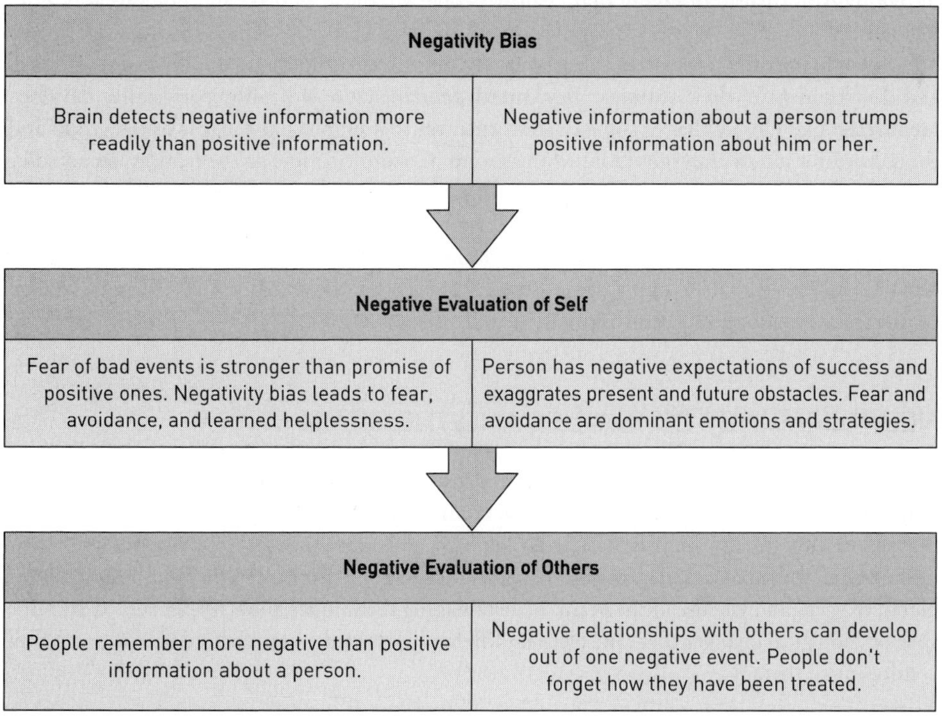

took place during this same time. If you are like most people, you will remember much more easily the insults that were directed toward you than the compliments. This situation occurs because negative events are inclined to resonate and be more memorable than positive or even neutral events.

It is important for parents to understand the negativity bias because it can influence their parenting techniques. Parents should realize that the negativity bias will cause their children to remember that one angry "You jerk!" much more easily than they will the hundreds of times that you give them a compliment. Understanding that a negative statement or act toward a child becomes much more figured or prominent in a child's memory may help parents to remember how important it is to try to keep their tempers under control. For positive experiences to be remembered, they have to take place frequently. Parents have to tell their children that they love them frequently in order for them to feel loved. They have to emphasize children's strengths many different times in a number of settings for children to believe that they have strengths.

MENTAL HEALTH FROM A NEUROSCIENTIFIC PERSPECTIVE

One way to think of mental illness is to say that one or more systems of the brain did not develop adequately and/or there is an absence of integration between various systems in the brain. In order to have a balanced mood, both the right and left hemispheres have to be actively involved in an equal or democratic way and reciprocally balance each other.

The environment assumes a prominent role in activation of the brain—especially a person's attachment pattern formed with a primary caretaker during infancy and early childhood. This, in turn, has a strong developmental influence on one's emotional regulation and one's feelings about oneself and others. If, during the attachment process, a child gets the message that he or she is not valued, shame and negativity will predominate.

Cozolino (2010) used the concept of the *social brain* to challenge the Western value of individualism. Instead of saying that healthy people are those who are autonomous and independent, he contends that because one's social brain is basically shaped in interaction with other people, healthy people are those who rely on others throughout their lives for strength and development of their abilities. This interdependent view of healthy personality development resembles closely that of some Eastern cultures that emphasize the role of the group and the subordination of the individual to the group. Cozolino's view of the healthy personality is consistent with several psychological theories, including relational theory (Mitchell, 1988) and attachment theory (Schore, 2001). Healthy relationships between people produce mentally healthy people. In contrast, disturbed relationships lead to mentally unhealthy individuals. Poor interpersonal relationships produce disorders of the social brain. One can change brain circuitry through relationships.

NEUROIMAGING TECHNIQUES AND THE BRAIN

Many of the significant findings about the brain and counseling have been made possible because of important improvements in neuroimaging. **Neuroimaging techniques** are based on the view that mental activity is primarily reflected in biological changes that take place in different parts of the brain. These biological changes include an increase or a decrease in the volume and flow of blood, oxygen, and glucose in the brain. Neuroimaging techniques allow researchers to examine specific biological changes that take place in different parts of the brain before, during, and after counseling or therapy.

NEUROSCIENCE: PSYCHOTHERAPY CHANGES YOUR BRAIN

Neuroscience has uncovered a number of aspects about our human life that may revolutionize how we conduct psychotherapy (LeDoux, 1996, 2002; Siegel, 1999, 2010). Nobel Prize winner Eric Kandel commented on how therapy affects clients' brains. According to Kandel (1998), "when a therapist speaks to a patient and the patient listens, the therapist is not only making eye contact and voice contact, but the action of neuronal machinery in the therapist's brain is having an indirect and one hopes, long lasting effect on the neuronal machinery in the patient's brain; and quite likely vice versa. Insofar as our words produce changes in our patient's mind, it is likely that these psychotherapeutic interventions produce change in the patient's brain. From this perspective the biological and sociopsychological approaches are joined" (p. 458).

Neuroscience research has shown how psychotherapy or "talking therapies" change the functions of the brain, its chemical operations, and its structure (Linden, 2006; Rossouw, 2013). For instance, Arthur Brody and his colleagues (2001) reported metabolic changes in clients with depression treated with interpersonal therapy. They found that subjects treated with interpersonal psychotherapy experienced a 38% decrease in their scores on the Hamilton Depression Rating Scale, while those treated with the drug paroxetine had a greater mean decrease in their scores. Both subgroups "showed decreases in normalized prefrontal cortex (paroxetine-treated bilaterally and interpersonal psychotherapy-treated on the right) and life anterior cingulate gyrus metabolism, and increases in normalized left temporal lobe metabolism" (Brody et al., 2001, p. 631). Similar findings supporting psychotherapy's impact on a client's brain were reported by Stephen Martin and his colleagues (Martin, Martin, Rai, Richardson, & Royall, 2001), who identified blood flow changes in depressed clients treated with interpersonal psychotherapy. The investigation showed interpersonal psychotherapy resulted in both limbic blood flow increase and basal ganglia blood flow.

Findings that support the belief that psychotherapy changes clients' brains present certain ethical and professional responsibilities for therapists and helping professionals. For instance: What are the fundamental basics that every ethical practicing therapist should know about neuroscience and clients' brains during therapy? How might practicing clinicians incorporate knowledge gained from neuroscience about the human brain in their everyday clinical practice? Counselors and therapists have tended to approach neuroscience from two perspectives. First, some have begun to incorporate basic neuroscience findings into established practices that are framed in psychoanalytic, cognitive-behavioral, humanistic, and social constructivist theoretical approaches (Davidson & Begley, 2012). Second, some clinicians are calling for a form of psychotherapy that is based primarily on neuroscience.

THE THERAPEUTIC RELATIONSHIP FROM A NEUROSCIENTIFIC PERSPECTIVE

Neuroscience offers a new conceptual framework for clinicians' understanding of what takes place during the counseling or therapy session. The process of psychotherapy uses the brain's plasticity for bringing about client change. The types of cognitive (problem-solving), emotional, psychological, and behavioral changes that counselors use in counseling and psychotherapy are dependent on the brain's producing new neurons and neural wiring that affect changes in different brain systems that also contribute to positive therapeutic outcomes.

Moreover, counseling often involves helping clients to shift their attention from a specific negative issue or situation (e.g., the problems that are causing distress) to positive outcomes. Counseling is about helping clients to shift their attention from negative thoughts and feelings to positive cognitions, emotions, and behaviors, which produces specific neurological changes that take only milliseconds to occur in different parts of the brain.

Therapy involves a clinician's assisting clients to restructure old neural pathways and to build new ones to help them deal with their challenges and to lead a more satisfying life. It is important to understand that the process of counseling and psychotherapy relies on clients' natural biological propensity for neuroplasticity and neurogenesis. Effective counseling often results in the generation of new neurons and neural networks that effect changes in a client's brain that produce a sense of well-being. When one uses the neuroscience conceptual framework, talk within the therapy hour becomes much more purposeful and intentional rather than hit-or-miss. The therapist is intentionally helping clients to engage in the process of neuroplasticity. Therapy may be considered successful to the extent that therapists are able to help create a therapeutic experience that results in creating neuroplasticity for clients.

Neuroscience can be used to help counselors and therapists conceptualize what is happening in their clients' brains. From the **neuroscience worldview**, psychotherapy is an interaction between two human brains and the neural pathways that therapist and client have created for themselves as a result of the interaction between their genetics and their life experiences. Additional support for this conceptualization is provided by Viamontes and Beitman (2006), who described the therapeutic relationship as "a relationship between two brains and their bodies" (p. 214). Both neuroscientists and clinicians have maintained that counselors and therapists can help a client develop new neural pathways as a result of establishing a caring and safe therapeutic relationship that communicates that they understand and accept him or her unconditionally (Hanson, 2010; Kandel, 1998, 2005; Siegel, 2010).

The therapeutic relationship can "enhance or replace an attachment relationship, based on how the right brain develops (the hemisphere that controls emotions) and continues to function in adulthood" (Farmer, 2009, p. 122). Therapeutic attachment facilitates neural restructuring in the right brain of clients (Farmer, 2009). In working with clients, counselors and therapists deal with more than just negative emotions, self-imposed limits, and bad memories. When therapists are engaged during the therapy hour, they deal with the very strategies that their clients use to encounter and cope with life. Clients generate neurological pathways of behavior in their brains. They even become addicted to their own brain chemicals as they repeat again and again life strategies that may not have been working for a long period of time. In essence, clients become addicted to the behavioral strategies they use for living. Neural restructuring can change a person's habitual neurological pattern of behavior.

The first step in helping clients to change their neural networks is to identify them. To achieve this goal, clinicians must engage in deep listening to what their clients are saying about their life situations and especially what they are saying about themselves, such as their having difficulty trusting others, problems in establishing and maintaining relationships, low self-esteem, or poor anger management. Helping professionals must understand that the already established neural networks in their clients' brains are based on their own life experiences. If clients do not have an established network for something, then they do not have a reference point for change. As clinicians identify clients' neural networks, they can then begin to consider experiences that might help them to build new neural networks that are more satisfying and less problematic. Clinicians might consider experimenting with brain sensory inputs such as art therapy, music therapy, therapeutic stories, and psychodrama. Sensory inputs tend to engage clients' neural networks to become active and open to learning new information. It is important that clients feel that they are in control of changing the neural networks in their brains.

How might a counselor or therapist help clients to see a connection between their own brains and what they are working on in therapy? Hanson (2010) has pointed out that when a therapist translates psychological issues into neural terms, such issues become demystified, normalized, and destigmatized. The client is taught to recognize how the neural networks associated with the amygdala, for instance, bring about states of fear and anger. It is not that the client is crazy or weird, but rather that the client might have to deliberately and intentionally change the wiring of his or her neural networks by having new affirming life experiences not built on fear (Arden, 2010).

CASE VIGNETTE 3.2
BRAD: A CASE OF STRESS

Brad had a history of responding negatively to stress. Every time he found himself in a stressful position, he would engage in nonproductive avoidance behaviors and "burying his head in the sand." Neuroscience suggests that an individual should address stress before it takes place. When a client buries his head in the sand, his problem-solving muscles begin to atrophy, similar to the way that one's body muscles atrophy when one does not use them sufficiently.

The therapist points out that Brad's brain becomes stuck in a rut of avoidance of problem-solving behavior. Brad wonders how he is going to deal with a situation, and his brain responds based on the neural pathways that he has established in the past.

The therapist tells Brad that instead of trying to avoid the situation, he might ask himself, "What can I do about this situation?" "Name just one small thing you can do about the problem," the therapist says.

Principles of neuroscience encourage change and the building of new neural pathways. The therapist informs Brad that because of the principle of neuroplasticity he can learn new ways of dealing with stress. In other words, Brad can change the way his brain is wired, and he can break out of his old, avoidance thinking ruts.

Brad's amygdala has sounded the panic alarm based on his past poor problem-solving ability. Instead of allowing his amygdala to go haywire, the therapist suggests that Brad begin to use more positive, strengths-based problem-solving skills. She encourages Brad to say to himself, "I can handle this. I have the skills to handle the problem. I don't have to run away."

The therapist has educated Brad about his brain's response to stress. She has helped him to understand what part of his brain is responding to stress. Brad learns that his amygdala's alarm signal is causing him to push the panic button. The therapist tells Brad that people "wire" their brains to respond to perceived threats either with uncontrollable emotions (such as fear and avoidance, or anger and aggression) or with a calm and resilient response. He can learn how to "rewire his brain" and

the neural pathways that govern his response to stress. The therapist directs Brad through a series of exercises designed to have him reflect on response and the situation. In addition, she indicates to Brad that she is going to help him go through a series of deep breathing exercises in order to calm the alarm signal given by his amygdala. The focus will be on using Brad's strengths-based problem-solving skills to more effectively deal with the stressful situation.

The therapist's task is to help Brad strengthen the neural connectivity to the cortex where rationality and the ability to reflect exist. Because the brain responds to its environment, the talking interaction (counseling) between a skilled and empathic counselor promotes a sense of safety in the therapeutic setting, making it easier for Brad to learn new ways of responding to stress. The therapist helps Brad to down-regulate the threat response and to learn new ways of responding and thinking that will help him to thwart being overwhelmed by negative emotional responses. Brad's commitment to practice the new skills he has learned from his therapist is very important. Learning new responses to stress takes time, and repetition is necessary to establish and maintain new neural pathways to override the old ineffectual ones.

Discussion Questions

1. Do you think that Brad is helped by understanding his brain's response to stress?

2. Would you feel comfortable teaching your client about the parts of the brain and how it responds to stress?

3. What additional activities might you use to down-regulate Brad's threat response to the stressful situation?

4. How might you go about teaching Brad new strengths-based problem-solving skills? Would you give Brad homework to complete to reinforce new neural pathways?

NEUROSCIENCE AND THE CULTURALLY RESPONSIVE COUNSELOR

Kandel (2005) suggested that therapists and counselors must develop an understanding of the neuropsychological principles that govern not only their own behavior but also that of their clients. Therapists and counselors whose practices are informed by neuroscience learn how to cultivate their clients' neuroplasticity. Therapy and counseling should produce new pathways of neural firing through the creation of a safe therapeutic environment and a corrective emotional experience (Allison & Rossouw, 2013). One role for a therapist or counselor is to help a client down-regulate his or her stress response so that new patterns of neural activation can take place. The therapist or counselor provides an environment in which a client's basic needs for safety and control are met so that a shift can take place from client patterns of avoidance and protection to patterns of approach. As Allison and Rossouw (2013) have stated,

> New neural patterns can be activated by down regulating the stress response and enhancing the basic needs of attachment and control. Safety is thereby facilitated through the development of new neural pathways that shift unhelpful patterns of thinking, feeling, and behaving. (p. 3)

MIRROR NEURONS AND COUNSELORS

Mirror neurons are specialized neurons in the brain that help us to understand the actions and intention of other people (Gallese & Goldman, 1998). Both clients and therapists/counselors experience neural activation when clients talk about their problems during therapy. When clients describe in detail their challenges or problems, mirror neurons are activated in the counselor's brain as he or she is engaged in deep listening and close observation of clients' behaviors. Schulte-Rüther, Markowitsch, Fink, and Piefke (2007) have pointed out that the "same neuronal activity patterns occur in the same areas of an observer's brain as in the brain of a closely observed and felt other person" (p. 1362). Neurological mirroring is facilitated when the interpersonal interactions between therapist and client are experienced as being nonjudgmental, positive-regarding, respectful, accepting, and empathic in nature (Schulte-Rüther et al., 2007).

Mirror neurons are part of the brain's mechanisms for attributing meaning to other people's actions. "Meaning," then, is established first in the brain. The meaning of persons, places, and things is defined in terms of their functional and psychological significance to a person. The ability of a therapist or counselor to be empathic may be dependent on his or her own system for understanding the intentions and emotional experiences of others (Iacoboni & Dapretto, 2006).

The **mirror neuron system (MNS)** includes the superior temporal cortex, which encodes a visual description of an observed action; the posterior parietal mirror neurons, which encode the kinesthetic of the action's movement sequence; the inferior frontal mirror neurons, which encode the perceived goal of the action; and the limbic circuitry, including the amygdala, which responds emotionally to the perceived goals. The ability to be empathic is partly dependent on the functioning of these related systems of circuits within a counselor and within a client. Mirror neurons connect visual and motor experiences and are involved in social functions such as learning, the development of gestures, and verbal language. According to Newberg and Waldman (2012), "the neurons that fire in someone's brain when they make a specific gesture also fire in your brain as you observe them" (p. 45).

The better therapists and counselors can mirror the neural activity in their clients' brains, the more likely they will be able to understand their clients (Newberg & Waldman, 2012). When therapists are able to accurately mirror their clients' feelings, they create neural resonance between them. As Newberg and Waldman (2012) have stated, "if you really want to understand what the other person is saying, you have to listen and observe the other person as deeply and fully as possible. Otherwise your brains won't mirror each other. If we can't simulate in our own brains what another person is thinking and feeling, we won't be able to cooperate with them" (p. 81).

A counselor can use neuroscientific principles to improve counseling by influencing the brain in multiple ways, choosing and combining different treatments, educating clients about brain functions, discussing the changeable nature of memory, and emphasizing optimism and growth as potential outcomes for relationships.

CASE VIGNETTE 3.3
THE CASE OF JUSTIN FROM A NEUROPSYCHOTHERAPY PERSPECTIVE

Justin greeted his counselor with his familiar "Hi, Doc. What are we going to do today? Didn't you tell me that we were going to be working on my brain? It's all messed up, Doc," Justin laughed. "We can go on to something else."

"I don't think that your brain is messed up, Justin," the counselor responded. "You've got a good brain. You're smart; you can draw; you can do a lot of different things with your brain, Justin. What I want us to work on today is increasing your knowledge of what is happening in your brain when it is functioning well and what's happening when it's not working so well. So, I brought in two things that I want to share with you. The first thing I want to do is to show you a brief video by Dr. Daniel Siegel on the teenage brain, even though you're not quite 13 yet. The video is about seven minutes long, and in it, Dr. Siegel uses his hand in a useful way to think about the brain. He also talks about what goes on in the brain of teenagers, why they make what seems like some crazy choices—doing things that if they had a moment to think about the situation, they might not do. Then, the second thing I'd like for us to do is to look at the model of the brain that I have on my desk and maybe engage in an exercise or two, depending on the time that we have left. How does that sound to you? Do you think you would like to do these things today?"

"Sure," Justin said. "I'm game. You know, Doc, I don't mind looking at a video and talking about it."

"Okay. But before we look at the video, I would like to get your thoughts about why there is sometimes friction and conflict between teenagers and their parents and teenagers and other aspects of our society—like school," the counselor said.

"Oh, that's easy," Justin replied. "It's like . . . it's like they're always telling us what to do—like do your homework, wash the dishes, stop watching so much TV, get up early enough so that you're not late for school, and so on and so on. It never stops. It's like we don't have a mind of our own. They don't trust us to do the right thing."

"So, you feel as if you are not given an opportunity to make up your own mind about things, that adults don't trust you to make the right decisions?" the counselor interjected.

"Exactly," Justin said, shaking his head. "I know that my mom doesn't trust me. I can look at her eyes and see that she is probably thinking, 'You're not going where you said you were going. You tell me anything just to get out of the house.' And sometimes she's right. I want to be with my friends. I don't want to be treated like some kind of a 'momma's boy.'"

"Well, Justin, the video raises some of the same issues that you just mentioned. Let's watch it for seven minutes and get your reaction to it," the counselor said.

The video showed Dr. Siegel putting his hand in a way to simulate the brain. He described how certain parts of the brain dealt with strong emotions, such as anger and fear. The amygdala was implicated for fear and angry responses to events. The video raised the question about why young people sometimes make such poor decisions. The video pointed out that during adolescence, the brain is experiencing a massive and necessary integration of functions that will have a long-term effect, and that a young person's solidarity with his peers was evolutionary insofar as young people banded together because they understood that down the line, they would be living in a world with their friends and peers. The shared experiences that adolescents have with each other enable their generation to become leaders. Adolescents are at the peak of their creative powers and courageousness. Further, Dr. Siegel mentioned the four qualities of the adolescent mind: novelty seeking, social engagement, increased emotional intensity, and creative exploration.

After viewing the video, Justin said, "Wow, I didn't know that's why I do some of the crazy things that I do."

The counselor responded, "What do you mean, Justin? Can you elaborate a little more about 'why you do the crazy things that you do'?"

"Well, things like what got me in trouble with the law and got me sent to you. My friends came by my house, and they wanted to go to the mall. I wanted to be with them. I didn't want to stay at home with my mom. We were going to go out and have some fun. I had no idea that that fun would land me in jail; otherwise, I would have stayed my butt at home.

"We were in Walmart, and one of my friends said, 'Let's see if we can steal something and get away with it.' None of us had any money. At first, I thought that it was crazy. I could see the cop standing near the exit of the store, and I thought, 'Are you crazy? We could get caught.'

"Then my friend said, 'Chick, chick, chick; you're just chicken, Justin.' So, he stole something. I'm not even sure what he stole, and a store detective told him to put it back. He didn't, and we all ran out of the store. The cop ran after us, and we were caught and put in jail."

"How are you connecting what happened to you at the mall and the video, Justin?"

"Well, just like the video said, young people like to be with their friends, and sometimes they will do things in groups that they wouldn't do if they were by themselves. I wanted my friends to like me. It was exciting that they invited me to go to the mall with them. I felt that I was finally doing something different than what I usually do at home." Justin sighed, remembering the sequence of events that landed him in trouble. "Maybe if I hadn't run,"

(Continued)

(Continued)

he said. "Maybe I should have told my friend that I was leaving because I didn't want any part of stealing. It all happened so fast."

"What you're saying to me is that if you had been alone, what happened would have never happened. You wanted your friends to like you, and you made the poor choice of sticking with them when you knew that one of them was going to steal something on a dare."

"You've got it, Doc. I should have never gone out with them that night. I knew that Darren had been caught stealing at the mall a year ago. Still I went with them."

"Choices," the counselor responded. "We all make some bad choices in our lives that we wish that we had never made. If you want to see what your life will be like in five years, review the choices you have made with your life during the last five years. You can't undo any of the choices you've already made. You have to move, forward, Justin."

"We're running out of time, and I want to make sure that you get an opportunity to look at the brain model on my desk. Remember, Dr. Siegel spoke about where fear is located in the brain. Well, here's where the amygdala is located, and when it is stimulated in fear or anger, our emotions can get out of control. This is the part of the brain that Dr. Siegel called our older brain, the reptilian brain. Here, put your hand on the reptilian brain. Sometimes when our emotions are out of control, it's because the reptilian brain has hijacked the front part of our brain—the prefrontal cortex. The next time you find yourself becoming so angry that you just want to hit someone, say to yourself, 'I'm not going to let my old brain hijack my thinking.'"

Justin sat back in his chair and put his hands behind his head, as if he had just received a new insight. "Before I thought that I couldn't do anything about my anger," he said. "Next time I get real angry, I am going to put my hand on the back of my brain, and say, 'You're not going to hijack me, not today.'"

Discussion Questions

1. How does Justin relate to Siegel's (1999) neuroscientific view of adolescent brain development?

2. Discuss how Siegel's model of the brain helped the counselor to explain to Justin what was happening to him with his choices of his friends and the incident at the shopping mall.

3. Explain how Justin's new understanding of his brain and its functions led to his feeling a sense of control over his anger and emotions.

4. What might be some additional techniques you, as a counselor, might use with Justin to help Justin understand better his complex reactions to stress and anger?

WHAT HAPPENS WHEN A COUNSELOR FOCUSES ON A CLIENT'S NEGATIVE LIFE EVENTS?

For decades, therapists and counselors have focused on their clients' problems and negative life events. The belief was that it was therapeutic for therapists and counselors to spend hours talking about a client's negative reactions to his father or about a client's feelings of being left out and ridiculed as a child and as an adolescent. Yet, recent research in neuroscience has indicated that such a focus may harm rather than help clients (Seligman, Steen, Park, & Peterson, 2005). The very moment that a person or a counselor expresses even the slightest degree of negativity, a sense of negativity is increased in both the speaker's and the listener's brains (Fredrickson, 2009).

Using negative words or even repeatedly uncovering or analyzing the negative events in a client's life may only serve to remind clients of their failures and inadequacies. Clients become mired down in the therapeutic quicksand of "my mother never loved me," "no one on both sides of my family liked me," or "I was always considered a problem child." When therapists and counselors have clients continually rehearse the negative circumstances of their lives, they send alarm messages to the client's brain—the amygdala. The quicker that therapists and counselors are able to stop talking about the client's negative life events, the more readily they are able to generate a sense of safety and well-being within the therapy hour. As Newberg and Waldman (2012) have explained, "if you intensely focus on a word like 'peace' or 'love,' the emotional centers in the brain calm down. The outside world has not changed at all, but you will still feel more safe and secure" (p. 27). This is the neurological power of positive thinking, and to date it has been supported by hundreds of well-designed studies.

When therapists and counselors work with clients to reframe negative thoughts and worries into positive affirmations, the therapeutic process improves, and the client regains self-control and confidence (Fossati et al., 2003). Therapists' and counselors' interpretations that emphasize the negative circumstances of a client's life stimulate anxiety, while positive statements stimulate relaxation. Put in an alternative way, if a counselor focuses on a client's strengths (strengths-based therapy), the client will begin to experience a sense of peacefulness in him- or herself, as well as toward others. The client's thalamus responds to the counselor's incoming message of strength instead of weakness, and it then relays this message to the rest of the brain. As a consequence of the strength message, the client is likely to experience the release of pleasurable brain chemicals such as dopamine, the reward system of the brain will be stimulated, and client anxiety and self-doubts are likely to dissipate (Brassen, Gamer, & Buchel, 2011; Fredrickson, 2009).

Concentrating on a client's strengths to deal with life challenges causes a client's body to relax. Strengths-based therapy stimulates a client's neocortex. Repeated highlighting of a client's strengths may even increase the thickness of the neocortex and shrink the size of a client's amygdala, the fight-or-flight mechanism in the brain (Newberg & Waldman, 2012). When therapists and counselors focus on clients' problems rather than on their strengths, they stimulate action in the amygdala. Worry or doubt also stimulates the amygdala.

NEUROSCIENCE AND MULTIPLE CULTURAL IDENTITIES

Thus far, cultural neuroscience has focused on a person's having a primary cultural identity. The emphasis has been on investigating differences in an American, Chinese, or other cultural identity. Yet, technology has changed the world so that many people are influenced by the world's different cultures. How does the brain reflect the fact that each person might have adopted aspects of different cultures? Can we adopt the practices of another culture without having any identification with that culture? Does adopting some cultural practice of a culture lower a person's prejudice toward people who originate from that culture? Although I raise these questions, cultural neuroscience has yet to progress to the point where it investigates the impact of our multiple cultural identities on the brain. Despite the lack of studies on the influence of multiple cultural identities on the brain, this section raises the issue of each person's multiple cultural identities.

A major theme of this section is that we all have multiple cultural identities; indeed, it is impossible for a person to have only one cultural identity. All people have multiple identities along a continuum of diversity. For example, people may have a racial or cultural identity, a sexual identity, a religious identity, a socioeconomic status identity, and so forth. These cultural identities are experienced within a social context, and depending on this context, one or more of these identities will come to the forefront and become salient in a person's life. The social meaning of individuals' various cultural and group identities is determined by the individuals themselves and by how others view their identities. A Japanese American female student who uses a wheelchair may find that her disability identity becomes salient when her wheelchair access is denied. In another setting with friends and relatives, her Japanese cultural heritage may figure more prominently (Hogg & Vaughan, 2002).

In the United States, our multicultural identities have been influenced by various patterns of immigration. According to "Language Use in the United States: 2011" (Ryan, 2013) about 381 languages are spoken or signed in the United States (U.S. Census Bureau, 2012), Latino, Asian and Pacific Islander, American Indian and Alaska Native, Middle Eastern, and African heritages make up over one-third of our population (Ortman & Shin, 2011). In terms of religious minorities, there are 2.6 million Jews, 1.3 million Muslims, 1 million Buddhists, and a half-million Hindus in the United States.

The number of LGBTQ individuals (those who identify as lesbian, gay, bisexual, transgender, or queer/questioning) is at best an estimate because it all depends on what one means by the term *gay*. The Williams Institute at the UCLA School of Law estimates that 9 million Americans (about 3.8%) identify as gay, lesbian, bisexual, or transgender (Johnson, 2016). In addition, approximately 19% of Americans have disabilities, and currently 13% of Americans are older adults (U.S. Census Bureau, 2011).

For many people, cultural identities are formed and incorporated as a result of their interactions with those from different cultural backgrounds. The ethnocultural influences of people who migrated from many different nations have a profound influence on American life. Following are some of the positive contributions of varying ethnocultural groups.

- Mindfulness practices from the Chinese and Japanese have now become incorporated into many theories of counseling and psychotherapy (Jones-Smith, 2016). In 1979, Jon Kabat-Zinn, the originator of mindfulness-based stress reduction (MBSR), brought mindfulness meditation back to an American hospital, the University of Massachusetts hospital.

  ○ "Today, more than 20,000 patients have participated in the University of Mass program, which has produced 1,000 certified MBSR instructors and MBSR in about 720 medical settings in more than 30 countries. MBSR—or mindfulness training . . . are now used for an almost unimaginable range of medical conditions, including cancer, heart disease, diabetes, brain injuries, fibromyalgia, HIV/Aids, Parkinson's organ transplants, psoriasis, irritable bowel syndrome, and tinnitus. Mindfulness has become central to the mental health profession and is commonly used in the treatment of attention-deficit hyperactivity disorder, depression, anxiety, obsessive-compulsive disorder, personality disorders, substance abuse, and autism. In addition, it's at the heart of psychotherap[y]" (Wylie, 2015).

- Dialectical behavior therapy, acceptance and commitment therapy, and mindfulness-based cognitive therapy have all made mindfulness part of the centerpiece of their theory (see Wylie, 2015).

- The healing practices of Hindu yoga, Chinese acupuncture, and tai chi are used by Americans of different ethnocultural backgrounds. According to a 2008 survey, the number of people who practiced yoga was 15.8 million; however, the latest figures suggest that 20.4 million Americans are now practicing yoga—about 8.7% of American adults. Why did Americans choose yoga? More than three-quarters of them said they were motivated to improve flexibility, overall conditioning, stress relief, and general health.

  ○ Americans have incorporated into their culture diverse music, such as African American jazz, blues, and rap; Caribbean reggae; pop music; and classical music (see YJ Editors, 2012).

- The American architectural landscape includes countless Japanese gardens and pagodas, synagogues, mosques, and Buddhist and Hindu temples.

Cultural Reflections

What, if any, cultural practices have you adopted or borrowed from other cultures?

What foods do you enjoy that are from another ethnic or cultural group?

Do you practice yoga, mindfulness, or meditation?

As demonstrated by the above incorporation of different aspects of culture in American life, multiculturalism has become a fact of life in the United States and in most nations of the world due to immigration. When people immigrate to countries outside their birth nation, other individuals are exposed to their cultures. Through the process of acculturation and assimilation, people assume a multicultural identity. Multicultural identities are oftentimes complex and are typified by individuals having conflicting values and loyalties.

WHAT IS A MULTICULTURAL IDENTITY?

In general, individuals who are mixed-race and mixed-ethnicity, those who have lived in more than one country, immigrants, and those raised with at least one other culture in addition to the culture of their birth may be considered multicultural (Berry, 2003; Padilla, 2006). Multicultural individuals tend to self-label themselves as such ("I am multicultural"), or they use compound self-descriptions, such as Chinese American, African American, and Latino American. A multicultural identity can be defined as the experience of having been exposed to and having internalized two or more cultures. It is an individual's attachment to and internalization of two cultures that matters in the definition of a multicultural identity. Although a person may have been exposed to more than one culture, it is only when the individual states an attachment and loyalty to these cultures that one can say he or she has a multicultural identity.

> **Cultural Reflections**
>
> *List four cultural identities you currently have. Consider such cultural factors as ethnicity/race, gender/sexual orientation, and so forth.*
>
> *Of the four cultural identities that you listed, place them in rank order from most important to you to least important to you.*
>
> *Are there conflicts in any of the four cultural identities you listed?*

Multicultural individuals have typically undergone a process of acculturation; that is, they have internalized some aspect of the dominant culture, even though they may subscribe to the ethnocultural values of their native culture. As Sparrow (2000) has maintained, "I think of myself not as a unified cultural being but as a communion of different cultural beings. Due to the fact that I have spent time in different cultural environments, I have developed several cultural identities that diverge and converge according to the need of the moment" (p. 190).

Increasingly, researchers will become less interested in one cultural, ethnic/racial identity and more concerned with multiple cultural group identities within a person.

Multiple cultural identities within a person can produce conflict, as the individual attempts to sort out the importance and salience of each identity. Feelings of cultural conflict tend to be common among mixed-heritage individuals and second-generation people. Conflict takes place when mixed-race and mixed-ethnicity individuals are often given (implicit or explicit) messages that suggest they are not "enough" of any one culture (e.g., a biracial person with Black and White background might be criticized for "not being Black enough" or "not being White enough"). Similarly, second-generation ethnic individuals might be criticized by their parents as not "ethnic" (Latino, for example) enough and by the White dominant society as not "American" enough. The process of dealing on a daily basis with two cultures can put a burden on the individual that results in stress and identity confusion (Root, 1998). As Phinney (2000) has stated, "increasing numbers of people find that the conflicts are not between different groups but between different cultural values, attitudes, and expectations within themselves" (p. 27). It is important to reiterate that multicultural identities can be formed by integrating other types of group identities. Sexual minorities, such as lesbian women, are multicultural because they must negotiate lesbian culture, mainstream heterosexual culture, and White culture (Fingerhut, Peplau, & Ghavami, 2005).

THE NEED FOR CLINICIANS TO ADOPT A MULTICULTURAL IDENTITY

It is not just the client who operates within a multicultural identity. Counselors also have a multicultural identity. It is important that counselors perceive and understand their own multicultural selves. How can counselors who are oblivious to their own various cultural, ethnic, socioeconomic, and other group identities counsel individuals if they are not even aware of their own various cultural and group identities? To act under the erroneous assumption that a multicultural identity is only important for clients and not for counselors sets the stage for counseling malpractice. Counselors must know who they are and what identities they have incorporated into their self-concepts before they can ethically work with clients. If they are unaware of their own cultural and group identities, they may be unwittingly guilty of racist or prejudicial attitudes detrimental to their clients (Gallardo, 2012). Counselors must develop a multicultural identity professionally if they are to succeed in understanding their clients' multiple cultural identities. According to Duan and Brown (2016),

> only those who are in the dominant group can afford the privilege of ignoring their cultural identity. An understanding of our cultural and social experiences as related to each of our group memberships, including membership in both privileged and disadvantaged positions, and the roles we play in others' social and cultural experiences is critical to our multicultural identity development. (p. 138)

Figure 3.3 illustrates what a culturally responsive identity for clinicians and counselors might look like.

As stated earlier in this chapter, it is impossible to have just one singular identity—being monocultural. At the very least, one is always bicultural as a result of one's gender. Table 3.2 consists of a worksheet that one might use to discover one's multicultural identity. It contains a selection for geographical or place identity, a cultural factor that is not contained in some multicultural dimensions. Geographical identity or place is extremely important to some individuals who label themselves as Northerner, Southerner, New Yorker, Middle Easterner, and so forth. Included in the chart is a column for salience, in which participants are to indicate how important the multicultural dimension is in their lives. Finally, participants are to consider the positive and/or negative features about the multicultural identity. They indicate if the identity confers a special kind of privilege on them in the last column on positive/negative effects of identity.

FIGURE 3.3A ■ Culturally Responsive Identity for Counselors and Mental Health Therapists

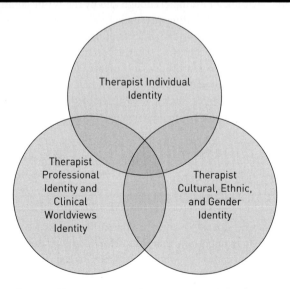

FIGURE 3.3B   ■   Levels of a Clinician's Identity and Cultural Competency

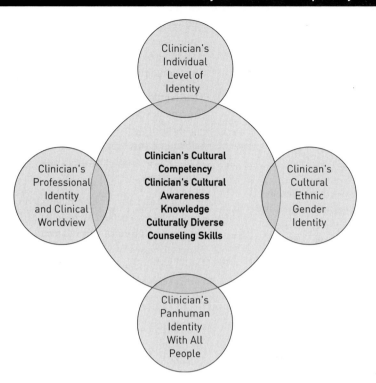

TABLE 3.2   ■   Multicultural Identity Worksheet

Multicultural Identity Dimension	Identity Salience or Importance (very important, important, somewhat important, not important at all)	Most Positive/Negative Thing About Multicultural Identity Dimension
Culture		
Ethnicity/race		
Gender		
Sexual orientation		
Religion/spirituality		
Social and economic status		
Geographical or place identity		
Age/generation		
Ability/disability		
Indigenous heritage/language		
National origin		

SUMMARY OF KEY POINTS

Cultural identity helps people to answer the question, "Who am I?" We construct our own identities through interactions with family, peers, organizations, institutions, media, and other connections we make in our everyday life. Oftentimes, when we focus on our identity, we emphasize what we can see—the external characteristics or markers of our identity, such as our ethnicity/race or where we were born. Yet, our identities are also composed of ideas, ideologies, and ways of seeing the world around us.

Important aspects of our cultural, racial, or ethnic identity include our gender, social class, sexual orientation, race, and ethnicity. These features have significant roles in determining how we understand and experience the world, as well as shaping the kinds of opportunities and challenges we encounter. Our understanding of our identities means determining how we fit in (or don't) with other groups of people. Our cultural values influence our cultural identity because they help us to create meaning and define who we are. Cultural values have power because we internalize them as part of our identity. Cultural identities shape our life experience, determining how we are treated, whom we meet and become friends with, what kind of education and jobs we get, where we live, what opportunities we are given, and what kinds of inequities or social injustice we may encounter.

The therapist or counselor must take into account a person's cultural identity because it forms the filter through which the person sees life and his or her life circumstances. Clinicians should understand that within any given person, various layers of identity exist, sometimes in harmony with each other and sometimes in conflict. It is important for clinicians to test for the significance of a person's cultural or racial identity and to understand that within any given cultural group, there are wide variations in cultural identity. Clinicians should also recognize that they are not immune from being affected by the impact of culture during therapy or counseling. Whereas clients may experience cultural transference, clinicians may undergo a process of countertransference wherein they transfer unto clients their cultural views and ethnic or racial or cultural identity.

The chapter offers the following points for clinicians:

1. Cultural identity formation is an important biological and social process necessary for a person's survival and adaptation, which, in turn, influences a person's cultural attachment pattern, self-integration, motivation reward systems, and emotional functioning.

2. The self does not develop in isolation, but instead develops within the context of cultural relationships that may be perceived to be affirming, soothing, and protective for the person. Our relationships with others shape our neural connections.

3. Cultural identity development is a process that involves a person's repeated participation in completing culturally related tasks and in interacting with various artifacts, as well as in observing other people as they interact with each other within a given culture. The cultural or ethnic self does not develop optimally in isolation, but rather develops within the safety and security of a cultural community of relationships that affirm and soothe a person so that he or she can learn information and various cultural roles. Cultural attachment facilitates the process of cultural identity. Cultural identity is formed in neural pathways of the brain.

4. We all have multiple cultural identities, and clinicians should recognize the interaction of a client's various cultural identities—being from a specific ethnic or cultural group, being a male or female, and so forth.

5. The brain has a negativity bias, which may influence a person's ability to solve problems. Counselors should work to help clients deal effectively with the brain's negativity bias.

6. Strengths are well-traveled neural pathways in the brain. Each counseling session should focus on a client's strengths and how a client might use his or her strengths to solve life challenges and problems.

7. Counselors should become knowledgeable about their clients' cultural strengths.

8. Counseling should work to help clients create new, positive neural brain pathways that help them to solve effectively their problems or life challenges.

DISCUSSION QUESTIONS

1. In groups of three to five, discuss how you have used the concept underlying mirror neurons to work with a client.

2. What role do you think cultural neuroscience will have in the next 10 years in counseling?

3. Discuss how the negativity bias operates in your own life.

KEY TERMS

Brain: a complex interwoven structure of billions of neurons that are described as the central nervous system.

Cultural Formulation Interview (CFI): an interview schedule created by the American Psychiatric Association (2013) as part of the *DSM-5* that presents questions for the systematic assessment of five categories dealing with a person's cultural background.

Cultural identity development: a process that involves a person's repeated participation in completing culturally related tasks and in interacting with various cultural artifacts. Cultural identity is facilitated by observing other people as they interact with each other within a given culture.

Cultural identity formation: an important biological and psychological process that is necessary for a person's survival and adaptation to the world.

Cultural mapping: a research strategy that involves mapping cognitive or neural differences across cultures. It involves determining which cognitive or neural processes vary across cultures without determining whether the differences are learned or innate.

Cultural neuroscience: an interdisciplinary field of study that investigates interrelations among culture, mind, and the brain.

Mind: emerges from the brain, and it is shaped by interpersonal relationships. The mind can be *defined* as a process that regulates the flow of energy and information. Human relationships shape the neural connections from which a person's mind emerges.

Mirror neuron system (MNS): includes the superior temporal cortex, which encodes a visual description of an observed action; the posterior parietal mirror neurons, which encode the kinesthetic of the action's movement sequence; the inferior frontal mirror neurons, which encode the perceived goal of the action; and the limbic circuitry, including the amygdala, which responds emotionally to the perceived goals.

Mirror neurons: connect visual and motor experiences. Mirror neurons help individuals to have empathy for each other and to experience similar feelings as another person when one is observing that person.

Negativity bias: negative experiences, or the fear of bad events, have a far greater impact on people than do neutral experiences or even positive ones. Human beings are biased toward behaving in a manner that will avoid negative experiences. Negative experiences are much more likely to be recalled, and people tend to be influenced by negative experiences in the past.

Neural net profile: patterns of neurons that fire together.

Neurogenesis: a process by which new nerve cells are generated. In neurogenesis, there is active production of new neurons.

Neuroimaging techniques: procedures based on the view that mental activity is primarily reflected in biological changes that take place in different parts of the brain. These biological changes include an increase or a decrease in the volume and flow of blood, oxygen, and glucose in the brain.

Neurons: the electrically excitable cells that process and transmit information within the brain by electrical-chemical signaling.

Neuroplasticity: the brain's ability to change and adapt as a result of life experiences; the brain continues to create new neural pathways throughout one's life, and it modifies existing neural pathways in order to adapt to new experiences, learn new information, and create new memories.

Neuroscience: an interdisciplinary science that integrates knowledge from psychology, computer science, mathematics, physics, philosophy, and medicine to study the nervous system.

Neuroscience worldview: psychotherapy is an interaction between two human brains and the neural pathways that counselor and client have created for themselves as a result of the interaction between their genetics and their life experiences.

Neurotransmitter: a chemical that is released from a nerve cell, which transmits an impulse from one nerve cell to another nerve, muscle, or organ or other tissue. It is essentially a messenger of neurologic information from one cell to another.

Synapse: the structural space between neurons in the nervous system. The word *synapse* comes from the Greek and means "point of contact." Synapses, or specialized connections between neurons, allow for signaling from one neuron to another.

REFERENCES AND SUGGESTED READING

Aitkenhead, D. (2017, February 25). Rachel Dolezal: "I'm not going to stoop and apologise and grovel." *The Guardian*. Retrieved from https://www.theguardian.com/us-news/2017/feb/25/rachel-dolezal-not-going-stoop-apologise-grovel

Allison, K. L., & Rossouw, P. J. (2013, August 27). The therapeutic alliance: Exploring the concept of "safety" from a neuropsychotherapeutic perspective. *The Neuropsychotherapist*. Retrieved from http://www.neuropsychotherapist.com/the-therapeutic-alliance-exploring-the-concept-of-safety-from-a-neuropsychotherapeutic-perspective/

Ambady, N., & Bharucha, J. (2009). Culture and the brain. *Current Directions in Psychological Science, 18*(6), 342–345.

American Mental Health Counselors Association. (2016). *AMHCA standards for the practice of clinical mental health counseling.* Retrieved from http://connections.amhca.org/HigherLogic/System/DownloadDocumentFile.ashx?DocumentFileKey=e6b635b0-654c-be8d-e18c-dbf75de23b8f

American Psychiatric Association. (2006). *Diagnostic and statistical manual of mental disorders* (4th ed., text rev.). Washington, DC: Author.

American Psychiatric Association. (2013). *Diagnostic and statistical manual of mental disorders* (5th ed.). Washington, DC: Author.

Applegate, J. S., & Shapiro, J. R. (2005). *Neurobiology for clinical social work: Theory and practice.* New York, NY: Norton.

Arden, J. B. (2010). *Rewire your brain: Think your brain to a better life.* New York, NY: Wiley.

Aspinwall, L. G., & Staudinger, U. M. (2003). *A psychology of human strengths: Fundamental questions and future directions for a positive psychology.* Washington, DC: American Psychological Association.

Baumeister, R. F., Bratslavsky, E., Finkenauer, C., & Vohs, K. D. (2001). Bad is stronger than good. *Review of General Psychology, 5*(4), 323–370.

Berry, J. W. (2003). Conceptual approaches to acculturation. In K. Chun, P. Balls-Organista, & G. Marin (Eds.), *Acculturation: Advances in theory, measurement and applied research* (pp. 17–37). Washington, DC: American Psychological Association.

Blanding, M. (2010). The brain in the world. *Tufts Magazine.* Retrieved from www.tufts.edu/alumni/magazine/winter2010/features/the-brain.html

Brassen, S., Gamer, M., & Buchel, C. (2011). Anterior cingulate activation is related to a positivity bias and emotional stability in successful aging. *Biological Psychiatry, 70*(2), 131–137.

Brickman, P., Coates, D., & Janoff-Bulman, R. (1978). Lottery winner and accident victims: Is happiness relative? *Journal of Personality and Social Psychology, 36*, 917–927.

Brody, A., Saxena, G., Stoessel, P., Gillies, L. A., Fairbanks, I. A., Alborzian, S., . . . Baxter, L. R., Jr. (2001). Regional brain metabolic changes in patients with major depression treated with either paroxetine or interpersonal therapy: Preliminary findings. *Archives of General Psychiatry, 58*(7), 631–640.

Buckingham, M., & Clifton, D. O. (2001). *Now, discover your strengths.* New York, NY: Simon & Schuster.

Busacca, L. A., & Sikorski, A. M., & McHenry, B. (2015). Infusing neuroscience within counselor training: A rationale for an integrally-informed model. *Journal of Counselor Practice, 6*(1), 39–55.

Butz, M., Worgotter, F., & van Ooyen, A. (2009). Activity-dependent structural plasticity. *Brain Research Reviews, 60*(2), 287–305.

Caine, G., Nummela-Cain, R., & Crowell, S. (1999). *Mindshifts: A brain-based process for restructuring schools and renewing education* (2nd ed.). Tucson, AZ: Zephyr Press.

Caplan, P. J. (1995). *They say you're crazy: How the world's most powerful psychiatrists decide who's normal.* Reading, MA: Addison-Wesley.

Carver, C. S., & Scheier, M. F. (1990). Principles of self-regulation: Action and emotion. In E. T. Higgins & R. M. Sorrentino (Eds.), *Handbook of motivation and cognition* (Vol. 2, pp. 3–52). New York, NY: Guilford Press.

Chiao, J., & Ambady, N. (2007). Cultural neuroscience: Parsing universality and diversity across levels of analysis. In S. Kitayama & D. Cohen (Ed.), *The handbook of cultural psychology* (pp. 237–254). New York, NY: Guilford Press.

Chiao, J. Y., Cheon, B. K., Pornpattananangkul, N., Mrazek, A. J., Blizinsky, K. D. (2013). Cultural neuroscience: Progress and promise. *Psychological Inquiry, 24*(1), 1–19.

Chiao, J. Y., Harada, T., Komeda, H., Li, Z., Mano, Y., Saito, D. N., . . . Iidaka, T. (2009). Neural basis of individualistic and collectivistic views of self. *Human Brain Mapping*, *30*(9), 2813–2820.

Chiao, J. Y., Harada, T., Komeda, H., Li, Z., Mano, Y., Saito, D. N., . . . Iidaka, T. (2010). Dynamic cultural influences on neural representations of the self. *Journal of Cognitive Neuroscience*, *22*(1), 1–11.

Council for Accreditation of Counseling and Related Educational Programs. (2009). 2009 standards. Retrieved from http://www.cacrep.org/wp-content/uploads/2017/07/2009-Standards.pdf

Cozolino, L. (2010). *The neuroscience of psychotherapy: Healing the social brain* (2nd ed.). New York, NY: Norton.

Curtis, M. E., & Bharucha, J. J. (2009). Memory and musical expectation for tones in cultural context. *Music Perception*, *26*, 365–375.

Danner, D., Snowdon, D., & Friesen, W. (2001). Positive emotions in early life and longevity: Findings from the nun study. *Journal of Personality and Social Psychology*, *80*, 804–813.

Davidson, R. J. (2004). Well-being and affective style: Neural substrates and biobehavioral correlates. *Philosophical Transactions of the Royal Society*, *359*, 1395–1411.

Davidson, R. J., & Begley, S. (2012). *The emotional life of your brain*. London, England: Hodder & Stoughton.

Duan, C., & Brown, C. (2016). *Becoming a multiculturally competent counselor*. Thousand Oaks, CA: Sage.

Dweck, C. S. (2006). *Mindset: The new psychology of success*. New York, NY: Random House.

Eriksen, K., & Kress, V. E. (2006). The DSM and the professional therapy identity: Bridging the gap. *Journal of Mental Health Therapy*, *28*, 202–217.

Farmer, R. L. (2009). *Neuroscience and social work practice: The missing link*. Thousand Oaks, CA: Sage.

Fingerhut, A. W., Peplau, L. A., Ghavami, N. (2005). A dual-identity framework for understanding lesbian experience. *Psychology of Women Quarterly*, *29*(2), 129–139.

Fossati, P., Hevenor, S. J., Graham, S. J., Grady, C., Keightley, M. L., Craik, F., & Mayberg, H. (2003). In search of the emotional self: An fMRI study using positive and negative emotional words. *American Journal of Psychiatry*, *160*(11), 1348–1345.

Fox, N. S., Calkins, S. D., & Bell, M. A. (1994). Neuroplasticity and development in the first two years of life: Evidence from cognitive and socioemotional domains of research. *Development and Psychopathology*, *6*, 677–696.

Fredrickson, B. L. (2001). The role of positive emotions in positive psychology: The broaden-and-build theory of positive emotions. *American Psychologist*, *56*, 218–226.

Fredrickson, B. L. (2003). The value of positive emotions. *American Scientist*, *91*, 330–335.

Fredrickson, B. (2009). *Positivity*. New York, NY: Three Rivers Press.

Gallardo, M. E. (2012). Therapists as cultural architects and systemic advocates: Latina/o skills identification stage model. In M. E. Gallardo, C. J. Yeh, J. E. Trimble, & T. A. Parham (Eds.), *Culturally adaptive counseling skills: Demonstrations of evidence-based practices* (pp. 77–112). Thousand Oaks, CA: Sage.

Gallese, V., & Goldman, A. (1998). Mirror neurons and the simulation of mind-reading. *Trends in Cognitive Science*, *2*(12), 493–501.

Giedd, J. N., Blumenthal, J., Jeffries, N. O., Castellanos, F. X., Liu, H., Zijdenbos, A., . . . Rapoport, J. L. (1999). Brain development during childhood and adolescence: A longitudinal MRI study. *Nature Neuroscience*, *2*, 861–863.

Giedd, J. N., Clasen, L.S., Lenroot, R., Greenstein, D., Wallace, G. L., Ordaz, S., . . . Chrousos, G. P. (2006). Puberty-related influence on brain development. *Molecular and Cellular Endocrinology*, *254–255*, 154–162.

Goldstein, H. (1990). Strength or pathology: Ethical and rhetorical contrasts in approaches to practice. *Families in Society*, *71*, 267–275.

Gopnik, A., Meltzoff, A. N., & Kuhl, P. K. (1999). *The scientist in the crib: Minds, brains, and how children learn*. New York, NY: William Morrow.

Gottman, J. (1995). *Why marriages succeed or fail: And how you can make yours last*. New York, NY: Simon & Schuster.

Grossman, K., Grossman, K. E., Spangler, G., Suess, G., & Unzner, L. (1985). Maternal sensitivity and newborns' orientation responses as related to the quality of attachment in northern Germany. In I. Bretherton & E. Waters (Eds.), *Growing points of attachment theory and research. Monographs of the Society for Research in Child Development*, *50*(1–2), Serial No. 209.

Han, S., & Northoff, G. (2008). Culture-sensitive neural substrates of human cognition: A transcultural neuroimaging approach. *Nature Reviews Neuroscience*, *9*, 646–654.

Hansen, J. T. (2009). On displaced humanists: Counselor education and the meaning-reduction pendulum. *Journal of Humanistic Counseling, Education and Development*, *48*, 65–76.

Hansen, J. T. (2012). Extending the humanistic vision: Toward a humanities foundation for the counseling profession. *Journal of Humanistic Counseling*, *51*, 133–144.

Hansen, J. T. (2014). *Philosophical issues in counseling and psychotherapy: Encounters with four questions about knowing, effectiveness, and truth*. Lanham, MD: Rowman & Littlefield.

Hanson, R. (2010). The brain: So What? The benefits and pitfalls of applying neuroscience to psychotherapy. *The Wise Brain Bulletin*, 4(2).

Hanson, R., & Mendius, R. (2009). *Buddha's brain: The practical neuroscience of happiness, love & wisdom*. Oakland, CA: New Harbinger.

Harada, T., Li, Z., & Chiao, J. Y. (Special Eds.). (2010). Differential dorsal and ventral medial prefrontal representations of the implicit self modulated by individualism and collectivism: An fMRI study. *Social Neuroscience*, 22, 1–15.

Hebb, D. O. (1949). *The organization of behavior*. New York, NY: Wiley.

Hecht, D. (2013). The neural basis of optimism and pessimism. *Experimental Neurobiology*, 22(3), 173–199.

Hogg, M., & Vaughan, G. (2002). *Social psychology* (3rd ed.). Englewood Cliffs, NJ: Prentice Hall.

Holtmaat, A., & Svoboda, K. (2009). Experience-dependent structural synaptic plasticity in the mammalian brain. *Nature Reviews Neuroscience*, 10, 647–658.

Hoshmand, L. T. (Ed.). (2006). *Culture, psychotherapy, and counseling: Critical and integral perspectives*. Thousand Oaks, CA: Sage.

Houts, A. C. (2003). Discovery, invention, and the expansion of the modern *Diagnostic and Statistical Manuals of Mental Disorders*. In L. E. Beutler & M. L. Malik (Eds.), *Rethinking the DSM: A psychological perspective* (pp. 17–65). Washington, DC: American Psychological Association.

Iacoboni, M., & Dapretto, M. (2006). The mirror neuron system and the consequences of its dysfunction. *Nature Review of Neuroscience*, 12, 942–951.

Ingersoll, R. E., & Rak, C. F. (2016). *Psychopharmacology for mental health professionals* (2nd ed.). Boston, MA: Cengage.

Ivey, A. E., Ivey, M. B., Zalaquett, C., & Quirk, K. (2009, December). Counseling and neuroscience: The cutting edge of the coming decade. *Counseling Today*, 53, 44–48. Retrieved from https://ct.counseling.org/2009/12/reader-viewpoint-counseling-and-neuroscience-the-cutting-edge-of-the-coming-decade/

Ivey, A. E., & Zalaquett, C. P. (2011). Neuroscience and counseling: Central issues for social justice leaders. *Journal for Social Action in Counseling and Psychology*, 3, 103–116.

Johnson, R. (2016). Gay population statistics in the United States: How many gay people are there? *LiveAbout*. Retrieved at https://www.liveabout.com/gay-population-statistics-in-the-united-states-1410784

Jones-Smith, E. (2011). *Spotlighting the strengths of every single student: Why U.S. schools need a strengths-based approach*. Santa Barbara, CA: ABC-CLIO/Praeger.

Jones-Smith, E. (2014). *Theories of therapy and psychotherapy: An integrative approach*. Thousand Oaks, CA: Sage.

Jones-Smith, E. (2016). *Theories of counseling and psychotherapy: An integrative approach* (2nd ed.). Thousand Oaks, CA: Sage.

Kandel, E. R. (1998). A new intellectual framework for psychiatry. *American Journal of Psychiatry*, 155, 457–469.

Kandel, E. R. (2005). *Psychiatry, psychoanalysis, and the new biology of mind*. Washington, DC: American Psychiatric Association.

Katz, M. (1997). *On playing a poor hand well*. New York, NY: Norton.

Kaut, K. P. (2011). Psychopharmacology and mental health practice: An important alliance. *Journal of Mental Health Counseling*, 33, 196–222.

Kindsvatter, A., & Geroski, A. (2014). The impact of early life stress on the neurodevelopment of the stress response system. *Journal of Counseling & Development*, 92, 472–480.

Kitayama, S., & Park, H. (2010). Cultural neuroscience of the self: Understanding the social grounding of the brain. *SCAN*, 5, 111–129. Retrieved from http://www.facstaff.bucknell.edu/jvt002/BrainMind/Readings/KitayamaAndPark.pdf

Lambert, K. G. (2005). The clinical neuroscience course: Viewing mental health from neurobiological perspectives. *The Journal of Undergraduate Neuroscience Education*, 3, 42–52.

LeDoux, J. (1996). *The emotional brain: The mysterious underpinnings of emotional life*. New York, NY: Simon & Schuster.

Le Doux, J. (2002). *Synaptic self: How our brains become who we are*. New York, NY: Penguin Books.

LeDoux, J. E. (2003). *How our brains become who we are*. New York, NY: Penguin.

Linden, D. E. J. (2006). How psychotherapy changes the brain—the contribution of neuroimaging. *Molecular Psychiatry*, 11, 528–538.

Lopez, S. J., & Snyder, C. R. (2002). *Handbook of positive psychology*. New York, NY: Oxford University Press.

Luke, C. C. (2016). *Neuroscience for counselors and therapists: Integrating the sciences of mind and brain*. Thousand Oaks, CA: Sage.

Lutz, A. L., Greischar, N., Rawlings, M., Ricard, M., & Davidson, R. (2004). Long-term meditators self-induce high-amplitude gamma synchrony during mental practice. *Proceedings of the National Academy of Sciences*, 10111, 16369–16373.

Lyubomirsky, S. (2008). *The how of happiness*. New York, NY: Penguin Press.

Maguire, E. D., Gadian, I., Johnsrude, C., Good, J., Ashburner, R., Frackowiak, R., & Frith, C. (2000). Navigation-related structural change in the hippocampi of taxi drivers. *Proceedings of the National Academy of Sciences, 97*, 4398–4403.

Magyar-Moe, J. L., Owens, R. L., & Conoley, C. W. (2015). Positive psychological interventions in counseling: What every counseling psychologist should know. *The Counseling Psychologist, 43*(4), 508–557.

Magyar-Moe, J. L., Owens, R. L., & Scheel, M. J. (2015). Applications of positive psychology in counseling psychology: Current status and future directions. *The Counseling Psychologist, 43*(4), 494–507.

Main, M. (1995). Attachment: Overview, with implications for clinical work. In S. Goldberg, R. Muir, & J. Kerr (Eds.), *Attachment theory: Social, developmental and clinical perspectives* (pp. 407–474). Hillsdale, NJ: Analytic Press.

Main, M., Kaplan, N., & Cassidy, J. (1985). Security in infancy, childhood, adulthood: A move to the level of representation. In I. Bretherton & E. Waters (Eds.), *Growing points of attachment theory and research. Monographs for the Society for Research in Child Development, 50*(2–3), 66–104.

Makinson, R. A., & Young, J. S. (2012). Cognitive behavioral therapy and the treatment of posttraumatic stress disorder: Where counseling and neuroscience meet. *Journal of Counseling & Development, 90*(2), 131–140.

Malik, M. L., & Beutler, L. E. (2002). The emergence of dissatisfaction with the DSM. In L. E. Beutler & M. L. Malik (Eds.), *Rethinking the DSM: A psychological perspective* (pp. 3–15). Washington, DC: American Psychological Association.

Maluccio, A. N. (1981). Competence-oriented social work practice: An ecological practice. In A. N. Maluccio (Ed.), *Promoting competence in clients: A new/old approach to social work practice* (pp. 1–24). New York, NY: Free Press.

Maracek, J. L. (1993). Disappearance, silences and anxious rhetoric: Gender in abnormal psychology textbooks. *Journal of Theoretical and Philosophical Psychology: Journal of Division, 24*(13), 115–123.

Martin, S. D., Martin, E., Rai, S. S., Richardson, M. A., & Royall, R. (2001). Brain blood flow changes in depressed patients treated with interpersonal psychotherapy of venlafaxine hydrochloride. *Archives of General Psychiatry, 58*, 641–648.

Matsumoto, D., Yoo, S. H., Fontaine, J., Anguas-Wong, A. M., Arriola, M., Ataca, B., . . . Zengeya A. (2008). Mapping expressive differences around the world: The relationship between emotional display rules and individualism v. collectivism. *Journal of Cross-Cultural Psychology, 39*, 55–74.

McGoldrick, M., Giordano, J., & Garcia-Preto, N. (2005). *Ethnicity and family therapy.* New York, NY: Guilford Press.

McHenry, B., Sikorski, A. M., & McHenry, J. (2013). *A counselor's introduction to neuroscience.* New York, NY: Routledge.

Mitchell, S. (1988). *Relational concepts in psychoanalysis.* Cambridge, MA: Harvard University Press.

Modell, A. H. (2003). *Imagination and the meaningful brain.* Cambridge, MA: MIT Press.

Moser, J. S., Hartwig, R., Moran, T., Jendrusina, A. A., & Kross, E. (2014). Neural markers of positive reappraisal and their associations with trait reappraisal and worry. *Journal of Abnormal Psychology, 123*(1), 91–105.

Myers, J. E., & Young, J. S. (2012). Brain wave biofeedback: Benefits of integrating neurofeedback in counseling. *Journal of Counseling & Development, 90*(1), 20–28.

Nauert, R. (2013). Are you hardwired to see the glass as half-empty? *PsychCentral.* Retrieved from http://psychcentral.com/news/2013/10/11/are-you-hardwired-to-see-the-glass-as-half-empty/60576.html

Newberg, A., & Waldman, M. (2012). *Words can change your brain. 12 conversational strategies to build trust, resolve conflicts and increase intimacy.* New York, NY: Penguin.

Nutt, A. E. (2015, June 16). Black like her: Is racial identity a state of mind? *The Washington Post.* Retrieved from https://www.washingtonpost.com/national/health-science/black-like-her-is-racial-identity-a-state-of-mind/2015/06/16/765b5a42-142d-11e5-9518-f9e0a8959f32

Oluo, I. (2017, April 19). The heart of whiteness: Ijeoma Oluo interviews Rachel Dolezal, the White woman who identifies as Black. *The Portland Mercury.* Retrieved from https://www.portlandmercury.com/feature/2017/04/19/18960329/the-heart-of-whiteness-ijeoma-oluo-interviews-rachel-dolezal-the-white-woman-who-identifies-as-black

Omer, I. (2013). Are genetic differences at the root of the Tutsi-Hutu Rwandan conflict. *Genetic Literacy Project.* Retrieved from https://geneticliteracyproject.org/2013/08/05/are-genetic-differences-at-the-root-of-the-tutsi-hutu-rwandan-conflict/

Ortman, J. M., & Shin, H. B. (2011). *Language projections: 2010 to 2020.* Population Division, U.S. Census Bureau. Presented at the Annual Meetings of the American Sociological Association, Las Vegas, NV, August 20–23.

Padesky, C. A., & Mooney, K. A. (2012). Strengths-based cognitive-behavioural therapy: A four-step model to build resilience. *Clinical Psychology & Psychotherapy, 19*, 283–290.

Padilla, A. (2006). Bicultural social development. *Hispanic Journal of Behavioral Sciences, 28*, 467–495.

Park, D., & Gutchess, A. (2006). The cognitive neuroscience of aging. *Current Directions in Psychological Science, 15*(3), 105–108.

Phinney, J. S. (2000). Identity formation across cultures: The interaction of personal, societal, and historical change. *Human Development, 43,* 27–31.

Quirk, G., Repa, J. S., & LeDoux, J. E. (1995). Fear conditioning enhances short-latency auditory responses of lateral amygdala neurons: Parallel recordings in the freely behaving rat. *Neuron, 15,* 1029–1039.

Rapp, C. A. (1998). *The strengths model: Case management with people suffering from severe and persistent mental illness.* New York, NY: Oxford University Press.

Rashid, T. (2009). Positive interventions in clinical practice. *Journal of Clinical Psychology, 65*(5), 461–466.

Rashid, T., & Ostermann, R. F. (2009). Strength-based assessment in clinical practice. *Journal of Clinical Psychology, 65*(6), 488–498.

Restak, R. (2006). *The naked brain: How the emerging neuro-society is changing how we live, work, and love.* New York, NY: Harmon Books.

Rizq, R. (2007). Tread softly: Counseling psychology and neuroscience. *Counseling Psychology Review, 22,* 5–18.

Root, M. P. P. (1998). Preliminary findings from the Biracial Sibling Project. *Cultural Diversity and Mental Health, 4,* 237–247.

Rossouw, P. J. (2013, January/February). The end of the medical model? Recent findings in neuroscience regarding antidepressant medication: Implications for neuropsychotherapy. *Neuropsychotherapy in Australia, 19,* 3–10. Retrieved from http://mediros.com.au/wp-content/uploads/2013/01/Neuropsychotherapy-in-Australia-EJournal-Edition-19.pdf

Ryan, C. (2013). Language use in the United States: 2011. *American Community Survey Reports.* U.S. Department of Commerce, U.S. Census Bureau. Retrieved at https://www.census.gov/prod/2013pubs/acs-22.pdf

Saleebey, D. (1996). The strengths perspective in social work practice: Extensions and cautions. *Social Work, 41,* 296–305.

Saleebey, D. (2006). *The strengths perspective in social work practices* (4th ed.). Boston, MA: Allyn & Bacon.

Schore, A. N. (2001). Effects of a secure attachment relationship on right brain development, affect regulation, and infant mental health. *Infant Mental Health Journal, 22*(102), 7–66.

Schulte-Rüther, M., Markowitsch, H. J., Fink, G. R., & Piefke, M. (2007). Mirror neuron and theory of mind mechanisms involved in face-to-face interactions: A functional magnetic resonance imaging approach to empathy. *Journal of Cognitive Neuroscience, 8,* 1354–1372.

Schwartz, J. M. (2002). *The mind and the brain: Neuroplasticity and the power of mental force.* New York, NY: HarperCollins.

Seligman, M. E. (1991). *Learned optimism.* New York, NY: Knopf.

Seligman, M. E. (2002). *Authentic happiness.* New York, NY: Free Press.

Seligman, M. E., Steen, T. A., Park, N., & Peterson, C. (2005). Positive psychology progress: Empirical validation of interventions. *American Psychologist, 60*(5), 410–421.

Seligman, M. E. P., Walker, E. E., & Rosenhan, D. L. (2001). *Abnormal psychology.* New York, NY: Norton.

Shore, R. (1997). *Rethinking the brain: New insights into early development.* New York, NY: Families and Work Institute.

Siegel, D. (1999). *The developing mind: How relationships and the brain interact to shape who we are.* New York, NY: Guilford Press.

Siegel, D. J. (2010). *The mindful therapist: A clinician's guide to mindsight and neural integration.* New York, NY: Norton.

Siegel, D. J. (2012). *The developing mind: How relationships interact with the brain to shape who we are.* New York, NY: Guilford Press.

Singh, A. A., Boyd, C. J., & Whitman, J. S. (2010). Counseling competencies with transgender and intersex persons. In J. A. Erickson Cornish, B. A. Schreier, L. I. Nadkarni, L. H. Metzger, & E. R. Rodolfa (Eds.), *Handbook of multicultural counseling competencies* (pp. 415–441). New York, NY: Wiley.

Sparrow, L. M. (2000). Beyond multicultural man: Complexities of identity. *International Journal of Intercultural Relations, 24,* 173–201.

Sperry, L. (2002). DSM-IV: Making it more clinician friendly. *Journal of Individual Psychology, 58,* 434–441.

Sroufe, L. A. (1996). *Emotional development: The organization of emotional life in the early years.* New York, NY: Cambridge University Press.

Stanley, D. A., Sokol-Hessner, P., Fareri, D. S., Perino, M. T., Delgado, M. R., Banaji, M. R., & Phelps, E. A. (2012). Race and reputation: Perceived racial group trustworthiness influences the neural correlates of trust decisions. *Philosophical Transactions of the Royal Society of London B: Biological Sciences, 367*(1589), 744–753. doi: 10.1098/rstb.2011.0300

Takahashi, K. (1990). Are the key assumptions of the "Strange Situation" procedure universal? A view from Japanese research. *Human Development, 33,* 23–30.

Tancredi, L. (2005). *Hardwired behavior: What neuroscience reveals about morality.* New York, NY: Cambridge University Press.

Tang, Y., Zhang, W., Chen, K., Feng, S., Ji, Y., Reiman, E. M., & Liu, Y. (2006). Arithmetic processing in the brain shaped by culture. *Proceedings of the National Academy of Sciences of the United States (PNAS), 103*(28), 10775–10780

Todd, R. M., Müller, D. J., Lee, D. H., Robertson, A., Eaton, T., Freeman, N., . . . Anderson, A. K. (2013, September 20). Genes for emotion-enhanced remembering are linked to enhanced perceiving. *Psychological Science* [Advance online publication]. doi:10.1177/0956797613492423.

U.S. Census Bureau. (2012). The two or more races population. *2010 Census Briefs*. Retrieved from https://www.census .gov/prod/cen2010/briefs/c2010br-13.pdf

Vaish, A., Grossmann, T., & Woodward, A. (2008). Not all emotions are created equal: The negativity bias in social-emotional development. *Psychological Bulletin, 134*, 383–403.

van IJzendoorn, M. H., & Sagi, A. (1999). Cross-cultural patterns of attachment. In J. Cassidy & P. R. Shaver (Eds.), *Handbook of attachment: Theory, research, and clinical applications* (pp. 713–734). New York, NY: Guilford Press.

Viamontes, V. I., & Beitman, B. D. (2006). Neural substrates of psychotherapeutic change part II: Beyond default mode.

Psychiatric Annals, 36, 238–247. Retrieved from http:// www.healio.com/psychiatry/journals/psycann

Walsh, W. B. (Ed.). (2003). *Counseling psychology and optimal human functioning*. Mahwah, NJ: Erlbaum.

Warnick, J. E., & Landis, D. (Eds.). (2016). *Neuroscience in intercultural contexts*. New York, NY: Springer.

Wylie, M. S. (2015). The mindfulness explosion. *Psychotherapy Networker*. Retrieved from https://www.psychotherapynetworker .org/magazine/article/66/the-mindfulness-explosion

Yang, E., Zald, D., & Blake, R. (2007). Fearful expressions gain preferential access to awareness during continuous flash suppression. *Emotion, 7*, 882–886.

YJ Editors. (2012, December 5). *Yoga Journal* Releases 2012 Yoga in America Market Study. *Yoga Journal*. Retrieved from https://www.yogajournal.com/press-releases/yoga-journal-releases-2012-yoga-in-america-market-study

Zhu, Y., Zhang, L., Fan, J., & Han, S. (2007). Neural basis of cultural influence on self-representation. *Neuroimage, 34*, 1310–1317.

4 STRENGTHS-BASED DEVELOPMENT, CULTURE, AND CLINICAL PRACTICE

CHAPTER OBJECTIVES

- Describe the process of strengths development within people and the narrative process that takes place about strengths in the mind.

- Understand the process of cultural attachment and the relational aspects of strengths development.

- Discuss Eastern and Western views on human strengths and how each cultural perspective believes strengths should be manifested.

- Explain the differences between a strengths approach to counseling and psychotherapy and a deficit approach.

- Demonstrate how to implement five general strengths-based themes during counseling.

- Explain how to create a culturally responsive strengths-building counseling environment.

- Illustrate how to conduct an initial culturally responsive interview.

> - *"It's time for parents to teach young people early on that in diversity there is beauty and there is strength."* —Maya Angelou
>
> - *"All healing practices are embedded in an inescapable web of moral agreements and political activities."* —Philip Cushman

INTRODUCTION

A major goal of this chapter is to integrate strengths-based therapy theory with basic concepts in multicultural counseling. Strengths-based therapy changes the way we think about people and the way we try to help them. Our strengths help us to overcome adversity; therefore, they should become the focus of counseling and therapy, rather than a client's problems or weaknesses (Flückiger, Wuesten, Zinbarg, & Wampold, 2010; Magyar-Moe, 2009; Walsh, 2003). A second goal is to present basic concepts in strengths practice. A third goal is to lay the groundwork for this author's presentation of the strengths-based therapy model (Jones-Smith, 2014).

Chapter 4 begins by examining the process of strengths development in people. It highlights the neurobiology of human strengths and the role that attachment and attention assume in forming our strengths. A comparison is made between the Eastern and Western cultural views of strengths. Chinese culture is used to represent Eastern culture. Yip (2005, 2008), a prominent Chinese researcher, has done extensive work to articulate the Chinese view of strengths-based practice. As researchers in other countries present their views on human strengths, their works will also be examined. Chapter 4 concludes with clinical practice skills related to creating a strengths-based environment and conducting an initial interview to determine clients' cultural attachment and preference for working with culturally different therapists or counselors.

CULTURE, THE BRAIN, AND STRENGTHS DEVELOPMENT

Definition of Strength

Aspinwall and Staudinger (2003) have noted the difficulties involved in defining human strength. *Strength* may be defined as that which helps a person to cope with life or that which makes life more fulfilling for oneself and others. Strengths are not fixed personality traits; instead, they develop from a dynamic, contextual process rooted deeply in one's culture. Our strengths are the lenses we use to process information, to experience others, to view time and structure, to accommodate or to make change in our lives, and to communicate with others (Smith, 2006).

Characteristics of Strengths

Strengths possess a number of characteristics. They may be internal or external; they may be valued intrinsically or extrinsically; and they are usually culturally bound, contextually based, and/or development and life span oriented. Strengths also have characteristics involving adaptability and functionality; they have a normative quality because they exist in comparison with other states, and each society tends to establish both enabling and limiting structures that permit individuals to move from one strength level to another. Strengths are characterized by a certain transcendent quality; they often develop out of polarities and are associated with good life outcomes (Smith, 2006).

Culturally Bound Strengths

Strengths are almost inevitably culturally expressed. Characteristics regarded as strengths in one culture may be viewed as weaknesses in another culture (Smith, 2006). Ethnic groups may be said to have particular cultural strengths (Chang, 2001). The strength for one culture may be its emphasis on the family, whereas the strength of another culture may be its ability to save and to engage in profitable commerce. The importance of strengths differs among cultures. For example, in cultures labeled as individualistic, autonomy is highly valued (Magyar-Moe, Owens, & Conoley, 2015). Conversely, in cultures described as collectivist, relational skills may be emphasized more. Helping professionals are faced with the challenge of learning and understanding individual and cultural strengths. A counselor might consider examining the following cultural strengths with a client:

- Art
- Celebrations
- Dance
- Elders
- Heroes
- Identity
- Music
- Past struggles and accomplishments
- Stories

THE NEUROBIOLOGY OF HUMAN STRENGTHS DEVELOPMENT

Strengths development is a three-prong process. First, it is *brain-based and physiological* in nature. Second, strengths development is *relational*. When relationships affirm one's strengths, one tends to feel good about oneself. When relationships disconfirm a person's strengths, one may not feel validated as a person. Third, strengths development is a process of *dialogic conversations with the self and with one's significant audiences.*

The Brain and Strengths Development

The brain is the seat of all human action. It is the computer, the hard drive for the rest of the human body. Infants come into the world with billions of neurons, which are largely unconnected to each other (Caine, Nummela-Caine, & Crowell, 1999; Gopnik, Meltzoff, & Kuhl, 1999; Shore, 1997; Siegel, 1999). Almost immediately after birth, an infant's brain begins to form trillions of connections and pathways between neurons. These pathways are critical because they permit the infant to see, smell, hear, learn, and reason (Shore, 1997; Siegel, 1999). The brain cells or neurons need to be activated, and the connections between neurons either are weak or have not been formed. As the neurons form synapses, they begin firing, which may be described as sending electrical impulses and layering the networks in the brain (Shore, 1997). First, the brain makes the networks that are necessary for survival (heartbeat, breathing, etc.). These survival functions are controlled by the hindbrain and the midbrain (Luke, 2016).

Children learn and develop strengths in the areas that produce the most synaptic connections in the brain (Luke, 2016). This situation occurs because the brain is the biological organ for learning. It contains the basis of mental processes that underlie mental functioning, often referred to as thought or mind. Learning is a function of the effectiveness of synapses to produce signals and initiate new signals along connecting neurons. As the brain learns and masters new skills or content, it needs less energy. Attachment has a significant influence on a person's emotions and behavior (Siegel, 1999).

Brain development is based on a complex interaction between genes and the environment. Most of what a child inherits is brought to fruition by his or her environmental experiences. The richer a child's environment and the more intentional a parent's planned interactions and experiences, the greater the number of neurological connections the child is able to develop. While experience wires a child's brain, repetition strengthens the brain's wiring. A child who practices playing the piano every day for three hours is more likely to develop a strength in piano playing than one who practices playing a piano for one hour a week. There are fertile times when the brain is capable to wire specific skills, and these fertile times are called "windows of opportunities." When positive life experiences occur during the windows of opportunities for a child, he or she will tend to have positive learning outcomes. Just the opposite is likely to become true for a child who has negative life experiences during these same time periods.

Culture affects learning. Researchers have found that language and music are interconnected. A child's native tongue affects the way in which he or she perceives music. All languages have been said to manifest a melody that is unique to a specific culture. At an early age, infants echo the inherent melodies of their native language when they cry and later when they speak. When working with clients, counselors might notice the tonal quality of their clients' language (Deutsch, 2010).

Moreover, the *brain looks for patterns* so that it does not have to work as hard when similar information is presented to it. Patterns constitute one of the brain's primary ways to process new information. As a child ages, the brain cells begin to specialize to complete different tasks. The brain eliminates a system or a neuron path if a particular skill or function is not used (Luke, 2016). Figure 4.1 provides a diagrammatic representation of how strengths develop within the brain. The diagram points out that strengths development is an interactive process.

FIGURE 4.1   ■   Strengths Development: The Brain, Relationships, and the Environment

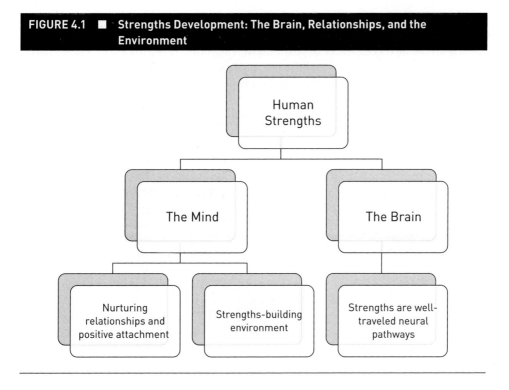

STRENGTHS AND THE BRAIN'S PRUNING PROCESS

The brain operates on a "use it or lose it" principle, meaning only those neural connections and neural pathways that are frequently activated are retained. Other brain connections that are not used consistently are pruned or discarded, thereby enabling the active connections to become stronger. According to the psychologist Donald Hebb (1949), when neurons fire together, they wire together—mental activity actually creates new neural structures (see also LeDoux, 2003).

For instance, studies have found that taxicab drivers in London have an enlarged hippocampus (a key brain area for making visual-spatial memories) because that part of their brains gets a great deal of workout (Maguire et al., 2000). People who say that they are happy tend to have more activity in the left frontal region of their brain (Davidson, 2004). When Tibetan practitioners go into deep meditation, their brains create powerful gamma brain waves of electrical activity (Lutz, Greischar, Rawlings, Ricard, & Davidson, 2004).

As pruning increases after 10 years of age, those synapses that have been reinforced because of repeated use tend to become permanent (Siegel, 1999). Conversely, the synapses that were not used often enough in the early years tend to become eliminated. The types of experiences children have influence how their brains and strengths will be wired as adults.

Individuals develop talents and strengths as a result of the repeated formation of synaptic connections in neural networks. As a child ages, stronger synapses within the network of brain connections continue to strengthen, whereas weaker connections tend to wither. After a young person reaches about age 15, his or her unique network of synaptic brain connections remains fairly stable and does not change (Luke, 2015). The scientific discovery provides support for the belief that talents and strengths do not change significantly over time (Luke, 2015).

Cultural Reflections

What impact has your multicultural background had on your development of strengths?

Can you trace your strengths to those associated with your ethnic or cultural group?

Is there a relationship between your gender and your strengths development?

RELATIONAL COMPONENTS OF STRENGTHS DEVELOPMENT

There is a relational component of strengths development. Strengths are developed partly out of the experiences one has and the interactions one has with others and the environment. Attachment is an important concept for helping people to develop their personal strengths. A trusted relationship is significant in helping individuals to develop their personal strengths. The strengths individuals develop are those that are usually highly prized in their culture (see Figure 4.2). When individuals become psychologically and emotionally attached to their culture, they are more inclined to develop strengths that are highly valued in their culture. The next section begins with a discussion of attachment theory and how this theory is relevant for people to develop their strengths. More attention needs to be focused on individual (personal) and cultural strengths in the multicultural counseling literature.

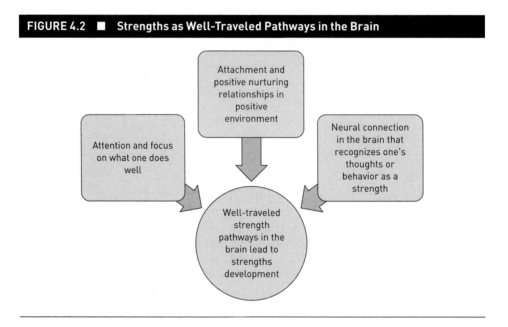

FIGURE 4.2 ■ Strengths as Well-Traveled Pathways in the Brain

ATTACHMENT THEORY AND STRENGTHS DEVELOPMENT

Attachment theory originated in evolutionary psychology to study the infant–mother bond of primates, and therefore, it is neither a Western nor an Eastern conceptualization of parenting styles (Jones-Smith, 2014). John Bowlby, the late British psychoanalyst, developed attachment theory as a result of applying ethology to infant behaviors. Bowlby believed that an infant's responses to his or her caregiver are evolved responses that promote the infant's survival.

Bowlby's theory of attachment was influenced by Harry Harlow's attachment experiments on Rhesus monkeys during the 1950s and 1960s. Attachment theory challenged the then conventional belief that attachment formed in response to a child's physical needs (e.g., food) by studying the caregiver's emotional responsiveness to an infant (Bowlby, 1969). In *The Developing Mind*, David Siegel (1999) has updated Bowlby's theory of attachment with neuroscience research. According to Siegel, "'attachment' is an inborn system in the brain that evolves in ways that influence and organize motivational, emotional, and memory processes with respect to significant caregiving figures" (p. 67). Attachment has a significant influence on a person's emotions and behavior (Siegel, 1999). Similarly, McLeod (2009) has stated that "the behavioral theory of attachment would suggest that an infant would form an attachment with a caregiver that provides food. In contrast," the evolutionary theory would suggest that "infants have an innate (biological) need to touch and cling to something for emotional comfort. . . . The determinant of attachment is not food but care and responsiveness."

BOWLBY'S THEORY OF ATTACHMENT: THE FOUNDATION FOR UNDERSTANDING INDIVIDUAL STRENGTHS DEVELOPMENT

A major theme of this section is that attachment forms the basis of our first strengths-building relationship. According to Bowlby (1969), an infant's relationship with a parent begins as a set of innate signals that summon an adult to the baby's side. Bowlby proposed that attachment develops in four phases: (1) preattachment (birth to 6 weeks), in which the infant's signals of crying, smiling, and grasping bring the infant into close contact with a parent or primary caregiver; (2) attachment-in-the-making (6 weeks to 6–8 months), during which infants respond differently to their primary caregiver than they do to others and a sense of trust is developed that the caregiver will respond when signaled; (3) clear-cut attachment (6–8 months to 18 months), in which babies display separation anxiety; and (4) formation of a reciprocal relationship (18 months to 2 years and on), in which children begin to negotiate with their parents—asking to be read a story before the parent leaves for a meeting.

Bowlby (1980) maintained that during the four phases of attachment, children create a lasting tie to a caregiver that they can use as a secure base in their parents' absence. As time passes, a true affectionate bond develops that is supported by new cognitive skills and emotional capacities. One consequence of the infant's attachment efforts is that he or she develops a set of expectations about the availability of attachment figures and the likelihood of their providing support during stressful situations. The infant's internal attachment model becomes an important part of his or her personality, and it functions as a guide for all future close relationships (Bretherton & Munholland, 1999). An infant's attachment system predisposes him or her to seek proximity to primary caregivers. At the behavioral level, an infant's attachment behaviors help to ensure his or her survival.

Attachment is important for the development of the infant's mind. It establishes an interpersonal relationship between the infant's mind and that of his or her caregiver or parent (Siegel, 1999). The infant uses the mature brain of the parent to help him or her survive. When children are securely attached to a parent, the parent has been emotionally responsive to the child's emotions (crying, hunger, fears, etc.) such that the parent is able to amplify the child's positive emotional states and to modulate or soothe the child's negative states (Ainsworth, Blehar, Waters, & Wall, 1978; Bowlby, 1988; Sroufe, 1996). These repeated positive or negative experiences become encoded into the child's implicit memories, and then they serve as mental models or schemata of attachment.

Researchers have found that an attachment relationship formed during infancy is associated with that child's or that adult's later emotional regulation, social relatedness, and development of self-reflection and narrative (Fox, Calkins, & Bell, 1994; Main, 1995; Main, Kaplan, & Cassidy, 1985; Siegel, 1999). Attachment relationships lead to specific changes in an infant's behavior and brain.

SIGNIFICANCE OF ATTACHMENT RELATIONSHIPS AND STRENGTHS DEVELOPMENT

Attachment relationships are significant for a child's strengths development because they provide the central foundation from which a child's mind develops, and it is within the mind that a child first develops the idea that he or she has strengths and talents. Contained within the child's mind are pictures of the parent or primary caregiver and the child's relationship to that person, and when children develop secure attachment relationships with their parents or primary care- givers, they are able to go out into the world to explore and to develop satisfying relationships with others. Whereas secure attachments appear to confer a type of psychological resilience on children and adults, insecure attachments may serve as an important risk factor for psychological maladjustment.

In general, children who experience secure attachments with their primary caregiver feel safe enough to develop a sense of separateness from their parents so that they can focus their atten- tion on their unique strengths and abilities. As children develop their strengths, they become aware that they are separate from their parents and that quite possibly they may have strengths and talents that their parents do not possess. Children who do not develop their own strengths do not tend to establish the means for their later separation from parents (Danner, Snowdon, & Friesen, 2001).

This author believes that the most important strength a parent can give a child is the strength of attachment—that is, the ability to form and maintain a healthy emotional bond with another person. All families must nurture young children and give them a secure sense of acceptance and belongingness. People who have formed secure attachments are more able to develop their strengths. Healthy attachments allow a child to love, to become a good friend, and to have within his or her head a model for future relationships. A family must meet a child's needs for both attachment and separateness. As children grow older, the developmental task of the family shifts from nurturing to preparing them for successful emancipation (separateness) that includes continuing familial ties and responsibilities and training them for independence.

Problems in forming an attachment or relational bond within the family can lead to fam- ily members being disconnected from one another. Such disconnectedness between parent and child reduces the child's ability to develop his or her strengths.

STRENGTHS DEVELOPMENT AND THE IMPORTANCE OF A TRUSTED RELATIONSHIP

We form attachment relationships throughout our lives. For older children, strengths develop- ment also takes place most easily within the context of a trusted relationship in which they express their intentions to grow in a particular area. For instance, a young girl tells her father that she wants to become an artist. The father buys his daughter numerous art supplies, comments positively on her paintings, and takes her to art shows. He arranges for art lessons and a mentor in the type of paintings that she likes painting the most. The girl's artwork becomes important to her and a source of pride for both her and her father. Strength development is almost inevi- tably relationship based. Someone, somewhere along the line, encourages the development of the strength, expresses support for it, and assists the person while he or she is in the process of improving and perfecting the strength.

More often than not, our ability to develop our strengths lies in our perceived social or rela- tional support for our strengths. Parents can provide emotional and instrumental support for the development of their children's strengths. Dustin Carter's life story provides an example of how parents can emphasize their children's strengths rather than their weaknesses. A high school wrestler from Hillsboro, Ohio, Dustin suffered a life-threatening infection at age 5 that required partial amputation of all four of his limbs. Despite this handicap, he made it all the way to the state wrestling quarter-final championships in 2008. As his parents told a reporter, Dustin had a determination to do things for himself and "had always been competitive and very strong-willed and determined—always." Even before his illness, "he was stubborn and strong-willed. Thank

God he got those qualities," said his mother. Dustin, who uses prosthetic legs when he is not wrestling, maintains that he can do the same things as other people and works hard to carry out that assertion (Katzowitz, 2008).

STRENGTHS DEVELOPMENT AND ATTENTION

The mind can change the structure of our brains through the process of intentional focus. Our intentional focus of the mind on positive or negative emotions directs our energy flow. Our minds are healthy when we use our mind energy to integrate positive and negative experiences such that there is a balance. As Hanson and Mendius (2009) have stated, "what flows through your attention sculpts your brain. Therefore, controlling your attention may be the single most important way to shape your brain and thus your mind" (p. 189).

> **Cultural Reflections**
>
> *Do you know your clients' strengths?*
>
> *How much time in counseling do you spend discussing your clients' problems and your clients' strengths?*
>
> *Is counseling for you problem focused or possibility and strengths focused?*

Strengths development deals with the issue of attention and what we choose to focus on. As information-processing individuals, we choose what we will attend to. We can choose to focus on our strengths or our weaknesses. Often, what we focus on is guided by significant others in our environment, especially our parents. Individuals must come to recognize their talents and the value that accrues to them as they engage in activities involving their strengths. When people gain awareness of their strengths, some make a conscious effort to seek out opportunities to use them. Awareness of our strengths usually is based on our own evaluation of our performance of certain activities or feedback that we gain from those in our inner and outer circles—parents, friends, and teachers. As people gain strengths awareness, they sometimes share information about their strengths with family members, friends, classmates, or coworkers. To improve upon their strengths, they may add practice, knowledge, and other skills (Hanson & Mendius, 2009).

Strengths development affects our relationships with others because it increases both our own self-awareness and our awareness of others. As we become aware of our strengths, we also begin to notice the strengths that others have. We all go through a strengths progression that entails self-awareness of strengths, awareness of others' strengths, and self-management of our strengths (Jones-Smith, 2014). One objective is to help clients become familiar with what strength feels like in their bodies so that they can call upon the same strength at a later point in therapy. When a counselor or therapist helps clients to simulate feelings of strength, the clients' neural pathways for strength are deepened and engaged.

By intentionally focusing on our clients' strengths, we can help them rewire their brains and change their mindsets. The counselor or therapist helps clients to place their attention on what is working in their lives—on what they have, rather than on what they don't have. Strengths-based therapy is directed partly at the negativity bias inherent in most people. It is designed to weaken the causes of suffering and to strengthen the causes of happiness (Padesky & Mooney, 2012).

ATTACHMENT PATTERNS ACROSS CULTURES

Culture influences what attachment styles or patterns are encouraged. Keller and Bard (2017) points out that the primacy of the mother–infant bond for attachment may only be the norm "in Western middle-class families which compose less than 5% of the world's population" (p. 114). In other cultures and socioeconomic groups, people may have limited resources that require shared responsibilities for caregiving with different and multiple roles and bonds forming.

FIGURE 4.3 ■ Cultural Identification, Attachment, and Cultural Competency

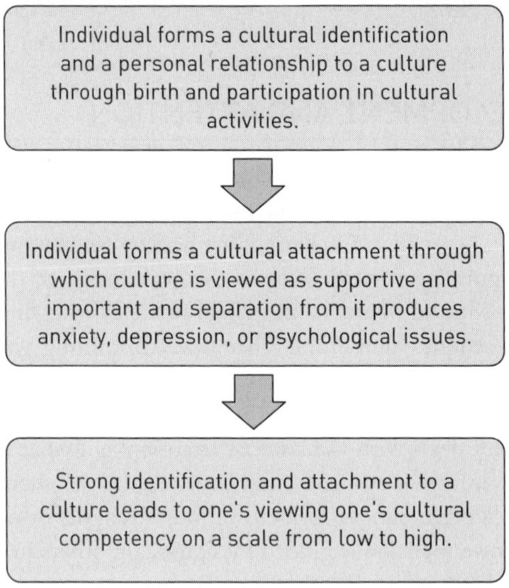

Individual forms a cultural identification and a personal relationship to a culture through birth and participation in cultural activities.

⬇

Individual forms a cultural attachment through which culture is viewed as supportive and important and separation from it produces anxiety, depression, or psychological issues.

⬇

Strong identification and attachment to a culture leads to one's viewing one's cultural competency on a scale from low to high.

Cross-cultural studies indicate that attachment patterns in Europe and in Asia differ from those in the United States and North America (Keller & Bard, 2017). For example, German infants display a great deal more avoidant attachment than do American infants. This may reflect the cultural fact that German parents value independence and encourage their infants to be nonclingy (Grossman, Grossman, Spangler, Suess, & Unzner, 1985). Likewise, Japanese infants rarely show avoidant attachment patterns. Japanese mothers rarely leave their babies in others' care (Takahashi, 1990). Despite these cultural patterns, the secure attachment relationship is the most common attachment pattern in all societies studied (van IJzendoorn & Sagi, 1999).

Moreover, just as people become attached to their caregivers, they likewise become attached to the cultures in which they have been raised. Thus, **cultural attachment** can be conceptualized as the degree to which an individual has an attachment relationship to the culture in which he or she has been raised (Keller & Bard, 2017). Such cultural attachment relationships may run along a continuum from very strong, to weak, to no attachment at all. Individuals who have a strong cultural attachment might, for instance, strictly abide by the values of that culture, in matters related to cultural dress, food, and religion—to name just a few indices (Hong, Fang, Yang, & Phua, 2013). I remember having two friends who were Jewish, one of whom ate ham during the high holy days while the other considered such behavior blasphemous and disrespectful of the Hebrew tradition. While one friend saw interfaith marriage as a challenge to the continuation of Jewish/Hebrew tradition, the other had no such cultural attachment. Each friend was attached differently to the Jewish culture. Figure 4.3 provides a way of conceptualizing the relationship of cultural identification and attachment.

SIGNIFICANCE OF CULTURAL ATTACHMENT, MIGRATION, AND ACCULTURATION

Individuals' cultural attachment might have an important influence on their responses to migration and acculturation in a different, cultural host country. For instance, Hong et al. (2013)

conducted a study in which they postulated that the adaptive solution of acculturation is analogous to infants' attachment to their caretakers. They maintained that forming secure attachment to the native and/or host cultures can help individuals cope with anxiety and stress to gain a sense of safe haven in a new country. To test their theory, the researchers recruited 57 Indonesian students studying in Singapore and measured their quality of cultural attachment in two ways: (1) self-reported cultural attachment styles with the native and host culture and (2) positive affective transfer from Indonesian (native) and from Singaporean (host) cultural icons. The "participants' self-reported attachment styles of native and host cultures and their positive affective transfer from the Indonesian (native) cultural icons were linked to better adjustment in the host culture (as indicated by less perceived discrimination and acculturation stress, and greater subjective well-being)" (p. 1024).

This author proposes the following relationships between cultural attachment and acculturation (see also Figure 4.3):

1. Individuals vary on a continuum from weak to strong cultural attachment, and such cultural attachment or the lack thereof is related to their subsequent acculturation level and/or acculturation experiences in a new host country.

2. Strong cultural attachment to one's native culture is related to the individual's perception that he or she has significant native cultural strengths and/or that the native country has recognized his or her cultural strengths, whereas weak cultural attachment is associated with fewer perceived cultural strengths.

3. Strong cultural attachment to one's native culture is inversely related to positive acculturation in a new culturally different host culture.

4. Weak cultural attachment to one's native culture is associated with positive acculturation in the new culturally different host culture.

STRENGTHS DEVELOPMENT, THE NARRATIVE PROCESS, AND THE MIND

Our minds engage in an autobiographical narrative process—a process that is based partly on our memories. Memories color our perceptions of ourselves and others. They also assume an important role in developing a strengths-based or deficit-based mindset. The internalized stories we tell ourselves about ourselves lead us toward either strength recognition or weakness recognition. A counselor might say to a client, "Tell me about a time when you felt the strongest in your life. What happened? Who was there with you?" Each one of us engages in a process of self-surveillance—a process of monitoring and judging ourselves in relationship to others. We engage in internal dialogues about our strengths and weaknesses. We develop a picture of ourselves being strong—the strong self—and a picture of ourselves as weak—the weak self. Our narrative stories help us to make sense out of our lives.

STRENGTHS AS DIALOGIC CONVERSATIONS WITH THE SELF

Strengths development and strengths recognition take place within our inner and outer conversational worlds. We all engage in internal dialogues about our strengths—for instance, how proficient we are in certain areas of our lives. We say to ourselves, "I'm really good in music,"

Cultural Reflections

How competent are you within the culture within which you have been raised?

What cultural strengths do you have?

Name one personal strength that you possess.

What do you tell yourself about your strengths and weaknesses?

or "Math is not my best suit." These internalized stories are essentially **strengths dialogues** with the self. When our inner strengths dialogues are positive and we act on our strengths, we experience a sense of self-satisfaction—possibly even happiness. When our inner dialogues are plagued by repeated surveillance and recognition of weakness, we can become discouraged.

Moreover, each of us engages in **strengths surveillance**, which is a two-prong process consisting of internalized self-dialogues and audience dialogues. Our internalized self-surveillance—that is, the process of monitoring and judging ourselves—leads to either our recognition, minimizing, or unawareness of our strengths. We are the dominant character in our inner world, while parents, siblings, teachers, friends, and others form the substance of our outer world. Almost inevitably, other people are involved in our strengths progress. People serve as part of the audience that comments to us and that helps to judge our abilities as strengths.

Strengths dialogues may also come from external sources. In this instance, they are said to be audience oriented. Usually, the audience consists of the significant people in our lives—our parents, siblings, extended family members, friends, teachers, coworkers, and neighbors. The outer world forms the **strengths audience**, which reflects to us how we are perceived by them. Sometimes the audience gives us praise in the form of positive hand clapping, while on other occasions, it boos our performance as poor or inadequate. The audience may also treat us with an air of indifference, thereby leading us to feel invisible or disposable as a person—as if we do not matter, or do not belong where we are.

WESTERN AND EASTERN VIEWS ON HUMAN STRENGTHS: THE CHINESE PERSPECTIVE

Culture conditions how strengths are viewed by a people. This section describes a Chinese application of the strengths perspective. Most presentations of the **strengths perspective in counseling and therapy** use a Western or Eurocentric cultural framework that stresses individual attainment and change of adverse situations. Although my own model of strengths-based therapy can be used in many different cultures, it was developed primarily from a Western rather than from an Eastern cultural framework.

The strengths-based therapy model has found its way to China, much in the same way that Americans have embraced the Buddhist meditation practice of mindfulness. Majority Chinese culture, however, conditions how the strengths perspective can be applied. In American culture, an individual has ownership of his or her own talents and strengths. In contrast, in Chinese culture, ownership of an individual's strengths rests with the collective group rather than with the individual (Yip, 2008).

In the chapter "Searching the Chinese Cultural Roots of the Strengths Perspective," Kam-shing Yip (2008) articulated the differences between the strengths perspective in the United States and in China. Yip points out that because the cultures of China, Japan, Korea, India, and many Arabic/Muslim nations share the value of collectivism over individualism, counselors and therapists should advocate strengths in terms of mutual acceptance, mutual respect, support, and dependence among members within families and within the ethnic communities. After reviewing a great deal of Chinese literature, Yip concluded that the Chinese evidence a cultural system that stresses the value of (1) family, (2) relations, (3) authority, and (4) "others."

Strengths as Possessions of the Collective Group Rather Than of the Individual

In Chinese culture, the family predominates over its members in virtually all domains. Great importance is placed on harmony and solidarity within the family, and behaviors of modesty, conformity, endurance, self-suppression, mutual dependence, and in-group loyalty are valued. Because the culture places strong emphasis on the family's reputation and wealth, members are willing to subordinate their personal goals, interests, and welfare for the sake of the family. The Chinese family orientation makes it important to develop collective strengths rather than individual strengths for individual members.

According to Yip (2008), therapists should avoid criticizing Chinese clients' strengths systems. Instead, they should treat Chinese clients' strengths as part of a family's honor. Likewise, clients' weaknesses may be viewed as shame for the entire family. For instance, if a Chinese student does well on an examination, he or she brings honor to the entire family. The family shares in the strengths of individual family members. Likewise, if a family member suffers from substance abuse, this weakness is reflected on the entire family.

A culturally different counselor or therapist should recognize that many Chinese clients may choose to contribute their ability, talents, and strengths for the sake of family honor as well as for family continuity (Yip, 2008). Clients' talents and strengths should be interpreted in such a manner as to glorify their parents and families. Clients' strengths should be regarded as assets of the collectives to which the client belongs.

Moreover, Chinese culture places greater value on some strengths than others. Clients' interpersonal strengths, such as showing respect to parents and seniors, are considered critical strengths and far more important than individual talents and abilities, such as high academic grades. In general, Chinese people put a premium on interpersonal strengths that demonstrate a person's ability to show respect and to develop harmony in a relationship.

The Chinese Authority Orientation and Permission to Demonstrate Strengths

Chinese culture values the strength of humility (Yip, 2008). In practical terms, this means that a person should express and display his or her strengths, talents, and abilities only with permission from an authority figure (Yip, 2008). If individuals display their strengths without first receiving permission, others will interpret this as "egocentric" and a challenge to the supremacy of the authority figure. For instance, if a student demonstrates academic talents in front of a class without first seeking the permission of his or her teacher, the student's behavior is regarded as belittling to the teacher. Yip (2008) points out that the next time, the teacher will probably not call on the student—with the goal of teaching the student to become humble enough to follow the social order of teachers and students.

Likewise, one must obtain approval to display one's strengths or talents at work. A company will not consider an employee's strengths to be beneficial to the organization if the demonstration of such talents is not first approved by supervisors. On the contrary, if an employee demonstrates his or her strengths without first seeking supervisor approval, the organization will consider the employee to be a threat and adopt a policy of ignoring him or her. Yip (2005, 2008) explains that in order to gain the approval of one's supervisors, one needs to be humble and to attribute one's strengths and talents to the graces and caring of supervisors. Moreover, the employee should let the supervisor take the glory and the benefits from his or her strengths (Yip, 2005, 2008).

Chinese Relational Orientation and Strengths

Relationships in Chinese culture depend very much on family, including extended family and ancestral ties. This also extends to social contacts; for example, the parent or grandparent of a friend or coworker is accorded a high level of respect due to the family relationship with that friend or coworker. Interpersonal distance varies depending on whether one is a close family member, close friend, or stranger. The Chinese hold in high regard relational strengths that are used between people. A person's ability to be sensitive to the needs of others, to show them respect, to be submissive to others, and to express one's views in a humble manner are considered prized strengths.

Chinese Other Orientation and Strengths

Yip (2005, 2008) indicates that in Chinese strengths-based development, it is more important for people to assert a responsibility and obligation within their social status than it is for them to demand their rights.

Western and Eastern cultures also have different views on weakness and what individuals should do about their weaknesses. Chinese views on weakness and suffering can be traced to the Taoist philosophy, which originated during the fourth century BCE in China. Together with Confucianism and Buddhism, Taoism is one of China's major religious traditions, which all endorse the concept of yin and yang, the sense of relativity, and the belief that suffering is part of the normal life of people. The strengths-based Chinese counselor or therapist helps clients to develop a sense of relativity and a coexistence with hardship and suffering. Clients come to perceive that everything happens in a relative way, and this strength helps clients to tolerate and endure adversity.

Chinese people perceive a strength in freeing themselves from the strong desire to control—a concept that forms part of the cornerstone of mindfulness as a psychotherapeutic approach. Instead, they place a high value on inner peace, and perhaps this is the reason that mindfulness as a psychotherapeutic approach has lasted for hundreds of years in China. The Chinese also value the strength of transcendence—of not being controlled by secular things such as wealth and prestige. As Dahlsgaard, Peterson, and Seligman (2005) have reported, transcendence is one of the strengths valued across six historical, philosophical, and cultural groups.

Some Considerations for Cultural Strengths

Although the preceding section has emphasized similarities and differences between Eastern and Western strengths, a counselor might consider examining the following strengths-based areas:

- Identity
- Past struggles and accomplishments

HOW DO I MAKE CULTURALLY RESPONSIVE COUNSELING STRENGTHS-BASED?

Strengths-based therapy may provide a good theoretical framework for cross-cultural counseling. This theoretical approach can be applied to a number of cultures because of the following factors:

- All people have strengths.
- Our strengths provide the means for helping people to deal with adversity, problems, or life changes. Generally speaking, our weaknesses cannot help us to deal with problems.
- Each culture outlines or prescribes the acceptable ways to use our strengths.

- In Eastern cultures, focusing on clients' strengths rather than on their weaknesses or diseases helps them not only to "save face" but also to use their resources to deal effectively with life issues.

- In Western culture, focusing on clients' strengths reaffirms the cultural value and belief in hope as well as the notion that the individual can overcome most difficulties.

- In Eastern culture, strengths can be used to help restore a harmonious balance in a person's life, especially as the strengths are directed toward the benefit of the collective group. In contrast, human deficits can rarely restore an out-of-balance relationship in clients' lives.

- The strengths perspective and strengths-based therapy have universal appeal because they cause the therapist to search for the best rather than the worst in human beings.

- The strengths approach emphasizes the importance of relationships in developing human strengths.

- Strengths-based therapy has appeal for both Eastern and Western cultures because on the one hand, the focus is on inner searching of self for strengths (Western- and Eastern-valued strength). On the other hand, the search for clients' strengths can be used in service of others (Eastern cultural value system).

- Human beings have the capacity to grow and to learn.

- The entire community is considered a potential resource to enlist on behalf of the client.

THE PHILOSOPHY OF STRENGTHS-BASED THERAPY

Strengths-based therapy asserts that we are the heroes of our own lives. At the heart of strengths-based therapy is the idea that whether people succeed in life or have frustrating lives of muddling through and quiet desperation depends a great deal on whether they have a strengths or a deficit mindset (Padesky & Mooney, 2012). Individuals with a **deficit mindset** focus on what is missing in themselves and in other people. They emphasize what they don't want instead of what they do want. Learning to look for another person's strengths—be it your partner, child, or friend—involves a process of noticing what's right about a person. Nora is an attractive woman in her late 50s. As we renewed our friendship over lunch, Nora began to provide me a report on each of the important people in her life and to indicate how they were not meeting her needs and expectations. One of her long-standing friends had not invited her to a house-warming party, and she felt slighted. Her son and daughter-in-law had stopped coming over on Sundays, and therefore she did not see her grandchildren as much as she used to see them. Worse yet, her son sent her a Mother's Day card two days late. Her husband only remembered her birthday when nudged by Nora's friend.

Nora has pictures in her head about what a good son, a good friend, a loving husband, and so on should say, think, feel, and give to her. Each day, she searches her experiences for instances wherein those with whom she comes into contact fail to meet her ideal pictures. She has mastered the recipe for the deficit mindset, for depression, and for lifelong disappointment—if she does not change the lenses that she uses to view the world. Those with a deficit mindset notice what's missing rather than what is there.

When we narrow our vision to focus on only the gap between what we want and what we have, we lose. The deficit mindset misses out on quite a bit because it fails to notice what is there. It fails to acknowledge life's gifts that lie amid our pain. An important concept and technique in strengths-based therapy involves helping clients to direct their attention so that they "notice

TABLE 4.1 ■ Therapy as Strengths Based or Pathology Based	
Strengths-Based Therapy	**Pathology—Medical Model Therapy**
The person is unique with talents and resources to be tapped for therapy.	The person is a "case" or a "diagnosis," such as bipolar, schizophrenic.
Therapy intervention is possibility focused.	Therapy intervention is problem focused.
The therapist comes to appreciate the person through personal narratives. Therapy is a collaborative process.	The therapist is the "expert" who interprets the individual's personal narrative for the purpose of arriving at a diagnosis.
Childhood trauma may contribute to a person's strengths or weaknesses.	Childhood trauma predicts later pathology.
The focus is on what is right about the person and on the person's strengths.	The focus is on the client's deficits and emphasizes what is wrong or abnormal.
Individuals, families, and communities are viewed as the experts, and their input is valued.	The professional is the expert on clients' lives. Input from clients may not be sought.
A client's strengths, skills, and abilities are resources for the work to be accomplished.	The knowledge and skills of the professional are the resources for the work to be accomplished.
The person's behavior is viewed as the problem.	The person is viewed as the problem.
Therapy focuses on strengths development and on finding one's place in the family and communities.	Therapy involves reducing symptoms and consequences of problems.

Source: Jones-Smith, 2014.

what is there for them." Nora was so hurting from not getting her Mother's Day card on time that she failed to notice that her son had remembered her. A **strengths mindset** generates a positive energy field, while those who maintain a deficit mindset generate a negative energy field. Those who are closest to us can influence our strengths and energy fields.

Strengths-based counseling adheres to the belief that even the most challenging life stories that clients bring to therapy contain examples of their exercise of strengths in their struggle with adversity (See Table 4.1). For instance, the addict's or substance abuser's maladaptive responses may also contain within them the seeds of a struggle for health. Oftentimes, when clients report their pain, they mention healthy things they have done to help them through their addiction. For instance, Gail's struggle with alcoholism revealed a destructive pattern at work and in other areas of her life; but when she was granted visitation rights with her son, she did not drink. I call this phenomenon the **client's struggle perception** (Ward & Reuter, 2011).

It is within a client's struggle with the presenting problem that practitioners search for strengths (Smith, 2006). What internal strength allowed Gail to refrain from drinking both prior to and during her visitation with her son? If a practitioner can help a client to see and understand the strength that allowed him or her to obtain some reprieve, however brief, from the painful struggle with the problem that brought him or her to therapy, this can create an opportunity for him or her to learn how to muster that source of strength in other areas of his or her life.

Cultural Reflections

When we focus on clients' problems rather than their strengths, we stimulate action in the amygdala.

Clients' worry or doubt stimulates the amygdala.

CULTURAL MINDSETS

Each culture tends to promote a particular mindset. In the United States, Carol Dweck (2006) maintains that people develop mindsets as they age. She defines a mindset as a fixed mental attitude that predetermines a person's responses to and interpretations of life and situations. Dweck outlines two mindsets: (1) a fixed mindset and (2) a growth mindset. The fixed mindset holds the belief that our abilities, intelligence, talents, and personality are fixed and cannot change. Within this purview, a person's talents and abilities are not developed but merely documented. People who hold this type of mindset tend to shy away from trying something new and may become anxious when presented with new challenges and tasks. In contrast, the growth mindset espouses the belief that our most basic abilities, intelligence, talents, and personality can change over time. People can accomplish their goals through hard work and dedication.

When a person with a fixed mindset is presented with a new problem, he or she tends to view the problem according to what he or she has been able to accomplish in the past. If the person has struggled with this type of problem, he or she is inclined to respond with anxiety. In contrast, a person with a growth mindset tends to view the new problem in terms of what he or she can learn from the experience and how he or she can grow to meet the challenge. A person with a growth mindset tends to say, "I can solve this problem if I try hard." A dominant theme in Dweck's (2006) book is that our limitations in life are learned rather than imposed upon us. If children believe they cannot learn, they will not learn.

Strengths-based therapy maintains that there are two additional types of mindsets: a deficit mindset and a strengths mindset (Jones-Smith, 2014). These two mindsets have a major impact on how we view the world, ourselves, and others. Our major institutions and organizations are constructed on one of these two perspectives. A major issue is that most of us are not consciously aware of the mindset that we carry around with us and teach to our children. Our mindsets are the gorillas in the room with us, either enabling or limiting what we can do in life. A mindset refers to the way we see ourselves and the manner in which we embrace the world and others. A mindset is built on a cognitive and an emotional map of oneself, other people, and the world. Mindset development takes place as part of our autobiographical narrative.

Strengths Mindset

For the most part, mindsets are learned from one's interactions with others. Based on one's life experiences, one develops either a strengths or a deficit mindset or attitude toward life. Why do some people seem to crumble from their adversities, while others grow stronger? Although each person is different, there are clearly mindsets that separate the winners from the losers, the strong from the weak. When people possess the mindset of resilience, they are able to deal with their life experience so that they are not defeated. Young people can be taught that they have a choice in how they view difficult or traumatic events in their lives. Their lives can change from one of beating the odds to one of changing the odds.

What is the strengths mindset? The strengths mindset is positive awareness. It is a resilient mindset. Such a mindset consists of positive attitudes that sustain one's optimism and one's efforts toward achievement and excellence in one's areas of talent. It involves behavior patterns that make one effective and beliefs that empower a person to succeed. The strengths mindset helps a person to become or stay motivated to take action and to sustain the energy necessary for his or her life journey. It represents a positive way of perceiving the world. A person looks for the opportunity that exists, even in a negative situation. Some questions to ask yourself about whether you have a strength or a deficit mindset are: Do you fight change or embrace it? Do you know your strengths? Do you use your strengths, talents, and skills with confidence, or do you shrink from using them?

There is also another side of the strengths mindset. The strengths mindset acknowledges and understands the weaknesses within the self. The strengths mindset does not run away from acknowledging one's own weaknesses. Do you know, acknowledge, and accept your imperfections or weaknesses? I can remember working with one client who had exceptional strengths in several areas. When he was firing on all cylinders, there was no stopping him. But he never learned how to manage his weaknesses. On the contrary, his limitations seemed to trip him up right at the time that he was poised for success. "I kept promising myself that I wasn't going to engage in that behavior again," he lamented. "But there I was again doing the very thing that I had promised myself I would not do again." An important issue for this young man was to learn how to take steps to prevent his demons, his weaknesses, from interfering with his strengths.

Deficit Mindset

A deficit mindset is negative awareness. Based on research on the negativity bias, people tend to perceive the world in terms of negative expectations and negative perceptions. Typically, the deficit mindset is focused on what is missing, what is lacking, or what is wrong with a situation or a person. If you have ever had a friend who is deficit based, you know the type. You ask her how the party was, and she recites every negative thing that she remembers about the party. "Well, it was okay, but this was missing, or this was lacking."

The mindsets of those who have been an intimate part of our lives—our parents—often take up residence within us. Deficit mindset parents are hard to live with if you are their child. They ignore the two As on your report card and spend a half hour lecturing you about the B and C you received. If you dread having your mother come to visit you because she has something to criticize, you have been raised with a deficit parenting mindset. If you have been raised by a parent who tended to see the glass as half empty, most likely you have incorporated into your mindset a major component of the deficit mindset. Conversely, if you have been reared by a parent who is inclined to look for the best in you and others, you have probably incorporated into your mindset that same tendency. Mindsets are a choice; they can be changed.

CULTURALLY RESPONSIVE STRENGTHS-BASED PRACTICE

This section is intended for practitioners who want to adopt strengths-based practices, while still maintaining a different theoretical orientation—for instance, a cognitive behavioral orientation (Padesky & Mooney, 2012). It provides the reader with general strengths-based guidelines and techniques. Chapter 5 is designed for the reader who desires to adopt the strengths-based therapy model developed, which contains various phases of psychotherapy.

Helping Clients Manage Weaknesses and Negative Self-Limiting Thoughts

The mantra for strengths-based therapy is to promote strengths and manage weaknesses that may sabotage our strengths. The goal is to learn how to use your strengths to manage your weaknesses (Padesky & Mooney, 2012). The strengths perspective maintains that spending most of your time in your areas of weakness will only improve your weakness to a level of average (Buckingham, 2007). Focusing on weaknesses blocks our goal achievement (Rashid & Ostermann, 2009).

Managing our weaknesses includes partnering with others, delegating to others, and developing new techniques to use our strengths in positive ways. We often focus on improving our weaknesses, as if fixing what is weak is actually going to help us to become excellent. Instead of trying to make our weaknesses our strengths, we should bring the area of weakness to one of functional competence.

Creating a Culturally Responsive Strengths-Building Therapy Environment

A culturally responsive therapy environment is one in which the therapist demonstrates an understanding and appreciation of a client's cultural background. It means acknowledging that every culture has specific values that can be used in treatment, such as the support of extended families and of religious or spiritual communities. As a result of appreciating a client's culture, a therapist can tap into the most effective treatment strategies—those based on the personal and cultural strengths of each individual (Rashid, 2009).

CASE VIGNETTE 4.1

MARISSA: FROM NOTICING WHAT'S MISSING TO NOTICING WHAT'S THERE

As Marissa sat on her couch, deep in thought, she tried to make sense of what was happening in her life. Her boyfriend, Eric, had just broken off their relationship, and she felt like she had been hit by a ton of bricks.

"I'm having trouble being around you," Eric had told her earlier that day. "You depress me. No matter how good a time we're having, you always seem to point out that something is wrong, missing, or not quite right. I never feel as if I can measure up to what you want. I tell you I've got a new job opportunity, and you caution me to stay where I am, even though you know I want to advance my career. You're always negative, and I'm upbeat, positive, happy, and ready to take life by the horns. I really care about you, Marissa, but I don't think we belong together. Let's give ourselves some space."

Until this conversation, Marissa had thought everything was working out with Eric. She wondered if what Eric had said about her was correct. Was she always negative about things? Maybe, she thought, she did have a tendency to see the glass as half empty.

Marissa then tried to unravel where her glass-half-empty attitude had begun. Was it something in her Roman Catholic upbringing or her Irish American family background? She recalled reading a statement by the Irish American senator Patrick Moynihan after the assassination of President Kennedy—another Irish American—which said, "I don't think that there is any point being Irish if you don't know that the world is going to break your heart someday" (McGoldrick, Giordano, & Garcia-Preto, 2005). Her parents had often said that although the Irish will fight against all odds, they still have a strong sense of human powerlessness in relation to nature (McGoldrick et al., 2005). Marissa had learned that Irish culture places great value on conformity and respectability. She had experienced what many Irish people call Irish guilt. She recalled being told in the Catholic school she attended that people are inherently bad and will suffer deservedly for their sins. Marissa came from a large family, but did not feel a close connection with her parents or siblings. Instead, in a pattern often seen in Irish families, they were taught to keep their feelings private and to be self-reliant. She recalled browsing in a book in the library that described members of Irish families as being isolated from one another. According to that book, when things go wrong in the family, members become sullen and puritanically rigid (McGoldrick et al., 2005).

For the next few weeks, Marissa pondered what Eric had said to her. She had thought he would call her, but he didn't, and she hadn't called him. Finally, she decided to go to therapy to find out why she tended to see the glass as half empty and why she appeared negative to Eric.

The first meeting with the therapist went quite well. The two talked about Marissa's background and the impact that she felt her family's interpretation of Irish culture had on her growing up.

Marissa: "I'm wondering if what Eric was talking about—my negativity—could be traced to my upbringing as a good Irish Catholic girl. Every time Eric and I had sex, I would enjoy it, but afterwards, I would have feelings about whether or not I should have done it—a good Irish Catholic girl like me. What would the nuns say? And it was not just sex. I was raised with the belief that people are bad, and that I, too, was imperfect—badly flawed. I was raised not to take chances—stick with the job you have, because you might lose it and something worse could happen to you. We never really discussed feelings in my family. All of my deep emotional feelings were just kind of walled off from the rest of me. When I grew older, I saw how other families lived, and I learned the phrase that I was 'talking Irish' when I appeared to be communicating and still not communicating at the same time."

Therapist: "I understand what you are saying, Marissa. I was raised with an Irish mother and an Italian father, so our house used to have heated discussions about what was possible and what people were really like. My father was the type who had to speak his mind, and my mother rarely spoke hers. Can we talk for a moment about what it felt like growing up as a good Irish Catholic girl in your family?"

The therapy discussion focused on Marissa's cultural story and what it felt like growing up as a "good Irish Catholic girl." Marissa said she felt a load was being taken off her chest because she could now talk about what she had walled off for years—her feelings about things in her life.

The therapist and she agreed to spend more time talking about her Irish background in the next session. Marissa had mentioned that her family members were out of touch with their feelings, and there appeared to be some hint that her being out of touch with her feelings was connected to her negative outlook on life.

Marissa was relieved that the therapist didn't suggest that she be placed on medication, nor did she give her a diagnosis, even though one was required for insurance reimbursement. Much to her surprise, the therapist had asked Marissa what she thought in her gut was

(Continued)

(Continued)

causing her to feel upset about what Eric had said. The therapist had also asked Marissa about her strengths. "Strengths?" Marissa mocked, "What strengths?"

The therapist responded by complimenting Marissa on her looks and on the fact that she was able to secure a job as an assistant professor at Donner Community College. Marissa smiled half-heartedly when the therapist complimented her on her looks. It appeared that even though she liked the therapist's compliments, she felt uncomfortable.

Therapist: "Tell me something good about you. It could be anything."

Marissa: "I'm not sure what to say. I was raised not to brag, and that would be like bragging for me."

To help Marissa, the therapist gave her a Positive Checklist, which asked her to just check off the qualities she thought she possessed. Marissa was also given a one-page statement that asked her to fill in the blanks about her strengths in specific areas. Marissa seemed pleased to find that she possessed several of the positive qualities on the checklist.

Marissa: "Am I just going to come here to tell you what's good about me? How is that going to help me?" she asked. "I think Eric has a point. Many times I turn down opportunities because I am afraid that things won't work out. In fact, I convince myself that things won't work out and that it is best to keep doing whatever I'm doing. I get this fear in the pit of my stomach that says, 'Slow down, Marissa!'"

The therapist reserved the last 10 minutes of the session to talk with Marissa about some findings in neuroscience related to the brain. She indicated that part of Marissa's tendency to see the glass as half empty was formed years ago—probably in childhood. The therapist pointed out that the glass-half-empty view wasn't Marissa's fault because negative experiences are registered immediately in the brain. In contrast, positive experiences generally have to be held in awareness for 5 to 10 or 20 seconds for them to register in emotional memories. Negative experiences register more strongly than positive ones, and the brain responds to negative events because such registering is related to our survival.

Therapist: "What do you want to do, Marissa? Do you want to change how you see and respond to the world?"

Marissa's response was made clear by her tears and quivering voice. "I want to change. I'm sick of being afraid of making changes. I'm sick of not believing that things can work out for me. I want to have some kind of hope. I want to be happy and meet a man who enjoys being with me and have a stable relationship that lasts."

Therapist: "I'm glad you want to make changes so that you can respond to the opportunities life has for you, Marissa. As I said earlier in our session, in order to change how you see the world, we have to change your brain—because it is your brain, your neural pathways, that are signaling to you 'Danger! Danger! Danger!' In order for you to start seeing the glass as half full, we'll have to consciously and deliberately help your brain register positive experiences so that they sink into the deepest layers of your mind.

"First we'll do some experiences in my office, and I'll give you homework assignments to help you take in the good about your life, even your situation with Eric. There's good with what happened with Eric. If Eric hadn't spoken about your being negative and depressing him, would you even be here? You came to see me because what Eric said registered true for you and you wanted to change that. So I compliment you for deciding to take a big step to change your life for the better.

"We are going to have exercises to help you focus on the emotional and body sensation aspects of your positive experiences. These will help you free up your attention and build self-confidence. The experiences and exercises I have used previously will help the positive experiences soak into your brain and body, registering deeply in your emotional memory. We will be using sensory imagining exercises where you will be asked to relax your body and absorb the positive experience. After the third session, I'm going to teach you the technique of mindfulness. Gradually, you will be able to replace old feelings of shame or inadequacy with current feelings of being cared about and loved.

"Does what I am proposing for the next 7 to 10 sessions sound like something you would like to do and that you feel would help you?"

Marissa: "It sounds great, like something I have needed to do for most of my life."

Therapist: "Okay. Let's get started on your homework for the next week. I want you to write some affirmations 10 times in the morning and 10 times right before you go to bed. By writing them right before you go to bed, the affirmations will stand a better chance of changing your unconscious mind. And it is in your unconscious mind that your negative views on life are located. Your conscious mind says, 'I want to make a change,' but your unconscious mind is the gatekeeper or the critical factor, and it says, 'Whoa there, you sure you want to do that?' Our work in therapy will focus on aligning your conscious desires with your unconscious ones, so that the gatekeeper won't keep you stuck in old, self-defeating patterns of behavior."

Marissa: "I guess I'm not as crazy as I thought. I need to change how I think about things, and you are going to be helping me to do that. I don't think I could change the way I see things on my own."

Therapist: "No, you're not 'crazy,' Marissa. This week I want you to keep a journal of the positive experiences in your life. Try to take in the good about a list of experiences that I am going to give you. For instance, I want you to write down whenever you felt gratitude and appreciation. Don't be afraid to write down even the smallest bit of good news or good fortune. You can feel gratitude for a sunset, or a smile from your neighbor or work colleague. Reflect on the good things at the end of each day. Then I am going to ask you to reflect on your strength as a survivor and your resiliency. I want you to notice when you feel loved, cared about, liked, and included. And here's the list of affirmations and the directions for completing them. I am also giving you a list of everyday experiences that I want you to take notice of so that they become registered in your brain as positive experiences."

Marissa: "Thank you. I don't know where I will find time . . ." Then, as if catching her negative response, Marissa said, "I'm open to doing what will help me have a positive outlook on life."

Therapist: "Take care."

Marissa: "See you next week."

Culturally responsive environments should convey an atmosphere that is welcoming to clients, including decorating one's office so that it reflects the culture of the clients one serves (McAuliffe, 2013). For instance, one might carry the flags of the clients' countries (including of course, the U.S. flag), pictures of well-known cultural symbols associated with the therapist's clientele, and other diversity artifacts that might symbolize one is receptive and open to different cultures. In addition, therapists might include symbols of social justice or pictures or quotations about social justice on their office wall. The following are some social justice quotations that clinicians might want to put on their wall to demonstrate their stance and beliefs about individual differences.

THE CULTURALLY RESPONSIVE THERAPY PHYSICAL ENVIRONMENT: SOCIAL JUSTICE QUOTATIONS FOR POSTERS IN THERAPISTS' OFFICE

"I wish I could say that racism and prejudice were only distant memories. We must dissent from the indifference. We must dissent from the apathy. We must dissent from the fear, the hatred and the mistrust . . . We must dissent because America can do better, because America has no choice but to do better." —**Thurgood Marshall** (U.S. lawyer and Supreme Court justice, 1908–1993)

"What a country needs to do is be fair to all its citizens—whether people are of a different ethnicity or gender." —**Chinua Achebe**

"Returning hate for hate multiplies hate, adding deeper darkness to a night already devoid of stars. Darkness cannot drive out darkness; only light can do that. Hate cannot drive out hate; only love can do that." —**Martin Luther King Jr.,** *Strength to Love*

The Initial Culturally Responsive Interview

In a culturally responsive therapy environment, therapists broach cultural differences with the client during the initial interview. The therapist listens for any client statements about his or her culture. When therapists have a different dominant language from their clients, they may either offer to obtain a translator (if this is feasible) or refer the client to another therapist. Therapists should have a working knowledge of the cultural background of their clients, including their preferred communication styles, artifacts, and values.

TABLE 4.2 ■ Culturally Responsive Clinical Skill Development: Skills for the First Therapy Session

Therapists might ask clients culturally related questions to determine their preference for working with a therapist.

- What type of characteristics or qualities are you looking for in a therapist?

- On a scale of 1 to 10, with 10 being *highly comfortable*, how comfortable would you feel in addressing issues of race, ethnicity, culture, gender, or sexual orientation with me?

- Do you think that your therapist needs to be similar to you on the dimension of ethnicity, culture, sexual orientation, or age?

- What would you like for me to know about you and your culture that might help me understand your situation better?

Therapists might ask themselves the following questions prior to, during, or after the first session.

- Do I understand my own cultural background in relation to this case?

- Do I understand my client's cultural background?

- Do I understand my client's worldview?

- Do I comprehend my client's cultural values for the following dimensions: (1) individualistic vs. collectivist—to what extent the culture places a greater value on the individuals versus the group; (2) high versus low uncertainty—how the client's culture handles uncertainty; (3) high-context cultures (high-context cultures are built on trust, relationships are important, and one's identity is rooted in groups; there is high use of nonverbal communication patterns; communication is indirect) vs. low-context cultures (relationships begin and end quickly—relationship boundary is not clear; one's identity is rooted in oneself; message is carried by words; communication is direct).

- Do I know how to create a strong transcultural therapeutic relationship? How is trust developed between individuals within my client's culture?

- What words can I use to convey that I understand the client's situation?

- Am I familiar with the words in a client's culture that reflect the client's feelings about his or her presenting issue? A person from Latino culture might use the words *desesperado* or *sin esperanza* to indicate a helpless feeling. In Jewish culture, a person might describe his feelings as *nebbish*.

- Can I comfortably use culturally relevant terms to describe a client's emotional state to help a client self-disclose? For instance, if a person quotes the Bible during a session, a therapist might state, "It sounds as if you find comfort in your religious faith. Can you tell me how your faith is helping you to deal with the situation?"

- What might be some positive ways my client might deal with or resolve the current issue in his or her culture?

TABLE 4.3 ■ Culturally Responsive Clinical Skill Development: Intervention Skills

The culturally responsive strengths-based clinician uses the following clinical intervention skills:

1. Asks clients about their strengths
2. Helps clients to see their strengths and positives in themselves
3. Focuses on clients' strengths as a therapeutic way of increasing client motivation
4. Helps clients to locate their strengths in their struggle with their presenting problems
5. Instills hope in clients so that they can make desired change
6. Highlights progress clients are currently making in therapy
7. Reframes clients' experiences in a positive manner
8. Assesses the resiliency of clients
9. Helps clients to develop their strengths-based plan
10. Helps clients to rewire their brains so that the focus is on their strengths and positives
11. Helps clients to deconstruct negative and "weakness" neural pathways based on fear and worry
12. Asks about the need to have a therapist with a similar cultural background or one who speaks the client's language

In addition to the multicultural competencies, a culturally responsive strengths-based therapist or counselor should demonstrate some basic skills. These skills are not exhaustive, but rather they can be used as a means to develop culturally responsive strengths-based competencies for clinicians. These competencies are listed in the Clinical Intervention Skills feature (See Table 4.3). There is some overlap with questions that might be asked during the first interview.

SUMMARY OF KEY POINTS

Counselors bring with them to counseling their own cultural baggage. The effective counselor is one who can adapt counseling theories and techniques to the individual needs of the client. The counselor must be able to see the client both as an individual and as a member of a particular cultural group. A client's cultural group membership should not be used to obscure the client. Culturally responsive counseling requires that the counselor understand (1) the importance of cultural, racial, or ethnic group membership on the socialization of the client and (2) the importance and uniqueness of the individual. To counsel a client solely on the basis of his or her cultural or gender group membership results in stereotyping.

A clinical focus on client strengths is necessary if clients are to deal effectively with their presenting issues. Many people experience strengths estrangement such that they have lost contact with their strengths and their potential to accomplish their goals.

Strengths begin in the brain, and they are characterized by well-traveled brain neural pathways. Strengths development is a process that involves both the development of positive (I can) neural pathways in the brain and the influence of a close nurturing relationship. Children's attachment relationship with a caregiver helps to develop their strengths.

As noted in Chapter 3 and in the present chapter, the brain has a negativity bias in that it remembers negative events more so than positive experiences. The negativity bias is part of the human survival mechanism. The bad predominates over the good because a so-called bad experience might be life-threatening. It takes three to five positive experiences to overcome one mildly negative experience.

- Clinicians, mental health practitioners, and counselors can only become as culturally competent as our brains will permit. The neural pathways that we have created in response to ourselves and to other cultures and ethnic groups will create either a fear or a comfort response in our brains.

- If there are deep neural pathways that were created and sustained by negative cultural experiences with those who are different from us, our brains will put limits on us by sending danger signals to the **amygdala**. As clinicians, we have to retrain the implicit biases locked into our brain's neural pathways.

- Culturally competent counseling involves a process of making known to ourselves the implicit biases padlocked into our brains about people who come from different cultures.

- Clinicians and therapists have become accustomed to a client assessment and therapy process that emphasizes negative client emotions and failures. To rehearse a client's problems in therapy is a process that reinforces neural pathways in the brain that focus on a person's deficits.

- The goal of therapy is to help a person develop neural pathways in the brain that ignite hope, positive relationships, and self-efficacy.

- It is important that clinicians help clients take notice of the good or the positive events that are happening in their lives.

- Clinicians must help clients to consciously and deliberately register positive experiences in the brain so that such events sink into the deepest neural pathways of the brain.

- Therapy should be about learning new positive experiences and using new positive experiences to counterbalance old negative ones. Therapy should be focused on helping clients to develop a strengths mindset.

- Therapists must learn how to construct a culturally responsive counseling environment that conveys an atmosphere that is welcoming to clients. Therapists should ask clients culturally related questions to determine their preference for working with a therapist.

DISCUSSION QUESTIONS

Discussion Question set 1: Cultural Self-Awareness

A. What is your primary culture, ethnicity, or racial category of identification?

B. What is your primary reference group (i.e., ethnic/racial, gender, sexual orientation, or religious group affiliation)?

C. What do you like most and least about your primary cultural reference group?

D. What are the values of your cultural group that have influenced you the most? The least?

E. Describe your earliest experiences with feeling different from others in your environment.

F. What are your feelings about being White or a person of color?

Discussion Question set 2: Culturally Diverse Counseling Strategies

List and discuss four strategies that you will use to overcome your personal challenges in working clinically with culturally diverse individuals.

Discussion Question set 3: Multicultural Training Activities

Create a list of three multicultural training activities (e.g., workshops, conferences, or online courses) you would like to engage in. Discuss how these activities will lead to your acquisition of knowledge, belief, attitude change, and clinical skills needed to work with individuals who are culturally different from you.

Discussion Question set 4: Finding Clients' Strengths

Think about a cultural group that you feel "challenged" to work with in a culturally competent manner. Research that group's cultural strengths and then list five different cultural strengths that members of this cultural group have been found to have. How might you use your awareness and knowledge of this group's cultural strengths to counsel members of this group?

KEY TERMS

Amygdala: A brain structure that is "responsible for detecting and responding to threats" (LeDoux, 2015) and has an influence on emotions, emotional behavior, and motivation.

Client's struggle perception: The exercise of strengths in a client's struggle with adversity; awareness of healthy things clients have done to rise above their problems.

Cultural attachment: The psychological relationship individuals form with their culture.

Deficit mindset: The mindset that focuses on the negative events in a person's life.

Pathology model (medical model): A counseling approach that emphasizes what's wrong with the client and looks for disorders and problems rather than strength.

Strengths audience: The reflection of how we are perceived by the significant people in our lives (our parents, siblings, extended family members, friends, teachers, coworkers, and neighbors).

Strengths dialogues: Stories we tell ourselves about ourselves that recognize our strong characteristics and behaviors.

Strengths mindset: The mindset that focuses on the positive events in a person's life and on a person's strengths.

Strengths perspective in counseling and therapy: The perspective that focuses on the positives and hope in a client's life.

Strengths surveillance: A two-prong process consisting of internalized self-dialogues and audience dialogues.

REFERENCES AND SUGGESTED READING

Ainsworth, M. D. S., Blehar, M. C., Waters, E., & Wall, S. (1978). *Patterns of attachment*. Hillsdale, NJ: Erlbaum.

Allison, K. L., & Rossouw, P. J. (2013, August 27). The therapeutic alliance: Exploring the concept of "safety" from a neuropsychotherapeutic perspective. *The Neuropsychocounselor*.

Retrieved from https://www.neuropsychotherapist.com/the-therapeutic-alliance-exploring-the-concept-of-safety-from-a-neuropsychotherapeutic-perspective/

Ambady, N., & Bharucha, J. (2009). Culture and the brain. *Current Directions in Psychological Science, 18*(6), 342–345.

American Psychiatric Association. (2006). *Diagnostic and statistical manual of mental disorders* (4th ed., text rev.). Washington, DC: Author.

Arakawa, D. (2008). Cultural strengths? *Positive Psychology News.* Retrieved from http://positivepsychologynews.com/news/dana-arakawa/20080314657

Aspinwall, L. G., & Staudinger, U. M. (2003). *A psychology of human strengths: Fundamental questions and future directions for a positive psychology.* Washington, DC: American Psychological Association.

Baumeister, R. F., Bratslavsky, E., Finkenauer, C., & Vohs, K. D. (2001). Bad is stronger than good. *Review of General Psychology, 5*(4), 323–370.

Blanding, M. (2010). The brain in the world. *Tufts Magazine.* Retrieved from www.tufts.edu/alumni/magazine/winter2010/features/the-brain.html

Bowlby, J. (1969). *Attachment and loss: Vol. 1. Attachment.* New York, NY: Basic Books.

Bowlby, J. (1980). *Attachment and loss: Vol. 3: Loss: Sadness and depression.* New York, NY: Basic Books.

Bowlby, J. (1988). *A secure base: Parent–child attachment and healthy human development.* New York, NY: Basic Books.

Brassen, S., Gamer, M., & Buchel, C. (2011). Anterior cingulate activation is related to a positivity bias and emotional stability in successful aging. *Biological Psychiatry, 70*(2), 131–137.

Bretherton, I., & Munholland, K. A. (1999). Internal working models in attachment relationships: A construct revisited. In J. Cassidy & P. R. Shaver (Eds.), *Handbook of attachment* (pp. 89–111). New York, NY: Guilford.

Brickman, P., Coates, D., & Janoff-Bulman, R. (1978). Lottery winner and accident victims: Is happiness *Journal of Personality and Social Psychology, 36,* 917–927.

Buckingham, M., & Clifton, D. O. (2001). *Now, discover your strengths.* New York, NY: Simon & Schuster.

Buckingham, M. (2007). *Go put your strengths to work: 6 Powerful steps to achieve outstanding performance.* New York: Free Press.

Caine, G., Nummela-Cain, R., & Crowell, S. (1999). *Mindshifts: A brain-based process for restructuring schools and renewing education* (2nd ed.). Tucson, AZ: Zephyr Press.

Caplan, P. J. (1995). *They say you're crazy: How the world's most powerful psychiatrists decide who's normal.* Reading, MA: Addison-Wesley.

Carver, C. S., & Scheier, M. F. (1990). Principles of self-regulation: Action and emotion. In E. T. Higgins & R. M. Sorrentino (Eds.), *Handbook of motivation and cognition* (Vol. 2, pp. 3–52). New York, NY: Guilford Press.

Chang, E. C. (2001). Cultural influences on optimism and pessimism: Differences in Western and Eastern conceptualizations of the self. In E. C. Chang (Ed.), *Optimism and pessimism: Theory, research, and practice* (pp. 257–280). Washington, DC: American Psychological Association.

Chiao, J., & Ambady, N. (2007). Cultural neuroscience: Parsing universality and diversity across levels of analysis. In S. Kitayama & D. Cohen (Eds.), *The handbook of cultural psychology* (pp. 237–254). New York, NY: Guilford Press.

Dahlsgaard, K., Peterson, C., & Seligman, M. E. (2005). Shared virtue: The convergence of valued human strengths across culture and history. *Review of General Psychology, 9*(3), 203–213. doi:10.1037/1089-2680.9.3.203.

Danner, D., Snowdon, D., & Friesen, W. (2001). Positive emotions in early life and longevity: Findings from the nun study. *Journal of Personality and Social Psychology, 80,* 804–813.

Davidson, R. J. (2004). Well-being and affective style: Neural substrates and biobehavioral correlates. *Philosophical Transactions of the Royal Society, 359,* 1395–1411.

Deutsch, D. (2010, July/August). Speaking in tunes. *Scientific American Mind, 21*(3), 36–43.

Dweck, C. S. (2006). *Mindset: The new psychology of success.* New York, NY: Random House.

Eriksen, K., & Kress, V. E. (2006). The DSM and the professional therapy identity: Bridging the gap. *Journal of Mental Health Therapy, 28,* 202–217.

Flückiger, C., Wuesten, G., Zinbarg, R. E., & Wampold, B. (2010). *Resource activation: Using clients' own strengths in psychotherapy and counseling.* Cambridge, MA: Hogrefe.

Fossati, P., Hevenor, S. J., Graham, S. J., Grady, C., Keightley, M. L., Craik, F., & Mayberg, H. (2003). In search of the emotional self: An fMRI study using positive and negative emotional words. *American Journal of Psychiatry, 160* (11), 1348–1345.

Fox, N. S., Calkins, S. D., & Bell, M. A. (1994). Neuroplasticity and development in the first two years of life: Evidence from cognitive and socioemotional domains of research. *Development and Psychopathology, 6,* 677–696.

Fredrickson, B. L. (2001). The role of positive emotions in positive psychology: The broaden-and-build theory of positive emotions. *American Psychologist, 56,* 218–226.

Fredrickson, B. L. (2003). The value of positive emotions. *American Scientist, 91,* 330–335.

Fredrickson, B. L. (2009). *Positivity*. New York, NY: Three Rivers Press.

Goldstein, H. (1990). Strength or pathology: Ethical and rhetorical contrasts in approaches to practice. *Families in Society, 71*, 267–275.

Gopnik, A., Meltzoff, A. N., & Kuhl, P. K. (1999). *The scientist in the crib: Minds, brains, and how children learn*. New York, NY: William Morrow.

Gottman, J. (1995). *Why marriages succeed or fail: And how you can make yours last*. New York, NY: Simon & Schuster.

Grossman, K., Grossman, K. E., Spangler, G., Suess, G., & Unzner, L. (1985). Maternal sensitivity and newborns' orientation responses as related to the quality of attachment in northern Germany. In I. Bretherton & E. Waters (Eds.), *Growing points of attachment theory and research. Monographs of the Society for Research in Child Development, 50*(1–2), Serial No. 209.

Han, S., & Northoff, G. (2008). Culture-sensitive neural substrates of human cognition: A transcultural neuroimaging approach. Author Reply. *Nature Reviews Neuroscience, 9*, 646–654.

Hanson, R. (2010). The brain: So what? The benefits and pitfalls of applying neuroscience to psychotherapy. *The Wise Brain Bulletin, 4*(2).

Hanson, R., & Mendius, R. (2009). *Buddha's brain: The practical neuroscience of happiness, love & wisdom*. Oakland, CA: New Harbinger.

Hebb, D. O. (1949). *The organization of behavior*. New York, NY: Wiley.

Hecht, D. (2013). The neural basis of optimism and pessimism. *Experimental Neurobiology, 22*(3), 173–199.

Hong, Y., Fang, Y., Yang, Y., & Phua, D. Y. (2013). Cultural attachment: A new theory and method to understand cross-cultural competence. *Journal of Cross Cultural Psychology, 44*(6), 1024–1044.

Hoshmand, L. T. (Ed.). (2006). *Culture, psychotherapy, and counseling: Critical and integral perspectives*. Thousand Oaks, CA: Sage.

Houts, A. C. (2003). Discovery, invention, and the expansion of the modern *Diagnostic and Statistical Manual of Mental Disorders*. In L. E. Beutler & M. L. Malik (Eds.), *Rethinking the DSM: A psychological perspective* (pp. 17–65). Washington, DC: American Psychological Association.

Ivey, A., Ivey, M., Zalaquett, C., & Quirk, K. (2011). *Essentials of intentional interviewing: Counseling in a multicultural world* (2nd ed.). Belmont, CA: Brooks/Cole.

Ivey, A., & Zalaquett, C. (2010). Neuroscience and counseling: Central issue for social justice leaders. *Journal for Social Action in Counseling and Psychology, 3*(1), 103–116.

Jones-Smith, E. (2011). *Spotlighting the strengths of every single student: Why U.S. schools need a strengths-based approach*. Santa Barbara, CA: ABC-CLIO/Praeger.

Jones-Smith, E. (2014). *Theories of therapy and psychotherapy: An integrative approach*. Thousand Oaks, CA: Sage.

Kandel, E. R. (2005). *Psychiatry, psychoanalysis, and the new biology of mind*. Washington, DC: American Psychiatric Publishing.

Katz, M. (1997). *On playing a poor hand well*. New York, NY: Norton.

Katzowitz, J. (2008, February 29). With an iron will, he finds a way. *The New York Times*. Retrieved from http://www.nytimes.com/2008/02/29/sports/othersports/29wrestler.html?mcubz=0

Keller, H., & Chaudhary, N. (2017). Is the mother essential for attachment? Models of attachment in different cultures. In J. Keller and K.A. Bard (Eds.), *The cultural nature of attachment: Contextualizing relationships and development* (pp. 109–138). Cambridge, MA: MIT Press.

LeDoux, J. E. (2003). *How our brains become who we are*. New York, NY: Penguin.

LeDoux, J. E. (2015, August 10). The amygdala is NOT the brain's fear center [Blog post]. *Psychology Today*. Retrieved from https://www.psychologytoday.com/blog/i-got-mind-tell-you/201508/the-amygdala-is-not-the-brains-fear-center

Lopez, S. J., & Snyder, C. R. (2002). *Handbook of positive psychology*. New York, NY: Oxford.

Luke, C. C. (2016). *Neuroscience for counselors and therapists: Integrating the sciences of mind and brain*. Thousand Oaks, CA: Sage.

Lutz, A. L., Greischar, N., Rawlings, M., Ricard, M., & Davidson, R. (2004). Long-term meditators self-induce high-amplitude gamma synchrony during mental practice. *Proceedings of the National Academy of Sciences, 10111*, 16369–16373.

Lyubomirsky, S. (2008). *The how of happiness*. New York, NY: Penguin Press.

Maguire, E. D., Gadian, I., Johnsrude, C., Good, J., Ashburner, R., Frackowiak, R., & Frith, C. (2000). Navigation-related structural change in the hippocampi of taxi drivers. *Proceedings of the National Academy of Sciences, 97*, 4398–4403.

Magyar-Moe, J. (2009). Therapist's guide to positive psychological interventions. New York: Elsevier.

Magyar-Moe, J. L., Owens, R. L., & Conoley, C. W. (2015). Positive psychological interventions in counseling: What every counseling psychologist should know. *The Counseling Psychologist, 43*(4), 508–557.

Magyar-Moe, J. L., Owens, R. L., & Scheel, M. J. (2015). Applications of positive psychology in counseling psychology: Current status and future directions. *The Counseling Psychologist, 43*(4), 494–507.

Main, M. (1995). Attachment: Overview, with implications for clinical work. In S. Goldberg, R. Muir, & J. Kerr (Eds.), *Attachment theory: Social, developmental and clinical perspectives* (pp. 407–474). Hillsdale, NJ: Analytic Press.

Main, M., Kaplan, N., & Cassidy, J. (1985). Security in infancy, childhood, adulthood: A move to the level of representation. In I. Bretherton & E. Waters (Eds.), *Growing points of attachment theory and research. Monographs for the Society for Research in Child Development*, *50*(2–3), 66–104.

Malik, M. L., & Beutler, L. E. (2002). The emergence of dissatisfaction with the DSM. In L. E. Beutler & M. L. Malik (Eds.), *Rethinking the DSM: A psychological perspective* (pp. 3–15). Washington, DC: American Psychological Association.

Maluccio, A. N. (1981). Competence-oriented social work practice: An ecological practice. In A. N. Maluccio (Ed.), *Promoting competence in clients: A new/old approach to social work practice* (pp. 1–24). New York, NY: Free Press.

Marecek, J. L. (1993). Disappearance, silences and anxious rhetoric: Gender in abnormal psychology textbooks. *Journal of Theoretical and Philosophical Psychology: Journal of Division 24*, 13, 115–123.

McAuliffe, G. (2013). *Culturally alert counseling: A comprehensive introduction*. Thousand Oaks, CA: Sage.

McGoldrick, M., Giordano, J., & Garcia-Preto, N. (2005). *Ethnicity and family therapy*. New York, NY: Guilford Press.

McLeod, S. (2009). Attachment theory [Blog post]. *Simply Psychology*. Retrieved from http://www.simplypsychology.org/attachment.html

Moser, J. S., Hartwig, R., Moran, T. P., Jendrusina, A. A., & Kross, E. (2014). Neural markers of positive reappraisal and their associations with trait reappraisal and worry. *Journal of Abnormal Psychology*, *123*, 91–105.

Nauert, R. (2013). Are you hardwired to see the glass as half-empty? *PsychCentral*. Retrieved from http://psychcentral.com/news/2013/10/11/are-you-hardwired-to-see-the-glass-as-half-empty/60576.html

Newberg, A., & Waldman, M. R. (2013). *Words can change your brain: 12 conversation strategies to build trust, resolve conflict, and increase intimacy*. New York, NY: Plume.

Padesky, C. A., & Mooney, K. A. (2012). Strengths-based cognitive-behavioural therapy: A four-step model to build resilience. *Clinical Psychology & Psychotherapy*, *19*, 283–290.

Quirk, G., Repa, J. S., & LeDoux, J. E. (1995). Fear conditioning enhances short-latency auditory responses of lateral amygdala neurons: Parallel recordings in the freely behaving rat. *Neuron*, *15*, 1029–1039.

Rapp, C. A. (1998). *The strengths model: Case management with people suffering from severe and persistent mental illness*. New York, NY: Oxford University Press.

Rashid, T. (2009). Positive interventions in clinical practice. *Journal of Clinical Psychology*, *65*(5), 461–466.

Rashid, T., & Ostermann, R. F. (2009). Strength-based assessment in clinical practice. *Journal of Clinical Psychology*, *65*(6), 488–498.

Saleebey, D. (1996). The strengths perspective in social work practice: Extensions and cautions. *Social Work*, *41*, 296–305.

Saleebey, D. (2006). *The strengths perspective in social work practices* (4th ed.). Boston, MA: Allyn & Bacon.

Seligman, M. E. (1991). *Learned optimism*. New York, NY: Knopf.

Seligman, M. E. (2002). *Authentic happiness*. New York, NY: Free Press.

Seligman, M. E., Steen, T. A., Park, N., & Peterson, C. (2005). Positive psychology progress: Empirical validation of interventions. *American Psychologist*, *60*(5), 410–421.

Seligman, M. E. P., Walker, E. E., & Rosenhan, D. L. (2001). *Abnormal psychology*. New York, NY: Norton.

Shore, R. (1997). *Rethinking the brain: New insights into early development*. New York, NY: Families and Work Institute.

Siegel, D. (1999). *The developing mind: How relationships and the brain interact to shape who we are*. New York, NY: Guilford Press.

Singh, A. A., Boyd, C. J., & Whitman, J. S. (2010). Counseling competencies with transgender and intersex persons. In J. A. Erickson Cornish, B. A. Schreier, L. I. Nadkarni, L. H. Metzger, & E. R. Rodolfa (Eds.), *Handbook of multicultural counseling competencies* (pp. 415–441). New York, NY: Wiley.

Smith, E. J. (2006). The strengths-based counseling model. *The Counseling Psychologist*, 34,(1), 13–79.

Sperry, L. (2002). DSM-IV: Making it more clinician friendly. *Journal of Individual Psychology*, *58*, 434–441.

Sroufe, L. A. (1996). *Emotional development: The organization of emotional life in the early years*. New York, NY: Cambridge University Press.

Sroufe, L. A., & Siegel, D. (n.d.). *The verdict is in: The case for attachment theory*. Retrieved from http://www/drdansiegel.com/uploads/1271-the-verdict-is-in.pdf

Stanley, D. A., Sokol-Hessner, P., Fareri, D. S., Perino, M. T., Delgado, M. R., Banaji, M. R., & Phelps, E. A. (2012), Race and reputation: Perceived racial group trustworthiness influences the neural correlates of trust decisions. *Philosophical Transactions of the Royal Society of London B Biological Sciences*, *367*(1589), 744–753. doi:10.1098/rstb.2011.0300.

Takahashi, K. (1990). Are the key assumptions of the "Strange Situation" procedure universal? A view from Japanese research. *Human Development*, *33*, 23–30.

Tang, X., Zhang, W., Chen, K., Feng, S., Ji, Y., Shen, J., & Reiman, E. (2006). Arithmetic processing in the brain shaped by cultures. *National Academy of Sciences, 28*, 10775–10780.

Vaish, A., Grossmann, T., & Woodward, A. (2008). Not all emotions are created equal: The negativity bias in social-emotional development. *Psychological Bulletin, 134,* 383–403.

van IJzendoorn, M. H., & Sagi, A. (1999). Cross-cultural patterns of attachment. In J. Cassidy & P. R. Shaver (Eds.), *Handbook of attachment: Theory, research, and clinical applications* (pp. 713–734). New York, NY: Guilford Press.

Walsh, W. B. (Ed.). (2003). *Counseling psychology and optimal human functioning.* Mahwah, NJ: Erlbaum.

Ward, C. C., & Reuter, T. (2011). *Strength-centered counseling: Integrating postmodern approaches and skills with practice.* Thousand Oaks, CA: Sage.

Yang, E., Zald, D., & Blake, R. (2007). Fearful expressions gain preferential access to awareness during continuous flash suppression. *Emotion, 7,* 882–886.

Yip, K. S. (2005). Chinese concepts of mental health: Cultural implications for social work practice. *International Social Work, 48,* 391–407.

Yip, K. S. (2008). Searching the Chinese cultural roots of the strengths perspective. In K. S. Yip (Ed.), *Strengths-based perspective in working with clients with mental illness: A Chinese cultural articulation* (pp. 21–36). Hauppauge, NY: Nova Science.

5

THE STRENGTHS-BASED THERAPY MODEL AND CULTURALLY RESPONSIVE COUNSELING

- *"What would it be like to have not only color vision but culture vision, the ability to see the multiple worlds of others?"* —Bateson

- *"Fall down seven times, get up eight."* —Japanese Proverb

- *"We do. There is no try."* —Yoda, *Star Wars*

CHAPTER OBJECTIVES

- Identify the significance of neurocultural consonance and dissonance.

- Understand the relationship between culture and neuroplasticity.

- List the seven phases of the strengths-based therapy model.

- Describe both the neuroscience and power of belief.

- Use the model of compassionate strengths-based communication in therapy (CLUES).

- Implement strengths-based talk, setting a strengths-based intention and a therapist-based psychotherapy intention.

INTRODUCTION

Chapter 5 examines the strengths-based therapy model as a means for providing culturally appropriate clinical services. Strengths-based therapy is designed to create new positive neural pathways in the brain and to deconstruct negative neural pathways based on individuals' self-limiting thoughts. Five steps are provided that clinicians can use to promote neuroplasticity for clients who want to change their lives.

This chapter also presents a cultural listening framework that clinicians can use with the strengths-based therapy model or with other theoretical models of helping. Clinical skill development regarding opportunity awareness is included as well.

Neurocultural Dynamics: Cultural Consonance and Cultural Dissonance

There are neurocultural dynamics—that is, how the brain has been organized culturally—in feelings of agreement or disagreement with our culture of origin and our acculturated cultural framework. Culture is more than skin deep or a simple difference in worldview; rather, culture is brain based. Each culture establishes brain-based or neurocultural dynamics. These neurocultural dynamics have to do with what the brain perceives as good or bad, desirable or undesirable, ego syntonic or ego dystonic. Culture shapes individuals' brains and perceptual fields and affects the alarm system in the brain—the amygdala. Therapists can violate a person's sense of cultural consonance during therapy, such that the therapy relationship becomes one of cultural dissonance. For instance, in working with Asian American clients, counselors must be sensitive to the cultural implications of silence and limited participation in group activities.

Neurocultural dynamics—that is, how the brain has been organized culturally—affect a person's feelings of cultural consonance or cultural dissonance. Cultural consonance is a model created by Dressler, Mauro, Ribeiro, and Santos (2007) to measure how closely individuals' behaviors are consonant or in agreement with their guiding awareness of their culture. The model is developed from Goodenough's (1996) definition of culture: "that which one needs to know in order to function adequately in a given society" (p. 291). Dressler et al. (2007) define cultural consonance as the extent to which people approximate in their own personal belief or behaviors the cultural patterns from the culture with which they identify or from which they come or were born. In simplest terms, it is people's agreement with the major tenets of their culture. Cultural consonance measures the level at which people consistently behave within a specified cultural framework or model. When people experience cultural consonance, they tend to feel a sense of neuro-equilibrium, rest, or peace. The brain is at rest. There is a sense that one is in harmony with one's culture and with the environment in which one was raised.

Studies have found that cultural consonance is a predictor of one's physical and psychological health (Dressler, 2007; Dressler et al., 2007). Lende and Downey (2012) propose that neurocultural dynamics vary among sufferers, depending on genetic differences and the individual's relationship to his or her cultural group. People who are experiencing

---

TABLE 5.1 ■ Culturally Responsive Clinical Skill Development: Neurocultural Consonance and Dissonance

Important clinical questions a clinician might seek to answer:

- Is the client experiencing cultural consonance or cultural dissonance?

- What is the impact of such *cultural consonance* (agreement with the major tenets of his or her cultural group) or *cultural dissonance* (significant differences or emotional departures from the major tenets of his or her cultural group) on the client's presenting problem?

- How does the client manifest cultural consonance or cultural dissonance?

- How has culture organized the client's perceptual field?

- What body of cultural knowledge provides an important reference point for the client?

- What psychological distress is created by the client's feelings of cultural consonance or cultural dissonance?

- What beliefs, values, or behaviors of the client's culture are creating cultural consonance or cultural dissonance?

- How would the client like to resolve the cultural dissonance he or she is feeling?

Some questions the clinician might ask to deal with a client's feelings of cultural consonance or dissonance:

- "How can you help me to understand what you are feeling about your sense of conflict or disagreement with your culture?"

- "How do you feel that your cultural conflict or differences in your cultural values are creating difficulties in your personal happiness and in your relationships with other people?"

- "On a scale of 1 to 10, what is your comfort level—with 1 being *not comfortable at all* and 10 being *extremely comfortable*—with adopting the cultural values, cultural beliefs, or cultural behaviors of your native culture?"

- "On a scale of 1 to 10, what cultural values, beliefs, or behaviors are you most comfortable with from your native culture?"

- "On a scale of 1 to 10, what cultural values, beliefs, or behaviors are you least comfortable with from your native culture?"

- "What values, beliefs, or behaviors do you feel most comfortable adopting from the culture in which you are currently living?"

- "What values, beliefs, or behaviors do you feel least comfortable adopting from the culture in which you are currently living?"

- "How might I help you to use your individual strengths and cultural strengths to deal positively with cultural consonance or cultural dissonance?"

cultural consonance (agreement with the major tenets of their culture) are less likely to experience depression because cultural consonance precipitates the release of serotonin in the brain. In contrast, **cultural dissonance**—differences or emotional departures from the major tenets of one's cultural group—produces problems for individuals. Cultural dissonance most likely results in the release of stress hormones, such as cortisol, in the brain (Lende & Downey, 2012). Individuals' relationships with their culture are very important in therapy, because such relationships alone may be the source of their emotional distress. Table 5.1 includes a list of questions counselors may consider to better understand their clients' cultural consonance or dissonance.

Clinicians must also understand their own neurocultural dynamics. How have their brains been culturally organized? How are their brains responding to their clients' cultural differences? To what extent are there elements of agreement or disagreement between clinicians' culture and the cultures of their clients?

Cultural conflict takes place in therapy when there is a high level of cultural dissonance between the therapist and the client; conflicts arise due to the differences in values and norms between the therapist's culture and the client's culture. Cultural dissonance in counseling takes place when there are complex combinations of expectations about these cultures. When cultural dissonance and conflicts occur during counseling or therapy, it is important that (1) the individuals describe what they find offensive in each other's behavior, (2) they reach an understanding of each other's cultural perceptions, (3) they seek to find out how the problem would be handled or solved in each other's culture, and (4) they develop conflict solutions.

Strengths-Based Therapy and the Law of Neuroplasticity

A critical part of the revised strengths-based therapy model is built on the law of **neuroplasticity**, which says in simplified language that the brain can change throughout one's life. In this type of therapy, the clinician helps clients to change their brains and minds to focus on their strengths so that they are healthier and happier. Wexler (2011) has provided a more scientific definition of neuroplasticity: "Neuroplasticity is the quality of neural structures to change, primarily through change in the interconnections of the nerve cells that constitute the structure" (p. 1). Neuroplasticity is, then, the ability of the brain to reorganize itself. It is a gift from the process of neurogenesis (creating new brain cells), and it refers to the brain's ability to adapt to change.

Learning takes place when neurons communicate with each other. As the brain learns something new, neurons become clustered together to create a neural pathway. Neural pathways are important because they help move new learning into long-term memory, until such learning becomes automatic or deeply understood. When neurons in the brain fire together during a learning task, the neural pathways are linked and strengthened, thereby leading to the saying among neuroscientists that "neurons that fire together wire together" (Hebb, 1949). A person's attention is a critical factor in the formation of neural networks. Neuroplasticity requires focused attention. The mind takes the shape of whatever it rests upon—even depression if a person ruminates on the negative.

During the 1990s, Dr. Michael Merzenich (2013) performed a number of experiments that demonstrated the importance of attention in the formation of neural networks. In one experiment, he applied a tapping stimulus to the fingers of two groups of monkeys, changing the rhythm of tapping from time to time. For one group of monkeys, responding to a change in the tapping resulted in a reward of a sip of juice. In the other group of monkeys, responding to a change in the tapping did not result in any reward. Six weeks later, Merzenich examined the monkeys' brains and found that the monkeys who had been rewarded had significant changes in their brains because they paid close attention to the stimulus and waited for the rhythm change. There were no such changes in the brains of monkeys who did not pay attention to the tapping, despite the fact that the tapping on their fingers was exactly the same.

Merzenich (2013) concluded that experience coupled with attention leads to physical changes in the structure and future functioning of the nervous system, especially the brain. He observed that people choose and change how their minds will work in real time. If we want to change anything in our lives, we must first focus our attention on what we want to change. Without focused attention, connections in the brain are not made, and memory is not stored. Merzenich concluded that neuroplasticity is facilitated by the following conditions:

1. A person must train the brain to pay attention to or focus on something.

2. The brain's reward system has to be activated.

3. A person must learn *to evaluate positively his or her performance* of the activity on which attention is focused.

4. A person must participate in new learning activities that engage the brain.

One implication of Merzenich's (2013) work on neuroplasticity is that counselors and therapists who work with clients must teach clients how to focus their attention on what they want in their lives instead of what they do not want. When clients make even slight changes as a result of focusing on the positive changes they want in their lives, they must reward themselves in some kind of significant way.

Neuroplasticity and the power of visualization. Research has found that visualizing or think-ing about an activity is sufficient to create the neural connections related to that activity. For instance, Dr. Alvaro Pascual-Leone and his colleagues (1995) conducted experiments in which they demonstrated changes in the brains of individuals based solely on their visualization of completing a simple task. Individuals in one participant group were instructed to mentally visu-alize practicing a finger exercise, while the other group was instructed to physically practice on the piano as fluidly as they could, for two hours on five straight days. The volunteers who played the piano were given a brief transcranial-magnetic-stimulation (TMS) test that permitted the scientists to infer the function of neurons just beneath the TMS coil. After a week of practice, the researchers found that the stretch of motor cortex devoted to these finger movements had expanded. This finding was in agreement with a growing number of studies showing that greater use of a particular muscle causes the brain to devote more cortical real estate to it.

The law of neuroplasticity is important for strengths-based therapists because it provides a scientific basis for understanding how change is produced within clients. Most often when people come to counseling or therapy, the neural networks in their brains are filled with thoughts of failure and hopelessness. Healing the mind requires deconstructing neural pathways that con-tain an abundance of negative self-appraisal and instituting new neural pathways that carry posi-tive information about oneself and others (Hellerstein, 2011). For instance, many of the anxiety and depression disorders have been associated with negative, deficit thinking—that is, thinking that suggests negative expectations for success instead of positive ones (Hellerstein, 2011). If counselors and therapists can get clients to develop positive neural pathways that are lined with thoughts about their strengths, then these mental disorders might be reduced. To help any cli-ent, change must first begin in the brain—with establishing positive, new neural networks that say "I can." The more counselors and therapists can help clients focus on where they want to go instead of where they have been, the more likely they will be hope filled instead of depression filled (Scheel, Davis, & Henderson, 2012; Seligman, 2002).

The connection between strengths-based therapy and neuroplasticity can be conceptualized in terms of four steps (FAPS—focus on the client's strengths, activate the client's brain-based reward system, provide a positive appraisal of the client's therapy performance, and construct strengths-based activities). First, the clinician must help clients to train their brains to focus on their strengths and the positive aspects of their lives. Second, the therapist must learn how to activate the reward system located in their clients' brains. Third, clinicians must evaluate their clients' performance during therapy in a positive manner. Positive appraisal of a client's progress in therapy helps to keep that person working toward a goal. Fourth, the clinician helps the client to construct strengths-based activities that encourage the development of new neural pathways.

The Neuroscience of Belief

Although the power of belief was included in summary form in the introduction to the strengths-based therapy model, this concept is presented in detail for the current revised version of the strengths-based therapy model. Researchers have begun to analyze the power of belief—not just belief in religion, but also belief in other areas, including how we feel about people who are similar to and different from ourselves. According to Jordan Grafman (see Kapogiannis et al., 2009), prior director of cognitive neuroscience at the National Institute of Neurological Disorders and Stroke, the brain is primed for belief in much more than God or a higher power.

Kapogiannis and colleagues (2009) investigated why religion is a universal human feature, and found that a belief in God is deeply embedded in the human brain. Based on several research studies, scientists now believe that there is not just one "God spot" in the brain but rather several areas of the brain that form the biological foundations of religious belief (Kapogiannis et al., 2009).

> The researchers said their findings support the idea that the brain has evolved to be sensitive to any form of belief that improves the chances of survival, which could explain why a belief in God and the supernatural became so widespread in human evolutionary history.

> "Religious belief and behaviour are a hallmark of human life, with no accepted animal equivalent, and found in all cultures," said Professor Jordan Grafman, from the US National Institute of Neurological Disorders and Stroke in Bethesda, near Washington. "Our results are unique in demonstrating that specific components of religious belief are mediated by well-known brain networks, and they support contemporary psychological theories that ground religious belief within evolutionary-adaptive cognitive functions." (Connor, 2009)

The **law of belief** states that whatever is in individuals' belief system becomes their reality (Kapogiannis et al., 2009). Every belief is an interpretation of what has occurred in a person's life. It is not until individuals change their belief system that they can change their reality and their performance. Belief systems become a part of the fulcrum around which a person's self is located (Wu, 2015). When therapists and clients understand the law of belief, clients can be helped to manifest those things in life that they truly want. The first thing that clients have to understand is that they create their beliefs and, therefore, they can choose to create new beliefs. The following summarizes the power of belief (Kapogiannis et al., 2009):

- Belief changes the brain because it creates new neural pathways in the brain.

- Belief motivates people because it provides a reason for doing something.

- Belief gives hope to people, especially belief in the positive (Snyder, 2000; Snyder, Michael, & Cheavins, 1999).

- Belief directs a person's actions (Azar, 2010).

Neuroscience and belief. The brain filters all incoming sensory information against one's beliefs, and whatever doesn't fit in one's subconscious mind is discarded or de-emphasized. The subconscious mind chooses to act on what is in alignment with what one believes. If a person changes what he believes, he "rewires" his brain. The power of beliefs is that they often operate at the subconscious level of awareness. Beliefs reveal how a

---

Cultural Reflections

"I am no longer afraid of storms,
For I am learning how to sail my ship."

—*Louisa May Alcott*

"A ship is safe in harbor, but that's not what ships are for."

—*William Shedd*

person thinks life really is, and they tend to be deeply embedded in one's subconscious mind. A person's subconscious mind creates a life based on one's beliefs.

The Power of Cultural Beliefs and Dying: A Comparison of Chinese Americans and White Americans

The power of cultural beliefs has been associated with dying. Phillips, Ruth, and Wagner (1993) examined the death records of nearly 30,000 Chinese Americans and 412,632 White Americans. The researchers found that Chinese Americans, but not Whites, die significantly earlier (1.3–4.9 years) than average if they have a combination of disease and birth year that Chinese astrology and medicine consider ill fated. The results held for nearly all major causes of death studied. The researchers found that the more strongly the Chinese Americans believed traditional Chinese superstitions about birth year and other factors, the earlier they died. After examining the data, the researchers concluded that the reduction in life expectancy could not be explained by genetic factors, lifestyle choices, or behavior of the individuals; skill of the doctors; or any other variable. Phillips et al. theorized that negative emotions trigger the amygdala in the limbic brain to send out a red alarm that activates the fight-or-flight stress response. When the body's nervous system is in a fight-or-flight state, the body's self-repair mechanisms don't function properly, making the body susceptible to illness and death. When people think negative thoughts about their health, they are potentially poisoning their bodies with stress hormones that deactivate their bodies' natural self-repair mechanisms.

Cultural beliefs influence health behavior a great deal of the time. For instance, Jehovah's Witnesses often refuse blood transfusions because of their religious beliefs, while Seventh-day Adventists have been leaders in the "health food" movement and medical research because their teachings emphasize the idea that one's body is God's temple. Cultural beliefs, including religious ones, affect how and from whom a person will seek help, how health choices are made, and how a client responds to a given therapeutic approach.

Self-Limiting Beliefs

We all harbor self-doubts or self-limiting beliefs, yet the vast majority of a person's doubts are nothing more than memories from the past that are projected onto the present and the future. Self-limiting beliefs are negative thoughts about one's own abilities that make it difficult for clients to function in a healthy manner and to accomplish their goals. For instance, a person might state that he wants to earn a master's degree in finance. When he begins to think about this goal, the following thoughts might get in his way: "I'm not smart enough," "I'll never be able to pass the finance courses," and so forth.

Negative thoughts are often based on strongly held beliefs that are picked up by a person's subconscious mind. Beliefs are the assumptions (positive or negative) a person makes about him- or herself, about others in the world, and about how one expects things to be. When people create a belief, they create their reality. A person's brain adapts to his or her beliefs.

The "evidence" or excuse people present for not making a change in their lives is usually not the reason behind it. The evidence usually consists of recent or past circumstances that appear to substantiate their self-limiting belief. Some **self-limiting beliefs** include the following:

- I am unlovable.

- I am hopeless.

- I don't matter.

- I have no control over what is happening to me.

- I can't do this.

- I am a bad person.

- Something bad will happen if I pursue my dreams.

- The world is a dangerous place.

- People are out to get me.

- Something or someone must change before I will be okay.

- I am not good enough.

- No one understands me.

- Nothing ever works out for me.

- You have to strike people before they harm you.

Negative beliefs create fear because they tell people that they can't accomplish something, such as make a desired change in their lives. Most people don't recognize the negative beliefs that might be holding them back. It is important in counseling and therapy that clinicians help clients to clear the negative thinking blocks that prevent them from enjoying life. One way in which a counselor or therapist might assist clients in recognizing negative thoughts and blocks is to ask them to think of some of the goals they want to achieve or some of the changes they desire to make. Clients are then instructed to track the thoughts that appear. If they hear anything from themselves that says maybe they should give up, they are controlled by negative thoughts and beliefs. Examples of negative thoughts include "It's too difficult," "I don't know how to do it," "I've tried everything," "Yeah but . . .," and "What's the point?"

Self-limiting beliefs create anxiety.

For instance, a person might have the belief that "there is something basically wrong with me" or that "life is difficult." Self-limiting beliefs create anxiety or stress within individuals' emotional system and their bodies. People tend to use two basic ways of dealing with emotional stress or anxiety. The first way is to use distractions, such as alcohol, food, drugs, watching television, or listening to loud music, to block out their current reality.

The second way people tend to deal with anxiety is by developing **survival strategies**, unproductive mental "crutches" that help them deal with emotional stress or anxiety. For instance, Alicia is an aspiring actress who is quite beautiful. Her survival strategy is "Being beautiful makes me desirable." Recently, Alicia has noticed wrinkles forming around her smile and eyes because she is now over the age of 40. She is gradually losing her beauty—the one thing she believes makes her acceptable and desirable. People who live by survival strategies instead of their choices find that the need to fulfill the terms of their survival strategy determines their lives.

People become stuck in the life stories that define them. Our stories are about the past. Worry and fear tend to inhabit life stories in which people feel stuck.

Negative thinking causes pain.

Negative thinking can be compared to staring at a closed door. People have to learn how to find the silver lining in the situation. They need to focus on the hidden and visible opportunities. To get over their pain, they need to focus on the open door. To generate positive energy out of a negative situation, one has to say, "Something great is going to come out of this situation."

Moreover, people tend to view themselves either as creators of their reality or as victims of circumstances. People who view themselves as victims are inclined to become permanently stuck in their victimhood and self-limiting beliefs (Azar, 2010). Strengths-based therapy maintains that any belief a client holds is just an interpretation of something or someone. The therapist asks a client, "Is this belief getting you what you want? Is it moving you away from or toward what you

TABLE 5.2 ■ Clinical Intervention Skill: Strengths-Based Therapy and Self-Limiting Beliefs
Step 1. Identify the self-limiting belief.
Step 2. Acknowledge that you created the belief and that the belief has no power over you, except that which you give it.
Step 3. Understand the technique you are using to deal with the self-limiting belief, either distraction, (e.g., drugs, food, watching TV, alcohol, listening to loud music) or survival (e.g., beauty, what makes one feel worthwhile) (may be personalized).
Step 4. Release (surrender) the self-limiting belief.
Step 5. Reprogram or substitute a new, self-empowering belief.

desire?" When clients understand that their self-limiting beliefs are just their own interpretations rather than truth or facts, they assume some power and control over their beliefs. They learn that a belief has no power or control over them, except what they give to it. As clients learn that they create their beliefs, they also realize that they can create new beliefs to replace the old ones. The hardest step in this process involves releasing the old belief systems so that clients can reprogram themselves with new, empowering beliefs (Azar, 2010).

After letting go of self-limiting beliefs, a person's subconscious mind may be given new, positive beliefs for living. To get at a client's self-limiting beliefs, a counselor or therapist might ask, "What's stopping you from achieving your goals? Or, perhaps even more honestly, what excuses are you giving yourself to continue with the same behavior you say that you want to change? What would happen if you could replace the excuses you give yourself about your current situation?" Sometimes clients are in therapy for years because the treatment has never focused on finding and releasing negative, dysfunctional, or self-limiting beliefs. Strengths-based therapy seeks to find, release, and replace self-limiting beliefs with those that are empowering and self-fulfilling to clients. Table 5.2 provides steps for working through this process.

Another approach clinicians can use to challenge a client's self-limiting beliefs is what has been termed the four-*R* process:

- **R1** = **Recognize** the negative thoughts and thought patterns that a client has.

- **R2** = **Reframe** the negative thoughts and memories.

- **R3** = **Release** the emotions underlying the negative thoughts and emotions; override the fear circuits that sustain the negative thoughts.

- **R4** = **Retrain** the brain with positive thoughts and affirmations and create an action plan to move toward a new, positive goal.

THE REVISED STRENGTHS-BASED THERAPY MODEL

New Concepts and Clinical Strategies

The strengths approach operates at two basic levels: (1) the micro level, which focuses primarily on the strengths of individuals; and (2) the macro level, which deals with the strengths of institutions, organizations, groups, and even nations. At the individual level, strengths begin in the brain, and then they proceed to be conceptualized in the mind, as part of the self-construal of basic competencies. As pointed out in Chapters 2 and 3, strengths are well-traveled pathways in the brain that are formed by one's genetics and relationships (including attachment relationships). Everything we do or think creates connections within the network of our brains, and the more we repeat something, the stronger the connections get. These brain connections gradually evolve into well-traveled neural pathways.

Strengths are more than what we do well. What we do well is an outward manifestation or a practical application of our strength. Our strengths are part of who we are; they provide a source of self-identification, and they give us a sense of internal power. Most people, however, do not focus on their strengths; instead, they emphasize correcting their weaknesses.

Basic Assumptions of Strengths-Based Therapy

Strengths-based therapy has universal appeal because all cultures have developed strengths that may be used to deal with life challenges. The next section outlines some basic assumptions of strengths-based therapy. These assumptions are contained in Table 5.3.

The Role of the Client in Strengths-Based Therapy

Clients are the heroes of their own lives. They decide if they will or will not embark on their own yellow brick road. The strengths-based approach to therapy endorses a Client Bill of Rights, which the therapist gives to the client during the process of arranging for treatment (see Table 5.4).

TABLE 5.3 ■ Basic Assumptions of Strengths-Based Therapy
• Each person's greatest room for growth is in the area of his or her strength or strength zones.
• Even when people have clear vulnerabilities, they also have strengths, which are revealed in their passions.
• Psychological treatment is about client competence building, as well as helping clients to start their own healing process.
• Psychotherapy should be about the installation of hope (Snyder et al., 2000).
• Practicing from a strengths perspective means believing that the strengths and resources necessary to resolve a difficult situation reside within the client and his or her ability to mobilize the environment on his or her behalf.
• Strengths-based therapy focuses on what the client is doing about the problem rather than on the problem itself—so that the client does not become mired down in the problem itself.
• Strengths-based therapy addresses a client's problems by focusing on his or her strengths, skills, interests, and support systems, which in turn provide a foundation for the client to resolve presenting issues.
• Strengths-based therapy focuses on how people survive the problems of life and what resources they can draw on to build their resilience.
• Strengths-based therapy emphasizes the protective factors that promote a positive resolution of clients' presenting issues.
• Strengths-based therapists do not deny that clients may have serious symptoms and problems. They understand that suffering, problems, and mental distress do exist for some clients, but these do not form the entire story of clients' lives.
• Whereas traditional therapy often emphasizes getting to the root of problems and spends a great deal of time examining the past, strengths-based therapy has more of an emphasis on arriving at desired present or future—six months from now.
• The therapist does not seek to engage the client into repeated recounting of the narrative of his or her suffering.
• Strengths-based therapy is about promoting clients' self-efficacy, helping them to believe in their own strengths, and taking control of the controls implementing the goals they want to achieve in their preferred life.
• Clients are encouraged to attribute their survival and recovery to their own strengths and capabilities, thereby enhancing their sense of self-efficacy.

TABLE 5.4 ■ Client Bill of Rights for Treatment
• I have a right to be treated with respect.
• I have a right to privacy and confidentiality.
• I have a right to be viewed as a person capable of changing, growing, and becoming positively connected to my community.
• I have a right to be considered a collaborative partner in the therapy process.
• I have a right to ask for services that build upon my strengths and teach me how to manage my weaknesses.
• I have a right to have my culture and ethnicity viewed as a strength and to request services that honor, respect, and take into consideration my beliefs.
• I have a right to ask that all clinical assessment of me include my strengths in addition to my needs, limitations, and challenges.
• I have a right to set my own treatment goals rather than to have them set for me.
• I have a right to learn from my past mistakes and not to be viewed only in terms of such mistakes.
• I have a right to have messages of hope infused throughout my therapy process.
• I have a right to have a therapist who knows how to help me build upon my competencies and strengths.

Source: Elsie Jones-Smith, 2014.

The Role of the Strengths-Based Therapist

The therapist and the client engage in therapeutic conversations that focus on the client's competencies and strengths. The therapist capitalizes on clients' strengths as a therapeutic intervention. When strengths become the focus, people are inclined to have higher levels of motivation, greater engagement, greater personal or life satisfaction, higher levels of productivity and performance, and deeper understanding of themselves and others (Clifton, Anderson, & González-Molina, 2016; McQuaide & Ehrenreich, 1997). Table 5.5 compares the roles of the client and therapist in traditional therapy and in strengths-based therapy.

TABLE 5.5 ■ Comparison of the Roles of the Client and Therapist	
Therapist as Expert	**Therapist and Client as Collaborators**
Therapist conceptualizes in terms of client problems and mental illness	Therapist and client think in terms of client solutions and mental health being relative rather than an absolute state of perfection
Therapist uses technical jargon of his or her profession	Therapist uses client's own language and metaphors
Therapist pathologizes the client—focuses on what is wrong with the client	Therapist avoids pathologizing the client—focuses on what is right about the client and places client's behavior along a continuum of mental health functioning
Therapist unilaterally sets goals for therapy	Therapist and client construct goals conjointly as collaborators
Therapist focuses on ridding client of pathology	Therapy focuses on client's strengths, survival and coping skills, and helping client to live his or her desired life, as well as on exceptions to problem state
Therapist defines the problem to be worked	Therapist accepts client's definition of the presenting problem

The Strengths-Based Therapy Model: Overview of Phases

The strengths-based therapy model is an integrative approach for treating people with mental health and addiction issues. It draws upon research and therapy interventions from the strengths-based literature, including research on phases of change and motivational enhancement, need theory, logotherapy, and the cognitive behavioral school of thought. The revised strengths-based therapy model (Jones-Smith, 2016). now has seven phases of therapy. SWOB (strengths, weaknesses, opportunities, and barriers) analysis in Phase 2 has allowed for the elimination of the previous Phase 3, which examined internal and external client barriers (see Figure 5.1).

The entire strengths-based therapy protocol involves the service provider's conceptualizing the therapeutic relationship in terms of the following areas: (1) the client's desired problem or issue resolution, (2) the client's strengths (internal and external) to be used in the therapy process, (3) the therapist's ways to ask questions of the client, (4) the success factors on which the therapist and client can build, (5) the barriers to the client's success (internal and external), (6) the needs the client must address to bring about the desired reduction or elimination of the presenting issue, and (7) the actual solutions that the client will implement. The client's needs category identifies those things that will be needed for reduction or elimination of the presenting problem, building a healthy new identity, or building healthy new connections with the family and the community (Scheel et al., 2012). For instance, one client's need was to find a permanent place to live; another client had financial needs that had to be met prior to issue resolution (Conoley & Conoley, 2008).

A major theme of strengths-based therapy is that service providers help clients not only to identify and build their strengths but also to manage their weaknesses. The failure of clients to use their strengths appropriately and to manage their weaknesses has resulted in their unrealized potential. During therapy, clients look inside themselves to identify their strongest areas. They are assisted in learning how to manage their weaknesses so that they do not sabotage their strengths. Another important theme is that to remain healthy, a person must have a goal—some purpose in life that he or she can respect and be proud to work toward. Hope, whether it is in the future or in a higher power, is an essential ingredient of strengths-based treatment. Finally, therapists engage in strengths building, which involves finding a meaningful way of helping clients to use a strength that brings them happiness.

FIGURE 5.1 ■ Phases of the Strengths-Based Therapy Model

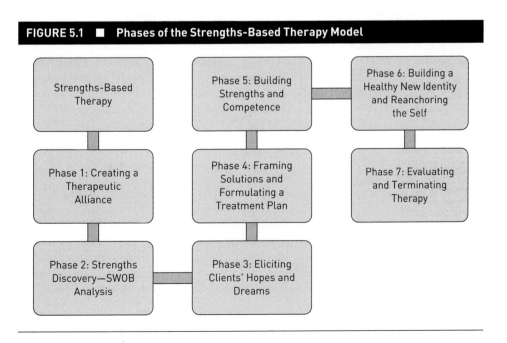

The strengths-based therapy model has four additional themes: (1) "Let Go," (2) "Let In," (3) "Let Be," and (4) "Move Forward." These themes suggest movement in therapy, and they are discussed briefly in the following sections. Although I have specified phases during which these themes may become more predominant, they occur throughout therapy in an ebb-and-flow fashion rather than in a linear manner. Most people have these themes in their lives, and their responses to them may make all the difference regarding whether or not they are living a fulfilled and meaningful life.

Acknowledge the client's pain.

Before engaging in the four therapeutic themes described below, it is important for the client to acknowledge that the therapist understands the client's pain. Clients come to therapy feeling intensely the pain in their lives. If a therapist jumps too quickly to strengths, some clients may feel that they are not being heard or their pain is unacknowledged. With this caveat in mind, let us examine the four major themes in strengths-based therapy.

"Let Go." The theme of "Let Go" is most evident in Phases 1 through 3 of the strengths-based therapy model. All too often in therapy, clients and therapists rehearse the past. They go over each detail of the client's suffering. This is what strengths-based therapy calls "rehearsing the pain." When clients talk about someone who has hurt them in the past, that offense is stirred up, and they start thinking about what happened. Yet, in that moment, both the therapist and the client have a choice to make. Instead of rehearsing the pain of past disappointments, they can express forgiveness for the person and let the hurt go. The therapist helps the client to understand that forgiveness and letting go of bitterness is for their own benefit rather than that of the perpetrator of pain. The therapist helps clients to see that bad memories, bad relationships, resentment, and anger need to be released—dumped into the trash can along with yesterday's garbage. Thinking about negative events brings up pain, makes clients feel sad, and blocks their forward movement.

Let go and surrender.

The "Let Go" phase of strengths-based therapy utilizes the surrender process. One function of surrender is that it tends to neutralize client resistance regarding a presenting problem. Resistance is staring at a closed door and doing nothing about a situation. The client surrenders to what is going on in his or her life that is causing a great deal of pain. In surrendering, the client accepts the life situation without the negative judgment because it is the negative judgment about the situation that causes distress and pain. A number of techniques can be used to surrender, ranging from simple statements such as "I surrender my worry and concern about this issue," "I put the matter in the hands of the universe [or in the hands of a higher power]," or "I surrender and let go of all negative energies about this issue." The therapist assists the client in identifying what needs to be surrendered and helps the client to challenge the triggering belief ("I'm not good enough; life is too hard").

Let go of fear.

Fears often bring people to therapy, especially gnawing unconscious fears. During the "Let Go" phase of therapy, the clinician encourages clients to deal with their fears about the situation that brought them to therapy. Fear is the brain's response to real or imagined threat. When fear circuits in the brain light up, a person's motivation is usually reduced. The client's unconscious fears are the most difficult to deal with; yet, they are often the silent killers of one's dreams. Fear paralyzes clients' actions. As noted earlier in this chapter (p. 138), practitioners use the four-*R* process: recognize the fear, reframe it, release the emotion dealing with the fear, and retrain the brain to deal with fear.

Let go of self-limiting beliefs.

The therapist might help the client to let go of self-limiting beliefs. The client asks, "Is this belief serving me or hurting me? Am I aware when this self-limiting belief shows up? What positive belief can I use to replace this self-limiting belief?"

According to Hanson and Mendius (2009), pain is inevitable, but suffering is a choice that we make. Clients suffer when they continually rehearse their pain—the experiences that hurt them and the people that hurt them. On the other hand, clients weaken their pain and suffering when service providers focus on their strengths.

The therapist can use guided imagery to acknowledge the pain and let it go. Clients are asked not to reexperience the pain but rather to notice its presence—what it feels like and where it is located in the body. Using body relaxation techniques, the therapist helps the client with letting go of the pain and the suffering. The pain travels from the place in the client's body where it hurts the most, outward to the toes. The client repeats, "I cannot stop all pain in my life any more than I can stop the rain. But I choose not to respond with the emotional response of suffering to the rain in my life. I acknowledge the rain and understand that it may be needed to bring the flowers in my life."

> **Cultural Reflections**
>
> *Thinking about your own life, what would you like to let in?*
>
> *What's keeping you from letting it in?*
>
> *Is it easier to think about what you want to get out of or let into your life?*

"Let In." The therapist asks the client, "What do you want to let in your life? Who or what is shutting the door on what you desire for yourself in life? What do you need to do to let your desired state or thing into your life? How can you open the door?" Clients can come up with things they can do to open the door and let in the opportunities they want. When therapist and client agree on what the client will do to let in realization of goals, and when the client is ready to take the necessary action, the client gets up and symbolically opens the door of the therapist's office. For some clients, letting in may be as simple as exercising three times a week. The client actively works to let in the positive in his or her life. To let in desires, the client engages in positive affirmations. The therapist emphasizes "letting in" during Phases 2 through 3 of the strengths-based therapy model (see Figure 5.1), although the therapeutic process of letting in may occur at any point during therapy.

"Let Be." This concept refers to the client's desire to be in harmony with him- or herself and the rest of the world—the good and the bad. The client struggles to reach a balanced state. One might say, "I will focus on my musical strengths," or "I will learn to manage my weight problem." Clients strive not only for internal balance but also for balance in their relationships with those they love—partner, mate, daughter, son, mother, father, brother, sister, work colleague, and so on. Clients learn to release their demand that other people be the way that they want them to be. For instance, instead of arguing about a partner's not doing the dishes, the person decides to take another step to keep harmony in the home.

> **Cultural Reflections**
>
> *If you could wave a magic wand to give you peace and harmony in your life, with whom would you like to establish a harmonious relationship?*
>
> *What's stopping you from establishing a harmonious relationship with this person?*
>
> *Of these three forces—power, control, and harmony—which force seems to characterize most of your relationships with others?*

Our need to control others oftentimes brings about disharmony in our lives. Strengths-based therapy seeks to help clients restore harmony in their lives and in their relationships with others. Yip (2008) has pointed out that one strength of Chinese culture is that the people seek harmony within their families, their relationships with others, and the government. Harmony is a prized cultural value and strength. Morita therapy, which is Japanese in origin, emphasizes discovering a new self and moving forward with life instead of searching for the reasons for suffering, anxieties, or fears (Jones-Smith, 2011). Strengths-based therapy does not try to uncover all the reasons for a person's challenging situation. Instead, it focuses on figuring out what needs to be done to change the situation. Strengths-based therapy maintains that when individuals establish harmonious relationships with themselves, others, and their environment, they have adaptive mental health.

"Move Forward." Life does not move backward, nor does it stand still. Life is energy. It always moves forward. Too much of traditional therapy has involved "digging among the dry bones of the past" with far too little benefit for the client. Strengths-based therapy places a major emphasis on moving forward in Phases 6 through 7. A backward movement in therapy is temporary and very brief—usually to help a client reach an understanding of how past decisions have impacted his or her life. Moving forward may entail supporting a client in constructing new goals and a new plan for living—typically called a treatment plan (see Phase 4), helping a client to develop new strengths-based competencies (Phase 6), or assisting one in developing a healthy new identity (Phases 6 and 7).

Building a therapeutic alliance is based on incorporating into treatment certain practice principles, as follows: (1) Respect clients as people who have worth as human beings, regardless of their present life circumstances; (2) establish a relationship with the person, not the problem, be it a mental disorder or drug addiction; and (3) learn what the client wants.

STRENGTHS-BASED THERAPY TECHNIQUES

Culturally Responsive Strengths-Based Therapist Communication

Strengths-based therapy has been revised to include a specific framework called therapeutic communication with clients. Compassionate therapeutic communication is adapted from Newberg and Waldman's (2012) 12 strategies for effective communication. When a therapist communicates with a client, a process of neural resonance should take place. Neural resonance is the process of mirroring the neural activity in another person's brain. The more therapists can mirror the neural activity in a client's brain, the better able they will be to establish a therapeutic alliance. If a therapist closely observes a client's face, gestures, and tone of voice, the therapist's brain will begin to align with the client's brain (Newberg & Waldman, 2012).

Neural resonance takes place when a therapist listens to and observes a client as deeply and fully as possible. Brain scan research has revealed that the more deeply we listen, the more our brain will mirror the activity in the client's brain. Compassionate therapeutic communication is designed to stimulate cooperation between the therapist and the client as they converse during the therapy hour. As Newberg and Waldman (2012) have stated,

> effective communication depends upon neural resonance. As researchers at Princeton University demonstrated in an fMRI brain-scan experiment, neural coupling vanishes when participants communicate poorly . . . . The researchers also discovered that good listeners—the ones who paid the closest attention to what was being said—could actually anticipate what the speaker was going to say the moment before they said it. (p. 82)

Compassionate Strengths-Based Communication in Therapy

Strengths-based therapy uses *CLUES* to convey the type of compassionate communication that a therapist should use during the therapy hour. The acronym is described below.

C = **Cultivate inner silence** when working with clients so that the "noise" from the therapist's own life is reduced. Most people have positive and negative inner speech. The therapist calms his or her inner speech to be able to give the fullest attention and to be present with the client during therapy. If you are thinking about what happened at breakfast this morning with your wife and kids or about the stock market, you have inner chatter rather than inner silence.

L = Listen deeply for the client's story, especially for the client's emotions, feelings, and cultural messages. Therapists listen deeply when they observe a client's nonverbal cues and when they do not interrupt the client. Listening deeply promotes mirror neurons. As mentioned previously in this chapter, the more deeply we listen, the more our brain will mirror the activity in the other person's brain. Mirror neurons allow us to understand another person. Listening deeply means not interrupting your client; it means temporarily putting yourself in your client's shoes; it means hearing his or her pain, the silent tears and cries.

U = Use positive words in talking with clients. Therapists who model using positive words when they talk with clients will find that the clients begin to observe and reflect their therapists' behavior. Remember the three-to-one ratio of Fredrickson's (2009) "broaden and build theory": If a therapist expresses fewer than three positive thoughts or behaviors for every negative one, the therapeutic relationship is likely to fail. If a therapist wants the relationship with a client to succeed, he or she should generate at least three positive messages for every negative statement. Find something positive to say to your clients, even if it's just "I really respect the fact that you're seeking help." Or, "I see hope in your situation. I believe that together we are going to find a way out of what must feel overwhelming right now. My father used to say that when two shoulders are put together to lift a problem, it becomes lighter. Let's put our shoulders together."

E = Express appreciation of client as a person, as well as show respect for the client's culture. The therapist expresses appreciation for the client's efforts and struggles with challenges. The appreciation must be genuine. Therapy should begin and end with the therapist's statements of client appreciation. For instance, the therapist might ask him- or herself, "What do I really value about this person? Which attribute about my client do I value the most?"

S = Speak warmly, slowly, and briefly during therapy. The therapist speaks warmly and sincerely to convey compassion and sensitivity to the client and his or her situation. Using a warm voice will increase the healing power of therapeutic treatment. A strengths-based therapist uses a warm, friendly voice; allows a few seconds of thoughtful silence; and then communicates confidence and positive expectation to the client. When a therapist speaks slowly, it increases a listener's ability to understand what is being said. A slow voice has a calming effect on a client, who may be experiencing anxious feelings. Whenever possible, the therapist should speak briefly—that is, limit his or her speaking to 30 seconds. If a therapist is trying to communicate a critical piece of information to a client, he or she should break down the information into smaller segments—a sentence or two—and then wait for the client to respond. Conscious minds can only retain 30 seconds or so of information.

Creating a Culturally Responsive Therapeutic Alliance

The strengths-based therapist gives the client a copy of the Client Bill of Rights (Table 5.4) to establish clearly that the client is respected as a human being, regardless of his or her presenting issues. The therapist asks the client to read over the Client Bill of Rights. If the client has known difficulty reading, then the therapist summarizes the content of this document. The therapist elicits the client's presenting problem and strengths story.

A culturally responsive therapy environment is one in which the therapist demonstrates an understanding and appreciation of a client's cultural background. It means acknowledging that every culture has specific values that can be used in treatment, such as the support of extended families and of religious or spiritual communities. As a result of appreciating a client's culture, a therapist can tap into the most effective treatment strategies—those based on the personal and cultural strengths of each individual (Rashid, 2009).

In a culturally responsive therapy environment, therapists broach cultural differences with the client during the initial interview. The therapist listens for any client statements about his or her culture. When therapists have a different dominant language from their clients, they may either offer to obtain a translator (if this is feasible) or refer the client to another therapist. Therapists should have a working knowledge of the cultural background of their clients, including their preferred communication styles, artifacts, and values.

Building Trust: Ways to Enhance the Therapeutic Alliance

What does the strengths-based therapist do to enhance a collaborative therapeutic alliance? First, the therapist must be able to create a sense of trust with the client. Trust suggests that the client will be able to rely and depend on the therapist; there is a belief that the therapist is competent and trustworthy. Trust is built in a therapeutic relationship when clients believe that their therapist (1) will be helpful and is capable of helping them resolve the issues that brought them to therapy, (2) will keep them safe from blame and hurtful comments, and (3) will provide them with positive, hopeful feelings that things will work out okay for them. In addition, the therapist must show that he or she believes in the client. The therapist takes a deep interest in the client's view of his or her situation. The therapist should never let a client leave his or her office demoralized after telling his or her story.

To develop a sense of client safety within the first few therapy sessions, the therapist should:

- *Provide early evidence of being helpful*. In the very first session, the therapist demonstrates to clients a sample of what they will do in therapy that will lead to an improvement of the client's presenting problem. For instance, the therapist might be able to show how improved communication skills might be helpful or how clients might view their situation in a different or new, nonthreatening manner. In individual therapy, clients sense early on if their therapist is judgmental or helpful.

- *Quickly generate a sense of safety for the client during therapy*. The therapist must avoid triggering a sense of real or imagined threats. A simple device to calm down a person's agitated sense of fight or flight is to first compliment him or her on making the decision to come to therapy. For example, "I want to compliment you on making a decision to obtain counseling. That's a wise decision because you are saying that you're tired of the way things have been in your life and you're ready to make a positive change." After waiting for a response from the client or asking for a response to the foregoing statement, the clinician continues by reassuring the client that he or she has come to the right place: "I'm here to help you make that change, and I am confident that by working together, we can address to your satisfaction the issues that brought you to counseling. I have helped a number of people using a strengths-based approach. Right now, I am going to ask you to take a few deep breaths just so that you can feel comfortable in our session." The client takes a few deep breaths, or the clinician can ask the client in what part of the body he or she is feeling stress. In that case, the clinician would ask the client to engage in basic muscle relaxation—that is, tensing the agitated body parts (neck, back, and stomach) and then releasing the tension. Whenever a client receives any type of positive relief from stress (however small the relief is), he or she is inclined to believe, "Hey, maybe this counselor can help me. I am feeling better already."

- ***Create a sense of safety and trust*** by shifting the client's language from worry to optimism. For instance, the therapist might say, "Tell me something good that happened to you today—however small that something might be. It can be something as simple as 'My coffee was good this morning' or 'I didn't encounter a whole lot of traffic on my way here.'" Optimism can also be created by the therapist talking about his or her skills and qualifications, the percentage of people helped by the therapist's approach to therapy, and so forth.

- ***Introduce a basic concept from strengths-based therapy***, which is that therapy focuses on what we want to create in our lives, not on what we *don't* want to happen. For instance, a woman might be threatened by the loss of her children to Child Protective Services. Instead of having therapy overshadowed by the threat of Child Protective Services, the therapist emphasizes what the woman wants—to keep her children, to raise her children in a responsible manner. The human tendency is to try to fix what is not working or to focus on what we don't want to happen—not so with strengths-based therapy. What is it that you want to happen? How would you like to raise your children so that they would grow up well taken care of? "Let's focus on the positive parenting skills that you do have and see where we can build on these skills to ensure that your children are raised in a healthy way."

- ***Assist clients to focus on the present and a future*** desired state rather than on the past. The therapist reorients clients from what they cannot change (the past) and what has not been working for them (the complaint or presenting problem) to what they can change (the present and the future) and what they would prefer to take place (their goal or desired life direction).

- ***Never allow a client to leave a therapy session without some sort of reassurance or compliment on their work in therapy***. "I want to compliment you on your work during therapy today. You showed great insights regarding some of the challenges you are facing." A client should not leave therapy wondering what the therapist thinks about him or her, now that the dark secret has been revealed or now that some self-disclosure has been made in therapy.

Additional strategies for establishing a relationship with a client can be found in Table 5.6.

Strengths Discovery: Using SWOB Analysis

Strengths-based therapy has been revised to include SWOB analysis, which is a way of analyzing a client's strengths, weaknesses, opportunities, and barriers. SWOB is based on the

TABLE 5.6 ■ Culturally Responsive Clinical Skill Development: Questions to Establish a Relationship With a Client
• Where would you like to begin in telling me your story?
• In your opinion, what is most important for me to know about you and the situation that brought you here?
• If you had to state one or two things that you want to be sure that we talk about, what would those things be?
• From your perspective, how might I best help you to reach your goals or to make the changes that you mentioned in telling your story?
• I've listened carefully to your story, but I did not hear much about your strengths. Tell me something good about you, something that you do well that I might not know about.
• I really admire your courage in coming to therapy—especially your honesty and openness in sharing your story with me.
• You deserve a lot of credit for _____.

TABLE 5.7 ■ SWOB Analysis	
STRENGTHS Strengths known to the client (what he or she does well, purpose in life) Strengths unknown to client (identified by therapist)	**WEAKNESSES** Weaknesses known to client (avoidance of issues) Weaknesses unknown to client (identified by therapist)
OPPORTUNITIES Opportunities hidden in the problem Opportunities readily apparent to client Hidden benefits of adversity	**BARRIERS** Internal barriers (those residing in the client) External barriers (social injustice, prejudice, cultural differences)

SWOT analysis. SWOT is an acronym for strengths, weaknesses, opportunities, and threats that a business or corporation might take into consideration when making a decision or forging a different course of action. **SWOT analysis** is used to conduct an audit and analysis of the overall strategic position of the business and its environment. Its primary purpose is to identify the strategies that will create a business model that will best align an organization's resources and capabilities to the requirements of the environment. SWOB analysis declines to use the word *threat* because it has the tendency to set off a fight-or-flight response within individuals. In place of *T* for *threats* in SWOT analysis, SWOB analysis uses *B* for *barriers*, which also may be either internal or external or both (see Table 5.7).

SWOB and Strengths Analysis

SWOB analysis focuses on the four elements of the acronym: strengths, weaknesses, opportunities, and barriers (Humphrey, 2005). The purpose of performing a SWOB analysis is to reveal the positive forces in a client's life and the potential problems that need to be addressed. A SWOB analysis can be used to explore a client's new efforts to solve a particular problem. It can help a client identify opportunities for success within the context of barriers to success. It can be used to determine where change is possible, especially if the client is at a turning point in life (see Figure 5.2).

Strengths analysis. The first part of SWOB analysis involves an analysis of the client's strengths. In Figure 5.2, strengths may be those known and unknown to the client. Quite often it is the therapist who helps the client detect or understand hidden strengths. In SWOB analysis, the client's strengths are used to take advantage of the opportunities that the problem presents. Although a strengths-based assessment takes place throughout the therapy relationship, it is accentuated in the first three sessions.

Strengths-based therapy maintains that early problems should not define a person's total identity (Bretton, 1993; Goldstein, 1990; Rapp, 1998). A person's identity is primarily described in terms of his or her talents and assets. Strengths-based therapy shifts focus from problems to assets for overcoming adverse circumstances. Finding a client's strengths may not be easy because we may not be seeking what is working and because strengths may be obscured by symptoms or oppressive circumstances (Bretton, 1993). The clinician helps the client uncover strengths at the biological, psychological, social, cultural, environmental, economic, material, and political levels (DeJong & Miller, 1995). Biological strengths can include rest, nutrition, and compliance with medication, health status, exercise, and adequate leisure time.

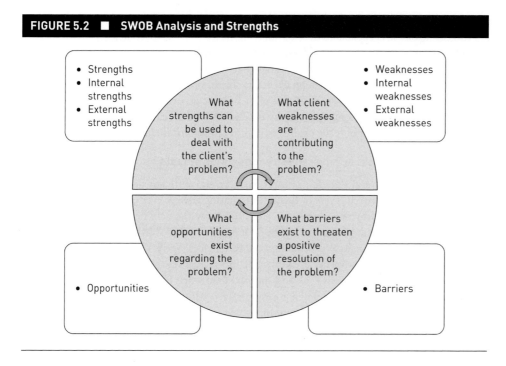

FIGURE 5.2 ■ SWOB Analysis and Strengths

Psychological strengths might be subdivided into such categories as cognitive strengths (e.g., intelligence, problem-solving abilities, and knowledge), emotional strengths (e.g., self-esteem, stable mood, optimism, good coping skills, self-reliance, and self-discipline), social strengths (e.g., belonging and support, friends, family, and mentors), cultural strengths (e.g., beliefs, values, and traditions), economic strengths (e.g., being employed, having sufficient money, and having adequate housing), and political strengths (e.g., equal opportunity and having a voice in decisions). The therapist helps identify client strengths by asking clients to describe what positives they would like to continue in their relationships (Durrant & Kowalski, 1992; Saleebey, 1992).

Strengths-Based Therapy and Opportunity Awareness

The brain's negativity bias keeps people stuck in survival mode. Therefore, a person might not be able to engage in opportunity awareness. The strengths-based therapy model involves helping clients change their brains so that they can see the opportunities available to them. Strengths-based therapy is about helping clients to develop neural pathways that allow them to focus on the opportunities before them and to develop ways to mitigate the barriers they face. There is a saying that what does not kill us makes us stronger (Goethe), that adversity is the mother of invention. In fact, Albert Einstein himself once said, "In the middle of difficulty lies opportunity." The great motivational writer Napoleon Hill has also stated, "Opportunity? Often it comes in the form of misfortune, or temporary defeat." Strengths-based therapy maintains that each problem has hidden within it the seeds of a new opportunity, if only our eyes are open to see it. Therapists need to spend at least 70% of therapy time looking for the opportunity hidden in the client's presenting problem instead of 90% of their time trying to fix a client's problem. Sometimes helping clients to fix their problems brings only temporary, superficial change.

A person's adversity, his or her presenting problem, or whatever one wants to call it in therapy oftentimes builds emotional muscle within a client. Once a person learns how to navigate a situation or realizes that he or she has survived an event once thought to be a death knell, a real life ruined, he or she is capable to develop survival muscle—what psychologists call resilience. Shattered dreams can produce new dreams that are even better than those destroyed. People have to learn that they can dream new dreams—that when one door closes, another may open.

There are at least two ways in which clients' problems or adversities may become "opportunities" for them. The first opportunity takes place because experiencing adversity may actually strengthen a person. The second opportunity may occur because clients perceive new things in their environment that might really change or improve things for them.

Opportunities exist because adversity strengthens individuals.

During the past several decades, researchers in several different fields have reported that people who have experienced severe or even incapacitating adverse events often report that they were positively changed by the experience—that somehow they are better persons as a result of the adverse experiences (McMillin, 1999). In an article titled "Whatever Does Not Kill Us: Cumulative Lifetime Adversity, Vulnerability, and Resilience," Seery, Holman, and Silver (2010) found that the benefits of adversity are very, very real. These researchers found that although people do suffer from mental, physical, and spiritual pain when bad things happen to them, in the process of suffering many develop a greater understanding of hardship and are better prepared for it when it comes knocking again. In a study involving more than 2,000 participants, Seery et al. found that

> exposure to adverse life events typically predicts subsequent negative effects on mental health and well-being such that more adversity predicts worse outcomes. However, adverse experiences may also foster subsequent resilience, with resulting advantages for mental health and well-being. In a multiyear longitudinal study of a national sample, people with a history of some lifetime adversity reported better mental health and well-being outcomes than not only people with a high history of adversity but also people with no history of adversity. (p. 1025)

The researchers concluded that adversity plays an important role in building resilience and that it also promotes mental health and well-being. When people develop resilience, they develop psychological and social resources that help them tolerate adversity (Rutter et al., 2007). In addition, coping with adversity may itself promote a person's development of subsequent resilience. Experiencing low but not zero levels of adversity actually teaches effective coping skills (Seery et al., 2010). People who have experienced little or no adversity may be worse off than those undergoing problems. Individuals who have navigated adversity successfully experience what Seery et al. (2010) term as "adversarial growth" after a specific subsequent major event.

Opportunities exist because clients become aware of other positives in the environment.

In a study of 1,054 college alumni, Aldwin, Sutton, and Lachman (1996) asked respondents two benefit-related questions about a low point in their lives. Ninety-eight percent stated that they had "learned something" from the adversity, and 79% said that they were able to "turn some aspect of the experience to their advantage." Moreover, adversity or problems may provide new opportunities because they result in changes in one's life structure.

Strengths-based therapy maintains that therapists should engage in assessing a client's adversity growth. Clients who have experienced little adversity in their lives may become overwhelmed when they experience major stressful life events. This conclusion is in keeping with Seery et al.'s (2010) finding that respondents with "no prior adversity were more negatively affected by recent adversity than were individuals with low lifetime adversity" (p. 1038).

Clients in the "no prior adversity" category may not be able to see the opportunity in their adversity situation. Strengths-based therapy teaches clients that problems are solvable and that there might be an opportunity—a silver lining—in the problem, if the client is willing to look for the opportunity. Table 5.8 contains some *opportunity questions* a therapist might ask of a client experiencing problems.

Eliciting Clients' Hopes and Dreams

Hopes and dreams keep people alive and motivated. Oftentimes, clients who are experiencing challenges in life have forgotten about their hopes and dreams. According to Jevne and Miller (1999), hope may be defined as "looking forward with both confidence and uncertainty to something good. When we hope, we anticipate that something we want to happen can indeed happen" (p. 10). Hope is typically experienced in relationship to someone or something, and there are at least two levels of hope: specific and general. Snyder (2000) has defined hope as the process of thinking about one's goals and motivation (agency) and ways to achieve those goals.

The importance of hope in the therapeutic relationship has been well documented (Edey, Jevne, & Westra, 1998; Snyder, 2000). Hubble, Duncan, and Miller (1999) have referred to hope as an "expectancy effect" or a "placebo effect." That is, the curative effects of therapy are not specifically the result of a given treatment procedure; rather, they are the result of the client's positive and hopeful therapeutic expectations. Clients have been known to show some improvement in their presenting problem immediately after making an appointment for therapy. What allowed them to improve was their expectation of hope—that they were going to get the help they needed to deal with the problem or situation.

Therapists use hope intentionally in the counseling relationship to help motivate clients for change. They ask questions about the client's hope or ask clients to reframe their stories from a hope perspective using their particular strengths.

TABLE 5.8 ■ Culturally Responsive Clinical Skill Development: Opportunity Awareness Therapist Questions

The following are questions therapists might ask clients to increase their awareness of the opportunities hidden in their problems:

- Let's suppose that you were told that a culturally valuable opportunity prize was located within the problem that you were bringing to therapy and that all you had to do to claim it was to find the opportunity prize and open it. What opportunity prize do you see as a result of the problem that brought you to therapy?

- What strengths might you use to take advantage of the opportunities presented by your problem?

- What barriers might trip you up in taking advantage of the opportunities contained within the difficulty that you mentioned?

- In terms of the crisis that you have experienced, what new relationship, work, or personal growth opportunities do you believe are available to you?

- There is a saying: "Never let a good crisis go to waste." What opportunities do you see now that would make your current crisis not go to waste?

- What opportunities are now possible for you because of the problems that caused you to seek therapy?

- How might your strengths help you to take advantage of the hidden opportunities in the problem you are facing?

- What weaknesses might prevent you from acting on the opportunities before you?

- What barriers might act as threats to realizing the opportunities contained in the problem that caused you to seek therapy?

Cultural Reflections

What might be some ways that you could assess if a client is experiencing cultural consonance or cultural dissonance?

How might factors such as migration or acculturation influence a client's perception of cultural consonance or cultural dissonance?

The strengths-based therapist uncovers a client's story while placing emphasis on the hope the client has for the future, feels in the present, or remembers from the past. The therapist uses what Edey et al. (1998) recommends—that is, using the word *when* to support hope (i.e., *when* you reach your desired harm reduction goal, *when* you get your children back, *when* you get a job).

Strengths Talk

A guiding principle of strengths-based therapy is to engage clients in strengths talk. **Strengths talk** may be strategies, beliefs, and personal assets used to accomplish goals, resolve challenges, or build resilience (Padesky & Mooney, 2012). Generally speaking, strengths involve areas of sustained client activity. Because any regularly practiced behavior will encounter challenges, strengths tend to exemplify a certain degree of resiliency on the part of a client. Most often, strengths can be described in terms of everyday language in daily activities.

The language of strengths focuses on what individuals do best. Some everyday strengths might be "I have a good sense of humor" or "I don't give up easily." Strengths talk may also be conceptualized as any client speech that shows past, present, or future capability and competency. Strengths talk consists of statements about the self (and other people) and what one is capable of doing. Any time the prefrontal cortex assesses a memory that carries with it a sense of "Yes, I can" or "I'm good at this," it can send an inhibitory transmitter, GABA, to the amygdala. The neurotransmitter GABA inhibits the firing of the amygdala, thereby signaling that the amygdala does not need to activate a survival response. Strengths identification involves the process of "noticing" and "attention." When a person's strength is kicking in, the person takes notice of it and recognizes it. "I sing well." "I can draw better than most people." Strengths talk has the following characteristics:

- It is achievement oriented.
- It is competency based.
- It is often preceded by "I can," "I am," or "I'm good at."
- It suggests a positive expectancy about one's talents or abilities.
- It is self-reflective and self-evaluative.
- It suggests that a person believes in himself or herself.
- It is hope filled.

How does a clinician recognize and encourage strengths talk in clients? Many people have been taught not to mention their strengths. Sharing their strengths with others is sometimes viewed as bragging, and some cultures discourage a focus on individual strengths. Strengths are for the glory of the group instead of the individual. There are various categories of strengths talk that range from individuals' complete denial that they have any strengths to their being able to articulate clearly their strengths (see Table 5.9).

Strengths talk produces a variety of benefits, both physical and psychological:

- It encourages client insight and client perspective taking.
- It generates optimism for the client.
- It provides a sense of direction.
- It develops confidence within clients.
- It buffers against client physical illness.
- It generates positive energy.

TABLE 5.9 ■ Strengths Talk Categories
Category 1: I don't have any strengths.
Category 2: I am not sure what my strengths are.
Category 3: No one has ever told me that I have any strengths. I am only aware of my weaknesses.
Category 4: Other people sometimes tell me that I have strengths, but I don't really feel them deep down inside.
Category 5: I have strengths, but I am not sure how to use them to make my life better.
Category 6: I have strengths, and others know my strengths.
Category 7: I have people who support my strengths and who help me to develop them.
Category 8: I use my strengths on a regular basis to make my life more fulfilling and happy.

Having a client talk about strengths might involve asking such questions as "What do you yearn to do? What do you enjoy doing the most? How have you been successful in the past? What traits, characteristics, or strengths help you to achieve your goals or to get things done? In what areas of your life have you experienced rapid learning? What comes to you easily? Describe some of your key achievements in life. Tell me something good about you; it could be anything that you feel good about or like about yourself. If you were given an important assignment, what personal qualities would you use to complete it?" It is important that clinicians encourage clients to elaborate on their strengths to create greater awareness of them so that they can be used to deal with the challenges that brought them to therapy. Table 5.10 includes a chart therapists can use in helping clients to become aware of their strengths.

Culturally Responsive Strengths Talk

Strengths talk varies based on one's culture. People who adopt a collectivist culture perspective will focus on strengths talk primarily for the group, and they will emphasize how one's strengths can be used to promote the welfare of a designated group. In collectivist cultures, strengths talk may focus on one's family, community, or work situation. In these cultures, people are valued if they are generous, helpful, dependable, and attentive to the needs of others. Some countries that are considered collectivist include Japan, China, Korea, Argentina, Brazil, and India. In contrast, Western countries emphasize an individualistic outlook on life; therefore, the strengths talk focuses on the independence, assertiveness, and accomplishments of the individual. Because a concept of the individual and the group exists in all cultures, even in collectivist cultures, people will engage in strengths talk that is individually oriented, and the converse is true for people living in individualistically oriented cultures. People in such countries will engage in strengths talk about their families. Throughout the Western world, there is a great deal of talk about the strengths of organizations.

Surrendering: Contributions From Chinese Culture and Mindfulness

The revised strengths-based therapy model has elaborated on the surrendering process contained in the "Let Go" part of the model. To release a self-limiting belief, one must surrender it to the universe. Surrendering means to stop your resistance to a situation or thought. It means giving up our sense of control over events for which we do not have complete control. Surrendering means allowing things to unfold and happen naturally instead of trying to make a certain situation happen. People try to control things because of what they think or fear will happen if they don't exercise control. Yet, for the most part, control is rooted in fear and worry.

The desire to control happens when we are attached to a particular outcome that we believe is best for us or best for another person. At the center of our desire to control are issues of trust. We do not trust that what happens will be best for us or for our loved ones. When we can trust

TABLE 5.10 ■ Culturally Responsive Intervention Skill: Strengths Talk

Things I like doing include . . .

1. _____
2. _____
3. _____

People tend to compliment me on . . .

1. _____
2. _____
3. _____

Obstacles I have overcome include . . .

1. _____
2. _____
3. _____

What I like most about me is . . .

1. _____
2. _____
3. _____

Accomplishments that I am proud of include . . .

1. _____
2. _____
3. _____

I'm at my best when I am . . .

1. _____
2. _____
3. _____

Times I have helped others or made a difference in someone else's life include . . .

1. _____
2. _____
3. _____

Cultural strengths I am proud of include . . .

1. _____
2. _____
3. _____

Cultural beliefs that strengthen me include . . .

1. _____
2. _____
3. _____

Cultural strategies that have helped me to succeed include . . .

1. _____
2. _____
3. _____

that things will work out, we do not have to try to micromanage our partner's life, our children's lives, or the universe. We simply let go. The energy of surrender is freeing, releasing, and peaceful. One gives up the struggle and the fight to have things the exact way in which he or she wants them to take place. In fact, the word *surrender* means to stop fighting—with oneself, with others, and with the universe. A person declares, "I surrender; I let go of all negative beliefs about this issue. I surrender, release, and let go of all negative energies about this situation, event, or person."

Eckhart Tolle, best known as the author of *The Power of Now* (1999) and *A New Earth: Awakening to Your Life's Purpose* (2005), has commented on human problems and the role that problems play in our lives. Tolle was listed by the Watkins Review in 2011 as the most spiritually influential person in the world. In 2008, a *New York Times* writer called Tolle "the most popular spiritual author in the United States" (McKinley, 2008). According to Tolle, we create and maintain problems because they give us a sense of identity. We hold onto our pain way beyond its ability to serve us. We tend to replay our past mistakes over and over again, so they serve to support our inner belief that we are "less than."

The surrender process is beneficial because one is able to acknowledge the negative circumstances in his or her life without engaging the amygdala, the fight-or-flight part of the brain. In fact, quite the opposite happens. The surrendering process provides immediate emotional relief and peace to a person because he or she no longer has to struggle with trying to win or prevail in the situation.

Understanding the power of surrender runs antithetical to Western culture, especially American culture. Americans are taught not to surrender. Much of the marketing messages that Americans are inundated with tells Americans to do exactly the opposite of surrender. On the contrary, Americans are encouraged to "fight to the very end" and to never give up, to "man up" and face reality. Americans are taught from a very early age to try to control their life circumstances and not to back down. Much of this sentiment is conveyed in the song popularized by Frank Sinatra, "My Way"—a client might reason that even though she tried to commit suicide and lost everything, at least "I did it my way." As Americans, our natural instinct in dealing with a problem is to try to regain control of it. Therefore, we fight and struggle to assert our power. In contrast to American culture that advocates fighting to the end, Chinese culture maintains that one ends a struggle by letting go. When one lets go of the string, the struggle is over.

The surrender concept is not new to strengths-based therapy. Decades ago, Alcoholics Anonymous (AA) adopted the surrender process. AA's first step states "We admitted we were powerless over alcohol—that our lives had become unmanageable." Yet, this important first step in AA has not been without its critics. AA has been challenged for its surrendering to the power of alcohol and to the spiritual power of God. Some argue that AA's emphasis on surrender is a "copout"; that alcoholics should just toughen up and find ways to control the drug addiction better.

Therapist "Surrender" Intervention Procedures

The strengths-based therapy model has adopted the following surrender outline for the "Let Go" part of its model.

First, the therapist examines the client's experience with the challenge and his or her final act of surrender. What qualities does the client have that helped him or her to continue fighting the problem or challenge?

Second, the therapist examines the precipitating factors that led to the surrender. What factor or set of circumstances finally forced the client to surrender to the issue?

Third, describe and understand the client's surrender as a psychological event.

Fourth, examine the positive phase (surrender response) that follows the client's surrender regarding the problem. For instance, surrender suggests cessation of a fight, and the ending of a fight is often followed by internal peace and quiet. The strengths-based therapy model labels the feeling of peace and relaxation that occurs after surrender as the "surrender response," which is a positive mental state.

Fifth, the client's surrender produces a change of a state of mind. The client is now able to release the old problems and to begin a new path of growth and maturation. The client is no longer psychologically encumbered by the past. He or she can now live in the present and forge a new identity. The identity of his or her old problems has now been shed.

The Surrender Process and Culturally Responsive Counseling

The surrender process varies according to one's cultural membership. In Western culture, suffering is something to be avoided and controlled, whereas in Eastern culture, Buddhism teaches that suffering is part of the human tradition (Santee, 2007). It is difficult for individuals in Western societies to surrender to any form of suffering. One does not make peace with the suffering or with a problem; one fights to the end to conquer the problem.

In contrast to Western societies, Buddhism uses the concept of the Four Noble Truths to deal with suffering and the process of surrendering. In this step-by-step approach to dealing with human suffering, Buddha outlines the problem, the cause of the problem, the removal of the problem, and the pathway to the removal of the problem. In the Western counseling model, a client comes to therapy because he or she has a problem that is causing him or her pain or suffering. The problem is compromising the client's ability to be happy. The therapist diagnoses the problem—for instance, anxiety, depression, and so forth—then develops clinical strategies specific to the problem that has been diagnosed.

In the Chinese Buddha model, the client's situation is viewed as part of the problem of universal suffering and dissatisfaction (Santee, 2007). The Second Noble Truth maintains that the cause of universal suffering and dissatisfaction is twofold: (1) ignorance of the nature of human existence and (2) human craving and desire. In the Western psychological world, the cause of a specific disorder or problem is based on the perspective of the psychotherapy framework. For instance, the medical model might diagnose a brain disorder, while the cognitive theoretical framework would focus on the client's irrational thoughts. The Western world views human suffering as caused by a specific disorder, while the Eastern world (Buddhism) sees suffering as part of the human condition that affects everyone. Buddhism says that suffering is caused by humans' craving and desire and their failure to accept suffering as part of the human condition.

Eastern culture uses the technique of mindfulness to acknowledge and surrender the suffering that a person is experiencing. Mindfulness involves a moment-to-moment awareness of what one is experiencing. It is about being nonjudgmentally in the present (Santee, 2007). In mindfulness practice, all feelings are experienced as being impermanent, interdependent, and nonsubstantial. Thoughts and beliefs are observed as thoughts and beliefs and not as absolute facts. The practice of mindfulness allows clients to surrender whatever thoughts and feelings they are experiencing to the universe. By viewing their situations nonjudgmentally and by acknowledging that what is upsetting to them are their thoughts and feelings, clients surrender the negative effects of their life situation to the universe.

Setting a Strengths-Based Intention: Contributions From India

Another new addition to the strengths-based therapy model is the concept and technique of setting a strengths-based intention. Setting a strengths-based intention can be traced to India and Hindu culture. According to the famous Indian American health guru Deepak Chopra, "Intention is the starting point of every dream. It is the creative power that fulfills all of our needs, whether for money, relationships, spiritual awakening, or love. Everything that happens in the universe begins with intention." On his website, Chopra (2017) traces the notion of setting an intention to the sages of India. He points out that thousands of years ago, Hindu sages said that our destiny is ultimately shaped by our deepest intentions and desires: "The classic Vedic text known as the Upanishads declares, 'You are what your deepest desire is. As your desire is, so is your intention. As your intention is, so is your will. As your will is, so is your deed. As your deed is, so is your destiny.'" Chopra maintains that an intention is "a directed impulse of consciousness that contains the seed form of that which you want to create."

A person's intentions can have powerful effects on his or her behavior. The regions of the brain involved in "intention" are connected to regions involved in motor action. As a result, when individuals set intentions, they fire up the action centers of their brains. Zschorlich and Köhling (2013) conducted an experiment to explore the idea that conscious intentions do exist, prior to motor actions, and that these intentions are accompanied by specific changes in brain activity. These investigators used transcranial magnetic stimulation on the motor cortex region of the brain and found that if people thought about their actions, it would prompt a stronger physical response. The researchers concluded that the brain's "intention network" prepares actions by increasing the excitability of the cells that produce the movement. Our intentions can lead us to take actions to accomplish that which we desire to do.

The revised strengths-based therapy model introduces the concept of setting a strengths-based intention as a means of helping clients to take specific actions toward what they say they desire—that is, their intentions. The underlying premise is that setting an intention alone creates change in individuals' brains, and that these brain-based changes cause individuals to move toward what they say they want in their lives. An intention exists for a person's behavior and feelings. An intention is in the most general area a thought. It is very enlightening and powerful to help a client bring an intention to the surface after a behavior has taken place or a feeling has been expressed. Further, clinicians might consider assisting clients to create a positive intention before one even has actually taken place so that clients' identified intention can guide their behavior.

A written intention helps clients to focus their attention more effectively than simply thinking about an intention. Moreover, intentions create a certain level of consciousness about what one wants or desires. If clients set a positive intention that they want to be more appreciative of the good things in life, they have directed themselves to a specific consciousness—one of appreciation or one of gratitude. Setting an intention suggests that a person will take certain actions. In fact, actions follow intentions even when one is unaware that one has set an intention. When one sets positive intentions designed to bring about the good in a person or a situation, what naturally follows are positive, empowering actions on the part of the intention setter. An example of a strengths-based intention might be as follows: "I intend to write a best-selling novel"; "I intend to become a millionaire in three years"; "I intend to find a suitable partner within the next nine months."

> ## Cultural Reflections
>
> *Intentions sometimes function outside of our immediate awareness.*
>
> *When you awakened this morning, what intentions did you set for yourself?*
>
> *Did your intentions succeed in the manner that you desired? Why or why not?*
>
> *Try writing an intention in longhand and examine how you feel once you've written it down.*

Having clients set a strengths-based intention is therapeutic because such intentions convey the belief that they have the power to manifest into their lives the things they want and need. It is the strength of a belief behind an intention that is significant. Intentions that are backed by unbelief or doubt have little chance of being manifested in clients' lives. In setting a strengths-based intention, the clinician works to help a client align his or her conscious and subconscious beliefs so that they are in alignment or harmony. If clients set a strengths-based intention in their conscious mind that their subconscious mind doubts they can achieve, it is likely that they will not be able to achieve that intention. For example, a person might say that she wants to lose 30 pounds. Soon, however, the person begins the internal battle between her conscious mind, which wants the loss of 30 pounds, and her subconscious mind, which is telling her that she is going to fail as she did in the past with dieting. Because the subconscious mind always directs the conscious mind, it will win the dieting battle.

Intention statements should describe the life a person wants to create. Some guidelines in setting strengths-based intentions are as follows:

1. Choose an intention that is for your greater good. Think of a statement that reflects or summarizes the change you want to make in your life or where you want to go.

2. Use meditation to put yourself in a very relaxed state of mind. The best time to plant your intentions is during meditation, when your awareness is centered in the realm of possibilities. In addition, intention is much more powerful when it takes place while you are feeling content instead of when you are feeling lack or need.

3. Be very clear about what you want to achieve or manifest in your life, and concentrate on the intention for at least five minutes.

4. Create an intention that is strengths based.

5. State the intention in a positive manner and make sure it is simple and something you can easily repeat over and over again to yourself. If you want friends, then an intention statement might be "I have an abundantly fulfilling life with the love and friends I want." If you want to write an intention statement about finances, you might state, "I have more than enough to invest, to live the life I want in the home I want, and to share my wealth with my children, grandchildren, friends, and family."

6. Recognize that the power of an intention is magnified when you write it in longhand.

7. Feel the intention as if it has already taken place—as if you have already completed your journey or reached your desired intention. Try to see who is there with you.

8. State the intention with strong, positive emotion. If you can't create strong positive emotions about your intention, there is no real desire, and the intention will probably not manifest itself.

9. Imagine the intention visually and picture what your life will be once it is manifested.

10. Let your intention go out to the universe with gratitude. Let go of any control you might want to have regarding the intention. Trust that your intentions will come to fruition.

Setting intentions is not just for clients. Therapists can also set their own strengths-based intentions for themselves (Table 5.11), as well as for each therapy session.

Culturally Responsive Strengths-Based Intention Setting

People from all cultures set intentions for their behavior. Major differences can be observed, however, in individualistic and collectivistic cultures. In individualistically oriented cultures, strengths-based intentions are inclined to focus on the individual. Conversely, in collectivistic cultures, strengths-based intentions focus on the welfare of the group. In reality, every culture has some aspects of individualism and collectivism, and this fact is demonstrated in the Olympics. During the Olympics competition, participants from collectivistic cultures tend to stress the importance of winning for their country. In Western countries, the emphasis is on individuals doing their very best and the accolades they will get from doing their best. The Olympics is also focused on the group accomplishments for nations, and therefore, each nation shares in the spotlight of a participant's individual achievement. Strengths-based intentions can be either group oriented or individually oriented. They can emphasize the needs and goals of the group as a whole over the needs and wishes of each individual, or they can focus primarily on the needs and accomplishments of the individual.

TABLE 5.11 ■ Culturally Responsive Clinical Intervention: Setting Therapist Intentions for Psychotherapy

- Therapists are encouraged to set intention(s) with their clients.

- Therapists write down the intention(s) they have for each phase of the counseling relationship. For example:
  - "During the initial interview, I listen for ways to establish a relationship with Robert. My therapeutic intention is to establish a positive, therapeutic alliance with him."
  - "My intention for my initial interview is to give my client the feeling that I have listened to her and that I have given her hope that by working together we can resolve the challenge that brought her to therapy."

- In writing a therapeutic intention, therapists consider how they want to be with their clients more so than what they will do or say during the therapy hour, although they also may choose to write intentions about what they will do or say.

- Therapists can also write intentions about being strengths based or about using a particular clinical technique.

- Therapists write therapeutic intentions that emphasize their being fully present, engaged, and listening at all levels to their clients. For instance, one therapeutic intention might be "When I am working with Jennifer, I am fully present, I listen deeply to what she is saying, and I consider the emotions behind her words. I am concerned with what she is feeling and what has prompted her feelings."

- Therapists can write culturally responsive intentions for therapy—for instance, "I make an intention to listen carefully for culture in my clients' stories."

SUMMARY OF KEY POINTS

The strengths-based therapy model provides a new framework that offers an opportunity for helping professionals to modify the psychiatric worldview that still dominates so much of therapy. Strengths-based development involves the identification of strengths, the integration of these strengths into our views of ourselves, and the resulting changes in behavior. To move toward this therapy model, clinicians must make a paradigm shift to a strengths emphasis.

- The strengths paradigm does not eliminate the need to address barriers in a client's life—barriers such as poverty, abuse, neglect, and other life challenges that can be devastating for people.

- Moreover, a strengths-based approach does not just focus on positives while ignoring real challenges or problems. Instead, it entails figuring out ways to recognize and use genuine strengths to allow for building on existing client competencies.

- The strengths-based therapist understands that if multifaceted client needs are to be addressed effectively during counseling, clinical interventions must be based on strengths and what works for clients. What people need is a balanced paradigm in which deficit-reduction efforts are matched with strength interventions.

- Although research is still in its beginning stages, the evidence is beginning to mount that a strengths-based program leads to a number of positive outcomes, including better function of families, improved mental health, greater life satisfaction, and improved educational performance. Strengths are the building blocks for change and form the primary focus in therapy. The strengths-based therapy model offers much to those professionals who desire to work from a positive psychological perspective.

DISCUSSION QUESTIONS

Discussion Question set 1

All people have strengths that can be identified and used to enhance their well-being. Ask your clients to identify two occasions when they have been at their best or when they have felt they were at their best.

A. Have your client talk about the experience and to relive it as vividly as possible.

B. Jot down each strength that the client shows as he or she talks.

C. After the client finishes talking, share with him or her the strengths that you observed as he or she talked.

Discussion Question set 2

Present a diagram of SWOB analysis to your clients. Discuss with your clients the following:

A. Does your client have strengths that are currently not being used or are currently being underused?

B. Are there strengths your client can use to achieve his or her goals?

C. Are there strengths your client can use to overcome his or her obstacles?

KEY TERMS

Cultural consonance: A model created by William Dressler and colleagues (2007) to measure how closely individuals' behaviors are consonant or in agreement with their guiding awareness of their culture. When people experience cultural consonance, they tend to feel a sense of neuro-equilibrium, rest, or peace.

Cultural dissonance: A model created by William Dressler and colleagues (2007) to measure how closely individuals' behaviors are not in agreement or are at odds with their guiding awareness of their culture. Cultural dissonance produces problems for individuals and most likely results in the release of cortisol (a stressor) in the brain.

Law of belief: States that whatever is in individuals' belief system becomes their reality.

Neurocultural dynamics: How the brain has been organized culturally affects a person's feelings of cultural consonance or cultural dissonance.

Neuroplasticity: The quality of neural structures to change, primarily through change in the interconnections of the nerve cells that constitute the structure.

Opportunity questions: Questions a therapist or counselor might ask clients that cause them to search for new possibilities, favorable situations, or positive outcomes in the negative life circumstances they are facing.

Self-limiting beliefs: Doubts about one's own abilities and strengths, firmly held negative self-beliefs that are picked up by a person's subconscious mind.

Strengths talk: Talk that focuses on clients' strengths and produces a sense of optimism.

Survival strategies: Unproductive mental "crutches" that help people deal with emotional stress or anxiety.

SWOB analysis: Strengths analysis for clients, where S = strengths, W = weaknesses, O = opportunities, and B = barriers.

REFERENCES AND SUGGESTED READING

Aldwin, C. M., Sutton, K. J., & Lachman, M. (1996). The development of coping resources in adulthood. *Journal of Personality*, *64*(4), 837–871. doi:10.1111/j.1467-6494.1996.tb00946.x

Arnold, E. M., Walsh, A. K., Oldham, M. S., & Rapp, C. A. (2007). Strengths-based case management: Implementation with high-risk youth. *Families in Society: The Journal of Contemporary Human Services*, *88*(1), 83–94.

Azar, B. (2010). A reason to believe. *Monitor on Psychology*, *41*(11). Retrieved from http://www.apa.org/monitor/2010/12/believe.aspx

Bretton, M. (1993). Relating competence-promotion and empowerment. *Journal of Progressive Human Services*, *5*, 27–44.

Chopra, D. (2017). *5 steps to setting powerful intentions*. The Chopra Center. Retrieved from http://www.chopra.com/articles/5-steps-to-setting-powerful-intentions#sm.001v9un0o17fbewpqsg1p238zmk8t

Clifton, D. O., Anderson, E., & González-Molina, G. (2016). *StrengthsQuest: Discover and develop your strengths in academics, career, and beyond*. New York, NY: Gallup Press.

Connor, S. (2009, March 10). Belief and the brain's "God spot." *The Independent*. Retrieved from http://www.independent.co.uk/news/science/belief-and-the-brains-god-spot-1641022.html

Conoley, C. W., & Conoley, J. C. (2008). *Positive psychology and family therapy: Creative techniques and practical tools for guiding change and enhancing growth*. Hoboken, NJ: Wiley.

Cox, K. F. (2006). Investigating the impact of strengths-based assessment on youth with emotional or behavioral disorders. *Journal of Child and Family Studies*, *15*(3), 287–301.

Crenshaw, D. A. (Ed.). (2010). *Reverence in healing: Honoring strengths without trivializing suffering*. Lanham, MD: Rowman & Littlefield.

DeJong, P., & Miller, S. D. (1995). Interviewing for client strengths. *Social Work*, *40*, 729–736.

Dressler, W. W. (2007). Cultural consonance. In D. Bhugra & K. Bhui (Eds.), *Textbook of cultural psychiatry* (pp. 179–190). Cambridge, MA: Cambridge University Press.

Dressler, W. W., Mauro, C. B., Ribeiro, R. P., & Santos, J. E. (2007). A prospective study of culture consonance and depressive symptoms in urban Brazil. *Social Science and Medicine, 65,* 2058–2069.

Durrant, M., & Kowalski, K. (1992). Enhancing views of competence. In S. Friedman (Ed.), *The new language of change* (pp. 107–137). New York, NY: Guilford Press.

Early, T. J. (2001). Measures for practice with families from a strengths perspective. *Families in Society, 82*(3), 225–232.

Edey, W., Jevne, R. F., & Westra, K. (1998). *Hope-focused counseling.* Edmonton: The Hope Foundation of Alberta.

Fitzpatrick, M. R., & Stalikas, A. (2008). Positive emotions as generators of therapeutic change. *Journal of Psychotherapy Integration, 18*(2), 137–154.

Fredrickson, B. L. (2009). *Positivity: Top-notch research reveals the 3-to-1 ratio that will change your life.* New York, NY: Three Rivers Press/Crown.

Galassi, J. P., & Akos, P. (2007). *Strengths-based school counseling: Promoting student development and achievement.* Mahwah, NJ: Erlbaum.

Goldstein, H. (1990). Strength or pathology: Ethical and rhetorical contrasts in approaches to practice. *Families in Society, 71,* 267–275.

Goodenough, O. R. (1996). Replication and the evolution of culture. *Anthropology News, 37*(1), 10–12. doi:10.1111/an.1996.37.1.10.2

Gray, M. (2011). Back to basics: A critique of the strengths perspective in social work. *Families in Society, 92*(1), 5–11.

Han, S., & Poppel, E. (Eds.). *Culture and neural frames of cognition and communication.* New York, NY: Springer.

Hanson, R., & Mendius, R. (2009). *Buddha's brain: The practical neuroscience of happiness, love & wisdom.* Oakland, CA: New Harbinger.

Harbin, J. M., Gelso, C. J., & Pérez Rojas, A. E. P. (2013). Therapist work with client strengths: Development and validation of a measure. *The Counseling Psychologist, 42*(3), 345–373.

Hebb, D. O. (1949). *The organization of behavior.* New York, NY: Wiley.

Hellerstein, D. (2011). *Heal your brain: How the new neuropsychiatry can help you go from better to well.* Baltimore, MD: Johns Hopkins University Press.

Hill, N. (1937). Think and grow rich. Wise, VA: Official publication of the Napoleon Hill Foundation, sponsored by Sound Wisdom.

Holzer, P. J., Bromfield, L. M., & Richardson, N. (2006). The effectiveness of parent education programs for preventing child maltreatment. *NCPC Issues* No. 24. Australian Institute of Family Studies. Retrieved from https://aifs.gov.au/cfca/publications/effectiveness-parent-education-and-home-visiting-chil

Hubble, M. A., Duncan, B., & Miller, S. (Eds.). (1999). *Heart and soul of change.* Washington, DC: American Psychological Association.

Humphrey, A. (2005). "SWOT" analysis for management consulting. *SRI Alumni Newsletter.* Menlo Park, CA: SRI International.

Jevne, R. F., & Miller, J. E. (1999). *Finding hope: Ways to see life in a brighter hope.* Fort Wayne, IN: Willowgreen.

Jones-Smith, E. (2011). *Spotlighting the strengths of every single student: Why schools need a strengths-based approach.* Santa Barbara, CA: Praeger.

Jones-Smith, E. (2014). *Strengths-based therapy: Connecting theory, practice, and skills.* Thousand Oaks, CA: Sage.

Jones-Smith, E. (2016). *Theories of counseling and psychotherapy: An integrative approach.* Thousand Oaks, CA: Sage.

Jones-Smith (2016). Revised strengths-based counseling model. Unpublished manuscript. Philadelphia, PA.

Kapogiannis, D., Barbey, A. K., Su, M., Zamboni, G., Krueger, F., & Grafman, J. (2009). Cognitive and neural foundations of religious belief. *Proceedings of the National Academy of Sciences, 106*(12), 4876–4881.

Lende, D. H., & Downey, G. (Eds.). (2012). *The encultured brain: An introduction to neuroanthropology.* Cambridge, MA: MIT Press.

Lipton, B. (2015). *The biology of belief* (10th anniversary ed.). Carlsbad, CA: Hay House.

Lounsbury, J. W., Fisher, L. A., Levy, J. J., & Welsh, D. P. (2009). Investigation of character strengths in relation to the academic success of college students. *Individual Differences Research, 7*(1), 52–69.

Magyar-Moe, J. L., Owens, R. L., & Conoley, C. W. (2015). Positive psychological interventions in counseling: What every counseling psychologist should know. *The Counseling Psychologist, 43*(4), 508–557.

Magyar-Moe, J. L., Owens, R. L., & Scheel, M. J. (2015). Applications of positive psychology in counseling: Current status and future directions. *The Counseling Psychologist, 43*(4), 494–507.

McMillen, J. C. (1999). Better for it: How people benefit from adversity. *Social Work, 44* (5), 455–468.

McKinley, J. (2008, March 23). The wisdom of the ages, for now anyway. *The New York Times.* Retrieved from https://www.nytimes.com/2008/03/23/fashion/23tolle.html

McQuaide, S., & Ehrenreich, J. (1997). Assessing client strengths. *Families in Society: The Journal of Contemporary Social Services, 78*(2), 201–212.

Merzenich, M. (2013). *Soft-wired: How the new science of brain plasticity can change your life* (2nd ed.). San Francisco, CA: Parnassus.

Newberg, A., & Waldman, M. (2010). *How God changes your brain.* New York, NY: Ballantine Books.

Newberg, A., & Waldman, M. R. (2012). *Words can change your brain.* New York, NY: Plume.

Padesky, C. A., & Mooney, K. A. (2012). Strengths-based cognitive-behavioural therapy: A four-step model to build resilience. *Clinical Psychology & Psychotherapy, 19*(4), 283–290. doi:10.1002/cpp.1795

Pascual-Leone, A., Nguyet, D., Cohen, L. G., Brasil-Neto, J. P., Cammarota, A., & Hallett, M. (1995). Modulation of muscle responses evoked by transcranial magnetic stimulation during the acquisition of new fine motor skills. *Journal of Neurophysiology, 74*(3), 1037–1045.

Phillips, D. P., Ruth, T. E., & Wagner, L. M. (1993). Psychology and survival. *Lancet, 342*(8880), 1142–1145.

Price-Robertson, R. (2010, December). Supporting young parents. *CAFCA Practice Sheet.* Australian Institute of Family Studies. Retrieved from https://aifs.gov.au/cfca/sites/default/files/publication-documents/ps3.pdf

Ralph, R. O., Lambric, T. M., & Steele, R. B. (1996). *Recovery issues in a consumer developed evaluation of the mental health system.* Presentation for the 6th Annual Mental Health Services.

Rapp, C. A. (1998). *The strengths model: Case management with people suffering from severe and persistent mental illness.* New York, NY: Oxford University Press.

Rashid, T. (2009). Positive interventions in clinical practice. *Journal of Clinical Psychology, 65*(5), 461–466. doi:10.1002/jclp.20588

Rutter, M., Kreppner, J., Croft, C., Murin, M., Colvert, E., Beckett, C., . . . Sonuga-Barke, E. (2007). Early adolescent outcomes of institutionally deprived and non-deprived adoptees. III. Quasi-autism. *Journal of Child Psychology and Psychiatry, 48*(12), 1200–1207. doi:10.1111/j.1469-7610.2007.01792.x

Saleebey, D. (1992). *The strengths perspective in social work practice.* New York, NY: Longman.

Sandage, S. J., Hill, P. C., & Vang, H. C. (2003). Toward a multicultural positive psychology: Indigenous forgiveness and Hmong culture. *The Counseling Psychologist, 31*(5), 564–593.

Santee, R. G. (2007). *An integrative approach to counseling: Bridging Chinese thought, evolutionary theory, and stress management.* Thousand Oaks, CA: Sage.

Scheel, M. J., Davis, C. K., & Henderson, J. D. (2012). Therapist use of client strengths: A qualitative study of positive processes. *The Counseling Psychologist, 41*(3), 392–427.

Seery, M. D., Holman, E. A., & Silver, R. C. (2010). Whatever does not kill us: Cumulative lifetime adversity, vulnerability, and resilience. *Journal of Personality and Social Psychology, 99*(6), 1025–1041. doi:10.1037/a0021344

Seligman, M. E. P. (2002). Positive psychology, positive prevention, and positive therapy. In C. R. Snyder, & S. Lopez (Eds.), *Handbook of positive psychology* (pp. 3–9). New York, NY: Oxford University Press.

Smith, E. J. (2006). The strengths-based counseling model. *The Counseling Psychologist, 34*, 13–79.

Smock, S. A., Trepper, T. S., Weltchler, J. L., McCollum, E. E., Ray, R., & Pierce, K. (2008). Solution-focused group therapy for Level 1 substance abusers. *Journal of Marital and Family Therapy, 34*(1), 107–120.

Snyder, C. R. (Ed.). (2000). *Handbook of hope: Theory, measures, and applications.* San Diego, CA: Academic Press.

Snyder, C. R. (2002). Hope theory: Rainbows in the mind. *Psychological Inquiry, 13*(4), 249–275.

Snyder, C. R., Ilardi, S. S., Cheavens, J., Michael, S. T., Yamhure, L., & Sympson, S. (2000). The role of hope in cognitive-behavior therapies. *Cognitive Therapy and Research, 24*(6), 747–762.

Snyder, C. R., Michael, S., & Cheavins, J. (1999). Hope as a psychotherapeutic foundation for nonspecific factors, placebos, and expectancies. In M. A. Hubble, B. Duncan, & S. Miller (Eds.), *Heart and soul of change* (pp. 179–200). Washington, DC: American Psychological Association.

Snyder, C. R., Parenteau, S. C., Shorey, H. S., Kahle, K. E., & Berg, C. (2002). Hope as the underlying process in psychotherapeutic change process. *International Gestalt Journal, 25*(2), 11–29.

Syka, J., & Merzenich, M. M. (2003). *Plasticity and signal representation in the auditory system.* New York, NY: Springer.

Tehan, B., & McDonald, M. (2010, September). Engaging fathers in child and family services. *CAFCA Practice Sheet.* Australian Institute of Family Studies. Retrieved from https://aifs.gov.au/cfca/publications/engaging-fathers-child-and-family-services

Tolle, E. (1999). *The power of now: A guide to spiritual enlightenment.* Novato, CA: New World Library.

Tolle, E. (2005). *A new earth: Awakening to your life's purpose.* New York, NY: Penguin Books.

Wexler, B. (2011). Neuroplasticity: Biological evolution's contribution to cultural evolution. In S. Han & E. Poppel (Eds.), *Culture and neural frames of cognition and communication* (pp. 1–17). Berlin, Germany: Springer-Verlag.

Wu, P. C. (2015, April 17). What we choose to believe—the power of belief. *Psychology Today.* Retrieved from https://www.psychologytoday.com/blog/jacobs-staff/201504/what-we-choose-believe-the-power-belief

Yip, K. S. (2008). Searching the Chinese cultural roots of the strengths perspective. In K. S. Yip (Ed.), *Strength-based perspective in working with clients with mental illness: A Chinese cultural articulation* (pp. 21–36). Hauppauge, NY: Nova Science.

Zschorlich, V. R., & Köhling, R. (2013). How thoughts give rise to action: Conscious motor intention increases the excitability of target-specific motor circuits. *PLoS One, 8*(12). doi:10.1371/journal.pone.0083845

6 CULTURALLY RESPONSIVE ASSESSMENT AND THE CULTURAL FORMULATION INTERVIEW

- *"Culture hides more than it reveals, and strangely enough what it hides, it hides most effectively from its own participants."* —Edward T. Hall

- *"Joy is what happens to us when we allow ourselves to recognize how good things really are."* —Marianne Williamson

CHAPTER OBJECTIVES

- Utilize models of assessment for culturally responsive counseling.

- Identify clinical issues in conducting a qualitative, culturally responsive assessment, such as learning how to listen for culture in a client's story and honoring the client's communication style for feelings, space, and contact.

- Acquire the basic clinical skills involved in using the four domains of the Cultural Formulation Interview of the DSM-5.

- Explain the criticisms and limitations of the Cultural Formulation Interview.

- Construct and use cultural genograms.

- Describe culture-bound syndromes and their assessment criteria.

- Attain competency in using the culturally responsive, strengths-based therapy model's assessment process.

- Conduct assessments of clients' external strengths, internal strengths, and relational strengths.

- Construct and use a strengths genogram.

INTRODUCTION

The previous chapters were foundational in that they provided important background knowledge for clinicians working with culturally diverse individuals. In this chapter, we transition to demonstrating how culturally responsive concepts can be integrated with strengths-based therapy and neuroscience to provide therapy to clients. To achieve this goal, clinicians must learn how to (1) conduct culturally responsive assessments, (2) engage in case conceptualization, and (3) collaborate with the client to form an effective treatment plan.

GENERAL ASSESSMENT PRINCIPLES IN COUNSELING AND PSYCHOTHERAPY

Psychological assessment is an important part of counseling and psychotherapy because it helps to "measure and observe the client's behavior to arrive at a diagnosis and guide treatment" (American Psychological Association, 2017c). **Psychological assessment** can be defined as a clinician's use of clinical procedures and instruments to determine the cause(s) or etiology of a client's presenting issues for the purpose of developing an effective treatment plan. Meehl's (1954) classic book, *Clinical Versus Statistical Prediction*, divided assessment into two basic categories: clinical and actuarial. Meehl noted that proponents of a **clinical assessment** (also known as **qualitative** or **idiographic assessment**) have described this approach as rich, contextual, sensitive, open-minded, deep, genuine, insightful, and meaningful. In contrast, the **actuarial** or **quantitative (nomothetic)** method uses instruments, tests, and statistical methods to assess a client's problems and progress during therapy.

Proponents of this actuarial, or quantitative, orientation have described their approach as communicable, testable, reliable, rigorous, precise, and empirical.

Clinical, or qualitative, assessment primarily uses idiographic, informal, impressionistic, and frequently unstructured procedures. In-depth interviews and autobiographies are two often used qualitative assessment procedures. The qualitative approach provides a quick, noninvasive method for assessing a client's worldview. The therapist simply listens to the values that the client expresses and then moves to place those values within a cultural framework. According to Koltko-Rivera (2004), worldviews may be defined as "sets of beliefs and assumptions that describe reality" (p. 3). The quantitative approach can also be used to measure a client's worldviews; see, for instance, the *Scale to Assess World View* (Ibrahim & Kahn, 1987; Ibrahim, Roysircar-Sodowsky, & Ohnishi, 2001).

Currently, however, psychology is moving toward **mixed methods** in research and counseling, which may be defined as using a combination of quantitative and qualitative assessment methods (Lonner & Ibrahim, 2008). Mixed methods help to evaluate what is normal and abnormal in specific cultural situations, and it is believed that this assessment approach helps reduce risks associated with misdiagnosis and **cultural malpractice**, which is the inappropriate use of Eurocentric values and cultural perspectives when counseling culturally different individuals. Cultural malpractice takes place when a counselor or therapist believes that his or her culture is superior to all other cultures, and involves exhibiting cultural bias against those who are culturally different from the counselor or therapist. It may even entail actual cultural destructiveness, where counselors or therapists make a conscious effort to destroy cultures different from their own. Cultural malpractice can also take the form of cultural denial and the so-called color-blind doctrine where counselors or therapists deny the importance of culture, race, and ethnicity. Cultural malpractice would also involve not following the APA Multicultural Guidelines (American Psychological Association, 2017b) and the APA Code of Conduct (American Psychological Association, 2017a) that deals with culture. Both the American Counseling Association (2005) and the American Psychological Association (2003) recommend using quantitative assessment instruments that have been normed on the population that one is assessing. One should make sure that if one is using an instrument or test for African American clients, for example, African Americans have formed part of the norming population.

Cultural Bias in Assessment

Sometimes bias occurs in the assessment of culturally diverse clients. In statistics, bias refers to systematic error in a test that systematically overestimates or underestimates the value of the variable it is assessing. **Cultural bias in assessment** takes place as a function of a nominal cultural variable, such as ethnicity or gender. According to He and van de Vijver (2012), "bias refers to nuisance factors that jeopardize the validity of instruments applied in different cultures" (p. 3). Van de Vijver and Leung (1997, 2011) have outlined three types of assessment bias: (1) construct, (2) method, and (3) item.

Construct bias takes place during cross-cultural assessments when

- A construct differs across cultures so that the construct does not completely overlap between the cultures. A test is measuring one construct that differs in the client's culture.

- There is an inadequate sampling of all relevant behaviors, so that some behaviors relevant in one culture may be sampled insufficiently. This type of construct bias has a greater chance of taking place when there are short questionnaires or scales.

- There is insufficient coverage of the construct. Sometimes only one or two dimensions of the construct may be assessed in the instrument.

Method bias can occur when

- The people taking a test are unequally familiar with the items. The test items may be more closely aligned with one culture, usually the dominant culture in a society.

- The assessment administrator or the person giving the test has differential effects on the participants. Research has shown that stereotype threat or having a White person administer a test to a person of color might cause the test taker to give a low performance on the assessment device.

- The samples are incomparable.

- The physical test conditions vary, or procedures differ from one assessment situation to another.

Item bias takes place when

- There are problems in the translation of one or more items.

- The wording of the items is too complex.

- The topic of an item is not represented in the culture or curriculum of the persons being assessed.

He and van de Vijver (2012) propose the concept of **equivalence and bias in assessment** as a way to minimize or reduce bias in cross-cultural assessment. These researchers assert that "equivalence refers to the level of comparability of scores across cultures" (p. 3). They use the comparison of the equivalence of miles and kilometers to demonstrate the differences between assessment bias and equivalence. One can convert miles to kilometers, and after such a conversion, the data in distance (miles and kilometers) can be compared across countries. He and van de Vijver note that "bias does not refer to random errors but to systematic measurement anomalies that are expected to be replicable if a study were to be repeated." In contrast, "equivalence is a characteristic of cross-cultural comparisons and not an intrinsic property of instruments; both kilometers and miles are adequate units to measure distances and any lack of equivalence issues arise only in the comparison of both" (He & van de Vijver, 2012, p. 3).

It is important that counselors and educators know how to use tests across cultures because the inappropriate use of tests or test bias may invalidate the results for people who come from a variety of cultural backgrounds (He & van de Vijver, 2012). Good assessment measures minimize the test biases discussed. When interpreting test scores, it is important to determine if the meaning derived from the original cultural group can be applied to the culturally different test taker. As Kwan, Gong, and Maestas (2010) have stated,

> before attributing meaning to test scores that deviate from the norm in the abnormality, deficiency, or psychopathology direction, researchers and clinicians should also consider a number of issues: whether the construct as measured by the test items exist in the test taker's culture, whether endorsing behavioral/attitudinal/affective items in the scored direction connote meanings different from the item's intended purpose, and whether there are subtle factors that influence test response systematically . . . It is imperative for clinicians to know the test norms of culturally different groups, as well as research that examined factors that contribute to significant differences between cultural groups. (pp. 410–411)

CASE VIGNETTE 6.1
CULTURALLY RESPONSIVE SKILL DEVELOPMENT: ASSESSMENT, EQUIVALENCE, AND BIAS IN ASSESSMENT INSTRUMENTS

Assume that you are a culturally responsive counselor interested in assessing the self-concepts of two female first-year college students at a local four-year college. The first student is an American Indian named Cha'risa (an American Hopi name meaning "elk") who has experienced some acculturation conflicts between her American Indian heritage and the social situations she is encountering at college. Cha'risa feels that she is an invisible person on campus, except for the few American Indian students with whom she socializes on campus (only one has a Hopi background). The Hopi Indians live primarily on the 2,531.773-square-mile Hopi Reservation in northeastern Arizona. According to the 2010 U.S. Census, there are 18,327 Hopi in the United States. The Hopi language is one of 30 in the Uto-Aztecan language family. Cha'risa misses her family, who live in a suburban community near the Hopi Reservation. For the most part, Cha'risa's grades are quite good—mostly Bs, a couple of As, and one C. The counselor has received permission from Cha'risa to administer a self-concept inventory, an acculturation instrument, and a college adjustment test.

Nayandini (her name means "she who has won the eye and is attractive") has also come to counseling because of acculturation conflicts; she misses her native Sri Lanka and her parents. The Democratic Socialist Republic of Sri Lanka, known previously as Ceylon, is an island country in Southeast Asia near India. Nayandini is doing well in all her college subjects, mostly As with a couple of Bs, and she has made some friends—mostly White American students connected with the International Student Office on campus. Although Nayandini speaks and writes at a proficient level, she is not entirely comfortable speaking English. She states that she would perform better if the tests were in her native language, Sinhala (also called Sinhalese or Singhalese). The counselor has also received permission from Nayandini to administer a self-concept inventory, an acculturation instrument, and a college adjustment test.

The counselor observes that Cha'risa's scores on the self-concept inventory are higher than those for Nayandini. Cha'risa's scores on the acculturation conflict test reveal less cultural conflict, and she has a better college adjustment score than does Nayandini.

Discussion Questions

If you were the college counselor, how would you respond to the following questions?

1. Of the three approaches to assessment outlined in this chapter—quantitative, qualitative, and mixed methods—which do you believe helps you to understand best the differences in the women's scores?

2. What do you think about the discrepancy between the scores of the two women?

3. Do you think that the counselor should learn more about Hopi and Sri Lankan culture?

4. Are there any other tests that you might consider giving?

5. How would you use data gathered from the initial interview?

6. What role, if any, might culture be playing in the young women's problems?

Models of Assessment for Culturally Responsive Counseling

Several researchers have constructed models of assessment for multicultural counseling. Richard H. Dana has developed a mixed-methods approach to cultural assessment called the Multicultural Assessment-Intervention Process (MAIP). Dana's model uses a seven-step procedure that allows the clinician to make frequent and careful selections among traditional and other appropriate psychometric tools. Using MAIP (Dana, 2005), the therapist

- Identifies the client's cultural identity

- Determines the client's level of acculturation

- Constructs a "culture-specific service delivery style" in which questions are phrased in terms of the client's culture

- Uses the client's preferred language, if possible

- Chooses the culturally appropriate assessment devices or modes to use
- Uses culturally appropriate strategies to share the results of the assessment with the client

Ridley, Li, and Hill (1998) have put forth what they have called the Multicultural Assessment Procedure (MAP). The primary goal of the MAP is to improve the cultural competence of mental health clinicians who are involved in culture-sensitive assessment. The MAP contains four phases: (1) collecting culturally pertinent data via multiple methodologies, (2) formulating a working hypothesis through accurate interpretation of the data gathered, (3) testing the hypothesis using available cultural and clinical data and refining the hypothesis as needed, and (4) providing an accurate assessment report (see McKitrick, Edwards, & Sola, 2007). The basic assessment used in the MAP is the clinical interview. The assessment model incorporates relevant cultural variables through all phases of the assessment process. The MAP model actually engages the client in the assessment process, and this client involvement serves to reduce the incidence of cultural misunderstandings and biases.

Neuropsychology and Cross-Cultural Assessment: Barriers to Client Change

Fear, the Human Brain, and Clinical Assessment

What is the relationship between culture, neuroscience, and clinical assessment? Mental stress is felt first in the brain and in the mind. Clients' fears often stand in the way of what they want out of life. Fear can block the change clients seek in counseling. The theory is that if clients understand what is happening in their brains when they respond to certain situations or events, they will be in a much better position to deal with obstacles, fear, and worry. Very often clients experience fear, worry, or panic without understanding how these emotions are recorded in the brain. If a client has an elementary understanding of the brain and various emotions, he or she might be able to say, "I'm upset because my amygdala is responding to a form of threat. What is the threat I am experiencing, and how can I calm my stress response?"

As observed in earlier chapters, culture organizes and conditions the brain. We perceive life through the lenses of our culture. On some occasions, a client's culture may actually mask neuropsychological conditions; therefore, clinicians should consider broadening their competency by becoming familiar with some of the following resources: *Handbook of Cross-Cultural Neuropsychology* (Fletcher-Janzen, Strickland, & Reynolds, 2000); *Assessment and Culture: Psychological Tests With Minority Populations* (Gopaul-McNicol & Armour-Thomas, 2002); *Neuropsychology and the Hispanic Patient: A Clinical Handbook* (Pontón & Leon-Carrión, 2001); *Minority and Cross-Cultural Aspects of Neuropsychological Assessment* (Ferraro, 2002); and the *International Handbook of Cross-Cultural Neuropsychology* (Uzzell, Pontón, & Ardila, 2007). Nell (2000) has presented an overview of culture-sensitive neuropsychological assessment.

Conducting a formal neuropsychological assessment of clients is usually beyond the scope of most clinicians and this text; however, it is important that clinicians understand the brain, how it functions, and what parts of the brain may be implicated in basic human emotions, such as fear, love, motivation, and attachment. Regardless of one's cultural background, worry and fear may produce similar responses in the brain. People need to understand that an important function of the brain is to keep people in their comfort zone. Worry and fear occur when a person's brain is taken out of its comfort zone.

According to Daniel Siegel (2010), harmony in the brain, or neural coherence as he calls it, gives us a sense of peace. People want to achieve peace in their lives. To achieve peace, people must quiet the brain, and they must seek harmony in their relationships because it is the disharmony in relationships with others that is often the cause of psychological pain. Fear is the brain's responses to real or imagined threat. When the fear circuits in the brain light up, the client's motivation or the motivational side of the brain gets lowered or reduced. Fear operates on both the conscious and the unconscious level.

Clients tend to have a fear response to the idea of undergoing assessment by their clinicians. Therefore, it is important that clinicians use positive words during the assessment process. Before counselors and therapists can help clients develop new neural pathways based on their strengths, they must first understand what happens in the brain related to negative and positive thoughts. Drs. Andrew Newberg and Mark Waldman, authors of *How God Changes Your Brain* (2010) and *Words Can Change Your Brain* (2013), have pointed out the brain can be changed by mindfulness meditation, spirituality, and self-compassion. According to these researchers, mindful meditation enhances blood flow and function in an area of the brain called the anterior cingulate cortex, which mediates our experience of empathy, social awareness, intuition, and compassion and our capacity to regulate emotion.

Practices that strengthen the anterior cingulate cortex help clients to regulate their emotions and to have enhanced empathy, social awareness, intuition, and compassion. The goal of counseling should be to strengthen the anterior cingulate cortex using meditation and other brain-calming techniques. Sometimes practicing a cultural ritual can help calm the brain. For instance, some cultures follow a ritual of setting a place at the dinner table for a family member who is absent as a way of cherishing hope that he or she will return safely, thereby reducing worry or fear about the absent loved one. Clinicians will be viewed as helpful by most clients if they can assist in calming their clients' brains, or in reducing fear and worry.

Anger is another negative emotion, one that impairs communication to the prefrontal cortex as mediated through the anterior cingulate cortex. As a result, emotion and fear take over in determining a person's behavior. Anger interrupts the functioning of a person's frontal lobes. Once anger takes over, a person loses the ability to be rational, and is often unaware that he or she is acting in an irrational way. When this happens, it's impossible to listen to someone else or to feel empathy or compassion—regardless of that person's cultural background.

The Role of Culture in Quieting the Brain

When people focus on their spiritual values and goals, they increase the blood flow to the frontal lobes and anterior cingulate cortex, which causes the activity in emotional centers of the brain to decrease (Newberg & Waldman, 2010, 2013). Every clinician should consider adopting healing rituals that have cultural resonance for clients. Therapeutic talk may be insufficient to engage the healing process for some clients (Moodley & West, 2005).

Clinicians need to be aware that the fear center in clients' brains controls their motivation. When clients feel fear, it stops their motivation. Conversely, when clients feel hope, their motivation to achieve or to change is increased (Welton & Kay, 2015). Counseling should be about using hope to build clients' motivation for change. During strengths-based therapy, clients are guided in how to use their strengths to talk to their fear and to quiet their fight-or-flight response to situations. Strengths-based therapy is designed to help clients strengthen their anterior cingulate cortex by teaching them brain-calming practices, such as meditation and strengths talk. Assessments of clients in strengths-based therapy should therefore be focused on hope and possibilities rather than on what is wrong with clients.

Assessment, Cultural Resonance, and Empathy

A clinician's assessment of culturally diverse clients is also influenced by the level of cultural resonance and empathy he or she establishes with clients. As discussed in Chapter 2, cultural empathy is the ability to understand and to feel compassion for a person who comes from a culture different from one's own (Welton & Kay, 2015). As described in Chapter 3, mirror neurons in the brain help individuals to have empathy for each other, and thus we can infer the relationship between cultural empathy and mirror neurons (Welton & Kay, 2015). One technique for training clinicians to increase their cultural empathy is by watching videos of practitioners counseling individuals from different cultures.

Cultural empathy causes a clinician to become attuned to his or her client. The clinician's internal state shifts such that his or her internal state resonates with the client's inner world. Cultural resonance results in a client's feeling deeply understood by the counselor or therapist. Conversely, intercultural problems can develop when a clinician's "lack of culturally resonant experience and knowledge, deeply held stereotypes, and preconceived notions interfere with the counseling relationship and impede counseling effectiveness" (Trimble, 2010, p. 252).

As pointed out in Chapter 3, the field of cultural neuroscience is revealing the deep roots of some of our cultural differences. People react strongly at the neural level to emotional signals from in-group members compared to out-group members. Chia et al. (2008) found greater activation in the amygdala to faces of people from participants' own cultural group than from another cultural group. In another study, Adams et al. (2010) found a similar pattern of activity in the superior temporal sulcus to facial cues on a mind-reading task to members of one's own culture as compared to members of other cultures. People in this study were found to be more accurate at mind-reading members of their own culture. The researchers concluded that we seem to be less attuned to people from other cultures and that such lack of attunement or cultural resonance may set the background for future misunderstandings and conflicts.

Yet, there is hope that through training and cultural exposure, clinicians may be able to become more attuned to their clients. As we know, experience and exposure shape the brain. With repeated exposure to other cultures, the brain can become more culturally attuned. Neuroscience holds the potential of clarifying answers to important questions: Are there critical periods during which the brain responds more positively to cultural exposure? What kind of neural reshaping in the brain takes place when people migrate from one culture to another?

Research in neuroscience might help researchers to better under ethnic/racial prejudice. Long before we become consciously aware of bias or prejudice, our brains develop neural pathways for cultural attunement and cultural resonance with others. Ethnic/racial prejudice consists of neural pathways in the brain. The good news is that neuroplasticity will allow us to develop new neural pathways that will, through clinician training in culturally diverse issues, help us to become more attuned with those who are culturally different from us.

> ## Cultural Reflections
>
> *For which cultural groups, other than your own, do you feel a moderate or high degree of cultural resonance?*
>
> *What factors have helped you to feel cultural resonance with members of these other cultural groups?*

Assessment and Cultural Knowledge About Clients

A clinician's cultural knowledge about a client may provide the groundwork for cultural resonance. To provide culturally responsive assessment of clients, clinicians need to acquire cultural knowledge regarding their clients' concepts of health, illness, and healing. Culture interacts with mental health issues. Clients' beliefs about counseling treatment, including their view of the role of the counselor and what treatment is supposed to accomplish, are extremely important. The following questions emphasize cultural issues that are relevant to assessment, treatment planning, case conceptualization, and case management. Table 6.1 presents a framework for assessing a clinician's cultural knowledge of a client.

CLINICAL ISSUES IN CONDUCTING A QUALITATIVE, CULTURALLY RESPONSIVE ASSESSMENT

During intake and assessment, clinicians should frame clinical issues in culturally appropriate ways (Comas-Díaz, 2012; Lynch & Hanson, 2011). For instance, if the client comes from a collectivist culture that places a high premium on family harmony and stability, the clinician might ask, "How is your family being affected by your substance abuse?" Or, "How is your family

TABLE 6.1 ■ Culturally Responsive Clinical Intervention Skill: Critical Cultural Knowledge for Assessing Culturally Diverse Clients
• How does the client view mental illnesses and healing practices within his or her culture?
• In the client's culture, what are acceptable behaviors for managing stress?
• How do the people from the client's culture express emotions and emotional distress?
• What specific words do people from the client's culture use to describe the client's presenting problem?
• How do members of the client's cultural group explain the origins or causes of the client's presenting problem or issue?
• Does the client's culture have culturally specific ways to describe the client's condition, and if so, how does the ethnocultural group explain the origins or causes of the client's condition?
• What cultural symptoms within the client's cultural membership group might predispose or lead the clinician to make a misdiagnosis of the client's condition?
• Are there specific therapeutic or clinical approaches that are appropriate for members of the client's ethnocultural group?
• How are caregiving practices manifested in the client's cultural group?
• Is honor attached to caring for family members with specific physical and mental health disorders?
• What role do family members assume in providing health care or mental health services for the client?
• How should assessment and screening be conducted for members of the client's culture?
• Are there culturally appropriate peer support groups available for the client?
• What traditional healing methods does the client's culture support?

dealing with your sadness and depression?" Or, "What concerns do you have for your family and your symptoms?" It is important to acknowledge the intricacies of the client's cultural context and life circumstances (Gallardo, Parham, Trimble, & Yeh, 2012).

Learning How to Listen for Culture in the Client's Story

Before clinicians can conduct a culturally responsive assessment, they must learn how to listen for the client's cultural story. It is also impossible for clients to talk about themselves or discuss what brought them to therapy without revealing some statement about their cultural identity (e.g., "As a woman, I experience . . ." or "As a man, I feel . . .") and their connection, conflict, or estrangement with some cultural group. Although sometimes clients come to counseling or therapy with the complaint that they are experiencing acculturation or cultural conflicts, others are only dimly aware of how culture might be impacting their presenting problem. Clients might not specifically use the word *culture*, but it is often implied in their descriptions about what is taking place in their lives. For instance, in relating his or her life story, does the client tend to express an individualistic or collectivist worldview? What is the role of the group or the family in the client's life? What cultural values does the client express in describing his or her presenting issues?

What is the person's orientation toward control and time? For instance, American culture emphasizes a high need for personal or individual control over life events. Americans tend to struggle with accepting life at face value or as things appear to be. On the whole, Americans value "being busy," "having a daily to-do list," multitasking, and getting things done as quickly as possible. From a cultural standpoint, Americans are likely to experience stress and anxiety when they cannot control their life events or when they cannot cross things off their "to-do list." In contrast to the more relaxed culture of Mexico, Americans would find it difficult to take a *siesta*, a nap during the middle of the day. From an American value standpoint, time must be used to achieve getting things done—not for sleeping. As a result, Americans tend to be sleep deprived.

Moreover, Americans value certainty rather than uncertainty. In contrast, many Asian clients are comfortable with uncertainty. In fact, Asians tend to have a strong belief that uncertainty is inherent in life and, therefore, that each day is to be taken as it comes. This value orientation is reflected in Asian attitudes toward health and sickness. For instance, Americans tend to talk about "beating" or "fighting" an illness—conquering a disease. In contrast, Asians are more inclined to reflect an attitude of acceptance of what life brings. They view fighting an illness as a negative approach to healing (Matsuda, 1989; Sue & Sue, 2013).

Research has found that clients' self-reports form the most reliable source of information about the impact of cultural factors on their lives (Rodriguez & Walls, 2000). A clinician's knowledge of clients' worldviews enriches the therapeutic relationship (Paniagua, 2014). When clinicians are not aware of the differences between their worldviews and those of their clients, misunderstandings and cultural impasses can take place. Therefore, clinicians must be prepared to ask questions about clients' worldviews and their cultural relationships. For instance, a clinician might ask, "What would you like for me to know about your experiences in your culture?" Showing interest in a client's culture helps to establish trust and to strengthen the therapeutic alliance (Duan & Brown, 2016).

During counseling and therapy, clinicians listen for evidence of clients' cultural values and the importance of such values to them. They also listen for the importance of religion in clients' lives, for their internal and external strengths, and for any evidence of internalized oppression. Clinicians help clients to understand when their problems are culturally centered conflicts, and they affirm clients' efforts to use culturally appropriate solutions to resolve their issues. The key is listening for cultural values and for the client's attitude toward his or her culture.

Assessment: Cultural Communication in High- and Low-Context Cultures

Problems arise during counseling when the cultural communication styles of the clinician and client conflict with each other. While the clinician communicates in a straightforward, direct manner, the client might prefer to use an indirect style of communication and silence as a way of revealing feelings and thoughts. Cultural impasses in counseling may occur because the clinician's communication style might be offensive to the client, and vice versa. Whereas some cultures perceive interruptions, corrections, and direct questions as rude, other cultures infer that the listener is actively involved in the conversation.

According to Hall (1976), major differences in communication and listening occur between cultures that may be categorized as high context or low context. Some examples of high-context cultures include China, Japan, North and South Korea, Vietnam, and many Arab and African countries. **High-context cultures** are more relational, collectivist, intuitive, and contemplative. Interpersonal relationships, group harmony, and consensus are highly valued in high-context cultures. In contrast, low-context cultures are generally linear, individualistic, and action oriented. People in **low-context cultures** value logic, facts, and directness. Interpersonal communications in these cultures are expected to be straightforward, concise, and precise. Some examples of low-context cultures include the United States, Germany, the United Kingdom, and France.

In assessing clients, clinicians need to be aware of their own cultural communicative style as well as that of their clients. How does the clinician respond to silence on the part of a client? The manner in which a clinician listens to a client's story can either promote or hinder cultural resonance between therapist and client (Trimble, 2010).

Honoring the Client's Communication Style for Feelings, Space, and Contact

Cultural Reflections

How would you rate yourself as a listener on a scale of 1 to 10, with 10 being an excellent listener?

How comfortable are you with silence when talking with family members and friends?

The following are some general guidelines for use with different cultural groups. These guidelines are given with the understanding that there are usually broad variations within each ethnocultural group on any given variable.

- Persons from some White/European cultural groups may be uncomfortable with extended silences and may feel that silences are an indication that nothing is being accomplished (Franks, 2000). In contrast, American Indians place great value and emphasis on listening. They tend to use extended silences for gathering their thoughts or for showing that they are open to another person's words (Coyhis, 2000).

- Latinos are inclined to value *personalismo* (i.e., warm, genuine communication) in their interactions with others. They value personal rapport in business dealings, and they prefer personal relationships to formal ones (Barón, Casas, 2008). Some Latinos begin their conversations with what is known as *plática* (small talk) prior to disclosing more personal information or dealing with serious issues (Comas-Díaz, 2012). Conversely, Asian Americans prefer a communication style that is not too personal or emotional; some may lack confidence in a professional whose communication style is too personal (Lee & Mock, 2005). In many American Indian and Latino cultural groups, cooperation and agreeableness (*simpatía*) are valued, and therefore, members of these groups may avoid disagreement, contradiction, and disharmony within the group.

- Learn the client's verbal and nonverbal ways of communicating with others.

- Become aware of the client's cultural feelings about personal space; preferred ways of moving, sitting, and standing; the meaning of gestures; and the degree of eye contact expected (Hall, 1976). For instance, Asian Americans come from high-context cultural groups that encode carefully sensitive messages so as to avoid offending others. A clinician who listens only to the content of an Asian American's message may miss the underlying message because what is not said may be more important than what is said (Fowler, Glenwright, Bhatia, & Drapeau, 2011; Lee & Mock 2005). Table 6.2 provides a framework for assessing differences in client/clinician communication styles.

Culturally Responsive Counseling and the Intake Process

Culturally responsive treatment is based on the clinician's having conducted culturally appropriate screening and assessment. In conducting a cultural assessment, clinicians should avoid addressing clients informally. They should not assume familiarity with a client until they have established a relationship with their client and they understand their client's cultural expectations and preferences. It is important to keep in mind that some clients may view the initial interview and evaluation as inappropriately intrusive if the clinician asks for too much personal information about family members or if the clinical content is a source of family dishonor or shame. In addition, some clients may resist or distrust the intake process if the clinician and client come from ethnocultural backgrounds that have a long history of racism and oppression. Then, too, some clients might be hesitant to participate in the intake process because they view the counselor as the absolute authority or sole expert, and therefore, they expect to be told what to do.

To deal effectively with these potentially negative influences on counseling, it is important that the clinician use the intake interview to explain what is going to take place during assessment and the treatment phase of therapy (Mohatt et al., 2008). The **LEARN** mnemonic provides a convenient way of conducting a culturally responsive intake interview (see Table 6.3).

TABLE 6.2 ■ Culturally Responsive Clinical Intervention: Assessing Differences in Client/Clinician Communication Styles

This intervention is intended to be used as a self-assessment tool and as a way to explore differences in communication styles among clinicians, clients, and supervisors. It is an informal rather than a formal assessment of communication styles. Place a check in the category that best represents your style and/or your client's style of communication.

Nonverbal Communication Patterns

1. **Eye Contact**

   When talking

Direct, sustained eye contact	Indirect or not sustained
Client _____	Client _____
Clinician _____	Clinician _____

   When listening

Direct, sustained eye contact	Indirect or not sustained
Client _____	Client _____
Clinician _____	Clinician _____

2. **Vocal Pitch/Tone**

High/loud	Low/soft
Client _____	Client _____
Clinician _____	Clinician _____
More expressive	Less expressive

3. **Speech Rate**

Fast	Slow
Client _____	Client _____
Clinician _____	Clinician _____

4. **Pauses or Silence**

Little use of silence in dialogue	Pauses; uses silence in dialogue
Client _____	Client _____
Clinician _____	Clinician _____

5. **Facial Expressions**

Frequent expression	Little expression
Client _____	Client _____
Clinician _____	Clinician _____

6. **Use of Gestures**

Frequent use of gestures	Infrequent use of gestures
Client _____	Client _____
Clinician _____	Clinician _____

(Continued)

TABLE 6.2 ■ (Continued)		
Verbal Patterns of Communication		
7. **Emotional Expression**		
	Does express and identify feelings in speech	Does not express or identify feelings in speech
	Client _____	Client _____
	Clinician _____	Clinician _____
8. **Self-Disclosure**		
	Frequent	Rarely or little self-disclosure
	Client _____	Client _____
	Clinician _____	Clinician _____
9. **Verbal Directness**		
	Verbally direct, explicit	Indirect, subtle, does not say everything
	Client _____	Client _____
	Clinician _____	Clinician _____
10. **Context**		
	Low context, relies on words to convey feelings rather than nonverbal	High context, high use of nonverbal parts of conversation
	Client _____	Client _____
	Clinician _____	Clinician _____
11. **Orientation to Self**		
	High use of "I" statements, orientation to self	Low use of "I" statements, orientation to others
	Client _____	Client_____
	Clinician _____	Clinician _____

TABLE 6.3 ■ Culturally Responsive Clinical Intervention: LEARN and the Intake Interview

- **Listen** to each client from his or her cultural worldview. Avoid interrupting or posing questions before the client finishes talking; instead, take time to learn the client's perception of his or her presenting problems and treatment, and preferences for treatment and healing practices.

- **Explain** the overall purpose of the interview and intake process. Describe the initial session and provide a reasonable rationale for asking about personal information.

- **Acknowledge** the client's concerns and discuss the cultural differences between you and your client. Make sure you understand your client's explanatory model of illness and health. Take into consideration the client's healing beliefs and practices and explore ways to incorporate these into the treatment plan.

- **Recommend** a course of action after collaborating with the client, and convey the importance of his or her participation in the treatment planning process. Point out to the client that his or her beliefs and traditions can serve as a framework for healing in treatment and understand that not all clients will be initially receptive to collaborating with the treatment process.

- **Negotiate** a treatment plan that incorporates the client's cultural norms and lifeways into a treatment plan that includes long-term and short-term goals and objectives. Demonstrate respect for the client's culture throughout the treatment process and honor the client's preferred way of communicating. Once the treatment plan and its modality are established and implemented, encourage regular feedback from the client and assess his or her treatment satisfaction (Dreachslin, Gilbert, & Malone, 2013; Ring, 2008).

Culturally appropriate assessment involves a clinician's asking and answering the following questions:

1. Has the client's culture/ethnicity been taken into consideration when formulating an assessment or diagnosis?

2. Are culturally relevant assessment tools available, and have these been used to augment the assessment/diagnosis process?

3. Has the client's culture/ethnicity been identified, described, and incorporated as part of the cultural assessment?

4. Has the client's level of acculturation been identified, described, and incorporated as part of the cultural assessment?

In working with clients, it is sometimes difficult to keep track of all that one is supposed to accomplish from a culturally responsive perspective. Table 6.4 presents a Culturally Responsive Intake Checklist that can be used to determine how well a clinician has taken into account the client's background. The clinician would simply check if the following information has been asked or obtained from the culturally responsive intake interview. Please note that this intake checklist has not been standardized on any population. It was developed by the author of this text, and researchers are welcome to use it for conducting research.

THE DSM-5 AND THE CULTURAL FORMULATION INTERVIEW

This section contains a description of the most widely used cultural assessment tool in the world—the Cultural Formulation Interview, or CFI (American Psychiatric Association, 2013). I predict that within five to seven years, knowledge and training related to this cultural assessment tool will be required for most counselors, therapists, psychologists, social workers, and psychiatrists. To provide culturally appropriate treatment, clinicians must use a method that permits them to systematically take culture into consideration when conducting a clinical assessment. Culturally responsive assessment acknowledges the unspoken words and the unexpressed emotions in a client's body language, as well as the unconscious attitudes and beliefs expressed in their behavior (Gallardo et al., 2012). Moreover, when clinicians use a systematic method for assessing cultural contributions to a client's mental distress presentation, they are in a better position to diagnose culturally patterned experiences of illness that are distinct from mainstream psychiatric diagnostic criteria. As Lewis-Fernández and Díaz (2002) have stated, "many societies around the world have developed folk mental health classification systems that are distinct from US psychiatric nosology. Patients from these societies and cultural backgrounds often express distress and psychopathology less in accord with US diagnostic categories than with their popular syndromes" (p. 272). Moreover, Lewis-Fernández and Díaz have maintained that there are differences in psychiatric disorders and their expressions among the various cultural groups. They point out, for example, that neurasthenia was originally a U.S. professional diagnosis but is no longer contained in the *Diagnostic and Statistical Manual* (DSM) system, and that in 1997, it was the most prevalent disorder among Chinese Americans in Los Angeles County. Clearly, there are culture-bound syndromes for various members of various ethnocultural groups.

The CFI is the most widely used cultural assessment tool throughout the world (DeSilva, Aggarwal, & Lewis-Fernández, 2015). It represents decades of work by the American Psychiatric Association, and it is the first attempt to construct a clinical model and an interview tool to help clinicians review culture in a systematic manner. The CFI can be described as a culturally focused idiographic approach to complement the nomothetic approach of the DSM. The CFI attempts to standardize how a cultural interview should be conducted by clinicians. The next section presents a brief history of the CFI, followed by a description of research on the effectiveness of this interview tool and an overview of its basic components (American Psychiatric Association, 2013).

TABLE 6.4 ■ Culturally Responsive Intake Checklist

DIRECTIONS: In conducting a culturally responsive intake interview, it is sometimes difficult to keep track of all the cultural issues that are discussed. The following Culturally Responsive Intake Checklist is designed to help the clinician become aware of what is discussed during the cultural interview.

The Culturally Responsive Intake Checklist might be used over two sessions so that time can be allotted to discuss each cultural factor listed. Depending on the client's presenting problem, not all issues will be discussed with each client. If an item has been discussed with the client, simply place a check.

Cultural Identity—Individual and Family

____ 1. Cultural identity (ethnocultural and religious groups with which the client self-identifies; other ethnocultural ground the client may not explicitly identify with)

____ 2. Family's ethnocultural background

____ 3. Father's ethnocultural and religious background

____ 4. Mother's ethnocultural and religious background

Languages Spoken

____ 5. Languages spoken while growing up

____ 6. Language client speaks with his or her family

____ 7. Language in which client feels proficient or literate

____ 8. Language client speaks at school or at work

Client's Worldview

____ 9. Collectivist culture—orientation toward the group

____10. Individualist culture—orientation toward the individual

____11. Communication—indirect, subtle, emphasis on nonverbal

____12. Communication—direct, meaning in words spoken

____13. High-context culture

____14. Low-context culture

Client's Past and Current Involvement With Country of Origin

____15. Client's past contact with family or friends in country of origin

____16. Client's current contact with family or friends in country of origin

____17. Client's current contact with community agencies

____18. Client's presence or lack of friends from his or her culture of origin

Migration

____19. Immigration history

____20. Migration trauma, if any

____21. Reason for migrating

____22. Losses associated with immigration and relocation history

Oppression and Social Justice/Injustice Experiences

____23. Addressing internalized oppression

____24. Challenging internalized oppression

____25. Discussing external oppression, ethnic/racial discrimination

Acculturation Issues and Conflicts

____26. Acculturation level

____27. Acculturation conflicts, intergenerational acculturation conflicts

____28. Acculturation stress, level of

Family, Intergeneration, Structure

____29. Intergenerational family history and concerns

____30. Family structure and values

____31. Birth order roles and expectations

____32. Gender roles and expectations

____33. Family views on help seeking

____34. Relationship and dating concerns

____35. Sexual and gender orientation

Health, Wellness, and Beliefs About Mental Illness

____36. Beliefs about health and wellness

____37. Health concerns

____38. Beliefs about substance use, abuse, and dependence

Mental Health Treatment Issues and Concerns

____39. Beliefs about mental illness and mental health treatment

____40. Cultural views of distress

____41. Client use of traditional, cultural healing practices

____42. Treatment concerns related to cultural differences between client and clinician

____43. Help-seeking patterns of client and client's family

____44. Cultural views on help seeking for mental health, and inclusion of family members

____45. Review of clinician–client confidentiality parameters and concerns

____46. DSM-5 culturally related V codes

Socioeconomic Factors and Background of Client and Family

____47. Education history and concerns

____48. Work history and concerns

____49. Socioeconomic status and financial concerns

Social Support and Community Concerns

____50. Cultural group affiliations

____51. Current network of social support

____52. Community concerns

_____ **Printed Name and Signature of Intake Interviewer**

_____ **Date of Interview**

_____ **Summary Comments**

_____

_____

Source: ©Elsie Jones-Smith.

Brief History of the Cultural Formulation Interview

In 1994, the DSM-IV contained within it the *Outline for Cultural Formulation*, which described in narrative form the components of a cultural assessment. This cultural assessment dealt with a client's cultural identity and cultural explorations for the client's illness. Since 1994, the Outline for Cultural Formulation has been revised in the DSM-5 as the CFI (American Psychiatric Association, 1994, 2013).

Usefulness and Effectiveness of the Cultural Formulation Interview

Cultural Reflections

Have you been trained in the use of the Cultural Formulation Interview?

Do you agree or disagree with the contents of the four components of the Cultural Formulation Interview?

To what extent would you feel comfortable using the Cultural Formulation Interview?

There is mounting evidence that the CFI is helpful to clinicians. DeSilva et al. (2015) have conducted evidence-based research on the CFI. Commenting on their research, these investigators have stated

in collaboration with institutions from around the world, our team at Columbia University and the New York State Psychiatric Institute led a multidisciplinary consortium that developed and tested the CFI for DSM-5. More than 300 patients and 75 clinicians in 6 countries found the CFI to be feasible, acceptable, and clinically useful when incorporated at the beginning of a diagnostic evaluation.

Description and Overview of the Cultural Formulation Interview

The CFI deals with the client's own narrative of his or her illness. It contains questions about the views of the client's social network. The theory behind the CFI is that all clients bring their own cultures, values, and expectations to the therapy relationship. Differences exist in client expectations about the relief therapy will bring to their lives, about payment for therapy services, about whether relatives or other health systems will be involved in the client's care, about whether an interpreter will be needed, and so forth (Brach & Fraser, 2000). The CFI is designed to be used in clinical encounters with all clients and not just clients from ethnocultural minority communities.

The CFI has three components. (1) *Component 1* is a core interview consisting of 16 open-ended questions divided into four domains: (a) cultural definition of the problem; (b) cultural perceptions of cause, context, and support (including cultural identity); (c) cultural factors that affect self-coping and past help seeking; and (d) cultural factors that affect current help seeking. (2) *Component 2* is an informant interview that evokes the views of family members, friends, and caregivers on the same four interview domains. (3) *Component 3* consists of 12 supplementary modules that elaborate on the four domains of the core and informant components of the CFI.

The CFI is particularly helpful when the clinician and the client do not share the same cultural background because it elicits cultural information that is potentially helpful in directing the clinical intervention. It highlights the influence of culture on the client's symptomatology, explanatory models of illness, help-seeking preferences, and expectations for distress relief (Lewis-Fernández & Díaz, 2002). Yet, the CFI may be helpful even for persons sharing the same race or ethnocultural background because persons sharing the same race or culture may differ in their cultural backgrounds their degree of acculturation, and be different in significant ways from each other. In other words, not all Asian Americans, American Indians, African Americans, White Americans, gays, or individuals with disabilities have encountered the same experiences in constructing their specific identity.

THE FOUR DOMAINS OF THE CULTURAL FORMULATION INTERVIEW

Domain 1: Cultural Definition of the Problem

This domain deals with the client's view of his or her illness or presenting problem. The questions in this domain first inquire about the client's reasons for the visit, with the understanding that the client's view of the presenting issues might not be the same as that of the clinician. The clinician focuses on the client's own way of understanding the presenting problem. The clinician raises the following three questions in Domain 1 of the CFI.

Clinician Questions for Domain 1 of the CFI

1. What brings you here today? How would you describe your problem?

2. How would you describe your issue or problem to a family member or friend?

3. What are you most concerned about?

Domain 2: Cultural Perceptions of Cause, Context, and Support

Questions in this domain seek to clarify what a person and support group consider the origin of the problem to be. The clinician tries to discover how the client's cultural identity is related to the presenting issue and whether or not the client's cultural background is causing problems.

Clinician Questions for Domain 2 of the CFI

4. Why do you think this is happening to you?

5. What do your family members, your friends, or others in your community think is causing your problem?

6. What kinds of support help with your problem?

7. What kinds of stress make your problem worse?

Role of Cultural Identity Questions

8. What are the most important aspects of your background or identity to you?

9. Are there any aspects of your background or identity that make your problem better or worse?

10. Are there any aspects of your background or identity that are causing other concerns or difficulties with your problem?

Domain 3: Cultural Factors Affecting Self-Coping and Past Help Seeking

Domain 3 explores what the person has done in the past to cope with the situation and to seek treatment for the presenting issue. Here the clinician might consider the multiple identities that a person has and the salience or importance of each. For instance, a Latino man may be a heroin user, but he identifies primarily as a gay man who has sought treatment for his substance abuse at a gay drug treatment center.

Clinician Questions for Domain 3 of the CFI

11. What have you done on your own to cope with your problem?

12. What kinds of treatment, help, advice, or healing have you sought for your problem?

Domain 4: Cultural Factors Affecting Current Help Seeking

Domain 4 explores the client's preferences for future care and any concerns he or she has about the clinician–client relationship. Does the person's cultural membership group have negative attitudes toward a person seeking mental health services?

Clinician Questions for Domain 4 of the CFI

13. Has anything prevented you from getting the help you need (e.g., money, work, family, stigma, or discrimination)?

14. What kinds of help do you think would be most useful to you at this time for your problem?

15. Are there other kinds of help that your family members, your friends, or other people have recommended would be helpful for you now?

16. Have you been concerned about the fact that sometimes clinicians and clients misunderstand each other because they come from different cultural backgrounds or have different expectations? Is there anything that we can do to provide you with the care you need?

Cultural Formulation Interview Summary Statements

The earlier version contained a section of the CFI that summarized the information derived from questions in the four domains—that is, integrating the material gleaned from questions 1 through 16—that have a bearing on diagnosis and treatment. The clinician concentrates on the role that cultural factors have had in determining the client's overall illness. The summary provided by Lewis-Fernández and Díaz (2002) demonstrates how cultural information could be used for a middle-age Puerto Rican woman who had been hospitalized:

> In this case, the overall assessment would mention that the patient's cultural identity is that of a rural Puerto Rican migrant with limited formal education, who speaks Spanish exclusively and has only lived for limited periods in the US, resulting in minimal acculturation. Her psychopathology is expressed in the traditional Puerto Rican idioms of *nervios* and *ataques de nervios*. She attributed the origin of these problems and her relapsing course to multiple past stressors and traumas, and especially to unresolved conflicts with her children resulting from her prolonged separation from them during childhood. (p. 291)

Data obtained from the CFI will help the clinician and the client to formulate a mutually acceptable, culturally responsive strengths-based treatment plan.

Supplementary Modules to the Core Cultural Formulation Interview

The third component of the CFI consists of 12 supplementary modules that expand on the core 16-item questionnaire. These modules are designed to help clinicians conduct a more comprehensive cultural assessment, focusing on populations with specific needs. The last module explores caregivers' experiences in order to clarify the nature and cultural context of caregiving. The areas included in the supplementary modules are as follows:

1. Explanatory Model
2. Level of Functioning
3. Social Network
4. Psychosocial Stressors
5. Spirituality, Religion, and Moral Traditions
6. Cultural Identity
7. Coping and Help Seeking
8. Clinician–Patient Relationship
9. School-Age Children and Adolescents
10. Older Adults
11. Immigrants and Refugees
12. Caregivers

Criticisms and Limitations of the Cultural Formulation Interview

The CFI is not without its critics. Aggarwal, Nicasio, DeSilva, Boiler, and Lewis-Fernández (2013) conducted a study designed to investigate perceived barriers to CFI implementation in clinical practice. The study involved 32 clients and 7 clinicians at a New York site within the DSM-5 international field trial. Using a fidelity paradigm to code debriefing interviews after each CFI session, the investigators found that the most frequent client threats were "lack of differentiation from other treatments, lack of buy-in, ambiguity of design, over-standardization of the CFI, and severity of illness" (p. 505). The most frequent threats were lack of relevance between intervention and problem, drift from the format, repetition, severity of patient illness, and lack of clinician buy-in. From the clients' perspective, lack of differentiation from other treatments was the most common theme in the fidelity paradigm study. About 12 in 32 interviews said that the CFI seemed to be closely related to other aspects of the standard interview, intake, or set of treatments. Clients were asked: "How different were these questions from those of your other clinicians?" (Aggarwal et al., 2013, p. 516). Clients tended to respond that the questions on the CFI were the same questions that other clinicians asked of them and that the CFI lacked novelty (Aggarwal et al., 2013). Lack of motivation/buy-in appeared in 8 out of 32 clients' responses. Clients were apprehensive in discussing the past and religion. They were uncomfortable talking about past coping patterns and religious supports and stressors as cultural factors contributing to their illness (Aggarwal et al., 2013).

An analysis of what clinicians found to be barriers to implementation of the CFI revealed that the most common theme was the lack of conceptual relevance between intervention and problem. The CFI's conceptualization of culture was deemed problematic in 15 clinician references. One clinician stated,

It's aimed at getting cultural information, but I haven't really been getting much cultural information from them unfortunately. I learned about them as people, but I'm not hearing themes of race, ethnicity, culture, religion. Those things aren't really coming out so much in my interviews, unfortunately. So it's not so much of a cultural interview as much as an interview about themselves, learning about them as people. (Aggarwal et al., 2013, p. 518)

From my perspective, the CFI does not sufficiently consider how embedded the client is in his or her traditional culture. Cultural embeddedness refers to the degree the individual is aligned with his or her native culture—how much cultural consonance or dissonance the individual experiences in terms of his or her native or adoptive culture. Here the clinician would consider such factors as how recently the client immigrated to the United States or any other country, whether the immigration was voluntary or not, and whether the client has lived in other countries. The clinician might ask such questions as the following: What country did you come from, and how different is that culture from the United States (or the country where you now live)? Whom do you associate with? What type of neighborhood do you live in; do you have to leave your current neighborhood to be with people from your native country? Do you follow traditional dietary habits of your culture? For some people, traditional dietary habits can be maintained for a number of generations. Do you dress in your country's traditional style? Do you use the services of a native healer?

For some people, the more recently they migrated, the less acculturation has taken place. If a person was forced to leave his or her native country and was detained in other countries, as has been the situation with some Southeast Asian immigrants, negative immigration experiences may hinder acculturation. The clinician might also inquire about how similar or different the client's native culture is from the client's current adopted culture and how the client would be treated for the illness or problem in the native culture.

To get a clearer idea of a client's cultural embeddedness, a clinician might ask about the client's current associations. Does the client associate with friends primarily from his or her membership ethnocultural group or with individuals from the new culture? In my opinion, the 16 questions contained within the CFI are too few; however, it is a major step forward in acknowledging the impact of culture on therapy assessment, diagnosis, and treatment.

Culturally Relevant V Codes in the DSM-5

The DSM-5 lists four V codes that are considered to be culturally relevant "conditions and problems that may be a focus of clinical attention or that may otherwise affect the diagnosis, course, prognosis, or treatment of a patient mental disorder . . . . These conditions and problems . . . are not mental disorders" (American Psychiatric Association, 2013, p. 715). The cultural V codes are Acculturation Difficulty, Nonadherence to Medical Treatment, Religious or Spiritual Problem, and Target of Perceived Adverse Discrimination or Persecution. Table 6.5 contains other pertinent V codes clinicians might take into account when conducting a culturally responsive assessment (American Psychiatric Association, 2013).

Culture-Bound Syndromes and Assessment

Sometimes standard diagnoses can be of limited value when working with culturally diverse clients. Each culture produces cultural concepts of distress, and therefore, expressions of psychological problems are partly culturally specific. Behavior that is unacceptable or aberrant in one culture may be considered acceptable in another. These cultural views of distress may or may not be represented in the DSM-5 diagnostic criteria (American Psychiatric Association, 2013). Disorders that are specific or unique to particular cultures are called culture-bound syndromes (Kwan et al., 2010) or cultural syndromes (American Psychiatric Association, 2013). Sometimes

TABLE 6.5 ■ The DSM-5 and Culturally Relevant V Codes

Recommended V Codes

1. Acculturation Difficulty (V62.4, p. 724)

2. Nonadherence to Medical Treatment (V15.81, p. 726)

3. Religious or Spiritual Problem (V62.89, p. 725)

4. Target of (Perceived) Adverse Discrimination or Persecution (V62.4, p. 724)

Additional V Codes With Cultural Relevance

5. Parent–Child Relational Problem (V61.20, p. 715)

6. Sex Counseling (V62.49, p. 725)

7. Sibling Relational Problem (V61.8, p. 716)

8. Social Exclusion or Rejection (V62.4, p. 724)

9. Relationship Distress With Spouse or Intimate Partner (V61.10, p. 716)

10. Identity Problem (presented throughout)

CASE VIGNETTE 6.2

CULTURALLY RESPONSIVE CLINICAL SKILL INTERVENTION: USING THE CULTURAL FORMULATION INTERVIEW WITH A CHINESE AMERICAN CLIENT

The Case of Mrs. Zang

The Cultural Formulation Interview

Domain 1: Cultural Definition of the Problem

Clinical notes: Elicit client's view of core problems and key concerns.

Clinical statement: "What brings you here today, Mrs. Zang?"

Mrs. Zang stated that her 10-year-old son was killed in a car accident by a drunken driver six months ago. Mrs. Zang also has a 7-year-old daughter with whom she is very close. Since her son's death, she has found it difficult to function at home and work. She has trouble eating and sleeping, is tormented by constant headaches and nausea, and can't seem to concentrate, such that she is making mistakes at work. Normally, she has had an excellent relationship with her boss, but her recent errors have caused him to reprimand her. Mrs. Zang works as a computer software expert at a midsize corporation. Her husband of 15 years (who works as a college engineering professor) has complained that she is neglecting her household duties, such as cleaning and the proper cooking of meals. Even her personal hygiene has declined, and their sexual relations have been nonexistent for the past six months. Mrs. Zang has tried to talk with her husband about how

upset she is over their son's death, but he just responds that "suffering comes to us all" and that "she must endure."

Domain 2: Cultural Perceptions of Cause, Context, and Support

Clinician: "Why do you think this is happening to you? Some people may say that their problem is the result of bad things that happen in their lives, a physical illness, a spiritual reason, or other causes. What do you think are the causes of your problem? What do you think that your family members are saying about what's causing your problems?"

In addition, the clinician used the following questions to elicit Mrs. Zang's explanatory model:

- "What do you call your problem in your culture? Does it have a specific name that you use?"

- "What does the problem do to you, and how does it cause you to react?"

- "What do you fear most about your problem?"

Mrs. Zang: "I think that I might also have an imbalance of energy in my system. I went for acupuncture, but that did not help for very long. I don't know what's wrong. When I go to my son's room, I hear him talking to me . . . his spirits are there."

(Continued)

(Continued)

Mrs. Zang's somatic complaints: According to Chan and Parker (2004), in Chinese culture people tend either to deny depression or to express it somatically. Moreover, Yeung, Chang, Gresham, Nierenberg, and Fava (2004) have reported that on average Chinese Americans do not consider depression to be a malady that needs to be reported to a physician, and further that some are unfamiliar with the concept of depression as a treatable disorder. When the clinician and client are from different cultural backgrounds, the diagnosis of depression might be missed. Hussain and Cochrane (2002) reported that Eastern culture assumes a holistic approach to the mind and body and that therefore an imbalance of energy can result in illness.

Domain 3: Cultural Factors Affecting Self-Coping and Past Help Seeking

Clinician: "In the past, how have you sought help from others, including doctors, friends, healers, and so forth?"

Mrs. Zang: Mrs. Zang adheres to the traditional Chinese family system. Her husband has forbidden her to talk with anyone about the problems she is having, as this might bring shame on the entire family. She says that it is bad luck that she lost her son and that people are controlled by forces outside of themselves, such as fate, luck, or chance—an Asian worldview (Pham, 2007). She has avoided seeking help so as not to "shame" her family. She states that her illness helps her to show others her grief for her son. She suggests that her stomach nausea may be due to her fears that something bad will also happen to her daughter.

Barriers to Treatment

Clinician: "Has anything prevented you from getting help with your problem?"

Mrs. Zang: "My husband has asked me not to talk about my problems with my family or with anyone. I have tried to obey him, but it is getting to be too much for me to bear alone. People in my culture resolve their own problems. We don't usually go to outsiders for help."

Domain 4: Cultural Factors Affecting Current Help Seeking

Clinician: "What kinds of help might be most beneficial to you right now? Are there other kinds of help that your family or other people might provide to you?"

Mrs. Zang: "I need you to tell me what is wrong with me—why I am sick all the time, why I can't concentrate at work. I am afraid I am going to lose my job. My husband says that I should just accept our fate that our son died. Our lives are determined by fate and outside forces that we cannot control. I don't want to be weak. I don't want to disappoint my husband. There is no harmony in our home because of how I am acting. People in my culture don't go to outsiders for help."

Domain 4: Clinician–Client Relationship

Clinician: "We are not from the same cultural background. Are you concerned about our cultural background differences, and is there anything I can do to provide you with the care you desire?"

Mrs. Zang: "At first, I wanted to speak with a Chinese woman counselor. You know women understand each other better. We know what it feels like deep down inside when our actions might bring dishonor to our families. But you seem to understand how I feel. I'm not sure you understand everything, but I will tell you what it is like to be a Chinese American woman in my situation. I've been in this country for 16 years, so I am part Chinese, part American. You treat me with respect and dignity, and now I am beginning to feel that maybe I will get better."

Summary of Cultural Factors in the Clinician and Client Relationship

The clinician may not be knowledgeable about the Chinese cultural view of "bad luck" and its relationship to the client's problem. Mrs. Zang seemed willing to share with the clinician some aspects of Chinese culture, and such sharing of cultural knowledge will help build the therapeutic alliance. The clinician might be inclined to discuss earlier on the five stages of grief, but if this information is presented too early, Mrs. Zang might see such a comment as "dismissive" of her cultural beliefs.

culture-bound syndromes may enter into a cultural assessment of clients. A **culture-bound syndrome**, also known as a **culture-specific disorder** or **folk illness**, is a combination of psychiatric and somatic symptoms that are specific to a particular culture, and usually the folk illness is not recognized in other cultures. The term *culture-bound syndrome* was included in both the fourth and fifth versions of the *Diagnostic and Statistical Manual of Mental Disorders* (American Psychiatric Association, 1994, 2013), and Table 6.6 provides a list of some of the most common culture-bound syndromes (Arredondo, Bordes, & Paniagua, 2008; Kwan et al., 2010; Lewis-Fernández et al., 2010). The DSM-5 provides a more extensive list of culture-bound syndromes.

TABLE 6.6 ■ Culture-Bound Syndromes

Culture-Bound Syndrome	Brief Description	Populations
Ataque de nervios	Involves uncontrollable shouting, attacks of crying, trembling, and verbal and physical aggression. Persons with this syndrome report a feeling of being out of control. *Ataques* can range from normal expressions of distress that are not associated with a mental disorder to psychiatric symptoms associated with anxiety, mood dissociative, or somatoform disorders.	Caribbean, Latin American, Latin Mediterranean
Dhat (*jiryan* in India, *skra prameha* in Sri Lanka, *shen-k'uei* in China)	A folk diagnosis for severe anxiety and hypochondriacal concerns associated with the discharge of semen, weakness, and exhaustion.	Asian Indian (India, Sri Lanka, and China)
Mal de ojo	A Spanish phrase meaning "evil eye." Symptoms include sleeping problems, crying for no clear reason, vomiting, and fever. Females are known to experience this syndrome.	Spanish and Caribbean
Maladi moun fe mal	A general Haitian Creole term for medical and mental disorders. If disorders are believed to be from the devil, the disorder is called Malady Satan (Satan's sicknesses). If the disease is thought to be from God, the sickness is termed Malady Iwa (disease of God).	Haitian
Taijin kyofusho	Guilt about embarrassing others; timidity resulting from the feeling that appearance, odor, and facial expressions are offensive to other people.	Asian
Shin-byung	Fear, dizziness, anorexia, and gastrointestinal problems suggesting anxiety.	Korean
Wacinko	Anger, withdrawal, mutism, and/or suicide resulting from reaction to disappointment and interpersonal problems.	American Indian

Paniagua (2014) has suggested that clinicians do not make much use of culture-bound syndromes because they lack knowledge about them and because a practitioner cannot expect to receive payment for the assessment and treatment of culture-related syndromes such as *ataque de nervios.*

Culture-bound symptoms are varied; consequently, there can be no single type of diagnostic or therapeutic approach. When working with a client from another culture who presents with symptoms that appear unfamiliar, it is helpful to find out what they and other concerned people believe is going on. For instance, an American Indian client might say to a clinician that he believes his weakness, loss of appetite, and fainting are the result of the action of witches and evil supernatural forces, or "ghost sickness." To a clinician unfamiliar with this cultural syndrome, the client's statements might be construed to suggest that the client is suffering from schizophrenia. However, if the clinician consults with the client's family members, he will discover that the client's symptoms are part of a culture-related syndrome (Paniagua, 2014; Westermeyer, 1993).

The DSM-5 does not distinguish between culture-bound syndromes and cultural variations (American Psychiatric Association, 2013, p. 758) in the client's report of symptoms, but it does note that clinicians' failure to identify "cultural variations" in the presentation of symptoms may lead them to "misjudge the severity of a problem or assign the wrong diagnosis" (American Psychiatric Association, 2013, pp. 758–759). The DSM-5 suggests that "spiritual explanations may be misunderstood as psychosis" (American Psychiatric Association, 2013, p. 759). Some African American and Hispanic populations subscribe to spiritual explanations for their maladies. There is no exact correspondence between culture-bound syndromes and DSM diagnoses. It is recommended that a therapeutic approach be used that includes both culture-specific and Western medical ways of responding to the illness or culture syndrome (Simons, 2001; Simons & Hughes, 1985).

Does culture influence only the culture-bound syndromes? Cultural factors haves been found to affect the presentation of such mental health disorders as schizophrenia, major depression, anxiety disorders, and attention deficit hyperactivity disorder (Canino & Alegría, 2008). Cultural influence can be found at multiple levels of mental disorders. First, culture and society mold or sculpt the meanings and expressions people give to different emotions (Paniagua, 2014). Second, cultural factors provide the yardstick for determining which symptoms or signs are normal or abnormal. Third, culture outlines what constitutes health and illness. Fourth, culture shapes both illness and help-seeking behavior (Paniagua, 2014). Therefore, culture influences mental disorders beyond culture-bound syndromes.

CULTURAL GENOGRAM: AN ASSESSMENT TOOL

The **genogram** is an assessment tool used by a number of mental health professionals, including clinicians, social workers, and therapists (Bean, Perry, & Bedell, 2002; Hardy & Laszloffy, 1995). The genogram is diagrammatical intergenerational map of three or more generations. As an assessment tool, it focuses on intergenerational patterns and relationships among family members (Goldenberg & Goldenberg, 2000). The genogram can bring forth a large amount of family information. For instance, it can illustrate family history, family strengths, family problems, and so forth (Hardy & Laszloffy, 1995). The **cultural genogram** can be used to gain cultural knowledge about a family (Bean et al., 2002). Genograms can provide a flexible assessment in that they can focus on religious and cultural beliefs, family traditions, spiritual issues, family history, and family strengths. Clinicians and clients must decide which aspects of culture are important, and they must choose symbols to represent those cultural features. The cultural genogram can be used as an educational tool to teach clinicians a structured way to elicit information about clients' cultural beliefs and practices (Shellenberger et al., 2007).

Hardy and Laszloffy (1995) have outlined several steps for preparing a cultural genogram. Their model for creating the cultural genogram was originally designed for students or trainees in the marriage and family therapy program at Syracuse University; however, it has been used with individuals and families.

1. ***Define one's culture of origin***. A person's culture of origin includes the major group(s) from which he or she has descended that were the first generation to come to the United States. For instance, if a person was born in the United States but his grandparents were German, then his culture of origin consists of German.

2. ***Identify organizing principles and pride/shame issues***. Identify the major organizing principles of each group that comprises the client's culture of origin. Hardy and Laszloffy (1995) gave an example regarding Jewish culture. According to these researchers, in Jewish culture, fear of persecution is an organizing principle, and educational achievement is a pride/shame issue.

3. ***Create symbols***. The clinician should create symbols to denote all pride/shame issues and to indicate their impact on family functioning.

4. ***Select colors***. The clinician and clients should select a different color to represent each group comprising a client's culture of origin. The configuration of colors gives a quick view of the overall cultural composition of the family system and of each individual's unique cultural identity. Genograms that are dominated by a single color indicate that the family system is characterized by a high degree of cultural homogeneity. Conversely, if genograms have a collage of colors, the family is most likely multicultural. After these observations based on selecting colors, the clinician can develop questions that direct further exploration of the client's unique cultural background.

5. ***Identify intercultural marriages***. Intercultural marriages represent a blending of cultures and thus a blending of pride and shame issues. In intercultural marriages, the parties must negotiate how different cultural heritage gets passed down, and they have to trace the intergenerational consequences of the intercultural marriage. The symbol ~ is used to denote intercultural marriages.

6. ***Construct a cultural framework chart***. The sixth step in the cultural genogram process involves establishing a cultural framework chart (CFC). The CFC constitutes the legend for the cultural genogram. Each person is given a CFC that lists the major organizing principles and the pride/shame issues with their corresponding symbols.

7. ***The genogram***. The final step involves constructing a three-generation (minimum) family genogram that contains symbols to identify intercultural marriages, colors to illustrate the cultural composition of each person's cultural identity, and symbols created to denote pride/shame issues.

Hardy and Laszloffy (1995) developed a long list of questions to consider while preparing for a cultural genogram discussion. Some of the questions are similar to those contained in the CFI; therefore, I have provided an abbreviated list of Hardy and Laszloffy questions in Table 6.7.

Both genograms in general and cultural genograms have been used with a number of culturally diverse groups, including Asian families of diverse cultural heritages (Lim & Nakamoto, 2008), African Americans (Thomas, 1998), and Latino Americans (Yznaga, 2008). Thomas (1998) has stated that a multicultural genogram can be used to assess the culture and world-view of family members as well as to establish rapport with diverse families. Thomas explored such cultural variables as race, ethnicity, gender, immigration, social class, and spirituality.

TABLE 6.7 ■ Questions to Consider in Preparing the Cultural Genogram
1. How are gender roles defined within the group? How is sexual orientation regarded?
2. What prejudices or stereotypes does the group have about itself?
3. What prejudices and stereotypes do other groups have about this cultural group?
4. What are the ways in which pride/shame issues of each group are shown in your family system?
5. If more than one group comprises your culture of origin, how did family members negotiate those differences?
6. What are your family beliefs and feelings about the group(s) that make up your culture of origin? What parts of the group(s) do you accept or reject?

Source: Hardy & Laszloffy (1995).

Lim and Nakamoto (2008) reported that genograms can be an effective psychosocial tool for Asians from three countries, Malaysia, Japan, and Cambodia. The authors delineated salient therapeutic themes and mapped changes from a transgenerational perspective with attention focused on sociocultural and political processes. Hardy and Laszloffy (1995) pointed out, however, that the cultural genogram may not be appropriate for Hindu Indians because of the large number of people considered a part of one's family:

> For example, a Hindu trainee from Southern India pointed out the cultural bias ingrained in our assumption that a complete family system can be mapped out in a single two dimensional diagram. She explained that in her culture, the definition of family is much more expansive than in Western society. In constructing her cultural genogram, she was forced by the limitations of the standardized genogram format to leave out many individuals who were significant in defining her cultural context and identity. As an example of how large familial networks are in her culture, she explained that 900 relatives attended her sister's wedding, and her mother and sisters personally wrote thank-you notes to all of them. (p. 236)

Clearly, the utility of a cultural genogram will vary according to the structure of some cultures. The next section focuses on both individual and cultural strengths.

THE STRENGTHS-BASED THERAPY MODEL'S ASSESSMENT PROCESS

Using the strengths-based therapy model, strengths discovery assessments are made individually with clients over a series of interviews because it is important to have "strengths chats" with clients instead of an interrogation (VanDenBerg & Grealish, 1996). The helping professional conducts strengths discovery in an informal, conversational manner. Typically, the helping professional does not first present the client with a checklist of positive qualities. As much as possible, the therapist engages in a conversation that appears to flow naturally about clients' strengths. The helping professional's follow-up questions can be used to focus on areas of strengths, to clarify clients' strengths, and to keep the conversation flowing.

Clinicians point out to the individual that their collaborative approach to strengths-based assessment is an ongoing process rather than a discrete event. As they engage in counseling, they might discover additional client strengths. Psychologists and social workers summarize periodically the strengths they have heard during therapy, even if the client has not

Cultural Reflections

We usually find what we are looking for. If we look for strengths in our clients, we find strengths, and if we look for deficits, we find those too.

STRENGTHS DISCOVERY TOPICS

- Client's interests and preferences (hobbies)
- Client's values and cultural traditions
- Client skills, abilities, and competencies
- Client's personal attributes, such as sense of humor and perspective taking

- Client's dreams and aspirations
- Strategies that have worked well for the client in the past
- Family members, relatives, friends, and other people who have supported or helped out the client in the past

explicitly stated these qualities as strengths. Helping professionals refrain from imposing their views of some characteristic as a strength. Instead, they ask the client to consider if it might be a strength. In the final analysis, it is the client's perception of a characteristic as a strength that is important.

Assessment of Clients' Internal Strengths

A strengths-based assessment is one that evidences a balance between the difficult life situations or problems that people have and the strengths (internal and external) and barriers (internal and external) they have for dealing with their life situations. As much as possible, the therapist, psychologist, or social worker looks for functional and usable strengths that might be used in the treatment process (Smith, 2006). Do the strengths carry over into other areas? Look at how strengths can help to build communities or contribute to where you live or work. The following list contains strengths discovery topics:

At the onset of assessment of the situation, clients may describe the problem as emanating from the environment, from inside themselves, or from an interaction between their inner selves and the environment (Jones-Smith, 2014). The bottom line is that clients come for help when they feel pain, vulnerability, or an inability to solve their problems on their own. When they come for help, clients experience a high need to have their problems understood by the therapist.

Moreover, many clients who are dealing with issues such as problematic substance use, mental health problems, and family challenges have a negative view of themselves, and they often share the stereotypes of them held by society. They are more likely to think of themselves as addicts, crazy, borderline, or worthless than to see themselves as having innate talents, skills, and abilities. Standard assessment techniques that focus primarily on documenting clients' symptoms continue this negative equilibrium. As a means of introducing strengths language into the assessment and treatment process, the author has developed several instruments, including the *Strengths Checklist* (Table 6.8).

A Word About Models of Strengths-Based Measurement

Many assessment strategies use a normative strategy. That is, a person's individual scores are compared to those of her or his peers for the purpose of obtaining a ranking. IQs are normative scores, as are scores on most screening tests for mental health and addiction problems. It is my belief that the normative approach may not be an appropriate basis for strengths evaluations. The process of ranking people in terms of their strengths immediately creates the likelihood that both the evaluator and the client will interpret "low" scores on strengths measures as indications of weakness or failure. This conclusion would defeat the purpose of the assessment. Second, there is no justification for ranking the expression of strengths along a continuum.

The strengths-based therapy model maintains that it is more appropriate to use an ipsative strategy. The ipsative approach focuses on the description of the individual without reference to norms or group values. This separates the individual's unique profile from those of others and removes the likelihood of spurious comparisons. Strengths-based assessment and the techniques

TABLE 6.8 ■ The Strengths Checklist

DIRECTIONS: The table that appears below consists of a number of words that can be used to describe yourself or to identify qualities that you have. You will notice that the words are all positive. This is not an accident. We want to know more about your personal strengths and abilities, and this is one way of quickly getting some information.

We would like you to go through the list and rate each word for how well it describes you. There are no right or wrong answers.

You can use this scale to rate each word.

5. This is really like me.

4. This is somewhat like me.

3. This is a little like me.

2. This is not really like me.

1. This is definitely not like me.

If you are not sure about the meaning of a word, your teacher or therapist will help you.

Spiritual	Nonjudgmental	Compassionate	Forgiving
Reflective	Trustworthy	Conscientious	Self-assured
Persuasive	Energetic	Perceptive	Friendly
Artistic	Insightful	Optimistic	Persistent
Good-natured	Flexible	Calm	Intelligent
Reasonable	Organized	Intuitive	Broad-minded
Enthusiastic	Perceptive	Detail-oriented	Good learner
Punctual	Hopeful	Discreet	Resourceful
Industrious	Empathetic	Tenacious	Courageous
Tactful	Sensible	Responsible	Fair-minded
Leader	Nurturing	Determined	Grateful
Tolerant	Assertive	Humble	Loyal
Reflective	Goal-oriented	Dependable	Confident
Patient	Team player	Persistent	Competent
Articulate	Creative	Cooperative	Communicator
Tactful	Self-reliant	Optimistic	Considerate

Source: ©Elsie Jones-Smith.

presented in this book are not meant to be used to compare individuals, establish group norms, or document the characteristics of groups or populations. Clearly, there is a role for normative strengths-based studies, and I do not discourage others from using the normative approach.

The Strengths Checklist is based on the Peterson and Seligman (2004) list of positive strengths. The checklist contains a set of words representing the Peterson and Seligman strengths categories. The words were chosen to provide a range of choices within each category and to increase the likelihood that the clients using the checklist would find words that capture their personal experiences.

The checklist (Table 6.8) is designed to be completed by the client privately. It can also be used interactively with the client. The client is asked to consider each word and rate how characteristic it is of him or her. If done interactively, the words are read aloud, and the client rates them on the form. If done individually, the client reads the words and assigns a value on the checklist. Either the client or the therapist identifies all descriptive words given a 5, then all words given a 4, 3, and so on. The items receiving the highest scores indicate the person's significant strengths. The benefit of the Strengths Checklist is that it gives both the client and the therapist a quick way of gaining insight about the client's perceived strengths in a nonthreatening manner.

Strengths Assessment and the Treatment Process

After clients feel they have been heard and understood, they are in a position to move from a problem-oriented, vulnerable self to a problem-solving self who has assets. It is part of the therapist's responsibility to help the client activate strengths that may have lain dormant for a period of time. The therapist points out to the client that activating strengths-oriented self-concepts is part of the treatment process. Hence, strengths-based assessment may help a client to solve his or her current issue, and it might also increase his or her ability to deal with future problems.

If a client is hesitant to discuss his or her strengths, then the practitioner might consider presenting him or her with a checklist of strength qualities (Smith, 2006). The clinician might say, "Clients have taught me that a number of strengths might be valuable to a person facing challenging life situations. Let's look over this list and see what fits for you." The clinician does not have to go over all strengths. The client checks those strengths that apply to him or her. If the practitioner does not present a checklist of strengths, then he or she writes down the strengths, assets, or skills that the individual mentions. It is important for the client to see the practitioner writing down the strengths or reviewing them from the checklist. The helping professional then gives the individual a copy of his or her strengths. During the process of strengths assessment, it might be necessary to gently refocus individuals back to examining their strengths and away from their usual pattern of discussing their problems and deficiencies. As clinicians do so, they indicate that they are not ignoring or denying important client problems.

Adversity Assessment: Coping Skills Strengths

All people encounter adversity in their lives. The degree to which individuals can overcome or successfully cope with their adversity provides an indication of their resiliency (Smith, 2006).

There is the long-standing belief that what does not kill us makes us stronger. The clinician asks questions about clients' overcoming adversities (Table 6.9) in order to reignite their sense of self-efficacy and competency. Once the clinician learns the kinds of coping skills clients have used to successfully overcome past adversities, he or she may suggest that clients use these same strengths, skills, or talents in their substance harm-reduction program.

Assessment of Clients' External Strengths

The strengths-based therapy model maintains that family members and friends often affect the course of clients' problems. Sometimes labels such as *codependent, rescuer, caretaker*, and

TABLE 6.9 ■ Culturally Responsive Clinical Intervention: Ways to Ask Strengths Questions About Overcoming Adversities
• How have you managed to overcome adversities?
• What adversity in your life has made you stronger?
• How did you manage to become stronger as a result of this adversity?
• What have you learned about yourself as a result of overcoming this adversity?

TABLE 6.10 ■ Culturally Responsive Clinical Intervention: Ways to Ask Questions About Family Strengths

- With whom in your family do you have a close relationship?
- Whom can you trust in your family? Who is the most dependable?
- Who in your family helps you when you are stressed?
- Do you visit your relatives? If so, whom do you visit?
- Where do you call home?
- Whom do you consider family?

enabler are used to describe how a family member or friend may unwittingly promote a person's presenting issue through ineffective but well-intentioned "help." It is recommended that therapists and agencies establish a treatment protocol for involving clients' families in the treatment process. Table 6.10 provides questions clinicians can use to assess family strengths.

Two success factors on which the helping professional can build are (1) family clearly has connections and a support system and (2) family members have bonded with the client and established positive communication patterns with each other.

Relational Strengths: Friends' Strengths

Friends assume an important role in both getting and sustaining an addiction. It is important, therefore, for the clinician to assess the kinds of friends with whom the client associates (Hwang & Cowger, 1998). Almost invariably, clients' decisions to enter treatment and to sustain either a harm-reduction program or abstinence result in their changing of friends. Table 6.11 provides ways a counselor can assess the strengths of friends for a client.

Cultural Reflections

Suppose you were given an opportunity to take a journey toward attaining the kind of life you would ideally like to lead.

Consider the three people whom you would like to take with you on your journey.

What qualities do they have that make you want to take them along with you?

TABLE 6.11 ■ Culturally Responsive Clinical Intervention: Ways to Ask Questions About the Strengths of Friends

- Is there anyone with whom you feel especially connected? (Note: It is very hopeful when youths feel connected to at least one other prosocial person.)
- Whom do you seek out when you feel stressed? Who provides a safe haven for you?
- How well liked are you by the people with whom you come into contact? (The ideal situation is that the client is well liked by others and has the ability to form and maintain positive relationships.)
- Do you have a best friend? (It is a very positive sign when the client has one "best friend" who plays a significant role in his or her life.)
- How would you describe your friends?

Ways to Ask Questions About General Social Support Strengths

- Who in your life helps you to reach your goals?
- Tell me about a time when you did something nice for another person, someone whom you helped out.
- Can you name two people who can help you to develop the competencies and skills you want?

CREATING A STRENGTHS GENOGRAM

In addition to tracing cultural factors, a genogram can be used to identify strengths that have been built up over the years in a person or in a family. The clinician can create a **strengths genogram** so that a family's skills can be reinforced. The clinician simply asks the family or the client to find a strength and trace it back or forward to others in the family who have that strength. The clinician might ask, "Has your family strength served to bond family members? How has your family strength helped your family deal with adversity? What did your family members do to pass this strength from one generation to another? What role has the family strength played in producing family pride or shame?"

ASSESS THE CLIENT'S POTENTIAL FOR SELF-HARM AND RISK TO OTHERS

As practitioners engage in strengths-based assessment, they do not ignore problems dealing with suicidal ideation or suicide attempts; the client's risk to do harm to others; physical problems associated with the presenting problem, such as risk of drug overdose; potential harm from others; abuse of children; and cognitive limitations (not being able to read or write) and physical disabilities (Rapp, 2006). These challenges are noted, and appropriate action is taken with regard to the established guidelines for assessment of clients' lethality or potential risk for suicide.

SUMMARY OF KEY POINTS

Assessment is a major part of culturally responsive strengths-based therapy. Clinicians should be trained so that they recognize what constitutes culturally fair assessment. They should understand what leads to cultural bias in assessment of all clients, and not just those who are culturally diverse.

Several major assessment approaches were reviewed in this chapter, including the DSM-5 Cultural Formulation Interview, the cultural genogram, and the strengths discovery and assessment process.

- This author predicts that the CFI and its supplementary modules will become standard procedure for a number of helping professionals, including psychologists, psychiatrists, counselors, therapists, social workers, and mental health counselors. Anyone who is interested in working with culturally diverse clients should become familiar with the CFI, even though I believe that it is not without its limitations.

- Cultural genograms provide another way to assess culturally diverse clients. I recommend that clinicians become knowledgeable about cultural genograms and how to use them with clients.

- One benefit of using a cultural genogram is that the assessment process becomes highly interactive, with the client making important contributions to the structure and content of the cultural genogram.

- I recommend using a strengths genogram, and this chapter provided some questions one might ask in constructing such a genogram. Every family and every person has strengths, and it is enlightening for a family to trace its major strengths across three generations. As families and individuals become more aware of their strengths, they feel better about themselves, and they become motivated to take positive action to resolve their problems. As stated throughout this book, focusing on a client's strengths relaxes the amygdala and the fight-or-flight response that is elicited when clients are fraught with fear and worry.

- Clinicians should learn about the brain so that they can communicate to clients what is happening to them when they are experiencing fear and worry.

- Clinicians need to understand how their words can either calm or excite a client's amygdala-related response.

DISCUSSION QUESTIONS

Discussion Question Set 1

Use "Strengths-Based Counseling Model's Assessment Process" to assess a client with whom you have been working. After conducting the assessment, cite three new facts, issues, or things you have learned about your client. Did focusing on your client's strengths help you to see him or her differently? Did you notice your client's effective coping skills? How might you use your client's strengths to develop your treatment plan?

Discussion Question Set 1

In groups of three or four, discuss how you intend to use the Cultural Formulation Interview to work with a client. What are two main concerns you have about using the CFI with a culturally diverse client? Pair off in pairs or dyads and use the 16 questions of the CFI to elicit the following cultural issues: cultural identity, cultural concepts of distress, cultural stressors and supports, and cultural features of the clinician–individual relationship.

KEY TERMS

Actuarial assessment (also known as **quantitative** or **nomothetic** assessment): Assessment that is usually quantitative in form and content, using standardized instruments to measure a client's worldviews or other constructs.

Clinical assessment (also known as **qualitative** or **idiographic** assessment): An assessment approach primarily using idiographic, informal, impressionistic, and frequently unstructured procedures to provide a quick, noninvasive method for assessing a client's worldview.

Cultural bias in assessment: In statistics, *bias* refers to systematic error in a test. A biased test is one that systematically overestimates or underestimates the value of the variable it is intended to assess. Cultural bias in assessment takes place as a function of a nominal cultural variable, such as ethnicity or gender. It can occur in relation to a construct, method, and/or item(s) in the assessment.

Cultural genogram: An educational tool used by mental health professionals to provide a structured way to address clients' and families' cultural beliefs and practices.

Cultural malpractice: The inappropriate use of Eurocentric values and cultural perspectives when counseling culturally different individuals.

Culture-bound syndrome (also known as a **culture-specific disorder** or **folk illness**): A combination of psychiatric and somatic symptoms specific to a particular culture and usually not recognized in other cultures. The term was included in both the fourth and fifth versions of the *Diagnostic and Statistical Manual of Mental Disorders* (American Psychiatric Association, 1994, 2013).

Equivalence and bias in assessment: He and van de Vijver (2012) propose the concept of equivalence as a way to minimize or reduce bias in cross-cultural assessment. These researchers assert that "equivalence refers to the level of comparability of scores across cultures."

Genogram: A type of family tree that records information about family members and their relationships over at least three generations.

High-context cultures: Cultures that are more relational, collectivist, intuitive, and contemplative. Interpersonal relationships, group harmony, and consensus are highly valued in high-context cultures. Some examples of high-context cultures include China, Japan, North and South Korea, Vietnam, and many Arab and African countries.

Idiographic Assessment: An assessment approach that has been described as rich, contextual, sensitive, open-minded, deep, genuine, insightful, and meaningful.

Low-context cultures: Cultures that are more literal, individualistic, and fact oriented. Some examples of low-context cultures include the United States, Germany, and the United Kingdom.

Mixed methods: A combination of quantitative and qualitative assessment methods in research and therapy (Lonner & Ibrahim, 2008).

Psychological assessment: A clinician's use of clinical procedures and instruments to determine the cause(s) or etiology of a client's presenting issues for the purpose of developing an effective treatment plan.

Qualitative or ideographic assessment: An assessment approach primarily using idiographic, informal, impressionistic, and frequently unstructured procedures to provide a quick, noninvasive method for assessing a client's worldview. See also, clinical assessment.

Quantitative assessment: Usually uses standardized instruments to measure a client's worldviews or other constructs.

See, for instance, the *Scale to Assess World View* (Ibrahim & Kahn, 1987).

Strengths genogram: A genogram format used to trace the strengths of families across at least three generations.

REFERENCES AND SUGGESTED READING

Adams, R. B., Jr., Franklin, R. G., Rule, N. O., Freeman, J. B., Yoshikawa, S., Kveraga, K., . . . Ambady, N. (2010). Culture, gaze, and the neural processing of fear expressions: An fMRI investigation. *Social Cognitive and Affective Neuroscience, 5*, 340–348.

Aggarwal, N. K., Nicasio, A. V., DeSilva, R., Boiler, M., & Lewis-Fernández, R. (2013). Barriers to implementing the DSM-5 Cultural Formulation Interview: A qualitative study. *Culture, Medicine, and Psychiatry, 37*(3), 505–533. Retrieved from https://www.ncbi.nlm.nih.gov/pubmed/23836098

American Counseling Association. (2005). *Code of ethics.* Alexandria, VA: Author.

American Psychiatric Association. (1994). Outline for cultural formulation. In *Diagnostic and statistical manual of mental disorders* (4th ed., pp. 845–846). Washington, DC: Author.

American Psychiatric Association. (2013). *Diagnostic and statistical manual of mental disorders* (5th ed.). Washington, DC: Author.

American Psychological Association. (2003). *Guidelines for multicultural education, training, research, practice and organizational change.* Washington, DC: Author.

American Psychological Association. (2017a). *Ethical principles of psychologists and code of conduct.* Retrieved from http://www.apa.org/ethics/code/

American Psychological Association. (2017b). *Multicultural guidelines: An ecological approach to context, identity, and intersectionality.* Retrieved from http://www.apa.org/about/policy/multicultural-guidelines.pdf

American Psychological Association. (2017c). *Understanding psychological testing and assessment.* Psychology Help Center. Retrieved from http://www.apa.org/helpcenter/assessment.aspx

Arredondo, P., Bordes, V., & Paniagua, F. (2008). Mexicans, Mexican Americans, Caribbean, and other Latin Americans. In A. J. Marsella, J. L. Johnson, P. Watson, & J. Gryczynski (Eds.), *Ethnocultural perspectives on disaster and trauma* (pp. 299–320). New York, NY: Springer-Verlag.

Barón, M. (2000). Addiction treatment for Mexican American families. In J. A. Krestan (Ed.), *Bridges to recovery: Addiction, family therapy, and multicultural treatment* (pp. 219–252). New York, NY: Free Press.

Bean, R. A., Perry, B. J., & Bedell, T. M. (2002). Developing culturally competent marriage and family therapist: Treatment guidelines for non-African American therapist working with African American families. *Journal of Marital and Family Therapy, 28*(2), 153–164.

Brach, C., & Fraser, I. (2000). Can cultural competency reduce racial and ethnic health disparities? A review and conceptual model. *Medical Care Research and Review, 57*(Suppl. 1), 181–217.

Braithwaite, C. A. (1990). Communicative silence: A cross-cultural study of Basso's hypothesis. In D. Carbaugh (Ed.), *Cultural communication and intercultural contact* (pp. 321–328). Hillsdale, NJ: Erlbaum.

Canino, G., & Alegría, M. (2008). Psychiatric diagnosis—is it universal or relative to culture? *Journal of Child Psychology and Psychiatry, 49*(3), 237–250. doi:10.1111/j.1469-7610.2007.01854.x

Casas, J. M., Raley, J. D., & Vasquez, M. J.T. (2008). ¡Adelante! Counseling the Latina/o: From guiding theory to practice. In P. B. Pedersen, J.G. Draguns, W. J. Lonner, & J. E. Trimble (Eds.). *Counseling across cultures* (6th ed.) (pp. 129–146). Thousand Oaks, CA: Sage.

Chan, B., & Parker, G. (2004). Some recommendations to assess depression in Chinese people in Australia. *Australian and New Zealand Journal of Psychiatry, 38*, 141–147.

Chia, J. Y., Harada, T., Komeda, H., Zhang, L. Mano, Y, Saito, D., Parrish, T. B., Sadato, N., & Lidaka, T. (2008). Neural basis of individualistic and collectivistic views of self. *Human Brain Mapping, 30*, 2813–2820.

Comas-Díaz, L. (2012). *Multicultural care: A clinician's guide to cultural competence* (pp. 33–56). Washington, DC: American Psychological Association.

Coyhis, D. (2000). Culturally specific addiction recovery for Native Americans. In J. Krestan (Ed.), *Bridges to recovery: Addiction, family therapy, and multicultural treatment* (pp. 77–114). New York, NY: Free Press.

Coyhis, D. L., & White, W. L. (2006). *Alcohol problems in Native America: The untold story of resistance and recovery—The truth about the lie.* Colorado Springs, CO: White Bison.

Dana, R. H. (2005). *Multicultural assessment: Principles, applications, and examples.* Mahwah, NJ: Erlbaum.

DeSilva, R., Aggarwal, N. K., & Lewis-Fernández, R. (2015). The DSM-5 Cultural Formulation Interview and the evolution of cultural assessment in psychiatry. *Psychiatric Times, 32*(6). Retrieved from http://www.psychiatrictimes.com/special-reports/dsm-5-cultural-formulation-interview-and-evolution-cultural-assessment-psychiatry

Dreachslin, J. L., Gilbert, M. J., & Malone, B. (2013). *Diversity and cultural competence in health care: A systems approach.* San Francisco, CA: Jossey-Bass.

Duan, C., & Brown, C. (2016). *Becoming a multiculturally competent counselor.* Thousand Oaks, CA: Sage.

Ferraro, F. R. (2002). *Minority and cross-cultural aspects of neuropsychological assessment: Enduring and emerging trends.* Lisse, Netherlands: Swets & Zeitlinger.

Fletcher-Janzen, E., Strickland, T. L., & Reynolds, C. R. (2000). *Handbook of cross-cultural neuropsychology.* New York, NY: Kluwer Academic.

Fowler, D. M., Glenwright, B. J., Bhatia, M., & Drapeau, M. (2011). Counselling expectations of a sample of East Asian and Caucasian Canadian undergraduates in Canada. *Canadian Journal of Counselling and Psychotherapy/Revue Canadienne de Counseling et de Psychotherapie, 45*(2), 151–167.

Franks, P. H. (2000, March 8). *Silence/listening and intercultural differences.* Presented at the Twenty-First Annual International Listening Association Convention, Virginia Beach, VA.

Gallardo, M. E., Parham, T. A., Trimble, J. E., & Yeh, C. J. (2012). Understanding the skills identification stage model in context. In M. E. Gallardo, C. J. Yeh, J. E. Trimble, & T. A. Parham (Eds.), *Culturally adaptive counseling skills: Demonstrations of evidence-based practices* (pp. 1–21). Thousand Oaks, CA: Sage.

Goldenberg, H., & Goldenberg, I. (2000). *Family therapy: An overview* (5th ed.). Pacific Grove, CA: Brooks/Cole.

Gopaul-McNicol, S., & Armour-Thomas, E. (2002). *Assessment and culture: Psychological tests with minority populations.* San Diego, CA: Academic Press.

Grieger, I. (2008). A cultural assessment framework and interview protocol. In L. A. Suzuki & J. G. Ponterotto (Eds.), *Handbook of multicultural assessment: Clinical, psychological and educational applications* (pp. 132–161). San Francisco, CA: Jossey-Bass.

Grieger, I., & Ponterotto, J. G. (1995). A framework for assessment in multicultural counseling. In J. G. Ponterotto, J. M. Casas, L. A. Suzuki, & C. M. Alexander (Eds.), *Handbook of multicultural counseling* (pp. 357–374). Thousand Oaks, CA: Sage.

Hall, E. T. (1976). *Beyond culture.* New York, NY: Anchor Press.

Hardy, K. V., & Laszloffy, T. A. (1995). The cultural genogram: Teaching for the future by learning the past. *Counselor Education and Supervision, 39*(3), 177–189.

Hartman, A., & Laird, J. (1995). Diagrammatic assessment of family relationships. *Families in Society, 76*(2), 111–122.

He, J., & van de Vijver, F. (2012). Bias and equivalence in cross-cultural research. *Online Readings in Psychology and Culture, 2*(2). doi:10.9707/2307-0919.1111.

Hofstede, G. (1980). *Culture's consequences: International differences in work-related values.* Beverly Hills, CA: Sage.

Hussain, F., & Cochrane, R. (2002). Depression in South Asian women: Asian women's beliefs on causes and cures. *Mental Health, Religion and Culture, 5*(3), 285–311.

Hwang, S. C., & Cowger, C. D. (1998). Utilizing strengths in assessment. *Families in Society, 79*(1), 25–31.

Ibrahim, F. A., & Kahn, H. (1987). Assessment of world views. *Psychological Reports, 60*, 163–176.

Ibrahim, F. A., Roysircar-Sodowsky, G., & Ohnishi, H. (2001). Worldview: Recent developments and needed directions. In J. G. Ponterotto, J. M. Casas, L. A. Suzuki, & C. M. Alexander (Eds.), *Handbook of multicultural assessment* (2nd ed., pp. 425–456). Thousand Oaks, CA: Sage.

Iwao, S. (1993). *The Japanese woman: Traditional image and changing reality.* Cambridge, MA: Harvard University.

Jones-Smith, E. (2014). *Theories of counseling and psychotherapy: An integrative approach.* Thousand Oaks, CA: Sage.

Koltko-Rivera, M. E. (2004). The psychology of world-views. *Review of General Psychology, 8*, 3–58.

Kwan, K.-L.-K., Gong, Y., & Maestas, M. (2000). Language, translation, and validity in the adaptation of psychological tests for multicultural counseling. In J. G. Ponterotto, J. M. Casas, L. A. Suzuki, & C. M. Alexander (Eds.), *Handbook of multicultural counseling* (3rd ed., pp. 397–412). Thousand Oaks, CA: Sage.

Lee, E., & Mock, M. R. (2005). Asian families: An overview. In M. McGoldrick, J. Giordano, & N. Garcia-Preto (Eds.), *Ethnicity and family therapy* (3rd ed., pp. 269–289). New York, NY: Guilford Press.

Lewis-Fernández, R., & Díaz, N. (2002). The cultural formulation: A method for assessing cultural factors affecting the clinical encounter. *Psychiatric Quarterly, 73*(4), 271–295.

Lewis-Fernández, R., Hinton, D. E., Laria, A. J., Patterson, E. H., Hofmann, S. G., Craske, M. G., . . . Liao, B. (2010). Culture and the anxiety disorders: Recommendations for DSM-V. *Depression and Anxiety, 27*(2), 212–229. doi:10.1002/da.20647

Lim, S., & Nakamoto, T. (2008). Genograms: Use in therapy with Asian families with diverse cultural heritages. *Contemporary Family Therapy, 30* (4), 199–219.

Lonner, W. J., & Ibrahim, F. A. (2008). Appraisal and assessment in cross-cultural counseling. In P. G. Pedersen, J. G. Draguns, W. J. Lonner, & J. E. Trimble (Eds.), *Counseling across cultures* (6th ed., pp. 37–56). Thousand Oaks, CA: Sage.

Lynch, E. W., & Hanson, M. J. (2011). *Developing cross-cultural competence: A guide for working with children and their families*. Baltimore, MD: Brookes.

Matsuda, M. J. (1989). Public response to racist speech: Considering the victim's story. *Michigan Law Review*, *87*(8), 2320. doi:10.2307/1289306

McGoldrick, M., & Gerson, R. (1985). *Genograms in family assessment*. New York, NY: Norton.

McKitrick, D. S., Edwards, T. A., & Sola, A. B. (2007). Multicultural issues. In M. Hersen & J. C. Thomas (Eds.), *Handbook of clinical interviewing with adults* (pp. 64–78). Thousand Oaks, CA: Sage.

McQuaide, S., & Ehrenreich, J. H. (1997). Assessing clients' strengths. *Families in Society*, *78*(2), 201–212.

Meehl, P. E. (1954). *Clinical versus statistic prediction*. Minneapolis: University of Minnesota Press.

Mohatt, G. V., Rasmus, S. M., Thomas, L., Allen, J., Hazel, K., & Marlatt, A. (2008). Risk, resilience, and natural recovery: A model of recovery from alcohol abuse for Alaska Natives. *Addiction*, *103*(2), 205–215. doi:10.1111/j.1360-0443.2007.02057.x

Moodley, R., & West, W. (Eds.). (2005). *Integrating traditional healing practices into counseling and psychotherapy*. Thousand Oaks, CA: Sage.

Nell, V. (2000). *Cross-cultural neuropsychological assessment: Theory and practice*. Mahwah, NJ: Erlbaum.

Newberg, A., & Waldman, M. (2010). *How God changes your brain*. New York, NY: Ballantine Books.

Newberg, A., & Waldman, M. (2013). *Words can change your brain*. New York, NY: Plume.

Paniagua, F. A. (2014). *Assessing and treating culturally diverse clients: A practical guide*. Thousand Oaks, CA: Sage.

Peterson, C., & Seligman, M. E. P. (2004). *Character strengths and virtues: A handbook and classification*. Washington, DC: American Psychological Association.

Pham, M. (2007, Spring). A brief cultural guide in working with Asian Pacific Islanders. *Cultural Connections*. Retrieved from http://www.ochealthinfo.com/newsletters/culturalconnection/2007/2007-spring.pdf

Pontón, M. O., & Leon-Carrión, J. (2001). *Neuropsychology and the Hispanic patient: A clinical handbook*. Mahwah, NJ: Erlbaum.

Pratt, S., & Weider, L. (1990). On being a recognizable Indian among Indians. In D. Carbaugh (Ed.), *Cultural communication and intercultural contact* (pp. 45–64). Hillsdale, NJ: Erlbaum.

Rapp, D. E. (2006). Integrating cultural competency into the undergraduate medical curriculum. *Medical Education*, *40*(7), 704–710. doi:10.1111/j.1365-2929.2006.02515.x

Ridley, C., Li, L., & Hill, C. (1998). Multicultural assessment: Reexamination, reconceptualization, and practical applications. *The Counseling Psychologist*, *26*, 827–910.

Ring, J. M. (2008). *Curriculum for culturally responsive health care: The step-by-step guide for cultural competence training*. Oxford, England: Radcliffe.

Rivera, M. M., Byrd, D., Saez, P., & Manly, J. (2010). Increasing culturally competent neuropsychological services for ethnic minority populations: A call to action. *Clinical Neuropsychology*, *24*(3), 429–453.

Rodriguez, R. R., & Walls, N. E. (2000). Culturally educated questioning: Toward a skills-based approach in multicultural counselor training. *Applied & Preventive Psychology*, *9*, 89–99.

Saleebey, D. (2006). *The strengths perspective in social work*. Boston, MA: Allyn & Bacon.

Shellenberger, S., Dent, M. M., Davis-Smith, M., Seale, J. P., Weintraut, R., & Wright, T. (2007). Cultural genogram: A tool for teaching and practice. *Families, Systems, & Health*, *25*(4), 367–381.

Siegel, D. J. (2010). *The mindful therapist: A clinician's guide to mindsight and neural integration*. New York, NY: Norton.

Simons, R. C. (2001). Introduction to culture-bound syndromes. *Psychiatric Times*. Retrieved from http://www.psychiatrictimes.com/cultural-psychiatry/introduction-culture-bound-syndromes-0

Simons, R. C., & Hughes, C. C. (Eds.). (1985). *The culture-bound syndromes: Folk illnesses of psychiatric and anthropological interest*. New York, NY: Springer.

Smith, E. J. (2006). The strengths-based counseling model. *The Counseling Psychologist*, *34*(1), 13–79.

Thomas, A. J. (1998). Understanding culture and worldview in family systems: Use of the multicultural genogram. *The Family Journal: Counseling and Therapy for Couples and Families*, *6*(1), 24–32.

Trimble, J. E. (2010). The virtues of cultural resonance, competence, and relational collaboration with Native American Indian communities: A synthesis of the counseling and psychotherapy literature. *The Counseling Psychologist*, *38*(2), 243–256.

Uzzell, B. P., Pontón, M., Ardila, A. (2007). *International handbook of cross-cultural neuropsychology*. Mahwah, NJ: Erlbaum.

van de Vijver, F. J. R., & Leung, K. (1997). *Cross-cultural psychology series, Vol. 1. Methods and data analysis for cross-cultural research.* Thousand Oaks, CA: Sage.

van de Vijver, F. J. R., & Leung, K. (2011). Equivalence and bias: A review of concepts, models, and data analytic procedures. In D. Matsumoto & van de Vijver (Eds.), *Cross-cultural cultural research methods in psychology.* Cambridge, England: Cambridge University Press.

VanDenBerg, J. E., & Grealish, E. M. (1996). Individualized services and supports through the wraparound process: Philosophy and procedures. *Journal of Child and Family Studies, 5*(1), 7–21. doi:10.1007/bf02234675

Welton, R., & Kay, J. (2015). The neurobiology of psychotherapy. *Psychiatric Times, 32*(10). Retrieved from http://www.psychiatrictimes.com/neuropsychiatry/neurobiology-psychotherapy

Westermeyer, J. J. (1993). Cross-cultural psychiatric assessment. In A. C. Gaw (Ed.), *Culture, ethnicity, and mental illness* (pp. 125–144). Washington, DC: American Psychiatric Press.

Yeung, A., Chang, D., Gresham, R., Nierenberg, A. A., & Fava, M. (2004). Illness beliefs of depressed Chinese American patients in primary care. *The Journal of Nervous and Mental Disease, 192*(4), 324–327.

Yznaga, S. D. (2008). Using the genogram to facilitate the intercultural competence of Mexican immigrants. *The Family Journal: Counseling and Therapy for Couples and Families, 16*(2), 159–165.

CULTURALLY RESPONSIVE CASE CONCEPTUALIZATION AND TREATMENT PLANNING

- *"Never look for a psychological explanation unless every effort to find a cultural one has been exhausted."*
  —Margaret Mead quoting William Fielding Ogburn, one of her mentors at Columbia University

- *"Diversity may be the hardest thing for a society to live with and perhaps the most dangerous thing for a society to be without.* —William Sloane Coffin Jr.

- *"Be the change you wish to see in the world."* —Mahatma Gandhi

CHAPTER OBJECTIVES

- Explain the process of case conceptualization for working with culturally diverse clients and recognize how cultural factors may impact case conceptualization.

- Identify cultural bias and cultural disparities in mental health service delivery systems, including the overdiagnosis of people of color.

- Implement the components of the Cultural Formulation Interview, including assessment of (1) cultural identity, (2) cultural explanations of the illness, (3) cultural factors related to the psychosocial environment and levels of functioning, (4) cultural elements of the clinician–patient relationship, and (5) the overall impact of culture on diagnosis and care.

- Apply the Cultural Formulation Interview for case conceptualization in working with culturally diverse clients.

- Apply strengths-based case conceptualization and strengths-based treatment plans for treating culturally diverse clients.

- Utilize culturally responsive strengths-based treatment counseling techniques, such as developing a strengths journal and strengths cards.

INTRODUCTION

This chapter focuses on case conceptualization, a very important part of a clinician's responsibility. Sperry (2010) has asserted that developing a conceptual framework for conducting therapy forms one of the most critical competencies for clinicians. Yet, for some beginning clinicians, case conceptualization is a difficult process to learn. **Case conceptualization** can be defined as the process of using good theoretical frameworks to organize assessment and interview data to formulate hypotheses that may explain the underlying dynamics of the client's presenting problem in order to formulate an appropriate treatment plan (Sperry, 2010).

A case conceptualization is based on the theoretical model a helping professional uses to organize his or her personal views as to what is happening to a client. A **theoretical framework** (or **theoretical model**) is a collection of beliefs or a unifying theory of what caused the client's presenting problem and what is needed to bring about positive change.

Case conceptualization is governed by a clinician's worldviews in two distinct areas: (1) a clinician's personal worldview or outlook on life and (2) a clinician's theoretical perspective that he or she uses in examining clients' personal problems. In terms of one's personal worldview, although many people maintain that a conceptual framework for psychotherapy is learned in graduate school, it is actually learned a great deal earlier. A conceptual framework unfolds when a person begins to adopt beliefs and attitudes about the causes of different situations and problems. A counseling theoretical framework alone is insufficient for a meaningful framework; all perspectives taken by the clinician are ultimately cultural in nature. All people are conditioned by their culture to have lenses through which they view the world and its problems. Culture is in itself a filter, a lens. Culture provides a framework for examining a client's presenting problems.

In terms of a theoretical perspective, a clinician might have a case conceptualization that is founded on a cognitive behavioral theoretical framework, a psychodynamic framework, or a strengths-based framework. It is beyond the scope of this chapter to present case conceptualization from the many different types of counseling or psychotherapeutic frameworks. This chapter first presents generic models of case conceptualization that can be tailored for a clinician's avowed theory of counseling or psychotherapy. The chapter concludes with a strengths-based case conceptual model that incorporates important dimensions of the Cultural Formulation Interview (CFI) (American Psychiatric Association, 2013).

Developing a good case conceptualization is extremely important because it is used to create a **treatment plan** for clients and guides what the clinician does during the process of therapy treatment. A clinician's awareness of culture or even his or her knowledge about a culture may prove to be insufficient for delivery of mental health services to a client. We need a systematic way of incorporating culture into the therapy relationship because culture is a primary force in the creation of a person's identity. A case conceptualization helps the clinician to construct a systematic way of incorporating culture into therapy.

White Clinicians and Culturally Diverse Clients

The United States has become a multicultural, multiracial, and multilingual society. Therefore, it is highly likely that the average American clinician will be working with clients from cultural backgrounds different from his or her own. This statement is buttressed by some of the latest data published by the U.S. Census Bureau. According to Humes, Jones, and Ramirez (2011), more than half of the growth in the total U.S. population between 2000 and 2010 was a result of the increase in the Hispanic and Latino population. The White group is still numerically and proportionally the largest racial and ethnic group in the United States, but it is also growing at the slowest rate (1% from 2000 to 2010). Conversely, the Hispanic and Asian populations have grown considerably, partly because of their high levels of immigration. Between 2000 and 2010, for example, the Hispanic population grew by 43%, increasing from 35.3 million in 2000 to 50.5 million in 2010 (Humes et al., 2011). By 2010, Hispanics comprised 16% of the total U.S. population of 308.7 million.

In that same year, the Black or African American population totaled 38.9 million and represented 13% of the total population. Approximately 14.7 million people identified their race as Asian (about 5% of all respondents). About 2.9 million people identified themselves as American Indian or Alaska Native (about 0.9% of the total population). Native Hawaiian and other Pacific Islanders comprised 0.5 million, which represented 0.2% of the total population (Humes et al., 2011).

Overall, census reports have projected that ethnic/racial minorities will become a numerical majority by the year 2050; other surveys have predicted that the demographic change will take place decades sooner. In the 2010 Census, a little over one-third of the U.S. population reported their race and ethnicity as something other than non-Hispanic White (i.e., "minority"). The so-called minority population grew from 86.9 million to 111.9 million between 2000 and 2010, representing a growth of 29% over the decade.

Cultural Reflections

Let's assume that you are a White American reading the statistics on the growing "browning" of America.

What thoughts and feelings are going through your head as you read these statistics?

Now imagine for a moment that you are a member of one of the five ethnic minorities discussed. What thoughts and feelings are going through your head as you read the same population statistics?

The geographic distribution of the population according to race and ethnicity is also significant. In the 2010 Census, a large number of areas, especially in the South and West, had large proportions of the total population that was minority. Nearly half of the West's population was minority (47%), numbering 33.9 million. Among the states, California had the largest minority population at 22.3 million. Between 2000 and 2010, a number of states had majority "minority" populations, including Texas, the District of Columbia, Hawaii, and New Mexico, where more than 50% of the population was part of a minority group. Among all the states, Nevada's minority population increased at the highest rate—by 78% (Humes et al., 2011).

A question that may come to mind related to these Census results is "What about people of mixed race or ethnicity?" Indeed, this is an important question, as many Americans are multiracial and/or multiethnic, and Chapter 3 of this book points out that every one of us actually has a multicultural identity. Yet it was not until 2000 that the Census Bureau offered an option for respondents to classify themselves in more than one racial category. The 2010 Census had six single-race categories (five "standard" races and a "some other race" category) and 57 combined-race categories, such as White–American Indian, White–Asian, and White–Black. In that year, 9 million Americans (2.9%) chose one of these combined-race categories (Patten, 2015).

The above statistics have important implications for the mental health clinician. The majority of clinicians are White American, while a growing number of clients are from so-called minority or culturally diverse backgrounds. The low percentage of people of color as clinicians and psychologists has been said to contribute to bias in the delivery of mental health services as well as to high attrition rates in counseling (Paniagua, 2014). Given the increasing diversity of the U.S. population, mental health service providers must become aware of the influences that culture has on psychological processes, mental illnesses, and help-seeking behavior.

Cultural Bias and Disparities in Mental Health Service Delivery Systems

Cultural bias and disparities in mental health practice have long been reported in the literature (Blake & McAuliffe, 2011; Sue & Sue, 2013). For instance, in 2001, the Surgeon General of the United States published a report on the mental health status of ethnic/racial minorities. Some key findings summarized in that report were that (1) the mental health needs of members of racial and ethnic minorities are unmet, (2) there is a strong need to understand both cultural and sociopolitical factors affecting the life experience of people of color, and (3) cultural competency in the delivery of services is critical to the psychological and physical well-being of persons of color. The report also noted that the mental health practitioner is not immune from inheriting the prejudicial attitudes, biases, and stereotypes that exist in the broad American society (U.S. Department of Health and Human Services, 2001). The Surgeon General's report *Mental Health: Culture, Race, and Ethnicity* stated that compared to White Americans, members of racial and ethnic minority populations are

- Less likely to have access to available mental health services

- Less likely to receive necessary mental health care

- Often provided with a poorer quality of treatment

- Significantly underrepresented in mental health research

Cultural Reflections

A clinician without a case conceptualization is like an airplane being flown without a pilot, drifting aimlessly in space.

Perhaps as a consequence of the disparities in mental health services, members of American racial minority groups are more likely to delay seeking treatment, and when they do seek mental health services, it is often not until they are at an acute stage of illness. Although generally rates of mental disorders among people in most ethnic minority groups are similar to rates for Caucasians, members of minority populations are more likely to experience factors, such as racism, discrimination, violence, and poverty, that may exacerbate mental illnesses (U.S. Department of Health and Human Services, 2001).

What Happens When Clinicians Are Biased Against Their Clients?

Clinician bias is a very real problem when working with culturally diverse clients (McAuliffe, 2013). Although most clinicians are inclined to view themselves as objective and nonbiased, this is seldom the case. A clinician's worldviews, which are often entrenched and sometimes outside of his or her immediate awareness, color the therapeutic relationship such that clinicians are inclined to view differences in presentation of mental issues as pathology (Dana, 2002). In quoting the comments of prominent clinicians on clinician bias in a *Washington Post* article, Vedantam (2005) reported that over a two-year period, psychiatrist Heather Hall had to correct the diagnoses of nearly 40 culturally diverse clients. Clearly, there are culture-related issues in **diagnosis**, especially when the client and clinician are not from the same cultural and socioeconomic background. Misdiagnosis sometimes takes place because the clinician lacks knowledge about the client's cultural idioms of distress.

Research on some ethnic groups has demonstrated that culture has a critical role in individuals' expression of depression. For instance, Fry and Nguyen (1996) conducted a comparative study of Australian and Vietnamese nursing students' perceptions of depression and found that Vietnamese students believed that a "superior person" would not allow troubling thoughts or emotions to affect them as greatly. In contrast, Australian students identified with the Western worldview and believed their emotions were beyond their control, and sought help for their suffering. Fry and Nguyen concluded that culture can influence a person's understanding and experience of depression.

Schreiber, Stern, and Wilson (2000) conducted a study to discover how women from West Indian culture address feelings of depression. The investigators conducted semistructured interviews with 12 Black West Indian Canadian women who experienced depression. The researchers found that Black West Indian Canadian women managed their depression in culturally defined ways by not showing vulnerability. From their perspective, suffering from depression was a symptom of life as a woman. In contrast, White Canadian women did not attribute depression symptoms to being a woman, but rather acknowledged that they were experiencing a type of mental disorder.

Nicolas and colleagues (2007) investigated the expression and treatment of depression among Haitian immigrant women in the United States. These investigators reported that Haitian immigrant women experienced three distinctive types of depression ("pain in the body," "relief through God," and "fighting a winless battle"). For Haitian American women, culture had a deep and enduring impact on how they experienced depression. Nicolas et al. stated, "Haitian immigrant women's experiences of depression may be unique to their culture. . . . Studying mental health conditions from a perspective other than that of the native culture of clients may produce inaccurate findings" (p. 96).

Cultural Reflections

Have you ever encountered cultural biases in a mental health delivery system? If so, what biases did you find?

If your mental health delivery system seems to be void of cultural bias, to what do you attribute this lack of bias?

In a different study that investigated the influence of culture on depression, Brown, Schulberg, and Madonia (1996) compared the psychiatric history and presenting symptoms of African Americans and European Americans suffering from major depression. While these investigators reported similarities between African Americans and Whites in primary mood symptoms and condition severity, they also found important differences between these two groups. African Americans tended to talk about their depression in terms of physical symptoms and psychosocial stressors, whereas White clients were more inclined to describe their depression as mood disturbances.

Clinicians must understand how clients' culture can influence their expression of a mental health condition or mental disorder. In addition, they must become aware of how their cultural worldviews impact their diagnoses of clients. It is important that clinicians examine themselves to see if they have biases against clients of color or against culturally diverse clients. Paniagua, O'Boyle, Tan, and Lew (2000) have proposed an instrument, the Self-Evaluation of Biases and Prejudices Scale, to assist clinicians in determining if they have unintended biases and prejudices against various clients.

Overdiagnosis of People of Color: Seeing Greater Pathology Than There Is in a Client

Another consequence of clinician bias toward clients is shown in the literature of diagnosis of members of racial and ethnic minorities. Research has shown that people of color and other members of a wide range of "minority" cultures are often overdiagnosed (Duan & Brown, 2016). **Overdiagnosis of minority clients** sometimes results from clinicians seeing pathology or mental health problems in members of culturally diverse groups (Duan & Brown, 2016) when, in fact, the client might be responding appropriately within his or her cultural framework. For decades, studies have shown that African Americans are more likely to be misdiagnosed with schizophrenia than any other ethnic group. Although research on American Indians and Alaskan Indians is limited, existing studies suggest that members of these populations experience a disproportionate percentage of mental problems and disorders (Paniagua, 2014).

Counseling Attrition Rate for Members of Ethnic/Racial Minorities

Clinician bias and lack of multicultural counseling skills have also been associated with high **psychotherapy attrition rates for ethnic/racial minorities**. The necessity for clinicians to acquire culturally responsive competency for counseling clients is highlighted when one considers the attrition rate for members of racial, cultural, and ethnic minority groups. Nearly 50% of racially and ethnically diverse clients terminate treatment or therapy after just one visit with a mental health practitioner (Paniagua, 2014). At the beginning of treatment, such clients are at high risk for feeling apprehensive and uncertain as to whether treatment will be helpful. The first meeting between client and clinician is usually their first encounter with the counseling profession; therefore, it is important during counseling that clients feel hopeful and understood by their clinician. The first client visit can become the last (Paniagua, 2014). It is important that clients feel understood, respected, and hopeful about the therapy treatment from the very moment they enter the therapy room (Asnaani & Hofmann, 2012; Taber, Leibert, & Agaskar, 2011).

Attrition has a negative impact in that it not only prevents culturally diverse clients from receiving mental health services they need to deal with their problems but also represents a major threat to the internal validity of studies that require a representative sample from participants (Awad & Cokely, 2010). One way to prevent attrition with clients is to use cultural variables that are important to clients. This chapter maintains that the therapist's ability to communicate with a client in a culturally sensitive manner, to exhibit cultural competence during assessment, and to establish a therapeutic alliance is more important than similarity of race or ethnicity between therapist and client (Duan & Brown, 2016).

Clinicians are challenged to reach beyond cultural differences to work effectively with clients. They have to endeavor to understand their clients' worldviews, cultural values, and life circumstances. In addition, they must understand their own cultural conditioning of what they believe is standard therapeutic practice. Three potential barriers to multicultural counseling include class-bound values, linguistic issues, and culture-bound variables. In general, counseling has been described as a White,

Cultural Reflections

Is there any ethnocultural group that you feel uncomfortable counseling?

Have you had any conversations with yourself about working with members of this ethnocultural group?

What do you think is the best way to deal with this issue?

middle-class activity that oftentimes ignores environmental conditions, such as poverty and racism (Lui & Pope-Davis, 2005). Clients with low incomes may find it difficult to pay a therapist and transportation costs for seeing one.

Cultural barriers that sometimes prevent individuals from culturally diverse groups from receiving appropriate mental health care include

- Mistrust of the clinician and fear of what the treatment might involve

- Different ideas about what constitutes mental illness and mental health

- Language barriers and ineffective communication on the part of both client and clinician

- Access barriers involving inadequate or no insurance coverage

- A lack of cultural and ethnic diversity in the mental health workforce, including the clinician

CASE CONCEPTUALIZATION: SOME GENERAL ELEMENTS

Case conceptualization skills have traditionally been viewed as crucial for establishing competency skills for clinicians, psychotherapists, social workers, and mental health professionals in general (Constantine & Gushue, 2003; Constantine & Ladany, 2000; D. Lee, Sheridan, Rosen, & Jones, 2013; D. Lee & Tracey, 2008; Schomburg & Prieto, 2011; Sperry & Sperry, 2012). Since the time of Freud, the formulation of cases has been crucial to the assessment, diagnosis, and treatment of clients. Case conceptualization models have been founded on the theories of psychotherapy. For instance, the psychodynamic model provided the foundation for the first case conceptualization model. The psychodynamic model was built on the assumption of the unconscious and that a client's problems can be understood as a result of conflicts that result in anxiety. The biological model, the behavioral model, and the cognitive model all followed the psychodynamic one. Any case conceptualization must be founded on a theory or model of psychotherapy.

Case conceptualization is the process in which clinicians make sense of a client's presenting concerns within the context of a psychotherapy theoretical framework (Constantine & Ladany, 2000). It addresses how clinicians explain or understand a client's symptoms, cognitions, feelings, strengths, challenges, and behaviors in terms of a specific theory or an integration of theories. Clinicians' understanding of these issues provides the basis for their formulating counseling goals and intervention strategies. After a clinician has conducted a culturally responsive assessment, he or she is then in a position to begin case conceptualization, which should be based on the clinical and quantitative data the clinician has been able to gather related to the client. There are generic or general components of case conceptualization as well as culturally responsive approaches to case conceptualization.

Case conceptualizations give clinicians a coherent treatment strategy for planning and directing treatment interventions to help clients achieve their goals. In addition, a case conceptualization helps therapists to experience a sense of confidence in their work (Hill, 2005). A good case conceptualization has explanatory power (meaning it has a compelling explanation for the presenting problem), and it also has predictive powers in that it anticipates obstacles that might militate against treatment success (Sperry & Sperry, 2012).

Cultural Reflections

How much training have you had with case conceptualization?

If you had to choose a psychotherapy theory as the basis for your case conceptualization, what theory would that be?

The Five *P*s of Case Conceptualization

Counselors sometimes look for simple formats for case conceptualization. Along such lines, Macneil, Hasty, Conus, and Berk (2012) have introduced the five *P*s of case formulation. According to Macneil et al., a case formulation serves a number of functions, including helping a clinician to understand significant factors that have influenced a client's presentation, identifying critical difficulties, outlining what interventions should be used, and anticipating challenges that may take place during counseling treatment. The five *P*s of case conceptualization can be used with a variety of psychotherapeutic frameworks.

1. **Presenting problem.** The clinician looks beyond diagnosis to what the client and clinician identify as difficulties and how the client's life has been impacted. For instance, a person may meet the criteria for a diagnosis of borderline personality disorder. The counselor and client may determine how that diagnosis is expressed. Is the person able to maintain employment, does he or she have erratic friendships, or has he or she engaged in self-harm attempts? Essentially, the clinician makes a diagnosis and makes a list of how the client expresses the disorder in everyday life.

2. **Predisposing factors.** The clinician asks the client, "What factors contributed to the development of your problem?" The clinician is encouraged to think from a biopsychological perspective; for instance, he or she identifies any organic brain injuries or birth difficulties; any genetic vulnerabilities, such as a family history of mental health difficulties; and any psychological factors that put the client at risk of developing a specific mental health difficulty.

3. **Precipitating factors.** The clinician examines significant events that preceded the onset of the disorder, such as substance abuse, legal difficulties, or loss of a job. The questions that the clinician seeks to answer are "Why now?" and "What are the triggers or events that brought on the problem?"

4. **Perpetuating factors.** What factors seem to maintain the client's problem(s)? For instance, does the client have a substance abuse problem, does the client have behavioral patterns such as avoidance or withdrawal that tend to perpetuate his or her problems? Are there any issues that will likely make the problem worse?

5. **Protective/positive factors.** What client strengths can be used to deal effectively with the problem? Are there available protective factors, such as social support or community resources, to assist in the client's recovery?

CULTURALLY RESPONSIVE CASE CONCEPTUALIZATION

Imagine that you are a recent master's-level graduate of a counseling psychology program in a large middle Atlantic city that has sizeable African American, Latino American, and Asian American populations. You (Jim Massina) come from a White Italian American background. You consider yourself to be a member of the millennial generation because you just turned 30 and because you have a deep commitment to social justice. You are excited that you just landed a job as a mental health counselor at National Health Association (NHA), a medium-size human service organization that provides mental health services to individuals recovering from mental health illnesses and alcohol addiction. After being hired, you are given a caseload of 20 clients, three of whom include the following: (1) an 18-year-old Puerto Rican lesbian who has been thrown out of her mother's home because of her sexual orientation and who is currently unemployed and homeless;

CASE VIGNETTE 7.1

EMILY: A YOUNG WHITE AMERICAN WOMAN OF GERMAN DESCENT

Emily is a White American of German ancestry. She came to counseling complaining that she had just lost her job due to the fact that the company was closing and moving to a new location overseas. She was not offered a new position, and even if she were, she could not afford to travel to an entirely new country—Mexico. Emily stated that she felt she was a failure because she was now unable to take care of herself, and her family—notably her parents and siblings—saw her as a failure.

Emily also confided that after losing her job, she broke up with her boyfriend of three years. For some time, he had been complaining about her being overweight.

Emily complains that she cannot sleep at night and that she has gained at least 20 pounds within the past three months because food is the only thing that seems to bring her any measure of comfort. Although, initially, Emily had applied for a number of positions as a general office manager in law firms, she stated that she did not want to try anymore and that she feared that no one would hire her because of her weight and because she was not very attractive.

Emily had considered going back to live with her parents because she was struggling to pay her rent, utilities, food, and so forth. Instead of offering Emily her "old bedroom" until she could get on her feet again, her parents gave her a loan for $800, but explained that she could not return home. She saw her parents as typical German parents. Rarely did their family talk openly about the struggles individual family members were facing. Emily's mother suffered in silence as her father dominated the entire family. At one time, Emily had asked her mother if maybe their family should enter counseling, but her mother's cold stare and terse response let her know that such would not be possible for them. "What family problems?" her mother asked. "We're good Germans. We work hard. Your father provides a good living for us. We don't need to go outside our family to resolve our issues."

Emily told the counselor that she could hardly ever remember her family talking about "feelings" around the dinner table. After Emily graduated from college with a BA in computer science, she did not feel "unwelcomed" at home, but it was clear that her parents expected her to move out on her own. Most of her friends who came from German backgrounds reported similar experiences as Emily had when she was considering when and how she was going to move out of her parents' home.

In German families, parents and children may give up contact with each other instead of experiencing the pain of discussing their feelings about each other. Not once had her parents talked with her about their feelings related to her leaving home and getting her own apartment. When Emily left home, she felt emotionally cut off from her family. It was no wonder that her parents did not want her back in their home again.

Emily said that she feels abandoned by her family and former boyfriend. As long as she had a job, everything seemed okay. "I feel like I've been kicked in the guts by my parents, my job, and my boyfriend. I don't know if I can go on. What's the use?"

Emily states that the only relief she gets is when she attends a weekly Bible study class. During those times, she feels hope. "Maybe God will turn things around for me." Although she has one close girlfriend, she has had second thoughts about that relationship. Her girlfriend has told Emily that she has her own set of problems and that Emily depresses her because her life never seems to get any better.

While in the first month of unemployment, Emily scheduled a number of job interviews; now she says it is getting harder and harder for her to crawl out of bed each day. She lacks energy to do very much, and as a result, she has stopped cleaning her apartment. "Everything's a mess," she told the clinician. "My house is a mess, I'm a mess, and my life is a mess."

This is not the first time that Emily has had a problem with depression. She recalled that about a year ago she went through a similar emotional breakdown because of a breakup with her old boyfriend. She says that she hates to deal with loss. Emily also informed the clinician that her mother had suffered from postpartum depression after she gave birth to her two children. Emily's mother is in her late 50s, while her father is in his late 60s and has retired from his job as a postal clerk.

Case Discussion

1. Provide a tentative DSM-5 diagnosis of Emily's mental health condition.

2. Use Macneil et al.'s (2012) five-*P*s case conceptualization approach for counseling Emily.

3. Why is Emily so depressed?

4. What are the predisposing factors that contributed to Emily's depression?

5. Identify the precipitating factors that Emily encountered.

6. What factors in Emily's life are likely to perpetuate her depression?

7. What strengths or positive factors does Emily have in her life that may serve as protective factors during counseling?

8. Are there any cultural factors in Emily's life that you would take into consideration for her assessment and treatment?

9. Do you think that Emily's German background has anything to do with her feelings of being abandoned by her parents and family?

10. Would you ever consider using the 16-item Cultural Formulation Interview as part of your counseling efforts with Emily? Explain.

(2) a 16-year-old African American girl who has been referred by her high school counselor for a possible bipolar disorder; and (3) a 68-year-old Irish American male suffering from depression and anxiety because his wife of 30 years has just had to be placed in a nursing home, leaving him all alone in their modest home.

Your CACREP (Council for Accreditation of Counseling and Related Educational Programs) internship in counseling was at a community counseling center in one of the outlying predominantly White suburbs. After the intake interview with each of these three clients, you wonder if you are qualified to work with these individuals. Their problems seem overwhelming, and except for the three-hour multicultural counseling course, little was ever mentioned during your two-year program about culturally responsive counseling. All your professors were White, and none specialized in cross-cultural psychology. In quiet moments in your office, you ask yourself, "Am I really competent to be working with these clients? Should I refer these clients because I know little about their culture?" As an Italian American, you can't imagine being all alone in your senior years. You decide to review your multicultural counseling book as a means to help you feel more competent. As a master's-level clinician, you are not sure where to begin. NHA requires you to write a case conceptualization and treatment plan for each client. You know how to make a clinical diagnosis, but you are not sure how culture fits into your case conceptualization and treatment plan.

Jim is right to be concerned about his level of multicultural competency in counseling culturally diverse individuals. Culture must be considered in every aspect of case conceptualization, including the interview, assessment, diagnosis, and treatment of culturally diverse individuals. As noted in Chapter 6, the assessment of culturally diverse clients produces additional layers of complexity, especially when the client has a different ethnocultural background than the clinician. For the most part, few studies have investigated case conceptualization from a cross-cultural perspective (D. Lee & Tracey, 2008). The studies that do exist have not shed a great deal of light on what constitutes culturally responsive case conceptualization. For instance, Constantine (2001a, 2001b, 2001c) conducted a series of studies on that topic. In general, her methodology involved providing psychotherapy trainees with a written vignette about a client of color trying to manage various culturally laden problems, and asking the trainees to write a conceptualization addressing the etiology of the client's problem and the steps they would take to address the complaints.

It is unclear what actual multicultural conceptualization skills were effective. Some studies found that actual multicultural conceptualization skills were not related to self-reported multicultural competence, after social desirability was taken into account (Constantine & Ladany, 2000). Researchers have found that multicultural case conceptualization skills were correlated positively with an eclectic/integrative therapeutic orientation (Constantine, 2001c). Several researchers found that multicultural case conceptualization skills were related positively to multicultural training (Constantine, 2001b, 2001c; Constantine & Gushue, 2003). Moreover, trainees of color exhibited higher multicultural case conceptualization abilities than White trainees in one study (Constantine, 2001b). Schomburg and Prieto (2011) found that "despite didactic, clinical, and extracurricular training in multiculturalism, marriage and family therapy trainees did not sufficiently incorporate cultural factors into their clinical case conceptualizations" (p. 223).

While the researchers need to be commended for their work, very little information has been uncovered regarding what exactly culturally responsive case conceptualization constitutes and how it differs from general case conceptualization. As it currently stands, the CFI provides the best structure for integrating multicultural concepts into case conceptualization.

Case Conceptualization, Diagnosis, and the Revisions in the DSM-5

Case conceptualization should take into consideration the *Diagnostic and Statistical Manual of Mental Disorders*, fifth edition (American Psychiatric Association, 2013). The DSM-5 lists various criteria for each mental disorder included in the book. When a person seeks the services of a mental health clinician, the clinician interviews the client, takes a medical history, and may subsequently administer psychological evaluations for the purpose of establishing a diagnosis. After the clinician has gathered all assessment data from the client, he or she makes a diagnosis based on the symptoms assigned from the DSM-5 (Sperry, 2014). Having a clinician make a diagnosis can be helpful because it can help clinicians raise hypotheses about the client's psychological dynamics, and it can help clinicians plan therapeutic actions to counteract or to deal effectively with the nature and severity of a client's distress. Other common advantages of using a diagnosis are that it provides

- A common language for helping professionals and clients to describe disorders, presenting issues, or challenges

- A framework that can be used in treatment planning, and that facilitates insurance reimbursement for counseling services

- A classification system that can be used in clinical research to determine which treatments are effective

- A classification system that allows individuals to find mental health support networks for people who share similar problems

In contrast, the downside of diagnosis is that sometimes people are viewed primarily in terms of their diagnosis. The truth is that a diagnosis is a social construction that people have created to better understand another person's behaviors and thoughts. Some *limitations* associated with diagnosis include the fact that it

- Provides a master status for identifying clients by their diagnosis instead of their multiple identities

- Focuses primarily on pathology rather than clients' strengths

- Leads to stigmatization of people and potential errors in conceptualizing individuals' problems

Cultural Reflections

Let's assume that you want to obtain therapy for depression or anxiety.

Looking at your own ethnocultural background, what, if anything, would you like a clinician to know about you from a cultural standpoint?

How would you feel about being counseled by a person from an American ethnic minority?

Diagnosis and culture. A clinical diagnosis is an expression of culture. The DSM-5 is written and produced by American psychiatrists, and thus the observations it reports for various mental disorders are completed within a Western cultural framework, using Western language and perspectives. There is some research that shows that the same basic patterns of mental disorders discussed in the DSM have been found around the world (Westermeyer, 1987).

Concern about the influence of culture on diagnosis should not just be considered an issue that affects ethnic minorities because that would deny the impact of cultural factors in the everyday life of majority populations in the United States and in countries throughout the world. Culture influences the expression of a client's symptoms. As Renato Alarcón (2009) has stated in reference to cultural psychiatry, cultural psychiatry should not be considered only a psychiatry of ethnic minorities or of exotic lands, because that would deny the impact of cultural factors in the everyday life of majority populations in any country or continent, or reduce them to existing only in places far from urban centers, developed countries or, more precisely, Western nations. While it is true that, due to clinical convenience, the presentation and discussion of cultural issues in health, disease, diagnosis and treatment may utilize examples of ethnic minorities, immigrants, refugees, or the so-called "special populations" (children, adolescents, the elderly, women, homosexuals, or members of cults and religious sects, all of them considered "minorities"), it would be a great mistake to assume that culture exists only in and for these groups. Actually, the recognition of cultural components in psychiatric diagnosis for all would be a great step forward in correcting this erroneous view. (p. 136)

Important Revisions in the DSM-5

The DSM-5 is the latest version of the *Diagnostic and Statistical Manual of Mental Disorders* (American Psychiatric Association, 2013). The basic purpose of revising the DSM-5 was to take into consideration two decades of scientific and clinical research. This section reviews some of the major changes in the DSM-5 that should be included in any case conceptualization and treatment plan. It does not provide an in-depth analysis of the DSM-5, but rather provides a very brief overview of changes contained in the DSM-5 (American Psychiatric Association, 1994, 2013).

Although the DSM-5 includes approximately the same number of disorders as were included in the DSM-IV (American Psychiatric Association, 1994), the DSM-5 has reordered the DSM-IV's sixteen chapters. Instead of grouping mental disorders categorically as did the DSM-IV, disorders are now grouped together based on underlying vulnerabilities. Most of the changes in the DSM-5 are now in alignment with the World Health Organization's (WHO) *International Classification of Diseases*, 10th edition (ICD-10) (1992). Making these changes improves communication between the DSM-5 and the ICD-10.

Understanding the DSM-5 is crucial for clinicians engaged in case conceptualization. To develop a culturally responsive treatment protocol for a person, clinicians must have some understanding of the DSM-5. It is unusual for cultural factors alone to be the sole cause for a client's distress or presenting problems. Cultural factors are taken into account when making a diagnosis.

The DSM-5 has modified the previous multiaxial system, presented new dimensional assessments, and made some revised cultural considerations. Because the DSM-5 is relatively recent, major revisions from the older DSM-IV are summarized so that the clinician can make an informed diagnosis for clients and an adequate case conceptualization and treatment plan.

What is different in the DSM-5 compared to the DSM-IV? The DSM-5 now consists of only three sections:

1. **Section 1** provides an introduction with information regarding how to use the revised manual of mental disorders.

2. **Section 2** outlines the categorical diagnoses according to a revised chapter organization.

3. **Section 3** includes conditions that require further research before being considered as formal disorders, as well as cultural formulations, a glossary, and the contributors to the text.

Dimensional Assessments. In the DSM-IV, a person either had or did not have a particular symptom. To be given a diagnosis, a person was required to have a certain number of symptoms. The DSM-5 now provides for clinicians to use dimensional assessments to reveal the severity of a specific diagnosis. The severity ratings are *very severe, severe, moderate,* and *mild.*

Changes to the Multiaxial System. In the DSM-IV, a system of five axes or dimensions was used for diagnostic and treatment purposes. These five axes were

1. Axis I: Clinical Syndromes/Disorders
2. Axis II: Personality Disorders/Mental Retardation
3. Axis III: Medical Conditions
4. Axis IV: Psychosocial and Environmental Stressors
5. Axis V: Global Assessment of Functioning

Cultural Reflections

Have you had training in making clinical diagnoses for people experiencing mental health problems?

Do you anticipate obtaining training regarding diagnosis and the DSM-5?

How comfortable do you feel making a DSM-5 diagnosis for a client?

The DSM-5 has adopted a nonaxial documentation approach, and it has combined the first three DSM-IV-TR (American Psychiatric Association, 2000) axes into one list. The first three axes have now been substituted with a list that contains all mental disorders, personality disorders, intellectual disability diagnoses, and other medical diagnoses. Separate notations for Axes IV and V have been adopted such that psychosocial factors, environmental factors, and disability factors are considered. Moreover, the term *general medical condition* has been replaced in the DSM-5 with *another medical condition* where relevant across all disorders (American Psychiatric Association, 2013).

The following diagnoses are new in the DSM-5: disruptive mood dysregulation disorder, hoarding disorder, excoriation disorder (individuals who compulsively pick their skin for no apparent reason), psychological factors affecting other medical conditions and factitious disorder, genito-pelvic pain/penetration disorder, and gender dysphoria (a new diagnostic class in the DSM-5 that emphasizes the phenomenon of "gender incongruence" rather than "cross-gender identification" as was the case in the DSM-IV with "gender identity disorder").

CASE CONCEPTUALIZATION AND THE CULTURAL FORMULATION INTERVIEW

The CFI of the DSM-5 should form an important part of the clinician's assessment and case conceptualization. Many of the cultural variables to be considered in a diagnosis have been outlined in the DSM-5 CFI, and the reader is referred to Chapter 6, where the 16 questions are presented to be used with the CFI. The cultural factors specifically outlined were (1) the client's identity with an emphasis on cultural identity, (2) cultural explanation of illness, (3) psychosocial environment level and intergenerational conflicts, (4) the therapeutic relationship with the client, and (5) the overall cultural assessment of the client.

Advantages of Using the CFI in Case Conceptualization

One major benefit of using the CFI for case conceptualization is that it promotes individualized assessments of culturally diverse clients. The CFI helps clients to talk about the influence of their culture on their lives, and it helps counselors to understand how they view their problems. The CFI can help clinicians to arrive at a better understanding of a person within the context of his or her culture.

Díaz, Añez, Silva, Paris, and Davidson (2017) conducted a CFI feasibility study that investigated (used an audio-recorded interview format) the usefulness of the CFI with monolingual Hispanic clients (18–70 years old) from several Latin American countries. The clients received outpatient services at the Hispanic Clinic of the Connecticut Mental Health Center, which provides services to individuals regardless of their legal immigration status or ability to pay. According to Díaz et al., the CFI is a personalized interview that "facilitates individualized assessments by clinicians instead of their relying on preconceived or stereotypic notions about race-ethnicity or country of origin. The CFI captures the patient's voice systematically and documents what is 'at stake' for the person" (p. 112). The researchers found that client trust and disruption of relationships were major themes elicited by the CFI. Díaz et al. stated,

> Disruption of relationships was a major theme. When participants could not get along with important people in their lives, such as family members or fellow churchgoers, they sought mental health care. "We do not treat each other like family anymore," "He cheated on me, he traumatized me," "I have problems with my children." Interpersonal harmony was crucial for participants, and disruption of relationships was a powerful motivation to seek help.

> The loss of trust—"confianza"—was a serious problem for some participants, requiring professional attention. "Confianza" is a Hispanic value related to feeling at ease about revealing personal experiences to others. "I do not trust." "I could not work" . . . Restoration of trust was critical. . . . As participants gained trust in the therapeutic relationship, they re-established social ties. In turn, restored relationships aided in healing. (p. 113)

Using the CFI, Díaz and colleagues (2017) also found that traumatic experiences caused some participants to seek counseling. The researchers noted that "for Hispanics, auditory hallucinations can be trauma related without meeting criteria for a psychotic disorder. 'I cannot find myself. I feel lost.' 'The memories made me nervous.' 'My mind is gone.' 'I want to stop remembering sad things. I want to stop thinking bad thoughts'" (p. 113).

The CFI questions were helpful in revealing participants' thoughts about whom or what caused their problems. Some of the participants revealed that they saw their problem as a consequence of their actions—as punishment, for instance, for not following God's purpose for their lives, because they did not obey their mother—or as a test from God. Clients were able to resolve their issues when the counseling treatment valued their religious beliefs. As Díaz et al. (2017) observed, "participants' perceptions were that they were not in good standing as church members were also a compelling reason to seek help. When their concerns were addressed, they often perceived a restored relationship with God and reconnected with their church" (p. 112).

The CFI also elicited themes related to participants' experiences of loss. Participants reported that the death of loved ones, leaving their country of origin, and leaving children and other family members behind were important factors that produced feelings of loss. "I left my children. I cannot eat. I just want to cry and cry thinking how could I eat when my children might be hungry" (Díaz et al., 2017, p. 113).

In the Díaz et al. (2017) study, immigrants expressed nostalgia and guilt for leaving their families behind, and they speculated that they would not be in the position they were currently in if they had not left their countries of origin. Answering questions on the CFI helped them to deal with the loss of family, language, food, and customs. Counseling helped the participants to mourn these losses so that they could develop a new identity while still respecting their old identity.

Advantages of Using the CFI to Assess Clients' Cultural Identity

This section of the CFI goes beyond the 16 questions described in Chapter 6. It presents actual interview questions clinicians might use during the interview. Understanding a person's identity is indispensable to assessment and evaluation. A cultural identity involves the following areas: ethnicity, race, geographical origin, language, acculturation, gender, age, and sexual orientation. A client may initially identify with broad racial, ethnic, and cultural groups.

Yet each person has a unique identity and history that informs the clinician about how he or she has practiced culture within the family unit. Clinicians should avoid overgeneralizations about clients' ethnicity and race. There is not just one Latino, African American, or American Indian culture. In other words, there are many features of a client's cultural identity that go beyond ethnicity and race. An African American from East Harlem, New York, might describe his experiences quite differently than one from Boise, Idaho. As another example, two Asian Americans may have come from China, but their identities may vary depending on their socioeconomic status (SES), their gender, and the geographical region from which they originated.

Clinicians are encouraged to ask about a person's multiple categories of identity, such as one's identity involved with race, ethnicity, country of origin, language, and acculturation. Other identity domains include gender, age, sexual orientation, religious and spiritual beliefs, geographic region, and SES (Alcántara & Gone, 2014). The cultural identity of a client includes such factors as ethnicity/race, country of origin, language, gender, age, religious/spiritual beliefs, SES, sexual orientation, migration history, disability status, and level of acculturation. To assess clients' ethnicity, a clinician might ask them to describe their grandparents' and parents' country of origin, their religion, traditional roles and work skills, and holidays and celebrations in which the family participated. The clinician should examine the intersection of a client's social identities and the ways in which these multiple identities influence or cause problems for him or her (Mezzich, Caracci, Fabrega, & Kirmayer, 2009). Cultural identity questions are provided in Table 7.1.

> ### Cultural Reflections
>
> *Some Americans believe that questions about cultural identity are only for members of ethnic/racial minorities and not relevant to White Americans' lives.*
>
> *What are your thoughts about this issue?*
>
> *Do you believe that culturally responsive therapy is for majority, or White, Americans, or is it primarily for members of ethnic/racial minorities? Please explain your response.*

Using the CFI to Reveal Clients' Immigration History

Migration history is another factor that can form an important part of a culturally diverse client's cultural identity in the case of clients who have emigrated from one country to another. Clinicians should assess two parts of a client's **migration history**: (1) the premigration history, which includes country of origin, position in the family, education, employment status, political issues, and experiences of war and traumatic events; and (2) the actual immigration journey of the client. The goal of taking a premigration history is to understand clients' former baseline life experiences in their native country prior to migration (DeSilva, Aggarwal, & Lewis-Fernández, 2015).

The migration history should contain the client's reasons for leaving, a notation of who was left behind, who paid for the trip, and any hardships or trauma that the client endured. Did the client experience torture, beatings, rape, or imprisonment in refugee camps? Should the client be described as a migrant, meaning one who left his or her country voluntarily, or would he or she be best categorized as a refugee? Migration constitutes a major change for the individual, as well as a stress factor (Roth, 2006). Migration is also a known risk factor for schizophrenia (Cantor-Grae, Pedersen, McNeil, & Mortensen, 2003; Cantor-Grae & Selten, 2005). Migration is an abrupt change that requires a person to make a series of adaptations to various stressors (Watters, 2001; Westermeyer, 1989). Although migration can induce stress, not everyone has the same

TABLE 7.1   ■   Culturally Responsive Clinical Skill Development: Cultural Identity Questions

A clinician might ask clients the following questions regarding ethnic or cultural reference group:

- Where are you and your parents from?
- How do you trace your ancestry? With what groups or nations do you most closely identify?
- How close or connected do you feel to your identified cultural group?
- What is your father's and mother's ethnocultural background?
- Do you maintain contact with your family or friends in your country of origin?
- Do you belong to a group containing people from your country of origin?
- Do you have friends from your country of origin?
- How would you describe your current involvement with community agencies in your neighborhood?
- Do you belong to a social group with people from your host culture (American)?
- What is your perception of American (or host) culture?
- Have you ever experienced any racism or ethnocentrism in America?
- Do you celebrate your culture's holidays?
- Do you eat the foods typical of your culture?
- What is considered most respectful in your culture?
- Have you ever been excluded because of your gender, race, or culture?
- Is there anything you would like me to know that we have not included here about you or your culture?

Language

Many culturally diverse individuals have fluency in more than one language. The counselor or therapist might ask clients what language they consider their primary language. In addition, as noted in Chapter 6, clinicians should take note of their client's communication style. The communication styles of individuals from high- and low-context cultures differ, especially in the way silence is treated.

Language Questions

- What language did you speak while growing up?
- What language do you currently speak with members of your family?
- In what language do you feel most comfortable speaking, reading, and writing?
- What language do you use in your community?
- What language do you prefer to use in our work together?
- Would you prefer for me to obtain an interpreter who speaks your language?

experiences prior to migration and after its occurrence. Clinicians need to pay attention to the client's coping strategies and strengths (Kleinman, 1996; Tseng, 2001).

Clinicians need to explore issues of loss of family members, and material possession losses—of jobs and of SES, as well as of their culture and community and religious support (Lewis-Fernández & Díaz (2002). A client with a migration history that indicates downward mobility in his or her occupational status might develop low self-esteem and insecurity, which might precipitate or bring on a mental disorder. A psychological assessment of a client who has migrated needs to include a narrative of the individual's migration history to provide the counselor with a better understanding of the client's prior living situation, family life and status, and reasons for flight (E. Lee, 1990).

Using the CFI to Help Clients Deal With Acculturation Issues

A client's **level of acculturation** is related to his or her migration history, but it is relevant for clients whose ancestors emigrated as well as for immigrant clients. Clinicians can assess a client's level of acculturation by using a numerative framework—that is, first generation, second generation, and third generation (Berry & Kim, 1988; E. Lee, 1990). Another way of addressing a person's degree of acculturation is to use such terms as *traditional, transitional, bicultural,* or *Americanized* (E. Lee, 1990). Traditional families are those that have been born and raised in their country of origin. Generally speaking, such immigrants speak only their native language, and they tend to live in ethnic enclaves, such as Chinatown in New York City.

Counseling and psychotherapy should address the multiple losses that individuals have encountered as a result of their immigration and subsequent acculturation. It should help them to mourn their losses involving family, language, food, and customs, while assisting them to develop a new life in their host country. Table 7.2 provides migration and acculturation questions a clinician can use in working with culturally diverse clients.

Cultural Explanations of the Individual's Illness

This part of the CFI refers to the client's symptoms, his or her severity of symptoms, and experiences with help seeking. This section focuses on the client's views on how the illness operates, meaning what caused it, why it presented at the time that it did, how it is affecting the client, and what are the possible outcomes with treatment. The cultural explanatory model involves what the client says or believes caused his or her problems.

TABLE 7.2 ■ Culturally Responsive Clinical Skill Development: Migration and Acculturation Questions

Migration Questions

- What caused you to leave your country?
- How would you describe your migration journey?
- Did you experience any trauma during the time that you migrated?
- How do you now feel about your decision to migrate to this country?
- Knowing what you know now about the United States, would you migrate here again?
- Did you migrate to this country on your own free will, or were you forced to come here because of circumstances in your country of origin?
- How has your life been affected by the move to the United States?
- What do you miss the most about your country of origin?
- What did you leave behind when you moved to the United States?
- What new relationships have you made in the United States?
- As a result of your immigration, what new opportunities have you had in the United States?
- Has the move to this country affected your health in any way?
- How has your family been affected by your move to this country?

Acculturation Questions

- How easy or difficult has it been for you to adjust to living in this country?
- How have members of your family adjusted to living in this country?
- Are there differences in your children's adjustment to this country and your adjustment?
- Have you experienced any conflicts with your children because they have adopted the values of this country?

The section about cultural explanations of illness refers to the importance of trying to understand the individual client's way of expressing and perceiving his or her illness. Depending on a client's situation, his or her way of communicating a need for support and help will change (Kleinman, 1996; Tseng, 2001). Different cultural groups establish cultural limits for normality. Illness can take on different explanations and meanings (Kleinman, 1996). Expectations of help and cure can also vary according to one's culture. For instance, in some cultures, a client who has visual and audio hallucinations with religious content is considered to be having normal religious experiences (Tseng, 2001). In Asian American cultures, depression may be experienced largely in somatic terms, rather than with sadness or guilt as exemplified by many White Americans (E. Lee, 1990). The clinician should try to find out what the individual client is trying to communicate and what meaning he or she gives to his or her problems and situation.

Even people with the same mental diagnosis may differ in the manner in which they express their mental disorder, largely due to their cultural background. For instance, anxiety disorders are some of the most prevalent mental disorders throughout the world. Yet these disorders are strongly affected by racial, ethnic, and cultural factors. Each culture establishes religious, spiritual, and moral values that govern how individuals within that culture can express their anxiety.

The prevalence rates for anxiety disorders within the United States, a multiracial and multiethnic country, reveal differences in diagnoses for these disorders across groups. For instance, a study by Asnaani, Richey, Dimaite, Hinton, and Hofmann (2010) reported a cross-ethnic comparison of lifetime prevalence rates of anxiety disorders in a sample of Hispanic Americans ($N = 3,615$), Asian Americans ($N = 1,628$), and African Americans ($N = 4,598$). The results revealed that Asian Americans consistently endorsed symptoms of all four major anxiety disorders (social anxiety disorder, generalized anxiety disorder, panic disorder, and posttraumatic stress disorder) less frequently than any of the other racial groups. In contrast, White Americans ($N = 6,870$) consistently endorsed symptoms of social anxiety disorder, generalized anxiety disorder, and panic disorder more frequently than African Americans, Hispanic Americans, and Asian Americans. These findings suggest a strong contribution of culture to anxiety disorders.

Hofmann and Hinton (2014) investigated individuals' expressions of anxiety across several ethnic groups. The investigators reported that Cambodians typically show multiple anxiety-related syndromes that are based on fears of disturbed "inner wind" and blood flow. These events are called "wind attacks." Whereas North Americans often complain of having "butterflies in their stomachs" when they feel anxious, Cambodians worry that these abdominal sensations indicate the occurrence of an "upward hitting wind" that will eventually lead to cardiac arrest (Hofmann & Hinton, 2014).

Chinese culture also expresses anxiety differently than White American culture. In traditional Chinese medicine, anxiety states are often linked to a person's organ dysfunction, such as to a "weak kidney," known as *shen xu*, or a "weak heart" (*xin su*). The DSM-5 lists *taijin kyofusho* (TKS) as a culturally specific version of social anxiety in Japanese and Korean culture. People who may be diagnosed with TKS are concerned about doing something that will offend or embarrass the other person, similar to social anxiety disorder.

Puerto Rican culture and Dominican culture also have their own specific twists on anxiety disorders. Individuals in these cultures may refer to anxiety as *ataque de nervios* (attack of nerves). Typical symptoms include a sense of loss of control, chest tightness, a feeling of heat in the body, palpitations, shaking of the arms and legs, and feelings of fainting. Fear and anger assume a prominent role in bringing on an attack of nerves. An attack of nerves is known as an idiom of distress, which is a known way of acting and reacting when one receives bad news or when something is upsetting.

For a more detailed listing of cultural idioms of stress, please refer to Chapter 6 (Table 6.6). Questions dealing with the meaning of an illness are provided in Table 7.3.

TABLE 7.3 ■ Culturally Responsive Clinical Skill Development: Cultural Explanation of Illness Questions
• How serious do you judge your symptoms to be?
• How would you describe your problem if you were talking with members of your family, relatives, or friends?
• Do you know other people who have had similar problems?
• What do you believe caused your problems?
• What sort of help and treatment do you think will make the problem go away?
• What sort of help and treatment have you previously sought?
• If you had stayed in your country, what kind of help and treatment would you have been given? What kind of treatment would you have asked for?
• What do your family members and friends think about the problems you are having? What kind of treatment do they recommend for you?

Cultural Factors Related to the Psychosocial Environment

The psychosocial environment can also affect an individual's psychological functioning. There may be social stressors in the environment that are affecting the client. The clinician attempts to get at the available social supports, and levels of functioning and disability. Psychosocial needs can often drive individuals to seek counseling services. For instance, some individuals might seek counseling because they have lost their papers and wallet, they are homeless and waiting for a place to live, and they have no money to provide for their basic needs. Part of their recovery may involve obtaining employment and providing for their families as a desirable counseling treatment outcome. Most individuals appreciate attention to their psychosocial needs and counselors helping them to cut through "red bureaucratic tape" (Díaz et al., 2017). What instrumental, emotional, and informational support does the client have? The client's description of everyday life provides important information about his or her actual living conditions, and from this information, the clinician is able to formulate follow-up questions aimed at assessing possible symptoms. The solutions to the client's problems are often located in the client's local neighborhood and life situation. Thus, the clinician explores the assistance the client needs and might be able to receive from his or her surrounding network (Kleinman, 1996; Tseng, 2001).

In working with culturally diverse individuals, counselors should consider helping them to restore social ties and supportive social networks as part of their case conceptualization and treatment plan. In developing a culturally responsive treatment plan, clinicians should consider the importance of the social networks available to their clients. Questions dealing with clients' psychosocial environment are provided in Table 7.4.

TABLE 7.4 ■ Culturally Responsive Clinical Skill Development: Psychosocial Environment Questions
• How do your problems affect you on a day-to-day basis?
• How do your problems affect your relationships with others?
• How do your problems affect your ability to be active?
• How do your problems affect your ability to cope at home?
• Are your problems affecting your ability to work?
• Is there anything in your daily life that adds to or sets the stage for your having problems?
• Is there anyone whom you trust and can talk with about your problems?
• Are you able to talk with your family and your relatives about your problems?
• Are there any difficulties in doing so?

Adapted from Bäärnhielm, 2009.

CASE VIGNETTE 7.2

ASTRID: A HAITIAN WOMAN EXPERIENCING CULTURAL PSYCHOSOCIAL ISSUES

Astrid is a 38-year-old Haitian mother of two children (5 and 7 years old) who immigrated to the United States about 8 years ago as a result of the earthquakes that struck Haiti. She immigrated to the United States with the assistance of a coalition of African American and White Protestant ministers. Within the past two years, she has become a naturalized U.S. citizen. She married a natural-ized Haitian; she works as a home health care aid.

Several months ago, Astrid's husband had an affair with one of the members of their predominantly Haitian church. The couple have had major arguments in front of their three children and talked about divorcing each other. The problem is that neither one earns enough money to get a separate apartment. They are living in a rather modest home in New York City.

The children have been concerned about the loud yell-ing fights between their parents. John, the youngest child, has started to experience problems at school. He was caught fighting another kid and suspended for three days. Upset at John's behavior, Astrid's husband gave John a "whipping." John told his teacher about the beating, and Child Protective Services showed up at the family's door-step. Astrid and Phillip (Astrid's husband) explained that the beating of children was accepted in their culture and that it was based on the Biblical statement that one should not spare the rod in disciplining children. They did not feel as if they had done anything wrong in giving John a good whipping. How else was he to learn to obey?

The couple is now required to go to counseling to learn different methods for disciplining their children. They feel resentful of Child Protective Services.

For the past month, Astrid has complained of head-aches. She went to counseling and explained that she had an "empty head" and that she felt that "her head was not there." The counselor was unfamiliar with what Astrid meant by having "an empty head"; and Astrid tried to explain what these phrases meant in Haiti. She com-plained of stomachaches and of not being able to sleep at night and poor appetite.

Astrid has strong religious views, and she belongs to a Haitian church that could be categorized as Protestant; however, its members also practice several voodoo ritu-als. Astrid believes that God would take away her prob-lems if she prayed long enough.

Astrid's problems are complicated because her mother and two siblings are still in Haiti. They have not recovered financially from the powerful earthquake(s) that devastated Haiti, and they are still living in portable homes that are unsafe. Astrid sends money to her mother and siblings once a month, and these money transfers have produced arguments with Phillip, who feels that Astrid should focus on taking care of their family.

Case Discussion

Based on the information presented in Chapters 6 and 7, use the DSM-5, the Cultural Formulation Interview, and other material to respond to the following questions.

1. What diagnosis would you give for Astrid's presenting symptoms and her description of her problems?

2. On what information would you base your diagnosis?

3. How would you assess Astrid's immigration and acculturation in the United States?

4. What psychosocial factors seem to be impacting Astrid's mental condition? To what extent does Astrid need to be given information about the impact of stress on her physical and mental health?

5. What cultural factors seem to be influencing how Astrid conceptualizes her problems—"empty head" or "my head is not there"?

6. What is your knowledge of Haitian culture?

7. Using the five *P*s, what tentative case conceptualization would you make of Astrid's difficulties and life situation?

8. How would you go about establishing a treatment plan for Astrid?

9. What steps would you take to integrate cultural factors into Astrid's treatment plan? What cultural factors have you identified that seem to be having an influence on her?

10. What kind of therapeutic relationship would you attempt to establish with Astrid? Would you consider family counseling?

Cultural Issues in the Counseling Relationship: Ethnocultural Transference and Countertransference

The clinician should note differences in culture and social status between the client and the clinician and indicate what problems, if any, these differences may create in diagnosis and treat-ment (e.g., difficulty in communicating in the client's first language, understanding the cultural

TABLE 7.5 ■ Culturally Responsive Clinical Skill Development: Therapeutic Relationship Questions

- What has it felt like describing and explaining your problems and your situation for me?

- What has it meant for you to be able/not be able to use your native language with me?

- How have you felt about me since you have had to have a language interpreter in the room with us?

- Have I asked you the right questions from your perspective?

- Is there anything important that you would like to tell me about your situation that we have not talked about?

- How well have I understood your problems and your situation?

- How well do you think that others at this agency have understood your problems and your situation?

- How comfortable do you feel talking about your situation with me?

Adapted from Bäärnhielm, 2009.

significance of client's presenting issues, developing an appropriate therapeutic relationship, or deciding if a client's behavior is normative or pathological for his or her culture).

Therapeutic factors such as *ethnocultural transference* and *ethnocultural countertransference* may also contaminate a culturally diverse therapeutic relationship. Comas-Díaz and Jacobsen (1991) have pointed out how cultural and ethnic factors affect emotional reactions in both the therapist and the patient in psychotherapy. A therapist who is from the same ethnic or racial group may overidentify with the client beyond that which would be healthy. In this instance, the clinician might be experiencing ethnocultural transference. **Ethnocultural countertransference** takes place when a clinician swings between overcompensation and exaggerated friendliness and suspicion with more or less concealed hostility. The reactions can put their stamp on the relationship. Comas-Díaz and Jacobsen suggest that an exaggerated suspicion, but also an exaggerated focus on differences in ethnicity, can hinder a functioning working alliance. Table 7.5 presents questions clinicians can ask when counseling culturally different clients.

Overall Cultural Assessment for Diagnosis and Treatment

The CFI highlights how cultural considerations can be used to inform a comprehensive diagnosis and treatment plan for the client. The clinician translates the client's narrative or story to his or her own professional language and theoretical framework. The summary is based on material gathered from the CFI and other assessment data. The summary should include the content areas explored in the CFI, as well as other important areas that have arisen during the interview. Using the various sections in the CFI, the clinician evaluates what cultural factors and social context mean for the client's illness and life situation. The client's perspective should be included in order to facilitate treatment planning. The clinician's summary statements should cover the current difficulties the client is facing and the possibility for social support and also the client's strengths, resources, and opportunities for support. The clinician should discuss the summarizing assessment with the patient.

STRENGTHS-BASED CASE CONCEPTUALIZATION

The strengths-based therapy model maintains that a good case conceptualization model should have four components: (1) a diagnostic formulation, which involves using all data gathered from assessment procedures; (2) cultural formulation, using the CFI; (3) a strengths component; and (4) a treatment formulation (Jones-Smith, 2014). In addition, such a case conceptualization

- Identifies precipitating and maintaining factors that contribute to the client's presenting problem

- Presents cultural factors that might be affecting the client's presenting concerns

- Identifies the client's individual, social, and cultural strengths, and examines evidence of the client's resilience

- Helps to establish collaboratively the short-term and long-term goals and the means by which such goals can be achieved

- Identifies, anticipates, and addresses potential individual, social, and systemic barriers that may interfere with and jeopardize treatment effectiveness

- Provides feedback to client and others on the treatment team

The strengths-based case conceptualization protocol shows how strengths can be used as part of a clinician's case conceptualization (see Table 7.6).

STRENGTHS-BASED TREATMENT PLANS

The strengths-based therapy model goes beyond simply administering a strengths-based instrument. One purpose of engaging in strengths discovery with clients is to collaborate with clients to develop a strengths-based treatment plan. A strengths-based treatment plan uses the strengths identified during therapy to establish resources to achieve a client's goals. From the strengths-based therapy model, a treatment plan is designed to motivate the individual or family to change. Clients' strengths will guide the treatment process (McQuaide & Ehrenreich, 1997).

How does a strengths-based practitioner use the information obtained from the strengths discovery process to develop a strengths-based treatment plan? Table 7.7 summarizes some of the similarities and differences between a traditional treatment plan and a strengths-based one. In depicting these differences, no effort is made to reduce the value of traditional treatment plans. Instead, the goal is to demonstrate how strengths assessment can be used in treatment planning.

A strengths-based treatment plan should not only identify a client's strengths but also specify how the strengths will be used to assist in dealing with the presenting issue. Typically, a treatment plan consists of three to five pages with detailed information about the client and his or her background, presenting issues, goals, and so forth. Such treatment plans are often written for the benefit of the counselor rather than the benefit of the client. Clients need something simple—perhaps only a page or a half page that summarizes goals, strengths to be used to accomplish goals, time frame, and some indication of how the client will know when he or she has achieved the desired goals.

CULTURALLY RESPONSIVE STRENGTHS-BASED THERAPY TECHNIQUES

Strengths-based therapy has an arsenal of techniques to use during therapy. This section describes therapeutic interventions therapists can use with their clients during strengths-based therapy. The intervention techniques are designed to help clients bring positive emotions into their lives. Clients are given exercises they can use at home to promote positive feelings.

Strengths Journal

Beginning with Phase 3, the therapist asks the client to keep a **strengths journal**, in which the client records on a daily basis the specific strength he or she uses to deal with everyday life issues. The client is asked to identify the strength used, how it was used, and any other thoughts or developments that have occurred related to his or her strengths.

TABLE 7.6 ■ Strengths-Based Case Conceptualization Protocol: Integration of the CFI

Clinician's name: _____ Date: _____

Component 1

1. Identify client's personal background: age, sex, race, marital/family status, school or job status, living situation, socioeconomic status, and so on.

2. Presenting problem: Use client's own words to describe the presenting problem.

3. Prioritize presenting problems.

4. History of presenting problem
   A. Duration of presenting problem
   B. Precipitating events for seeking therapy
   C. Previous help-seeking behavior and results of those efforts
   D. Attitudes about mental health
   E. Attitudes about presenting problem
   F. Resources used in prior help seeking

5. Medical concerns: illnesses/problems, medications

6. Alcohol and drug use

Component 2

7. Cultural factors—outline for cultural formulation
   - Cultural identity of individual—what does belonging in that ethnocultural group mean to the client?
   - Cultural explanation of illness
   - Psychosocial environment/level of intergenerational conflicts
   - Therapeutic relationship
   - Overall cultural assessment

Component 3

8. Strengths assessment
   A. Internal strengths
   B. External strengths and support groups
   C. Cultural strengths
      1. Pride and participation in one's culture
      2. Social skills, traditions, knowledge, and practical skills related to client's culture
      3. Bilingual or multilingual abilities
      4. Generational wisdom
      5. Culturally specific ways of coping with stress
      6. Extended families and nonblood kinships
      7. Spiritual practices and faith
      8. Cultural maintenance skills
      9. Coping skills for racism and oppression
   D. Resiliency and hope

Component 4—Treatment Plan With Obstacles Considerations

9. Treatment goals
10. Treatment strategy
11. Treatment interventions
12. Treatment obstacles
13. Treatment/cultural considerations
14. Treatment prognosis
15. Treatment evaluation and termination

Source: © Elsie Jones-Smith.

TABLE 7.7 ■ Strengths-Based Versus Traditional Treatment Plans		
Domain of Concern	Strengths-Based Treatment Plan	"Traditional," Deficit-Based, or Problem-Focused Treatment Plan
Treatment Plan	Use client strengths to deal with presenting issues and to help client reach or achieve identified goals. Treatment plan guides the treatment process and is a "living document" that can be changed to meet client's goals and needs.	Treatment plan focuses on list of identified client problems that the client must deal with. Treatment plan is largely inflexible, and items once written must be accounted for during the treatment process.
Client's Role in Constructing the Treatment Plan	Client is a collaborator in developing the treatment plan.	Treatment plan is largely created by the therapist or helping professional with little input from the client.
Client Presenting Problems	Client's presenting issues are addressed in the treatment plan, but they do not dominate the treatment plan. Commitment to a multilevel understanding of the client, including the client, family, community, helping systems, and culture.	Client's presenting problems form the entire basis of the treatment plan. Client's issues are conceptualized in terms of pathology. Often, only the client's problems are addressed. Belief that understanding of a single dimension is sufficient.
Client Strengths	Client's strengths become a focal point of a treatment plan. Treatment plan is based partly on client assessment. Client assessment is strengths based, while it also takes into account a client's presenting issue or problem. Client strengths are placed in the forefront or beginning of the treatment plan.	Client assessment is usually problem oriented rather than strengths oriented. Client's strengths are minimized. Assessments do not measure client's strengths. Client strengths assessment takes place usually at the end of a problem-oriented assessment.
Treatment Goals	Treatment goals represent an integration of client's presenting problems and his or her strengths. Indicate how client's strengths will be used to deal with treatment goals. Treatment goals are worded positively.	Treatment goals focus on client's presenting problems. Focus is usually on the techniques the therapist will use to help client rectify or change his or her problem. Treatment goals are often worded negatively—the client "will no longer" or "will stop" . . .
Use of Community Resources	Uses natural supports and resources (activities, community institutions, and key resource people outside the immediate family) available within the community. Professionals link family to community resources, and facilitate referrals as needed.	Overreliance on use of agency and institutional resources. Continuing overreliance on professional services instead of increasing use of normalizing community resources.

"What Is the Truth?" Question

Clients often say that they do not know what they want or they do not know what direction to take. Yet if they ask themselves a simple question—"What is the truth?"—their body almost provides an answer. Clients may not give their clinicians the answer that this question brings forth. For instance, a woman says that she has mixed feelings about a friend and that she

CASE VIGNETTE 7.3

MARIO: A PUERTO RICAN MALE AND STRENGTHS-BASED THERAPY

Mario is a 32-year-old Puerto Rican male who sat in the counselor's office looking as if he did not want to be there. He checked his cell phone for text messages right in front of the counselor, even though she had asked him previously not to do so.

Counselor: "Mario, we had an agreement that you would not text, receive calls, or use your cell phone in any way. Would you please put the cell phone away?"

Mario: "Yeah, yeah, I know . . . I'm expecting an important text."

Counselor: "Is someone ill, or is there a family emergency that you need to deal with?"

Mario: "No, nothing like that. A friend of mine has been going through some things, and I have been trying to help her out. I told her that I would be there for her, and I did not want her to feel that I was running out on her by not answering her text message."

The counselor paused, pondering where she was going to go next. She could emphasize Mario's breaking of their agreement about no cell phones to make sure that he never did it again, or she could take another route, and comment that despite the fact that he was going through his own share of difficulties, he was still concerned about other people, namely his friends.

Counselor: "I appreciate your putting away your cell phone, Mario, and I also want to point out that I believe that you have just shown a strength that you need to look at and give yourself credit for having."

Mario: "What's that?" Mario said in a sarcastic, half-laughing tone. "Me, with a strength? Yeah, right."

Counselor: "I've noticed several strengths in you, Mario. Although I disapprove of your checking your cell phone for text messages from your friend, I'm impressed with your strength of nurturing. You care about those people who are close to you, and you do your best to help them."

Mario: "And sometimes that gets me into trouble. Sometimes I care too much, and people rely on me too much."

Counselor: "Let's just focus for a brief time on the fact that you help others and others look to you for help. What good do you think that they see in you?"

Mario: "I hadn't thought of it like that . . . like what you are saying . . . I guess they see me as a caring person, as someone they can trust—who is not going to blab their business to other people— as someone who listens. Several of my closest friends have told me that I'm a good listener."

Counselor: "How does that make you feel when others look to you for help and compliment you for being a good listener or for being a caring person?"

Mario: "Like I said, I feel pretty good about it all. I hadn't thought about these areas being strengths . . . but then I look at myself. I've got problems of my own. Otherwise, I wouldn't be here. I drink too much. I've now been arrested for driving while intoxicated. I might lose my job because of this. There's a lot going on in my own life. I can't seem to get a handle on it all. Each time I say that I am not going to drink any longer, something happens that tees me off, and bam, I'm right back where I started."

Counselor: "We can talk about your drinking, Mario. I want to point out that your nurturing strength is still there, despite the drinking. I want you to let that fact sink in, and I don't want you to dismiss your strength as unimportant because you also have a weakness—drinking too much. We all have strengths and weaknesses, Mario. Each one of us has to figure out how to use our strengths to manage our weaknesses so that they don't trip us up, the way that your drinking did the other week and led to your arrest.

"What I would like to do is to learn more about your strengths—what people look up to you for and what you do best. I also want to learn what you want to do about your drinking. As your counselor, I use a harm-reduction approach, which says that I will work with you to help you deal with drinking on a broad range—from completely stopping drinking to having a life where you reduce the harm that drinking is currently producing in your life. I hope to learn about your strengths as you tell me how you have tried to deal with the harm that drinking has produced in your life—for instance, when you have been successful in reducing your drinking."

Case Analysis

From this point, Mario talked about his relationship with alcohol—what it seemed to help him do. He also indicated that although he wanted to stop drinking completely, he wasn't sure that he could do so on his own.

Treatment involved helping Mario to get in contact with his strengths, of which he had several. The counselor and Mario conducted an extensive strengths discovery process, as Mario wanted to learn as much as possible about his strengths. He seemed pleased that for the first time in his life, he was on a hunt for what was good about him, what he could do well, and what he seemed naturally gifted to do. Most of Mario's strengths were people oriented—interpersonal.

Mario's strengths were also assessed in terms of his environment, his culture, and his spirituality. He identified his spirituality as a key factor in helping him to remain sober. As the therapist and Mario assessed his internal and external strengths, Mario began to identify friends and family who might help him to remain sober. In addition, Mario took the CliftonStrengths assessment (Gallup, 2018) and the VIA Classification of Strengths (VIA Institute on Character, 2018)—two strengths instruments that provided him with elaborate printouts.

Mario also examined the cultural components of his alcoholism. He began to read about alcoholism and Latinos. He discovered that ethnic groups within the Latino community varied in their alcoholism rates. His ethnic membership group, Puerto Ricans, had the highest rate of alcohol dependence among Latinos. There were a number of factors associated with Latino alcoholism rates. The community in which he lived had a high rate of stores selling alcohol.

Another factor contributing to Latino drinking is acculturation, the partial or complete adoption of the beliefs and values of the American social system. Zemore (2007) conducted an exhaustive review of the literature to find out if acculturation was associated with drinking outcomes among Latinos in the United States. The results of the review of the literature revealed that higher acculturation was very consistently associated with higher odds of drinking among women, even controlling for demographic covariates. Some evidence suggested that highly acculturated men are more prone to drink than are their peers who are low in acculturation. As a result of acculturation, the original drinking pattern of an ethnic group tends to change to resemble more closely that of the majority population—in this instance, White Americans. Latinos are inclined to have a lower rate of alcoholism in their native country than in America. Greater acculturation to the American way of life (acculturative stress) has been hypothesized to lead to drinking problems for some Latinos (Zemore, 2007). Armed with this information, Mario reached out to several community organizations in his neighborhood that dealt with alcohol prevention and helping families that experience problems with substance abuse.

Mario established several goals with regard to reducing the harm that alcohol was having on his life. He agreed to attend Alcoholics Anonymous (AA) meetings, even though he had not completely stopped drinking. Treatment involved assisting Mario in reducing his triggers and responding to them differently. Mario had felt powerless once his triggers set in.

The counselor gave him strengths cards (see page 224) and an empowerment tool kit to help him deal with the negative thoughts that said he was powerless and could not control his drinking. The two worked on strengths memories (see page 224), especially using a strengths memory whenever Mario felt threatened by the urge to drink.

Nurturing others was a strength, and both Mario and the counselor believed that Mario might work well as an addiction counselor if he could stop drinking. For the first time in a long time, Mario felt that he could control life rather than be controlled by it. He had hope.

The counselor and Mario developed a brief seven-point treatment plan that he was given a copy of so that he could refer to it during the week. The harm reduction that he wanted in his life was to abstain completely from drinking. Gradually, Mario began to understand the relationship that he had established with drinking. Drinking was his close friend. He terminated his friendship with alcohol. Mario discovered that most of his barriers that kept him drinking were both internal and external. Whenever he felt inadequate or overwhelmed, he drank. He learned how to take small steps to avoid the feeling that he was overwhelmed. If a problem arose, he decided to do something about it within 24 hours of its occurrence. Waiting any longer led to his repeated postponement of resolving the problem and to his feeling of being overwhelmed by it.

Six months after his initial counseling visit, Mario had reached a decision to completely stop drinking. He enrolled in his local community college to obtain a certificate in alcoholism and substance abuse counseling. Mario is doing well in his courses, and he was accepted to complete an internship in alcoholism and substance abuse counseling at the Salvation Army. He continued attending weekly AA meetings at one of the churches in his neighborhood.

does not know what to do about their friendship. In response to this dilemma, she asks herself, "What is the truth about your feelings for your friend?" The answer may come more quickly than spending a half hour with the clinician trying to uncover the client's feelings about her friend. Have a wife or husband ask, "What is the truth about my feelings for my mate or partner?" The answer will almost always come to the person.

Cultural Reflections

Which of the strengths-based interventions or techniques would you feel most comfortable using?

Have you ever been trained in how to help a client use his or her strengths?

The Oracle: Conversations About Life Purpose

The number-one question people have is "Why was I created?" and, second, "What is my purpose in life?" I have worked with people who said they would give anything just to really know their real purpose in life. This intervention technique is designed to help clients answer the question about their life purpose.

The clinician says to the client:

- Suppose there was an Oracle that you could go to that would tell you why you were created and what your real purpose in life is.

- What do you think the Oracle would tell you about why you were created?

- What do you think the Oracle would say is your life purpose?

- How close does your life resemble what you think is your life purpose?

- After the Oracle tells you what your exact life purpose is, what, if anything, would you do to change your life?

The Gratitude Diary

Have clients keep a daily gratitude diary in which they must list two things for which they are grateful each day. At the end of the week, clients are asked to make a summary of their week that takes into account the daily gratitude entries. Clients must make a statement about the good they are noticing in their lives.

Cultural Reflections

Have you ever been in a situation where you had to use your strengths to help you out of a difficult situation?

What strengths memories do you have for yourself?

One technique is to pull out a strengths memory when you are faced with a difficult situation.

Strengths Memories

Ask clients to remember a time in their lives when they displayed good strength and to keep this image in mind while planning and working toward goals. For instance, one client had been an excellent swimmer during his youth, winning many medals. When he came to therapy and recounted swimming as one of his strengths, the counselor asked him to get a picture in his mind of winning one of his medals. Every time he went for a job interview or took a step toward reaching one of his goals, he was asked to first take a few seconds to ready himself with his strengths memory.

Strengths Cards

Strengths cards are used to remind clients of their strengths. A card is wallet sized, and it contains on it four affirmations about strengths:

- I will achieve the goals that I establish for myself, one by one, step by step.

- I am a survivor and an achiever.

- I am confident in using my strengths to achieve my goals and to deal with challenges.
- I manage my weaknesses in a successful manner.

Strengths Charts

The counselor or therapist can use strengths charts to help clients better understand their strengths. Strengths charts can vary, depending upon the client's presenting issue, age, and other challenges. For instance, a strengths chart can be created for college admissions. Issues such as the client's level of development should be taken into consideration. Strengths charts can be developed for clients dealing with issues of depression, anxiety, and so forth. Parents can be asked to complete strengths charts for their children. A basic format for a strengths chart is provided in Table 7.8.

TABLE 7.8 ■ My Child's Strengths Chart					
Strength	High Strength Level	Medium Strength Level	Low Strength Level	Functional Competency	Weakness
Academics:					
English					
Math					
Science					
Reading					
Social studies					
School Activities:					
School government					
School clubs					
School sports					
Art					
Drama					
Community Activities:					
Community service					
Religious					
Spiritual					
Family Bonding					
Teacher Relationships					
Problem-Solving Skills					
Interpersonal Skills					
Personal Appearance					

(Continued)

TABLE 7.8 ■ (Continued)

Strength	High Strength Level	Medium Strength Level	Low Strength Level	Functional Competency	Weakness
Communication Skills					
Inner Emotional Strengths:					
Sense of humor					
Coping skills					
Resilience					
Inner Circle of Support Strengths:					
Family					
School friends					
Community friends					
Church					
Cultural and Ethnic Strengths					
Spirituality					
Creativity					
Analytical and Cognitive					
Wisdom					
Relational and Nurturing					
Survival					
Other					

SUMMARY OF KEY POINTS

This chapter was designed to help you develop effective culturally responsive case conceptualization and treatment planning skills. Using 2010 U.S. Census population data, the first part of the chapter pointed out that the average clinician stands a good chance of working with a culturally diverse client. In fewer than 30 years, the numbers for members of ethnic minority groups are expected to exceed those for majority White Americans (Paniagua, 2014). Next, a general case conceptualization model was presented.

- White American clinicians are not the only ones who may have difficulty working with clients from ethnic minority backgrounds. We all have biases, but some of our biases carry more weight. The biases of the dominant group are infinitely more powerful than those of members of racial or ethnic minority groups. As Hays (2013) has commented, "if you are being discriminated against as the sole person of color in your workplace, but your White co-workers and supervisor all disagree with you, chances are high that the dominant White perspective with its particular bias will win" (p. 26).

- Comas-Díaz and Jacobsen (1991) have pointed out that even clinicians from the same ethnocultural group as their clients may experience difficulty working with these clients. The twin processes of ethnocultural transference and ethnocultural countertransference operate during same-ethnic-group psychotherapy as well as when the clinician and client are from different ethnic groups.

- When clinicians are of the same ethnocultural group as their clients, they may overidentify with their clients.

- Then, too, some clinicians may harbor hatred toward members of their own ethnocultural group. Internal ethnic group self-hatred is demonstrated by the fact that virtually every major ethnic group has negative names that members call each other; however, they would be offended if members of a majority or another minority group used those same ethnic/racial epithets.

- The point is that no one gets a free pass from hatred just because of the color of his or her skin or ethnic membership group.

- Whenever we work with clients, regardless of their ethnocultural membership group, we should ask ourselves, "What cultural and other barriers potentially exist between my client and me?"

- The CFI, first introduced in Chapter 3, forms a large part of Chapter 7 on culturally responsive case conceptualization. One implication the reader might draw is that the CFI will be refined and that it will become part of standard training for most psychologists, social workers, and psychiatrists.

- Another major trend in psychology and in mental health is the increasing emphasis on strengths. As it stands right now, most clinicians either give lip service to working with client strengths or tack it on to their primary theoretical approach. As neuroscience teaches us more about the brain and its responses to trauma and other life challenges, the strengths approach will grow.

DISCUSSION QUESTIONS

Discussion Question set 1

Culture determines

- Whether or not an experience is an illness

- How we communicate during a clinical encounter or a service

- How we support individuals

- How we structure our work settings

- The moral stance we take toward mental health care

In small groups of three, discuss the above five referenced points in terms of your own specific culture. How does your cultural background determine if an experience is an illness? How does your worldview affect how you see mental illness in terms of your clients?

Discussion Question set 2

In small groups of three or four, discuss one clinical situation in which a difference in cultural backgrounds affected the counseling relationship. How did you handle the situation? Based on what you have learned thus far in reading this book, what would you do differently?

KEY TERMS

Case conceptualization: The process of using good theoretical frameworks to organize assessment and interview data to formulate hypotheses that may explain the underlying dynamics of the client's presenting problem in order to formulate an appropriate treatment plan.

Diagnosis: The identification and labeling of a disease based on its signs and symptoms.

Ethnocultural countertransference: Takes place when a clinician swings between overcompensation and exaggerated friendliness and suspicion with more or less concealed hostility.

Level of acculturation (degree of acculturation): An assessment of a client's adjustment to the host culture that can use a numerative framework—first generation, second generation, and third generation—or such terms as *traditional, transitional, bicultural,* and *Americanized* (E. Lee, 1990).

Migration history: Assessment for clients who have emigrated from one country to another, including the premigration history (country of origin, position in the family, education, employment status, political issues, experiences of war and traumatic events, etc.) and the actual immigration journey. The goal is to understand the client's baseline life experiences in his or her native country prior to migration.

Overdiagnosis of minority clients: The tendency of counselors and therapists to give members of racial minority groups more serious mental health diagnoses than they give to members of the dominant or majority race.

Psychotherapy attrition rate for ethnic/racial minorities: Nearly 50% of racially and ethnically diverse clients terminate treatment or therapy after one visit with a mental health practitioner.

Strengths journal: The client records on a daily basis a specific strength he or she uses to deal with everyday life issues. The client is asked to identify the strength used, how it was used, and any other thoughts or developments that have occurred related to his or her strengths.

Theoretical framework (or **theoretical model; theory of psychotherapy**): A collection of beliefs or a unifying theory of what caused the client's presenting problem and what is needed to bring about positive change with the problem.

Treatment plan: Outlines goals, objectives, and counseling interventions, where goals are broad statements of desired outcomes, objectives are statements of observable and measurable outcome targets, and interventions are counseling techniques or strategies used to help the client reach the objective. A good treatment plan has a case conceptualization that includes an understanding of what the problem is, how it developed, and what steps should be taken to resolve/deal with the problem.

REFERENCES AND SUGGESTED READING

Alarcón, R. D. (2009). Culture, cultural factors and psychiatric diagnosis: Review and projections. *World Psychiatry, 8*(3), 131–139. Retrieved from http://www.ncbi.nlm.nih.gov/pmc/articles/PMC2755270/

Alcántara, C., & Gone, J. P. (2014). Multicultural issues in the clinical interview and diagnostic process. In F. T. Leong (Ed.), *APA Handbook of multicultural psychology: Applications and training* (Vol. 2, pp. 153–163). Alexandria, VA: American Psychological Association.

American Psychiatric Association. (1994). *Diagnostic and statistical manual of mental disorders* (4th ed.). Washington, DC: Author.

American Psychiatric Association. (2000). *Diagnostic and statistical manual of mental disorders* (4th ed., text rev.). Washington, DC: Author.

American Psychiatric Association. (2013). *Diagnostic and statistical manual of mental disorders* (5th ed.). Washington, DC: Author.

Asnaani, A., & Hofmann, S. G. (2012). Collaboration in culturally responsive therapy: Establishing a strong therapeutic alliance across cultural lines. *Journal of Clinical Psychology, 68* (2), 187–198.

Asnaani, A., Richey, J. S., Dimaite, R., Hinton, D. E., & Hofmann, S. G. (2010). A cross-ethnic comparison of lifetime prevalence rates of anxiety disorders. *Journal of Nervous and Mental Disease, 198,* 551–555.

Awad, G. H., & Cokely, K. O. (2010). Designing and interpreting quantitative research in multicultural counseling. In J. G. Ponterotto, J. M. Casas, J. M. Suzuki, & C. M. Alexander (Eds.), *Handbook of multicultural counseling* (3rd ed., pp. 385–398). Thousand Oaks, CA: Sage.

Berry, J. W., & Kim, U. (1988). Acculturation and mental health. In J. Dasen, J. W. Berry, & N. Sartorius (Eds.), *Health and cross-cultural psychology towards application* (pp. 207–235). London, England: Sage.

Blake, P. R., & McAuliffe, K. (2011). "I had so much it didn't seem fair": Eight-year-olds reject two forms of inequity. *Cognition, 120*(2), 215–224. doi:10.1016/j.cognition.2011.04.006.

Brown, C., Schulberg, H., & Madonia, M. (1996). Clinical presentations of major depression by African Americans and Whites in primary medical care practice. *Journal of Affective Disorders, 41,* 181–191.

Cantor-Grae, E., Pedersen, C. B., McNeil, T. F., & Mortensen, B. (2003). Migration as a risk factor for schizophrenia: A Danish population-based cohort study. *British Journal of Psychiatry, 182,* 117–122.

Cantor-Grae, E., & Selten, J. P. (2005). Schizophrenia and migration: A meta-analysis and review. *American Journal of Psychiatry, 162,* 12–24.

Carter, R. T. (2007). Racism and psychological and emotional injury: Recognizing and assessing race-based traumatic stress. *The Counseling Psychologist, 35*(1), 13–105.

Comas-Díaz, L., & Greene, B. (1994). *Women of color.* Guilford, NY: New York.

Comas-Díaz, L., & Jacobsen, F. (1991). Ethnocultural transference and countertransference in the therapeutic dyad. *American Journal of Orthopsychiatry, 61*(3), 392–402.

Constantine, M. G. (2001a). Counselor experience related to complexity of case conceptualization and supervision preference. *Counselor Education and Supervision, 40,* 203–220.

Constantine, M. G. (2001b). Independent and interdependent self-construals as predictors of multicultural case conceptualization in counselor trainees. *Counseling Psychology Quarterly, 14,* 33–42.

Constantine, M. G. (2001c). Multicultural training, theoretical orientation, empathy and multicultural case conceptualization ability in counselors. *Journal of Mental Health Counseling, 23,* 357–372.

Constantine, M. G. (2002). Predictors of satisfaction with counseling: Racial and ethnic minority clients' attitudes toward counseling and ratings of their counselors' general and multicultural counseling competence. *Journal of Counseling Psychology, 49,* 255–263.

Constantine, M. G., & Gushue, G. V. (2003). Examining individualism, collectivism, and self-differentiation in African American college women. *Journal of Mental Health Counseling, 25*(1), 1–15.

Constantine, M. G., & Ladany, N. (2000). Self-report multicultural counseling competence scales: Their relation to social desirability attitudes and multicultural case conceptualization ability. *Journal of Counseling Psychology, 47,* 155–164.

Dana, R. H. (2002). Culture and methodology in personality assessment. Mental health services for African Americans: A cultural/racial perspective. *Cultural Diversity and Ethnic Minority Psychology, 8,* 3–18.

DeSilva, R., Aggarwal, N. K., & Lewis-Fernández, R. (2015). The DSM-5 Cultural Formulation Interview and the evolution of cultural assessment in psychiatry. *Psychiatric Times.* Retrieved from http://www.psychiatrictimes.com/print/211891/page/0/1

Díaz, E., Añez, L. M., Silva, M., Paris, N., & Davidson, L. (2017). Using the Cultural Formulation Interview to build culturally sensitive services. *Psychiatric Services, 68*(2), 112–114.

Duan, C., & Brown, C. (2016). *Becoming a multiculturally competent counselor.* Thousand Oaks, CA: Sage.

Fry, A., & Nguyen, T. (1996). Culture and the self: Implications for the perception of depression by Australian and Vietnamese nursing students. *Journal of Advanced Nursing, 23,* 1147–1154.

Gallup. (2018). *CliftonStrengths 34.* Retrieved from https://www.gallupstrengthscenter.com/home/en-us/strengthsfinder

Hansen, N. D., Pepitone-Arreola-Rockwell, F., & Greene, A. F. (2000). Multicultural competence: Criteria and case examples. *Professional Psychology: Research and Practice, 31*(6), 652–660.

Hays, P. A. (2013). *Connecting across cultures.* Thousand Oaks, CA: Sage.

Hofmann, S. G., & Hinton, D. E. (2014). Cross-cultural aspects of anxiety disorders. *Current Psychiatry Reports, 16,* 450. Retrieved from https://link.springer.com/article/10.1007/s11920-014-0450-3

Humes, K. R., Jones, N. A., & Ramirez, R. R. (2011, March). Overview of race and Hispanic origin—2010. *2010 Census Briefs.* U.S. Census Bureau. Retrieved from https://www.census.gov/prod/cen2010/briefs/c2010br-02.pdf

Jones-Smith, E. (2014). *Theories of counseling and psychotherapy: An integrative approach.* Thousand Oaks, CA: Sage.

Kleinman, A. (1996). How is culture important for DSM-IV? In J. Mezzich, A. Kleinman, H. Fabrega, & D. Parron (Eds.), *Culture & psychiatric diagnosis: A DSM-IV perspective* (pp. 15–25). Washington, DC: American Psychiatric Press.

Lambert, M. J., & Barley, D. E. (2002). Research summary on the therapeutic relationship and psychotherapy outcome. In J. C. Norcross (Ed.), *Psychotherapy relationships that work: Therapist contributions and responsiveness to patients* (pp. 17–32). New York, NY: Oxford University Press.

Lee, D. L., Sheridan, D. J., Rosen, A. D., & Jones, I. (2013). Psychotherapy trainees' multicultural case conceptualization content: Thematic differences across three cases. *Psychotherapy: Theory, Research, Practice, Training, 50*(2), 206–212.

Lee, D. L., & Tracey, T. J. G. (2008). General and multicultural case conceptualization skills: A cross-sectional analysis of psychotherapy trainees. *Psychotherapy: Theory, Research, Practice, Training, 45*(4), 507–522.

Lee, E. (1990). Family therapy with Southeast Asian refugees. In M. P. Mirkin (Ed.), *The social and political contexts of family therapy* (pp. 331–354). Needham Heights, MA: Allyn & Bacon.

Lewis-Fernández, R., & Díaz, N. (2002). The cultural formulation: A method for assessing cultural factors affecting the clinical encounter. *Psychiatric Quarterly, 73*(4), 271–295. doi:10.1023/A:1020412000183

Lui, W. M., & Pope-Davis, D. B. (2005). The working alliance, therapy ruptures and impasses, and counseling competence: Implications for counselor training and education. In R. T. Carter (Ed.), *Handbook of racial-cultural psychology and counseling* (pp. 148–167). Hoboken, NJ: Wiley.

Macneil, C. A., Hasty, K. K., Conus, P., & Berk, M. (2012). Is diagnosis enough to guide treatment interventions in mental health? Using case formulation in clinical practice. *BMC Medicine, 10,* 111. Retrieved from https://bmcmedicine.biomedcentral.com/articles/10.1186/1741-7015-10-111

McAuliffe, G. (2013). *Culturally alert counseling: A comprehensive introduction* (2nd ed.). Thousand Oaks, CA: Sage.

McQuaide, S., & Ehrenreich, J. (1997). Assessing client strengths. *Families in Society: The Journal of Contemporary Social Services, 78*(2), 201–212. doi:10.1606/1044-3894.759

Mezzich, J. E., Caracci, G., Fabrega, H., Jr., Kirmayer, L. J. (2009). Cultural formulation guidelines. *Transcultural Psychiatry, 46*(3), 383–405.

Nicolas, G., Desilva, A. M., Subrebost, K. L., Breland-Noble, A., Gonzalez-Eastep, D., Manning, N., . . . Prater, K. (2007). Expression and treatment of depression among Haitian immigrant women in the United States: Clinical observations. *American Journal of Psychotherapy, 61*(1), 83–98.

Norcross, J. C. (2002). Psychotherapy relationships that work: Therapist contributions and responsiveness to patients.

In J. C. Norcross (Ed.), *Psychotherapy relationships that work: Therapist contributions and responsiveness to patients* (pp. 3–16). New York, NY: Oxford University Press.

Paniagua, F. A. (2014). *Assessing and treating culturally diverse clients: A practical guide.* Thousand Oaks, CA: Sage.

Paniagua, F. A., O'Boyle, M., Tan, V. L., & Lew, A. S. (2000). Self-evaluation of unintended biases and prejudices. *Psychological Reports, 887,* 823–829.

Patten, E. (2015, November). *Who is multiracial? Depends on how you ask: A comparison of six survey methods to capture racial identity.* Washington, DC: Pew Research Center. Retrieved from http://www.pewsocialtrends.org/2015/11/06/who-is-multiracial-depends-on-how-you-ask/.

Pedersen, P. B., & Pope, M. (2010). Inclusive cultural empathy for successful global leadership. *American Psychologist, 65,* 841–854.

Ponterotto, J. G., Utsey, S. O., & Pedersen, P. B. (2006). *Preventing prejudice: A guide for counselors, educators, and parents.* Thousand Oaks, CA: Sage.

Schomburg, A. M., & Prieto, L. R. (2011). Trainee multicultural case conceptualization ability and couples therapy. *Journal of Marital Family Therapy, 37*(2), 223–235.

Schreiber, R., Stern, P., & Wilson, C. (2000). Being strong: How Black West-Indian Canadian women manage depression and its stigma. *Journal of Nursing Scholarship, 32*(1), 39–45.

Sperry, L. (2010). *Core competencies in counseling and psychotherapy: Becoming a highly competent and effective therapist.* New York, NY: Routledge.

Sperry, L., & Sperry, J. (2012). *Case conceptualization: Mastering this competency with ease and confidence.* New York, NY: Routledge.

Sue, S. (2009). Ethnic minority psychology: Struggles and triumphs. *Cultural Diversity and Ethnic Minority Psychology, 15,* 409–415.

Sue, D. W., & Sue, D. (2013). *Counseling the culturally diverse: Theory and practice* (6th ed.). Hoboken, NJ: Wiley.

Taber, B. J., Leibert, T. W., & Agaskar, V. R. (2011). Relationships among client-therapist personality congruence, working alliance, and therapeutic outcome. *Psychotherapy: Theory, Research, Practice, Training, 48*(4), 376–380.

Tseng, W. S. (2001). *Handbook of cultural psychiatry.* San Diego, CA: Academic Press.

U.S. Department of Health and Human Services. (2001). *Mental health: Culture, race, and ethnicity—a supplement to mental health: A report of the Surgeon General.* Rockville, MD: U.S. Department of Health and Human Services, Substance Abuse and Mental Heal Service Administration, Center for Mental Health Services.

Vedantam, S. (2005, January 23). See no bias. *The Washington Post.* Retrieved from http://www.washingtonpost.com/wp-dyn/content/article/2005/01/23/AR2005040314622.html

VIA Institute on Character. (2018). *The VIA Classification of Strengths.* Retrieved from http://www.viacharacter.org/www/Character-Strengths

Watters, C. (2001). Emerging paradigm in the mental health care of refugees. *Social Science & Medicine, 52,* 709–1718.

Westermeyer J. (Eds.), *Psychiatric care of migrants: A clinical guide* (pp. 000–000). Washington, DC: American Psychiatric Publishing.

World Health Organization. (1992). *The ICD-10 classification of mental and behavioural disorders: Clinical descriptions and diagnostic guidelines.* Geneva, Switzerland: World Health Organization.

Zemore, S. E. (2007). Acculturation and alcohol among Latino adults in the United States: A comprehensive review. *Alcoholism-Clinical and Experimental Research, 12,* 1968–1990.

CULTURALLY RESPONSIVE STRENGTHS-BASED THERAPY FOR AFRICAN AMERICANS

- *"In the End, we will remember not the words of our enemies, but the silence of our friends."* —Martin Luther King Jr.

- *"Do not become the thing you fear. We did not come to fear the future. We came here to shape it."* —Barack Obama

- *"I have learned over the years that when one's mind is made up, this diminishes fear."* —Rosa Parks

CHAPTER OBJECTIVES

- Describe the demographics of the African American population in the United States.

- Explain how social class relates to African Americans in terms of the underclass, the middle class, and the upper class.

- Identify oppression, discrimination, and microaggressions against African Americans.

- Describe African American cultural values and worldviews.

- Identify the cultural strengths of African Americans.

- Implement psychotherapy approaches for working with African Americans.

- Evaluate clinical issues in counseling African Americans.

INTRODUCTION

This chapter explores the ethnocultural state of affairs for African Americans in the United States, and it discusses various approaches for counseling members of this large, heterogeneous group. It departs significantly from typical writings about the counseling of African Americans in that it does not focus on the negative, but rather deals with the upper and middle classes as well as the underclass. For the most part, researchers have focused on either the African American working class or the growing underclass, the poverty of the Black underclass, the lack of educational achievement of African American youth, the high crime and incarceration rate, and a host of other problems.

Clearly, some of these problems do exist for African Americans; however, that is not their entire story. There is more to African Americans than poverty statistics or a recounting of the history of American slavery. Focusing on what amounts to a group's victim status serves primarily to keep the public thinking of members of this group in negative terms. One should remember slavery as an attempt to denigrate and dehumanize an entire group of people. That African Americans have been able to overcome this is a strength that should be identified and affirmed. Further, the African American ethnocultural group is a heterogeneous one with members occupying the broad spectrum of social class, including people such as Barack Obama, a two-term president of the United States; Nobel Peace Prize winners Ralph Bunche and Martin Luther King Jr.; and Toni Morrison, a Nobel laureate in literature (Touré, 2011).

African Americans have achieved in virtually every major area in American society, but this fact seems to be overlooked in favor of painting them as perpetual victims of oppression who have achieved very little in life. Therefore, this chapter, in keeping with the strengths-based approach advocated throughout this book, focuses on the positive accomplishments of African Americans, while still acknowledging the negative life circumstances of what has become the permanent Black Underclass (Ellison, 2015). There must be balance in describing ethnocultural groups in America, and my goal in writing this chapter is to evidence a balanced perspective. The reader is referred to the author's tripartite model of identity developed some time ago (Smith, 1985, 1991), which maintains that each one of us has (1) an individual identity with our own identity footprints of unique life experiences; (2) a group-level identity in which we share similarities (similar footprints) with a particular group of people—often called our ethnocultural group (each person has multiple group identities—gender, sex, ethnicity, etc.); and (3) a universal level of identity—an identity as a human being that we share with all other human beings—the footprints of a human being. When we talk about African Americans, we are actually speaking about only one level of a person's identity, and for any given person, the African American identity may or may not be the most important aspect of his or her identity.

THE AFRICAN AMERICAN POPULATION: SOME BASIC DEMOGRAPHICS

According to the U.S. Census Bureau, in 2010, the entire U.S. population comprised 308.7 million people, and of this number, approximately 38.9 million people self-identified their race as Black or African American, constituting 12.6% of the total population (Humes, Jones, & Ramirez, 2011). The 2010 figure of 38.9 million self-identified African Americans represents an increase of 4.3 million over the 34.6 million reported in 2000 (Grieco & Cassidy, 2001. What's interesting is that 3 million additional African Americans reported their race as Black or African American in combination with one or more other races/ethnic groups (Humes et al., 2011). African Americans are part of the new U.S. Census–designated "mixed race" groups. This author predicts that within the next decade or so, the current designation of racial groups used by the U.S. Census Bureau will be modified so that only one race will be represented—the human race—and all other designations will be called ethnic or cultural groups.

The Overall Socioeconomic Status of African Americans

The socioeconomic status of African Americans is usually painted as extremely gloomy and negative, and for millions of African Americans, the negative portrait is accurate—especially for those located in the working class or what is now being called the "permanent Black Underclass." This section examines the socioeconomic status of African Americans from the so-called Black Underclass to the working class, to the middle class, and even to the Black upper class—although some people question whether there can be a socioeconomic category for African Americans called the "upper class." First, however, I will begin with the overall picture—that is, by lumping everyone together who is listed as African American—followed by an analysis of the working class and the underclass.

The 2010 U.S. Census reported that the median income of African American families was $33,578, far below the national U.S. median family income of $50,045. Among White families, the median income was $52,480 (U.S. Census Bureau, 2010). The poverty rate for the broad African American group is dire. Approximately 25.9% or 10.1 million of those who identified themselves as African American or Black (not in combination with other ethnic/racial groups) lived below the poverty level, whereas only 12.0% of individuals who identified as White, not in combination with other ethnic groups, had a similar economic income (U.S. Census Bureau, 2010). The 2010 poverty line statistics for African Americans represented an increase of 1.9 million over the figures for 2000, where 8.2 million lived below the poverty guideline level (Bishaw & Iceland, 2003).

The Black Underclass

One of the disturbing economic facts of life in the United States is that large numbers of African Americans live in poverty, either at or below the poverty line, and that this economic status has persisted for decades and generations, forming a social stratum at the bottom of the national class schema termed the **Black Underclass**. Recently, the Henry J. Kaiser Family Foundation reported data that show that within the United States, 10% of White Americans live in poverty, compared to 27% of African Americans, 24% of Hispanic Americans, and 14% of Americans in other ethnic/racial groups ("Poverty Rate by Race/Ethnicity," 2015). Various reasons have been given to explain the high rates of poverty among African Americans and Latinos, including racism, sexism, taking care of other relatives, lack of education, generational poverty, and personal choices.

More than 50 years ago, Michael Harrington published a book, *The Other America: Poverty in the United States* (1962), in which he wrote about the poverty of large numbers of African Americans and poor Whites. His book led to Presidents Kennedy and Johnson waging a war on poverty. Harrington called this class the underclass, a class grouping that was below the working class and that showed little chance of "pulling itself up by the bootstraps." In 2012, Peter Dreier wrote an article, "The Invisible Poverty of 'The Other America' of the 1960s Is Far More Visible Today," in which he stated the following:

> It is now a generation later and, thanks in part to Harrington, the poor are no longer invisible. The policies adopted as part of Lyndon Baines Johnson's (LBJ's) war on poverty (including Medicaid; subsidized housing; Head Start; legal services; raising the minimum wage; and, later, food stamps)—in combination with a strong economy—significantly reduced poverty. The nation's poverty rate was cut in half—from 22.4 percent in 1959 to 11.1 percent in 1973. The decline in poverty was particularly dramatic among the elderly, thanks to Medicare and cost-of-living increases for Social Security.

Dreier concluded that the programs of the 1960s and 1970s did work—at least somewhat. Harrington has pointed out, however, that the level of spending for antipoverty programs (less than 1% of the federal budget) was insufficient to truly address the high rates of poverty. The poverty rate in the United States is two to three times higher than that for most European countries, and Canada has a much lower "poverty rate and does not permit the level of sheer destitution and misery found in the United States, including hunger, slums and the growing army of homeless people sleeping on park benches and in vacant buildings" (Dreier, 2012). The problem seems to be getting worse. As Dreier (2012) has stated, "Even more startling is the fact that 100 million people comprise what the US Census calls the poor and the 'near poor,' based on a new definition of poverty that measures living standards, not just income. Almost one-third of the nation, in other words, can barely make ends meet."

Cultural Reflections

Imagine that you are all alone by yourself, meditating on your relationships with ethnocultural groups in America.

You have decided that you are going to be brutally honest with yourself in answering the following questions:

How comfortable would you feel counseling an African American from the Black Underclass?

How would you go about establishing a relationship with a Black person whose income is below the poverty line, who has little education, and who is living in dire circumstances?

Why does this chapter allot so much space to the economic problems of some African Americans, specifically those in the underclass? The problems of the Black Underclass are enormous, and they merit the attention of all Americans. If the average clinician works in a city, state, or federal agency that deals with counseling the poor, it is highly likely that he or she will be working with a member of the Black Underclass. It's important to know who is in the Black Underclass and what their unique circumstances are. It is also very important to treat such individuals with respect and dignity, and not just as representatives of an economic group.

Black Poverty: Implications for Counseling

Poverty may bring out the not-so-good aspects of individuals. People who feel trapped in irreversible poverty may be angry and hostile toward even those who try to help them. If the clinician is a White American, the client might respond, "What the hell do you know about me or my situation? You don't give a damn about me! You're just here to collect a check, and that's all." If the clinician is another African American, the client might respond, "And who do you think you are, Ms. Ann? You come here to see how the rest of us live, Ms. High and Mighty. You're no better than the White counselors."

In reality, the African American client may actually want help. Because of the history of slavery and racial oppression, plus ongoing poverty that is perceived at least in part to be caused by White racism, the average African American client from the underclass might have issues of trust with any clinician. The client may simply be transferring onto the clinician his or her own low self-worth feelings about being Black and poor and in need of help in a society that appears to be callous or indifferent to his or her suffering and plight. Sometimes it is difficult not to be overwhelmed by the circumstances or the anger and depression of those located what appears to be permanently in the Black Underclass.

Yet, it is not just poverty that seems to be affecting members of these groups, but rather issues related to family structure and cultural values. There is enough blame to go around for everyone—racists as well as the victims themselves. The belief has emerged that an entirely new culture of the underclass has been created (Kochhar & Fry, 2014).

Cultural Reflections

When clinicians look for different expressions of the same value in their clients who may be culturally different from them, they create within the therapeutic relationship an expectation of core similarities between them and their clients.

Let's suppose you were working with a Black and a White parent from the underclass, and both are having behavioral problems with their children in school.

What core value would you seek to use to establish a positive relationship with your client?

Would you give any consideration to the idea that a possible common value might be that "most parents want their children to do well in school," and "I'm here to help you accomplish that goal"?

The White Underclass

To be sure, African Americans are not the only ones in the underclass. A growing number of White Americans are finding that they have fallen into the underclass. Richard Florida (2012) has pointed out that income and wealth inequality have reached record levels in the United States and the inequalities are beginning to approach levels found in some third-world nations. American Whites are being pushed into the underclass because the ranks of the working class have shrunk due to automation and globalization. In 2012, Nicholas Kristof, an Op-Ed columnist for *The New York Times*, wrote an article titled "The White Underclass" that elucidated why there is a growing **White Underclass**. According to him, "historically, 'underclass' has often been considered to be a euphemism for race, but increasingly it includes elements of the white working class as well." Some of the factors mentioned for a rise in the White Underclass include the loss of good paying jobs, a largely service economy, the widespread use of drugs, and the breakdown of the White family. Richard Florida (2017) points out that more than

60 million Americans belong to the service class. In support of his position, Kristof cites the 2012 book by Charles Murray, *Coming Apart: The State of White America, 1960–2010*, where Murray examines family breakdown among working-class Whites and the decline of the traditional values of diligence. For instance, among White American women with only a high school education, 44% of births are out of wedlock, a sizeable increase from the 6% figure in 1970.

Kristof (2012) states,

> Today, I fear we're facing a crisis in which a chunk of working-class America risks being calcified into an underclass, marked by drugs, despair, family decline, high incarceration rates and a diminishing role of jobs and education as escalators of upward mobility. We need a national conversation about these dimensions of poverty, and maybe Murray can help trigger it.

We ought to listen to what Kristof has to say. In February 2016, PBS *Frontline* aired a two-hour television special on drug use in the state of New Hampshire. Incredibly and sadly, both rural and city residents in majority White New Hampshire considered their number-one problem to be heroin addiction and the breakdown of the family caused by drug addiction (Gaviria, 2016).

In summary, the underclass is not the sole province of African Americans. It is increasingly becoming a permanent home for some White Americans. Accordingly, clinicians will have to deal with some of the same problems described for African Americans with White Americans. Right now, the problem of the White Underclass is being hidden because of the mathematics involved in regression toward the mean and because of the high salaries of some Whites in the middle and upper classes. Large numbers of Whites are hurting, economically speaking, and no one seems to be paying much attention to their pain.

The African American Middle Class

Despite the enormous problems of the Black Underclass, there are more hopeful statistics regarding the African American middle class. The African American middle class has existed since the emancipation of slavery, although it usually involved freed slaves, most of whom had very fair skin. It was the African American middle class that formed the teachers and professors, created businesses, and created institutions of higher learning (Bowser, 2006; Franklin, 1993).

In contrast to the Black Underclass, the African American middle-class person tends to seek private counseling or psychotherapy voluntarily when problems arise. During the 1960s and 1970s, members of the African American middle class tended to be redlined to the inner city, and they lived in working-class neighborhoods (Cashin, 2000). The U.S. Census Bureau does not list specifically middle-class income guidelines. Instead, it looks at the median income of households, meaning the amount that divides the income distribution of a group into two equal groups—one half having income above the median and one half having income below the median. Although African American migration to the suburbs began in 1979, by the 1990s most middle-class African Americans had moved out of inner-city neighborhoods into the more White middle-class or affluent suburbs (Cashin, 2000).

The real disparity between the African American middle class and the White American middle class lies in the figures for net worth. According to a Pew study in 2009, the net worth of Whites compared to African Americans is almost 20 to 1 (Kochhar, Fry, & Taylor, 2011).

Because of the decline in housing value and stocks during 2008, "the typical black household had just $5,677 in wealth (assets minus debts) in 2009; the typical Hispanic household had $6,325 in wealth; and the typical white household had $113,149." According to a 2013 Pew report, "in 2013, the net worth of the typical white family was nearly 13 times that of the typical black family, and 10 times that of the typical Latino one. Both gaps have widened since the recession ended more than five years ago" (Kochhar & Fry, 2014).

Cultural Reflections

How do you feel about multimillion-dollar salaries that some African American professional athletes are earning?

Do you feel resentment at any level?

When you see an interracial couple—Black and White—how do you feel?

Do you ever think, "I wish everyone would stick to his or her own kind of race?"

Counseling Implications for Middle-Class African Americans

Counseling members of the Black middle class is likely to be easier than working with those who are in dire poverty. For one thing, their life circumstances might not be as overwhelming as those of a member of the underclass. As their basic needs are taken care of by family financial resources, members are able to relax a bit more and to focus their attention on their other needs. In general, members of the African American middle class have found some success in American life. Many have earned a degree in higher education and found success in other ventures. Thus, they may be more inclined to trust when it comes to a counselor either from their own ethnic membership group or from another ethnic group. Because the middle-class African American community may be small, members may know each other, and therefore, for privacy reasons (they may run in similar professional or social circles), they may actually choose a White clinician or a clinician in a nonmembership ethnic group (Smith, 1991). The goal may be to find a clinician who shares one's values and worldviews rather than one who is a member of the same ethnocultural group (Paniagua, 2014).

Is There an African American Upper Class?

Almost 20 years ago, Lawrence Otis Graham (1999) wrote a book, *Our Kind of People: Inside America's Black Upper Class*. Graham, himself a Princeton and Harvard Law School graduate, visited elite African American clubs and sororities to gain inside information on the Black elite or Black upper class.

If membership in a class is determined by how much money one earns, it is clear that an African American upper class exists. According to the U.S. Census Bureau (2010), 13.5% of Whites earned $100,000 and over, while 6.5% of African Americans fell into that household income category.

In 2010, 5.0% of White Americans earned $200,000 and over; only 1.1% of African Americans earned that salary. Increasing numbers of African Americans are attending Ivy League universities, but they still lack the generations of wealth in their families. At the heart of the question "Are there African Americans in the upper class of American society?" are unspoken racial attitudes. The answer is that it all depends on who's asking the question, what criteria are being used to evaluate said status, and what are one's underlying sentiments about race or ethnic groups in the United States.

HISTORICAL AND PSYCHOSOCIAL ISSUES FOR BLACKS: OPPRESSION, DISCRIMINATION, AND THE LEGACY OF SLAVERY

The African American Response to Slavery

It is beyond the scope of this book to present an overview of early, historical enslavement of African Americans. Slavery was designed to strip Africans of their culture and language by refusing to place individuals from the same tribe together. Such tactics were met with only limited success. Yet neither cultural diversity nor multiple languages blocked the development of African American cultures in the new world. Many of the African cultures, customs, dance, and values were preserved, including an African worldview. Despite slavery, African Americans have proved to be a very resilient people—from slavery to being the president (Parham, 2012).

The legacy of slavery is that it attributed a master status to White Americans simply on the basis of the color of their skin. White skin served as a type of "affirmative action calling card" that could be submitted to employers for employment and promotion, to schools and colleges for entrance into desired programs of study, and to builders of housing for the rental of apartments and the purchase of houses in the most desirable sections of a community. White skin was a status symbol that entitled one to privilege, and just one drop of Black blood could endanger one's White status. One had to protect one's White status at all costs because the absence of it could result in poverty and an undesirable life situation.

It was not until the emergence of Japan and China as world leaders that things began to go slightly downhill for White Americans. During the 1980s and 1990s, manufacturing jobs were lost to China and Mexico, and the Japanese challenged the Detroit automobile makers so much that plants were closed. I remember watching former White autoworkers attack at random Chinese and Japanese Americans because they felt that China and Japan had destroyed their way of life. The sun was beginning to set on parts of the American manufacturing industry in much the same way that the sunset was hovering over Great Britain. Everyone wanted someone to blame, and members of American ethnic minority groups proved to be easy targets.

Racism has passed through various stages in American society. Whereas Whites used to openly acknowledge their privileges for just being White people, it became fashionable for some to charge African Americans with "playing the race card." To be honest, there has been card playing on both sides. One person plays a White card, another plays a Black card—round and round we go, where it stops, nobody knows (Toldson, 2008).

According to Ridley (1995, 2005), White Americans engage in what he calls unintentional covert racism, in which the individual does not intend to be racist, but the bottom line is that the person's behavior culminates in negative consequences for an African American. Neville, Worthington, and Spanierman (2001) have similarly criticized the statements by some Whites that they don't see color—in other words, that they are **color blind**, or that they claim to not treat people differently based on how they appear. Looking directly at the face of an African American, some Whites have stated, "You know, I really don't see color when I'm talking with you." "Yeah, well, what do you see? Am I some sort of grayish or nude color?" All joking aside, a person may have the very best intentions when making such statements and may be only trying to say that their relationship with another person is beyond race, beyond color.

Neville and colleagues (2001) have asserted that when individuals claim that they are color blind, they are essentially denying the existence of race as a social issue, while at the same time maintaining their existing White privilege. People who claim to be color blind when evaluating college instructors or employees who are culturally different from themselves may be covertly asserting that their own status of entitlement is due to their own merit and not related to their ethnocultural heritage. On the other hand, the color-blind statements of some White Americans may only reflect their desire to say that "I see you as a human being and not as an African American," or "Your skin color is not the most important thing about you."

The legacy of slavery can be traced to current racist attitudes toward African Americans. Contemporary forms of racism in the 21st century include discriminatory practices in virtually every aspect of African American life, including severely reduced job opportunities, truncated educational and housing opportunities, and false imprisonment. Many White Americans bristle at being called racist, and some feel that they should not have to pay for the sins of their fathers.

Microaggressions and Prejudice Against African Americans

According to an Associated Press poll, racial attitudes did not improve in the four years after the United States elected its first African American president, Barack Obama, in 2008 (Capehart, 2012). The poll found that a slight majority of Americans expressed prejudice toward African Americans whether they recognized those feelings or not. Approximately 51% of Americans expressed explicit anti-Black attitudes, compared with 48% in a similar study conducted in 2008. The poll found that racial prejudice had increased regardless of whether the survey used questions that explicitly asked respondents about racist attitudes or an experimental test that measured implicit views toward race without asking questions about that topic directly. Another poll found that most Americans also expressed anti-Hispanic sentiments.

The same respondents were also given a survey that measured implicit racism, in which a photo of a Black, Hispanic, or White male flashed on the screen before a neutral image of a Chinese character. "The respondents were then asked to rate their feelings toward the Chinese character. Previous research has shown that people transfer their feelings about the photo onto the character, allowing researchers to measure racist feelings, even if a respondent does not acknowledge them" (Associated Press, 2012). All the surveys were conducted online because prior research has shown that people are more honest when responding to online surveys than when they are faced with a live interviewer. Researchers from Stanford University, the University of Michigan, and NORC at the University of Chicago conducted the survey. Although there was progress in Obama's election as president of the United States, there was also backlash. The poll noted that many Americans reported perceived antagonism toward them since Obama took office. The individuals pointed to events involving police brutality and to cartoons and protest posters that mocked the president with racist visuals and stereotypes, or lynching him in effigy (Associated Press, 2012).

The poll reported that racial prejudice was not limited to one group of Americans, with 79% of Republicans and 32% of Democrats expressing negative attitudes toward Blacks. The implicit test found little difference between the two political parties; however, a majority of both Democrats and Republicans held anti-Black feelings (55% of Democrats and 64% of Republicans, as well as 49% of political Independents).

The issue of racism toward African Americans has particular relevance for psychotherapy relationships. Negative racial attitudes toward a person of color are hard to conceal from that person. The issue is: What should clinicians do when they know that they have negative racist attitudes toward African Americans? Should they ignore their feelings and attempt to work with the client? Should the clinician inform a supervisor of his or her negative feelings against African Americans and ask for supervision of the counseling situation?

African American Population Mixed With Other Ethnic/Racial Groups: Microaggressions

> ### Cultural Reflections
>
> *If you were aware that you had negative racial attitudes toward African Americans, would you attempt to counsel members of this ethnocultural group? If so, do you think that you could counsel a client effectively for whom you harbored negative racial feelings?*
>
> *Would you tell your supervisor about your racial concerns and ask for his or her guidance?*

Do Americans treat African Americans of "mixed" racial ancestry better than they respond to those who claim Black ancestry? As of 2010, those who identify as Black in combination with those who identify as having mixed ancestry including Black heritage totaled approximately 42 million people. Thus, African Americans comprised approximately 14% of the total American population (Rastogi, Johnson, Hoeffel, & Drewery, 2011). The ethnic groups that were most commonly reported in combination with African Americans were White (1.8 million); American Indian and Alaska Native (269,421); White, American Indian, and Alaska Native (230,848); and Asian (185,595). It is important for clinicians to inquire about—or at the very least be aware of—the biracial identity of some African Americans. Although historically in the United States, one drop of African American blood made a person 100% Black, some mixed-blood

CASE VIGNETTE 8.1

TIGER WOODS AND MULTIRACIAL IDENTITY

Internationally recognized professional golfer Tiger Woods made headlines in 1997 when, after his groundbreaking victory in the U.S. Masters Tournament, Oprah Winfrey asked him on her show if it bothered him to be called African American. The 21-year-old golfer replied, "It does . . . I'm just who I am, whoever you see in front of you."

Woods continued by stating that as a child he had invented the term *Cablinasian* to describe his parents' multiethnic and nationality background—a mix of half Asian (Chinese and Thai), one-quarter African American, one-eighth Native American, and one-eighth Dutch. Woods had constructed the term as a way of honoring his mother Kultida (of Thai, Chinese, and Dutch ancestry), as well as respecting and acknowledging other aspects of his cultural and racial heritage. Woods further acknowledged that as a student, he would select both African American and Asian for his ethnic/racial background on official forms. Woods's statements about his ethnic/racial identity angered many African Americans who viewed him as the first African American winner of the Masters—a sports star who was one of their own, and whose success in breaking down racial barriers in golf was a real source of pride to them.

Woods had declared himself "unblack," which was not well received by the African American community. Another way of looking at this was that Tiger Woods's calling himself *Cablinasian* was a bold break with the "one drop of blood" rule. Tiger Woods was essentially saying that he had the right to self-identify, to call himself what

he felt he was, instead of allowing others to foist upon him an ethnic/racial identity based on their own thoughts and feelings about African Americans.

Cablinasian sparked a renewed debate in American society about people with parents of mixed ethnicity and nationality. Could these people create their own socioethnocultural category, and would the U.S. Census Bureau recognize mixed ancestry or continue the "one drop of blood" rule? Who has the right to determine a person's ethnocultural identity? Does the person have the right to say how he or she wants to be represented or categorized? What ethnic or racial identity forms a master status for that person?

Woods's statement about being *Cablinasian* put him at the forefront of the multiracial identity movement in the United States. In 2000, Tom Petri proposed legislation for a multiracial check box to be included in the 2000 U.S. Census. He called his proposal the "Tiger Woods Bill." In 2010, the Census Bureau made this change, allowing African Americans to designate themselves as African American or mixed with the ancestry of other ethnic groups. The 2010 U.S. Census responses suggest that the outdated and unscientific way of viewing race according to the "one drop of blood" rule is changing. Increasingly Asian Americans, Latino Americans, African Americans, and White Americans are checking more than one box for their self-identified ethnic/racial identity. Like Tiger Woods, these people are claiming their right to self-authorize, to declare who they are to the world.

African Americans want to be considered as biracial or bi-ethnic rather than as a member of only one ethnic group. When clinicians respond only to the African American part of a person's ethnocultural identity, they are using the "one drop of African American blood" rule and enforcing a master status ethnic identity. This may convey that the most important part of someone's identity is being Black, and very little else about the person's racial or ethnic identity matters. Being Black forms a master status that governs a person's entire life.

Cultural Reflections

Where there is no enemy within, the enemies outside cannot hurt you.

—African proverb

AFRICAN AMERICANS AND CULTURAL VALUES

The African American Worldview

Psychologists use the construct of worldview to describe beliefs and values about such variables as the nature of time (e.g., present, future), social relationships (e.g., individualism, collectivism), and the presence or absence of natural and supernatural entities (e.g., materialism, spiritualism) that are shared among ethnocultural groups (Koltko-Rivera, 2004). These cultural variables provide the framework for individuals to behave and think in a certain way, their attitudes toward mental health and healing, and the types of treatment or remedies they believe are helpful. For instance, European or White Americans are said to have a worldview reflecting the values of individualism, materialism, and future temporal orientation. In contrast, the worldviews of African Americans have been characterized by values that include interdependence and collective responsibility, spirituality, and present temporal orientation (Kambon, 1992; Morris, 2001; Toldson, 2008).

The African American worldview appears to be in a state of change, and it is tempered by the age of a person, the geographic area in which he or she lives, and his or her membership in a specific socioeconomic group. Young African Americans, who may or may not have experienced directly the same level of oppression and racism as their parents did, may feel less constricted by their ethnocultural membership group (Cose, 2011). The difference between young and older African Americans in their worldview was demonstrated in the attitudes of members of these two groups during the 2008 presidential election. Young African Americans, who were told that their votes would be "thrown away" by voting for Senator Barack Obama instead of Hillary Clinton, responded: *So what? I don't believe I am throwing away my vote. Times have changed. I am going to vote my hopes, not my fears* (McGuirt, 2009).

Older African Americans, those from 50 years of age on, are more inclined to have adopted a collectivist orientation toward life (we must help each other because we are all one group), while younger African Americans tend to adhere to an individualistic outlook on life, and they usually do not attend church at the same rate as their parents did. Older African Americans are appalled at the high rate of Black-on-Black crime in the inner cities across this country that is usually committed by young people ages 18 to 35 (Cose, 2011).

African American Ethnocultural Identity

Ethnocultural or ethnic/racial identity development can be conceptualized as a positive way that individuals develop a view of their own membership group, as well as of other ethnocultural groups. African American cultural identity has been the source of much research, and some of this research has already been cited in Chapter 3 of this book in the section on multicultural identity (Cross, 1991; Helms & Cook, 1999; Helms & Parham, 1985; Vandiver, Fhagen-Smith, Cokley, Cross, & Worrell, 2001). In the United States, ethnicity or race is usually a primary identity that carries with it some status symbol or a system of privileges.

As noted in Chapter 3, White Americans tend to say that ethnicity is unimportant to them, that they have so many different strands of ethnicity—Italian, Irish, and German, for instance—that it is difficult to identify with any one cultural group. Members of European ethnic groups generally have the privilege or right to choose when and how they will self-identify their ethnicity. European Americans can choose to be just "White" or a hyphenated White American, such as Italian American, Irish American, or German American, depending upon the circumstances surrounding any encounter. That is, for most White Americans, ethnicity is *symbolic* or *optional* in one's characterization of oneself. In contrast, people of color do not have the option of symbolic ethnic identification (Waters, 2004).

Herbert Gans (1979), a famous sociologist, coined the term *symbolic ethnicity* in 1979 to capture what he described as an ethnic identity that comes without cost to a person. Gans proposed that symbolic ethnicity began during the 1970s, and signaled that European Americans or White Americans were putting aside the old ethnic rivalries that used to divide various members of the White group so that these individuals could treat ethnicity as a "hobby," meaning a leisure activity. What really mattered was that one was included in the White ethnic category; all else was insignificant, as exemplified by the large amount of intermarriage among White ethnic groups. In general, European or White Americans (unless they are recent immigrants) are not identified publicly in terms of their ethnicity. For instance, a person who commits a crime is simply identified as "White"; no other ethnocultural group is attached to him or her.

In contrast, other ethnic groups, and especially people of color, are publicly identified as "non-White" and, hence, become racialized ethnic minorities. No one really keeps track of the number of Polish people or Irish or Italians who commit crimes in America. The only ethnocultural identity that really matters is their White American ethnocultural heritage—forget the hyphenated group designation. Moreover, many White Americans point to the poverty of some African Americans and say that there are few real barriers to their success. Why can't they become like the Italians and the Irish and other groups who have made it financially in America?

As Shapiro (2004) has commented, White Americans endorse a type of laissez-faire attitude concerning racism against people of color. White Americans see "African Americans as individuals just like themselves, rather than as members of a group who were forced to play by rigged rules used historically to ensure their disadvantage and white domination" (Shapiro, 2004, p. 101).

Cultural Reflections

Reflect on how you would describe yourself in a classroom situation involving small groups.

Would you describe yourself as a hyphenated American—American Indian, White American, Asian American, and so forth?

If you would not mention your ethnicity, race, or culture, why?

Is the mentioning of your ethnocultural identity "optional"?

White Americans do choose to have and to display a hyphenated White American identity when it is convenient for them to do so. Such self-identification is usually done in the privacy of their homes or in social situations such as family gatherings or during gatherings for designated holidays—for example, St. Patrick's Day for the Irish acknowledgment of their White ethnocultural identity or similar celebrations for Italians (Columbus Day) or Polish people (Kosciuszko Day). According to Manning Marable (2000), "racialized minorities are fundamentally different from other ethnic groups because they share a common history of oppression, residential segregation, economic subordination, and political disenfranchisement" (p. B34).

Racial identification for African Americans and other "people of color" is not optional; it is visible in most situations. Further, it is enforced by the American government in terms of how people are recognized and represented or counted by the U.S. Census Bureau, which incorrectly endorses the concept of multiple racial groups. Even the term *people of color* is used to designate that these are people who cannot be assimilated to "Whiteness." All people of color are simply lumped together because the color of their skin is made a key metric for identification and status in American life. The strengths-based therapy model (Jones-Smith, 2014) maintains that ethnicity and cultural identification can be a source of strength and comfort to people.

Research has shown that African American youth who have a positive identification with their ethnocultural group perform better academically (Smith, 2006). Ethnocultural bonding can be a source of support and healing for individuals from all ethnic groups—regardless of the color of skin for that ethnic group.

How have researchers conceptualized ethnic or **racial identity development models** for African Americans? William Cross (1971) is the father of the models of ethnic identity development. In 1971, Cross coined the idea of Nigrescence, and he developed a theoretical model that described the process of becoming Black, as opposed to being a Negro or colored. The early **Cross model of racial identity** served as the foundation for the subsequent sector identity development model he developed with Peony Fhagen-Smith. The early Nigrescence model made a major assumption that one proceeded from the preencounter stage (no meaningful contact with White racism) to an internalization stage that demonstrated a progression from psychological dysfunction to psychological health (Vandiver, 2001).

Because of criticisms of the 1971 Cross model, he revised his theory of Nigrescence in his book *Shades of Black* (Cross, 1991). The Cross and Fhagen-Smith (2001) model described the progression of identification of individuals as they move toward a healthy African American identity. The identity model conceptualized the life span model of African American identity in terms of six sectors, explained briefly in Table 8.1. Although Cross's revised Black identity model contains almost all the features from the early model, it departs from such in several significant ways.

First, Cross and Fhagen-Smith (2001) introduced the concept of race salience, which refers to the extent to which race is an important and integral part of a person's way of encountering life. The African American person may approach life with race consciousness having either a large or a small role in his or her life. Salience for "Blackness" can be manifested in terms of a positive (pro-Black) or negative (anti-Black) valence. The term *race salience* replaced Cross's previous use of the word *pro-White* in the earlier preencounter stage. The present Cross revised model now describes two new identities: (a) preencounter assimilation and (b) preencounter anti-Black. Previously, Cross had theorized that when a person rejected Blackness and accepted an American perspective, he or she was characterized by self-hate and low self-esteem. With the revised model, an African American at the preencounter stage who experiences the salience of race as small and whose identity is oriented toward an "American" perspective does not necessarily have to be consumed with self-hate and low-esteem. This revision of the Cross model seems to take into consideration the situation of middle-class or upper-class African Americans who acknowledge that they are Black, but whose living situation and environment might not have led to such negative experiences that they are filled with self-hate.

A person's sense of low self-esteem was linked to the *preencounter* anti-Black orientation. Cross explained the negative self-esteem evidenced in the preencounter stage is caused by the negative images about African Americans portrayed in the mass media, among people in one's environment, and in the educational literature. Negative images of African Americans in the media predispose an individual to internalize self-hatred. The major consequence is that the person incorporates negative racial images into his or her personal identity.

Cultural Reflections

To what extent do you believe that African Americans experience the ethnic/racial identity stages outlined by Cross?

In your opinion, has the revised Cross model changed substantially since his earlier 1971 model of identity?

The second major change in the revised Cross model occurs in the immersion–emersion stage, previously described as a fused anti-White/pro-Black identity. The immersion–emersion stage is now divided into two additional stages: anti-White alone and anti-Black alone.

The third major revision of the early Cross model combines the fourth and fifth stages (internalization and internalization–commitment) into one stage, internalization. During this last stage, an African American accepts himself or herself as Black. As a result of this self-acceptance, the individual can manifest three different types of identities: (1) Black nationalist (high Black positive race salience), (2) biculturalist (Blackness fused with an American identity), and (3) multiculturalist (multiple identity formation), which includes a consideration of ethnicity/race, gender, sexual orientation, and so forth. Despite Cross's revision of his early 1971 model of Nigrescence, many people continue to use the early theoretical model. Table 8.1 provides a summary of the revised Cross and Fhagen-Smith (2001) model of Black identity development.

Acculturation and African Americans

Cultural Reflections

Do you think that the term acculturation *applies to African Americans? Why or why not?*

Do the various socioeconomic classes of African Americans represent different levels of their acculturation to mainstream American values and culture? Explain your response.

Although acculturation has been traditionally associated with immigrants to a new country, it also can be applied to African Americans (Paniagua, 2014). Not all African Americans identify highly with being an African American. As Cross and Fhagen-Smith (2001) have stated in their revision of the 1971 Cross model, a person may have high or low salience for his or her African American identity. For instance, middle-class African Americans may identify more strongly with mainstream White American culture than they do with African American culture. Case Vignette 8.2 describes Natasha, an African American college student who moved from her almost all-White neighborhood in the Midwest to Baltimore, Maryland.

TABLE 8.1 ■ Culturally Responsive Clinical Skill Development: The Revised Cross Model of Black Identity Development

Cross (1971) adopted the idea of Nigrescence, which he labeled as the process of becoming Black—a journey that involved moving from negative, internalized Black self-hatred to a positive Black identity. The 1971 Cross model of Nigrescence forms the foundation for the later sector model developed with Fhagen-Smith. Cross and Fhagen-Smith (2001) created the life span model of Black identity in six sectors:

- **Sector 1: Infancy and Childhood in Early Black Identity Development**
  o Factors like families, social networks, and historical events play a role in the early socialization of Black children.
  o Parents, guardians, and other members of the child's community have routines and norms that reflect Black culture. Cross says that an individual is constantly being socialized into the Black culture at both a conscious and unconscious level.

- **Sector 2: Preadolescence**
  o Development is influenced by a number of factors, including parents and the type of ethnic identity enacted in the home and environment. The person can experience high race salience (positive, conscious), low race salience (neutral, unconscious), or internalized racism (negative, conscious). Cross and Fhagen-Smith suggested that an individual who has high race salience is most likely to develop both a positive self-concept and Black identity over the course of his or her ethnocultural identity journey.

- **Sector 3: Adolescence**
  o The person starts to develop a Black self-concept based on life experiences and may determine how important this is to his or her overall identity in this sector.
  o Developing a self-concept may be affected by the person's peer group, community, and/or school environment. How does the person demonstrate and present his or her Black identity to the world? Is the individual too Black or not Black enough?

- **Sector 4: Early Adulthood**
  o **Low/high race salience and internalized racism** reemerge in this stage and may cause the individual to see race as unimportant, highly important, or something to be proud or ashamed of.

- **Sector 5: Adult Nigrescence**
  o Four stages accompany Nigrescence:
  o **Preencounter**—Low-race-salience individuals may appreciate Black culture while adopting values of the dominant culture, while internalized racism individuals may become anti-Black.
  o **Encounter**—A person experiences some sort of conflict with members of the White American community (or another ethnic group) that causes racial conflict. As a result, the Black individual begins to question his or her Black identity.
  o **Immersion–Emersion**—Described as a fused identity (anti-White/pro-Black in the earlier model). Although Cross discusses two separate identities, he actually presents three possible combinations: anti-White, pro-Black, and anti-White/pro-Black combination.
  o **Internalization/Internalization Commitment**—Has three specific resolutions to dissonance that has been caused by negative racial contact.
  o **Black Nationalist**—Individuals believe being Black is the most salient identity. They use a Black Nationalist identity for sociopolitical purposes and to produce change in the broader American society and in the world.
  o **Bicultural**—Individuals integrate their Black identity with the dominant culture.
  o **Multicultural**—Individuals still identify as Black, but they also tend to use other cultural identities, such as gender and sexual orientation.

- **Sector 6: Nigrescence Recycling**
  o Sector is characterized by a continuous process of revising one's ethnic/racial identity.
  o **Nigrescence Recycling**—Individual is forced to call into question his or her Black identity. Those who have truly achieved a healthy self-concept deal with the situation by using wisdom, which is an understanding of Black identity in all parts of one's life.

What is the significance of the revised Cross model for clinicians and counselors?

In Cross and Fhagen-Smith's (2001) model, clinicians must deal with the identity stage in which their client is located. The clinician works to help the client develop a healthy African American identity. Lack of client trust may become a factor if the client is in the early stages of Black identity development. The clinician does not pretend that he or she is color blind when it comes to working with the African American client. Instead, the clinician engages the client in an honest discussion about his or her ethnic/racial differences and the impact that such differences might have on their therapeutic alliance. Clinicians can have a positive impact on African American clients' healthy ethnic identity development by providing them with the support and space to explore and find their own identity as it fits into the broad American society.

CASE VIGNETTE 8.2

NATASHA: A YOUNG BLACK GIRL WHO FOUND HER BLACK IDENTITY

Natasha had spent the majority of her life living in a predominantly White community in Idaho, where she felt accepted and treated fairly by White friends, teachers, and community residents. She hardly thought about being African American because "there was no reason for her to do so."

When her family moved to Baltimore, Maryland, she suddenly became deeply aware of her Blackness, and although she had mostly fond memories of her White friends in Idaho, she said she would never return there.

When I asked Natasha why she would not return to Idaho, she replied that she had found something much more precious than she had in her home state. First, she had been introduced to African American culture, including African American music, art, and the social clubs and sororities headed by members of her own ethnocultural group. She said that she had never really been exposed to much African American culture in Idaho. In Baltimore, she participated in social clubs that were run by other African American women, and she shared in a wonderful type of "sisterhood" that she had never experienced before.

"I'm not going back to Idaho because I have found something that I want more here in Baltimore. We share a bond that I did not have with my White friends in Idaho.

"I mean, I had a bond with my White friends in Idaho. I slept over at their homes, ate dinner with them, and attended the same school and the same social events. I had a lot of good times. But dating was a problem. Sometimes there were not enough Black boys to go around. When I was younger, it didn't seem to matter about my kissing some of my friends who were boys and White. But the older I got, things changed."

There was a long pause, as if Natasha were saying good-bye to an identity that she had outgrown. Her eyes filled with tears.

"I finally found me," she said. "I know who I am, and I am a beautiful young Black woman. I don't ever want to change my identity."

Case Analysis and Discussion

Natasha had spent the majority of her life in mainstream, White American culture. She became acculturated in Black culture when she moved to Baltimore.

Conversely, there are some African Americans who become acculturated to White American culture. As Paniagua (2014) has pointed out, "the fact that a client is an African American does not necessarily mean that the client identifies as African American" (p. 59). Identification with the African American culture may be reflected in music preferences, style of dress, language, and a host of other factors. For instance, African Americans sometimes use a vernacular style of speaking known as Black English or Ebonics to demonstrate their commitment to an African American identity.

1. During the first session with an African American client, the clinician should consider asking how the client perceives his or her racial identity.

2. In what Cross stage of Black identity development would you place Natasha? In the internalization stage, a person develops a long-term commitment to his or her ethnocultural membership group (Evans & George, 2008).

3. What part of the case vignette suggests that Natasha might be in the internalization-commitment stage?

4. How would you go about exploring with Natasha her newfound "Blackness" and what it means to her as far as dating, careers, and so forth?

Structure of the African American Family

The overall observation is that the African American family may be conceptualized as both a major strength and a major weakness within American society (Evans & George, 2008). It is a major strength in that it provides the training and social support necessary for young people to survive and thrive. It is a weakness in that a large number of African American families are headed by women and, for all practical purposes, fatherless. Approximately one-third of African American households are headed by married couples, compared with half of all U.S. households (Taylor, Larsen-Rife, Conger, Widaman, & Cutrona, 2010). On the other hand, for African Americans in the lower socioeconomic strata, the family has been characterized as matriarchal.

Among African Americans in the lower class, 63% are headed by women, compared to 33% of all U.S. households (Taylor et al., 2010). Moreover, African American children are less likely to be living with two married parents (35%) than are Asian children (84%), Hispanic children (64%), and White children (75%). More African American women give birth to out-of-wedlock children (72%) than non-Hispanic White women (29%) ("African American Population Report," n.d.).

The Extended African American Family

African Americans traced their use of the extended family network to West Africa. In general, the extended family network is used more extensively by members from the lower socioeconomic group than from those located in the middle class (Brown, Cohon, & Wheeler, 2002). Middle-class African Americans tend to put into operation the nuclear family used by White American families. The extended family network is used because it provides a flexible and adaptable financial and social support network. A family can use the extended family network to respond to adversity. In such families, members pool resources and build community as a means to cope with long-term poverty. Family members may provide economic support for each other and may absorb others into the household. The extended network provides support for family members in terms of taking care of children and sharing in household duties. African American families that use the extended kin network may include people who are not actually members of the family (Brown et al., 2002). A family member may call a nonrelated person a cousin when, in fact, no blood relations actually exist.

When counseling African American clients, it may be important to ask them about who is in the household and what role the persons are assuming. Sometimes households may be run more efficiently because there are a number of resources within the extended family network. On other occasions, there may be insufficient supervision of all extended family members, and problems may take place with abuse of children. Too many people in a household may also make it difficult for the family to have clear rules, or to allocate sufficient space for family members to conduct even simple tasks like completing homework. Insufficient space or high-density living arrangements may precipitate violence and aggression among family members. Many Americans from other ethnocultural groups also use an extended family framework.

CULTURAL STRENGTHS OF AFRICAN AMERICANS

The cultural strengths of African Americans are many and varied. The contributions of African Americans in the arts are legendary and include such people as Marian Anderson (concert singer), Leontyne Price (opera singer), Maya Angelou (poet and writer), and Lorraine Hansberry (playwright, *A Raisin in the Sun*); trumpet players Miles Davis, Dizzy Gillespie, and Wynton Marsalis; pop singing artists Michael Jackson, Whitney Houston, and Lionel Richie; and actors Sidney Poitier, Harry Belafonte, Cicely Tyson, and Denzel Washington. Some famous religious and/or political leaders, introduced at the beginning of this chapter, include Ralph Bunche, recipient of the Nobel Peace Prize for his work in the Middle East; Martin Luther King Jr. (also a Nobel Peace Prize winner); and two-term U.S. president Barack Obama (a third African American Nobel Peace Prize winner).

Although most African American people were denied opportunities for formal education during the slavery era, African American scientist Benjamin Banneker (1731–1806) made the first clock in America, created an almanac, and laid out the streets of Washington, DC. Then there were the following: Daniel Hale Williams, an American physician, surgeon, and medical researcher who was the inventor of the blood bank; Emmett Chappelle, a physician who performed the first prototype open-heart surgery; Garrett Morgan, who made both the first traffic signal invention and the first patented gas mask; and Mae Jemison, an American physician and NASA astronaut known for being the first Black woman to travel in space. Then consider the contributions of African American athletes—tennis stars such as Arthur Ashe, Althea Gibson, Serena Williams, and Venus Williams; basketball stars such as Kareem Abdul-Jabbar, Michael Jordan, and Stephen Curry; and football legends such as Jim Brown, Emmitt Smith, and a long list of others. The contributions of African Americans are numerous, and far too many to list in this small section. The entire African American population should not be judged by the poor behavior of some people in the underclass. Then, too, there is hope even in the underclass; there are good people in that group.

Some cultural strengths among African Americans include a positive ethnic identity, an extended family kin network, flexible family roles, achievement orientation, and spiritual beliefs and practices (Kaslow et al., 2010). Both the African American family and the Black church, with its inculcation of strong spiritual beliefs, have been said to account for the finding that African Americans have lower levels of heavy and binge drinking than any ethnic group, with the exception of Asian Americans (National Institute on Alcohol Abuse and Alcoholism, 1998).

Cultural Reflections

Ethnocultural identity theory has been said to be very important in counseling African Americans.

How might you determine a client's stage of Black identity development?

How would you use Black identity theory for counseling African American clients?

Parham and Parham (2002) have pointed out that a positive African American identity forms a source of strength for many members of this group. One strength of a positive African American identity is that it provides a framework for helping individuals to have a worldview that allows them to make certain assumptions about the reality that they face—in other words, who they are, where they fit into the world, and what their purpose in life is. For instance, the Cross (1971, 1991) model of African American identity really deals with a person's sense of African self-consciousness and cultural continuity. Cross's stages of Nigrescence outline a movement from a psychological mindset of self-degradation to a place of ethnocultural self-pride. If a person has a secure African American identity, as well as the factors that support and sustain that identity against racism and other destructive factors, he or she has incorporated a cultural strength.

In addition, a positive African American identity serves as a buffer against racism and oppression; it forms the foundation for bonding with other people that helps each person to form attachments with other people who share similar cultural practices and worldviews. Parham and Parham (2002) contend that identity provides a sense of individual pride and achievement in which one can vicariously share with others in that membership group. In fact, White and Parham (1993) have proposed that an African American's specific stage of ethnic identity can be used to help a clinician understand the potential difficulties in breaking down barriers with a client of this cultural descent. It is the sharing of the positive aspects of an ethnocultural identity that makes it a cultural strength.

African American Resiliency: The Greatest and Most Formidable Strength

Perhaps the greatest strength of African Americans is that they are a resilient people—able to survive and to endure so that they move over the decades from slavery to the presidency of the United States of America. When I consider the resiliency of African Americans, I remember the civil rights movement of the 1960s where African Americans responded nonviolently to taunts, insults, and the water hoses of the people; the national political campaign of George Wallace; the four children bombed and murdered while attending church; the nine people shot by a White man in Charleston, South Carolina, while they prayed; the taunting of President Obama with racial epithets; students and activists trying to appeal to the American public with signs that say "Black Lives Matter." I then think of the poem by Maya Angelou ringing in my head that says "And still I rise. I rise. I rise."

Religion and Spirituality

Religion and spirituality are often at the center of African American culture. According to Cook and Wiley (2000), **spirituality** is the "foundation of personal and communal life" for African Americans (p. 370). Grills (2002) has asserted that the essential ingredient in the African American worldview is spirit. Supporting Grills's statements, a Harris Poll (conducted online within the United States between November 13 and 18, 2013, among 2,250 adults of ages 18 and older) reported that a strong majority (74%) of U.S. adults say that they believe in God. Outside of specific religious samples, the groups most likely to be absolutely certain there is a God include African Americans (70%), Republicans (65%), and baby boomers (60%). The poll data revealed that people state that spiritual and religious beliefs give meaning and purpose to their lives; they provide a framework that helps them cope with the stressors of life (Oman & Thoresen, 2003).

Yet, the data show that in contrast to the general American population, most psychologists do not describe themselves as spiritual or religious (Bilgrave & Deluty, 2002; Delaney, Miller, & Bisono, 2007). There appears to be "a disconnect" between clinicians and clients in their spiritual/religious orientations. As Plante (2009) has stated,

> a significant disconnection exists between psychologists, who generally are nonreligious and nonspiritual, and their clients, who generally are religious and spiritual and are seeking professional mental health services about how best to live their lives and cope with various stressful and challenging life events. Furthermore, most psychologists have received essentially no training in how best to work with religious-spiritual clients or related themes during the course of their professional training. In fact, two thirds of psychologists report that they do not feel competent to integrate religious-spiritual matters into their clinical work. (Shafranske & Malony, 1990, p. 11)

Part of the gulf between therapists and clients in their orientation toward spiritual/religious issues can be traced to the actual training of clinicians. The vast majority of clinicians have been trained to provide professional psychological services in a secular manner that purports to be primarily scientific and unaffected by spiritual and religious beliefs (Plante, 2009). Few universities offer courses that would help graduate students learn how to deal with spiritual/religious issues that arise during therapy. In fact, 68% of all training directors in clinical psychology internship training programs said that they "never foresee religious/spiritual training being offered in their program" (Russell & Yarhouse, 2006, p. 434). The fact that many psychologists and other helping professionals do not feel comfortable integrating spiritual issues during therapy does not bode well for many African Americans who evidence a high percentage of religiosity.

The clinician is trying to conceptualize his or her clients' problems from a psychoanalytic or cognitive behavioral perspective. In contrast, the African American client may be thinking, "By His [meaning Jesus's] stripes I will be healed of this mental condition" or "I don't care what cognitive behavioral therapy says—the Bible says that a man is so he thinketh in his heart. The Bible dealt with a man's thought long before what you call it . . . cognitive behavioral therapy."

Historically, the Black church has loomed large in African American life, providing not only spiritual guidance and social support, but also collective political action and an opportunity for leadership (Toldson, 2008). For instance, George works by day as a laborer at one of the plants, but on Sunday, he becomes Mr. Williams because he is the Head Deacon of his church, in charge of 10 other deacons and a small group of ministers aspiring to become associate pastors. Mr. Williams heads up the church's fund for building a new church, and already that fund has

Cultural Reflections

How do you view African Americans as a group?

Do you distinguish among the various socioeconomic groupings for African Americans?

Do you have any African American friends? Why or why not?

If you are African American, do you have any White friends? How about Asian American or Latino friends? Why or why not?

grown to almost $2 million. In traditional White American society, George is just George, a common everyday laborer, but in the Black church, he is "somebody"; *his life matters*, and he makes important contributions to his community and ethnocultural group.

The Black church encourages the practice of collectivism where all adults are expected to assume some responsibility for caring for children in a community and in a church. The African proverb, "It takes a village to raise a child," is often reinforced in the church. It should be noted, however, that the value of collectivism varies among African American people. Older members of this ethnocultural group are inclined to adopt the value of collectivism; however, young people, especially those who may have been raised without a father, tend to adopt the value of "me against your gang" and a "what's in it for me?" attitude. The notion of collectivism is sometimes evident when middle-class African Americans "reach back" to help those less fortunate. Moreover, middle-class African Americans may slip back into poverty themselves when they use their resources and psychological energy to help those family members who appear to be struggling just to make ends meet.

In addition, the Black church has assumed responsibility for maintaining the cultural traditions of African Americans (Grills, 2002). Some of the traditions of the African American church include African heritage rituals, praise dancing, drumming, call and response preaching, and singing. It is important that a clinician inquire about an African American's religion or spirituality because such questions may form the foundation for the therapeutic alliance (Evans & George, 2008). Sometimes these individuals have already sought the advice of their pastors and attended pastoral counseling. Some African Americans believe that their problems are caused by evil spirits or by not living according to the Bible. Moreover, in keeping with their spirituality, many African Americans have the belief that God will take care of their problems. They will cite such Biblical quotations as "No weapon formed against me shall prosper." They may hold prayer services to cleanse themselves of any evil spirits.

It is important to remember that religion and spirituality are not important to all African Americans. To assess the importance of religion or spirituality, the therapist might ask a client, "Have you discussed the issues that brought you to counseling with anyone in your church?" "What would you like for me to know and understand about how your religion/ spirituality guides your life?" "Do any Biblical verses have very special meaning for you? Are you willing to share those verses with me?" "What Biblical verses give you special hope that you are going to be able to handle the problems that brought you to therapy?" "I'm not of your religious faith, but very often most religions share some common principles and values, such as one must have faith or hope that tomorrow will bring a new day. I believe that your coming here today is evidence of your faith that things can get better for you." The overall goal is to help the client to use his or her religion in a positive, supportive manner so that he or she feels spiritual strength.

Table 8.2 contains some clinical questions a therapist might consider using to integrate African Americans' high value on spirituality and traditional counseling theories. These questions can be used for working with any client for whom spirituality might be an important factor in his or her life.

Counseling and Psychotherapy Approaches for Working With African American Clients

There is no one African American view on mental health. Instead, there are broad within-group differences among African Americans on just about every counseling variable. In general, African Americans prefer to turn to God and the church for mental health issues. In fact, African Americans are inclined to view clinicians with what Paniagua (2014) calls a healthy cultural paranoia. Researchers have maintained that the mental health system's treatment of African Americans has left a lot to be desired (Constantine, 2007). As Parham and Brown (2003) have

TABLE 8.2 ■ Culturally Responsive Clinical Skill Development: Questions to Elicit Clients' Spiritual Life

1. Questions designed to elicit clients' past spirituality:
   a. How did you express your spirituality in the environment in which you grew up?
   b. When did you first discover your spirituality?
   c. When you were young, how did you conceptualize your spiritual/religious self?
   d. What, if any, spiritual milestones have you experienced in your life?

2. Questions designed to elicit clients' present or current spirituality:
   a. What do you believe is sacred in your life?
   b. Have your spiritual/religious beliefs changed over the years? How?
   c. What do you feel is God's purpose in your life?
   d. How do you think God views the pain you are currently experiencing?
   e. How do you experience the spiritual in your life?
   f. How has your spirituality/religion helped you understand or deal with the problems that brought you to therapy?
   g. How has your spirituality given your life meaning or pleasure?
   h. Who supports you spiritually?
   i. Who does not support you spiritually?
   j. How has your spirituality given you a sense of connection to others?
   k. What has been damaging to your spirituality?
   l. Do you feel comfortable talking about your religious views as a part of your therapy?
   m. How do you feel talking about your spirituality with me, your clinician?
   n. What support have you been able to obtain from your church or pastor?
   o. Should we try to enlist the support of your pastor during our work in therapy?

Source: Jones-Smith (2016).

asserted, "you cannot help an individual to achieve a level of mental health if you have no idea about what constitutes mental health for that people or that person" (p. 85). These researchers also define mental health as "a state of personal well-being where each person is able to successfully confront life's challenges, using cognitive, emotional and behavioral attributes in appropriate ways" (Parham & Brown, 2003, p. 86). Healthy African Americans have a positive sense of identity for themselves and in their ethnocultural people.

African Americans tend to believe that a mentally healthy person has a relationship with and connectedness to God. From the African American perspective, clinicians are viewed as people who will focus on what's wrong with you, not on what's right with you (Boyd-Franklin, 2002).

Role of the Therapist in Working With African American Clients

Parham and Brown (2003) maintain that clinicians should be thought of as healers. They posit that clinicians cannot nurture aspects of other people's humanness without first respecting their clients and their own culture. Moreover, these authors indicate that healers serve as a conduit for energy flow during the therapy hour. Using the "awareness," "knowledge," and "skills" framework provided by the multicultural competencies (Sue, Arredondo, & McDavis, 1992), Parham, White, and Ajamu (2011) have proposed counselor/therapist competencies for working with African American clients (see Table 8.3).

TABLE 8.3 ■ Counselor/Therapist Competency Skills for Counseling African American Clients
Awareness
• Counselors and therapists are cognizant of their own personal biases and assumptions about African American people.
• Counselors and therapists are aware of their role as "healers."
• Counselors and therapists are aware of their own spirituality.
• Counselors and therapists must have a vision for African Americans that embraces the transformative possibilities of the human spirit.
Knowledge
• Knowledge of African American psychology and history
• Knowledge of the components of an African American worldview
• Knowledge of the limitations of traditional Euro-American psychological frameworks to African Americans
• Knowledge of the limitations of the traditional theoretical approaches to therapy
• Knowledge of ethnic/racial identity development models and frameworks
• Knowledge of appropriate assessment instruments for African Americans
• Knowledge of racism and oppression, especially how individual, institutional, and cultural racism impacts the lives of African Americans
• Knowledge of the dynamics of family in the African American community
• Knowledge of individual, institutional, and community resources that provide social and financial support to the African American community
Skills
• Ability to connect and to establish therapeutic rapport with African American clients
• Ability to hear the surface (content) and deep structure (emotional meaning) of the client's message(s) during therapy
• Ability to advocate on behalf of clients to social agencies and institutions
• Ability to use theories and other constructs to form diagnostic impressions of the client

Clinical Issues in Counseling African Americans: Trust and Cultural Mistrust

In the therapeutic relationship, trust involves the absence of misgivings on the part of both the clinician and the client. Clinicians must be able to establish bonds of trust with their African American clients. The therapist asks the questions: Can my clients trust that I want the best for them? Are my clients' secrets safe with me? Do I respect my clients? Do I really want to establish a therapeutic relationship with my African American clients? Am I able to focus on the positive aspects of African American culture? Can I actually provide unconditional acceptance of my clients?

Research studies have found that client-perceived trustworthiness is based on factors such as sincerity, openness, honesty, and perceived lack of motivation for personal gain. Because African American clients may view the clinician as part of the establishment, they may be reluctant to trust. Challenges to a clinician's trustworthiness can cause ruptures during therapy.

Yet, in order for therapy to be effective, the client must be able to trust the clinician and have confidence that the clinician has his or her best interests in mind. Several decades ago, Terrell and Terrell (1981) stated that African Americans evidenced "healthy cultural paranoia" toward White Americans. Such mistrust benefits African Americans in that it serves as a protective armor against racial injustice (Bell & Tracey, 2006).

In an early study, Terrell and Terrell (1984) investigated whether a relationship existed between the race of a clinician, client sex, cultural mistrust level, and premature termination rates among African American clients. The participants completed standard agency forms and the Cultural Mistrust Inventory (CMI). The participants were then randomly assigned to either an African American or a White American clinician. During the intake interview, information was collected about the client's problem and its etiology, and a tentative treatment plan was established. The clients were expected to schedule a return visit within the following two weeks. Approximately 25% of the clients assigned to the African American clinician did not return (17 out of 68 clients); however 43% of the clients seen by the White clinician (29 out of 67) did not return.

Four years later, Watkins, Terrell, Miller, and Terrell (1989) studied the effects of cultural mistrust on (1) African American college students' perceptions of the clinician's credibility, (2) participant-perceived confidence in the clinician to help resolve different problem areas, and (3) participant-perceived willingness to return for a follow-up visit. The 60 African American female college students and 60 White American female college students were given identical counselor descriptions. Clients who were highly mistrustful perceived the White American clinician less favorably and less able to assist in dealing with general anxiety, shyness, dating difficulties, and feelings of inferiority. Bell and Tracey (2006) criticized the CMI because some of the items on the CMI seemed rather extreme in nature and there was no assessment of whether the respondents mistrusted other ethnocultural groups in addition to Whites.

One way to build trust with an African American client is for the clinician to demonstrate empathy toward the client. Clinicians must be able to "feel" some measure of what the client is experiencing and then have the ability to communicate and express that feeling during therapy in open and honest ways that the client understands and accepts.

How Therapists Drive Away African American Clients: Microaggressions

Some White clinicians are dismissive of the impact of racism on their ethnic minority clients. Because some have not been exposed to the minority experience, such clinicians may not consider that racism could be traumatic. Oftentimes, these therapists subscribe to the color-blind approach when working with people of color. Terwilliger, Bach, Bryan, and Williams (2013) have contended that a color-blind ideology for counseling is actually a form of racism because it provides an excuse for therapists to ignore the effects of racism and to remain ignorant about the cultures and customs of people of color. Offensive comments that some White clinicians make to African American clients are "I'm not racist; you're just too sensitive" and "Focusing on race will not help us to understand your depression." These statements provide some evidence that the counselor or therapist is uncomfortable with the idea that racism and mental health are connected (Chae, Lincoln, & Jackson, 2011; Chou, Asnaani, & Hofmann, 2012).

The majority of the mental health professionals in the United States are White, and cultural mistrust and past experiences with racism may predispose some African Americans to hold negative expectations about being counseled by White clinicians. Even in White therapists who have received extensive multicultural training, racism is often manifested unconsciously during counseling (Gushue, 2004).

Constantine (2007) conducted a study that investigated African American clients' perceptions of their White counselors with regard to (a) perceived racial microaggressions in cross-racial counseling relationships, (b) the clinical working alliance, (c) their clinicians' general and multicultural counseling competence, and (d) their counseling satisfaction. On the issue of White clinicians' microaggressions toward African American clients, Constantine reported that such incidents (e.g., racial slights or racial invisibility) had a negative effect on the clients' perceptions of the therapeutic working alliance and their perceptions of competence on the part of the clinician. This held true whether or not a White clinician's racial hostility was consciously recognized.

Clinician, "Do No Harm"

Clinicians, counselors, and therapists are supposed to *do no harm*. Yet the studies just described suggest that they may actually harm African American clients with their microaggressions, their supposedly innocent remarks that were not intended to insult anyone. When counselors make insensitive racial remarks, African American clients may feel doubly discriminated against by those who are placed in their lives in positions of trust. It is extremely difficult to reveal one's deepest secrets to a counselor who has just committed a racially insensitive microaggression. As Williams (2013) has stated, the power dynamics in therapy may make it difficult for minority clients to respond to racist comments during counseling. Clients may simply respond to such comments by remaining silent or by harboring anger toward the very one who is supposed to help them. It is important to remember that no one is completely immune from having negative stereotypes of disadvantaged groups, and clients from minority backgrounds might actually resent having to work with a counselor of a different ethnic or cultural background (Williams, 2013).

Clinician's Acknowledgment of Racism and Oppression

It is important that a client's race or ethnocultural membership does not become an elephant sitting in the therapy room with neither clinician nor client even mentioning it. No matter how much counselors and therapists try to avoid dealing with it, the factor of race inevitably challenges the therapeutic alliance (Parham, 2002). Lee (1995) has proposed three guiding principles for counseling African American clients. First, he maintains that clinicians should always inquire about the influences in clients' lives, including their involvement with African American culture and the church, as well as the time they spend in majority White culture. Second, Lee suggests that clinicians explore the extent to which oppression has been a part of clients' lives and their reactions to oppression. Third, he recommends that clinicians learn about clients' family relationships. Clinicians must be able to acknowledge oppression toward African Americans and give compassionate reassurance that things will get better and that they will overcome.

NTU: AN AFROCENTRIC MODEL FOR COUNSELING AFRICAN AMERICANS

Several models have been proposed for counseling African American clients. One such model, NTU psychotherapy, is an **Afrocentric** approach to working with Black clients. According to Phillips (1990), "NTU psychotherapy is based on the core principles of ancient African and Afrocentric world view, nurtured through African American culture, and augmented by concepts and techniques of Western psychology" (p. 55). The NTU approach consists of six characteristics that complete its conceptual framework. It is spiritually oriented, family focused, culturally competent, competency based, holistically oriented, and values driven (Gregory &

Harper, 2001). NTU is a Bantu (Central African) term meaning "essence"; it refers to a universal energy system. Therapy is conceptualized as vibrational healing.

NTU uses the principles of Nguzo Saba as a framework for harmonious living. The role of the NTU therapist is founded on a spiritual relationship with the client. The five phases of NTU psychotherapy are Harmony, Awareness, Alignment, Actualize, and Synthesis (Phillips, 1990). For more information on NTU, the reader is referred to Phillips (1990) and Gregory and Harper (2001).

Cultural Issues in Strengths-Based Therapy With "At-Promise Youth"

Cultural belief systems form the heart and soul of resilience. Each cultural belief system makes meaning out of adversity and challenge. Most cultural systems focus on transcending problems and life challenges. It is important for all service providers to understand the cultural belief systems of their clients.

Moreover, the helping professional assesses a youth's attachment to his or her ethnic group and culture. The service provider might ask, "How important is your cultural group to you? How does your cultural group help you to deal with challenges in your life? What important relationships have you formed with other members of your cultural group? How do members of your cultural group handle adversity?" Youth might find strengths, comfort, and guidance in adversity as a result of their connections with their cultural and religious traditions. Sometimes youth find spiritual nourishment with the signs and symbols of their culture. The important factor is that culture provides the youth with a belief system about how to handle adversity and how to come through it with a positive outcome. When youth see themselves as part of something bigger than themselves, they are able to put the crisis they are facing in perspective.

Another intervention that the therapist can make is to ask youth about the healing aspects of their culture. For many youth, music constitutes an important part of their cultural background. For instance, many African American youth relate to hip-hop music because it is the type of cultural music with which they have been raised. Having African American youth explore their feelings using hip-hop music could be a way to form a relationship with them.

Cultural values form a consistent source of protective factors in the development of resiliency. For example, the cultural value of collectivism or individualism has a major influence on how youth view themselves during their struggle with adversity. Youth with a collectivist cultural value system would be more inclined to deal with adversity by gathering the support of family members and cultural groups. In contrast, youth who have adopted an individualistic value system might be more inclined to believe that they alone are responsible for their problem and that they should come up with a solution to the challenge facing them. Moreover, within each culture, there are proverbs or sayings that guide members' behavior and their attitudes toward adversity and overcoming challenges.

CASE VIGNETTE 8.3

MORRIS: AN AFRICAN AMERICAN ADOLESCENT "AT PROMISE" INSTEAD OF "AT RISK"

Morris is a 17-year-old African American male who lives in North Philly. He is the third-oldest son in a family of four children. He lives with his mother, paternal grandmother, and younger sister, representing both promise and difficult challenges. For instance, one of Morris's older brothers, David, attended college for 2 years but dropped out because he lacked the money and could not concentrate on his courses. According to him, the pressures of having to take care of his girlfriend and their 2-year-old daughter were too much. David works in the meat department at a local supermarket. He hustles on the side, sometimes selling pocketbooks, body oils, and drugs (marijuana).

(Continued)

(Continued)

Morris's oldest brother, Robert, is currently serving 10 to 15 years in jail for possession and distribution of drugs. Robert used to supply cocaine to his mother. Morris's mother has struggled on and off with drug addictions over the years. His mom's father is a minister of a small Baptist church. Sometimes when Morris thinks about his grandfather, he wonders what happened to the rest of the family. Somehow the family manages to survive and to eke out a living from what Morris is able to give from his job as a clerk in a grocery store, his mom's monthly disability check, and his grandmother's Social Security check. His mom's older brother and sister have good jobs and live in a better section of Philly. Morris used to attend his grandfather's church, but he stopped going about a year ago when his grandfather told him that he was going to end up just like Robert.

Morris is in his junior year of high school. During the past year, his grades have begun to slip to mostly Cs and a couple of Ds. Morris's teachers describe him as a promising but troubled young person. Sometimes he comes to class unprepared, and he just daydreams out the window for the entire period. When he does complete his schoolwork, there are hints of potential. His English teacher said that Morris could actually get a B if he put more effort into his work. He needs to learn grammar and to work on his reading and spelling. Morris was absent from school for more than 45 days last year. His (paternal) grandmother is worried about the people he hangs around with. Sometimes on school nights, he does not get into the house until one or two in the morning, without any explanation of where he has been. If his grandmother continues to probe about his whereabouts, Morris becomes angry and shouts back at her. His grandmother attends church on a regular basis, and she has asked Morris to attend with her. She provides what structure and organization exists within their household. When Morris was 12 years old, his father was murdered during an argument with one of his friends. Prior to his father's murder, Morris had a fairly good relationship with him. He couldn't bring himself to cry at his father's funeral because he was angry with him over the fact that now the family had to find some way to take care of itself.

Morris states that he wants to go to college. A few months ago, he was picked up for possession of drugs (marijuana with the intent to sell), but he has a good chance of getting probation. Morris wants to turn his life around. He talks about looking out for his younger sister. He complains that he always feels that he has to "watch his back" in his neighborhood. One of Morris's close friends was killed last year in a fight over a girl. Although Morris wants to have a better life than his brother and mom, he feels that he will end up like his friend—dead before he is 30. The judge has referred Morris to counseling with a nonprofit agency in an effort to straighten out his life.

Discussion Questions

1. How would you evaluate and assess Morris from the perspective of risk factors, protective factors, resilience, strengths, and goals?

2. How would you develop a strengths-based assessment protocol for him and a strengths-based treatment plan?

3. What diagnosis would you make for Morris?

4. What strengths does Morris have that would help him to navigate successfully his current issues with the law and at school?

5. How would you help interject hope into Morris's situation?

6. How would you apply the strengths-based therapy model to Morris?

Further Discussion

Morris has a number of risk factors in his life. His mother is still using cocaine on an intermittent basis, his older brother is in jail, and his father was murdered. Moreover, Morris has important individual risk factors: He is doing poorly in school—his grades having slipped within the past marking period or so—and he was caught selling marijuana. The family's tight financial situation is another risk factor. Morris is hanging out with the wrong crowd, and this has caused him to stay out past midnight on school nights.

Morris also has some protective factors in his life. His (paternal) grandmother loves him and takes him to church with her. Therefore, there is some evidence that Morris has a spiritual component to his life. Spirituality is a definite strength in that his maternal grandfather is a pastor of a church. It would be important to reconnect Morris with his grandfather to see if the latter could find a mentor for him at his church.

Morris never got into any trouble with the law prior to his marijuana-selling conviction. Up to that point, he had a clean record. He also performed fairly well academically in school. Morris's English teacher believes that he has some writing ability, if he would just buckle down and learn some basic grammar and punctuation skills. Morris has some nurturing qualities. He wants to stay home to take care of his younger sister, and this is a positive sign that he still has elements of a prosocial character. There are people who care about Morris.

Strengths-Based Therapy Treatment Plan for Morris

Building a therapeutic relationship. During the first stage of counseling, the counselor works to develop a relationship with Morris. He compliments Morris for coming to the community counseling center, and he asks Morris what he would like to achieve from counseling. The counselor said, "What if the court did not order you to come to counseling? Let's say that you've come to a fork in the road and you're trying to figure out which way to go. This is an opportunity to get a new lease on life—to turn yourself around. I have on my desk right next to you a hope chest. You can make three hopes that will come true, but today I want you to think about making just one. If you could be granted one hope/wish, what would that be?"

"I'd like to change this court case so that it would be dismissed, and I would not have to deal with any more legal issues contaminating my life."

The counselor responded, "You're right, Morris, ending the court case would take a load off your mind. Would it bring you happiness, a sense of accomplishment?"

"I would get a big foot off my neck. But it wouldn't change my life a lot."

The counselor asked, "What would change your life, Morris? What would have to change in your life to give you a sense of hope about your future?"

First Morris said that money would make him happy and take a load off him. Then the counselor asked Morris to close his eyes for a few minutes, take a deep breath and count to five, and breathe in and out until he felt more relaxed than when he first came to the counselor's office. Although Morris felt hesitant to close his eyes before the counselor, he did so. Morris wasn't in the habit of closing his eyes before anyone, especially someone White. But here was this White counselor asking Morris to trust enough so that he would close his eyes.

Counselor: "Tell me about the first thing that stands in your way of having more money. What obstacle is blocking your path to getting more money?"

Morris: "I need a job. I need for someone to take a chance and hire me."

Counselor: "Where would you like to work part-time, Morris?"

Morris: "I don't know. Maybe at some place like Home Depot or Best Buy or maybe even Walmart in the electronics department, where I could sell electronic equipment and go over music with my customers."

Counselor: "Okay, Morris, that sounds like possibilities to me. Now I want you to close your eyes and imagine that you apply for a job at Walmart, and then imagine that every obstacle that might block your getting hired is removed. You remove the obstacles that prevent you from getting hired, Morris. Somehow, you manage to present yourself so well that there is an instant connection between you and the interviewer. You answer in a positive manner every question that has blocked you from getting hired in the past."

Morris: "Hey, that's powerful. I never felt so confident before. I was just ready—on my game. It felt like I was 'obstacle hurdling'—you know, like sprinters do in the Olympics. I was jumping over every obstacle that got in my way."

Counselor: "Life can be like that, Morris, if you make up your mind that you're an obstacle hurdler. You are either going to be defeated by the obstacles that you face in life, or you're going to find a way around the obstacles. Isn't that what some Black people have done who made it out of the inner city? Jay-Z went obstacle hurdling and look where he landed."

Morris paused to reflect on what he had just experienced with his counselor. He did not have to be overwhelmed by the obstacles in his life.

Gradually, the counselor steered the conversation toward Morris's strengths. "Tell me something good about you, Morris, something that I might not know, something that's not included in your file."

Morris mentioned that he wrote rap music and that he had won a writing contest at his church about Martin Luther King Jr. He also mentioned caring for his younger sister and making sure that everything was protected at home. He was the "only real man" in the house.

During the ensuing counseling sessions, Morris talked about using his writing strength to bring up his grade in English, and he also indicated that his social studies teacher had told him that he could write a research report on any topic and relate it to social studies. Morris chose to write an extra-credit report on the rap music movement and how it had a significant impact on American culture and the culture of the world. Rap music has spread to virtually every major country in the world. Rap music is the language and music of the young. Gradually, his grades began to improve.

Strengths discovery. Next, the counselor asked if it would be okay for him to ask his grandfather to join them for part or all of a counseling session. Surprisingly, Morris agreed, and a connection was made that reconnected Morris's relationship with his grandfather. Morris came back to the church, and he joined the choir. He even wrote a Christian rap song that was played for the entire congregation. Morris was beginning to find himself. Morris took the CliftonStrengths assessment, which helped him identify other strengths. Morris began to talk about himself in terms of his strengths. A change was taking place within Morris.

(Continued)

(Continued)

Letting go, letting in. Morris let go of his old friends that got him into trouble. He still saw them hanging out in the 'hood, but he said that he had to be home to take care of his sister, and they let him go. The people in the choir at his grandfather's church became his new friends.

Harmony at home and at school. Morris examined his life to determine what he could do to bring greater harmony at home. The counselor asked, "What is one small thing you could do to bring greater harmony at home?" Morris responded that if he stopped staying out late on school nights, the arguments with his grandmother would stop. Morris ended his relationships with his buddies by getting rid of his old cell phone and getting a new one with a different telephone number. He stopped sleeping in class because he was finally getting to bed at a proper hour on school nights. Paying attention in class instead of sleeping brought him higher grades on his midterm exams.

Building a healthy new identity. Morris is building a healthy new identity for himself, but it isn't easy. Some of his former buddies claim that he has sold out. Morris wrote a strength prayer that he presented to his

counselor and to his church. Morris is not finished. The environment in which he lives presents new challenges each day. The risk factors are there, but now Morris has learned how to use his strengths to deal with the risks that he encounters.

Finally, notice the power of the obstacle hurdling technique that the counselor used with Morris. The counselor taught Morris not to run away from the obstacles he was likely to encounter while working toward his goal, but rather to imagine the obstacles that he was likely to encounter and then find a way to hurdle over them. In essence, the counselor was teaching Morris to develop new neural pathways in the brain that reflected his competence. The more that Morris envisioned himself hurdling his obstacles, the more confident that he became. The technique of obstacle hurdling was powerful in that it taught Morris that he did not have to feel overwhelmed, that he could successfully deal with the obstacles strewn on the yellow brick road toward his goal. Obstacle hurdling is a powerful technique to use with African Americans whose day-to-day environment might be covered with numerous land mines trying to trip them up so that they do not accomplish their goals.

SUMMARY OF KEY POINTS

Counseling African American clients can be a very engaging and challenging process. If the clinician is from a different ethnocultural group, it is important to discuss ethnic/racial differences with the client. Be careful of making verbal microaggressions during therapy with Black clients. Avoid using phrases such as "One of my best friends is an African American," "I don't see color when I work with you," "You're playing the race card," and so forth.

1. Do not allow the racial difference between the clinician and the client to be the elephant in the room that both are trying not to acknowledge. Also, understand that African American clients may display a healthy type of *cultural paranoia* during counseling or psychotherapy, primarily because of their historical experience of having their culture devalued.

2. Many African American clients are protective of their families, and therefore, it would behoove the clinician not to provide a direct causal link between the client's behavior and the parenting practices of family members. No matter how desolate a client's situation is, reframe the

situation in terms of the client's strengths. To avoid engaging in biased assessments, conduct a culturally appropriate assessment of African American clients.

3. Therapeutic interventions with African American clients should take into consideration and weave throughout counseling African American values of spirituality, family, and a positive ethnocultural identity. The clinician might assess the ethnic/racial identity stage in which the client is located. A good technique to use with African Americans is to have them develop a list of three to five spiritual advisors or cultural heroes (who may be dead or alive) upon which they can call in times of decision making.

4. Another good technique to use with African American clients is the "obstacle hurdling" exercise, wherein clients are encouraged to establish goals and to imagine the obstacles that they think might prevent them from achieving their goals. As they consider their goal obstacles, they repeatedly envision themselves hurdling successfully those obstacles until they achieve

success. This technique can be helpful in combating clients' typical response to stay stuck in their old patterns because they have repeatedly envisioned themselves failing to achieve their goals.

5. To avoid developing cultural mistrust in the counseling relationship, the clinician should be genuine in his or her verbal and nonverbal communications. African Americans tend to communicate from a high-context framework, and therefore, they pick up quickly any discrepancies in what the counselor is saying and actually feeling during counseling.

6. Whenever possible, focus on the strengths of African American clients instead of their problems or their deficits, for only their strengths can provide solutions to the issues that brought them to therapy. The strengths-based therapy model comports with spiritual concepts that some African Americans might find compatible with their spiritual beliefs, such as the power of forgiveness, the benefit of surrendering one's problems, and the value of letting go of the past. Remember that African Americans form heterogeneous groupings. Focus on the positive in an African American client's life, and he or she will be more likely to become motivated to change.

DISCUSSION QUESTIONS

Discussion Question Set 1

The group leader provides a class handout sheet to each class member, which asks the following questions:

A. How might an African American's stage of racial identity affect his or her willingness to be counseled by a member of a different ethnic/racial group?

B. How would you go about assessing or determining an African American's stage or phase of racial identity development?

C. Where are you now on your journey of racial or cultural identity development?

D. What impact might your own stage of racial or cultural identity development have on the counseling process with an African American client?

Discussion Question Set 2

African Americans tend to place a high cultural value on spirituality and the church. How might you incorporate spirituality into working with members of this group? How would you go about emphasizing an African American's strengths over his or her deficits?

KEY TERMS

Afrocentric or African-centered: A worldview that places high value on interpersonal relationships between people, and in which the survival of the group holds great importance and spirituality and inner divinities hold significance. Other cultural beliefs are that all men are equal and share a common bond, and that all events are tied together with one another.

Black Underclass: A social group of African Americans that is located at the bottom of the class schema in the United States. The underclass has been described as those who have very little education, who for generations may be underemployed or unemployed, who live on welfare, and who may sometimes use criminal activity to support their families. Poverty is the defining characteristic of generations of family members. Although the underclass is frequently mentioned in terms of some African Americans

living in poverty-stricken inner cities, the underclass can be of any racial or ethnic group.

Color blind: The false claim that some Whites and others make when they profess not to see the color of a person standing before them.

Cross Model of Racial Identity: Cross (1971) adopted the idea of Nigrescence, the process of becoming Black, as the foundation for his later revised model of Black identity development. The Cross model looks at the progression of identification of individuals as they move toward a healthy Black identity.

Racial identity development models: The first racial identity model was developed by William Cross for African Americans during the early 1970s.

Spirituality: African Americans place a very high cultural value on spirituality and religion.

White Underclass: A social group of White Americans that is located at the bottom of the class schema in the United States. The underclass has been described as those who have very little education, who for generations may be underemployed or unemployed, who live on welfare, and who may sometimes use criminal activity to support their families. Poverty is the defining characteristic of generations of family members. The underclass can be of any ethnic group.

REFERENCES AND SUGGESTED READING

African American population report. (n.d.). Retrieved from http://blackdemographics.com/

APA Task Force on Resilience and Strength in Black Children and Adolescents. (2008). *Resilience in African American children and adolescents: A vision for optimal development.* Retrieved from https://apa.org/pi/families/resources/resiliencept.pdf

Associated Press. (2012, October 27). AP poll: U.S. majority have prejudice against Blacks. *USA Today.* Retrieved from https://www.usatoday.com/story/news/politics/2012/10/27/poll-black-prejudiceamerica/1662067/

Bell, T. J., & Tracey, T. J. G. (2006). The relation of cultural mistrust and psychological health. *Journal of Multicultural Counseling and Development, 34*(1), 2–4.

Bilgrave, D. P., & Deluty, R. H. (2002). Religious beliefs and political ideologies as predictors of psychotherapeutic orientations of clinical and counseling psychologists. *Psychotherapy, 39,* 245–260.

Bishaw, A., & Iceland, J. (2003). *Poverty: 1999-Census 2000 brief.* Washington, DC: U.S. Department of Commerce, Economic and Statistics Administration.

Bowser, B. P. (2006). *The Black middle class: Social mobility-and vulnerability.* Boulder, CO: Lynne Rienner Publishers.

Boyd-Franklin, N. (2002). *Black families in therapy.* New York, NY: Oxford University Press.

Brown, S., Cohon, D., & Wheeler, R. (2002). African American extended families and kinship care: How relevant is the foster care model for kinship care? *Children and Youth Services Review, 24*(1-1), 55–79.

Capehart, J. (2012, October 29). The AP poll. *Washington Post.* Retrieved from https://www.washingtonpost.com/blogs/post-partisan/post/the-rise-of-hate-in-the-age-ofobama/2012/10/29/2ed7c4c0-21ec-11e2-ac85-e669876c6a24_blog.html?utm_term=.d4e4c5104fa9

Cashin, S. D. (2000). Middle-class black suburbs and the state of integration: A post-integrationist vision for metropolitan America *(Georgetown Law and Economics Research Paper No. 241245).* Washington, DC: Georgetown University.

Chae, D. H., Lincoln, K. D., & Jackson, J. S. (2011). Discrimination, attribution, and racial group identification: Implications for psychological distress among Black Americans in the National Survey of American Life (2001–2003). *American Journal of Orthopsychiatry, 81*(4), 498–506.

Chou, T., Asnaani, A., & Hofmann, S. G. (2012). Perceptions of racial discrimination and psychopathology across three U.S. ethnic minority groups. *Cultural Diversity and Ethnic Minority Psychology, 18* (1), 74–81.

Constantine, M. G. (2007). Racial microaggressions against African American clients in cross-racial counseling relationships. *Journal of Counseling Psychology, 54*(1), 1–16.

Cook, D. A., & Wiley, C. Y. (2000). Psychotherapy with members of African American churches and spiritual traditions. In P. S. Richards & A. E. Bergin (Eds.), *Handbook of psychotherapy and religious diversity* (pp. 369–396). Washington, DC: American Psychological Association.

Cose, E. (2011). *The end of anger: A new generation's take on race and rage.* New York, NY: Ecco, an Imprint of HarperCollins Publishers.

Cross, W. E. (1971). The Negro to black conversion: Toward the psychology of Black liberation. *Black World, 209,* 13–27.

Cross, W. E. (1991). *Shades of black: Diversity in African American identity.* Philadelphia, PA: Temple University Press.

Cross, W. E., & Fhagen-Smith, P. E. (2001). Patterns of African American identity development: A life span perspective. In C. Wijeysinghe & B. Jackson (Eds.), *New perspectives on racial identity development* (pp. 243–270). New York, NY: New York University Press.

Delaney, H. D., Miller, W. R., & Bisono, A. M. (2007). Religiosity and spirituality among psychologists: A survey of clinician members of the American Psychological Association. *Professional Psychology: Research and Practice, 38,* 538–546.

Dreier, P. (2012, March 22). The invisible poverty of "The Other America" of the 1960s is far more visible today. *Truthout.* Retrieved from http://www.truth-out.org/news/item/8040-michael-harrington-and-deprivation-in-an-affluent-society

Ellison, C. D. (2015). Are we talking enough about the Black middle class? *Pacific Standard*. Retrieved from http://www.psmag.com/politics-and-law/are-we-talking-enough-about-the-black-middle-class

Evans, K. M., & George, R. (2008). African Americans. In Garrett McAuliffe & Associates (Eds.), *Culturally alert counseling: A comprehensive introduction* (pp. 146–187). Thousand Oaks, CA: Sage.

Florida, R. (2012, October 29). The 66% America's growing underclass. *CITYLAB*. Retrieved from https://www.citylab.com/life/2012/10/66-americas-growing-underclass/3618/

Florida, R. (2017). *The new urban crisis: How our cities are increasing inequality, deepening segregation, and failing the middle class—and what we can do about it*. New York: Basic Books.

Frank, J. H. (1993). *Racial equality in America*. Columbia: University of Missouri Press.

Gans, H. (1979). Symbolic ethnicity: The future of ethnic groups and cultures in America. *Ethnic and Racial Studies, 2*, 1–20.

Gaviria, M. (Producer). (2016, February 23). Chasing heroin [Television series episode]. In *Frontline*. PBS.

Graham, L. O. (1999). *Our kind of people: Inside America's Black upper class*. New York, NY: HarperCollins.

Gregory, W. H., & Harper, K. W. (2001). The NTU approach to health and healing. *Journal of Black Psychology, 27*(3), 304–320.

Grieco, E. M., & Cassidy, R. C. (2001). *Overview of race and Hispanic origin: Census 2000 brief*. Washington, DC: U.S. Department of Commerce, Economics, and Statistics Administration.

Grills, C. (2002). African centered psychology: Basic principles. In T. A. Parham (Ed.), *Counseling African descent people: Raising the bar of practitioner competence* (pp. 10–24). Thousand Oaks, CA: Sage.

Gushue, G. V. (2004). Race, color-blind racial attitudes, and judgments about mental health: A shifting standards perspective. *Journal of Counseling Psychology, 51*, 398–407.

Harrington, M. (1962). *The other America: Poverty in the United States*. New York, NY: Macmillan.

Helms, J. E., & Cook, D. A. (1999). *Using race and culture in counseling and psychotherapy*. Boston, MA: Allyn & Bacon.

Helms, J., & Parham, T. (1985). *The Racial Identity Attitude Scale (RIAS)*. Irvine: University of California Press.

Humes, K. R., Jones, N. A., & Ramirez, R. R. (2011). *Overview of race and Hispanic origin: 2010*. Washington, DC: U.S. Department of Commerce, Economics, and Statistics Administration.

Jones-Smith, E. (2014). *Strengths-based therapy: Connecting theory, practice, and skills*. Thousand Oaks, CA: Sage.

Jones-Smith, E. (2016). *Theories of counseling and psychotherapy: An integrative approach*. Thousand Oaks, CA: Sage.

Kambon, K. K. (1992). *The African personality in America: An African-centered framework*. Tallahassee, FL: Nubian Nation.

Kaslow, N. J., Leiner, A. S., Reviere, S., Jackson, E., Bethea, K., Bhaju, J., . . . Thompson, M. P. (2010). Suicidal, abused African American women's response to a culturally informed intervention. *Journal of Consulting and Clinical Psychology, 78*, 449–458.

Kochhar, R., & Fry, R. (2014, December 12). Wealth inequality has widened along racial, ethnic lines since end of great depression. *Pew Research Center*. Retrieved from http://www.pewresearch.org/fact-tank/2014/12/12/racial-wealth-gaps-great-recession/

Kochhar, R., Fry, R., & Taylor, P. (2011, July 26). Wealth gaps rise to record highs between Whites, Blacks, Hispanics. *Pew Research Center*. Retrieved from http://www.pewsocialtrends.org/2011/07/26/wealth-gaps-rise-to-record-highs-between-whites-blacks-hispanics/

Koltko-Rivera, M. E. (2004). The psychology of worldviews. *Review of General Psychology, 8*, 3–58.

Kristof, N. (2012, February 8). The white underclass. *The New York Times: Opinion Pages*. Retrieved from https://www.nytimes.com/2012/02/09/opinion/kristof-the-decline-of-white-workers.html

Lee, C. R. (1995). *Counseling for diversity: A guide for school counselors and related professionals*. Needham Heights, MA: Allyn & Bacon.

Marable, M. (2000, February 25). We need a new and critical study of race and ethnicity. *The Chronicle of Higher Education*, p. B34.

McGuirt, M. (2009, July 21). Young Black turnout a record in 2008 election. *ABC News*. Retrieved from https://abcnews.go.com/Politics/story?id=8140030&page=1

Morris, E. F. (2001). Clinical practices with African Americans: Juxtaposition of standard clinical practices and Africentricism. *Professional Psychology: Research and Practice, 32*, 563–572.

Murray, C. (2012). *Coming apart: The state of White America, 1960–2010*. New York, NY: Crown Forum, a division of Random House.

National Institute on Alcohol Abuse and Alcoholism. (1998). *Alcohol Use Among Special Populations, 22*(4). Can be retrieved from http://pubs.niaaa.nih.gov/publications/arh22-4/toc22-4.htm

Neville, H. A., Worthington, R. L., & Spanierman, L. B. (2001). Race, power, and multicultural counseling psychology: Understanding White privilege and color-blind racial attitudes. In J. Ponterotto, J. M. Casas, L. A. Suzuki, & C. M. Alexander (Eds.), *Handbook of multicultural counseling* (pp. 257–288). Thousand Oaks, CA: Sage.

Oman, D., & Thoresen, C. F. (2003). Spiritual modeling: A key to spiritual and religious growth? *The International Journal for the Psychology of Religion, 13*, 149–165.

Paniagua, F. (2014). *Assessing and treating culturally diverse clients*. Thousand Oaks, CA: Sage.

Parham, T. A. (1993). *Psychological storms: The African American struggle for identity*. Chicago, IL: African American Images.

Parham, T. A. (2002). *Counseling African descent people: Raising the bar of practitioner competence*. Thousand Oaks, CA: Sage.

Parham, T. A. (2012). Delivering culturally competent therapeutic services to African American clients: The skills that distinguish between clinical intention and successful outcomes. In M. E. Gallardo, C. J. Yeh, J. E. Trimble, & T. A. Parham (Eds.), *Culturally adaptive counseling skills: Demonstrations of evidence-based practices* (pp. 23–42). Thousand Oaks, CA: Sage.

Parham, T. A., & Brown, S. (2003). Therapeutic approaches with African American populations. In F. D. Harper & J. McFadden (Eds.), *Culture and counseling: New approaches* (pp. 81–98). Needham Heights, MA: Allyn & Bacon.

Parham, T. A., & Parham, W. D. (2002). Counseling African Americans: The current state of affairs. In T. A. Parham (Ed.), *Counseling African descent people: Raising the bar of practitioner competence* (pp. 1–10). Thousand Oaks, CA: Sage.

Parham, T. A., White, J. & Ajamu, A. (2011). The psychology of Blacks: Centering our perspectives in the African Consciousness (4th Ed.). Upper Saddle River, NJ: Prentice Hall.

Phillips, F. B. (1990). NTU psychotherapy: An Afrocentric approach. *The Journal of Black Psychology, 17*(1), 55–74.

Plante, T. G. (2009). *Spiritual practices in psychotherapy: Thirteen tools for enhancing psychological health*. Washington, DC: American Psychological Association.

Plante, T. G., & Thoresen, C. E. (Eds.). (2007). *Science, spirit, and health: How the spiritual mind fuels physical wellness*. Westport, CT: Praeger/Greenwood.

Poverty rate by race/ethnicity. (2015). Kaiser Family Foundation. Retrieved from http://kff.org/other/state-indicator/poverty-rate-by-raceethnicity

Rastogi, S., Johnson, T. D., Hoeffel, E. M., & Drewery, M. P. (2011). *The Black population: 2010*. Washington, DC: U.S. Census Bureau, U.S. Department of Commerce.

Ridley, C. R. (1995). *Overcoming unintentional racism in counseling and therapy*. Thousand Oaks, CA: Sage.

Ridley, C. R. (2005). *Overcoming unintentional racism in counseling and therapy* (2nd ed.). Thousand Oaks, CA: Sage.

Russell, S. R., & Yarhouse, M. A. (2006). Training in religion/spirituality within APA-accredited psychology predoctoral internships. *Professional Psychology: Research and Practice, 37*(4), 430–436. http://dx.doi.org/10.1037/0735-7028.37.4.430

Shafranske, E. P., & Malony, H. N. (1990). Clinical psychologists' religious and spiritual orientations and their practice of psychotherapy. *Psychotherapy: Theory, Research, Practice, Training, 27*(1), 72–78. http://dx.doi.org/10.1037/0033-3204.27.1.72

Shapiro, T. M. (2004). *The hidden cost of being African American*. New York, NY: Oxford University Press.

Smith, E. J. (1985). Ethnic minorities: Life stress, social support, and mental health issues. *The Counseling Psychologist, 12*, 537–579.

Smith, E. J. (1991). Ethnic identity development: Toward the development of a theory within the context of majority/minority status. *Journal of Counseling and Development, 70*, 181–188.

Smith, E. J. (2006). The strengths-based counseling model. *The Counseling Psychologist, 34*, 13–79.

Stockman, F. (2016, April 18). On crime bill and the Clintons: Young Blacks clash with parents. *The New York Times*. Retrieved from https://www.nytimes.com/2016/04/18/us/politics/hillary-billclinton-crime-bill.html

Sue, D. W., Arredondo, P., & McDavis, R. (1992). Multicultural counseling competencies and standards: A call to the profession. *Journal of Multicultural Counseling and Development, 20*, 64–88.

Taylor, Z. E., Larsen-Rife, D., Conger, R. D., Widaman, K. F., & Cutrona, C. E. (2010). Life stress, maternal optimism, and adolescent competence in single mother, African American families. *Journal of Family Counseling, 24*, 468–477.

Terrell, F., & Terrell, S. L. (1981). An inventory to measure cultural mistrust among Blacks. *The Western Journal of Black Studies, 5*(3), 180–184.

Terrell, F., & Terrell, S. (1984). Race of counselor, client sex, cultural mistrust level, and premature termination from counseling among Black clients. *Journal of Counseling Psychology, 31*, 371–375.

Terwilliger, J. M., Bach, N., Bryan, C., & Williams, M. T. (2013). Multicultural versus colorblind ideology: Implications for mental health and counseling. In A. Di Fabio (Ed.), *Psychology of counseling* (pp. 97–108). Hauppauge, NY: Nova Science.

Toldson, I. A. (2008). Counseling persons of Black African ancestry. In P. B. Pedersen, J. G. Draguns, W. J. Lonner, & J. E. Trimble (Eds.), *Counseling across cultures* (6th ed., pp. 161–179). Thousand Oaks, CA: Sage.

Touré. (2011). *Who's afraid of post-Blackness? What it means to be Black now.* New York, NY: Free Press.

U.S. Census Bureau. (2005). *Statistical abstract of the United States: 2004–2005.* Retrieved from https://www.census.gov/library/publications/2004/compendia/statab/124ed.html

U.S. Census Bureau. (2010). *Median income in the past 12 months: 2010 American community survey—1 year estimates.* Washington, DC: U.S. Government Printing Office.

Vandiver, B. J. (2001). Psychological Nigrescence revisited: Introduction and overview. *Journal of Multicultural Counseling and Development, 29,* 165–173.

Vandiver, B. J., Fhagen-Smith, P. E., Cokley, K. O., Cross, W. E., & Worrell, F. C. (2001). Cross's Nigrescence model: From theory to scale to theory. *Journal of Multicultural Counseling and Development, 29,* 174–200.

Waters, M. C. (2004). Optional ethnicities. In M. L. Anderson & P. H. Collins (Eds.), *Race, class, and gender* (pp. 418–427). Belmont, CA: Wadsworth/Thompson Learning.

Watkins, C. E., Jr., & Terrell, F. (1988). Mistrust level and its effects on counseling expectations in Black client-White counselor relationships: An analogue study. *Journal of Counseling Psychology, 35,* 194–197.

Watkins, C. E., Jr., Terrell, F., Miller, F. S., & Terrell, S. L. (1989). Cultural mistrust and its effects on expectational variables in Black client-White counselor relationships. *Journal of Counseling Psychology, 29,* 513–531.

Williams, M. T. (2013). How therapists drive away minority clients. *Psychology Today.* Washington, DC: American Psychological Association. https://www.psychologytoday.com/blog/culturally-speaking/201306/how-therapists-drive-away-minority-clients

9

CULTURALLY RESPONSIVE STRENGTHS-BASED THERAPY FOR AMERICAN INDIANS AND ALASKA NATIVES

CHAPTER OBJECTIVES

- Describe the demographics and population statistics of American Indians and Alaska Natives.

- Evaluate the theory of historical trauma among American Indians and Alaska Natives.

- Analyze ethnic/racial stereotypes and microaggressions against American Indians.

- Explain the worldview of American Indians and the tribe as family.

- Identify the cultural values associated with American Indians, including sharing and generosity, time orientation, spirituality, noninterference, and communication style.

- Enumerate the cultural strengths of American Indians and Alaska Natives.

- Describe some common mental health challenges and acculturation conflicts for American Indians and Alaska Natives.

- Implement counseling approaches for American Indians and Alaska Natives.

- *"A frog does not drink up the pond in which it lives."*
  —American Indian proverb

- *"He who would do great things should not attempt them all alone."* —Seneca proverb

- *"Hold on to what is good,*
  Even if it's a handful of earth.
  Hold on to what you believe,
  Even if it's a tree that stands by itself.
  Hold on to what you must do,
  Even if it's a long way from here
  Even if it's easier to let go.
  Hold on to my hand,
  Even if someday I'll be gone away from you."
  —Pueblo prayer

INTRODUCTION

This chapter examines the American Indian and **Alaska Native** population as an overall cultural group. This group merits attention because of its indigenous historical significance to the development of this country. It is a group that has demonstrated its resilience throughout the ages, yet it is often a "forgotten" ethnic/racial group in the United States.

DEFINING GROUP MEMBERSHIP

The American Indian population has been known by several names, including *Native Americans, American Indians*, and *Native people* (Garrett, 2008; Trimble & Gonzalez, 2008; Witko, 2006), while the U.S. Census Bureau uses the category *American Indian and Alaska Native* (Grieco &

Cassidy, 2001; LaFromboise & Dizon, 2003). Witko (2006) has pointed out that "many Indians raised in urban areas prefer to call themselves 'Native Americans,' whereas those who grew up on a reservation tend to call themselves 'American Indians'" (p. 10). Garrett (2008) has pointed out that other terms used to describe members of this group have included *First Nations people*, *Aboriginal people*, and *Indigenous people*. The clinician should ask the client what term he or she prefers the clinician to use during counseling or therapy.

DEMOGRAPHIC AND POPULATION STATISTICS

The 2010 U.S. Census found that there are approximately 5.2 million people in the United States (about 1.7% of the population) who identified themselves as American Indian and Alaska Native. Out of this total, 2.9 million people self-identified as American Indian and Alaska Native alone, while nearly half of the American Indian and Alaska Native population, or 2.3 million people, reported being American Indian and Alaska Native in combination with one or more other ethnic groups or races. The American Indian and Alaska Native population is projected to be approximately 8.6 million by July 1, 2050 (U.S. Census Bureau, 2012). The median age of the American Indian and Alaska Native population is 29.0 years compared to 37.2 years for the population as a whole.

Of the five race groups designated on the U.S. Census Bureau form (American Indian or Alaska Native, Asian, Black or African American, Native Hawaiian or Other Pacific Islander, and White), the American Indian and Alaska Native population had the second-largest percentage (44%) reporting more than one race (Humes, Jones, & Ramirez, 2011). The Native Hawaiian and Other Pacific Islander population had the largest percentage (56%) reporting more than one race. American Indians and Alaska Natives who reported more than one race grew at a faster rate than the population of American Indians and Alaska Natives alone. Of the 2.3 million American Indians and Alaska Natives who reported more than one race, the most frequent race in combination was White (1.4 million or 63%), followed by Black (269,000) and another category that combined Black and White (231,000). Together, these three combinations accounted for approximately 84% of all American Indians and Alaska Natives who reported multiple races (Norris, Vines, & Hoeffel, 2012).

The majority of American Indians and Alaska Natives lived in the West, with the South having the second-largest proportion followed by the Midwest and the Northeast. The multiple-race American Indian and Alaska Native population was more geographically dispersed than the population of American Indians and Alaska Natives alone, with the majority of all people in these two groups living in 10 states, California, Oklahoma, Arizona, Texas, New York, New Mexico, Washington, North Carolina, Florida, and Michigan.

The U.S. Census uses the term *American Indian areas* to include such geographic locations as "federal **reservation** and/or off-reservation trust land, Oklahoma tribal statistical areas, [and] state reservation or federal-or-state-designated American Indian areas" (Norris et al., 2012, p. 13). A higher proportion of the American Indian and Alaska Native alone population (31%) lived inside American Indian areas (i.e., federal reservation and/or off-reservation trust land, Oklahoma tribal statistical area, state reservation, or federal- or state-designated American Indian statistical area) than did the American Indian and Alaska Native in combination population (20%) (Norris et al., 2012). The Navajo Nation had the largest American Indian and Alaska Native population living on reservations. Garrett (2008) has commented that some people "might find it surprising to realize that approximately 50 percent of the Native American population resides in urban areas" (p. 226).

The Cherokee (819,105) tribal grouping had the largest American Indian population in 2010, followed by Navajo (332,129), Choctaw (195,764), Mexican American Indian (175,494),

Chippewa (170,742), Sioux (170,110), Apache (111,810), and Blackfeet (105,304). The Yup'ik tribal grouping and the Iñupiat tribal grouping had the largest Alaska Native alone and Alaska Native alone-or-in-any-combination populations, and the Yup'ik tribal grouping had the largest Alaska Native population (Norris et al., 2012).

Why is it important to know demographic information about American Indians and Alaska Natives? Many clinicians may have had little contact with members of this population; therefore, it is important to provide baseline data so that they can begin to understand who these people are. Clinicians are likely to see American Indians from the 10 states noted above. Most American Indians live in urban areas rather than on reservations. Further, many American Indians living in urban areas have a mixed ethnic/racial heritage, with either White or Black combinations (Norris et al., 2012).

WHO IS AN "AUTHENTIC" OR "REAL INDIAN"?

Barcus (2003) has observed that in comparison with the four major culturally diverse groups in the United States, (African American, Latino/a American, Asian American, and American Indian/Native American), American Indians are the only group that has a legal definition of race. A legal definition of an **American Indian** was constructed to determine who had certain rights to land, especially on the reservations, and who was eligible for federal assistance in specific programs. People who want to be considered an American Indian prove their status in terms of the legal definition established by the Bureau of Indian Affairs, an agency of the U.S. Department of the Interior. This status is conferred through membership in a **tribe**, which is an indigenous social grouping connected by heritage, history, and culture. According to this Bureau of Indian Affairs definition, a person must have an Indian "blood quantum" of at least 25% to be considered an Indian and must have proof of tribal status. According to Garrett (2008), "blood quantum refers to the percentage of ancestry that can be traced to people from [a given] tribe; it is not literally a measure of blood" (p. 223). The same researcher has discussed the "Indian card," a physical card that members of American Indian tribes carry to prove that they are what they say they are. While some American Indians view the Indian card as a form of oppression, others see it as a source of tribal pride.

Each tribe, however, has a voice in what it considers enough ancestry to be called an American Indian. While some require a person to have at least 50% Indian ancestry, others only require 12% (Witko, 2006). Ken Hansen, then chairman of the Samish tribe, supported the right of Indian nations to decide who is and who is not an American Indian, and stated: "It is a fundamental right of any nation, including tribal nations, to define their own membership. If a person meets the criteria for membership in a tribe, they are Indian" (Shukovsky, 2001, p. A13). It is considered rude to ask an American Indian if he or she meets the federal definition of an American Indian. Barcus (2003) has suggested that the "blood quantum" formula is racist.

> ### Cultural Reflections
>
> *American Indians are required to carry the "Indian card" to demonstrate that they are a recognized American Indian.*
>
> *How would you feel if you were required to carry a card showing that you are a "full-blooded American" or that you are a "full-blooded Italian American," "full-blooded German American," or any other ethnic grouping?*
>
> *Should the United States have cards to distinguish between those who were born Americans and those who have naturalized? Explain your answer.*

Although the U.S. Census Bureau and federal regulations define "Indianness," other criteria have also been used to identify who is an American Indian. Cameron and Turtle-Song (2003) have identified three additional criteria to determine who is an American Indian. The first important question is "Are you an enrolled member of a specific tribe?" A person's citizenship within a tribe gives one voting powers within the tribe, the right to directly petition the U.S. government on behalf of the tribe, and the right to obtain whatever tribal resources are available. The individual's involvement in Indian culture is a second criterion. The significant question here is "Have you been raised in and/or do you understand the cultural norms and mores of the tribe?" The third criterion deals with biology: "Are you a biological descendant of a given tribe?" (Cameron & Turtle-Song, 2003).

SOCIOECONOMIC STATUS

The U.S. Census Bureau (2010b) reported the average annual household income for those self-identified as American Indian and Alaska Native not in combination with other races was $35,060. In contrast, the median annual income for U.S. households as a whole was $50,046 (U.S. Census Bureau, 2010b). In 2010, the U.S. Census Bureau reported that the average annual household income for Asians was $67,022; Whites, $52,480; African Americans, $33,578; and Hispanics, $40,165. In 2010, 15.3% of the total U.S. population and 12.5% of Whites lived below the poverty level. The percentage of American Indians and Alaska Natives who were in poverty in 2010 was 28.4% (U.S. Census Bureau, 2010a).

Approximately 77% of American Indians and Alaska Natives age 25 and older had at least a high school education. Within this group, 13% had earned a bachelor's degree or higher. In comparison, the overall American population had an 86% high school completion rate, and 28% of Americans had earned a bachelor's degree or higher. Approximately, 67,644 American Indians and Alaska Natives age 25 and older had a graduate or a professional degree (U.S. Census Bureau, 2010a).

THEORY OF HISTORICAL TRAUMA AMONG AMERICAN INDIANS

The theory of historical trauma among American Indians has been used to explain why members of this group are at a greater risk of developing feelings of psychological distress and more likely to have poor or less favorable overall physical and mental health than the rest of the American population (Barnes, Adams, & Powell-Griner, 2010). Using the literature on the Jewish Holocaust survivors and their decedents, Brave Heart and Debruyn (1998) proposed the concept of historical trauma to explain American Indians' current difficulties in American life. According to these researchers, American Indians' problems are the result of "a legacy of chronic trauma and unresolved grief across generations" enacted on them by the European dominant culture (Brave Heart & Debruyn, 1998; Gone, 2014).

This historical trauma has been theoretically transferred to subsequent generations through biological, psychological, environmental, and social means, resulting in a cross-generational cycle of trauma (Sotero, 2006). Although a number of researchers believe that the theory of historical trauma is clinically applicable to American Indians (Brave Heart, Chase, Elkins, & Altschul, 2010; Goodkind, LaNoue, Lee, Freeland, & Freund, 2012; Myhra, 2011), there is scant empirical research to support the basic concepts underlying the theory (Evans-Campbell, 2008; Gone, 2009). There has been little research regarding how the past atrocities are connected to the present plight of American Indians (Gone, 2014).

The historical trauma experienced by American Indians is reflected in the policies and treaties that the U.S. government held toward each tribe (BigFoot & Schmidt, 2010). Each tribe had its own special history with the U.S. government that influenced how the government policy of assimilation affected historical trauma and cultural identity within the specific tribe. According to Gray and Rose (2012), this relocation policy was replaced in the late 1880s by a policy of compulsory assimilation into the dominant White American society, which disrupted American Indian societies in many ways and prevented their cultures from being passed on to younger generations.

For many American Indians, the impact of historical trauma on their communities was felt psychologically. *Historical trauma* is the term used to convey the legacy of social and cultural suffering related to harmful policies that the U.S. government imposed on American Indian communities. For instance, one policy mandated the forced removal of American Indian children from their homes and their placement in boarding schools away from their families. American Indians maintained that this policy has had a lasting impact on the mental

Cultural Reflections

How much do you know about American Indian and/or Alaska Native history?

Do you believe the notion of historical trauma is valid for American Indians? Explain your answer.

Should American Indians forget about what happened to them, including claims of genocide, and just "get on with their lives"?

Explain.

health of American Indian communities. The suffering that was caused by this policy has been transmitted from generation to generation (Gone, 2014; Salzman, 2001).

Other historical trauma includes the dispossession of American Indians from their lands and property, the deliberate disruption of indigenous language and culture and the forced assimilation of American Indians into White American society, federal relocation programs of American Indians to cities, and American Indian wars and massacres. It is important that the clinician understand the systemic intergenerational trauma that American Indians and their communities have experienced because such knowledge provides the basis for the underlying mental stress that sometimes manifests itself in terms of alcohol and drug addiction, as well as psychological disorders. Cultural understanding of American Indians is critical for effective counseling and psychotherapy because it provides opportunities for integrating American Indian perspectives into a treatment model (Gone, 2014).

Trimble and Gonzalez (2008) have posited that American Indian culture has served as a buffer against historical trauma that members of these groups have suffered throughout their experience in the United States. As a result of historical trauma and unresolved grief, "cultural recovery movements are occurring among indigenous people throughout the world to reconstruct a world of meaning to act in . . . and to recover ceremonies and rituals that address life's problems" (Salzman, 2001, p. 173). Individuals in favor of the recovery movement have encouraged the use of tribal and community rituals to promote a sense of safety and continuity.

ETHNIC/RACIAL STEREOTYPES, RACISM, AND MICROAGGRESSIONS

American Indians and Alaska Natives form one of the least understood ethnic groups in the United States, primarily because many are isolated on reservations and other lands from the general American population. Much of what Americans know about American Indians comes from limited sources, such as the movies or an occasional television program. Some common stereotypes of American Indians are as follows:

- All American Indians and Alaska Natives have black hair, tan skin, and brown eyes.
- All are given an Indian name.
- Indians are confined to reservations, wear braids, and ride horses.
- Indians are alcoholics.
- Indians are primitive, lazy, and undeserving of assistance from the American government.

Cultural Reflections

What is your position on using American Indian names and symbols for various athletic teams, such as Redskins or Chiefs for a football team? Explain.

Why do you think that many athletic teams choose American Indian names?

Do you believe that the use of American Indian names for team mascots is an example of racism or microaggression?

WORLDVIEW

There is no one worldview for American Indians and Alaska Natives. There are more than 560 federally recognized American Indian tribes and Alaskan villages existing in the United States (Gray & Rose, 2012). Depending on one's tribal membership, there are probably several worldviews for American Indians. The worldviews of American Indians change as their cultural identity group changes.

Although there is not one definitive worldview that comprises all American Indian cultures, many American Indians appear to agree on certain values and ways of seeing and experiencing the world. *Worldview* refers to the core beliefs and values of a people. It includes a culture's view of the nature of reality, the nature of people and of God, and the way that the universe operates. The worldview of American Indians has been compared with that of the dominant majority White American culture. In general, American Indian culture is a collectivist culture. Whereas White American culture tends to exert a strong need to control nature, American Indian culture is said to seek harmony with the environment. American Indians view the earth as their Mother, and as having a sacred bond with their creation. The natural environment is conceptualized as gifts from the Creator (BigFoot & Schmidt, 2010). People were created not to "lord" over other beings, but rather to cooperate and share the bounty of the earth with other people and animals as well. The core of the American Indian worldview is to be in tune with the creation, with Mother Earth, and with all that is around one. The American Indian's religious views use a pluralistic religious life based on nature as living and sacred. In contrast, the dominant European religious view seeks power in a deity. Table 9.1 compares the individualistic White American culture with the collectivist American Indian culture.

TABLE 9.1 ■ Comparing and Contrasting American Indian and White American Worldviews

Individualistic (American White)	Collectivist (American Indian)
• Dominant over nature	• Equal to nature
• Control over environment; one is the master of the universe	• In harmony with environment; one does not master the universe
• Emphasis on the welfare of the individual over the group	• Emphasis on the welfare of the group over the individual
• One's being in the world is independent, autonomous; self-sufficiency is stressed	• One's being in the world is interdependent; focus on being part of a group, cooperation
• Personal and independent control is emphasized	• Control is by the collective (i.e., by the tribe, clan)
• Nuclear family structure	• Extended family structure
• Elders are sent to senior citizens' homes; value of youth over elders	• Elders are valued for their wisdom; elders are respected and held in high esteem
• Communication is direct and highly verbal, with a fair amount of verbal confrontation	• Communication is indirect and nonverbal; silence is an important part of communication
• Spirituality is optional	• Spirituality is a core part of the individual
• Spiritual life is centered on church	• Spiritual life is centered on nature
• People rely on business contacts, government	• People rely on elders, ceremonies
• Materialism and acquisition of things	• Sharing of resources
• Time orientation is toward the future and gets objectified as a commodity	• Time orientation is on the present; no effort to control time
• Competition is valued, some boasting about one's performance against others	• Cooperation is valued; competition is positive when it benefits the whole group
• Economics—individual property	• Economics—communal property
• Derive an understanding of the world from the order the people create	• Derive an understanding of the world from the natural order's rhythms and cycles of life
• Ownership of the land one occupies	• Does not have a sense of ownership of the land
• No real sacred places; churches bought, sold	• Sacred places, especially burial places
• Procedurally oriented	• Relationally oriented
• Conflict is direct, with focus on winning	• Conflict is indirect, with focus on harmony

FAMILY STRUCTURE: THE TRIBE AS FAMILY

Similar to the values held by African Americans, Hispanics, and Asians, American Indians hold the family to be of great importance (Garrett, 2008). American Indians add one additional layer: the importance of the tribe to which one belongs. In American Indian culture, the individual is also of secondary importance to the tribe. American Indian culture emphasizes the administration of the family by the father and the older relatives. There must be mutual respect among all family members and among the tribal leaders. The father is viewed as the administrator of the family and not as an absolute authority. American Indian children are taught to be independent and to make up their own minds. American Indian culture emphasizes familism, which espouses the primacy of the family over the individual. Moreover, it is hard to describe the "typical" American Indian family. Family structure varies according to one's tribe. The Navajo Indians range from matriarchal structures where women govern the family to patriarchal structures where men are the primary authority figures. Most American Indians use the extended family structure, and children are sometimes raised by relatives, including aunts, uncles, and grandparents (Garrett, 2008). The extended family may go beyond blood relatives to friends and other tribal and clan members who are sometimes given a family relationship—for instance, being considered a brother or sister based on the closeness and the role they have in another person's life (BigFoot & Braden, 1998).

In American Indian culture, the tribe is also considered family. Tribal leaders and elders are consulted by family members when marital conflicts and other problems occur within the family, especially if the husband and wife come from different tribes. Tribal membership is central to an individual's identity in American Indian communities. Accepting responsibility for family obligations has traditionally been central to an American Indian identity.

CULTURAL IDENTITY

The topic of American Indian identity development has been written about by several researchers (Horse, 2005; Trimble, 2012; Trimble & Thurman, 2002). In a special issue of *New Directions for Student Services: Serving Native American Students*, Perry Horse (2005) stated that an American Indian identity is multifaceted. American Indians are citizens of America's indigenous nations and are viewed as having an evolving culture. Their ethnocultural identity is influenced by how they choose to identify themselves, encounters with negative racial attitudes and White privilege, and their unique legal and political statuses within the United States. The spectrum of American Indian identity is broad.

Some of the broad diversity within the American Indian community is caused by the fact that individuals have married and mixed intertribally for numerous generations. In addition, the cultural identity of American Indians is sometimes blurred because of the high rate of interracial mixing with White Americans and African Americans during the past 500 years. For instance, Russell (1997) has estimated that at least 98% of the American Indian population is tribally mixed, and approximately 75% are racially mixed. Currently, the term *full-blooded Indian* is used to refer to American Indians who consider themselves to be 100% descended from one tribe (Garrett, 2008). Most American Indian tribes do not permit a person to be registered in two tribes.

One indicator of an American Indian identity is the extent to which an individual understands or is competent in an Indian language. Some American Indians have learned English as a second language; therefore, they tend to see the world differently than those who were raised in an English-speaking environment. The names of American Indians may also reflect their level of their cultural identity.

American Indian cultural orientations have been placed into four basic categories: (1) traditional, (2) acculturated, (3) bicultural, and (4) marginalized (Garrett and Pichette, 2000). Cultures that are philosophically very close to the traditional past of a tribe are referred to as "traditional," and those that are closer to Western culture are designated as "acculturated." Those who walk in two worlds are called bicultural, whereas those that are marginalized may not identify with either culture. Individual tribal members may vary along the continuum from traditional, to acculturated, to bicultural, to marginalized.

Gray and Rose (2012) point out that those "who may have grown up with Western or no cultural identity may choose as adults to rediscover their Native American cultural roots and find teachers to guide their journey. This makes it important for the therapist to determine how their client may relate to culture and identity" (pp. 82–83). In their model of American Indian cultural identity, discussed later in this chapter, Garrett and Pichette (2000) call those in recovery the pantraditionals.

Perry Horse (2005) has proposed an ethnic identity model for American Indians. According to him, American Indian identity is very personal and has five primary influences on a person's consciousness, including levels of connection to culture and language, validity of American Indian genealogy, the extent of holding a related spiritual worldview, one's self-concept as an American Indian, and enrollment status in a tribe. Horse maintains that within a racially stratified, White-privileged American society, American Indians must struggle to maintain an ethnocultural identity, all the while encountering racism. In addition, this researcher asserts that American Indians do not share just one ethnic identity—that there is broad diversity within this community. A key concern is forced acculturation by the dominant White culture. Horse's perspective on American Indian identity development is centered on the idea of American Indian consciousness. This consciousness is reflected in

Cultural Reflections

Do you feel that the four categories of cultural orientations for American Indians are accurate?

Describe your contact with an American Indian and/or Alaska Native.

In what cultural grouping would you place the American Indian(s) with whom you have had contact?

Was your contact with an American Indian positive or negative? Please describe.

- An American Indian's knowledge of language of his or her culture
- The increase in an American Indian's awareness and comprehension of his or her tribe's history
- An American Indian's adoption of a worldview that is consistent with the traditions and culture of his or her heritage
- The amount of emphasis an individual places on his or her American Indian heritage

Trimble (2000) proposed a four-part ethnic identity measurement model that includes four domains: natal (ethnic origins), subjective (attitudes and identities), behavioral (language, preferences, activities), and situation (settings). Research on Trimble's model had assessed primarily the behavioral domain of American Indian identity.

Gonzalez and Bennett (2011) have suggested that previous research on American Indian identity has focused primarily on bicultural ethnic identity. These researchers developed a new measured called the Native Identity Scale (NIS) that assesses various determinants of an ethnic minority experience. Their exploratory study resulted in a four-factor model of American Indian ethnic identity: Centrality, Humanism, Public Regard, and Oppressed Minority. The results of the NIS study suggest that there are underlying dimensions of an American Indian identity that are not captured by current assessment measures.

CULTURAL VALUES

Researchers have described American Indian values that appear to cut across tribal nations. Some of these traditional values include "the importance of community contribution, sharing, acceptance, cooperation, harmony and balance, noninterference, extended family, attention to nature, immediacy of time, awareness of the relationship, and a deep respect for elders" (Garrett, 2008, p. 235).

Sharing and Generosity

Traditional American Indians esteem the values of **sharing and generosity**. Possessions are considered a way for helping others. Although people from a Western worldview may feel that they have lent an American Indian something, the indigenous person may consider the so-called "loaned object" a gift that does not necessitate repayment or return. Materialism and ownership of "things" is far less important than being a good person (Gray & Rose, 2012). Generosity is considered evidence of a person's wisdom and humility (Jumper-Reeves, Dustman, Harthun, Kulis, & Brown, 2014). The respected American Indian is not one who has large savings, but instead the person who gives generously. Moreover, many indigenous cultures do not emphasize status and getting ahead, as is the case in Western culture. Such cultures do not prize putting away for the future, collecting large quantities of food or possessions, and financial security. Indigenous people believe that nature will provide whatever is needed, and therefore, excess goods are given away during ceremonies. Whatever one needs is located in the present; the belief is that the future will take care of itself.

Time Orientation

American Indian traditions maintain that people do not have to live by the clock. Things happen when they are ready to happen. Mother Earth will signal when it is time to begin and end a thing or a task. Time is relatively flexible. Natural rhythms dictate time rather than the clock. Most American Indians orient themselves to the present and the immediate tasks at hand. Such a present time orientation is based on the deep philosophical emphasis on being instead of becoming (Jumper-Reeves et al., 2014).

Cultural Reflections

Generosity and gifting are cultural values for American Indians.

Suppose you have worked with an American Indian client, and at the close of your eight-week counseling session, he gives you a gift, a beautiful ring with an emerald set in it.

Given the American Psychological Association's warning against accepting gifts, would you accept your client's gift, or would you return it to him, telling him about the APA position? Explain your answer.

Spirituality

Many American Indian tribal languages have no word for religion; instead, spiritual practices form an integral part of a person's everyday life. Because of their history of trauma and other factors, American Indians may ascribe to and practice various religious belief systems along with their traditional tribal systems (Garcia, 2000). The traditional spirituality of American Indians involves a way of honoring one's connection with Mother Earth. Traditional American Indians believe that people exist on earth to be helpers and protectors of life and that there is a single higher power known as Creator, Great Creator, Great Spirit, or Great One (Locust, 1998).

Although the definition of **spirituality** varies from tribe to tribe, Garcia's (2000) definition can be applied to most American Indians:

> Spirituality is giving credit and honor to the Great Spirit, the Creator, and Grandfather of all Indian people. Spirituality means living the life that the Great Spirit has blessed people with. It means being respectful of all things, especially the elders and the children. It means taking care of the Mother Earth and not abusing the gifts She has provided. It means acknowledging the Creator in every aspect of one's life. Spirituality is sometimes demonstrated through prayer. (p. 47)

American Indians believe that all things in nature are for the good of all and cannot be owned by people. One must live in balance and in cooperation with nature, taking only what one needs (BigFoot & Braden, 1998). In contrast to the Western cultural view that mandates what constitutes religion—for instance, a set dogma that one may recite and a specific day on which one may practice one's religion (Sunday or Saturday)—in American Indian spiritual practice, everything may be imbued with the divine, and there is no separation of religion from everyday life. People are viewed as caretakers of the desired life. "Therefore, from the perspective of a traditionalist, to see oneself as a caretaker is to accept responsibility for the gift of life by taking good care of that gift, the gift of life that others have received, and the surrounding beauty of the world in which one lives" (Garrett, 2008, p. 239).

Cooperation and Harmony

Cooperation and harmony are highly valued in American Indian life. Because of a strong emphasis on the importance of a group, competition within the group is rare (Garrett & Portman, 2011). As a result, individuals can feel secure in being a member of the group and not being singled out or placed in a position above or below fellow members. One can, however, compete with one's own past performance. Sometimes when an American Indian student does not answer a question in class, other American Indian children may say that they also do not know the answer, when in reality they actually do know the answer.

American Indians believe that every living organism has a purpose or reason for being. There is a belief in the "straight path" (Cruz & Spence, 2005; Katz, 1993). Life is a gift from the Creator. Therefore, one must live in a humble way and give thanks for all gifts one receives each day (Jumper-Reeves et al., 2014). Locust (1985) emphasizes that "Native American Indians believe that each individual chooses to make himself well or to make himself unwell. If one stays in harmony, keeps all the tribal laws and the sacred laws, one's spirit will be so strong that negativity will be unable to affect it. Once harmony is broken, however, the spiritual self is weakened and one becomes vulnerable to physical illness, mental and/or emotional upsets, and the disharmony projected by others" (p. 4).

The straight path provides the individual traditional American Indian principles and guidelines for living a life free of emotional turmoil, confusion, and poor health.

Noninterference

Noninterference means that an individual is not to interfere with the choices of others because such actions would be disrespectful. American Indians are raised not to interfere with others and to observe instead of reacting impulsively. They respect the rights of others. The value of noninterference is especially observed in the parenting practices of individuals. Others should not interfere with one's parenting styles (Trimble & Gonzalez, 2008).

Communication Style and Silence

American Indians and Alaska Natives have a communication style that differs from that of the average American. In general, Americans are very talkative, while American Indians are usually a quiet and reserved people. Silence is a way of communicating that has long been embedded in American Indian culture. If American Indians are angry or upset in a social situation, they usually do not express those emotions. Instead, they are silent. A major American Indian cultural value is the dictum "Listen before you speak." American Indians rarely talk simply for the sake of talking, and neither do they tend to engage in small talk, except between close friends or family.

American Indians may often speak in a soft or low voice and avoid direct eye contact to demonstrate respect for a listener (BigFoot & Funderburk, 2010). The goal is to engage in careful listening so that one understands what a person means rather than what one actually says. Storytelling may be used to make a point to another person. The indirect and cooperative communication style of American Indians differs from that of most Westerners who may ask a series of questions, interrupt, tell others what to do, or argue their points. Listening rather than speaking is important in American Indian culture.

TABLE 9.2 ■ Some General Communication Rules Adopted by American Indians
• Honor silence; instead of talking, let your actions speak.
• Do not engage in lengthy conversations to get to know someone; wait until you know the person well.
• Regulate your emotions and do not express strong emotions in words or actions.
• Avoid direct questions; instead, observe and wait to receive information.
• Avoid displaying superior knowledge or correcting someone.
• Children should be silent in the presence of adults, and adults should neither reprimand nor praise a child in public.
• Direct eye contact (staring or extended gaze) is considered rude.

Adapted from Heit, M. (1987).

Storytelling is a major way of communicating in American Indian culture. In fact, from an early age, children are taught to listen, observe, and memorize. Whereas European culture tends to emphasize the written word, American Indians use storytelling as an oral way of passing their history and stories down from one generation to the next. In this respect, American Indian culture is quite similar to African culture, which also uses the oral tradition of storytelling to pass the culture of its people onto the next generation (BigFoot & Funderburk, 2010).

It should be noted that these are general guidelines for communication with American Indians; however, some of the communication styles described may not represent all American Indian tribes. According to Mary Heit (1987), American Indians have certain general unwritten rules for communication, which are summarized in Table 9.2.

It is easy to see how problems could develop between clinicians who are non-Native peoples and clients who are American Indian. Clinicians value self-disclosure, sometimes on the first interview. Clinicians may also not know how to deal with silence from their clients. The first question they might ask is "What does the client's silence mean?" Or, worse yet, "What's wrong with this client? Doesn't he know that he's supposed to talk? How am I supposed to help him if he does not talk?"

Cultural Reflections

How comfortable are you with silence during counseling?

How would you feel if a client said absolutely nothing for five minutes during therapy?

When you are in a group of friends, do you tend to be the one doing the most talking?

Do people seem to seek your opinion because you are silent most of the time?

CULTURAL STRENGTHS

Clients are best served when clinicians help them solve their problems by means of their strengths. A major strength of American Indian cultures is the extensive and rich informal resources that are available to deal with family problems. Some of the cultural values of American Indians also function as their strengths, including their allegiance to family and tribe, respect for elders, respect for the land and the environment, and strong resilience (Aronowitz, 2014). A strong identification with American Indian and Alaska Native culture, traditional healing practices, and the wisdom of elders are additional cultural strengths.

American Indians developed strength symbols across various tribes. The bear is one of the strength symbols created in American Indian culture. The bear symbol was supposed to represent a protector, and it symbolized physical strength and leadership. Bears are large and agile. The black bear and the Grizzly were native to North America, and the American Indians strongly associated them with strength (Office of Minority Health, 2012).

Other strength symbols were represented in colors, especially the color red, which was used in war paint. The eagle symbol was also used to indicate strength and courage. Currently, some of the symbols of strength are reflected in American Indian tattoos (Alter, 2016).

HEALING: THE CIRCLE AND MEDICINE WHEEL IN INDIAN LIFE

You have noticed that everything an Indian does is in a circle, and that is because the power of the world always works in circle, and everything tries to be round . . . Everything the power of the world does is done in a circle . . . Our tepees were round like the nests of birds, and these were always set in a circle, the nation's hoop, a nest of many nests, where the Great Spirit meant for us to hatch our children. (Black Elk, Oglala Sioux Holy Man [1863–1950], quoted in Moodley & West, 2005, p. 298)

We see in the world around us as many symbols that teach us the meaning of life . . . The Indian's symbol is the circle, the hoop . . . The bodies of human being and animals have no corners. Our circle is timeless, flowing; it is new life emerging from death—life winning out over death. (Halfe, 1993, p. 7)

Much of American Indians' life is based on their knowledge of the rhythm of life, which they obtain through the observation of nature. What American Indians have observed is that there are no straight lines in nature. Nature expresses itself in circular patterns. The wheel represents the cycle of life, such as birth, death, and rebirth. The circle or wheel represents *Wakan Tanka*—"The Great Everything" or the universe itself.

In traditional American Indian life, the **circle** is a symbol of equality; it indicates that no person is more important than any other person. In circle meetings, all people are permitted to speak, and the words spoken are accepted and respected on an equal basis. There is no break in the circle, and it holds or contains that which cannot be broken. The circle is an important symbol in American Indian life, and oftentimes gatherings in powwow were organized in a series of circles. Dancing also occurred in the center of a circle formed by the drums and the audience.

Medicine. American Indians do not use medicine in the same manner as do White Americans. When American Indians use the term *medicine*, they are referring to the vital power or force within nature and to the personal power that each person has, which helps him or her to become whole or complete. The American Indian equation is medicine = energy = power = knowledge.

Medicine wheel. What is a medicine wheel, and how can it be used? A **medicine wheel** is a circle that illustrates the balance between natural and personal powers to show that everything in life is interconnected. A medicine wheel contains four directions, which are represented as points on the circle. These directions are often linked with different animals, colors, or characters in specific traditions. The wheel symbolizes the need for harmony and balance within oneself and with all creatures and people on earth.

The medicine wheel is a symbol of balance for American Indian and Alaska Native communities, which represents four areas of balance: physical, emotional, intellectual, and spiritual (Harris & McFarland, 2000; Whitekiller, 2004). The medicine wheel represents the way American Indians approach life, not in a linear fashion, but instead in a circular way.

The center of the wheel symbolizes the center of one's life, and the perfect balance of all that surrounds one. The wheel represents the circle of awareness of the individual self, and it can be used as a philosophical system that helps a person to find his or her way. It can be used to determine which direction one should go in life and for aligning physical, mental, emotional, and spiritual aspects of one's life. The medicine wheel

Cultural Reflections

What parts of American Indian culture and values do you like the most? The least?

How competent do you feel counseling an American Indian who lives in urban America? Who lives on Indian territory, such as a reservation?

suggests that change is inevitable, that life is a process of development, and that the ultimate goal is wholeness. Medicine wheel designs are frequently used as the logo for Indian agencies and organizations. The wheel is a reminder that people should strive for balance, wholeness, and harmony in life.

COUNSELING APPLICATIONS OF THE CIRCLE AND MEDICINE WHEEL

The medicine wheel has been used in mental health settings to help American Indians heal from their problems. One therapeutic use of the medicine wheel is the **talking circle**, a type of group therapy in which individuals sit in a circle. Sage is sometimes used in talking circles. According to Gray and Rose (2012), "the burning of sage can create a positive, culturally friendly environment for [American Indian] clients because sage is used for blessing and purifying and helps create a peaceful, calming, positive, and sage environment for the client. Sage also communicates an acceptance of the culture and openness to providing comfort in this difficult experience. . . . Alternatives to this may be providing dried sage that the client can take to breathe in the science and sprinkle over them instead of smudging with the smoke of the burning sage" (p. 89). After giving group members sage to put on themselves, the group leader opens the meeting by sharing a personal experience, which is followed by group members talking about their own experiences and feelings. The unspoken rule is that only one person can speak at a time, and others are not permitted to crosstalk or question the speaker. Moodley and West (2005) quote a participant in a talking circle who said, "Talking circles helped me because I could talk and hear myself and decide whether this was a true thing or a passing state of being. . . . I could clarify this by hearing myself speaking about my feelings and by having other people witness it. . . . There were a lot of times when I crumbled and just let go of the pain" (p. 299).

Another counseling application of the medicine wheel is the **circle of courage**, which is used in working with young people. The circle of courage is a model of positive youth development that maintains that all youth need a sense of belonging, mastery, independence, and generosity to become mentally healthy and to thrive (Brendtro, Brokenleg, & Van Bockern, 1990, 2002). The belonging quadrant (which affirms "right now I belong here") is based on American Indian culture and Maslow's (1943) theory of human needs and motivation. In traditional American Indian society, treating others as relatives and drawing them into one's circle of belonging was used to show respect, concern, and good will. The mastery (achievement) quadrant of the circle of courage model carries something of the sentiment "I will try to do my very best." This quadrant is based on the belief that every child has a need to feel competent and that when this need is satisfied, the child is motivated to achieve in other areas. The independence quadrant (we become independent by building trust) is based partly on the research in early child development and neuroscience that says that every child has a need to become attached, yet independent. The generosity quadrant of the circle of courage (altruism) is based on the principle that helping others improves our own self-esteem and helps us to deal with the stress in our lives.

The circle of courage model integrates American Indian worldviews on childhood development and modern strengths-based approaches to address the needs of children by creating cultures of respect (Brendtro et al., 1990, 2002). In traditional tribal societies, the central purpose is the education and empowerment of children (Gilgun, 2002). The American Indian circle of courage model provides a powerful alternative to narrow, deficit-focused views. Professionals in various nations have applied circle of courage constructs to fields of youth development including education, juvenile justice, child welfare, faith-based settings, and health care (Brendtro et al., 1990, 2002).

Numerous authors have discussed the benefit of introducing American Indian beliefs and ceremonies within the conventional counseling setting (Dufrene & Coleman, 1992; Heilbron & Guttman, 2000; LaFromboise, Trimble, & Mohatt, 1990). Heilbron and Guttman (2000) found that using a healing circle with First Nations, or Native Canadian, women who are survivors of child sexual abuse was effective treatment and beneficial. A modification of the "sacred circle" has been proposed for group therapy (Garrett, Garrett, & Brotherton, 2001). However, other researchers have cautioned against incorporating American Indian techniques and approaches into counseling members of their group—without proper training by tribal leaders. Thomason (2012) has stated that

> there has been much discussion in the literature on incorporating traditional Native American healing techniques into counseling in order to make it more culturally appropriate (Herring, 1999; McCabe, 2007; Trujillo, 2000). Some of these methods involve Native spiritual traditions and typically have been used primarily by sanctioned tribal healers. . . . [T]raditional healing methods, such as talking circles, may be used by non-Native counselors who are culturally competent and have been trained in the methods, but they [respondents] say that it would be better to find a Native counselor or refer the client to a tribal healer. (p. 7)

Trimble (2010) has cautioned clinicians against integrating American Indian healing techniques into traditional counseling approaches. According to him,

> advocating an integration of the traditional with the conventional is not without its problems. For many Indians and Natives, the idea of sharing their traditional healing and spiritual traditions with outsiders would not be acceptable and would be met with fierce resistance. . . . [T]here are a few Indian and Native communities who are willing to establish collaborative relationships with mental health practitioners. Moreover, there are a few Indian and Native healers who work with outsiders to promote health, well-being, and spiritual balance. Numerous Indian and Native community leaders demand that collaboration with mental health specialists occur under their direction and control. Practitioners should be prepared to collaborate with the communities, share results that have practical value, and accept the conditions imposed by the community in gaining access to those in need of psychological assistance. (Trimble, 2010, p. 253)

Debate has also centered on what counselor characteristics most facilitate a positive, effective counseling relationship with American Indian and Alaska Native clients. Along such lines, Reimer (1999) collected information from Iñupiat members of an Alaska Native village concerning the characteristics they found desirable in a healer. Her participants responded that they desired a healer who (a) was virtuous, kind, respectful, trustworthy, friendly, gentle, loving, clean, giving, helpful, and not one who wallows in self-pity; (b) was strong mentally, physically, and spiritually; (c) worked well with others by becoming familiar with people in the community; (d) had good communication skills and knew how to listen; (e) was respected because of his or her knowledge; (f) was substance free; (g) knew how to follow the culture; and (h) had faith and a strong relation with the Creator. These are counseling skills most trainees are imbued with during the training process to become a counselor. Counselors need to be willing to listen without judging the American Indian culture.

Cultural Reflections

How comfortable do you feel using some of the American Indian healing techniques described herein, such as talking and healing circles?

Do you think it is appropriate to include training in American Indian healing techniques for counselors who are not American Indians? Explain.

Who should provide the actual training? College professors? American Indian healers?

MENTAL HEALTH CHALLENGES

American Indians face a number of mental health issues that have been connected to their experience of historical trauma (Gone, 2014). These include acculturation conflicts, alcohol abuse, and substance abuse (Thomason, 2000). American Indians experience depression, anxiety, and several other psychological disorders at a higher rate than the general American population (Zahran et al., 2004), but they underutilize mental health services (Greer, 2004; McCormick, 1997). As Thomason (2012) has pointed out,

> it would be very useful to know how best to encourage Native Americans to use the services available to them; how to make such services culturally appropriate; and how to conduct effective counseling and mental health services with members of this population. It is particularly important for counselors in urban areas to know how to serve Native Americans effectively, since at least half of all Native Americans live in urban areas and they are more likely to seek counseling than those who live in rural and reservation areas. (Witko, 2006, p. 1)

Traditional Healing

Traditional American Indian and Alaska Native healing systems emphasize a holistic balancing of mind, body, and spirit. Such systems do not isolate one part of the person and then heal that part. Members of the American Indian and Alaska Native population who meet the criteria for depression/anxiety or substance abuse tend to seek help from traditional or spiritual healers rather than from a psychological or medical source. Studies have reported that approximately 34% to 49% of American Indian and Alaska Native people with diagnosed behavioral disorders used traditional healers, and 16% to 32% of those using biomedical services for emotional problems had also contacted a traditional healer (Beals et al., 2005).

Although the American Indian population has problems similar to and different from other groups, this section focuses primarily on acculturation conflicts, alcohol and substance abuse, and suicide.

Acculturation Conflicts

American Indian young people may experience acculturation conflicts over their exposure to two very different cultures. Some youth feel trapped between the expectations of their parents to uphold traditional American Indian values and the need to adjust to the values of the broad American society. Young male Indians said that their Indianness or being an Indian was a problem (Bee-Gates, Howard-Pitney, LaFromboise, & Rowe, 1996; Flynn, Olson, & Yellig, 2014).

American Indians' level of acculturation can be assessed using the Native American Acculturation Scale (Garrett & Pichette, 2000). The degree of American Indians' and Alaska Natives' acculturation needs to be evaluated because this is a variable that can affect the counseling process. Recall the four cultural orientations identified by Garrett and Pichette (2000) earlier in this chapter: (1) traditional, (2) marginal, (3) bicultural, (4) assimilated, and (5) pantraditional (acculturated/assimilated but seeking to reconnect with one's American Indian identity). Many American Indians and Alaska Natives are fully acculturated and assimilated; consequently, they ascribe to the values of the broad American society. Clinicians should avoid making assumptions about American Indians' cultural identities. Instead, they should learn what level of acculturation the clients are at and what their specific needs are. Mental health professionals should assess for any tribal affiliations, language(s) spoken, where the person was raised, and his or her current level of tribal affiliation. During the initial interview, Garrett (2008) suggests that the clinician might ask such questions as "Tell me about your family," "How do you identify yourself culturally?" and "Tell me about how you see yourself as a person, culturally and spiritually."

When counseling American Indian clients, clinicians should assess the effect of oppression on the client's life experience and presenting issues (Lee, 2014). To assess the impact of oppression on a client, a clinician might broach the topic of oppression with a client. Clinicians might ask, "Do you feel you have had any experiences with being oppressed? If so, what is that like?" (Flynn et al., 2014).

Alcohol Abuse

Substance abuse is a major mental health issue encountered by American Indian and Alaska Native populations (American Psychiatric Association, 2010; Espy et al., 2014; Office of Minority Health, 2012). Research has found that the rates of alcohol use vary across tribes and nations, but that American Indians evidence the highest weekly alcohol consumption of any ethnic group (Chartier & Caetano, 2010; Hasin, Stinson, Ogburn, & Grant, 2007). According to data from the Centers for Disease Control and Prevention (CDC), 1 in 10 American Indian deaths are alcohol related (Associated Press, 2008). Nearly 12% of the deaths of American Indians and Alaska Natives are alcohol related—more than three times the percentage in the general American population. The report released by the CDC found that 11.7% of deaths among American Indians and Alaska Natives between 2001 and 2005 were alcohol related, compared with only 3.3% for the U.S. population as a whole (Associated Press, 2008).

The two leading causes of alcohol-related deaths among American Indians involved traffic accidents and alcohol liver disease, each of which caused more than a quarter of the 1,514 alcohol-related deaths over the four-year period. Homicide caused 6.6% and suicide 5.5% of the alcohol-related deaths. About a third of the tribal alcohol-related deaths took place in the Northern Plains, where reservations are remote and often destitute. The study reported that 68% of the Indians whose deaths were alcohol related were men, 66% were younger than 50 years old, and 7% were younger than 20 years old.

A study was conducted on alcohol-attributable mortality among American Indians and Alaska natives in the United States from 1999 to 2009 (Landen, Roeber, Naimi, Nielsen, & Sewell, 2014). The objective of the study was to describe the relative burden of alcohol-attributable death among American Indians and Alaska Natives in the United States. Cross-referencing National Death Index records with Indian Health Service registration records, the researchers calculated age-adjusted alcohol-attributable death rates from 1999 to 2009 for American Indian/Alaska Native and White persons by sex, age, and geographic region. American Indian and Alaska Native persons had a substantially higher rate of alcohol-attributable death than Whites from 2005 to 2009 in Indian Health Service delivery areas. The Northern Plains had the highest rate of American Indian/Alaska Native deaths (123.8/100,000), and the East had the lowest (48.9/100,000). The researchers concluded that proven strategies that reduce alcohol consumption and make the environment safer for excessive drinkers should be established in American Indian and Alaska Native communities.

A number of factors have been said to be associated with the high rates of alcoholism among the American Indian and Alaska Native population, including genetics, social and cultural influences, and personal attitudes toward alcohol. Some Indian people believe that the loss of their culture is the primary cause of their existing problems, including alcoholism. Individuals in this category believe that the loss of Indian culture has resulted in culture not being a protective factor against alcoholism (Beauvais, 1998).

Suicide Rates for American Indians and Alaska Natives

American Indians and Alaska Natives experience a high rate of suicide compared to the general U.S. population. Herne, Bartholomew, and Weahkee (2014) assessed national and regional suicide mortality for American Indian and Alaska Native people. These researchers found that death rates from suicide were approximately 50% higher among American Indian and Alaska Native persons (21.2%) than among Whites (14.2%).

When region was examined, rates for American Indian and Alaska Native people were highest in Alaska (rates = 65.4% and 19.3% for males and females, respectively) and in the Northern Plains (rates = 41.6% and 11.9% for males and females, respectively). The disparities in suicide rates between American Indians/Alaska Natives and Whites were also highest in these geographical regions. Herne and colleagues (2014) concluded that a coordinated multidisciplinary effort at a number of levels was needed to address suicide among American Indians and Alaska Natives.

COUNSELING APPROACHES FOR AMERICAN INDIANS AND ALASKA NATIVES

To develop a positive therapeutic relationship with an American Indian or Alaska Native, a clinician must have an understanding of the psychological aspects of his or her cultural experience. As noted earlier in the section on historical trauma, American Indians experienced systematic—and, in many cases, violent—attempts to extinguish their tribal culture and language, and some were forced to assimilate to the values and ways of the dominant culture (Bichsel & Mallinckrodt, 2001). Perhaps one consequence of this type of historical trauma is that victims mistrust outsiders and mental health clinicians. American Indians underutilize counseling services, and when they do engage such services, they have one of the highest dropout rates for any group (Bichsel & Mallinckrodt, 2001). In a study of American Indian women, Bichsel and Mallinckrodt (2001) found that counselor attitude and value similarity were among the most important features of counseling. Women who were committed to American Indian culture preferred female counselors of the same ethnicity because presumably such a counselor would be able to help them with the ethnic identity status they assume in relating to their family members. Yet the study concluded that it is more important for a counselor to be sensitive to the client's culture than it is to have a counselor from that culture who is insensitive to its values.

It has been suggested that clinicians display American Indian and Alaska Native art in the therapeutic environment, including paintings, pottery, dolls, dream catchers, or beadwork, to demonstrate an appreciation and acceptance by the clinician (Gray & Rose, 2012). When the clinician works with grief and loss issues, he or she should be aware of the specific tribe's taboos, traditions, and cultural practices. Some tribes have cultural taboos against speaking aloud a person's name who has died because speaking the names of the dead pulls the individuals back from the spirit world and will not let them move forward in their journey. As an alternative to saying the deceased individual's name, the clinician might involve the grieving person(s) in artwork (Gray & Rose, 2012).

What causes problems when working with American Indians and Alaska Natives? According to Trimble and Gonzalez (2008), "the counselor may lack basic knowledge about the client's ethnic and historical backgrounds, the client may be driven away by the professional's counseling style, the client may sense that his or her worldview is not valued, the client may feel uncomfortable talking openly with a stranger, or the ethnic background of the counselor may create client apprehension" (p. 95).

Knowledge of the American Indian's culture is an absolute requirement (LaFromboise, Berman, & Sohl, 1994). The clinician must not ask questions prior to establishing some basis of a relationship with the client. It is helpful if the clinician offers the client something to drink (Garrett, 2008).

Cultural Reflections

Does it surprise you that American Indian women prefer a culturally sensitive clinician over one who may also be American Indian, but not culturally sensitive? Explain.

What are your thoughts about your ability to relate to an American Indian client, even though you may be from a different culture?

Let's assume that you were going to be counseled by a person from an ethnic group different from your own. How would you feel? Would you ask for a counselor from your ethnic background?

TABLE 9.3 ■ Practices for Establishing a Trust Relationship With American Indian and Alaska Native Clients

Greeting—Many traditional American Indians prefer a gentle handshake, because the firm handshake might be viewed as an aggressive show of power or a personal insult. To avoid difficulties with the greeting, the clinician might consider following the client's lead.

Hospitality—Because of American Indians' emphasis on generosity, kindness, and gifting, it might be helpful to offer the client a beverage or snack as a sign of good relation. In traditional Indian culture, not offering some form of hospitality to a visitor or guest is to bring shame on oneself and one's family.

Silence—Traditional American Indian culture says that when two people meet, very little should be said between them during the beginning moments of the encounter. The clinician should observe "quiet time" at the beginning of a therapy session and then transition into the therapeutic process after giving the client time to adjust to the therapy situation. This brief transition time (usually two to five minutes) allows the client to be put at ease and shows respect, understanding, and patience.

Space—The clinician should be aware of space and should not always attempt to fill space with words. In addition, the clinician should respect the physical space of the client by not sitting too close to him or her and by not sitting directly across from the client. The clinician might consider sitting side by side with the client at an off angle.

Eye contact—American Indian clients who may be considered traditional tend to avert their eyes as a show of respect, and the clinician should use the same type of eye contact. Because the eyes are believed to be the pathway to the spirit, to persistently look someone in the eye suggests aggression. In contrast to White American society, listening is done with the ears more so than with the eyes.

Intention—Intention deals with trust, and the clinician should offer respect and humility. Moreover, he or she should not try to control or influence the client, which is considered "bad medicine."

Collaboration—The clinician should approach healing as a collaborative process and give helpful suggestions or alternatives without being pushy or trying to control the client.

Suggestions have been made regarding how to establish a trustworthy counseling relationship with an American Indian or Alaska Native client. For instance, Garrett et al. (2013) maintain that the clinician should consider the practices listed in Table 9.3.

Herring (1999) has proposed that clinicians should provide a "culturally affirmative environment" for American Indian clients. It might be helpful to know that some past studies have found that clinician ethnicity is not an important factor that affects the outcome of counseling American Indian clients (LaFromboise & Dixon, 1981; Lokken & Twohey, 2004). Herring suggests the following guidelines for clinicians:

Address openly the issue of dissimilar relationships rather than pretending that no differences exist;

Schedule appointments to allow for flexibility in ending the session;

Use flexibility in allowing for the end of a session;

Be open to allowing the extended family to participate in the session; Consider inviting the extended family to participate in the counseling session;

Allow time for trust to develop before focusing on problems; spend time developing trust before dealing with client problems;

Respect the use of silence; respect client's use of silence;

Demonstrate honor and respect for the [client's] culture(s); and

Maintain the highest level of confidentiality. (pp. 55–56).

CASE VIGNETTE 9.1
JOHNATHAN: AN AMERICAN INDIAN MAN CAUGHT BETWEEN TWO CULTURES

Description

This is a case study about Johnathan Johnson (or JJ, as he is known to his friends), a young American Indian college student from the Seneca Nation in Western New York outside of Buffalo. Johnathan is a second-semester college student at one of the nearby State University colleges. He sought counseling because he is considering dropping out of college and returning to the Seneca Nation, where he formerly had a job working in one of the stores on the Seneca Nation reservation. Johnathan is deeply committed to his Seneca Nation and its culture—especially to the spiritual aspects of his culture.

Johnathan speaks quietly, as if he is giving thoughtful consideration to whatever he is trying to get across. Sometimes when the counselor speaks, Johnathan is simply silent, for what appears to be a long time for the counselor. In the first few counseling sessions, the counselor would interrupt and punctuate Johnathan's silences with statements such as "Is something wrong?" or "Did I say something to offend you?" Now the counselor has learned to accept Johnathan's silences and not to interfere by trying to fill the room with nervous, professional chatter and additional questions. She waits for Johnathan to gather his thoughts, and when he is silent, she sometimes gets up to fix him a cup of coffee, with three sugars and no cream.

The problem is that there are few American Indians on campus, and Johnathan is lonely, especially at night when he misses his family—mother, father, sister, and brother. Trying to help the counselor understand his dilemma, Johnathan said, "We used to sit around the dining room table at night, with a sage candle burning in the center of the table. The sage candles would relax and clear the negative energy in the room. We would wait for someone to speak, and sure enough, there was always someone who had something on his or her mind. I'd listen, and then I might say something. Usually, my dad would begin telling a story in response to whatever the person would say, and everything would seem much clearer—at least to me. I used to love listening to my father's stories. They always seem to make a point without his saying, 'I think you should do this or that, or maybe you should try this.'

"I miss the smells of my culture. No one here burns sage candles. I burned a sage candle, and when my roommate came into our room, he said, 'What the hell's going on in here? Are you doing something weird with Indian spirits?' I felt insulted, blew out the candle, and never answered him. Everybody here tries to tell me what to do, as if I don't have the sense to make my own choices. I miss my father's stories. There's no stories here to guide me—just a set of rules everyone is supposed to follow."

The counselor assigned to Johnathan had never worked with an American Indian before. She had read a brief sketch about his culture, but she felt inadequate to counsel Johnathan. She had checked with her supervisor and asked if there was a counselor who had experience counseling American Indians, but the answer was no. She was told that "people are just people," "do the best you can," "go on the Seneca Nation website," and "just don't worry about his background." American Indian students had a fairly high dropout rate at the college. No one had been able to exactly figure out why, because some had come in with the same standardized test scores of most students who were admitted at the college.

The counselor visited the Seneca Nation of Indians website, where she saw the word *Nya:weh sgeno*, which means welcome. The counselor was surprised to find so many Christian references. Events were planned for Christmas, Valentine's Day, and Easter. The thought occurred to her, "What was Johnathan really missing?" Was Johnathan's talk about missing the spirituality of the Seneca Nation just a way of covering up wanting to avoid the challenge of college work? Besides, most college students felt a little homesickness from their parents.

The Seneca Nation website said that its nation has a proud and rich history and that it was the largest of six American Indian nations comprising the Haudenosaunee or Iroquois Confederation, or Six Nations, a democratic government that predated the U.S. Constitution. The Senecas described themselves in the following manner: "We are known as the 'Keeper of the Western Door,' for the Seneca are the westernmost of the Six Nations. In the Seneca language we are also known as *O-non-dowa-gah* (pronounced: Oh-n'own-dough-wahgah) or 'Great Hill People'" (https://sni.org/). Currently, the Seneca Nation of Indians has over 8,000 members, and they are the fifth-largest employer in western New York.

Further investigation revealed that the Seneca Nation had just sent a $31.6-million quarterly payment to New York State as part of its revenue share agreement. Since its 2002 agreement with New York State, the Seneca Nation has paid more than $1.1 billion to New York State.

"Wow!" the counselor exclaimed. She didn't realize the financial contributions of the Seneca Nation to New York.

The counselor began to investigate the topic of American Indian students on campuses throughout the United States. She discovered that spirituality permeates American Indian culture in comparison to the more secular dominant society (Gilgun, 2002). Given this fact, it is important to understand the beliefs that are relevant to the student—regardless of whether these beliefs are traditional or otherwise. Colleges should consider providing American Indian students opportunities to express their beliefs and to engage in cultural activities as a form of coping.

Moreover, the counselor found that the research revealed that the most successful American Indian students have a least one strong relationship related to their education (Light, 2003). American Indians are a relational people, so relationships built with a faculty member, an advisor, or other students outside the classroom can be extremely valuable. Many of the problems American Indian students face are not academic but rather personal and relational (Garrod & Larimore, 1997).

American Indian students have the lowest retention rate of all minority students, and tribal colleges suffer from high remedial education (Garrod & Larimore, 1997). A four-component model has been developed for American Indian college students on predominantly White college campuses, and this model includes financial support, academic counseling, spiritual and cultural opportunities, and mentoring (Ambler, 2003).

The overwhelming data seem to support that American Indian college students are successful in their academic endeavors when colleges offer programs that deal with American Indian cultural identity, spirituality, and extended family support (Garcia, 2000; HeavyRunner & DeCelles, 2002; Kerbo, 1981; Martin, 2005). For instance, Guillory (2009) conducted a qualitative study on retention strategies for American Indian college students. Based on his findings, Guillory recommended that colleges and universities establish programs that encourage American Indian students to maintain a strong connection between the campus community and their tribal community. Guillory indicated that fostering a positive American Indian cultural identity was a major factor leading to improved college retention for members of this group. According to him, "university programs which directly connect Native American students to their native communities prove successful for both recruitment and retention" (Guillory, 2009, p. 18).

In addition, mentoring and academic counseling can enhance Native American students' overall educational experience and increase retention rates (HeavyRunner & DeCelles, 2002; Martin, 2005). College courses should cover content that recognizes American Indian contributions to American society. Although much work has been done in higher education to implement programs for American Indian students, more is still needed; Kanu (2006) and HeavyRunner and DeCelles (2002) concluded that the retention rates of American Indian students will remain low unless more attention is given to the financial, academic counseling, mentoring, spiritual, and relational aspects of college life (Guillory, 2009).

Strengths-Based Therapy and Johnathan: American Indian College Student

Johnathan has a number of strengths that the counselor should consider in working with him. First, he is highly spiritual, which means that he has an internal system for guiding his behavior. Second, he has a strong family whose members meet to support each other on a regular basis at their home. Third, he is doing fairly well with academics in school. Fourth, his family is supporting him financially, even though it is a challenge for them to do so. Fifth, he has a strong cultural identity with his American Indian culture, and this identity may be used to support his efforts in college.

Johnathan also has some risk factors that should be taken into account. He is living in a predominantly White college environment for the second time in his life (he is a second-semester freshman). He has not made many friends at the college, and he feels that the college not only does not care about his culture, but disrespects it. The fact that his roommate suggested he was doing something wrong by lighting a sage candle has upset him. He wants to change roommates, and he has asked if there is another American Indian student on campus with whom he can share a dorm room. Yet, it's also something else. Johnathan has not been able to connect with any of his faculty. He attends class, hands in his papers, and gets a grade. There's nothing else to make him feel connected to the professor or to the college.

Building a Therapeutic Relationship

In the beginning of their first counseling session, the counselor's relationship with Johnathan was a bit strained. She had a more Type A personality, while Johnathan was definitely a Type B person. Even their speech patterns clashed. The counselor spoke in a direct New York style, while Johnathan seemed to speak much more slowly, and he did not directly say what was on his mind. She was definitely task oriented, while Johnathan was more process oriented.

Finally, the counselor began to relax because she felt that she and Johnathan were butting heads, culturally speaking. She decided to slow down, stop focusing on how she wanted Johnathan to get on the right track and to stay in school, and really listen to him. She asked Johnathan if he would like a cup of coffee, and he said yes.

They sat there sipping coffee, saying nothing for a few minutes. The counselor decided to take Johnathan's lead in trying to establish a relationship with him. She deliberately slowed down her speech to match his, and she came around from behind her desk to sit in the chair beside him. Johnathan seemed to respond positively to this move on her part.

(Continued)

(Continued)

The counselor began to talk with Johnathan about his American Indian culture. The counselor said, "Before you came, I was reading about American Indian culture, and there's a lot to learn. Your culture is a rich culture; there are so many different aspects to it. I don't know a great deal about the Seneca Nation, except for what I read in the newspapers. I know that the casino at the Seneca Nation has added about $1.2 billion to the New York State treasury, and some of my friends go there to fill up their cars with gas because it's cheaper. The Seneca Nation is actually doing a lot of good for New York State, and you should be proud of its accomplishments."

Johnathan: "I am proud of what we do at the Seneca Nation. We say 'welcome' to the rest of the world. We want to share what we have with you. Maybe if I taught you one word, 'welcome,' we could begin to get to know each other."

Counselor: "That would be great. How do you say 'welcome' in your native language?"

Johnathan: "The word is *Nya:weh sgeno*, which means 'welcome.'"

The counselor practiced saying *Nya:weh sgeno*.

Johnathan smiled, and continued: "As the farthest west of the Six Nations, the Seneca Nation is considered the Keeper of the Western Door. We are also known as the Great Hill People—or, in our language, *O-non-dowa-gah* [pronounced: Oh-n'own-dough-wahgah]."

Counselor: "You must be very proud of your American Indian culture and what the people at the Seneca Nation are doing for you and others."

Johnathan: "Yes. We are a humble people. We give thanks to our Creator for all that we have been able to accomplish."

The counselor began to understand that Johnathan was trying to establish a relationship with her. He wanted her to know who he was and what was important to him; it was clear that being a Seneca Indian was important to him. As they began to talk, she asked if it was all right to call him JJ, and he responded that was what most of his friends called him.

Counselor: "Tell me something about you, JJ. I know that you're a Seneca Indian, that your culture is important to you. I know that you have strengths; otherwise, you wouldn't be here at the State University. I've just glanced at your academic record, and you have done quite well for your first semester here."

Strengths Discovery

Although Johnathan seemed reluctant to talk about his strengths, he did mention his grades, and he also talked about his work at one of the stores at home. He had just been promoted because the store manager liked the fact that he was always on time and ready to do whatever was necessary. Johnathan was working on the weekly news journal for young people. He was involved in working on various groups for the upcoming Easter holiday.

Letting Go, Letting In

During the second counseling session, the counselor again offered Johnathan coffee, and he accepted such. This time she sat next to him, right from the beginning. In fact, she had rearranged the chairs in her office to make it more hospitable for him. She cut out a few pictures of Seneca Nation art and posted it on the wall of her office.

The counselor was surprised to learn that Johnathan actually celebrated Easter, which was part of the Christian religion. The Seneca Nation used a blending of Christianity with American Indian spiritual rituals.

Johnathan turned his attention to one of the two posters that the counselor had on the wall of her office. The poster had a picture of an American Indian and next to it the following words: *"The souls of my ancestors peer out from behind my mask of skin and through my memories, they live again."*

Counselor: "I displayed that picture, JJ, because it reminded me somewhat of you. You're trying to make your way in two worlds—honoring your Seneca Nation culture and traditions and at the same time living in what must appear to be the White man's world. Do you feel any such conflicting loyalty feelings?"

Johnathan: "Sure, sometimes I would just like to flunk out of college so that I could go back home. No one would blame me if I said I tried my best."

Counselor: "But the grades you earned last semester and the grades that you're earning now say loud and clear that you can do the work. So, you don't have lack of academic ability as a reason for your quitting the State University and returning home."

Johnathan: "Why does that quotation on that poster remind you of me? What's it saying to you about me?"

Counselor: "It's saying to me that you are concerned about what a college degree might mean for you and your attachment to your culture. For me, the poster is reassuring because it says,

JJ, that you don't leave your Indian culture behind because you attend State University. Your ancestors are also with you; they are in your memories that cannot be taken from you; they are an indivisible part of you as they peer out from you."

Johnathan: "Hey, that's almost Indian—what you just said. I don't have to leave State University because I carry my culture. I carry the drum inside of me."

Counselor: "Yes, that's exactly it. You're feeling conflict because of conflicting cultural loyalties. You want an education, but you don't want to lose your cultural identity. You don't want to become White. You just want an education so that you might help yourself, your family, and your Seneca Nation."

Johnathan: "That's exactly how I feel. Now I am sensing that I don't have to feel this conflict because the choices I've given myself are artificial. No person can make me less than a Seneca Indian. I am Senecan, and I will be such all my life—regardless of whether or not I get a college degree. And what is the second poster saying about me to you?"

Counselor: "This poster is another American Indian saying that reminded me of you. It says, *'When a storm is coming all other birds seek shelter. The eagle alone avoids the storm by flying above it. May your heart soar like an eagle.'* I am just wondering, JJ, if you need to fly above the storm that you are currently experiencing about State University, quitting the university, and returning home without your degree. I am wondering if you might consider letting go of your fear of selling out. You actually might let your dream about becoming a teacher take hold in your life."

Johnathan took a sip from his coffee cup, put it down very slowly, and said, "I'm going to talk with my family about what we talked about this weekend when I go home. I'm also going to consult one of the tribal leaders. They're always saying that we need more teachers who have their degrees so that we can teach our own children."

Johnathan: "We Senecas have a ceremony for letting go and letting in. Everything moves in a circle. There are always new beginnings and endings. That's how we see life."

Counselor: "I believe that the circle and the medicine wheel are beautiful parts of American Indian culture. It takes courage—from you and from me—to continue on our journey around the circle."

Harmony at Home and at College

The counselor moved during the therapy sessions to help Johnathan have a sense of internal peace and harmony—both within himself and at college. With Johnathan's permission, the counselor obtained a mentor who was a professor in Johnathan's major—teacher education. A meeting was scheduled between the two, and Johnathan seemed pleased that he had someone with whom he could establish a relationship at the university. She also put an ad in the university newspaper seeking people who might be interested in establishing an American Indian club on campus. She reached out to the tribal leader of the Seneca Nation to see if he would consider speaking at the university about the Seneca Nation's culture. Johnathan's family was also invited to attend the counseling sessions and to spend time with the counselor.

Because of his new mentor and other activities that the counselor has been instrumental in arranging, Johnathan has reported feeling less stressed and less confused. He feels more connected to the university, and his focus now is on how earning his college degree might help himself, his family, and the Seneca Nation.

Building a Healthy New Identity

Johnathan is well on his way to building a healthy new identity. He has organized a college support group at the Seneca Nation so that college students can express their concerns about attending a predominantly White university and leaving their Indian culture behind. He feels good about himself, and he periodically visits his counselor to tell her about his progress around his own specific circle of life. Johnathan is even talking about earning a PhD degree.

SUMMARY OF KEY POINTS

Clinicians working with American Indians and Alaska Natives must first learn their culture, values, and degree of cultural identity before attempting counseling. The majority of American clinicians do not have the cultural expertise to counsel American Indians and Alaska Natives from a deeply Indian perspective. Instead, it is recommended that non-Native clinicians use a blending of American Indian cultural techniques (those with which they feel comfortable) and conventional psychological interventions in an effort to empower members of this population (LaFromboise et al., 1990). The following are some counseling interventions clinicians might use:

- Promote cultural connections between what one does in the clinical interview with American Indians and Alaska Natives and their culture. For instance, the clinician might have pictures of Indian art in his or her office and use sage or have it available for clients to use.

- Address or examine the historical context of a client's problem. The clinician should become knowledgeable about cultural and financial resources within the community for American Indian people.

- Encourage positive cultural identity, using the cultural themes of spirituality, belonging, mastery, independence, and generosity (Brendtro et al., 1990). Some questions the clinician might ask are as follows:

Where do you belong? (belonging); What are you good at? (mastery); What are your strengths? What limits you? (independence); and What do you offer to others? (generosity).

- Become knowledgeable about the long history of trauma and oppression of American Indians and Alaska Natives.

- Become aware of problems, such as alcoholism and substance abuse, suicide, and domestic violence.

- Deal effectively with generational issues in acculturation.

- Work to increase the client's coping measures.

DISCUSSION QUESTIONS

Discussion Question set 1

Describe how historical events related to American Indians continue to have an impact on their communities today.

Discussion Question set 2

Identify three cultural challenges that confront non–American Indian counselors who work with American Indian clients. How can such counselors meet these challenges?

KEY TERMS

Alaska Native: A member of the aboriginal people of Alaska, including American Indians, Eskimo, and Aleut peoples.

American Indian: Someone who wants to be considered an American Indian must prove his or her status in terms of the legal definition established by the Bureau of Indian Affairs, an agency of the U.S. Department of the Interior. A person must have an Indian blood quantum of at least 25% to be considered an Indian and must have proof of tribal status. Garrett (2008) has stated, "Blood quantum refers to the percentage of ancestry that can be traced to people from [a given] tribe; it is literally a measure of blood" (p. 223).

Circle: In traditional American Indian life, the circle is a symbol of equality; it indicates that no person is more important than any other person. In circle meetings, all people are permitted to speak, and the words spoken are accepted and respected on an equal basis. There is no break in the circle, and it holds or contains that which cannot be broken. The circle is an important symbol in American Indian life, and oftentimes gatherings in pow-wow were organized in a series of circles. Dancing also occurred in the center of a circle formed by the drums and the audience.

Circle of courage: A counseling application of the medicine wheel used in working with young people. The model

integrates American Indian worldviews on childhood development and modern strengths-based approaches to address the needs of children by creating cultures of respect.

Cooperation and harmony: Highly valued in American Indian life. Because of a strong emphasis on the importance of a group, competition within the group is rare. Individuals can feel secure in being a member of the group and not being singled out or placed in a position above or below fellow members. One can, however, compete with one's own past performance.

Medicine wheel: A circle that represents natural and personal powers in complete balance and shows that everything is interconnected and part of the whole. It contains four directions, which are represented as points on the circle. These directions are often linked with different animals, colors, or characters in specific traditions. The wheel symbolizes the need for harmony and balance within oneself and with all creatures and people on earth.

Noninterference: An American Indian value associated with living.

Reservation: Land designated and set aside by the U.S. Bureau of Indian Affairs as a place where American Indians live.

Sharing and generosity: Traditional American Indians esteem the values of sharing and generosity. Possessions are considered a way for helping others. Generosity is considered evidence of a person's wisdom and humility. The respected Indian is not one who has large savings, but instead the person who gives generously.

Spirituality: The traditional spirituality of American Indians involves a way of honoring one's connection with Mother Earth. Traditional American Indians believe that people exist on earth to be helpers and protectors of life and that there is a single higher power known as Creator, Great Creator, Great Spirit, or Great One (Locust, 1998).

Talking circle: A type of group therapy in which individuals sit in a circle. Sage is sometimes burned to create a peaceful, calming, positive environment. Sage also communicates an acceptance of the culture and openness to providing comfort. The group leader opens the meeting by sharing a personal experience, which is followed by group members talking about their own experiences and feelings. Only one person talks at a time.

Tribe: An indigenous social grouping of American Indians connected by heritage, history, and culture. The tribe forms an important part of identity for many American Indians.

REFERENCES AND SUGGESTED READING

Alter, T. (2016). Native American tattoos: Turtle and dream-catcher. *Native Net*. Retrieved from http://www.native-net.org/na/native-american-tattoos.html

Ambler, M. (2003). Putting a name to cultural resilience. *Tribal College Journal, 14*(4), 8–9.

American Psychiatric Association. (2010). *Mental health disparities: American Indians and Alaska Natives*. Retrieved from https://www.integration.samhsa.gov/workforce/mental_health_disparities_american_indian_and_alaskan_natives.pdf

Aronowitz, N. W. (2014). Proud heritage: Mentors teach Native students about their pasts. *NBC News*. Retrieved from http://www.nbcnews.com-mentors-teach-native-students-about-their-pasts-n184271

Associated Press. (2008, August 28). 1 in 10 Native American deaths alcohol related. *NBC News*. Retrieved from http://www.nbcnews.com/id/26439767/ns/health-addictions/t/native-american-deaths-alcohol-related/#.VuU5UfkrKUk

Barcus, C. (2003). Recommendations for the treatment of American Indian population. In Council of National Psychological Associations for the Advancement of Ethnic Minority Interests (Ed.), *Psychological assessment of ethnic minority populations* (pp. 24–28). Washington, DC: Association of Black Psychologists.

Barnes, P. M., Adams, P. F., & Powell-Griner, E. (2010). Health characteristics of the American Indian or Alaska Native adult population: United States, 2004–2008. *National Health Statistics Reports, No. 20*. Hyattsville, MD: National Center for Health Statistics.

Beals, J., Manson, S. M., Whitesell, N. R., Spicer, P., Novins, D. K., & Mitchell, C. M. (2005). Prevalence of DSM-IV and attendant help-seeking in 2 American Indian reservation populations. *Archives of General Psychiatry, 62*(1), 99–108.

Beauvais, F. (1998). Cultural identification and substance abuse: An annotated bibliography. *Substance Use and Misuse, 33*, 1315–1336.

Bee-Gates, D., Howard-Pitney, B., LaFromboise, T., & Rowe, W. (1996). Help-seeking behavior of Native American Indian high school students. *Professional Psychology: Research and Practice, 27*, 495–499.

Bichsel, R. J., & Mallinckrodt, B. (2001). Cultural commitment and the counseling preferences and counselor perceptions of Native American women. *The Counseling Psychologist, 29*, 858–881.

BigFoot, D. S., & Braden, J. (1998). *On the back of a turtle*. Oklahoma City: University of Oklahoma Health Sciences Center.

BigFoot, D. S., & Funderburk, B. W. (2010, August). Honoring children, making relatives: Indigenous traditional parenting practices compatible with evidence-based treatment. *Communique*. Retrieved from http://www.apa.org/pi/oema/resources/communique/2010/08/indigenous-parenting.aspx

BigFoot, D. S., & Schmidt, S. (2010). Honoring children, mending the circle; Cultural adaptation of trauma-focused cognitive-behavioral therapy for American Indian and Alaska Native children. *Journal of Clinical Psychology, 66*, 847–856.

Brave Heart, M., Chase, J., Elkins, J., & Altschul, D. B. (2010). Historical trauma among indigenous peoples of the Americas: Concepts, research, and clinical considerations. *Journal of Psychoactive Drugs, 43*(4), 282–290.

Brave Heart, M., & Debruyn, L. M. (1998). The American Indian holocaust: Healing historical unresolved grief. *American Indian and Alaska Native Mental Health Research, 8*(2), 60–82.

Brendtro, L., Brokenleg, M., & Van Bockern, S. (1990). *Reclaiming youth at risk: Our hope for the future*. Bloomington, IN: National Education Service.

Brendtro, L., Brokenleg, M., & Van Bockern, S. (2002). *Reclaiming youth at risk: Our hope for the future* (Rev. ed.). Bloomington, IN: National Educational Services.

Cameron, S. C., & Turtle-Song, I. (2003). Native American mental health: An examination of resiliency in the face of overwhelming odds. In F. D. Harper & J. McFadden (Eds.), *Culture and counseling: New approaches* (pp. 66–80). Boston, MA: Allyn & Bacon.

Chartier, K., & Caetano, R. (2010). Ethnicity and health disparities in alcohol research. *Alcohol Research & Health*, *33*(1–2), 152–160.

Cruz, C. M., & Spence, J. (2005, August 7). *Oregon tribal evidence based and cultural best practices*. Retrieved from http://library.state.or.us/repository/2007/200710220 927381/index.pdf

Dufrene, P., & Coleman, V. D. (1992). Counseling Native Americans: Guidelines for group process. *Journal for Specialists in Group Work*, *17*(4), 229–234.

Espy, D. K., Jim, M. A., Cobb, N., Bartholomew, M., Becekr, T., Haverkamp, D., & Plescia, M. (2014). Leading causes of death and all-cause mortality in American Indians and Alaska Natives. *American Journal of Public Health, 104*(Suppl. 3), S303–S311.

Evans-Campbell, T. (2008). Historical trauma in American Indian/Native Alaska communities: A multilevel framework for exploring impacts on individuals, families, and communities. *Journal of Interpersonal Violence, 23*(3), 316–338.

Flynn, S. V., Olson, S. D., & Yellig, A. D. (2014). American Indian acculturation: Tribal lands to predominating White postsecondary settings. *Journal of Counseling and Development, 92*, 280–293.

Garcia, F. (2000). Warriors in education: Persistence among American Indian doctoral recipients. *Tribal College, 11*(3), 46–50.

Garrett, M. T. (2008). Native Americans. In M. T. Garrett (Ed.), *Culturally alert counseling: A comprehensive introduction* (pp. 220–254). Thousand Oaks, CA: Sage.

Garrett, M., Garrett, J., & Brotherton, D. (2001). Inner circle/outer circle: A group technique based on Native American healing circles. *Journal for Specialists in Group Work, 26*, 17–30.

Garrett, M. T., Garrett, J. T., Grayshield, L., Williams, C., Portman, T. A. A., Rivera, E. T., . . . Kawulich, B. (2013). Culturally alert counseling with Native Americans. In G. McAuliffe & Associates, *Culturally alert Counseling: A comprehensive introduction* (2nd ed., pp. 185–230). Thousand Oaks, CA: Sage.

Garrett, M. T., & Pichette, E. F. (2000). Red as an apple: Native American acculturation and counseling with or without reservation. *Journal of Counseling & Development, 78*(1), 3–13.

Garrett, M. T., & Portman, T. A. A. (2011). *Counseling Native Americans*. Belmont, CA: Cengage.

Garrod, A., & Larimore, C. (Eds.). (1997). *First persons, first peoples: Native American college graduates tell their life stories*. Ithaca, NY: Cornell University Press.

Gilgun, J. F. (2002). Completing the circle: American Indian medicine wheels and the promotion of resilience of children and youth in care. *Journal of Human Behavior in the Social Environment, 6*, 65–84.

Gone, J. P. (2009). A community-based treatment for Native American historical trauma: Prospects for evidence-based practice. *Journal of Counseling and Clinical Psychology, 40*(4), 468–478.

Gone, J. P. (2014). Reconsidering American Indian historical trauma: Lessons from an early Gros Ventre war narrative. *Transcultural Psychiatry, 51*, 387–406.

Gonzalez, J., & Bennett, R. (2011). Conceptualizing native identity with a multidimensional model. *American Indian and Alaska Native Mental Health Research, 17*(2), 22–42. Retrieved from http://www.ucdenver.edu/academics/col leges/PublicHealth/research/centers/CAIANH/journal/ Documents/Volume%2017/17(2)_%20Gonzalez_Native_ Identity_Multidimensional_Model_22-42.pdf

Goodkind, J., LaNoue, M., Lee, C., Freeland, L., & Freund, R. (2012). *Journal of Community Psychology, 40*(4), 466–478.

Gray, J. S., & Rose, W. J. (2012). Cultural adaptation for therapy with American Indians and Alaska Natives. *Journal of Multicultural Counseling and Development, 40*, 82–92.

Greer, M. (2004). Statistics show mental health services still needed for native populations. *APA Monitor on Psychology, 35*(9), 23.

Grieco, E. M., & Cassidy, R. C. (2001). *Overview of race and Hispanic origin: Census brief*. Washington, DC: U.S. Department of Commerce, Economics and Statistics Administration.

Guillory, R. (2008). It is about family: Native American student persistence in higher education. *Journal of Higher Education, 79*(10), 58–87.

Guillory, R. (2009). American Indian/Alaskan Native college student retention strategies. *Journal of Developmental Education, 33*(2), 12–21.

Halfe, L. (1993). Healing from a native perspective. *Cognica, 26*(1), 7–10.

Harris, E., & McFarland, J. (2000). *The assessment of cultural protective factors among Native Americans: The survey of Nez Perce culture*. Paper presented at the Annual Meeting of the American Evaluation Association, Honolulu, HI.

Hasin, D. S., Stinson, F. S., Ogburn, E., & Grant, B. F. (2007). Prevalence, correlates, disability, and comorbidity of DSM-IV alcohol abuse and dependence in the United States: Results from the National Epidemiologic Survey on alcohol and related conditions. *Archives of General Psychology, 64*, 830–842.

HeavyRunner, I., & DeCelles, R. (2002). Family education model: Meeting the student retention challenge. *Journal of American Indian Education, 41*(2), 29–37.

HeavyRunner, I., & Marshall, K. (2003). Miracle survivors: Promoting resilience in Indian students. *Tribal College Journal, 14*(4), 15–17.

Heilbron, C., & Guttman, M. (2000). Traditional healing methods with First Nations women in group counseling. *Canadian Journal of Counselling, 34*, 3–13.

Heit, M. (1987, March). Communication styles of Indian peoples. *AWASIS Journal*.

Herne, M. A., Bartholomew, M. L., & Weahkee, R. L. (2014). Suicide mortality among American Indians and Alaska Natives, 1999–2009. *American Journal of Public Health, 104*(Suppl. 3), S336–S342.

Herring, R. D. (1999). *Counseling with Native American Indians and Alaska Natives: Strategies for helping professionals.* Thousand Oaks, CA: Sage.

Horse, P. G. (2005). Native American identity. Wiley Online, Retrieved at https://doi.org/10.1002/ss.154.

Humes, K., Jones, N., & Ramirez, R. (2011). Overview of race and Hispanic origin: 2010. *2010 Census Briefs* (C201BR-02). U.S. Census Bureau. Retrieved from http://www.census.gov/prod/cen2010/briefs/c2010br-02.pdf

Jumper-Reeves, L., Dustman, P. A., Harthun, M. L., Kulis, S., & Brown, E. F. (2014). American Indian cultures. How CBPR illuminated intertribal cultural elements fundamental in an adaptation effort. *Prevention Science, 15*, 547–556.

Kanu, Y. (2006). Getting them through the college pipeline: Critical elements of instruction influencing school success among Native Canadian high school students. *Journal of Advanced Academics, 18*(1), 116–145.

Katz, R. (1993). *The straight path: A story of healing and transformation in Fiji.* Reading, MA: Addison-Wesley.

Kerbo, H. (1981). College achievement among Native Americans: A research note. *Social Forces, 59*(4), 1275–1280.

LaFromboise, T., Berman, J., & Sohl, B. (1994). American Indian women. In L. Comas-Díaz & B. Greene (Eds.), *Women of color: Integrating ethnic and gender identities in psychotherapy* (pp. 30–71). New York, NY: Guilford.

LaFromboise, T. D., & Dixon, D. N. (1981). American Indian perception of trustworthiness in a counseling interview. *Journal of Counseling Psychology, 28*, 135–139.

LaFromboise, T., Dizon, M. R. (2003). American Indian children and adolescents. In J. T. Gibbs & L. N. Huang (Eds.), *Children of color: Psychological interventions with culturally diverse youth.* San Francisco, CA: Jossey-Bass.

LaFromboise, T., Trimble, J. E., & Mohatt, G. (1990). Counseling intervention and American Indian tradition: An integrative approach. *Counseling Psychologist, 18*, 628–654.

Landen, M., Roeber, J., Naimi, T., Nielsen, L., & Sewell, M. (2014, June). Alcohol-attributable mortality among American Indians and Alaska Natives in the United States, 1999–2009. *American Journal of Public Health, 104*(Suppl. 3), S343–9.

Lee, C. C. (Ed.). (2002). *Multicultural issues in counseling: New approaches to diversity* (3rd ed.). Alexandria, VA: American Counseling Association.

Lee, C. C. (2014). Multicultural issues in counseling: New approaches to diversity (4th ed.). Hoboken, NJ: Wiley.

Light, R. (2003). Enhancing students' college experience with specific advising suggestions. *Academic Advising Today: Quarterly Newsletter.* Retrieved from http://www.nacada.ksu.edu/AAT/NW26_2.htm#light

Locust, C. (1985). Apache Beliefs about Unwellness and Handicaps". *Monograph.* Native American Research and Training Center, University of Arizona, Tucson.

Locust, C. (1998, September/October). Split feathers. *Pathways, 13*(4). National Indian Child Welfare Association Inc.

Lokken, J. M., & Twohey, D. (2004). American Indian perspectives of Euro-American counseling behavior. *Journal of Multicultural Counseling and Development, 32*, 320–331.

Martin, R. (2005). Serving American Indian students in tribal colleges: Lessons for mainstream colleges. *New Directions for Student Services, 109*, 79–86.

Maslow, A. H. (1943). A theory of human motivation. *Psychological Review, 50*(4), 370-396.

McCormick, R. M. (1997). First Nations counselor training in British Columbia: Strengthening the circle. *Canadian Journal of Community Mental Health, 16*(2), 91–99.

Moodley, R., & West, W. (2005). *Integrating traditional healing practices into counseling and psychotherapy.* Thousand Oaks, CA: Sage.

Myhra, L. L. (2011). "It runs in the family": Intergenerational transmission of historical trauma among urban American Indians and Alaska Natives in culturally specific sobriety maintenance programs. *American Indian and Alaska Native Mental Health Research, 18*, 17–40.

Norris, T., Vines, P. L., & Hoeffel, E. M. (2012, January). The American Indian and Alaska Native population: 2010. *2010 Census Briefs* (C2010BR-10). U.S. Census Bureau. Retrieved from http://www.census.gov/prod/cen2010/briefs/c2010br-10.pdf

Office of Minority Health. (2012). *Mental health and American Indians/Alaska Natives*. Retrieved from http://minority health.hhs.gov/omh/browse.aspx?lvl=48lvllD=39

Paniagua, F. A. (2014). *Assessing and treating culturally diverse clients: A practical guide* (4th ed.). Thousand Oaks, CA: Sage.

Reimer, C. S. (1999). *Counseling the Inupiat Eskimo*. Westport, CT: Greenwood.

Russell, G. (1997). *American Indian facts of life*. Phoenix, AZ: Russell. http://dx.doi.org/10.1037/h0054346

Saltzman, M. (2001). Cultural trauma and recovery: Perspectives from terror management theory. *Trauma, Violence, and Abuse, 2*, 172–191.

Salzman, P. C. (2001). *Understanding culture: An introduction to anthropological theory*. Prospect Heights, IL: Waveland Press.

Shukovsky, P. (2001, March 29). "Urban Indians" are going home. *Seattle Post Intelligencer*, pp. A1, A13.

Sotero, M. M. (2006). A conceptual model of historical trauma: Implications for public health practice and research. *Journal of Health Disparities Research and Practice, 1*(1), 93–108.

Thomason, T. C. (2000). Issues in the treatment of Native Americans with alcohol problems. *Journal of Multicultural Counseling and Development, 28*, 243–252.

Thomason, T. (2012). Recommendations for counseling Native Americans: Results of a survey. *Journal of Indigenous Research, 1*(2), Article 4. Retrieved from http://digitalcom mons.usu.edu/kicjir/vol1/iss2/4

Trimble, J. E. (2010). The virtues of cultural resonance, competence, and relational collaboration with Native American Indian communities: A synthesis of the counseling literature. *The Counseling Psychologist, 38*(2), 243–256.

Trimble, J. E. (2012). Working with North American Indian and Alaska Native clients: Understanding the deep culture within. In M. E. Gallardo, C. J. Yeh, J. E. Trimble, and T. A. Parham (Eds.), *Culturally adaptive counseling skills: Demonstrations of evidence-based practices* (pp. 181–200). Thousand Oaks, CA: Sage.

Trimble, J. E., & Dickson, R. (2005). Ethnic identity. In C. B. Fisher & R. M. Lerner (Eds.), *Encyclopedia of applied developmental science* (Vol. *1*, pp. 415–420). Thousand Oaks, CA: Sage.

Trimble, J. E., & Gonzalez, J. (2008). Cultural considerations and perspectives for providing psychological counseling for Native American Indians. In P. B. Pedersen, J. G. Draguns, W. J. Lonner, & J. E. Trimble (Eds.), *Counseling across cultures* (6th ed., pp. 93–111). Thousand Oaks, CA: Sage.

Trimble, J. E., Helms, J., & Root, M. (2003). Social and psychological perspectives on ethnic and racial identity. In G. Bernal, J. Trimble, K. Burlew, & F. Leong (Eds.), *Handbook of racial and ethnic minority psychology* (pp. 239–275). Thousand Oaks, CA: Sage.

Trimble, J. E., & Thurman, P. (2002). Ethnocultural considerations and strategies for providing counseling services for American Indians. In P. Pedersen, J. Draguns, W. Lonner, & J. Trimble (Eds.), *Counseling across cultures* (5th ed., pp. 53–91). Thousand Oaks, CA: Sage.

U.S. Census Bureau. (2010a). *American Community Survey (ACS): Race/ethnicity and American Indian and Alaska Native data*. Retrieved from https://www.census.gov/pro grams-surveys/acs/data/race-aian.2010.html

U.S. Census Bureau. (2010b). *Median income in the past 12 months: 2010 American Community Survey—1 year estimates*. Washington, DC: U.S. Government Printing Office.

U.S. Census Bureau. (2012, October 25). American Indian and Alaska Native Heritage Month: November 2012. *Profile America: Facts for Features*. Retrieved from https://www .census.gov/newsroom/releases/archives/facts_for_fea tures_special_editions/cb12-ff22.html

Whitekiller, V. (2004). *Cultural resilience: Factors that influence the graduation of Native American college students* (Doctoral dissertation, Oklahoma State University). Retrieved from http://asu.edu/etd/

Witko, T. M. (2006). *Mental health care for urban Indians: Clinical insights from native practitioners*. Washington, DC: American Psychological Association.

Zahran, H. S., Kobau, R., Moriarty, D. G., Zack, M. M., Giles, W. H., & Lando, J. (2004). Self-reported frequent mental distress among adults—United States, 1993–2001. *Morbidity and Mortality Weekly Report, 53*(41), 963–966.

10 CULTURALLY RESPONSIVE STRENGTHS-BASED THERAPY FOR ASIAN AMERICANS, NATIVE HAWAIIANS, AND PACIFIC ISLANDERS

- *"A nation's treasure is in its scholars."* —Chinese proverb

- *"Life is for one generation; a good name is forever."* —Japanese proverb

- *"The person who knows himself and his opponent will be invincible. Carve a peg only after you have observed the hole."* —Korean proverb

- *"Every kind of animal can be tamed, but not the tongue of man."* —Filipino proverb

- *"When eating a fruit, think of the person who planted the tree."* —Vietnamese proverb

- *"Life is like a lamp flame; it needs a little oil now and then."* —Asian Indian proverb

- *"The way to authority is through service."* —Samoan proverb

CHAPTER OBJECTIVES

- Become knowledgeable about the demographics and population statistics of Asian Americans and Pacific Islanders.

- Analyze ethnic/racial stereotypes and microaggressions against Asian Americans and Pacific Islanders.

- Understand the worldviews of Asian Americans and Pacific Islanders.

- Recognize the cultural values of Asian Americans and Pacific Islanders, including the values of collectivism, family, education, hard work, and communication style.

- Learn the cultural strengths of Asian Americans and Pacific Islanders.

- Comprehend Asian American and Pacific Islander mental health challenges, acculturation conflicts, help-seeking attitudes, and expectations about counseling.

- Learn the cultural factors to take into consideration for counseling Asian Americans and Pacific Islanders.

INTRODUCTION

This chapter addresses the cultural, demographic, political, and counseling issues associated with Asian Americans and Pacific Islanders living in the United States. Members of this large group trace their original background to the Far East, Southeast Asia, the Indian subcontinent, and the islands of the Pacific Ocean. In recent years, Asians have surpassed Hispanics as the largest group of new immigrants to the United States. Almost three-quarters (74%) of Asian American adults were born abroad, and of this group, about half state that they speak English very well (see "The Rise of Asian Americans," 2013, p. 2).

Asian American ethnic and cultural groups differ vastly in their history, language, traditions, customs, religion, values, immigration history, and exposure to war trauma. Each country of an Asian subgroup has its own unique history, culture, language, religious beliefs, and pathways to the United States. Because of their common geographic origins, Asian American and Pacific Islander ethnic groups are often treated as a single ethnocultural group (B. Kim & Park, 2008), notably as a single category in U.S. Census Bureau data. As Nadal, Escobar, Prado, David, and Haynes (2012) have stated, "when Asian Americans are described in counseling and psychology, they are often lumped as a homogeneous group with similar values, family systems, and mental health experiences. This assumption can be problematic because of the heterogeneity of the Asian American community" (p. 156). Yet, despite their considerable differences between groups and within groups, Asian Americans are distinctive as a whole when compared with all U.S. adults, "whom they exceed not just in the share with a college degree (49% vs. 28%), but also in median annual household income ($66,000 versus $49,800) and median household wealth ($84,500 vs. $68,529)" ("The Rise of Asian Americans," 2013, p. 3).

Although this chapter is about Asian Americans and Pacific Islanders as a group, the Asian American population contains at least 43 individual ethnic groups with varying cultural backgrounds (Asian & Pacific Islander American Health Forum, 2011). Space limitations for this chapter make it impossible to write in depth about any one member of this broad ethnic/racial category, and therefore, it is recommended that the reader consider obtaining additional information about specific groups within the Asian American and Pacific Islander category. It is difficult to place so many different ethnic groups under the homogeneous heading of Asian American when, in fact, some of the groups have historically engaged in wars against each other. Yet there are important similarities that they share, including their geographic origin in the Asia-Pacific region of the globe. The intent of this chapter is to reach a middle ground in describing Asian Americans and Pacific Islanders—that is, to present an overview of their similarities while acknowledging the differences between and within ethnic groups.

DEMOGRAPHIC AND POPULATION STATISTICS

Who Are Asian Americans and Pacific Islanders? A Census Definition

The definition of Asian used in the 2010 U.S. Census is as follows: "'Asian' refers to a person having origins in any of the original people of the Far East, Southeast Asia, or the Indian subcontinent, including, for example, Cambodia, China, India, Japan, Korea, Malaysia, Pakistan, the Philippine Islands, Thailand, and Vietnam. The Asian population includes people who indicated their race(s) as 'Asian' or reported entries such as 'Asian Indian,' 'Chinese,' 'Filipino,' 'Korean,' 'Japanese,' and 'Vietnamese' or provided other detailed Asian responses" (Hoeffel, Rastogi, Ouk Kim, & Shahid, 2012, p. 2).

From the above, it is clear that the Asian American and Pacific Islander category includes a broad range of different nationalities and ethnic groups. However, six major ethnic groups account for more than 95% of the Asian American and Pacific Islander population: Chinese, Filipino, Japanese, Asian Indian, Korean, and Vietnamese. In many contexts, "East Asian" refers to the various ethnic groups with origins in China, Korea, and Japan; "Southeast Asian" refers to people with origins in Vietnam through Burma (the region historically known as Indochina) and the Malay archipelago; "Asian Indian" refers to the various ethnic groups with origins in India and neighboring nations; and **Pacific Islander** refers to Melanesian, Micronesian, Native Hawaiian, and Polynesian ethnic groups.

The 2010 U.S. Census defined Asian American and Pacific Islander individuals in terms of two categories: "Asian alone"—that is, those who reported only a single detailed Asian group such as "Chinese" or "Japanese"—and Asian in combination with one or more other ethnic groups/races such as Chinese and White or Filipino and African American (Hoeffel et al., 2012).

The 2010 Census data revealed that 14.7 million people, or 4.8% of U.S. residents, were Asian American alone. Another 2.6 million people reported that they were Asian in combination with one or more other races or ethnic groups. When combined, these two groups totaled 17.3 million people, or approximately 5.6% of all people in the United States ("The Rise of Asian Americans," 2013).

The Asian American population increased more than four times faster than the total U.S. population in the early 21st century. In the decade from 2000 to 2010, while the total U.S. population grew from 281.4 million to 308.7 million (a 9.7% increase), the Asian alone population grew from 10.2 million to 14.7 million (a 43% increase), and the overall Asian American alone-or-in-combination group grew by 46%. Three years later, by April 2013, the Asian American and Pacific Islander population had grown from 17.3 million to 19.4 million, including both the "alone" and "combined" U.S. Census Bureau designations ("The Rise of Asian Americans," 2013).

Multiple-Race Reporting for Asian Americans

Nearly 15% of the Asian American population reported multiple races. The largest multiple-race combination was Asian and White, with this group forming 1.6 million people (9% of the overall Asian population). The next-largest Asian combinations were "Asian and Some Other Race" (9%), "Asian and Black" (7%), "Asian and Native Hawaiian and Other Pacific Islander" (6%), and "Asian and White and Native Hawaiian and Other Pacific Islander" (5%). These five combinations accounted for almost 90% of all Asian Americans who reported multiple races. The Asian and White multiple ethnic/racial group combination had the greatest increase in growth (an 87% increase between 2000 and 2010), followed by the Asian and Black population, which increased from 6% to 7% (Hoeffel et al., 2012).

The Asian American population is heavily concentrated in the western part of the United States, with 46% living in the West, 22% in the South, 20% in the Northeast, and 12% in the Midwest. In the West, Asian Americans constitute 11% of the total population, compared to 6% in the Northeast and 3% in both the South and the Midwest.

In 2010, about three-quarters (75%) of all Asian Americans lived in 10 states: California (5.6 million), New York (1.6 million), Hawaii (0.8 million), New Jersey (0.8 million), Texas (0.7 million), Illinois (0.7 million), Washington (0.6 million), Florida (0.6 million), Virginia (0.5 million), and Pennsylvania (0.5 million). The proportional representation of Asian Americans is growing in key states. In Hawaii, Asian Americans represented over 50% of the total population. In the following five states, they constituted 8% or more of the total population: California (15%), New Jersey (9%), Nevada (9%), Washington (9%), and New York (8%).

Subgroup Representation of Asian American Groups

According to the 2010 Census, the detailed Asian groups with one million or more responses for the Asian alone-or-in-any-combination population were Chinese, Filipino, Asian Indian, Vietnamese, Korean, and Japanese. The Chinese population was the largest in-combination Asian group, with 4.0 million people who reported Chinese alone with no additional identified Asian group or race category. The Filipino (3.4 million) and Asian Indian (3.2 million) populations were the second- and third-largest detailed Asian groups. Of the identified Asian groups with one or more alone-or-in-any-combination populations, Japanese, Filipino, Chinese, Vietnamese, and Korean populations were more heavily concentrated in the West. The largest proportion of each group lived in California ("The Rise of Asian Americans," 2013).

Cultural Reflections

What are your thoughts and feelings about Asian Americans and Pacific Islanders?

Do you have or have you ever had any Asian American or Pacific Islander friends?

Would you ever choose an Asian American or Pacific Islander as a friend?

Cultural Reflections

Most Americans believe that Hispanics are the fastest-growing ethnic minority group in the United States.

What are your thoughts and feelings about Asian Americans and Pacific Islanders being the fastest-growing ethnic minority category within this country?

HISTORICAL CHANGES IN THE ASIAN AMERICAN PROFILE

With immigration comes a complex societal drama that plays out in the social, economic, religious, political, and cultural realms among the immigrants themselves, their descendants, and the United States as a whole. The current profile of Asian Americans differs drastically from the one they had a century ago. In the early years, Asian Americans were initially drawn to this country by opportunities to work in low-skilled occupations. In the early 20th century, a series of racially motivated anti-immigration laws blocked Asian American and Pacific Islander immigration (except those from the Philippines, which was then an American territory), and culminated in the National Origins Act of 1924. The majority of Japanese Americans in the United States today are the descendants of Japanese who migrated to Hawaii or to the continental United States before 1924.

In 1965, Asian Americans constituted less than 1% of the American population, primarily because their numbers were restricted by an entire century of exclusionary immigrant policies based on their ethnic group/race membership (B. Kim & Park, 2013). That year is noteworthy because it was the height of the civil rights movement and a robust economy, and as a result, the U.S. government opened the doors to immigration from all over the globe, including Asia. The decision to permit Asians the right to immigrate to the United States was transformative. The Immigration and Nationality Act of 1965 resulted in new opportunities for immigrants from Asian countries, especially for high-skilled workers, and it led to the immigration of a large number of Chinese, Korean, and Filipino citizens.

The end of the Vietnam War in 1975 brought about a large number of Southeast Asian refugees. In 1978, another wave of Asian Americans came to the United States to escape persecution, including the Vietnamese, Chinese-Vietnamese, Cambodians, Laotians, Hmong, and Mien.

The situation of Asian Americans and Pacific Islanders improved when, in 1978, a joint congressional resolution established Asian/Pacific American Heritage Week. The congressional resolution chose the first 10 days of May to coincide with two important milestones in Asian/Pacific American history: the arrival in the United States of the first Japanese immigrants (May 7, 1843) and the contributions of Chinese workers in building the transcontinental railroad, which was completed on May 10, 1869.

Some 14 years later in 1992, Congress expanded the Asian/Pacific American History Week to a monthlong observance. In 1997, a U.S. Office of Management and Budget directive mandated that the Asian or Pacific Islander racial category be separated into two categories: (1) Asian and (2) Native Hawaiian or Other Pacific Islander.

From their 1% population representation in the United States in 1965, Asian Americans currently make up nearly 6% of the U.S. population. In a computer age and technology economy, Asian Americans and Pacific Islanders are the "highest-income, best-educated and fastest-growing" American ethnic/racial group in the country ("The Rise of Asian Americans," 2013, p. 1). Recent Asian immigrants are about three times more likely as are recent immigrants from other parts of the world to receive their green cards—or permanent resident status—on the basis of employment instead of through family sponsorship.

By 2010, Asians had become the largest group of new immigrants to the United States. Many Asian immigrants come to the United States with master's degrees, PhDs, and medical degrees without the staggering student loan debt many American students bear. The difference in educational attainment by Asian Americans and Pacific Islanders has resulted in a huge income disparity or difference between Asian and White Americans—and, in fact, an income disparity in their favor with all other American ethnic groups.

Intermarriage and the Asian American Population

The tendency toward interethnic/interracial marriage is another factor that may have contributed to the success of Asian Americans in U.S. society. In 2016, Asian Americans were the most likely of any major ethnic or racial group in this country to live in mixed neighborhoods and to marry across racial lines. Consider this: When Priscilla Chan, a medical school graduate, married Facebook founder Mark Zuckerberg, she joined the ranks of the 37% of all recent Asian brides who wed a member of a non-Asian ethnic group. Intermarriage, especially with White Americans, has been one way that Asian Americans have been able to gain acceptance by the dominant society, and most likely contributes to the high percentage of them living in either mixed neighborhoods or predominantly White communities (see "The Rise of Asian Americans," 2013).

SOCIOECONOMIC STATUS OF ASIAN AMERICANS AND PACIFIC ISLANDERS: 2013

In 2013, the median income for the Asian alone population grew to $72,474, approximately $6,000 more than that reported in the 2010 Census data. The median household income differed according to one's subgroup membership. For instance, for Asian Indians, the median income in 2013 was $100,547, but for those from Bangladesh, it was $51,331 (U.S. Census Bureau, 2015). Please note that most of the data presented in the section on socioeconomic status comes from an April 29, 2015, U.S. Census Bureau report.

In general, Asian American and Pacific Islander ethnic groups tended to have higher annual incomes than the overall U.S. population, including annual incomes for White Americans. Asian Indians and the Taiwanese had the highest median household and family, as well as per capita, incomes, and other Asian groups had consistently high median household, median family, and per capita incomes—much higher than the national figures for White Americans, African Americans, Hispanics (Latinos), and Native Americans.

The Asian American and Pacific Islander ethnic groups with the lowest median family, median household, and per capita incomes were Bangladeshi, Hmong, and Cambodian; their incomes were also lower than those for the U.S. population.

In 2013, the poverty rate for the Asian alone population was 12.7%. The percentage of the Asian alone population 25 and older who had a bachelor's degree or higher level of education was 51.3%, compared with 29.6% for all Americans 25 and older. The percentage of 25-and-older Asian alone population who had a graduate or professional degree was 21.6%, compared with 11.2% for all Americans 25 and older (U.S. Census Bureau, 2015).

Native Hawaiians and Other Pacific Islanders: Socioeconomic Issues

Recently, the White House conducted an initiative to disaggregate U.S. Census data on Asian Americans and Pacific Islanders after a campaign from Native Hawaiian and Other Pacific Islander citizens argued grouping the ethnic groups together masked the true needs of the Native Hawaiian and Other Pacific Islander community. The White House initiative reported that the Native Hawaiian and Other Pacific Islander population had high rates of smoking, drinking, and obesity, with the leading causes of death in the Native Hawaiian and Other Pacific Islander community including heart disease, cancer, stroke, diabetes, and accidental injuries.

According to the U.S. Census Bureau, 17.6% of the Native Hawaiian and Other Pacific Islander community lived below the poverty line in comparison to a national poverty rate of 11.7% for Asians and 11.0% for Whites (Macartney, Bishaw, & Fontenot, 2013).

ASIAN AMERICANS AS THE "MODEL ETHNIC MINORITY": MYTH OR REALITY?

According to a 2013 Pew Research Center study, "Asian Americans are the highest-income, best-educated and fastest-growing racial group in the United States. They are more satisfied than the general public with their lives, finances, and the direction of the country, and they place more value than other Americans do on marriage, parenthood, hard work and career success" ("The Rise of Asian Americans," 2013, p. 1). The success of Asian Americans, as indicated by findings such as these, has led researchers and the dominant White American society to label them the "**model minority**" (Bell, Harrison, & McLaughlin, 1997; Hsia & Peng, 1998). William Peterson (1966) first coined the term, generalizing that Asian Americans function well in society, are relatively free from negative racial discrimination, and experience few adjustment difficulties (B. Kim & Park, 2013). Support for the "model minority" thesis can be found in the Asian cultural values of diligence, frugality, emphasis on educational and occupational achievement, and the ability to maintain "**face**" in the light of adversity (Crystal 1989; B. Kim, Atkinson, & Yang, 1999).

Some, however, object to the use of the label of model minority (Sandhu, Leung, & Tang, 2003). For instance, they point out that poverty rates are especially high among Hmong, Guamanian, Indonesian, and Cambodian immigrants. According to the U.S. Department of Labor (2015), "the [Asian American and Pacific Islander] community has the second highest share of unemployed workers who are long-term unemployed (30.2 percent) . . . The Vietnamese community has the highest share of long-term unemployed workers (41.5 percent)."

Moreover, the high educational attainment described earlier does not apply to all Asian American and Pacific Islander groups. Only 40% of the Hmong have completed high school, and less than 14% of Tongan, Cambodian, Laotian, and Hmong adults have a bachelor's degree (U.S. Census Bureau, 2015).

In many major cities in the United States, there are Asian American enclaves (e.g., Chinatown in New York, Japantown in San Francisco) where problems of unemployment, poverty, and juvenile delinquency are endemic. Asian Americans from lower-income groups and recently arrived refugees are experiencing limited access to health care as well as linguistic, cultural, financial, and systemic barriers. Critics of the Asian American "model minority" label argue that this label prevents Asian Americans from receiving the amount of assistance and opportunities they need in governmental aid and programs (Sandhu et al., 2003).

Cultural Reflections

Do you believe that Asian Americans and Pacific Islanders form the model minority group in the United States? Explain your thoughts and feelings.

Is the "model minority" label something that reflects positively on Asian Americans and Pacific Islanders, or is it a stereotype that harms members of this group?

ETHNIC/RACIAL STEREOTYPES, RACISM, AND MICROAGGRESSIONS

As noted in the section on historical changes in the Asian American profile, people of Asian descent have historically been subjected to racism and discrimination in the United States. In *Discrimination in America: Experiences and View of Asian Americans*, based on a survey conducted for National Public Radio, the Robert Wood Johnson Foundation, and the Harvard T.H. Chan School of Public Health (2017), it was reported that Asian Americans born in the United States report more discrimination than Asian immigrants. Overall, Asian Americans reported numerous personal experiences of discrimination across many areas. According to the report, "a quarter or more of Asian Americans say they have been personally discriminated against because they are Asian when applying for jobs (27%), when being paid equally or considered for promotions (25%), and when trying to rent or buy housing (25%)" (p. 1).

Some Americans commit microaggressions when they falsely assume that every Asian American they meet has just recently arrived to this country or cannot speak English very well (Sue, Bucceri, Lin, Nadal, & Torino, 2009). They may express surprise that an Asian American speaks English without a foreign accent, or ask such questions as "When did you come to this country?" of a native U.S. citizen who can trace his family heritage to three generations born in the United States (Ong, Burrow, Fuller-Rowell, Ja, & Sue, 2013).

Sue and colleagues (2009) investigated racial microaggressions against Asian Americans using a focus group analysis of 10 self-identified Asian American participants utilizing a semistructured interview format. The participants identified eight major microaggression themes directed toward Asian Americans: (1) alien in one's own land, (2) the attribution of intelligence to them, (3) exoticizing Asian women, (4) invalidation of interethnic differences, (5) denial of racial reality, (6) pathologizing cultural values and communication styles, (7) second-class citizenship, and (8) invisibility. Participants reported that racism directed toward them was often subtle rather than overt. As Sue et al. stated,

> Asian Americans, for example, may be more likely to experience microaggressions with themes that revolve around "alien in own land," "invisibility," and "invalidation of interethnic differences" than African Americans. This statement is not meant to suggest that Blacks may not also be victim to these racial microaggression themes, but they may be more prone to experience racial microaggressions around other themes like "assumption of criminal status" and "color blindness" than Asian Americans. (p. 98).

CULTURAL ISSUES OF ASIAN AMERICANS AND PACIFIC ISLANDERS

Worldviews of Asian Americans and Pacific Islanders

Each culture espouses a worldview, which can be conceptualized as shared beliefs, values, and assumptions that a person uses to make sense of his or her life experiences that are hidden deep within the norms, customs, and traditions of the surrounding society. A worldview influences how we see ourselves (Triandis, 1989). It gives us messages about who we are, who we should strive to become, and how we should relate to others. Worldviews give our lives a sense of coherence, a sense of meaning, connection, and purpose. The worldviews of the many Asian American and Pacific Islander cultures generally involve a collectivistic orientation, a strong family bond, a time orientation that is long-term, and a high-context communication style (Duan & Wang, 2000). Asian American worldviews are discussed in the following sections that deal with the values of this broad and varied group.

Collectivistic Versus Individualistic Orientation

Most Western cultures, including the U.S. dominant culture, are individualistically oriented, while most Eastern cultures (Asian Americans and Pacific Islanders) have a **collectivistic orientation** (Triandis, 1995). The most relevant feature of individualism is valuing one's independence and putting an emphasis on personal responsibility and freedom of choice, personal autonomy, and achieving self-fulfillment (Sandhu et al., 2003). People who advocate an individualistic worldview or value are inclined to ask the following questions or statements: "What do I gain from completing this service or act?" "What are my individual rights in this situation?" "How is this going to benefit me?" They emphasize that they are distinct and unique, versus "I am a member of a family or tribe." They emphasize their duty to themselves rather than their duty to the group, and they are more concerned about how their behavior will affect themselves instead of how it will affect others.

In individualistic cultures, people are taught to be self-reliant, creative, and assertive (Duan & Wang, 2000). Members of individualistic cultures tend to belong to many groups, but their affiliation with them is short-lived because they are designed to enhance their self-worth (Triandis, 1995). People with an individualistic perspective give priority to their own personal goals over the collective ones of the group. They tend to honor horizontal interpersonal relationships more so than vertical ones.

In contrast, collectivistic cultures suppress individual rights, needs, and desires for the benefit and welfare of the group. Members of such cultures feel a strong sense of commitment to and obligation in satisfying the interests and goals of the group, especially the interests of one's family or one's work group. They place family members' needs, the needs of the work group, and the needs of their nation ahead of their own individual desires (Duan & Wang, 2000).

A collectivistic or group orientation helps to maintain family and work group solidarity. For instance, in Asian and Pacific Islander cultures, people reconcile differences of opinion in order to retain harmony within the group. Asian Americans who adopt a collectivistic perspective put a great value on showing respect for other people's feelings, and in doing so, they foster a spirit of cohesiveness. Individuals understand the reciprocity that results from submitting one's goals and wishes for the benefit of the family or work group (E. Lee, 1997). People with a strong collectivistic view subordinate their personal goals for collective ones; they are concerned about the effect of their behavior on others. One often sees the collectivistic orientations of Olympic athletes from Asian countries when they respond that they practiced and exceled for the honor of their nation—much more so than for their own individual honor.

Cultural Values of Asian Americans and Pacific Islanders

Although this section examines Asian American and Pacific Islander cultural values, it must be pointed out that the cultural values described below apply mainly to Chinese, Filipino, Japanese, and Korean Americans (B. Kim & Park, 2013). Furthermore, even with these groups, there are significant differences in terms of such values as collectivism, emotional self-control, family honor through achievement, filial piety, and humility. In particular, Filipino Americans demonstrate less adherence to emotional self-control than the other three major Asian American groups, less adherence to filial piety than Japanese and Korean Americans, and less adherence to collectivism than Japanese Americans (B. Kim & Park, 2013). It is with these differences in mind that the following sections on Asian American values are presented.

Cultural Reflections

Would you label your worldview as collectivistic (oriented toward the group) or individualistic (oriented toward the individual)?

What are the benefits of a collectivistic and an individualistic point of view?

High Value on Education and Hard Work

In traditional Asian cultures, people with advanced education are held in high esteem. For instance, teachers are treated with great respect—contrast this cultural value with the oft-quoted quip by George Bernard Shaw, "Those who can, do. Those who can't, teach." In general, Asians do not evaluate their teachers at the end of the year the way that Americans do. Most Asian families make educational and occupational achievement a top priority (E. Lee, 1997; Sue & Sue, 2003).

Family Hierarchical Structure, Family Values, and Parenting Styles

The family structure of the majority of Asian Americans and Pacific Islanders is patriarchal and **hierarchical**, with males and older family members having a higher status (B. Kim & Park, 2013). Traditional Asian families place a high value on the family unit instead of the individual. A family member is viewed as the product of all the generations of his or her family (E. Lee, 1997). Family rituals such as ancestor worship, family celebrations, funeral rights, and genealogy records support the view that Asians hold the family in great regard. One's actions reflect on the family unit.

Family members are expected to live according to their clearly defined roles and positions in the family hierarchy, based on age, gender, and social class. Favoritism exists toward males, and there may be specific roles for the oldest son (especially the Chinese oldest son and brother) and the oldest daughter. The traditional role of a mother is to provide support, while the father's role is to discipline. There are, however, some differences in Asian families. Of the six major Asian American groups identified in this chapter, Japanese are the most acculturated; they trace their heritage for more than four generations in the United States. Whereas Filipino American families tend to be more egalitarian in nature, Korean, Southeast Asian, and Chinese American families are more patriarchal and collectivist in outlook. Communication in traditional Asian families is also of a hierarchical nature, in that communication flows downward from parents to children (Lau, Fung, & Yung, 2010).

> ## Cultural Reflections
>
> *In your opinion, what are the strengths of an Asian American family? Disadvantages?*
>
> *Is there any particular Asian American or Pacific Islander ethnic group that you feel especially drawn to in a positive manner? Explain.*

Five Types of Asian American Families

E. Lee (1997) has proposed that Asian American families are in transition and that there are five types or categories of such families. She points out that these five types of Asian American families are hypothetical constructs, rather than evidence-based findings, that help to elucidate the various family acculturation experiences in this country.

Type 1—The Traditional Asian American Family. These types of Asian American families ascribe to and maintain the traditional family values of their ethnocultural heritage. These families may have recently immigrated to the United States, or they may live in ethnic enclaves, such as Chinatown or Koreatown, and have limited contact with mainstream American society.

Type 2—The "Cultural Conflict" Asian American Family. In this type of family, members may ascribe to different cultural values. The cultural conflict Asian American family is characterized by different rates of acculturation regarding the dominant American societal values. Differences are also observed in the values and expectations of their parents. As E. Lee (1997) has explained, whereas traditional Asian American parents expect their children to share their own values of hard work and respect for elders, their children may have picked up American values that emphasize autonomy and assertiveness. In the culturally conflicted Asian American family, parents and their children may argue over dating, marriage, school, and jobs. Conflict may also arise when children are more closely connected with American culture or speak better English than their parents and have to assist their relatives with navigating traditional American society.

Type 3—The Bicultural Asian American Family. A large proportion of these Asian American families have well-acculturated parents who immigrated to the United States several decades ago. Members of these families often hold professional degrees, have relatively high incomes, and live in mixed interethnic/interracial neighborhoods. Usually, family members are bilingual and bicultural, and they have transitioned from a patriarchal to an egalitarian relationship between parents and children. Many of these families have adopted the nuclear family structure of the dominant American society, and they may visit extended family members on weekends and holidays.

Type 4—The Americanized Family. Americanized families have at least two generations of parents and children who were born in the United States. These families communicate in English only, tend not to maintain their ethnocultural identities, adopt an egalitarian family structure, and hold an individualistic worldview.

Type 5—The Interracial Asian Family. As noted in the section on demographics, the percentage of interracial marriages among Asian Americans is steadily increasing. Japanese Americans lead this trend with more than half marrying outside their ethnic group, followed by Filipino, Chinese, Vietnamese, and Korean Americans (E. Lee, 1997). Whereas some

Cultural Reflections

Of the five Asian American family types, which do you feel closest to? Why?

How might you consider using the Asian American family in counseling treatment?

interracial families are able to integrate both cultures, others may experience conflicts in values, religious beliefs, communication styles, and relationships with in-laws.

The Suppression of Family Problems: Self-Control, Emotional Restraint, and Shaming

Asian Americans endorse the values of self-control and restraint of emotionality (Sue & Sue, 2003). Self-control is demonstrated by showing poise and calmness during highly emotional experiences, maintaining dignity when confronted with pain or suffering, and sustaining **humility** and appropriate behavior for the situation. It is expected that family members will demonstrate their inner stamina and strength to tolerate crisis and stress. One consequence of the emphasis on self-control is that Asians may be unwilling to acknowledge or own strong emotion, including grief or pain, due to their family actions and cultural values. Some Western or American psychologists may find the stoic demeanors of Asian people difficult to penetrate and to interpret (Kramer, Kwong, Lee, & Chung, 2002). Humility may be manifested not by emphasizing one's own accomplishments, but instead by pointing out the contributions of others.

Moreover, most Asian families have unwritten rules about discussing or divulging family problems outside the family (Leong, Lee, & Chang, 2008). Problems are to be shared only among family members. Asians tend to use the technique of **shame** and shaming to help enforce societal expectations and proper behavior in their culture (Leong et al., 2008). If a person is shamed by his actions or by the treatment of family members, he loses "face" with others. The fear of **losing face**, or of not having a high enough status in the eyes of one's significant others, prevents many Asians from acknowledging their problems in public or to anyone outside their families.

Asian Americans tend to give deference to authority figures, age, and intelligence. They assume that their ancestors and elders have more wisdom than they do. In many traditional Asian American families, members feel a strong sense of obligation to the family unit. Honor and duty to one's family is extremely important. Children are raised to have unquestioning obedience to their parents; they should never challenge their parents' authority. Chinese and Chinese American citizens in particular have adhered to the doctrine of filial piety, which is based on Confucian philosophy. **Filial piety**, or respect for one's parents, elders, and ancestors, is manifested in rules of conduct such as "only speak when spoken to" or "speak only if one has something important to say." Great importance is placed on the family unit, and children are expected to care for their parents in their old age (Teon, 2016). Confucianism also has a long history in Korea. Korean culture maintains that younger members of a family are obligated to care for their aging parents and family members. Outside the family unit, Koreans are raised to respect and show deference to older individuals and authority figures.

Shame is used to discourage inappropriate behaviors that might have a negative impact on a family's reputation. The failures of any one family member impact the family as a whole (Sue & Sue, 2003). Family reputation is important. One of the worst things a person can do is to disgrace his or her family (Louie, 2014).

The threat of a potential loss of face or loss of status, and the resulting shame, may cause distress, resulting in depression and anxiety. Asians' desire to avoid a loss of face and shame has been linked with their high sense of self-control and self-discipline (B. Kim & Park, 2008; Leong et al., 2008). In counseling Asian American clients, clinicians should explore if they feel they will lose face and bring about shame on themselves and their families if they talk about their problems in public. To help a client **save face**, clinicians should use questions that don't emphasize the fact that a client may be experiencing problems. They might ask the client, "How are you feeling today?" and not "Do you feel depressed or anxious about your situation?"

Gender Issues in Asian American Families

Traditional roles for men and women prevail among some Asian American groups. To maintain harmony within the family and to avoid spousal conflict, women usually defer to their husbands in final decisions. Traditional Asian expectations of women conflict with the values in the dominant American society that emphasize independent thinking, achievement, and self-sufficiency of women, even at the expense of others' feelings and needs (Kramer et al., 2002). These conflicting values can lead to mental health disorders.

Children and Adolescents in Asian American Families

In Asian American families, children are highly valued. They are taught to be polite, quiet, humble, and deferential to parents, teachers, and their elders. Conformity to expectations is emphasized, and emotional outbursts are discouraged. Failure to meet the family's expectations brings shame and loss of face to both the children and their parents. Asian American parents are not usually forthcoming with affection and praise because of fear that such praise will lead to laziness. Children who do not do well in school bring shame to their families (Kramer et al., 2002).

Asian American culture does not view adolescence in the same way that the dominant American culture does. There is little or no emphasis on young Asian American teenagers' individuating/separating from their parents and families, and seeking a definition of self outside the family is not encouraged. Moreover, Asian children and adolescents usually acculturate more readily than their parents and elders, and as a result, they serve as interpreters for their parents and grandparents. Children may experience acculturation conflict because parents want their children to embrace cultural skills and values that will allow them to succeed in American society, but don't want them to completely assimilate and lose their connections to their native culture. For example, parents may encourage their children to learn English, but then turn around and criticize them for abandoning their native language. Such confusing messages to children and adolescents promote transgenerational acculturation conflict (B. Kim & Park, 2013; Kramer et al., 2002).

Young Adult Asian Americans

As Asian American adolescents grow to adulthood, they may become immersed in Western cultures and values. As a result, they may experience conflict between Western peer pressure on the one hand and traditional Asian family expectations on the other. In some cases, Asian American adults develop a dual identity—they may have an Asian (Chinese, Korean, etc.) identity at home and a Western identity when out in public. In addition, Asian young adults often feel an obligation to follow their parents' preference over their own career choice. They may sometimes lose emotional and financial support if they diverge from their parents' career choice for them.

Conflict may be exacerbated if Asian young adults become involved in an interracial romantic relationship. They may feel pressured to date only people from their specific ethnic group because of parental fears that biracial children will diffuse the family lineage and culture.

Following is a list of some stresses Asian American young adults may face that conflict with traditional Asian family expectations:

- Pressure from American peers to smoke, drink, and have sex

- Pressure from American peers to separate and individuate from their parents

- Reconciling traditional Asian modes of communication with more assertive modes of communication within the majority American culture

- Resolving new immigrant acculturation conflicts and trauma associated with war in their native country

- Anti-Asian sentiment or racial microaggressions against members of their ethnic group (Kramer et al., 2002)

The Elderly Asian American Community

In contrast to elderly White Americans, who stress their independence and the desire not to become burdens to their children, elderly Asians may look forward to having their adult children care for them. For example, most traditional elderly Chinese prefer to have their children move in with them. When they live separately, they do so in an effort to avoid conflict over family roles (E. Lee, 1997).

> ### Cultural Reflections
>
> *How would you describe your communication pattern? Is it high context or low context?*
>
> *Have you ever communicated by just using silence? Explain.*
>
> *Can a look convey as much as words? Elaborate.*

In Chinese families that have adopted an extended family structure, grandparents often are responsible for the care of grandchildren. In contrast, Japanese American older adults frequently maintain separate households from their children and grandchildren. Korean and Vietnamese elders are welcomed to live with their children. Elderly Asians who live with children and grandchildren view such living arrangements as a reward for everything they have provided to younger generations.

ASIAN AMERICAN AND PACIFIC ISLANDER COMMUNICATION: HIGH-CONTEXT CULTURE

As noted in earlier chapters, high-context cultures tend to be more relational, collectivistic, and intuitive. Communication in Asian American cultures is usually high context. Asians tend to favor an intentional lack of directness in conversation because preserving harmony between people is considered more important than being "right" or arriving at the exact "truth." Typically, Asian cultures are high-context cultures; they use gesture, body language, eye contact, intonation, word stress, and silence in conversations more so than actual spoken words.

In high-context Asian cultures, using few words can sometimes communicate an important message (Hall, 1976). Asians tend also to use silence and lack of eye contact to communicate with others. Silence is a sign of respect and politeness; it may also indicate that a client wants to continue speaking after having made a point in the conversation (Sue & Sue, 2003). Asians view eye contact as a sign of disrespect and aggression from the person making eye contact (Leong et al., 2008). Hence, clinicians need to become aware of the meanings that Asians may attribute to direct eye contact and silence. If a clinician considers lack of eye contact and silence as negative client behavior, he or she may stop the client from exploring a clinical issue any further and create the basis for a premature termination of counseling.

In general, Asian people tune in to the moods of others during conversation, and they expect others to also exemplify such behavior (Leong et al., 2008). During counseling, Asian clients may expect therapists to sort out their concerns, confusions, and hesitance, while therapists may desire more precise descriptions of the problem. Smiling oftentimes means something different in Asian culture than it does in American or Western culture. A therapist might mistake Asian clients' head nodding, smiles, and apparent verbal assent as clear indications of their understanding and agreement with the therapist when, in fact, just the opposite may be true. Asians tend to smile when confused or embarrassed, and therefore, it is important for the therapist to ask clarifying questions about the client's head nodding and smiles (B. Kim & Park, 2013).

CULTURAL IDENTITY OF ASIAN AMERICANS: NO ONE IDENTITY MODEL FOR ALL

There have been several models of Asian American identity development; however, most of these were constructed decades ago, and they have important shortcomings (J. Kim, 1981; Kitano, 1982; Sue, 1973). For example, models of ethnic or cultural identity development for Asian Americans are flawed because most dealt with just one or two groups—primarily Chinese (Sue, 1973) and Japanese (J. Kim, 1981; Kitano, 1982). Given that there are more than 40 Asian American groups, all with different cultural values and different migration histories, it is impossible to have one ethnic or cultural identity model represent them all.

The Pew Research Center's report "The Rise of Asian Americans" (April 2013) is a survey of over 3,500 Asian Americans. It provides some insight regarding how Asian Americans see themselves. According to the survey's findings, Asian Americans' identity correlated with their nativity and duration of time in the United States. The report stated that about two-thirds of Asian Americans who were born in the United States describe themselves as feeling like "a typical American," but fewer than one-third of Asian immigrants say the same. For immigrants who arrived in 2000 or later, the proportion was fewer than one-fifth. In terms of referring to their ethnic heritage, most Asian Americans prefer to identify themselves by their country of origin (e.g., Chinese or Chinese American, Indian or Indian American), and a significant minority (more than 10%) simply refer to themselves as American.

As is the case with many other ethnic minority groups, Asian and Pacific Islander Americans experience a series of identity transformation. Various stage models have been proposed to describe Asian Americans' identity transformation process, such as Sue and Sue's (2003) Racial/Cultural Identity Development (R/CID) Model (see Sue & Sue, 2016 for more information about this model).

CULTURAL STRENGTHS AND CONTRIBUTIONS OF ASIAN AMERICANS

The cultural strengths of Asian Americans are many and varied. Their family structure and values about hard work and achievement in education and careers have contributed a great deal to their success in this country. In addition, Asians are notable for their resilience and strength in the face of adversity (B. Kim & Park, 2008; Sue & Sue, 2003). Asian Americans' ability to maintain elements of their culture serves as a protective factor against prejudice and discrimination (Hwang, Wood, & Fujimoto, 2010). Although Pacific Islanders face a number of challenges with regard to discrimination, their collective orientation, strong families, and sense of community have worked to their benefit. Their families form not only a source of support but also a strong economic unit. The educational and career achievements of Asian Americans have been outstanding, and they have made contributions to this nation since their arrival.

Asian Americans have made a number of contributions to the United States, far too many to list in a single chapter. The following list includes some notable contributions of Asian Americans across several different identified Asian groups:

- Dr. Daniel Chee Tsui, a Chinese-born American citizen, shared the Nobel Prize in Physics in 1998 with Horst Störmer and Robert Laughlin for their discovery of the fractional quantum effect (Nobel Media AB, 2014).

- Kim Hyung-son and Kim Ho, two Korean immigrants, founded the Kim Brothers Co., a fruit wholesale business. Their experiments breeding fruit produced the nectarine, a cross between a peach and a plum.

- Ajay V. Bhatt is an Asian Indian American computer architect who is the co-inventor of the USB port (Universal Serial Bus technology) found on most personal computers.

- Dr. Kenneth Matsumura, a Japanese American, invented the bioartificial liver using live rabbit cells. *Time* magazine designated the bioartificial liver 2001's "Invention of the Year."

- Duke Kahanamoku, a Native Hawaiian, was a gold medal Olympic swimmer and is credited with popularizing the sport of surfing in the modern age.

- Dalip Singh Saund was the first Asian American to be elected to the U.S. House of Representatives in 1956.

- Steven Chu, a Chinese American, received the Nobel Prize in Physics in 1997 for his work on cooling atoms. He also served as the U.S. Secretary of Energy from 2009 through 2013.

- Maya Lin, daughter of Chinese immigrants, won a contest to design the Vietnam Veterans Memorial in Washington, DC, when she was just 21 years old. Almost a decade later, Lin designed another famous structure: the Civil Rights Memorial in Montgomery, Alabama.

In addition to the list above, Asian Americans have contributed in many ways to the U.S. military. During World War II, the 100th Infantry Battalion and the 442nd Regimental Combat Team was a segregated army unit of Japanese Americans that fought in Italy and Germany. Because of their heroics, they became known as the most decorated unit in U.S. military history for their size and length of service. What is most amazing is that many of these men volunteered to serve despite being placed in concentration camps by the U.S. government due to fears that they would side with the Japanese during the war. Japanese Americans served in the Pacific against Japan, and they used their knowledge of the Japanese language and culture in critical ways that benefited the U.S. Military Intelligence Service. As a result of their contributions in military intelligence, General Douglas MacArthur stated that never in the history of combat has one side known so much about the enemy, prior to actual combat.

As previously mentioned, in 1992, the U.S. Congress passed a law designating the month of May as Asian/Pacific American Heritage Month. As former U.S. Secretary of the Interior Sally Jewell stated on May 9, 2013,

> Asian Americans and Pacific Islanders have long been leaders in every aspect of our social fabric—in government, business, science, medicine, the arts, education and our armed forces . . .
>
> From Angel Island, where more than 1 million Asian immigrants arrived on these shores, to the Chinese immigrants who helped build the railroads across the country, to the Japanese American internment camps of World War II, these stories are all important threads in the great American tapestry. ("Asian Americans, Pacific Islanders Important to U.S. History," 2013)

Cultural Reflections

Have you ever had to acculturate in American society?

What was that experience like for you?

Have you ever assisted anyone who was going through acculturative stress? Describe the situation.

Discuss factors that contribute to acculturative stress of Asian and Pacific Islander Americans.

ACCULTURATION AND CULTURAL ISSUES AFFECTING MENTAL HEALTH

Acculturation Conflicts

Asian American immigrant clients experience a process of acculturation in the United States. According to Bryan S. K. Kim and Yong S. Park (2008), acculturative stress is a major factor associated with the development of mental health problems for Asian Americans living in the United States. For instance, an Asian American client who has immigrated to this country might feel that his traditional values (e.g., indirect form of communication, silence, lack of eye contact, and emphasis on collectivism instead of individualism) are not respected by Americans. As a result, such a client might develop depression and anxiety that is related to his or her acculturative stress. Acculturative conflicts may take place across the generations, when young people acculturate at a faster rate than their parents and grandparents. Acculturative stress has been associated with a number of problems, including perceived discrimination, cultural incompatibilities, and intergenerational conflicts (Leong & Lau, 2001). Some psychological symptoms of psychological stress are anxiety, depression, hypersensitivity, heightened psychosomatic symptoms, and in some instances suicidal ideation.

Acculturation Level and Counseling

Individuals' level of acculturation and enculturation can also influence the effectiveness of multicultural counseling. Whereas acculturation can be conceptualized as the extent to which the individual integrates the American culture into his or her values, attitudes, and behaviors, enculturation is the degree to which a person retains and identifies with his or her culture of origin (Maki & Kitano, 2002). Generally speaking, Asian clients who have acculturated to mainstream American society have spent a longer time in the United States functioning in integrated, mainstream settings. Therefore, they are more likely to be responsive to therapy than those who are highly enculturated with regard to their native culture. Conversely, clients with a strong adherence to ethnic values may adopt a role in counseling that protects the family honor.

An Asian American's level of acculturation can influence his or her mental health and help-seeking behavior. Individuals who are more acculturated into the mainstream American society are more likely to seek professional psychological help, while those who are less acculturated are inclined to seek help from community elders, religious leaders, student organizations, and church groups (Leong et al., 2008). One possible reason for this difference is that those who are more acculturated may believe that there is no stigma in looking for professional counseling, whereas less acculturated individuals embrace the shame and stigma associated with getting outside assistance with problems. A client's acculturation, age, and cultural adjustment difficulties predict the effects of mental health symptoms (Yeh, 2003).

Help-Seeking Attitudes of Asian Americans

Asian Americans have been reported to have a low rate of mental health utilization but a high rate of premature termination of counseling services (Yeh & Wang, 2000). Scholars have reported that they prefer to seek help from family and social relations, religious, and spiritual authority (Yeh & Wang, 2000). Some reasons that have been used to explain the low mental health utilization rates include the lack of bilingual therapists, cultural prescriptions against revealing family secrets, discrimination against members of their ethnic group, and therapists' inability to design culturally appropriate forms of treatment (Leong, 1996).

Mental Health and Asian Americans

Culture helps to shape individuals' mental health beliefs, their coping strategies, their help-seeking behaviors, and their views of mental illness. Asian Americans who have been acculturated and who subscribe to Western-oriented mental health beliefs may not have the same mental health orientation as recent immigrants who tend to endorse their culture's traditional religious and mental health beliefs. As pointed out in earlier chapters, culture conditions the brain in certain ways, and hence it influences individuals' views and orientations toward mental health. It is noteworthy that not all Asian Americans will endorse the mental beliefs discussed in this section. A great deal will depend on the cultures from which they come and their level of acculturation.

In an early study, E. Lee (1997) pointed out that cultural factors affect Chinese views on schizophrenia. According to her, schizophrenia may be conceptualized in several different ways—for instance, as an imbalance of *yin* and *yang* and disharmony in the flow of **qi** (or **chi**). Chinese culture conceptualizes that the energy (*qi*) within each human being is connected to the energy of the universe. Emotional problems result, then, from an imbalance of *yin* and *yang* (bipolar life forces) or from an overabundance of *qi* (life force energy). Moreover, a mental illness such as schizophrenia may be conceptualized as "karma" caused by deeds from past lives or as punishment from God. Chinese citizens may also view schizophrenia as physical and emotional strain and exhaustion, or as an organic disorder where mental illness is seen as a manifestation of such physical diseases as brain disorders, liver diseases, or hormonal imbalances. Finally, Chinese culture supports the view that mental illness is related to a person's character weakness. In contrast, mental health is gained by self-discipline, use of one's own willpower, and the avoidance of negative thoughts (Banerjee, Mullainathan, & Hanna, 2012).

Asian culture tends to use somatization as an expression of mental distress. Hence, a person will describe symptoms of physical illness when no organic cause for the illness is found. Different body organs are associated with different emotions. For instance, joy comes from the heart, while sorrow emanates from the lungs, anger from the liver, and fear from the kidneys (E. Lee, 1997). It is important, however, that clinicians do not overgeneralize that all Asian Americans' organic expressions of illness are unfounded. Some individuals who report physical symptoms may actually be experiencing real organic problems instead of a somatic expression of psychological distress. Individuals who subscribe to a traditional Chinese view on mental health may not report a problem as one dealing with depression. Instead, traditional Chinese individuals tend to describe depression as neurasthenia—a syndrome of exhaustion, weakness, and diffused bodily complaints that are caused by inadequate physical energy in the central nervous system. According to S. Lee et al. (2000), neurasthenia is an official diagnosis in China and is popular in Chinatowns across this nation.

Mental Health of Native Hawaiians and Other Pacific Islanders

Many cultures in the Pacific do not have a formal word for mental illness because they view emotional and psychological problems as integrated with biological, cognitive, and spiritual components. Native Hawaiian culture does not use the term *mental illness*, but instead uses the word *pilikia* (trouble). Having poor mental health is seen as an imbalance in family, natural, or spiritual areas. Micronesian culture tends to conceptualize depression as related to the loss of important relationships. People in Micronesia use the word *ialomweiu*, which translates to loneliness or sadness from the loss of a loved one, to describe the Western idea of major depression (Leong & Kalibatseva, 2011).

In a study dealing with Asian American and Pacific Islander mental health, Itti and Narasaki (2014) summarized a recent report by the National Alliance on Mental Illness (NAMI). These authors point out that because of social stigmas and cultural and language barriers, mental illnesses among American Pacific Islanders are largely undiagnosed, untreated, and not discussed. According to the NAMI report, suicide is one of the top five leading causes of death for American Pacific Islanders, with Asian American women over age 65 having the highest suicide rate among members of this group. Itti and Narasaki state,

> According to the National Asian American Pacific Islander Mental Health Association (NAAPIMHA), young Asian American women have the highest rates of depressive symptoms and suicide ideation for their age group. Native Hawaiians and Pacific Islanders had proportionally the most suicides in Honolulu. Due to war time trauma cultural dislocation, racism, poverty and other environmental reasons, nearly three-quarters of Southeast Asians reportedly meet the criteria for an affective disorder, which

includes depression, anxiety, and post-traumatic stress disorder, with high percentages among Cambodians and Vietnamese. (p. 2)

Mental Illness and Substance Use Among Asian Americans and Pacific Islanders

There are important differences in substance use and mental health issues between Asian Americans and Other Pacific Islanders. In 2014, according to the Substance Abuse and Mental Health Services Administration (see RTI International, 2015),

- For individuals ages 12 and up, the rate of illegal drug use was 4.1% among Asian Americans and 15.6% among Native Hawaiians and Other Pacific Islanders.

- Binge alcohol use was lowest among Asian Americans ages 12 and up (14.5%) and 18.3% among Native Hawaiians and Other Pacific Islanders.

- Binge alcohol use rate for youth ages 12 to 20 was 6.7% for Asian Americans, compared to a national American average of 13.8%.

- The rate of substance dependence or abuse was 4.5% for Asian Americans and 10% for Native Hawaiians and Other Pacific Islanders.

Asian Americans' Expectations About Counseling

Some Asian American clients, especially those from the major Asian cultures (Chinese, Japanese, and Korean), initially come to counseling expecting that the clinician will tell them what is wrong with them and what steps they can take to resolve their problems. That is, they tend to view therapists as authority figures (B. Kim & Park, 2013). To increase the likelihood that Asian clients will return to therapy, the clinician should demonstrate both clinical expertise and authority during the very first session. This situation exists because in Asian culture, people ascribe higher status to those who have high expertise in an area or those who have authority (Sue & Sue, 2013).

> **Cultural Reflections**
>
> *What expectations do you have about counseling?*
>
> *Do you view the counselor as the expert in the clinical relationship?*
>
> *How would you go about telling a client what to expect during counseling?*

Research studies have reported that Asian Americans expect that clinicians will take an active role in structuring the session and in producing guidelines on the client's and clinician's roles during therapy. While the therapist is expected to take the role of being the expert, clients are told that they are the experts on their own lives (Chen & Davenport, 2005). Asian American clients are inclined to expect that their role in therapy is to be respectful and obedient. Because they view the therapist as the expert, he or she should avoid making jokes or becoming too familiar with Asian American clients—especially during the first therapy session. The therapist should maintain a type of formalism, addressing the client as "Mr." or "Ms." rather than by his or her first name.

To exemplify therapeutic expertise, the therapist might mention prior experiences wherein he or she has successfully helped a client to resolve a problem similar to that of his or her current client. The therapist's office should contain visible displays of his or her professional credentials, and he or she should introduce him- or herself as "Dr. So-and-So." Throughout the first session, the therapist should mention clear and specific goals that can be resolved in a short amount of time (B. Kim & Park, 2008).

As just one example of a particular therapeutic approach applied with a particular Asian ethnic group, Chen and Davenport (2005) conducted a review of the literature on cognitive behavioral therapy (CBT) treatment outcomes for Chinese American clients. They concluded that using CBT with Chinese Americans may not be effective if it isn't adjusted to address certain cultural differences. Based on their review, they suggest that clinicians make the following modifications to improve CBT treatment outcomes for Chinese American clients:

- In the very beginning of therapy, counselors should explain their role, and they should stress that while they are the expert in the therapeutic process, the client is the expert on his or her life.

- Listen carefully and take into consideration the client's physical complaints because oftentimes Asian American clients may use somatic complaints to express their emotional distress. Having emotional problems is associated with shame and stigma.

- Frame questions in a way where there is no true "correct" response. Asian American clients may feel challenged to provide a specific answer to questions opening with "what" and "why."

Chen and Davenport (2005) state that, in working with Chinese American clients, techniques such as sentence stem, guided imagery, or dream analysis may help bring out the client's deep emotions. These researchers note that it is crucial for the therapist to spend time communicating the concept of psychotherapy to the client and to assess the client's readiness for emotional explorations.

Cultural Healing and Indigenous Practices

Asian Americans tend to have a holistic view of mind and body (Ryder, Yang, & Heine, 2002). They believe that physical problems are the source of psychological and emotional stress, and that once the physical illness is treated all will be well. Hence, Asian American clients might not mention anxiety or depression. Instead, they will focus on describing headaches, fatigue, and disturbances in sleep and appetite (Wong, Tran, Kim, Kerne, & Calfa, 2010). In working with Asian American clients, clinicians should consider somatic complaints as real problems that merit their attention. By talking about a client's physical complaint, the therapist legitimizes what the client is actually feeling. This approach also provides a way to deal with both the somatic complaint and any underlying psychological problems (Leong et al., 2008).

Many Asian American and Pacific Islander people adhere to indigenous and native cultural healing practices. Bryan S. K. Kim and Yong S. Park (2013) point out that therapists working with Asian American clients may use Western conventional treatment approaches or refer clients to practitioners who use indigenous healing approaches. Some of the common treatment modalities include (1) acupuncture, which entails inserting needles into specific pressure points in the body to release pressure and pain; (2) yoga, which involves controlled movements of the body during meditation; (3) herbal medicine, which consists of herbs and foods used for specific illnesses; and (4) mindfulness meditation and prayer (Grey & Hall-Clark, 2015).

CULTURAL FACTORS IN COUNSELING ASIAN AMERICANS

It is important that clinicians understand the role of culture in their psychological treatment of Asian Americans. The cultural values of members of this vast heterogeneous group include an emphasis on the connection between the mind and the body, interpersonal harmony, and the focus on the family. Factors such as shame, embarrassment, and loss of face also have major influences on whether or not a person will acknowledge that he or she is experiencing psychological difficulties.

Moreover, Asian Americans have been found to underutilize mental health services because of cultural values, such as not going outside of the family to discuss personal issues or problems, or feeling that one is being disloyal when one discusses issues related to another family member. The cultural value of shaming might also cause Asian American clients not to seek counseling; one feels ashamed that one cannot solve his or her own problem. Clinicians need to demonstrate some level of interest in the client's culture in order to present themselves as being culturally responsive. Zhang and Dixon (2001) conducted a study that found that culturally responsive counselors who displayed pictures and crafts from the client's native land, who had a world atlas with a map of Asia visible, who used greetings in the client's own language, and who expressed interest in knowing more about the client's culture were rated more positively than were clinicians who did not evidence these behaviors.

Study participants responded that these clinician behaviors demonstrated the clinicians' openness to different cultures, their capability of relating to people of different cultures, and their capability of being more helpful in resolving problems than culturally neutral counselors. The study showed that being culturally responsive does not have to involve a clinician's comprehensive knowledge of each culture. Instead, the clinician must convey an interest in and respect for other cultures, evidence an eagerness to learn about other cultures, and show appreciation of the client's heritage (Zhang & Dixon, 2001).

Eliciting Clients' Views About Their Presenting Problem

Culturally competent assessment and treatment of mental health problems for Asian Americans mandates that the clinician ask clients and their family members to share their cultural views on the cause of the problem, reveal past coping patterns and health care–seeking behaviors, and discuss treatment expectations. Because the clinician is viewed as an authority figure, Asian clients will answer questions from the therapist, but they are unlikely to raise issues during treatment. Instead they will tell the clinician what they think he or she wants to hear. To deal with Asian Americans' reluctance to raise clinical issues, the clinician must reassure clients that when they talk about their problems, no judgments about them or their family will be made.

To arrive at an understanding of the client's problems, the clinician might ask questions that will elicit clients' understanding of the causes of presenting issues. Some questions might be "What do you think caused your problem?" "Why do you think it started when it did?" "What does your problem do to your body?" "Does your issue/problem interfere with your daily routines?" The reader is referred to the Cultural Formulation Interview for additional questions that reveal a client's problem (American Psychiatric Association, 2013; see also Chapters 3 and 7).

Focus on Clients' Cultural and Group Strengths

In addition to focusing on the client's problems, the clinician should identify sources of support and strength to the individual, family, and community network and in the cultural teachings. During a crisis, a clinician might identify social support strengths from extended family members, friends, and community members. Clinicians should be aware that generally speaking, Asian Americans use individual strengths for the benefit of the family or for the group, and that it might be embarrassing to focus on the individual strengths of their client without relating them to the group.

E. Lee (2002) has suggested a number of culturally responsive steps a counselor or therapist might take with a client:

- Understand the cultural differences and similarities between the counselor and the client in terms of appropriate goals and strategies that take into account Asian American cultural values such as collectivism, hierarchical family relationships, and patriarchal orientation of Asian families.

- Discuss cultural factors related to shame (if appropriate) related to seeking counseling. Discussing shame may help the client to discuss his or her feelings about needing counseling and may build the necessary trust and rapport between counselor and client.

- Integrate Eastern and Western mental health and health approaches. The clinician should consider adopting a holistic model of health prevalent in Eastern cultures and integrate this model with Western psychological approaches. For instance, in the treatment of a Chinese or Korean American client with depression, it might be helpful to provide psychoeducation on the Western biological and psychological views of depression. In addition, the clinician considers exploring Eastern approaches to treatment, including the use of Chinese herbal medicine, acupuncture, *qigong*, mindfulness, or yoga. The clinician might point out Western views on biological causes of depression and the Chinese cultural outlook on energy depletion. Practiced in China for over 3,000 years, *qigong* is a form of gentle exercise that consists of repeated movements, often stretching the body and increasing fluid movement (blood, synovial, and lymph) and building awareness of how the body moves in space. A *qigong* exercise has both internal and external movement. The internal movements or flows in China are called *neigong* or "internal power." *Qigong* can be helpful in the treatment of depression and physiological disorders. It is useful in producing inner tranquility because it helps to manage stress, anger, depression, and morbid thoughts when *chi* (energy) is not regulated. *Qigong* has also been found useful in the treatment of cancer, internal organ ailments, poor circulation, nerve pain, and back and joint problems. *Chi* or *qi* is a basic Chinese cultural value that refers to the energy and the flow of the life force that pervades all living things (see www.energyarts.com/what-qigong). When family members are dealing with death or unpredictable changes, philosophical teachings from Asian cultures can be therapeutic.

- Activate the family's cultural strengths. Strengths in Asian and Asian Pacific families include social support from the extended family, a strong sense of family obligation and loyalty, filial piety, heavy emphasis on educational achievement, and strong work ethic.

- Understand the family's communication style. Determine the Asian American's primary language and dialect. Typically, Asian Americans use indirect styles of communication, and they avoid confrontation with others. The clinician may have to read between the lines. If the clinician is too direct, Asian Americans might view him or her as too pushy or insensitive.

Native Hawaiian Values and Cultural Healing Practices

Native Hawaiians have developed a rich culture and language. Most people have become familiar with the saying *aloha*. *Aloha* represents an important Native Hawaiian cultural value. *Aloha* consists of two words, *alo* (which means one's face, presence, or being) and *ha* (one's breath, life). Native Hawaiians believe that by saying and feeling *aloha*, a person shares his or her spiritual essence through one's breath. Native Hawaiians like to feel that they are respected and cared for if they are willing to enter a counseling relationship. They also have internalized a strong sense of responsibility to take care of their family members and loved ones. This cultural value is summarized in the saying *aloha aku, aloha mal* ("give love, get love").

Another value in Hawaiian culture is *lokahi*, which means "unity, agreement, accord, unison, and harmony." *Lokahi* represents a state of delicate balance and harmony with oneself, others, nature, and God. A person is healthy when his or her physical, mental, and spiritual components are all in harmony. Hawaiians view themselves as interconnected with the vast universe. The *lokahi* triangle is a holistic view of physical and mental health. *Lokahi* also includes the environment around an individual and relationships with others, especially family members, ancestors, and god(s), as well as mental and emotional states. The physical body cannot be healed without setting right any problems within the mental or spiritual realms. An individual or client must be willing to take responsibility for his or her own healing, including making amends for any wrongs he or she might have caused in the past. The word *ha'aha* means "humble, unpretentious, unassuming, and modest," and *olu'lu* means "pleasant, nice, amiable, satisfied, and agreeable" (Brightman & Subedi, 2007).

The *Ho'oponopono*: A Native Hawaiian
Culturally Based Intervention for Resolving Conflict

Native Hawaiians have a rich culture for resolving mental health issues and family and interpersonal conflict. Instead of using outside professionals, Native Hawaiians have traditionally relied on their *'ohana* or family. When problems exceed a family's capability to resolve them, the family selects a family leader or *po'o*, or they may chose a *haku*, or medium, trained within and accepted by the *'ohana*. A family can also consult a *kahuna* when the *'ohana* is unable to resolve its difficulties and problems. Both the *haku* and the *kahuna* are usually very highly trusted and respected family members. Using the *'ohana*, a *kaku*, or a *kahuna*, a family is able to keep its emotional and psychological problems with the family (Chun, 2011).

The *ho'oponopono* is a culturally based intervention developed by Native Hawaiians. It was originally used to "discuss and settle arguments, assuage hurt feelings, mediate angry words, and deal with other types of interpersonal problems" (Hurdle, 2002, p. 187). The *ho'oponopono* conflict resolution model is grounded in the traditional Hawaiian values involving the importance of the extended family, the need for harmonious relationships, and the restoration of good will, or *aloha* (Hurdle, 2002).

The *ho'oponopono* is opened with a prayer. Next, the family's problem is identified with a description of the *hala* or transgression and the negative effect (*hihia*) that the problem has caused. Each individual who has been affected by the problem shares his or her feelings (*mana'o*) about the problem. The *ho'oponopono* is used to reveal who did what to whom, and when. The goal of the *ho'oponopono* is to seek self-scrutiny, honest communication, and the avoidance of blaming the other person(s). A cooling-off period (*ho'omalu*) may be called if the participants become too emotional.

Following the discussion phase, the resolution phase is initiated with the *mihi* or a confession of wrongdoing and the seeking of forgiveness. To establish an atmosphere of mutuality, "the wronged party also asks forgiveness for his or her reactions to the offense" (Hurdle, 2002, p. 187). Because all parties to the conflict ask for forgiveness of each other, an equal status is established between them. If necessary, during the resolution phase, a plan for restitution for the offense may be adopted. The *kala* concludes the forgiveness and restitution phase, and all conflict and hurt are released so that the negative entanglement is broken. The closing phase is called the *pani*, and it includes a "summary of the process, a reaffirmation of the family's strengths and enduring bonds, and a final prayer" (Hurdle, 2002, p. 187). The problem that has been worked out is then declared closed and should not be brought up again. Following the completion of the *ho'oponopono*, a meal is often shared by all involved. The *ho'oponopono* represents a traditional Hawaiian conflict resolution process with clear roles for all participants. It has a healing and spiritual focus that is designed to restore family harmony.

Other traditional Native Hawaiian healing practices include dream and vision analysis and *pikai*, or the removal of evil spirits by using the ritual *pi* (sprinkling with tea water or salted water).

For Native Hawaiians and Other Pacific Islanders, E. Lee (2002) suggests that clinicians should

- Demonstrate understanding and knowledge of their native history and circumstances, including the political history and affiliation of the United States to the Pacific islands

- Be competent in using a range of both Native and Western treatment interventions

- Utilize a family's strengths in terms of extended family support and community networking

In Hawaii, the Department of Human Services uses an intervention called *'Ohana* (family). It might be helpful to bring together the extended family and the neighborhood support system to collectively deal with family issues (Hurdle, 2002).

CASE VIGNETTE 10.1
EVE ZHANG: MULTICULTURAL ISSUES IN STRENGTHS-BASED RECOVERY

There are a number of multicultural issues in the recovery process. Each ethnic group tends to have its own views on what constitutes mental health and maladaptive health. Each ethnic group also has views about what constitutes an appropriate relationship with service providers and whether it is acceptable to seek mental health treatment. Multicultural issues may also be present in the mental health agency through which the client seeks treatment. Part of the assessment process might include questions about a client's cultural attitudes toward mental health issues—especially being diagnosed with a disability and seeking treatment for it.

This section applies the strengths-based therapy model to the case of Eve Zhang, a Chinese American woman suffering from bipolar disorder. There are multicultural issues involved in this case. Therapy expanded across 12 sessions for Eve. A case discussion follows. This case is adapted from Chapter 7 of the author's book, Jones-Smith, E. (2014). *Strengths-based therapy: Connecting theory, practice, and skills.* Thousand Oaks, CA: Sage.

Case Description

Eve Zhang is a 28-year-old director of computer services at a major university. In this position, she manages the day-to-day computer system for faculty and students. She was diagnosed as having bipolar disorder at age 16. She has been hospitalized for bipolar disorder four times since her initial diagnosis. Eve's family is originally from Hong Kong. They have rejected her on the grounds that she has brought great shame to the family. Eve has an older brother who is a medical doctor and who has said that he is too busy with his clients to visit her. No one else in the family has ever been diagnosed with a mental illness. Because of her family's ostracizing her, Eve has turned to her work. Oftentimes she works 12-hour days, and much of this overwork is unnecessary. Eve has few friends. At times she struggles with her disability. She has consented to enter a recovery program, but she has done so reluctantly. She is afraid that if she receives another hospitalization, she might lose her job, which pays her health insurance and a good salary. How might you work with Eve using the strengths-based therapy model?

Case Discussion and Treatment Plan

Eve entered the therapist's office in a hesitant manner. She wondered if the therapist would ever be able to understand her feelings. She and the therapist were from two completely different cultures. The therapist came from a European background, and Eve had been raised as the dutiful Chinese daughter. The two cultures were vastly different. The therapist's culture was individualistic in orientation and focused on individual achievement. In contrast, Chinese culture was collectivist in orientation, where group solidarity and harmony were far more important than individual achievement. Chinese culture emphasized getting along with family members, saving face, and respect of elders. Eve doubted if the therapist could ever truly understand what it meant to be a Chinese daughter and to have an older brother who was so successful—a medical doctor.

Forming a Therapeutic Alliance

Eve's initial presentation to the therapist was as a "shy" young woman who was ashamed to be sitting there in his office. She stated that she came to therapy because she did not want to have to be placed in the hospital again because of her bipolar disorder. She indicated that her entire family was ashamed of her and had cut off virtually all contact with her. The loss of her family grieved Eve deeply. In Chinese culture, the family was everything. Now Eve was without a family, and she felt worthless.

After the therapist listened to Eve's story, he complimented her. He said: "Despite your family's rejection of you, Eve, I see a lot of strength in you." Eve lifted her eyes slightly to meet his for a brief moment. "You seem surprised that I see strength in you, Eve." Eve remained silent. The therapist continued. "Your family has rejected you because of your mental disability. You live alone without many friends. You've been in the hospital four times, but somehow despite all you've experienced alone, you have managed to survive and to be productive at work in a rather challenging position. It hasn't been easy, Eve. Some people would have been crushed under such rejection and illness, but you managed to pull yourself together, get up in the morning, get dressed, go to work, perform at a reasonable level, and come home again. That takes strength, Eve, and I think we should begin by acknowledging and respecting the strengths that you've shown under difficult circumstances."

Eve's eyes filled with tears, and she covered her mouth so as to prevent herself from sobbing. The therapist watched Eve's struggle with crying before him. "It's okay to cry here, Eve. You've been through a lot. You have a right to cry about what has happened to you."

Eve finally responded, "Thank you. Everybody tells me what's wrong with me. I have this illness. I didn't ask for it. I don't want it. Why did it have to happen to me? It's not fair. My brother doesn't have a mental illness. No one in my family has this illness except for me."

The therapist looked kindly toward Eve and her search for justice in the world. He did not have a quick answer for her question about justice. "I don't have an easy answer for you, Eve. Sometimes, the thorns in our lives are there to make us stronger."

"In Chinese culture, we are not supposed to complain about our struggles. We're supposed to endure. I wouldn't mind enduring my bipolar disorder. It's just that enduring it all by myself is too much for me. The last time I had to go to the hospital, I sat in my hospital room hoping that my mother or my brother would come to see about me. But no one ever did."

The therapist responded, "I don't mean to minimize the pain that you've experienced, Eve, because it has been great. But if I just focus only on the pain that you have endured without dealing equally with your strengths, I don't think we're going to get very far. I'm counting on the strengths you've already shown to pull you through this all. I want to stop focusing on what has gone wrong in your life and start emphasizing what's working for you and what you are doing to make things work for you."

From this point on, Eve and the therapist agreed to take a closer look at her strengths. The therapeutic alliance between Eve and the therapist had been forged. She did not have to fear that the therapist was going to spend session after session dissecting the causes of her illness. During the therapy session, Eve and the therapist had acknowledged the mental disability and the pain that it had caused her. Now the issue was to find her strengths to deal with the illness so that she could have a more personally satisfying life.

The therapist gave Eve a copy of the *SBT and Your Recovery Journey* handout to get her acquainted with the concept of recovery and to inform her about the recovery process that the two would be engaged in. In addition, he gave her a copy of *Strengths-Based Therapy's Circle of Support for Clients.* The therapist asked Eve if she would be willing to complete the circle of support diagram so that she would have a better idea of where she needed to strengthen support for her recovery from the bipolar disorder. The rest of the case discusses critical issues that were addressed during the first 12 sessions of Eve's mental health recovery.

Eve's Strengths

As the therapist pointed out, Eve has several strengths that could prove helpful in her recovery. Eve completed the *Personal Strengths* form. Eve said that her best qualities as a person were that she was persistent, determined, and capable of enduring issues. Eve took several instruments that measured her strengths, including the CliftonStrengths assessment (Gallup, 2018).

Strengths Perception

As strengths-based therapy recovery progressed, Eve's perception of her strengths increased. In fact, she began to take notice of her strengths and those of others. The therapist was instrumental in keeping Eve's strengths as the focal point of recovery. She would deal successfully with her bipolar disorder by using her strengths.

Strengths Within the Struggle

The therapist's comments on Eve's strengths within the struggle were critical for helping her to engage in recovery. Prior to therapy, Eve had not thought about her strengths, most likely because Chinese culture emphasized modesty and using strengths for the collective good. In Chinese culture, it is considered poor manners to tout one's strengths before others. Gradually, Eve reconciled her need to feel that she had individual strengths that she could use to better her life and to make contributions to others.

"Let Go" Desires

Eve let go of some of her fears about not being good enough and about others finding out about her illness. She let go of staying in her apartment all by herself and her own self-imposed isolation. She let go of the stigma of having a bipolar disorder.

Hope

Hope dominates Eve's current life. She sees a future for herself in which she is a contributing member of her neighborhood community. Recently, Eve was invited to speak on having a bipolar disorder at a Hong Kong university. Her family felt that Eve's newfound fame reflected well on the family, and her father and mother are encouraging her to accept the Hong Kong university invitation.

Harvesting the Good

Never in Eve's wildest dreams did she feel that she would be able to harvest any good out of her bipolar disorder. Yet her struggle with the disorder has helped her to find her true self. It is not just the speaking engagements on having a bipolar disorder that have changed her life. Instead, it is the sense that her life has some purpose. She's not just working at a job for a salary. She has dedicated her life to helping others learn about the many different twists and turns of a bipolar disorder.

Let In

Perhaps the most important part of therapy was finding out about her strengths and learning how to use them to deal appropriately with the bipolar disorder as well as other problems. Eve had been living her life as a closed system. She was now an open system interacting with the rest of the world. The fact that she had actively sought positive outside relationships had changed her life for the better.

(Continued)

(Continued)

Eve's Goals and Barriers

As therapy progressed, Eve began to tackle her goals with her analytical strengths, her strengths of persistence, organization, and endurance. Some of Eve's goals were to end her virtual isolation from the rest of the world and to become a participating member capable of making contributions to others. She also wanted to reconnect with her family and to achieve more positive self-esteem. Eve's primary barriers continue to be her shyness and tendency to try to go it alone.

Building Strengths and Competencies

As Eve began to engage in the recovery process, she talked about what happened to her during her illness and what life is like now for her. Gradually, she was able to transcend the stigma that has been attached to her mental illness. She started a process of confronting and exorcising the stigma of having a bipolar illness. Confronting the stigma of her illness helped her to heal. At one point, Eve requested an appointment with her family—mother, father, and brother. She asked them to take into account the fact that she was not her illness.

Eve stated, "I am asking you to love me because I am your child and your sister—because I am a member of this family and because I did not do anything wrong to bring on this illness. My illness just exists, the same way that rain exists, the same way that most people experience some pain in their lives. Don't blame me for this illness. I did not cause it. If someone ran over you with a car by accident, would I abandon you? Would I be ashamed of you? I don't think so. I would treat you with compassion, kindness, and support. I shouldn't have to earn your love. You should give it willingly to me because I am a member of this family and because I have tried to achieve to bring honor to this family."

Eve made some inroads with her family. Her mother walked over to her and hugged her. At first, her brother tried to deny that he had rejected and avoided her; then, suddenly, he said, "I'm sorry, Eve. Will you forgive me?"

Instead of running away from her illness and avoiding others because of it, Eve joined two support recovery groups. In one group, she was assigned a buddy whom she could call if she felt stressed. They became close friends. As Eve became more confident in her newfound self-respect, she began speaking at Asian-sponsored events on mental health issues.

"Let Be" Harmony

Eve has been able to achieve some sense of harmony in her life. She embraced Buddhism and began meditating on a daily basis. She even changed her diet so that she would have greater internal stability. The therapist used the Wheel of Life exercise with Eve so that she could see where she wanted greater balance in her life. Eve chose to spend less time at work and more time meeting with her support groups and occasionally having dinner with her family. Her efforts to remove the stigma of bipolar disorder helped in reducing the triggers that were brought on by feelings of shame and rejection by her family. In addition, Eve has started to better manage her medication. She has changed her medications several times because she said that her mood was changing to become more positive in outlook.

Moving Forward and Acting As If It Is Impossible to Fail

Eve is moving forward with her life. For the most part, her bipolar illness is being well managed and controlled. Eve has not had another hospital placement incident. The therapist was instrumental in helping Eve overcome many of her fears. He suggested that whenever she wanted to achieve a goal, she should act as if it were impossible to fail. There might be barriers and problems along the way, but the stones that she encountered would be treated as *stepping-stones*. Eve continues her participation in two mental recovery groups.

SUMMARY OF KEY POINTS

Prevalence rates of mental illness for Asian Americans and Pacific Islanders are approximately the same for other Americans. Researchers have found that attitudinal similarity between the clinician and the Asian client and agreement on the cause and treatment of a disorder are more important than ethnic/racial match in increasing clinician credibility and the working alliance (Meyer, Zane, & Cho, 2011). Similarly, clinicians who address the cultural beliefs of their Asian clients are perceived as more competent by their clients (Wang & Kim, 2010).

The following are a number of implications for culturally competent counseling for Asian Americans.

1. Mental health clinicians need to understand the great interethnic variations among Asian Americans and Pacific Islanders.

2. Because mental health problems are influenced by cultural, generational, and acculturation levels, clinicians must assess these specific

cultural factors when working with Asian Americans and Pacific Islanders.

3. Culturally responsive strengths-based therapists understand the role of such Asian cultural values as interpersonal harmony, shame and loss of face, and filial piety in affecting Asian Americans' and Pacific Islanders' beliefs about psychological distress.

4. Successful treatment of mental health problems for the Asian American or Pacific Islander client is based on

   A. The clinician's awareness of the client's cultural background, immigration history, and acculturation history and conflicts, if any
   B. The clinician's comprehension of the client's beliefs about health, mental health, and healing
   C. The clinician eliciting from the client his or her views on what caused the presenting problem

   D. The clinician's use of the family support system to increase the client's adherence to treatment regimens and to reduce barriers to counseling
   E. The clinician's focus on the family's strengths including the resources within the client's extended family and the community

5. Culturally competent clinicians should be aware of their Asian American and Pacific Islander clients' cultural beliefs related to psychological distress, and they should have knowledge about how they may influence their client's symptoms of distress.

6. Clinicians should assess their clients to determine if oppression is influencing their clients' well-being.

7. Clinicians should be knowledgeable about Asian Americans' and Pacific Islanders' indigenous healing practices.

DISCUSSION QUESTIONS

Discussion Question Set 1

Discuss the following factors that might have an impact on counseling an Asian American or Pacific Islander:

- Adherence to traditional Asian values
- Acculturation level
- Immigration experience
- High-context/low-context communication style
- Family dynamics and interdependence
- Shame

Discussion Question Set 2

Discuss the pros and cons of Asian Americans being considered the "model minority."

KEY TERMS

Collectivistic orientation: A worldview that values the group over the individual. One's identity resides in the family or in the work group, and so forth.

Face: A combination of social standing, reputation, dignity, and honor.

Filial piety: The cultural value that one should honor one's parents and elders and take care of one's parents during old age.

Hierarchical: A family structure that gives greater status to males and older adults and where women and children defer to men and their elders.

Humility: A cultural value of some Asian Americans, which espouses that one does not brag or tout one's accomplishments.

Losing face: A person loses social standing, dignity, or reputation due to some action by the individual or by others.

Model minority: A term often used to suggest that Asian Americans achieve great success in the United States and that they might serve as a model for all other ethnic groups.

'Ohana: In Hawaii, the Department of Human Services uses an intervention called 'Ohana (family). Clinicians bring together the extended family and the neighborhood support system to collectively deal with a family's issues.

Pacific Islanders: The largest ethnic subgroups of Pacific Islander Americans are Native Hawaiians, Samoans (Guam, the Northern Mariana Islands), Chamorros, Fijians, Marshallese, Tongans, Micronesian Americans, Polynesian Americans, and French Polynesians.

Qi* or *chi: The Chinese belief that life is pervaded by energy called a life force.

Qigong: Alternatively spelled *chi gung* or *chi kung*; a form of gentle exercise consisting of movements that are repeated a number of times, such that the body is stretched, thereby increasing fluid movement and building a person's awareness of how the body moves in space.

Save face: Taking steps to prevent the loss of honor; in Japanese culture, some individuals may commit suicide to save face.

Shame: An intense feeling that one is flawed and has failed to live up to the expectations of one's family, friends, or community.

REFERENCES AND SUGGESTED READING

American Psychiatric Association. (2013). *Diagnostic and statistical manual of mental disorders* (5th ed.). Washington, DC: Author.

Asian Americans, Pacific Islanders important to U.S. history. (2013, May 19). *Mission of the United States: Geneva, Switzerland*. Retrieved from https://geneva.usmission.gov/2013/05/10/asian-americans-pacific-islanders-important-to-u-s-history/

Asian & Pacific Islander American Health Forum. (2011, July). *Demographic and socioeconomic profiles of Asian Americans, Native Hawaiians, and Pacific Islanders in the United States*. Retrieved from http://www.apiavote.org/sites/apiavote/files/APIAHF%20July%202011.pdf

Banerjee, A., Mullainathan, S., & Hanna, R. (2012). *Corruption* (Working paper no. 17968). National Bureau of Economic Research. doi:10.3386/w17968

Bell, M. P., Harrison, D. A., & McLaughlin, M. E. (1997). Asian American attitudes toward affirmative action in employment: Implications for the model minority myth. *Journal of Applied Behavioral Science, 33*, 356–377.

Brightman, J. D., & Subedi, L. A. (2007). Hawai'i. *AAPI Culture Brief, 2*(7). Retrieved from http://www.ntac.hawaii.edu/downloads/products/briefs/culture/pdf/ACB-Vol2-Iss7-Hawaii.pdf

Chen, S.-W.-H., & Davenport, D. S. (2005). Cognitive-behavioral therapy with Chinese American clients: Cautions and modifications. *Psychotherapy: Theory, Research, Practice, Training, 42*(1), 101–110.

Chen, T., & Hsu, C.-C. (2016, March 18). Asian Americans. *Encyclopedia of Public Health*. Retrieved from http://www.encyclopedia.com/topic/Asian_Americans.aspx

Chun, M. N. (2011). *No nā mamo: Traditional and contemporary Hawaiian beliefs and practices*. Honolulu: University of Hawai'i Press.

Crystal, D. (1989). Asian Americans and the myth of the model minority. *Social Casework, 70*, 405–413.

David, E. J. R., & Okazaki, S. (2006). The Colonial Mentality Scale (CMS) for Filipino Americans: Scale construction and psychological implications. *Journal of Counseling Psychology, 53*, 241–252.

Duan, C., & Brown, C. (2016). *Becoming a multicultural competent counselor*. Thousand Oaks, CA: Sage.

Duan, C., & Wang, L. (2000). Counseling in the Chinese context: Accommodating both individualistic and collectivist values. *Asian Journal of Counseling, 7*(1), 1–20.

Gallup. (2018). *CliftonStrengths 34*. Retrieved from https://www.gallupstrengthscenter.com/home/en-us/strengths finder

Grey, H., & Hall-Clark, B.N. (2015). *Cultural considerations in Asian and Pacific Islander American mental health*. New York: Oxford University Press.

Haque, A. (2010). Mental health concepts in Southeast Asia: Diagnostic considerations and treatment implications. *Psychology, Health, & Medicine, 15*, 127–134.

Hall, E. T. (1976). *Beyond culture*. New York, NY: Anchor Press.

Hoeffel, E. M., Rastogi, S., Ouk Kim, M., & Shahid, H. (2012, March). The Asian population: 2010. *2010 Census Briefs*. U.S. Census Bureau. Retrieved from http://www.census.gov/prod/cen2010/briefs/c2010br-11.pdf

Hsia, J., & Peng, S. S. (1998). Academic achievement and performance. In L. C. Lee & N. W. S. Zane (Eds.), *Handbook of Asian American psychology* (pp. 325–358). Thousand Oaks, CA: Sage.

Hurdle, D. E. (2002). Native Hawaiian traditional healing: Culturally-based interventions for social work practice. *Social Work, 47*(2), 183–192.

Hwang, W.-C., Wood, J., & Fujimoto, K. (2010). Acculturative family distancing (AFD) and depression in Chinese American families. *Journal of Consulting and Clinical Psychology, 78*, 655–667.

Itti, M., & Narasaki, D. (2014, July 10). Let's talk about Asian American and Pacific Islander mental health. *Washington State Commission on Asian Pacific American Affairs*. Retrieved from http://capaa.wa.gov/wp-content/uploads/2014/06/Mental-Health-Article.pdf

Iwamasa, G. (n.d.). *Recommendations for the treatment of Asian American/Pacific Islander populations*. Scottsdale, AZ: Asian American Psychological Association. Retrieved from http://www.apa.org/pi/oema/resources/ethnicity-health/asian-american/psychological-treatment.pdf

Kim, B., Atkinson, D., & Umemoto, D. (2001). Asian cultural values and the counseling process: Current knowledge and directions for future research. *The Counseling Psychologist, 29*(4), 570–603.

Kim, B. S. K., Atkinson, D. R., & Yang, P. H. (1999). The Asian values scale: Development, factor analysis, validation, and reliability. *Journal of Counseling Psychology, 29*, 570–603.

Kim, B. S., & Park, Y. S. (2008). Culturally alert counseling with East and Southeast Asian Americans. In Garrett McAuliffe & Associates (Eds.), *Culturally alert counseling: A comprehensive introduction* (1st ed., pp. 188–219). Thousand Oaks, CA: Sage.

Kim, B. S., & Park, Y. S. (2013). Culturally alert counseling with East and Southeast Asian Americans. In Garrett McAuliffe & Associates (Eds.), *Culturally alert counseling: A comprehensive introduction* (2nd ed., pp. 157–183). Thousand Oaks, CA: Sage.

Kim, J. (1981). The process of Asian American identity development: A study of Japanese-American women's perceptions of their struggle to achieve personal identities as Americans of Japanese ancestry. *Dissertation Abstracts International, 42*, 155IA. (University Microfilms No. 81-18080)

Kitano, H. H. L. (1982). Mental health in the Japanese American community. In E. E. Jones & S. J. Korchin (Eds.), *Minority mental health* (pp. 149–164). New York, NY: Praeger.

Kleinman, A., Eisenberg, L., & Good, B. (1978). Culture, illness and care: Clinical lessons from anthropologic and cross-cultural research. *Annals of Internal Medicine, 88*, 251–258.

Kramer, E. J., Kwong, K., Lee, E., & Chung, H. (2002). Cultural factors influencing the mental health of Asian Americans. *Western Journal of Medicine, 176*(4), 227–231.

Lau, A. S., Fung, J. J., & Yung, V. (2010). Explaining elevated social anxiety among Asian Americans: Emotional attunement and a cultural double bind. *Cultural Diversity and Ethnic Minority Psychology, 15*, 77–85.

Lee, E. (1997). *Working with Asian Americans: A guide for clinicians*. New York, NY: Guilford Press.

Lee, E. (2002, February). *Cultural diversity series: Meeting the mental health needs of Asian and Pacific Islander Americans*. National Technical Assistance Center for State Mental Health Planning (NTAC).

Lee, S., Yu, H., Wing, Y., Chan, C., Lee, A. M., Lee, D. T. S., . . . Weiss, M. G. (2000). Psychiatric morbidity and illness experience of primary care patients with chronic fatigue in Hong Kong. *American Journal of Psychiatry, 157*, 380–384.

Leong, F. (1996). Toward an integrative model for cross-cultural counseling and psychotherapy. *Applied and Preventive Psychology, 5*, 189–209.

Leong, F. T. L., & Kalibatseva, Z. (2011). Effective psychotherapy for Asian Americans: From cultural accommodation to cultural congruence. *Clinical Psychology: Science and Practice, 18*(3), 242–245.

Leong, F., & Lau, A. (2001). Barriers to providing effective mental health services to Asian Americans. *Mental Health Services Research, 3*, 201–214.

Leong, F. T., Lee, S., & Chang, D. (2008). Counseling Asian Americans. In P. B. Petersen, J. G. Draguns, W. J. Lonner, & J. E. Trimble (Eds.), *Counseling across cultures* (pp. 113–128). Thousand Oaks, CA: Sage.

Louie, S. (2014). Asian honor and suicide: The difference between East and West. *Psychology Today*. Retrieved from https://www.psychologytoday.com/blog/minority-report/201406/asian-honor-and-suicide

Macartney, S., Bishaw, A., & Fontenot, K. (2013, February). Poverty rates for selected detailed race and Hispanic groups by state and place: 2007–2011. *American Community Survey Briefs*. U.S. Census Bureau. Retrieved from https://www.census.gov/prod/2013pubs/acsbr11-17.pdf

Maki, M., & Kitano, H. (2002). Counseling Asian Americans. In P. Pedersen, J. Draguns, W. Lonner, & J. Trimble (Eds.), *Counseling across cultures* (pp. 109–131). Thousand Oaks, CA: Sage.

Meyer, O., Zane, N., & Cho, Y. I. (2011). Understanding the psychological processes of the racial match effect in Asian Americans. *Journal of Counseling Psychology, 58*, 335–345.

Nadal, K. L., Escobar, K. M. V., Prado, G. T., David, E. J. R., & Haynes, K. (2012). Racial microaggressions and the Filipino American experience: Recommendations for counseling and development. *Journal of Multicultural Counseling and Development, 40*(3), 156–173.

National Public Radio, Robert Wood Johnson Foundation, & Harvard T.H. Chan School of Public Health. *Discrimination in America: Experiences and views of Asian Americans*. (2017, November). Retrieved from https://www.rwjf.org/content/dam/farm/reports/surveys_and_polls/2017/rwjf441733

Nobel Media AB. (2014). The Nobel Prize in Physics 1998. *Nobelprize.org*. Retrieved from www.nobelprize.org/nobel_prizes/physics/laureates/1998/

Okazaki, S. (2000). Assessing and treating Asian Americans: Recent advances. In I. Cuéllar & F. Paniagua (Eds.), *Handbook of multicultural mental health: Assessment and treatment of diverse populations* (pp. 237–248). Washington, DC: American Psychiatric Association.

Ong, A. D., Burrow, A. L., Fuller-Rowell, T. E., Ja, N. M., & Sue, D. W. (2013). Racial microaggression and daily well-being among Asian Americans. *Journal of Consulting Psychology, 60*, 188–199.

Peterson, W. (1966, January 9). Success story: Japanese American style. *The New York Times Magazine*, pp. VI–20.

The rise of Asian Americans, updated edition. (2013, April 4). *Social & Demographic Trends*. Pew Research Center. Retrieved from http://www.pewsocialtrends.org/2012/06/19/the-rise-of-asian-americans/

RTI International. (2015, September 10). *Results from the 2014 National Survey on Drug Use and Health: Detailed tables*. Rockville, MD: Substance Abuse and Mental Health Services Administration, Center for Behavioral Health Statistics and Quality. Retrieved from https://www.samhsa.gov/data/sites/default/files/NSDUH-DetTabs2014/NSDUH-DetTabs2014.pdf

Ryder, A. G., Yang, J., & Heine, S. J. (2002). Somatization vs. psychologization of emotional distress: A paradigmatic example for cultural psychopathology. *Online Readings in Psychology and Culture*, *10*(2). https://doi.org/10.9707/2307-0919.1080

Sandhu, D. S., Leung, S. A., & Tang, M. (2003). Counseling approaches with Asian Americans and Pacific Islander Americans. In F. Harper & J. McFadden (Eds.), *Culture and counseling: New approaches* (pp. 99–114). Boston, MA: Allyn & Bacon.

Sue, D. W. (1973). Ethnic identity: The impact of two cultures on the psychological development of Asians in America. In S. Sue & N. Wagner (Eds.), *Asian Americans: Psychological perspectives* (pp. 140–149). Palo Alto, CA: Science and Behavior Books.

Sue, D. W., Bucceri, J., Lin, A. L., Nadal, K. L., & Torino, G. C. (2009). Racial microaggressions and the Asian American Experience. *Asian Journal of Psychology*, *S*(1), 88–101.

Sue, D. W., & Sue, D. (2003). *Counseling the culturally different: Theory and practice* (4th ed.). Hoboken, NJ: Wiley.

Sue, D. W., & Sue, D. (2013). *Counseling the culturally diverse: Theory and practice* (7th ed.). Hoboken, NJ: Wiley.

Teon, A. (2016). Filial piety in Chinese culture. *The Greater China Journal*. Retrieved from https://china-journal.org/2016/03/14/filial-piety-in-chineseculture/

Triandis, H. C. (1989). The self and social behavior in differing cultural contexts. *Psychological Review*, *96*, 506–520.

Triandis, H. C. (1995). *Individualism and collectivism*. Boulder, CO: Westview Press.

U.S. Census Bureau. (2015, April 29). Asian/Pacific American Heritage Month: May 2015. *Facts for Features*, Release Number: CB15-FF.07. Retrieved from https://www.census.gov/newsroom/facts-for-features/2015/cb15-ff07.html

U.S. Department of Labor. (2015, April 29). *The economic status of Asian Americans and Pacific Islanders*. Retrieved from https://www.dol.gov/_sec/media/reports/AsianLaborForce/2016AsianLaborForce.pdf

Wang, S., & Kim, B. S. K. (2010). Therapist multicultural competence, Asian American participants' cultural values, and counseling process. *Journal of Counseling Psychology*, *57*, 394–401.

Wong, Y. J., Tran, K. K., Kim, S.-H., Kerne, V. V. H., & Calfa, N. A. (2010). Asian Americans' lay beliefs about depression and professional help-seeking. *Journal of Clinical Psychology*, *66*, 317–322.

Yeh, C. J. (2003). Age, acculturation, cultural adjustment, and mental health symptoms of Chinese, Korean, and Japanese immigrant youths. *Cultural Diversity and Ethnic Minority Psychology*, *9*(1), 34–48.

Yeh, C. J., & Wang, Y. W. (2000). Asian American coping attitudes, sources, and practices: Implications for indigenous strategies. *Journal of College Student Development*, *41*(1), 94–103.

Zhang, N., & Dixon, D. N. (2001). Acculturation and attitudes of Asian international students towards psychological help. *Journal of Multicultural Counseling and Development*, *31*(3), 205–222.

11 CULTURALLY RESPONSIVE STRENGTHS-BASED THERAPY FOR HISPANIC AND LATINO/A AMERICANS

- *Dime con quién andas, y te diré quién eres.*

  Tell me who you hang out with, and I'll tell you who you are.

- *Al mal tiempo, buena cara.*

  Put a good face to the bad times.

- *Si Dios quiere.*

  If it's God's will.

- *Cuando una puerta se cierra, otra se abre.*

  When one door closes, another one opens.

CHAPTER OBJECTIVES

- Describe the demographics and population statistics of Hispanic and Latino/a Americans.

- Analyze racial and ethnic stereotypes and microaggressions against Hispanic and Latino/a Americans.

- Describe the worldviews of Hispanic and Latino/a Americans.

- Identify the cultural values associated with Hispanic and Latino/a Americans, including *familismo, fatalismo, machismo, marianismo, personalismo, respeto*, and spirituality.

- Describe the acculturation conflicts of Hispanic and Latino/a Americans.

- Identify the cultural strengths of Hispanic and Latino/a Americans.

- Apply your understanding of the mental health issues of Hispanic and Latino/a Americans to counseling approaches for working with members of this ethnic group.

INTRODUCTION

This chapter examines the cultures of the ethnic group classified by the U.S. Census Bureau as Hispanic and Latino or Latina Americans. It describes how Hispanic and Latino/a cultures that are bound largely by language and geographic location distinguish themselves from other cultures. These ethnocultural groups form the largest ethnic minority in the United States, and it is predicted that by 2060, one out of every four Americans will be Hispanic or Latino/a (Colby & Ortman, 2015).

This chapter describes approaches to culturally responsive strengths-based therapy with individuals who are part of the emerging Hispanic/Latino majority in the United States. It begins by examining the terms *Hispanic* and *Latino/a*. Who developed these terms, and what do they represent? Which term do members of this ethnocultural population prefer to describe themselves? Do they see their race and ethnicity as different sides of a coin?

During the 1970s, the U.S. government adopted the term *Hispanic* to describe people who can trace their heritage to Mexico, Cuba, other Spanish-speaking nations in Central and South America, and Spain. In contrast, the term *Latino/a* was introduced during the 1970s as a shortened version of "Latin American," used to refer to individuals from Mexico, Spanish-speaking Caribbean Islands, and other Spanish-speaking countries in Central and South America. Latino/a Americans are people of Latin American descent. Since *Hispanic* refers to the Spanish language, individuals of Portuguese and/or Brazilian heritage are generally not considered Hispanic, but Brazilian Americans are often included in the category *Latino/a*.

How do members of this ethnocultural group prefer to describe themselves? A survey by the Pew Research Center has found that among Hispanics and Latinos, many are ambivalent about using the two terms (Passel & Taylor, 2009). About half of those Hispanic/Latino individuals surveyed said they had no preference for either term; instead, most preferred to be identified with their country of origin. Of those who did indicate a preference, twice as many said they preferred the term *Hispanic* as opposed to *Latino*.

The U.S. Census Bureau (2011) emphasizes that Hispanic or Latino ethnicity is not a racial category: "Hispanic origin can be viewed as the heritage, nationality group, lineage, or country of birth of the person or the person's parents or ancestors before their arrival in the United States. People who identify their origin as Hispanic, Latino, or Spanish may be any race." Thus, Americans who identify as Hispanic or Latino/a may be Black/African American, White/Caucasian, Asian, American Indian, some other race, or mixed race.

If race is not the defining factor for Hispanics and Latinos, then what ethnocultural factors link members of this broad population group that traces its heritage from a wide geographic swath of countries? The Spanish language and culture constitute the common bonds for many Hispanic and Latino Americans, regardless of whether they trace their genetic origins to Africa, Europe, or the Americas. Another common bond formed among members of this ethnocultural group is the immigrant experience. In working with individuals from a Hispanic or Latino background, it is important to ask the client what cultural designation he or she prefers and then use such when counseling the client. As Comas-Díaz (2001) asserted, "the mediating factors in self-designation are gaining a voice and power to name one's identity and to define one's reality" (p. 116).

Hispanic/Latino Americans are very heterogeneous in terms of their immigration, acculturation experiences, and other cultural perspectives. Because of the heterogeneous nature of the Hispanic/Latino American population, this chapter will examine primarily the shared experiences of this population as a whole. To a lesser extent, it will also describe some of the unique features of different subgroups of Hispanic/Latino Americans.

Overall Hispanic/Latino American Population

One of the notable characteristics of the Hispanic/Latino American population is its rapid growth, which is observed among a number of Hispanic/Latino subgroups. According to the 2010 Census, Hispanic or Latino origin accounts for 50.5 million people, or 16% of the U.S. population. This figure represents an almost 3% increase from the 2000 Census figures, where the Hispanic/Latino population constituted 35.3 million people, or 13% of the total American population. The majority of the growth in the total American population came from increases in those who reported their ethnicity as Hispanic or Latino. More than 50% of the total growth in the American population from 2000 to 2010 was due to the increase in the Hispanic/Latino population (U.S. Census Bureau, 2011).

Historical Changes in the Hispanic/Latino Demographic Profile

There have been historical changes in the Hispanic/Latino profile. Since 1960, the Hispanic/Latino population has increased almost ninefold, from 6.3 million to 55.3 million in 2014. By 2060, it is projected to grow to 119 million (Colby & Ortman, 2015). The increase in the Hispanic/Latino population comes from both those who are foreign born and those who are born in the United States. During the past 50 years, the foreign-born Hispanic/Latino population has increased by more than 20 times—from fewer than 1 million in 1960 to 19.4 million in 2014. In contrast, the U.S.-born Hispanic/Latino population has only increased sixfold over this same time period. There are approximately 30 million more U.S.-born Hispanics and Latinos in the United States today (35.9 million) than there were in 1960 (5.5 million) (Colby & Ortman, 2015). Immigration, then, is a primary source of the growth of the Hispanic/Latino population.

Recent demographic data on the Hispanic/Latino population in the United States have revealed that in 2014 there were 55.3 million Hispanics and Latinos and that they now constitute 17.3% of the total U.S. population. Based on the latest projections from the U.S. Census Bureau, the Hispanic share of the U.S. population is expected to reach 28.6% by 2060 (Colby & Ortman, 2015).

There is a growing Hispanic/Latino presence in the United States that is driving tremendous demographic changes. Whereas some researchers have predicted that the total Hispanic/Latino population in the United States will be 28.6% of the total U.S. population in 2060, others have estimated that by 2050, 30% of the American population will consist of Hispanics and Latinos. The Hispanic/Latino population is a very young one. While currently one in five children under the age of 18 is Hispanic or Latino, by 2050, it is predicted that two in five children under the age of 18 will be Hispanic or Latino (Cárdenas & Kerby, 2012).

Hispanic/Latino Subgroup Percentages

An analysis of Hispanic/Latino subgroups indicates that about three-quarters of Hispanics and Latinos in the United States are of Mexican, Puerto Rican, or Cuban origin. In 2010, people of Mexican origin formed the largest Hispanic/Latino group, representing 63% of the total Hispanic/Latino population in the United States. People of Puerto Rican origin constituted the second-largest group, and they formed 9% of the Hispanic/Latino population in 2010, down from 10% in 2000. From 2000 to 2010, Cubans remained at 4% of the total Hispanic/Latino population (U.S. Census Bureau, 2011).

In 2010, the Mexican American population was by far the largest Hispanic/Latino population; it increased by 54% and demonstrated the largest numeric change (11.2 million). The Mexican American population was 20.6 million in 2000 and 31.8 million in 2010 (U.S. Census Bureau, 2011). The Puerto Rican population increased by 36%, from 3.4 million in 2000 to 4.6 million in 2010. The Cuban American population increased by 44%, from 1.2 million in 2000 to 1.8 million in 2010 (U.S. Census Bureau, 2011). Although the Mexican population is still numerically and proportionally the largest Hispanic/Latino group in the United States, this group grew at a rate slower than many of the "Other Hispanic" subgroups (U.S. Census Bureau, 2011).

The "Other Hispanics"

The U.S. Census Bureau uses the designation of "Other Hispanic" to represent those Hispanics and Latinos who are not Mexicans, Puerto Ricans, or Cubans. Among the 12.3 million "Other Hispanics" in 2010, 1.4 million were of Dominican origin; 4.0 million were of Central American origin; 2.8 million reported South American origin; 635,000 were Spaniard; and 3.5 million reported general terms such as *Hispanic* or *Latino* (U.S. Census Bureau, 2011). Salvadoran origin formed the largest group of Central American origin Hispanics at 1.6 million, followed by Guatemalans (1.0 million) and Hondurans (633,000). The South American Hispanic population consisted of the following groups: Colombian (909,000), Ecuadorian (565,000), and Peruvian (531,000). The Spaniard population in 2010 was more than six times larger than that reported in 2000, increasing from 100,00 to 635,000. Similarly, other Hispanic groups from Central and South America (e.g., Honduras, Guatemala, El Salvador, Bolivia, and Venezuela) evidenced large percent increases from 2000 to 2010, sometimes doubling their population sizes.

Cultural Reflections

How do you feel about Hispanics and Latinos becoming 30% of the total American population by 2050?

Do you think that American society would change if Hispanics and Latinos formed one out of every six Americans by 2050?

Why or why not?

Geographical Location of Hispanics and Latinos in the United States

More than 75% of the Hispanic/Latino population lived in either the West or the South. In 2010, 41% of Hispanics and Latinos lived in the West, while 36% lived in the South. The Northeast accounted for 14% of the Hispanic/Latino population, while the Midwest accounted for 9%. Although the Hispanic/Latino population grew in every region of this country, it increased most significantly in the South and Midwest. In 2010, over half of the Hispanic/Latino population resided in just three states: California, Texas, and Florida. The states that have the highest numbers of Mexican Americans are, in rank order: California, Texas, Arizona, Illinois, and Colorado. The states with the highest number of Puerto Ricans from the largest to smallest number include New York, Florida, New Jersey, Pennsylvania, and Massachusetts. The states with the largest Cuban American representation are Florida, California, New Jersey, New York, and Texas (U.S. Census Bureau, 2011).

Racial Identification(s) for the Hispanic/Latino Population

In responding to the 2010 Census, members of the Hispanic/Latino population predominantly identified their race as either "White" or "Some Other Race." As noted earlier, Hispanic/Latino origin can apply to any race. Beginning in 1997, the Office of Management and Budget required federal agencies to use a minimum of five race categories: White, Black or African American, American Indian or Alaska Native, Asian, and Native Hawaiian or Other Pacific Islander. For respondents who declined to identify with any of these five race categories, OMB approved the Census Bureau's adding of a sixth category—"Some Other Race"—on the 2010 Census questionnaire. Approximately 94% of Hispanic/Latino respondents (47.4 million) reported one race. About 53% of the Hispanic/Latino population identified as White and no other race, while about one-third (37%) gave responses that were classified as Some Other Race alone when answering the question on race. Nearly 3 million Hispanics and Latinos (6%) gave multiple races, and within this group, a large proportion gave race combinations involving Some Other Race. In terms of Hispanic/Latino subgroups, Mexican origin respondents reported predominantly as White alone (53%) and Some Other Race alone (39%). Likewise, both South American Hispanics (66%) and those of Cuban origin (85%) were much more likely than the total Hispanic/Latino population to report White alone as their racial identity (U.S. Census Bureau, 2011).

Paniagua (2014) has provided insight regarding the response to color on the part of Hispanic or Latino individuals. He points out that Hispanics use a broad range of racial denominations, noting that "many Hispanics refer to other Hispanics who have dark skin as *morenos* or *prietos* and those with olive skin or dark complexions are *trigueños*. Hispanics with light skin or kinky hair are known as *grifos, jabaos,* or *albinos*; Hispanics who have Indian features are called *indios*" (p. 92).

Ho (1992) has observed that some Hispanics and Latinos (particularly Mexican American parents) prefer children with light skin color because they believe that "if one looks and acts European, one is more acceptable" in American society (p. 105). As Paniagua (2014) has observed, "the therapist should also explore with the client any preference concerning skin color in the client's family and how this preference may affect the assessment, diagnosis, and treatment of the client" (p. 93). Hispanic/Latino skin preference for children and others may be related to their level of acculturation into American society, and the extent to which they believe that White is the desired color.

Subgroup Migration History of Some Major Hispanic/Latino Groups

Hispanics and Latinos are heterogeneous in the circumstances of their migration as well as in other characteristics. It is important to note some of the historical events that have brought

Hispanics and Latinos to the United States. Many key differences among the four major Hispanic/Latino groups are connected to the different circumstances involved in their migration to this country. Let us examine these circumstances for several of the major Hispanic and Latino population groups.

Mexican Americans

Mexicans have been residents of this country longer than any other Hispanic/Latino group. In fact, St. Augustine in what is now Florida was established as a Spanish fort in 1565, and Santa Fe and Taos in what is now New Mexico were settled by Spaniards in the early 1600s. At the time of the Mexican War (1846–1848), when the United States took over large territories from Texas to California, many Mexicans chose to remain in their "new" American communities. The Mexican Revolution (1910–1917) also contributed to the growth of the Mexican population in the United States because both economic hardships brought on by the war and the need for laborers north of the border led to increased Mexican immigration. What distinguishes many immigrants from Mexico is that many arrived "unauthorized" (without appropriate documentation) (U.S. Department of Health and Human Services, 2001).

Puerto Ricans

After World II, high unemployment among displaced agricultural workers on the island of Puerto Rico resulted in large-scale emigration to the mainland United States that continued through the 1950s and 1960s. In the 1980s, the migration pattern became more circular as many Puerto Ricans chose to return to the island. Puerto Ricans can be distinguished from other Hispanic/Latino groups in that they are U.S. citizens, whether they live in Puerto Rico or in one of the 50 United States. Their migration is governed by the second Organic Act, or Jones Act of 1917, which granted Puerto Ricans U.S. citizenship.

> ### Cultural Reflections
>
> *Of the Hispanic/Latino subgroups presented in this chapter, which one(s) do you feel the closest to? Why?*
>
> *From which group(s) do you feel the most social distance—in other words, you would not like to live next door to them or have a member of your family marry a member of this group? Explain.*

Cubans

Although a small influx of Cubans immigrated to the United States during the second half of the 19th century and in the early part of the 20th century, the largest number of Cuban immigrants came after the communist revolution led by Fidel Castro overthrew the Fulgencio Batista government of Cuba in 1959 (Bernal & Shapiro, 1996). Initially an elite group of highly educated Cubans immigrated, but in later years immigration continued with *balseros* (boat people), lower-income Cubans who made the dangerous crossing to the United States by makeshift watercraft. The educated Cuban professionals who immigrated in the early 1960s have become well established, but those who arrived with few economic resources did not fare as well. In contrast to Mexican immigrants, many Cubans have gained access to citizenship and federal support because of their status as political refugees (Cattan, 1993).

Central Americans

Immigrants from Central American countries (Belize, Costa Rica, El Salvador, Guatemala, Honduras, Nicaragua, and Panama) constitute the most recently settled Hispanic/Latino subgroup in the United States. An important distinguishing feature of Central Americans' immigration is that many fled their countries *por la situación* (roughly, "because of the situation"), a phrase that references the political terror and atrocities they faced in their homelands (Farias, 1994; Jenkins, 1991; M. Suarez-Orozco, 1990) due to political conflicts and human rights abuses related to the "drug wars" beginning in the 1980s. Approximately 21% of foreign-born Central Americans arrived in the United States between 1970 and 1979, and the large majority (about 70%) arrived between 1980 and 1990 (Lesser & Batalova, 2017).

During the 2010s, Central American immigrants to the United States received significant media attention because of the number of unaccompanied children fleeing gang violence and poverty. In 2015, 3.4 million Central Americans lived in the United States, representing approximately 8% of the 43.3 million immigrants. The vast majority of the Central Americans came from El Salvador, Guatemala, and Honduras. During 2016, U.S. Customs and Border Protection intercepted approximately 46,900 unaccompanied children. The majority of Central Americans who have achieved lawful residence in the United States did so as a result of acquiring a green card and through family reunification channels (Lesser & Batalova, 2017).

In contrast to Cubans, relatively few Central American immigrants are recognized as political refugees, despite war-related trauma and terror that precipitated their immigration and subsequently placed them at high risk for posttraumatic stress disorder. Moreover, many Hispanics/Latinos who arrive in this country without proper documentation have difficulty obtaining jobs and getting promoted. They also live with the constant immobilizing fear of being deported.

Immigration Status, Naturalization, and Pathways to Citizenship

The circumstances that caused various Hispanic/Latino groups to immigrate to the United States influenced their immigration status and treatment by the government and by American society in general. As noted previously, Puerto Ricans, whether born on the mainland or in Puerto Rico, are by definition U.S. citizens and, as a result, have access to government-sponsored support services. In the case of Cubans, because they fled a communist government, the U.S. government provided support through refugee or entrant status work permits (Gil & Vega, 1996), giving Cuban immigrants the opportunity to obtain citizenship. With this support, more than half (51%) of Cuban immigrants have become U.S. citizens, compared to only 36% of Mexican immigrants. About two-thirds of all undocumented immigrants are from Mexico (Marrero, 2011). Additionally, almost half of all Hispanic/Latino adults have expressed concern that they, a family member, or someone they know personally will be deported (Pew Research Center, 2007).

The Development, Relief, and Education for Alien Minors (DREAM) Act was first introduced in the Senate in August 2001. It aims to provide minors who entered the United States illegally, often referred to as "Dreamers," with conditional residency and eventually a path to permanent citizenship (Krogstad, 2017). This piece of legislation has been proposed numerous times but has lacked support to pass as law as of this writing. On June 15, 2012, President Obama signed an executive order titled Deferred Action for Childhood Arrivals, or DACA, that permits "Dreamers" to stay in the United States provided that they meet the following criteria.

You may request DACA if you:

1. Were under the age of 31 as of June 15, 2012;

2. Came to the United States before reaching your 16th birthday;

3. Have continuously resided in the United States since June 15, 2007, up to the present time;

4. Were physically present in the United States on June 15, 2012, and at the time of making your request for consideration of deferred action with USCIS;

5. Had no lawful status on June 15, 2012;

6. Are currently in school, have graduated or obtained a certificate of completion from high school, have obtained a general education development (GED) certificate, or are an honorably discharged veteran of the Coast Guard or Armed Forces of the United States; and

7. Have not been convicted of a felony, significant misdemeanor, or three or more other misdemeanors, and do not otherwise pose a threat to national security or public safety.

If undocumented residents are able to meet these criteria, they will be permitted to obtain a driver's license and Social Security number and a two-year work authorization, but no formal path to U.S. citizenship exists through this program. Approximately 800,000 undocumented youth were enrolled in DACA as of 2017. President Trump ended DACA on September 5, 2017.

Many Americans oppose giving Dreamers and other undocumented immigrants a path to legal citizenship. They contend that undocumented workers violated the law by coming to this country illegally, that they did not adhere to immigration policy followed by other immigrants, and that, further, they have produced a drain financially with welfare and educational expenses. Others have argued that businesses and communities have benefited from the contributions of undocumented individuals who provide labor for undesirable jobs, pay taxes, and engage in various civic activities. According to Murray (2013), a majority of American citizens and Latinos are in favor of some path to naturalized citizenship for undocumented individuals.

Having a pathway to U.S. citizenship for Hispanic and Latino/a immigrants is extremely important. The Pew Research Center has estimated that 56% of all legal foreign-born individuals, not just those from Spanish-speaking countries, became naturalized citizens in 2011, the highest percentage in three decades, and an 18-percentage-point increase since 1990. Another 12.4 million are green card holders who could eventually become naturalized and American citizens (Barrera, Lopez, Passel, & Taylor, 2013). In 2011, naturalized citizens made up 39% of the 39.6 foreign-born individuals living in the United States, up from 34% of the 32.1 immigrants in 2000.

According to the Pew Research Center's publication on Hispanic trends in naturalization (2000–2011), Mexican Americans formed 3.5 million of the 9.7 million immigrants who were eligible for naturalization but who had not been naturalized. After the 1990s, the naturalization rate for Mexicans has flattened such that in 2011, Mexicans had a 36% rate of naturalization compared to that of 61% for all immigrants. In comparison with immigrants from other Latin American countries and the Caribbean, Mexicans had the lowest naturalization rate in 2011 (Barrera et al., 2013).

There are several explanations given for the low rate of naturalization of Mexican citizens. Because of the close proximity to Mexico, Mexicans are more likely to maintain close ties to their home country. Some Mexicans might hesitate to become an American citizen because they are not aware that they can hold dual citizenship in Mexico and in the United States. The benefit of becoming an American citizen should not be undervalued. That status confers such benefits as the right to vote, to participate in federal programs, and to become eligible for federal employment.

Socioeconomic Status of Hispanic/Latino Americans

The socioeconomic status of Hispanic/Latino Americans is improving. Yet, according to the 2010 U.S. Census, the median household income for all Hispanic/Latino families was $40,165, well below the national median incomes of $50,046 for all families and $52,480 for non-Hispanic White families. In 2010, nearly 13.3 million Hispanic/Latino individuals or 26.7% of the Hispanic/Latino population lived in poverty, in comparison with 15.2% of the total U.S. population. The high poverty rate for Hispanics and Latinos can be partly attributed to the respondents' educational level and to the fact that many arrived in this country impoverished (Short, 2011; U.S. Census Bureau, 2011).

According to Cárdenas and Kerby (2012), as of June 2012, Hispanics and Latinos represented 16% of the U.S labor force at nearly 25 million workers. It is projected that Hispanics and Latinos will constitute 18% of the workforce by 2018. The educational attainment of Hispanics and Latinos as a group is a matter of concern. As Cárdenas and Kerby (2012) have asserted,

> employed Latinos are less likely to hold a college degree than either whites or African Americans, and are heavily concentrated in certain industries and sectors. Only one in six employed Latinos above the age of 25 holds a college degree, which is less than half the portion of employed whites.

Although Hispanic and Latino/a American college attendance rates have improved dramatically during the past decade (nearly doubling from 2009 to 2010—from 13% to 27%) among 18- to 24-year-olds, they continue to lag (32%) in comparison to all other racial and ethnic groups. "African Americans (38 percent), Asians (62 percent), and young white adults (43 percent) continue to be more likely to attend college than Hispanics" (Cárdenas & Kerby, 2012).

Approximately 41% of the adult Hispanic/Latino population did not earn an official high school diploma (Fry, 2010). The low educational achievement of Hispanic and Latino Americans has been linked to their unemployment rate, which was 11.5% in 2011, compared to 7.9% for non-Hispanic Whites.

Because many Mexicans, Puerto Ricans, Central Americans, and recent Cuban immigrants immigrated to the United States as unskilled laborers or displaced agricultural workers, they lack the computer skills and economic resources to make their adjustment without great psychological stress. In addition, Hispanics and Latinos experience a higher unemployment rate than some other groups because they are overrepresented in industries such as construction and manufacturing, both of which lost the most jobs during the Great Recession of 2008. They are underrepresented in job sectors that reported job growth during the recession, such as education and health services (Cárdenas & Kerby 2012).

Ethnic/Racial Stereotypes, Racism, and Microaggressions

Recently, discrimination has been reconceptualized in terms of chronic stressors or everyday experiences with discrimination that affect adversely individuals' physical and psychological health (Araújo & Borrell, 2006). Racial and ethnic microaggressions have been found to negatively impact people of color (i.e., Hispanics/Latinos, Asian Americans, and African Americans) (Nadal, 2011; Rivera, 2012; Rivera, Forquer, & Rangel, 2010; Sue, Bucceri, Rivera, Forquer, & Rangel, 2010). Racial microaggressions have been defined as "brief and commonplace daily verbal, behavioral, and environmental indignities, whether intentional or unintentional, that communicate hostile, derogatory, or negative racial slights and insults to the target person or group" (Sue, Capodilupo, et al., 2007, p. 273). Microaggressions have been found to have a negative impact on mental health of people of color (Nadal, 2011).

Nadal, Mazzula, Rivera, and Fujii-Doe (2014) conducted a study of microaggressions experienced by Hispanic/Latino Americans to determine if such discrimination was manifested differently based on participants' gender, ethnicity, or nativity. The results indicated that "women experienced more microaggressions in the workplace or school settings; self-identified Dominicans were more likely to experience being exoticized; and Puerto Ricans more likely to be treated as second-class citizens or as criminals. The results also found younger Latinos/as, and those with lower levels of education, were more likely to experience microinvalidations" (p. 67). The researchers concluded that there are important within-group differences in Hispanic/Latino Americans' experiences of microaggressions.

Hispanic and Latino/a Americans' Worldviews

Cultural Reflections

How do you feel about Hispanic/Latino people?

Do you have positive or negative stereotypes of Hispanic/Latino people?

Would you choose a Hispanic/Latino person as a friend?

There is no one worldview of Hispanic and Latino/a Americans. Members of this broad, heterogeneous group do share similar outlooks on the world, as well as differences. This section focuses on the shared worldviews of members of these groups. The Hispanic/Latino culture holds a relatively collectivist worldview; that is, those who belong to this culture are highly oriented toward the welfare of the group rather than the individual. Both responsibility and accountability are shared among members of the family and the group. Because Hispanics and Latinos emphasize the collective good over individualistic concerns, they promote an atmosphere of harmony and cooperation among group members (Casas, Raley,

& Vasquez, 2008). Interpersonal relationships are crucial in the lives of Hispanics and Latinos (Hernandez, Garcia, & Flynn, 2010; Kuhlberg, Pena, & Zayas, 2010). Having a collectivist orientation, Hispanics and Latinos often look to one another for opinions, instead of seeking the opinion of an expert. Collectivist values pervade virtually all aspects of Hispanic/Latino life.

A person's ability to speak the Spanish language is another aspect of the Hispanic/Latino worldview (Hernandez et al., 2010). One does not have to be proficient in speaking Spanish, as many third- and fourth-generation Hispanic/Latino young people cannot speak Spanish. Speaking Spanish has less to do with competency and more to do with the cultural meanings people attach to language. For Hispanics/Latinos in the United States, Spanish is an important part of their personal, social, and political identity (Casas et al., 2008). People feel connected to each other because they share a common language (Hernandez et al., 2010; Kuhlberg et al., 2010). A critical issue facing Hispanics/Latinos is teaching their children to be able to communicate in Spanish. The adults in Hispanic/Latino culture must be able to enculturate their children toward their culture. Enculturation is the process of communicating a group's culture from one generation to another. Changes within Hispanic/Latino culture have and will continue to take place through a family's interaction with the twin processes of enculturation and acculturation.

Hispanics and Latinos also tend to have a worldview that espouses a "present time" perspective over a future one. Hispanics and Latinos tend to focus on present needs, and therefore, clinicians would be wise to first emphasize short, immediate goals that can be set and reached (Gallardo, 2012). Hispanic/Latino culture has a relaxed approach to time; it does not tend to respond to culture where minutes or hours are critical factors. Whereas those from North American and Northern European cultures are very exact about time and being present at the designated time, Hispanics and Latinos tend to give a person more leeway if he or she is a half-hour late for an appointment (Delgado-Romero, Nevels, & Capielo, 2013).

Communication Style of Hispanics and Latinos

The communication style of Hispanics and Latinos is also reminiscent of that for other collectivist cultures; that is, they prefer to interact at an emotional or spiritual level with friends and others in their community. In most interpersonal encounters, Hispanics and Latinos rely on nonverbal communication and gut feelings. As Ricardo López (2009), a reporter with *Latino Opinion*, has stated,

> many of you will know that Latinos are also keen on physical connection. Hugs and kisses are normal in everyday interactions. It is normal for Latino men to greet females with a kiss; even if they do not know each other well. Men also hug each other as a sign of affection. In fact, a very common closing for a business letter in Latino correspondence is "un abrazo" or "a hug." In interviewing Latinos I sometimes use touch to communicate that I understand and care about what they have to say. Simple gestures like a hand on the shoulder or a handshake are effective. In some instances when a respondent became very emotional I have offered a hug. I don't know that I have ever used touch in non-Hispanic interviewing.

In general, Hispanics and Latinos tend to have a highly respectful way of communicating, and formal titles are used when addressing people. Hispanics and Latinos also communicate by touching and by showing affection toward friends whom they may kiss; males may be hugged and kissed. Sometimes the politeness of Hispanics and Latinos is interpreted as being subservient or servile. Some of the polite phrases that Hispanics and Latinos tend to use are *a sus órdenes* ("at your command") and *con permiso* ("with your permission"); people may also refer to *mi reina* ("my queen") or *mi rey* ("my king") when speaking of wives and girlfriends or husbands and boyfriends Delgado-Romero et al., 2013).

Hispanics/Latinos tend to use their hands and body when they are talking—much more so than is the case for Northern Europeans (Paniagua, 2014). As López (2009) has stated, "I find myself using hand movements even when I talk on the phone and nobody sees me! I have said many times that if you tie my hands I am unable to speak. Voice pitch and volume is also used extensively among Latinos."

HISPANIC/LATINO AMERICAN CULTURAL VALUES

A clinician's failure to understand and to respond appropriately to Hispanic/Latino clients' cultural values can lead to a number of adverse clinical consequences, including premature termination of counseling, noncompliance with clinical recommendations, and decreased satisfaction with counseling. A major challenge in working with individuals from Hispanic and Latino backgrounds is to be able to use cultural generalizations appropriately without stereotyping the individual client. To avoid stereotyping Hispanic/Latino clients, or any client for that matter, clinicians must remember that there are important differences between Hispanic/Latino subgroups and within specific groups (Gallardo, 2012). That is, each Hispanic/Latino client may resemble other members of his or her group in value orientation, while at the same time having his or her own unique interpretation of this culture. Factors such as the individual's socioeconomic status, education, degree of acculturation, and proficiency in English mediate a Hispanic/Latino client's thoughts and behavior (Delgado-Romero et al., 2013).

The Hispanic/Latino Family and the Cultural Value of *Familismo*

Hispanic/Latino culture is a collectivist culture with strong family values and loyalties. The family or group takes precedence over the needs of the individual. In this culture, ***familismo*** is the value of family over individual or community needs and the expression of strong loyalty, reciprocity, and solidarity among family members (Gallardo, 2012). In Hispanic/Latino culture, the family is the major source of a person's identity, and the sense of family belonging is strong. For example, when a couple marries, the parents of the bride and groom welcome the opposite side's aunts, uncles, and cousins as members of their own extended family. Conversely, individuals are slow to trust nonfamily members. Clinicians should consider including the family, meaning the nuclear and extended family, when working with Hispanic/Latino clients. Cooperation and sacrifice among family members is emphasized. Decisions should not be made by individuals without consulting the family. Clinicians can gain the trust of the Hispanic/Latino client by eliciting the opinions, recommendations, and thoughts from other family members who may or not be present (Delgado-Romero et al., 2013).

Cultural Reflections

To what extent is the Hispanic/Latino worldview similar to your worldview?

Do you believe that your worldview is compatible with that of Hispanic/Latino people?

Do you have any thoughts about the Hispanic/Latino family?

Family Structure of Hispanic/Latino Americans: *Machismo, Respeto,* and *Marianismo*

Hispanic/Latino households frequently contain members of the extended family, and they live in households containing five or more members (U.S. Census Bureau, 2010). The family structure is stratified so that it is hierarchical in nature, with special authority given to parents, males, and the elderly. Usually, Hispanic/Latino families observe a type of generational hierarchy in which the elderly are given a place of esteem and power. The father is the ultimate symbol of power within the family.

The Role of Men in the Hispanic/Latino Family. Typically, men tend to be dominant in Hispanic/ Latino families, and family members attribute to them a quality called ***machismo***. The characteristics associated with *machismo* include physical strength, sexual attractiveness, masculinity, aggressiveness, and the ability to drink alcohol without getting drunk (Gallardo, 2012). According to Delgado-Romero, Galvan, Hunter, and Torres (2008), *machismo* "can also include positive characteristics such as pride, honor, responsibility to be a good provider, and assertive behavior" (p. 338). *Machismo* plays an important role in the Puerto Rican, Mexican, and other Hispanic/ Latino groups. In general, *machismo*

- Is a positive attribute

- Influences Hispanic/Latino adolescent males during ethnic identity formation

- Implies certain rights and privileges specific to men

- Refers to a male's manhood, honor, dignity, and protecting one's name

Hispanic/Latino men are expected to be financial providers for the family, to maintain the integrity of the family unit, and to uphold the honor of family members. Hispanic/Latino men are given *respeto* (respect) from family members. **Respeto** means that people are given the appropriate deferential behavior based on their sex, age, social position, or economic status. Women show respect by being submissive to their husbands.

Hispanic/Latino Children. Parents are obligated to raise their children so that they show *respeto* for authority figures, and if they achieve this feat, the child is said to be *una persona bien educada* (a well-educated person)—someone whose parents have taught him or her the importance of acting with respect and dignity (*con respeto y dignidad*). If a child does not show the proper respect, he or she is described as *mal educada* (poorly educated) (Paniagua, 2014). If a Hispanic/Latino father says that his son does not have education, he is conveying the idea that his son does not show the proper *respeto* to authority figures or to people in the community. In early life, Hispanic/Latino children learn (1) a deep sense of family responsibility, (2) rigid definitions of sex roles (usually in traditional families), (3) respectful treatment of the elderly, (4) the male's position of respect and authority in the family, and (5) the female's position of homemaker, symbolized by the cultural value of *marianismo*, discussed below.

> ### Cultural Reflections
>
> *Of the Hispanic/Latino cultural values discussed thus far in this chapter, which value are you in most agreement with?*
>
> *Which value would you have difficulty adopting as your own?*
>
> *What are your thoughts about Hispanic/ Latino adolescents constituting one in six adolescents in the United States?*

Hispanic/Latino Adolescents and Young Adults. Hispanic/Latino adolescents constitute one in six adolescents in the United States (Pew Research Center, 2016). The rapid growth in communities among Hispanics and Latinos has created a significant racial-generational gap in the United States. In 2010, 34.9% of Hispanics and Latinos were under the age of 18, compared to 20.9% of non-Hispanic Whites (Cárdenas & Kerby, 2012; López, 2009).

The situation of Hispanic/Latino adolescents is important because they deal with both acculturation and ethnic identity conflicts, which bring on stress and maladaptive behaviors. Hispanic/Latino adolescents have a high risk of such behaviors as alcohol and tobacco consumption, aggression toward others, and suicide (Smokowski, Rose, & Bacallao, 2010). Those who are born in this country have been reported to have high rates of juvenile delinquency and substance abuse (Pew Research Center, 2009). According to Baumann, Kuhlberg, and Zayas, 2010, Latina adolescents have the highest rate (15%) of attempted suicide in comparison with other adolescent groups. Acculturation stress has been found to be a significant factor in Hispanics' and Latinos' alcohol-use patterns (Chartier & Caetano, 2010).

Hispanic/Latina Women. In general, Hispanic/Latina women are expected to show respect and submission to their husbands; however, their submission to their husbands tends to vary along the lines of the degree of their acculturation in American society. Women subscribe to **marianismo**, the high value Hispanic/Latina women put on being dedicated, loving, and supportive wives and mothers (Delgado-Romero et al., 2008). The word *marianismo* refers to the Virgin Mary, the much revered mother of Jesus Christ in the Bible. According to Delgado-Romero et al. (2008), "there are strengths in the value of *marianismo*, such as dedication to the family and being a keeper of tradition" (p. 338).

The Cultural Value of *Personalismo*

Whereas Americans are more time and task oriented, Hispanics and Latinos are inclined to emphasize the importance of a relationship (Arredondo, Bordes, & Paniagua, 2008; Casas et al., 2008). They subscribe to **personalismo** (personalism) in their interactions with others, including mental health professionals. They seek a sense of warmth from those with whom they interact. A related term to *personalismo* is **simpatía**, which translates as "kindness" (not "sympathy") and suggests that there should be politeness and pleasantness even when one is confronted with stress. If counselors assume a businesslike attitude toward Hispanic/Latino clients, they might perceive the relationship as negative. Clinicians should be attentive, show respect, and exhibit some degree of confidence that indicates that they know what they are doing.

Comas-Díaz (2012) has observed that the value of *personalismo* extends to the client's gift-giving during therapy. She maintains that "these gifts usually consist of inexpensive souvenirs, books, consumables, flowers, [or] handmade items" Comas-Díaz, 2012, p. 116). If a counselor rejects such gifts, the Hispanic/Latino client may feel offended in that the value of *personalismo* was not appreciated, and therefore terminate prematurely from therapy. Gifts that are offered as a form of payment for counseling or therapy are inappropriate according to the American Psychological Association (2010) ethical principle 6.06, which deals with bartering with clients or patients. Clinicians should note that Asian American and American Indian clients also tend to give gifts during counseling and therapy.

The Cultural Value of *Fatalismo*

Hispanics and Latinos tend to believe that uncertainty is inherent in life and that people should take each day as it comes rather than spending a great deal of time worrying or trying to control external forces. **Fatalismo** (fatalism) is the belief in a person's destiny, the idea that a person can do little to change fate or to control or prevent adversity (Ho, 1992). While some clients might use the belief of *fatalismo* to suggest there are no protections against their problems (it was fate that things happened the way they did), others might use *fatalismo* to become involved in various religious activities and to connect spiritually with God.

Spiritual and Religious Values

The majority of Hispanics and Latinos are religious; they believe that God is involved in their everyday lives. More than two-thirds of Hispanics/Latinos are Catholic (68%); 20% are Protestant (20%), 8% secular, 3% "Other Christians," and 1% other faiths (Pew Forum on Religion & Public Life & Pew Hispanic Project, 2007). Two-thirds of Hispanic/Latino worshippers attend churches presided over by Hispanic/Latino clergy, where services are given in Spanish and most worshippers are also Hispanic/Latino (Pew Forum on Religion & Public Life & Pew Hispanic Project, 2007).

Many Hispanics and Latinos have deeply spiritual values, demonstrated by their habits of praying every day, having a religious object in their home, and attending a religious service at least once a month (Pew Forum on Religion & Public Life & Pew Hispanic Project, 2007).

Faith and church are intricate parts of family and community life. Hispanics and Latinos use religion to derive an understanding of physical and mental illnesses and the healing process (Kemp & Rasbridge, 2004).

ACCULTURATION CONFLICTS FOR HISPANIC/LATINO AMERICANS

Acculturation is a controversial issue in the treatment of Hispanic/Latino clients because stress is created when a person is forced to choose between two cultures. Acculturative stress can be expressed in family discord, intergenerational conflict, and ethnic/racial identity conflict (McAuliffe & Associates, 2013). Most individuals who immigrate to a new country experience acculturation conflicts as they attempt to adjust to new societal values, beliefs, and ways of interacting. For instance, as new arrivals of Hispanic/Latino men and women begin to adjust to American life, they may find that the cultural values of *machismo* and *marianismo* conflict with the American values related to egalitarian relationships between men and women. If a Latina woman acculturates to the role of an independent American woman who wants to work outside the home, conflicts may take place over her husband's demand that she adhere to the Latina value of *marianismo*.

Acculturation conflict and pressure is a risk factor for Hispanic/Latino clients if they live in an environment that lacks sufficient social support from family, teachers, friends, and counselors. It often creates stress and loss of self-esteem as the individual attempts to juggle a clash of values. As Casas and colleagues (2008) have pointed out, "when acculturation pressures confront especially strong ethnic identification, a person's mental health may be put at increased risk. In relation to resilience, other researchers contend that, with support from significant others, an individual's choice to maintain important aspects of his or her sociocultural background can create a 'healthy aware' individual who can function effectively across cultures and settings" (p. 140).

Clinicians should be aware of how cultural conflicts over gender roles in families may lead to family disharmony and problems. For example, E. Flores, Tschann, Dimas, Pasch, and de Groat (2010) investigated the potential effect of acculturation on marital conflicts in a group of Mexican American husbands and wives and found that "more acculturated husbands and wives experience more direct marital conflicts than less acculturated husbands and wives" (p. 49).

Miranda and Umhoefer (1998) investigated the relationship between Hispanic/Latino acculturation and mental health. These investigators found that both high- and low-acculturated Mexican Americans scored high on social dysfunction, alcohol consumption, and acculturative stress. In contrast, bicultural Latinos obtained significantly higher scores on social interest and lower scores on depression, suggesting that a bicultural acculturation is the least detrimental stage of acculturation as far as Hispanics' and Latinos' mental health is concerned. Latinos who evidenced a bicultural acculturation maintained elements of the Mexican culture while incorporating practices and beliefs of American culture. The researchers concluded that a bicultural orientation to Mexican and American life may be the "healthiest" route for acculturation because individuals with bicultural values accept and negotiate features of both cultures.

Acculturation conflicts often occur between adolescent Hispanics and Latinos and their parents, especially in the area of rules and procedures that govern teen dating. Traditional Hispanic/Latino families may subscribe to a dating process that involves the chaperoning of adolescent females by parents or relatives (e.g., uncles and aunts). The Hispanic/Latino tradition of chaperoning young female adolescents is in stark contrast to the dating process for American teenagers.

> **Cultural Reflections**
>
> *Have you ever experienced an acculturation conflict with the mainstream values of American society?*
>
> *If so, what type of conflict did you experience?*
>
> *How did you go about resolving the acculturation conflict?*

Acculturated Latina adolescents create problems for their traditional Latino families when they demand to date a young man (particularly one who is not Latino) without a chaperone (Bernal & Gutierrez, 1988).

Likewise, acculturation conflicts can be linked with a Hispanic/Latino adolescent's attempt to forge an ethnocultural identity. During adolescence, Hispanic/Latino young people must decide if they are going to adhere to mainstream American or traditional Hispanic/Latino values. Acculturation on their parts raises the questions, "Who am I?" "Where do I belong?" "Should I adopt the cultural values that American teenagers endorse, or should I cling to my Mexican or Hispanic cultural values?" "Am I a Chicano," "Latino," or "Hispanic"? Hispanic/Latino adolescents' acculturation process is influenced by their search for an ethnocultural identity (Bernal & Gutierrez, 1988). Researchers have found that parent–adolescent conflict is associated with lower self-esteem among acculturated adolescents whose families have a minimal focus on *familismo*—that is, the importance of family ties (Smokowski, Rose, & Bacallao, 2010). Hispanic/Latino clients' degree of acculturation has practical implications for counseling. Those with low degrees of acculturation might find it difficult to self-disclose to counselors and therapists because of a lack of trust. Clinicians should inquire about potential acculturation conflicts with Hispanic/Latino clients.

CULTURAL IDENTITY OF HISPANICS AND LATINOS

Models of ethnic and racial identity are useful in assessing, conceptualizing, and providing counseling to clients. Ruiz (1990) developed a specific Chicano/Latino model of ethnic identity to address the process of enculturation and acculturation related to Hispanic/Latino populations. The model outlines the development, transformation, and resolution of ethnic identity conflicts that Hispanics and Latinos may encounter. The model has four key assumptions: (1) Marginality correlates highly with a Hispanic/Latino person's maladjustment, (2) negative experiences of forced assimilation are detrimental to a Hispanic/Latino person, (3) having pride in one's Hispanic/Latino ethnic identity is positively correlated with good mental health, and (4) having pride in one's Hispanic/Latino identity gives the person freedom to choose in the acculturation process. According to Ruiz, the identity process involves five stages: causal, cognitive, consequence, working through, and successful resolution.

1. During the ***causal stage***, the individual receives messages from the surrounding environment; significant others ignore, negate, or otherwise denigrate the Hispanic/Latino heritage. Positive affirmation of the person's Hispanic/Latino identity is absent. Because the person may experience deeply humiliating and sometimes traumatic experiences connected to being of Hispanic/Latino heritage, he or she may fail to identify with Hispanic/Latino culture.

2. The ***cognitive stage*** involves the individual's incorporation of three erroneous belief systems that come about as a result of the negative ethnic stereotypes he or she hears. The three distorted belief systems are intended to influence the behavior of the Latino individual, and they are as follows: (1) Ethnic group membership is associated with poverty and prejudice; (2) assimilation into the dominant White society is the means of escape from poverty and prejudice; and (3) assimilation into the mainstream society is the only pathway to success.

3. During the ***consequence stage*** of identity development, the fragmentation of the Hispanic/Latino person's ethnic identity intensifies, and as a result, he or she may reject the Chicano/Latino heritage. The person feels ashamed and embarrassed by his or her ethnic characteristics, such as name, accent, skin color, cultural customs, and so forth. The person becomes estranged from his or her ethnocultural identity and therefore rejects it.

4. The ***working through stage*** is characterized by two major dynamics. Increasingly, the Hispanic/Latino person is unable to cope with the psychological stress of the ethnic identity conflict. In addition, the person decides not to continue being a "pretender" by identifying with an alien identity. The working through stage forces the individual to reclaim and to reintegrate disowned ethnic identity fragments. It encourages a person to integrate a healthier Chicano/Latino identity. The individual experiences ethnic consciousness as he or she attempts to reclaim, reintegrate, and reconnect with his or her ethnic identity.

5. The fifth and final ***successful resolutions stage*** is typified by the person's increased acceptance of self, culture, and ethnicity. The person experiences improved self-esteem as he or she now believes that the Hispanic/Latino ethnic identity is positive and can lead to success.

The Ruiz (1990) model is notable because it was developed by using a clinical population. Another plus associated with this model is that it suggests interventions and directions the counselor might take for each of the five stages. For instance, Ruiz recommends for the cognitive stage that the counselor use strategies to attack the client's faulty beliefs. During the consequence stage, the counselor helps the client to reintegrate ethnic identity fragments in a positive manner. The counselor emphasizes ethnocultural identification during the working through stage, and for the successful resolutions stage, the counselor works to help the client develop a positive ethnic identity.

HISPANIC/LATINO CULTURAL STRENGTHS

Hispanic/Latino Americans have important cultural strengths. Focusing on Hispanic/Latino clients' strengths promotes their mental health. Strengths can be conceptualized as protective factors that can be used to combat distress.

Clinicians should focus on strengths to promote Hispanic/Latino clients' well-being. The family constitutes a powerful strength for Hispanic/Latino families. All too often, psychological studies focus on the deficits of Hispanics and Latinos rather than on their strengths. For instance, many Hispanic/Latino immigrants come to this country poor, seeking a better economic life for themselves and family members. Yet recent research is beginning to show that despite the fact that a large number of Hispanic/Latino children are poor, they enter school with some of the same social skills as do White American children. A study published in the American Psychological Association journal *Developmental Psychology* states, "The majority of Latino children arrive at kindergarten with social competencies that are comparable to those held by middle-class White children" (Galindo & Fuller, 2010, p. 591). The article is one of seven dealing with factors leading to the success or lack of success of Latino children. Overall, the studies showed that Latino children are inclined to start school with some strong assets, but those early gains are likely to soon disappear if they attend low-quality schools and live in low-income neighborhoods. The articles concluded that Latinos appear to have some cultural practices that make their children ready to learn. As noted in the section on Hispanic/Latino children, an important social skill that Hispanic/Latino children learn at an early age is *respeto* and acting *con respeto y dignidad*. As a result of learning *respeto* in Hispanic/Latino culture, children go to school ready to learn and eager to show respect for the teacher and all who are in positions of authority at their school.

A recent Child Trends Hispanic Institute paper examined some of the assets that Latina mothers bring to parenting and their children's education. Researcher Manica Ramos (2014) interviewed 43 immigrant Latina

Cultural Reflections

What are your thoughts about the strengths of Hispanic/Latino Americans?

Is there any one Hispanic/Latino strength that you especially admire? Explain.

mothers with pre-K-age children whose annual family incomes were under $35,000. Ramos concluded that the mothers were willing to make sacrifices for their children and they were able to state how their efforts might improve their children's lives. All mothers agreed that education was the key to a better life and being "better" or "great" (Ramos, 2014).

In most societies around the world, the family is the crucible from which all else comes. The Hispanic/Latino American family is faring well in comparison to other American families. Over 62% of Hispanic/Latino children live with two married parents. The divorce rate is lower for Hispanic/Latino families than for many ethnic minority groups. The low educational achievement rate for Hispanic/Latino adolescents is related to their families' poverty and to the fact that they attend poor schools that lack appropriate resources and skilled teachers. It is predicted that as the socioeconomic status of Hispanic/Latino families improves, so will the educational achievement of their children.

The cultural strengths of Hispanic/Latino Americans are numerous. Their spirituality is a major strength for them. Clinicians who explore individual and family religious practices in the present and in the past can reveal successful coping mechanisms for clients. For instance, during times of stress, Latinas may invoke the Virgin Mary, Jesus, the Virgin of Guadalupe, or a patron saint. Common Hispanic/Latino cultural expressions are ¡Ay, Dios mio! ("Oh my God!") and Si Dios quiere ("If it's God's will") (M. Flores & Carey, 2000). Hispanic/Latino music is sung all over the world, and Hispanics and Latinos have made significant contributions to the cuisine available in American life. Cinco de Mayo parades have brought pleasure to thousands of Americans. Yet the greatest strength of Hispanics and Latinos rests in the close-knit loyalty of their family.

HISPANIC/LATINO PHYSICAL AND MENTAL HEALTH ISSUES

The mental health of Hispanic/Latino Americans has been associated with their recent immigrant status versus their birth in the United States. Hispanic/Latino adults who are immigrants have lower prevalence rates of mental disorders than those born in the United States. One factor that contributes to their resilience is what C. Suarez-Orozco and M. Suarez-Orozco (1995) refer to as a "dual frame of reference." Investigators found that Hispanic/Latino immigrants in middle school frequently compare their or their family's life in their native country to their life in the United States, while U.S.-born Hispanic/Latino children compare their situation with that of their American peers. Hispanic/Latino American children may be more aware of what they do not have and thus may experience more distress. The Suarez-Orozcos also referenced high aspirations for immigrants to succeed in America, often to support their families instead of just themselves. Relatively recent immigrants' dual frame of reference and collective achievement goals are part of a complex set of factors that may explain why some Hispanic/Latino immigrants function better than Hispanics and Latinos of later generations.

Guarnaccia, Parka, Deschamps, Milstein, and Argiles (1992) also found that some Hispanic/Latino families use spiritual strength to cope with a relative's serious mental illness. Family members' strong belief in God gave them a sense of hope. For example, in reference to her brother's mental illness, one of the participants stated, "We all have an invisible doctor that we do not see, no? This doctor is God. Always when we go in search of a medicine, we go to a doctor, but we must keep in mind that this doctor is inspired by God and that he will give us something that will help us. We must also keep in mind that who really does the curing is God, and that God can cure us of anything that we have, material or spiritual" (Guarnaccia, Parka, et al., 1992 p. 206).

Recent national data have revealed that the mental health of Hispanics is affected by poverty and acculturation ("Mental Health and Hispanics," 2017). Hispanics' poverty level affects their mental health status. "Hispanics below the poverty level, as compared to Hispanics over twice the poverty level, are three times more likely to report psychological distress" ("Mental Health and Hispanics," 2017). Surveys excerpted from the Centers for Disease Control and Prevention's Summary Health

Statistics for 2010 revealed that among American adults 18 years of age and over, a larger proportion of Hispanic men than non-Hispanic men said that they experienced feelings of sadness (3.8% vs. 2.5%), hopelessness (2.8% vs. 1.9%), and worthlessness (2.0% vs. 1.6%), and that everything is an effort all of the time (6.2% vs. 4.9%) (National Center for Health Statistics, 2018).

Similar patterns held for Hispanics and White women, with Hispanic women evidencing greater sadness, hopelessness, and worthlessness than White women. Hispanic men did evidence lower suicide rates than White men. The suicide rate for Hispanics is half that of the non-Hispanic White population. However, suicide attempts for Hispanic girls in Grades 9–12 were 70% higher than for White girls in the same age group in 2011. Despite the higher rates of sadness and hopelessness for Hispanics, non-Hispanic Whites received mental health treatment two times more than Hispanics in 2008 (see "Mental Health and Hispanics," 2017).

Moreover, Hispanics and Latinos share a worldview related to health, mental health, and health habits. Oftentimes, they rely on culturally approved traditional healing systems because of the lower costs involved and because expensive modern medical care is unaffordable for many (Comas-Díaz, 2012). Religious leaders, including Catholic priests and Protestant ministers, help Hispanic/Latino clients to deal with their mental health problems. Hispanic and Latino people are a deeply religious and spiritual people; therefore, they believe that prayers will take away or cure a physical or mental health problem (Comas-Díaz, 2012). Generally speaking, Hispanics and Latinos (usually those who are not fully acculturated) only seek the services of a mental health professional after they have (1) sought the assistance of their priest or minister, (2) engaged in prayers to ask a higher being to take away the problem, or (3) discussed the problem with family members and friends (Comas-Díaz,, 2012).

Hispanics and Latinos believe that certain behaviors can cause mental health issues and problems (Comas-Díaz, 2012; Delgado-Romero et al., 2008). For instance, Mexicans believe that *envidia* (envy) causes illness and bad luck and that *mal de ojo* (the evil eye) is caused when someone looks with jealousy at another person (Kemp & Rasbridge, 2004).

In addition, some Hispanics and Latinos believe that a mental disorder (*enfermedad mental*) is less serious than being insane (*estar loco*). If a person believes that he or she is experiencing a mental disorder, he or she will seek help from a friend, relative, or clergy (Kemp & Rasbridge, 2004). A client who suffers from a mental disorder may be experiencing a *crisis nerviosa* or *ataque de nervios* (nervous breakdown). Conversely, a person who is *loco* may require hospitalization. If a client is brought to a mental health clinic, family members may believe that he or she is *loco*.

In an early study, Jenkins (1988) found that many Mexican Americans attributed their relatives' schizophrenia to *nervios*, which suggests that the client is not blameworthy; hence, family members were more inclined to be accepting and less critical of the illness. Their warmth and accepting attitude toward their relative's *nervios* helped to protect the relative with schizophrenia from relapse. The spirituality of Hispanic/Latino families when combined with their conceptions of mental illness and their warmth provided critical support to family members.

> ### Cultural Reflections
>
> *How comfortable would you feel counseling a Hispanic/Latino American?*
>
> *Do you feel that you have acquired sufficient knowledge and skills to work with a Hispanic/Latino client? If so, where did you gain your cultural knowledge?*
>
> *If you do not think that you have sufficient cultural knowledge to work with Hispanic/Latino clients, would you decline working with clients from this cultural background? Would you seek to become more knowledgeable about Hispanic/Latino culture?*

COUNSELING APPROACHES FOR WORKING WITH HISPANIC/LATINO CLIENTS

Making a Culturally Responsive Strengths-Based Diagnosis for Hispanic/Latino Clients

As noted earlier in this book, the Cultural Formulation Interview (American Psychiatric Association, 2013) has assisted in providing a cultural framework for diagnosing culturally diverse clients. McAuliffe and associates (2013) have recommended using a three-step process to culturally responsive diagnosis: (1) assess client's cultural identity and the salience of such identity prior to diagnosing, (2) consider the ethnocultural group's or local descriptions of mental distress, and (3) work through the *Diagnostic and Statistical Manual of Mental Disorders* in an Axis IV-III-I-II order. With the publication of the DSM-5, McAuliffe et al.'s (2008) three recommendations need to be modified because the axis system has been discontinued in the new manual.

Paniagua (2014) has suggested that the clinician consider the following points for counseling practice. The clinician should focus on the current events of the client's life, as opposed to engaging in an extensive review of the client's past.

1. The clinician should use a problem-solving approach for working with clients.

2. Consideration should be given to including the family in the counseling process by intentionally mentioning this possibility to the client and his or her family.

3. The clinician should talk about spiritual issues, including the *mal puesto*, or the hex, and *mal de ojo*, or the evil eye. These beliefs may control the manner in which the client sees the problem, and consequently, they should be explored during the first session.

4. Listen for the client's individual and cultural strengths and honor the client's struggle with the presenting problem.

5. Listen for culture in the client's story.

6. Use more *personalismo* and less formalism—during the first session, the clinician should initially emphasize formality; however, for the ensuing sessions, the clinician should use *personalismo*, including close physical proximity, handshaking, and self-disclosure by the clinician.

7. The clinician should avoid insight-oriented and rational emotive therapy because insight-oriented therapy "blames" the client for his or her own problems, and rational emotive therapy is too argumentative.

8. Do not recommend that the client take actions against his or her cultural values, especially the values of *machismo* and *marianismo*.

9. Before the client leaves the first session, provide him or her with recommendations or steps that can be taken to alleviate his or her presenting issue.

10. Acknowledge prejudice and racism, and where appropriate challenge any internalized oppression.

11. Create a culturally responsive therapy environment that will make the client feel welcome. Include pictures related to the client's culture.

12. Consider using the Cultural Formulation Interview.

13. Be prepared to conduct culture-based assessment that includes information about gender socialization, religious and spiritual orientation, ethnic identity, and language preferences.

14. Understand the client's worldview.

15. Become acquainted with factors that contribute to acculturation stress, and learn about family migration history.

16. Understand when it is appropriate to use language interpreters.

17. Know when it is appropriate or inappropriate to involve an indigenous healer.

CASE VIGNETTE 11.1

ENRIQUE: STRENGTHS-BASED THERAPY AND THE JUVENILE JUSTICE SYSTEM

This section provides a case study involving a Latino client using the strengths-based therapy model. At the end of the case study, I have provided a strengths-based treatment plan for correctional settings.

Multicultural Issues in Juvenile Correction Systems

Minority youth are overrepresented at every level of the juvenile justice system. Why is the number of minority youth in the juvenile justice system so out of proportion to their representation in the general population?

Disproportionate minority contact is the disproportionate representation of minority youth in the juvenile justice system. This first came to national attention in 1988, when the Coalition for Juvenile Justice mentioned the topic in its annual report to Congress. In response to the report, Congress required that all states receiving formula grant funds address disproportionality among those in the juvenile justice system.

Clinical and Treatment Issues for Youth in the Juvenile Justice System

When youth become involved in the juvenile justice system, they become disempowered, stigmatized, and devalued. The strengths-based therapy model gives power, strengths, and value to these youth. The strengths-based therapy model is designed to restore youth to healthy, productive, and competent lifestyles. Treatment issues involve assessing a youth's and a family's strengths and helping the youth to make positive connections with the community. Emphasis is also placed on repairing the harm that the youth has created and building a youth's competencies. How does one go about developing prosocial activities to engage youth? Other questions to ask include, "Does the juvenile need substance use disorder treatment? Residential services? Mental health services? What educational services are necessary?" Generally, transitional programming begins at the disposition stage for youngsters in juvenile detention. Disposition may be long or short term or may be an informal adjustment handled in or outside of the court system.

The strengths-based therapy model is applied to the case of Enrique, a Mexican American youth. The case is one that is modified, and the entire case can be found at the Detention Diversion Advocacy Program (DDAP). The case study is part of the government domain; therefore, it can be used by other authors with appropriate citation.

Case Analysis Using the Strengths-Based Therapy Model: Enrique

Enrique was a 17-year-old Mexican immigrant who ran with a street gang in San Francisco when he was first referred to DDAP. He lived with his mother in a predominantly Hispanic neighborhood. His mother, who was in poor health and spoke very little English, was the only family member with whom he had regular contact. Enrique was referred to DDAP through the Public Defender's Office after being arrested for involvement in a shooting between rival gang members. Both Enrique and his mother faced the possibility of deportation as a result.

Enrique's case manager was Mario Sanchez. Upon interviewing Enrique and his mother, Mario assessed Enrique's strengths and those of his mother. Despite Enrique's involvement in a gang, he had performed fairly well in school, earning mostly Cs and Bs in all subjects. Enrique also attended Mass on a weekly basis with his mother.

Together, Mario, Enrique, and his mother developed a release plan. Though the charges against Enrique were serious, it was only Enrique's first offense; therefore, the judge accepted Mario's release plan.

Assessment of strengths. Enrique's strengths were in the area of math and finances. He was fascinated by Wall Street and the stock market after having seen a movie about a man played by Will Smith who went from being homeless to earning millions in the stock market (*The Pursuit of Happyness*, 2006). Mario sought to capitalize on Enrique's interest in the stock market by getting a mentor for him from a local investment firm. With the court's approval, the mentor set up a small investment in stocks for Enrique and his mother for approximately $300.

Enrique was to monitor the stocks he chose and to indicate to the mentor any action he wanted to take regarding the stocks he had chosen. Enrique chose two stocks in the biomedical field. Each share was approximately $7. After doing considerable research, he discovered that one stock was in the area of getting approved by the Food and Drug Administration for novel cancer treatments, while the other one was developing an obesity drug. Enrique was excited that he could stay at home and earn money by choosing and monitoring the progress of stocks.

Based on self-reported and tested strengths, Mario, Enrique, and his mother decided that Enrique needed to be back in school. Because of the arrest and potential

(Continued)

(Continued)

sentencing hanging over his head, Enrique was not permitted to return to his home school until the matter was adjudicated.

The release plan. During the first 30 days of the release plan, Mario was able to place Enrique into an alternative school, an after-school program, tutoring, and a part-time job that paid him a small stipend at his mentor's financial investment firm. Enrique was encouraged because his stock was improving. Both stocks reported impressive results for their clinical trials, and there was a small rally. Despite the small amount of money that Enrique had available to him for investment purposes, his stock doubled at the report of the successful clinical trials, and Enrique's original $300 investment was now $600. Enrique said that he wanted to become an investment expert. It was certainly less risky than selling drugs or participating in gangs.

Mario engaged Enrique and his mother in various extracurricular activities, including many new and valuable experiences for Enrique, making him realize that he had a future after these incidents. Mario and the financial mentor started to serve as the male role models Enrique had never had.

After the first 30-day trial period, Mario showed the court Enrique's progress, and the judge permitted another 6 months with Mario's diversion agency, to eventually be followed by another 6 months, and thereafter Enrique was put on formal probation. The diversion agency helped Enrique and his mother move from their old neighborhood to a new city to give them both a fresh start.

Let go. Enrique had gradually let go of his gang behavior. He wanted a new identity for himself and for his mother. At each step of the treatment process, Enrique was receptive to positive change—working with his mentor, attending events with prosocial kids his age, and finally securing living arrangements away from the gang.

Enrique wanted to remove all vestiges of his past life with the gang. He asked Mario and the diversion agency if they would assist him in removing tattoos from his face and arms, officially ending his relationship with his gang. Enrique's mentor gave him an internship with his company so that he could improve his knowledge of stocks. Enrique learned that if he wanted to be in the investment world, he needed to do well in math and the rest of his subjects. He had to go to college, because no firm would hire him without a degree.

Let in. Mario suggested that Enrique might want to repair the harm that had been done, even though he was only a silent bystander. In his new neighborhood, Enrique volunteered to mentor boys aged 9 to 12. For the first time, Enrique became concerned about understanding the feelings of others who had been harmed by crime. Sessions with Mario, Enrique, and Teresa (Enrique's mother) helped to forge a greater understanding between the parent and son. As a result, there was greater harmony in their home.

Developing competencies. What has really helped Enrique is his development of new competencies related to his work with his financial investment mentor. Enrique has used the money that he has earned from his part-time job to help his mother buy stock. The money they earned was critical in providing income to help their family move out of their old neighborhood. Enrique has also developed competencies in counseling as a result of his volunteer work at the Boys Club in his new neighborhood. His greatest competencies have been developed in his academic subjects at his new high school. Enrique is doing exceptionally well in his courses—mostly As and Bs.

Moving forward. Enrique and his mother developed a goal of his attending college, and Mario expedited the college application and college enrollment process for him. Enrique began studying to be a financial advisor. His close relationship with Mario helped him to understand that he has potential, and how important it was to have someone to help him navigate the juvenile justice system. Enrique maintained close ties with Mario, and he continues to have a healthy relationship with his mother.

SUMMARY OF KEY POINTS

In counseling Hispanic/Latino clients, clinicians must take into consideration the cultural and individual dimensions of the client's life. An important first step is to recognize the heterogeneity of the Hispanic/Latino culture and the differences between the various subgroups. Understand that there are different Hispanic/Latino worldviews that are related to a person's country of origin, education, and socioeconomic status.

- In general, Hispanic/Latino culture is largely a collectivist culture, meaning that individuals value the group over the individual. The emphasis is on benefiting the welfare of the group, especially the family, over the rights of the individual.

- Although there are important differences in the Hispanic/Latino subgroups, clinicians should familiarize themselves with such terms as *familismo, respeto, simpatía*, and *machismo* and their implications for working with clients from this ethnocultural group.

- In working with clients from Hispanic/Latino backgrounds, the clinician should understand the heterogeneity of the culture in addition to individual differences between clients and members of their group.

- The clinician should recognize that there are varying worldviews within members who adhere to the Hispanic/Latino culture based on differences in places of origin, historical political relations with the United States, and socioeconomic and educational background.

- The clinician should be knowledgeable about acculturation stressors, family immigration, ethnic and racial identity models, and sociopolitical forces that restrict social justice. He or she should also know when it is appropriate to involve an indigenous healer or to refer the client to another referral source. Counselors and therapists should understand their own culture and the impact that such has on their clients and others.

DISCUSSION QUESTIONS

Discussion Question Set 1

In small groups of three or four people, discuss what you perceive as two potential barriers and two cultural factors you might experience in counseling Hispanic/Latino clients.

Discussion Question Set 2

Discuss two cultural strengths you believe are important in counseling clients from Hispanic/Latino backgrounds.

KEY TERMS

Familismo: In Hispanic or Latino/a culture, the high value placed on both the nuclear and the extended family over the individual; identity of the individual comes largely from the family.

Fatalismo: In Hispanic or Latino/a culture, the belief that uncertainty or destiny is inherent in life and that people should take each day as it comes.

Machismo: In Hispanic or Latino/a culture, a defined gender role for males that signifies male authority and responsibility to be a provider for the family.

Marianismo: In Hispanic or Latino/a culture, a defined gender role for females inspired by the perceived example of the Virgin Mary; it signifies that a woman should be subservient to her husband and serve as a dedicated, loving, and supportive wife and mother.

Personalismo: In Hispanic or Latino/a culture, the high premium placed on relationships instead of material things and the desire for establishing an emotional bond with those with whom one interacts on a regular basis.

Respeto: In Hispanic or Latino/a culture, the value that holds elders and those in authority in high esteem.

Simpatía: In Hispanic or Latino/a culture, the desire for kindness and pleasantness even when confronted with stress; nonconflictural and pleasant interpersonal relationships with others.

REFERENCES AND SUGGESTED READING

American Psychiatric Association. (2013). *Diagnostic and statistical manual of mental disorders* (5th ed.). Washington, DC: Author.

American Psychological Association. (2010). *Ethical principles of psychologists and code of conduct*. Washington, DC: Author.

Araújo, B. Y., & Borrell, L. N. (2006). Understanding the link between discrimination, mental health outcomes, and life chances among Latinos. *Hispanic Journal of Behavioral Sciences, 28*, 245–266.

Arredondo, P., Bordes, V., & Paniagua, F. A. (2008). Mexicans, Mexican Americans, Caribbean, and other Latin Americans. In A. J. Marsella, J. L. Johnson, P. Watson, & J. Gryczynski (Eds.), *Ethnocultural perspectives on disaster and trauma: Foundations, issues, and applications* (pp. 299–320). New York, NY: Springer.

Barrera, A. G., Lopez, M. H., Passel, J. S., & Taylor, P. (2013, February 4). *Recent trends in naturalization, 2000–2011*. Pew Research Center. Retrieved from http://www.pewhispanic.org/2013/02/04/ii-recent-trends-in-naturalization-2000-2011-2/

Baumann, A. A., Kuhlberg, J. A., & Zayas, L. H. (2010). Familism, mother-daughter mutuality, and suicide attempts of adolescent Latinas. *Journal of Family Psychology, 24,* 616–624.

Bernal, G., & Gutierrez, M. (1988). Cubans. In L. Comas-Díaz & E. E. H. Griffith (Eds.), *Clinical guidelines in cross-cultural mental health* (pp. 233–261). New York, NY: Wiley.

Bernal, G., & Shapiro, E. (1996). In M. McGoldrick, J. Giordano, & J. K. Pierce (Eds.), *Ethnicity and family therapy* (2nd ed., pp. 155–168). New York, NY: Guilford Press.

Cárdenas, V., & Kerby, S. (2012, August 8). *The state of Latinos in the United States*. Center for American Progress. Retrieved from https://www.americanprogress.org/issues/race/report/2012/08/08/11984/the-state-of-latinos-in-the-united-states/

Casas, J. M., Raley, J. D., & Vasquez, M. J. T. (2008). Counseling the Latina/o from guiding theory to practice. In P. B. Pedersen, J. G. Draguns, W. J. Lonner, & J. E. Trimble (Eds.), *Counseling across cultures* (6th ed., pp. 129–146). Thousand Oaks, CA: Sage.

Cattan, P. (1993). The diversity of Hispanics in the U.S. work force. *Monthly Labor Review, 116,* 3–15.

Chartier, K., & Caetano, R. (2010). Ethnicity and health disparities in alcohol research. *Alcohol Research & Health, 33*(1–2), 152–160.

Colby, S., & Ortman, J. M. (2015, March). Projections of the size and composition of the U.S. population: 2014 to 2060. *Population Estimates and Projects: Current Population Reports*. U.S. Department of Commerce, Economics & Statistics Administration, U.S. Census Bureau. Retrieved from https://www.census.gov/library/publications/2015/demo/p25-1143.html

Comas-Díaz, L. (2001). Hispanics, Latinos, or Americanos: The evolution of identity. *Cultural Diversity and Ethnic Minority Psychology, 7,* 115–120.

Comas-Díaz, L. (2012). *Multicultural care: A clinician's guide to cultural competence*. Washington, DC: American Psychological Association.

Delgado-Romero, E. A., Galvan, N., Hunter, M. R., & Torres, V. (2008). Latino/Latina Americans. In G. McAuliffe & Associates (Eds.), *Culturally alert counseling: A comprehensive introduction* (pp. 323–352). Thousand Oaks, CA: Sage.

Delgado-Romero, E. A., Nevels, B. J., & Capielo, C. (2013). Culturally alert counseling with Latino/Latina Americans. In G. McAuliffe & Associates (Eds.), *Culturally alert counseling:*

A comprehensive introduction (2nd ed., pp. 293–315). Thousand Oaks, CA: Sage.

Farias, P. (1994). In A. J. Marsella, T. Bornemann, S. Ekblad, & J. Orley (Eds.), *Amidst peril and pain: The mental health and wellbeing of the world's refugees* (pp. 101–113). Washington, DC: American Psychological Association.

Flores, E., Tschann, J. M., Dimas, J. M., Pasch, L. A., & de Groat, C. L. (2010). Perceived racial/ethnic discrimination, posttraumatic stress symptoms, and health risk behaviors among Mexican American adolescents. *Journal of Counseling Psychology, 57,* 264–273.

Flores, M. T., & Carey, G. (2000). *Family therapy with Hispanics: Toward appreciating diversity*. Boston, MA: Allyn & Bacon.

Fry, R. (2010). *Hispanics, high school dropouts and the GED*. Pew Research Center. Retrieved from http://pewhispanic.org/reports/report.php?ReportID=122

Galindo, C., & Fuller, B. (2010). The social competence of Latino kindergartners and growth in mathematical understanding. *Developmental Psychology, 46*(3), 579–592.

Gallardo, M. E. (2012). Therapists as cultural architects and systemic advocate: Latina/o Skills identification stage model. In M. E. Gallardo, C. J. Yeh, J. E. Trimble, & T. A. Parham (Eds.), *Culturally adaptive counseling skills: Demonstrations of evidence-based practices* (pp. 77–112). Thousand Oaks, CA: Sage.

Gil, A., & Vega, W. A. (1996). Two different worlds: Acculturation stress and adaptation among Cuban and Nicaraguan families in Miami. *Journal of Social and Personal Relations, 13,* 437–458.

Guarnaccia, P. J., Canino, G., Rubio-Stipec, M., & Bravo, M. (1993). The prevalence of *ataques de nervios* in the Puerto Rico study: The role of culture in psychiatric epidemiology. *Journal of Nervous and Mental Disease, 181,* 157–165.

Guarnaccia, P. J., Parka, P., Deschamps, A., Milstein, G., & Argiles, N. (1992). *Si dios quiere*: Hispanic families experiences of caring for a seriously mentally ill family member. *Culture, Medicine and Psychiatry, 16*(2), 187–215. doi:10.1007/bf00117018

Hernandez, B., Garcia, J., & Flynn, M. (2010). The role of familism in the relation between parent-child discord and psychological distress among emerging adults of Mexican descent. *Journal of Family Psychology, 24,* 105–114.

Ho, M. K. (1992). *Minority children and adolescents in therapy*. Newbury Park, CA: Sage.

Jenkins, J. H. (1991). The state construction of affect: Political ethos and mental health among Salvadoran refugees. *Culture, Medicine & Psychiatry, 15,* 139–165.

Jenkins, J. H. (1988). Conceptions of schizophrenia as a problem of nerves: A cross-cultural comparison of Mexican Americans and Anglo-Americans. *Social Science and Medicine, 26,* 1233–1243.

Jones-Smith, E. (2014). *Strengths-based therapy: Connecting theory, practice, and skills.* Thousand Oaks, CA: Sage.

Kemp, C., & Rasbridge, L. A. (2004). Mexico. In *Refugee and immigrant health: A handbook for health professionals* (pp. 260–270). Cambridge, England: Cambridge University Press.

Krogstad, J. M. (2017, August 3). U.S. Hispanic population growth has leveled off. *Pew Research Center.* Retrieved from http://www.pewresearch.org/fact-tank/2017/08/03/u-s-hispanic-population-growth-has-leveled-off/

Kuhlberg, J. A., Pena, J. B., & Zayas, L. H. (2010). Familism, parent-adolescent conflict, self-esteem, internalizing behaviors and suicide attempts among adolescent Latinas. *Child Psychiatry and Human Development, 41*(4), 425–440.

Lesser, G., & Batalova, J. (2017, April 5). *Central American immigrants in the United States.* Migration Policy Institute. Retrieved from https://www.migrationpolicy.org/article/central-american-immigrants-united-states

López, R. A. (2009, March 25). Nonverbal Latino communication & social networking. *Latino Opinion.* Retrieved from http://www.latinoopinion.com/category/language-and-communication/

Marrero, P. (2011, August 8). Migración Mexicana permanence estable. *La Opinión.* Retrieved from http://www.impre.com/laraza/nticias/2011/8/3/migracion-mexicana-permanece-e-266040-2.html

McAuliffe, G., & Associates. (2013). *Culturally alert counseling: A comprehensive introduction* (2nd ed.). Thousand Oaks, CA: Sage

Mental health and Hispanics. (2017, February 24). Office of Minority Health, U.S. Department of Health and Human Services. Retrieved from https://minorityhealth.hhs.gov/omh/browse.aspx?lvl=4&lvlid=69

Miranda, A. O., & Umhoefer, D. L. (1998). Depression and social interest differences between Latinos in dissimilar acculturation stages. *Journal of Mental Health Counseling, 20,* 159–171.

Motel, S., & Patten, E. (2012). Hispanic origin profiles, 2010. *Pew Research Center.* Retrieved from http://www.pewhispanic.org/2012/06/27/country-of-origin-profiles/

Murray, M. (2013). NBC/WSJ poll: Majority supports citizenship, believes immigration strengthens nation. *NBC News.* Retrieved from http://nbclatino.com/2013/04/11/nbcwsj-poll-strong-majority-backs-citizenship-for-undocumented-immigrants/ http://nbclatino.com/2013/04/11/nbcwsj-poll-strong-majority-backs-citizenship-for-undocumented-immigrants/

Nadal, K. L. (2011). The Racial and Ethnic Microaggressions Scale (REMS): Construction, reliability, and validity. *Journal of Counseling Psychology, 58,* 470–480. doi:10.1037/a0025193

Nadal, K. L., Griffin, K. E., Wong, Y., Hamit, S., & Rasmus, M. (2014). Racial microaggressions and mental health: Counseling clients of color. *Journal of Counseling & Development, 92,* 57–66. doi:10.1002/j.1556-6676.2014.00130.

Nadal, K. L., Mazzula, S. L., Rivera, D. P., & Fujii-Doe, W. (2014). Microaggressions and Latina/o Americans: An analysis of nativity, gender, and ethnicity. *Journal of Latina/o Psychology, 2*(2), 67–78.

National Center for Health Statistics. (2018, April 11). Tables of Summary Health Statistics. *Centers for Disease Control and Prevention.* Retrieved from https://www.cdc.gov/nchs/nhis/shs/tables.htm

Paniagua, F. A. (2014). *Assessing and treating culturally diverse clients: A practical guide* (4th ed.). Thousand Oaks, CA: Sage.

Passel, J. S., & Taylor, P. (2009, May 28). Who's Hispanic? *Hispanic Trends.* Pew Research Center. Retrieved from http://www.pewhispanic.org/2009/05/28/whos-hispanic/

Pew Forum on Religion & Public Life & Pew Hispanic Project. (2007). *Changing faiths: Latinos and the transformation of American religion.* Washington, DC: Pew Research Center.

Pew Research Center. (2007). 2007 *National Survey of Latinos: As illegal immigration issue heats up, Hispanics feel a chill.* Retrieved from http://pewhispanic.org/reports/report.php?ReportID=84

Pew Research Center. (2009). *Between two worlds: How young Latinos come of age in America.* Retrieved from http://pewresarch.org/pubs/1438/young-latinos-coming-of-age-in-america

Pew Research Center. (2016, January 19). *Millennials make up almost half of Latino eligible voters in 2016.* Retrieved from http://www.pewhispanic.org/2016/01/19/millennials-make-up-almost-half-of-latino-eligible-voters-in-2016/

Ramos, M. (2014, June). The strengths of Latina mothers in supporting their children's education: A cultural perspective. *Child Trends Hispanic Institute* (Publication #2014–29).

Rivera, D. P. (2012). Microaggressions and health outcomes for Latina/o Americans: Understanding the influences of external characteristics and psychological resources Doctoral dissertation, Columbia University, New York.

Rivera, D. P., Forquer, E. E., & Rangel, R. (2010). Microaggressions and the life experience of Latina/o Americans. In D. W. Sue (Ed.), *Microaggressions and marginality: Manifestations, dynamics, and impact* (pp. 59–83). New York, NY: Wiley.

Ruiz, A. (1990). Ethnic identity: Crisis and resolution. *Journal of Multicultural Counseling and Development, 18,* 29–40.

Short, K. (2011). *The research supplemental poverty measure: 2010.* Washington, DC: U.S. Department of Commerce.

Smokowski, P. R., Rose, R. A., & Bacallao, M. (2010). Influence of risk factors and cultural assets on Latino adolescents' trajectories of self-esteem and internalizing symptoms. *Child Psychiatry and Human Development, 41*, 133–135.

Stephen, R., & Brown, A. (2015, May 12). *Statistical Portrait of Hispanics in the United States 1980–2013*. Pew Research Center. Retrieved from http://www.pewhispanic.org/2015/05/12/statistical-portrait-of-hispanics-in-the-united-states-2013-key-charts/

Suarez-Orozco, C., & Suarez-Orozco, M. M. (1995). *Transformations: Immigration, family life, and achievement motivation among Latino adolescents*. Stanford, CA: Stanford University Press.

Suarez-Orozco, M. M. (1990). Speaking of the unspeakable: Toward a psychosocial understanding of responses to terror. *Ethos, 18*, 353–383.

Sue, D. W., Bucceri, J. M., Lin, A. I., Nadal, K. L., & Torino, G. C. (2007). Racial microaggressions and the Asian American experience. *Cultural Diversity and Ethnic Minority Psychology, 13*, 72–81. doi:10.1037/1099-9809.13.1.72

Sue, D. W., Capodilupo, C. M., Torino, G. C., Bucceri, J. M., Holder, A. M. B., Nadal, K. L., & Esquilin, M. (2007). Racial microaggressions in everyday life: Implications for clinical practice. *American Psychologist, 62*, 271–286. doi:10.1037/ 0003-066X.62.4.271

U.S. Census Bureau. (2010). Poverty status in the past 12 months: 2010 American community survey-1 year estimates. Washington, DC: U.S. Government Printing Office.

U.S. Census Bureau. (2011). *The Hispanic population: 2010, 2010 Census Briefs*. U.S. Department of Commerce, Economics and Statistics Administration. Retrieved from file:///C:/Users/E/Downloads/Documents/The%20Latino%20Population,%202010,%20Bureau%20of%20the%20Census,%20c2010br-04.pdf

U.S. Census Bureau. (2014). Table 11. Percent distribution of the projected population by Hispanic origin and race for the United States: 2015 to 2060. Retrieved from https://www.census.gov/data/tables/2014/demo/popproj/2014-summary-tables.html

U.S. Department of Health and Human Services. (2001). *Mental health: Culture, race, and ethnicity—a supplement to mental health: A report of the Surgeon General*. Rockville, MD: U.S. Department of Health and Human Services, Substance Abuse and Mental Health Services Administration, Center for Mental Health Services.

12 CULTURALLY RESPONSIVE STRENGTHS-BASED THERAPY FOR ARAB AND MUSLIM AMERICANS

- *"Palestine is the cement that holds the Arab world together, or it is the explosive that blows it apart."* —Yasser Arafat

- *"If you have much, give out your wealth. If you have little, give out your heart."* —Arab proverb

- *"Open your mouth only if what you are going to say is better than silence."* —Arab proverb

- *As-salāmu 'alaykum* ("Greetings, peace be unto you"); *wa 'alaykumu s-salām* ("And peace be upon you, too") —Arabic greeting

CHAPTER OBJECTIVES

- Discuss the demographics and population statistics of Arab Americans and Muslim Americans.

- Analyze ethnic/racial stereotypes and microaggressions against Arab Americans and Muslim Americans.

- Describe the worldviews of Arab Americans and Muslim Americans, while acknowledging the differences between these two groups.

- Recall the cultural values of Arab Americans and Muslim Americans.

- Describe the cultural strengths of Arab Americans and Muslim Americans.

- Describe Arab American and Muslim American mental health challenges, acculturation conflicts, help-seeking attitudes, and expectations about counseling.

- List cultural factors to take into consideration for counseling Arab Americans and Muslim Americans.

INTRODUCTION

This chapter explores the cultural, social, and political issues involved in counseling Arab and Muslim Americans. Despite the continued growth of these populations within the United States, few textbooks have examined cultural issues related to counseling such individuals (Abi-Hashem, 2008; Abudabbeh, 1996; Abudabbeh & Aseel, 1999; Ajrouch, 2007; Ajrouch & Jamal, 2007; Dwairy, 2006; Fakih, 2013).

A major issue that must be confronted in this chapter is fear. Whereas the Arab and Muslim populations were previously accepted in many areas of American life, the rise of radical Islamist terrorism has meant that some are now feared and hated because of the horrific actions of a few (W. Ali et al., 2011). In some circles, the words *Arab* and *Muslim* have almost become synonomous with the term *potential terrorist*, resulting in the irrational fear known as *Islamophobia*. It is not the purpose of this chapter to debate the political issues surrounding terrorism, but it is important to acknowledge the fearful, tense situation surrounding Arab and Muslim Americans and Muslims in the United States. Fear causes people to make decisions that they later regret; it is the seed for hatred between people, and it paralyzes us when we need to take action to correct a situation.

This chapter addresses the following questions: Who are Arab and Muslim Americans? When did they come to this country, and why? What are their contributions to American society? How does one go about counseling members of these groups? In addition, the chapter reviews some of the special challenges Arab and Muslim Americans face because of the current political climate in the United States and around the world.

Who Are Arab and Muslim Americans?

Arab Americans include a broad group of people from different nations and ethnic origins (Lipka, 2017; Nassar-McMillan & Hakim-Larson, 2003). The first issue related to counseling Arab and Muslim Americans is a knowledge issue: Counselors need to educate themselves about these populations and the fact that, while they overlap, they are not synonymous. The ethnocultural designation of Arab includes a diversity of ethnic groups that span the continents of Asia and Africa and the transcontinental region of the Middle East (Hakim-Larson, Nassar-McMillan, & Paterson, 2013). There are 22 Arab countries in the world, including Algeria, Bahrain, the Comoro Islands, Djibouti, Egypt, Iraq, Jordan, Kuwait, Lebanon, Libya, Mauritania, Morocco, Oman, Palestine, Qatar, Saudi Arabia, Somalia, Sudan, Syria, Tunisia, the United Arab Emirates, and Yemen. Arab Americans, therefore, can trace their ancestry to any of these nations.

Distinguishing Between the Terms *Arab* and *Muslim*

Part of the problem in American society and throughout the world is that many people confuse Arabs with Muslims, but they are not one and the same. As Nydell (2012) has stated,

> we must not confuse Arabs with Muslims. . . . There are 1.8 billion Muslims in the world and they are a majority in fifty-six countries. There are currently about 360 million Arabs, 5 percent of whom are Christians or practice other religions. Owing primarily to immigration, Islam has become the second-largest religion in both the United States and Europe. (p. xxv)

Arabs. One of the defining features of an **Arab** identity is a shared language: Arabic. However, within Arab countries, there are distinct groups whose language is not Arabic (Berbers, Kurds, etc.) but who have absorbed the prevailing Arab culture (Nydell, 2012). There are about 300 million Arabs worldwide ("Facts About Arabs," 2009). Most Arabs live in the Middle East. The Arab Middle East consists of countries that belong to the League of Arab States and speak Arabic as a national language (Hakim-Larson et al., 2013). In addition, some immigrants from the Middle East are not considered Arab because they do not speak Arabic (for instance, Turks speak Turkish, and Iranians speak Farsi).

> **Cultural Reflections**
>
> *What are your feelings about Muslim Americans?*
>
> *Do you believe that Muslims are stereotyped on television or in the movies?*

A second major characteristic that some Arabs share is the Islamic religion. **Islam** emerged in Mecca in the early 7th century (AD 610) through the life and work of the Prophet **Muhammad**, who created the **Qur'an**, the holy book that sets forth the basic beliefs and tenets of the Islamic religion (Dwairy, 2006).

Muslims Worldwide. According to Lipka (2017), **Muslims** constitute the fastest-growing religious group in the world. It has been a major force in influencing Arab culture. However, it is important to note that not all Muslims are Arabs and that some Arabs are not Muslims. Islam spread to a number of non-Arab countries, and today the majority of Muslims live outside the Arab world. Many people in the United States and elsewhere tend to confuse Arabs with Muslims, but they are not one and the same. A large proportion of Muslims are neither Arabic speaking nor Middle Eastern in their heritage, with ancestors from Indonesia, India, Pakistan, Bangladesh, Iran, and Turkey. Indonesia is the country that contains the world's largest Muslim population; however, the Pew Research Center has projected that India will have that distinction by the year 2050 (Lipka, 2017). India (160,945,000) has the third-largest Muslim population in the world. China has more Muslims than Syria, and Russia has more Muslims than Jordan and Libya combined. The Pew Research Center has also projected that the Muslim population in Europe will reach 10% of all Europeans by 2050 (Lipka, 2017).

Muslim Subgroups. Within Islam, there are two basic groups: **Sunni** and **Shiite**. Sunnis form about 90% of Muslims worldwide, while Shiites make up the rest of the 10% and form the overwhelming majority in Iran (Renard, 1998). Some of the conflicts in the Middle East have been between Sunni and Shiite Muslims.

About 30% to 40% of Muslims in the United States are African American; they form the largest single cultural group in the Islamic community (Smith, 1999; Younis, 2009). Although many Americans associate African American Muslims with the Nation of Islam headed by Louis Farrakhan, that group speaks for only a small portion (about 50,000) of African American Muslims (Hodge, 2005). Virtually all African American Muslims are mainstream Sunnis (Melton, 1999; Smith, 1999; Younis, 2009).

Three Waves of Arab Migration to the United States

It is important for counselors and therapists to understand the immigration history of individuals they seek to counsel because their reason(s) for leaving their homeland reveal much about what they were seeking in coming to this country. While there is some disagreement over whether Arabic peoples migrated to the United States in two (Abudabbeh, 1996) or three distinct waves (Erickson & Al-Timimi, 2004), this section presents Arab migration in terms of three waves.

The first wave of Arab immigrants arrived between the 1870s and the 1920s and consisted mostly of poor, uneducated males from the regions that today are Syria, Lebanon, and Yemen. They were predominantly Christian in religious faith, and some came to America because they were experiencing religious discrimination. They assimilated easily into the culture of the United States because they shared the religion endorsed by the majority of Americans and because they evidenced a relative lack of Arab identity (Nydell, 2012). Most of the first wave of Arab immigrants left their families in their native countries and worked in factories, such as those in the newly emerging automobile industry in Detroit, to earn enough money to improve their families' lives back home (Abu-Laban & Suleiman, 1989; Kayyali, 2006; Naff, 1993; Orfalea, 2006). There was a high rate of intermarriage because Arab men outnumbered Arab women at least four to one. The Arab immigrants who came during this time period produced several noted poets, artists, and writers (e.g., Kahlil Gibran) who became permanent residents of the United States.

The immigration of Arabs was slowed from the late 1920s to the late 1940s because of restrictive quotas and the Great Depression (Orfalea, 2006). The second wave of Arab immigration to the United States was spurred on by several political factors, including the 1948 Arab-Israeli War, which produced a mass migration of primarily Palestinian Arabs as well as many from Egypt and others from Iraq. Whereas 90% of the Arab immigrants in the first wave were Christians, in this second wave only 40% were of this faith; the majority were Muslim, and they came with a sense of Arab identity that centered on Arab–Israeli conflicts and a rejection of secular Western behavior. This group was much more affluent than the first wave of Arab immigrants, comprising many highly educated professionals and precipitating what became known as the "brain drain" problem throughout the Middle East (Orfalea, 2006). This second wave did not assimilate to American life as easily as the first, as these immigrants wanted to retain their cultural identity, and they affirmed their culture by establishing cultural clubs, political committees, and Arabic language schools.

> **Cultural Reflections**
>
> *Debate has centered on not admitting any more Muslims into the United States.*
>
> *What are your thoughts on this issue?*
>
> *Should American Muslim neighborhoods be patrolled by the police?*

The third wave of Arab immigrants has occurred from the 1960s to the present time, motivated by events such as the 1975 Lebanese Civil War, the ongoing Israeli–Palestinian conflict, and political turmoil in Egypt, Syria, and Yemen (Orfalea, 2006). As the American public began to associate Arabs and Muslims with terrorist attacks such as the 1983 bombing of the Marine barracks in Beirut, Lebanon, and the 1993 car bombing that damaged the World Trade Center, immigrants from this culture were met with a negative reception. As a result, instead of assimilating, the new immigrants frequently opted to live in separate enclaves and on the fringes of American society, even though they adopted many American cultural mores. The third wave of Arab immigrants has provided the impetus for the establishment of many Muslim schools, mosques, charities, and Arabic language classes.

In 2017, the anti-Arab and anti-Muslim sentiment of some U.S. policymakers was embodied in a presidential executive order denying entry to citizens of several predominantly Muslim nations, whether as travelers or as refugees. After the executive order was blocked by federal courts, President Donald Trump issued a second, more limited executive order. However, "critics have noted that major attacks such as the 9/11 New York attacks, the Boston marathon bombing and the Orlando nightclub attack were carried out by people from countries not on the list, such as Saudi Arabia, Egypt and Kyrgyzstan, or by US-born attackers" ("Trump Travel Ban," 2017).

Demographic Data on Arab Americans

The demographics of Arab Americans are difficult to pin down—perhaps because they are the least studied ethnic group in the United States (Asi & Beaulieu, 2013; Lipka, 2017). How is Arab ancestry determined by the U.S. Census Bureau? Its American Community Survey (ACS) contains an ancestry question that asks each person his or her "ancestry or ethnic origin." From these responses, anyone who reported being Algerian, Bahraini, Egyptian, Emirati, Iraqi, Jordanian, Kuwaiti, Lebanese, Libyan, Moroccan, Omani, Palestinian, Qatari, Saudi Arabian, Syrian, Tunisian, or Yemeni was considered to be of Arab ancestry. The Census Bureau

> defines ancestry as the ethnic origin, descent, roots, heritage, or place of birth of the person or of the person's ancestors. Ancestry is a broad concept. The ancestry question was not intended to measure the degree of attachment to a particular group, but simply to establish the ethnic group(s) with which the respondent self-identifies. (Asi & Beaulieu, 2013, p. 1)

Asi and Beaulieu (2013) conducted an analysis of ACS briefs for Arab households in the United States from 2006 to 2010. Data reported in their brief were based on the ACS five-year estimates from the 2006–2010 Selected Population Tables. Arab households were defined as households that reported an Arab ancestry response. The five-year estimates for 2006–2010 revealed that these households included an estimated 1.5 million people, or 0.5% of the total American population. This figure represented a 76.0% increase since 1990. Although the Arab population is a distinct ancestry group, it is also one of the most heterogeneous ethnic/cultural groups in the world, including White and dark-skinned individuals. As a result of their migration histories and individual choices, many Arab Americans are of mixed ancestry; there are Arab-Irish Americans, Arab-Italian Americans, and Arab-German Americans. Approximately 80% of Arabs identify as White, while 17% say they are White and another race (Orfalea, 2006).

Asi and Beaulieu's (2013) study focused on selected Arab ancestry groups—Lebanese, Egyptian, Syrian, Palestinian, Moroccan, Iraqi, Jordanian, and Yemeni. Their data showed that the median household income was $56,433, about $4,500 higher than the median household income for all American households ($51,914). Individuals from Arab ancestry had lower home ownership percentage (59.6%) (with home ownership being defined as the percentage of all occupied housing units that are owner occupied) than the rate for all Americans (66.6%). The Lebanese and Syrians had home ownership rates above the national level at 71.6% and 69.2%, respectively. The Arab American population is concentrated primarily in five cities: Detroit/Dearborn area, Los Angeles, the New York metropolitan area, Chicago, and Washington, DC.

Socioeconomic Status of Arab Americans

The socioeconomic status of Arab Americans is above that for the average American. On average,

- Arab Americans are more educated than the rest of the American population.

- The average income of Arab Americans is higher than that for the rest of the American population.

- Many of those who immigrated in the second and third waves of Arab immigration have degrees in engineering, law, and medicine.

According to the U.S. Census Bureau, Arab Americans, both native born and immigrants, have a higher level of achievement than the average U.S. population, with over 46% of Arab Americans having earned a bachelor's degree in comparison to 28% of the U.S. population (Arab American Institute, 2011). Approximately 79% of Arab Americans are in managerial, professional, sales, or administrative fields. Arab Americans subscribe to a variety of religions. About 33% are Roman Catholic, 25% are Muslim, 18% are Eastern Orthodox, and 10% are Protestant (Arab American Institute, 2003).

Denying Arabs immigration to the United States will not eliminate the immigration of members of the Muslim faith to this country because so many come from countries that the United States considers either friendly or allies (Dwairy, 2006).

American Muslims: Some Demographics

The Pew Research Center has conducted some of the most current studies on the number of American Muslims living in this country. It has been estimated that there were approximately 3.45 million Muslims living in the United States in 2015 (Mohamed, 2016). On the whole, Muslim Americans are much younger than the overall U.S. population. A little over a third (35%) of Muslim American adults are between 18 and 29 years old—a much larger group than the general population that falls within that age bracket (21%). While just 14% of Muslim Americans are ages 55 and over, about 36% of the overall U.S. adult population falls within this age bracket (Pew Research Center, 2017b). About half of the Muslim population is married, with the majority noting that they married a spouse who is Muslim. On average, Muslim Americans have 2.4 children, while the rate is 2.1 for the general American public.

Muslims, African Americans, and Jews

In 2016, there were fewer American Muslims than American Jews (5.7 million), but more Muslims than Hindus (2.1 million). African Americans constitute approximately 30%–35% of Muslims in the United States (Fakih, 2013; Younis, 2009). Hence, they form the largest single cultural group in the American Islamic community (Richards & Bergin, 1997; Smith, 1999). As previously noted, although the Nation of Islam's Louis Farrakhan is often portrayed as the representative of all African American Muslims, he is not. The Nation of Islam is estimated to have approximately 50,000 members. When African Americans are excluded, it is estimated that about 75% of adult Muslims in this country are foreign born (Haddad, 1997; Nydell, 2012). Although recent Muslim immigrants have come from countries around the world, most have immigrated from the Middle East/North Africa and South/Southeast Asia (Nydell, 2012).

Socioeconomic Status of Muslim Americans

The educational attainment levels of Muslim Americans closely resemble those of the general American public. About 31% of Muslim Americans are college graduates, with 11% having earned a postgraduate degree. Muslim immigrants tend to be more highly educated than U.S.-born Muslims.

<table>
<tr><td>

Cultural Reflections

African Americans form a large percentage of Muslims in the United States.

What are your thoughts and feelings about African American Muslims?

How comfortable would you feel counseling an African American Muslim?

</td><td>

Despite similar levels of education to Americans, they report lower incomes and higher underemployment rates. Moreover, Muslims are just as likely as Americans to have a household income over $100,000, but they are more likely than members of the general American public to have an income under $30,000. Muslims are three times as likely as the average American to be unemployed and looking for work (Pew Research Center, 2017a).

</td></tr>
</table>

Muslim adults report a low full-time employment rate (44%), and 29% state that they are underemployed in that they work part-time or would prefer full-time work. In comparison, only 12% of U.S. adults in general are underemployed (Mohamed, 2016).

Muslims and Immigration

About 75% of U.S. Muslims are immigrants or the children of immigrants. Among the U.S. Muslim adults who were born abroad, the largest percentage comes from South Asia (Pakistan, India, Afghanistan, and Bangladesh) (35%), with an additional 23% having been born in other parts of the Asia-Pacific region (such as Iran and Indonesia).

It has been projected that by 2040 the U.S. Muslim population will have grown faster and larger than the Jewish and Hindu populations because of two primary factors: (1) immigration and (2) higher fertility or natural births (Lipka, 2017; Mohamed, 2016).

Immigration of Muslims has been responsible for a little over half of the Muslim population growth from 2010 to 2015. Muslim immigrants now represent approximately 10% of all legal immigrants in this country.

MICROAGGRESSIONS AGAINST ARAB AND MUSLIM AMERICANS

For several decades, Arab/Muslim Americans have been bombarded with negative stereotypes of their ethnocultural group. For instance, Shaheen (1984) analyzed more than 100 popular entertainment programs, cartoons, and major documentaries that related to Arabs and found that all channels portrayed Arabs as billionaires, bombers, belly dancers, or unfriendly desert dwellers with veiled harems. While most of these stereotypes have lost their appeal, that of the terrorist and bomber has persisted to the present day.

Recent research on bias against members of ethnic minority groups has focused on microaggressions. Unlike a direct racial attack that uses racial epithets, a racial microaggression is an indirect and veiled insult that tends to leave a person feeling angry and confused, sometimes wondering if race was the cause of the remark. When individuals encounter microaggressions, they may feel psychologically and physically drained, which may lead to higher stress levels and poor mental health outcomes (Nadal, Wong, et al., 2011; Sue, Bucceri, Lin, Nadal, & Torino, 2007). A number of researchers have claimed that Muslims in the United States and abroad are faced with **Islamophobia** (López, 2011; Nadal, Issa, Griffin, Hamit, & Lyons, 2010). There has been a reported increase in hate crimes against Muslims in the United States and elsewhere since 9/11 (Council on American-Islamic Relations, 2003, 2008; Rippy & Newman, 2006).

Using a qualitative approach, Nadal, Griffin, et al. (2012) investigated religious microaggressions against Muslims and found that they could be divided into six categories:

1. Endorsing Religious Stereotypes

2. Exoticization

3. Pathology of Different Religious Groups

4. Ethnocentrism

5. Assumption of Religious Homogeneity

6. Denial of Religious Prejudice

Nadal, Griffin, et al. (2012) noted that the Muslim community in the United States is diverse racially (with the largest populations being Arab, Asian, and Black) and ethnically (with people from various countries including Syria, India, the Philippines, and Spain). Thus, Muslim Americans may experience microaggressions that may be due not only to religion, but also to race, ethnicity, gender, or some combination of these. Microaggressions can be complicated and result from any number of factors associated with an individual.

Nadal, Griffin, et al. (2012) concluded that the examples of religious microaggressions experienced by the participants in his study were described as both intentional and unintentional. In some cases, the enactor was aware of the connotation and implications of her or his words or actions (e.g., someone using Islamophobic language to hurt someone's feelings), but other enactors were likely unaware of their actions. For example, an individual who stares at a Muslim woman wearing a *hijab* (head scarf) out of curiosity may not recognize the hurtful message that is communicated. According to these researchers, although racism is said to have diminished, Islamophobia is still rampant, and Muslim Americans still experience blatant discrimination on a regular basis.

> ### Cultural Reflections
>
> *Have you ever engaged in a microaggression against an Arab American or a Muslim American?*
>
> *Have you ever stood by silently while another person made offensive and/ or ethnocentric remarks about Arab or Muslim Americans?*

Arab and Muslim Americans and "Passing"

Participants in the Nadal, Griffin, et al. (2012) study reported how they used "passing" to avoid dealing with microaggressions. Some participants reported fewer microaggressions when they did not wear identifying Muslim garments. The concept of "passing" was introduced in the literature on multiracial microaggressions (Johnston & Nadal, 2010) to convey that when a person is mistaken or "passes" for the dominant group, she or he may be given more privilege than those who do not (or cannot) pass. Muslims who do "pass" as non-Muslim may not encounter the same types, or amounts, of microaggressions as people who are easily identified as Muslim.

Nadal, Griffin, et al. (2012) concluded that it is important for the counseling literature to focus on the mental health and lived experiences of Muslim Americans. Microaggressions may have negative consequences for Muslim Americans' mental health, and clinicians need to both understand the impact of microaggressions their Muslim clients may experience and be conscious of their own biases and stereotypes and how they may unintentionally manifest in psychotherapy.

Despite the microaggressions and ethnocentric acts that Arabs and Muslims were faced with in the wake of the 9/11 attacks, many seemed strengthened in their ethnic identity. A Zogby poll conducted in October of that year showed that 88% responded that they were proud of their heritage, and 84% said that their ethnic heritage is important in defining their identity. Approximately 80% responded that gaining Palestinian rights is personally important to them (Zogby, 2001).

CULTURAL VALUES AND
WORLDVIEW OF ARABS AND MUSLIMS

Both Arabs and Muslims come from culturally and racially diverse groups. Younis (2009) has stated that Muslim Americans are the most racially and culturally diverse religious group in the world. Because of the wide ethnic and racial diversity among Arabs and Muslims, it is difficult to distinguish cultural values that apply to all groups. The **Muslim religion** or Islam is oftentimes a core cultural value of some Arabs (not all Arabs are Muslim) and Muslims. The term *Muslim culture* encompasses many different Muslim cultural groups, including Asian Muslims, Middle Eastern Muslims, African Muslims, and European and American Muslims. Each of these groups has its own variation on Muslim traditions and customs; however, some features of the religion are accepted by all Muslims, including the **Five Pillars of Islam**, giving to charity, and emphasizing the duty to care and love older adults and the elderly.

The Religion of Islam

Muslims believe that Allah is the supreme God of all Abrahamic religions and that Islam represents a continuation and culmination of Judaism and Christianity. Islam is a way of life. The world *Islam* means "submission," specifically submission to Allah (Fakih, 2013; Haddad, 1997; Haddad & Smith, 1996). Out of gratitude for Allah's goodness, Muslims seek to follow the straight path, called the *shari'a*, which governs all aspects of life. Islam is based on the Five Pillars of Faith (Bowker, 2000). It is generally agreed that these Five Pillars are held in common by all Islamic groups:

1. *Shahada*: The profession of faith ("There is no God but Allah, and Mohammad is His Messenger")

2. *Salat*: Praying five times a day

3. *Zakat*: A tax designed to give financial help to the poor

4. *Sawm*: Fasting in the holy month of Ramadan

5. *Hajj*: The pilgrimage to Mecca

Shahada. The first pillar mandates that Muslims submit and pray to one God (Pillar of Shahada). Muslims are required to take a declaration of faith—"There is no god but Allah, and Mohammad is His Messenger" (El Azayem & Hedayat-Diba, 1994).

Salat: Ritual Prayers. There is also the tenet regarding ritual prayers, *salat* or *salah*, in which the person faces Mecca, the holy city of Islam, as the second pillar of faith. Muslims are required to pray five times a day, and men are encouraged to pray in mosques rather than at home in order to forge community bonds. Women are permitted to pray at home in order to take care of their family responsibilities. The schedule of many men may not permit them to pray in mosques; therefore, they may pray at home, in the work setting, or during travel in a car, train, or airplane if the time for one of the five daily prayers approaches.

Islam Prayer Rituals: *Wudhu*

Muslims are required to observe specific rituals during their daily prayer. Worshippers must be dressed modestly in clean clothing. Islamic teaching mandates that worshippers engage in what is known as ***wudhu***, which is a ritualistic washing of one's hands, feet, arms, and legs. After the *wudhu* has been performed, individuals must find a quiet place to pray.

Cultural Reflections

How much knowledge do you have about Arab/Muslim culture?

Would you feel comfortable counseling a Muslim woman who wore a hijab, or headscarf?

How comfortable would you feel counseling a person who is an American Muslim?

Any quiet place can be used for prayer, as long as the prayers are said while facing in the direction of Mecca, the birthplace of the Prophet Muhammad.

Traditionally, Muslims say prayers while standing, sitting, or kneeling on a small rug. The *sujud* ritual requires worshippers to kneel with their palms, knees, toes, forehead, and nose touching the ground, repeating three times "Glory be to God, the highest." For Muslims, the five daily prayer times constitute important requirements of the Islamic faith because they serve to remind individuals of Allah, and they serve as a bond uniting Muslims throughout the world.

During early times, Muslims looked to the sun to determine the various times of the day for prayer. In modern times, individuals may be given printed daily prayer schedules, or they may use apps. Missing a prayer is considered to be a lapse of faith, and all missed prayers should be made up as soon as possible.

The Imam: Prayer Leader. The word **imam** is an Arabic word, meaning "stand in front of." The imam's role is to lead a group in prayer, guide it in worship, and perform services such as marriage or funeral rites. An imam is usually any Muslim community member who is in good standing or hired for this purpose. An imam is usually selected because of his deep spiritual understanding and knowledge of the different Islamic teachings. If no imam is present at prayer time in a mosque, any member (usually an elder) can step up to assume an imam's role (Bowker, 2000).

Zakat. The third pillar is *zakat* (for those who can afford giving), or almsgiving and giving help to the poor. A percentage of a person's wealth, usually 2.5% of one's accumulated wealth and assets, is given to the community to correct economic inequalities and to promote the general welfare (Husain, 1998).

The fourth pillar is the yearly fast, *sawm*, held during the month of **Ramadan**. During this time, healthy adults abstain from eating, drinking, smoking, and sexual activity, from sunrise to sunset, in order to engage in spiritual renewal. The degree to which individuals practice the five pillars of Muslim faith shows the importance of Islam in their lives.

The final pillar of faith is the pilgrimage, **hajj**, to Mecca. Each person who has the financial means is expected at least once in his or her lifetime to take a pilgrimage to Mecca.

Collectivist Worldview of Arabs and Muslims

Individuals from Arab and Muslim cultures tend to subscribe to a collectivistic instead of an individualistic approach to life (Dwairy, 2006). Members of this group value interdependence among members of their group (Sayed, Collins, & Takahashi, 1998). The goals of the group are more important than those of the individual. Sayed et al. (1998) quote an Arab proverb to represent their view on collectivism: "The believer is for his brother—like connecting building blocks supporting each other; if one part falls ill, the whole body crumbles of fever and sleeplessness" (p. 444). According to Budman, Lipson, and Meleis (1992), Arabs do not see themselves primarily as individuals, but rather consider themselves members of groups, especially family groups.

The Arab and Muslim Family

In Arab and Muslim cultures, the individual is submissive to the family and to the norms of the society. The family is governed by a patriarchal hierarchical authority. In many Arab and Muslim countries, the people must depend on the family or tribe for their survival rather than on the state. Because the state does not provide for the needs of the individual, Arabs and Muslims must rely on the family for matters related to child care, education, jobs, houses, and protection (Dwairy, 2006). A family has power and control over its individual members, and members may be pressured to abide by acceptable behavior patterns at the cost of development of their own personality.

All major decisions in life are determined by the family. For instance, the family makes decisions regarding clothing, social activities, career, marriage, housing, size of the family, and child-rearing. The individual has very limited opportunity for individual personal choices. The individual's expression of feelings is not welcome; instead one is expected to express what family members anticipate (Ibrahim & Dykeman, 2010; Keshavarzi & Haque, 2013). This method of communication in Arab/Muslim families is directed by the values of respect (*ihtiram*), fulfilling social duties (*wajib*), and pleasing others and avoiding conflict (*mosayara*) (Dwairy, 2006). Parents seldom encourage independence and like to remain involved in their children's lives for as long as possible. It is not uncommon for Arab parents to make such major decisions for their children regarding choice of a career or marital partner (Budman et al., 1992). For the average Arab/Muslim, family is considered a priority, even with work obligations. Arab employers will excuse an employee's absence or tardiness if family obligations or duties are involved. In Arab/Muslim culture, a family member's behavior reflects on the reputation of the entire family. As El Saadawi (1993) has stated, "one's family name is a ready-made identification which reveals to all both one's reputation and one's access to assistance" (p. 14).

Honor (*sharaf*) is an important feature of family life. Under *sharaf*, the actions of an individual can bring shame to the entire family. Hence, a person might choose to ignore a potential health concern such as drug addiction, mental illness, sexually transmitted infection, or pregnancy out of fear that the family would consider the condition to be shameful (Ahmad, 2004).

The Extended Patriarchal Family Structure and the Eldest Son

Most Arab/Muslim children grow up in an extended family where members share in caretaking responsibilities (Nydell, 2012). In traditional Arab culture, members of two or more generations live in a single household, and in wealthier families, the families live in a family compound. The extended Arab family usually consists of a married man and some of his adult sons and their families, plus grandparents. Although a number of people are viewed as adult authority figures, most are male. In Arab culture, there is a preference for male over female offspring because Arabs believe that men contribute more to their families' influence. As Arab/Muslim families acculturate and assimilate into mainstream American culture, they tend to form nuclear families with grandparents and an unmarried child living with them sometimes.

Cultural Reflections

How would you compare Arab/Muslim families to your family?

Are there any similarities that your family shares with Arab/Muslim families?

What are the differences between your family and Arab/Muslim families?

Arab children tend to have a loving attachment to their mothers, while viewing their father as an authoritarian figure regarded with respect and fear. Nydell (2012) maintains that Arabs are inclined to give more corporal punishment to their children than do Americans. This tendency may get them into difficulty with Child Protective Services in the United States. Arab children are faced with great pressures to conform to their family members' wishes. Some Arab children may even believe that nonconformity to their parents' wishes is a sin (Nydell, 2012).

The oldest son is given a position of privilege in Arab/Muslim society (Nydell, 2012). The oldest son is trained at an early age to become the head of the extended family. According to Najjar (1994),

he [the eldest son] is given every privilege, according to the means of the family, with the expectation that, as an adult, he will care for his aging parents and younger siblings, especially any unmarried sisters. (p. 41)

Adolescents. Arab/Muslim cultures tend to support an early, brief, and far less "storm and stress" adolescent period than is typical in Western or American culture. American society supports a process of separation and individuation in which young people develop their own separate identities and form strong peer relationships. In contrast, Arab culture requires that adolescents adjust themselves to fit their family environment (Nobles & Sciarra, 2000). They remain under the control of their parents for a much longer time than do American adolescents.

Arab American parents do not want and do not expect their adolescent children to challenge them or their authority, or to become self-centered rather than family-centered. When Arab/Muslim American parents demand obedience and conformity to the family from their adolescent children, they may experience negative discrimination from mainstream American culture that has a different set of expectations for puberty, dating, marriage, and attitudes toward parents and elders than their own culture (Nobles & Sciarra, 2000). Arab/Muslim parents seldom encourage their adolescent children's independence, and they seek to remain active in their lives for as long as possible. Arab/Muslim adolescents are caught between the demands of two very different cultures—Arab/Muslim culture that places supreme priority on the family and conformity to it, and American culture that views adolescence as a period of storm and stress, individuation and separation from one's parents, and emphasis on forming relationships with peers (Nydell, 2012).

Arab/Muslim parents who fear losing their adolescents to the American culture sometimes become overprotective, thereby preventing the child from developing his or her own identity (Nobles & Sciarra, 2000). Arab/Muslim adolescents may become confused in this tug of cultural wars. They may develop guilt feelings and anxiety if they choose to not follow their family's traditions and rules.

Challenges in Arab/Muslim Families. Arab American parents seek balance in helping their children maintain their ethnic identity while at the same time adjusting to the demands of the broad American culture. In a study of 30 Christian Jordanian mothers of adolescents in the Los Angeles area, Pollara and Meleis (1995) found that their greatest source of stress was trying to raise their children within a cultural context that challenges some of their basic values. The mothers said that they were engaged in persistent worry, despair, guilt, and confusion about the welfare of their children, and that they feared losing their children's respect and control over parenting. The parents felt that the general American public did not understand their feelings as Muslim mothers (Ahmed & Reddy, 2007; Amri & Bemak, 2013; Ibrahim & Dykeman, 2010).

Community

Community, or *ummah*, is an important cultural value for Arabs and Muslims (Nydell, 2012). The need for affiliation is very strong among Arabs and Muslims. They thrive on a large number of relationships. It is believed that a relationship exists between individual freedom and the community's responsibility to the individual. Individual freedom is abridged so as not to harm other members of the community, because it is the community that protects and empowers the individual. The value on community causes some Muslims to emphasize cooperation, caring, equality, interconnectedness, and social support (Kelly, Aridi, & Bakhtiar, 1996). As a result of a community orientation, some individuals seek to address their problems within the community instead of seeking outside assistance. Sometimes community status can become more important than personal well-being, and clients may have significant connections within their community network (Kelly et al., 1996).

Communication Patterns and Arab and Muslim Americans

High-Context Culture. Arab and Muslim culture is highly contextual, meaning that people seek an understanding of events by examining the entire context of circumstances in which they take place. An Arab/Muslim wants to know more about another person than an American typically needs to know for a relationship to develop (Lipson & Meleis, 1983).

Body language and social distance are important factors in establishing rapport with Arab American clients. Individuals of the same gender typically touch each other repeatedly during a conversation; it is common to see two women or two men holding hands as a sign of friendship. Moreover, kissing on both cheeks is customary in greeting a person of the same sex.

In speech, Arabs tend to repeat the same idea or issue for emphasis. Such repetitions are used to make a point or to give reassurance to another person. If a person makes a statement softly and does not repeat it, an Arab may wonder if the speaker really means what he or she is saying. This kind of repetition is found in the Arabic language, which uses many different phrases that have the same meaning.

Time and Space

Arabs and Muslims are similar to Latinos and Native Americans in that they do not place a strong emphasis on punctuality. A client might be late for an appointment or not come at all because something else was considered more important. Arabs and Muslims like to take time to establish a relationship before attending to the business at hand (Nydell, 2012).

Arabs and Muslims tend to use a smaller conversational distance (2 feet) whereas Americans are more comfortable using a 5-foot conversational spatial distance. The closer proximity helps Arabs and Muslims to read more carefully the other person's reactions in a conversation. Differences in conversational distance may influence how Arabs and Muslims respond to clinicians. If a clinician puts a great spatial distance between the client and him or her, the client may feel rejected (Kelly et al., 1996).

The Cultural and Racial Identity of Arab/Muslim Americans: White?

Ajrouch and Jamal (2007) have maintained that immigration to the United States for some Arab Americans and Muslims has been a case of assimilating to a White identity. These researchers have stated that

> immigration to the United States includes the experience of being placed into a racial hierarchy, which becomes one of the primary means by which identity is established. Yet, the defining characteristics of racial categories are complicated, and open to negotiation. Immigration policy in the U.S. historically employed whiteness as a precondition for citizenship (Gaultieri, 2001; Hale, 2002), and so the saliency of race to adaptation among immigrants is a deep-rooted phenomenon that implicitly organizes the migrant experience. A key issue to consider in the analysis of immigrant adaptation is the definition of "whiteness." Whiteness represents a sociological category that demarcates unspoken privilege and power. (Ajrouch & Jamal, 2007, p. 860)

In general, Arab and Muslim immigrants have been legally placed in the White category; however, Ajrouch and Jamal (2007) have argued that the United States' racial classification system affects one's identity upon arrival in this country. Those people who are legally classified as a minority upon arrival, such as immigrants from the Dominican Republic (Itzigsohn, Giorguli, & Vazquez, 2005) or Somalia (Kusow, 2006), may reject the ascribed racial label that designates them as a Black minority. Conversely, immigrants who benefit from the U.S. racial classification system by being labeled White tend to embrace that identity because of the power and benefits that it provides (Ajrouch & Kusow, 2007).

Skin color is one of the three factors that affect the acculturation and assimilation of immigrants to the United States (Kusow, 2006; Portes & Rumbaut, 1996). Immigrants from the Middle East and Arab countries may be treated differently based on their skin color and their migration history in this country. For instance, the Lebanese and Syrians have a migration history to the United States that predates the 1800s. They also have a physical appearance that resembles other Mediterranean immigrants, such as those from Italy, Greece, or Spain. During the early 1900s, Lebanese and

Cultural Reflections

Were you aware that the U.S. government considers Arabs and Middle Easterners as "White"?

What are your thoughts on this issue?

In your opinion, what defining characteristics make a person "White" in the United States?

Syrian immigrants secured a White identity for Middle Eastern immigrants (Gaultieri, 2001). Based on their long migration history, people who have Lebanese and Syrian national origins will be more likely than other Arab Americans to state that they have a White racial identity. In contrast, Arab/Muslim immigrants who arrived after 9/11 and the attacks by Muslim terrorists tend to be less accepted by the broad American society, and hence, they demonstrate a strong affinity with a group (such as a non-White) status.

What does all of the foregoing mean for an Arab/Muslim ethnic or cultural identity? According to Ajrouch and Jamal (2007), American society has established a racial hierarchy in which being White is at the top of the hierarchy. As Phyllis McIntosh (1989) has observed, being White in America gives one access to White privilege and benefits denied to those who place within a minority category. Arab Americans may identify strongly with their Arab and Muslim identity, but they may reject the minority status identity that American society may give them.

To gather information regarding how immigration status influences Arab/Muslim identity, Ajrouch and Jamal (2007) conducted a study on Arab/Muslim Americans in Michigan—home to the largest and most visible concentration of Arabic-speaking people in this country. The study posed four basic questions: "1) Will long-standing immigrants be more likely to identify as white than recent immigrants or the U.S. born? 2) Will white identity announcements vary by national origin? 3) Will Muslims be less likely to subscribe to a white identity? 4) Will those who identify with a pan-ethnic (Arab-American) label and who hold strong ethnic feelings be less likely to identify as white?"

The results showed that individuals who were Lebanese/Syrian or Christian, and those who felt that the term *Arab American* did not describe them, tended to identify as White. In addition, individuals who used the pan-ethnic term *Arab American* to describe themselves were associated with a greater likelihood of identifying as White. The findings of Ajrouch and Jamal's (2007) study revealed different patterns of assimilation among Arab Americans. Whereas some Arab American respondents reported both strong ethnic and White identities, others reported a strong White identity, yet they distanced themselves from the pan-ethnic term *Arab American*. In both instances, Arab Americans embraced a White identity, even though some may have rejected an Arab American identity.

ACCULTURATION: PATTERNS AND CONFLICTS

Three Patterns of Acculturation and Conflicts. Many Arabs and Muslims have experienced cultural marginalization in mainstream American society. Arab Americans tend to cope with their marginality by (1) denying their ethnic identity, (2) withdrawing into an ethnic/religious enclave, and (3) engaging mainstream American society through information campaigns directed toward the news media, book publishers, politicians, and schools. As a result of such efforts, the cable television network TNT announced that it would no longer show movies that blatantly bashed Arabs and Arab Americans. Included in this category were the films *Shadow Warriors 2: Assault on Death Mountain* and *Thunder in Paradise*.

Arab Americans who deny their ethnic background range from recent arrivals, to assimilated immigrants, to those who are American born. These individuals often opt for a White identity (Ajrouch & Jamal, 2007). American-born Arabs deny their ethnic identity by making a complete break with their ethnicity; they adopt American culture completely. Immigrants who deny their Arab ethnicity may point out their distinctiveness from Arab and Islamic culture (Nobles & Sciarra, 2000). Abu-Laban and Suleiman (1989) maintain that some Arab Americans never reveal their ethnic background because of widespread stereotyping. One famous person in the denial category is Ralph Nader, who seldom refers to his Arab Lebanese heritage.

Arab Americans in the withdrawal pattern category tend to live in ethnic enclaves and to be recent immigrants (both skilled and unskilled professionals) who prefer to live in ethnic neighborhoods, or close to other members of the same group in the suburbs. They believe that their ethnic culture and religious traditions are not respected in American culture, and therefore, they seek to minimize acculturation and assimilation. Members of this group take the position that cultural marginalization is the price of living in American society. As Nobles and Sciarra (2000) have asserted,

> they are able to stay in touch with their country of origin through advances in telecommunications; this reinforces their sense of Arab community and tradition, intensifying a preference for living in ethnic Arab neighborhoods or near other Arab Americans in the suburbs. Finding their ethnic identity and religious traditions alien to the dominant American culture, they prefer to stay withdrawn in order to prevent assimilation. (p. 185)

Those who advocate engaging American society seek to win societal acceptance of Arab Americans into mainstream American society. This third group of Arab Americans can be called integrationists because they emphasize the common bonds between Arab or Islamic values and American values. Arab integrationists focus on the commonalities between Christianity and Islam. They confront anti-Arab stereotyping and racism by emphasizing that they are Americans who happen to be of Arab ancestry. According to Nobles and Sciarra (2000), "Arab Americans who engage with the dominant culture tend to have distant ancestral ties, be successful, have high leadership positions, advocate secularism, or identify with Christianity. . . . They identify themselves as Americans who happen to be of Arab ancestry" (p. 185).

Cultural Strengths of Arab and Muslim Americans

The cultural strengths of Arab and Muslim Americans include their family values and their numerous contributions in many fields of American life, including entertainment, politics, business, the arts, and sports. Some renowned Americans of Arab descent include Steve Jobs, former CEO of Apple Inc., whose biological father was Syrian; Ralph Nader, Lebanese American whose book, *Unsafe at Any Speed*, prompted the U.S. Congress to pass the National Traffic and Motor Vehicle Safety Act of 1966; Kahlil Gibran, Lebanese American author of *The Prophet*; John Sununu, the first Arab American governor of New Hampshire and former chief of staff to President George W. Bush; Donna Shalala, Lebanese American and former secretary of health and human services; Lucie Salhany, an American of Jordanian and Lebanese descent, the first woman to head a broadcast television network; Dr. Michael DeBakey, inventor of the heart pump; and Rony Seikaly, former NBA player for the New Jersey Nets.

MENTAL HEALTH ISSUES FOR ARAB AND MUSLIM AMERICANS

Arabs and Muslims tend to view mental health differently than Westerners. For the most part, Western psychology conceptualizes psychopathology as an intrapsychic disorder that can cause suffering and impairment in one's overall functioning. Westerners value such constructs as separation and individuation from parents, and entire theories are based upon this process—see, for instance, psychodynamic and psychoanalytic approaches to psychotherapy (Jones-Smith, 2016). In contrast, Arabs and Muslims rarely have personalities that are individuated from parents and their families.

Many Arabs and Muslims believe that visions and dreams are highly significant. They may make decisions on the basis of dreams and visions (Dwairy, 2006).

Moreover, mental illness is a major stigma for both Arab and Muslim Americans (Ciftci, Jones, & Corrigan, 2012). A person with mental distress or illness is inclined not to seek counseling from professionals. Although there are differences among various Arab and Muslim communities, there are also some common practices and beliefs across Muslim groups. Many Muslim groups believe that Allah causes illnesses. As Ciftci, Jones, and Corrigan (2012) have stated,

> there are contextual differences among practices and beliefs about health and illness and important commonalities across Muslim groups. A fundamental tenet of Islam is that there is one God (the Arabic word for God, Allah, is used universally by Muslims, regardless of ethnic group or language of origin) and Allah causes everything including illnesses. According to some religious leaders, illness is one method of connection with God and should not be considered as alien, but "rather . . . an event, a mechanism of the body, that is serving to cleanse, purify, and balance us on the physical, emotional, mental and spiritual planes" (Rassool, 2000, p. 1479).

Concerns about family social standing predispose some Arab and Muslim individuals not to disclose mental illness because to do such would be shameful (Aloud & Rathur, 2009; Amer, 2006; Erickson & Al-Timimi, 2001). In a study analyzing 67 immigrant women who reported experiencing domestic abuse, Abu-Ras (2003) found that approximately 70% reported shame and 62% felt embarrassment for obtaining formal mental health services. Muslim women tend to express a higher level of need for mental health services, while men express more negative attitudes toward help seeking (Khan, 2006). Aloud and Rathur (2009) also found significant levels of self-reported shame among Muslims with regard to using formal mental health services.

Mental Health, Religiosity, Arab Elders, and Posttraumatic Stress Disorder

Several studies have investigated the impact of discrimination and trauma on Arabs and Muslims. One study showed that self-reports of recent discrimination were positively correlated with psychological distress and negatively correlated with self-esteem and environmental mastery (Moradi & Hasan, 2004). Another study involved Arab Americans from 19 states and the District of Columbia and found that among Christian Arab Americans less integration and more marginalization were associated with lower family dysfunction (Amer & Hovey, 2007). Greater family dysfunction and greater Arab religious/family values and acculturative stress were predictors of depression. In the same study, however, among Muslim Arabs, less Arab religious/family values, less religiosity, and greater marginalization were associated with family dysfunction.

Ajrouch (2007) investigated the psychological well-being of Arab American elders and found that immigrant status was associated with lower life satisfaction and more frequent feelings of depression. Another study reported that Iraqi clients were more likely to be diagnosed with posttraumatic stress disorder (PTSD), more likely to have physical complaints, and more inclined to have full remission after care than other Arab American clients (Jamil, Hakim-Larson, et al., 2006). Jamil, Nassar-McMillan, and Salman (2005) investigated the mental health of 32 Gulf War refugees and found that 59% of the respondents met the threshold for PTSD.

COUNSELING ARAB AND MUSLIM AMERICANS

Arab and Muslim Americans tend not to be "psychologically minded." The Arab language has few words describing psychological concepts, and therefore, Arab/Muslim clients are not inclined to be predisposed to seeking counseling. Erickson and Al-Timimi (2004) have asserted that Arab Americans are generally wary about mental health services. They question the potential value of therapy and express concern that their cultural values may be dismissed or challenged.

More specifically, Arab/Muslim Americans expressed concerns about (1) the American cultural value of raising children to be independent and self-sufficient; (2) the American tendency to intermix the genders, thereby leading to immorality; and (3) the American emphasis on materialism instead of spirituality and caring for others. They view modern psychotherapy as a Western enterprise (Dwairy, 2006). Arab Americans who are most inclined to seek psychotherapy are those who are educated and acculturated to mainstream American values, or who are experiencing a trauma of crisis.

Because of widespread prejudice against them and acculturative stress, Arab Americans are at risk for developing challenges to their psychological health (Ciftci, Jones, & Corrigan, 2012). Many Muslim individuals live in fear of hate crimes, and they experience anxiety about the future, threats to their safety, loss of community, and isolation (Abu-Ras & Abu-Bader, 2008). A qualitative study of Muslim American college women wearing a hijab revealed that participants had both fears of disapproval from their parents for not wearing the hijab and fears of disapproval from society for wearing the hijab when deciding whether to visibly identify with the Muslim community (Ciftci, Shawahin, Reid-Marks, & Ellison, 2013).

Counselors must take into consideration the contextual factors involving the interaction of identity, stigma, and discrimination. As with the other ethnic groups who have immigrated to the United States, acculturating to a second culture can be stressful as one attempts to maintain one's cultural roots. Moreover, as pointed out earlier, Arab parents face a great deal of stress as they attempt to maintain Arab values at home, in the face of great pressure for their children to conform to the American way of doing things (Ahmed & Reddy, 2007; Amri & Bemak, 2013; Ibrahim & Dykeman, 2010).

> ## Cultural Reflections
>
> *On a scale of 1 (incompetent) to 10 (very competent), how competent do you feel you would be in counseling an Arab/ Muslim American?*
>
> *What would make you feel comfortable and/or uncomfortable in counseling members of this ethnic and religious group?*

Role of Family, Friends, and Religious Leaders With Mental Health Concerns

Arab and Muslim individuals have been found to display a greater willingness to seek help from families and religious leaders than from formal mental health services (Al-Darmaki, 2003; O. Ali, Milstein, & Marzuk, 2005). This finding is supported with Hamdan's (2009) emphasis on the significance of the collectivist nature of Muslims. Hamdan points out that in Muslim culture mental illness is a "private family matter" and that *imams* (religious leaders) have important roles in dealing with mental illness in a Muslim community. Therefore, Hamdan recommends that clinicians integrate religion into treatment. Even though *imams* spend time counseling congregants, they rarely have formal education in counseling or in mental health issues. Analyzing a survey that examined the imam's role in servicing Muslim communities in the United States, O. Ali and colleagues (2005) concluded that "although Imams have little formal training in counseling, they are asked to help congregants who come to them with mental health and social service issues. Imams need more support from mental health professionals to fulfill a potentially vital role in improving access to services for minority Muslim communities in which there currently appear to be unmet psychosocial needs" (p. 202). The researchers noted that following the aftermath of September 11, 2001, there was an increased need to counsel Muslims who face discrimination from the American public.

COUNSELING ARAB AND MUSLIM AMERICANS: SOME RECOMMENDATIONS

Clinicians working with Arab and Muslim Americans must take into consideration the issue of the stigma associated with seeking mental health services. Arab families request mental health counseling only as a last resort, and they tend to telephone for help rather than to come in person for treatment (Nydell, 2012). In general, counselors and therapists tend to encounter six types of barriers in providing mental health counseling for Muslims. These barriers are mistrust of mental health counselors, religious beliefs about the causes of mental issues, fear of racism and discrimination, language barriers, differences in communication, and other issues of culture and religion (Amri & Bemak, 2013; Keshavarzi & Haque, 2013).

Erickson and Al-Timimi (2004) have proposed other recommendations for providing counseling and mental health services to Arab/Muslim clients. Counselors and therapists must consider carefully the applicability of these recommendations for their individual clients.

1. To reduce Arab/Muslim clients' apprehension about counseling/therapy, clinicians should carefully explain what can be expected from counseling/therapy. An orientation to counseling/therapy should explain the role of the clinician and the client. Clinicians should also show an interest in learning about Arab American culture and values and respect for the client's religion and worldviews.

2. Many Arab/Muslim Americans would most likely respond best to a clinician with a directive style, offering concrete advice for specific concerns in the beginning of counseling/therapy.

3. Clinicians should consider including family with any form of treatment, if only including them indirectly. Clinicians should not encourage family members to openly express anger toward each other because such confrontations might challenge the family structure and honor system.

Other recommendations include the following:

4. Clinicians should not criticize or challenge the Islamic religion or its tenets.

5. Clinicians should not encourage the open expression of feelings against family members.

6. Clinicians should take a few minutes to warm up before delving into the business of the appointment. A client might be offered tea.

7. Clinicians should conduct a self-assessment to determine their attitudes and feelings toward Arab/Muslim Americans.

CASE VIGNETTE 12.1
NADIA: STRENGTHS-BASED THERAPY FOR ARABS AND MUSLIMS

Muslims respond positively to present-oriented strengths-based approaches in counseling in which their positive attributes and environments are emphasized and used to solve problems (Al-Abdul-Jabbar & Al-Issa, 2000; Al-Radi & Mahdy, 1994; S. Ali, Liu, & Humedian, 2004; Azhar & Varma, 2000; Daneshpour, 1998). This approach aligns closely with Islamic values of spirituality, family, and community, legitimizing the client's values and building trust with the counselor.

Nadia: An Arab/Muslim Teenager

Nadia is a 17-year-old Arab American girl who has recently begun to experience stomachaches and headaches because she says that she can't wait to get out of her father's house. She complains that her father is a dictator in the home, that she is afraid to challenge him, and that she wants to attend college in a different city than the one in which she lives. She feels conflicted because she wants to honor her father and to respect his position

(Continued)

(Continued)

of authority in the family. Her mother just wants her to get along with her father and to honor his wishes that she attend college in New York City. Nadia resents her older brother because she says that he is favored by her father and mother. Nadia says that her family's favoritism toward her brother is unfair. She states that she feels American, while her parents feel that they are Arabic, and they want to honor all Arabic values and traditions.

Other than her rebellion about attending college out of town, Nadia's father considers her a good girl because she has almost straight As in her school subjects. He refuses to allow her to date. Nadia believes that if she attends college out of town she will be able to date and to develop her own identity apart from that of her family. She does not completely reject her heritage as an Arab American. In fact, she is quite proud of it, but she says that she was raised in America and she wants to become accepted as an American. Nadia was referred to counseling by her school counselor because she was found crying silently in class on two separate occasions. The school counselor called Nadia's parents and recommended that they seek counseling as a family.

The therapist at the clinic was aware and knowledgeable about some aspects of Arab and Muslim culture. He therefore asked Nadia's father to come in individually before he spoke with the entire family. The invitation acknowledged the father's authority in the family. When the father appeared, the therapist greeted him respectfully and offered him a cup of tea. The therapist had on his wall the Arabic greeting. The father saw the greeting and asked: "Do you speak Arabic?" The therapist responded no but that he liked the Arabic greeting because it resonated with him spiritually—that he wished peace on all who cross his office threshold.

Assurance of Confidentiality. During their initial private meeting, the clinician reviewed the limits of confidentiality and reassured the father that their confidentiality would be maintained. The therapist introduced himself more formally by giving the father information about his professional background. The therapist showed the proper respect to the father as the head of his family.

After the meeting with the father, the entire family came in during the following week for their initial therapy consultation. Based on the earlier meeting with the therapist, the father was more receptive to therapy. The therapist had made it clear that the family's values related to Islam would be respected, and that if anything were said that was offensive to Islamic teachings, the family members would bring these incidents to the therapist's attention.

Assessment of Strengths. Instead of beginning the therapy session talking about Nadia's problems, the therapist went around and complimented each family member to demonstrate that there was "honor" in their

coming to therapy. Their actions demonstrated they were a strong family. The fact that Nadia's father came in early to speak with the therapist indicated that they could go forward with honor in counseling.

The therapist inquired about how their faith or spirituality might be used. The question was raised: "Perhaps it's fate that you are here together as a family. Maybe your being here is a sign that something good might come out of what appeared initially to be a negative situation."

In the assessment interview with the family, several themes emerged. First, the parents said that immigrating to the United States had been difficult for them, but Nadia was born in this country. Both the father and the mother worked, and both stated that they encountered daily little digs or insults about their Muslim background. These insults and microaggressions had led the parents to reject American society as unsafe. In fact, they feared that Nadia would also be hurt, even though she was well liked by her classmates.

The second problem centered on Nadia's withdrawal to her room and her lack of engagement during family meetings. The father and mother felt that they were losing control of their daughter and that she was rejecting them. Youssef, Nadia's brother, said that he felt hostility coming from his sister each time that his family did something special for him.

The therapist initially had Nadia speak about what she admired about her father, mother, and brother. She was asked to speak about one "strength" that she had observed about each one of them. She was also asked to describe what she was most grateful about living in her family.

Nadia's words touched everyone in the room. She spoke about how grateful she was for her parents' dedication to their employment, which enabled her to attend one of the better schools in New York City. She said that she felt grateful for Youssef, who always seemed to appear just when she needed him most. When she talked about her mother's working and sacrifices for her, Nadia's eyes filled with tears.

The family was reassured that Nadia was not rejecting members because she did not want to be Arabic. In fact, Nadia stated that she was proud of her Arabic heritage. Nadia then went on to explain that the headaches started when she began to apply to the colleges for admission, especially the colleges that were far away. "No matter where I go," Nadia explained, "my family will always be carried with me in my heart."

The therapist then asked each person in the family to think of two strengths that their family possessed. In go-around fashion, each family member stated two strengths for which he or she was grateful that the family had. Nadia's parents were encouraged to talk about the strengths they used in dealing with their immigration to the United States and in the seemingly daily microaggressions they faced. Talking about their family strengths and the strengths that their parents had used in making it each day buoyed up the family's hope. Smiles came over their faces, and the family seemed to relax.

Let Go. The parents were asked how they could best deal with Nadia's "problem" and what they wanted to let go surrounding it. Soon the family said that Nadia's situation was not just Nadia's problem, but rather the entire family might consider ways to solve her desire to attend a college away from home and her father's desire to keep her in New York. Youssef suggested that she live in the dorms in New York City, so that she could begin to develop her own education and career. Her mother recommended that she might consider colleges and universities just outside of New York City, so that the commute would not be more than an hour. Her father asked to be assured about her "chastity," if she lived away from home.

Both the father and the mother said that they wanted to let go of their fears that Nadia was rejecting them and her Arabic identity. Nadia's expressions of love for them had reassured them. Youssef said that he wanted to let go of the competition and the conflict between the two of them. Nadia stated that she wanted to let go of her resentment toward her father because she knew that deep down inside he wanted the best for her. Nadia told her father that she loved him.

The therapist suggested that to restore harmony and balance, the family members might consider forgiving each other so that they could let go of hurts. Nadia's stomach problems and headaches disappeared.

Let In. During the next therapy session, the family focused on letting in. The therapist asked the family members to consider what spiritual directions Islam gave them regarding the problems they faced. Nadia's father mentioned that one of the moral traits recommended in the Qur'an is forgiveness. He recited the following lines from the Qu'ran by heart:

> In one verse, Allah commands: "They should rather pardon and overlook. Would you not

love Allah to forgive you? Allah is Ever-Forgiving, Most Merciful" [Qur'an, 24:22]. Those who do not abide by the moral values of the Qur'an find it very difficult to forgive others because they are easily angered by any error committed. However, Allah has advised the faithful that forgiveness is more proper.

> "The repayment of a bad action is one equivalent to it. But if someone pardons and puts things right, his reward is with Allah" [Qur'an, 42:40]. "But if you pardon and exonerate and forgive, Allah is Ever-Forgiving, Most Merciful" [Qur'an, 64:14]. It has also been revealed in the Qur'an that forgiveness is a superior moral trait: "But if someone is steadfast and forgives, that is the most resolute course to follow" [Qur'an, 42:43]. For that reason, believers are forgiving, compassionate, and tolerant people who, as revealed in the Qur'an, "control their rage and pardon other people" [Qur'an, 3:134].

After the father reviewed those verses/statements contained in the Qu'ran, the family felt that it was on the right course. Allah was pointing the way for their family. It was destined that they should be in counseling.

Developing Competencies. The therapist used the next session to begin helping the family to develop competencies for dealing with family issues. Family biweekly meetings were established that were to be run by the father. Any family member could bring a concern.

Moving Forward. The final therapy session signaled that the family had moved forward. Nadia had earned a scholarship, which included the costs of a dorm room and food, at a prestigious university in New York City. She and her parents agreed upon days when they would be visiting her.

SUMMARY OF KEY POINTS

Arab and Muslim Americans are a diverse group coming from more than 22 different countries. In general, clinicians have very little cultural knowledge about Arab and Muslim culture. The following implications for practice have been drawn from the literature (Ahmed & Reddy, 2007; S. Ali, Liu, & Humedian, 2004; Amri & Bemak, 2013; Ibrahim & Dykeman, 2010; Keshavarzi & Haque, 2013).

1. Assess your cultural, ethnic, and racial attitudes toward Arab and Muslim Americans.

2. The clinician's office should reflect some knowledge and understanding of Middle Eastern culture. It should project professionalism with diplomas and credentials framed and available for clients' inspection.

3. The clinician should use a warm and personable demeanor to promote trust with the client.

4. First assess the client's presenting problem; then assess the client's history of immigration, generation status, and ethnic identification.

5. Know that some Arab and Muslim clients may present their problem as a natural and supernatural will of God, and the clinician should not challenge this religious view of the client's problem.

6. The clinician should provide positive validation and normalization of the individual's or family's coming to therapy/counseling for assistance in order to reduce the shame associated with seeking help. Compliment the father on his wisdom in coming in for consultation and therapeutic assistance.

7. Help the client to understand the process of acculturation and the stressors that family members face as they work toward a bicultural ethnic identity.

8. Understand that many Arab and Muslim Americans face discrimination and prejudice because of their ethnocultural background.

9. When counseling Arab and Muslims, it is important to provide a clinician of the same gender as the client.

10. If the clinician experiences any difficulties in communicating with Arab/Muslim clients, he/ she should consider referring the client/family to a practicing Arab/Muslim counselor/therapist.

11. Consider including members of the client's family when counseling individuals from Arab and Muslim American backgrounds.

12. Become aware that Arab and Muslim Americans may have different interactional styles that are rooted in their culture involving such factors as time, space, and communication.

13. When faced with value conflicts with Muslim clients, consider consulting with an imam, a Muslim religious leader, or a respected member of the local community.

14. Clinicians should explore the client's spiritual belief system when working with Muslims. A clinician's assessment of spiritual beliefs and practices can help to activate Islamic values. For instance, prayer, fasting, and rituals are believed to be effective measures for dealing with distress.

15. Be aware that Arabs and Muslims tend to have a pattern of somatization of anxiety or depression, and that they may be apprehensive about seeking counseling or psychotherapy.

DISCUSSION QUESTIONS

Discussion Question Set 1

What are some important differences that you see between Arab Americans and Muslim Americans? What are some similarities between members of these two groups?

Discussion Question Set 2

There is a history of heated debate about Muslim immigration to the United States. Discuss three strengths that you believe that Arab Americans and Muslim Americans have in common. How might you consider using these strengths in counseling? On a scale of 1 (*not culturally competent at all*) to 10 (*culturally competent*), rate the degree to which you feel qualified to counsel either an Arab American or a Muslim American. Discuss the factors that led to your self-rating.

KEY TERMS

Arab: A person who originates from countries situated in the Middle East and parts of North Africa, and whose primary language is Arabic.

Five Pillars of Islam: Five core Islamic spiritual teachings/principles to which all Muslims must subscribe and adhere, including professing faith to Islam and the Prophet Muhammad.

Hajj: The Muslim pilgrimage to Mecca that all Muslims (with the means to do so) are expected to make.

Hijab: Head covering that some Muslim women use. In some Muslim countries, wearing the hijab is a sign of devotion and commitment to the Muslim faith.

Imam: Arabic word meaning "stand in front of," a person who is usually considered a spiritual leader. An imam leads a group in prayer at a mosque, guiding the mosque members in matters of Islamic worship. There are no clergy in Islam, and an imam can be any Muslim community person in good standing—usually an elder. An imam is chosen for his deep spiritual understanding of the Qu'ran and Islamic teachings.

Islam: The religion of Muslims; it is a monotheistic faith revealed through Muhammad as the Prophet of Allah. The Arabic word *salaam* (English translation, "peace") has the same root as the word *Islam*, with one interpretation maintaining that individual personal peace is attained by utterly submitting to God.

Islamophobia: An irrational fear and dislike of Muslims, often based on inaccurate stereotypes.

Muhammad: The messenger of the Muslim God, Allah, according to the Muslim religion and the Qur'an.

Muslim: A person who believes in Allah and the Prophet Muhammad as his messenger and who testifies to the beliefs of the Qur'an.

Muslim religion: Muslims are followers of Islam or the Qur'an, the Muslim holy book.

Qur'an: The Islamic holy book that was revealed in stages to the Prophet Muhammad over 23 years. Muslims view Qur'anic revelations as the sacred word of God.

Ramadan: The ninth month of the Muslim year, during which strict fasting is observed from sunrise to sunset. Throughout the entire month, Muslims fast, from sunrise until sunset, every single day. Fasting during Ramadan is regarded as a compulsory religious duty (it is one of the so-called Five Pillars of Islam, each of which is incumbent upon all Muslims to abide by).

Shiites: Make up 10% of Muslims worldwide, and they form the overwhelming majority in Iran. Some of the conflicts in the Middle East have been between Muslims who call themselves Sunni and those who say they are Shiite.

Sujud: The position assumed during daily prayers in the Islamic faith.

Sunnis: Form about 90% of Muslims worldwide.

Wudhu: A ritualistic washing of one's hands, feet, arms, and legs prior to engaging in prayer. After the *wudhu* has been performed, individuals must find a quiet place to pray.

REFERENCES AND SUGGESTED READING

Abi-Hashem, H. (2008). Arab Americans: Understanding their challenges, needs, and struggles. In A. Marsella, J. Johnson, P. Watson, & J. Gryczynski (Eds.), *Ethnocultural perspectives on disaster and trauma* (pp. 115–173). New York, NY: Springer.

Abudabbeh, N. (1996). Arab families. In M. M. McGoldrick, J. Giordano, & J. K. Pearce (Eds.), *Ethnicity and family therapy* (pp. 333–346). New York, NY: Guilford Press.

Abudabbeh, N., & Aseel, H. A. (1999). Transcultural counseling and Arab Americans. In J. McFadden (Ed.), *Transcultural counseling* (pp. 283–296). Alexandria, VA: American Counseling Association.

Abu-Laban, S. (1989). Identity and adaption among Arab American Muslims. In B. Abu-Laban & M. W. Suleiman (Eds.), *Arab Americans: Continuity and change* (pp. 45–63). Belmont, MA: Association of Arab American University Graduates.

Abu-Laban, B., & Suleiman, M. (1989). *Arab Americans: Continuity and change*. Belmont, MA: Association of Arab American University Graduates.

Abu-Ras, W. (2003). Barriers to services for Arab immigrant battered women in a Detroit suburb. *Social Work Research and Evaluation, 3*(4), 49–66.

Abu-Ras, W., & Abu-Bader, S. H. (2008). The impact of the September 11, 2001, attacks on the well-being of Arab Americans in New York City. *Journal of Muslim Mental Health, 3*(2), 217–239.

Ahmad, N. M. (2004). *Arab-American culture and health care*. Retrieved from http://www.cwru.edu/med/epidbio/mphp 439/Arab-Americans.htm

Ahmed, S. (2012). Adolescents and emerging adults. In S. Ahmed & M. M. Amer (Eds.), *Counseling Muslims: Handbook of mental health issues and interventions* (pp. 251–280). New York, NY: Routledge.

Ahmed, S., & Reddy, L. (2007). Understanding the mental health needs of American Muslims: Recommendations and considerations for practice. *Journal of multicultural Counseling and Development, 35*(4), 207–218.

Ajrouch, K. J. (2000). Place, age, and culture: Community living and ethnic identity among Lebanese American adolescents. *Small Group Research, 31*, 447–469.

Ajrouch, K. J. (2004). Gender, race, and symbolic boundaries: Contested spaces of identity among Arab-American Adolescents. *Sociological Perspectives, 47*(4), 371–391.

Ajrouch, K. J. (2007). Resources and well-being among Arab-American elders. *Journal of Cross Cultural Gerontology, 22*(2), 67–82.

Ajrouch, K. J., & Jamal, A. (2007). Assimilating to a White identity: The case of Arab Americans. *International Migration Review, 41*(4), 860–879.

Ajrouch, K. J., & Kusow, A. M. (1999). Family and ethnic identity in an Arab American community. In M. W. Suleiman (Ed.), *Arabs in America: Building a new future* (pp. 129–139). Philadelphia, PA: Temple University Press.

Ajrouch, K. J., & Kusow, A. M. (2007). Racial and religious contexts: Situational identities among Lebanese and Somali Muslim immigrants. *Ethnic and Racial Studies*, *30*(1), 72–94. doi:10.1080/01419870601006553

Al-Abdul-Jabbar, J., & Al-Issa, I. (2000). Psychotherapy in Islamic society. In I. Al-Issa (Ed.), *Al-Junun: Mental illness in the Islamic world* (pp. 277–293). Madison, CT: International Universities Press.

Al-Darmaki, F. R. (2003). Attitudes towards seeking professional psychological help: What really counts for United Arab Emirates University students? *Social Behavior and Personality*, *31*, 497–508.

Ali, O. M., Milstein, G., & Marzuk, P. M. (2005). The Imam's role in meeting the counseling needs of Muslim communities in the United States. *Psychiatric Services*, *56*, 202–205.

Ali, S., Liu, W., & Humedian, M. (2004). Islam 101: Understanding the religion and therapy implications. *Professional Psychology: Research and Practice*, *35*(6), 635–642.

Ali, W., Clifton, E., Duss, M., Fang, L., Keyes, S., & Shakir, F. (2011). Fear, Inc. The roots of the Islamophobia network in America. *Center for American Progress*. Retrieved from https://www.americanprogress.org/issues/religion/reports/2011/08/26/10165/fear-inc/

Aloud, N., & Rathur, A. (2009). Factors affecting attitudes towards seeking and using formal mental health and psychological services among Arab Muslim populations. *Journal of Muslim Mental Health*, *4*, 79–103. http://dx.doi.org/10.1080/15564900802487675

Al-Radi, O., & Mahdy, M. A. (1994). Group therapy: An Islamic approach. *Integrative Psychiatry*, *10*(3), 106–109.

Amer, M. M. (2006). *When multicultural worlds collide: Breaking down barriers to service use.* Paper presented at the annual meeting of American Psychological Association, New Orleans.

Amer, M., & Hovey, J. D. (2007). Socio-demographic differences in acculturation and mental health for a sample of second generation/early immigrant Arab Americans. *Journal of Immigrant and Minority Health*, *9*, 335–347.

American Psychiatric Association. (2013). *Diagnostic and statistical manual of mental disorders* (5th ed.). Washington, DC: Author.

Amri, S., & Bemak, F. (2013). Mental health help-seeking behaviors of Muslim immigrants in the United States. *Journal of Muslim Mental Health*, *7*(1), 43–59. Retrieved from https://quod.lib.umich.edu/j/jmmh/10381607.0007.104/—mental-health-help-seeking-behaviors-of-muslim-immigrants?rgn=main;view=fulltext

Arab American Institute. (2003). *Religious affiliations of Arab Americans*. Retrieved from http://www.aaiusa.org

Arab American Institute. (2011). *Arab American demographics*. Retrieved from http://www.aaiusa.org/pages/demographics/

Asi, M., & Beaulieu, D. (2013, May). Arab households in the United States: 2006–2010. *American Community Survey Briefs*, published by the U.S. Census Bureau, U.S. Department of Commerce, Economics and Statistics Administration. Retrieved from http://www.census.gov/prod/2013pubs/acsbr10-20.pdf

Azhar, M. Z., & Varma, S. L. (2000). Mental illness and its treatment in Malaysia. In Ihsan Al-Issa (Ed.), *Al-Junun: Mental illness in the Islamic world* (pp. 163–186). Madison, CT: International University Press.

Bowker, J. (2000). Five pillars of Islam. In *The concise Oxford dictionary of world religions*. New York, NY: Oxford University Press.

Budman, C. L., Lipson, J. G., & Meleis, A. I. (1992). The cultural consultant in mental health care: The case of an Arab adolescent. *American Journal of Orthopsychiatry*, *62*, 359–370.

Byng, M. D. (1998). Mediating discrimination: Resisting oppression among African American Muslim women. *Social Problems*, *45*, 473–487.

Ciftci, A., Jones, N., Corrigan, P. W. (2012). Mental health stigma in the Muslim community. *Journal of Muslim Mental Health*, *7*(1). Retrieved from http://quod.lib.umich.edu/j/jmmh/10381607.0007.102?rgn=main;view=fulltext

Ciftci, A., Shawahin, L., Reid-Marks, L., & Ellison, Z. (2013). *Campus experience for Muslim women wearing hijab.* Paper presented at the National Multicultural Summit, Houston, TX.

Council on American-Islamic Relations. (2003). *The status of Muslim civil rights in the United States: Guilt by association.* Washington, DC: CAIR.

Council on American-Islamic Relations. (2008). *The status of Muslim civil rights in the United States 2008.* Washington, DC: CAIR. Retrieved from http://www.cair.com/Portals/0/pdf/civilrights2008.pdf

Daneshpour, M. (1998). Muslim families and family therapy. *Journal of Marital and Family Therapy*, *24*(3), 355–368. doi:10.1111/j.1752-0606.1998.tb01090.x

Dwairy, M. (2006). Counseling Arab and Muslim clients. In P. B. Pedersen, J. G. Draguns, W. J. Lonner, & J. E. Trimble (Eds.), *Counseling across cultures* (6th ed., pp. 147–160). Thousand Oaks, CA: Sage.

El Azayem, G. A., & Hedayat-Diba, Z. (1994). The psychological aspects of Islam: Basic principles of Islam and their psychological corollary. *International Journal for the Psychology of Religion*, *4*(1), 41–50. http://dx.doi.org/10.1207/s15327582ijpr0401_6

El-Badry, S. (n.d.). Arab American demographics. *Arab American Market*. McLean, VA: Allied Media Corp. Retrieved from http://www.allied-media.com/Arab-American/Arab%20american%20Demographics.html

El Saadawi, N. (1993). Women and sex. In D. L. Bowen & E. A. Early (Eds.), *Everyday life in the Muslim Middle East* (pp. 81–83). Bloomington: Indiana University Press.

Erickson, C. D., & Al-Timimi, N. R. (2001). Providing mental health services to Arab Americans: Recommendations and considerations. *Cultural Diversity and Ethnic Minority Psychology, 7*, 308–327.

Erickson, C. D., & Al-Timimi, N. R. (2004). Counseling and psychotherapy with Arab American clients. In T. Smith (Ed.), *Practicing multiculturalism: Affirming diversity in counseling and psychology* (pp. 234–254). Boston, MA: Pearson.

Facts about Arabs and the Arab world. (2009, November 29). American-Arab Anti-Discrimination Committee. Retrieved from http://www.adc.org/2009/11/facts-about-arabs-and-the-arab-world/

Fakih, R. R. (2013). *Ethnic identity among Arab Americans: An examination of contextual influences and psychological well-being*. Wayne State University Dissertations, Paper 881. Retrieved from http://digitalcommons.wayne.edu/oa_dissertations/881

Gaultieri, S. (2001). Becoming White: Race, religion and the foundations of Syrian/Lebanese ethnicity in the United States. *Journal of American Ethnic History, 20*(4), 31–38.

Haddad, Y. Y. (1997). Make room for the Muslims? In W. H. Conser Jr. & S. B. Twiss (Eds.), *Religious diversity and American religious history* (pp. 277–284). New York, NY: Oxford University Press.

Haddad, Y. Y., & Smith, J. I. (1996). Islamic values among American Muslims. In B. C. Aswad & B. Bilge (Eds.), *Family and gender among American Muslims* (pp. 19–40). Philadelphia, PA: Temple University Press.

Hakim-Larson, J., Nassar-McMillan, S., & Paterson, A. D. (2013). Culturally alert counseling with Middle Eastern Americans. In Garrett McAuliffe & Associates (Ed.), *Culturally alert counseling: A comprehensive introduction* (2nd ed., pp. 263–292). Thousand Oaks, CA: Sage.

Hamdan, A. (2009). Mental health needs of Arab women. *Health Care for Women International, 30*(7), 593–611. doi:10.1080/07399330902928808

Hodge, D. R. (2005). Social work and the house of Islam: Orienting practitioners to the beliefs and values of Muslims in the United States. *Social Work, 50*, 162–173.

Hodge, D. R., & Nadir, A. (2008). Moving toward culturally competent practice with Muslims: Modifying cognitive therapy. *Social Work, 53*(1), 31–41.

Hourani, A. (1989, February 1). *Islam in European thought*. The Tanner Lectures on Human Value. Delivered at Clare Hall, Cambridge University, England.

Husain, S. A. (1998). Religion and mental health from the Muslim perspective. In H. G. Koenig (Ed.), *Handbook of religion and mental health* (pp. 279–290). San Diego, CA: Academic Press.

Ibrahim, F., & Dykeman, C. (2010). Counseling Muslim Americans: Cultural and spiritual assessments. *Journal of Counseling & Development, 89*(4), 387–396.

Itzigsohn, J., Giorguli, S., & Vazquez, O. (2005). Immigrant incorporation and racial identity: Racial self-identification among Dominican immigrants. *Ethnic and Racial Studies, 28*(1), 50–78.

Jamil, H., Hakim-Larson, J., Farrag, M., Kafaji, T., Duqum, I., & Jamil, L. H. (2002). A retrospective study of Arab American mental health clients: Trauma and the Iraqi refugees. *American Journal of Orthopsychiatry, 72*(3), 355–361.

Jamil, H., Nassar-McMillan, S. C., & Salman, W. A. (2006). Iraqi gulf war veteran refugees in the US: PTSD and physical symptoms. *Social Work Health Care, 43*(4), 85–98.

Johnston, M. P., and Nadal, K. L. (2010). Multiracial microaggressions: Exposing monoracism in everyday life and clinical practice. In D. W. Sue (Ed.), *Microaggressions and marginality: Manifestation, dynamics, and impact* (pp. 287–310). New York, NY: Wiley.

Jones-Smith, E. (2016). *Theories of counseling and psychotherapy: An integrative approach*. Thousand Oaks, CA: Sage.

Kayyali, R. (2006). *The Arab Americans*. Westport, CT: Greenwood Press.

Kelly, E. W., Aridi, A., & Bakhtiar, L. (1996). Muslims in the United States: An exploratory study of universal and mental health values. *Counseling and Values, 40*, 206–218.

Keshavarzi, H., & Haque, A. (2013). Outlining a psychotherapy model for enhancing Muslim mental health within an Islamic content. *The International Journal for the Psychology of Religion, 23*(3), 230–249.

Khan, Z. (2006). Attitudes toward counseling and alternative support among Muslims in Toledo, Ohio. *Journal of Muslim Mental Health, 1*, 21–42.

Kusow, A. M. (2006). Migration and racial formations among Somali immigrants in North America. *Journal of Ethnic and Migration Studies, 3*(32), 533–551.

Lipka, M. (2017). Muslims and Islam: Key findings in the U.S. and around the world. *Pew Research Center*. Retrieved from http://www.pewresearch.org/fact-tank/2017/08/09/muslims-and-islam-key-findings-in-the-u-s-and-around-the-world/

Lipson, J., & Meleis, A. I. (1983). Issues in health care of Middle Eastern patients. *Western Journal of Medicine, 139*(6), 854–861.

López, F. B. (2011). Towards a definition of Islamophobia: Approximations of the early twentieth century. *Ethnic and Racial Studies, 34*, 556–573.

Mahmoud, V. (1996). African American Muslim families. In M. McGoldrick, J. Giordano, & J. K. Pearce (Eds.), *Ethnicity and family therapy* (2nd ed., pp. 122–128). New York, NY: Guilford Press.

Mapping the global Muslim population. (2009, October 7). Experts: Demographic study. *Pew Research Center.* Retrieved from http://www.pewforum.org/2009/10/07/mapping-the-global-muslim-population/

McIntosh, P. (1989, July/August). White privilege: Unpacking the invisible knapsack. *Peace and Freedom*, pp. 10–12.

Mohamed, B. (2016). A new estimate of the U.S. Muslim population. *Pew Research Center.* Retrieved from http://www.pewresearch.org/fact-tank/2016/01/06/a-new-estimate-of-the-u-s-muslim-population/

Moradi, B., & Hasan, N. T. (2004). Arab American person's reported experiences of discrimination and mental health: The mediating role of personal control. *Journal of Counseling Psychology, 51*(4), 418–428.

Muslim population in the US: New poll shows none of us have any idea. (2014, November 6). Retrieved from www.idigitaltimes.com/muslim-population-us-new-poll-shows-none-us-have-any-idea-392930

Nadal, K. L. (2008). Preventing racial, ethnic, gender, sexual minority, disability, and religious microaggressions: Recommendations for promoting positive mental health. *Prevention in Counseling Psychology: Theory, Research, Practice and Training, 2*(1), 22–27.

Nadal, K. L. (2011). The Racial and Ethnic Microaggressions Scale (REMS): Construction, reliability, and validity. *Journal of Counseling Psychology, 58*, 470–480.

Nadal, K. L., Griffin, K. E., Hamit, S., Leon, J., Tobio, M., & Rivera, D. P. (2012). Subtle and overt forms of Islamophobia: Microaggressions toward Muslim Americans. *Journal of Muslim Mental Health, 6*(2), 16–37.

Nadal, K. L., Issa, M., Griffin, K. E., Hamit, S., & Lyons, O. B. (2010). Religious microaggressions in the United States: Mental health implications for religious minority groups. In D. W. Sue (Ed.), *Microaggressions and marginality: Manifestation, dynamics, and impact* (pp. 287–310). New York, NY: Wiley & Sons.

Nadal, K. L., Wong, Y., Griffin, K., Sriken, J., Vargas, V., Wideman, M., & Kolawole, A. (2011). Microaggressions and the multiracial experience. *International Journal of Humanities and Social Sciences, 1*(7), 36–44.

Naff, A. (1993). *Becoming American: The early Arab immigrant experience.* Carbondale: Southern Illinois University Press.

Najjar, R. (1994). A Palestinian's struggle with cultural conflicts. In J. M. Bystydzienski & E. P. Resnick (Eds.), *Women in cross-cultural transitions* (pp. 39–44). Bloomington, IN: Phi Delta Kappa Educational Foundation.

Nassar-McMillan, S. C., & Hakim-Larson, J. (2003). Counseling considerations among Arab Americans. *Journal of Counseling & Development, 81*, 150–159.

Nobles, A. Y., & Sciarra, D. T. (2000). Cultural determinants in the treatment of Arab Americans: A primer for mainstream therapists. *American Journal of Orthopsychiatry, 70*(2), 182–191.

Nydell, M. (2012). *Understanding Arabs: A contemporary guide to Arab society.* Boston, MA: Intercultural Press.

Orfalea, G. (2006). *The Arab Americans: A history.* Northampton, MA: Olive Branch Press.

Pargament, K. I. (1997). *The psychology of religion and coping.* New York, NY: Guilford Press.

Pew Research Center. (2017a, April 5). *The changing global religious landscape.* Retrieved from http://www.pewforum.org/2017/04/05/the-changing-global-religious-landscape/#global-population-projections-2015-to-2060

Pew Research Center. (2017b, July 26). *Demographic portrait of Muslim Americans.* Retrieved from http://www.pewforum.org/2017/07/26/demographic-portrait-of-muslim-americans/

Pollara, M., & Meleis, A. (1995). Parenting their adolescents: The experience of Jordanian immigrant women in California. *Health Care for Women International, 16*, 195–211.

Portes, A., & Rumbaut, R. G. (1996). *Immigrant American: A portrait.* Berkeley: University of California Press.

Rassool, G. H. (2000). The crescent and Islam: Healing, nursing, and the spiritual dimension: Some considerations towards an understanding of the Islamic perspectives on caring. *Journal of Advanced Nursing, 32*, 1476–1484.

Renard, J. (1998). *Responses to 101 questions on Islam.* Mahwah, NJ: Paulist Press.

Richards, P. S., & Bergin, A. E. (1997). *A spiritual strategy for counseling and psychotherapy.* Washington, DC: American Psychological Association.

Richards, P. S., & Bergin, A. E. (2005). *A spiritual strategy for counseling and psychotherapy* (2nd ed.). Washington, DC: American Psychological Association.

Rippy, A. E., & Newman, E. (2006). Perceived religious discrimination and its relationship to anxiety and paranoia among Muslim Americans. *Journal of Muslim Mental Health, 1*, 5–20.

Rippy, A. E., & Newman, E. (2008). Adaptation of a scale of race-related stress for use with Muslim Americans. *Journal of Muslim Mental Health, 3,* 53–68.

Sayed, M., Collins, D., & Takahashi, T. (1998). West meets East: Cross-cultural issues in inpatient treatment. *Bulletin of the Menninger Clinic, 62,* 439–454.

Shaheen, J. G. (1984). *The TV Arabs.* Bowling Green, OH; State University Popular Press.

Smith, J. I. (1999). *Islam in America.* New York, NY: Columbia University Press.

Sue, D. W., Bucceri, J., Lin, A. I., Nadal, K. L., & Torino, G. C. (2007). Racial microaggressions and the Asian American experience. *Cultural Diversity and Ethnic Minority Psychology, 13*(1), 72–81. doi:10.1037/1099-9809.13.1.72

Trump travel ban: Questions about the revised executive order. (2017, July 14). *BBC News.* Retrieved from http://www.bbc.com/news/world-us-canada-39044403

Younis, M. (2009). *Muslim Americans exemplify diversity, potential.* Retrieved from http://news.gallup.com/poll/116260/Muslim-Americans-Exemplify-Diversity-Potential.aspx

Zogby, J. J. (2001, October). *Arab Americans attitudes and the September 11 attacks.* Retrieved from http://www.aaiusa.org/PDF/attitudes.pdf

13

CULTURALLY RESPONSIVE STRENGTHS-BASED THERAPY FOR WHITE AMERICANS OF EUROPEAN ANCESTRY

CHAPTER OBJECTIVES

- Describe the demographics of White Americans of European heritage.

- Describe the worldviews and values of White Americans of European heritage.

- Evaluate theories related to White ethnocultural identity development.

- Implement counseling strategies and solutions to mental health issues associated with White Americans.

- Identify cultural strengths of White Americans and how these strengths can be applied to the clinical setting.

- *"You've got to do your own growing, no matter how tall your grandfather was."* —Irish proverb

- *"Starting is easy, persistence is an art."* —German proverb

- *"A candle loses nothing by lighting another candle."* —Italian proverb

- *"A man is not old until his regrets take the place of his dreams."* —Jewish proverb

- *"The greatest oaks have been little acorns."* —Polish proverb

INTRODUCTION

This chapter examines the cultural foundations of Americans who have European ancestry, a group referred to as Euro-Americans or White Americans in this chapter. Although White Americans are grouped into one large ethnocultural category, there are important cultural differences among them. This broad category includes individuals from the following backgrounds (listed in approximate order of proportion in the U.S. population): German, British (i.e., English, Welsh, Scottish, and Irish), Italian, Scandinavian, Greek, Slavic, other Western European (Portuguese, Spanish, Basque, French, Dutch, etc.), Central European (Swiss, Polish, Austrian, etc.), and Eastern European (Baltic, Ukrainian, Russian, etc.). It should be noted that in this book, the heading of White Americans excludes various categories of ethnic groups that also identify as White, such as Hispanic (people from Spain) and Middle Eastern White. Moreover, because of length limitations, this chapter provides only very brief descriptions of White Americans of European ancestry.

White Americans who identify as Jewish constitute a cross section of geographic connections, as European, or Ashkenazi, Jews trace family roots to countries from Russia to England, from Scandinavia to Italy. Sephardic Jews are those with ancestry in the Iberian peninsula (i.e., Spain and Portugal). Identifying as Jewish typically refers to ethnicity and culture as well as religion, and many who describe themselves as Jewish may also say they are not religious.

White Americans of European ancestry form the largest ethnic category in the United States, making up about two-thirds of the American population (Hixson, Hepler, & Kim, 2011). Despite their numbers, however, these ethnocultural groups are excluded from many multicultural counseling books (Richmond & Guindon, 2013). When White Americans are mentioned in multicultural books, (1) their ethnocultural backgrounds are often ignored, (2) they are treated as a homogeneous entity rather than the heterogeneous groups that form them, and (3) they are sometimes treated as if White privilege and an individualistic culture are the only significant cultural facts about them. Too many of the multicultural textbooks emphasize White privilege without talking about White empathy or even acknowledging that it took a substantial number of White Americans to vote into office the first African American president of the United States.

In writing a chapter that deals broadly with 53 White ethnic groups, there is an inherent danger of overgeneralizing—of stereotyping the very groups we seek to explain—when we lump all members of any one ethnic group together. Imagine the dangers of stereotyping when we merge 53 White ethnic groups under one general heading of White people of European ancestry. As pointed out in Chapter 1 under my theory of ethnic identity development, all people are like some specific group of people, like no other person, and like all other people in the world—my tripartite model of ethnic identity development put forth in an early article (E. Smith, 1985). Yet, despite the potential dangers of overgeneralizing about White people of European ancestry, one must use the group level of ethnocultural analysis in this chapter.

A major goal of this chapter is to present Euro-Americans sensitively, including both their strengths and their challenges. All ethnic groups, including those who have European ancestry, merit a balanced presentation of their ethnocultural group.

Historical Perspectives and Immigration of White Europeans to the United States

American Indians were the original people on the land currently known as the United States of America. All other populations have immigrated to this geographical area. The White population formed the first settlers to the original 13 American colonies, and White ethnic groups can be analyzed in terms of their waves of immigration to the United States. From 1830 to 1930, nearly 32 million people from various parts of Europe left their homes and immigrated to the United States to start a new life. Clearly, the United States is a country of immigrants from people throughout the world. The immigrants who came to this country were motivated by various factors, including famine, wars or conflicts within their country, religious persecution, and a search for work and new opportunities for their families (Zinn, 2003).

Demographics and Population Statistics

The federal Office of Management and Budget provided a definition of what constitutes a White person in the United States for the 2010 Census:

> "White" refers to a person having origins in any of the original peoples of Europe, the Middle East, or North Africa. The White racial category includes people who marked the "White" checkbox. It also includes respondents who reported entries such as Caucasian or White: European entries, such as Irish, German, and Polish; Middle Eastern entries, such as Arab, Lebanese, and Palestinian; and North African entries, such as Algerian, Moroccan, and Egyptian. (Hixson et al., 2011, p. 2)

The 2010 Census revealed that the U.S. population was 308.7 million. Of this, 223.6 million people, or 72%, identified as White alone. This figure included White Hispanics as well as Whites from Middle Eastern countries. Moreover, 7.5 million people, or 2%, reported White in combination with one or more other races. Combined, these two groups totaled 231.0 million people. Approximately 75% of all people in the United States identified as White, either alone or in combination with one or more other races.

Cultural Reflections

How would you rate your knowledge about White Americans of European ancestry?

Do you know, for instance, where the early White settlers were from and what their cultural contributions were?

When you view a White client, in what ways do you take into consideration his or her ethnocultural background?

Just five years after the 2010 report, the U.S. Census Bureau reported that minorities constituted 38% of the total American population. It was also projected that the non-Hispanic White population in this country was 198 million. Part of the 2015 projection of 38% minority population is based on the expected growth in the numbers of minority children. The U.S. Census Bureau (2015) reported that

around the time the 2020 Census is conducted, more than half [50.2%] of the nation's children are expected to be part of a minority race or ethnic group. This proportion is projected to continue to grow until by 2060, just 36 percent of all children (people under age 18) will be single-race non-Hispanic White, compared with 52 percent today.

In addition, the Census Bureau projected that 50.3% of all Americans will be minorities in 2044. "The minority U.S. population is projected to increase to 56% of the total in 2060, compared with 38% in 2014" (U.S. Census Bureau, 2015).

The demographic data presented as follows represent a summary of some of the data retrieved from the U.S. Census Bureau's (2014) American Community Survey 1-year estimates and from O'Connor, Lubin, and Spector (2013). In general, the data are presented from the largest White ethnocultural groups to the smaller ones.

German Americans: 46,047,113

The largest wave of Germans came to America during the 1850s because they were encountering civil unrest and high unemployment at home. Thirty-nine percent live in the Midwest, 25% in the South, 19% in the West, and 17% in the Northeast, most densely settled in Wisconsin, Minnesota, North Dakota, South Dakota, Nebraska, and Iowa—in the traditional "German belt."

Irish Americans: 33,147,639

Poverty was a fact of life in Ireland for centuries. The great potato famine of the 1840s, precipitated by overdependence on this single crop, as well as land ownership policies of the English government, precipitated a mass exodus from Ireland (Kennedy, 1983; Scally, 1995). Between 1820 and the 1920s, an estimated 4.5 million Irish immigrated to the United States, with many settling in large cities such as New York, Boston, Philadelphia, Chicago, and San Francisco.

English Americans: 24,382,182

The majority of the founders of the United States of America were of English descent and lived throughout the 13 British colonies. English Americans are found in large numbers in the Northwest and West. Since the 1980 U.S. Census, the number of people who reported English ancestry decreased by at least 20 million, partly because more citizens of English descent have started to list themselves as "American."

American Ancestry: 22,097,012

A large number of people claim American ancestry, either as a political statement or because their pre-American ancestry is mixed or uncertain.

Italian Americans: 17,558,604

Between 1880 and 1920, approximately 4 million Italians immigrated to the United States. These immigrants tended to form "Little Italy" neighborhoods in many large northeastern cities, as well as in some rural areas of California and Louisiana.

Scandinavian Americans: 10,920,197

Scandinavia, also known as the Nordic nations, is the region of northern Europe comprising Finland, Sweden, Norway, Denmark, and Iceland (formerly ruled by Denmark). The U.S. population includes 677,272 Finnish Americans; 4,293,208 Swedish Americans; 4,444,586 Norwegian Americans; 1,453,897 Danish Americans; and 51,234 Icelandic Americans (McGoldrick, Giordano, & Garcia-Preto, 2005). The largest wave of Scandinavians immigrated to the United States during the 19th century. Today, Scandinavian Americans are most prevalent across the northern Midwest and the northern-tier western states, including Washington, Utah, and Alaska.

Polish Americans: 9,249,392

Polish Americans comprise the largest Slavic group in the United States. Polish immigration peaked between the mid-19th century and World War I, when an estimated 2.5 million Polish people immigrated to the United States. Looking for an improved economic life, they mostly settled in industrial urban areas.

French Americans: 9,136,092

The Census category for French ancestry excludes those from the Basque region, located in western France and northeastern Spain. Many French families immigrated to the United States after first living in other parts of the Americas, so French immigrants are sometimes divided into more specific categories such as French Canadian, Acadian, or Louisiana Creole. States with the largest French communities include California, Louisiana, Massachusetts, Michigan, and New York.

Scottish Americans: 5,365,154

More than 1 million Scots immigrated to the United States in the 19th century. As economic conditions worsened in Scotland, Scottish immigrants continued to arrive through the 1920s. States that have large Scottish populations include California, Florida, Texas, New York, and Michigan.

Scotch-Irish: 2,978,827

In the 17th and 18th centuries, thousands of Scottish residents lost their homes and farms due to the English government's land use policies known as the highland clearances. Many of these impoverished Scots emigrated to Ireland, and because they were Protestants, they tended to settle in the northern region of Ireland known as Ulster. Between 1717 and 1775, hundreds of thousands of Scotch-Irish left Ireland to seek a better life in the United States. While many settled in New England, some settled in Appalachia or farther west. Although Scotch-Irish descendants can be found throughout the country, they are mostly located on the East Coast.

Jewish Americans: 4,200,000

Jewish identity refers to ethnicity and culture as well as religion. There are about 4.2 million Jews in the United States, and another 1.1 million who label themselves as cultural Jews—who say that they have no religion but who consider themselves to be Jewish (Liu, 2013). The earliest Jewish presence in North America dates from the 1600s; religious freedom in the English colonies enabled the establishment of synagogues in many cities. In the 19th century, Eastern European Jews immigrated to the United States because of poverty and persecution. Between 1880 and 1942, more than 2 million Jews immigrated from Russia, Austria, Hungary, and Romania. During World War II, the United States closed its borders to refugees from enemy countries, meaning that Jews fleeing the Nazi Holocaust could not immigrate; however, after the war, some 80,000 Jews from Germany and neighboring countries were granted visas. In the late 1980s and early 1990s, thousands of Soviet Jews were granted political asylum in the United States. Today, nearly 85% of Jewish Americans were born in the United States. The number of Jews declined from 5.5 million in 1990 to 4.2 million in 2010; this decline is attributed to an aging population and low birth rates among Jewish women (Saxe & Tighe, 2013).

Dutch Americans: 4,243,067

New York City was established by Dutch immigrants in the early 17th century. A new wave of Dutch immigrants came to America following World War II. Dutch Americans are concentrated in several counties in Michigan and Ohio, and many also live in California, New York, and Pennsylvania.

Russian Americans: 2,762,830

The Russians originally settled in and controlled Alaska, and many remained after the United States purchased Alaska from Russia in 1867. States with the highest number of people who claim Russian ancestry include Maryland, New York, North Dakota, and South Dakota.

Slovak Americans: 2,000,000

Not to be confused with Slavic (those from the vast region of Slavic countries extending from Ukraine and Belarus to the former Yugoslavia and Bulgaria), Slovaks are a subgroup with ancestry in Slovakia, a Slavic country that was formerly part of Czechoslovakia. There are about 2 million ethnic Slovaks living in the United States, compared to about 5 million people living in Slovakia.

Greek Americans: 1,319,188

Records of Greeks immigrating to the United States date back to the 1600s; however, the most substantial number of Greek immigrants came to the United States between the mid-1800s and Greece's admission to the European Union in 1981. Currently, there are more Greeks in the United States than in any other country outside of Greece (Killian & Agathangelou, 2005).

SOCIOECONOMIC STATUS OF WHITE AMERICANS

It is beyond the scope of this chapter to report the socioeconomic status of each of the 53-plus White American ethnic groups. Instead, this section reports the socioeconomic status of White Americans of European ancestry as a group. The socioeconomic status of White Americans is linked to their numerical majority in American society. White culture is the dominant subculture in this country because White Americans have greater power to control resources and establish rules for their benefit in comparison to other ethnic groups. In the United States, as well as in many societies throughout the world, the numerical majority group, the most powerful group, prevails.

The median income for White Americans as a group in 2011 was $55,412, compared with $32,068 for African Americans (DeNavas-Walt, Proctor, & Smith, 2012). Although Asian Americans have a higher median income ($66,000) than White Americans, some scholars have pointed out that more members of an Asian family are working—hence, the larger median family income (Liu, 2013).

The White Population, Intermarriage, and Multiple-Race Identification

In the 2010 Census, 7.5 million people (an increase of 37%) reported White in combination with one or more additional races. The multiple-race White population grew at a faster rate than the White-alone population, and the largest multiple-race combination was White and Black.

Among people who reported they were White and one or more additional races, one-fourth identified as White and Black, and nearly one-fourth identified as White and Some Other Race; over one-fifth reported White and Asian, and nearly one-fifth reported White and American Indian and Alaska Native. These four combinations represented 89% of all Whites who reported multiple races (see Hixson et al., 2011).

ETHNIC GROUP SALIENCY FOR WHITE AMERICANS

The salience of an ethnic identity varies according to a person's level of acculturation and assimilation (E. Smith, 1991). European Americans are a step higher on the ladder of assimilation and acculturation than most other ethnic groups discussed in this book. The intermarriage among White American ethnic groups has led to a blurring of distinctions among European Americans, and as a consequence, the majority of European Americans have a mixed European heritage. As a result of intermarriage, ethnic distinctions among Americans of European ancestry have faded and blurred, while those of ethnic groups of color have become prominent.

Ethnicity does not just apply to people of color. In one of the author's multicultural classes, a student said, "My father is German and English, but my mother is Italian and Irish. None of these groups have any great pull on me. I can't write that paper you've assigned because in my family, no one culture stands out. I'm an American. We don't celebrate any holidays other than American holidays." From this point, we began to examine what this student valued in life and to whom she could trace those values. Reluctantly, she began to acknowledge the cultural influences of her multicultural family. The family is the crucible for ethnocultural identity, and when the family fails to impart an ethnocultural identity, the community usually provides some direction.

White Americans do have cultural traditions and norms that have become largely invisible to them, except when they congregate socially with members of their own specific ethnocultural group. Some White European holidays have become American holidays. Consider, for instance, St. Patrick's Day. During the St. Patrick's Day parades, one will see African Americans, Asian Americans, and Hispanic Americans, as well as members of other ethnic groups, all wearing green and some singing a version of "Danny Boy."

Ethnic identity awareness often comes from freedom of choice. In America, Whites have the option of being aware or unaware of their race (McGoldrick et al., 2005). Yet, when people are oppressed, they may not have an option to become unaware of their ethnicity, color, or race. In America, it is difficult to avoid being aware that one is an African American, an Asian American, or an American Indian.

Oppression of American ethnic minority groups increases the saliency of their ethnicity. Saliency refers to the degree to which an ethnocultural group is important (a highlighted feature of one's life) to a person and the extent to which one identifies with that group and adopts the values and worldviews of a specific culture.

The concept of ethnic group saliency is relevant for both minority and majority groups, and it may be affected by three factors. First, researchers have asserted that there is a correlation between ethnic identity salience and oppression (Sue & Sue, 2013). Groups that are oppressed because of their ethnicity or culture evidence high ethnic identity because their ethnocultural heritage is the source of prejudice, discrimination, and oppression. Second, where an ethnic group stands on the continuum of immigrant-to-acculturation-to-assimilation is another factor that affects a person's ethnic identity (Giordano & McGoldrick, 2005). In general,

Cultural Reflections

What are your thoughts about White intermarriage with other White ethnic groups?

What ethnic group or groups are salient in your life? In your ethnic identity?

What thoughts do you have about the substantial intermarriage of Whites and Blacks, Whites and Asians, and Whites and American Indians and Alaska Natives?

Cultural Reflections

Do you believe that oppression has anything to do with the saliency of ethnicity in a person's life?

Why do you think that White Americans might not give conscious thought to their racial membership group?

White Americans have lived in this country for at least two to four generations; therefore, they are far along on the continuum of assimilation. A third factor affecting the ethnic identity of White Americans is that a new, superordinate identity has emerged that is more powerful than the individual ethnic identities (that is, whether one is Irish, German, Italian, and so forth). This superordinate identity has been labeled **Whiteness** and includes the set of privileges that Whiteness brings to its members.

Racial Stereotyping of White European Americans

Racial stereotyping of White Americans has become part of the multicultural literature. Some textbooks highlight the racism of some Whites, while failing to give adequate attention to the fact that millions of White Americans have been at the forefront of the social justice movement for members of ethnic minorities (Sue & Sue, 2013). Sometimes American Whites may be put off by members of ethnic minorities stereotyping them in the very same way that they claim they are stereotyped. Kathyrn Alessandria (2002), a doctoral student in a counselor education program, has commented on how insulted, disrespected, and unacknowledged she felt while attending a multicultural session within the counseling profession:

> Within the counseling profession, it is not uncommon to hear professionals speak about multicultural issues by comparing specific racial and ethnic groups to Whites, thus making the assumption that all European Americans are alike. As an individual who self-identifies as a first-generation Italian American, I often find myself leaving conferences frustrated after attending seminars on multicultural issues. The descriptions of White do not describe many of the European American people I know, my family, or me. I leave with the impression that the field thinks White people do not have distinct cultures. (p. 57)

Yet the issue goes beyond knowing that one needs to understand the individual ethnic cultures within Americans who share a White European ancestry. Just as it is *not okay* to stereotype, for example, all African Americans or Asian Americans, neither is it okay for members of ethnic minority groups to stereotype all White European Americans as WASPs, or as insensitive people who cling to **White privilege**. All White Americans are not alike. There are important historical, geographical, and cultural backgrounds that distinguish them from one another. As Alessandria (2002) has asserted, some multicultural scholars "minimize the value White ethnics place on their ethnicities and how they identify themselves. In other words, because they are White, have they been told that they have no culture and thus come to believe it?" (p. 58).

Moreover, not all White Americans endorse and subscribe to racism or White privilege. History has recorded that White Americans have played prominent roles as abolitionists and as civil rights advocates down through the ages. The lives of White Americans, African Americans, Asian Americans, Native Americans, and Hispanic Americans are intricately interwoven throughout the history of this country, if only exemplified by the fact that White Americans have intermarried with members of most racial minorities in this nation. White Americans contribute to the "mixed-race population" more so than any other group.

Racism has generational connection, age, and social class dimensions, which may be changing in this country. For instance, one characteristic of "millennials" is that they believe strongly in social justice. As Helen Fox (2011) has stated in her book, *Their Highest Vocation: Social Justice and the Millennial Generation,*

> according to polls, today's millennial college students are the most politically progressive generation in U.S. history. They are deeply concerned about social and economic inequality, they support egalitarian relationships among nations and peoples, and they believe that the government should do whatever it takes to protect the environment. They have a strong desire to change the world for the better, and are volunteering in record numbers to do so.

Ethnic and racial diversity is a hallmark of this generation, both because of the group's sheer size and because of the impressive number of immigrants arriving in the United States since the 1990s. Because of the increasing mix of ethnicities and the explosion of the Internet, Millennials are "the world's first generation to grow up thinking of itself as global" (Howe & Strauss, 2000, p. 16). (pp. 7–8)

Is an American Identity Synonymous With a White Identity?

According to the U.S. Census Bureau data described earlier, some White Americans of European ancestry claim that they have an **American identity**. And one must ask: What is this American identity? When used by Whites, is the term *American identity* just a politically correct way of saying a "White identity," where being American is almost equated with being White?

Some researchers have suggested that an American identity does not extend to all Americans. Historian Ronald Takaki (2002) has maintained that "in the creation of our national identity 'American' has been defined as 'white'" (p. 2). Labeling one's ethnic identity as "American" is simply a way of embracing a White identity without having to use the word *White*. It is a way of wrapping one's ethnic group in the red, white, and blue American flag in a manner that ethnic groups of color cannot choose to do. The "American as White" image is so deeply embedded in our society. Explaining the symbolic connection between an American identity being synonomous with a White identity, McGoldrick and colleagues (2005) have stated that

> European Americans in this country became "Americans" and learned "American" values of freedom, democracy, the rights of the individual, and a society based on the common man. Nothing in this self-definition says anything about whiteness. By naming themselves as only "American," European immigrants and their descendants could avoid thinking of themselves as White, for America itself was defined by its whiteness (Hitchcock, 2002).
>
> The American as White image is deeply embedded in our society, so much so that it is difficult to determine what is really American in terms of the cultural elements that apply to all citizens. This confusion of imagery, White as American and American as White, permeates our educational system. . . . Ask most people to imagine a "typical" American, and they will see the image of a White person. (pp. 509–510)

By invoking an "American identity," White Americans are either consciously or perhaps unconsciously laying claim to a superordinate White identity that unites the various White ethnic groups—a superordinate identity that is far more powerful in this country than just having an Irish, German, or Polish identity. A White American identity carries with it certain benefits and a sense of implicit power and control. According to David Roediger (1999), there is a benefit or a "wage" for simply being White in the United States. In the book *The Great Wells of Democracy*, Manning Marable (2002) describes the benefits of Whiteness:

> Whites . . . have an important material asset that allows them to escape the greatest liabilities and disadvantages of poverty—their whiteness. White Americans who are homeless, unemployed and/or uneducated for the most part still believe in the great American master narrative of opportunity and upward mobility. If they scrape together enough money to buy a new suit, they will find it relatively easy to obtain employment, albeit at subsistence wages. They know with the same set of skills and level of educational attainment as the Black householders across the street, they stand a superior chance of being hired. Whiteness creates a comfortable social and psychological safety net for the white poor. Every day may not be a lucky day, but nobody has to sing the blues for long. (p. 210)

Cultural Description of White American Ethnic Groups

White Americans of European ancestry are not a monolithic group. There are important cultural distinctions between them. It is not feasible to describe the cultural background and contributions of the 53 White European ethnic groups. Putting all White Europeans in one large category conceals important cultural differences among White ethnic groups.

This section presents a brief outline of the culture of three White American cultural groups of European ancestry: English Americans, Italian Americans, and American Jews. These descriptions are, at best, generalizations based on broad characteristics; therefore, they may not apply to some individuals within these subgroupings. A number of factors influence whether or not the generalizations apply to an individual member of a specific White ethnic group, including one's generational membership; one's enculturation or acculturation to the mainstream or dominant Anglo American culture; the importance one assigns to cultural practices, customs, and influences; the manner in which one's family engaged in specific ethnic practices; and the degree to which there are multiple White ethnics or other ethnic heritage within one's family.

Cultural Description of Anglo or English Americans

The history of Anglo or English Americans is often taught in American schools as the history of the United States. English Americans have the distinction of having their history taught in most grammar and high schools in the United States, while that of other White ethnocultural groups is often ignored or relegated to only a few paragraphs. Part of the emphasis on English Americans' history in our schools is based on the actual overall influence that this group has had in developing this nation and in influencing mainstream American culture. The tremendous influence that English Americans have had on the development of the United States is reflected in the fact that members of this group have now begun to designate their cultural background as American instead of English American. The U.S. Census Bureau has reported that 24 million people have listed "American" as their cultural ancestry.

Who are English Americans, and what were their early cultural values? Moreover, to what extent have their values been revised and maintained in modern-day U.S. culture? The immigration of English Americans to this country is usually traced to two major groups: (1) the Puritans and (2) the Cavaliers.

The **Puritans** came to this country first in the 1620s and later in the 1630s. The Puritans were Protestant people in England who were persecuted because they wanted to interpret the Bible for themselves, instead of having religious clergy do so for them. In England, Queen Elizabeth mocked them and gave them the nickname "Puritans" because they argued that the Church of England should be purified of any liturgy ceremony or practices not found in Biblical scripture. Puritans maintained that the Bible was their sole authority, and they applied the Bible to every area of their lives. The Puritans' goal was to establish a Biblical society, a holy commonwealth that would serve as an example to England.

The Puritans settled in the northeastern area of this country, specifically in Massachusetts. They established schools for their children so that they could learn to read the Bible. In 1636, they established Harvard College to train ministers. Work was an important value for the Puritans. They believed that God called each person to a specific vocation or occupation. Working in one's calling was a way to honor God, and it was considered a sin not to work. The Puritans had a profound influence on English American culture. The Puritan emphasis on hard work was instrumental in leading to capitalism.

Because of their religious belief that each person had the right to interpret the Bible for him- or herself, the Puritans placed a high cultural value on individualism. As McGill and Pearce (2005) have maintained, the cultural value of individualism was transferred and superimposed on the manner in which the Puritans dealt with other areas of their lives, including finances, politics, and family relationships. Gradually, what initially started out as religious individualism—meaning the right to interpret the Bible for themselves—developed into a psychological cultural orientation that made the individual rather than the group the center of focus. The emphasis on psychological individualism meant that people were responsible for what happened to them and should accept responsibility for whatever life dealt them. If they were poor, they had to accept responsibility for their limited financial means.

The Puritan culture evolved into a broader English American culture. On average, Anglo/English Americans prefer not to complain about their problems. Instead, they value holding up under pressure or shouldering pain silently. They also tend "not to waste words" (McGill & Pearce, 2005). In a study involving Kluckhon's value orientation of basic cultural choices, Anglo Americans evidence "a strong future orientation, prize individual achievement, and see themselves as dominant in their relationship to the natural world. . . . Above all, Anglo Americans value work . . . An Anglo American's identity, relationships, self-esteem, and sense of adequacy and well-being are likely to be tied to work" (McGill & Pearce, 2005, p. 520). English Americans tend to talk about "working on relationships, love, sex, fulfillment, and identity" (McGill & Pearce, 2005, p. 457).

The major contributions that the Puritans made to American culture were spreading Protestantism throughout the colonies, advocating the value of hard work and the duty to profit from one's labor (capitalism), and insisting on the importance of the individual or individualism.

Another English influence involved the Anglicans or the Cavaliers. The Anglicans brought with them many of the customs they had subscribed to in their old country. Unlike the Puritans, the Anglicans settled in the South (Richmond & Guindon, 2013). The Anglicans established an internal class system (based on the feudal system in England) that involved owning large plantations and slaves. Also in contrast to the Puritans, the Anglicans did not place a high value on education. As a result, for a long time, the South had only a few elite colleges and universities. Moreover, even today, the academic achievement in southern states is much lower than that in northern American states.

Microaggressions, English American Culture, and the Designation of "WASP" Culture

The culture of English Americans has changed over the past 350 to 400 years. No one claims to be a Puritan in modern-day America, unless one wants to establish that he or she is a "blue-blood" American—one who can trace his or her history to colonial days. As time progressed, the Puritan designation was renamed to reflect an English American culture.

During the 1960s, researchers described the English American culture as "WASP," which was short for White Anglo-Saxon Protestant. The WASP culture has been described as having old money, a deep sense of entitlement, and an emphasis on good manners (often described as "good taste"). Members of this category established the right way to act in virtually every situation. Manners included knowing which fork to use at the dinner table, how to introduce people, how to clap at an opera, and how to dress properly for different events and situations. For instance, women should wear sleeveless dresses only in certain situations, and men should wear brown, dark blue, or gray suits for job interviews. WASPs tended to believe that education should lead to a person being "cultured" rather than smart. Good manners were far more important than one's academic achievement. They also usually voted Republican and joined country clubs that restricted membership along racial and gender lines. Even today, one may hear another person saying that one comes from "old" money. Currently, the designation of WASP has fallen into some measure of disrepute. The emphasis now is on labeling one's ancestry as American instead of English, even though one might trace his or her ancestry to England.

Cultural Strengths of English Americans

English American culture is characterized by an emphasis on individual responsibility for one's situation. The typical American from an English ancestry background shows emotional restraint, a high value for work, and a nuclear family. These cultural features are usually positive; however, in some instances, they may also be a double-edged sword. Other important cultural values include a strong emphasis on individualism, autonomy, achievement, and punctuality. For instance, the first question a person of English descent might ask is "What do you do for a living?" If you are late for a job interview with a person of English culture, consider that job lost. Individuals have a strong sense of internal rather than external control. Individuals create separate households as soon as they graduate from high school or college. There is an emphasis on "launching" one's children so that they can live on their own.

Communication Style and Attitudes Toward Talk and Psychotherapy

Communication in families of English ancestry tends to be largely instrumental—that is, words are used to accomplish one's goals. This instrumental attitude toward language is reflected in the movie *Ordinary People*, where the son talks about his brother's death. He says, "What's the point of talking about it? It doesn't change anything."

Counseling English Americans

The majority of English Americans are amenable to some form of counseling or therapy. In keeping with the work metaphor, they may speak of the "work" involved in therapy. Issues in therapy may involve conflict with dependency and autonomy needs. Because the emphasis is on the nuclear family, members of one's extended family may be kept at bay. English Americans may be reluctant to seek help from family members and others. Therapy becomes effective when the counselor helps the individual to achieve a balance between getting help from others and being independent.

According to McGill and Pearce (2005), English Americans tend to identify as problems those situations that disrupt their autonomous functioning: "Usually, they attempt to avoid dependency and direct expressions of anxiety that would elicit caretaking. They may, even when suffering, prefer emotional isolation and withdrawal. Lack of contact, separation from others, difficulty in communicating, and blandness are not likely to be regarded as problems" (p. 523).

White English Americans value insight and reason and meaningful discussion. They want to define clearly the problem they are facing, and they believe that hard work in counseling or therapy will be beneficial to them. Once problems are defined, clients are ready to engage in therapy. English American clients believe that the real struggles in life are usually within the self, and with the right amount of effort, therapy will have a successful outcome (Kaufmann, 2004).

English American clients come to therapy with a sense of strong individualism that may actually hamper their help-seeking behavior. Counselors and therapists should take into account English clients' strong belief in individualism. The goal of therapy might be to help English clients to reach out of their personal isolation to others, to reclaim important emotional experiences, and to devise a plan to go forward in the future (McGill & Pearce, 2005).

English American children often feel pressured to meet their parents' high expectations of academic achievement, and they sometimes feel that their parents' love is conditional rather than unconditional. English American families that have a strong emphasis on independence and achievement may feel that the family is hardly ever together because of independent conflicting schedules. As a result, they may rarely eat together or share sufficient time to deal with family issues.

On the adult level, the English male or father is often a workaholic. Alcohol is used to deal with anxiety over one's economic or financial situation. Women may face conflicts over working and staying at home to take care of their children.

Notable English Americans

Presidents of the United States (most have English ancestry)—George Washington, John Adams, John Quincy Adams, James Madison, Gerald Ford

Astronauts—John Glenn, Alan Shepard

Inventors—Thomas Edison, Eli Whitney

Directors/Writers—Ron Howard, Orson Welles

Entertainers—Ben Affleck, Clint Eastwood

Cultural Description of Italian Americans

Many Italians immigrated to the United States from what is generally known as the Mediterranean area of Europe; they were largely from southern Italy. Most were unskilled laborers and Catholics. They settled primarily in New England (Rhode Island, Massachusetts) and in the Middle Atlantic states (New York, Pennsylvania, Delaware).

Italian immigration to the United States took place from the 1800s to the late 1960s. For the most part, Italians formed what is known as the "New Immigration," which was the third and largest wave of immigration. Whereas the "Old Immigration" consisted of Germans, Irish, British, and Scandinavians, the "New Immigration" was largely formed by Italians, Slavs, and Jews. Between 1870 and 1930, more than 5 million Italians immigrated to the United States. More than two-thirds of the Italian immigrants were laborers, or *contadini*. Later, a small population of Italian craftsmen, including carpenters, brick layers, masons, tailors, and barbers, immigrated to the United States.

Italians immigrated with the intent to earn money and to return home, but instead of returning to Italy, some brought their families to the new country. Between 1901 and 1920, about 50% of Italians repatriated to Italy. Italians worked in mining, textile, and clothing manufacturing. In the United States, Italians settled into a "Little Italy," and many stayed within the confines of their communities for two generations (Giordano, McGoldrick, & Klages, 2005). Italians were not initially accepted by other Catholics and Americans. They encountered ethnic prejudice in their new country. It was not until the 1920s that Italians began to be integrated into the American labor force.

What forces helped to shape southern Italian cultural values? Political oppression was critical in forging the cultural beliefs of Italians. Centuries of invading armies and governmental injustice taught them that they could count only on their families and a few of their closest friends and townspeople. As a result, Italians developed a fear of outsiders. They developed a complex code of obligations that regulated relationships both inside and outside of the family called *l'ordine della familigia* (Gambino, 1974). This code not only represented a mistrust of outsiders, but family members who violated it were considered disloyal and a shame to their families (Mangione & Morreale, 1992). Sometimes outsiders are given a special position because of their closeness to the family. Italians call close male friends *gumba*, which is a slang term used to designate friends close enough to be in the inner circle. *Goomba* is a term often used for an Italian godfather and *goomma* for godmother.

Because many of their lives seemed to be based on the precarious whims of outsiders, Italians developed a belief system in fate called *destino*. One's life was controlled by fate, and therefore, it was important to enjoy the moment. Hence, Italians developed family gatherings that were characterized by music and food (Cleary & Demone, 1988).

Italian families are usually headed by the father, who may be authoritarian. The Italian mother is usually deeply loved and the heart of the family. Although Italian women were expected to be faithful to their husbands, the husbands were given a great deal of latitude in sexual behaviors. One spoken rule was that family members were never to do anything to bring disgrace to the family. Moreover, they were asked not to talk about the family to outsiders. Italians turn to their families for solving problems rather than seek mental health services (Cleary & Demone, 1988).

It has been said that Italian Americans never really "launch" their children. Instead, they send them out to marry and to bring their partners back to the Italian family circle. Parents and children tend to live in reasonably close proximity to each other (within a few blocks), and there may be multiple contacts and telephone calls between them each day. Italians raise their children to be supportive of the family and to contribute to its economic well-being, even after they have married and left the family household (Giordano et al., 2005).

Italian culture clashed with the dominant Anglo American values that emphasized individualism, independence, and personal achievement over the group (Gambino, 1974). Italian culture is a very emotionally and verbally expressive culture while English American culture is more restrained and conservative. Italians are known for gesturing with their hands; however, their emotionality may only be short-lived. The "Little Italy" residential enclaves that they formed helped them to preserve their Italian traditions.

Moreover, the type of Catholicism practiced by Italians contained a mixture of pagan customs. The religious practices of Italians clashed with the beliefs of the Irish who dominated the Catholic Church and ran the parochial schools where Italians sent their children to be educated (Giordano et al., 2005).

In Italy, villages developed their own saints to fend off evil. One of the most popular Italian beliefs is the *malocchio* (*mal* = "bad," *occhio* = "eye"). Italians believe that those who give the **evil eye** can cause harm to a person. The evil eye is what individuals give to each other when they are jealous of a person. Giving a person the evil eye is similar to putting a curse on him or her (Giordano et al., 2005). Many Italians wear a horn amulet (*cornetto, corno, cornicello*). The horns are usually made of gold, and they are worn as a necklace or hung in one's home to ward off evil spirits.

Microaggressions and Italians

Italians are often stereotyped negatively as members of the Mafia (*Mafioso*) or organized crime; however, FBI statistics have shown that there may be no more than 1,500 Mafia members throughout the United States (Giordano et al., 2005).

Communication Style and Attitudes Toward Talk and Psychotherapy

As noted, the communication style of Italian Americans is quite expressive. Italians use colorful language, and they use their hands a lot when they talk. Around friends, Italians may become quite loud and highly emotional. Italians use words to express the emotional intensity of an experience or situation. They may become baffled when others hold them to their words because it is the emotionality that the words convey rather than the words themselves that have the most important meaning. Some Italian Americans have coined pithy statements, such as famous and beloved baseball player Yogi Berra's "It ain't over until the fat lady sings."

Cultural Strengths of Italian Americans

The greatest cultural strengths of Italian Americans are the family and their wide range of expressiveness in language and emotions. Italians are well known for their cuisine; pizza and spaghetti have become American dishes as much as Italian ones. In addition, Italians have made outstanding contributions in music, especially in opera, and in the movies (e.g., *The Godfather*) (Mangione & Morreale, 1992). Italians maintain that Christopher Columbus, an Italian, discovered the United States of America. Americans celebrate this holiday on or about October 12 each year. The influences of Italian American culture on this country are pervasive.

Counseling Italian Americans

Because Italians tend to keep their problems within their families, by the time they decide to enter counseling or therapy, the problem may have become severe. During counseling, they may be quite passionate and loud. Counselors who are unfamiliar with the high degree of expressiveness of Italian culture might become alarmed when family members shout at each other or voice strong emotions (Giordano et al., 2005).

Counselors have to be careful of making pathological definitions of family enmeshment when they hear Italians talk about calling their mother three times a day or spending every Sunday eating at their grandmother's house.

Notable Italian Americans

Academia—A. Bartlett Giamatti, former (1977) president of Yale and former commissioner of the National (Baseball) League

Business—Lee Iacocca, former president of the Ford Motor Company

Arts and Entertainment—Martin Scorsese, film director and screenwriter (*Rocky, Taxi Driver*)

Music—Frank Sinatra; Mario Lanza, opera tenor

Politics—Antonin Scalia, first Italian American to sit on the U.S. Supreme Court

Explorer—Christopher Columbus, who Italians maintain discovered the United States of America

Cultural Description of American Jews

Jewish Americans: Cultural Values and Counseling Issues

Jewish Americans are a diverse group. This ethnic group includes people who practice Judaism and have a Jewish heritage, as well as people who have converted to this faith but lack Jewish parents or family members. The ethnic grouping also includes people who have a Jewish cultural background but do not practice Judaism (Schlosser, 2006). There are different degrees of adherence to Judaism and its cultural traditions. **Orthodox Jews** are considered traditional because they maintain all Jewish traditions. Conservative Jews preserve Jewish cultural traditions, but they tend to give broader interpretations of religious law. Reform Jews allow their members the freedom to make choices about which Jewish traditions (especially dietary) to follow (Altman, Inman, Fine, Ritter, & Howard, 2010).

One does not have to practice Judaism to identify as a Jew. According to Schlosser (2009), the cultural dimensions of identifying as a Jew may include having pride in being Jewish, maintaining the importance of marrying a Jew, adhering to Jewish values (*tikkun olam*), having a strong connection to Israel, contributing to Jewish causes, and being active in a Jewish organization. For individuals in this category, having a Jewish identity means having a common history and set of experiences.

Although many American Jews now experience White privilege, this has not always been the case. Throughout the decades, Jews have experienced great prejudice and discrimination, known as **anti-Semitism**. Prior to the 19th century, Jewish ghettos (*pogroms*) were established in many European cities. **Pogroms** were residential enclaves in which Jews were restricted to live. Jewish ghettos were surrounded by walls that separated Jews' living quarters from the rest of the city's residents. Although pogroms were abolished (for the most part) during the 19th century, the Third Reich (during World War II) resurrected pogroms and created a new Jewish ghetto system for the purpose of persecuting Jews. Extreme religious bias against Jews resulted in the **Holocaust**, which killed 6 million Jews. To add insult to the heinous crimes committed against them during the Holocaust, there are history revisionists who either deny that the Holocaust actually took place or minimize its effects on millions of Jews.

Prior to World War II, Jews were viewed racially as non-White (Schlosser, 2009). Many multicultural textbooks fail to mention Jews as a distinct cultural group that has suffered centuries of oppression and discrimination. Jewish cultural identity consists of religious and cultural dimensions. Some of the religious dimensions of Jewish identity include the degree to which individuals adhere to Jewish religious orthodoxy, whether or not they observe the Sabbath and maintain a kosher eating household, if they celebrate all Jewish holidays, fasting during **Yom Kippur** (Day of Atonement), following dietary laws of *Pesach* (Passover), and observing Jewish rituals.

Despite the fact that many Jews have been at the forefront of many social movements for members of ethnic minorities, they are often excluded from many multicultural textbooks. Stephen Weinrach (2002), an important counselor educator who was proud of his Jewish identity, criticized counseling organizations for ignoring the situation of Jewish Americans:

> Issues that have concerned Jews have failed to resonate with the counseling profession, including for the most part, many of the outspoken advocates for multicultural counseling. . . . The near universal failure of those committed to multicultural counseling to rail against anti-Semitism and embrace the notion of Jews as a culturally distinct group represents the most painful wound of all. (p. 310)

Weinrach's (2002) criticism is well taken if one considers the Jewish value of *tikkun olam*, defined as acts of kindness performed to perfect or repair the world. The Jewish cultural value of *tikkun olam* maintains that it is important for Jews to participate in repairing the world. Jews have often participated in social action—for instance, the civil rights movement in this country during the 1960s. Michael Schwerner (Jewish), Andrew Goodman (Jewish), and James Chaney (African American) were three young civil rights workers acting to register Black voters in Mississippi. They were killed by a Ku Klux Klan lynch mob near Meridian, Mississippi. The deaths of these young men sparked a national outrage and led to increased White support for the civil rights movement.

Jewish Americans vary in their cultural identity, depending on their religious views. Orthodox Jewish communities are usually closely knit, and they may seek counseling from their rabbi rather than a professional counselor (Rich, 2011). Men and women have more egalitarian roles in homes of Reform Jews or in homes where Judaism is not practiced. Schlosser (2009) has developed a religious and cultural/ethnic identity for Jewish Americans. According to her, Jews move from a lack of awareness of their Jewish identity to an emerging awareness of a Jewish identity to an assessment of Jewish identity in terms of other religious and cultural groups. Next the individual moves either toward or away from Jewishness (cultural Jews who say that Judaism is not important to them), and finally to an integration of their Jewish identity with their other identities.

On the whole, Jewish Americans are inclined to have families in which children are encouraged to discuss and express opinions on family issues. Members of this ethnic group place a high value on educational and career success. Hence, one hears the phrase "my son, the doctor" in some Jewish satires or television programs.

Microaggressions and American Jews

Jewish Americans are often targeted for hate crimes and discrimination. Some Americans may only notice that Jews may be well educated and financially secure; they may ignore or be unaware of anti-Semitism against Jews. Anti-Semitism is prejudice or discrimination against people of Jewish descent.

Cultural Strengths of American Jews

A major cultural strength of Jews is their religious traditions, faith in God, and historical experiences that give them an enduring sense of community and bonding with other Jews. In addition, Jews have been at the forefront of most social justice movements in this country, including the civil rights movement and the women's movement. Because of the Holocaust, Jews as a group serve as a reminder of what happens when ethnic hatred and religious hatred are taken to the extremes. The most important Jewish holidays are Passover, Yom Kippur, Rosh Hashanah, and Hanukkah.

Communication Style and Attitudes Toward Talk and Psychotherapy

In Jewish culture, individuals value analyzing and discussing their experiences. Jews place a high value on cognitive clarity. From their perspective, analyzing and sharing feelings and ideas helps them to clarify themselves in relation to others and to make sense out of what has happened to them. Part of this Jewish cultural value can be traced to their historical experiences of discrimination and persecution. How does one make sense of Jewish ghettos (*pogroms*) or the Holocaust? Part of the Jewish emphasis on understanding our human development is evident in their contributions to the field of psychology. Jews have led the world in analyzing people's relationships with themselves and others. Consider, for instance, the work of Sigmund Freud, who is considered the father of modern psychology, and the contributions of Erich Fromm, who wrote about the psychosocial development of human beings (Jones-Smith, 2014).

Counseling American Jews

Noting the diversity of Jewish Americans, Langman (1999) has recommended some guiding principles for counseling Jewish Americans. According to him, counselors should first be respectful and knowledgeable about Jewish culture. He points out that many counselors come from a Christian background and might not be aware of Jewish traditions, values, and religious rituals. Second, counselors should become aware of the many different types of Jewish identities—religious and nonreligious. Counselors should become knowledgeable about the history of anti-Semitism and its effects on Jewish identity, as well as the consequences of internalized anti-Semitism (Rosen, Rebeta, & Zalman Rothschild, 2014). Third, counselors should become aware of their own biases, if any, toward Jewish people. For Orthodox Jews and other deeply religious Jews, it may be desirable to consult a rabbi, or religious leader of the Jewish religion.

Notable American Jews

Scientist—Albert Einstein

Developer of Microsoft—Bill Gates

Developer of Polio Vaccine—Jonas Salk

Politics—U.S. Supreme Court Justice Ruth Bader Ginsburg

THE WHITE AMERICAN WORLDVIEW

Despite the many differences between and among White American ethnic groups, researchers often present what they describe as the White American worldview. It might be more accurate to speak of a Western rather than a White worldview. The fact that White American culture is the dominant culture in this country is not necessarily an indictment of individual White people. As McGoldrick et al. (2005) have stated, "it is to say that White culture holds greater power to control resources, set rules, and influence events in comparison to other subcultures" (p. 510).

The traditional European worldview has been extracted from the values associated with the countries of origin for American Whites. In truth, however, there is no one White American worldview, but instead multiple worldviews that have core similarities. Most European American groups have acculturated to the dominant Anglo culture, and they have also influenced that same culture. For instance, one core White American worldview is the strong belief in individualism as opposed to collectivism, and the strong belief in autonomy for the individual. White Americans tend to be future oriented; they adhere to rigid time schedules; and they tend to hold a strong work ethic, believing that hard work should result in personal, occupational, and financial achievement. Other values included in the worldviews of White Americans include a belief in freedom and individual rights, the nuclear family, individual achievement, and free market competition.

Cultural Reflections

What are your thoughts about an American identity instead of an ethnic identity?

Is an American identity the same as a national identity, or is it something different?

Many Whites state that they have an American identity instead of an ethnic identity. Why do you think this is? Do you feel that this position is a "copout," or does it reflect the reality of White intermarriage?

The White American worldview can also be conceptualized along the lines of high- and low-context cultures. As noted in earlier chapters, Edward T. Hall (1976) popularized the concept of high-context and low-context cultures. Cultures that encode a message in an explicit code are labeled as low context. For instance, an American White person tends to engage in highly explicit verbal communications. The speaker assumes nothing. Everything is conveyed in the explicit verbal message. In low-context cultures, a person's message tends to be highly detailed and explicit; it may also be redundant for emphasis. Verbal abilities are highly valued in the White American worldview. In contrast, high-context cultures are more sensitive to nonverbal messages; there is far less dependence on the spoken word. The White American view is that success is within the control of the person, and individual achievement is more important than group achievement. People have a responsibility to act on their own behalf.

Finally, another important worldview for White Americans has been a belief in the superiority of White people. The White American male is presented as the epitome of success. The worldview of White Americans of European ancestry has emphasized the alleged racial superiority of White men over men from other ethnocultural cultures (Richmond & Guindon, 2013).

Whiteness and White Privilege

Clinicians sometimes question: Why is it important that I learn about the culture of Whiteness and White privilege when I am counseling individuals of varying cultural backgrounds? Isn't White privilege a political rather than a clinical concern? Aren't we just highlighting our differences and becoming more divisive when we as clinicians take into consideration racism and White privilege as part of the counseling package?

Racism is not just a problem for people of color. Both racism and White privilege have very real negative consequences for all involved. White privilege limits the potential contributions of people of color, and thus the world has a skewed view of human potential. White privilege gives White Americans a false sense of superiority, and it allows them only a distorted view of the world. As Kivel (2002) has asserted,

> racism distorts our senses of danger and safety. We are taught to live in fear of people of color. We are exploited economically by the upper class and unable to fight or even see this exploitation because we are taught to scapegoat people of color. . . . we have been taught that people of color are the real danger, never the white men we live with. (p. 46)

In the clinical relationship, racism is sometimes the proverbial "elephant in the room." Both the client and the clinician avoid talking about the impact of social and racial injustice on the client. They dance around the topic, and as a result, both fail to understand the broad ramifications of the client's problem. Both client and clinician must come to an understanding of what it means to be White. They must come to know from an internal sense the meaning of "Whiteness" in their respective lives.

Whiteness refers to the light skin color of European Americans and the all-encompassing privilege that accompanies being a member of the so-called White race. For many people of color, Whiteness is connected to unearned privilege, advantages, and benefits that American society confers on White individuals (Sue & Sue, 2013). Some of those privileges and unearned advantages include (1) having the power to define reality for themselves and for people of color, (2) having both conscious and unconscious stereotypes of people of color, and (3) being oblivious to the advantage that they have simply by virtue of the color of their skin (Hays, 2014).

It is overly simplistic to label all White Americans as racists or ethnocentric. It is true, however, that it is difficult to escape one's socialization as a White person or to avoid the racial biases and prejudices of one's forebears or family members (Cokely, 2006). Yet this process is not just limited to Whites. All people are influenced to varying degrees by their ethnocultural upbringing. All people are raised with varying degrees of prejudice toward members of groups who are different from them.

White privilege impacts a person's vision. The following are some of the guidelines that McGoldrick et al. (2005) have used in training mental health practitioners:

- White privilege may dim or distort our vision. The more privilege one has, the more difficult it is to consider how one's own actions affect others with less privilege.

- Those who have White privilege may take their privilege for granted—rights such as being heard, being treated fairly, and having access to time, space, and resources.

- The more power and privilege one has, the more difficult it is to think about the rage of those who lack such privilege.

> **Cultural Reflections**
>
> *Has anyone ever called you a racist? If so, describe the circumstances under which this took place.*
>
> *If you were deeply honest with yourself, would you say that you are a racist?*
>
> *Can individuals who are members of ethnic minority groups also be considered racists? Explain.*

DECENTERING WHITENESS

According to Hitchcock and Flint (2015), one can resolve the issue of White privilege not by rallying against White people but rather by **decentering Whiteness**. These authors maintain that there exists in the United States a mainstream culture that is less White than it used to be, but still "Whiteness" forms the mainstream or the center of American society and culture. Hitchcock and Flint have stated that "those in the center, those who occupy a dominant status, such as whiteness, experience the center not so much as a consciously acknowledged status, but rather as a complex of features in their social experience that have surrounded them since inception. . . . If whiteness or white culture, is at the center of American society, then color and cultures of color are at the margins. . . . Cultures of color erect defensive barriers to protect themselves from white culture, and to a lesser extent, other cultures of color" (pp. 1, 3).

Hitchcock and Flint (2015) recommend that Whiteness needs to be removed out of the center of American society to join other racial/cultural groups who are located at the margins. They point out, however, that simply attacking Whiteness is not enough to accomplish decentering Whiteness. In their opinion, "assaults on whiteness, depending on their nature, may have the effect of confirming and solidifying the central position of whiteness in American society. Like a prize fighter who by defeating all contenders expands their reputation and retinue, whiteness may find its position reinforced while those who attack it are relegated further to the margins. Thought must be given to how whiteness itself can be more marginal. . . . It will take a multiracial effort to displace whiteness, one that includes people from all racial/cultural groups" (p. 5).

MODELS OF WHITE RACIAL IDENTITY DEVELOPMENT

Brief Historical Overview of White Racial Identity Models

The discussion of racial identity development is significant because it attempts to get at the question of who we are and what we stand for. Each society gives messages to individuals about who they are based on their ethnocultural group membership. Since the 1970s with the construction of the Cross (1971) model for African American identity development, scholars have constructed models of racial identity. From a historical perspective, White racial identity development models were developed following those that were created for members of various minority groups. Current models of White racial identity development have forced the issue about Whiteness and what it means in American society.

The early White identity development models were created by Rita Hardiman (1982) and Janet Helms (1984). Other White identity models were also developed by Ponterotto (1988). Whereas the Black identity models focused on the oppression of individuals who were in a numerical minority and had been subjected for centuries to racism and even slavery, the White racial identity models emphasized the psychological conditions of the "oppressors"—individuals who were in the numerical majority and had numerous unearned life privileges and far greater power and access to money, wealth, and material resources; who had power, resources, and countless unearned life privileges; and who were responsible for racism in the United States (Richmond & Guindon, 2013).

Both Janet Helms (1984, 1990), who is of African American ancestry, and Rita Hardiman (1982), who is of European ancestry, maintained that if American society were ever to achieve true racial equality and appreciative interracial interaction, White Americans would have to examine themselves regarding their own racial attitudes and racial behavior toward people of color. These researchers believed that the development of White identity in the United States was closely related to the development of racism in this country. Earlier, J. M. Jones (1972, 1997) had identified three types of racism: (1) individual racism that consists of the personal attitudes, beliefs, and behaviors people use to convince themselves of the superiority of Whites and the inferiority of people of color; (2) institutional racism that involves the social policies, laws, and regulations within American society to maintain the economic and social advantages of Whites over non-Whites; and (3) cultural racism that includes the societal beliefs and customs that promote the superiority of White culture over the cultures of other people.

Both Hardiman (1982) and Helms (1984, 1990) theorized that each of these types or levels of racism becomes part of a White person's racial identity. To develop a healthy White racial identity, defined as a **nonracist** or **anti-racist** identity, White Americans would have to come to terms with one or all three types of racism that Jones (1991) had identified. Hardiman and Helms were asking White Americans to look deeply within themselves to see what was really there about race, instead wearing a false nonracist mask. Too many White American counselors and therapists were claiming that they were "color blind": that they did not see color when they were working with clients (Neville, Gallardo, & Sue, 2016). Too many were simply not accepting any responsibility for the oppression of members of ethnic minority people in the United States. To go forward and work effectively with clients of color, White American clinicians would have to accept responsibility for their historical legacy of oppression by passively accepting the racist status quo or by direct action to ensure White dominance (Neville, Gallardo, & Sue, 2016).

THE HARDIMAN WHITE RACIAL IDENTITY MODEL

(*Note*: The following is excerpted from Ponterotto et al, 2006, with permission from the publisher.)

One of the first models for White racial identity development was created by Rita Hardiman (1982) as part of her doctoral dissertation. Hardiman examined White racial identity development through social identity theory. She studied six autobiographies written by White authors describing their life experiences as White Americans. Each author discussed her or his growth and development regarding racial issues and racism. The six authors consisted of four women and two men from various regions of the United States. Hardiman reviewed the following autobiographies in order to develop her model of White identity development: *Killers of the Dream* (L. Smith, 1963); *The Wall Between* (Braden, 1958); *Confessions of a White Racist* (King, 1971); *The Education of a WASP* (Stalvey, 1970); *Hey, White Girl!* (Gregory, 1970); and *White on White: An Anti-Racism Manual for White Educators in the Process of Becoming* (Edler, 1974).

The greatest strength of the **Hardiman model of White identity development** is its sheer creativity and descriptive methodology. The overwhelming majority of identity research in psychology has relied on quantitative methods involving the use of survey instruments. Hardiman (1982) used qualitative methods admirably to integrate major themes, insights, and experiences from the six autobiographies. Based on her analysis of the books, she developed a five-stage model comprising (1) lack of social consciousness, (2) acceptance, (3) resistance, (4) redefinition, and (5) internalization. Let us examine these stages.

Stage 1: Naivité or Lack of Social Consciousness

During this stage, individuals are unaware of the complex codes of appropriate behavior for White people. Stage 1 White individuals naïvely operate from their own needs, interests, and curiosity, and as a consequence, they break many social rules and may be reprimanded or rebuked for their thoughts and behaviors. During this time, White people begin to learn what it means to be White and what other Whites consider appropriate attitudes and behaviors regarding racial issues. In support of Stage 1, the lack of social consciousness stage, Hardiman (1982, p. 159) cites the autobiography of Anne Braden (1958), in which the author remembers a conversation with her mother when she was a child. As the two talked, Anne happened to use the term *colored lady*, at which point her mother quickly retorted, "'You never call colored people ladies. . . .' I can hear her voice now. 'You say colored woman and white lady—never a colored lady'" (Braden, 1958, p. 21). Hardiman's Stage 1 covers birth to about 4 or 5 years of age. It is the stage in which awareness of racial differences first begins. Confusion about race and one's role as a "racial" human being is one characteristic of Stage 1. White children are taught the privileges associated with being White, and they may not yet feel hostile, fearful, or superior to African Americans. Racial curiosity is another dominant characteristic of Stage 1 of the Hardiman model.

> ### Cultural Reflections
>
> *Do you think that race really matters in the United States? Explain your response.*
>
> *In what ways, if any, does race matter to you personally?*
>
> *Would you intermarry with a person from a different ethnic group? With what ethnic groups might you consider intermarriage?*
>
> *In what ways, if any, does race matter in the counseling relationship?*

Stage 2: Acceptance

Acceptance takes place as a result of racial socialization by parents, educators, peers, the church, the media, and the larger surrounding community (Hardiman, 1982). During this transition period, White children quickly learn White racial ideology, as they are taught White people's shared opinions and behaviors with regard to racial issues and interactions—that is, which actions for White people are acceptable and unacceptable—which will be met with punishment and derision and which will be met with approval and support from other Whites.

As a result of the White racial socialization process, White children accept the behavior and beliefs that support White social codes. The dominant White belief system becomes internalized, and the individual no longer needs conscious reminders regarding what thoughts, actions, and behaviors are appropriate for White people. Braden's (1958) autobiography captured the prevailing unspoken attitude with regard to Black and White racial beliefs.

> It was most regrettable that the Negroes had ever been brought to this country in the first place and slavery had certainly been wrong. The presence of the Negroes in the South today was probably our punishment for the sins of our forefathers in bringing them here as slaves. . . . Negroes were really not bad creatures and certainly they had their uses, as they were available as domestic servants so white women could be freed from the burden of housework. . . . The point was to treat them kindly, not only because this was of course right according to Biblical teaching but also because if you treat a Negro with kindness he is also good to you—somewhat in the way a pet dog is

good to the master who is good to him. And of course, the Negro people are happy in this relationship, there is not a reason to feel sorry for them—goodness, they are more carefree and there's nothing they like better than having some white folks who will take care of them. (pp. 19–21, cited in Hardiman, 1982, pp. 170–171)

According to Hardiman (1982), Stage 2 can last many years, even a lifetime. Most of the autobiographies describe Stage 2, acceptance, in great detail, and many authors of the autobiographies were in their adult years before encountering situations that would facilitate their transition to Stage 3, resistance.

Stage 3: Resistance

The transition from Stage 2 to Stage 3 was described as confusing and agonizing by the White autobiographers as they began to acknowledge the reality of the Black experience in America. The movement to Stage 3, resistance, is often precipitated by interaction with people of color, social events, or information presented in the media or in books. For instance, King (1971) said that reading a library book challenged his acceptance stage belief system:

I was a grown man before discovering that George Washington and Thomas Jefferson (those wise, saintly men whose pronouncements on liberty and justice leaped from my textbooks and echoed from the mouths of our Independence Day orators . . .) had owned slaves. It was shocking to learn that demigods who had influenced documents affirming the thrilling, limitless doctrine that all men are created equal had been otherwise capable of holding men in bondage for the profit from their sweat. I well remember discovering these new lessons in the Midland County Library, in my twenty-first year, and then standing outside, looking up at the windswept streets, and thinking, "Hell, if they lied to me about that, they've lied to me about everything." (p. 17, cited in Hardiman, 1982, p. 180)

During the transition to Stage 3, Hardiman (1982) points out that Whites experience painful emotions, ranging from guilt and embarrassment at having been gullible enough to believe the racist messages they received to anger and disgust at the racist system and at the people who lied to them. Stage 3 people acknowledge their Whiteness, and they comprehend that they have been socialized by institutional racism within mainstream American society. For perhaps the first time, Stage 3 White Americans understand minority group anger at White American society, and they conclude that all minority groups are victimized along a continuum by White racism. White people in Stage 3 are unclear about what their role should be in dealing with racism. They experience "White guilt" about the treatment of people of color as they review their previous racial attitudes. As they contemplate the privilege status of their Whiteness, they begin to feel angry both at themselves and at other Whites. One tactic of resistance stage people is to re-educate themselves and other Whites about the harmful effects of racism, and some engage in learning information about cultures different from their own. Some may even participate in challenging and confronting racist institutions via letter writing and demonstrations. The dominant motif is that they attempt to resist White racism, and such resistance may lead them to feel estranged from other Whites, while at the same time feeling uncertain about whether or not they will be accepted by people of color.

Stage 4: Redefinition

Stage 4 White individuals find themselves in search of a new White identity. During the redefinition stage, White individuals not only acknowledge the reality and pervasiveness of racism, but they also act to change difficult racial situations. Their efforts to change White American society to become less racist promote within themselves a positive White identity—one that is not based on having to feel superior to people of color. Whites in redefinition begin to search out the positive features of White identity not based on racism. For instance, they learn more about their culture (e.g., Western philosophy, art, and music), and they develop a sense of pride in their group that is not founded on debasing other ethnic groups. Stage 4 White individuals recognize that while cultures differ in values, no culture is superior to another, and they all contribute to the enrichment of human life. They acknowledge both the strengths and the limitations of White history and culture. They also seek to help other Whites to redefine themselves as Whites and as human beings. They experience true empathy for Whites stuck in the earlier stages of White identity development, and maintain that it is in White people's own self-interest to eliminate racism. As the limitations of racism are removed in their attitudes, Stage 4 White people develop a sense of pride in their new revised positive White identity.

Stage 5: Internalization

During Stage 5, internalization, White people integrate and incorporate their new racial identity into their overall social identity, which is positive and healthy. Internalized White individuals have balanced their racial identity with other aspects of their identity. Such individuals direct their energy and efforts toward liberating other Whites from racism and educating themselves about other forms of oppression (e.g., sexism, homophobia, and ageism). They begin to examine the interaction of race with other group identities (e.g., the interaction of racism and sexism). Internalized Whites voluntarily alienate themselves from some aspects of the social environment and actively engage with other aspects.

THE HELMS MODEL OF WHITE IDENTITY DEVELOPMENT

Helms (1984) introduced a model of White identity development that has become the source of much research in the psychological literature. Since 1984, Helms has modified her model several times, and she has developed an instrument to measure White identity development (e.g., Helms, 1990, 1995, 2005; Helms & Cook, 1999). Helms originally identified stages of White identity, but she subsequently labeled them as statuses because statuses were viewed as more fluid than stages.

Both Helms (1990, 1995, 2015) and Hardiman (1982) maintain that racism is an integral part of being a White American. Both scholars view the process of White racial identity development as one that entails abandoning one's racism and developing a realistic and self-affirming White racial identity. The **Helms model of White identity development** focuses on White privilege and the socialization of Whites.

Helms proposed that Whites internalize a sense of entitlement and learn to maintain their unearned privilege by misrepresenting and distorting the features and contributions of other ethnic groups—specifically those involving people of color. A primary thrust of Helms's work was to examine how the racial identity developmental process differed between ethnic/racial groups due to differences in their respective power. Helms (1995) maintained that the "issue for whites is abandonment of entitlement, whereas the general development issue for people of color is surmounting internalized racism" (p. 184). Helms (1990, 1994) asserted that White Americans must accept (1) their own Whiteness, (2) the cultural implications of being White, and (3) a nonracist view of themselves that does not depend on the perceived superiority of one racial group over another.

Helms's model of White racial identity development consists of two major phases (abandonment of racism and defining a nonracist identity) and six different statuses (contact, disintegration, and reintegration—part of the abandonment phase; and pseudo-independent status, immersion/emersion status, and autonomy status—part of the nonracist identity phase).

Phase 1: Abandonment of Racism

1. Contact Status

In the Helms model, contact is an initial White racial status characterized by denial or obliviousness to White privilege. White people in this status tend to believe that everyone has an equal chance for success, and they are usually oblivious to racial discrimination against members of ethnic minority groups. They have few experiences with people of color. They tend to make such statements as "I really don't see color when I am talking to an African American." They minimize the importance of race. They accept uncritically the superiority of Whites and the inferiority of people of color. They react to racial stimuli with avoidance and denial behaviors. They use White criteria automatically without actual awareness that other criteria are possible. White individuals in the contact stage take no action to understand their own privilege or work toward creating a more just society. As Peggy McIntosh (1989) has commented on her White racial identity development,

> my schooling gave me no training in seeing myself as an oppressor, as an unfairly advantaged person, or as a participant in a damaged culture. I was taught to see myself as an individual whose moral state depended on her individual moral will. . . . Whites are taught to think of their lives as morally neutral, normative, and average, and also ideal, so that when we work to benefit others, this is seen as work which will allow "them" to be more like "us." (p. 8)

During the contact status, the White individual might minimize racism, especially institutional racism. "Racism is a thing of the past," a person might say; "I'm trying to stop talking about the whole race issue because talking about it separates and segregates people." The person engages in the myth of meritocracy—that is, the belief that everyone starts on an even-level playing field: "Hard work is what matters, not the color of one's skin."

2. Disintegration Status

The disintegration status is characterized by disorientation, guilt, and anxiety as the realities of racism seem to pierce the obliviousness of the contact stage. The individual is caught between wanting to be accepted by the normative (White) group and simultaneously being conflicted over viewing and treating people of color as inferior to Whites. Moreover, the person might be conflicted over polar opposites—that is, one wants to be seen as nonracist, but at the same time, one does not want one's son or daughter to marry a person of color.

The individual feels conflicted about his or her loyalty to White people and his or her humanistic feelings that all people should be treated fairly and equally. For instance, one believes that Trayvon Martin was murdered unjustly, but at the same time, he supports George Zimmerman on technical issues.

During the disintegration status, people become conscious of their Whiteness. They may utter statements such as "I disagree with the way people of color are treated, but I am only one person." Helms has asserted that people try to resolve their conflicting racial feelings, and that they may do so by (1) avoiding contact with persons of color, (2) not thinking consciously about race, and (3) obtaining reassurance from others that White people did not cause racism; the problem lies in some failure by the person of color.

Cultural Reflections

Looking at the Hardiman and Helms models of White racial identity development, which model do you find offers more credence and usefulness for you?

Do you think that White Americans undergo a White identity development? If so, what causes this development?

3. Reintegration Status

This status represents a regression that has the person accepting the beliefs of White superiority over people of color. It is characterized by denigration of and intolerance toward people of color and by the forceful protection of one's White privilege and the racial status quo. In the Helms model, reintegration represents the purest or strongest White racist status. White people justify racist treatment of people of color by "blaming the victim" for their conditions. White people in this stage believe that people of color should "pull themselves up by their bootstraps." They use stereotypes to describe an entire group of people, and they refuse to acknowledge social class differences with regard to people of color. Poverty, unemployment, and low academic achievement associated with minority individuals are thought to reflect their own failings or lack of effort. This status may be characterized as a regression because the person idealizes his or her own socioracial group and is intolerant of other minority groups. Whatever residual feelings of anxiety and guilt from the previous status White people might still possess, they are now transformed into anger toward and fear of minority group individuals.

Phase 2: Defining a Nonracist Identity

4. Pseudo-Independent Status

The pseudo-independent status precipitates the second phase of the Helms White racial identity model. A person transitions into this phase due to a jarring event that shakes him or her from the reintegration status. The individual begins to move beyond Whiteness to arrive at an understanding of racial, cultural, and sexual orientation differences and may reach out to interact with minority group members. Yet the White individual tends to choose people of color based on how "similar" they are to him or her. Some Whites treat other Whites in the pseudo-independent status as if they have violated White loyalty.

5. Immersion/Emersion Status

This status differs from the pseudo-independence status in that it is characterized by focusing on changing oneself instead of people of color or other Whites. If one is reinforced in one's personal exploration of oneself as a racial being, questions are directed toward understanding what it means to be White. The person begins a quest to answer such questions as "Who am I racially?" and "How do I want to live as a White person?" The person may want to truly confront his or her own biases, to redefine Whiteness, and to become more actively engaged in combating racism and oppression.

The White individual may immerse him- or herself in biographies or autobiographies of Whites who have explored their racial identity. Some participate in White consciousness-raising groups that are designed to help one discover one's individual self-interest in abandoning racism. The person confronts his or her own biases.

6. Autonomy Status

Autonomy is the most advanced status of racial identity development for White Americans. It is characterized by reduced feelings of guilt, acceptance of one's role in perpetuating racism, and increased efforts to abandon White privilege. The autonomous person is cognitively complex and flexible and seeks not to engage in racial oppression. Such individuals have the capacity to relinquish White privilege. The autonomous person has finally arrived at a nonracist White identity, and does not become offended when members of minority groups talk about White racism. The autonomous person may be conceptualized as having arrived at a self-actualized White racial identity.

James Edler was one of the individuals whom Hardiman used in developing her theory of White identity. Reflecting on his journey to develop a nonracist White identity, Edler, who is a White male, states that while the genuine struggle to understand one's White culture and the emotional poison we've ingested is valuable, what is more important is for White individuals to take action and implement change based on the insights they have gained. He calls such action constructive antiracist behavior.

Criticism of the Helms Model of White Racial Identity

Cultural Reflections

How easy or difficult do you believe it is for White Americans to achieve a nonracist White identity?

What are some examples of "constructive anti-racist behavior" that those who have attained autonomy status might engage in?

There have been criticisms of the Helms model of White racial identity. For instance, Rowe, Bennett, and Atkinson (1994) have argued that it is based on minority identity development models and that identity development for Whites does not develop under the same conditions as it does for minorities. They contend that too much attention is focused on the development of White attitudes toward minorities and insufficient attention is focused on the development of White attitudes toward themselves and their own identity. Other objections are that the Helms model errs in taking a developmental stance and in advocating a linear progression from an unhealthy racial identity to a healthy or nonracist White identity. Finally, Rowe (2006) has challenged Helms's model on the grounds that it is based on her White Racial Identity Attitude Scale (Helms & Carter, 1990), which Rowe characterizes as "pseudoscience" because the scale's psychometric properties are not supported by the empirical literature.

Significance of the White Identity Models

White racial identity models provide a means for White people, including counselors and therapists, to examine and explore where they are developmentally in their interactions with people of color. The construction of White identity development models was especially important because the overwhelming majority of mental health professionals and educators were White. Researchers maintained that because of their privileged status in society (Helms, 1995; Neville, Worthington, & Spanierman, 2001), Whites have not been predisposed to examine their own roles in race relations in this country. White racial identity development models proposed that White Americans engage in an honest self-examination of their roles in maintaining the oppressive racial status quo. The end goal of the White identity development process was to achieve a balanced identity perspective characterized by self-awareness, racial awareness, and commitment to social justice for all groups. The White identity process involved having individuals examine how they perceive themselves and process their lives as racial beings. Toward the end of the White racial identity development process, individuals accept their status as White persons in a racist society and redefine their racial identity and live their lives in a nonracist manner.

Research Findings and White Identity Development Models

Cultural Reflections

Looking back on your life, did you ever go through periods or phases in which your ethnic identity was changed or modified?

Do you believe that ethnic identity development takes place in most human beings? If so, when does it start, and what influences its development?

If suddenly you were told that you could magically no longer have an ethnic identity, what difference, if any, would the absence of an ethnic identity make in your life?

In general, studies have found that the level of White racial identity awareness is predictive of racism and internal interpersonal characteristics (Miville, Darlington, Whitlock, & Mulligan, 2005; Neville, Awad, Brooks, Flores, and Bluemel, 2013; Perry, Dovidio, Murphy, & van Ryn, 2015; Spanierman, Todd, & Anderson, 2009; Vinson & Neimeyer, 2003). Some of the findings of these studies were that (1) the less aware participants were of their White identity, the more inclined they were to display increased levels of racism; (2) the higher the level of participants' White identity development, the more likely participants were able to evidence multicultural competence, to establish a multicultural, therapeutic alliance, and to express more positive opinions toward members of ethnic minority groups; (3) women were more likely than men to manifest higher levels of White consciousness and to be less racially biased; and (4) multicultural therapy competence is correlated with White racial identity attitudes.

White Dialectics: The Promising Research of White Multicultural Scholars on White Identity Development

In place of the Hardiman and Helms models of White racial identity, White multicultural scholars have proposed a new theory called White dialectics. Nathan Todd and Elizabeth Abrams (2011) defined White dialectics as "the tensions that White people experience as dominant group members in the United States" (p. 353). These scholars have proposed White dialectics as a "new framework to understand and intervene with White students and White counselor trainees" (Todd & Abrams, 2011, p. 383). An underlying premise of their theory of White dialectics is that White Americans experience ambiguities about race relations in this country and about their own personal White identity.

Based on their research, Todd and Abrams (2011) identified six major dialectics (areas of tensions) that White individuals may experience as they develop their personalized White identity, and these involve coming to terms with (1) Whiteness and sense of self, (2) closeness and connection in multiracial relationship, (3) color blindness, (4) minimization of racism, (5) structural inequality, and (6) White privilege. At the heart of these White dialectics are questions: How does a White person come to terms with his or her own specific White identity? How does a White person develop an authentic nonracist identity (*authentic* is used in Carl Rogers's definition of being congruent with oneself) rather than a false identity? What issues does a White person have to confront successfully in developing an authentic White identity? For instance, how does a White person deal authentically and honestly with the notion that "I don't see color with African Americans or Asian Americans"? How does one go beyond merely voicing insincere, politically correct platitudes?

Using 22 White, non-Hispanic undergraduate students to form their sample, Todd and Abrams (2011) found that

> White authenticity is a process and not an outcome and is found at the intersection of the dialectics where an individual moves toward (a) self-understanding as White; (b) close and deep relationships with people of color; (c) an understanding of structural inequality and White privilege; and (d) an understanding of the importance of race through color consciousness and a close personal engagement with racism. (p. 385)

Todd and Abrams (2011) maintained that individuals who strive for an authentic White identity "have an integrated sense of self, enabling them to hold the tensions of a privileged position while engaging in antiracist behaviors" (p. 385). They recommended that counseling programs should develop interventions for Whites to deal with the ambiguity they may experience related to race. The ultimate goal is to develop nonracist identities for all people.

White Americans of European Ancestry and Mental Health Issues

Culture influences how mental illnesses are identified, defined, and interpreted—how they vary with respect to timing and onset, presenting symptoms, course, outcome, and treatment utilization and responses (Duan & Brown, 2016). There is very little information on the mental health of various White American ethnic groups of European ancestry. Most studies lump all Whites together and do not clarify whether the so-called White group under study contains only individuals from European ancestry. Within the multiculturally diverse literature, much of the research has focused on ethnic minority groups, and little attention has been focused on White American ethnic groups (Richmond & Guindon, 2013).

Studies have reported significant differences in individuals' attitudes toward mental illness among ethnic groups in the United States. Studies consistently find that African Americans and Latinos are significantly less likely than Euro-Americans to use and to receive mental health care (Sue & Sue, 2013).

COUNSELING WHITE AMERICANS OF EUROPEAN ANCESTRY

In the United States, theories about emotional health are generally based on studying the lives and experiences of people of White European ancestry. Most of the ideas put forth in current theories of counseling and psychotherapy are based on a White European worldview, which emphasizes the values of individualism and the importance of self-development. As Duan and Brown (2016) have asserted, "while society promotes mental health, what is considered as 'normal' or healthy does not represent or reflect the cultures and experiences of American minorities to the same degree as it does the majority" (p. 10). Behaviors that are similar to those of the dominant culture tend to be perceived as normal, healthy, or desirable. For instance, most counseling theories emphasize the desirability of client self-actualization and assume that "self-understanding or insight, freedom for self-actualization, and individuals' happiness or lack of negative emotions/symptoms are universally utmost important and desirable human conditions" (Duan & Brown, 2016, p. 13).

For instance, counseling's focus on verbalizing feelings is a very Euro-American value. Not all cultures speak directly about feelings. Some cultures are more inclined to talk about physical symptoms as a way of expressing how they are feeling. In some Asian cultures, for example, people talk about having stomach pains when they are experiencing mental health issues, such as depression. The entire idea of sharing very personal problems with a complete stranger is not considered normal in many ethnocultural communities.

Although this chapter has discussed the White European worldview, not all White groups share this same outlook. Worldviews change and differ depending on a group's ethnocultural history and life experiences. Despite the fact that all the groups discussed in this chapter came from White European ancestry, those ancestries differ, as also did their specific geographic locations and challenges. When one speaks about a "White European worldview," one is essentially participating in the same kind of ethnic/racial stereotyping to which members of ethnocultural groups of color object. No one likes being stereotyped simply on the basis of the color of one's skin.

At the same time that I make this observation, I note that what some call the White worldview has some basis in fact—especially if one examines the values to which many Whites subscribe. The major factor that makes American Whites of varying European ancestry more similar than different is their subscription to a "White identity" that contains within it a myriad of White privileges in comparison to other ethnocultural groups. To get the benefits of White privilege, many American Whites have sought to erase the cultural boundaries that previously separated one group from another and that sometimes caused groups to hurl ethnic epithets at each other.

Most White Americans are not monocultural (as they are often presented in multicultural textbooks), but rather they are, at the very least, bicultural—White identity and Irish, White identity and Italian, and so forth. Moreover, because of decades of intermarriage, many White Americans are multicultural—White, Irish, and Italian; White, Jewish, and American English; and so on. Multicultural scholars need to recognize that White Americans also have a multicultural identity worthy of inclusion and discussion in their counseling textbooks. During counseling, it would be important for a counselor to discover the White American's salient cultural identity. "Tell me, how do you see yourself as a person, as a cultural human being. With what groups do you identify? Who's important in your life to you? How have you been raised to deal with problems?"

In terms of counseling, White Americans of European ancestry vary in what they label as problematic behavior. It all depends on what the cultural group values. While English Americans may view dependency or emotionality as undesirable, the Irish become upset because a family member makes a scene. Italians consider it unacceptable when a family member is disloyal to the family, and Jews may become distressed because their children are not being "successful."

White ethnocultural groups also choose different ways to respond to problems. When family problems occur, English Americans may seek solace in work and in their jobs. They tend to face life difficulties with a certain amount of stoicism. English Americans may delay seeing a counselor because they want to solve their own problems by themselves. In contrast, Jews who value analyzing and discussing problems may consult a therapist to gain understanding and insight. Italians may prefer to seek help from within their own families, and they are inclined to engage in eating as a way to deal with problems. On the other hand, Irish Americans might first seek confession to a Catholic priest. They use prayers and drink to bring relief from their problems.

Counselors need to understand the cultural factors that impact how members of White Americans of European ancestry view their lives and their problems. When White American clients of European ancestry claim that culture has no impact on their lives, one might ask them, "What is your ideal marriage ceremony?" "What kind of goodbye funeral service would you like to have?" "What type of music do you listen to?" or "Who are your heroes?" Answers to these questions can reveal a great deal about a person's attachment, or lack thereof, to a specific ethnocultural group. For instance, one client said he wanted to say goodbye with everyone singing "Danny Boy" with a drink in hand. Clearly, Irish culture was important to him—right to the very end.

Cultural Reflections

How comfortable would you feel counseling a White American of European descent?

What background information would you like to know about your White client?

CASE VIGNETTE 13.1
JESSIE AND A STRENGTHS-BASED THERAPY APPROACH

The case study of Jessie is excerpted from an article by the author on the strengths-based counseling model published in *The Counseling Psychologist* (Smith, 2006). This case study emphasizes risk factors and protective factors as well as client strengths. Risk factors are those factors that may potentially undermine or threaten the well-being of a client. Protective factors are those factors that may cushion, reduce, or ameliorate threats in a person's life. Most young people have a combination of risk and protective factors, regardless of their socioeconomic status or ethnocultural heritage. In the later revision of strengths-based therapy, protective factors are considered to be on a continuum of client strengths. Protective factors are conceptualized as internal or external client strengths.

Jessie is a 15-year-old, White, second-generation, Polish American young woman who lives with her mother in a low socioeconomic, high-crime urban area. Her parents divorced three years ago. Although her father visits her frequently, he typically ends up fighting with her mother over her failure to raise Jessie properly. Jessie spends some weekends with her father and his new wife. The father works, but he is just barely solvent. Jessie's sister and brother also live with her mother. All three children argue with each other and with their mother frequently. Jessie's mother works two part-time jobs, so she is unavailable to supervise Jessie and her siblings

most of the time. The family is part of the working poor. Jessie's mother is fairly isolated from her larger family. Rarely does the mother attend any family gatherings, and when she does, conflict erupts between the mother and the mother's sisters.

Up until about a year ago, Jessie was attending public school on a regular basis; recently, however, she was picked up by the school truant officer and was charged with truancy. The truancy charge led to Jessie's being taken to family court, where she was ordered to undergo counseling for six months. Therefore, Jessie is an involuntary client at a community counseling center located outside her neighborhood.

Jessie's mother is upset, and she is afraid that her former spouse will seek custody of Jessie to bring Jessie's behavior under control. Jessie's mother has not consulted with the father about Jessie's truancy, although the other children have told him what happened. Jessie's mother is ashamed to tell her extended family about the problem. She is fairly isolated from her neighbors and relies primarily on herself.

Jessie sometimes babysits for her aunts (her mother's sisters) to earn extra money for going to the movies and to the downtown mall. Her aunts feel that she does a good job taking care of the younger children. Recently, Jessie's mother found a journal in which Jessie had written about concerns about having sex with her boyfriend.

(Continued)

(Continued)

Jessie's peers have pressured her to become sexually active, "to just do it and get it over with." Jessie cannot make up her mind about what she will do regarding having sex with her boyfriend. She feels alienated from some of her friends because one crowd has begun to smoke marijuana and drink. Jessie does not want to smoke, but she is considering doing so, just so her friends will not reject her. Although Jessie has friends who are both prosocial and delinquent, she feels depressed, lonely, and isolated. She feels that neither her father nor her mother really loves her.

Within the past three months, Jessie's grades have dropped; she earned three Ds and two Cs. Jessie is discouraged about school and does not expect to do well. She is concerned that she will never be able to graduate or to make anything of herself. Jessie reports interests in music and drama, and she had a minor singing role in one of the school plays.

Jessie is having difficulty figuring out who she is and what she wants to be. She constantly obsesses over her weight gain and her occasional zits. She feels as if she does not really belong in either peer group with which she goes out occasionally. Jessie is only marginally involved in the church's youth group.

What are Jessie's risk factors in each of the five domains of individual, family, school, neighborhood or community, and peers? Indicate what you believe to be the severity of Jessie's risk factors. Considering only Jessie's risk factors, at what level of risk would you place her (low, medium, high, or imminent danger)? What is Jessie's most critical or threatening risk factor? What risk factor might serve as a tipping point for her?

What are Jessie's protective factors in each of the same five domains? What is Jessie's strongest protective factor? In what domain is this protective factor located? To what extent do Jessie's protective factors moderate her level of risk for increased development of problematic behavior? What protective factor might slow or decrease Jessie's engagement in further risky behavior? In what areas of Jessie's life does she need protective factors? How resilient is Jessie? What evidence do you have of her resiliency? What kinds of experiences, knowledge, or skills must Jessie possess to make her more resilient? In what kinds of programs might you get Jessie involved?

Concerning developmental issues, where would you place Jessie along the developmental continuum for her age? What developmental tasks has she mastered? With what developmental tasks is she having difficulty? To what extent do her risk factors impede her mastery of the developmental tasks outlined for her age group? What are Jessie's developmental assets?

What are Jessie's personal strengths? How do you know that these are personal strengths for her? What is Jessie's strongest strength? To what extent is Jessie aware of her strengths? What support has she ever received from significant others for her strengths? How might you help Jessie to become aware of her strengths? How might you help Jessie to reframe problematic areas of her life? What are Jessie's hopes? Her fears? What are Jessie's family strengths? How well has the family bonded? What are the family competencies? To what extent is Jessie bonded to an ethnic culture? Does Jessie have an achieved ethnic identity? How might Jessie's culture help her and her family to heal and move forward? What cognitive and social competence skills must Jessie develop, and how might you assist her in achieving these skills?

Strengths-based clinicians understand on a deeply human level that part of their mission is to extend to clients like Jessie a "hope lifeline" (Snyder, n.d.). Just as one therapist once described psychotherapy as the purchase of friendship, strengths-based counseling psychologists know they sell hope in the counseling relationship, hope that the client can change, and hope that the client's life will improve.

Case analysis: Jessie. An in-depth analysis of Jessie's case is beyond the scope of this chapter; however, this section highlights training directions for understanding the case. Jessie's individual risk factors deal with how she processes information, interprets her life situation, and responds to her environment. Individual risk factors are also related to her lifestyle decisions (e.g., smoking, drinking, and becoming sexually active) and to her genetic makeup, including her intelligence. Jessie's individual risk factors involve her decision to become truant from school, her indecision about whether to become sexually active or to smoke, her physical appearance (e.g., zits), her depressed mental state (e.g., feeling lonely and isolated), her feelings of not being loved by both parents, her discouragement and low expectations about her school performance, and her inability to form independent positions for her own value system. Jessie has interests in music and drama.

Jessie's risk factors in the family domain are related to insufficient parental monitoring and supervision, behavior of friends, divorce of parents, lack of economic resources, family's lower socioeconomic status, lack of family bonding and caring (e.g., sibling conflict and arguing with mother), and lack of communication between divorced parents regarding the child. Moreover, the mother as custodial parent is isolated from her extended family and from neighbors.

Jessie's risk factors in the peer domain are significant because she appears to be at the crossroads for deciding whether to become involved in delinquent behavior. Her peers have favorable attitudes toward alcohol and marijuana, and some of her friends are delinquent. Her truancy from school may have been influenced by truant peers. Jessie seems to have greater peer than parental influence.

The case study does not present in detail Jessie's school risk factors; it states that Jessie had low individual academic achievement. Her grades dropped recently to three *D*s and two *C*s. The fact that Jessie's mother works two jobs suggests that the mother may have little parental involvement in Jessie's school. Community risk factors include a neighborhood with low socioeconomic and high crime levels. Jessie's involvement in family court is another critical area. The fact that Jessie has to attend a community counseling center outside her neighborhood suggests that the community may have few resources to help neighborhood residents.

Jessie's risk assessment is medium or moderately severe. Her most critical risk factor is involvement with delinquent friends. Strengths-based counseling maintains that the people with whom one associates have a more powerful force on one's behavior than does one's intelligence or family background. Highly intelligent individuals have been persuaded by their friends to break the law. The risk factor that might serve as a tipping point is Jessie's continued conflict with her mother and siblings and her contact with family court.

Protective factors have been conceptualized as conditions that interact with risk factors to reduce the latter's negative impact on the individual, thereby preventing the appearance of problem behavior. A major individual protective factor for Jessie is that she appears to be of average intelligence, as evidenced by the fact that previously she was getting grades higher than *C*s and *D*s. Average or above-average intelligence indicates that Jessie has good information-processing skills. She has not established negative educational self-fulfilling prophecies for herself. One may infer that Jessie has reasonable interpersonal and communication skills because she has friends.

Jessie's family protective factors are that she has two parents who evidence prosocial behavior (noncriminal record) and who appear to be concerned about her welfare. Her father visits her frequently, and Jessie spends some weekends with him and his new wife, suggesting that despite the divorce, he still wants to be active in her life. Despite the low socioeconomic level of the family, her parents provide the basic needs of the children, without assistance from the state. Both parents are employed, implying their acceptance of a work ethic. The concern of Jessie's mother for her daughter is reflected partly by her fear that her former spouse will seek custody of Jessie. Despite family conflict, both parents care about Jessie's welfare. The fact that the family has survived is a strength. The family still communicates significant developments among themselves, as shown by the siblings' informing the father about Jessie's truancy. There is an extended family from which Jessie's nuclear family may seek assistance. Jessie's mother's feelings of shame about the truancy suggest that the extended family is primarily prosocial or conventional in its adherence to norms.

A major school protective factor is the evidence that Jessie has bonded with her school, as seen through her minor singing role in a school play. Moreover, Jessie was attending school regularly up until about a year ago; therefore, her truancy is not long-standing. Jessie's protective factors in the peer realm are that she has prosocial peers. A significant counseling issue will be how to increase her contact with the prosocial peers. Jessie's involvement with her church's youth group is a protective community factor. The church may serve to provide spiritual counseling and support for the family. Moreover, Jessie's Polish American ethnic membership may be advantageous by offering the opportunity to be involved in cultural events related to her ethnic group. Finally Jessie's involvement with family court may be a blessing in disguise because it forces the family to examine itself, to get help, and to chart a more responsible course of action for Jessie.

Jessie's strongest protective factor is that she has two parents who care about her welfare, and the next strongest protective factor is her prosocial friends. Jessie's protective factors have moderated her risk factors. For instance, although she lives in a crime-ridden neighborhood, she has two parents who work and who want the best for her. Jessie's father offers the greatest possibility for decreasing her engagement in further risky behavior, primarily because he appears to have clear ideas about how she might be raised properly. Jessie's weekends with her father and his new wife provide an opportunity for a new supportive family setting without the conflict with her siblings.

Family isolation is a critical factor in Jessie's life. She must have additional positive role models and influences in her life, especially in the area of school and community. An effort should be made to contact the guidance counselor for assistance in helping Jessie to join activities such as the school choir, drama club, or newspaper. Greater prosocial involvement with the school might reduce any available time for socializing with delinquent friends. Ways to increase Jessie's academic achievement must be explored. What has caused her grades to drop? Greater involvement with the church might function to buffer the negative effects of Jessie's neighborhood.

Jessie is moderately resilient because she has been able to survive and function reasonably well in school despite the family's low socioeconomic level, the crime-ridden neighborhood, and the divorce of her parents three years ago. There is no evidence that she has adopted maladaptive behavior in response to the family breakup. On the contrary, Jessie appeared to bounce back from her parents' divorce until recently.

(Continued)

(Continued)

Developmentally, Jessie is reasonably on track. For most of her years, she has been able to succeed academically in school. She has mastered the developmental task of industry and making friends outside the family. She is having some difficulty with the developmental tasks relating to personal identity and sexual behavior. She is trying to forge a personal and sexual identity for herself. At this point, her peers have an undue influence on her decision to engage in problematic behaviors. Jessie needs help in clarifying her value system and the type of people with whom she wants to spend time. She is having difficulty with the developmental task of discovering what she wants to do in life. This situation may have occurred because of the financial limitations of her family and because she may have few role models in her neighborhood. Poverty may force Jessie to grow up fast and may not give her the chance to try different interests and behaviors in a safe environment.

Jessie has creative and relational or nurturing strengths. Evidence of her creative strengths is found in her journal, her participation in a school play, and her singing. Nurturing and strengths are found in her ability to care for children and in her making of friends. Jessie is in danger of not recognizing her strengths because there is no evidence that she has identified any of her creative pursuits as strengths. Her awareness of her creative and nurturing strengths might be increased by pointing out her involvement in activities that require these strengths. One might ask Jessie the "miracle questions," such as "What would you do with your life if tomorrow you awakened and no longer lived in the neighborhood in which you are now living? What would your life be like?" One might also use the "hope chest" technique: "Let's suppose that there was a magical hope chest, Jessie, and you could be anything that you wanted. What would be your first wish out of the hope chest?" Another approach might be "Tell me about what you perceive as your greatest strength," or "When you are at your best, what are you doing?"

Additional information might have to be provided to answer other questions related to Jessie's family competencies and the influence of her ethnic culture. This case study demonstrates, however, that strengths can be found in most individuals and in most families, despite their challenging situations. Families require help in understanding how they have survived and what family strengths have helped them survive.

Source: Smith, Elsie J (2006). "The Strenghts-Based Counseling Model." *The Counseling Psychologist*, 34(1), p. 13–79.

SUMMARY OF KEY POINTS

1. White Americans of European descent are not a homogeneous group. All Whites are not alike, nor are all African Americans, Asian Americans, American Indians, or members of any other group "all alike." Stereotyping of White Americans is just as objectionable as is stereotyping members of other ethnocultural minority groups.

2. Clinicians who provide clinical services to White Americans of European heritage need to understand their worldviews, what motivates them, and what approach to counseling they find acceptable.

3. Privilege is not equally distributed among White Americans. White privilege is influenced by ethnic origin, gender, social class, and sexual orientation.

4. Clinicians need to consider their own ethnic/racial identity development in working with others.

5. White racial identity development models have been useful in examining how a privileged majority can learn to become nonracist and socially just.

DISCUSSION QUESTIONS

Discussion Question 1: In groups of 3-5 people, discuss 2 counseling experiences you have had with a White American. To what extent did the person's ethnic group membership have on the client's presenting problem? How did you raise the influence of culture on the client's presenting problem?

Discussion Question 2: White Americans of European ancestry are often lumped together and treated as a monolithic group. Discuss briefly the pros and cons of raising the issue of ethnic group membership and culture with White American clients. Are there some White American ethnic groups that you feel closer to than others? Explain your answer.

KEY TERMS

American identity: An identity that many White Americans say they have when asked what is their cultural identity.

Anti-racist White identity: The identity that Helms and others propose that takes place within White Americans that will help them to eradicate racism in American society. See *nonracist White identity*, a synonym.

Anti-Semitism: Prejudice or discrimination against people of Jewish descent.

Decentering Whiteness: The belief that American society is centered around Whiteness and that Whiteness should be taken out of the center of American life and that there should be movement to embrace cultural groups in the margins. Decentering Whiteness entails a movement toward a multicultural central identity for the United States.

Destino: An Italian belief system in the role of fate in controlling one's life. One's life is controlled by fate, and therefore, it is important to enjoy the moment.

Evil eye: One of the most popular Italian beliefs is the *malocchio* (*mal* = "bad," *occhio* = "eye"). Italians believe that those who give the evil eye can cause harm to a person. Giving the evil eye is similar to putting a curse on a person. Italians use a horn amulet called the *cornetto, corno*, or *cornicello*. The horns are usually made of gold, and they are worn as a necklace or hung in one's home to ward off evil spirits.

Goomba: An Italian term often used for an Italian godfather; **goomma** is used for an Italian godmother.

Gumba: An Italian slang term used to designate friends close enough to be in the inner circle.

Hardiman model of White identity development: The White racial identity development model formulated by Rita Hardiman.

Helms model of White identity development: The White racial identity development model proposed by Janet Helms.

Holocaust: A period in Nazi Germany where Nazis killed approximately 6 million Jews because of their Jewish faith.

L'ordine della familigia: A complex code of Italian family obligations that regulated relationships both inside and outside of the family. This code not only represented a mistrust of outsiders, but family members who violated it were considered disloyal and a shame to their families.

Nonracist White identity: An identity that occurs when White Americans recognize their own racial biases against other groups; a person has a commitment to eradicate racial prejudice. See *anti-racist White identity*, a synonym.

Orthodox Jews: Jews who follow closely the rules and rituals of Judaism.

Pogroms: Residential enclaves in which Jews were restricted to live throughout Europe largely prior to the 19th century. *Pogroms* were surrounded by walls that separated Jews' living quarters from the rest of the city's residents.

Puritans: The members of an English religious group that immigrated to America during the 1620s and settled in Massachusetts—known for their insistence on individualism and their right to read and interpret the Bible for themselves. Established Harvard College in 1636 and a number of now elite northeastern universities. The Evangelicals in American society adhere to many of the Puritan religious beliefs.

Tikkun olam: A Jewish value and concept that means "world repair." It has become synonymous with the value and necessity of social action and the pursuit of social justice.

White privilege: The unearned advantages or privileges that are automatically given to people of White European descent.

Whiteness: The skin color or tone of people of European descent, their dominating status in the United States, and the implicit belief that White culture is the standard culture in American society and that all other cultures should be evaluated against it.

Yom Kippur: A major Jewish holiday, known as the Day of Atonement, that comes once a year and allows Jews to atone for their sins during the past year.

REFERENCES AND SUGGESTED READING

Alessandria, K. P. (2002). Acknowledging White ethnic groups in multicultural counseling. *The Family Journal: Counseling and Therapy for Couples and Families, 10*(1), 57–60.

Altman, A. N., Inman, A. G., Fine, S. G., Ritter, H. A., & Howard, E. R. (2010). Exploration of Jewish ethnic identity. *Journal of Counseling and Development, 88*, 163–173.

Axtell, J. (1985). *The invasion within: The contest of cultures in colonial North America*. New York, NY: Oxford University Press.

Berenbaum, M. (2006). *The world must know: The history of the Holocaust as told in the United States Holocaust Memorial Museum*. Baltimore, MD: Johns Hopkins University Press.

Braden, A. (1958). *The wall between*. New York, NY: Monthly Review Press.

Carpenter-Song, E., Chu, E., Drake, R. E., Ritsema, M., Smith, B., & Alverson, H. (2010). Ethnocultural variations in the experience and meaning of mental illness and treatment: implications for access and utilization. *Transcultural Psychiatry*, *47*(2), 224–251.

Cleary, P. D., & Demone, N. W. (1988). Health and social service needs in a Northeastern metropolitan area: Ethnic group differences. *The Journal of Sociology & Social Welfare*, *15*(4), 63–76.

Cokely, K. (2006). The impact of racialized schools and racist (mis)education on African American students' academic identity. In M. G. Constantine & D. W. Sue (Eds.) *Addressing racism* (pp. 127–144). Hoboken, NJ: Wiley.

Cross, W. E. (1971). The Negro-to-Black conversion experience. *Black World*, *20*(9), 13–27.

DeNavas-Walt, C., Proctor, B. D., & Smith, J. C. (2012, September). Income, poverty, and health insurance coverage in the United States: 2006–2011. *Current Population Reports*. U.S. Census Bureau. Retrieved from https://www.census.gov/prod/2012pubs/p60-243.pdf

Duan, C., & Brown, C. (2016). *Becoming a multiculturally competent counselor*. Thousand Oaks, CA: Sage.

Edler, J. (1974). *White on White: An anti-racism manual for White educators in the process of becoming*. Unpublished doctoral dissertation, University of Massachusetts.

Fine, L. (2016). Tikkun: A Lurianic motif in contemporary Jewish thought. In J. Neusner (Ed.), *From ancient Israel to modern Judaism, vol. 4. Intellect in quest of understanding: Essays in honor of Marvin Fox* (pp. 35–53). Classic Reprint. Charleston, SC: Forgotten Books.

Fox, H. (2011). *Their highest vocation: Social justice and the millennial generation*. New York, NY: Lang.

Gambino, R. (1974). *Blood of my blood: The dilemma of Italian Americans*. Garden City, NY: Doubleday.

Giordano, J., & McGoldrick, M. (2005). Families of European origin: An overview. In M. McGoldrick, J. Giordano, & N. Garcia-Preto (Eds.), *Ethnicity & family therapy* (pp. 501–519). New York, NY: Guilford Press.

Giordano, J., McGoldrick, M., & Klages, J. G. (2005). In M. McGoldrick, J. Giordano, & N. Garcia-Preto (Eds.), *Ethnicity and family therapy* (3rd ed., pp. 616–628). New York, NY: Guilford Press.

Gregory, S. (1970). *Hey, white girl!* New York, NY: Norton.

Hall, E. T. (1976). *Beyond culture*. New York, NY: Doubleday.

Hardiman, R. (1982). White identity development: A process-oriented model for describing the racial consciousness of White Americans (Doctoral dissertation). *Dissertation Abstracts International*, *43*, 104A. (University Microfilms No. 82–10330)

Hays, P. (2014). Finding a place in the multicultural revolution. In M. E. Gallardo (Ed.), *Developing cultural humility* (pp. 49–59). Thousand Oaks, CA: Sage.

Helms, J. E. (1984). Toward a theoretical explanation of the effects of race on counseling: A Black and White model. *The Counseling Psychologist*, *12*, 153–165.

Helms, J. E. (1990). *Black and white racial identity: Theory, research, and practice*. Westport, CT: Greenwood Press.

Helms, J. E. (1994). How multiculturalism obscures racial factors in the therapy process: Comment on Ridley et al. (1994), Sodowsky et al. (1994), Ottavi et al. (1994), and Thompson et al. (1994). *Journal of Counseling Psychology*, *41*, 162–165.

Helms, J. E. (1995). An update of Helms' White and people of color racial identity models. In J. G. Ponterotto, J. M. Casas, L. A. Suzuki, & C. M. Alexander (Eds.), *Handbook of multicultural counseling* (pp. 181–191). Thousand Oaks, CA: Sage.

Helms, J. E. (2005). Stereotype threat might explain the Black-White test-score difference. *American Psychologist*, *60*(3), 269–270. http://dx.doi.org/10.1037/0003-066X.60.3.269

Helms, J. E. (2015). Taking action against racism in a post-racism era: The origins and almost demise of an idea. *The Counseling Psychologist*, *43*, 138–145.

Helms, J. E., & Carter, R. T. (1990). Development of the White racial identity attitude inventory. In J. E. Helms (Ed.), *Black and White racial identity: Theory, research, and practice* (pp. 67–80). Westport, CT: Greenwood Press.

Helms, J. E., & Cook, D. A. (1999). *Using race and culture in counseling and psychotherapy: Theory and process*. New York, NY: Allyn & Bacon.

Hitchcock, J., & Flint, C. (2015). *Decentering Whiteness*. Roselle, NJ: Center for the Study of White American Culture.

Hixson, L., Hepler, B. B., & Kim, M. O. (2011, September). The White population: 2010. *2010 Census Briefs*. U.S. Census Bureau. Retrieved from http://www.census.gov/prod/cen2010/briefs/c2010br-05.pdf

Howe, N., & Strauss, W. (2000). *Millennials rising: The next great generation*. New York, NY: Vintage Books.

Jones, J. M. (1972). *Prejudice and racism*. Reading, MA: Addison Wesley.

Jones, J. M. (1991). Psychological models of race: What have they been and what should they be? In J. D. Goodchilds (Eds.), *Psychological perspectives on human diversity in America* (pp. 3–46). Washington, DC: American Psychological Association.

Jones, J. M. (1997). *Prejudice and racism* (2nd ed.). New York, NY: McGraw-Hill.

Jones-Smith, E. (2014). *Strengths-based therapy: Connecting theory, practice, and skills*. Thousand Oaks, CA: Sage.

Kaufmann, E. P. (2004). *The rise and fall of Anglo-America*. Cambridge, MA: Harvard University Press.

Kennedy, R. E. (1983). *The Irish: Marriage, immigration and fertility*. Berkeley: University of California Press.

Killian, K. D., & Agathangelou, A. M. (2005). Greek families. In M. McGoldrick, J. Giordano, & N. Garcia-Preto (Eds.), *Ethnicity and family therapy* (3rd ed., pp. 573–585). New York, NY: Guilford Press.

King, L. (1971). *Confessions of a white racist*. New York, NY: Viking Press.

Kivel, P. (2002). *Uprooting racism: How White people can work for racial justice*. New York, NY: New Society.

Langman, P. F. (1999). *Jewish issues in multiculturalism: A handbook for educators and clinicians*. Northvale, NJ: Aronson.

Liu, J. (2013, October 1). A Portrait of Jewish Americans. *Pew Research Center*. Retrieved from http://www.pewforum.org/2013/10/01/jewish-american-beliefs-attitudes-culture-survey/

Mangione, J., & Morreale, B. (1992). *La Storia: Five centuries of Italian American experience*. New York, NY: HarperCollins.

Marable, M. (2002). *The great wells of democracy: The meaning of race in American life*. New York, NY: Basic Civitas Books.

McFeatters, A. (2000, March 17). 10 U.S. presidents had Irish ancestors. *Post-Gazette National Bureau*. Retrieved from http://old.post-gazette.com/magazine/20000317irish9.asp.

McGill, D. W., & Pearce, J. K. (2005). American families with English ancestors from the colonial era: Anglo Americans. In M. McGoldrick, J. Giordano, & N. Garcia-Preto (Eds.), *Ethnicity and family therapy* (3rd ed., pp. 520–533). New York, NY: Guilford Press.

McGoldrick, M., Giordano, J., & Garcia-Preto, N. (Eds.). (2005). *Ethnicity and family therapy* (3rd ed.). New York, NY: Guilford Press.

McIntosh, P. (1989, July/August). White privilege: Unpacking the invisible knapsack. *Peace and Freedom Magazine*, 10–12.

Philadelphia, PA: Women's International League for Peace and Freedom.

Miville, M. L., Darlington, P., Whitlock, B., & Mulligan, T. (2005). Integrating identities: The relationship of racial, gender, and ego identities among White college students. *Journal of College Student Development, 46*, 157–175.

Neville, H. A., Awad, G. H., Brooks, J. E., Flores, M. P., & Bluemel, J. (2013). Color-blind racial ideology: Theory, training, and measurement implications in psychology. *American Psychologist, 68*, 455–466.

Neville, H. A., Gallardo, M. E., & Sue, D. W. (Eds.). (2016). *The myth of racial color blindness: Manifestation, dynamics, and impact*. Washington, DC: American Psychological Association.

Neville, H. A., Worthington, R. L., & Spanierman, L. B. (2001). Race, power, and multicultural counseling psychology: Understanding white privilege and color-blind racial attitudes. In J. G. Ponterotto, J. M. Casas, L. A. Suzuki, & C. M. Alexander (Eds.), *Handbook of multicultural counseling* (pp. 257–288). Thousand Oaks, CA: Sage.

O'Connor, L., Lubin, G., & Spector, D. (2013, August 13). The largest ancestry groups in the United States. *Business Insider*. Retrieved from http://www.businessinsider.com/largest-ethnic-groups-in-america-2013-8

Perry, S. P., Dovidio, J. E., Murphy, M. C., & van Ryn, M. (2015). The joint effect of bias awareness and self-reported prejudice on intergroup anxiety and intentions for intergroup contact. *Cultural Diversity and Ethnic Minority Psychology, 21*, 89–96.

Ponterotto, J. E. (1988). Racial consciousness development among White counselors' trainees: A stage model. *Journal of Multicultural Counseling and Development, 16*, 146–156.

Ponterotto, J. G., Utsey, S. O., & Pedersen, P. B. (2006). European American (White) Racial Identity Development, Mental Health, and Prejudice. In *Preventing Prejudice* (pp. 89–93). Thousand Oaks, CA: SAGE Publishing.

Rich, T. R. (2011). *Judaism 101*. Retrieved from http://www.hewfaq.org/

Richmond, L. J., & Guindon, M. H. (2013). Culturally alert counseling with European Americans. In Garrett McAuliffe & Associates (Eds.), *Culturally alert counseling: A comprehensive introduction* (2nd ed., pp. 231–262). Thousand Oaks, CA: Sage.

Ridley, C. (1995). *Overcoming unintentional racism in counseling and psychotherapy*. Thousand Oaks, CA: Sage.

Roberts, S. (2004). *Who are we: The changing face of America in the twenty-first century*. New York, NY: Time Books.

Rodriguez, R. (2002). *Brown: The last discovery of America*. New York, NY: Penguin.

Roediger, D. (1999). *The wages of Whiteness: Race and the making of the American working class*. New York, NY: Verso.

Rosen, D. D., Rebeta, J. L., & Zalman Rothschild, S. Z. (2014). Culturally competent adaptation of cognitive-behavior for psychosis: Cases of Orthodox Jewish patients with Messianic delusions. *Mental Health, Religion & Culture, 17,* 703–713.

Rowe, W. (2006). White racial identity; Science, faith and pseudoscience. *Journal of Multicultural Counseling and Development, 34,* 235–243.

Rowe, W., Bennett, S., & Atkinson, D. R. (1994). White racial identity models: A critique and alternative proposal. *The Counseling Psychologist, 22,* 120–146.

Saxe, L., & Tighe, E. (2013). Estimating and understanding the Jewish population in the United States: A program of research. *Contemporary Jewry, 33*(1/2) (April-July 2013), 43–62.

Scally, R. J. (1995). *The end of hidden Ireland: Rebellion, famine and emigration*. New York, NY: Oxford University Press.

Schlosser, L. Z. (2006). Affirmative psychotherapy for American Jews. *Psychotherapy: Theory, Research, Practice, Training, 43,* 424–435.

Schlosser, L. Z. (2009). *A multidimensional model of American Jewish identity*. Retrieved from https://www.bc.edu/content/dam/files/schools/lsoe_sites/isprc/pdf/Schlosser.pdf

Smith, E. J. (1985). Ethnic minorities: Life stress, social support, and mental health issues. *The Counseling Psychologist, 13,* 537–579.

Smith, E. J. (1991). Ethnic identity development: Toward the development of a theory within the context of majority/minority status. *Journal of Counseling and Development, 70,* 181–188.

Smith, E. J. (2006). The strengths-based counseling model. *The Counseling Psychologist, 34*(1), 13–79.

Smith, L. E. (1963). *Killers of the dream*. Garden City, NY: Doubleday.

Snyder, C. R. (n.d.). *Handbook of hope: Theory, measures, & applications*. Cambridge, MA: Academic Press.

Spanierman, L. B., Todd, N. R., & Anderson, C. J. (2009). Psychosocial costs of racism to Whites: Understanding patterns among university students. *Journal of Counseling Psychology, 56,* 239–252.

Stalvey, L. M. (1970). *The education of a WASP*. New York, NY: William Morrow.

Sue, D. W., & Sue, D. (2013). *Counseling the culturally diverse: Theory and practice* (6th ed.). Hoboken, NJ: Wiley.

Takaki, R. (2002). *Debating diversity: Clashing perspectives on race and ethnicity in America* (3rd ed.). New York, NY: Oxford University Press.

Todd, N. R., & Abrams, E. M. (2011). White dialectics: A new framework for theory, research, and practice with White students. *The Counseling Psychologist, 39*(3), 353–395.

U.S. Census Bureau. (2014). *American Community Survey (ACS): 2014 ACS 1-year estimates*. Retrieved from https://www.census.gov/programs-surveys/acs/technical-documentation/table-and-geography-changes/2014/1-year.html

U.S. Census Bureau. (2015, March 3). *New Census Bureau report analyzes U.S. population projections*. Retrieved from https://www.census.gov/newsroom/press-releases/2015/cb15-tps16.html

U.S. Diplomatic Mission to Germany. (2008). German Americans. *U.S. Embassy & Consulates in Germany*. Retrieved from http://www.euroamerican.org/

U.S. State Department. (2008, December). *German Americans*. Retrieved from https://usa.usembassy.de/germanamericans.htm

Vinson, T., & Neimeyer, G. J. (2003). The relationship between racial identity development and multicultural counseling competence: A second look. *Journal of Multicultural Counseling and Development, 31,* 262–277.

Weinrach, S. (2002). The counseling profession's relationship to Jews and the issues that concern them: More than a decade of selective awareness. *Journal of Counseling and Development, 80,* 300–314.

WonPat-Borja, A. J., Yang, L. H., Link, B. G., & Phelan, J. C. (2012). Eugenics, genetics, and mental illness stigma in Chinese Americans. *Social Psychiatry Epidemiology, 47*(1), 145–156.

Zinn, H. (2003). *A people's history of the United States*. New York, NY: HarperCollins.

14 CULTURALLY RESPONSIVE STRENGTHS-BASED THERAPY FOR WOMEN

- *"We ask justice, we ask equality, we ask that all the civil and political rights that belong to citizens of the United States, be guaranteed to us and our daughters forever."* —Susan B. Anthony

- *"I've come to believe that each of us has a personal calling that's as unique as a fingerprint—and that the best way to succeed is to discover what you love and then find a way to offer it to others in the form of service, working hard, and also allowing the energy of the universe to lead you."* —Oprah Winfrey

- *"I could not, at any age, be content to take my place by the fireside and simply look on. Life was meant to be lived. Curiosity must be kept alive. One must never, for whatever reason, turn his back on life."* —Eleanor Roosevelt

- *"If women are healthy and educated, their families will flourish. If women are free from violence, their families will flourish. If women have a chance to work and earn as full and equal partners in society, their families will flourish. And when families flourish, communities and nations will flourish."* —Hillary Clinton

CHAPTER OBJECTIVES

- Describe the demographics and population statistics of women in American society.

- Identify examples of gender inequalities and microaggressions against women.

- Analyze the biological and sociological bases of women's mental health issues.

- Apply feminist psychology approaches in counseling women.

- Learn feminist therapy techniques, including gender role analysis and gender role intervention.

- Identify strengths of female clients and how they can be harnessed in counseling and therapy.

INTRODUCTION

This chapter addresses the economic, political, and mental health circumstances surrounding women in the United States. Although American women constitute a majority group in terms of actual population numbers, they have been historically subjected to the kinds of prejudice, discrimination, and social injustice typically experienced by minorities. The disadvantaged status of American women in terms of power, jobs, and socioeconomic equality is the major reason that this book includes a separate chapter on them. Moreover, it is important to bear in mind that this chapter applies to women of all racial and ethnocultural groups, many of whom may experience additional discrimination and social injustice by virtue of being non-White.

Feminists have constructed their own approaches for counseling both women and men, and this chapter presents feminist approaches as appropriate for culturally responsive strengths-based therapy with female clients.

DEMOGRAPHICS OF AMERICAN WOMEN

In 2010, there were 156,964,211 females (50.8%) and 151,781,326 males (49.2%) in the United States. The sex ratio, or proportion of males to females, is an established measure used to describe the balance between males and females in the population. In 2010, there were 96.7 males per 100 females, an increase from 2000 when the sex ratio was 96.3 males per 100 females. All four regions of the United States had a sex ratio of less than 100, indicating more females than males. The sex ratio varied across regions. The Northeast had the lowest sex ratio (94.5 males per 100 females), followed by the South (96.1), the Midwest (96.8), and the West (99.3). Women live longer than men; therefore, the ratio of women to men increases as both sexes age. At age 85, there are twice as many women as men (U.S. Census Bureau, 2011a).

SOCIOECONOMIC STATUS OF U.S. WOMEN

Socioeconomic status (SES) is often measured as a combination of education, income, and occupation. It is commonly used to refer to a person or group's social standing or class. Social class refers to an individual or group's privilege, power, and control. SES affects everyone. It influences a person's functioning across the life span, as well as his or her physical and mental health. Disparities in income and wealth affect people, especially women. Women's SES is of great concern because they are usually the ones to raise children alone. When women are homeless, so are their children.

Women in Poverty

American women are more likely to be poor than American men. More than half of the 37 million Americans living in poverty are women (Cawthorne, 2008). Moreover, the gap in poverty rates between men and women is wider in the United States than anywhere else in the Western world. In 2007, approximately 13.8% of females were poor in contrast to 11.1% of males.

American women are poorer than American men in all ethnic and racial groups. A higher percentage of African American women are poor (26.5%) compared to African American men (22.3%); "23.6 percent of Hispanic women are poor compared to 19.6 percent of Hispanic men; 10.7 percent of Asian women are poor compared to 9.7 percent of Asian men; and 11.6 percent of White women are poor compared to 9.4 percent of White men" (Cawthorne, 2008). African American and Hispanic women encounter the highest rates of poverty, with over a quarter of African American women and almost a quarter of American Latina women living in the poor category. A Black woman or a Latina is at least twice as likely as a White woman to be living in poverty.

Gender differences in poverty rates increase with age. For children under age 18, the poverty rate for girls was not statistically different from the poverty rate for boys (approximately 21%) (DeNavas-Walt & Proctor, 2014). However, the poverty rates for women increase during their childbearing years and again in old age. The poverty gap between American women and men widens significantly between ages 18 and 24—20.6% of women are poor at that age, compared to 14.0% of men. The poverty rate for women aged 65 and older was 12.1%, while the poverty rate for men aged 65 and older was just 7.4%.

Why are more American women living in poverty than men? Women face a greater chance of poverty for several interrelated reasons. First, women are paid less than men, even when they have the same qualifications and work the same hours. Discrimination is the culprit in women's lower salaries, not lack of training or education. Women constitute 55% of college students, and they earn a greater percentage of associate's, bachelor's, and master's degrees; yet they earn less than their male counterparts across all racial groups. When one examines White men and women, women earn 80 cents for each dollar earned by men (U.S. Census Bureau, 2017).

Cultural Reflections

In your opinion, is gender equality real? Explain your answer.

What do you think can be done to equalize the salaries of males and females who work the same job?

A second reason for women's higher poverty rates is that they are often segregated in so-called pink-collar jobs, which are occupations traditionally held by women, that typically pay less than jobs in male-dominated industries. In 2007, almost half (43%) of the 29.6 million employed women in the United States were clustered in about 20 occupational categories, where the average annual median earnings were $27,383 (Cawthorne, 2008). For example, women make up 79% of elementary school teachers but only 44% of higher education faculty members (National Center for Education Statistics, 2017). As another example, women are underrepresented in science, technology, engineering, and mathematics (STEM) occupations, as well as in managerial and executive-level jobs (de Pillis & de Pillis, 2008) where their scarcity is referred to as the "glass ceiling."

A third reason for women's higher poverty rate is rooted in discrimination against women in the workplace. Women are often stereotyped and criticized when they do not conform to stereotypical sex role expectations. Although women in positions of authority are expected to be assertive and in control, they are also criticized for these same characteristics. According to Lyness and Thompson (2000), women can be made to feel excluded from the workplace due to a "boys' club" mentality and often aim to perform at a much higher level than male counterparts to be taken seriously. This exclusion may also discourage them from seeking mentorship from their superiors and can make them feel that they were hired due to "token" hiring practices.

Another reason why more women than men are in poverty is that women spend more time than men providing unpaid caregiving. Domestic and sexual violence sometimes traps women in a cycle of poverty too. "It is estimated that victims of intimate partner violence (IPV) collectively lose almost 8 million days of paid work each year because of the violence perpetrated against them by current or former husbands, boyfriends, or dates. Half of the cities surveyed by the U.S. Conference of Mayors identified domestic violence as a primary cause of homelessness" (Cawthorne, 2008).

MICROAGGRESSIONS AGAINST WOMEN AND GENDER INEQUALITY

Women are often subjected to microaggressions that sometimes are given as backhanded compliments made to a woman in passing, like telling a woman that she did a good job "for a woman" or labeling a female manager or CEO as a "bitch" while her male counterpart is described as a good or forceful leader. Another favorite microaggression used against women is the word *qualified*. "Marilyn may be a woman, but I think she is qualified for the job." A female professor's academic credentials are scrutinized, while her male counterpart gets a pass. The word *qualified* is hardly ever used to suggest that a male assistant professor's credentials don't match a woman's academic credentials. Both tenure review boards and even students assume that male professors/instructional staff are more qualified than women.

Students' bias against women faculty has been documented in the research. Therese Huston (2005) reported that White female faculty receive lower student evaluations than similarly situated male faculty. There were some gender preferences that indicated female students tend to give higher ratings to female instructors. Students sometimes rate professors on their own gender-biased expectations. There is the expectation that female faculty will be warm and friendly, while the same may not be expected of males. According to Huston, "female faculty who are rated as being low on warmth, interpersonal contact, and interest in their students were penalized on their course evaluation, . . . whereas male faculty who were rated as being low on these same interpersonal qualities did not receive lower course evaluations" (p. 3). Summarizing the research on race and gender influence on student evaluations, she stated that

> researchers found lower final course evaluation ratios for female minority faculty members, but not for male minority instructors. In their study, women instructors received significantly lower course evaluations than male instructors (nearly 1/2 standard deviation lower), and faculty of color received lower course evaluations than white faculty. There was also an interaction of race and gender such that female faculty of color received particularly low course evaluations. (p. 1)

Cultural Reflections

Have you ever engaged in microaggression against a woman?

What did you say, and how did the person respond?

Do you tend to rate male faculty higher than female faculty? Explain your answer.

What is the purpose of microaggressions? Microaggressions are used to exclude women, to make them feel inferior, and to suggest that they somehow don't measure up to what one is seeking. Microaggressions against women attempt to marginalize them. Most microaggressions operate at the unconscious level, or at the very least at the subconscious level, of awareness. Microaggressions can affect a woman's standard of living and quality of life. For instance, although White American males constitute only 33% of the American population, they occupy 80% of tenured positions in higher education, 80% of the U.S. House of Representatives and 80%–85% of the U.S. Senate, 90% of public school superintendents, and 100% of the U.S. presidents.

These statistics did not just happen by accident. They are supported by many Americans, some of whom are women. There are women who will not vote for another woman. For instance, Geraldine Ferraro was the first American woman to be selected as a presidential candidate. When she ran for Senate office in New York state, many women, including some who were Italian, wrote in to the local newspapers stating that they would not vote for a female senator from New York City. Microaggressions reflect the hidden or silent feelings of the general American public.

Sometimes when people use microaggressions against women, they are annoyed when a woman calls them on the remark. "Gee, you're really sensitive—maybe too sensitive," a person might say. "I didn't really mean anything by what I said." Microaggressions against women are used to remind them that they still aren't really equal. Usually, people using microaggression against a woman feel that they have some sort of privilege that she does not have. A microaggressor seldom takes the time to consider how his passing comments and actions might actually impact a woman. Women can take the microaggressions of men, but some have said that it really hurts when another woman "tries to insult you or to bring you down." Gender inequality is a fact in American life. Microaggressions are used to reinforce gender inequality or to remind American women of days gone by when they were even more oppressed.

THE MENTAL HEALTH ISSUES OF WOMEN

Mental illness is no respecter of a person's race, gender, or age. Nearly 50 million Americans suffer from mental illness (National Institute of Mental Health [NIMH], 2016). The Substance Abuse and Mental Health Services Administration (SAMHSA, 2010) estimates that nearly 23.8% of American women have experienced a diagnosable mental health disorder during the past year, compared to the estimated 15.6% of men who have experienced mental illness.

Research studies have found that gender and biological factors play critical roles in women's mental illness. The World Health Association found that women are two times more likely than men to experience depression, panic attacks, and eating disorders. Compared with men, women have a 70% greater lifetime risk of experiencing a major depressive disorder (Kessler, Chiu, Demler, & Walters, 2005).

Biological Factors Related to Mental Illness in Women

Biological differences alone can be prime factors in the development of some mental health issues (Graziottin & Serafini, 2009). Women have lower serotonin levels (Albert, 2015) than men, and they also process this chemical at slower rates, a factor that can lead to fluctuations in mood. In addition, females are more predisposed to hormonal fluctuations. Further, women with a family history of depression (genes, biological factors) may be more prone to develop depression than those whose families do not have the illness. Brain chemistry and hormones may precipitate depression in women. People with depression have different brain chemistry than people who do not have the illness. During different periods of a woman's life, her hormones may be changing, which in turn influences her brain chemistry. After giving birth, women may experience postpartum depression as a result of the levels of estrogen and progesterone hormones in her body quickly dropping. The hormonal change involved in menopause may increase a woman's risk for depression as well (NIMH, 2016).

Sex Roles and Sexualization

From a cultural perspective, American women have historically been the subordinate gender whose primary roles have been as nurturers and caregivers for children and the elderly (Dedovic, D'Aguiar, & Pruessner, 2009). A great deal of stress is placed on women who attempt to work a full-time job outside the home and come home to assume traditional nurturing, caretaking, and homemaking (cooking, cleaning, and so forth). Mental health issues develop in women when they feel overwhelmed and overburdened by their responsibilities at work and at home. The stress that women feel as a result of trying to assume their traditional homemaking and career roles can lead to depression and panic attacks.

As mentioned earlier, women tend to be concentrated in low-status pink-collar occupations. Such jobs are not only poorly paid; they also often involve chronic stress and provide few decision-making opportunities (Bonde, 2008; Verboom et al., 2011). The stress of working in such an occupation can be an aggravating factor in mental illness.

Moreover, the sexualization of women has also been associated with the development of negative self-images and mental health problems. Many women try to develop thin bodies to look like the models and actresses featured in the media. According to the American Psychological Association (2007), the negative sexualization of females can cause problems with their healthy development of self-esteem and self-image. Unhealthy bodily self-images can lead to shame, depression, anxiety, and stress.

Another message from society and the media is that a relationship with a man is essential for a woman's fulfillment in life. Women who internalize this message tend to blame themselves when relationships end with men. They may attempt to preserve a relationship with a male, even though their needs are not being met.

Intimate Partner Violence and Sexual Abuse

Women may experience mental disorders because of violence and sexual abuse (Chen et al., 2010; Vigod & Stewart, 2009). A new national study revealed that although 44% of women experience domestic violence, 76% say they have never been asked about domestic violence during a medical exam (Family and Youth Services Bureau, 2016).

National data from the Centers for Disease Control and Prevention (2017) have revealed some startling statistics:

Cultural Reflections

Domestic violence is a major mental health issue in the United States.

Why do you think that women and some men stay in abusive relationships where they are hurt physically?

How would you rate your ability to counsel a woman who is in a physically abusive environment?

Are you familiar with the reporting requirements for domestic violence when children are abused?

- Nearly 1 in 4 adult women and approximately 1 in 7 adult men report having experienced severe physical violence from an intimate partner in their lifetime.

- 16% of women and 7% of men have experienced contact sexual violence from an intimate partner (this includes rape, being made to penetrate someone else, sexual coercion, and/or unwanted sexual contact).

- 10% of women and 2% of men report having been stalked by an intimate partner.

On average, 24 people per minute are victims of rape, physical violence or stalking by an intimate partner in the United States—more than 12 million women and men over the course of a year (Truman & Rand, 2010).

Women's Strengths

Despite the problems presented up to this point in this chapter, women also exhibit considerable strengths in many areas. According to Susan Nolen-Hoeksema and R. L. Atkinson (2009), women have mental strengths that help them to find creative solutions to problems and focus on getting things done, instead of doing things their way. Women have a strong sense of identity that helps them deal with change and uncertainty quite well. Women's emotional and relational strengths allow them to create strong social networks that support them during times of crisis.

Women have a number of strengths that have been recognized by the broad American public. They are good communicators. Women have strong affiliative qualities such as being able to form strong relationships and displaying sensitivity toward the situations of others.

Writing in *Forbes* magazine, Glenn Llopis (2011) asserted that women have four critical skills to offer corporations. First, women are opportunity experts. They see opportunity in everything. Second, women are networking professionals. Third, they are relationship specialists; they cultivate relationships that are purposeful, genuine, and meaningful. They facilitate connections between people. Fourth, women are natural givers and socially conscious leaders.

Cultural Reflections

Think about the important women in your life. What strengths do they have?

What strengths does your mother have that you admire?

How have your mother's strengths been beneficial to your life?

COUNSELING APPROACHES FOR WOMEN: FEMINIST THERAPY

Feminist therapy is a school of thought that combines elements of the social constructivist and social justice movements. It emphasizes both psychological and sociological factors that have an impact on the development and mental health of clients (Enns, 1993, 2004). Feminist therapy is concerned with the different ways in which women and men develop throughout the life span. Feminist therapists focus on helping women and men understand the influence of gender roles and power differentials on families and on a given society.

There is no one major feminist therapeutic approach. There are, however, a number of key figures in feminist therapy, including Mary Ballou, Sandra Bem, Laura Brown, Bonnie Burstow, Lillian Comas-Díaz, Carolyn Enns, Oliva Espín, Carol Gilligan, Jean Baker Miller, Pam Remer, and Judith Worrell.

Feminist therapy grew out of the women's movement during the 1970s. The movement has had a profound impact on psychology and on the helping professions, as it shed light on the common experiences and problems associated with the social roles that women were made to endure. During the 1970s, Phyllis Chesler (1972) asserted that the traditional therapeutic relationship was patriarchal, arguing that women were often misdiagnosed in therapy because they did not conform to male therapists' gender role stereotypes. Female clients received higher rates of depressive diagnoses, and they were hospitalized more frequently than were men. In her book, *Women and Madness* (1972), Chesler gave many examples of **sexism** in therapy. Some 20 years later, she wrote an article (Chesler, 1997) stating that much progress had been made with women clients in therapy.

In the 1970s, a great deal of research was conducted on gender bias and on organizational development with an emphasis on women within the field of psychology. During this decade, the Association for Women in Psychology and the American Psychological Association's (APA) Division 35, Society for the Psychology of Women, were created. Several organizations, including the APA, established nonsexist guidelines for publication and for treatment of women clients (Enns, 1993).

During the 1980s, the profession made a concerted effort to define feminist therapy. Individual therapy was the most frequent modality used in working with women. Feminist therapists began to criticize the traditional systems of psychotherapy. They challenged the intrapsychic focus in psychotherapy. The overrepresentation of women within certain diagnostic categories, such as depression and eating disorders, was another major issue addressed. Feminists also began to examine issues related to body image, abusive relationships, eating disorders, and sexual abuse (Enns, 1993, 2004).

Four Main Philosophies of Feminists

By the end of the 1980s, the feminist movement had changed considerably, and so had the feminist philosophies that guided the practice of therapy. Researchers have identified four major feminist philosophies, which are sometimes termed the "second wave" of **feminism**. These philosophical positions are (1) liberal feminism, (2) cultural feminism, (3) radical feminism, and (4) socialist feminism. These philosophic views overlap; however, a point of commonality is their focus on equality.

Liberal feminism emphasizes helping individual women to transcend the limits of their gender socialization patterns. Individuals in this philosophical category contend that women deserve equality with men because they have the same abilities as men. The major goals of liberal feminist therapy are personal empowerment, dignity, self-fulfillment, and equality.

Cultural feminism asserts that oppression originates from society's devaluation of women's strengths. Feminists in this group stress the differences between women and men and contend that the society would benefit from the feminization of the culture so that it becomes more nurturing, intuitive, cooperative, and relational (Herlihy & Corey, 2005).

Radical feminism emphasizes that women are oppressed in patriarchal societies. Their goal is to change society by activism. Radical feminist therapists conceptualize therapy as a political enterprise. They identify the ways in which patriarchy dominates a person's everyday life, including household chores, paid employment, violence, and parenting (Herlihy & Corey, 2005).

Enns (2004) has made a distinction between radical and liberal feminist therapy. According to her, nonsexist therapy does not focus on social change, anger, or power issues but focuses on the therapist's awareness of his or her own values and on an egalitarian approach when working with female clients. In contrast, radical feminist therapists emphasize the political nature of the client and the role of social institutions. Radical feminists become involved in changing social issues, while liberal feminist therapists may or may not do so. Radical feminist therapists state that men should not be feminist therapists because they cannot serve as role models for women. Men can, however, be pro-feminist. Currently, feminist therapists accept men as clients.

Socialist feminism shares with radical feminism the goal of change in institutional and social relationships. Instead of focusing just on gender, however, socialist feminists emphasize multiple oppressions in a woman's life. The major goal is to change social relationships and institutions.

Cultural Reflections

To what extent do you believe feminist therapy is relevant to your life and to your clients' lives?

Have the issues of sexism in society largely been resolved or not resolved?

Since the 1980s, feminist women of color and postmodern feminists have challenged the underlying assumptions of traditional theories of psychotherapy. **Postmodern feminism** constitutes the "third wave" of feminist therapy. Postmodern feminists offer a framework for comparing and contrasting traditional therapies with feminist therapy. Several trends in postmodern feminism include an increasing role for women of color; an inclusion of lesbian feminists, who share many commonalities with radical feminists; and global international feminists who maintain that women throughout the world live under oppression.

Rationale for a Specialization in Therapy for Women

Taking a historical view of the decades and generations before the existence of a specialization in a therapeutic approach for women, several factors emerge as contributing to its development. First, two epidemiological surveys of community samples (Brown, 1992, 1994) sponsored by NIMH showed that a high proportion of people with signs of depression, anxiety, panic, simple phobia, and agoraphobia were women. These surveys also revealed that women had a higher utilization rate than men for health and community mental health agencies. Moreover, women were prescribed a disproportionate share of psychoactive drugs that had deleterious or unknown side effects (Brown, 1994, 2000). There was also concern about the increasing medicalization of women's psychological problems, including issues of diagnosis and prescriptive drugs (Worell & Remer, 2003).

DISSATISFACTION WITH EXISTING PSYCHOLOGICAL THEORIES

As early as the 1970s, feminists who were dissatisfied with existing theories, the psychological knowledge base, and the treatment approaches motivated a call for change (Worell & Remer, 2003). Discussion groups among women led to their awareness that the personal problems of individual women were rooted in their subordinate status in their families and society. These *consciousness-raising groups* were instrumental in the demand for an end to the sexist and oppressive social structures that characterized a male-dominated society (Enns, 2004).

There was unhappiness with traditional theories of female and male development that depicted stereotypical male traits as the norm and females as deficient because they differed from such norms. In addition, there was frustration with the continuing omission of women from the knowledge base of psychology (Brown, 2000). Women questioned the relevance of the existing therapy theories because they all located the problem within the mind of the woman (intrapsychic) instead of within broad societal injustices. Feminists argued that women's problems originated from external rather than internal sources. They demanded greater representation in the APA.

DISSATISFACTION WITH DIAGNOSTIC CATEGORIES AND MOTHER BLAMING

Feminists claimed that mainstream, male-dominated psychological theories and treatment engaged in "mother-blaming" for a host of disorders in children (Caplan & Hall-McCorquodale, 1985). In 1989, Paula J. Caplan wrote *Don't Blame Mother*, which focused on the difficult relationships between mothers and daughters.

Ballou and West (2000) have discussed a number of ways that gender issues and sexism are entrenched in therapy and psychotherapy. As recently as the 1980s, most therapists were White males. Women's responses to inequitable power struggles were often viewed as aberrations and as failures to fulfill a proper adult role. It was not so much that women were more insane than men; instead, it was a case that men had the naming power. They could label a woman as hysterical if she seemed emotional. Male therapists rarely took into consideration the societal injustices that may have led to a woman's depression. In contrast, feminist therapists not only recognize these injustices; they also consider how gender interacts with other diversity variables such as religion, race, ethnicity, and culture. For example, Arab women may have different issues confronting them than do African American women. Gender is usually tempered with other social factors.

TRADITIONAL THEORIES VERSUS FEMINIST THERAPIES: SIX CHARACTERISTICS

Feminist therapists view the traditional therapies as being fundamentally different in outlook and in underlying assumptions than the feminist therapies. Such critics point out that most of the extant theories of psychotherapy were developed during a time that women and men were seen as having different personality characteristics. Moreover, it was believed that biological differences between males and females resulted in their different outlooks on life and work. Worell and Remer (2003) have outlined six characteristics of traditional theories that indicate obsolete ideas about gender in people's lives:

1. *Androcentric theories* use male-centered constructs to reach conclusions about human life.

2. *Gendercentric theories* articulate separate developmental paths for men and women.

3. *Ethnocentric theories* make the incorrect assumption that their view of human development and interactions is valid for all races, cultures, and countries.

4. *Heterosexist theories* conceptualize a heterosexual orientation as normative and desirable, while devaluing same-sex relationships.

5. An *intrapsychic orientation* emphasizes a client's impulses, ideas, conflicts, or other psychological phenomena that take place within his or her mind, as opposed to an interpersonal orientation, which sometimes results in blaming the victim.

6. *Determinist theories* maintain that personality patterns are fixed at an early stage of development.

KEY CONCEPTS OF FEMINIST THERAPY

View of Human Nature

Feminist therapists challenge the masculine interpretation of human behavior. Feminist approaches to human nature present an androgynous view of human nature. Feminists argue that there are few truly biological differences between men and women. Most of the differences that we come to accept are socially constructed and influenced by culture. Human nature is neither male nor female.

Sex Role Stereotypes and Androgyny

In 1974, Sandra Bem constructed the Bem Sex Role Inventory, which is one of the most widely used gender measures. Based on their responses to this instrument, individuals are categorized as having one of four gender role orientations: masculine, feminine, androgynous, or undifferentiated. A *masculine* person is high on instrumental traits (making use of people for pleasure or profit, or having an attitude about an event or outcome that depends on one's perception of how that outcome is related to the occurrence of other desirable or undesirable consequences) but low on expressive traits (showing and sharing one's emotions and feelings). A feminine individual is high on expressive traits and low on instrumental traits. *Androgyny* is a term derived from the

Cultural Reflections

What gender roles have you adopted for your life?

Are the gender roles you have adopted working or not working for you?

Greek words *andras*, meaning "man," and *gyné*, meaning "woman," and refers to the mixing of masculine and feminine characteristics, a kind of hermaphroditism. An *androgynous* individual is simply a female or male who has a high degree of both feminine (expressive) and masculine (instrumental) traits. An *undifferentiated* person is low on both feminine and masculine traits (Bem, 1974). The ideal therapist is gender neutral.

Gender Schema Therapy

Based on her work on androgyny, Sandra Bem (1981, 1993) developed gender schema theory. A *schema* is an organized set of mental associations used to interpret what one sees. Gender schema theorists examine people in terms of how likely they are to view a situation in terms of gender issues. Bem observed that children learn to apply gender schemas fairly early. For instance, girls wear nail polish, and boys do not. Boys are not supposed to cry, whereas girls can and do cry. Adults who are gender focused tend to see behaviors as unmanly or unfeminine. Gender schema is a very strong schema. Bem proposes that parents teach their children an *individual difference* approach. If one child calls another a sissy because he likes ballet, the mother might point out that both males and females engage in ballet. Clients need to become aware of their own gender schema, especially as such a schema relates to how they view themselves. What factors enter into how a person might view him- or herself as a man or a woman?

GENDER ROLE STEREOTYPING ACROSS CULTURES

Although research reveals that males and females do not differ significantly from each other on most variables, gender role ideology is rather consistent across the world, and it is patterned by cultural factors. Typically, Western and developed nations that have a higher number of educated women employed have more egalitarian beliefs than do less developed countries (Williams & Best, 1990). Despite these differences, there is remarkable agreement across cultures about what men and women are like; therefore, researchers have concluded that gender stereotyping may be universal (Berry, Poortinga, Segall, & Dasen, 1992).

Claude Steele's (2003) seminal research has demonstrated the effect of racial and gender stereotypes on a person's performance. Steele and his colleagues began investigating the underperformance of women in difficult math classes and the underperformance of African Americans in higher educational settings compared to classmates who were intellectually equal. The researchers asked the following question: If two people are equally prepared for a challenging task, what is getting in the way for those who are performing below their ability? Using a series of experiments, the researchers identified a factor they called *stereotype threat*. Stereotype threat could be "felt by anyone who cared about a performance and yet knew that any faltering at it could cause them to be reduced to a negative group stereotype" (Steele, 2003, p. 316). The researchers' subtle activation of a negative stereotype consistently resulted in the participants' decreased performance on difficult tasks.

THE SOCIAL CONSTRUCTION OF GENDER

Feminists provide distinctions between the terms *sex* and *gender*. In general, the term *sex* refers to a biological variable to distinguish between females and males (Worell & Papendrick-Remer, 2001). In contrast, the term *gender* usually refers to culturally and socially constructed beliefs and attitudes about the traits and behaviors of females and males (Worell & Papendrick-Remer, 2001).

Societies and cultures construct their own meanings about gender that represent culturally shared agreements about what behavior is appropriate for males and females. The personal characteristics typically attributed to gender are not "true" attributes of females and males but are socially constructed categories that help to maintain female–male dichotomies and dominant-group power structures.

Gendered beliefs and practices vary across cultures and differ according to who makes the observations and judgments. In any given society, gender constructions vary within and across groups in a society. For example, White women in the United States might have different concepts of womanhood and femininity than Asian women, and African American women may have gender constructions different from those of Latina women. In each of these ethnic groups, subcultures retain their own distinctive gender expectations. When the social construction of gender intersects with other social status identities, it creates a self-image of who we are as females and males and how we should behave.

Our social construction of gender intersects with other social status identities to create a self-image of who we are and how we should act. The understanding that "I am a woman" functions to activate a person's experience of femaleness in society and serves as a general framework that shapes one's actions (Bem, 1981, 1983, 1993). The cognition that "I am a Latina American woman" generates different images as each person constructs personal and social identities from the intersection of his or her culture and experience. Gender also influences the expectations and behaviors of those with whom we interact, and these expectations result in self-fulfilling prophecies. Our social construction of gender influences the socialization practices we use with children and plays a big part in the diagnosis of women's illness, in the expression of symptoms, in the treatment strategies, and in theoretical explanations.

GENDER AND POWER DIFFERENTIALS

Feminist therapy has developed from the recognition that a great deal of human suffering takes place because of the unequal distribution of power in society based on a variety of factors such as race and ethnicity, class, disability, sexual orientation, and so on. Not only have these power differentials resulted in physical assaults against individuals, but also the end product may be psychological and economical, including limited educational and professional options. Power differentials are also linked to gender role expectations. For instance, feminist therapists maintain that societal gender role expectations greatly affect a person's identity from birth onward. Such expectations become deeply ingrained in one's personality and persist throughout one's life. The practice of feminist therapy is politicized in its understanding of the causes of psychological injury. In addition, feminist therapy has influenced postmodern psychotherapy's concept of power (Enns, 2004).

Most feminist approaches to therapy share a core group of beliefs that influence therapeutic practice (Enns, 2000; Worell & Papendrick-Remer, 2001), which are presented in the box that follows.

CORE FEMINIST BELIEFS

1. Males and females develop in different ways related to language, worldview, values, and perceptions, and such differences should be taken into consideration and respected in therapy.

2. Historically, women and minorities have been marginalized, and therefore dealing with issues related to power is an integral part of the therapeutic process for those who feel powerless.

3. Political/social/cultural variables are at the core of many presenting complaints for women.

4. The current diagnostic system is biased against both nontraditional and traditional female behavior.

Sometimes women's behavior is considered maladaptive when it might not be. The *Diagnostic and Statistical Manual of Mental Disorders* (DSM-5; American Psychiatric Association, 2013) and its earlier versions were developed primarily by White male psychiatrists. This diagnostic manual focuses on psychological symptoms and not on the social factors that caused them. Some feminist therapists have acknowledged these weaknesses, but they use the *DSM-5* in working with clients and assess the cultural context of clients' problems to prevent them from being blamed for their own problems.

FEMINIST THERAPY APPROACHES

The four major approaches of feminist therapy include consciousness raising, social and gender role analysis, social activism, and the therapeutic relationship. Let us examine each of these.

Consciousness Raising

Typically, **consciousness raising** is done in small groups, discussing women's individual and shared experiences. Consciousness raising empowers individuals to participate in social action to fight oppression. Consciousness-raising groups were held very effectively during the 1970s, 1980s, and 1990s. Similar to group therapy, therapists frequently incorporate consciousness raising into their practices because it helps women understand shared experiences and makes them feel less isolated.

Social and Gender Role Analysis

In social and **gender role analysis**, the therapist helps the client to identify his or her own experiences in regard to social and gender role norms. Together, the therapist and the client analyze how implicit and explicit sex roles may have contributed to the client's problems. This helps the client explore possible origins of psychological distress. Together the therapist and the client come up with ways to bring about social change and gain self-knowledge.

Women from ethnic minority backgrounds are often doubly oppressed by ethnicity/race and gender, which affect clients' role perceptions. The "deleterious effects of sexism, racism, and elitism" (Espin, 1994, p. 272) must be dealt with in sessions. When working with clients from ethnic minority backgrounds, Comas-Díaz (1994) recommends using "ethnocultural assessment" as outlined by Comas-Díaz and Jacobsen (1991), which is a diagnostic tool used to assess a client's level of ethnocultural identity. This social and gender role analysis should then be used during therapy to help clients find solutions to their problems.

Social Activism

Social activism is a third approach that some therapists use. This approach is founded on the premise that "the personal is political" and that the client's problems originate from the structural inequalities of a given society. The feminist therapist who adopts the philosophy of social activism advocates that clients speak out, organize protests, and engage in letter-writing campaigns. Feminists maintain that social change supports the mental health of all individuals.

The Therapeutic Relationship

The therapeutic relationship is based on empowerment of clients and the equalizing of power between therapist and client. The therapeutic relationship is structured to help the client identify gender-delimiting schema. Therapists teach clients to recognize how they define themselves and how they relate to others (gender role expectations). The therapist demystifies the counseling process.

The client is treated as an equal during feminist therapy. Clients are expected to participate actively in their own therapy. They may be asked to attend workshops and to engage in reading that explicates their situation. Clients become empowered as a result of participating in the therapeutic process.

GOALS OF FEMINIST THERAPY

Feminist therapists assert that the goals of therapy should include not only changes in the client's own personal life but also changes in society's institutions. Enns (2004) has proposed five goals for feminist therapy: equality, balancing independence and interdependence, empowerment, self-nurturance, and valuing diversity. The final goal of feminist therapy is to work to eliminate sexism and oppression within the broad society (Worell & Remer, 2003).

Political awareness and social action are important objectives in feminist therapy. Feminist theoretical approaches stress the need for women to become aware of gender role stereotyping, sexism, and discrimination (Ballou & West, 2000). Women are encouraged to become involved politically in such organizations as the National Organization for Women (NOW).

Whereas traditional theories of therapy and psychotherapy place little emphasis on the ways in which power affects the mental health of clients, feminist therapy considers the analysis of power differentials to be important to the therapeutic process (Hill & Ballou, 2005). Feminist therapists avoid fostering a sense of victimology among the clients they serve. *Victimology* refers to the belief that a person is a helpless victim of his or her environmental or contextual circumstances.

Feminist therapists stress the importance of intentionally using a strengths-based approach with women and men. Brown (2000) states that women should not be assessed primarily from a pathological perspective. Feminist therapy refers clients to women's support groups, community action work, and legal aid. Clinicians should help clients to realize their strengths. Most feminist clinicians combine feminist concepts with the traditional models of therapy. Worell and Remer (2003) maintain that feminist therapists help clients to

- Become cognizant of their own gender role socialization process

- Identify their internalized messages and replace them with positive, self-enhancing messages

- Learn how sexist and oppressive societal beliefs and practices influence them in negative ways

- Develop skills needed to effect changes in the environment

- Restructure institutions to eliminate discriminatory practices

- Assess the impact of social factors on their lives

- Construct a sense of personal and social power

- Learn to trust their experience and intuition

THE ROLE OF MEN IN FEMINIST THERAPY

Men can benefit from feminist therapy. Just as women deal with gender constraints, men are also constrained by gender-related expectations, such as the demands for strength and autonomy and the belief that they should not express vulnerability, sensitivity, or empathy. Men can benefit from feminist therapy by working on these issues and by learning new relationship skills to help them understand and explore issues involved with emotions, intimacy, and self-disclosure.

Feminist therapists can and do treat male clients. Levant (2001) has pointed out that feminist therapy might be helpful for men who feel overwhelmed about society's demands for achievement and performance. Ganley (1988) has described several issues and techniques for counseling men from a feminist perspective. For instance, men might desire assistance with intimacy issues.

The jury is still out on the effectiveness of men practicing as therapists using a feminist approach. Some experts maintain that men can be effective pro-feminist therapists when they embrace the principles and incorporate the practices of feminism in their therapy (Kahn, 2010).

Cultural Reflections

How relevant is feminist therapy to your life?

What parts, if any, of feminist therapy would you incorporate into your integrative approach to psychotherapy?

TECHNIQUES OF FEMINIST THERAPY

Feminist therapists address many life issues, including—among others—family and marriage relations, reproduction, career concerns, physical and sexual abuse, body image disorders, self-esteem, and empowerment of women. According to Bohan (1992), feminist practitioners should follow six guidelines:

1. Therapists should be knowledgeable concerning gender role socialization and the impact these standards have on what it means to be a woman or a man.

2. Therapists should be cognizant of the impact of the distribution of power within the family and power differentials between men and women in terms of decision making, child-rearing, career options, and division of labor.

3. Therapists must understand the sexist context of the social system in which men and women live and its impacts on both the individual and the family.

4. Therapists must be committed to promoting roles for both women and men that are not limited by cultural or gender stereotypes.

5. Therapists must acquire intervention skills that assist clients in their gender role journey.

6. Therapists must be committed to work toward the elimination of gender role bias as a source of pathology throughout society.

These principles are based on a gender-fair ideology for counseling that may be applied to family therapists as well. Worell and Remer (2003) have described six feminist therapeutic techniques from a cognitive-behavioral framework, gender role analysis, gender role intervention, assertiveness training, power analysis, and bibliotherapy.

Gender Role Analysis

Gender role analysis is used to help clients understand the influence of gender role expectations. The first step is to have the client identify various gender role messages that she has experienced during her lifetime. Second, the counselor helps the female client to identify positive and negative consequences of gender-related messages. Third, the clinician and the client identify the statements that the client makes to herself based on these gender role messages. Fourth, the clinician and the client decide which messages they want to change. Fifth, the clinician and the client construct a plan to implement the client's desired change and to have the client follow through. As a result of identifying and analyzing gender role messages, the client starts the process of freeing herself from such messages (Enns, 2004).

Gender Role Intervention

A counselor does not go through a detailed gender role analysis but instead helps the client to understand and to deal with the impact of gender role and other social expectations on her or him (Enns, 2000). The therapist helps the client achieve insights about social role expectations. For instance, an older woman may feel that she is not qualified to obtain a job. The counselor works with the woman to understand the societal basis of such beliefs; however, the counselor keeps the focus on identifying positive worker abilities that the client possesses.

Assertiveness Training

Feminist therapists sometimes recommend assertiveness training for their clients. Therapists believe that teaching assertiveness skills helps to reduce a sense of helplessness and depression among clients. Assertiveness training teaches people how to stand up for themselves without violating the rights of others. It stands in contrast to aggressiveness, which entails insisting on one's rights without consideration for the rights of others.

Power Analysis

Throughout much of history, especially American history, White men have exercised more power than women in making and enforcing decisions about family life, work, laws, and interpersonal relationships. Worell and Remer (2003) assert that therapists can help women clients to make changes when their lack of power has prevented change in the past. The first step in **power analysis** is to have the client provide a definition that fits for her and to apply it to different kinds of power (Enns, 2004). For instance, if a woman wants the power to express herself to her partner without being interrupted, she and the therapist examine ways for her to demonstrate communication power in her relationship with her partner. Second, the therapist and the client discuss differential access to power—legal, financial, and interpersonal. Third, the therapist and client discuss different ways power can be used to bring about the desired change. Fourth, clients reexamine the gender role messages they have been raised with that deal with power. Finally, the client and counselor develop power strategies to be used to obtain change.

Bibliotherapy

Bibliotherapy is the practice of therapy through books and reading. A therapist might refer clients to nonfiction books, autobiographies, self-help books, and movies. For instance, a therapist might give a reading assignment for a woman who is very concerned about her weight or body image. She might recommend reading some medical summaries related to weight gain or loss, as well as autobiographies of women who successfully dealt with their weight issues. In addition, therapists give clients reading assignments that address such issues as coping skills, gender role stereotypes, power differentials between men and women, gender inequality, and society's obsession with thinness. Reading assignments may serve to bridge cultural gaps between the client and therapist.

Relational-Cultural Theory: The New Feminist Psychotherapeutic Approach

Feminist therapy is still in the process of developing. **Relational-cultural theory (RCT)** is the most current form of feminist therapy. Comstock, Hammer, et al. (2008) trace the history of relational-cultural theory to Jean Baker Miller's (1986) book, *Toward a New Psychology of Women*. In that book, Miller noted the centrality of relationships in women's lives, while the traditional, male-dominated models of psychotherapy emphasized individuation, separation, and autonomy as markers of emotional maturity and psychological health (Comstock, Hammer, et al., 2008). She suggested that mental health professionals' lack of understanding of the contextual and relational experiences of women, people of color, and marginalized men has led to their devaluing important factors that contributed to such clients' psychological well-being.

RCT identifies how certain challenges impede individuals' ability to create, sustain, and engage in relationships in therapy and life and examines relational competencies over the life span. It complements the social justice movement by providing an alternative theoretical framework for mental health professionals to explore how these issues influence the mental health and development of all people.

The RCT approach to therapy is founded on the idea that healing takes place within the context of mutually empathic, growth-fostering relationships. It identifies and deconstructs obstacles to mutuality that individuals encounter in diverse relational contexts and networks (Comstock, 2005; Comstock & Qin, 2005). Although people may want a connection with others, they often develop an entire repertoire of behavior that alienates them from such connections. For instance,

Cultural Reflections

To what extent, if any, does relational-cultural theory add to feminist theory in psychotherapy?

instead of loving others, they withhold love and affection. They withdraw from others and criticize loved ones (Comstock, 2005). Negative interpersonal strategies keep individuals out of relationships and contribute to their maladjustment in living.

RCT therapists contend that the manner in which people navigate through their lifelong relational changes affects their mental health significantly. Comstock, Duffey, and St. George (2002) have asserted,

according to this model, understanding one's relational capacities in a sociocultural context allows one to move out of a place of shame and frustration and into the possibility for more mutually empathic and authentic connections (Hartling et al., 2000; Walker, 2001). As such, the relational model can be used with both women and men from diverse backgrounds and in therapy settings that address a multitude of issues (Jordan & Dooley, 2000). (p. 256)

RCT is based on the belief that the experiences of isolation, shame, humiliation, oppression, and marginalization are relational violations and traumas that are at the heart of human suffering (Comstock, Hammer, et al., 2008). The theory asserts that therapy that is not founded on relational, multicultural, or social justice ideology has the potential to perpetuate oppression. The core RCT principles, provided in Table 14.1, highlight the process of psychological growth and relational development.

FEMINIST THERAPY AND MULTICULTURAL THERAPY

Feminist therapists and multiculturalists have had a long working relationship. Although at times multiculturalists have accused feminists of being insensitive to the issue of race (Ivey, D'Andrea, Ivey, & Simek-Morgan, 2007), feminism and multiculturalism share more similarities than differences. For instance, both perspectives are social constructivist in orientation. Both approaches place a high priority on examining the impact of societal and cultural factors on their clients' lives. For instance, both theoretical frameworks give a place of importance to external forces such as power and dominance. Both feminist therapy and multicultural therapy have focused attention on the negative effects of discrimination and oppression. In addition, culturally competent feminist therapists search for ways to work within clients' cultures. Many of

TABLE 14.1 ■ Relational-Cultural Theory Principles	
1.	Throughout their life spans, people grow through and move toward relationships.
2.	Mature functioning is marked by movement toward mutuality rather than separation.
3.	Psychological growth is characterized by a person's ability to participate in increasingly complex and diversified relational networks.
4.	Mutual empathy and mutual empowerment are at the core of growth-fostering relationships.
5.	Authenticity is required for real engagement in growth-fostering relationships.
6.	People grow as they contribute to the development of growth-fostering relationships.
7.	The goal of development is an individual's realization of increased relational competence over the life span.

the techniques feminists have developed can easily be modified to work with a variety of ethnic and cultural groups. In recent years, these two approaches have worked on developing linkages between them. Both schools have called attention to the fact that therapy theories should be gender fair, multicultural in orientation, and life span oriented.

Contributions and Criticisms of Feminist Therapy

Feminist therapists have made a major contribution to therapy and psychotherapy by leading the way for gender-sensitive practice. Another noteworthy contribution is that feminist therapists have increased public awareness of the impact of culture and multiple oppressions on people. They have also helped the therapy field to understand how important it is to become aware of the gender role messages under which therapists and clients have been raised. Feminist therapists should be credited with helping the world to understand power relationships in families and between men and women.

Another contribution of feminist therapists is that they have been an important voice in questioning the traditional therapy theories. Most therapy theories put the cause of problems within the individual rather than within the external circumstances that exist in the environment or the society. Feminist therapists examine clients' problems in terms of the social context in which they live, and they have advocated an egalitarian relationship between the therapist and the client. They have worked to establish policies that reduce discrimination involving gender, race, culture, sexual orientation, and age. Feminist therapists have also demanded action in cases of sexual misconduct when male therapists abused the trust of female clients.

One criticism of feminist therapy is that instead of taking a neutral stance, therapists may strongly advocate a certain way of looking at gender roles and appropriate behavior for men and women, such that they interfere with their clients' autonomy. The therapist's task should be to provide support and information to challenge the client to choose for herself which road to take, not to convince the client to adopt certain attitudes or beliefs.

Other critics maintain that feminism originated and was developed by middle-class, White women who were overly represented in the lesbian tradition. As such, feminists have excluded other races and cultures in developing their theoretical approach. Recently, however, there has been a concerted effort to include women from other cultures and ethnic groups, and feminists have become much more inclusive.

INTEGRATION OF FEMINIST THERAPY WITH OTHER APPROACHES

There is a high potential for integrating feminist therapy principles with other therapeutic practices. Worell and Remer (2003) have indicated that before a theory of psychotherapy can be integrated with feminist therapy, feminists should look for sources of bias in the theory by analyzing its historical development, its key theoretical concepts, the use of sexist language, and bias in diagnosis and therapeutic techniques. They can work to eliminate sexist features of the theory to see whether the theory is compatible with feminist principles. That some principles of feminist therapy, such as gender equality, can be incorporated into other therapies is a strength because it can broaden the theoretical base of other models and therapies.

Feminist therapy has been integrated with behavior and cognitive therapy. To make cognitive and behavior therapies more consistent with feminist therapy, Worell and Remer (2003) have recommended changing diagnostic labels that emphasize the pathology of people, focusing on feelings and integrating concepts from gender role socialization. Enns (1987) has recommended that through Gestalt emphasis on awareness and self and choices, women may expand their options in the world. The Gestalt emphasis on taking responsibility may not take into consideration the social and economic factors that also influence clients' choices—issues that are an important part of feminist therapy.

CASE VIGNETTE 14.1
CASE ANALYSIS USING THE STRENGTHS-BASED THERAPY MODEL: MCINTOSH FAMILY

A brief case study is provided for the reader's own analysis. How would you use a strengths approach in working with Jennifer and her family? What, if any, strengths do you see in Jennifer, and in the family? How might these strengths be used in strengths-based family therapy?

The Case of the McIntosh Family

Jennifer is a 47-year-old White female. She and her husband Robert and son Jason have come to therapy because the "family is falling apart" and because Jennifer has filed for divorce. The family has come to counseling because they want to explore whether their marriage and family can be saved. Jennifer is depressed and has low self-esteem. Jennifer claims that her husband, Robert, is having an affair with a member of her church. In reaction to this situation, Jennifer has moved all her belongings into a tiny room of the house because she refuses to sleep with her husband. She has stated that she feels she is a prisoner in her own home because she lives in this tiny room that is just a little larger than a closet, while her husband lives in their large master bedroom and comes and goes whenever he wants.

Lately, Robert has been coming into the house at 2 and 3 in the morning. He eats, sleeps, works, and goes out bike riding with Cindy, who he claims is only a friend. Cindy broke up with her husband last year. Robert says that he has been trying to help her through this difficult period. Jennifer has given him an ultimatum to give up Cindy and stop coming in at all hours or else. Robert has said that he does not want a divorce, but he still goes out on bike rides with Cindy.

Jennifer is the third youngest in a family of four siblings. Her ethnic background is Italian American mixed with Irish. Her father is Irish and her mother Italian. She came from a working-class to middle-class background. For most of her life, Jennifer established a fairly close relationship with her mother. She calls her daily to see about her father (who is seriously ill) and just to check in and let her mother know what's happening between her and Robert. Jennifer is athletic; she swims and goes rafting when she can. Despite her athleticism, she is about 40 pounds overweight—about 5' 9" and 210 pounds. She loves to cook. Jennifer works as a marketing specialist at a major advertising firm.

Jennifer and her husband have one child, a 16-year-old, Jason, who has a speech impediment and who has been performing below his tested ability in school for the past several years. The couple has placed him in a private school for boys, hoping that he will focus on his academic work. Jason is distant from both parents, feeling that he cannot communicate with either; however, he gets along better with his father, even though his mother takes him on camping trips that he really enjoys, and his father spends comparatively little time with him.

This is Robert's second marriage, the first one having ended in divorce. Robert suddenly stated that he no longer felt fulfilled in the marriage after three children, one of whom was adopted. Robert is a sheriff with the highway patrol for the county. He is older (55) than Jennifer, and he is considering retiring within the next 2 years. Robert's father was an alcoholic who died a couple of years ago. His mother died a year before her husband's death. Robert is an only child who, at times, states in a matter-of-fact kind of way that he had to take care of his parents rather than the other way around. If you looked at Robert, you might guess that he was involved in law enforcement. He wears his hair in a short crew cut, and he seems to enjoy giving orders to others, including Jennifer. Although Jennifer would be the last to admit it, she's a little afraid of Robert because he has a gun—his sheriff revolver. She covers up her hidden fear of Robert by saying that she doesn't want to make him angry because he might be thinking about their argument and not be alert on the job.

Jennifer is secretly hoping that the therapist will help Robert see his mistakes and give up meeting with Cindy so that the two of them can go back to being a family again. She wants to know if she should proceed with the divorce and what, if anything, she could do to put her family back together again. According to Jennifer, Robert blames her for the present poor state of their marriage. He claims that she is overly dependent on him and that he has difficulty confiding in her and feeling as if he wants to protect her. Previously, the couple did have a mutually satisfying sex life, although they had begun to engage in sexual behavior less and less during the past year. Jennifer said she is losing all that is meaningful to her: her father (who is quite ill), job, husband, and marriage. She is unsure what steps to take to protect herself financially. She does not know how to reach out to Jason or what to say to him. Robert has agreed to attend two therapy sessions with Jennifer and Jason. He wants to feel that he did put some effort into saving his marriage.

Case Discussion of the McIntosh Family

The strengths-based therapist spent much of the first session trying to get to know the McIntosh family as a family and the intricate set of relationships that had been formed among the three family members. After listening to the family's story and Jennifer's plea to help save the marriage, the therapist asked each member two questions: In their opinion, was the family worth saving? Was the marriage worth saving? If the family were worth saving, could they elaborate on this point?

Robert, Jennifer, and Jason all agreed that the family was worth saving. They were less certain about whether the marriage could be saved. In an effort to get at the heart of why the family was worth saving, the therapist asked each member what were some of the strengths of their family. Some of the responses were "We tend to get things done when we work together." "We go to church together, and church is important to each one of us." The family was well provided for because both Jennifer and Robert worked. It wasn't clear what would happen if they got a divorce. Would Jason still be able to go to his private school? Finally, Jason mentioned that they all cared about each other.

Robert became uncomfortable at Jason's declaration that the family members loved each other, and he shifted in his chair, looked down at the floor, and then looked out the window. Jennifer picked up on Robert's discomfort about his loving her, and she confronted him with her suspicions. Robert responded that if she were going to start accusing him again about Cindy, he was leaving the session. Power was in Robert's hands. Jennifer had given him that power over her emotions and feelings. If Robert did not love her, she felt worthless.

The session ended with all members of the family agreeing that the family had strengths and should be saved because of Jason; however, there was less consensus about saving the marriage. Jennifer and Jason wanted to save the marriage. Robert was less enthusiastic about saving it. At the end of the therapy session, Robert said to Jennifer, "I guess we didn't mess up with everything. We did some things right. We've got family strengths. How about that?"

Robert did not show up for the second session as he had indicated he would. Only Jennifer and Jason were present. The therapist continued to emphasize both individual and family strengths. Jennifer was asked to describe some of the strengths that she saw in Jason and vice versa. They were given a two-word statement, "I appreciate . . . ," and then they were to tell each other what they appreciated about each other. Jason's relationship toward his mother softened. He asked, "Why didn't you ever tell me that you appreciated the way I come home on time and straighten the house? I wasn't even sure that you really noticed at all. You never said anything to me about it. The only time that you said anything was when I didn't clean up the kitchen."

"I'm sorry, Jason," Jennifer said, recognizing the hurt and anger in his voice. "You take me for granted, too. Last week, I had my hair cut, and no one said one thing to me. I got better responses from people who barely even know me. To my own family, I am . . . invisible. I'm this person who gets up in the morning and cooks and works all day and then comes home to cook and clean, but that's about all I am."

At the heart of Jason's and his mother's relationship were hurt feelings, anger, and the feeling that they were taken for granted. Both Jason and Jennifer completed Let Go cards—things that they would like to let go of in their relationship with each other. They wanted to let go of not being appreciated, being taken for granted, angry words, and a relationship that had grown strained. A good part of the second session was spent reestablishing a loving relationship between Jason and his mother. Their relationship grew more positive as Jennifer began to learn more about what mattered to Jason, and as she learned about some of the nonacademic strengths that he was demonstrating at school.

By the third session, Jason said that he could not miss any more of basketball practice, and he asked to be excused from attending therapy sessions. Quite a bit had been accomplished in improving the relationship between him and his mother. Robert had moved out of the house into his own small apartment, which had the effect of "releasing" Jennifer from the small room she had moved into. Jennifer decided to come in to work on what her life was going to be like without Robert. She wanted to be tested to discover her strengths. The therapist gave her the CliftonStrengths and VIA Virtues and Character Strengths assessments. Jennifer and the therapist discussed what she would like to let go of and to let in. Although she still loved Robert, she decided that she would have to let go of his being her husband. Cindy had won him over, and he spent most of his nonwork time with her.

Jennifer had to begin to think about the people she wanted to let in to become a part of her life. She joined several organizations for professional women that held seminars on different topics. She became more involved in her church, and she made a concerted effort to have dinner with Jason at least three nights a week—those nights when he did not have basketball practice. She and Jason experienced greater harmony as they spent more time listening to each other and talking about their feelings and what mattered to them. Gradually, Jennifer and her therapist developed a strengths-based treatment plan that had goals and a preferred future for her.

Jennifer's self-esteem increased as she became more aware of her strengths and how to apply or capitalize on them. Her meetings with other women who were going through similar experiences also helped her to let go of Robert, whom she eventually divorced.

(Continued)

(Continued)

Jennifer is happier now that she is divorced, and she has begun dating—nothing serious, dinner and a movie here and there. Her self-esteem is no longer dependent on how Robert treats her. She has forgiven Robert, and she is grateful that she found the strength to let him go and to move on with her life. Jason has continued to live with his mother, and he is preparing to go to college next year. Although he has a mainly positive relationship with his father, sometimes he says that he feels betrayed by him. Cindy's son is one of his close friends, and when he is with his father, Cindy, and his friend, he feels as if he is being disloyal to his mother—even though she has reassured him that it's okay for him to be around his dad and Cindy. Both Jennifer and Robert have continued to function as a family for Jason. They both helped him to select colleges for sending applications for admission. What died was the marriage between Jennifer and Robert, not their family for Jason.

SUMMARY OF KEY POINTS

It is important that both female and male clinicians assess themselves to identify any sexist beliefs, attitudes, and behaviors they may have. Clinicians should gain knowledge about the similarities and differences in the biological development of mental disorders in men and in women. There are both sex and gender differences between men and women that influence their mental health and/or substance use disorders. Moreover, clinicians need to become knowledgeable and to develop skills for dealing with trauma in women's lives. Women clients should be encouraged to recognize their unique strengths.

1. Clinicians should understand relational approaches in working with women and girls. They should gain knowledge about the relational context of the lives of women and girls, including the role of positive, nurturing relationships.

2. Women and girls may decide to express their gender roles in a variety of ways. Some may decide to enact traditional gender roles, while others may decide to act in nontraditional ways.

3. It is important that clinicians recognize that being female means there is an increased likelihood of intimate partner violence—that women and girls are significantly more likely to be victimized by someone they know and love, rather than by a stranger.

4. The clinician should be able to identify and respond to a client's trauma disclosures and to react appropriately when such disclosures are made, including making referrals when necessary.

5. Young girls should be encouraged to take math and science courses and to consider nontraditional careers in order to earn more money.

6. Clinicians should help women and girl clients to understand how society's sexualization of them may influence their self-esteem and sense of self-worth.

7. Clinicians should help women and girl clients learn about gender stereotypes and how such stereotypes may impact their lives.

8. Clinicians should help educate women and girls about potential gender/power dynamics in intimate partner relationships that could pose a risk of trauma or abuse.

9. Clinicians should work with women and girls to develop their self-esteem and self-efficacy so that they come to believe that they are deserving of mutual, positive, and supportive relationships.

10. Clinicians should help women and girl clients become aware of the signs of depression, including postpartum depression.

11. Clinicians should assess or screen for eating disorders, malnutrition, and other conditions.

DISCUSSION QUESTIONS

Discussion Question Set 1

In groups of three or four, discuss what you feel are the three most significant contributions feminist therapy has made in the counseling or treatment of women in psychotherapy.

Discussion Question Set 2

Do you believe that gender role analysis and power role relationship examinations should be a part of counseling women? Explain your answer. Is feminist therapy primarily for women, or is it appropriate also for men? Explain your answer.

KEY TERMS

Consciousness raising: Women in groups examine how oppression and socialization contribute to their personal distress and dysfunction. Consciousness raising helps women feel empowered to take steps against oppression by participating in social action.

Cultural feminism: Asserts that oppression originates from society's devaluation of women's strengths.

Feminism: A philosophical position endorsed by women that is designed to achieve gender equality and that advocates for women's equal rights involving economic, social, political, and marital issues.

Feminist therapy: An eclectic counseling approach that is based in feminist political analyses and feminist scholarship on the psychology of women and gender. It involves consciousness raising, gender role analysis, and resocialization of women and men.

Gender role analysis: The therapist helps the client to identify his or her own experiences in regard to social and gender role norms. Together, the therapist and the client analyze how implicit and explicit sex roles may have contributed to the client's problems.

Liberal feminism: Emphasizes helping individual women to transcend the limits of their gender socialization patterns.

Postmodern feminism: Constitutes the "third wave" of feminist therapy and offers a framework for comparing and contrasting traditional therapies with feminist therapy.

Power analysis: A technique in which therapists help their clients understand the type of power they want to have, the barriers to having that power, and steps to harness said power to bring about change.

Radical feminism: Emphasizes that women are oppressed in patriarchal societies.

Relational cultural theory (RCT): A type of therapy developed from the early work of Jean Baker Miller, MD, exploring the importance of dominance and subordination in human relationships and reframing the psychology of women as a psychology centered in relationships.

Sexism: The inequality and unfair treatment of women in American society and throughout the world.

Socialist feminism: Shares with radical feminism the goal of change in institutional and social relationships. Instead of focusing just on gender, however, socialist feminists emphasize multiple oppressions in a woman's life. The major goal is to change social relationships and institutions.

REFERENCES AND SUGGESTED READING

Albert, P. R. (2015). Why is depression more prevalent in women? *Journal of Psychiatry & Neuroscience, 40*(4), 219–221.

American Psychiatric Association. (2013). *Diagnostic and statistical manual of mental disorders* (5th ed.). Washington, DC: Author.

American Psychological Association. (2007). Guidelines for the psychological practice with girls and women. *American Psychologist, 62,* 949–979.

American Psychological Association. (2018). Fact sheet: Women & socioeconomic status. Retrieved from http://www.apa.org/pi/ses/resources/publications/women.aspx

Andrade, P., Noblesse, L. H., Temel, Y., Ackermans, L., Lim, L. W., Steinbusch, H. W., & Visser-Vandewalle, V. (2010). Neurostimulatory and ablative treatment options in major depressive disorder: A systematic review. *Acta Neurochirugia, 152,* 565–577.

Anthony, S. B. (1874). Declaration of the rights of women of the United States. *National Women Suffrage Association.* Retrieved from http://ecssba.rutgers.edu/docs/decl.html

Ballou, M., & West, C. (2000). Feminist therapy approaches. In M. Biaggio & M. Hersen (Eds.), *Issues in the psychology of women* (pp. 273–297). New York, NY: Kluwer Academic/Plenum.

Bem, S. L. (1974). The measurement of psychological androgyny. *Journal of Consulting and Clinical Psychology, 42,* 155–162.

Bem, S. L. (1981). Gender schema theory and its implications for child development. *Signs, 8,* 598–616.

Bem, S. L. (1983). Gender schema theory and its implications for child development: Raising gender-aschematic children in a gender-schematic society. *Signs, 8*(4), 598–616. http://dx.doi.org/10.1086/493998

Bem, S. L. (1993). *The lenses of gender.* New Haven, CT: Yale University Press.

Berry, J. W., Poortinga, Y. H., Segall, M. H., & Dasen, P. R. (1992). *Cross-cultural psychology: Research and applications.* New York, NY: Cambridge University Press.

Bohan, J. S. (1992). *Replacing women in psychology: Readings toward a more inclusive history.* Dubuque, IA: Kendall Hunt.

Bonde, J. P. (2008). Psychosocial factors at work and risk of depression: A systematic review of the epidemiological evidence. *Occupational and Environmental Medicine, 65,* 439–445.

Brown, L. S. (1992). A feminist critique of the personality disorders. In L. S. Brown & M. Ballou (Eds.), *Personality and psychopathology: Feminist reappraisals* (pp. 206–228). New York, NY: Guilford Press.

Brown, L. S. (1994). *Subversive dialogues: Theory in feminist therapy.* New York, NY: Basic Books.

Brown, L. S. (2000). Discomforts of the powerless: Feminist constructions of distress. In R. Neimeyer & J. Raskins (Eds.), *Constructions of disorder* (pp. 287–308). Washington, DC: American Psychological Association.

Caplan, P. J. (1989). *Don't blame mother.* New York, NY: Harper & Row.

Caplan, P. J., & Hall-McCorquodale, I. (1985). Mother-blaming in major clinical journals. *American Journal of Orthopsychiatry, 55,* 345–353. Retrieved from http://onlinelibrary.wiley.com/doi/10.1111/j.1939-0025.1985.tb03449.x/full

Cawthorne, A. (2008, October 8). The straight facts on women in poverty. *Center for American Progress.* Retrieved from http://www.americanprogress.org/issues/women/report/2008/10/08/5103/the-straight-facts-on-women-in-poverty/

Centers for Disease Control and Prevention. (2017). Preventing intimate partner violence: Fact sheet. *National Center for Injury Prevention and Control, Division of Violence Prevention.* Retrieved from https://www.cdc.gov/ViolencePrevention/pdf/IPV-FactSheet.pdf

Chen, L. P., Murad, M. H., Paras, M. L., Colbenson, K. M., Sattler, A. L., Goranson, E. N., . . . Zirakzadeh, A. (2010). Sexual abuse and lifetime diagnosis of psychiatric disorders: Systematic review and meta-analysis. *Mayo Clinic Proceedings, 85*(7), 618–629.

Chesler, P. (1972). *Women and madness.* New York, NY: Doubleday.

Chesler, P. (1997, November/December). Women and madness: A feminist diagnosis. *Ms.,* pp. 36–42.

Clinton, H. (1995, September 5). *Women's rights are human rights.* Speech, Beijing. Retrieved from https://kr.usembassy.gov/education-culture/infopedia-usa/famous-speeches/hillary-rodham-clinton-womens-rights-human-rights/

Comas-Díaz, L. (1994). *Women of color: Integrating ethnic and gender identities in psychotherapy.* New York, NY: Guilford Press.

Comas-Díaz, L., & Jacobsen, F. M. (1991). Ethnocultural transference and countertransference in the therapeutic dyad. *American Journal of Orthopsychiatry, 61,* 392–402.

Comstock, D. L. (Ed.). (2005). *Diversity and development: Critical contexts that shape our lives and relationships.* Belmont, CA: Brooks/Cole-Thomas Learning.

Comstock, D. L., Duffey, T. H., & St. George, H. (2002). The relational cultural model: A framework for group process. *Journal for Specialists in Group Work, 23,* 254–272.

Comstock, D. L., Hammer, T. R., Strentzsch, J., Cannon, K., Parsons, J., & Salazar, G. H. (2008). Relational-cultural theory: A framework for bridging relational, multicultural, and social justice competencies. *Journal of Therapy and Development.* Retrieved from http://www.highbeam.com/doc/1g1-1800000861154

Comstock, D. L., & Qin, D. (2005). Relational-cultural theory: A framework for relational development across the lifespan. In D. L. Comstock (Ed.), *Diversity and development: Critical contexts that shape our lives and relationships* (pp. 25–46). Belmont: CA: Brooks/Cole-Thomson Learning.

de Pillis, E. G., & de Pillis, L. (2008). Are engineering schools masculine and authoritarian? The mission statements say yes. *Journal of Diversity in Higher Education, 1,* 33–44.

Dedovic, K., D'Aguiar, C., & Pruessner, J. C. (2009). What stress does to your brain: A review of neuroimaging studies. *Canadian Journal of Psychiatry, 54,* 5–15.

DeNavas-Walt, C., & Proctor, B. D. (2014). Income and poverty in the United States: 2013. U.S. Census Bureau, *Current Population Reports,* P60–249. Washington, DC: U.S. Government Printing Office.

Enns, C. (1987). Gestalt therapy and feminist therapy: A proposed integration. *Journal of Counseling and Development, 66*, 93–95.

Enns, C. Z. (1993). Twenty years of feminist counseling and psychotherapy: From naming biases to implementing multifaceted practice. *The Counseling Psychologist, 21*, 3–87.

Enns, C. Z. (2000). Gender issues in therapy. In S. D. Brown & R. W. Lent (Eds.), *Handbook of counseling psychology* (3rd ed., pp. 601–638). Hoboken, NJ: Wiley.

Enns, C. Z. (2004). *Feminist theories and feminist psychotherapies: Origin, themes, and diversity* (2nd ed.). New York, NY: Haworth.

Espin, O. (1994). *Latina realities: Essays on healing, migration, and sexuality.* New York, NY: Dover.

Family and Youth Services Bureau. (2016). *Domestic violence and homelessness: Statistics.* Retrieved from https://www.acf.hhs.gov/fysb/resource/dv-homelessness-stats-2016

Ganley, A. L. (1988). Feminist therapy with male clients. In M. A. Dutton-Douglas & L. E. Walker (Eds.), *Feminist psychotherapies: Integration of therapeutic and feminist systems* (pp. 91–117). Norwood, NJ: Ablex.

Graziottin, A., & Serafini, A. (2009). Depression and the menopause: Why antidepressants are not enough. *Menopause International, 15*, 76–81.

Herlihy, B., & Corey, G. (2005). Feminine therapy. In G. Corey (Ed.), *Theory and practice of counseling and psychotherapy* (7th ed.). Belmont, CA: Brooks/Cole.

Hill, M., & Ballou, M. (2005). *The foundation and future of feminist therapy.* New York, NY: Haworth.

Huston, T. (2005). *Research report: Race and gender bias in student evaluations of teaching.* Center for Excellence in Teaching & Learning, Seattle University.

Ivey, A., D'Andrea, M., Ivey, M. B., & Simek-Morgan, L. (2007). *Theories of counseling and psychotherapy: A multicultural perspective* (5th ed.). Boston, MA: Allyn & Bacon.

Jones-Smith, E. (2016). *Counseling and psychotherapy: An integrative approach.* Thousand Oaks, CA: Sage.

Kahn, J. S. (2010). Feminist therapy for men: Challenging assumptions and moving forward. *Women & Therapy, 34*(1–2), 59–76. doi:10.1080/02703149.2011.532458

Kessler, R. C., Chiu, W. T., Demler, O., & Walters, E. E. (2005). Prevalence, severity, and comorbidity of 12-month DSM-IV disorders in the National Comorbidity Survey Replication. *Archives of General Psychiatry, 62*, 617–627.

Levant, R. F. (2001). Context and gender in early adult relationships. *Prevention and Treatment, 4*, art. 14.

Llopis, G. (2011, August 22). 4 skills that give women a sustainable advantage over men. *Forbes.* Retrieved from http://www.forbes.com/sites/glennllopis/2011/08/22/4-skills-that-give-women-a-sustainable-advantage-over-men/#2122d726c973).

Lyness, K. S., & Thompson, D. E. (2000). Climbing the corporate ladder: Do female and male executives follow the same route? *Journal of Applied Psychology, 85*, 86–101.

Miller, J. B. (1986). *Toward a new psychology of women* (2nd ed.). Boston, MA: Beacon Press.

National Center for Education Statistics. (2017). Fast facts: Race/ethnicity of college faculty. *U.S. Department of Education.* Retrieved from https://nces.ed.gov/fastfacts/display.asp?id=61

National Domestic Violence Hotline. (2014). *Get the facts & figures.* Retrieved from http://www.thehotline.org/resources/statistics/?gclid=CjwKEAjw86e4BRCnzuWGlpjLoUcSJACaHG55NlonSvWtio3TRawlTXbhjJy6dqQ7s_D8ob_2KGSTqhoC8Z3w_wcB

National Institute of Mental Health. (2016, July). *Depression in women: Five things you should know.* Retrieved from https://infocenter.nimh.nih.gov/nimh/product/Depression-in-Women-5-Things-You-Should-Know/TR%2016-4779

Nolen-Hoeksema, S., & Atkinson, R. L. (2009). *Atkinson & Hilgard's introduction to psychology.* Andover, MA: Wadsworth Cengage Learning.

Steele, C. (2003). Through the back door to theory. *Psychological Inquiry, 14*, 314–317.

Substance Abuse and Mental Health Services Administration. (2010). How many Americans experienced mental illness in the past year? *SAMHSA News.* Retrieved from http://media.samhsa.gov/samhsaNewsletter/Volume_18_6/MentalHealthR

Truman, J. L., & Rand, M. R. (2010, October 13). Criminal victimization, 2009. *Bureau of Justice Statistics.* Retrieved from https://www.bjs.gov/index.cfm?ty=pbdetail&iid=2217

U.S. Census Bureau. (2011a). *Age and sex composition: 2010.* Retrieved from http://www.census.gov/prod/cen2010br-03.pdf

U.S. Census Bureau. (2011b). *Women's history month: March 2011.* U.S. Department of Commerce. Washington, DC: U.S. Government Printing Office.

U.S. Census Bureau. (2017, August 10). *Historical income tables: People.* Retrieved from https://www.census.gov/data/tables/time-series/demo/income-poverty/historical-income-people.html

Verboom, C. E., Sentse, M., Sijtsema, J. J., Nolen, W. A., Ormel, J., & Penninx, B. W. (2011). Explaining heterogeneity in disability with major depressive disorder: Effects of personal and environmental characteristics. *Journal of Affective Disorders, 132,* 71–81.

Vigod, S. N., & Stewart, D. (2009). Emergent research in the cause of mental illness in women across the lifespan. *Current Opinion in Psychiatry, 22,* 396–400.

Williams, J. E., & Best, D. L. (1990). *Sex and psyche: Gender and self viewed cross-culturally.* Newbury Park, CA: Sage.

Worell, J., & Papendrick-Remer, P. (2001). *Feminist perspectives in therapy.* New York, NY: Wiley.

Worell, J., & Remer, P. (2003). *Feminist perspectives in therapy: Empowering diverse women* (2nd ed.). Hoboken, NJ: Wiley.

15

CULTURALLY RESPONSIVE STRENGTHS-BASED THERAPY FOR LGBTQ INDIVIDUALS

- *"A person once asked me, in a provocative manner, if I approved of homosexuality. I replied with another question: 'Tell me: When God looks at a gay person, does he endorse the existence of this person with love, or reject and condemn this person?' We must always consider the person."* —Pope Francis

- *"Openness may not completely disarm prejudice, but it's a good place to start."* —Jason Collins, first openly gay athlete in U.S. pro sports

- *"I was raised around heterosexuals, as all heterosexuals are. That's where us gay people come from . . . you heterosexuals."* —Ellen DeGeneres

CHAPTER OBJECTIVES

- Define terms related to the LGBTQ community.

- Describe demographic and socioeconomic data about LGBTQ individuals.

- Identify examples of discrimination and microagressions against LGBTQ individuals.

- Describe LGBTQ identity development and gender dysphoria.

- Summarize mental health issues and strengths related to LGBTQ individuals.

- Implement counseling considerations for LGBTQ clients.

- Comprehend the mental health challenges of the LGBTQ population.

- Learn about gay affirmative psychotherapy, barriers to assessment of LGBTQ clients, and so-called reparative therapy.

- Understand the implications for counseling members of the LGBTQ population.

INTRODUCTION

This chapter deals with counseling individuals who identify as lesbian, gay, bisexual, transgender, or queer/questioning. Although the acronym **LGBTQ** is used as an umbrella term, each letter represents the concerns, issues, and hopes of specific subpopulation groups. The letters *L* and *G* stand for *lesbian* and *gay*; they refer to a person's sexual orientation toward a person of the same sex: Females are attracted to other females, and males are attracted to other males. The term **gay** can be used to refer to men or women who are sexually and affectionally attracted to members of their same sex (Pope, 2008); however, although some women who are affectionally and sexually attracted to other women identify with the word *gay*, many others prefer the term **lesbian**. Throughout this chapter, the term *gay* will be used to refer to males, and the term *lesbian* will be used to refer to females (Gates, 2011). The *B* in the LGBTQ acronym refers to **bisexual**, a term that refers to a person who is sexually attracted to individuals of both sexual groups. Bisexuals evidence an affectional or sexual attraction toward both sexes. The *T* in LGBTQ represents transgender individuals, those whose **gender** identification is inconsistent with their biological sex (Pachankis & Goldfried, 2004). **Transgender** refers to anyone whose gender identity does not conform to society's expectations of gender roles as determined by the sex assigned at birth. The term includes, but is not limited to, preoperative, postoperative, and nonoperative individuals, who may or may not use hormones, and individuals who exhibit gender characteristics or identities that are perceived to be incompatible with their birth or biological sex (Lev, 2004). In contrast, individuals who identify with the gender that corresponds to the sex assigned to them at birth are called **cisgender**. Cisgender describes the vast majority of people in that it refers to a person whose biological gender is consistent with the way the person views his or her gender.

The *Q* in the acronym LGBTQ represents individuals who identify as **queer** or who question their sexual identity (Duan & Brown, 2016). The word *queer* is often used as a blanket term for this community and for the acceptance of **genderqueer** or **nonbinary** identities. According to Pope (2008), "queer . . . is a political statement of difference from the majority culture" (p. 203). Proponents of queer theory maintain that gender identity is not a rigid or static identity, but rather it can change over time. Queer theory was constructed in response to those who perceive gender identities to be consolidated or stabilized, believing, for instance, that one becomes gay or straight for a lifetime (Duan & Brown, 2016).

In past decades, the terms *heterosexual* and *homosexual* were used both in research and in everyday conversation. *Heterosexual* referred to a person affectionally and sexually attracted to the opposite sex, and **homosexual** referred to a person affectionally and sexually attracted to his or her same sex. A related term, *homophobia*, refers to an irrational fear or hatred of homosexuality. Persons who assume that heterosexuality is the norm or the "right" way to live are referred to as **heterosexist**.

Gender is one of the few human characteristics that people are conditioned to view as a binary construct. Other human characteristics, such as height, weight, IQ, and hair length, are all viewed along various continua. Yet most societies in the world, including the United States, are deeply rooted in a binary discourse concerning gender. We recognize only two sexes in the world, and our religion, cultural traditions, and language keep us locked in the view that both sex and gender are binary—male and female.

As we investigate the neuroscience of sexual orientation, we might gain greater insight regarding how the brain is organized to reflect our gender and sexual identity. Neuroscience may help us to conceptualize a nonbinary view of gender identity and development. Imagine neuroscientists asking, "What is love?" and "How does one seek to express his or her love for another person?" Instead, thus far, the focus of gender identity research has been on a person's genitals and the use of those to express sexual gratification and love. Could it be that the brain and the way it conceptualizes and responds to sexual gratification and love is the real place researchers should be looking for answers to some of the questions posed in LGBTQ research and gender identity? Where are love and sexual gratification really located—in the brain or in our genitals?

Along such lines, one might also consider that love is not a binary concept—that each one of us has a continuum for love. We love differently based on a number of factors such as our biological (family) relationships, our friendships, and other factors. Viewing our continuum of love and its expression toward others might provide us with some direction about acknowledging a continuum for gender identity. Feminist psychologists, especially Sandra Bem (1993), have already asserted that each person has both masculine and feminine traits, characteristics, and attitudes. Researchers talk about the androgynous person (containing both male and female attitudes and values). Could there be something similar with our gender identity?

DEMOGRAPHIC AND LGBTQ POPULATION DATA

Accurate data on the LGBTQ population is subjective. The most widely accepted statistic is that 1 in 10 individuals is LGBTQ; however, research suggests that the number might be closer to 1 in 20. Recent population surveys in the United States have included questions that help one to make an estimate of the size of the LGBTQ population. The Williams Institute at the UCLA School of Law, a sexual orientation law and public policy think tank, estimates that 9 million (about 3.85%) Americans identify as gay, lesbian, bisexual, or transgender (Gates, 2011). The institute reported that bisexuals make up 1.8% of the population, gays and lesbians 1.7%, and transgender adults 0.3%. According to Gates (2011), a Senior Research Fellow at the Williams Institute, women are more likely than men to identify as bisexual. In eight of the nine surveys conducted by the institute, bisexuals constitute more than half of the lesbian and bisexual population among women.

Cultural Reflections
When did you first learn about gays and lesbians?
How did you first learn about heterosexuality, homosexuality, and bisexuality?
What stereotypes exist in your ethnic group about gays and lesbians?

Individuals who have participated in same-sex behavior do not always identify as gay or bisexual. An estimated 19 million Americans (8.2%) state that they have engaged in same-sex sexual behavior, and almost 25.6 million Americans (11%) state that they have experienced same-sex sexual attraction (Gates, 2011).

SOCIOECONOMIC STATUS

Inequalities in education, income, and occupation affect the health and well-being of individuals. According to an American Psychological Association (American Psychological Association, n.d.) fact sheet on socioeconomic status (SES), lesbian, gay, bisexual, and transgender persons "are especially susceptible to socioeconomic disadvantages. Thus, SES is inherently related to the rights, quality of life, and general well-being of LGBT persons." Although LGBTQ persons are inclined to have more education on average than the general population, evidence suggests that they earn less money than their heterosexual and cisgender counterparts (Egan, Edelman, & Sherrill, 2008; Factor & Rothblum, 2007). According to studies on income for LGBTQ individuals,

- Gay men earn up to 32% less than similarly qualified heterosexual men.

- Approximately 64% of transgender people report incomes below $25,000.

- Although 5.9% of the general population earns less than $10,000, 14% of LGBTQ individuals earn within this income bracket (Maskovsky, 2001).

Part of the low income for the LGBTQ population may be attributed to the public's discrimination against them in the workplace. Nearly 68% of individuals identifying as LGBTQ stated that they have experienced employment discrimination (American Psychological Association, n.d.). The Williams Institute aggregated several surveys (Gates, 2011) to determine the degree to which gay and transgender workers experience discrimination and harassment in the workplace. The institute's findings indicate that discrimination and harassment are pervasive against LGBTQ people.

The Center for American Progress (Burns & Krehely, 2011) produced a report on workplace discrimination against LGBTQ individuals that included comments by LGBTQ individuals regarding their work experiences. The following cases are two examples of LGBTQ discrimination.

Brook Waits was gainfully employed in Dallas, Texas until her manager fired her immediately after she saw a picture on Brook's cell phone of Brook and her girlfriend kissing on New Year's Eve:

"I didn't lose my job because I was lazy, incompetent, or unprofessional. Quite the contrary, I worked hard and did my job very well. However that was all discarded when my boss discovered I am a lesbian. In a single afternoon, I went from being a highly praised employee, to out of a job."

And Officer Michael Carney was denied reinstatement as a police officer in Springfield, Massachusetts because he told his supervisors that he was gay:

"I'm a good cop. But I've lost two and a half years of employment fighting to get that job back because I'm gay . . . I'm proud to be Irish-American. I'm proud to be gay, and I'm proud to be a cop in Springfield, MA." (Burns & Krehely, 2011)

There are economic consequences of sexual orientation and gender discrimination. Gay and transgender people experience socioeconomic inequalities because of widespread discrimination in the workplace. Sexual orientation discrimination results in greater unemployment and poverty rates for gay and transgender people. U.S. federal law does not give LGBTQ people the same full workplace protections as are given to women, people of color, veterans, seniors, and the disabled. To correct this situation, in 2011, Congress introduced legislation called the Employment Non-Discrimination Act (ENDA), which would give workplace protections to LGBTQ workers similar to those afforded to women and minority groups. ENDA's premise is that all Americans merit equal treatment in the workplace regardless of sexual orientation or gender identity (Burns & Krehely, 2011). However, as of this writing, ENDA or similar legislation has not passed into law.

DISCRIMINATION AND THE GAY RIGHTS MOVEMENT

LGBTQ individuals form part of a sexual minority. Members may experience sexual prejudice, in the form of attitudes and beliefs reflecting negative assumptions and stereotypes about sexual orientation and gender identity. Just a few decades ago, gays and lesbians were subjected to widespread societal discrimination throughout the world. During the 1960s, law enforcement conducted raids on gay bars, and the names of those present at the raid were sometimes provided to local newspapers as a way of shaming the individuals. Many gay and lesbian individuals kept their sexual orientation hidden from their families and work colleagues—a pattern known as "being in the closet."

In 1969, gays and the New York City police engaged in a series of violent conflicts known as the Stonewall riots. On June 28, 1969, police raided the Stonewall Inn, a bar in the West Village of New York (Franke-Ruta, 2013). The Stonewall conflicts lasted several days and drew a crowd of 400 gay protesters. Never before had gay people stood up for themselves publicly to resist police harassment that targeted their community. Stonewall created a sense of solidarity and community and went down in history as a defining moment in the gay community's struggle for acceptance.

In 1970, the American Psychiatric Association's annual meeting was disrupted by protesters from a group called the Gay Liberation Front, an action that led to a 1973 position paper in which the APA called for full civil rights for gay and lesbian individuals. In 1986, the APA's new revision of the *Diagnostic and Statistical Manual of Mental Disorders* (DSM-III-R) no longer considered it a "disorder" to be gay or lesbian ("Panelists Recount Events," 1998).

In December 2010, President Barack Obama signed a bill repealing the U.S. military's "Don't ask, don't tell" policy, which had been in effect since 1994. Prior to 1994, the military had the prerogative to "ask" or require a person to "tell" whether he or she was gay and followed a policy of excluding non-heterosexuals from service. With the repeal of the "Don't ask, don't tell" policy, gay men and lesbian women were able to serve openly and with honor in the armed forces for the first time in history.

Increasingly, countries throughout the world are giving gays and lesbians the right to marry: Canada, Europe, Norway, the Netherlands, Belgium, Spain, Portugal, Iceland, and South Africa. In June 2015, the U.S. Supreme Court ruled that same-sex couples can marry nationwide, establishing a new civil right and giving gay rights advocates a historic victory.

Nearly 46 years to the day after the Stonewall riots ushered in the modern gay rights movement, this Supreme Court decision settled one of the major civil rights fights of this era—the right for members of the LGBTQ community to marry and have a family. Justice Anthony Kennedy's majority opinion spoke eloquently of the most fundamental values of family, love, and liberty:

> No union is more profound than marriage, for it embodies the highest ideals of love, fidelity, devotion, sacrifice and family. In forming a marital union, two people become something greater than they once were. . . .
>
> Their hope is not to be condemned to live in loneliness, excluded from one of civilization's oldest institutions. They ask for equal dignity in the eyes of the law. The Constitution grants them that right. (*Obergefell v. Hodges*, 576 U.S. ___, 2014)

When Kennedy said the key sentence that same-sex couples should be able to exercise the right to marry in all states, people in the Court's public gallery broke into smiles, and some cried. President Obama called gay marriage case plaintiff Jim Obergefell and congratulated him. "I just wanted to say congratulations," Obama said. "Your leadership on this has changed the country." Later on in the morning at the White House, Obama said, "Americans should be very proud, because small acts of courage slowly made an entire country realize that love is love" (de Vogue & Diamond, 2015). With this landmark decision, the United States became the 21st country in the world to legalize same-sex marriage nationwide, including territories. Married same-sex couples will now have the same legal rights and benefits as married heterosexual couples throughout the nation, and their marriage will be recognized on official documents such as birth and death certificates.

Despite these milestones, however, lesbian and gay discrimination continues to exist within the United States and throughout the world. In a study by Herek, Cogan, and Gillis (2002), more than 94% of LGBTQ adults stated they were the victim of a hate crime. Hate crimes committed against LGBTQ individuals make up the third-highest category of hate crimes reported to the FBI—forming 16.7% of all hate crimes reported nationally (U.S. Department of Justice, 2011). A study on victimization over the life span found that 12% of gay men and 13% of bisexual men, compared to 2% of heterosexual men, had been sexually victimized. Among women, sexual victimization rates were 16% for lesbians, 17% for bisexual women, and 8% for heterosexual women (Balsam, Rothblum, & Beauchaine, 2005).

> **Cultural Reflections**
>
> *Where would you place yourself on a homophobia continuum—from very little homophobia to a great deal of it?*
>
> *Have you ever been guilty of being hetero-sexist in your interactions with others?*
>
> *For instance, do you assume that a male has a girlfriend?*

Homophobia Persists

As noted earlier in the chapter, homophobia is an irrational fear and hatred of LGBTQ individuals. Gay and lesbian people sometimes experience *internalized homophobia*, a process by which a member of the LGBTQ community comes to accept and live out disparaging myths and stereotypes about LGBTQ persons.

The social and cultural context within which gays and lesbians live is extremely important. Environments, especially family environments, that view a same-sex or bisexual orientation as negative and as a disgrace produce individuals who experience internalized homophobia and sexual identity conflict. Homophobia can be summarized as containing the following elements:

- Irrational hatred of, fear of, and contempt for LGBTQ people

- Persecution or violence toward LGBTQ people

- Internalized hatred when one believes he or she is a gay man or lesbian

Cultural Reflections

What stereotypes do you have of LGBTQ individuals?

Have you ever witnessed a hate crime against a gay or lesbian person? If so, what did you do as you observed the bullying?

- The belief that if LGBTQ people touch you, they are making sexual advances
- The belief that LGBTQ people are asking to be treated "special" because they demand basic civil rights
- Changing your seat when an LGBTQ person sits next to you
- Repulsion by public displays of affection between LGBTQ people, while affection displayed between heterosexuals is acceptable

Heterosexism

Heterosexism is the belief that every person is heterosexual; therefore, it marginalizes or disregards persons who do not identify as heterosexual (Croteau, Lark, Lidderdale, & Chung, 2005). It is also the belief that heterosexuality is superior to homosexuality and other sexual orientations. Heterosexism pervades societal customs and institutions. When you first meet a person, do you naturally assume that the person is heterosexual? Why or why not? From my perspective, heterosexism exists because "normal" sexual development is thought to be heterosexual instead of homosexual. Stereotypes and negative attributions are at the heart of heterosexist attitudes (Kashubeck-West, Szymanski, & Meyer, 2008).

Microaggressions Against LGBTQ People

Microaggressions against members of the LGBTQ community are commonplace. Kevin Nadal, a professor at the John Jay College of Criminal Justice of the City University of New York, who is gay and Asian, described his experiences with microaggressions and bullying as a high school student:

When I was a teenager, there were a few boys at my high school who ridiculed me, almost every day. When I walked by them in the halls, they called me a "faggot" or screamed my name in a flamboyant tone. I learned to walk by without showing any reaction; I could not let them know that it bothered me, or else I would be proving to them that I was indeed gay. I didn't tell anyone about the bullying (not my parents, teachers, or anyone) because admitting that I was being teased for being gay would mean that I was admitting to being gay. I had never felt so alone in my life.

In college, it got a little better. While I was no longer harassed about my closeted sexual orientation, I didn't have any friends that were openly gay and most of my friends didn't have any either. Some of my friends and family members still made occasional homophobic jokes in front of me. While many loved ones later told me that they suspected that I was gay, no one gave me any reason to believe that they were gay-friendly. So I just remained in the closet a few more years until I couldn't take it anymore. (Nadal, 2014)

Nadal continued by saying that he had a difficult time accepting his gay identity because of the microaggressions that he had experienced throughout his life (Sue, Bucceri, Lin, Nadal, & Torino, 2007). The following are six types of microaggressions that Nadal (2014) states harm members of the LGBTQ community:

1. **Use of heterosexist or transphobic terminology**. Such expressions include "That's so gay"; for transgender people, it would involve saying "tranny" or "she-male." Hip-hop music sometimes uses the word *faggot* in its lyrics (Kashubeck-West et al., 2008).

2. **Endorsement of heteronormative culture and behaviors**. This occurs when an LGBTQ person is presumed to be heterosexual, or when he or she is asked or encouraged to act in gender-conforming ways. For instance, a person is told to "act like a man." An LGBTQ male may be asked if he has a girlfriend, and a female may be asked if she has a boyfriend. These kinds of questions or statements suggest that the average person is expected to be heterosexual.

3. **Assumption of universal LGBTQ experience**. These types of microaggressions occur when heterosexual people make the assumption that all LGBTQ persons have the same traits, beliefs, and experiences (Nadal, Issa, et al., 2011).

4. **Discomfort or disapproval of LGBTQ experience**. Microaggressions in this category take place when individuals make it clear that they do not approve of the gay and transgender experience. For instance, someone may express disgust at seeing two gay men kissing or two lesbian women kissing.

5. **Assumption of sexual pathology or abnormality**. This involves the perception of LGBTQ people as sexual deviants or overly sexual. Another fairly common microaggression occurs when people are leery about LGBTQ teachers, coaches, or babysitters. A third type of microaggression in this category is when straight men or straight women assume that a gay man or lesbian woman would "hit" on them as a possible mate.

6. **Denial of bodily privacy**. People may feel entitled or comfortable in objectifying transgender bodies (for example, asking trans people about their genitals when one would never ask such a personal question of a cisgender person).

Microaggressions have a significant negative impact on LGBTQ people's lives. Some studies have reported that the more LGBTQ people experience microaggressions, the more likely they are to report symptoms of depression, psychological distress, and even physical health issues (Nadal, Wong, et al., 2011). Repeated microaggressions are believed to be related to the higher prevalence of substance abuse, homelessness, and suicide among LGBTQ people (see Nadal, 2013, for a review). In the interest of social justice, it is important for clinicians to work toward making our schools, our workplaces, and society in general less homophobic. Microaggressions produce challenges to a person's positive sense of self. Microaggressions are not harmless. On the contrary, they hurt sometimes more than a physical punch.

LGBTQ IDENTITY DEVELOPMENT

Defining Sex, Sexual Orientation, and Gender Identity

Sex is what each person is assigned at birth; it refers to a person's biological status as either male or female, and it is usually determined by physical attributes. In contrast, gender connotes the socially constructed roles, behaviors, activities, and attributes that each society believes is appropriate for boys and men or girls and women. One may assume a gender role that is in agreement with one's biological sex or that is different from one's biological sex.

Gender identity refers to an individual's internal sense of being male, female, or something else. Gender reflects a society's social norms about what is appropriate feminine and masculine behavior (Carroll, Gilroy, & Ryan, 2002). Whereas sex refers to biological, chromosomal, and anatomical

Cultural Reflections

Have you ever used any one of the six identified microaggressions against a LGBTQ person?

Which one of the microaggressions did you use, and under what circumstances did you use it?

How did the individual respond after you used the microaggression against him or her?

Reflecting on the situation, how would you respond if given a chance to "redo" the interaction?

Cultural Reflections

Looking back on your own life, how would you describe your gender identity development?

Who helped you to negotiate the various stages involved in your gender identity development?

How would you like for your child to experience gender identity development?

determinants of male and female, gender deals with how people identify themselves as masculine or feminine. In this regard, gender identity involves a person's self-identification as a man, a woman, transgender, or some other categorization. **Gender expression** refers to the manner in which a person communicates gender identity to others through behavior, clothing, hairstyles, voice, or body characteristics (Central Counseling Services, 2017).

Psychologists do not completely understand how gender identity is formed, and therefore, they have identified many factors that might influence its development, including biological factors, social factors, language, and social and economic power (American Psychological Association, 2018). For instance, social learning theory maintains that children develop their gender identity through being taught gender roles explicitly by their parents, and through observing and imitating the gender-linked behaviors of others. For instance, boys may imitate their fathers in playing basketball, and girls may imitate their mothers in cooking. Children are often rewarded or punished depending on what behaviors they imitate or display. In many families, a boy who plays with dolls would not be rewarded for his behavior. Children also develop gender identity through interacting with their peers, especially in a school environment.

Children begin to learn about gender identity during their toddler and preschool years. They develop gender constancy, the understanding that sex is biologically based and remains the same even if clothing, hairstyle, and play activities change (American Psychological Association, 2018). Once children tend to reflect on gender roles, their gender-typed self-image and behavior strengthen.

Gender schema theory represents an information-processing approach to gender typing that combines social learning theory and cognitive development theory. It details how environmental pressures and children's cognitive abilities function together to determine gender role development (American Psychological Association, 2018; Berk, 2007). Children organize their experiences into gender schemas, or masculine and feminine categories to make sense of their world. When preschoolers learn how to label their own sex, they choose gender schemas consistent with it. For instance, a boy's gender schema may contain cognitions that men become president of the United States, while young girls' gender schema may consist of cognitions that women become fashion models.

Sexual orientation is an enduring emotional, romantic, or sexual attraction that a person feels toward men, toward women, or toward both. There are several forms of sexual orientation (Pope, 2008). One can be heterosexual, where the object of one's affection and sexual attraction is a member of the opposite sex. One can be homosexual or gay, where the object of one's sexual attraction is a person of the same sex that one was born with. The third option is that one can be transgender; one changes one's sexual biology. Research has not conclusively found sexual orientation to be determined by any particular factor or factors, and the timing of the emergence, recognition, and expressions of one's sexual orientation differs across people (Pope, 2008).

The term *sexual orientation* cannot necessarily be used interchangeably with *sexual activity*. Some adolescents and adults identify themselves as lesbian, gay, or bisexual, but they do not have sexual encounters with a person of the same sex. Likewise, other individuals do have sexual experiences with persons of the same sex, but they do not consider themselves lesbian, gay, or bisexual. During adolescence, for instance, many young people participate in a period of sexual experimentation and discovery.

Gender Dysphoria in Children and Adolescents

Gender dysphoria deals with individuals' discontent with the biological sex they have been born with. Recently, the topic of gender identity disorder has received attention in the lay and academic press. Some movie stars, for example, have stated publicly that they were allowing their children to choose how they wanted to express their own gender identity.

According to the American Psychiatric Association (2013), the diagnosis of gender identity disorder has changed (much in the same way that the diagnosis of homosexuality changed during the 1970s). In the *Diagnostic and Statistical Manual of Mental Disorders* (5th ed.), the condition formerly called gender identity disorder has been changed to gender dysphoria. For a person to be diagnosed with gender dysphoria, he or she must exhibit strong and persistent cross-gender identification, not just a desire for the perceived cultural advantages of being the other sex (American Psychiatric Association, 2013; Bressert, 2017). For young children, the disturbance is manifested by six (or more) of the following symptoms for at least a six-month duration:

- A repeatedly stated desire to be of the opposite sex, or an insistence that one is of the other sex

- For boys, a preference for cross-dressing or simulating female clothing; for girls, an insistence on wearing only stereotypical masculine clothing

- Strong and persistent preferences for cross-sex roles in make-believe play or persistent fantasies of being the other sex

- A strong rejection of typical toys/games typically played by one's sex

- A strong desire to participate in the stereotypical games and pastimes of the other sex

- A strong preference for playmates of the other sex

- A strong dislike of one's sexual anatomy

- A strong desire for the primary (e.g., penis, vagina) or secondary (e.g., menstruation) sex characteristics of the other sex (Bressert, 2017)

Gender dysphoria causes clinically significant distress or impairment in a person's social, occupational, or other important areas of functioning.

> ## Cultural Reflections
>
> *Until the 1970s, homosexuality was classified by the American Psychiatric Association as a mental disorder. This view was discarded, and homosexuality is no longer listed as such.*
>
> *How do you think the mental disorder called gender dysphoria will fare?*
>
> *Do you think that the DSM-6 will no longer consider gender dysphoria a mental disorder?*
>
> *Explain your answer.*

TRANSGENDER IDENTITY DEVELOPMENT

Transgender identity merits special attention because there are so many negative views on this form of gender identity and so little understanding of what it means to be transgender.

Although there is research exploring childhood cross-gender behaviors, few studies have explored what it means to grow up transgender in a binary gender world. Recent research has suggested that transgender people typically go through a process of dissonance, exploration, and disclosure that, if successful, leads finally to identity resolution (Lev, 2004). Transgender people have indicated that feelings of difference started in early childhood and the feeling that something was wrong or out of balance between the biological body and mind started as early as age 3. Still other children report a dissonance between mind and body as late as age 12 or 13. This gender identity discord is usually precipitated by physical changes during puberty—changes that may be unwanted by the youth (Grossman & D'Augelli, 2006).

After experiencing the initial feelings of gender dissonance, transgender people usually experience a period of identity confusion and exploration. A transgender person may experience a sense of excitement and struggle while on the road to developing a true sense of self. Conversely, transitioning transgender people may also have feelings of shame and guilt; they may encounter pressures to conform, and they may manifest efforts to keep their transitioning process a secret from family, their peers, and the school. Transgender people may immerse themselves in transgender communities, and they may begin to use cross-gender pronouns or gender-neutral pronouns to describe themselves (Grossman & D'Augelli, 2006). Identity development is complete when the person achieves a stable, healthy sense of self.

A young person's progress in developing a successful, healthy transgender identity may be compromised and thwarted by discrimination, harassment, and fear of rejection by parents or friends. The middle and high school years are critical transitioning years for transgender youth. During this time period, parents may reject them out of shame, and some may rush to have operations for their children before puberty sets in (Grossman & D'Augelli, 2006). Violence that is directed toward the self and from others is also experienced; 60% of transgender youth report having experienced violent assaults (Moran & Sharpe, 2004), and another 32% attempt suicide (Fitzpatrick, Euton, Jones, & Schmidt, 2005).

Transgender youth are often marginalized by the mainstream society, by their parents, and even by lesbian, gay, and bisexual support groups. This marginalization can be a contributing factor to suicide attempts. For instance, Fitzpatrick and colleagues (2005) reported that transgender college students were more likely to feel hopeless (32%), experience suicidal ideations, and attempt suicide. Although there are similarities between the experiences of gay, lesbian, and bisexual youth and transgender youth, there are important differences to consider. Transgender youth are less likely to be supported or accepted by their family, authority figures, or communities, and policies and practices that support gay, lesbian, or bisexual youth may not be extended to transgender youth (Kim, 2009).

There is some good news regarding transgender youth. Those who have connectedness to their family, school, and community tend to become resilient and stronger for the adversities they encounter—in other words, what does not kill us makes us stronger.

This section has dealt primarily with the issues that transgender people, especially transgender youth, experience during their identity development process. The next section examines the "coming out" process for gays, lesbians, and bisexuals. There is a certain amount of overlap in the two sections.

COMING OUT AND GENDER IDENTITY DEVELOPMENT FOR GAYS, LESBIANS, AND BISEXUALS

There have been some questions about whether or not gays and lesbians experience the same type of gender identity development as do individuals with heterosexual orientation. For the most part, identity development for gays and lesbians has focused on the process of **coming out**. When individuals have conflict about their sexual identity or they are forced to hide their true sexual identity because of fears of being ostracized, harmed, or demeaned in some way, their identity development is arrested or impaired.

Coming out is one of the most important developmental processes in the lives of LGBTQ people. Coming out *to others and to oneself* is a unique process that differentiates lesbians and gay men from other minority cultures. It can be defined as a process of recognizing, accepting, expressing, and sharing one's sexual orientation with oneself and others. The phrase *coming out* means to publicly affirm one's homosexual identity, sometimes to one person in conversation, sometimes by an act that puts one in the public eye.

Coming out, however, is not a single event but rather a lifelong process. Altman (1979) has defined coming out as

> the whole process whereby a person comes to identify himself/herself as a homosexual, and recognizes his/her position as part of a stigmatized and semi-hidden minority.
> The development of a homosexual identity is a long process that usually begins during

adolescence, though sometimes considerably later. Because of the fears and ignorance that surround our views of sex, children discover sexual feelings and behavior incompletely, and often accompanied by great pangs of guilt. [Many of us] manage to hide into our twenties a full realization that [we are] not like [them]. (pp. 15–16)

Part of the reason that individuals experience a coming-out process is because they have already been socialized into a male or a female role (Rosario, Schrimshaw, Hunter, & Braun, 2006). Each culture provides a definition of what is masculine and what is feminine. The traditional definition of masculinity has implications throughout the life span for boys and men. Kindlon and Thompson (2000) have asserted that there is a rigid male gender role that is based on "emotional illiteracy" (p. 5) and a culture of cruelty among young boys. Teenage boys who agreed with traditional gender roles for men were more inclined to "drink beer, smoke pot, have unprotected sex, get suspended from school, and 'trick' or force someone into having sex" (Kindlon & Thompson, 2000, p. 16). In contrast, a traditional female identity development for young girls is likely to focus on "sugar and spice and everything nice." It is assumed that the favorite color of young girls is pink and that they are submissive rather than assertive.

> **Cultural Reflections**
>
> *Has anyone close to you—a family member or a friend—come out as lesbian, gay, bisexual, transgender, or queer?*
>
> *If so, what was your response to his or her coming out?*
>
> *If you had a friend who appeared to be "gay" but who was still in the closet, would you encourage that person to come out? Explain your answer.*

COMING OUT FOR PEOPLE OF COLOR: A "TRICULTURAL EXPERIENCE"

Coming out for a member of an ethnic/racial minority can be extremely challenging. Students who come from ethnic minority backgrounds encounter what has been called a "tricultural experience." First, youth of color may experience the same type of homophobia or transphobia that White LGBTQ youth encounter. Second, they may undergo the racism that heterosexual students of color face. Third, and perhaps most hurtful, they may experience exclusion from both the LGBTQ and the ethnic minority communities with whom they identify. In general, LGBTQ youth of color may endure alienation/racism from the predominantly White LGBTQ community and alienation/homophobia from the predominantly heterosexual communities of color.

The third leg of the tricultural experience makes the situation of youth of color unique and risky because youth need a support base. For some LGBTQ youth, their families provide that source of support; for others, it's the school/community peer or social group. Consider how sources of support may be jeopardized for minority youth. A National Education Association report by Robert Kim (2009) highlighted the special circumstances of LGBTQ youth of color:

- An African American parent or law guardian rejects his or her child's homosexuality on grounds that it is against his or her community and religious values—a sin against God.

- A LGBTQ community center is located in an affluent White neighborhood, far away from predominantly ethnic minority communities.

- A youth of color does not feel comfortable joining an LGBTQ organization at school because it is predominantly White.

- A youth attends a church, synagogue, temple, or mosque that preaches against homosexuality as a sin.

- An Asian American parent or guardian rejects a LGBTQ son or daughter because "LGBTQ people do not exist in our culture."

Cultural Reflections

What does it mean to say that LGBTQ individuals who are also members of an ethnic cultural group have a unique kind of experience?

Do you know any LGBTQ individuals who are members of an ethnic minority group?

In your opinion, are these individuals well received by members of their ethnic group?

- A Latino parent tells his or her son that he must demonstrate *machismo* if he wants to be considered Latino.

The consequences of youth of color not having a reliable support base from home, school, or the community are formidable. They may include high rates of homelessness, dropping out of school, and severely compromised mental and physical health. As Kim (2009) has pointed out,

> for many GLBT youth of color, the integration of racial, sexual, and other identities calls for skilled navigation. Homophobia within ethnic minority communities, media images of GLBT people, and even terminology within the predominantly White GLBT community reinforce the stereotype that all gay people are White . . .

GLBT youth of color experience "shifting hierarchies" within their "multiple affiliations," sometimes expressing one over the other. . . . Says [University of Toronto] Professor [Lance] McCready, "We need to develop teachers' ability to observe, interpret, and understand the relationship between multiple social and cultural identities of queer youth of color." (p. 11)

African American and Latino gay and lesbian youth tend to be more reluctant to reveal their sexual orientation than are their White counterparts (Rosario, Schrimshaw, & Hunter, 2004). Usually, there does not have to be a coming-out process about one's ethnicity. The client's skin color, hair texture, and other defining features have been with him or her throughout life. Research suggests that the coming-out process for a gay ethnic/cultural minority person may be especially difficult because the individual may have to face two sources of prejudice and oppression (Estrada, Rigali-Oiler, Arciniega, & Tracey, 2011; Rosario et al., 2004). For instance, gay Mexican American males are inclined to have a greater degree of internalized homophobia because of the cultural value of *machismo*.

Coming out is a continuous process. Each time a gay man or lesbian woman meets a new person, he or she must make a decision to come out or not. Individuals use different strategies in the coming-out process, including using the correct gender-specific pronouns when mentioning love relationships or introducing themselves as members of the LGBTQ community (Pope & Schecter, 1992). However, coming out has its costs. Gonsiorek (1993) has described some consequences of delaying to accept one's sexual orientation. It may cause a developmental domino effect such that other developmental tasks—choosing a mate, choosing a career—are delayed.

LGBTQ YOUTH AND SCHOOLS

LGBTQ young people are becoming more visible in our schools. Recent studies have revealed that, on average, lesbian and gay youth first become aware of their same-gender attractions at an average of 9–10 years old and first identify as lesbian or gay at an average of 14–16 years old. LGBTQ students are subjected to many of the same problems experienced by adult gays and lesbians. According to a 2007 survey by the Gay, Lesbian and Straight Education Network (GLSEN), 86.2% of LGBTQ students reported being verbally harassed. More than half of the students surveyed stated that they felt unsafe in schools because of their sexual orientation, and a third said they felt unsafe due to their gender expression (Kosciw, Diaz, & Greytak, 2008).

Cultural Reflections

Have you been taught gender identity development in college?

To what extent is gender identity development different from and similar to identity development for heterosexuals?

LGBTQ youth embark upon developmental pathways that are both similar to and different from those of heterosexual adolescents (Cianciotto & Cahill, 2003). The majority of LGBTQ youth are healthy persons who make significant contributions to their families and schools. LGBTQ youth face additional hurdles in that they may have to cope with prejudice, discrimination, and violence both in their families and within the general society. Such marginalization negatively affects their mental and physical health. In one study, for example, LGBTQ students were more likely than heterosexual students to report missing school because of fear, being threatened by other students, and having their property damaged at school (Kosciw et al., 2008). "One result of the isolation and lack of support experienced by some lesbian, gay, and bisexual youth is higher rates of emotional distress, suicide attempts, and risky sexual behavior and substance use" (Just the Facts Coalition, 2008, p. 4). The following statement is from Ebonii Warren-Watts, a former student at the Chicago Public Schools:

> I started transitioning when I was sixteen. I started wearing my hair in a ponytail and wearing unisex clothes, arching my eyebrows. [People] called me a faggot, called me a cross-dresser, called me a queer . . . I started missing a lot of classes because of all this impact. I think that if my high school instructors had intervened, I would have made it through high school and not dropped out in the ninth grade. The combination of homophobia, transphobia, racism, classism, and age discrimination attacks GLBT youth of color who are struggling with instability and homelessness. (Kim, 2009, p. 13)

In order to provide an open and safe school environment, school personnel must understand the nature of sexual orientation development and support the healthy development of all students. When school environments become more positive for LGBTQ youth, the youths' higher rates of depression, anxiety, and substance abuse will most likely decrease.

LGBTQ FAMILIES: SOME FACTS

In past generations, when homosexuality was considered a mental disorder, it was thought that LGBTQ couples should not form families and raise children because such children would have mental problems and/or would grow up to be homosexual themselves. Since that time, millions of children in the United States have grown up with LGBTQ parents. While some of these children were conceived in heterosexual marriages or relationships, an increasing number of LGBTQ parents have conceived their own children through either surrogate relationships, foster parenting, or adoption. In 2008, the American Academy of Child & Adolescent Psychiatry published a summary that shows that children with gay and lesbian parents do not differ from children with heterosexual parents in their emotional development or in their relationships with peers and adults (Telingator & Patterson, 2008). It is important for parents to understand that it is the quality of the parent–child relationship and not the parent's sexual orientation that has an effect on a child's development.

In contrast to some concerns about LGBTQ parents, the American Academy of Child & Adolescent Psychiatry (2013) stated that children of lesbian, gay, or transgender parents

- Are not more likely to be gay than children with heterosexual parents

- Are not more likely to be sexually abused

- Do not show differences in whether they think of themselves as male or female (gender identity)

- Do not show differences in their male and female behaviors (gender role behavior)

The academy recommended that parents help their children cope with discrimination about their families by preparing them to handle questions and comments about their background or family. They should establish a supportive network for their children and consider living in a community where LGBTQ diversity is accepted, and help their children by practicing appropriate answers to questions.

MENTAL HEALTH ISSUES AND THE LGBTQ COMMUNITY

LGBTQ and gender-variant people have a broad range of concerns for which they might seek the help of counselors and mental health professionals. In addition to the usual problems that cause individuals to seek counseling, LGBTQ and gender-variant people often seek professional help in understanding their gender identities and their patterns of gender expression. They not only want to know how to deal with their "coming out," but they also want to learn how to deal with the concerns of their family members, especially their parents (Barret & Logan, 2002).

LGBTQ clients are first of all individuals with their own stories about what it means to grow up with their specific sexual orientation (Rothblum & Factor, 2001). They are both similar to and different from heterosexual clients. Despite this observation, their group membership (LGBTQ) predisposes them to share some common mental health concerns.

In one study, lesbians and their heterosexual counterparts were compared on demographic variables and mental health subscales (Rothblum & Factor, 2001). Lesbians were significantly more educated, more likely to live in urban areas, and more geographically mobile than their heterosexual counterparts. The heterosexual participants were more likely than lesbians to be married and homemakers, to have children, and to identify with a religion. Rothblum and Factor (2001) did not find any difference in mental health, but lesbians had higher self-esteem. Bisexual women evidenced significantly poorer mental health than did lesbians and heterosexual women.

Other researchers have examined the role of perceived discrimination and mental health of LGBTQ people. Cochran (2001) found that "recent improvements in studies of sexual orientation and mental health morbidity have enabled researchers to find some elevated risk for stress-sensitive disorders that is generally attributed to the harmful effects of anti-homosexual bias" (p. 932).

Mays and Cochran (2001) investigated the mental health correlates of perceived discrimination among lesbian, gay, and bisexual adults in the United States. The researchers found that gay and bisexual individuals more frequently than heterosexual individuals stated they had lifetime and day-to-day experiences with discrimination. About 42% attributed the discrimination against them to their sexual orientation. Perceived discrimination was positively correlated with both harmful effects of quality of life and indicators of psychiatric morbidity in the entire sample. The researchers concluded that higher levels of discrimination may form the basis of greater psychiatric morbidity risk among lesbian, gay, and bisexual individuals. Similarly, McLaughlin, Hatzenbuehler, and Keyes (2010) found that perceived discrimination based on sexual orientation, especially among those who kept silent about what happened, increased their risk of depression. Clearly, the higher mental illness rates for LGBTQ individuals can at least partially be attributed to the discrimination that they encounter because of their sexual orientation.

Some common mental health problems experienced by LGBTQ individuals include

- Posttraumatic stress disorder from living in an hostile environment to gay men and lesbian women

- Damaged self-image due to stigmatization, oppression, and the coming-out process

- Fragmented identity that comes from living a double life

- Developmental issues that result from a focus on sexual orientation and insufficient attention to other developmental tasks unrelated to sexual orientation

TOP 10 PHYSICAL AND MENTAL HEALTH CONCERNS OF LGBTQ COLLEGE STUDENTS

Pace University's *Spotlight* newsletter identified the "top ten physical and emotional health concerns of LGBT students" in its fall 2008 issue. These issues are particularly prevalent with college-aged LGBTQ individuals due to the number of life transitions they are experiencing at this time in their lives:

1. *Access, Comfort, and Trust.* LGBTQ students take notice and appreciate when college programming involves them and when the college has policies of nondiscrimination to protect their rights as members of the LGBTQ community.

2. *Coming Out.* Many LGBTQ students "come out" while at college. They may contemplate the risks and benefits of accepting their sexual orientation and revealing it to others.

3. *Healing From Oppression.* When LGBTQ students experience anti-LGBTQ discrimination, they may develop physical and mental health problems.

4. *Coping with Stress, Anxiety, and Depression.* Individuals who are LGBTQ are more likely to experience depression and anxiety than are their heterosexual counterparts, particularly if they feel isolated in a new setting.

5. *Surviving Suicidal Thoughts, Plans, or Attempts.* Decades of research have reported a link between LGBTQ young people and suicide. College students who report having gender characteristics usually associated with their opposite sex tend to be at greater risk for suicidal symptoms, regardless of their sexual orientation (D'Augelli, 1993).

6. *Sexual Health Concerns.* Sexually transmitted diseases have increased among members of the LGBTQ group.

7. *HIV/AIDS.* After 13 years of declining rates of new HIV infection, studies have found that rates of new HIV infection among men who have sex with men have recently increased.

8. *Smoking.* Approximately 43% of gay men and lesbians ages 18–24 smoke, in comparison to 17% of the rest of the population.

9. *Drinking and Other Drug Use.* It has been estimated that 20% to 25% of gay men and lesbians are heavy alcohol users. Gay and bisexual men have a higher addiction rate than heterosexual men with such drugs as marijuana, cocaine, and ecstasy.

10. *Body Image.* Both gay men and lesbians struggle with issues regarding their body images. Women in the gay community may become overweight, while gay men may struggle to achieve an exaggerated sense of male beauty.

STRENGTHS OF LGBTQ POPULATIONS

Despite the fact that LGBTQ individuals have encountered prejudice, discrimination, and microaggressions, they have as a group shown great strength and resiliency (Singh, Hays, & Watson, 2011). Among the strengths identified with this population are belonging to a supportive community, being involved in the fight for social justice, and having freedom from externally imposed gender roles (Riggle, Whitman, Olson, Rostosky, & Strong, 2008). Some LGBTQ people point to the benefit of their identity search for who they really are (Akerlund & Cheung, 2000), and others mention the egalitarian relationship that many LGBTQ couples have been able to establish in their homes (Bos & Gartrell, 2010).

Cultural Reflections

What are some strengths that you see in LGBTQ individuals?

Have you ever mentioned these strengths to an LGBTQ person as something that you admire in him or her?

Singh and colleagues (2011) explored the lived experiences of resilience of 21 transgender individuals. Using individual semistructured interviews, the researchers identified five common resiliency themes: evolving a self-generated definition of self, embracing self-worth, awareness of oppression, connection with a supportive community, and cultivating hope for the future. Two additional themes were social activism and being a positive role model for others.

Another study investigated the positive aspects of a bisexual self-identification. Rostosky, Riggle, Pascale-Hague, and McCants (2010) conducted an online survey that asked bisexual-identified individuals to respond to an open-ended question about the positive aspects of bisexual identity. The findings from an international sample of 157 adult participants (ages 18–69; 67% female; 25% Canadian; 19% British; 51% American; and 5% other) revealed "11 positive identity aspects: freedom from social labels, honesty and authenticity, having a unique perspective, increased levels of insight and awareness, freedom to love without regard for sex/gender, freedom to explore relationships, freedom of sexual expression, acceptance of diversity, belonging to a community, understanding privilege and oppression and becoming an advocate/activist" (Rostosky et al., 2010, p. 131). In contrast to the negative stereotypes about bisexual and gay individuals, this study found that the 11 aspects of a bisexual identity took place at three levels: first at the level of the self (intrapersonal), second at the level of interpersonal relationships, and third at the level of society or the community at large.

Rostosky and colleagues (2010) compared the findings of their study with those of Riggle et al. (2008) and reported that "common to both study samples were the positive aspects of living authentically and honestly, exploring sexuality and relationships, developing empathy for others, forging strong connections to others and to the larger community and engaging in social justice activism. . . . For LGB individuals, positive coping with stigma may involve actively making meaning of experiences and creating positive relationships and a positive self-view" (p. 140). The authors provided suggestions for including these findings in bisexual-affirmative counseling and therapy.

One takeaway from the studies cited in this section is that clinicians can promote and support a positive self-view for LGBTQ individuals by helping them to deconstruct internalized negative stereotypes and to co-construct personal narratives that focus on their strengths and resiliencies (Jones-Smith, 2014).

Moreover, LGBTQ scholars have made several important contributions to psychotherapy. For instance,

1. LGBTQ therapeutic approaches acknowledge the role of an oppressive environment and its forces on people, both females and males.

2. The LGBTQ perspective has helped therapists to understand the use of power in relationships and the role that power plays in heterosexual and homosexual contexts.

3. LGBTQ therapists encourage change and not just adjustment to one's circumstances.

COUNSELING MEMBERS OF THE LGBTQ COMMUNITY

Counseling LGBTQ individuals is a difficult process that requires that a therapist have strong multicultural counseling competencies (Barret & Logan, 2002; Hancock, 2000; Pope, 2008). Four important documents that discuss the competence of counselors and therapists who work with LGBTQ people are (1) *Report of the APA Task Force on Appropriate Therapeutic Responses to Sexual Orientation* (American Psychological Association, 2009b); (2) *Report of the APA Task Force on Gender Identity and Gender Variance* (American Psychological Association, 2009c); (3) Association for Lesbian, Gay, Bisexual, and Transgender Issues in Counseling's (ALGBTIC's)

"Competencies for Counseling Transgender Clients" (Burnes et al., 2009); and (4) "Guidelines for Psychotherapy With Lesbian, Gay, and Bisexual Clients" (American Psychological Association, 2012).

In order to counsel LGBTQ individuals effectively, therapists must have a basic understanding of the social, cultural, and historic context in which lesbian women and gay men, as well as those who identify as bisexual, transgender, or queer, live. Counselors and therapists should become aware of the history, language, traditions, and sense of community that characterize LGBTQ cultures (Lyons, Bieschke, Dendy, Worthington, & Georgemiller, 2010).

THE THERAPEUTIC PROCESS IN GAY AND LESBIAN PSYCHOTHERAPY

Except for issues that emanate from the first five stages of the Cass gender identity model, treatment for gay men and lesbians is similar to that for heterosexuals. In terms of mood disorders, anxiety disorders, relationship concerns, stress, and sexual issues, gay men and lesbian women present at about the same rate as their heterosexual counterparts, and treatment should be the same for both groups (Heffner, 2003). For adolescents who are struggling with gender identity issues, depression is significantly higher, and the suicide rate is double that of their straight friends. Suicidal ideation, depression, and anxiety tend to be higher among clients who have not accepted their sexuality or who are struggling for sexual orientation acceptance from friends and family. Heffner (2003) points out that couples therapy for gays should be treated no differently than marital therapy for straights, except for the obvious legal and social issues.

> ### Cultural Reflections
>
> *To what extent would you feel comfortable counseling a person who is a member of the LGBTQ community?*
>
> *Are you familiar with the counseling competencies required to work ethically with LGBTQ clients?*
>
> *What kinds of training have you had that might prepare you to counsel effectively an LGBTQ client?*
>
> *What kind of training would you like to have for working with LGBTQ clients?*

ROLE OF THE THERAPIST IN WORKING WITH LGBTQ CLIENTS

Counselors and therapists who work with LGBTQ clients should first take a personal inventory of their own sexual orientation attitudes. How does the counselor or therapist feel about LGBTQ people? Are there any negative or positive feelings for members of these groups? Does the counselor or therapist have any religious beliefs that would suggest that it might be better that he or she did not work with members of the LGBTQ community? If counselors or therapists have prejudices against members of the LGBTQ community, then they should refer the client to someone else. Heffner (2003) also states, "If a therapist believes homosexuality is wrong, sinful, immoral, or a mental illness, he or she should NOT work with gay clients. Refer this client to someone who is able to provide the necessary components of a therapeutic relationship." Both the American Counseling Association (2014) and the American Psychological Association (2009b, 2009c) have ethical codes that provide guidelines for working with clients around issues of their sexual orientation.

Second, before beginning treatment with an LGBTQ client, counselors and therapists are responsible for making sure that they are knowledgeable on issues related to sexuality and that they have the clinical skills needed to create a positive and nonjudgmental counseling relationship and will not feel uncomfortable discussing issues related to homosexuality (Heffner, 2003).

Third, counselors and therapists should be knowledgeable about the gender identity development of LGBTQ people. When counseling gay or lesbian clients, it is important to understand where they are in terms of their own sexual identities. Clients who state that they are trying to convert to a "straight lifestyle" are most likely in Stage 2 or 3 of the Cass sexual identity model. They have not accepted themselves as gay and most likely have not experienced strong love and acceptance from those who know their sexual orientation. Clients in Stages 4 and 5 are usually trying to reinvent themselves with their newly found acceptance of their sexuality. They may be looking for gay friends. Although they have accepted their sexuality, they have not learned how to integrate their sexuality into their overall sense of self. As Heffner (2003) has stated, "in treatment, the strength these individuals feel should be embraced and treatment should be focused on what they can do, not to make the world accept them, but to show the world that they are worthy of acceptance." Clients in Stage 6 of the Cass gender identity model present as no different from most other clients in therapy. Because they have accepted their sexuality and have developed relationships, they don't see being gay as the issue in their lives. Instead, they view their gayness as just one of the many issues they must contend with. They may also see their gayness in a positive light.

Morgan and Brown (1991) found that age cannot be a predictor of lesbian or gay identity development because people discover their sexual orientation at a variety of ages. To counsel LGBTQ individuals effectively, counselors and therapists must be aware of the stages of the clients' gender identity development in addition to their overall psychosocial development.

Fourth, counselors and therapists should be familiar with the LGBTQ culture, as well as the status of LGBTQ people within other cultural communities. If clinicians are lacking in knowledge regarding LGBTQ issues, there are a number of sources that can provide the missing information. For instance, the American Counseling Association has the Association for Lesbian, Gay, Bisexual, and Transgender Issues in Counseling; the American Psychological Association has Division 44—the Society for the Psychology of Sexual Orientation and Gender Diversity.

GAY AFFIRMATIVE PSYCHOTHERAPY

A number of theoretical approaches can be used with gay men and lesbians as long as some of the principles enunciated in the APA guidelines are maintained. The critical issue is respect for gay rights and issues in psychotherapy. Since the 1980s, psychotherapists have begun to use **gay affirmative therapy**, which encourages gay and lesbian clients to accept their sexual orientation (Landridge, 2007). This practical approach does not attempt to change gay men or lesbians to eliminate or to reduce their same-sex desires and behaviors. Gay affirmative psychotherapy states that homosexuality or bisexuality is not a mental illness. In fact, it encourages psychotherapists to assist clients in overcoming the stigma of homosexuality rather than the orientation itself. Gay affirmative therapy recognizes that many LGBTQ individuals are rejected by their families and therefore must form their own families (Milton & Coyle, 1999). It states that embracing and affirming a gay identity can be a key component to recovery from a mental illness or substance abuse.

Gay affirmative therapy is viewed as the appropriate answer to conversion therapy, which focused on trying to change the client's sexual identity from homosexual to heterosexual. Psychotherapy for LGBTQ clients appears to be still in the process of developing, as researchers, clinicians, and theorists learn more about homosexuality and identity development for LGBTQ people. Specific counseling techniques need to be identified for gay affirmative psychotherapy.

The counselor or therapist should work to create an accepting therapeutic environment. In order to achieve this goal, the following suggestions are offered (Buhrke & Douce, 1991):

- Do not assume that every client is heterosexual.

- Create an atmosphere of acceptance by using inclusive language during therapy. You might want to have magazines and brochures that are inclusive of gender orientation.

- Work at feeling comfortable talking about sex, gender, and sexual orientation.

- Do not assume that being LGBTQ is the cause of the client's problem.

- On the other hand, do not assume that being LGBTQ does not matter. It just might be part of the client's issue(s).

Barriers to Assessment of LGBTQ Clients

It is important to consider barriers to assessment of LGBTQ clients, which may include both attitudinal and knowledge issues as well as behavioral issues (Barret & Logan, 2002). LGBTQ individuals might feel hesitant to disclose their sexual orientation to a counselor or therapist. Therefore, the clinician must work to create a safe environment for an LGBTQ client to disclose (Pope, 2008).

Other barriers to accurate assessment of LGBTQ clients include

- Personal biases of providers

- The client's own internalized homophobia

- The counselor or therapist's lack of information and knowledge about an LGBTQ population

Positive Clinical Assessment of LGBTQ Clients

To conduct a meaningful assessment of LGBTQ clients, the counselor or therapist assesses along several dimensions, including medical or physical health, mental health concerns, and LGBTQ concerns (Anderson, Croteau, Chung, & DiStefano, 2001). Medical assessments should include specific questions for LGBTQ clients. The client is informed of the limits of his or her confidentiality and his or her right to refuse to answer any question. Some sample assessment questions that a counselor or therapist might ask about the client's LGBTQ status include (Barret & Logan, 2002) the following:

- How do you feel about your sexual orientation?

- Are you currently sexually involved—with males, females, or both?

- Describe your past sexual involvements.

- Have you come out about your sexual orientation? If so, to whom?

- When did you come out?

- Why did you come out?

- What was the coming-out process like for you? Would you say that it was primarily positive or negative?

- How does your family respond to you about your sexual orientation?

- How would you describe the sexual orientation of your closest friends?

- What is your culture's response to LGBTQ individuals?

- To what extent are sex and drugs linked together in your life?

- To what degree have you experienced shame, depression, anxiety, and low self-image due to your sexual orientation?

Reparative Therapy and Sexual Orientation Conversion Therapy

The terms *reparative therapy* and *sexual orientation conversion therapy* refer to psychotherapy whose goal is to eliminate or suppress a person's homosexuality. Reparative therapists and sexual conversion therapists claim that they can change one's sexual orientation. Both these therapeutic approaches are founded on a view of homosexuality that has been rejected by all the major mental health professions.

For the most part, conversion therapy is rejected in most circles, except when clients have strong religious sanctions against homosexuality. The general consensus among mental health organizations and professions is that both heterosexuality and homosexuality are normal expressions of human sexuality. The DSM-5 (American Psychiatric Association, 2013), which defines the standards of the mental health field, does not include homosexuality as a disorder. "Thus, the idea that homosexuality is a mental disorder or that the emergence of same-sex attraction and orientation among some adolescents is in any way abnormal or mentally unhealthy has no support among any mainstream health and mental health professional organizations" (Just the Facts Coalition, 2008, p. 5).

The nation's leading mental health organizations have all issued statements indicating that they do not support efforts to change individuals' sexual orientation through therapy and that they have serious concerns about the potential harm from such efforts. The American Psychiatric Association, American Psychological Association, and American Academy of Pediatrics have denounced conversion and reparative treatment because of the high number of negative outcomes and questionable success rate (Heffner, 2003). The National Association of Social Workers (n.d.) is similarly opposed and endorses acceptance of every individual of every sexual orientation.

CASE VIGNETTE 15.1
SAL AND THE STRENGTHS-BASED THERAPY MODEL

Sal spent his early years attending school in Florida, in a medium-sized football town where every Friday it seemed like the entire town met to cheer at a game. Sal was a White male of Italian descent. His family was middle class, with his mother working as a schoolteacher and his father as a postal clerk. Sal himself was a skinny, rather effeminate-looking boy. He didn't look anything like his brother, who played on the football team and was a star with the girls at school.

Everyone called Sal "gay," even though he didn't feel gay. They said that he just looked gay. Sal felt that he was an embarrassment to his brother, and they rarely talked during the school day or even acknowledged each other. Sal stayed on the sidelines, watching all the fun that his brother, Dom, was having. There was a part of him that wished he were Dom, that wished he weren't so skinny and "gay" looking.

It seemed that the kids at Sal's high school recognized that he was gay before Sal himself did. Sal was miserable. Most of the time he wished that he didn't exist, that somehow he could just leave his body and all his problems behind.

Then, without much warning, Sal's parents moved to New York City where his mother had applied for a job as a school principal. His father was also offered a promotion to supervisor at one of the New York postal substations. Initially, Sal didn't adjust. New York was just too big, and he did not know many people there. It was as if he had become invisible. Then one day Sal heard about an after-school program at Harvey Milk High School, a school that openly accepted gays and a lot of other people who were not gay. At Harvey Milk High School, Sal went to see the guidance counselor because he needed someone to talk with and to help him sort things out.

The counselor was very receptive to Sal. In fact, he sensed why Sal had come without his having to say anything. Sal confided to the counselor that the kids at his other high school had called him gay and a whole lot of other names that he would like to forget.

The counselor said: "I've listened to you tell me what the kids at your old school used to say about you. They called you gay, and you felt hurt because you didn't feel gay, and you didn't know what you were doing to make them call you gay."

"Yeah," Sal said with a sigh of relief that someone understood what he was feeling. "That's right. It was not as if I was wearing a stamp on my forehead that said, 'I'm gay, look at me.' I felt ashamed. I didn't know what to do."

Counselor: "Feeling ashamed of something that you really don't know a lot about must have been somewhat overwhelming for you. Did you try to talk with anyone about what was happening at school?"

Sal: "No, I just kept it all inside, turning it over and over again inside my head until it felt as if my head were going to burst."

Counselor: "And you're here now, Sal, because you are tired of turning it over and over again inside

Sal: "You've got it. If I'm gay, I need to know that and to face it."

Counselor: "And how do you find out if you're gay, Sal? Did you come here expecting me to tell you—to deliver a gay or not gay verdict? What do you think? Are you gay?"

Sal: "I don't know. Maybe I am. Maybe I'm not. I came here to sort everything out. I feel bad about myself. In fact, I hate myself. I hate the way I look. I hate being me."

The counselor and Sal agreed to meet again to discuss his concerns about possibly being gay.

Strengths Discovery. Sal had expected that the next session would be all about his problem, his unresolved question, but instead, the counselor said he wanted to spend time getting to know him. Much to his surprise, the counselor asked him about his strengths. Initially, Sal thought to himself, "Didn't you hear what I said to you last week? I said that I hated myself, and now you ask me about my strengths. What strengths? I don't have any, case closed."

The counselor told Sal that he saw a strength in him as he walked in the door of his office. "What strength did you see?" Sal asked.

The counselor said, "I saw the strength of a young man who was tired of living in the confusion that had dominated his life for a while, and now he was ready to do something about it. The very fact that you came back this week said to me that you weren't running away any more, that you were ready to explore with me your gender identity."

From that point on, the counselor began to explore Sal's other strengths. They discussed a side of Sal that seemed almost hidden and forgotten by him—his strengths. Except for his quarterly report card, no one had ever talked about his strengths. Most of the session was spent on examining Sal's strengths, in getting him in touch with what he did right and what he enjoyed doing. For the first time in years, Sal felt motivated to do something about his life. He had strengths. He had the power to figure things out for himself. There was no rush to pronounce himself "gay" or "not gay."

Let Go. The following two sessions were spent on examining the internalized homophobic statements Sal heard repeated in his head. The counselor helped him to distance himself from other people's opinions and negative statements. Gradually, Sal was able to let go of the internalized hurtful and negative statements of his former classmates. He learned that he had a choice either to let other people's opinions have an effect on him or to simply say to himself, "Delete, delete. I delete your message and opinion."

Let In. Sal's attendance at the after-school program led to his applying formally for acceptance at Harvey Milk High School. He felt that by enrolling in that school he could finally be himself. He could be free to learn and to sort things out about his own gender identity in a friendly atmosphere. Sal formed new friends at Harvey Milk High School, and he is now doing quite well.

Let Be. He feels a sense of harmony with himself because he has quieted the battle going on inside of himself. His grades have improved tremendously. Sal has decided that he is gay, but this decision doesn't frighten him anymore, because he has found a group of supportive teachers and friends at school.

He wasn't sure how his parents would take his coming out, so he texted them that he was gay. The text message that said "I'm gay" ended his fear of his parents' disappointment. While they did not accept his announcement of gayness with any kind of happiness, they did say that they had wondered themselves for a long time, and now they didn't have to wonder and worry. All cards were on the table, and the family could now heal and move forward. His parents reassured him that they still loved him and that they would always love him.

Move Forward. Sal is applying for admission to several colleges in New York City. For the first time he can remember, he is experiencing a sense of his own power and strengths, and he is happy.

SUMMARY OF KEY POINTS

LGBTQ treatment is not something one should embark upon without specific training for working with individuals of this group. This section contains a summary of some of the clinical implications for the various areas discussed in this chapter.

1. Before working with LGBTQ clients, clinicians should examine their own worldviews about heterosexuality and homosexuality and then examine the influence of such worldviews on a counseling relationship with an LGBTQ client.

2. Clinicians should familiarize themselves with the official American Psychological Association documents that deal with competent practice with LGBTQ individuals, including *Report of the APA*

Task Force on Appropriate Therapeutic Responses to Sexual Orientation (American Psychological Association, 2009b); *Report of the APA Task Force on Gender Identity and Gender Variance* (American Psychological Association, 2009c); and ALGBTIC's "Competencies for Counseling Transgender Clients" (Burnes et al., 2009).

3. LGBTQ is a very diverse community. A clinician should treat LGBTQ clients as individuals first and avoid making assumptions. Do not assume that because a client is LGBTQ that his or her presenting issues are related to his or her sexual orientation. He or she may have problems that are related to issues not involving his or her sexual orientation.

4. Clinicians should recognize *LGBTQ-specific issues* raised either explicitly or implicitly by the client during therapy. Such issues might include coming out, homophobia (internalized or externalized, leading to suicide, self-injury, and self-medication), leading a double life, drugs, alcohol, and HIV.

5. Clinicians should not assume that clients are heterosexual just because they have not indicated otherwise.

6. Clinicians should not assume that LGBTQ clients do not have children.

7. Clinicians offer psychotherapy services that are geared to address LGBTQ issues as they arise during the therapeutic relationship.

8. Clinicians should understand that LGBTQ clients may have been exposed to homophobia and heterosexism and may have internalized negative views of themselves based on such internalizations. Clinicians might have to use strategies that include identifying and removing negative cognitive distortions and then helping clients to develop positive affirming messages about their gender identity.

9. Competent clinicians help a client locate support within a given community to deal with LGBTQ issues.

10. Competent clinicians help an LGBTQ client recognize, understand, and deal with internalized and externalized homophobia.

11. Clinicians understand that the presence of a single, supportive adult in the life of an LGBTQ young person is a critical factor in increasing the youth's sense of safety and academic achievement and in decreasing the youth's risk of truancy or of dropping out of school.

12. The competent clinician helps schools to develop school district policies that specifically define and prohibit bullying, discrimination, and harassment based on a youth's sexual orientation and gender identity or expression. Generic anti-bullying or anti-discrimination policies do little to help those who are LGBTQ or who appear to be LGBTQ.

13. There are "risky" school environments that make it unsafe for LGBTQ youth and other marginalized students. Risky environments are defined as those in which students, staff, and administrators are unaware of or resistant to dealing with homophobic bullying and prejudice, and in which students feel unsafe if they are LGBTQ or gender-noncomforming, or perceived as such.

14. Current research has found that children with gay and lesbian parents do not differ from children with heterosexual parents in their emotion development or in their relationships with others. Moreover, their children are not more likely to be gay than children with heterosexual parents, and they are not more likely to be sexually abused.

15. Competent clinicians help LGBTQ clients to discover their strengths and to use such strengths in dealing with their life challenges.

16. Clinicians should ensure that their intake forms and office is free of heterosexist bias. Include questions on your intake forms that ask information about sexual orientation and gender identity.

DISCUSSION QUESTIONS

Discussion Question Set 1

In groups of three or four, discuss how comfortable you would feel counseling a member of the LGBTQ population. What kind of specific training has your university or institution provided in helping you to counsel effectively with members of the LGBTQ community?

Discussion Question Set 2

List three qualifications that you believe a person should have in counseling a member of the LGBTQ community.

What is your position on the bathroom issues related to transgender people? Should transgender people be required to use the bathroom of their birth sexuality or their identified sexuality?

KEY TERMS

Bisexual: A term that describes people who have an affectional and/or sexual attraction to members of both sexes.

Cisgender: A term that describes the vast majority of people in that it refers to a person whose biological gender is consistent with the way the person views his or her gender. For instance, most people who are born a female grow up to identify with other females.

Coming out: To publicly affirm one's homosexual identity, sometimes to one person in conversation, sometimes by an act that puts one in the public eye. Coming out, however, is never a single event but rather a lifelong process.

Gay: A term that describes a man who has a sexual attraction to another man.

Gay affirmative therapy: Does not attempt to change gay men or lesbians to eliminate or to reduce their same-sex desires and behaviors. It states that homosexuality or bisexuality is not a mental illness. It encourages psychotherapists to assist clients in overcoming the stigma of homosexuality rather than the orientation itself.

Gender: The socially constructed roles, behaviors, activities, and attributes that each society believes is appropriate for boys and men or girls and women. One may assume a gender role that is in agreement with one's biological sex or that is different from one's biological sex.

Gender dysphoria: Deals with individuals' discontent with the biological sex they are born with.

Gender expression: The manner in which a person communicates gender identity to others through behavior, clothing, hairstyles, voice, or body characteristics.

Gender identity: An individual's internal sense of being male, female, or something else. Gender reflects a society's social norms about what is appropriate feminine and masculine behavior.

Gender schema theory: An information-processing approach to gender typing that combines social learning theory and cognitive development theory. Children organize their experiences into gender schemas, or masculine and feminine categories to make sense of their world. When preschoolers learn how to label their own sex, they

choose gender schemas consistent with it. For instance, a boy's gender schema may contain cognitions that men become president of the United States, while young girls' gender schema may consist of cognitions that women become models.

Genderqueer/nonbinary: Terms used by some people who experience their gender identity and/or gender expression as falling outside the categories of man and woman. They may define their gender as falling somewhere in between man and woman, or they may define it as wholly different from these terms.

Heterosexism: The belief that every person is heterosexual; therefore, it marginalizes or disregards persons who do not identify as heterosexual. It is also the belief that heterosexuality is superior to homosexuality and other sexual orientations.

Heterosexist or transphobic terminology: Microaggressions that occur when a person uses negative or disparaging heterosexist language toward LGBTQ people. Some of these expressions include "That's so gay" and, for transgender people, saying "tranny."

Heterosexual: A term that is used to describe a person who has an affectional bond or attraction to a person of the opposite sex.

Homophobia: Fear of people attracted to the same sex.

Homosexual: A term that is used to describe a person who has an affectional bond or attraction to a person of the same sex. This term is considered to be outdated.

Lesbian: A woman who has an affectional and/or sexual attraction to another woman.

LGBTQ: The acronym that stands for lesbian, gay, bisexual, transgender, and queer (or questioning).

Queer: A term that includes many categories of sexual minorities that has been reclaimed by the LGBTQ community.

Sex: What each person is assigned at birth; it refers to a person's biological status as either male or female, and it is usually determined by physical attributes, such as chromosome, hormone prevalence, and external and internal anatomy. Whereas sex refers to biological, chromosomal, and anatomical determinants of male and female, gender deals with how people identify themselves as masculine or feminine.

Sexual orientation: An enduring emotional, romantic, or sexual attraction that a person feels toward men, women, or both.

Transgender: A broad range of sexual behaviors, identifications, and expressions that challenge the binary gender system.

REFERENCES AND SUGGESTED READING

Akerlund, M., & Cheung, M. (2000). Teaching beyond the deficit model: Gay and lesbian issues among African Americans, Latinos, and Asian Americans. *Journal of Social Work Education, 36,* 279–291.

Altman, D. (1979). *Coming out in the seventies.* Sydney, New South Wales, Australia: Wild & Woolley.

American Academy of Child & Adolescent Psychiatry. (2013, August). Lesbian, gay, bisexual and transgender parents. *Facts for families.* Retrieved from http://www.aacap.org/aacap/fffprint/article_print.aspx?dn=Children-with-Lesbian-Gay-Bisexual-and-Transgender-Parents-092

American Counseling Association. (2014). *ACA code of ethics.* Alexandria, VA: Author.

American Psychiatric Association. (2013). *Diagnostic and statistical manual of mental disorders* (5th ed.). Arlington, VA: Author.

American Psychological Association. (2009a, August 5). *Insufficient evidence that sexual orientation change efforts work.* Retrieved from http://www.apa.org/news/press/releases/2009/08/therapeutic.aspx

American Psychological Association. (2009b). *Report of the American Psychological Association Task Force on Appropriate Therapeutic Responses to Sexual Orientation.* Retrieved from http://www.apa.org/pi/lgbc/publications/therapeutic-resp.html

American Psychological Association. (2009c). *Report of the American Psychological Association Task Force on Gender Identity and Gender Variance.* Washington, DC: American Psychological Association.

American Psychological Association, Division 44/Committee on Lesbian, Gay, and Bisexual Concerns Joint Task Force. (2012). Guidelines for psychotherapy with lesbian, gay, and bisexual clients. *American Psychologist, 67,* 10–42.

American Psychological Association. (2018). *Transgender people, gender identity and gender expression.* Retrieved from http://www.apa.org/topics/lgbt/transgender.aspx

American Psychological Association. (n.d.). *Sexual orientation, gender identity & socioeconomic status.* Retrieved from http://www.apa.org/pi/ses/resources/publications/factsheet-lgbt.pdf

American School Counselor Association. (2016). *The school counselor and LGBTQ youth* (Adopted 1995, revised 2000, 2005, 2007, 2013, 2014, 2016). Retrieved from https://www.schoolcounselor.org/asca/media/asca/Position Statements/PS_LGBTQ.pdf

Anderson, M. S., Croteau, J. M., Chung, B., & DiStefano, T. M. (2001). Developing an assessment of sexual identity management for lesbian and gay workers. *Journal of Career Assessment, 9,* 243–260.

Balsam, K. F., Rothblum, E. D., & Beauchaine, T. P. (2005). Victimization over the life span: A comparison of lesbian, gay, bisexual, and heterosexual siblings. *Journal of Consulting and Clinical Psychology, 73,* 477–487.

Barret, B., & Logan, C. (2002). *Counseling gay men and lesbians: A practice primer.* Belmont, CA: Brooks/Cole.

Bem, S. (1993). *The lenses of gender.* New Haven, CT: Yale University Press.

Berk, L. E. (2007). *Development through the lifespan* (4th ed.). Boston, MA: Allyn & Bacon.

Bos, H., & Gartrell, N. (2010). Adolescents of the USA National Longitudinal Lesbian Family Study: Can family characteristics counteract the negative effects of stigmatization? *Family Process, 49,* 559–572.

Bressert, S. (2017). Gender dysphoria symptoms. *Psych Central.* Retrieved from https://psychcentral.com/disorders/gender-dysphoria-symptoms/

Buhrke, R. A., & Douce, A. (1991). Training issues for counseling psychologists in working with lesbians and gay men. *The Counseling Psychologist, 19,* 216–234.

Burnes, T. R., Singh, A. A., Harper, A., Pickering, D. L., Moundas, S., Scofield, T.,. . . Hosea, J. (2009). ALGBTIC competencies for counseling transgender clients. Retrieved from https://www.tandfonline.com/doi/abs/10.1080/15538605.2010.524839

Burns, C., & Krehely, J. (2011). *Gay and transgender people face high rates of workplace discrimination and harassment.* Center for American Progress. Retrieved from https://www.americanprogress.org/issues/lgbt/news/2011/06/02/9872/

gay-and-transgender-people-face-high-rates-of-workplace-discrimination-and-harassment/

Carroll, L., Gilroy, P. J., & Ryan, J. (2002). Counseling transgendered, transsexual, and gender-variant clients. *Journal of Counseling & Development, 80*(2), 131–139.

Cass, V. C. (1979). Homosexual identity formation: A theoretical model. *Journal of Homosexuality, 4*, 219–235.

Central Counseling Services. (2017, July 13). *What does transgender mean?* Retrieved from http://www.central counselingservices.net/beneficialblogs/2017/7/13/fxpkv07yub1pw4rrf8ywk28t79k5l0

Cianciotto, J., & Cahill, S. (2003). *Education policy: Issues affecting lesbian, gay, bisexual, and transgender youth.* New York, NY: National Gay and Lesbian Task Force Policy Institute.

Cochran, S. D. (2001). Emerging issues in research on lesbians and gay men's mental health: Does sexual orientation really matter? *American Psychologist*, pp. 932–947.

Croteau, J., Lark, J., Lidderdale, M., & Chung, Y. B. (Eds.). (2005). *Deconstructing heterosexism in the counseling professions.* Thousand Oaks, CA: Sage.

de Vogue, A., & Diamond, J. (2015, June 27). Supreme Court rules in favor of same-sex marriage nationwide. *CNN Politics.* Retrieved from http://www.cnn.com/2015/06/26/politics/supreme-court-same-sex-marriage-ruling/index.html

DeAngelis, T. (2002). A new generation of issues for LGBT clients. *APA Monitor, 33*, 42–44.

Duan, C., & Brown, C. (2016). *Becoming a multiculturally competent counselor.* Thousand Oaks, CA: Sage.

Egan, P. J., Edelman, M. S., & Sherrill, K. (2008). *Findings from the Hunter College poll of lesbians, gays, and bisexuals: New discoveries about identity, political attitudes, and civic engagement.* Washington, DC: Human Rights Campaign.

Estrada, F., Rigali-Oiler, M., Arciniega, M., & Tracey, T. J. G. (2011). Machismo and Mexican American men: An empirical understanding using a gay sample. *Journal of Counseling Psychology, 58*, 358–367.

Factor, R. J., & Rothblum, E. D. (2007). A study of transgender adults and their non-transgender siblings on demographic characteristics, social support, and experiences of violence. *Journal of LGBT Health Research, 3*, 11–30.

Fitzpatrick, K. K., Euton, S. J., Jones, J. N., Schmidt, N. J. (2005). Gender role, sexual orientation, and suicide risk. *Journal of Affective Disorders, 87*, 35–42.

Franke-Ruta, G. (Jan. 24, 2013). An amazing 1969 account of the Stonewall uprising. *The Atlantic.* Retrieved at https://www.theatlantic.com/politics/archive/2013/01/an-amazing-1969-account-of-the-stonewall-uprising/272467/.

Gainor, K. A. (2009). Including transgender issues in lesbian, gay and bisexual psychology. In B. Greene & G. L. Croom (Eds.), *Psychological perspectives on lesbian and gay issues, vol. 5: Education, research, and practice in lesbian, gay, bisexual, and transgendered psychology* (pp. 131–160). Thousand Oaks, CA; Sage.

Gates, G. J. (2011, April). How many people are lesbian, gay, bisexual and transgender? *The Williams Institute, UCLA School of Law.* Retrieved from https://williamsinstitute.law.ucla.edu/research/census-lgbt-demographics-studies/how-many-people-are-lesbian-gay-bisexual-and-transgender/

Gonsiorek, J. C. (1993). Threat, stress, and adjustment: Mental health and the workplace for gay and lesbian individuals. In L. Diamont (Ed.), *Homosexual issues in the workplace* (pp. 243–264). Washington, DC: Taylor & Francis.

Grossman, A. J., & D'Augelli, A. R. (2006). Transgender youth: Invisible and vulnerable. *Journal of Homosexuality, 51*(1), 111–128.

Hancock, K. A. (2000). Lesbian, gay, and bisexual lives: Basic issues in psychotherapy training and practice. In B. Greene & G. L. Croom (Eds.), *Education, research, and practice in lesbian, gay, bisexual, and transgendered psychology: A resource manual* (pp. 91–130). Thousand Oaks, CA: Sage.

Heffner, C. L. (2003, August 12). Counseling the gay and lesbian client: Treatment issues and conversion therapy. *AllPsych.* Retrieved from http://allpsych.com/journal/counselinggay.html

Herek, G. M., Cogan, S. C., & Gillis, J. R. (2002). Victim experiences of hate crimes based on sexual orientation. *Journal of Social Issues, 58*, 319–399.

Huang, Y., Brewster, M. E., Moradi, B., Goodman, M. B., Wiseman, M. C., & Martin, A. (2010). Content analysis of literature about LGB people of color: 1998–2007. *The Counseling Psychologist, 38*, 363–396.

Jones-Smith, E. (2014). *Strengths-based therapy: Connecting theory, practice, and skills.* Thousand Oaks, CA: Sage.

Just the Facts Coalition. (2008). *Just the facts about sexual orientation and youth: A primer for principals, educators, and school personnel.* Washington, DC: American Psychological Association. Retrieved from https://www.apa.org/pi/lgbt/resources/just-the-facts.pdf

Kashubeck-West, S., Szymanski, D., & Meyer, J. (2008). Internalized heterosexism: Clinical implications and training considerations. *Counseling Psychologist, 36*, 615–630.

Kim, R. (with D. Sheridan & S. Holcomb). (2009). *A report on the status of gay, lesbian, bisexual and transgender people in education: Stepping out of the closet, into the light.* Washington, DC: National Education Association of the United States.

Kindlon, D. J., & Thompson, M. (2000). *Raising Cain: Protecting the emotional life of boys.* New York, NY: Ballantine Books.

Kosciw, J. G., Diaz, E. M., & Greytak, E. A. (2008). *2007 National School Climate Survey: The experiences of lesbian, gay, bisexual and transgender youth in our nation's schools.* New York, NY: GLSEN.

Landridge, D. (2007). Gay affirmative therapy: A theoretical framework and defense. *Journal of Gay & Lesbian Psychotherapy, 11*(102), 27–43.

Lev, A. (2004). *Transgender emergence: Therapeutic guidelines for working with gender-variant people and their families.* Binghamton, NY: Haworth Clinical Practice Press.

Lyons, H. Z., Bieschke, K. J., Dendy, A. K., Worthington, R. L., & Georgemiller, R. (2010). Psychologists' competence to treat lesbian, gay and bisexual clients: State of the field and strategies for improvement. *Professional Psychology: Research and Practice, 41*, 424–434.

Maskovsky, J. (2001). Sexual minorities and the new urban poverty. In I. Susser & Thomas C. Patterson (Eds.), *Cultural diversity in the United States: A critical reader* (p. 322–342). Oxford, England: Blackwell. Reprinted in Baker, L. D. (Ed.). (2004). *Life in America: Identity and everyday experience* (pp. 227–239). Oxford, England: Blackwell.

Mays, V. M., & Cochran, S. D. (2001). Mental health correlates of perceived discrimination among lesbian, gay, and bisexual adults in the United States. *American Journal of Public Health, 91*(13), 1869–1876.

McLaughlin, K. A., Hatzenbuehler, M. L., & Keyes, K. M. (2010). Responses to discrimination and psychiatric disorders among Black, Hispanic, female, and lesbian, gay, and bisexual individuals. *American Journal of Public Health, 100*(8), 1477–1484. doi:10.2105/ajph.2009.181586

Milton, M., & Coyle, A. (1999). Lesbian and gay affirmative psychotherapy: Issues in theory and practice. *Sexual and Relationship Therapy, 14*, 43–59.

Moran, L., & Sharpe, A. (2004). Violence, identity and policing: The case of violence against transgender people. *Criminal Justice, 4*(4), 395–417.

Morgan, K. S., & Brown, L. S. (1991). Lesbian career development, work behavior, and vocational counseling. *The Counseling Psychologist, 19*, 273–279.

Nadal, K. L. (2013). *That's so gay? Microaggressions and the lesbian, gay, bisexual, and transgender community.* Washington, DC: American Psychological Association.

Nadal, K. L. (2014, February 7). Stop saying "That's so gay!": 6 types of microaggressions that harm LGBTQ people. *Psychology Benefits Society.* Retrieved from https://psychologybenefits.org/2014/02/07/anti-lgbt-microaggressions

Nadal, K. L., Issa, M., Leon, J., Meterko, V., Wideman, M., & Wong, Y. (2011). Sexual orientation microaggressions: "Death by a thousand cuts" for lesbian, gay, and bisexual youth. *Journal of LGBT Youth, 8*(3), 1–26.

Nadal, K. L., Skolnik, A., & Wong, Y. (2012). Interpersonal and systemic microaggressions: Psychological impacts on transgender individuals and communities. *Journal of LGBT Issues in Counseling, 6*(1), 55–82.

Nadal, K. L., Wong, Y., Griffin, K., Sriken, J., Vargas, V., Wideman, M., & Kolawole, A. (2011). Microaggressions and the multiracial experience. *International Journal of Humanities and Social Sciences, 1*(7), 36–44.

Nadal, K. L., Wong, Y., Issa, M., Meterko, V., Leon, J., & Wideman, M. (2011). Sexual orientation microaggressions: Processes and coping mechanisms for lesbian, gay, and bisexual individuals. *Journal of LGBT Issues in Counseling, 5*(1), 21–46.

National Association of Social Workers. (n.d.). *Lesbian, gay, bisexual and transgender.* Retrieved from https://www.socialworkers.org/Practice/LGBT

Pace University. (2008, Fall). *Spotlight newsletter.* Retrieved from https://www.pace.edu/sites/default/files/files/Counseling/spotlight-on-lgbt.pdf

Pachankis, J. E., & Goldfried, M. R. (2004). Clinical issues in working with lesbian, gay, and bisexual clients. *Psychotherapy: Theory, Research, Practice, Training, 41*(3), 227–246.

Panelists recount events leading to deleting homosexuality as a psychiatric disorder from DSM. (1998, July 17). Professional News, *Psychiatric News.* Retrieved from http://www.psychiatricnews.org/pnews/98-07-17/dsm.html

Pope, M. (2008). Culturally appropriate counseling considerations for lesbian and gay clients. In P. Pedersen, J. G. Draguns, W. J. Lonner, & J. E. Trimble (Eds.), *Counseling across cultures* (6th ed., pp. 201–222). Thousand Oaks, CA: Sage.

Pope, M., & Barret, B. (2002). Counseling gay men toward an integrated sexuality. In L. D. Burlew & D. Capuzzi (Eds.), *Sexuality counseling* (pp. 149–176). Hauppauge, NY: Nova Science.

Pope, M., & Schecter, E. (1992, October). *Career strategies: Career suicide or success?* Paper presented at the Second Annual Lesbian and Gay Workplace Issues Conference, Stanford, CA.

Riggle, E. D. B., Whitman, J. S., Olson, A., Rostosky, S. S., & Strong, S. (2008). The positive aspects of being a lesbian or gay man. *Professional Psychology: Research and Practice, 39*, 210–217.

Rosario, M., Schrimshaw, E. W., & Hunter, J. (2004). Ethnic/racial differences in the coming out process of lesbian, gay, and bisexual youths: A comparison of sexual identity development over time. *Cultural Diversity and Ethnic Minority Psychology, 10*, 215–228.

Rosario, M., Schrimshaw, E. W., & Hunter, J., & Braun, L. (2006). Sexual identity development among lesbian, gay, and bisexual youths: Consistency and change over time. *Journal of Sex Research, 43*, 446–458.

Rostosky, S. S., Riggle, E. D. B., Pascale-Hague, D., & McCants, L. E. (2010). The positive aspects of a bisexual self-identification. *Psychology & Sexuality, 1*(2), 131–144.

Rothblum, E. D., & Factor, R. (2001). Lesbians and their sisters as a control group: Demographic and mental health factors. *Psychological Science, 12*(1), 63–69.

Singh, A. A., & Chun, K. S. Y. (2010). From "margins to the center": Moving towards a resilience based model of supervision with queer people of color. *Training and Education in Professional Psychology, 4*(1), 36–46.

Singh, A. A., Hays, D. G., & Watson, L. S. (2011). Strength in the face of adversity: Resilience strategies of transgender individuals. *Journal of Counseling & Development, 89*, 20–27.

Spadaro, A, S. J. (2013, September 30). A big heart open to God: An interview with Pope Francis. *America: The Jesuit Review.* Retrieved from https://www.americamagazine.org/faith/2013/09/30/big-heart-open-god-interview-pope-francis

Sue, D. W., Arredondo, P., & McDavis, R. J. (1992). Multicultural competencies/standards: A call to the profession. *Journal of Counseling and Development, 70*(4), 477–486.

Sue, D. W., Bucceri, J., Lin, A. I., Nadal, K. L., & Torino, G. C. (2007). Racial microaggressions and the Asian American experience. *Cultural Diversity and Ethnic Minority Psychology, 13*, 72–81.

Telingator, C. J., & Patterson, C. (2008). Children and adolescents of lesbian and gay parents. *American Academy of Child Adolescent Psychiatry, 47*(12), 1364–1368.

U.S. Department of Justice, Federal Bureau of Investigation. (2011). *Hate crime statistics.* Retrieved at https://ucr.fbi.gov/hate-crime/2011

Vaughan, M. D., Miles, J., Parent, M. C., Lee, H. S., Tilghman, J. D., & Prokhorets, S. (2014). A content analysis of LGBT-Themed Positive psychology articles. *Psychology of Sexual Orientation and Gender Diversity, 1*(4), 313–324.

Voss, B. (2012, January 18). The A-list interview: Nick Jonas. *The Advocate.* Retrieved from http://www.advocate.com/arts-entertainment/best-broadway/2012/01/18/nick-jonas-stage-brother

Whitman, J. S., & Boyd, C. J. (2003). *The therapist notebook for lesbian, gay, and bisexual clients.* Binghamton, NY: Haworth.

Windmeyer, S. L. (2006). *The* Advocate *college guide for LGBT students.* New York, NY: Alyson Books.

Witten, T. M. (2014). It's not all darkness: Robustness, resilience, and successful transgender aging. *LGBT Health, 1*, 24–33.

16

CULTURALLY RESPONSIVE STRENGTHS-BASED THERAPY FOR INDIVIDUALS WITH DISABILITIES

CHAPTER OBJECTIVES

- Define disability from the legal (ADA) perspective and from the perspective of disability advocates.

- Describe the demographics of persons with disabilities.

- Summarize models of disability, categories of disability, and what it means to have an invisible disability.

- Analyze disability as a multicultural issue and examine models of disability, major categories of disabilities, and invisible disabilities.

- Understand microaggressions toward people with disabilities, ableism, and spread.

- Become knowledgeable about identity development for people with disabilities.

- Learn the cultural strengths of individuals with disabilities.

- Comprehend the mental health challenges of individuals with disabilities, including interaction strain.

- Understand the implications for counseling individuals with disabilities, including disability affirmative therapy and Olkin's model of disability and counseling approach.

- *"A true friend knows your weaknesses but shows you your strengths; feels your fears but fortifies your faith; sees your anxieties but frees your spirit; recognizes your disabilities but emphasizes your possibilities."* —William Arthur Ward

- *"Pain is Pain. Broken is Broken. FEAR is the Biggest Disability of all. And will PARALYZE you More Than Being in a Wheelchair."* —Nick Vujicic

- *"I am not handicapped by my condition. I am physically challenged and differently able."* —Janet Barnes, recognized as the longest-living quadriplegic

INTRODUCTION

Disability can happen to anyone—young/old, male/female, Black/White, and rich/poor. People with disabilities occupy a unique position in American society. On the one hand, they are not an ethnic minority group, and on the other, they encounter prejudices, discrimination, barriers, oppression, and marginalization similar to those encountered by people from the ethnic/cultural groups presented in this book. Moreover, ethnic minorities and women often find themselves included and over-represented in the population comprising people with disabilities. People with disabilities are often hidden, ignored, neglected, or forgotten. For all of these reasons, this group merits attention as a distinct population.

What does it mean to be disabled, especially in the United States? It depends on the person and the circumstances. For example, each time I watch Nick Vujicic, the Australian Christian evangelist, I am motivated to stop complaining about minor things. Nick was born with phocomelia, a rare disorder characterized by the absence of legs and arms (Vujicic, n.d.). As a child, Nick struggled mentally, emotionally, and physically, but eventually he came to terms with his disability. On television, Nick said that initially he asked God, "Why did You do this to me? Why did You make me a freak?" Then one day Nick said that the answer came to him that God wanted to use him to show His love to the world. From that time forward, Nick became an evangelist traveling the world and speaking to thousands of people. Nick has said that if suddenly he could change to have arms and legs, he would choose to remain as he is—without arms or legs. Nick responded that once he stopped feeling sorry for himself for what he was missing, he began to focus on what he did have and on his strengths. He now has a wife and a child (Vujicic, n.d.). Nick symbolizes a person who overcomes barriers and who uses his strengths to deal with disabilities. In addition, he manifests what a person can accomplish when he focuses his attention on what he can do rather than on what he cannot do.

This chapter addresses culturally responsive strengths-based therapy for individuals experiencing various types of disabilities.

DEFINITION OF DISABILITY AND THE AMERICANS WITH DISABILITIES ACT

Congress provided a legal definition in the **Americans with Disabilities Act (ADA)** of 1990 that describes an individual with a disability as a person who has "a physical or mental impairment that substantially limits one or more major life activities, a person who has a history or record of such an impairment, or a person who is perceived by others as having such an impairment" (U.S. Department of Justice, n.d.). The ADA protects people with intellectual impairment, hearing or vision impairment, orthopedic conditions, learning disabilities, speech impairment, HIV/AIDS, and other health or physical conditions that limit one's life activities.

The ADA deals with four basic areas. First, it requires that local, state, and federal governments and programs be made accessible for individuals with disabilities. Second, it requires employers with more than 15 employees to make "reasonable accommodations" for workers with disabilities and to refrain from discriminating against qualified workers with disabilities. Third, the law mandates that public buildings, accommodations, and facilities (e.g., bathrooms) make reasonable modifications to enable individuals with disabilities to use those buildings and facilities. (Note that "public" in this sense includes privately owned places that are open to the general public, such as stores and restaurants—not just government buildings such as courts and town halls.) Fourth, it requires that individuals with disabilities be given access to public transportation, communication, and other areas of public life (Fleischer, 2001; Murdick, Gartin, & Crabtree, 2007).

In terms of hiring and employment, although the ADA allows employers to inquire about a candidate's ability to perform a job, it places limitations on questions an employer can ask related to the disability. Moreover, if a person is qualified to perform a job, an employer cannot use tests that would cause him or her to be screened out because of a disability. In addition, employers are required to make "reasonable" accommodations for people with disabilities. For instance, an employer might accommodate an employee who has a chronic illness by changing the work schedule to allow time off for medical appointments so that the employee completes work assignments during other hours.

> **Cultural Reflections**
>
> *Does anyone in your family have a disability, as defined by the Americans with Disabilities Act?*
>
> *What are the attitudes in your family toward disability and toward individuals with disabilities?*
>
> *Reflecting on how you were raised, what attitudes about persons with disabilities were you exposed to?*

DEMOGRAPHICS OF PEOPLE WITH DISABILITIES

About 56.7 million people (18.7% of the U.S. population) reported having a disability in 2010. Included in this group are about 38.3 million people (12.6% of the total U.S. population) who had a severe disability. Approximately 12.3 million people aged 6 years and older (4.4% of the U.S. population) required assistance with one or more activities of daily living, which include bathing, dressing, grooming, feeding oneself, and toileting (Brault, 2012). People who have disabilities form the largest minority group within this country.

The risk of having a disability increases as individuals grow older. People in the oldest age group (80 years and older) had a 70.5% prevalence rate for a disability, whereas those in the youngest age group (under 15 years of age) had a prevalence rate of 8.4%. Severe disability increases with age. The probability of severe disability was 1 in 20 for those aged 15 to 24, and 1 in 4 for those aged 65 to 69. More than half (55.8%) of the oldest group (80 years and older) had a severe disability (Brault, 2012).

In addition to the U.S. Census Bureau reports on Americans with disabilities, which are published every few years, Cornell University conducts an annual *Disability Status Report*. The data used in the yearly studies come from the American Community Survey (ACS). Data reported in this section are taken from Cornell University's yearly *Disability Status Report*. In 2016, the overall percentage (prevalence rate) of people with a disability in the United States was 12.8%. In 2016, 40,890,900 of the 319,215,200 people in the United States reported one or more disabilities. For that same year, among the six types of disabilities identified in the ACS (discussed on page 455), the highest prevalence rate was for "Ambulatory Disability," 7.1%. The lowest prevalence rate was for "Visual Disability," 2.4% (Erickson, Lee, & von Schrader, 2018). Each individual's experience of disability is molded by his or her culture and community.

Although disability affects people of all ethnicities, sexual orientations, and gender identities, impairment does not take place uniformly across all groups. The traumatic brain injuries from the wars in Iraq and Afghanistan have resulted in a higher incidence of individuals with disabilities, especially among White Americans (Terrio, Nelson, Betthauser, Harwood, & Brenner, 2011). A U.S. Census Bureau report, "Americans With Disabilities: 2010," has provided an age-adjusted profile that reports disability according to gender and race (Brault, 2012). In general, age-adjusted rates give a much smaller prevalence rate. Age adjustment revises estimates to what they would have been if all groups had the same age distribution. In 2010, the age-adjusted disability rate for males was 17.6% and for females 18.3%; for non-Hispanic Whites, the age-adjusted rate was 17.4%, for Blacks alone 22.2%, for Asians alone 14.5%, and for Hispanics or Latinos alone 17.80%. According to Brault (2012), the Asian-alone population had the lowest rate, while the Black-alone population had the highest rate.

The lower prevalence rate for disabilities among Hispanic and Asian Americans is attributed to the fact that these population groups are much younger, and therefore, they have fewer members who are over the age of 65.

SOCIOECONOMIC STATUS

People with disabilities face significant challenges in employment and in the ability to support themselves; therefore, their socioeconomic status (SES) is lower than that of their nondisabled counterparts. The federal disability policy has used two primary approaches to improve the SES of people with disabilities. First, it has attempted to reduce or eliminate barriers to participation in the workforce. However, despite these attempts, people with disabilities continue to face discrimination in employment, and when they are hired, their pay is considerably below that of their counterparts who do not have disabilities. Second, the government has provided either cash or in-kind benefits to those who experience material hardship as a result of disability.

According to Brault (2012), less than half of individuals aged 21 to 64 with a disability were employed during the interview month (41.1%). In comparison, 79.1% of people in this age group without disabilities were employed. If one examines the data by severity of disability, 27.5% of adults with severe disabilities were employed compared with 71.2% of adults with nonsevere disabilities (Brault, 2012).

The Cornell University *2016 Disability Status Report* has revealed the following quick statistics about the employment status of people with disabilities (Erickson et al., 2018).

- In 2016, the employment rate of working-age people with disabilities in the United States was **36.2%**.

- In 2016, the employment rate of working-age people without disabilities in the United States was **78.9%**.

- The spread between the employment rates of working-age people with and without disabilities was **42.7 percentage points**.

- For the six categories of disabilities reported in the ACS, the people with a hearing disability had the highest employment rate (**52.1%**), and the lowest employment rate was for people identified with a self-care disability (**15.4%**).

Cultural Reflections

Do you believe people with disabilities should have the same employment opportunities as their able-bodied counterparts? Explain your answer.

Have you ever worked with a person who had a disability? If so, how would you describe that experience?

In your opinion, should people with disabilities be considered "oppressed minorities"? Why or why not?

People with disabilities experience great disparity in employment and in median income when compared with those without disabilities (Erickson et al., 2018). In 2016, the median income of households that included any working-age people with disabilities in the United States was $40,300, whereas the median income of households that did not include any working-age people with disabilities was $45,300—a $5,000 disparity. Among the six types of disabilities reported in the ACS, the highest median income was for persons with a hearing disability ($46,300), and the lowest was for households containing persons with a cognitive disability ($35,000).

MAJOR CATEGORIES OF DISABILITIES

The ADA definition is not the only way to define disability. The U.S. Census Bureau, in its annual ACS, collects data on six types of disability: (1) mobility and physical disabilities; (2) sensory disabilities; (3) health disabilities; (4) psychological disabilities; (5) intellectual disabilities, including learning disabilities; and (6) disorders of attention.

Mobility and physical disabilities involve those related to mobility as well as upper and lower limb disability. A person with a physical disability may have difficulty walking and use a cane, walker, or wheelchair. Physical disability also includes difficulties in stair climbing, which may be due to a heart condition or to a neurological or orthopedic condition, and difficulties in reaching, lifting, and carrying objects. Some causes of physical and mobility disabilities include spinal cord injuries, amputations, muscular dystrophy, Parkinson's disease, multiple sclerosis, and restriction of limb movement due to stroke (Bowe, 2000).

The Census categories of self-care, "go-outside-home," and employment disabilities are determined by the limitations experienced by the person, not by what causes the disability. A **self-care disability** involves difficulty with dressing, grooming, bathing, feeding oneself, and toileting. A **go-outside-home disability** means that the person has difficulty shopping, going to medical appointments, or performing other activities that involve leaving the home. An **employment disability** is defined by difficulty working at a job or business.

Sensory disabilities include vision and hearing disabilities. Visual impairment is examined along a continuum of loss of sight and/or blindness. People with hearing impairments are classified as being either hard of hearing or deaf. **Health disabilities** are impairments that limit endurance or may be life threatening. Some examples of health impairments are asthma, sickle-cell anemia, cancer, and kidney disease; attention deficit hyperactivity disorder is sometimes listed under this category (Bowe, 2000).

Psychological disabilities are evidenced in people who experience difficulties in their relationships with others, in their views of the world, and in their attitudes toward the self. Some examples of psychological or mental disabilities include anxiety disorders, depression, bipolar disorder, schizophrenia, and eating disorders. The American Psychiatric Association's (2013) *Diagnostic and Statistical Manual of Mental Disorders* (DSM-5) defines a mental disorder as a syndrome marked by important disturbance in a person's cognition, emotional regulation, or behavior that shows or reveals a dysfunction in his or her psychological, biological, or developmental processes. Typically, mental disorders lead to significant distress in a person's social, occupational, or other life activities. A reasonable or culturally approved response to a stressor, such as the death of a family member, is not a mental disorder.

Intellectual disabilities are those disabilities that influence the way people learn, perceive, and process information. More often than not, they involve what one labels as cognitive disabilities. In the past, individuals with cognitive disabilities were labeled as mentally retarded; however, this term has been outdated for the past couple of decades, and it has been replaced with the term *intellectual disability* (Schalock et al., 2007).

Under the rubric of intellectual disabilities are learning disabilities and disorders of attention (ADD—attention deficit disorder; ADHD—attention deficit hyperactivity disorder). An intellectual disability is one that develops before the age of 18 and is characterized by significant limitations in both intellectual functioning and behavior. Intellectual functioning (intelligence) includes a person's capacity to engage in general mental activities, general reasoning, problem-solving skills, and learning (Schalock et. al., 2007). The law that contains the relevant definition of learning disabilities is known as the Individuals with Disabilities Education Improvement Act of 2004:

> The term "specific learning disability" means a disorder in 1 or more of the basic psychological processes involved in understanding or in using language, spoken or written, that may manifest itself in the imperfect ability to listen, think, speak, read, write, spell, or to do mathematical calculations. . . Such term includes such conditions as perceptual disabilities, brain injury, minimal brain dysfunction, dyslexia, and developmental aphasia. (Section 1401.30)

Cultural Reflections

Have you ever worked with a child, adolescent, or adult who has attention deficit hyperactivity disorder?

If so, what challenges did you encounter?

Are you familiar with the signs of ADHD?

What do you know about adults with ADHD and their personal and work relationships?

Two primary characteristics of intellectual learning disabilities include (1) problems in information processing (McNamara, 2007) and (2) problems with the brain's ability to handle the phonology or sounds of language. Difficulties in information processing affect a person's ability to learn information, plan his or her time, organize information, or remember things (McNamara, 2007). Instead of viewing their learning difficulties as "problems in information processing," many young people and adults label themselves as "dumb" or not smart. School counselors and clinicians can help such individuals by providing knowledge or information about the learning disability and its impact on their performance and by helping them to self-manage their disability using cognitive behavioral and strengths-based approaches.

Some Invisible Disabilities

Millions of Americans suffer with **invisible disabilities**—that is, health issues that may not meet the legal requirements of a disability as defined by the ADA. An invisible disability is primarily neurological in nature. A person might have extreme fatigue, pain, dizziness, cognitive impairments, or a sleep disorder. These invisible disabilities might not be apparent to others, but they affect the individual's happiness and satisfaction with life. It has been estimated that nearly one in two people in the United States has a chronic medical condition, but most of these conditions do not qualify under the ADA as a "legal disability." Some invisible disabilities include allergies, asthma, fibromyalgia, diabetes, depression, lupus, narcolepsy, and Lyme disease (Invisible Disabilities Association, 2018). Invisible disabilities constitute the most common type of disability among college students. For instance, students with learning disabilities, ADHD, and/or psychiatric disabilities may request accommodations, even though they do not appear to have a disability (Invisible Disabilities Association, 2018).

Some Facts About People With Disabilities

Although people with disabilities constitute the world's largest minority, facts about their lives and existence are largely unknown. The following list of facts about disabilities has been adapted from various sources, including the Convention on the Rights of Persons with Disabilities ("10 Facts on Disability," 2017).

- Approximately 15% of the world's population, or more than a billion people, live with some form of a disability, making this group the world's largest minority.

- In countries where people have life expectancies over 70 years, people spend an average of about 8 years, or 11.5% of their life span, living with disabilities.

- Women with disabilities may be multiply disadvantaged, in that they may experience prejudice, discrimination, and oppression on the basis of their gender, ethnicity, and disability.

- Children with disabilities are less likely to attend school.

- Women and children with disabilities are frequently the victims of violence at school and at home, in the United States and throughout the world.

- Disabled people are vulnerable to poverty because they are more likely to be unemployed, and they often do not receive needed health care.

In general, individuals with disabilities have poorer health prognoses, lower education achievements, less economic participation, and higher rates of poverty than people without disabilities.

MODELS OF DISABILITY

Three major models have been used to conceptualize disability, and these include (1) the moral model, (2) the medical model, and (3) the social/minority model. The **moral model of disability** is the oldest, dating back centuries, and maintains that disability occurs because of a person's or a family's sin (Artman & Daniels, 2010; Olkin, 1999). Under this model, a disability is conceptualized as a test of one's faith (an affliction that will be endured on earth and rewarded at some later time—for instance, in heaven). There is something of the Biblical message that "God only puts on us what we can bear" and that those who help the person with the disability will be blessed by God.

Conversely, in some countries, people may regard those with disabilities as shameful and as proof that an evil spirit lies within them. Disability

---

Cultural Reflections

Have you ever observed a seemingly healthy person drive into a handicapped parking space, get out, and show no visible signs of a disability?

If so, what did you do? Did you say anything to the person, especially if that person looked healthy and was relatively young-looking?

Did it ever cross your mind that the individual might have an invisible disability?

Do you or anyone in your family have an invisible disability? What impact does the invisible disability have on your life?

Cultural Reflections

Taking into account the various categories of disabilities, which category would pose the greatest difficulty for you? Why?

Which disability category would you feel most comfortable working with? Why?

If you were asked to counsel an individual with a disability, how comfortable would you feel doing so?

Do you think that your professional training program has sufficient courses dealing with individuals with disabilities?

Cultural Reflections

Which of the three models of disability (moral, medical, sociopolitical/minority) do you subscribe to? Explain your answer.

What is the relevance of a model of disability for counseling a client?

How would you go about using a client's model of disability for counseling him or her?

happens because of a family's wrongdoing, and entire communities may be stigmatized because of the disability. The moral model conceptualizes disability as living within the individual and as having a certain amount of stigma associated with it; disability is the embodiment of evil, a punishment for a family member's transgression, a divine gift, or a test of faith and opportunity to overcome a challenge (Mackelprang & Salsgiver, 1999).

The **medical model of disability** has been the most dominant framework in modern times (Palombi, 2010). This model removed the moral or sin feature and substituted the perspective that disability emanates from the person's physical and mental limitations. Disability is a failure of a person's physical body, and therefore, it represents an abnormal and pathological condition. The medical model focuses on people's deficits and the elimination of the pathology or restoration of a person's functional capacity. Thus, it changed the conversation from "disability is a sin" to "disability is a medical condition" (Palombi, 2010). The medical model views disability as a defect or loss of function that resides within the individual. One benefit of the medical model is that it has been able to target treatment for a variety of health and mental health conditions.

Many people with disabilities have rejected the medical model and its emphasis on abnormality. In contrast, the **sociopolitical model**, also known as the **minority model**, maintains that disability is a product of the interaction between an individual and an environment (DePoy & Gilson, 2004). This model emphasizes the individual's strengths in negotiating interactions with the environment, including issues related to accessibility, accommodations, and social attitudes. According to this view, attitudinal barriers restrict the full participation of individuals with disabilities (Olkin, 1999). Using the approach provided by the civil rights movement in American history, the social model of disability focuses on advocating for the rights of individuals with disabilities (Olkin, 2002). Within this worldview, clinicians are encouraged to perceive a client's disability status as a special type of minority status. This view also maintains that the disability is only one aspect of a person's identity. Individuals within this category have multiple identities, including ethnic/racial, gender/sexual orientation, and so forth. The social model emphasizes the role that oppression, prejudice, discrimination, and social injustice play in the lives of individuals with disabilities. Under this model, a clinician can promote a client's positive disability identity and self-advocacy skills, or consult with others to make sure that the client has adequate accommodations or opportunities for participation.

DISABILITY AS A MULTICULTURAL ISSUE

Many negative barriers encountered by individuals with disabilities are attitudinally imposed.

Disabilities can be best understood as an interaction between a person and his or her environment. For instance, a person who uses a wheelchair may be confronted with unemployment not because of the disability but rather because of environmental barriers in the workplace that prevent, limit, or obstruct wheelchair access. Children with learning disabilities who are mainstreamed into classrooms may encounter barriers that have to do with teachers' and children's attitudes toward them. According to the World Health Organization (WHO), people with disabilities are some of the most marginalized people not only in the United States but throughout the world. The WHO goes on to say that

> disability is now understood to be a human rights issue. People are disabled by society, not just by their bodies. These barriers can be overcome, if governments, nongovernmental organizations, professionals and people with disabilities and their families work together. ("10 Facts on Disability," 2017)

Ableism

Ableism is a form of discrimination against individuals with disabilities based on their disability status alone. Ableism operates on varying levels, including individual, institutional, and societal. Ableism is "disability oppression" similar to gender, sexual orientation, and ethnic oppression. Ableism suggests that people with disabilities are deficient, not equal, to their able counterparts and unable to meet successfully their social and economic roles. Reduced expectations of people with disabilities limit their levels of educational and work achievement. Ableism suggests that people with disabilities are somehow inferior. Individuals with disabilities may internalize others' negative evaluations of them, and they may develop low self-esteem (Zascavage & Keefe, 2004).

Some examples of ableism include the belief that people with disabilities cannot perform the duties of a job or that they are inadequate in their mental functioning. Abelism is revealed in the comments that people make about individuals with disabilities. For instance, an insensitive person might remark about a blind person, "Why does he bother writing a play that he will never be able to see performed?" As another example, when a person with a deafness disability appeared on the television show *Dancing With the Stars*, each week the dancer was met with some kind of comment on his ability to dance even though he could not hear the music. Many capable individuals with disabilities are denied job opportunities because of ableism attitudes toward members of their group. According to Keller and Galgay (2010), ableism

> favors people without disabilities and maintains that disability in and of itself is a negative concept, state, and experience. Implicit within ableism is an able-centric worldview which endorses the belief that there is a "normal" manner in which to perceive and/or manipulate stimuli and a "normal" manner of accomplishing tasks of daily living. Disability represents a deviation from these norms. (p. 242)

PRIVILEGE AND PEOPLE WITH DISABILITIES

Able-bodied people have privileges that they take for granted. In an article by Peggy McIntosh (1998) on White privilege, an "Able-Bodied Privilege Checklist" was presented as a way to make able-bodied people realize the many advantages they enjoy in contrast to disabled individuals. For example, able-bodied individuals can go shopping alone, turn on the television and see people who "look like me," and work at a job without having people assume they were hired because of their disability rather than their employment qualifications.

Cultural Reflections

If you are able-bodied, which privilege would you be most distressed at losing, if you had to give one up?

Which able-bodied privilege, if any, is less important to you?

MICROAGGRESSIONS TOWARD PEOPLE WITH DISABILITIES

Microaggressions cause people with disabilities to be reminded of their disability first, even though the person unintentionally using a microaggression may be trying to be polite. In essence, the person is unable to see past the disability when interacting with people with disabilities. Disability microaggressions present an ableist worldview, which conveys a lack of value and respect for people with disabilities (Keller & Galgay, 2010). The ableist worldview contains negative assumptions about people with disabilities. The truth of the matter is that able-bodied individuals have unearned privileges.

Carrie Ann Lucas (2015), who identifies as a queer disabled woman, has provided a very insightful discussion of both microaggressions and macroaggressions against people with disabilities. Microaggressions are the little digs and thoughtless comments one receives from able-bodied individuals that get under the skin of people with disabilities and leave them wondering, "Was that remark really offensive, or am I just too sensitive?" To avoid committing microaggressions, one must be sensitive to the other person's situation and how one's words can hurt or strengthen the other person. There are few laws against the daily microaggressions one comes into contact with as a person with a disability.

In contrast, macroaggressions are actions that are meant to exclude by either direct acts or acts of omission. As Lucas (2015) has stated,

> not complying with disability rights laws is a macro aggression. The Americans with Disabilities Act has been law for more than 25 years, the Fair Housing Act for more than 27, the Individuals with Disabilities Education Act for more than 40 years, and Section 504 of the Rehabilitation has been law for more than 42 years. At this point, decades after all these laws were passed, any failure to comply is either a willful attempt to evade the law, or due to willful ignorance.

Lucas (2015) provides examples of the microaggressions and macroaggressions she faces on a daily and weekly basis. Microaggressions include using the accessible restroom stall when one could just as easily use the nonaccessible stalls, complaining about having to accommodate a person's disability, or asking a disabled person "what is wrong" with him or her. Macroaggressions include parking illegally in a handicapped parking space, refusing to allow a service animal to enter a store, or protesting a group home for people with disabilities being opened in one's neighborhood.

Cultural Reflections

Have you ever engaged in a microaggression against a person with a disability?

Describe the microaggression and its effect on the person.

Let's assume that you are at a restaurant and a person with a disability spills a drink on the table and has difficulty telling the server her order.

The server responds angrily, saying, "Now look what you have done, you. . ." and then catches him- or herself.

What, if anything, would you say or do?

SPREAD: A FORM OF ABLEISM

Ableism takes many different forms; these include spread and interaction strain. **Spread** takes place when people without disabilities respond as if the individual's disability has a more pervasive impact than it actually does (Henderson & Bryan, 2011; Wright, 1983). Some examples of spread include treating a blind person as if he or she also has a hearing disability, or responding to a person in a wheelchair as if the person is also limited intellectually. Whenever people respond to individuals with a disability as if all other aspects of the person are affected by the disability when such is not the case, spread or generalization of the disability takes place.

When spread occurs for a person with a disability, it denies that person his or her individuality. The fact that a person has a mobility disability or a visual disability is just one aspect of who that person is. We should accommodate the individual disability and not generalize the disability to all features of a person's life. A person is not his or her disability. Spread takes place when clinicians and others believe that the disability encompasses unrelated aspects of the person. To avoid spread, a clinician should ask if a disability is part of the presenting problem. When recent disabilities have occurred, a clinician might assess a client's coping strategies, whether the client blames him- or herself or others for the injury and the degree of social support available for the client (Rabasca, 1999).

INTERACTION STRAIN AND PEOPLE WITH DISABILITIES

Interaction strain takes place when people without disabilities become uncomfortable and anxious when they interact with people who have disabilities (Wright, 1983). For instance, a person might say to a blind person, "Can you see what I mean?" or, to a wheelchair user, "Let's go for a walk." After making such statements, the person might become anxious and explain that he or she did not mean anything by using the word *see* or *walk*. Clinicians need to understand that words such as *see, walk*, and *hear* are common expressions and "are not taken literally by individuals with disabilities during the course of a conversation" (Getch & Johnson, 2013, p. 521).

IDENTITY DEVELOPMENT AND PEOPLE WITH DISABILITIES

As noted in Chapter 3, the term *identity* refers to the self on three different levels, expressions of (1) individuality, (2) group identity, and (3) universal identity (Jones-Smith, 2016; Smith, 1985). Our identities define who we are in different contexts; they highlight social roles that we play, and they can be used to emphasize our past (who we used to be), our present (who we are now), and our future selves (who we hope to become).

Disability constitutes a specific identity context that distinguishes individuals as part of a group and that may subject them to marginalization, discrimination, microaggressions, and macroaggressions. Disability identity may be positive or negative, as is the case with gender identity and ethnic/racial identity. Positive disability identity takes place when individuals have an affirmative sense of self and feelings of connection to or solidarity with the disability community (Dunn & Burcaw, 2013). A negative sense of self takes place when one feels negative about one's disability identity.

Dunn and Burcaw (2013) reviewed the disability literature and identified six primary themes about a disability identity: (1) communal attachment, (2) affirmation of disability, (3) self-worth, (4) pride, (5) discrimination, and (6) personal meaning. A frequent theme in the formation of disability identity is the importance of community, such that people with disabilities are actively engaged with their peers based on their common disability experience. The affirmation of disability takes place when a person affirms the disability and asks that he or she be included in society with the same rights as able-bodied citizens. Self-worth, pride, and discrimination are grouped under the heading of disability identity politics and activism. As one engages in disability identity politics, one develops a sense of pride and self-worth. The person also becomes more aware of discrimination.

Finally, Dunn and Burcaw (2013) maintain that a major theme in the disability narratives was personal meaning making out of the disability. People search to find meaning in their disability, and this search often represents their personal acceptance of their situation. When individuals accept their life situations, they can then solidify the meaning of disability while still asserting a favorable disability identity. Individuals who search for meaning after the onset of disability often discover a "silver lining" for their disability.

Besides Dunn and Burcaw's (2013) disability identity model based on narratives, Olkin (1999) has presented a conceptual model for disability identities that features a five-point continuum ranging from (a) not disabled, to (b) disabled but no identity as a person with a disability, to (c) identifies as a person with a disability, to (d) feels a part of the disability community, to (e) disability rights activist. According to Olkin (1999), people who are located at the first two points (a and b) of the continuum are vulnerable to stigma, prejudice, and discrimination, whereas the end points of the continuum (d and e) indicate those whose disability is part of their self-identity. These individuals tend to have friends and partners with disabilities, and they seek services from counselors and therapists with disabilities.

EXPERIENCING A DISABILITY IDENTITY AFTER TRAUMA

Individuals who experience major life changes, such as car accidents, war trauma, and sickness and disease, must adjust their sense of identity when such changes leave them with permanent disabilities (Zola, 1982). Sometimes I watch veterans from the Iraq or Afghanistan war playing

Cultural Reflections

Do you personally know anyone who has experienced a disability as a result of some recent trauma, such as a car accident, war, violence, and so forth?

What adjustments did the person have to make as a result of the trauma?

If your boyfriend or girlfriend, who was previously able-bodied, came back home from war as a paraplegic, would you still marry the person (if the two of you were engaged to be married)? Explain.

basketball in wheelchairs or running races on metal legs, and I feel deep compassion for them and their families. I have deep respect for these people as they make a decision to adjust to their new physical disability, oftentimes with little complaint (Karp, 1999). Reconciling one's identity as a disabled person with previously held views about what being disabled means is a major task. As Carol Gill, a polio survivor, has stated:

> when you become a member of the group that you have previously felt fear or pity for, you can't help but turn those feelings on yourself. (quoted in Karp, 1999, p. 127)

When a person experiences a disability as a result of a traumatic injury or disease, there is a change in his or her identity. According to Karp (1999), "a traumatic injury or diagnosis of disease that suddenly makes you a member of the disabled community is a shock to your sense of self. Whatever image you had of disability will be the image you first apply to yourself. Before you were disabled, what were your reactions to people you saw or heard about who had a disability? How did you react when you saw a person in a wheelchair? Did you feel pity?" (p. 139).

For most individuals, the sudden onset of disability precipitates an intensive self-evaluation. A person goes from seeing him- or herself as an able-bodied adult to one who has a disability. One remembers his or her previous identity, and a part of that identity is always retained. Initially, one resists accepting the new identity of a person with a disability. There is usually a contradiction between one's disabled and nondisabled identities. However, gradually one makes a series of adjustments and adapts to the new identity of being a person with a disability.

As one makes adjustments to the disability and accepts what it entails, a person begins to rethink his or her self-esteem. As Karp (1999) has said,

> if you think your self-esteem relies on whether or not you can walk, you limit yourself. Your self-esteem is more truly related to your compassion, generosity, and doing your best in any situation. You don't have to be able to walk to take pride in yourself, or to be recognized and appreciated by the people you care about and who care about you. . . .
>
> In the ways that really matter, disability does not change you. Rather, disability threatens concepts you have held about who you are. . . . Who you are impacts your adjustment to disability. (p. 140)

Zola (1982) argues that many people make their disability a scapegoat for issues that would have shown up in their lives anyway. During the period of adjustment to the disability, people learn that there is a great deal more to them than their disability and the difficulties surrounding it. They begin to explore different parts of themselves, such as their sexual identity. Related to one's sexual identity, Zola wrote,

> while I agree that sex involves many skills, it seems to me limited and foolish to focus on one organ, one ability, one sensation, to the neglect and exclusion of all others. The loss of bodily sensation and function associated with many disorders, and its replacement with a physical as well as psychological numbness, has made sexuality a natural place to begin the process of reclaiming some of one's selfhood. (p. 219)

One way that some individuals attempt to deal with their sudden disability is by what Karp (1999) calls passing—trying as hard as possible to function as if one's disability does not exist. Passing becomes detrimental when one acts as if one is not disabled. There is a fine line between challenging oneself within reasonable boundaries and acting as if one does not have a disability. Passing is usually an attempt to make up for the losses one experienced as a result of the accident, disease, or trauma that caused the disability. In the words of Zola (1982), who recovered from polio but was left with a physical disability, "an uncomfortable assessment of my last twenty years was that they represented a continuing effort to reclaim what I had lost" (p. 214).

Individuals who develop disabilities suddenly or over a short period of time may find themselves experiencing depression, anger, anxiety, fear, and a deep sense of loss in the early stages of the disability experience. Clearly, their identities change from able-bodied to a person with a disability. They might have questions such as "Will I be able to find work?" "What will my disability do to my romantic relationship(s)?" or "Why did this happen to me?" Dealing with a disability, especially one that is brought on with sudden onset, typically means that a person discovers that adjustments can be made to deal with the disability and that even the most severe disability need not preclude a person from having a meaningful life (Karp, 1999). The disability might cause the person to spend time learning who he or she really is. "If I am not my disability, who am I?"

Cultural Reflections

The suicide rate for people with severe disabilities is higher than that for able-bodied people.

Let's assume that a person with a severe physical disability came to you and said that he was tired of living life in a wheelchair and that he was going to "end it all someday" with a gun.

What would be your response to the person?

What ethical responsibilities or obligations would you have as a counselor or mental health professional regarding the situation described or the potential suicide?

STRENGTHS OF PEOPLE WITH DISABILITIES

The strengths of people with disabilities are varied, depending on the type of disability, and most deal with individuals' personal qualities or compensatory strategies to replace the lost function, limb, or ability. An important strength of many people with disabilities is perspective taking and an enhanced ability to adapt and to persevere. Unlike their able-bodied counterparts, individuals with disabilities are able to take different perspectives of their life situations, largely because their disability has forced them to look at life differently. A person with cerebral palsy who cannot walk without assistance might say, "I am not just my legs." "I am more than my ability to walk or not walk." "My name is not cerebral palsy." Individuals should avoid calling people by their disabilities.

People with disabilities are able to focus on what they have instead of what they do not have. They are extremely creative in using different parts of the body that an able-bodied person might not consider. For instance, a person might not have arms, but he uses his feet and legs to type on the computer or to play an instrument. Mark Goffeney is an amazing guitar player with no arms. He plays the guitar with his feet and has been featured on YouTube and other media forms (Kelly, 2015; Ripley, 2016).

People with disabilities are often sources of inspiration to able-bodied people because of their creative adjustments to their circumstances. Instead of complaining, they learn how to make the most of what is possible for them.

Many individuals with disabilities who have lived through natural disasters show resiliency and adaptation. Instead of responding, "Where were they when we needed them?" they were more likely to think, "What are my possibilities? What options do I have?"

Other strengths of people with disabilities include the ability to make connections with others, finding meaning in life, meeting challenges, good coping strategies, and optimism and hope (Shallcross, 2011). People with disabilities also may evidence a greater sense of spirituality (Dunn & Brody, 2008). In addition, their disabilities sometimes make them more empathic and understanding of the difficulties that others face (Shallcross, 2011).

Researchers have found that individuals with learning disabilities also have strengths in related areas (Horowitz, 2013). For instance, in *The Dyslexic Advantage*, authors Brock and

Fernette Eide (2011) list four MIND aptitudes common in individuals with dyslexia: material or special reasoning, interconnectedness, narrative reasoning, and dynamic reasoning.

- *Material or spatial reasoning*: increased ability to solve problems with navigation or with the visualization of faces, scenes, and objects, skills that can be useful for designers, engineers, and filmmakers—such as Steven Spielberg, who has revealed that he is dyslexic.

- *Interconnectedness*: verbal reasoning ability to connect seemingly disconnected ideas.

- *Narrative reasoning*: great memory for personal experiences—this skill can be helpful for poets such as Philip Schultz, who has said that words first failed him and then saved him.

- *Dynamic reasoning*: ability to reason in new situations, especially in business or the scientific field.

COUNSELING APPROACHES FOR INDIVIDUALS WITH DISABILITIES

This section examines counselors' attitudes, training, and models for counseling people with disabilities. It also considers some potential issues that people with disabilities may bring to therapy. Disability affirmative therapy and strengths-based therapy are two therapy models that are identified for working with individuals with disabilities.

Counselor Attitudes and Training. Before counseling individuals with disabilities, it is important that clinicians search their own attitudes and beliefs about members of this population. Research suggests that mental health professionals often do not have sufficient knowledge of disability issues and have little experience working with clients who have disabilities (Strike, Skovholt, & Hummel, 2004). When clinicians have little understanding of a client's disability experience, they may feel uncomfortable and anxious when working with such clients (Olkin, 1999). Studies have found that rehabilitation professionals and mental health counselors have negative biases against people with disabilities (Rosenthal, Chan, & Livneh, 2006; Rosenthal & Kosciulek, 1996; W. Sullivan et al., 2011). Smart and Smart (2006) have observed that most graduates of counseling programs do not possess competencies to provide services to clients with disabilities.

Clinicians who lack experience with clients with disabilities may be guilty of implementing the "spread" effect—assuming that because a client has a disability, he or she must also have other things wrong that have nothing to do with the disability. A clinician might also err by focusing on a client's disability while ignoring other important areas of his or her life. On the other hand, a clinician can mistakenly assume that a client is using his or her disability as an excuse not to work or to engage in relationships.

Counselors' inability to identify disability-related themes may be considered an ethical issue (Hosie, Patterson, & Hollingsworth, 1989). To work ethically with people with disabilities, clinicians must be familiar with developmental issues as well as any medical conditions related specifically to the client's condition (Olkin, 2002). In working with people with disabilities, counselors may need to take into account the effects of social stigma, ableism, and relationship issues. Counselors must understand that the client's disability is only one part of his or her identity and that people with disabilities have multiple identities and roles. Individuals who are disabled and who hold multiple minority statuses have the experience of being "a minority within a minority" (McDonald, Keys, & Balcazar, 2007). Counselors need to work toward achieving a complete comprehension of such clients' multiple identities and interacting roles.

Cultural Reflections

Think about someone who you know has a disability.

What strengths does that person have?

Have you ever complimented the person for any of the strengths you see in him or her?

Ethical counselors arrive at an understanding of what it means to hold multiple minority statuses, such as being a person with a disability, African American, gay, and female. Together counselors and clients must determine which identities are most important to individuals with disabilities.

Palombi (2010) has pointed out that counseling professionals may find it difficult to incorporate disability factors in treatment services because they have not received instruction or training in disability issues and because they may be unaware of their own biases and attitudes toward people with disabilities. Additionally, he notes that counselors tend to have limited interaction with people with disabilities, and therefore do not feel competent to work with such clients. Counselors who know little about disability may not be aware that it is important for them to learn information about the onset, duration, and experiences associated with a client's disability.

Counseling with people who have disabilities should deal with their cultural history and multiple identities, the discrimination they have encountered as a result of their disability, and their self-esteem issues, as well as the difficulties that the disability brings to their lives.

Counseling Issues and the Effects of Disability

People with disabilities seek counseling for the same reasons as do their able-bodied peers, and they also seek counseling for issues related to barriers to independence, health separation, prejudice, and ableism. The effects of a disability or a chronic illness can be mentally challenging. Disabled clients may harbor feelings of anger and depression or feel frustrated or discouraged by frequent questions or expressions of pity about their condition. Young people who are affected by a disability sometimes experience depression and resentment when they are unable to participate in the same events and activities as their peers, and when they are subjected to teasing or bullying (Bailey et al., 2006).

Moreover, adults who are suddenly faced with newly acquired disabilities as a result of an accident, war, crime, or illness may experience confusion, frustration, or fear. If a client experiences lifestyle changes because of the disability, he or she may feel stressed, resentful, or overwhelmed. The support of a counselor or therapist can help a client to explore ways to address the new disability and to resolve any feelings about the disability. In counseling, a therapist can help a client clarify and address concerns about his or her new life. The counselor or therapist can help the individual to maintain a positive view of self that is separate from the disability (Olkin, 1999).

People with disabilities are frequently more socially isolated than those without disabilities, and the situation may be especially distressful for women (Nosek, Foley, Hughes, & Howland, 2001). When individuals with disabilities experience discrimination and stigmatization, they may be left with a feeling of being ostracized and different. Limited contact with other people who have disabilities may exacerbate the feeling of being isolated and different.

Women with disabilities have reported experiencing high levels of depression and low self-esteem (Nosek, Howland, Rintala, Young, & Chanpong, 2001). Men with disabilities are inclined to experience psychological distress from threats to their sexual identity and masculinity, as well as issues about their financial independence and employment (Marini, 2001).

Similarly, individuals who have disabilities who are also gay, lesbian, bisexual, or transgender encounter unique problems. Their own families and the broad American society are more likely to ostracize them than members of other minority groups (Olkin, 1999).

PEOPLE WITH DISABILITIES AND RISK FOR ABUSE

People with disabilities have a high risk for abuse and violence (Horner-Johnson & Drum, 2006; Hughes, 2005). In comparison to youth without disabilities, children and adolescents with disabilities are 3 to 10 times more likely to be abused or neglected (P. Sullivan & Knutson, 2000).

People with disabilities are at risk for abuse because able-bodied people and others view them as powerless, physically helpless, socially isolated, emotionally deprived, and sexually naïve. People who perpetrate violence and abuse against people with disabilities have less risk of being discovered, and the authorities are less likely to believe abuse reports from people with disabilities (Andrews & Veronen, 1993; Nosek, Foley, et al., 2001).

Moreover, women with disabilities are at an especially high risk for abuse (Brownridge, 2006), and they experience abuse for longer periods of time than women without disabilities (Nosek, Foley, et al., 2001). In contrast, society may tend to ignore the type of abuse that men with disabilities face (Saxton, McNeff, Powers, Curry, & Limont, 2006).

Yet violence and sexual abuse are not the only types of abuses that people with disabilities experience. Violence against individuals with disabilities can take such forms as withholding a client's medications or administering to him or her excessive dosages of prescribed medications. Other forms of abuse include involuntary confinement; withholding or damaging, breaking, or disabling assistive equipment (e.g., a wheelchair); and refusing to provide personal assistance for essential daily living activities such as eating and personal hygiene (Hughes, 2005; Nosek, Foley et al., 2001; Saxton et al., 2001). Another abuse tactic involves the behavior of personal assistants in community settings who may neglect people with disabilities, subject them to verbal and/or physical abuse, and exploit them financially by theft and other means (Oktay & Tompkins, 2004; Powers, Curry, & Oschwald, 2002).

Clinicians should recognize the signs and symptoms of disability-related violence and abuse, and further they should screen for abuse when working with clients with disabilities. Nosek, Hughes, and Taylor (2004) suggest that the psychologists

- Learn the signs, symptoms, and client/perpetrator dynamics of disability-related violence

- Screen on a regular basis for abuse and neglect, and intervene appropriately if it occurs

- Document the history of client abuse and neglect

- Discuss with clients plans for a safe retreat, backup personal care assistance, and social supports

- Establish contact information with local domestic violence/sexual assault programs and disability service providers

- Learn the pertinent state mandatory reporting requirements for violence against people with disabilities, elders, and dependent adults

EMPOWERMENT

Empowerment may be defined as a multidimensional social process that promotes a person's ability to exercise control over his or her life. When people have power, they can make decisions regarding their lives. Empowerment is influenced by individuals' perceptual views and sense of authority or agency about a situation. Although people may have many options in life, their perceptions of low control over their lives may predispose them not to act on their options.

According to Sales (2007), people with disabilities have been denied power throughout their lives: "They have dealt with the medical model all their lives where they've been told what they can do and cannot do. Because of mobility issues, they've been denied access. All of those things feed into being in a lower power position. They come to counseling with a need to be more 'empowered'" (p. 7).

Clinicians should consider using therapy or counseling models that seek to empower their clients. The strengths-based therapy model is one that seeks to empower clients (Jones-Smith,

2014). People with disabilities have strengths. A client whose strengths are recognized and celebrated tends to have a positive self-image and a greater ability to deal with life challenges than one who does not know his or her strengths (Dunn & Dougherty, 2005; Dykens, 2006). Some personal strengths include one's education, personality traits, creativity, social relationships, and social support system. Interventions that take into account the personal strengths of a client with a disability enhance that client's sense of self-esteem. As a result, the person feels empowered and develops a sense of resiliency (Dykens, 2006). A counselor helps clients with disabilities to identify the strengths they have to accomplish their goals. For instance, a client with a physical disability affecting his or her mobility might have intellectual and computer strengths that would be instrumental in achieving a goal of employment.

In addition, a clinician may work with a client to develop his or her self-advocacy skills because the person who advocates for his or her own social, economic, and political opportunities gains a greater sense of empowerment and well-being (Goodley & Lawthom, 2006; Reeve, 2000).

FAMILY COUNSELING AND PEOPLE WITH DISABILITIES

Family counseling may be desirable for individuals with disabilities. Families are significant because oftentimes they are the caretakers for individuals with disabilities, and because many of the individuals with disabilities are children and adolescents. Clinicians support their clients with disabilities by involving the family in intervention and educational planning (Gill, Kewman, & Brannon, 2003). For instance, a clinician working with an adolescent who has an intellectual or learning disability might work with the student and family to develop an individualized education program (IEP) (Combes, Hardy, & Buchan, 2004).

DISABILITY AFFIRMATIVE THERAPY AND DISABILITY ORIENTATION

Disability affirmative therapy is the most recent approach to working with individuals with disabilities, and therefore, it is presented first in this section. The affirmative model of disability was first presented by Swain and French (2000), who described people who adopt it as having a

> non-tragic view of disability and impairment which encompasses positive social identities, both individual and collective. . . grounded in the benefits of life style and life experience of being impaired and disabled. (p. 569)

A primary goal of the **affirmative disability model** is to challenge the underlying premise that impairment is a personal tragedy and to question the notion that people with disabilities should be treated as victims of misfortune. The affirmative model of disability has formulated a view of disability that could "enhance life or provide a lifestyle of equal satisfaction and worth" (Swain & French, 2000, p. 570). This **disability orientation** maintains the view that disabled people's beliefs and feelings about themselves and their impaired bodies can be an affirmation and statement of the benefits of such a life experience. Within the affirmative disability model, impairment is considered a characteristic of human difference rather than as a defective part of the body.

The affirmative disability model advocates a positive self-image and a nontragic view of a person with a disability. It challenges the negative discourse typically associated with a person with a disability. Cameron's (2007, 2010) research has shown that disabled people do affirm disabled lifestyles and that such lifestyles provide a counternarrative to the lives of nondisabled people. People with disabilities engage life positively through disability arts, art forms, and artwork. Affirmative disability therapy extends the social model of disability to the level that maintains there may be benefit in disability in keeping with the saying, "What does not kill us makes us stronger."

At the heart of the disability affirmative model of therapy is the concept of disability orientation. Darling and Heckert (2010) have outlined two dimensions of disability: *disability participation* and *disability orientation*. Disability participation refers to a person's access to an engagement with activities. *Disability orientation* includes three different aspects: (1) disability identity, (2) adherence to a particular model of disability, and (3) involvement in disability rights activism. It is important for a counselor/therapist to assess a client's disability orientation.

Darling (2003) has outlined a typology of disability orientations, which include (1) normalization, (2) resignation, (3) crusadership, and (4) affirmation. Table 16.1 presents a summary of disability orientations; it is adapted from McCormack and Collins (2012).

Normalization disability orientation. People with disabilities accept the norms of the cultural majority—that is, the view that disability is an undesirable feature. They seek lifestyles similar to nondisabled people by embracing rehabilitative activities, technology, and supportive employers (Darling & Heckert, 2010).

Resignation disability orientation. People who adopt this orientation accept the norms of the cultural majority. Although they desire to achieve a lifestyle similar to nondisabled individuals, they do not have the resources to achieve normalization, and at the same time, they do not have knowledge of, or access to, disability culture, advocacy, or affirmation (Darling & Heckert, 2010).

Crusader disability orientation. People with the crusader disability orientation accept the norms of the cultural majority, but they do not have access to a normalized lifestyle. They

TABLE 16.1 ■ Summary of Disability Orientations

Orientation	Norms Accepted	Wishes for Own Lifestyle	Access to Normalization	Access to Disability Culture
Normalization	Person accepts the norms of the cultural majority—disability viewed as undesirable	Person desires a lifestyle similar to nondisabled individuals	Person embraces rehabilitation, technology, and support of others	Person does not wish to embrace disability culture
Resignation	Person accepts the norms of the cultural majority—disability is undesirable	Person desires a lifestyle similar to nondisabled individuals	Person does not have resources to normalize	Person does not have knowledge to embrace disability culture
Crusader	Person accepts the norms of the cultural majority—disability is undesirable	Person desires social inclusion within society	Person does not have resources to normalize	Person has knowledge of and access to disability culture, strives to promote social change and inclusion in majority culture
Affirmation	Person accepts the norms of the cultural minority—disability is viewed in positive terms	Person desires that society recognize disability as a facet of human diversity, not necessarily social inclusion	Person does not wish to normalize; instead, he or she embraces disability	Person has knowledge of and access to disability culture; he or she takes pride in disability and views disability culture as something to celebrate

Adapted from McCormack & Collins, 2012.

have knowledge of and access to disability culture, and they may even engage in self-advocacy campaigns for social change to achieve greater social inclusion (McCormack & Collins, 2012).

Affirmative disability orientation. People who adopt an affirmative disability orientation do not accept the norms of the cultural majority, but rather they consider disability as their primary identity and view it in positive terms. Similar to crusaders, they become involved in disability culture; however, their focus is on embracing disability as a form of human diversity. They see their disability as something to be rejoiced in and celebrated with their cultural minority (McCormack & Collins, 2012).

> ### Cultural Reflections
>
> *Which model of counseling would you be most comfortable using with a client with a disability?*
>
> *To what extent do you believe that clients with disabilities can affirm their disability as a positive occurrence?*

Understanding a person's identity is crucial for counseling and therapy. Therapists must take into consideration a client's disability orientation as part of clinical practice with people with disabilities. Disability affirmative therapy focuses on the positive aspects of a client's disability. The following section presents Olkin's approach to counseling clients by learning their model of disability.

OLKIN'S MODEL OF DISABILITY AND COUNSELING APPROACH

Olkin (1999) has indicated that it is important to know a client's model of disability during the process of counseling. According to her, the model of disability that a client predominantly endorses shows (1) how the problem is perceived, (2) how the disability is presented, (3) the locus of the problem, and (4) goals for treatment. Olkin has suggested that clients and their families be provided with a copy of a table of various models of disability and asked questions about where the client would locate him- or herself. Olkin (1999) has indicated that the goal of the counselor or therapist is to remember that "there is no such thing as complete adjustment to disability. One is never there, only traveling there. Thus, clients' thoughts about disability will constantly change and evolve" (p. 172). She has recommended that counselors provide the following explanatory statement for clients:

> How you think about yourself as a person with a disability will affect greatly how you think about yourself overall. You may not even be aware that you have a model of disability. Take a few minutes to ask yourself some questions that can help bring your model to light. Use the questions in this table to help you, but also feel free to think of other questions or situations that the table doesn't address. (Olkin, 1999, p. 170)

For a complete listing of Olkin's table for assessing the client's model of disability, the reader is referred to her book *What Psychotherapists Should Know About Disability* (1999). Some relevant questions she presents under the moral model of disability are: Do you feel shame or embarrassed about your disability? Do you think your disability is punishment for your family's failing? Other questions a clinician might include under the moral model of disability are: Do you think that your disability is a punishment from God because of some sin that either you or your family committed? Do you believe that you are struck with your disability because God intends to use you in some special way?

Clients who take a medical model of disability might be asked questions that deal with medical issues: Do you believe that your disability can be best treated by a medical doctor? To what extent is your disability related to your family's medical history? Has a medical professional told you what you can and cannot achieve given your disability? Under the social model of disability, clients might be asked: Do you identify with being part of a minority group of persons with disabilities? Do you feel that you are a target of injustice because of your disability? Other questions a clinician might ask a client with a disability are: How were you raised with regard to the disability? What messages did your parents give you about your disability?

APA's Guidelines for Assessment of and Intervention With Persons With Disabilities

In the January 2012 issue of the *American Psychologist*, the American Psychological Association published its *Guidelines for Assessment of and Intervention With Persons With Disabilities*. This document lists 22 practice guidelines for psychologists who work with people who have disabilities. The guidelines state that to work effectively with people with disabilities, psychologists should "become familiar with how disability influences a client's psychological well being and functioning" (American Psychological Association, 2018). The guidelines are not exhaustive and do not take precedence over a therapist's well-informed judgment.

Guidelines for Disability Awareness, Accessibility, and Diversity (1–10)

The first five guidelines guide the counselor/therapist to learn about disability paradigms, examine his or her own beliefs and reactions toward individuals with disabilities, increase his or her knowledge about working with persons with disabilities, learn the federal laws that support and protect people with disabilities, and provide barrier-free services.

Guidelines 6–10 encourage counselors/therapists to understand the experiences common to disabilities, recognize social and cultural diversity in the lives of persons with disabilities, learn how attitudes and misconceptions can influence the particular nature of a person's disability development across the life span, strive to recognize the strengths and challenges of families of individuals with disabilities and that people with disabilities are at increased risk for abuse, and address abuse-related situations appropriately.

Guidelines Related to Assessment and Testing of Individuals With Disabilities (11–16)

Guidelines 11–16 guide the counselor/therapist to learn about technological opportunities and challenges for people with disabilities, consider disability as a dimension of diversity along with other dimensions, apply the assessment approach that is most psychometrically sound and appropriate for clients with disabilities, determine whether accommodations are appropriate for clients to yield a valid test score, find appropriate perspectives and articulate both the strengths and limitations of assessment, and maximize fairness and relevance in interpreting assessment data of clients with disabilities by applying approaches that reduce potential bias and integrate data from multiple sources.

Guidelines That Cover Interventions (17–22)

The final guidelines, 17–22, cover interventions. Counselors/therapists should recognize that there is a broad range of individual responses to disability and, when appropriate, plan and implement psychological interventions; they are aware of the impact of their interventions and work on clients and their families; they recognize that interventions may focus on enhancing clients' well-being; they advocate for client self-determination; they recognize and address health promotion issues for individuals with disabilities; and they strive to increase their knowledge and skills about working with individuals with disabilities through training, education, and expert consultation.

CASE VIGNETTE 16.1

ELIZABETH: STRENGTHS-BASED THERAPY AND A YOUNG TEENAGER SUFFERING TRAUMA FROM A CAR ACCIDENT

Elizabeth is a 16-year-old teenager living at home with her mother, father, and younger brother. At age 14, both she and her mother were involved in an accident with a drunk driver. As a result, Elizabeth is paralyzed from the waist down, and she uses a wheelchair for mobility. Elizabeth has had difficulty adjusting to her new physical reality.

Prior to the car accident, Elizabeth had no physical disability. In fact, she loved running and being physically active. She took great pride in her athleticism. During her freshman year of high school, Elizabeth was a cheerleader and one of the star floor gymnasts. For most of her middle school and high school years, Elizabeth was an honor student who said that her career goal was to become a pediatrician.

During the first year after her accident, Elizabeth was in and out of the hospital and in therapy support groups that were designed to help her slowly regain better control of her upper-body movements. She learned how to leverage herself in and out of her wheelchair onto the living room couch and onto her bed. Because Elizabeth spent so much time in the hospital and in rehab, she did poorly in most of her academic subjects. She said that she couldn't face going to basketball games and watching the cheerleaders perform cheers and jumps that she used to do without a great deal of effort.

For the two years since the accident, Elizabeth has been experiencing symptoms of depression, suicidal thoughts, and low self-esteem. Oftentimes she complains that "I might as well be dead. I'm tired of sitting in this wheelchair. I'll never get married or have children. I'm sick of my life. I don't want to live anymore." Elizabeth has found it difficult to stay in contact with her former friends. They occasionally come by her house, but Elizabeth says that it is mostly out of pity that they come.

Elizabeth has been placed on various antidepressants, including Cymbalta and Lexapro, both of which had side effects. For instance, Lexapro left her with headaches, jittery feelings, and nausea right after a dose. The doctor felt that Cymbalta might be increasing her suicidal thoughts because this is one of the side effects for young people.

A decision was made to place Elizabeth in both individual and group therapy that emphasized a strengths-based approach. She is also attending a support group with other young people who use wheelchairs. Elizabeth's entire focus was on her physical losses as a result of the accident. Therapy was designed to help her recognize the many strengths that she still possessed. She needed to feel good about herself again, to feel empowered that she could still do things to make her life worth living.

Strengths Discovery

One goal of strengths-based therapy was to help Elizabeth understand that she was not her disability, that she still had an identity that was uniquely Elizabeth, and that she had strengths that could help her achieve new goals. The first part of therapy involved strengths discovery for Elizabeth. She was given a strengths inventory and asked to evaluate what strengths she had before the accident and after it. Elizabeth identified the strengths she had in working with children and in relating to people who were having problems. Her friends had always said that she was a good listener. The therapist asked Elizabeth how the car incident had harmed her ability to be a good listener and how it had damaged her love for children.

Much to her surprise, Elizabeth came to realize that she still had most of the same strengths before the accident, except for her mobility strengths. True, she was no longer able to engage in gymnastics or be a cheerleader, but she still had her nurturing strengths, her interpersonal strengths, and her intellectual strengths. The therapist used strengths cards to help Elizabeth see visually the strengths that she still had. Elizabeth was asked to place her strengths in two card piles—pile 1, those strengths she had lost, and pile 2, those strengths she had remaining. The pile was much higher for the strengths that remained with Elizabeth. Elizabeth was encouraged, and gradually she began to feel better about herself.

The therapist asked Elizabeth if she saw any silver lining in her situation. Were there any positive takeaways? She replied that she felt the accident had sensitized her to the plight of others and that she no longer took anything for granted.

Strengths-based therapy continued over the next 15 weeks. Session 2 was spent engaging in SWOB (strengths, weaknesses, opportunities, and barriers) analysis, which is a form of strengths analysis (see Chapter 5). Using SWOB analysis, the therapist and Elizabeth used a four-quadrant square in which Quadrant 1 contains the strengths known to the client ("what I do well") and also strengths unknown to the client

(Continued)

(Continued)

(strengths identified by the therapist). Quadrant 2 deals with client weaknesses (weaknesses known to the client and weaknesses unknown to the client, or those identified by the therapist and others). Quadrant 3 deals with opportunities, both those hidden in the problem (benefits of adversity) and opportunities readily available to the client. Quadrant 4 deals with barriers to the client, including internal client barriers, such as avoidance or procrastination, and external barriers, such as social injustice and cultural differences. Session 3 focused on continuing Elizabeth's strengths search and identifying ways that she might use those strengths to have a more meaningful life and a possible career. Elizabeth decided that she wanted to become a school counselor.

Let Go. Elizabeth was asked if she needed to let anything go, if there was anything holding her back from embracing life. She said that she was angry with God for allowing the accident to take place, but that she was grateful that He allowed her to survive with most of her strengths. She decided to let go of her anger toward God and even toward the drunk driver.

The therapist engaged Elizabeth in a strengths meditation journey where she saw herself achieving many of the goals that she had identified in the first session. The therapist had Elizabeth identify the self-limiting thoughts that she had that were holding her back and making her think that her entire identity was wrapped up in her wheelchair.

Let In. The therapist asked Elizabeth to set a strength intention. The therapist shared with Elizabeth the belief that an intention is the starting point of every dream. One must say what he or she intends to do; otherwise, the subconscious mind might derail one's efforts. The therapist and Elizabeth decided that she was to place that strength intention on her wheelchair where she could see it. For the first time in years, Elizabeth felt hopeful. The therapist helped Elizabeth to shift her language from worry to optimism. She was told that every time she felt overwhelmed by a negative, self-limiting thought, she was to say to herself, "I let go of that thought."

Framing Solutions. The therapist spent two sessions on helping Elizabeth to frame solutions and to establish a treatment plan that she wanted to guide her journey. Elizabeth is now working toward achieving her goals. She has been able to rebuild her self-esteem by focusing on the many strengths that she still has. As a result of her support group of friends, she has even started to date again. Elizabeth has stopped taking the antidepressant because her mood has changed to become much more positive.

Harmony and Moving Forward. She now understands the accident did not end her ability to have children and to have a wonderful family. Elizabeth has been accepted into college, and she intends to become a high school counselor. There is harmony in her life again. Thoughts of suicide are now things of the past. She is moving forward in life.

SUMMARY OF KEY POINTS

The following are some principles and suggestions for working with individuals with disabilities that have been discussed within this chapter.

1. Clinicians should assess and identify their beliefs and attitudes about individuals with disabilities.

2. Clinicians need to make the environment disability affirmative by including posters, pictures, or other art forms that include people with disabilities in empowered situations. Make sure your office is barrier free and is physically accessible for clients.

3. It is important to understand clients as individuals with disabilities, not disabled individuals. Do not address the individual as his or her disability.

4. Each person with a disability has his or her own unique disability identity.

5. Do not assume that a client is seeking therapy for issues related to his or her disability. A client's disability should not be the sole focus of counseling. The clinician should determine if the disability is related to the presenting problem, and if not, assessment should focus on the problem instead of the disability.

6. Disability is a biopsychosocial construct that takes place as a dynamic interaction of individuals with their various environments.

7. Clinicians can help individuals with disabilities become self-determined people within a society. Counseling should help to empower people with

disabilities. Clinicians recognize that they may have to function as advocates for the client and family members to bring about changes in the environment and within institutions, including academic and work settings. They promote equal access and equal opportunity for people with disabilities in their practice and work environments.

8. Clinicians must become aware of the American Psychological Association's *Guidelines for Assessment of and Intervention With Persons With Disabilities* and understand how to implement those guidelines in practice.

9. It is important that clinicians understand the various models of disability (moral, medical, or social model) and with which model of disability the client identifies. Determining the client's model of disability indicates how the client perceives his or her disability or the meaning that the client gives to the disability.

10. Clinicians should also consider the four disability orientations to which an individual might subscribe (the normalization disability orientation, the resignation disability orientation, the crusader disability orientation, and the affirmative disability orientation). These orientations represent new directions in working with individuals with disabilities.

11. Clinicians need to understand that clients with disabilities have multiple identities and that the salience of any one identity will vary depending on the circumstances in which they find themselves. Clients with disabilities may experience multiple microaggressions and macroaggressions because of prejudice toward their disability.

12. Ethnic/racial minorities and gender minorities who are also individuals with disabilities may encounter multiple sources of prejudice and discrimination. Ethnic/racial minorities and those of various gender orientations are inclined to experience discrimination based on both their ethnicity and disability.

13. People of color (with the exception of Asian/Pacific Islanders), women, and older adults are more likely to have a disability than their counterparts. Such higher rates of disability may be attributed to their higher rates of poverty, lack of education and employment opportunities, violence, limited access to health care, and their own personal behaviors (Centers for Disease Control and Prevention, 2018; Drum, McCain, Horner-Johnson, & Taitano, 2011; Flack et al., 1995).

14. Different cultural, minority, and religious groups tend to attribute different causes and meanings to disability (Bryan, 2007).

15. Two counseling theoretical approaches that hold promise for working with individuals with disabilities include the strengths-based therapy model and affirmative disability counseling.

16. Clinicians must ensure the validity, fairness, and appropriateness of tests and assessments and interventions by assessing their own possible biases and ideas about disability.

17. Clinicians should not just focus on a client's disability alone, but rather they should help the client to balance personal strengths and limitations.

18. Clinicians who work with clients with disabilities maintain their skills and knowledge by actively seeking disability-related training, education, and consultation.

DISCUSSION QUESTIONS

Discussion Question Set 1

Discuss the three models of disability presented in this chapter and state which model is most in alignment with your own personal experience and beliefs.

Discussion Question Set 2

A disabled female in a wheelchair came to your office and stated that she wanted to end it all because she was sick and tired of being in a wheelchair and watching all her able-bodied friends having fun and enjoying life. How might you go about counseling this individual? Which counseling theoretical framework would you use? Explain your rationale and then begin to outline a therapy plan to respond to her despair and her desire to end her life.

KEY TERMS

Ableism: A form of discrimination against individuals with disabilities based on their disability status alone. Ableism operates on varying levels, including individual, institutional, and societal. Ableism is "disability oppression," similar to gender, sexual orientation, and ethnic oppression. Ableism suggests that people with disabilities are deficient, not equal to their able counterparts, and unable to meet successfully their social and economic roles.

Affirmative disability model: Challenges the underlying premise that impairment is a personal tragedy and questions the notion that people with disabilities should be treated as victims of misfortune. The affirmative model of disability has formulated a view of disability that could "enhance life or provide a lifestyle of equal satisfaction and worth." Disabled people's beliefs and feelings about themselves and their impaired bodies can be an affirmation and statement of the benefits of such a life experience.

Americans with Disabilities Act (ADA): Signed into law in 1990, providing a federal mandate of nondiscrimination to individuals with disabilities for state and local governments and the private sector of American society.

Disability orientation: Portrays a person's interpretation of his or her disability experience as well as his or her perceptions of what it means to be disabled.

Employment disability: Defined by difficulty working at a job or business.

Go-outside-home disability: Means that the person has difficulty shopping, going to medical appointments, or performing other activities that involve leaving the home.

Health disabilities: Impairments that limit endurance or may be life threatening. Some examples of health impairments are asthma, sickle-cell anemia, cancer, and kidney disease; attention deficit hyperactivity disorder is sometimes listed under this category.

Intellectual disabilities: Disabilities that influence the way people learn, perceive, and process information.

Interaction strain: Takes place when people without disabilities become uncomfortable and anxious when they interact with people who have disabilities (Wright, 1983). For instance, a person might say to a blind person, "Can you see what I mean?" or, to a person in a wheelchair, "Let's go for a walk." After making such statements, the person might become anxious and explain that he or she did not mean anything by using the word *see* or *walk*.

Invisible disabilities: Health issues that do not meet the legal requirements of a disability as defined by the Americans with Disabilities Act. An invisible disability is a hidden disability or challenge that is primarily neurological in nature. A person might have extreme fatigue, pain, dizziness, cognitive impairments, or a sleep disorder.

Medical model of disability: A model of disability that removed the moral or sin feature and substituted the perspective that disability emanates from the person's physical and mental limitations. Disability is a failure of a person's physical body, and therefore, it represents an abnormal and pathological condition. The medical model focuses on people's deficits and the elimination of the pathology or restoration of a person's functional capacity.

Mobility and physical disabilities: Disabilities related to mobility as well as upper and lower limb disability. For example, a person with a physical disability may have difficulty walking and use a cane, walker, or wheelchair.

Moral model of disability: The oldest model related to disability, it maintains that disability occurred because of a person's or a family's sin or moral failure.

Psychological disabilities: Evidenced in people who experience difficulties in their relationships with others, in their views of the world, and in their attitudes toward the self.

Self-care disability: Involves difficulty with dressing, grooming, bathing, feeding oneself, and toileting.

Sensory disabilities: Include vision and hearing disabilities. Visual impairment is examined along a continuum of loss of sight and/or blindness. People with hearing impairments are classified as being either hard of hearing or deaf.

Sociopolitical model, also known as the **minority model:** Maintains that disability is a product of the interaction between an individual and an environment. According to this view, attitudinal barriers restrict the full participation of individuals with disabilities. The sociopolitical model of disability focuses on advocating for the rights of individuals with disabilities.

Spread: Takes place when people without disabilities respond as if the individual's disability has a more pervasive impact than it actually does.

REFERENCES AND SUGGESTED READING

10 facts on disability. (2017, November). *World Health Organization*. Retrieved from http://www.who.int/features/factfiles/disability/en/

American Psychiatric Association. (2013). *Diagnostic and statistical manual of mental disorders* (5th ed.). Washington, DC: Author.

American Psychological Association. (2018). *Guidelines for assessment of and intervention with persons with disabilities*. Retrieved from http://www.apa.org/pi/disability/resources/assessment-disabilities.aspx

Andrews, A. B., & Veronen, L. I. (1993). Sexual assault and people with disabilities. *Journal of Social Work and Human Sexuality, 8*(2), 137–159.

Artman, L. K., & Daniels, J. A. (2010). Disability and psychotherapy practice: Cultural competence and practical tips. *Professional Psychology: Research and Practice, 41*(5), 442–448.

Bailey, D. B., Jr., Bruder, M. B., Hebbeler, K., Carata, J., Defosset, M., Greenwood, C., . . . Barton, L. (2006). Recommended outcomes for families of young children with disabilities. *Journal of Early Intervention, 28*(4), 227–251.

Bowe, F. (2000). *Physical, sensory, and health disabilities: An introduction*. Upper Saddle River, NJ: Merrill/Prentice-Hall.

Brault, M. W. (2012, July). Americans with disabilities: 2010. *Current Population Reports*. Retrieved from https://www.census.gov/library/publications/2012/demo/p70-131.html

Brownridge, D. A. (2006). Partner violence against women with disabilities. *Violence Against Women, 12*(9), 805–822. doi:10.1177/1077801206292681

Bryan, W. V. (2007). *Multicultural aspects of disabilities: A guide to understanding and assisting minorities in the rehabilitation process* (2nd ed.). Springfield, IL: Thomas.

Cameron, C. (2007). Whose problem? Disability narratives and available identities. *Community Development Journal, 42*(4), 501–511.

Cameron, C. (2008). Further towards an affirmation model. In T. Campbell, F. Fontes, L. Hemingway, A. Soorenian, & C. Till (Eds.), *Disability studies: Emerging insights and perspectives* (pp. 14–30). Leeds, England: Disability Press.

Cameron, C. (2010). *Does anybody like being disabled? A critical exploration of impairment, identity, media and everyday experience in a disabling society*. Unpublished PhD thesis. Edinburgh, Scotland: Queen Margaret University. Retrieved from http://etheses.qmu.ac.uk/258/

Centers for Disease Control and Prevention. (2018, June 27). *Disability and Health Data System (DHDS)*. Retrieved from https://www.cdc.gov/ncbddd/disabilityandhealth/dhds/index.html

Combes, H., Hardy, G., & Buchan, L. (2004). Using q-methodology to involve people with intellectual disability in evaluating person-centered planning. *Journal of Applied Research in Intellectual Disabilities, 17*(3), 149–159.

Cornish, J. A. E., Gorgens, K. A., Olkin, R., Palombi, B. J., & Abels, A. V. (2008). Perspectives on ethical practice with people who have disabilities. *Professional Psychology: Research and Practice, 39*(5), 488–497.

Darling, R. B. (2003). Toward a model of changing disability identities: A proposed typology and research agenda. *Disability and Society, 18*(7), 881–895.

Darling, R. B., & Heckert, D. A. (2010). Orientations toward disability: Differences over the life course. *International Journal of Disability, Development and Education, 57*(2), 131–143.

DePoy, E., & Gilson, S. F. (2004). *Rethinking disability: Principles for professional and social change*. Belmont, CA: Thomson/Brooks/Cole.

Drum, C. M., McCain, M. R., Horner-Johnson, W., & Taitano, G. (2011, August). *Health disparities chart book on disability and racial and ethnic status in the United States*. Institute on Disability, University of New Hampshire. Retrieved from http://www.iod.unh.edu/pdf/Health%20Disparities%20Chart%20Book_080411.pdf

Dunn, D. S., & Brody, C. (2008). Defining the good life following acquired physical disability. *Rehabilitation Psychology, 53*(4), 413–435.

Dunn, D. S., & Burcaw, S. (2013, November). Thinking about disability identity. *Spotlight on Disability Newsletter*. Retrieved from http://apa.org/pi/disability/resources/publications/newsletter/2013/11/disability-identity.aspx

Dunn, D. S., & Dougherty, S. B. (2005). Prospects for a positive psychology of rehabilitation. *Rehabilitation Psychology, 50*(3), 305–311.

Dykens, E. M. (2006). Towards a positive psychology of mental retardation. *Journal of Orthopsychiatry, 76*, 385–393.

Eide, B. L., & Eide, F. F. (2011). *The dyslexic advantage: Unlocking the hidden potential of the dyslexic brain*. New York, NY: Plume.

Erickson, W., Lee, C., & von Schrader, S. (2018). *2016 disability status report: United States*. Ithaca, NY: Cornell University Yang-Tan Institute on Employment and Disability (YTI).

Flack, J. M., Amaro, H., Jenkins, W., Kunitz, S., Levy, J., Mixon, M., . . . Yu, E. (1995). Panel I: Epidemiology of minority health. *Health Psychology, 14*(7), 592–600.

Fleischer, D. (2001). *The disability rights movement.* Philadelphia, PA: Temple University Press.

Fox, M. H., White, G. W., Rooney, C., & Cahill, A. (2010). The psychosocial impact of Hurricane Katrina on persons with disabilities and independent living center staff living on the American Gulf Coast. *Rehabilitation Psychology, 55*(3), 231–240.

Getch, Y., & Johnson, A. L. (2013). Counseling individuals with disabilities. In Garrett McAuliffe & Associates (Ed.), *Culturally alert counseling: A comprehensive introduction* (2nd ed., pp. 505–542). Thousand Oaks, CA: Sage.

Gill, C. J., Kewman, D. G., & Brannon, R. W. (2003). Transforming psychological practice and society: Policies that reflect the new paradigm. *American Psychologist, 58*(4), 305–312.

Goodley, D., & Lawthom, R. (2006). *Disability and psychology.* London, England: Palgrave.

Henderson, G., & Bryan, W. V. (2011). *Psychosocial aspects of disabilities.* Springfield, IL: Thomas.

Horner-Johnson, W., & Drum, C. E. (2006). Prevalence of maltreatment of people with intellectual disabilities: A review of recently published research. *Mental Retardation and Developmental Disabilities Research Reviews, 12*(1), 57–69.

Horowitz, S. (2013). Strengths of students with learning disabilities and other disorders [Video file]. *YouTube.* Retrieved from https://www.youtube.com/watch?v=CYHzJGTA6KM

Hosie, T. W., Patterson, J. B., & Hollingsworth, D. K. (1989). School and rehabilitation preparation: Meeting the needs of individuals with disabilities. *Journal of Counseling & Development, 68*(2), 140–144.

Hughes, R. B. (2005). Violence against women with disabilities: Urgent call for action. *The Community Psychologist, 38,* 28–30.

Invisible Disabilities Association. (2018). What is an individual disability? Retrieved from https://invisibledisabilities.org.

Jones-Smith, E. (2014). *Strengths-based therapy: Connecting theory, practice, and skills.* Thousand Oaks, CA: Sage.

Jones-Smith, E. (2016). *Theories of counseling and psychotherapy: An integrative approach.* Thousand Oaks, CA: Sage.

Karp, G. (1999). *Life on wheels: For the active wheelchair user.* Sebastopol, CA: O'Reilly & Associates.

Keller, R. M., & Galgay, C. E. (2010). Microaggressions experienced by people with disabilities in U.S. society. In H. E. Yuker (Ed.), *Attitudes toward persons with disabilities* (pp. 47–57). New York, NY: Springer.

Kelly. (2015). Amazing musician born with no arms plays guitar with his feet. *Elite Readers.* Retrieved from https://www.elitereaders.com/mark-goffeney-musician-born-with-no-arms-plays-guitar-with-feet/

Lucas, C. A. (2015, September 19). Microaggressions, macroaggressions and disability [Blog post]. *Disability Culture.* Retrieved from http://www.disabilitypride.com/2015/09/19/microaggressions-macroaggressions-and-disability/

Mackelprang, R., & Dell Orto, A. (1999). *The psychological and social impact of disability.* New York, NY: Springer.

Mackelprang, R. W., & Salsgiver, R. O. (1999). *Disability: A diversity model approach in human service practice.* Belmont, CA: Brooks/Cole.

Marini, I. (2001). Cross-cultural counseling issues of males who sustain a disability. *Journal of Applied Rehabilitation Counseling, 32,* 36–41.

McCormack, C., & Collins, B. (2012). The affirmative model of disability: A means to include disability orientation in occupational therapy? *British Journal of Occupational Therapy, 75*(3), 156–158.

McDonald, K. E., Keys, C. B., & Balcazar, F. E. (2007). Disability, race/ethnicity and gender: Themes of cultural oppression, acts of individual resistance. *American Journal of Community Psychology, 39,* 145–161.

McIntosh, P. (1998). White privilege: Unpacking the invisible knapsack. In M. McGoldrick (Ed.), *Re-visioning family therapy: Race, culture, and gender in clinical practice* (pp. 147–152). New York, NY: Guilford Press.

McNamara, B. E. (2007). *Learning disabilities: Bridging the gap between research and classroom practice.* Upper Saddle River, NJ: Merrill/Prentice Hall.

Murdick, N. L., Gartin, B. C., & Crabtree, T. (2007). *Special education law* (2nd ed.). Upper Saddle River, NJ: Merrill/Prentice Hall.

Nosek, M. A., Foley, C. C., Hughes, R. B., & Howland, C. A. (2001). Vulnerabilities for abuse among women with disabilities. *Sexuality and Disability, 19*(3), 177–189.

Nosek, M. A., Howland, C., Rintala, D. H., Young, M. E., & Chanpong, G. F. (2001). National study of women with physical disabilities: Final report. *Sexuality and Disability, 19*(1), 5–40.

Nosek, M. A., Hughes, R. B., & Taylor, H. B. (2004). Violence against women with disabilities: The role of physicians in filling the treatment gap. In S. L. Welner & F. Haseltine (Eds.), *Welner's guide to the care of women with disabilities* (pp. 333–345). Philadelphia, PA: Lippincott, Williams, and Wilkins.

Oktay, J. S., & Tompkins, C. J. (2004). Personal assistance providers' mistreatment of disabled adults. *Health and Social Work, 29*(3), 177–189.

Olkin, R. (1999). *What psychotherapists should know about disability*. New York, NY: Guilford Press.

Olkin, R. (2002). Could you hold the door for me? Including disability in diversity. *Cultural Diversity and Ethnic Minority Society*, 8(2), 130–137.

Palombi, B. J. (2010). Disability: Multiple and intersecting identities—Developing multicultural competencies. In J. A. E. Cornish, B. A. Schreier, L. I. Nadkarni, L. H. Metzger, & E. R. Rodolfa (Eds.), *Handbook of multicultural counseling competencies* (pp. 55–92). Hoboken, NJ: Wiley.

Powers, L. E., Curry, M. A., & Oschwald, M. (2002). Barriers and strategies in addressing abuses: A survey of disabled women's experiences. *Journal of Rehabilitation*, 68, 4–13.

Rabasca, L. (1999). Guidelines for spinal cord injuries don't go far enough. *APA Monitor*, 30, 1–2.

Reeve, D. (2000). Oppression within the counseling room. *Disability & Society*, 15(4), 669–682.

Ripley. (2016). *Ripley's believe it or not: Unlocking the weird*. Orlando, FL: Author.

Rosen, G. D. (2017). *The dyslexic brain: New pathways in neuroscience discovery*. New York, NY: Psychology Press.

Rosenthal, D. A., Chan, F., & Livneh, H. (2006). Rehabilitation students' attitudes toward persons with disabilities in high- and low-stakes social context: A conjoint analysis. *Disability and Rehabilitation*, 28, 1517–1527.

Rosenthal, D. A., & Kosciulek, J. F. (1996). Clinical judgment and bias due to client race or ethnicity: An overview with implications for rehabilitation counselors. *Journal of Applied Rehabilitation Counseling*, 27(3), 30–36.

Sales, A. (2007). *Rehabilitation: An empowerment perspective*. Sioux Falls, SD: Pro Ed.

Saxton, M., Curry, M. A., Powers, L. E., Maley, S., Eckels, K., & Gross, J. (2001). "Bring my scooter so I can leave you": A study of disabled women handling abuse by personal assistance providers. *Violence Against Women*, 7(4), 393–417.

Saxton, M., McNeff, E., Powers, L., Curry, M., & Limont, M. (2006). We are all little John Waynes: A study of disabled men's experience of abuse by personal assistants. *The Journal of Rehabilitation*, 72, 3–13.

Schalock, R. L., Luckasson, R. A., Shogren, K. A., Borthwick-Duffy, S., Bradley, V., Buntinx, H. E. . . . Yeager, M. H. (2007). The renaming of mental retardation: Understanding the change to the term *intellectual disability*. *Journal of Intellectual & Developmental Disability*, 45(2), 116–124.

Shallcross, L. (2011). Seeing potential, not disability. *Counseling Today*, 54, 28–35.

Smart, J. F., & Smart, D. W. (2006). Models of disability: Implications for the counseling profession. *Journal of Counseling & Development*, 84, 29–40.

Smith, E. J. (1985). Ethnic minorities: Life stress, social support, and mental health issues (Major contribution). *The Counseling Psychologist*, 13, 537–579.

Strike, D., Skovholt, T., & Hummel, T. (2004). Mental health professionals' disability competence: Measuring self-awareness, perceived knowledge, and perceived skills. *Rehabilitation Psychology*, 49(4), 321–327.

Sullivan, P. M., & Knutson, J. F. (1998). The association between child maltreatment and disabilities in a hospital-based epidemiological study. *Child Abuse & Neglect*, 22(4), 271–288.

Sullivan, P. M., & Knutson, J. F. (2000). Maltreatment and disabilities: A population-based epidemiological study. *Child Abuse & Neglect*, 24(10), 1257–1273.

Sullivan, W. F., Berg, J. M., Bradley, E., Cheetham, T., Denten, R., Heng, J., . . . McMillan, S. (2011). Primary care of adults with developmental disabilities: Canadian consensus guidelines. *Canadian Family Physician*, 57, 541–553.

Swain, J., & French, S. (2000). Towards an affirmation model of disability. *Disability and Society*, 15(4), 569–582.

Terrio, H. P., Nelson, L. A., Betthauser, L. M., Harwood, J. E., & Brenner, L. A. (2011). Postdeployment traumatic brain injury screening questions: Sensitivity, specificity, and predictive values in returning soldiers. *Rehabilitation Psychology*, 56, 26–31.

Tips for interviewing people with disabilities (n.d.). *National Center on Disability and Journalism*. Retrieved from http://ncdj.org/resources/reporters/interviewing-tips/

U.S. Department of Justice. (n.d.). Introduction to the ADA. *Information and Technical Assistance on the Americans with Disabilities Act*. Retrieved from https://www.ada.gov/ada_intro.htm

Vujicic, N. (n.d.). Bio. *Life Without Limbs*. Retrieved from https://www.lifewithoutlimbs.org/about-nick/bio/

Wright, B. (1983). *Physical disability* (2nd ed.). New York, NY: Harper & Row.

Zascavage, V. T., & Keefe, C. H. (2004). Students with severe speech and physical impairments: Opportunity barriers to literacy. *Focus on Autism and Other Developmental Disabilities*, 19, 223–234.

Zola, I. K. (1982). *Missing pieces: A chronicle of living with a disability*. Philadelphia, PA: Temple University Press.

17 CULTURALLY RESPONSIVE STRENGTHS-BASED THERAPY FOR OLDER ADULTS

CHAPTER OBJECTIVES

- Summarize the demographics of older adults, especially those receiving services in the home or in the community.

- Discuss cultural and societal factors related to older adults.

- Describe and give examples of ageism and microaggressions experienced by older adults.

- Define and assess mental health issues commonly seen in older adults, including dementia.

- Implement the strengths-based therapy model with older adults.

- *"Life is a succession of lessons which must be lived to be understood."* —Unknown

- *"For age is an opportunity no less than youth itself, though in another dress, and as the evening twilight fades away, the sky is filled with stars, invisible by the day."* —Henry Wadsworth Longfellow

- *"Nobody grows old merely by living a number of years. We grow old by deserting our ideals. Years may wrinkle the skin, but to give up enthusiasm wrinkles the soul."* —Samuel Ullman

INTRODUCTION

This chapter focuses on therapy with older adult clients, particularly those age 65 and older. The study of older adults is referred to as *gerontology*, and the medical field focusing on older adults is called *geriatrics*. Both terms come from the Greek *geron* ("old man"). Gerontologists often categorize older adults by **chronological age**, referring to individuals aged 65–74 as young-old, 75–84 as middle-old, and 85 and older as old-old.

However, a person's **functional age** is determined much less by chronology than by sociocultural and physiological influences. For example, the way a person views the aging process may determine how well he or she is able to function at a given chronological age. In other cases, a person may have one or more medical conditions that impair his or her functioning so that his or her functional age is older than what is ordinarily seen at a given chronological age. In addition to functional age, another way of looking at age is **subjective age**—the way a person assesses his or her own progress on the journey toward old age. For example, Axelson (1985) found that Mexican Americans tend to see themselves as "old" earlier in life (e.g., at about age 60) as compared with African Americans (age 65) and White Americans (age 70).

Aging also depends a great deal on the culture to which one subscribes. Views on aging vary from one culture to another. Some cultures value old age as an accumulation of wisdom and status, while others see aging as undesirable and try to deny and delay it as long as possible.

Although the United States has many laws mandating equal treatment for its citizens, ageism remains a common form of discrimination. **Ageism** includes negative stereotypes and discrimination against older adults. It is observed in counseling and therapy settings, in employment opportunities and the workplace, and in myriad other areas of life. For instance, after the age of 60, it is difficult for an American to find a good-paying job. People sometimes make thoughtless comments about older people, such as "You don't look bad for your age" or "Do the elderly really think about sex?"

For some counselors working with older adults, there is an unspoken question: Does it really matter what approach one uses, since these clients are not going to live that much longer anyway? This chapter maintains that it does indeed matter what treatment philosophy and model one uses for responding to the needs of older people. Older people deserve the same standard of care as that given to those who are younger. Because one is advancing in age, it does not mean that one's life is over. As the famous baseball coach Yogi Berra used to say, "It ain't over 'til it's over."

Thanks to advances in medical treatment and proactive health modalities, older Americans today are healthier than they were a generation ago. The average American will live about 12 to 25 years after retirement at age 65. The overall life expectancy rate for all Americans was 78.74 in 2015; for White males, 76.6, and White females, 81.3; and for Black males, 72.2, and Black females, 78.5 (Centers for Disease Control and Prevention, 2017b).

Since the mid-1990s, practitioners and researchers have proposed using a strengths-based approach with an older or aging population (Perkins & Tice, 1995). The strengths-based model represents a shift from traditional models of helping that are founded primarily on dealing with an older person's medical issues to one of addressing the whole person in his or her environment. The medical model is based on the fact that older adults tend to suffer from chronic conditions such as heart disease, cancer, stroke, diabetes, and chronic pulmonary disease (Balcázar, Alvarado, Hollen, Gonzalez-Cruz, & Pedregón, 2005).

This chapter describes how the strengths-based therapy model can be used in working with older adults, particularly those who are receiving home- and community-based services. The first part of the chapter provides basic statistics on the aging American population and the challenges that older adults face. The strengths-based therapy model is applied to an older adult group. A case example of an older adult using the strengths-based therapy model is provided.

DEMOGRAPHICS FOR OLDER ADULTS

Numbers of Older American Adults

In 2014, 46 million people age 65 and over lived in the United States, making up about 14.1 percent of the total population. Nearly 1 in every 7 or about 14.1% of the population is an older American. In 2030, the older population is projected to be more than twice as large as in 2000, growing to 74 million and representing 21% of the total U.S. population. According to Ortman, Velkoff, and Hogan (2014), the older American population will have significant growth. In a U.S. Census Bureau report, "An Aging Nation: The Older Population in the United States," these researchers state that

> between 2012 and 2050, the United States will experience considerable growth in its older population. In 2050, the population aged 65 and over is projected to be 83.7 million, almost double its estimated population of 43.1 million in 2012. The baby boomers are largely responsible for this increase in the older population, as they began turning 65 in 2011. By 2050, the surviving baby boomers will be over the age of 85.

The aging of the population will have wide-ranging implications for the country. By "aging," demographers often mean that the proportion of the population in the older ages increases. As the United States ages over the next several decades, its older population will become more racially and ethnically diverse. The projected growth of the older population in the United States will present challenges to policy makers and programs, such as Social Security and Medicare. It will also affect families, businesses, and health care providers. (Ortman et al., 2014, p. 1)

The growth in both the number and proportion of older adults in this country is unprecedented for our nation, and it is being driven by two realities: first, the fact that Americans are living longer than in previous decades, and second, the post–World War II baby boom. The aging of the baby boomers will continue to have profound effects on our nation's public health, social services, and health care systems. In addition, certain states and counties will have higher proportions of older adults than others. Mather (2016) has pointed out that in many parts of the country, especially in counties located in the rural Midwest, people are "aging in place" because a large number of young people have moved to different locations.

There are a number of potential policy implications for the growth in the older population. The aging of the baby boom generation could provide the impetus for an increase in the number of Americans age 65 and older requiring nursing home care to 2.3 million in 2030—up from 1.3 million in 2010. The increased longevity of the baby boomers also means that Social Security and Medicare expenditures will increase from a combined 8% of gross domestic product to 12% by 2050.

Racial Composition of Older Adults

Although the older population is not as racially and ethnically diverse as the younger population, its diversity is projected to increase substantially over the next four decades. The White population is projected to decrease by approximately 10 percentage points among those age 65 and older between 2010 and 2050. In contrast, all other ethnic/racial groups are projected to see an increase in population. The minority population is projected to make up 42% of the older adult population in 2050, up from 20% in 2010 (Administration on Aging, 2012). The changing ethnic/racial composition of the American population under age 18, compared to those age 65 and older, has created a "diversity gap" between generations (Mather, 2016). In 2013, 21.2% of persons age 65 and older were members of ethnic or racial minority populations—8.6% were African Americans (not Hispanic), 3.9% were Asian or Pacific Islander (not Hispanic), 0.5% were American Indian (not Hispanic), 0.1% were Native Hawaiian or Pacific Islander (not Hispanic), and 0.7% identified as being of two or more races. Persons of Hispanic origin (who may be of any race) represented 7.5% of the older population.

Projections indicate that by 2060, the older population will be 55% non-Hispanic White alone, 22% Hispanic alone, 12% non-Hispanic Black alone, and 9% non-Hispanic Asian alone. The Hispanic older population is projected to grow the fastest, from 3.6 million in 2014 to 21.5 million in 2060. The Asian American population is also projected to experience significant growth. In 2014, there were about 2 million older single-race non-Hispanic Asians, and by 2060, this population is projected to be about 8.5 million.

Labor Force Participation and Socioeconomic Conditions

Older adults are working longer, and this may be attributed to their improved health (Mather, 2016). The labor force participation rate for individuals ages 65–69 increased dramatically from 1985 through 2015. For men in this age group, the labor force participation rate increased from 24% to 37%, and for women it increased from 14% to 28% (Purcell, 2016).

The median income of older persons in 2013 was $29,327 for males and $16,301 for females. Households containing families headed by persons age 65 and older reported a median income in 2013 of $51,486. The major sources of income as reported by older persons in 2013 were Social Security (reported by 86% of older persons), income from assets (reported by 51%), private pensions (reported by 27%), government employee pensions (reported by 14%), and earnings (reported by 28%). Social Security constituted 90% or more of the income received by 36% of beneficiaries in 2012 (22% of married couples and 47% of nonmarried beneficiaries).

Differences were also found in the income of older White and African American families. In 2013, the median net worth of households headed by White people age 65 and older ($255,000) was almost five times that of households headed by older Black people ($56,700) (Federal Interagency Forum on Aging-Related Statistics, 2016).

The poverty rate for older adults has decreased. Whereas 29% of people age 65 and over lived below the poverty threshold in 1966, by 2014, the proportion of the older population living in poverty had decreased to 10% (Federal Interagency Forum on Aging-Related Statistics, 2016).

Marital Status

In 2015, older men were much more likely than older women to be married. Approximately 74% of men ages 65–74 were married, compared to only slightly over half (58%) of women in the same age group. For men and women, the proportion who were married at older ages decreased; however, women experienced a lower rate. Even when researchers examined marital status for men age 85 and older, the majority of men (59%) were married in 2015 (Federal Interagency Forum on Aging-Related Statistics, 2016).

Older non-Hispanic White women and Black women were more likely than women of other races to live alone. In 2015, 37% of non-Hispanic White women and 43% of African American women lived alone, compared with about 20% for older Asian women and 23% of older Hispanic women.

Health Status of Older Adults

The majority of older adults are healthy and capable of living independent lives. Only 3.3% of adults ages 65–74 require assistance with personal care from others. This percentage increases with age, with 10.5% of adults age 75 and older needing such help (Federal Interagency Forum on Aging-Related Statistics, 2016). From 1999 to 2014, age-adjusted death rates for all causes of death among people age 65 and older declined by 20%. Death rates declined for heart disease, cancer, chronic lower respiratory disease, stroke, diabetes, and pneumonia (Federal Interagency Forum on Aging-Related Statistics, 2016).

From 2012 to 2014, older non-Hispanic White people were more likely to report good to excellent health than their non-Hispanic Black and Hispanic counterparts (80% vs. 65% and 66%, respectively). In 2014, 22% of the population age 65 and older reported having a disability as defined by limitations in vision, hearing, mobility, communication, cognition, and self-care. Women tended to report a disability more so than men (24% vs. 19%) (Federal Interagency Forum on Aging-Related Statistics, 2016).

In 2013, approximately 3% of the Medicare population age 65 and older lived in community housing with at least one service available. About 4% lived in long-term care facilities. Among those age 85 and older, 8% lived in community housing with services, and 15% lived in long-term care facilities. For those ages 65–74, about 98% lived in traditional community settings (Federal Interagency Forum on Aging-Related Statistics, 2016).

Cultural Reflections

Reflecting on the older adults in your life—those 65 and older—in what socioeconomic health and living categories would you place them?

Projecting yourself into the future, where would you place yourself in these categories?

Are you living alone, with families, or in some form of assisted living accommodations? Explain.

The need for elder care is projected to be fueled by a steep increase in the number of Americans living with Alzheimer's disease, which could almost triple by 2050 to 14 million, up from 5 million in 2012 (Mather, 2016). In 2014, about 1.2 million people age 65 and older lived in nursing homes. Nearly 780,000 people of that age lived in residential care communities, such as assisted living facilities. In both settings, individuals age 85 and older formed the largest age group among residents.

WESTERN AND EASTERN CULTURAL VIEWS ON AGING

This section examines the contrast between how aging is viewed in mainstream U.S. (Western) culture versus Asian (Eastern) cultures (Fung, 2013). Western views on aging are very different from Eastern perspectives.

Whether we recognize it or not, older adults are the transmitters of a culture. They preserve a culture's values, meaning, tools, rituals, and practices. Aging is a dialectical process in which the negatives of growing older are often balanced with the positive features (Cicirelli, 2003). Research has discussed how conceptions and experiences of well-being vary across cultural contexts (Christopher, Christopher, & Dunnagan, 2000; Diener & Suh, 2000; Kitayama & Markus, 2000). These studies reveal that much cultural variation in well-being is linked with basic cultural differences in conceptions of self and relationships. Western culture is oriented toward individualism; a high value is placed on a person's independence, self-reliance, and hard work. Western culture encourages families to strike a balance between loyalty to one's own nuclear family and loyalty to one's aging parents. Life may become hard for older adults living in a Western culture because as they age, they inevitably lose their independence, self-reliance, and ability to work.

In the United States, "aging gracefully" suggests that people should maintain their physical beauty, remain self-sufficient, and stay as active as ever. The suggestion, in other words, is that Americans shouldn't age at all. Our media spotlights people of advanced age accomplishing remarkable feats, such as former president George H. W. Bush skydiving on his 90th birthday. We celebrate high-functioning elders like Barbara Walters and Regis Philbin, who continued to host major television shows into their 80s; video gamer Doris Self, who won championships at age 81; and former president Jimmy Carter, who continued to write, travel, and engage in social and diplomatic projects into his 90s.

Generally speaking, in Western cultures, youth is revered, while the signs of aging on older adult people are viewed with distaste. The cultural values of a society assume an important role that colors the aging process. When people age in Western societies and especially in the United States, they may feel that they are losing their value as human beings because of the high premium placed on work. The fear of death contaminates the entire aging process in Western societies.

Aging has more positive meanings in Japan than in the United States. In Japanese culture, the pressure to stay young forever does not exist (Ryff & Singer, 2008). Japanese views of aging are based in Buddhist, Confucian, and Taoist philosophies that describe aging as maturity. As a consequence, old age is considered a socially valuable part of life, even a time of "spring" or "rebirth" after years of working and raising children (Kitayama, 2000, 2002). As one ages, he or she is expected to gain transcendental understanding, including an accepting attitude toward death and the ability to function impartially in social interactions (Lock, 1998). In Japanese culture, there is the image of the older person as a *sen-nin* ("wise from experience"). The widespread Confucian norm of filial piety, in which children honor their parents, facilitates the continued respect for and care of aging parents (Hwang, 1999).

In contrast to Western cultures, Eastern cultures are collectivistic and oriented toward the group; individuals place a high value on family, relationships with others, and the older adult.

Eastern cultures tend to view taking care of older adults as part of a family's responsibility. Elder care in the United States focuses on providing independent care. In China, the cultural value of filial piety mandates deference and respect to one's parents and ancestors (Fung, 2013). Whereas Western countries primarily provide financial support for older adults by programs like Social Security, traditions in Asian countries call for the family to care for its elders. However, Fung, (2013) has pointed out that rapid industrialization and movement from rural areas to cities may be reducing the cultural value of filial piety in China (Liu, Ng, Loong, Gee, & Weatherall, 2003).

Differences are also evident in the types of roles older adults are able to assume in Western and Eastern cultures. Japanese culture has more age-graded roles and tasks than U.S. culture. For instance, Japanese women participate in age-specific neighborhood groups that are organized by the city government (Karasawa et al., 2011). Japan has special celebrations that mark a person's 60th birthday (the completion of a life-calendar cycle), as well as the 77th, 88th, and 99th birthdays. In addition, Japan celebrates a Revere the Elder Day, on which city mayors give money to people over 80 years old (Karasawa et al., 2011). Japanese culture uses age-specific terminology to address older people for the purpose of showing respect. Although Japan is rapidly changing to become more Westernized in its treatment of its elders, such as placing aging parents in retirement homes, there are still marked differences between aging in Japanese and American culture.

Similar to Japanese and Chinese culture, the Korean value for elders is based on the Confucian principle of filial piety. Koreans are socialized to give deference and respect not only to their own family members but also to other elderly people in their community (Sung, 2004). Korean culture traditionally marks a person's 60th and 70th birthdays with special celebrations. The *hwan-gap*, or 60th birthday, is a festive time when children celebrate their parents' passage into old age. *KohCui* ("old and rare") is the family celebration for an elder's 70th birthday (Sung, 2004).

> **Cultural Reflections**
>
> *How does your ethnocultural membership group view the aging process?*
>
> *At what age does your ethnocultural membership group consider that a person becomes old?*
>
> *Are older adults within your ethnocultural group revered?*
>
> *Does your ethnocultural membership group hold any special celebrations as a person ages?*

AGEISM

Robert Neil Butler coined the term *ageism* in 1969 to describe discrimination against seniors, defining three connected elements: *prejudicial attitudes* toward older people, old age, and the aging process; *discriminatory practices* against older people; and *institutional practices and policies* that perpetuate stereotypes about them (Achenbaum, 2015).

Research on age-related attitudes in the United States consistently finds that negative attitudes exceed positive attitudes toward older people because of their looks and behavior. In his study *Aging and Old Age*, Posner (1995) discovered "resentment and disdain of older people" in American society. Negative stereotypes, age discrimination, and the broad, general devaluing of older adults can have an important impact on their self-esteem, emotional well-being, and behavior.

MICROAGGRESSIONS AND THE OLDER ADULT

According to the Center on Aging and Work at Boston College, older adult workers may experience age discrimination and microaggressions directed against them because of their age (James, Pitt-Catsouphes, & Besen, 2013). Ageism is illegal; yet, older workers between the ages of 45 and 74 reported that they have been turned down for a job, and about 1 in 10 state that they were passed up for a promotion, laid off, or denied access to career development because of their age.

Cultural Reflections

Have you ever committed a microaggression against an older adult?

What did you say, and who was that older adult?

What are your true feelings about older adults, say, age 70 and older?

At what age should a person be required to retire? Explain your answer.

In addition, older adults may experience microaggressions, sometimes intentional and sometimes unintentional, that communicate hostile, derogatory, or negative slights against members of the targeted group. Microaggressions may include expressing surprise that an older person is able to use a smartphone or even a computer, tapping one's foot or rolling one's eyes when an older person is slow giving an order in a restaurant, or, when driving, giving a dirty look while passing an older driver on the road.

Another form of microaggression is **elderspeak**, language that tends to treat older adults as if they are children—for instance, "Be a good girl and take your medicine now" or "Let's see if you can be a good boy and. . ." Elderspeak is oftentimes demeaning to older adults, and such communications may function as barriers to their successful treatment (Lombardi et al., 2014; Williams, Herman, Gajewski, & Wilson, 2009).

Regarding older adults in the workplace, the Center on Aging and Work (James et al., 2013) has reported findings that indicate negative attitudes toward older workers do influence these workers' engagement with their jobs and ultimately their mental health. Such negative attitudes decrease older adults' productivity, so employers should pay attention and weed out the microaggressions for the good of the company as well as the older employees.

Prevention of Chronic Physiological Disease

The increasing number of older Americans poses significant challenges for our nation's public health system. The current focus is to promote health and functional independence to help older adults stay healthy and to remain in their homes. When older adults practice healthy behaviors, make use of clinical preventive services, and continue to engage with family and friends, they are likely to remain healthy and to live independently (Centers for Disease Control and Prevention & Merck Company Foundation, 2007).

Cultural Reflections

Imagine that you have lived for 80 years. How do you picture yourself?

How would you evaluate your physical and mental health status? Explain.

Who is around you? Are you living in your own home or apartment, or are you living with family and friends? Explain.

The Centers for Disease Control and Prevention (2015) has reported that the majority of older adults are healthy and are capable of living independently. Only about 3.3% of adults ages 65–74 require personal care help from other individuals, and this percentage increases to 7% for those age 75 and older. The percentage of adults needing nursing home care is about 1% for those age 65–74, 3% for those age 75–84, and 9% for those age 85 and older (U.S. Department of Health and Human Services, 2016).

To keep older adults healthy, it is important to prevent chronic diseases. Approximately 80% of older adults have one chronic condition, and 50% have at least two. The Centers for Disease Control and Prevention & Merck Company Foundation (2007) identified five priorities or challenges for improving older adults' health and quality of life: (1) promote healthy lifestyle behaviors to improve the health of older adults, (2) increase older adults' use of clinical preventive services, (3) address cognitive impairment issues, (4) deal with issues related to mental health, and (5) provide education on planning for serious illness.

MENTAL HEALTH ISSUES OF THE OLDER ADULT

Older adults often face a number of mental health issues, including depression, Alzheimer's disease, elder abuse, and substance abuse. This section begins by examining depression among older adults.

DEPRESSION AND OLDER ADULTS

Depression is a major mental health challenge for older Americans. It is one of the conditions most frequently associated with suicide in older adults (Conwell, 2001; Conwell & Brent, 1995; Hybeis & Blazer, 2003). The National Institute of Mental Health (n.d.) considers depression in people age 65 and over to be a major public health problem. Studies of nursing home patients with physical illnesses have found that the presence of depression substantially increases the likelihood of death from those illnesses.

Among older adults, depression is a widely underrecognized and undertreated medical illness. Some health professionals mistakenly believe that persistent depression is an acceptable response to a person's serious illness or loss and financial difficulties that accompany aging (APA, 2009). Yet, depression is not a normal part of aging and interferes significantly with a person's ability to function. Factors that increase the risk of depression in older adults are being female; being single, divorced, or widowed; loneliness; stress; illnesses; medications; family history; fear of death; substance abuse; and elder abuse.

Depression in older adults may be overlooked because sadness may not be the main symptom. Their symptoms of depression may not be obvious, or they may not be willing to talk about their feelings. Some symptoms of depression include feeling sad or empty; feeling hopeless, irritable, anxious, or guilty; loss of interest in favorite activities; feeling very tired; not being able to concentrate or remember details; not being able to sleep or sleeping too much; overeating or not wanting to eat at all; and thoughts of suicide and suicide attempts (W. Cox, Abramson, Devine, & Hollon, 2012).

> **Cultural Reflections**
>
> *Have you ever come into contact with an older adult suffering from depression?*
>
> *What was your response to the older adult?*
>
> *What impact, if any, has this chapter had on your views about depression and older adults?*

Treatment for Depression Among Older Adults

Although late-life depression affects about 6 million Americans age 65 and older, only 10% actually receive treatment for depression. One reason that older adults have a low percentage rate for treatment of depression is that they often show symptoms of depression differently than do younger age groups. In older adults, a number of life changes often predispose them to depression. Because of changes in an elderly person's life situation and the fact that older adult people are expected to slow down, doctors and families may miss the signs of depression. Consequently, treatment gets delayed, and seniors find themselves using alcohol to self-treat depression; however, this may make the situation worse.

Depression and Physical Illness in Older Adults

Depression in older adults may also be a sign of a physical illness. It can also be a psychological reaction to an illness. Physical illnesses that increase the risk for depression include thyroid disorders, Parkinson's disease, heart disease, cancer, and stroke.

For older adults, depression tends to last longer; it doubles their risk of cardiac diseases and increases their risk of death from illness. It also reduces an older adult person's ability to rehabilitate. Because of this risk, an older adult person should be evaluated and treated even if the depression is mild (National Institute of Mental Health, n.d.).

To manage depression at home, older adults should exercise regularly, seek out pleasurable activities, and maintain good sleep habits. They should also be taught the early signs of depression and learn how to react if sad feelings get worse. Older adults should minimize use of alcohol because this substance can make depression worse and may impair judgment about suicide (National Institute of Mental Health, n.d.).

Suicide and Depression in Older Adults

Older Americans are disproportionately likely to die by suicide. Although they form only 12% of the U.S. population, people age 65 and older accounted for 16% of suicide deaths in 2004 (Centers for Disease Control and Prevention & Merck Company Foundation, 2007). In 2004, 14.3 of every 100,000 people age 65 and older died by suicide, higher than the rate of about 11 per 100,000 in the general population. Non–Hispanic White men age 85 and older were most likely to die by suicide. Suicide rates for people age 65 and older were, for non–Hispanic Whites, 15.9 per 100,000; for Asians and Pacific Islanders, 10.6; for Hispanics, 7.9; and for non–Hispanic Blacks, 5.0. Usually, the first person that older adults turn to for help with problems that require mental health treatment is their primary care physician, who may have limited training with older adults or a strengths-based approach. Hence, neither the client nor the physician may recognize the symptoms of depression. Older adults tend to assume that complaints about sleep disturbances, changes in appetite, and mood differences are related to physical problems (W. Cox et al., 2012).

Both antidepressant medications and psychotherapy are treatment approaches for depression with older adults. For some older adults who are in good physical health, the combination of medication and psychotherapy provides the most benefit or relief. Studies have found that nearly 80% of older adults with depression recovered with the combined treatment and had lower recurrence rates than with psychotherapy or medication alone (Little et al., 1998; Reynolds et al., 1999). It helps when older adults spend time with other people and talk to a relative or a friend about their feelings. It is also important for them to do the things they used to enjoy before they had depression. Studies have found that doing these things, even when the person does not expect to enjoy them, can help lift his or her spirits (National Institute of Mental Health, n.d.).

Elder Abuse

According to the National Council on Aging (2017), **elder abuse and neglect** includes physical abuse, emotional abuse, sexual abuse, financial exploitation, neglect, and abandonment. Physical abuse involves inflicting physical pain or injury upon an older person. Emotional abuse means humiliating verbal assaults, threats of abuse, harassment, or intimidation, while passive neglect takes place when a caregiver fails to provide an older adult with life's necessities, including food, clothing, shelter, and medical care. Willful deprivation entails denying an older adult medication, medical care, shelter, food, a therapeutic device, or other physical assistance, resulting in exposing that person to the risk of physical, mental, or emotional harm. Nearly 1 in 10 Americans age 60 and older have experienced some form of elder abuse. It has been estimated that as many as 5 million elders are abused each year, but only 1 in 14 cases of abuse are reported to the authorities.

Who are the abusers of older adults? In almost 90% of elder abuse cases, the perpetrator is a family member, with two-thirds of perpetrators being the elder's adult children or spouses. Social isolation and mental impairment (such as dementia or Alzheimer's disease) are two factors that contribute to elder abuse. The National Council on Aging (2017) has reported that nearly half of those with dementia experienced abuse or neglect. Older adults with disabilities also have a higher rate of elder abuse.

Elder abuse can come in the form of physical abuse, emotional abuse, financial abuse, and neglect, and the effects of elder abuse can be quite devastating. Older people who have been abused have a 300% higher risk of death in comparison to those who have not been mistreated. It has been estimated that elder financial abuse and fraud costs older Americans $36.5 billion a year. Elders tend to report financial exploitation at a higher rate than they do emotional, physical, and sexual abuse or neglect (Acierno et al., 2010; Sewell, 2013).

ALZHEIMER'S DISEASE AND OTHER COGNITIVE IMPAIRMENTS

Mental deterioration and dementia are often associated with older persons. Some people perceive adults age 65 and older to be mentally incompetent. Research has found that there is some cognitive slowing with normal aging that sometimes results in the forgetting of names and phone numbers or the misplacement of such objects as keys, wallets, and so forth (Salthouse, 2012). The majority of older adults do not experience dementia or a significant cognitive impairment as a result of aging. Even though they may score lower on cognitive tests, their overall cognitive performance in real-life situations remains about the same.

What is dementia? **Alzheimer's** is a disease that attacks the brain, and it is the most common form of **dementia**. It is a general term for memory loss and other intellectual disabilities serious enough to interfere with daily life. Alzheimer's disease accounts for 60%–80% of dementia cases (Alzheimer's Association, 2016). Alzheimer's disease usually develops slowly, and it becomes worse over time. Although the greatest risk factor for Alzheimer's disease is increasing age, it is not a normal part of aging, and younger people can have early onset of Alzheimer's disease. Nearly 5% of people have the early onset of the disease, and the symptoms may appear in a person's 40s or 50s.

The number of Americans living with Alzheimer's disease is growing, with an estimated 5.4 million Americans of all ages living with Alzheimer's disease in 2016. Of the 5.4 million Americans with Alzheimer's, an estimated 5.2 million people are age 65 and older. Some important facts about Alzheimer's disease and older adults provided by the Alzheimer's Association (2016) are as follows:

- One in nine people age 65 and older have been reported to have Alzheimer's disease.
- By 2050, someone in the United States will develop the disease every 33 seconds.
- Among Americans age 70, 61% of those with Alzheimer's are expected to die before the age of 80 compared with 30% of those without Alzheimer's.
- Alzheimer's disease is the sixth-leading cause of death in the United States and the fifth-leading cause of death for people age 65 and older.
- It has been estimated that in 2016, 700,000 people with Alzheimer's will die.
- Alzheimer's disease worsens over time.
- Alzheimer's has no current cure, but treatments for its symptoms are available.
- Family caregivers spend more than $5,000 a year caring for someone with Alzheimer's.
- One in three seniors die with Alzheimer's or another dementia each year.
- In 2015, more than 15 million caregivers provided an estimated 18.1 billion hours of unpaid care.
- In 2016, Alzheimer's and other dementias cost the United States $236 billion.
- Complications from Alzheimer's kill more than breast and prostate cancer combined.

People with memory loss and other signs of Alzheimer's may find it difficult to recognize they have a problem. However, signs of dementia-like symptoms may be crystal clear to family members or friends. Early diagnosis and intervention treatments are critical to slowing the progress of Alzheimer's. Studies have found that cognitive decline in older adults can be delayed or postponed by exercising on a regular basis, by using cognitive activities to stimulate the mind (e.g., chess, crossword puzzles, reading, and computer games), and by changing to a lifestyle that involves healthy eating and nutrition (Williams & Kemper, 2010).

According to the National Council on Aging (2017), elder abuse includes physical abuse, emotional abuse, sexual abuse, financial exploitation, neglect, and abandonment. Older adults with disabilities also have a higher rate of elder abuse (National Council on Aging, 2017). Elder abuse is illegal. Counselors who work with older adults might consider using a mental status exam, such as the Mini-Mental State Examination (MMSE). The MMSE takes about 5 to 10 minutes, and it consists of 11 items that measure a person's orientation, attention and calculation, recall, language, and visual motor integrity.

SUBSTANCE ABUSE AND OLDER ADULTS

Substance abuse has become an increasing problem among members of the older adult population. Recent census data estimate substance abuse among those age 60 and older (including misuse of prescription drugs) currently affects about 17% of this population. The increase in substance abuse among people in their early 60s and 70s has been attributed in part to the aging of the baby boomers, who have tended to have higher rates of illicit drug use than those of previous generations (National Institute on Drug Abuse, 2015).

Ruth did not drink when she was younger; however, as she grew older, her children moved away, leaving her feeling lonely and unneeded. Her husband also died, and so did many of the people with whom she had been friends for decades. Ruth turned to alcohol to escape the pain of loneliness. Currently, she has just turned 80, and she has been diagnosed as an alcoholic.

Similarly, John has been using drugs on and off for years. It started with marijuana in the late 1960s, and continued intermittently for years. Like Ruth, John drinks just to make it through the night. He is in his late 70s, and his physician has informed him that his use of alcohol interacts with several of his medicines. His children are concerned that one day they will come to visit him and find him dead from an interaction between his medications and his alcoholism.

Both Ruth and John illustrate what has been labeled one of the fastest-growing health problems in the United States—substance abuse among the older population, meaning people age 60 and older. It has been estimated that about 17% of the population age 60 and older misuse prescription drugs, alcohol, and even cocaine. It has been estimated that some of the abuse of prescription drugs may be attributed to lack of understanding about taking the proper dosage of the medication. Some of the medications abused by older Americans include benzodiazepines, opiates, and muscle relaxants.

Older adults who abuse alcohol or drugs can find themselves in dangerous situations because the combination of their age and physical challenges puts them at risk for mental problems, kidney and liver disease, and injuries from falls. In addition, because many older adults tend to take a lot of different medications, their drugs may react with alcohol to cause serious problems, which might mistakenly be viewed as normal signs of aging, even though they are not. Even small dosages of drugs can result in older people responding with drug tolerance—meaning that their bodies may require increasingly higher doses to get the original effect, or they may feel withdrawal symptoms when they no longer take the drug.

For older people, some of the commonly misused drugs include anxiety pills, sleeping medications, and pain medications. Oftentimes, older adults who become addicted to drugs have a serious medical condition that results in chronic pain, and therefore, they take the medication to ease the physical pain they experience on a daily basis.

Alcohol and Pain Medications

It is recommended that older people should be extremely careful of the amount of alcohol they consume because of their bodily physical changes. For women and men over the age of 65 years, it has been suggested that the amount of alcohol considered to increase health risks is either more than seven standard drinks per week on average or more than three drinks on any day. Exceeding these recommended amounts of alcohol can result in stomach and liver problems, increased risk of stroke, interference with prescribed medications, increased falls and injuries, impairment to sleep and/or memory, and the increased instance of car accidents.

> Approximately three out of five older adults take painkillers regularly. More than one in five take a medication that affects their central nervous system and about 11% use benzodiazepines (a type of sedative). Older women are much more likely to use benzodiazepines than men. (Health in Aging, 2016)

Nearly 50% of adults over age 65 consume alcohol. Among these, 14.5% drink more than the recommended weekly allowance (more than seven drinks per week) or drink in binges. When accounting for older adults' other medical problems, a survey classified 53% of older drinkers as having harmful or hazardous drinking patterns (Bogunovic, 2012).

The social and physical changes that accompany aging may well increase vulnerability to drug-related problems. The slowing down of older adults' rate of metabolism can increase sensitivity to the effects of drugs (U.S. Department of Health and Human Services, 2005; Substance Abuse and Mental Health Services Administration, 2010).

Although greater percentages of older men have substance abuse problems than do older women, women are more inclined to begin drinking heavily later in life. Older women are more vulnerable to the negative effects of alcohol because of their small size and the decrease in water in their body. Substance abuse among the older population is more prevalent when they suffer a number of losses, including death of loved ones, retirement, and loss of health. Gender differences in substance abuse between men and women can be attributed to the fact that women are more likely to be widowed or divorced, to have experienced depression, and to have been prescribed psychoactive medications that increase the negative effects of their heavy use of alcohol late in their lives (Lowry, 2013). Clinicians need to become knowledgeable about the patterns of drug abuse among older people and alert to the possibility that some physical problems of older adults—for example, falls and other accidents—may stem from illicit drug use.

Primary care physicians have a key role in screening older people for drug abuse and related issues. The U.S. Department of Health and Human Services (2005) has published a comprehensive treatment manual using evidence-based cognitive behavioral group therapy for substance abuse in older adults. One contribution of the manual is that it helps to provide specific interventions to a group or individual modality, and it has therapy approaches that incorporate physiological, cognitive, and social changes that relate to the older adult.

SEXUALITY AND THE OLDER ADULT

Sexuality continues to have a role in the lives of older adults because people are living longer and healthier lives. Therefore, it is important for physicians, psychologists, and counselors to assess and treat sexual issues in the older adult. In the past, people have been inclined to view sexuality among older adults as humorous or disgusting. Clinicians have tended to view sexual dysfunction as a normal and untreatable part of aging. Such distorted attitudes have changed widely, however, starting with the sexual and feminist revolutions in the 1960s and 1970s and buoyed by the widespread use of hormone replacement therapy and then the advent of oral erectogenic agents for erectile dysfunction (Steffens, Blazer, & Mugdha, 2015).

For many people, discussing sexuality among adults over the age of 65 is a taboo topic. The prevailing belief in American societies and in many countries around the world is that older adults don't participate in sex. This perception is inaccurate for many men and women who live in the age of Viagra (sildenafil). Bob Dole, former Republican candidate for president of the United States, made a commercial praising the virtues of Viagra, which, according to him, had given him back his sex life. The 2006 film *Away From Her* brought to the forefront issues of sexuality in couples dealing with dementia. Julie Christie starred as an older woman with Alzheimer's disease whose sexuality remained vibrant. When working with older adults, counselors, psychologists, social workers, and mental health practitioners tend not to take into consideration the sexuality of older adults. Instead, they assume that sexuality is no longer an issue for older adults.

Yet, in reality, sexual activity continues into the eighth decade for many elders. Some factors that impede an older person's discussion of his or her sexuality include the age of the counselor, the client's sexual orientation, and the client's cultural background. Moreover, the sexual concerns of men and women often differ in their focus. While men are more inclined to focus on performance, women may emphasize cuddling, caring, and love. Gradually, people all over the world have come to understand that a person's sexuality continues throughout his or her lifetime (Buttaro, Koeniger-Donohue, & Hawkins, 2014).

Although sexuality is important for both men and women as they age into their 60s, 70s, and 80s, sexuality is still a difficult topic for many psychologists, counselors, and physicians to discuss with their clients. It is only relatively recently that researchers have begun to investigate carefully the sexual behavior of older adults. For instance Lindau et al. (2007) reported on a survey of 3,005 respondents ages 57–85 who were questioned about their sexual activity. The majority of older Americans are sexually active, and they consider intimacy an important part of their lives. Some of the findings of the study were as follows:

- About half of the men and women surveyed said they had at least one sexual problem, and about a third reported at least two problems. Sexuality among respondents declined with age. A large percentage of respondents indicated that they were sexually active in the preceding 12 months, but this percentage decreased with age—from 73% of those ages 57–74, to 53% of those ages 65–74, to 26% of those ages 75–85.

- Healthier people were more inclined to report being sexually active. Approximately 81% of men and 51% of women reporting excellent or very good health said they had been sexually active within the past 12 months. In contrast, 47% of men and 26% of women who reported fair or poor health said that they had sexual activity in the previous year. Both diabetes and hypertension were strongly associated with individuals' sexual concerns.

- The majority of older adults have not discussed sex with their medical doctors, despite the high prevalence of sexual problems. Only 38% of men and 22% of women said they had discussed sex with a physician after age 50.

In 2013, Northrup, Schwartz, and Witte conducted a survey that found that among the survey respondents, who were all age 50 or older, 59% of men and 56% of women reported that their partners were not fulfilling their needs. In addition, more than 25% of the men said they were not having enough sex, while 25% of the women said they were not living the lifestyle they had hoped for. Thirty-one percent of couples have sex several times a week, 28% a couple times a month, 8% once a month, and 33% rarely or never. The happiest couples said "I love you" at least once a week. The most prevalent problems mentioned by women were a lack of desire, difficulty with vaginal lubrication, and inability to experience orgasm. Older men discussed sexual concerns that were focused primarily on erectile difficulties. Health issues had a major impact on older adults' sexual activity, with those in poor health becoming less likely to be sexually active and more likely to experience sexual problems.

Block, Smith, and Segal (2014) have maintained that seniors can continue to enjoy sex if they are open to new ideas, try different positions, vary times of day, and incorporate sex toys into sex play. These researchers summarized studies that indicate that erectile dysfunction (ED) is associated with medication side effects, diabetes, coronary artery disease, and other disorders; therefore, men should be routinely screened for ED in the primary care setting.

Women experience both physical and psychological problems that affect their sexuality as they age. It has been estimated that women have a sexual dysfunction rate ranging from 25% to 63% of older women (Adenivi, Brindley, Pryor, & Ralph, 2007). After reviewing the literature on sexual function in older women, Ambler, Bieber, and Diamond (2012) concluded that the prevalence of sexual dysfunction may be as high as 68%–86.5%. According to these researchers, the most common problems for older women are lack of estrogen, frequent lower urinary tract infections, problems with arousal and achieving orgasm, lack of libido, pain with intercourse, negative body image, and a sense of diminished desirability and attractiveness.

Cultural representations of aging and sexuality influence how women perceive their sexuality as they age. According to Loe (2004), most women still see sex as men's territory, with women functioning as silent partners. In addition, research on the sexuality of older lesbian, gay, bisexual, transgender, and questioning (LGBTQ) individuals is notably missing in the literature (Watters & Boyd, 2009). Heaphy, Yip, and Thompson has asserted that American society tends to support the cultural heteronormative stigma in which the only kind of sexuality to be valued and condoned is that among healthy heterosexual males. Identifying these factors is vital to examining and addressing the concerns and needs of aging female adults.

The LGBTQ Older Adult

LGBTQ older adults represent an important part of American society. They are defined as the population of sexual and gender minorities over the age of 50. There is no census count available for LGBTQ older adults living in the United States as of this writing, but it has been estimated that there are over 2.4 million LGBTQ adults over age 50 in the United States, and this number is expected to increase to over 5 million by 2030.

This section on LGBTQ older adults uses an **intersectionality** approach for examining this population group. Adams (2016) has advocated an intersectional approach to services and care for LGBTQ older adults. Such an approach takes into account the heterogeneity of the experiences and cultural backgrounds of LGBTQ older adults. Many LGBTQ older adults live at the intersection of two or more identities—for instance, being lesbian and Mexican American. There are LGBTQ older adults who are African American, Latino American, Asian American, and American Indian, to just mention the diverse ethnicity and cultural experiences of LGBTQ older adults. Practitioners in the field of aging should consider incorporating an intersectional approach to their work that weaves in race, gender, ability, and/or disability, as well as other social considerations that affect an elder LGBTQ person's life.

Soon Kyu Choi and Ilan H. Meyer (2016) conducted a review of LGBTQ research findings in 2014. The key findings from this report are summarized below:

- Compared to heterosexual adults, LGBTQ older adults are more likely to be single or living alone. Studies have reported that resilient LGBTQ older adults often rely on "families of choice" for support.

- Many LGBTQ older adults state that their primary health care providers do not know about their sexual orientations, and many say they are reluctant to discuss their sexual orientations or gender identity with health care providers.

- LGBTQ older adults are more likely to face poverty or economic difficulty, and they deal with significant physical health and mental health disparities.

- In contrast to their non-LGBTQ counterparts, LGBTQ older adults have experienced and continue to experience discrimination due to their sexual orientation and gender identity.

Overall, as a group, LGBTQ elders are at high risk for severe social isolation because they are four times less likely to be parents, twice as likely to be single and living alone, and more inclined to be disconnected from their families of origin. Their reduced absence of partners, adult children, and other family members has led to thin social and care networks (Adams, 2016). However, it is important to note that LGBTQ older adults do not have a homogeneous aging experience.

Intimate Partner Abuse of Older LGBTQ Adults

Little has been written about intimate partner abuse among older LGBTQ adults. The New York State Office for the Prevention of Domestic Violence (n.d.) has summarized the following important considerations for examining intimate partner abuse of older LGBTQ adults:

- Outing: LGBTQ older adults are often threatened with "outing of their sexual identity" by their intimate partners in return for money, sex, or other demands.

- Shame or Embarrassment: Older LGBTQ individuals have often internalized homophobia.

- Control of Finances and Assets: Many LGBTQ older adults are not protected by marriage and/or community property laws; thus, it can become easy for an abuser to gain and control all of a couple's finances.

THE STRENGTHS-BASED THERAPY MODEL AND THE OLDER ADULT

Strengths-Based Therapy's Philosophy About Older Adults

The goal of strengths-based therapy for older adults is to help them live long and productive lives and to enjoy a good quality of life. The strengths-based therapy model maintains that older adults have an ongoing potential to grow, heal, and learn. Older adults have individual and environmental strengths. They also possess the ability to determine what is best for them. They can use existing competencies to identify and address their own concerns, and their strengths can be involved in the process of healing and self-health. In strengths-based therapy, the therapist or case manager helps to identify the older individual's strengths and to locate situations in which those strengths can be used. Individuals are the acknowledged experts on their lives. A strengths-based approach to working with older adults is collaborative and reduces the power differential between professionals and individuals/families (Anuradha, 2004; Rashid & Ostermann, 2009). The strengths-based therapy model uses such guiding concepts as empowerment and social justice.

The strengths-based therapy model asserts that there is a need to discover what has helped the older adult get to where he or she is in life. In this model, the focus is on the individual instead of the problem. The therapist balances problems with the strengths of individuals and their environments (Chapin & Cox, 2001; Perkins & Tice, 1995; Rashid, 2009). The strengths-based therapy approach focuses on what is working well and emphasizes the promotion of mental wellness in older adults with mental illness or with a disability. For instance, Yarry, Judge, and Orsulic-Jeras (2010) used a dyadic approach that identified and built upon both care partners' current strengths to deal with mild to moderate memory loss.

The strengths-based therapy model adopts the philosophy of empowering older adults by helping them to reestablish bonds with their community and neighborhood. All too often, older women and men are isolated and hidden away from the communities in which they live. They become the invisible people of a community. Older adults have a great deal to offer their communities. For instance, many older adults help operate and deliver the Meals on Wheels program to shut-ins. Others volunteer for reading and math programs in schools. Senior Volunteers in

Broward County, Florida, provides volunteering opportunities in three different federal programs: Senior Companions, Foster Grandparents, and RSVP. The Retired and Senior Volunteer Program (RSVP) engages individuals age 55 and older in volunteer service to meet critical community needs. The interests of volunteers are matched with nonprofit and public organizations seeking assistance. In an attempt to attract seniors, the organization states, "You can connect to others, share the years of your experience, and make an impact in your community! Whatever your experience and abilities, we have a senior volunteer position for you." There are numerous state volunteering programs for seniors throughout this nation.

Role of the Strengths-Based Therapist and Older Adults

Although some older adults do seek out private, individual therapy, many do not. Instead, therapy for older adults is usually offered under the structure of case management. Older adults, especially those experiencing some form of physical and mental disability, tend to have multiple medical and nonmedical needs. For instance, a client may fall and be hospitalized for a hip replacement. Although the medical needs of the person may have been met, the person must then deal with instrumental issues such as transportation to and from medical appointments, shopping, and worship services; basic meal preparation and housekeeping; financial assistance; and social isolation.

Other older individuals may suffer from a chronic heart condition or a chronic disease and may require the services of a home care health aide to help them bathe and take care of their personal hygiene needs, as well as a personal care aide to prepare certain meals, help with the shopping, and so on. Older adults with serious or chronic disabilities require the involvement of medical professionals to protect them from further injury and debilitation, as well as health and personal care aides at home. Still other aging individuals may encounter acute illnesses that last several months. The stress involved in obtaining and providing emotional support from medical doctors and caregivers with the personal hygiene and household tasks may take its toll on older adults and their families. Similar to younger persons with disabilities, some older adults require only minimal assistance to arrange and manage supports to enable them to remain in their homes and communities.

The involvement of so many people with older adults (medical doctors, personal caregivers, etc.) necessitates using a case management framework. Within either the individual therapy or the case management approach, a major goal is to help the person manage the aging process, especially with his or her family. For instance, most older adults want to remain in their homes as long as they can. Family members, however, may not support an older parent living in his or her home because of inadequate care or because of concerns about the parent's security and well-being. One role of the therapist or case manager is to provide the older adult client with options and include the client in the decision-making process about whether he or she will remain at home or be placed in some form of assisted living.

Older adults may find it difficult to voice their need for help from family members and others. Oftentimes, they may remain silent about their needs, not wanting to acknowledge their need for help. Many older people state that they value their freedom, privacy, and independence much more than they value living in a safe and protected environment. For instance, when Rose broke her hip and had to be hospitalized, she stated that upon her release from the hospital, she wanted to return to her own home. Rose's case manager assisted her by helping her to make meaningful choices about her care at home. She helped contact the senior citizens' jitney to obtain transportation to and from the doctor and to other places that Rose wanted to attend—church, for instance. She assisted Rose by helping her to arrange for a personal care aide and a health aide to assist her with her rehabilitative exercise.

Case managers help older clients to successfully manage their aging process and the emotional and physical losses they encounter. They assist older adults to manage their strengths, their needs, and their risks and security issues.

CASE VIGNETTE 17.1

REBECCA GERVASE

Rebecca Gervase had worked as a teacher for more than 40 years. When she retired 4 years ago from teaching, she lost her sense of purpose and identity, became depressed, fell in the shower, and was hospitalized briefly for her injury. Her son and daughter felt that she was depressed over the loss of her husband of 42 years during the past year. Her children took her to a therapist to deal more effectively with her loss and depression. The therapist gave Rebecca a depression checklist, and the findings indicated that she was depressed.

Talking about her depression was the first step for Rebecca. She had felt guilty that she was whining about her losses while others who had endured greater losses had said very little. The therapist began to focus on Rebecca's teaching strengths and recommended that she volunteer to help the first-grade teacher at the school where she taught previously with her reading groups.

Rebecca responded affirmatively, and gradually her sense of purpose came back to her. She was doing what she loved without having the responsibility of teaching an entire grade.

Arrangements were made to have a cleaning service come in once every two weeks to assist Rebecca with her household chores. Rebecca's son and daughter were happy that their mother had returned to teaching for two hours, four days a week. They purchased an emergency response bracelet that she could use to summon help if she ever fell again. With the additional help, the part-time teaching work, and the emergency bracelet, plus therapy for her depression, Rebecca was able to deal with her losses and to move on with her life.

Discussion Questions

1. How do you conceptualize Rebecca's major mental health issues?

2. What other possible interventions might be helpful to alleviate Rebecca's depression?

3. Would you recommend medication to help deal with Rebecca's depression?

4. How might family members become an important part of Rebecca's treatment?

5. Do older adults still need a sense of purpose in living—even at their age?

PHASES OF STRENGTHS-BASED THERAPY FOR OLDER ADULTS

The seven phases of the strengths-based therapy model outlined in this section apply mainly to moderately to high-functioning older adults. They may not be as appropriate for older adults experiencing Alzheimer's disease, facing significant cognitive deficits in their day-to-day functioning, or entering the frail stage of the aging process.

Cultural Reflections

Does your counselor or mental health training program have a component that involves counseling the older adult?

Do you feel your training program has prepared you adequately to counsel older adults?

What kinds of background material or training exercises would you like to have to better prepare you for counseling older adults?

Phase 1: Establishing a Therapeutic Alliance

Establishing a therapeutic alliance with older adults is governed by the same principles as for younger clients. The therapist or case manager is respectful of the older person. He or she asks how the person would like to be addressed—such as "Mr.," "Mrs.," "Ms.," or "Dr."—instead of assuming it is acceptable to call the client by his or her first name. It is also important to know or to understand how the client's culture views the aging process. Are older people revered within the client's culture? How does the client's culture respond to or deal with the aging process?

It is important to determine what the older client wants from therapy and what his or her expectations are of the therapist. During the first meeting, the therapist might spend some time clarifying what the issue is for the client. For instance, some older clients tend to present their issues in medical terms. In fact, physicians are usually the first to hear an older person's primary complaint. Older people should be encouraged not to dismiss their feelings on the grounds that they are part of the aging process. The repeated loss and death of some friends and family members can be the underlying cause of depression; however, as noted earlier, depression does not have to be part of the normal aging process.

During therapy, the therapist should turn the conversation to the client's strengths and to having the client understand that he or she will be using strengths to deal with whatever issue prompted him or her to seek therapy. Vaillant and Mukamal's (2001) research on successful aging asserted that one can predict before the age of 50 if a person will age successfully by using the following indicators: parental social class, family cohesion, major depression, ancestral longevity, childhood temperament, and physical health at age 50. The authors defined successful aging in terms of the following factors:

1. Retaining intellectual curiosity and creative abilities
2. Seeing meaning in life, even late-stage adulthood
3. Remaining physically active to remain healthy
4. Being more spiritual in their outlook on life than are those who grow older less well
5. Retaining friendships and satisfaction with spouses, children, and family life
6. Engaging in volunteer work and civic involvement.

Phase 2: Strengths Discovery

The therapist or case manager seeks to get a holistic picture of the older client (Nelson-Becker, Chapin, & Fast, 2006). In general, assessments of older adults are directed mainly to establish eligibility for reimbursable services. The strengths-based therapy model maintains that assessment should include successful aging concepts that take into consideration five goals voiced by older adults, mainly, the goals of independence, participation, care, self-fulfillment, and dignity (Galambos & Rosen, 1999). Assess strengths in all areas: physical, mental, social, and spiritual. Specifically, the therapist or case manager assesses how the client is coping with the physical and emotional stresses of aging, how he or she wishes to maintain control over his or her life, who is crucial in the person's support system, and what is meaningful to this person for maintaining a desired quality of life. The strengths assessment process is not designed to replace existing standardized assessments to determine health care benefits for older adults.

Table 17.1 provides an assessment tool that mental health professionals can use with older adults to determine their strengths. As the clinician raises these questions during counseling, the older adult begins to sense his or her strengths. The questions are designed to encourage older adults to consider what is going on in their lives and to give them a sense of empowerment for the future.

The strengths-based therapy model consists of 12 strengths components that are categorized into three thematic categories: physical health, mental health and spirituality, and relationships and social support. This model is an adaptation of the model created by the Denver Regional Council of Governments (DRCOG) in 2004. The DRCOG model was based on a survey of more than 8,300 senior citizens throughout the state of Colorado. The mental health and spirituality component consists of assessing older clients' mental health, their sense of self-efficacy, their feelings of being valued by members of their community, and their spirituality or sense of spiritual being. The physical health component also contains three subcomponents, including the older person's physical well-being, nutrition and food, and security. The relationships and social support component consists of identifying a person's practical support, social support, engagement in life, and leisure and hobby activities.

TABLE 17.1 ■ Strengths-Based Assessment Questions for Older Adults
1. What is going well for you right now?
2. What would your preferred future look like?
3. What do you like about your current living situation?
4. What things would you like to change about it?
5. What type of housing situation would you ideally like to have?
6. How do you get to where you want or need to go?
7. How would you like to expand your transportation or your ability to get around?
8. Tell me some ways that your family provides social and emotional support for you.
9. How does your family help you to feel good about yourself?
10. What, if any, role does spirituality or religion play in your life?
11. How would you describe your health?
12. What are two personal desires of your life that make your life meaningful?

12-Component Model of Strengths Assessment for Aging Well

Table 17.2 describes a 12-component strengths assessment approach for working with older adults. The model takes into consideration areas such as physical activity, nutrition and food, security strengths, daily living strengths, mental health, culture and spirituality, relationships and social support, and engagement in life. These strengths provide a starting point for assessment and can be used as a checklist. For instance, for each item to which the client responds affirmatively or has a strength, the therapist/case manager gives him or her one point. The therapist/case manager then sums the total number of strengths that the older client has. Clients with a high number of strengths may be said to be aging well. Therapists/case managers are encouraged to add or delete strengths based on the aging category in which the client is placed—that is, new senior citizen, frail older adult, and so forth. Many more strengths could have been included. For older adults in the DRCOG study, possessing a greater number of strengths was related to higher self-ratings of quality of life. Those with four or fewer strengths had an average quality-of-life rating of 63, while those with nine or more had an average rating of 90 on the 100-point scale. Other findings were that (1) those who lived with others were more likely to have nine or more strengths, (2) the number of strengths generally increased with education and income, and (3) those who were limited physically were less likely to possess nine or more strengths.

Identifying barriers to solving problems/reaching goals. During Phase 2, the therapist and the client identify barriers to resolving the current issue that brought the client to therapy. The therapist asks, "What are the internal barriers you've created in your life that prevent you from solving this challenge?" Quite often, fear serves as an internal barrier or a paralyzing force that prevents a person from taking the necessary action to solve a particular issue or problem. There may also be external barriers—the lack of supportive people in one's life or living in a violent community.

The therapist/case manager and the client identify the external barriers blocking the resolution of a client's problem. For instance, one older adult woman lived alone in her apartment, and her son and grandchildren lived several hundred miles away in another city. The prospect of

TABLE 17.2 ■ 12-Component Strengths-Based Therapy Assessment Model for Older Adults	
Physical Health Category of Strengths	
Physical Activity Nutrition and Food Security Strengths ADL or Daily Living Strengths Transportation Strengths	_____ Client has had no problem in last 12 months that limited him or her physically. _____ Client has engaged in moderate exercise 3 or more days per week. _____ Client is able to perform heavy-duty housework, including yard work and snow shoveling, without any help. _____ Client has had no problem in last 12 months having enough food to eat. _____ Client has not needed help in past 2 months in getting enough food or the right kinds of food to eat. _____ Client can afford food and healthy meals. _____ Client eats two or more complete meals a day. _____ Client has not lost 10 or more pounds in the past 6 months without intending to do so. _____ Client can do all of the following without any assistance: walk, eat, dress, bathe, use the toilet, get in and out of bed or a chair. _____ Client can perform all of the following without assistance: prepare meals, shop for personal items, do light housework, manage medications, manage money, use a telephone. _____ Client can use available transportation or has access to transportation.
Mental Health and Spirituality Category of Strengths	
Mental Health	_____ Client has had no major problem in feeling lonely, sad, or isolated within past 12 months. _____ Client has not evidenced any emotional or mental illness that limited his or her daily activity. _____ Client strongly agrees that "I am usually a happy person" and "I usually feel peaceful and calm."
Self-Efficacy Valued by Community (Older people valued and cultural traditions) Spirituality	The client agrees with most of the following statements: __ I feel as if I have control over the things that happen to me. __ I take responsibility for my own actions. __ I have planned for my financial future. __ I have a sense of life purpose. __ I can handle most things that life throws at me. __ I still have goals that I want to achieve. __ I believe I have the ability to accomplish my goals. _____ Client strongly agrees that "My community values older people" and that "My community values my language and cultural traditions." _____ Client strongly agrees that "Religion or spirituality is important in my life" or "I receive a lot of practical or social support from my church or spiritual group." _____ Client states that spirituality or religion provides a moral base for him or her to make decisions about living. _____ Client maintains that spirituality or religion provides a comforting way for him or her to conceptualize this last phase of his or her life. _____ Client believes in a spiritual or a religious afterlife that provides victory over death.

(Continued)

TABLE 17.2 ■ (Continued)

Relationships and Social Support Category of Strengths

Practical Support Social Support Engagement in Life Leisure or Hobby	_____ Client has received a lot of practical support from family, friends, neighbors, a club or social group, or a nonprofit community agency. _____ Client has received a lot of social support from family, friends, neighbors, a club or social group, or a nonprofit community agency. _____ Client has either participated in a club or civic group 6 or more hours per week or performed volunteer work 1 or more hours per week. _____ Client has visited with family 6 or more hours per week or visited with friends 6 or more hours per week. _____ Client has provided help to friends or relatives 1 or more hours per week. _____ Client spent at least 1 hour per week participating in a hobby such as art, gardening, or music.

death was frightening to the older woman. Was she to face death all alone? Didn't her son care about her?

Another woman was placed in a nursing home because the daughter and her family could no longer take care of her. The mother pleaded with the daughter, "Didn't I bake you cookies when you were young? Didn't I attend all your plays? Am I just a mother of convenience for you? Now that I can't do things for you, you don't want me around anymore. You want to get rid of me. Why put me in a home to die?"

Tears filled the daughter's eyes as she recalled the haunting questions that her mother raised about being placed in an "old folks' home." It wasn't that she didn't love her mother. She did appreciate everything her mother had done for her. It was simply that she, too, was getting older, and she had obligations of her own such as her job, which involved frequent travel. Her husband and children also had commitments and plans. The family knew it was unsafe to leave the mother alone in her own home for days at a time with no one to help her with activities of daily living. The letting go part of Phase 3 can be quite challenging for both the client and the therapist.

Phase 3: Letting Go, Harvesting the Good, Eliciting Clients' Hopes and Dreams, and Letting In the Good/Change

The strengths-based therapist/case manager works with clients to identify internal and external barriers to the presenting issue/problem or the client's strengths, to let go of the past, and to harvest the good out of a long life. For many people, growing older oftentimes means that one has had to let go of a number of things in life that one has treasured, including the loss of one's parents, spouse, and close friends; the separation from work associates and from work itself when one retires; the gradual diminishing of one's physical prowess; and impairments of one's health. In fact, letting go can form a dominant theme of an aging person's life.

Letting go. The critical question is, How does one let go? Does one let go begrudgingly? Does one fight it, or accept it? Does one welcome it as a relief from responsibility? Does one resent it as "robbing" one of earlier happiness? How does one let go of one's youth and all that accompanies youth? One person said, "Now that I am retired, I can speak my mind. I don't have to worry about keeping up with the Joneses or waking up to my 6 a.m. alarm clock. The alarm clock doesn't control me anymore. I control it." Other aging individuals have expressed appreciation for the quality time they now have to spend with sons, daughters, and grandchildren. It all depends on how you see the glass—as half empty or half full. During Phase 3 of the strengths-based therapy model, the therapist/case manager spends time talking about the client's "letting go" process and how it has affected him or her. Letting go is a necessary first step in "letting in" the good in a person's life.

Harvesting the good. Harvesting the good out of life is another theme related to aging. Every life has both good and bad. Every life has decisions one wishes one had made or had not made. Every life has mistakes, pitfalls, victories, triumphs, and transcendence. The strengths-based therapist helps the older adult to sort out, on balance, the life he or she has led. "Overall," the therapist might say, "how would you rate your life on a scale of 1 to 10, with 10 being highly satisfying?" Another way of asking this question is "How satisfied are you with the life that you have led?" or "If you could live your life over differently, what would you change? What would you leave the same?"

Cultural Reflections

Do you think that older adults—those age 75 and older—should consider counseling if they have a mental health issue?

How do you feel about counseling older adults?

Would you ever consider having a clinical practice that focused on counseling older adults? Explain your answer.

Harvesting the good means taking the good out of even bad or negative circumstances. An older client might say, "I am sorry that I married my spouse, but I am happy for the three children that he gave me." Another reflects on career choices, and he or she asserts, "Looking back, I wish I had had the guts to become the singer that I really wanted to become instead of settling for teaching elementary school. Teaching, however, has been good to me. I was able to take care of my family and to put my kids through college." During moments dealing with harvesting the good out of life and out of negative circumstances, the therapist/case manager focuses on helping the client to realize the strength(s) that pulled him or her through the negative situation. "Despite all the negative life challenges you face, you always managed to survive. Can you tell me about one or two of the strengths that helped you to survive what you went through?"

Instilling hope—letting in. Older people have hope for their lives, just as do those who are younger. Some differences do occur in what they hope for and in the life-and-death struggles that they face. Dufault and Martocchio (1985) have proposed the existence of two different types or spheres of hope. They labeled one type of hope generalized hope and the other type particularized hope.

Older people may have both generalized hope and particularized hope. They may hope that they live longer (generalized hope), and they may hope that they recover from a specific illness (particularized hope).

The power of hope. Researchers have found a therapeutic value of hope to health, healing, well-being, and quality of life (Moore, 2005; Snyder, Irving, & Anderson, 1991). During the past three decades, interest in hope has intensified, as shown by a surge in qualitative and quantitative studies—many of which have occurred in health care settings. Research has linked hope and healing (Snyder et al., 1991), hope and coping (Hall, 1990; Herth, 1990; Snyder, 2000), hope and goal setting (Snyder, 1994), hope and finding meaning in suffering and illness (Herth, 1990; Jevne & Miller, 1999), and hope as an antidote to hopelessness (Duggleby, 2001). Helping professionals have identified hope as a fundamental necessity (Hall, 1990), being vital to both life and living (Jevne & Miller, 1999), and an essential human need—particularly among older adults (Forbes, 1994). Research has emphasized the relational nature of hope, exploring in particular the centrality of caregivers, family, and friends to fostering hope (Herth, 2000).

The power of spirituality and religion. Spirituality and faith have also been found to be factors influencing hope (Duggleby, 2001). Most religions encourage people to have hope. Religious beliefs, including faith in a higher power, life after death, and the power of prayer, can increase a person's sense of hope. Davis's (2005) study involving people ages 60–89 found positive correlations between hope and spirituality, hope and well-being, and spirituality and well-being. Research studies have reported that hope is a life force and is something that individuals rely on in times of crisis, tragedy, or illness (Cutcliffe & Grant, 2001; Davis, 2005; Herth, 1990). Several studies have explored the potential for hope to be instilled or encouraged among depressed older persons living in nursing homes. Still other studies have examined hope among persons with specific afflictions, such as cancer (Duggleby & Wright, 2004; Fehring, Miller, & Shaw, 1997) and stroke (Bays, 2001).

The strengths-based therapy model subscribes to the view that hope is a life force that provides important benefits to people. Most important, hope gives people the desire to live and to continue seeking the accomplishment of their goals and life purpose. Hope is essential for older adults to continue living after having experienced so many losses in their lives. Table 17.3 provides hope questions a therapist might use with older adults.

Strengths-based therapy case managers instill hope in older adults by reminding them of their strengths and what they have accomplished in life. They assist older clients by having them focus on what remains rather than on what is lost or what is missing. For instance, one may have lost one's parents due to death but still have grandchildren or great grandchildren. The focus is always on the positive, on what remains with the older adult instead of what is missing or gone.

Phase 4: Framing Solutions and Strengths-Based Treatment Plans

During Phase 4 of strengths-based therapy, the goal is to create a strengths-based treatment plan. Older adults usually require a highly individualized treatment plan because they tend to have different health situations and physical strengths. For instance, a strengths-based treatment plan for a healthy older adult is quite different from that for a person suffering from the early or late stages of dementia (Yarry et al., 2010). A person suffering from the early stages of dementia

TABLE 17.3 ■ Hope Questions for Older Adults

We have been discussing your support systems. I was wondering, what is there in your life that makes you feel strong and able to deal with different situations?

- What are your sources of hope, strength, comfort, and peace?
- What do you hold on to during difficult times?
- What sustains you and keeps you going?
- For some people, religion or spiritual beliefs provide comfort and strength in dealing with life's ups and downs; is this true for you?
- Do you look forward to the future?
- Do you consider yourself part of an organized religion?
- How important is your religion or spirituality to you on a scale of 1 to 10, with 10 being important?
- Are you a member of a religious or spiritual community?
- What parts of your religion or spirituality do you feel help you the most—prayer, meditation, reading scripture, attending religious services, listening to church music, or another factor?
- What promises or hopes does your religion or spirituality provide to you?
- How does your religion or spirituality help you to cope with loss and disappointment?

might have a treatment plan that contains strategies to help him or her remember items. A person might use a calendar to record taking his or her medications. Another technique used with clients suffering from dementia is to display a sign reading "Remember Your Safe Return Necklace," printed on bright paper with bold lettering, in a conspicuous place.

Framing a life plan and "bucket list." Older adults who have reasonably good health might develop a life plan that includes a "bucket list" of things they want to accomplish and experience before they leave. Others might be encouraged to write the book, paint the work of art, or compose the music that they always promised themselves they would do. Still others create treatment plans for dealing with a disability or a loss. For instance, a treatment plan may be developed for dealing with heart disease, cancer, vision loss, or any other disability or problem the older individual faces.

Whenever possible, the client's treatment plan focuses on his or her preferred picture of the future. For example, a client states that he wants to remain living independently at home. The treatment plan would outline the older person's strengths, the internal and external barriers to his or her remaining in the home, and the strategies he or she plans to use to accomplish this goal. All goals in the treatment plan should be stated affirmatively or positively.

Components of a treatment plan. The treatment plan identifies client needs. As the client and the case manager consider the identified goal, they ask, What needs to happen for the person to achieve this goal? What is currently getting in the way of the person's achieving this goal? What could trip the person up as he or she moves toward the goal? What kinds of resources/help does the older person need to achieve the goal(s)? What functional strengths do the older person and his or her family have to accomplish the identified goals? The treatment plan should specify the steps the older adult is to take toward accomplishing his or her goal.

The client's treatment plan specifies what he or she would like to let into his or her life. For example, the individual may need to permit others to help him or her with household chores. It is difficult for some older adults to ask for and to receive assistance taking care of the things that they used to take care of alone. For some women, it is very difficult to have another woman in their kitchen cooking meals.

Harmony. The older adult moves toward obtaining a sense of harmony in his or her life. The treatment plan is designed to bring about a greater sense of harmony. Some older adults move to create harmony in their relationships with family members. For instance, one woman was forced to move in with her daughter because of ill health. Both the daughter and the mother acknowledged that they had not had a good relationship. The case manager's treatment plan involved developing strategies to build a new mother–daughter relationship between the two.

Moreover, sometimes an older person has to make peace or develop a sense of harmony about who he or she is. As Popeye the Sailor Man used to say, "I am what I am." The issue is how one reconciles the diverse strands of one's life to find a sense of harmony. Still further, some older adults must make peace and develop a sense of harmony despite the many health and physical challenges they face. "I am not my heart disease, even though I recognize that it is slowly taking my life."

Phase 5: Building New Competencies

It is rarely too late to build competencies. Older adults can develop new competencies. For instance, some older adults suffering from pain become trained in and develop competencies in mindfulness or meditation techniques for the purpose of dealing positively with such pain. In other cases, acquiring new competencies involves taking up a hobby or volunteering. It's been said that Grandma Moses began painting at age 80. People who are actively involved in creating new competencies create a sense of self-efficacy and something of the feeling that "I've still got what it takes."

An older client's treatment plan should be forward looking and identify competencies that would strengthen him or her. New competencies keep a person feeling that life is not over for him or her. Hopefully, clients learn that although they might retire from a specific job, they do not retire from life—instead, retirement from a career can be a time to make changes to continue the race. Life goes on after retirement, and so should people.

Phase 6: Building a Healthy New Identity

People work on their identities—on who they are—for most of their lives. Therefore, it is possible for older adults to continue building a healthy new identity. Some may pick up new hobbies such as aerobics, athletics, or social activities that keep them active. In recent years, a growing number of older men and women are engaging in plastic surgery (Ellin, 2011). Experts suggest that this trend will likely increase as the baby boomer generation continues to age, and speculations about the reason behind this trend include longer and healthier life spans, interest in dating or seeking new careers and wanting to update their appearance accordingly, or simply a desire to reverse or minimize the visible effects of aging.

Phase 7: Moving Forward and Terminating Treatment

Together, the therapist/case manager and the older client determine when treatment should be ended. For some older adults, death or illness terminates treatment. Others have achieved the goals they set out to accomplish. In terminating treatment, the therapist/case manager and the client evaluate the progress they have made toward achieving goals.

ADDITIONAL STRENGTHS ASSESSMENT ISSUES

Strengths-based assessment varies according to the circumstances of the older adult's health and mental status. Several strengths-based inventories have been constructed for working with older adults. Judge, Yarry, and Orsulic-Jeras (2006) have developed a strengths-based inventory for assessing individuals with dementia and their caregivers' current strengths. Kivnick and Murray (2001) have constructed a life strengths interview guide to assess older individuals' strengths. Another strengths-based tool is the Care-Receiver Efficacy Scale (CRES) (E. Cox, Green, Seo, Inaba, & Quillen, 2006). This scale assesses self-efficacy in older adults who are care receivers.

Strengths-based assessment should also contain spiritual and cultural assessment of older adult clients. On average, older adults value the importance of religion and spirituality in their lives. They rely on their faith to sustain them as they deal with illness and challenges and as they attempt to build competence in new areas. The question the therapist should ask is, How can the client's religion or spirituality be engaged to build on personal strengths or to cope with challenging issues?

A FINAL NOTE ON CLINICAL INTERVENTION AND TREATMENT ISSUES

Strengths-based clinical interventions with older adults are varied and based on the type of challenges they face. For instance, Yarry et al. (2010) have developed dementia-management interventions to positively impact mental health outcomes for caregivers and care receivers. They used a strength-based, dyadic intervention that identifies and builds on both care partners' current abilities to address their special care needs. Yarry et al. constructed a strengths-based intervention called Acquiring New Skills While Enhancing Remaining Strengths (ANSWERS) for caregiving dyads coping with the symptoms of mild to moderate dementia.

A strengths-based approach to treatment for frail older adults should build on those activities or strengths they can still do. For example, a frail older adult may still be able to make a call to a grandchild, send a birthday card, sit on the porch, or sing a favorite song. One therapist wheeled a frail, retired music teacher to her piano and watched her fingers delicately touch the keys as she played a favorite piece by Brahms. An elder client's strengths may be the last to leave. Older adults should be given every opportunity to use whatever meaningful strengths remain. The older person's strengths may provide a source of solace or a sense of self-efficacy.

CASE VIGNETTE 17.2
USING THE STRENGTHS-BASED THERAPY MODEL WITH SARAH

Sarah is a 70-year-old retired buyer for a major department store. She retired at the age of 65 because she said that she wanted to devote more time to being with her husband, two children, and four grandchildren. For the most part, Sarah was a vibrant woman when she retired. She didn't look 70, and she still dressed attractively.

Within two years after her retirement, Sarah's husband, Ben, filed for divorce. Sarah was devastated. Although she realized that there were difficulties in the marriage, she had not thought they were sufficiently severe to warrant a divorce. Ben told her that he had been seeing someone else for the past year and a half and wanted to make a commitment to the new woman in his life. The woman was 12 years younger than Ben, who was also 70. Ben told Sarah that he did not know how much longer he had to be around, but that he wasn't going to waste any of it being unhappy. They had been married for 35 years, and their children were grown and doing well with their own children. There was no reason to stay or to keep hiding the truth from Sarah.

The divorce was made final two months before Sarah's 71st birthday. Sarah felt drained. She and Ben had argued over the finances involved with his business, the house, and everything else that involved money or memorabilia. Although some of her friends had congratulated her on what she was able to get in terms her financial settlement, Sarah really wanted her marriage back. For the past 35 years of her life, she had been Ben's wife. She and Ben used to go out to dinner, see movies, and attend art shows and concerts together. Now there was no one—just her and her friends. The divorce left Sarah feeling like a failure. She kept asking herself what she had done wrong to cause the divorce. She didn't deserve to be alone in her later years. The pictures in her head said that she was supposed to grow old with Ben and her family.

To fill the void created by Ben's moving out and leaving her for a younger woman, Sarah volunteered her services with her own children and her grandchildren.

Where she used to call them once or twice a week, she was now calling her son and daughter every day—sometimes twice a day.

Both her son and daughter accused her of intruding in their lives, especially with their children. They resented the fact that Sarah often brought gifts for the children without asking them first. Sarah sometimes contradicted rules her children had set for her grandchildren. Put simply, she was overstepping her boundaries with her children and the running of their lives.

Sarah began complaining to her girlfriends that she was not feeling well, and upon their suggestions, she visited her primary care physician to find out what was wrong. She had begun to lose weight, and everything she cooked tasted bland. Sarah asked her doctor for medication to help her sleep at night. She had a hard time getting to sleep, and she was awakening three to four times a night. By the time morning arrived, she was exhausted from tossing and turning all night.

Realizing that Sarah had just gone through a bitter divorce, the medical doctor asked Sarah if she were depressed. Although Sarah claimed that she was not depressed or "crazy" in any way, she took the prescription for depression. The depression medication helped, but Sarah still felt empty inside. Upon her third trip to her doctor for a refill of the prescription dealing with depression, the doctor recommended that she see a psychologist or a social worker for psychotherapy.

The therapist recommended that Sarah also join a self-help group dealing with depression of older adults. Sarah joined the group. Sarah needed to make new connections and relationships with others.

The therapist conducted a 12-component, strengths-based assessment of Sarah, and Sarah took the VIA Classification of Strengths online (www.viacharacter .org/www/Character-Strengths). Based on the strengths assessment, Sarah and her therapist began to outline goals and a life plan for her. For the first time in a

(Continued)

(Continued)

long time, Sarah felt hopeful that there was a future for her. After assessing Sarah for personal and spiritual strengths, the therapist recommended that Sarah renew her connection with the Lutheran Church, which she had stopped attending three years ago.

The therapist also engaged Sarah in Pearls, a program for dealing with depression in older adults. The therapist visited Sarah in her home when they began to implement the Pearls program. Sarah found new friends in her support group—people who had the same issues as she. She adopted the mantra of service to others as a way to help her to deal positively with her depression. She volunteered her expertise as a retail buyer to the Women's Business Center. She also became involved in an organization that was dedicated to getting suits and business attire for lower-income women entering the workforce. Sarah's many contacts in the retail community were influential in getting many new suits donated to the organization.

For the past couple of months, Sarah has begun to have dinner with Matthew, a widower at her church. She claims that their relationship is just for companionship. Sarah is questioning if she is too old to get married. Still, she says that she would like to have someone to cuddle up to at night. She has practical concerns about finances. Would she have to change her will to include her new husband? How would her children feel about a new man in her life?

Sarah is well on her way to a full recovery from depression. Her medical doctor has reduced the dosage of her medication and has indicated that he will gradually wean her from the medication. Sarah's relationship with her children has improved. In fact, both children have complained that she doesn't come around very much and that the grandchildren miss her. They were disappointed that she no longer served as an "on-call babysitter." Sarah has responded that her life is full, that she is enjoying her life, and that she is looking forward to each day.

Case Discussion

Establishing a therapeutic alliance. Sarah approached the first session with her therapist with some apprehensions about whether the therapist would deem her crazy. Her energy was focused on what the therapist might think about her rather than on getting well from whatever had brought on the depression. The therapist reassured Sarah that she was not crazy and encouraged her to examine some of the events in her life that might have precipitated the depressive reaction.

Sarah is similar to many other older adults who discover that retirement often brings the realization that they are alone and that their life journey has hit a real turning point. They have lived more of their life than what lies ahead in the future. Sarah had been a very successful buyer in a large retail store. She still had many strengths, but she found it difficult to seek help from others—especially therapy, which had a negative connotation in her mind. The therapist helped Sarah examine some of the precipitating life events that might have been triggers for her depression—her retirement, Ben's affair with a younger woman, the stressful divorce, her children's rejection of her daily involvement in their lives. Instead of denying that she was depressed, Sarah began to make peace with her depression as a signal that she needed to make changes in her life. The therapist asked Sarah, "What is your depression saying to you? What is it telling you about your life?"

Sarah responded, "It's telling me that my life sucks, that I thought I had everything planned out—how I was going to live, the type of man I would marry, the number of children I would have, the house I would buy, my job . . . It all worked for a while, and now the time of these things working for me has changed. I'm stuck in the past, stuck with what was rather than what is. If my life is to have any new meaning, I have to reach out for other people, other things, other meanings in my life. And I'm scared. I'm scared that I might be too old to begin new things, to start over. There's a part of me that wants to start over, and there's a part of me that says give me my old life back."

The 12-component model of strengths assessment for aging well. The therapist and Sarah conducted a 12-component model of strengths assessment for aging well. They agreed that Sarah did not have to fear growing older. Instead, she could embrace it. This outlook on life was quite a change for Sarah. In the past, she didn't want to get old. She feared losing her mental faculties. Sarah decided that she could either spend her life fearing the inevitability of aging or enjoy each aspect of it. "I'm old enough that I don't have to spend my life trying to please everyone. I say and do what I feel is right. What is anyone going to do to me? Fire me? I don't think so. I'm freer now than I have ever been in my life."

During ensuing sessions, Sarah examined the three components of aging well: (1) mental health and spirituality, (2) physical health, and (3) relationships and support. Sarah discovered that in comparison with some older adults, she fared quite well, having more than 15 strengths. For instance, in the physical health category, she had had no problem in the last 12 months that limited her physically, she had no problem in the last 12 months having enough food to eat, and she was able to perform heavy-duty housework. She had strengths in daily living skills.

Sarah had the fewest strengths in the mental health area, but she was working hard in this area. Her sense of self-efficacy was growing, and slowly she adopted the outlook that her life had purpose. Although Sarah did not feel valued by her community, she believed that her service to others could change this negative response to older people in her community. A big change took place in Sarah's strengths in spirituality. She went back to church and joined a prayer group that met once a week. As Sarah listened to the prayers of others, she felt more gratitude for the blessings that she had in her life. Sarah began to keep a gratitude journal, and she remarked that this journal helped her to focus on what was positive in her life rather than on what was missing or absent. Sarah became aware of her strong nurturing strengths.

The third aging well category that Sarah was assessed in was relationships and social support. Sarah began to make changes in this area. For one thing, she stopped forcing herself on her children and on her grandchildren. There was a big world out there and other people with whom she could place her energy. Sarah's volunteer work with a women's group that provided suits to lower-income women was rewarding for her. Not only was she able to help others, but also she used her old contacts in the retail industry. In fact, as a result of her volunteer efforts, one retail establishment hired Sarah as a part-time consultant for community service. The volunteering efforts proved extremely helpful, as the focus was changed from emphasizing her problems to helping others who were less fortunate. Sarah had begun to engage life more fully. There was now greater balance in her life. The emphasis was not solely on her family.

Letting go. Life for Sarah was not without experiencing some pain. It was difficult for her to let go of Ben, especially during special family gatherings that her children held and to which they invited Ben with his new partner. The first time that Sarah met Ben's new partner at a gathering at her son's house, she went home and cried. In the morning, she took out her gratitude journal and began to write. "I'm grateful," she wrote, "for the years that Ben and I had together. I would have liked spending the rest of my life with Ben, but that time has passed. I thank Ben for providing for his family and for leaving me financially secure in my later years."

The therapist and Sarah processed "letting go" of Ben in their next session. The therapist focused on forgiveness and what Sarah's forgiveness of Ben might bring to her own life. At first, Sarah did not want to forgive Ben. He had done her wrong, and he should be punished. The therapist encouraged Sarah to write a letter to him expressing her forgiveness. She could either decide to keep the letter or send it to him.

Harvesting the good. The gratitude journal helped Sarah to harvest the good of her life experiences. For each negative event that she remembered, she forced herself to harvest one good. Instead of feeling bitter toward her children for calling her intrusive in their lives, Sarah began to harvest the good out of their relationships with each other. Sarah began to see that perspective was everything. What really mattered was the view of things that she took.

Developing a strengths-based life plan. At first, Sarah was hesitant to create a life plan, especially at her age, but the therapist had been gradually instilling hope in Sarah. The depression had sapped Sarah's feelings of hopefulness, and now she was taking it all back. Sarah's life plan focused on her making greater connections with others and with those who were less fortunate than she. She felt needed at the women's organization—New Careers—that provided clothing for lower-income women. People at New Careers relied on her contacts for donations from major women's clothing stores.

Sarah decided that she would work part-time as a consultant for one of the stores that contributed to New Careers. She felt good that she had some place that she absolutely had to be three days a week. Sarah's life plan also involved reconnecting positively with her children. In fact, her children began to complain that her schedule was so filled that they saw her infrequently and that they missed their babysitter.

Sarah also decided to make some changes regarding her health. She began an exercise program at her church for senior women. Thus, she was able to prevent negative health issues caused by the lack of exercise while at the same time enjoying the companionship of other women her age.

Building new competencies. Over the course of eight months, Sarah had begun to build new competencies. Her work with New Careers had helped her to develop competencies in the area of connecting businesses with community needs. Yet the greatest competency she developed was in the area of managing her own mental health. Sarah had participated in the Pearls program for depression, and she learned new skills for detecting signs of depression and for taking action to prevent its onset. Pearls is a federal program for treating depression in older adults. It has both a Chronic Care model and a Collaborative Care model that involves dealing with individuals' problems, goal setting, and a continuum of self-management training and follow-up. The Pearls program is evidence based and has been found to be highly effective in treating depression in older adults (Centers for Disease Control and Prevention & National Association of Chronic Disease Directors, 2009).

Creating a healthy new identity and moving forward. Sarah is no longer depressed. Her life is full of meaningful activity and relationships. She believes that her life matters to others, and she has gained a newfound sense of purpose. Sarah has created a healthy, positive, new identity for herself. She is even beginning to date, although she prefers not to call her dinner and lunch engagements dates. Sarah is now deciding to what extent she wants to let a new man into her life and into her family's life. She took Matthew to a family gathering held by her son. It was interesting to watch how Ben responded to Matthew. He seemed a bit put off that another man found Sarah attractive and wanted to be with her—even at her age.

SUMMARY OF KEY POINTS

This chapter has explored strengths-based therapy for the older adult. The first part of the chapter presented basic statistics on the aging population within the United States. This nation has a rapidly aging population—meaning those who are nearing or who have reached age 65 and over. An important issue is whether or not helping professionals, including psychologists, social workers, and mental health workers, are prepared to address appropriately the issues and needs of this aging population. The challenges facing this population include the prevention of chronic diseases and depression due to loss and changing life situations. The National Institute of Mental Health has stated that depression among older adults is a major challenge for this country.

A 12-component model of strengths assessment for aging well was presented, along with a checklist of strengths and an inventory of strengths assessment for the older adult. The strengths-based therapy model was applied to treatment of the older adult. Using strengths-based therapy, a case study of an older adult woman, Sarah, was presented, plus a discussion of treatment issues for her. Multicultural issues in counseling the older adult were explored. Emphasis was placed on comparing and contrasting attitudes and perspectives on aging between the United States and Japan. It was concluded that Japan has a more positive, age-friendly approach to aging than that evidenced in the United States. Japanese people celebrate the aging process with specific holidays and presentations to mark a long life. In Japan, old age is considered a socially valuable part of life, even a time of "spring" or "rebirth" after years of working and raising children.

The American Psychological Association (2004, 2014) Division 12 (Clinical Psychology) has developed competencies for work with older adults, "Guidelines for Psychological Practice With Older Adults." The 20 guidelines address attitudes; general knowledge about adult development, aging, and older adults; clinical issues; assessment, intervention, consultation, and other service provisions; and education. Guideline 5 is relevant to multicultural issues. It states, "Psychologists strive to understand diversity in the aging process, particularly how sociocultural factors such as gender, ethnicity, socioeconomic status, sexual orientation, disability status, and urban/rural residence may influence the experience and expression of health and of psychological problems in later life" (American Psychological Association, 2004, p. 242). Many of these guidelines are summarized in the clinical practice section of this chapter. Finally, it is important to

1. Use an intersectional framework when working with older adults that takes into consideration their ethnicity, gender, sexual orientation, and immigration status, as well as other factors

2. Help older adults to establish support systems in their communities

3. Assist older adults to cope with loss, both physical and mental, and depression, a symptom of their multiple losses

4. Take into consideration an older adult's lifetime need for affection, love, and sexual interaction—touching, kissing, hugging, and so forth

5. Ask about an older adult's substance use

DISCUSSION QUESTIONS

Discussion Question Set 1

1. Interview a person over 65, using either your own strengths inventory (based on questions presented in this chapter) or a strengths inventory in the research literature. Complete the inventory and write a brief summary of it. In your summary, include answers to the following questions:

   - How did you feel interviewing the older adult?

   - How did the older adult respond to you?

   - What did you learn about the older adult's strengths?

   - Based on what you learned from your interview, what recommendations would you make in treatment for the older adult?

2. Make several impairment cards that state *hearing loss, vision impairment, cognitive deficits*, and so on and then find a partner. One student selects a card and becomes a client with the impairment, and the other student becomes the interviewer. The interviewer asks questions such as the following:

   - What are your goals in life?

   - Who are the important people in your life?

- What are you most proud of accomplishing?
- What gives life meaning for you?

3. Look into your pocket or book bag and give up three things that are important to you. In pairs, describe what you gave up and what it meant to you to give up the item or representation of something that is important to you. For instance, a person may give up keys to a car because the car has meaning for him or her. The student describes what it feels like to give up the car. The purpose

of this exercise is to demonstrate how an older person might feel as he or she experiences the loss of physical prowess or loved ones.

Discussion Question Set 2

Discuss in small groups of five the following:

1. The kind of older person you want to be
2. What your younger self wants to say to your older self
3. Two major goals you have for your older self

KEY TERMS

Ageism: A biased attitude or belief that the normal process of aging is largely negative and that older people are characterized as being prone to depression, forgetfulness, and other disorders and that as a consequence they will not benefit from treatment of mental disorders.

Alzheimer's: A disease that attacks the brain, and the most common form of dementia. Alzheimer's disease usually develops slowly, and it becomes worse over time. Although the greatest risk factor for Alzheimer's disease is increasing age, it is not a normal part of aging, and younger adults can have early onset of Alzheimer's disease.

Chronological age: The number of years a person has lived.

Dementia: A general term for a decline in mental ability severe enough to interfere with a person's daily life.

Elder abuse and neglect: The abuse of an older adult person that might include financial abuse, physical abuse, and sexual abuse, as well as verbal and psychological abuse.

Elderspeak: A derogatory and patronizing way of speaking to older adults that often treats them like older children.

Functional age: Determined much less by chronology than by sociocultural and physiological influences. For example, the way a person views the aging process may determine how well he or she is able to function at a given chronological age.

Intersectionality: The view that people must be examined from multiple perspectives that reflect their multiple identities and realities experienced as part of the living process.

Subjective age: The way a person assesses his or her own progress in aging.

REFERENCES AND SUGGESTED READING

7 cultures that celebrate aging and respect their elders. (2014). *Huffington Post*. Retrieved from https://www.aplacelikehomealf.com/our-care-and-services/respect-your-elders/healthy-living-02252014-0220-pm-et-updated-may-18-2015/

Achenbaum, W. (2015, October 19). A history of ageism since 1969. *American Society on Aging*. Retrieved from http://www.asaging.org/blog/history-ageism-1969

Acierno, R., Hernandez, M. A., Amstadter, A. B., Resnick, H. S., Steve, K., Muzzy, W., & Kilpatrick, D. G. (2010). Prevalence and correlates of emotional, physical, sexual, and financial abuse and potential neglect in the United States: The National Elder Mistreatment study. *American Journal of Public Health, 100*, 292–297.

Adams, M. (2016). An intersectional approach to services and care for LGBT elders. *Generations: Journal of the American Society on Aging*. Retrieved from http://www.asaging.org/blog/intersectional-approach-services-and-care-lgbt-elders

Adenivi, A. A., Brindley, G. S., Pryor, J. S., & Ralph, D. J. (2007). Yohimbine in the treatment of orgasmic dysfunction. *Asian Journal of Andrology, 9*, 403–407.

Administration on Aging. (2012). *A profile of older Americans: 2011*. Retrieved from http://www.cdc.gov/nchs/data/databriefs/db64.pdf

Alzheimer's Association. (2016). 2016 Alzheimer's disease facts and figures. *Alzheimer's & Dementia, 12*(4), 459–509. doi:10.1016/j.jalz.2016.03.001

Ambler, D. R., Bieber, E. J., & Diamond, M. P. (2012). Sexual function in elderly women: A review of current literature. *Reviews in Obstetrics and Gynecology, 5*(1), 16–27.

American Psychological Association. (2004). Guidelines for psychological practice with older adults. *American Psychologist, 59*(4), 216–260.

American Psychological Association. (2009). Aging in the 21st Century: Psychologists say longer lives can still lead to happier golden years. Retrieved at http://www.apa.org/news/press/releases/2009/08/aging-21st.aspx.

American Psychological Association. (2014). Guidelines for psychological practice with older adults. *American Psychologist, 69*(1), 34–65.

Anuradha, K. (2004). Empowering families with mentally ill members: A strengths perspective. *International Journal for the Advancement of Counseling, 26,* 383–391.

Auldredge, A., & Espinoza, R. (2013). *Health equity and LGBT elders of color: Recommendations for policy and practice.* New York, NY: Services and Advocacy for GLBT Elders.

Axelson, J. A. (1985). *Counseling and development in a multicultural society.* Monterey, CA: Brooks/Cole.

Balcázar, H., Alvarado, M., Hollen, M. L., Gonzalez-Cruz, Y., & Pedregón, V. (2005, July). Evaluation of *Salud Para Su Corazón* (Health for Your Heart)—National Council of La Raza *Promotora* outreach program. *Preventing Chronic Disease.* Retrieved from http://www.cdc.gov/pcd/issues/2005/jul/04_0130.htm

Bays, C. L. (2001). Older adults' descriptions of hope after a stroke. *Rehabilitation Nursing, 26*(1), 18–27.

Block, J., Smith, M., & Segal, J. (2014). Better sex over 50: Tips for enjoying a healthy sex life as you age. *HelpGuide.* Retrieved from http://www.helpguide.org/elder/sexuality_aging.htm

Bogunovic, O. (2012). Substance abuse in aging and elderly adults. *Psychiatric Times, 29*(8). Retrieved from http://www.psychiatrictimes.com/geriatric-psychiatry/substance-abuse-aging-and-elderly-adults

Buttaro, T. M., Koeniger-Donohue, R., & Hawkins, J. (2014). Sexuality and quality of life in aging: Implications for practice. *The Journal for Nurse Practitioners, 10*(7), 480–485.

Centers for Disease Control and Prevention (2017a, May 3). *Disability and functioning (noninstitutionalized adults aged 18 and over).* Retrieved from http://www.cdc.gov/nchs/fastats/disability.htm

Centers for Disease Control and Prevention. (2017, June 28). *Chronic disease overview.* Retrieved from https://www.cdc.gov/chronicdisease/overview/

Centers for Disease Control and Prevention & Merck Company Foundation. (2007). *The state of aging and health in America: 2007.* Whitehouse Station, NJ: Merck Company Foundation. Retrieved from http://www.cdc.gov/Aging/pdf/saha_2007.pdf

Centers for Disease Control and Prevention and National Association of Chronic Disease Directors. The state of mental health and aging in America, 2013. Atlanta, Georgia: National Directors of Chronic Disease. Retrieved at https://www.cdc.gov/aging/pdf/State-Aging-Health-in-America-2013.pdf.

Centers for Disease Control and Prevention & National Association of Chronic Disease Directors. (2009). *The state of mental health and aging in America: Issue brief #2: Addressing depression in older adults: Selected evidence-based programs.* Atlanta, GA: National Association of Chronic Disease Directors.

Chapin, R., & Cox, E. O. (2001). Changing the paradigm: Strengths-based and empowerment-oriented social work with frail elders. *Gerontological Social Work Practice: Issues, Challenges, and Potential, 36,* 165–179.

Choi, S. K., & Meyer, I. H. (2016). *LGBT aging: A review of research findings, needs, and policy implications.* Los Angeles, CA: Williams Institute.

Christopher, S., Christopher, J. C., & Dunnagan, T. (2000). Culture's impact on health risk appraisal psychological well-being questions. *American Journal of Health Behavior, 24*(5), 338–348.

Cicirelli, V. G. (2003). Older adults' fear and acceptance of death: A transition model. *Ageing International, 28*(1), 66–81. https://doi.org/10.1007/s12126-003-1016-6

Conwell, Y. (2001). Suicide in later life: A review and recommendations for prevention. *Suicide and Life Threatening Behavior, 31*(Suppl.), 32–47.

Conwell, Y., & Brent, D. (1995). Suicide and aging: I: Patterns of psychiatric diagnosis. *International Psychogeriatrics, 7*(2), 149–164.

Cox, E. O., Green, K. E., Seo, H., Inaba, M., & Quillen, A. A. (2006). Coping with late life challenges: Development and validation of the care-receiver efficacy scale. *The Gerontologist, 46,* 640–649.

Cox, W. T., Abramson, L. Y., Devine, P. G., & Hollon, S. D. (2012). Stereotypes, prejudices, and depression: The integrated perspective. *Perspectives in Psychological Science, 7*(5), 427–429.

Cutcliffe, J. R., & Grant, G. (2001). What are the principles and processes of inspiring hope in cognitively impaired older adults within a continuing care environment? *Journal of Psychiatric and Mental Health Nursing, 8*(5), 427–436.

Davis, B. (2005). Mediators of the relationship between hope and well-being in older adults. *Clinical Nursing Research, 14*(3), 253–272.

Delamater, J., & Moorman, S. M. (2007). Sexual behavior in later life. *Journal of Aging and Health, 19,* 921–965.

Denver Regional Council of Governments. (2004, October 5). *Strengths and needs assessment of older adults in the Denver metro area*. Boulder, CO: National Research Center.

Diener, E., & Suh, E. M. (2000). *Measuring subjective well-being to compare the quality of life*. Boston, MA: MIT Press.

Dufault, K., & Martocchio, B. C. (1985). Hope: Its spheres and dimensions. *Nursing Clinics of North America*, *20*, 379–391.

Duggleby, W. (2001). Hope at the end of life. *Journal of Hospice and Palliative Nursing*, *3*(2), 1–57.

Duggleby, W., & Wright, K. (2004). Older adult palliative care cancer patients' descriptions of hope-fostering strategies. *International Journal of Palliative Nursing*, *10*(7), 352–359.

Ellin, A. (2011, August 8). The golden years polished with surgery. *The New York Times*. Retrieved from http://www.nytimes.com/2011/08/.9/health/09plastic.html

Espinoza, R. (2014). *Out & visible: The experiences and attitudes of lesbian, gay, bisexual and transgender older adults, ages 45–75*. New York: Services and Advocacy for GLBT Elders.

Federal Interagency Forum on Aging-Related Statistics. (2016, August). *Older Americans 2016: Key indicators of well-being*. Washington, DC: U.S. Government Printing Office. Retrieved from https://agingstats.gov/docs/LatestReport/Older-Americans-2016-Key-Indicators-of-WellBeing.pdf

Fehring, R. J., Miller, J. F., & Shaw, C. (1997). Spiritual well-being, religiosity, hope, depression, and other mood states in older adult people coping with cancer. *Oncology Nursing Forum*, *24*(4), 663–671.

Forbes, S. B. (1994). Hope: An essential human need in the older adult. *Journal of Gerontological Nursing*, *20*(6), 5–10.

Fredriksen-Goldsen, K. I., Hoy-Ellis, C. P., Goldsen, J., Emlet, C. A., & Hooyman, N. (2014). Creating a vision for the future: Key competencies and strategies for culturally competent practice with lesbian, gay, bisexual, and transgender (LGBT) older adults in the health and human services. *Journal of Gerontological Social Work*, 57(2–4), 80–107.

Fung, H. H. (2013). Aging in culture. *The Gerontologist*, *53*(3), 369-377.

Galambos, C., & Rosen, A. (1999). The aging are coming and they are us. *Health and Social Work*, *24*(1), 73–77.

Hall, B. A. (1990). The struggle of the diagnosed terminally ill person to maintain hope. *Nursing Science Quarterly*, *3*(4), 177–184.

Health in Aging. (2016, November). *Aging & health A to Z: Drug and substance abuse*. Retrieved from http://www.healthinaging.org/aging-and-health-a-to-z/topic:drug-and-substance-abuse/

Heaphy, P., Yip, A., & Thompson, D. (2004). Ageing in a heterosexual context. Ageing and Society, 24, (6), 881–902.

Herth, K. A. (1990). Relationship of hope, coping styles, concurrent losses, and setting to grief resolution in the older adult widow(er). *Research in Nursing & Health*, *13*(2), 109–117.

Herth, K. (2000). Enhancing hope in people with a first recurrence of cancer. *Journal of Advanced Nursing*, *32*(6), 1431–1441.

Horstman, A. M., Dillon, E. L., Urban, R. J., & Sheffield-Moore, M. (2012). The role of androgens and estrogens on healthy aging and longevity. *The Journals of Gerontology Series A: Biological Sciences and Medical Sciences*, *67*(11), 1140–1152.

Hwang, K. (1999). *Filial piety and loyalty: Practice and discourse in contemporary East Asia*. Stanford, CA: Stanford University Press.

Hybeis, C. F., & Blazer, D. G. (2003). Epidemiology of late-life mental disorders. *Clinics in Geriatric Medicine*, *19*, 663–696.

James, J. B., Pitt-Catsouphes, M., & Besen, E. (2013, May 15). The costs of age-related "microaggressions" and what employers can do to avoid them. *AGEnda*. Retrieved from http://agingandwork.bc.edu/blog/the-costs-of-age-related-microaggressions/

Jevne, R. F., & Miller, J. E. (1999). *Finding hope: Ways to see life in a brighter light*. Fort Wayne, IN: Willowgreen.

Judge, K. S., Yarry, S., & Orsulic-Jeras, S. (2006). *Strengths-based inventory for assessing individuals with dementia and their caregivers' current strengths*. Cleveland, OH: Cleveland State University.

Karasawa, M., Curhan, K. B., Markus, H. R., Kitayama, S. S., Love, G. D., Radler, B. T., & Ryff, C. D. (2011). Cultural perspectives on aging and well-being: A comparison of Japan and the United States. *International Journal of Aging and Human Development*, *73*(1), 73–98.

Kitayama, S. (2000). Cultural variations in cognition: Implications for aging research. In P. C. Stern & L. L. Carstensen (Eds.), *The aging mind: Opportunities in cognitive research* (pp. 218–237). Washington, DC: National Academy Press.

Kitayama, S. (2002). Culture and basic psychological processes: Toward a system view of culture. *Psychological Bulletin*, *128*, 189–196.

Kitayama, S., & Markus, H. R. (2000). The pursuit of happiness and the realization of sympathy: Cultural patterns of self, social relations, and well-being. In E. Diener & E. M. Suh (Eds.), *Culture and subjective well-being* (pp. 113–161). Cambridge, MA: MIT Press.

Kivnick, H., & Murray, S. (2001). Life strengths interview guide: Assessing elder clients' strengths. *Journal of Gerontological Social Work*, *34*(4), 7–31.

Levy, B. R., Chung, P. H., Bedford, T., & Navrazhina, K. (2014). Facebook as a site for negative age stereotypes. *Gerontologist*, *54*, 172–176.

Lindau, S. T., Schumm, P., Laumann, E. O., Levinson, W., O'Muircheartaigh, C. A., & Waite, L. J. (2007). A study of sexuality and health among older adults in the U.S. *New England Journal of Medicine, 357,* 762–774.

Little, J. T., Reynolds, C. F., III, Dew, M. A., Frank, E., Begley, A. E., Miller, M. D., . . . Kupfer, D. J. (1998). How common is resistance to treatment in recurrent, nonpsychotic geriatric depression? *American Journal of Psychiatry, 155*(8), 1035–1038.

Liu, J. H., Ng, S. H., Loong, C., Gee, S., & Weatherall, A. (2003). Cultural stereotypes and social representations of elders from Chinese and European perspectives. *Journal of Cross-Cultural Gerontology, 18*(2), 149–168. https://doi.org/10.1023/A:1025108618426

Lock, M. (1998). Deconstructing the change: Female maturation in Japan and North America. In R. A. Shweder (Ed.), *Welcome to middle age! (and other cultural fictions)* (pp. 45–74). Chicago, IL: University of Chicago Press.

Loe, M. (2004). Sex and the senior woman: Pleasure and danger in the Viagra era. *Sexualities, 7,* 303–328.

Lombardi, N. J., Buchanan, J. A., Afierbach, S., Campana, K., Sattler, A., & Lai, D. (2014). Is Elderspeak appropriate? A survey of certified nursing assistants. *Journal of Gerontological Nursing, 40,* 44–52.

Longfellow, H. W. (1825). Morituri Salutamus: Poem for the fiftieth anniversary of the class of 1825 in Bowdoin College. *Poetry Foundation.* Retrieved from https://www.poetryfoundation.org/poems-and-poets/poems/detail/44639

Lowry, F. (2013). Opioid abuse in the older adult, an urgent concern. *Medscape.* Retrieved from http://www.medscape.com/viewarticle/776128

Markus, H. R., & Kitayama, S. (1991). Culture and the self: Implications for cognition, emotion, and motivation. *Psychological Review, 98*(2), 224–253.

Mather, M. (2016). The affective neuroscience of aging. *Annual Review of Psychology, 67,* 213–238.

McDonnall, M. C. (2011). Physical status as a moderator of depressive symptoms among older adults with dual sensory loss. *Rehabilitation Psychology, 56,* 67–76.

Mills, T., & Henretta, J. G. (2001). Racial, ethnic, and sociodemographic differences in the level of psychosocial distress among older Americans. *Research on Aging, 23*(2), 131–152.

Miniño, A. M. (2011, July). *Death in the United States, 2009* (NCHS data brief no 64). Hyattsville, MD: National Center for Health Statistics. Retrieved from http://www.cdc.gov/nchs/data/databriefs/db64.pdf

Moore, S. L. (2005). Hope makes a difference. *Journal of Psychiatric and Mental Health Nursing, 12*(1), 100–105.

National Council on Aging. (2017, August 8). *Elder abuse statistics & facts.* Retrieved from https://www.ncoa.org/public-policy-action/elder-justice/elder-abuse-facts/

National Institute on Drug Abuse. (2015, June). *Drug facts: Nationwide trends.* Retrieved from https://www.drugabuse.gov/publications/drugfacts/nationwide-trends

National Institute of Mental Health. (n.d.). *Older adults and depression.* Retrieved from https://www.nimh.nih.gov/health/publications/older-adults-and-depression/index.shtml

Nelson-Becker, H., Chapin, R., & Fast, B. (2006). The strengths model with older adults: Critical practice components. In D. Saleebey (Ed.), *The strengths perspective in social work practice* (4th ed., pp. 148–169). Boston, MA: Pearson Education.

New York State Office for the Prevention of Domestic Violence. (n.d.). *Intimate partner abuse of older adults: Special considerations for the LGBTQ community.* Retrieved from http://www.opdv.ny.gov/professionals/elderabuse/lgbtqcommunity.html

Nicholson, N. R. (2012). A review of social isolation: An important but underassessed condition in older adults. *Journal of Primary Prevention, 33,* 137–152.

Northrup, C., Schwartz, P. P., & Witte, J. (2013). *The normal bar.* New York, NY: Random House.

Ortman, J. M., Velkoff, V. A., & Hogan, H. (2014, May). An aging nation: The older population in the United States. *Current Population Reports.* Retrieved from https://www.census.gov/prod/2014pubs/p25-1140.pdf

Perkins, K., & Tice, C. (1995). A strengths perspective in practice: Older people and mental health challenges. *Journal of Gerontological Social Work, 23*(3/4), 169–185.

Purcell, P. (2016). Employment at older ages and social security benefit claiming. *Social Security Bulletin, 76*(4), 1–18.

Rashid, T. (2009). Positive interventions in clinical practice. *Journal of Clinical Psychology, 65,* 461–466.

Rashid, T., & Ostermann, R. F. (2009). Strength based assessment in clinical practice. *Journal of Clinical Psychology: In Session, 65,* 488–498.

Reynolds, C. F., III, Perel, F. E., Imber, S. D., Comes, C., Miller, M. S., Mazumdar, S., . . . Kupfer, D. J. (1999). Nortriptyline and interpersonal psychotherapy as maintenance therapies for recurrent major depression: A randomized controlled trial in patients older than 59 years. *Journal of the American Medical Association, 28*(1), 39–45.

Rowland, D. (1992). A five-nation perspective on the older adult. *Health Affairs, 11*(3), 205–215.

Ryff, C. D., & Singer, B. H. (2008). Understanding healthy aging: Key components and their integration. In V. Bengtson, D. Glans, N. M. Putney, & M. Silverstein (Eds.), *Handbook of theories of aging* (2nd ed., pp. 117–144). New York, NY: Springer.

Salthouse, T. (2012). Consequences of age-related cognitive declines. *Annual Review of Psychology, 63,* 201–226.

Schaie, K., Willis, S., & Caskie, G. (2004). The Seattle longitudinal study: Relationship between personality and cognition. *Neuropsychology of Cognition, 11*, 304–324.

Sewell, D. (2013). Aging America: Elder abuse on the rise. *NBC News.* Retrieved from http://vitals.nbcnews.com?Z_news/2013/01/27/16725913-aging-america-elder-abuse-on-the-rise?

Snyder, C. R. (1994). *The psychology of hope: You can get there from here.* New York, NY: Free Press.

Snyder, C. R. (2000). Hypothesis: There is hope. In C. R. Snyder (Ed.), *Handbook of hope: Theory, measures, and applications* (pp. 3–21). San Diego, CA: Academic Press.

Snyder, C. R., Irving, L. M., & Anderson, J. (1991). Hope and health: Measuring the will and the ways. In C. R. Snyder & D. R. Forsyth (Eds.), *The handbook of social and clinical psychology: The health perspective* (pp. 285–307). Elmsford, NY: Pergamon Press.

Steffens, D., Blazer, D. G., & Mugdha, E. T. (2015). *Sexuality and aging: The American Psychiatric Publishing textbook of geriatric psychiatry* (5th ed.). Washington, DC: American Psychiatric Publishing.

Substance Abuse and Mental Health Services Administration. (2010). *New nationwide study shows a dramatic rise in the proportion of older Americans admitted for substance abuse treatment from 1992 to 2008.* Retrieved from http://www.samhsa.gov/newsroom.press-announcemtns/201006161100

Sung, K.-T. (2004). Elder respect among young adults: A cross-cultural study of Americans and Koreans. *Journal of Aging Studies, 18*, 215–230. 10.1016/j.jaging.2004.01.002.

Takagi, E., Silverstein, M., & Crimmins, E. (2007). Intergenerational co-residence of older adults in Japan: Conditions for cultural plasticity. *Journal of Gerontology: Social Sciences, 62B*, S330–S339.

U.S. Department of Health and Human Services. (2005). *Substance abuse relapse prevention for older adults: A group treatment approach.* Rockville, MD: Substance Abuse and Mental Health Services Administration.

U.S. Department of Health and Human Services. (2016). *A profile of older Americans: 2016.* Retrieved from https://www.giaging.org/documents/A_Profile_of_Older_Americans__2016.pdf

Vaillant, G. E., & Mukamal, K. (2001). Successful aging. *American Journal of Psychiatry, 158*(6), 839–847.

Watters, Y., & Boyd, T. V. (2009). Sexuality in later life: Opportunity reflections for health care providers. *Journal of Sexual and Relationship Therapy*, 24, 307-315.

Williams, K. N., Herman, R., Gajewski, B., & Wilson, K. (2009). Elderspeak communication: Impact on dementia care. *American Journal of Alzheimer's Disease and Other Dementias, 24*, 11–20.

Williams, K. N., & Kemper, S. (2010). Interventions to reduce cognitive decline in aging. *Journal of Psychosocial Nursing and Mental Health Services, 48*, 42–61.

Yarry, S. J., Judge, K. S., & Orsulic-Jeras, S. (2010). Applying a strength-based intervention for dyads with mild to moderate memory loss: Two case examples. *Dementia, 9*, 549–557.

18 CULTURALLY RESPONSIVE STRENGTHS-BASED THERAPY FOR IMMIGRANTS AND REFUGEES

CHAPTER OBJECTIVES

- Recall demographics and population statistics of immigrants, refugees, and asylees.

- Analyze stereotypes, microaggressions, and hate crimes against immigrants, refugees, and asylees.

- Recognize immigrants and refugees as contributing members of American society.

- Understand the mental health issues specific to immigrants and refugees.

- Examine the Triple Trauma Paradigm for working with immigrants and refugees.

- Become familiar with counseling and therapy models for working with refugees and immigrants.

- *"Remember, remember always, that all of us, and you and I especially, are descended from immigrants and revolutionists."* — Franklin D. Roosevelt

- *"It is estimated that one in every 122 individuals in the world is a refugee, internally displaced, or seeking asylum."* —United Nations High Commissioner for Refugees

- *"I was not born a refugee. I was forced to become one."* —Unknown

- *"Refugees present perhaps the maximum example of the human capacity to survive despite the greatest of losses and assaults on human identity and dignity."* —Marjorie Muecke

INTRODUCTION

Immigrants and refugees have become a worldwide concern. Virtually every major country in the world has been affected by what appears to be a global pattern of migration. The major purposes of this chapter are (1) to understand the demographics and characteristics of immigrants and refugees who come to the United States, (2) to identify and review issues in counseling members of these two categories, (3) to examine the strengths of immigrants and refugees, and (4) to review models of counseling them. While this chapter focuses primarily on immigrants and refugees in the United States, it begins with summarizing some startling facts about displaced people worldwide.

Forcibly displaced people is the term used for several categories of immigrants and refugees. There are three types of forced migration: (1) conflict-induced displacement, (2) development-induced displacement, and (3) disaster-induced displacement. Conflict-induced forced migration occurs when people are forced to flee their homes because the authorities are unable or unwilling to protect them. Such conflict might take place as a result of civil war, generalized violence, or persecution on grounds of nationality, race, religion, or social group. People become forcibly displaced as a result of developments within their countries, such as when their country builds a dam in a rural area, constructs new highways or airports, or engages in other large-scale infrastructure projects. People usually remain within the borders of their own country when they are forcibly displaced by development projects. Natural disasters such as tsunamis, flooding, or earthquakes can also result in large-scale migrations of people. Millions of people are displaced by disasters each year.

The majority of the free world nations have people who have migrated there from other parts of the world—from Africa, Asia, and the Middle East. For instance, one will see in Denmark and Sweden people who have migrated from Africa, Asia, and the Middle East. Even Iceland, which is 90% White Christian, indicated in 2015 that it was willing to accept more refugees than its current policy of accepting only 50 individuals (up to 200 over 2016 and 2017) (Dearden, 2015; Hafstad, 2015).

What should one make of the new worldwide migration patterns? António Guterres, then United Nations High Commissioner for Refugees, stated in 2015 that "we are witnessing a paradigm change, an unchecked slide into an era in which the scale of global forced displacement as well as the response required is not clearly dwarfing anything seen before" (UNHCR, 2015a, p. 3). According to the UNHCR (2015a), there were a reported 59.5 million forcibly displaced persons worldwide in 2014. Of this number, 19.5 million were refugees, 38.2 million were internally displaced persons, and 1.8 million were asylum seekers. The year 2014 saw the highest displacement on record with 8.3 million persons being added to the 2013 year total (51.2 million).

Approximately 53% of the refugees worldwide in 2014 came from three countries: Syrian Arab Republic (3.88 million), Afghanistan (2.59 million), and Somalia (1.11 million). On average, 24 people worldwide were displaced from their homes every minute during 2015—amounting to some 34,000 people per day (UNHCR, 2016). If we summed up the 2014 total numbers of forcibly displaced people, they would make up the 24th-largest nation in the world.

Wars and internal disputes have constituted the primary cause for such large numbers of forcibly displaced persons. Globally forced displacement increased in 2015 with record high numbers of people traveling from their native homes. There were higher numbers of displaced people for 2015 because of crises in Syria and throughout Central and East Africa. By the end of 2015, 65.3 million people were forcibly displaced because of persecution, conflict, generalized violence, or human rights violations. This number is 5.8 million more than the prior year. If 65.3 million people were a nation, they would constitute the 21st-largest country in the world.

REFUGEE, ASYLEE, AND *IMMIGRANT:* SOME WORKING DEFINITIONS

Before providing statistics on the number of immigrants and refugees in the United States, it is important to provide basic definitions of these terms. *Migration* and *migrants* are general, nonjudgmental terms referring to people who have relocated from their home country to another country. To immigrate is to enter a new country, while to emigrate is to leave the former country.

According to the U.S. Department of Homeland Security (2016), "A **refugee** is a person outside his or her country of nationality who is unable or unwilling to return to his or her country of nationality because of persecution or a well-founded fear of persecution. An **asylee** is a person who meets the definition of refugee and is already present in the United States or is seeking admission at a port of entry."

The president of the United States, in consultation with Congress, determines the numerical ceiling for refugee admissions on a yearly basis. After September 11, 2001, the number of refugees admitted into the United States decreased drastically, but annual admissions have steadily increased due to improved means of conducting background security checks. About 85,000 refugees were admitted to the United States in 2016 (American Immigration Council, 2016).

A little over a third of the refugees who were admitted into the United States in fiscal year 2016 (37%) were religious minorities in their home countries. Of those, 61% were Christians, according to a Pew Research Center analysis of data from the State Department's Refugee

Cultural Reflections

What are your thoughts and feelings about admitting refugees, asylees, or immigrants to the United States? Do you think that numerical limits should be placed on the number of people admitted to this country in each of these three categories? What admission criteria would you use to admit immigrants or to deny them access to this country?

Processing Center (Connor, 2016). Muslims, the next-largest group, made up 22% of the religious minority refugees who were admitted to the United States. Hindus and members of other, smaller world religions made up the bulk of the remaining religious minority refugees (9% and 6%, respectively) (Connor, 2016; Connor & Krogstad, 2016).

The United States grants asylum to people already in the United States who are seeking protection based on the same five protected grounds (race, religion, nationality, membership in a particular social group, and political opinion) upon which refugees are evaluated. Asylees may apply at a port of entry at the time they seek admission or within one year of having arrived in this country. The United States does not place a limit on the number of individuals who may be granted asylum in a given year, and there are not specific categories for determining who may seek asylum. In fiscal year 2014, 23,533 individuals were granted asylum. Refugees and asylees are eligible to become legal permanent residents one year after they are admitted to the United States as a refugee or one year after receiving asylum (American Immigration Council, 2016).

An **immigrant** is a person who has moved from his or her country of origin to the United States or another nation, and who currently resides in that nation. The term *illegal immigrant* is not a legal term; it is popularly used jargon that refers to a person who has failed to go through the established immigration procedures established by the host country. An **undocumented immigrant** is a foreign-born person who does not have a legal right to be or to remain in the United States. All undocumented immigrants do not sneak across the border. A large number of immigrants originally came to this country legally as tourists or on a temporary visa and then failed to leave (American Immigration Council, 2016; Pew Research Center, 2018). Both the U.S. Department of Homeland Security (2016) and the Pew Research Center (2018) estimate that the number of undocumented immigrants in the United States is approximately 11.4 million.

Large numbers of undocumented immigrants have been able to remain in this country largely because U.S. enforcement resources are insufficient to keep up with the number of undocumented immigrants. The Center for American Progress has estimated that it costs $23,480 to deport just one person, including the costs of legal proceedings, apprehension, detention, and transportation (Fitz & Martinez, 2010). In 2010, it was estimated that it would cost $158 billion for apprehension, $29 billion for detention, $7 billion for legal processing, and $6 billion for transportation. The estimated total cost over five years (at that time, from 2010 to 2015) was $285 billion (Fitz & Martinez, 2010).

A major difference between immigrants and refugees is that immigrants are viewed as having made their change in location voluntarily, whereas refugees are deemed to change their location involuntarily to escape persecution, terrorism, war, or some other life-threatening situation. **Naturalization** is the state-approved process that foreign-born individuals go through to become a citizen of a country (Migration Policy Institute, 2016).

The **migration process** has been conceptualized as taking place in broadly three stages (Bhugra, 2004). The first stage is premigration, which involves a person's decision and preparation to move. The second stage, migration, refers to the actual physical relocation of individuals from one place to another. The third stage is called postmigration, and it takes place when an immigrant has been absorbed within the social and cultural tapestry of the new country (Bhugra, 2004). Social and cultural rules and new roles may be learned at this stage (Bhugra, 2004). It has been found that the initial stage of migration may have comparatively lower rates of mental illness and health problems than the later stages, because people tend to migrate at a younger age. During the postmigration stage, individuals tend to have problems with acculturation and the potential discrepancy between attainment of goals and actual achievement in the latter stages (Bhugra, 2004).

Demographics and Population Statistics: Some Key Facts About the World's Refugees

The Pew Research Center has published important facts about the world's refugees, of which the most compelling are mentioned as follows (Connor & Krogstad, 2016):

1. Almost *1 in 100 people worldwide or 60 million people* are forcibly displaced from their homes. This figure changes drastically depending on what part of the world one lives in. For instance, more than 1 in 20 people living in the Middle East are displaced. About 1 in 60 people living in continental Africa are displaced.

2. As of 2015, nearly *6 in 10 Syrians* were forcibly displaced from their home—whether migrating to another country or internally displaced in Syria—a number unprecedented in recent history for a single country.

3. About half of refugees in 2015 trace their origin to just three countries: Syria (378,000), Afghanistan (193,000), and Iraq (127,000).

4. European countries received a record 1.3 million refugees in 2015.

5. Europe has witnessed a rise in the number of unaccompanied minors seeking asylum, with almost half coming from Afghanistan.

6. By a large margin, Europeans disapprove of how the European Union is dealing with the refugee issue.

7. Almost half of refugees entering the United States in 2016 were Muslim. A slightly lower share of 2016's refugees were Christian (44%).

8. Americans have consistently opposed admitting large numbers of refugees. During 1958, Hungarians (65,000) were accepted as refugees to the United States; in 1979, the Indochinese (14,000) came; in 1980, the Cubans came; and in 1999, a large group of ethnic Albanians came. In each of these time periods, the vast majority of Americans disapproved of the country's acceptance of refugees.

Foreign-Born in the United States

Both the United States and the world are changing because of forced displacement of people around the globe. Nearly one out of every six people in the United States are foreign-born (Zeigler & Camarota, 2014). In 2014, the U.S. immigrant population stood at more than 42.4 million, or 13% of the U.S. population (Zong, Batalova, & Hallock, 2018).

Immigrants and their U.S.-born children now number approximately 72 million people, or 26% of the overall U.S. population. The largest group of immigrants came from Mexico (12 million), while 10.5 million are from South and East Asia, 4 million from the Caribbean, 3.2 million from Central America, 3 million from South America, 1.6 million from the Middle East, and another 7.5 million from other countries. Although Mexican immigrants make up about 30% of all U.S. immigrants, Asians are the fastest-growing group of immigrants in the United States (Pew Research Center, 2015). In 2014, the top five U.S. states by number of immigrants were California (10.5 million), Texas and New York (4.5 million each), Florida (4 million), and New Jersey (2 million). Mexican immigrants are primarily concentrated in the West and Southwest, and more than half live in California or Texas (Zong & Batalova, 2016).

Undocumented Immigrants

In the United States, undocumented immigrants draw a high degree of controversy. For the most part, the terms *illegal immigrant* and *undocumented immigrant* are synonomous. Many of the undocumented immigrants arrived in this country prior to the year 2000, and a 2014 study found that they are well settled into American life, with most working and crime free (Center for American Progress Immigration Team, 2014). Another study found that the crime rate for immigrants is not higher than that for native-born Americans (Ewing, Martinez, & Rumbaut, 2015). More than half of the undocumented immigrant population has a high school degree or higher. Because most immigrants work, they pay billions of dollars in taxes each year, and almost half of those who have lived in the United States for more than 10 years are homeowners (Center for American Progress Immigration Team, 2014). Many undocumented immigrants live in states with large agricultural industries, where they provide much needed hard labor on farms and orchards.

The Pew Research Center (2018) has published five facts about illegal immigration in the United States:

1. There were 11.1 million undocumented immigrants in the United States in 2015, accounting for 3.4% of the nation's population. The estimated number of unauthorized immigrants in the U.S. labor force has stabilized since 2009.

2. The U.S. civilian workforce contained 8 million unauthorized immigrants in 2015, accounting for 5% of those who were working or were unemployed and looking for work.

3. Mexicans constituted 52% of all unauthorized immigrants in 2014, but their numbers have been declining in recent years. In contrast, the number of unauthorized immigrants from nations other than Mexico grew from 5 million in 2009 to 5.4 million in 2015. The numbers increased for unauthorized immigrants from Asia, Central America, and sub-Saharan Africa.

4. Six states accounted for 59% of unauthorized immigrants in 2015: California, Texas, Florida, New York, New Jersey, and Illinois. In six states (Louisiana, Massachusetts, New Jersey, Pennsylvania, Virginia, and Washington), the unauthorized immigrant population grew from nations other than Mexico.

5. An increasing proportion of unauthorized immigrants have resided in the United States for at least a decade. In 2014, unauthorized immigrant adults had lived in the United States for a median of 13.6 years. Only 7% of Mexican unauthorized immigrants had been in the United States for less than five years in 2014, compared with 22% of those from all other countries.

DACA: Deferred Action for Childhood Arrivals

The American reaction to immigration and undocumented immigrants has become crystallized in the fight both for and against **DACA**, which stands for Deferred Action for Childhood Arrivals. In 2012, then president Barack Obama used an executive order to authorize DACA, which provided temporary deportation protection for more than 800,000 undocumented or unauthorized young immigrants who were brought to this country illegally by their parents. This executive order permitted these young unauthorized immigrants, also called "Dreamers," to apply for work permits.

In 2018, the U.S. Department of Homeland Security provided on its website a brief explanation of DACA:

On June 15, 2012, the Secretary of Homeland Security announced that certain people who came to the United States as children and meet several guidelines may request consideration of deferred action for a period of two years, subject to renewal. They are also eligible for work authorization. Deferred action is a use of prosecutorial discretion to defer removal action against an individual for a certain period of time. Deferred action does not provide lawful status.

The Department of Homeland Security also listed the basic guidelines for determining if a person is eligible for DACA consideration. The following list contains the basic guidelines for DACA; for additional information on eligibility requirements for DACA, the reader is referred to the Department of Homeland Security's web page. Refer to page 322 of Chapter 11 for a list of DACA recipient qualifications.

Recent polls have reported that a large majority of Americans support maintaining DACA. A CBS News poll conducted during January 2018 reported that 70% of Americans favor allowing those who benefit from the program to remain in the United States (Samuels, 2018). President Donald Trump has stated that he would rescind the program, and he gave Congress six months to come up with a solution.

> **Cultural Reflections**
>
> *What are your feelings about DACA? Should DACA be continued? Federal judges have blocked efforts to end the DACA program. Do you agree or disagree with their rulings? What are your thoughts about the financial cost ($23,380 for each person) of removing DACA recipients?*

The Forces of Migration

People leave their countries for different reasons. Forced or involuntary migration may take place because of internal conflict within a country or disaster-induced displacement (Negy, Schwartz, & Reig-Ferrer, 2009). Conflict-induced displacement refers to those who are forced to flee their homes because of civil war, generalized community violence, or threat and persecution based on one's nationality, race, religion, political opinion, social group, or sexual orientation. Disaster-induced displacement refers to national disasters (floods, earthquakes, landslides, or rising sea levels). Counselors need to vary their intervention strategies depending on the type of forces that produced the client's migration. Individuals who have been displaced because of natural disasters may present a different set of circumstances than those who migrated because of internal conflict and war.

Unaccompanied children and teenagers from Central American countries such as Guatemala, Honduras, and El Salvador came to public attention in 2013 and 2014 when media reported that increasingly large numbers of such young people were arriving in the United States. Unaccompanied minors are given full court hearings, and they are treated as those seeking asylum (Lind, 2014; Restrepo & Garcia, 2014).

Educational Levels and Socioeconomic Status of Immigrants

There is a broad range of educational achievement among immigrants. According to Ji and Batalova (2012), immigrants make up nearly 28% of American physicians, 31% of computer programmers, and 47% of medical scientists. Almost 75% of foreign-born Americans with college degrees are Asian or White, while 17% are of Latino origin (Ji & Batalova, 2012). More than 50% of Asian immigrants have a college degree (López & Bialik, 2017). Research has found that children of immigrant families have high rates of poverty (35%) and nearly 50% are uninsured (Wright, Chau, & Aratani, 2011).

Immigrants as Contributing Members of American Society

Immigrants have made important contributions to American society. From 1995 through 2005, 25.3% of all engineering and technology companies in the United States had at least one key immigrant founder. Further, these immigrant-founded companies amassed more than $52 billion in sales and created almost 450,000 jobs by the end of 2005 (Wadhwa, Saxeniam, Rissing, & Gereffi, 2007).

Citizenship status matters for displaced people in the United States. Citizenship provides a level of legitimacy in the United States, protections under the law, and access to financial and social resources that are critical for integrating into a new country. American citizenship also helps to produce a sense of identity and belonging (Zeigler & Camarota, 2014).

Griswold (2002) has pointed out that, contrary to popular myth, immigrants do not push Americans out of jobs. Instead, immigrants tend to fill jobs that Americans cannot or will not fill, usually at the high and low ends of the skill spectrum. "Immigrants are disproportionately represented in such high-skilled fields as medicine, physics, and computer science, but also in lower-skilled sectors such as hotels and restaurants, domestic service, construction and light manufacturing" (Griswold, 2002, p. 2). Griswold continued by stating that

nowhere is the contribution of immigrants more apparent than in the high-technology and other knowledge-based sectors. Silicon Valley and other high-tech sectors would cease to function if we foolishly were to close our borders to skilled and educated immigrants. The immigrants represent human capital that can make our entire economy more productive. Immigrants have developed new products, such as the Java computer language, that have created employment opportunities for millions of Americans.

Immigrants are not a drain on government finances. The NAS [National Academy of Sciences] study found that the typical immigrant and his or her offspring will pay a net $80,000 more in taxes during their lifetimes than they collect in government services. For immigrants with college degrees, the net fiscal return is $198,000. (Griswold, 2002, p. 2)

Griswold (2002) also asserted that successive waves of immigrants have kept our country demographically young and enhanced our influence in the world. More recently, MacDonald and Sampson (2012) have also pointed out the positive benefits of immigration.

Similarly, Peri (2013) has highlighted the economic benefits of immigration and emphasized the importance of highly educated immigrants:

Highly educated immigrants are a huge asset for the U.S. economy, which attracts scientists and engineers from all over the world. One-quarter of the U.S. based Nobel laureates of the last 50 years were foreign-born, and highly educated immigrants account for about one-third of U.S. innovation. In 2006, immigrants founded 25 percent of new high-tech companies with more than $1 million in sales, generating income and employment for the whole country. Innovation and technological growth are the engines of economic growth in technologically advanced countries like the United States, where attracting and training new scientists and engineers is key to continued economic success. (p. 3)

MICROAGGRESSIONS, HATE CRIMES, AND DISCRIMINATION AGAINST IMMIGRANTS AND REFUGEES

Cultural Reflections

What are your thoughts about the benefits of admitting immigrants to the United States? Do you think there should be educational requirements for admitting new immigrants to this country? What admission requirements would you impose on admitting new immigrants to this country?

In a *Slate* article, Jamelle Boule (2015) made an insightful comment about American attitudes toward immigrants and refugees: "We are a nation of immigrants and refugees. Yet we always fear who is coming next." Many Americans oppose immigrants coming to the United States and reject creating a path to citizenship for illegal immigrants. Such individuals assert that undocumented immigrants violated the law by not adhering to immigration policy and that further they are a drain on financial resources of each state. In contrast to these anti-immigrant attitudes, other Americans point out that businesses rely on the labor provided by undocumented workers, many of whom have lived in the United States for decades, paying taxes and making important contributions to their communities. Polls have reported that

72% of the broad American public and 83% of Hispanics surveyed indicated that they would support a policy permitting "foreigners who have jobs but who are staying illegally in the United States the opportunity to eventually become legal American citizens if they pay a fine, any back taxes, pass a security background check, and take other required steps" (Hart Research Associates, 2014).

Although the United States has a history of admitting refugees dating back to the Displaced Persons Act of 1948, refugees often encounter discrimination in this country. Undocumented immigrants are often the targets of emotional and physical harassment, and they also experience economic abuse at the hands of their employers (Yakushko, Watson, & Thompson, 2008).

> **Cultural Reflections**
>
> *Imagine that you were asked by an interviewer to describe your feelings about immigrants, refugees, and asylees. You have decided that you are going to be honest with the interviewer. What would you say about your feelings related to people who are immigrants, refugees, and asylees?*

MENTAL HEALTH ISSUES OF IMMIGRANTS AND REFUGEES

Social adjustment and mental illness in migrants may be influenced by the duration of their relocation, the similarity or dissimilarity between the culture of origin and the culture of settlement, language and social support systems available to them, acceptance by the "majority" culture, access and acceptance by the expatriate community, employment, and housing (Bhugra, 2004). Yakushko et al. (2008) reported that the stress that immigrants and refugees face is directly related to acculturative stress. Prolonged exposure to high levels of stress can lead to cognitive impairments, depression, heart disease, compromised immune systems, and **posttraumatic stress disorder (PTSD)**. It is important to examine acculturative stress in terms of the individual's migration stage.

The migrations of people of many different cultural, racial, and ethnic backgrounds have caused mental health workers to work with people from many different cultural, racial, and ethnic backgrounds. This diversity of cultures, religious groups, and ethnicities can make diagnosis and treatment of illness challenging in people whose background and experience differ significantly from that of the clinician. Culture is the lens through which people view their world. Culture has an important role in the presentation of illness and one's experience of mental disturbance.

In working with immigrants and refugees, a clinician must deal not only with the cultural differences but also with stressors involved during the process of migration. Depending upon the type and cause of migration, the migration process itself can be stressful. The migration process alone can affect the mental health of migrating individuals and their families as they encounter issues of cultural bereavement and cultural identity (Short et al., 2010).

Cultural Bereavement: Migrants and Refugees

Researchers have labeled the phenomenon of loss experienced by migrants and refugees as **cultural bereavement**. In his work with Southeast Asian refugees, Eisenbruch (1991) devised a cultural bereavement interview as a way to clarify the structure of the grief reaction and to begin the process of healing for the individual. Cultural bereavement may be reduced if the immigrant or refugee is able to maintain ties to the culture of origin. Cultural bereavement will be influenced by the refugee's cultural identity.

Cultural Identity and Stress for Immigrants and Refugees

Identity is the totality of how a person perceives him- or herself. Bhugra (2004) has noted that the components of cultural identity include religion, rites of passage, language, dietary habits, and leisure activities. Religious rituals and beliefs one was raised with, even if not practiced as an adult, make up key parts of a person's cultural identity. Leisure activities include music, movies, sports, and literature. Social and cultural identities are usually more resistant to change, and they are typically the last to adjust during a period of acculturation.

Immigrants and refugees undergo a process of assimilation, during which time their cultural differences lessen as they adapt to the value system of the host culture. A person may experience loss of individual cultural identity to some degree during the process of assimilation into the host society. The immigrant or refugee may experience changes in attitudes, family values, generational status, and social affiliations. Different levels of acculturation can affect relations between first-, second-, and third-generation family members. Changes in one's cultural identity can be stressful and lead to mental health problems. The acculturation process may help the individual to gain a new sense of belonging in his or her new culture.

MENTAL HEALTH ISSUES AND PRE- AND POSTMIGRATION

It is important to explore new arrivals' pre- and postmigration experiences because there is often a direct connection between their experiences and their adjustment in their new home (Neuner, Schauer, Klaschik, Karunakara, & Elbert, 2004). Fazel (2005) has reported that refugees who remained longest in camps had higher rates of psychopathology and that refugees who resettled in Western countries were approximately 10 times more likely to develop posttraumatic stress symptoms than was the general population. Other studies have found that the rates of developing schizophrenia and other psychoses were high for those immigrants who experienced a significant level of psychological stress during the first two years of their resettlement (Kisely, Terashima, & Langille, 2008). These researchers concluded that stress in the initial resettlement period could have far-reaching health effects; therefore, immediate services and resources to combat postmigration stress are extremely important. The questions in Table 18.1 allow the practitioner to understand the client's premigration experiences in his or her native country.

Acculturative Stress: A Postmigration Mental Health Issue

Symptoms related to having survived torture are only heightened by acculturative stress when survivors settle in their new country (Gorman, 2001). Simple daily tasks such as dressing, meal preparation, laundry, shopping, housekeeping, childcare, eating customs, use of electricity and technology, fast pace of life, and occupational change may prove to be too much for some

TABLE 18.1 ■ Culturally Responsive Clinical Questions on Client's Premigration Experiences
1. What was it like in your home country?
2. How would you describe your life in your native country?
3. What did you like and dislike about your country?
4. What factors led you to leave your home country?
5. Where did you go after leaving your country? What was it like in your first host country?
6. What was it like coming to the United States?
7. Did you have any expectations or assumptions of what it would be like in America? What matched your expectation, and what was surprising?
8. What was the most rewarding part of your migration experiences?
9. What was the most challenging part of your migration experience?

refugees (Whiteford, 2005). Language barriers and discrimination add to the mistrust of refugee torture survivors, and such mistrust may have a negative impact on the counseling relationship.

Acculturative stress is a fact of life for many immigrants and refugees (Bemak & Chung, 2014). Acculturative stress is that stress that immigrants face as a result of resettlement from their country of origin to their host culture. Acculturative stress sometimes involves depression, anxiety, feelings of marginality, and alienation. Immigrants must learn about the American educational system; they must develop proficiency in English; and they must seek work. In addition, they have to adapt to new cultural mores and customs (Bemak & Chung, 2014). They may feel marginal to American society, and oftentimes they restrict their social activities to a small group of other immigrants and friends.

Birman and Tan (2008) have pointed out that it is important for immigrants and refugees to have a sense of belongingness and feeling comfortable in American culture. When individuals do not experience being a part of American culture, they may feel **cultural alienation**, which is defined as the degree of estrangement or apartness one feels from the surrounding culture. Studying Vietnamese immigrants, Birman and Tan (2008) reported positive correlations between depression and alienation, and between American acculturation and reduced alienation.

In addition, many refugees experience relational stress within their nuclear and extended families (Bemak & Chung, 2014). Sometimes intergenerational conflicts take place as younger family members acculturate to American culture faster than do their parents. Young immigrants may feel the pressure of the educational system to learn the academic and social language of this country in order to gain acceptance from their American counterparts. Parents sometimes feel that their children are abandoning both them and their culture (American Psychological Association, Presidential Task Force on Immigration, 2013).

What postimmigration events cause stress in immigrants and refugees? Immigrants experience higher levels of distress and adverse mental health symptoms when they learn their credentials from their home country are not recognized or when they experience a decrease in socioeconomic status because of an inability to find positions that match those positions previously held (Dow, 2011).

New arrivals' loss of economic status and housing can also lead to mental health adjustment problems. A study has found that poor derelict housing in areas understood as unsafe increased mental health problems (Porter & Haslam, 2005). Neighborhoods perceived as unsafe or violent militate against a sense of social cohesion (Beiser, Hou, Hyman, & Tousignant, 2002), thereby increasing mental health difficulties. Immigrants who experience discrimination have higher levels of isolation and risk behaviors, such as alcohol and drug use and involvement in fights (Flores, Tschann, Dimas, Pasch, & de Groat, 2010; Pumariega, Rothe, & Pumariega, 2005). In addition, immigrants and refugees may experience **survivor's guilt** because they survived while others were killed or died along the way.

Moreover, immigrants and refugees experience high levels of stress when they feel that the host country or community is unwelcoming or when they feel that they have been targeted based on negative portrayals of members of their group in the media (Pickering, 2001) or when their ethnic group has been linked to terrorism (Hugo, 2002). An unwelcoming host community can lead to higher levels of stress that may serve as a precursor to more substantial physical and mental health problems in the future. Targeting based on negative portrayals in the media (Pickering, 2001) and national security concerns tied to terrorism (Hugo, 2002) have led to higher rates in adjustment stress that correlate with higher levels of depression, anxiety, and other mental health problems (Finch, Kolody, & Vega, 2000; Yeh, 2003). It is important for a therapist to ask about clients' experiences with discrimination in their homeland and whether or not family members were separated.

Cultural Reflections

If you had a magic wand and could immediately stop all immigration to the United States from foreigners, would you exercise the power of your magic wand to prevent all further immigration to this country?

If you would not eliminate all immigration to this country, what category of individuals would you still permit to immigrate to this country so that they would be on a path to American citizenship?

Postmigration: Helping Clients With Basic Resettlement Needs

The first primary step practitioners take with new arrivals is to help them with their resettlement needs, such as acquiring stable housing, gaining employment, securing food and clothing, and obtaining access to medical facilities and other community agencies. It is important to meet the basic safety needs of immigrants and refugees before dealing with their mental health needs.

After assisting individuals with their basic safety needs, the practitioner can then turn his or her attention to issues involving their premigration and resettlement experiences. Table 18.2 lists culturally sensitive questions a counselor or practitioner might ask new arrivals about their resettlement experiences.

After individuals' basic needs are met, they may be more inclined to utilize mental health services (Chen, Kazanjian, & Wong; 2009; Derr, 2016; Wong et al., 2006). Issues in counseling or therapy are likely to deal with premigration and postmigration stresses and the experiences of cultural bereavement, profound loss, and trauma. The ensuing section discusses torture as a mental health issue for refugees, immigrants, and asylees.

Torture Experiences: A Key Mental Health Issue for Refugees, Immigrants, and Asylees

According to the United Nations, torture may be defined as "any act by which severe pain or suffering, whether physical or mental, is intentionally inflicted on a person for such purposes as obtaining from him or a third person information or a confession, punishing him for an act he or a third person has committed or is suspected of having committed, or intimidating or coercing him or a third person, or for any reason based on discrimination of any kind, when such pain or suffering is inflicted by or at the instigation of or with the consent or acquiescence of a public official or other person acting in an official capacity" (United Nations Office of the High Commissioner for Human Rights, 1984). This definition excludes "pain or suffering arising only from, inherent in or incidental to lawful sanctions," such as the death penalty that exists in many countries (United Nations Office of the High Commissioner for Human Rights, 1984).

Torture tends to create within individuals a sense of complete dependency, helplessness, unpredictability, and isolation. Although the specific methods of torture vary, they include both physical and psychological techniques designed to terrorize people. Both Amnesty International (2014b) and the American Psychological Association (2007) have given the following as examples of torture: beating, shoving, squeezing/pressure techniques, pinching, insertion of objects into bodily orifices, exposure to extreme or prolonged physical exertion, strangulation, obstruction of airways, near drowning, chemical exposure, exposure to extreme temperature, electrocution, sensory deprivation or overstimulation, waterboarding, sexual humiliation, mock executions, rape, cultural or religious humiliation, exploitation of phobias or psychopathology, hooding, forced nakedness, stress positions, the use of dogs to threaten or intimidate, isolation,

TABLE 18.2 ■ Culturally Skilled Questions Related to Postmigration of Immigrants and Refugees
1. How are you adjusting to your new home?
2. Is there anything about the current place you live that reminds you of your home country? What is it?
3. How might I help you to make your way better with your new community?
4. What information or skills do you need at this time to help you feel more comfortable in your new community?
5. What concerns you the most as you begin a new chapter of your life in America?

and the threatened use of any of the above techniques to the individual or to members of the person's family.

Torture is a secretive practice, and therefore, it is difficult to obtain a true torture prevalence rate. In 2014, 141 countries practiced torture, but the practice of torture is not associated with a particular ethnic, religious, or geographic area (Amnesty International, 2014a). Instead, torture tends to be more common in countries that are economically disadvantaged and struggling to develop, and in any country undergoing social unrest and stress (McDonald & Sand, 2011).

Willard, Rabin, and Lawless (2014) recently conducted a study on the prevalence of torture in U.S. Iraqi refugees. The study reported that Iraqi refugees face difficulties resettling in the United States, due partially to their experiencing high rates of torture. The researchers conducted a retrospective review in 2011 on the postarrival health screens of Iraqi refugees resettled in Utah in 2008 and 2009. The measures used in the study included reports of torture experience as defined by the United Nations, reports of physical and mental health symptoms at the time of screening, and association of torture to the existence of symptoms on arrival. Of the 4,979 Iraqi refugees screened, 56% had experienced torture before arrival in the United States. Willard et al. found that torture was the most significant predictor of mental illness symptoms. The researchers concluded that "Iraqi refugees in the US have a high prevalence of torture, and torture is associated with the presence of both mental and physical symptoms on the post-arrival screen" (Willard et al., 2014, p. 1069). Torture was also associated with the presence of both physical and mental health symptoms within the first 90 days of these Iraqi refugees' arrival within the United States. The authors concluded that the prevalence of torture in Iraqi refugees has huge implications not only for the individual Iraqi but also for his or her family, community, and future generations.

A large number of studies have found that torture survivors suffer long-term physical consequences and mental health conditions (Ahmadi, Hajsadeghi, Mirshkarlo, & Ebrahim, 2011; Basoglu, 1992; Berliner, Mikkelsen, Bovbjerg, & Wiking, 2004; Birck, 2001; Dedert, Calhoun, Watkins, Sherwood, & Beckham, 2010; Holtz, 1998; Shrestha et al., 1998). Studies have found an association between stress, depression, and the future development of chronic diseases such as hypertension, coronary vascular disease, metabolic syndrome, and diabetes mellitus.

The Refugee/Asylee Experience: The Triple Paradigm

To help the provider understand common phases of the refugee/asylee experience, the Center for Victims of Torture (2005) has developed the Triple Trauma Paradigm. The Triple Trauma Paradigm describes three phases of traumatic stress that apply to torture survivors in exile who may or may not enter the United States with refugee status. These stages correspond roughly to the premigration, migration, and postmigration phases of the migration narrative. They are described as follows because of the emphasis on torture.

Preflight: This period covers the series of events, sometimes occurring over years, that results in the person's decision to flee. This period deals with events in the survivor's life, as well as the broader sociopolitical context within his or her country, that created a climate of fear. Typically, harassment and intimidation threats, brief arrests, and monitoring take place over a period of time. These incidents are usually followed by the infliction of suffering, the disappearance of friends or relatives, public display of atrocities, loss of job or property, detention, and torture.

Flight: The flight period entails the refugee's escape and flight to the country of desired refuge. It lasts from one day to years. At the psychological level, refugees may experience profound uncertainty and fear of being caught and a deep sense of insecurity. They may live in refugee camps that have conditions of squalor, crime, unemployment, and malnutrition (Center for Victims of Torture, 2005).

Postflight: Postflight is composed of the period of resettlement. The challenges of postflight include cultural shock, cultural acculturation, and assimilation. Survivors may feel marginalized, and they may experience poverty, racism, or anti-refugee or anti-immigrant prejudice. Torture survivors encounter barriers to accessing health care services. Some find that they are ineligible for assistance services due to lack of insurance, and they may face psychological misdiagnosis and the stigma of needing mental health care.

The Triple Trauma Paradigm provides a useful way of examining the refugee migration experience. The next section describes the strengths-based therapy model for working with refugees (Jones-Smith, 2014).

Core Counseling Competencies for Working With Torture Survivors

Trauma is defined as a deeply distressing or disturbing experience that robs a person of a sense of power and control over his or her own life. The guiding principle of recovery from trauma is to restore power and control to the survivor. One major goal of trauma-focused therapy is to help the client to reestablish a sense of safety and to reconstruct his or her life so that it is not dominated by the traumatic memories experienced in the homeland or en route to the new host country. Therapy for immigrants and refugees should be collaborative. The therapist emphasizes the client's ability to bounce back and to be resilient in the face of severe challenges. The therapist attends to the client's trauma stories, but he or she does not dwell on them. The therapist helps clients to see that despite the horrible conditions that they underwent, they are still standing. Strengths-based therapy helps clients to get in touch with the strengths that kept them alive.

Counselors and therapists who are familiar with and who respect their clients' culture, language, and trauma experiences create pathways for understanding. The Center for Victims of Torture (2005) has maintained that when working with refugees and immigrants who have been tortured, helping professionals should acquire expertise in the following four core fields of competency:

KNOWLEDGE of the life experiences and resettlement issues of refugees, asylum seekers and asylees before, during, and after the violence;

COMPREHENSION of torture and its long-term effects on survivors, their families, their community, and professionals who work with them;

CULTURAL COMPETENCE with traumatized people;

WORKING EFFECTIVELY with interpreters. (p. 20)

To conduct a clinical assessment for knowledge of refugees' and immigrants' life experiences and resettlement issues, practitioners inquire about life before torture (see Table 18.3). The Center for Victims of Torture (2005) recommends that the following information be assessed regarding the refugee's or immigrant's home country, including his or her

- Social, economic, educational, and political status
- Cultural beliefs, cultural values and practices, rituals, ceremonies, significant achievements, or milestones that gave life meaning
- Family, social, and community roles (e.g., how was this family regarded within its native intact community? What were the responsibilities associated with various family roles, such as oldest son or daughter?)
- Pretrauma functioning, or highest level of functioning in the home country (e.g., who was the refugee, immigrant, or family before the torture?)

TABLE 18.3 ■ Culturally Responsive Therapist Questions About Clients' Trauma Experiences

- Did you witness or experience directly any deeply disturbing situations in your home country or during your journey to get to the United States?

- Can you share some of those experiences and memories with me?

- What memories are the most difficult for you to handle?

- Were you forced to leave any family member behind?

- What do people do in your culture when they experience major losses and survive horrific events?

- How would your culture help you to heal from the trauma that you have experienced?

- How would you like to heal from the experiences that you described to me?

- What supports in this country would help you to heal from the trauma you experienced?

Cultural Humility and Clinical Practice With Refugees and Immigrants

What is cultural humility? Traditionally, the word *humility* has been used to convey meekness or humbleness, yet it can also be used to express a willingness to accurately assess oneself and one's limitations, or to indicate that there are gaps in one's knowledge and an openness to new ideas. In the case of counseling, humility takes on the connotation that counselors must acknowledge the limitations of their cultural worldview and work toward overcoming this perspective to provide better mental health care for those whom they serve. Cultural humility represents an acknowledgment of one's own limitations to true intercultural understanding. When a therapist realizes that his or her worldview is just a perspective or an outlook and therefore limited, it becomes much easier to acknowledge one's own biases in terms of other groups' worldview.

Why is cultural humility important? An attitude of cultural humility is important because it means not pigeon-holing all people in one or several categories. Instead of assuming that all members of a certain culture conform to a certain cultural stereotype, a therapist will understand that each person remains an individual and should be treated as such. Cultural humility is also an important step in helping to redress the imbalance of power inherent in therapist–client relationships or other relationships between care providers/researchers and those they serve.

Therapists realize as they approach clients who are culturally different from them that their own perspective is full of assumptions and prejudices. Therapists must be aware that even extensive knowledge about a given culture is not the same as having assimilated oneself into that culture, and therefore one must be aware of the differences that will still exist between their own perspective and the perspective of the members of that culture.

To provide effective mental health services to immigrant and refugee populations, clinicians must have an awareness of their limitations. Instead of searching for cultural competence, clinicians might better strive for cultural humility. As Levi (2009) has stated,

> the approach of cultural humility goes beyond the concept of cultural competence to encourage individuals to identify their own biases and to acknowledge that those biases must be recognized. Cultural competency implies that one can function with a thorough knowledge of the mores and beliefs of another culture; cultural humility acknowledges that it is impossible to be adequately knowledgeable about cultures other than one's own. (p. 97)

Cultural humility denotes a willingness to accurately assess oneself and one's limitations. Cultural humility is an acknowledgment of one's own barriers to true intercultural understanding. It is an approach that understands one's own perspective is full of assumptions and prejudices. The doctrine of cultural humility addresses the power imbalance between clinician and client. It maintains that having extensive knowledge about a client's culture is not the same as having been assimilated oneself into that culture. Cultural humility is extremely important in counseling immigrants and refugees.

Culturally responsive practice with non-Western, multicultural populations requires that mental health professionals evaluate the relevance of treatment approaches and their applicability to the migrant or refugee's cultural background and experience. Such practice also demands that practitioners develop a treatment plan that integrates client expectations and culture. Moreover, the culturally responsive clinician understands that no one theory can explain all human suffering or functioning. An integrative approach to practice will most likely have to be adopted when working with immigrants and refugees.

To assume a posture of cultural humility, clinicians need to take into consideration their clients' definition of mental health and mental health services. The stigma that surrounds the term *mental illness* exists in most countries; therefore, most clients will be hesitant to attribute any of their symptoms to a mental disorder based on the negative cultural repercussions that affect the individual and family members as well (Whitley, Kirmayer, & Groleau, 2006; Wong et al., 2006). Moreover, a culture describes mental health symptomatology based on its own history and reasoning for why symptoms appear as they do.

What is understood as "normal" varies dramatically between cultures (Sadock & Sadock, 2007); hence the clinician must inquire about the client's cultural definitions of typical/atypical mental behavior. He or she must then treat the client given what he or she has learned about mental health and mental disorder in the client's culture. Table 18.4 is a clinical skill chart based on questions asked in the *Cultural Formulation Interview, 1. Explanatory Model* (American Psychiatric Association, 2013).

Use of Interpreters With Immigrants and Refugees

A mental health worker might consider the use of interpreters if the immigrants or refugees are not fluent in English. The interpreter must communicate accurately the content of the client's and therapist's statements, as well as the affect or emotion shared between them. Interpreters

TABLE 18.4 ■ Culturally Responsive Clinical Skill in Exploring Cultural Definitions of Mental Health and the Client's Problem
• Can you tell more about how you understand your problem?
• How do people in your culture or home country understand mental health?
• How might your culture explain the symptoms you are describing?
• Can you tell me what you think caused your problem?
• Has living in this country led you to think differently about the causes of your problem?
• How serious do you consider your problem to be?
• What kind of treatment for the problem would a person in your culture receive?
• What do you believe is the best way to treat your problem?
• How concerned are people in your family about your having this problem?
• What would your family members and friends say is the best way to deal with the problem that you described?

serve as cultural brokers who help clients and providers understand differences in the meaning of the words used in therapy. They also offer suggestions regarding how to bridge the linguistic and cultural divide between client and therapist. Interpreters can help the therapist understand the nonverbal communication messages that are present in treatment, thereby increasing the therapist's awareness of cultural factors that may support or hinder the therapeutic process. Kirmayer et al. (2011) have maintained that the effectiveness of treatment can be greatly enhanced when trained interpreters and cultural brokers can address "any linguistic or cultural differences that impede communication and mutual understanding" (p. 959). Further, the interpreter's communications can help forge or solidify therapeutic alliance between the client and the therapist, as he or she communicates the feelings of both. Moreover, the interpreter's very presence provides some measure of support for the client. Interpreters should identify any incongruence between client statement and body/facial cues.

Conversely, interpreters may also present certain challenges. For instance, sometimes several service agencies may use the interpreter throughout the agency, so interpreters may be spread across multiple programs and serve multiple roles within the organization. Having the same interpreter for a client across such different settings as therapy, career counseling, and marital and family counseling can create issues with trust and confidentiality. Further, the interpreter may be a member of the client's community, thereby raising added areas of confidentiality and boundaries that must be addressed. Studies have reported that inadequate interpreters and linguistic and cultural barriers faced by new immigrants have been a major deterrent in accessing quality mental health services with long-term implications (Bauer, Rodríguez, Szkupinski Quiroga, & Flores-Ortiz, 2000; Ku & Waidmann, 2003).

The interpreter should assume the role of a conduit of information. He or she should not change what is being said. The interpreter should clarify what is being said so that both parties understand the information shared in the conversation. The interpreter plays the role of the cultural broker, providing the therapist with relevant cultural context and clarifying cultural concerns that could impede mutual understanding. Therapists should meet with the assigned interpreter prior to and after sessions to ensure the format and goals of therapy are consistent and there is clear understanding of what was exchanged in the session.

Miller, Zoe, Pazdirek, Caruth, and Lopez (2005) have indicated that many interpreters have no training in working with distressed or traumatized people, and they themselves may become traumatized as they interpret for clients. In the beginning, clients may form a stronger attachment to their interpreter than to their therapist. Sometimes interpreters may interject their own feelings, or they may question the therapist's interventions because they have insufficient knowledge of the therapeutic approach (Miller et al., 2005).

In addition, it is important to discuss the issue of confidentiality because many immigrant and refugee clients believe that speaking to someone outside of the family about personal issues is culturally inappropriate (Center for Victims of Torture, 2005). Moreover, many refugees have had negative experiences with government officials; therefore, they may be concerned that any information that they provide to the therapist will be used against them. The clinician informs the client that no information will be shared with anyone, including his or her spouse and other family members.

If possible, the mental health worker should provide information in the client's language. During the initial intake, the clinician asks if the client feels comfortable in the therapy space. He or she also pays attention to any nonverbal cues emitted by the client and takes time to explain why the client's personal details are needed. After asking how problems are typically addressed in the client's culture, the therapist inquires if the client

Cultural Reflections

"An Oromo man sits quietly, saying very little in his psychotherapy session. He is wary of his interpreter, an Ethiopian who speaks his language but is not Oromo. He does not mention his past involvement with a resistance movement and subsequent imprisonment and torture" (Center for Victims of Torture, 2005, p. 32).

What steps, if any, should you take as a counselor to prevent the difficulties described with the Oromo man and his Ethiopian interpreter? Is it sufficient just to make sure that the client and the interpreter speak the same language? What other factors might you have to take into consideration?

would be more comfortable with family or community members present (Centers for Victims of Torture, 2005). To put a client at ease, the therapist might have him or her describe common traditions and special cultural events that are important to him or her.

Secondary Trauma for Mental Health Therapists and Counselors

Service providers often experience unanticipatedly strong feelings or shock when discussing torture or listening to survivors' stories. When a mental health practitioner feels the effects of being exposed to trauma indirectly through others, he or she is said to have experienced secondary, or vicarious, trauma. **Secondary trauma** is considered to be an occupational hazard for therapists. It is conceptualized as an experience that can be reduced and managed, but not avoided completely (Center for Victims of Torture, 2005). It is essential that providers who work with torture survivors receive training on secondary trauma and have access to professional consultation regularly. Training should cover the following subjects: (1) signs and symptoms of secondary trauma, (2) contributing factors in the work itself, (3) contributing factors in the work environment, (4) contributing factors in the individual, and (5) methods for addressing secondary trauma (Centers for Victims of Torture, 2005).

As the Center for Victims of Torture (2005) has asserted, "organizations or clinics providing services to torture survivors can implement policies and procedures that prevent or ameliorate secondary trauma at the organizational level. Many contributing factors to secondary trauma are connected to the workplace and may be outside the control of the individual worker. Organizational strategies that deal openly with secondary trauma help reduce the sense of isolation, stigma, and shame that workers may experience" (p. 31).

COMPETENCY ASSESSMENT FOR PRACTITIONERS WORKING WITH REFUGEES AND IMMIGRANTS

Most counseling and clinical psychology training programs provide little or no training for working with refugees and immigrants. Table 18.5 is designed to help counselor and helping professional trainees to assess areas related to their competency for working with refugees and immigrants who may have experienced great trauma and torture during the migration process.

Because few counseling training programs have courses or practicums that focus on working with refugees and immigrants, counselor trainees tend to have limited knowledge or experience in working with refugees and immigrants. The questions in Table 18.6 are designed to get training programs thinking about providing specific training in working with refugees who have experienced unspeakable trauma and torture. The questions are designed to start a conversation within training programs about appropriate courses and training for helping professionals who expect to work with victims of torture and great trauma.

COUNSELING AND THERAPY MODELS FOR WORKING WITH REFUGEES WITH PTSD

This section reviews recent theoretical approaches to counseling individuals. Three approaches are discussed: (1) psychoeducational approach to demystify counseling, (2) narrative exposure therapy, and (3) strengths-based therapy. Clearly, there are other approaches for dealing with refugees and immigrants who have faced torture and violence in their homelands.

Refugees and immigrants are frequently the victims of multiple traumas, and traditional counseling approaches may not be very helpful. Among some of the hundreds of thousands of people fleeing war-torn Syria, Afghanistan, and Iraq, as well as other areas in Africa, significant

TABLE 18.5 ■ Practitioner's Knowledge and Skills Assessment for Working With Refugees and Immigrants

(1) Very limited (2) Limited (3) Average (4) Good (5) Excellent

How would you rate your knowledge and understanding about

1. The current worldwide situation for refugees and immigrants?

2. The migration process for many refugees and immigrants?

3. The various legal statuses of immigrants in the United States?

4. Torture, including the types of torture used against refugees, asylees, and immigrants?

5. How torture affects refugee and immigrant families?

6. How to provide culturally competent counseling services for refugee torture survivors?

7. Narrative exposure therapy?

8. Psychoeducational approach to counseling refugees and immigrants?

9. Adapting current models of psychotherapy and counseling to meet the needs of refugee torture survivors?

10. Using mental health assessments and interventions in a culturally responsive manner when working with refugee torture survivors?

11. Co-creating a treatment plan with a refugee survivor or client who has experienced torture?

12. Working with interpreters during counseling refugees or immigrants?

TABLE 18.6 ■ Counseling Training Programs and Provision of Training for Working With Refugees and Immigrants

1. Does your counseling or human service training program currently offer a course in working with refugees and immigrants?

2. Does your training program offer a practicum that deals with counseling or providing mental health services to refugees and immigrants?

3. Has your training program ever discussed with students refugees' and immigrants' experiences with torture?

4. Has your training program ever required you to read empirical or nonempirical articles dealing with refugee survivors of torture?

5. Do you feel that your training program has adequately prepared you to counsel or otherwise work with refugees and immigrants?

6. Has your training program ever provided you with information about self-care in working with refugees and immigrants?

7. What kinds of training do you think your training program should make available or require you to complete with regard to refugees and immigrants?

8. To what extent do you believe that members of your faculty are competent to offer courses in providing mental health services to refugees and immigrants?

9. Has your training program ever offered courses or instruction on the newer forms of psychotherapy for treatment of refugees and immigrants, such as narrative exposure therapy or trauma focused therapy?

10. On a scale of 1 to 10, with 10 being *excellent* and 1 being *poor*, how would you rank the training that your department has provided for providing mental health services to refugees and immigrants?

numbers may be prone to having severe mental illnesses, including a complex form of PTSD. Working with Médecins Sans Frontières (Doctors Without Borders) in makeshift arrival camps in Sicily, Italian psychotherapist Aurelia Barbieri gives what she calls "psychological first aid" to migrants arriving in Italy after months or years making their escape from their war-torn countries (Kelland, 2015).

Refugees who have fled from war-torn regions of the world often say that they have been subjected to physical and psychological torture, merciless shelling, rape, and sexual violence, as well as other atrocities. Given these reported conditions, there exists a high prevalence of PTSD (Turrini, et al, 2017). PTSD is associated with elevated rates of mood changes, anxiety, nightmares, and symptoms involving dissociation, intrusive thoughts, and hypervigilance (Chung & Bemak, 2007).

The existing knowledge about effective treatment of PTSD in civilian populations who have been scarred by war is only in its infant stages. Very little clinical research has been conducted on how to adequately support and treat refugees and immigrants who have experienced great atrocities. The majority of refugees who have survived war and torture may have been forced to flee to places that were also wrought with danger and persecution. Many of these refugees are not only poor and living under desperate human conditions, but also they may be dependent on humanitarian aid and suffering from malnourishment. The life conditions that many refugees and immigrants have faced reduce the applicability of psychotherapeutic treatment approaches that have been developed for Western PTSD populations. Maslow's (1968) hierarchy of needs maintains that treatment for psychological problems cannot be addressed properly as long as the individual is confronted with safety issues and lack of food.

Several counseling approaches have been modified to deal with PTSD in refugees and immigrants. It is usually recommended that therapists first use a psychoeducational approach to deal with refugees and immigrants suffering from PTSD. In addition, a relatively large number of studies have found that cognitive behavioral therapy, especially exposure and cognitive techniques, are highly effective when treating trauma victims (Neuner, Schauer, Klaschik, et al., 2004; Nickerson, Bryant, Silove, & Steel, 2011). The following two sections describe both a psychoeducational and new theoretical approach called narrative exposure therapy.

The Psychoeducational Counseling Model for Refugees and Immigrants

Mental health practitioners might consider using an initial psychoeducational approach to the treatment of immigrants and refugees. They would discuss what mental health is and the kinds of clinical interventions they would use to address the client's problem. It might be helpful to use a neuroscientific explanation of trauma—that is, an explanation that focuses on the brain and its responses to trauma, including such responses as hypervigilance, flashbacks, and insomnia. A practitioner's discussion of the brain's responses to trauma helps to normalize the experiences as those that the average person would experience under the conditions that the client described. Such an approach frees the client of shame and self-blame.

Psychoeducational approaches to counseling refugees and immigrants are designed to increase the client's understanding of mental health and to have the client prioritize mental health as a means of supporting overall well-being. As Neuner, Schauer, Klaschik, et al. (2004) have stated,

> a common element in brief interventions for the assistance of large numbers of
> traumatized refugees is psychoeducation, thought to cause some relief for traumatized
> people by explaining the nature of the symptoms caused by traumatic experiences and
> by demonstrating that this response is normal. Psychoeducation has been used as an
> add-on element with various treatment approaches (Foa & Rothbaum, 1998;

WHO/UNHCR, 1996). Some therapists suggest using psychoeducation as an economical and effective large-scale intervention to reduce the suffering of populations affected by war. (p. 580)

Narrative Exposure Therapy and PTSD

Neuner, Schauer, Elbert, and Roth (2002) developed **narrative exposure therapy (NET)** as a standardized short-term approach based on the principles of cognitive behavioral exposure therapy by adapting the classical form of exposure therapy to meet the needs of traumatized survivors of war and torture. Exposure therapy requires the client to repeatedly talk about the worst traumatic event in detail while reexperiencing all emotions associated with the event. During the sessions of NET, a client is first assessed to determine the presence and level of the PTSD, and then he or she is asked to start depicting his or her own lifeline with regard to happy and unhappy events (Neuner, Schauer, Elbert, et al., 2002). The lifeline is represented by a rope, and the client is asked to use flowers to mark happy events and rocks to indicate unhappy ones. After the client makes this graphic representation, he or she is then asked to explain all the events outlined on the rope line and to describe some potential dreams and hopes for the future.

NET is designed to be carried out for a small number of sessions per week for a few weeks. The goal of NET is to make the client experience all the unhappy events from the past and to focus on the most unhappy event(s). As the client is repeatedly exposed to the unhappy event that may have caused the PTSD, the client gets used to experiencing the event and thus experiences some relief from it.

The majority of clients experience a habituation of the emotional response to the traumatic memory, which subsequently leads to a remission of PTSD symptoms. As most refugees have experienced many traumatic events, it is often difficult to identify the worst event before treatment. Instead of defining a single event as a target in therapy, the client creates a narrative about his or her whole life from birth up to the present situation while focusing on the detailed report of the traumatic experiences. Thus, the first step of NET is to reduce the symptoms of PTSD by confronting the client with the memories of the traumatic event. A second step must be taken that involves the reconstruction of the client's autobiographic memory and a consistent narrative. Therefore, NET focuses on the habituation of emotional responding to reminders of the traumatic event and the construction of a detailed narrative of the event and its consequences.

The efficacy of narrative exposure for the treatment of PTSD for refugees is quite high. Robjant and Fazel (2010) conducted a literature review on the efficacy of narrative therapy for the treatment of PTSD for refugees. The researchers concluded that NET was highly effective in the treatment of PTSD in both adults and children. They stated that

> results from treatment trials in adults have demonstrated the superiority of NET in reducing PTSD symptoms compared with other therapeutic approaches. Most trials demonstrated that further improvements had been made at follow-up—suggesting sustained change. Treatment trials of Kidnet have shown effectiveness in reducing PTSD amongst children. Emerging evidence suggests that NET is an effective treatment for PTSD in individuals who have been traumatized by conflict and organized violence, even in settings that remain volatile and insecure. (Robjant & Fazel, 2010, p. 1030)

Counseling Refugees and Immigrants Using a Strengths-Based Approach

Strengths of Migrants and Refugees

Individuals and families with migrant and refugee backgrounds have strengths that can be used to promote positive counseling outcomes. Parents might have endured inconceivable circumstances to protect their children and families in order to take them to a safe place. Oftentimes, the family structure and cohesiveness and family members' belief in their ability to cope provide a firm foundation for them to live in the new host country. In American society, immigrants have a high level of engagement in the labor market (American Psychological Association, Presidential Task Force on Immigration, 2013).

Moreover, many immigrants come from collectivist cultures, and their families usually display a strong sense of cohesiveness and cooperation. Immigrants usually identify with other immigrants, and they may be supportive of each other. Moreover, migrants who experience the loss of their culture and guilt over leaving their homeland may grow stronger, as the acculturation process proceeds and as they develop a sense of belonging in their new homeland. The majority culture may seem less threatening and more inviting as the individual becomes more linguistically and socially fluent in this new culture. His or her integration and assimilation into the broad American society can help reduce feelings of loss and grief. In acculturation, the migrant's culture interacts with the majority culture of the new homeland, and thus, a dynamic and reciprocal process results that produces changes in the broader cultural group, enhancing the ability of people of the dominant American culture to better appreciate and understand aspects of the immigrant's culture (American Psychological Association, Presidential Task Force on Immigration, 2013).

CULTURALLY RESPONSIVE STRENGTHS-BASED THERAPY

An important part of strengths-based therapy is resilience. According to Luthar, Cicchetti, and Becker (2000), **resilience** is the maintenance of positive adaptation and development in the face of significant adverse experiences. Resilience helps people to move forward in the face of great tragedy and struggle; it is a valuable quality that is recognized across a broad range of human service disciplines (Howe, Smajdor, & Stöckl, 2012; Kaminsky, McCabe, Langlieb, & Everly, 2007; Luthar, 2006; Prilleltensky, 2005). People who survive life-threatening illness or massive personal losses (family, country, culture) and who remain alive and hopeful are said to be resilient.

Digging down deep for resilience is an important component of many immigrants' and refugees' migration narrative. One wonders how some refugees and immigrants have been able to summon the wherewithal to continue living. It takes resilience to leave a war-torn country in search of a new life for oneself and one's family. It takes resilience to be willing to rebuild one's life after one has experienced the murder and death of family members and after one has been beaten mercilessly and tortured (Jones-Smith, 2014). Strengths-based therapy focuses on clients' resilience, their strengths, and their ability to go forward into a country that is largely unknown. Therapists should acknowledge that it takes a great deal of strength and dedication to explore immigration options, file applications, and settle in a new country (Jones-Smith, 2014). When a therapist recognizes a client's strengths, the client feels empowered and affirmed as a human being. Table 18.7 lists some strengths-based questions to address to trauma-exposed clients.

TABLE 18.7 ■ Strengths-Based Therapy Questions for Trauma-Exposed Clients
• Tell me what it is about you that kept you fighting, that allowed you to withstand the trauma that would have crushed other people.
• What are some of your strengths that kept you alive during those horrible moments?
• If you had to choose one strength that you have that helped you survive the trauma, what would that strength be?
• How did you keep hope alive? What is it about you that helped you to get up every day and face the trauma, but still keep moving forward?

TABLE 18.8 ■ Culturally Responsive Strengths-Based Skills With Immigrants and Refugees

1. Document and validate the client's resilience and strengths.

2. Document events and circumstances when the client demonstrated strength and resilience during each of the following periods: premigration, migration, and postmigration, or arrival at the host country.

3. Ask the client to describe a time when he or she felt strong or used his or her strengths to overcome adversity during his or her migration narrative.

4. Validate and affirm the immigrant or refugee's survivor narrative.

5. Help the client to reframe the negative torture experiences as survivor experiences.

6. Validate and encourage the client's belief in his or her ability to succeed in the new host country.

7. Validate and encourage the client's beliefs regarding his or her ability to achieve goals.

In culturally responsive strengths-based therapy, the first step is to acknowledge the trauma that the person endured. The next step is to get the person to see the internal strengths that allowed him or her to survive the traumatic ordeal. The focus is almost always on the client's strengths, for only strengths can be used to help one endure the pain or to move forward, despite the debilitating situation. The skills listed in Table 18.8 are designed to help the practitioner to explore experiences of trauma and loss while identifying culturally appropriate responses and methods of healing/recovering from trauma and loss.

CASE VIGNETTE 18.1
USING A CULTURALLY RESPONSIVE STRENGTHS-BASED APPROACH WITH MOHAMMED

Mohammed is a 36-year-old male refugee from Iraq. He was permitted to seek refuge in the United States because he was an interpreter for the U.S. armed forces in Iraq. Prior to coming to the United States, he was a physician's attendant, providing services to war-torn Iraq. Before the war in Iraq, he was a respected member of his Sunni community. Sunnis had greater power and ruled over the much larger group of Shiites in Iraq. The assassination of Saddam Hussein resulted in greater conflict between these two Muslim groups.

Mohammed risked his life and the lives of his family members to be an interpreter for the U.S. armed forces. He came to therapy sessions because he reported not being able to sleep, eat, or get any enjoyment out of his new home. Although he understood the terminology around mental health, he felt that he should be stronger for his family, especially his two young children. Mohammed was placed on medication to help reduce his depression symptoms.

During therapy, Mohammed discussed his feelings about not belonging in America. He missed his sister, brother, and mother—all still living in Iraq. Sometimes he experienced flashbacks about the bomb shelling near his work and home and nightmares that he might be attacked by his own people because he was helping the United States. Moreover, Mohammed missed his Iraqi culture and being around his friends. He also complained that when he told Americans where he came from, people looked at him with deep suspicion and distrust. In the United States, his first job was as a laborer in a plant, and Mohammed viewed his job as a step down from his position in Iraq.

Treatment for Mohammed focused on an integration of psychoeducational counseling, trauma-focused cognitive behavioral approaches, and narrative and strengths-based therapy. The therapist helped him to see that many of his reactions were normal responses to the trauma that he had experienced in Iraq. His sleeplessness and

(Continued)

(Continued)

depression were connected to the loss of his country, extended family, and friends.

Mohammed's diagnosis was posttraumatic stress disorder, characterized by symptoms of hypervigilance, depressed mood, and flashbacks. He agreed to attend biweekly 50-minute sessions using an integrated treatment approach involving cognitive behavior therapy (thoughts). Medical case management services were given to him for the medication and other health issues he was facing. The therapist assisted him with such adjustment needs as food stamps, bus cards, and housing.

The therapist integrated narrative exposure therapy to help Mohammed alter his migration narrative from one who felt powerless to a survivor. Coming to the United States allowed Mohammed to rewrite his narrative so that he would not be defined by his losses in his native country. It was recommended that he seek the support of American Iraqi organizations to help him form new friends and contacts.

The therapist lifted Mohammed's spirits by asking him about his strengths. The therapist asked Mohammed to recall one day in his life when he felt in control of his life and strong. "Now remember that image, Mohammed," he said. "Whenever you are challenged, I want you to get the picture in your head that shows you using your strengths and other people commenting favorably on your strengths." The therapist worked with Mohammed to help him describe his narrative experience so that it contained more strengths-based language that showed his resilience. Deep breathing exercises were used to help him let go of some of the painful experiences that still dominated his memories. The therapist asked Mohammed to think about some goals he would like to achieve in the United States and to spend some time each day visualizing his accomplishing those goals. The therapist focused on helping Mohammed to identify instances in which he demonstrated resilience both prior to coming to the United States and postarrival.

SUMMARY OF KEY POINTS

To deliver culturally responsive therapeutic services, clinicians must have an awareness of the major differences and similarities between Western models of mental health treatment and non-Western beliefs around mental health and the role of culture. Many such clients will require the help of an interpreter to communicate with the therapist, and the role of any such interpreter needs to be made clear. The interpreter becomes part of a therapeutic triangle (therapist, client, interpreter) that links the therapist and client in purposeful, therapeutic communication.

1. Practitioners engaged in therapy services with immigrants and refugees should be knowledgeable about their premigration, migration, and postmigration experiences and the impact of trauma, cultural identity, loss, and cultural bereavement on their lives.

2. During the initial intake or first counseling session, make sure that the client feels comfortable in the therapy room.

3. At the conclusion of a session, ask the client how he or she felt about how the session went and what can be done to make him or her feel more comfortable during therapy.

4. Therapists should meet with the interpreter both prior to and after a session is completed to ensure

that there is a clear understanding of what took place during therapy.

5. After a counseling session, the therapist should ask if there was anything he or she did not understand or respond to appropriately or to reflect a lack of understanding of the client's culture.

6. The therapist might also ask the interpreter, "Did this session bring up any difficult feelings for you?"

7. Practitioners should also have an intentional and purposeful recognition of their refugee and immigrant clients' resilience and strength that is developed through their narration of their migration experience. They should understand how clients' strengths and resilience can help them deal with challenges they encounter in the destination or host country.

8. Effective counseling with immigrant and refugees requires clinicians to practice from a place of cultural humility regarding a client's cultural history and traditions. The therapeutic process with refugees and immigrants creates opportunities for learning and growth in both the client and the practitioner.

9. As clients take time to learn the culture of their new host country, the therapist should also start a journey that involves learning about the clients' culture and the meaning that their culture has for their lives.

10. Trauma-experienced immigrants and refugees oftentimes may have a deep mistrust in government and their neighbors because they have experienced the worst side of humanity, which has engrained a deep mistrust in their government, their community, and their neighbors. As a result of culturally sensitive, responsive, and compassionate counseling with individuals, therapists can help clients to rebuild lives and to strengthen life skills for a brighter future in the new host country.

11. Literature on best practices with refugees maintains that clinicians must understand the cultural background and individual values, beliefs, and practices associated with healing and health for each client (Short et al., 2010). They must understand how individual refugee clients view their own mental health and how they conceptualize help seeking and therapy.

12. For the most part, therapy is largely a Western phenomenon, and it may feel strange and uncomfortable to refugees from different cultures and different parts of the world (Gorman, 2001).

13. Narrative exposure therapy is a new therapeutic approach for counseling refugees based on the principles of cognitive behavioral exposure therapy. It adapts the classical form of exposure therapy to meet the needs of traumatized survivors of war and torture.

14. During the resettlement process, counselors should acquire knowledge regarding the legal systems relevant to various migrant statuses as it can impact access to services and employment, as well as how trusting and honest a refugee feels that he or she can be in counseling (Piwowarczyk, 2007).

15. Culturally accurate diagnosis and assessment are critical to providing competent services to refugee torture survivors; however, most of our clinical assessment tools are culturally biased. Clinicians must interpret clients' assessment results with caution and take into account the multiple contexts that influence clients' mental health symptoms and assessment responses (Gorman, 2001).

16. Focus on the complex layers of identity (intersectionality) for each torture survivor or immigrant, exploring intersectionality in terms of how a counselor might respond with a relevant theoretical framework for mental health services. The concept of intersectionality provides a way to identify the refugee's or immigrant's gender, race, culture, disability, sexual orientation, age, ethnicity, religion, familial orientation (collective and/or individualistic), and sociopolitical position (and so forth). The importance of overlapping identities and intersectionality must be integrated in the treatment framework for refugees and immigrants.

17. Refugees and asylum survivors confront challenges different from those that the average American citizen experiences. Not only do they face the prospect of indefinite separation from family members and friends who were not able to come with them, but also they may have witnessed the killings of loved ones, or worse, they may have been tortured or maimed themselves. Survivors endure huge emotional and cultural losses, and they may require treatment for physical as well as psychiatric wounds (Center for Victims of Torture, 2005).

18. Despite experiencing many stressors, refugees and asylees are unlikely to present for counseling. Instead, the family is viewed as the first support system. When refugees or immigrants do seek counseling, some may come because they are mandated by the court because of their child-rearing practices or because of domestic violence. Given that family and child-rearing practices may be different in their native country, refugees and immigrants might not have a clear understanding of why their traditional cultural behaviors are not acceptable in their new host country. Counselors may have to spend time familiarizing themselves with family child-rearing practices within the American cultural system.

19. Counselors should strive to understand the parenting and discipline norms from the refugee's home culture. They should educate parents about the norms, laws, and expectations in the United States. They should provide information about what behavior is acceptable and unacceptable within the American cultural system.

20. Torture and cumulative trauma are the strongest predictors of PTSD in refugees and asylees.

Refugees and asylum seekers (refugee claimants) are at higher risk than other immigrants due to their experiences of traumatic losses and stressors, including uncertainty about their refugee status.

21. Practitioners should develop their own supportive system of self-care to decrease the negative effects of secondary torture or trauma.

DISCUSSION QUESTIONS

1. Describe the impact of premigration trauma on the mental health of refugees.

2. Discuss how differing rates of acculturation contribute to mental health issues for migrants.

3. Explain how a counselor might put into practice cultural humility when working with a refugee or recent migrant.

4. Discuss what counseling theoretical approaches you might use in developing a treatment plan for a refugee who was raped repeatedly during the premigration journey.

KEY TERMS

Asylee: a person who meets the definition of refugee and is already present in the United States or is seeking admission at a port of entry.

Cultural alienation: the degree of estrangement or apartness one feels from the surrounding culture—sometimes experienced by immigrants in a new host country.

Cultural bereavement: the experience of the refugee, asylee, or immigrant resulting from the loss of social structures, cultural values, and self-identity. The person experiences grief over the loss of his or her culture and may suffer guilt feelings over abandoning the homeland culture.

DACA: Deferred Action for Childhood Arrivals. In 2012, President Obama used an executive order to authorize DACA, which provided temporary deportation protection for more than 800,000 undocumented or unauthorized young immigrants who were brought to this country illegally by their parents.

Forcibly displaced people: the term used for several categories of immigrants and refugees. There are three types of forced migration: (1) conflict-induced displacement, (2) development-induced displacement, and (3) disaster-induced displacement.

Illegal immigrant: a lay term for an individual who has failed to go through the established immigration procedures established by the host country.

Immigrant: a person who has moved from his or her country of origin to the United States or another nation, and who currently resides in that nation. Immigrants are viewed as having made their change in location voluntarily.

Migration process: takes place in broadly three stages. The first stage is premigration, which involves a person's decision and preparation to move. The second stage, migration, refers to the actual physical relocation of individuals from one place to another. The third stage is called postmigration, and it has been framed as the "absorption of the immigrant within the social and cultural framework of the new society."

Narrative exposure therapy (NET): a new theory developed for working with refugees, asylees, and immigrants who have faced torture and great trauma during the immigration process. Neuner, Schauer, Elbert, and Roth (2002) developed narrative exposure therapy as a standardized short-term approach based on the principles of cognitive behavioral exposure therapy by adapting the classical form of exposure therapy to meet the needs of traumatized survivors of war and torture.

Naturalization: An immigrant or refugee becomes a naturalized citizen after he or she has met the criteria and gone through the U.S. government process for becoming a citizen of the United States.

Posttraumatic stress disorder (PTSD): a mental health disorder that results because an individual has suffered or witnessed extreme violence or torture that led him or her to believe that he or she was going to die.

Refugee: a person outside his or her country of nationality who is unable or unwilling to return to his or her country of nationality because of persecution or a well-founded fear of persecution; refugees are deemed to change their location involuntarily.

Resilience: the maintenance of positive adaptation and development in the face of significant adverse experiences; it helps people to move forward in the face of great tragedy and struggle.

Secondary trauma: when a mental health practitioner feels the effects of being exposed to trauma indirectly through others, he or she is said to have experienced secondary, or vicarious, trauma. Secondary trauma is considered to be an occupational hazard for therapists.

Survivor's guilt: the guilt refugees and immigrants may feel about surviving torture and atrocities in their homeland while friends and family members may have to be left behind.

Trauma: a deeply distressing or disturbing experience that robs a person of a sense of power and control over his or her own life.

Undocumented immigrant: an individual who is not born in the United States and who has immigrated to this country without following the country's immigration laws.

REFERENCES AND SUGGESTED READING

Ahmadi, N., Hajsadeghi, F., Mirshkarlo, H., & Ebrahim, R. (2011). Post-traumatic stress disorder, coronary atherosclerosis and mortality. *American Journal of Cardiology, 108*(1), 29–33.

American Immigration Council. (2016, August 12). *How the United States immigration system works.* Retrieved at https://www.americanimmigrationcouncil.org/research/how-united-states-immigration-system-works

American Psychiatric Association. (2013). *Diagnostic and statistical manual of mental disorders* (5th ed.). Washington, DC: Author.

American Psychological Association. (2007, August 19). *Reaffirmation of the American Psychological Association position against torture and other cruel, inhuman, or degrading treatment or punishment and its application to individuals defined in the United States Code as "enemy combatants."* Retrieved from http://www.apa.org/about/policy/torture.aspx

American Psychological Association, Presidential Task Force on Immigration. (2013). *Crossroads: The psychology of immigration in the new century.* Washington, DC: American Psychological Association.

Amnesty International. (2014a, May 14). *Torture in 2014: 30 years of broken promises.* Retrieved from https://www.amnesty.org.au/torture-2014-30-years-broken-promises

Amnesty International. (2014b, May 14). *Torture: Our legacy, our future.* Retrieved from https://www.amnesty.org/en/latest/campaigns/2014/05/torture-our-legacy-our-future/

Basoglu, M. E. (Ed.). (1992). *Torture and its consequences: Current treatment approaches.* Cambridge, UK: Cambridge University Press.

Bauer, H. M., Rodríguez, M. A., Szkupinski Quiroga, S., & Flores-Ortiz, Y. G. (2000). Barriers to health care for abused Latina and Asian immigrant women. *Journal of Health Care for the Poor & Underserved, 11*(1), 33–44.

Beiser, M., Hou, F., Hyman, I., & Tousignant, M. (2002). Poverty, family process, and the mental health of immigrant children in Canada. *American Journal of Public Health, 92*(2), 220–227.

Bemak, F., & Chung, R. C. Y. (2014). Immigrants and refugees. In F. T. Leong, L. Comas-Díaz, G. C. Nagayama Hall, V. C. McLoyd, & J. E. Trimble (Eds.), *APA handbook of multicultural psychology, Vol. 1: Theory and Research* (pp. 503–517). Washington, DC: American Psychological Association.

Berliner, P., Mikkelsen, E. N., Bovbjerg, A., & Wiking, M. (2004). Psychotherapy treatment of torture survivors. *The International Journal of Psychosocial Rehabilitation, 8,* 85–96.

Bhugra, D. (2004). Migration and mental health. *Acta Psychiatrica Scandinavica, 109,* 243–258.

Birck, A. (2001). Torture victims after psychotherapy—a two-year follow-up. *Torture, 11*(2), 55–58.

Birman, D., & Tan, N. (2008). Psychological distress and adjustment of Vietnamese refugees in the United States: Association with pre-and postmigration factors. *American Journal of Orthopsychiatry, 78,* 109–120.

Boule, J. (2015). When people flee to America's shores. *Slate.* Retrieved at http://www.slate.com/articles/news_and_politics/history/2015/11/america_s_long_tradition_of_fearing_refugees_the_united_states_has_always.html

Center for American Progress Immigration Team. (2014). *The facts on immigration today.* Retrieved from https://www.americanprogress.org/issues/immigration/reports/2014/10/23/59040/the-facts-on-immigration-today-3/

Center for Victims of Torture. (2005). Working with torture survivors: Core competencies. In *Healing the heart: A guide for developing services for torture survivors* (pp. 20–49). Retrieved from http://www.cvt.org/main.php/HealingtheHurt

Chung, R. C.-Y., & Bemak, F. (2007). Immigrant and refugee populations. In M. G. Constantine (Ed.), *Clinical practice with people of color* (pp. 125–142). New York, NY: Teachers College Press.

Connor, P. (2016). U.S. admits record number of Muslim refugees in 2016. *Pew Research Center.* Retrieved from http://www.pewresearch.org/fact-tank/2016/10/05/u-s-admits-record-number-of-muslim-refugees-in-2016

Connor, P., & Krogstad, J. M. (2016). Key facts about the world's refugees. *Pew Research Center.* Retrieved from http://www.pewresearch.org/fact-tank/2016/10/05/key-facts-about-the-worlds-refugees/

Dearden, L. (2015, September 1). More than 11,000 Icelanders offer to house Syrian refugees to help with European crisis. *Independent.* Retrieved from http://Icelandreview.co.uk/new/world/europe/more-than-11000-icelanders-offer-to-house-syrian-refugees-to-help-european-crisis-10480505.html

Dedert, E. A., Calhoun, P. S., Watkins, L. L., Sherwood, A., & Beckham, J. S. (2010). Posttraumatic stress disorder, cardiovascular, and metabolic disease: A review of the evidence. *Annals of Behavioral Medicine, 39*(1), 61–78.

Dow, H. D. (2011). An overview of stressors faced by immigrants and refugees: A guide for mental health practitioners. *Home Health Care Management & Practice, 23*(3), 210–217. doi:10.1177/1084822310390878

Eisenbruch, M. (1991). From post-traumatic stress disorder to cultural bereavement: Diagnosis of Southeast Asian refugees. *Social Science and Medicine, 33,* 673–680.

Ewing, W. A., Martinez, D. E., & Rumbaut, R. G. (2015, July 13). The criminalization of immigration in the United States. *American Immigration Council.* Retrieved from http://immigratonpolicy.org/speial-reports/criminalization-immigration-united states

Fazel, M. (2005). Prevalence of serious mental disorder in 7000 refugees resettled in western countries: A systematic review. *Lancet, 365,* 1309–1314.

Finch, B., Kolody, B., & Vega, W. (2000). Perceived discrimination and depression among Mexican-origin adults in Calif. *Journal of Health and Social Behavior, 41*(3), 295–313.

Fitz, M., & Martinez, G. (2010). The costs of mass deportation: Impractical, expensive, and ineffective. *Center for American Progress.* Retrieved at https://cdn.americanprogress.org/wp-content/uploads/issues/2010/03/pdf/cost_of_deportation.pdf

Flores, E., Tschann, J. M., Dimas, J. M., Pasch, L. A., & de Groat, C. L. (2010). Perceived racial/ethnic discrimination, posttraumatic stress symptoms, and health risk behaviors among Mexican American adolescents. *Journal of Counseling Psychology, 57*(3), 264–273.

Gorman, W. (2001). Refugee survivors of torture: Trauma and treatment. *Professional Psychology: Research and Practice, 32*(5), 443–451.

Griswold, D. (2002). Immigrants have enriched American culture and enhanced our influence in the world. *CATO Institute.* Retrieved from https://www.cato.org/publications/commentary/immigrants-have-enriched-american-culture-enhanced-our-influence-world

Hafstad, V. (2015, October 16). Red Cross: 200 refugees 2016 and '17. *Iceland Review.* Retrieved from http://icelandreview.com/news/2015/10/16/red-cross-200-refugees-2016-and-17

Hart Research Associates. (2014). *NBC News/Wall Street Journal survey.* Retrieved from http://www.migrationpolilcy.org/article/college-educated-immigrants-united-states

Holtz, T. (1998). Refugee trauma versus torture trauma: A retrospective controlled cohort study of Tibetan refugees. *Journal of Nervous Mental Disorders, 186,* 24–34.

Howe, A., Smajdor, A., & Stöckl, A. (2012). Towards an understanding of resilience and its relevance to medical training. *Medical Education, 46*(4), 349–356.

Hugo, G. (2002). Australian immigration policy: The significance of the events of September 11. *International Migration Review, 36*(1), 37–40.

Ji, Q., & Batalova, J. (2012). College-educated immigrants in the United States. *Migration Policy Institute.* Retrieved from http://www.migrationpolicy.org/article/college-educated-immigrants-united-states

Jones-Smith, E. (2014). *Strengths-based therapy: Connecting theory, practice, and skills.* Thousand Oaks, CA: Sage.

Kaminsky, M., McCabe, O. L., Langlieb, A. M., & Everly, G. S., Jr. (2007). An evidence-informed model of human resistance, resilience, and recovery: The Johns Hopkins' outcome-driven paradigm for disaster mental health services. *Brief Treatment and Crisis Intervention, 7*(1), 1.

Kelland, K. (2015, December 3). Psychologists are designing refugee-focused therapies for migrants. *Huffington Post.* Retrieved from https://www.huffintonpost.com/entry/refugee-psychological-trauma_us_56660c8bc4b072c9d1c41f2a

Kirmayer, L. J., Narasiah, L., Munos, M., Rashid, M., Ryder, A. G., Guzer, J., . . . Pottie, K. (2011). Common mental health problems in immigrants and refugees: General approach in primary care. *Canadian Medial Association Journal, 183*(12), E959–E967. doi:10.1503/cmaj.090292

Kisely, S., Terashima, M., & Langille, D. (2008). A population-based analysis of the health experience of African Nova Scotians. *Canadian Medical Association Journal, 179,* 653–658.

Ku, L., & Waidmann, T. (2003). *How race/ethnicity, immigration status, and language affect health insurance coverage, access to care and quality of care among the low-income population.* Washington, DC: Kaiser Commission on Medicaid and the Uninsured.

Levi, A. (2009). The ethics of nursing student International clinical experiences. *Journal of Obstetric, Gynecologic, and Neonatal Nursing, 38*(1), 94–99.

Lind, D. (2014, July 29). 14 facts that help explain America's child-migrant crisis. *Vox.* Retrieved from https://www.vox.com/2014/6/16/5813406/explain-child-migrant-crisis-central-america-unaccompanied-children-immigrants-daca

López, G., & Bialik, K. (2017, May 3). Key findings about U.S. immigrants. *Pew Research Center.* Retrieved from http://www.pewresearch.org/fact-tank/2017/05/03/key-findings-about-u-s-immigrants/

Luthar, S. S. (2006). Resilience in development: A synthesis of research across five decades. In D. Cicchetti & D. J. Cohen (Eds.), *Developmental psychopathology, Volume 3: Risk, disorder, and adaptation* (2nd ed., pp. 739–795). Hoboken, NJ: Wiley.

Luthar, S. S., Cicchetti, D., & Becker, B. (2000). The construct of resilience: A critical evaluation and guidelines for future work. *Child Development, 71*(3), 543–562. doi:10.1111/1467-8624.00164

MacDonald, J. M., & Sampson, R. J. (2012, June 19). Don't shut the golden door. *The New York Times.* Retrieved from http://www.nytimes.com/2012/06/20/opinion/the-beneficial-impact-of-immigrants.html

Maslow, A. (1968). *Toward a psychology of being* (2nd ed.). Princeton, NJ: Van Nostrand.

McDonald, T. W., & Sand, J. N. (2011). *Post-traumatic stress disorder in refugee communities: The importance of culturally sensitive screening, diagnosis, and treatment.* Hauppauge, NY: Nova Science.

Migration Policy Institute. (2016). *Largest U.S. immigrant groups over time, 1960–present.* Retrieved from https://www.migrationpolicy.org/programs/data-hub/charts/largest-immigrant-groups-over-time

Miller, K. E., Zoe, L. M., Pazdirek, L., Caruth, M., & Lopez, D. (2005). The role of interpreters in psychotherapy with refugees: An exploratory study. *American Journal of Orthopsychiatry, 75,* 27–39.

Negy, C., Schwartz, D., & Reig-Ferrer, A. (2009). Violated expectations and acculturative stress among U.S. Hispanic immigrants. *Cultural Diversity and Ethnic Minority Psychology, 15,* 255–264.

Neuner, F., Schauer, M., Elbert, T., & Roth, W. T. (2002). A narrative exposure treatment as intervention in a refugee camp: A case report. *Journal of Behavioural and Cognitive Psychotherapy, 30,* 205–209.

Neuner, F., Schauer, M., Klaschik, C., Karunakara, U., & Elbert, T. A., (2004). A comparison of narrative exposure therapy, supportive counseling, and psychoeducation for treating posttraumatic stress disorder in African refugee settlement. *Journal of Consulting and Clinical Psychology, 72*(4), 579–587.

Nickerson, A., Bryant, R. A., Silove, D., & Steel, Z. (2011). A critical review of psychological treatments of posttraumatic stress disorder in refugees. *Clinical Psychology Review, 31,* 399–417.

Paunovic, N., & Ost, L. G. (2001). Cognitive–behavior therapy vs exposure therapy in the treatment of PTSD in refugees. *Behavioral Research and Therapy, 39,* 1183–1197.

Peri, G. (2013). The economic benefits of immigration. *Berkeley Review of Latin American Studies.* Retrieved from https://clas.berkeley.edu/research/immigration-economic-benefits-immigration

Pew Research Center. (2015, September 28). *Modern immigration wave brings 59 million to U.S., driving population growth and change through 2065.* Retrieved from http://www.pewhispanic.org/2015/09/28/chapter-2-immigrations-impact-on-past-and-future-u-s-population-change/

Pew Research Center. (2016, November 3). *Unauthorized immigrant population trends for states, birth countries, and regions.* Retrieved from http://www.pewhispanic.org/interactives/unauthorized-trends/

Pew Research Center. (2018). *Unauthorized immigration.* Retrieved at http://www.pewresearch.org/topics/unauthorized-immigration/

Prilleltensky, I. (2005). Promoting well-being: Time for a paradigm shift in health and human services [Supplemental material]. *Scandinavian Journal of Public Health, 33*(66), 53–60.

Pickering, M. (2001). *Stereotyping: The politics of representation.* New York, NY: Palgrave.

Piwowarczyk, L. (2007). Asylum seekers seeking mental health services in the United States: Clinical and legal implications. *Journal of Nervous and Mental Disease, 195,* 715–722.

Porter, M., & Haslam, N. (2005). Predisplacement and postdisplacement factors associated with mental health of refugees and internally displaced persons: A meta-analysis. *Journal of the American Medical Association, 294,* 602–612.

Pumariega, A. J., Rothe, E., & Pumariega, J. B. (2005). Mental health of immigrants and refugees. *Community Mental Health Journal, 41*(5), 581–597. doi:10.1007/s10597-005-6363-1

Restrepo, D., & Garcia, A. (2014, July 24). The surge of unaccompanied children from Central America. *Center for American Progress*. Retrieved from https://www.americanprogress.org/issues/immigration/reports/2014/07/24/94396/the-surge-of-unaccompanied-children-from-central-america-root-causes-and-policy-solutions/

Robjant, K., & Fazel, M. (2010). The emerging new evidence for narrative exposure therapy: A review. *Clinical Psychology*, *30*(8), 1030–1036.

Sadock, B. J., & Sadock, V. A. (2007). *Kaplan & Sadock's synopsis of psychiatry: Behavioral science/clinical psychiatry* (10th ed.). Alphen aan den Rijn, Netherlands: Wolters Kluwer.

Samuels, B. (2018, January 14). Poll: Most Americans support DACA. *The Hill*. Retrieved from http://thehill.com/homenews/administration/368959-poll-most-americans-support-daca

Short, E. L., Suzuki, L., Prendes-Lintel, M., Furr, G. P., Madabhushi, S., & Mapel, G. (2010). Counseling immigrants and refugees. In J. G. Ponterotto, J. M. Casas, L. A. Suzuki, & C. M. Alexander (Eds.), *Handbook of multicultural counseling* (3rd ed., pp. 201–212). Thousand Oaks, CA: Sage.

Shrestha, N. M., Sharma, B., Ommeren, M. V., Regmi, S., Makaju, R., Komproe, I., Shrestha, G. B., & DeJong, J. T. V. (1998). Impact of torture on refugees displaced within the developing world: Symptomatology among Bhutanese refugees in Nepal. *JAMA*, *280*, 443–448.

Turrini, G., Purgato, M., Ballette, F. , Nosé, M., Ostuzzi, G., Barbui, C. (2017). Common mental disorders in asylum seekers and refugees: Umbrella review of prevalence and intervention studies. International Journal of Mental Health Systems, 11, 51. Published online 2017 Aug 25. doi: 10.1186/s13033-017-0156-0.

United Nations High Commissioner for Refugees. (2015a). *Global trends: Forced displacement in 2014*. Retrieved from http://www.unhcr.org/556725e69.html

United Nations High Commissioner for Refugees. (2015b). *Midyear trends 2015*. Retrieved from https://www.scribd.com/document/293588937/UNHCR-2015-Mid-Year-Trends-report

United Nations High Commissioner for Refugees. (2016). *Global trends: Forced displacement in 2015*. Retrieved from https://reliefweb.int/report/world/unhcr-global-trends-forced-displacement-2015

United Nations Office of the High Commissioner for Human Rights. (1984, December 10). *Convention against torture and other cruel, inhuman or degrading treatment of punishment*. Retrieved at https://www.ohchr.org/EN/ProfessionalInterest/Pages/CAT.aspx

U.S. Department of Homeland Security. (2016). *Refugees and asylees*. Retrieved from https://www.dhs.gov/immigration-statistics/refugees-asylees

U.S. Department of Homeland Security. (2018). *Estimates of the unauthorized immigrant population residing in the United States*. Retrieved from https://www.dhs.gov/immigration-statistics/population-estimates/unauthorized-resident

Wadhwa, V., Saxeniam, A., Rissing, B., & Gereffi, G. (2007, January 4). America's new immigrant entrepreneurs. *UC Berkeley School of Information*. Retrieved from http://people.ischool.berkeley.edu/~anno/Papers/Americas_new_immigrant_entrepreneurs_I.pdf

Whiteford, G. E. (2005). Understanding the occupational deprivation of refugees: A case study from Kosovo. *Canadian Journal of Occupational Therapy*, *72*, 78–88.

Whitley, R., Kirmayer, L. J., & Groleau, D. (2006). Understanding immigrants' reluctance to use mental health services: A qualitative study from Montreal. *Canadian Journal of Psychiatry*, *51*, 205–209.

Willard, C. L., Rabin, M., & Lawless, M. (2014). The prevalence of torture and associated symptoms in United States Iraqi refugees. *Journal of Immigrant and Minority Health*, *16*(6), 1069–1076.

Wong, E. C., Marshall, G. N., Schell, T. L., Elliott, M. N., Hambarsoomians, K., Chun, C. A., & Berthold, S. M. (2006). Barriers to mental health care utilization for U.S. Cambodian refugees. *Journal of Consultation Clinical Psychology*, *74*, 1116–1120.

Wright, V. R., Chau, M., & Aratani, Y. (2011, March). *Who are America's poor children?* Retrieved from http://www.nccp.org/publications/pub_1001.html

Yakushko, O., Watson, M., & Thompson, S. (2008). Stress and coping in the lives of recent immigrants and refugees: Considerations for counseling. *International Journal for the Advancement of Counselling*, *30*, 167–178.

Yeh, C. J. (2003). Age, acculturation, cultural adjustment, and mental health symptoms of Chinese, Korean, and Japanese immigrant youths. *Cultural Diversity and Ethnic Minority Psychology*, *9*(1), 34.

Zeigler, K., & Camarota, S. A. (2014). *U.S. immigrant population record 41.3 million in 2013*. Washington, DC: Center for Immigration Studies.

Zong, J., & Batalova, J. (2016, April 14). Frequently requested statistics on immigrants and immigration in the United States. *Migration Policy Institute*. Retrieved from http://www.migrationpolicy.org/article/frequently-requested-statistics-immigrants-and-immigration-united-states/

Zong, J., Batalova, J., & Hallock, J. (2018, February 8). Frequently requested statistics on immigrants and immigration in the United States. *Migration Policy Institute*. Retrieved at https://www.migrationpolicy.org/article/frequently-requested-statistics-immigrants-and-immigration-united-states

19 CULTURALLY RESPONSIVE STRENGTHS-BASED THERAPY FOR MULTIRACIAL PEOPLE

- *"Some people are positively thrilled that the number of mixed-race Americans appears to be soaring. These individuals even have the idealistic notion that race-mixing will lead to bigotry's end. But these people ignore the obvious: ethnic groups in the U.S. have been mixing for centuries, yet racism hasn't vanished. Racism even remains a factor in a country such as Brazil, where a wide swath of the population identifies as mixed-race."*
—Nadra Kareem Nittle, author

- *"I have the right*

- *Not to keep the races separate within me.*

- *Not to justify my ethnic legitimacy.*

- *To identify myself differently than strangers expect me to identify.*

- *To create a vocabulary to communicate about being multiracial or multiethnic."* —Maria P. P. Root, "Bill of Rights for People of Mixed Heritage"

CHAPTER OBJECTIVES

- Recall the demographics and population statistics related to individuals with multiracial heritage.

- Define the "one drop rule" and the sense of not quite belonging.

- Identify bias and microaggressions against people with multiracial backgrounds.

- Discuss multiracial identity development and the intersectionality of race with other factors, such as gender, sexual orientation, age, and (dis)ability.

- Identify the cultural strengths of individuals with multiracial heritage.

- Analyze the mental health challenges of individuals with multiracial heritage.

- Implement culturally responsive strengths-based competencies for counseling multiracial individuals.

INTRODUCTION

America is changing, racially and culturally speaking. This country is not only becoming less White and more culturally diverse, but also is slowly embracing the idea that traditional methods of racial categorization are obsolete and self-serving for those in power (Renn, 2012; Robinson-Wood, 2017). We are moving gradually toward accepting the fact that few of us are racially "pure." A growing number of Americans now identify as multiracial or multiethnic (Bailey, 2013; Pew Research Center, 2015). For instance, many White Americans can be classified as multiethnic because their ethnic heritage might include Irish, Polish, German, or Italian heritage due to a pattern of intermarriage among members of these groups. The author of this book belongs to a family that includes African American, White, Puerto Rican, and American Indian members. As a nation, we appear to be abandoning the notion that people should have to choose only one primary ethnic/racial identity—White or African American, Asian or American Indian—and recognizing that they may embrace the various strands of their ethnicity or racial heritage (Bailey, 2013; Pedrotti, Edwards, & Lopez, 2008).

The experiences of multiracial persons came to the forefront of American society in 1967 with the U.S. Supreme Court decision mandating legalization of interracial marriages nationwide as a result of the *Loving v. Virginia* case. Prior to that decision, 16 U.S. states had laws prohibiting marriage between Caucasians and African Americans. Some 50 years later, intermarriage between Americans of different backgrounds has changed and continues to change our concept of race and ethnicity (Bailey, 2013), which brings me to the point made in Chapter 3 of this book. There is only one race in the world, and that is the human race. We are all just variations on what it means to be human.

Race: A Social Construction

Race is a social construction based on physical appearance (skin color, hair color and texture, facial features, ancestry, nationality, and culture) (Shih, Bonam, Sanchez, & Peck, 2007). As Renn (2012) has pointed out, in America and throughout the world, race is used for identification, to place people into demographic groups; however, **identity** is the meaning people ascribe to their membership in racial categories. Whereas identification comes about as a result of external assignment or categorization, racial or ethnic identity stems from internal processes mediated by individuals' encounters with external influences in their environment (Root, 1996).

What factors or social processes have sustained the social construction of race? In order to have racial categories in a society, we have to agree either tacitly or explicitly on what constitutes a race (Sanchez, 2010; Shih et al., 2007). Thus, the continued existence of the social construction of race is contingent on the collective agreement of social groups and the widespread acceptance of such constructions (Smedley & Smedley, 2005). Although many people give lip service to the concept that there is only one human race, and not five human races, they still categorize people into the various "racial groups." Based on this observation, it would appear that Americans and the rest of the world's people are not yet ready to stop categorizing people into five racial groups (Sanchez & Garcia, 2009). The inclusion of this chapter on people with multiethnic/multiracial heritage makes this book complicit with the rest of the world in using artificial, unscientific classifications of people into five different racial groups. This chapter is devoted to examining the life situation of multiethnic or multiracial individuals. Although the two terms are used interchangeably, the author believes that *multiethnic* is the more accurate term for people who can trace their ancestral heritage to different groups (Bailey, 2013).

Cultural Reflections

Do you believe there are five races? If so, what are those races?

How do you define race?

In what race would you place yourself?

What are your feelings about the United States becoming more multiracial?

To what extent, if any, has your family become multiracial?

Definition of *Multiracial*

In recent generations, the term ***multiracial*** has changed because people have begun to take charge of how they are described racially (Robinson-Wood, 2017). The U.S. Census Bureau's decennial census contains the single largest data collection on Americans' racial identity. As explained in Chapter 13, the Census Bureau's survey categorizes people as White, Black or African American, American Indian or Alaska Native, Asian, Native Hawaiian or Other Pacific Islander, and "Some Other Race." Prior to 2000, individuals were required to choose only one racial category to describe themselves. Beginning with the 2000 census, respondents had the option of choosing more than one race. The Census Bureau places individuals who select two or more races into the multiple-race population category.

Several different terms have been used to describe a multiracial population, including *biracial, mixed race, multiracial, multicultural,* and *mixed heritage* (Aspinall, 2009; Henriksen & Paladino, 2009; Jackson, Yoo, Guevarra, & Harrington, 2012; Root & Kelley, 2003). Since the early 2000s, the term *multiracial* has been the most frequently used (Henriksen & Paladino, 2009; Root & Kelley, 2003). More recently, however, scholars have begun using the terms *mixed race* and *multiple heritage* (Henriksen & Paladino, 2009). These terms and another term that combines them (*mixed heritage*) acknowledge the intersectionality and multiple dimensions of a person's identity, including race, culture, and lived experiences (Edwards & Pedrotti, 2004). Throughout this chapter, the term *multiple heritage* is used synonymously with *interracial, mixed heritage*, and *multiracial*.

In contrast to the word *multicultural*, the term *bicultural* describes a person who is a product of two distinct cultural groups and lives between two sets of cultural norms and expectations (Gibbs, Huang, & Associates, 1989; Root, 1990). Similarly, the term **biracial** refers to a person whose parents are of two distinct socially constructed racial groups. The term **monoracial** describes a person who has parents of the same socially constructed racial group. A person who is biracial may have one or both parents who are biracial or may have a multigenerational family history of racial mixing.

Demographic and Population Data on the Multiracial Population in the United States

The multiracial population in the United States has grown significantly since the 2000 census. Between 2000 and 2010, the number of White and Black biracial Americans more than doubled, while the population of adults with a White and Asian background increased by 87% (Jones & Bullock, 2013). In light of such statistics, one might conclude that multiracial people are a new phenomenon in the United States. The truth is, however, that multiracial people have been a part of the country's fabric for centuries. Consider anthropologist Audrey Smedley's finding that the first child of mixed Afro-European ancestry was born in the United States as early as 1620 (Smedley & Smedley, 2011). Even some well-known historical figures such as Crispus Attucks, Jean Baptiste Point du Sable, and Frederick Douglass were mixed race.

In 2010, the U.S. Census Bureau reported that about 9.1 million people, or 2.9% of the total American population, chose two or more racial categories when asked about their race (Jones & Bullock, 2012a and b). Approximately 92% of the people reporting multiple races reported exactly two races. Only 7.5% said that three or more racial groups contributed to their racial heritage, and less than 1% reported more than four races (Jones & Bullock, 2012a and b). The biggest increase in the number of races reported since 2000 was seen in the proportion of people who reported three races.

The Pew Research Center reported in 2015 that the Census Bureau's estimate that 2.1% of the U.S. adult population is multiracial may be inaccurately low. Based on its own survey, the Pew Research Center estimates that 6.9% of the U.S. adult population could be considered multiracial. The Pew study used several different categories to arrive at the 6.9% multiracial composition of the United States. The study was based on a nationally representative survey of 1,555 multiracial Americans ages 18 and older that was conducted online from February 6 to April 6, 2015. A major reason for the disparity in the estimated multiracial population rests in the questions the Census Bureau asked and in how it collected data. The Pew Research Center survey estimated that 2.6% of Americans are multiracial based on their grandparents' racial background, 2.9% based on the racial background of their parents, and 1.4% because they used two or more races to describe themselves (Jones & Bullock, 2012, 2013).

Four multiple-race groups formed the largest race combinations in 2010. The 2010 census reported that of the individuals who identified as more than one race, (1) 20.4% selected Black and White—approximately 1.8 million; (2) 19.3% chose White and "Some Other Race," representing the second-largest multiracial group at 1.7 million; (3) 18% chose Asian and White—approximately 1.6 million, representing an increase in growth of 87% since 2000; and (4) American Indian and White constituted the fourth-largest category (15.9%), numbering around 1.4 million with an increase of 32% since 2000 (Jones & Bullock, 2012a and b). Almost half of the American Indian and Alaska Native population (43.8%) and more than half of the Native Hawaiian and Other Pacific Islander population (55.9%) reported more than one race (Jones & Bullock, 2012a and b).

Multiracial self-identification in the United States varies depending on the racial mixture. As noted in the preceding paragraph, American Indians, Native Hawaiians, and Pacific Islanders are the most likely to state they are of more than one race. African Americans and Whites are the least likely to report they are of more than one race—yet, the most common multiracial combination in the United States is African American and White (Jones & Bullock, 2012a and b).

Among all of the "two or more races" individuals, 83% included White as one of the race groups. Besides the White race combination, the three most frequently reported race groups among all race combination groups were Black, Some Other Race, and Asian. African Americans formed 34% of the multiple-race population, followed by Asians (29%) and American Indians and Alaska Natives (25%). Native Hawaiians and Other Pacific Islanders constituted 7.6% of the multiple-race population (Jones & Bullock, 2012a and b).

Age of Multiracial Population

According to the U.S. Census Bureau (2010), the fastest-growing population in the United States is multiracial youths. Currently, the United States has more than 4.2 million children identified as multiracial, an increase of nearly 50% since the 2000 census. In general, the multiracial population is much younger than the overall U.S. population. For those reporting two or more races, the median age was 23.4 compared with 35.4 for the total U.S. population. Among those reporting two or more races, 25.5% were under the age of 10 in contrast with 14.1% in the total population. The people who reported as mixed White and Black/African American were very young, with 71% of this population under the age of 18 compared with 25% in the overall population. The median age for people reporting a combination of White and Black races was

TABLE 19.1 ■ "Two or More Races" Population by Racial Composition: 2010		
Two or More Racial Groups	**Population Total**	**Population %**
White and African American	1.83 million	20.4%
White and Some Other Race (SOR)	1.74 million	19.3%
White and Asian	1.62 million	18.0%
White and American Indian/Alaska Native	1.43 million	15.9%
African American and SOR	314,571	3.5%
African American and American Indian/Alaska Native	269,421	3.0%
Asian and SOR	234,462	2.6%
African American and Asian	185,595	2.1%
White and Hawaiian/Pacific Islander	169,991	1.9%
Asian and Hawaiian/Pacific Islander	165,690	1.8%

Source: US Census Bureau, 2010.

9.7 years, and those claiming a White/Asian heritage had a median age of 18.1 years. Table 19.1 summarizes the "two or more races" population for 2010 (Jones & Bullock, 2012a and b, 2013; U.S. Census Bureau, 2010).

Interracial Marriage in the United States

From the founding of this nation, most U.S. states had laws of **miscegenation** (mixing of races) that banned marriages and sexual relationships between White and African Americans. As a result of miscegenation laws, biracial and multiracial children were considered illicit results of such illegal marriages and relationships (Root, 1996). Miscegenation laws were ruled unconstitutional in 1967 by the U.S. Supreme Court in *Loving v. Virginia*. The term *miscegenation* was first used in 1863, during the American Civil War, by journalists seeking to disgrace the abolitionist movement by creating debate over the prospect of interracial marriage after the abolition of slavery. Since 1967, interracial marriages have been legal in the United States, and the number of such marriages has increased steadily.

In 2010, the Census Bureau reported that approximately 15% of all new marriages in the United States were between individuals of different races or ethnicities. Approximately 9% of Whites, 17% of African Americans, 26% of Latino/as, and 28% of Asians married people from a different racial group. More African American males married outside their group (24%) than did African American females (9%). In contrast, 36% of female Asian Americans married outside their ethnic group compared to 17% of Asian males (U.S. Census Bureau, 2010).

The "One-Drop Rule"

Do the many contributing parts of a person's ethnicity really matter? The answer to this question is rather straightforward. Yes, race and ethnicity still matter in today's world. However, we have come a long way from the time when, legally and socially, it was believed that "one drop of "African American blood" meant that a person was Black. The "**one-drop rule**" is an American class-based social system that supports the myth of "racial purity" by assigning the individual of mixed racial heritage to the least desirable racial status—a practice known as *hypodescent*. The "one-drop rule" was institutionalized by *Plessy v. Ferguson*, an 1896 Supreme Court decision that ruled that a person who was seven-eighths White and one-eighth Black and "maintained that he did not look Negro" was still to be classified as Black (Davis, 1991). Many prominent multiracial Americans—Tiger Woods, for instance—are refusing to be classified by the "one-drop rule." Instead, they are embracing their entire ethnic/racial heritage.

Although the hypodescent rule would logically apply to other ethnic/racial minority groups, it is used predominantly with African Americans (Root, 1996). When Asian women intermarry with Whites, their children are typically considered multiracial. In contrast, when African Americans intermarry with Whites, their children are often considered Black. The "one-drop rule" has a greater impact for those who have darker skin than for those who have lighter skin.

When Barack Obama started to run for the presidency of the United States in 2007–2008, major newspapers—*Time* magazine, the *New York Times*, and a number of other papers—all carried stories about his mixed ethnic/racial heritage. People were fascinated by the fact that his mother was a White Kansan and his father a Black Kenyan.

As noted in Chapter 8 of this book, Tiger Woods's invention of the word *Cablinasian* to describe his ethnic heritage speaks to a number of issues. First, Woods raises the question of who has the right to decide what part of one's ethnic heritage is more important than another. Second, he puts forth for consideration the futility of trying to discern the relative contributions of the various strands of his ethnicity. Third, he brings forth the question: Does one's race really matter? The answer is an undeniable yes. Race matters not only in the United States, but also throughout the world (Brunsma, 2006).

Cultural Reflections

To what extent do you subscribe to the "one-drop rule"?

How would you describe the racial heritage of former president Barack Obama?

Should people intermarry with other cultural and ethnic groups? Explain.

Despite much progress in the area of civil rights, the "one-drop rule" is still alive and well in the United States; the major difference is that it is less acceptable than it used to be (Rockquemore, 2002). American society tends to make people choose one ethnic/racial identity over another, and Americans across the board have not been very receptive to individuals who claim more than one racial identity. These attitudes are complex, however. For example, contrary to the "one-drop rule," some maintain that people of mixed heritage are not "really" African American. A Pew Research Center study in 2014 found that a majority of Americans chose to describe President Obama as "mixed race" and that only 25% described him as "Black." Among African Americans, however, 55% referred to the president as "Black" (Cillizza, 2014).

Microaggressions Directed Toward Multiracial Individuals

As explained in previous chapters, racial microaggressions are subtle or indirect statements or behaviors (intentional or unintentional) that communicate hostile or denigrating messages toward the target group. Racial microaggression research has tended to focus exclusively on monoracial people of color, leaving the experiences of multiracial people unexplored (Nadal et al., 2011).

Previous literature has revealed that multiracial individuals experience common forms of discrimination, including isolation and disapproval from extended family (Root, 1998), social isolation (Brown, 1995), a lack of social recognition (Nakashima, 1996), and exclusion from one's neighborhood and community (Kerwin & Ponterotto, 1995). Jackson's (2010) study found that multiracial people describe their experiences with racism as being direct (e.g., being called a racial epithet) or indirect (e.g., overhearing a joke about one of their racial groups). Root's (1998) study reported that multiracial individuals who are of mixed Asian/Black heritage encounter more discrimination than those who are of mixed Asian/White heritage. Multiracial Black/White students experienced more prejudice compared to their monoracial Black and monoracial White peers (Brackett et al., 2006).

Individuals of mixed racial heritage face microaggressions as a result of their contact with others. To clarify the kinds of microaggressions that multiheritage individuals face, Johnston and Nadal (2010) proposed a theoretical taxonomy with five categories of microaggressions experienced by members of this population:

- *Exclusion or isolation* takes place when a multiracial person is excluded or isolated based on his or her mixed race. For example, a biracial White/Black girl is told "You aren't Black enough" by her Black friends or family, or "You act too White." As another example, a person of Asian/White heritage may be excluded from extended-family group gatherings; family members refuse to accept the individual because he or she is not fully Japanese, Chinese, or Korean.

- *Exoticization and objectification* occur when a multiracial person is made to feel dehumanized or when he or she is treated like an object. A biracial White/Asian person may be repeatedly asked, "What are you?" Some people also consider mixed-heritage people to be exotic and sexually appealing. A person might comment, "I love the way that you seem to have taken the best of both the White and the Hispanic races."

- *Assumption of monoracial or mistaken identity* takes place when a multiracial person is assumed or mistaken to be monoracial or of a different racial group. This kind of experience invalidates one's complete racial identity. One Latino/African American student reported that his teacher singled him out for a program that was designed for Middle Easterners. A biracial White/Latino male feels insulted when he is told a joke about Latinos among White colleagues because they do not know he is also Latino.

- *Denial of multiracial reality* happens when a monoracial person invalidates or makes little of a multiracial person's experiences (e.g., a person is told that he should stop being so sensitive about race). "Come on," a person might say to a multiracial friend, "sometimes you're just too sensitive about race. I'm sure the person meant nothing by serving you last."

- *Pathologizing of identity and experiences* occurs when a multiracial person is told that he or she has psychological issues because he or she is mixed; a multiracial person's identity or experiences are viewed as psychologically abnormal. Although Johnston and Nadal's (2010) taxonomy was derived from conducting a literature review, empirical research needs to be conducted to provide evidenced-based research.

In a study investigating microaggressions and the multiracial experience, Nadal and colleagues (2011) found that multiracial people experience microaggressions that are both similar to and unique to monoracial people of color. The authors asserted that like monoracial people of color, multiracial people experience themes of feeling exoticized, being treated like a second-class citizen, or being assumed to be a foreigner. Similar to participants in prior studies, participants developed coping skills and strategies in order to prevent microaggressions (e.g., avoiding dating certain types of people) or to be prepared to respond to microaggressions when they occur. Participants described being excluded or isolated by their own family. One participant shared how she felt her grandfather favored her other cousins because of their "lighter skin tones, monoracial identities, or both" (Nadal et al., 2011, p. 43).

Forcing an Ascribed Identity on Multiracial Individuals

Another threat to a multiracial individual's being sometimes takes place when the government and school officials require multiracial students to choose only one race on demographic forms (Renn, 2009; Sanchez, 2010; Sanchez & Garcia, 2009). They are denied the basic right to self-identify as they choose. Researchers have found that this lack of control in being able to properly self-identify affects one's mental health (Townsend, Markus, & Bergsieker, 2009).

Racism, Skin Color, and Multiracial Backgrounds

Moreover, Whites have developed a social distance scale for each of the so-called racial minorities in the United States. The original Bogardus (1947) study was designed to measure the level of acceptance that White Americans feel toward members of the most common ethnic groups in the United States. Whites had the greatest amount of social distance from African Americans. Social distance was measured by having respondents respond to statements regarding if they would marry or want to live next door to a person from a given ethnic/racial background. A 2005 study found that the mean level of "social distance towards all ethnic groups, as well as the spread between the groups with the highest and lowest levels of social distance, decreased since 1977" (Parrillo & Donoghue, 2005, p. 257).

The level or amount of racism that multiracial individuals experience varies, depending on what racial groups constitute their mixed racial heritage. On average, multiracial individuals with an African American background tend to encounter racial attitudes that are usually directed toward members of the African American community in general. When individuals have a biracial Asian and White American heritage, they are more likely to be accepted and treated as White, whether or not they have traditional Asian features. Similarly, biracial individuals who are White and American Indian say that they feel the most connected to the White race.

Skin color is an important issue for multiracial individuals living in the United States. Researchers have found that Americans across and within racial or ethnic groups tend to attribute more favorable characteristics to individuals who have lighter skin tones and they generally believe that others also consider light skin as more attractive than dark skin. These researchers also found that dark-skinned African Americans in this country have "lower socioeconomic status, more punitive relationships with the criminal justice system, diminished prestige, and less likelihood of holding elective office compared with their lighter counterparts" (Hochschild & Weaver, 2007, p. 643).

According to the Pew Research Center's (2015) survey of multiracial individuals, about 55% say they have been subjected to racial slurs or jokes. Whereas 40% of the mixed-race individuals with an African American background said that they were stopped by the police, only 15% of the White and American Indian population and 6% of biracial Asian and White Americans said that they were stopped by the police. In general, the amount of racial discrimination most biracial or mixed-race individuals reported tended to be similar to that of the racial group that the persons most resembled in appearance.

The "What Are You?" Question

Robinson-Wood (2017) has reported that many biracial people have encounters with or experiences of racism that have caused them to think deeply about their racial heritage. Biracial children are often asked, "What are you?" Sometimes the comments of others can be quite painful. For instance, one young person reported that she was told that she did not look like any member of her family: "Your father is Black and your mother is White, but you don't look like either of them."

At the heart of the "What are you?" question is the idea that the person does not look as if he or she really belongs to any established racial group; the person is a misfit of some sort. Sometimes the parents of multiracial young people may not be viewed as sympathetic to their children's issues around being multiracial. They may dismiss a young person's multiracial concerns as being "too sensitive" to the issues of race. One African American college student often insisted that her mother (who was White) accompany her whenever she was trying to rent an apartment, apply for credit, or make a big purchase. "You come with me, Mom," she would say. "Then I know that I will get what I want." Once the mother tried to reassure her daughter that it was not racism that she was encountering but instead she was experiencing other people's rudeness. The daughter responded, "Take your head out of the sand, Mom. Stop trying to excuse other people's racism. When you do that, Mom, you deny my everyday reality. It's like you're telling me that the racism I experience as a multiracial person is all in my head." Maria Root offers a cultural reflection from her book titled *The Multiracial Experience*.

Marginality and Mixed Heritage

According to Root (1990), mixed-heritage people begin life as "marginal individuals" because American society rejects viewing children who have both a Black and White heritage as unequal. Whites may reject a biracial child as not White, and a similar situation may also exist with African Americans. Neither ethnic/racial group may accept the multiracial children. Therefore, the children exist at the outer edges of marginality. Their internal racial identity may be distinctly different from that of their parents. When people ask a biracial or multiracial person, "What are you?"

Cultural Reflections

Answering the Question: What Are You? (Maria Root's Reflections)

From the time I started elementary school to the time I started junior high, strangers, teachers, and friends' parents often let me know I was different by asking "Where are you from?" I would name my street, my city, or a geographic marker near my house. But I knew these answers, although they sometimes stopped the inquiry, were not replying to the question they intended. Sometimes if the inquiry continued, I would give my birth country, the Philippines, a place I could no longer remember. For some strange reason, this of all answers seemed to satisfy them. Some would go further and knowingly ask, "Your dad in the military?" a question I dreaded and disliked. Then sometime in my teens in the era of ethnic and racial pride movements the question about my difference more frequently became "What are you?" By then I understood that the question was mostly about my physical ambiguity, asked by someone wondering "whose side was I on." I gave various fractions and explanations, trying to hurry my explanation away from this difference. Demographic changes require that the question must change again. It must move from an individual on to a societal one. The larger question increasingly facing this nation is, "Who are we?" (Excerpted from Maria P. P. Root, The Multiracial Experience, 1995, p. xiii).

the question almost inevitably asks the person to justify his or her existence based on concepts of racial purity and monoracialism.

Feelings of marginality with regard to one's mixed racial heritage may be caused by a number of factors. To ease feelings of marginality, some multiracial individuals do not consider themselves to be multiracial. As noted earlier, the vast majority of individuals (61%) with a multiracial background do not consider themselves to be multiracial. The Pew Research Center (2015) has reported a number of reasons individuals might not consider themselves to be multiracial:

- They look like one race (47%), which was the reason former president Obama gave.

- They were raised as members of one racial group (47%).

- They closely identify with only one race (39%).

- They never knew the family member or ancestor who was a different race from the one in which they were raised (21%).

- They received pressure from family, friends, or the American society to identify with only one race (21%).

The next section presents a case example of the hurdles multiple-heritage people experience. It reviews some models of multiracial identity development.

CASE VIGNETTE 19.1

MULTIPLE-HERITAGE CASE EXAMPLE: NORWEGIAN FATHER, AFRICAN AMERICAN MOTHER

Richard C. Henriksen Jr., Norwegian and African American--I was born in 1952 to parents who were from different backgrounds. My father had roots that led to Norway, and my mother was African American. They got married when such a marriage was still illegal in 16 states. I grew up not knowing my father's family because they disapproved of my mother, and my grandparents let it be known that they never wanted to meet their grandchildren. I did get to meet my uncles and a few cousins, but no lasting relationships were built. My mother's family was different. Although there were questions about my mother's marriage to a White man, he was accepted, and my siblings and I developed long-lasting relationships with most of the family, especially my grandfather, my two grandmothers, and my uncles. I felt accepted by most of the family but knew that there were family members who never believed I was Black enough.

Source: Excerpted from Richard C. Henriksen Jr. and Derrick A. Paladino: *Counseling Multiple Heritage Individuals, Couples, and Families* (2009). Alexandria, VA: American Counseling Association.

The Sense of Not Quite Belonging, of Being Different

This section presents a case example of the hurdles multiple-heritage people experience. It reviews some models of **biracial/multiracial identity development**. Many multiracial individuals report a sense of not quite belonging—of sometimes even being told that they don't belong—of being different from others, and oftentimes such feelings of being different and not belonging start at an early age. For instance, Leah Brew, who is half White and half Japanese, reported in an article that she felt that she just did not belong (Meyers, 2016).

CASE VIGNETTE 19.2
WHERE DO I BELONG?

"When I was young, I didn't know I was different," says licensed professional clinical counselor Leah Brew, who is half White and half Japanese. "Then we moved, and I was made fun of [at her new school] because they said I was Chinese."

Brew didn't know what being Chinese meant, but based on the teasing she was subjected to, she assumed it was something horrible. "So I asked my mom if I was Chinese, and she said, 'No, you're Japanese.'" . . . She was relieved but soon found that when she corrected her tormentors, it made no difference. Although Brew was also white, it was her Japanese appearance that mattered to her classmates.

As she grew older, Brew . . . traveled to Japan. . . . Although she loved experiencing the culture and the people, she didn't feel quite at home there either. For one thing, . . . she inherited her White father's height and towered over everyone on the street. . . . Today, . . . when it comes to her own identity and culture, Brew says she at times sees herself as mostly white and at other times mostly Japanese. She acknowledges that she is always moving back and forth between the two.

Source: Excerpted from Meyers (2016).

The stress of being treated differently because of one's multiracial makeup can affect individuals' well-being (Salahuddin & O'Brien, 2011). Being part of a community consisting of mixed ethnic/racial background improves multiracial young people's well-being (Sanchez & Garcia, 2009).

MODELS OF MULTIETHNIC/ MULTIRACIAL IDENTITY DEVELOPMENT

During the 1990s, controversy arose about the applicability of monoracial identity development models for multiracial and biracial people. Previously, in the 1980s, it was believed that multiracial and biracial individuals should adopt the race of the parent of color. This position was based on the historical "one-drop rule," or the doctrine of racial hypodescent. It was previously assumed that if a biracial person opposed being categorized as Black, then he or she was somehow not mentally well adjusted. When increasing numbers of multiracial individuals began to challenge this assumption, researchers began to develop models of biracial identity development. Research on multiracial identity development was influential in getting the U.S. Census Bureau to include a biracial category on the census.

Pedrotti et al. (2008) maintain that multiracial individuals face unique issues (Root, 1996), and that the identity development process differs in multiracial clients in comparison with monoracial individuals (Gillem, Cohn, & Throne, 2001; Miville, Baysden, & So-Lloyd, 1999). These differences may be due to the fact that monoracial models of identity "do not recognize the social complexity of adopting a biracial identity in a monoracially defined social world" (Miville, 2005, p. 303). Individuals who are multiracial often describe experiences of feeling alienated, unsure about self-identification, and frustrated with others' attempt to ascribe a racial identity to them (Root, 1996). Clinicians working with multiracial individuals must understand the challenges that they face and recognize that models of racial identity designed for monoracial individuals may not be appropriate for use with this population.

Poston (1990) and Root (1990, 1998) were early scholars to publish models that outlined healthy biracial identity development. These authors challenged the view that having a biracial identity would be fraught with problems; they based their models on their clinical experience and in the case of Root on personal experience. Poston (1990) maintained that the current models of racial identity development (Cross, 1971; Cross & Vandiver, 2001; Helms, 1984, 1995) did not accurately reflect biracial individuals' identity experiences, and therefore he proposed a "new and positive model" (p. 153) that emphasized five levels of experiences of biracial people.

Level 1 focuses on an individual's personal identity that is independent of either parent's ethnic/racial background. Young children hold a personal identity that is independent of their parents' ethnic/racial identity.

Level 2 deals with a person's choice of group categorization wherein an individual chooses a multicultural existence that includes both parents' heritage groups or the person chooses a culture from one parent's background. A number of variables may influence a person's decision to identify primarily with one parent's ethnic/racial group membership, including the social status of the parent's ethnic/racial group and level of support for the chosen identity.

Level 3 involves enmeshment/denial. The person feels guilty at not being able to identify with all aspects of his or her heritage, and these feelings may lead to anger, shame, or self-hatred. Enmeshment/denial takes place because the individual feels guilty and disloyal for choosing one group over another. He or she then denies the differences between the racial groups and identifies with both racial groups. The individual has to resolve the guilt and anger to move beyond this level.

Level 4 is appreciation. Individuals broaden their ethnic/racial reference group by learning about all aspects of their backgrounds, even though they may choose to identify with one group more than with others. The individual learns to appreciate the other group with which he or she has chosen not to identify.

Level 5 focuses on integration. At this final level, the individual is able to integrate all aspects of his or her multiracial identity. The individual values all of her or his ethnic identities. Although Poston (1990) acknowledged that this model resembled the earlier ones (Cross, 1971), he maintained that his model was different in that it dealt with biracial experience instead of just monoracial experience.

Root (1990) proposed four potentially positive resolutions for the tensions that biracial or multiracial individuals encounter in American society:

1. **Acceptance of the identity society assigns.** The individual's family and the strong acceptance and support of a racial group (usually minority) results in the individual accepting the identity that the society assigns. For instance, if individuals have a multiethnic culture of Asian and White American, they will be inclined to identify with the group that looks most like them.

2. **Identification with both racial groups.** Depending on societal support and personal ability to maintain this identity in the face of potential resistance from others, the biracial (or multiracial) individual attempts to identify with both (or all) heritage groups.

3. **Identification with a single racial group.** The individual chooses one group, independent of social pressure, with which to identify himself or herself.

4. **Identification as a new racial group.** Regardless of the person's specific ethnic/racial background, he or she identifies most strongly with other biracial people. Root's (1990) fourth position accounted for the impact of racism on identity. She introduced the possibility of a new identity group: biracial or multiracial. She also proposed a kind of situational saliency in racial identity. An individual might self-identify in more than one way at the same time or move fluidly among identities.

More recently, Renn (2003) has asserted that the linear models proposed by Poston and Root do not work well for biracial or multiracial individuals and, therefore, ecological models should be used to explain factors contributing to multiracial identity development. Renn proposed the following five patterns of identity among multiracial college students: (1) monoracial identity;

(2) multiple monoracial identity—consciousness of more than one racial identity, but each identity has a separate place in the individual's overall self-construal; (3) multiracial identity—the individual integrates all identities as one positive self-concept; (4) extraracial identity—the individual chooses to identify with a race that is different from his or her mixed heritage; and (5) situational identity—the individual chooses one race with which to identify based on the events or circumstances.

Researchers have also investigated biracial identities involving primarily White and Black biracial individuals. Rockquemore (1999) found four racial identities:

1. Singular identity (either a Black or a White identity)

2. Border identity (exclusively biracial)

3. Protean identity (sometimes Black, sometimes White, sometimes biracial)

4. Transcendent identity (no racial identity)

Brunsma and Rockquemore (2001) conducted a study involving 177 White and Black biracials (individuals with one Black and one White parent) to measure their racial identity. They asked respondents, "Which of the following statements best describes you exclusively?"

1. I consider myself Black (or African American).

2. I sometimes consider myself Black, sometimes my other race, and sometimes biracial depending on the circumstances.

3. I consider myself biracial, but I experience the world as a Black person.

4. I consider myself exclusively as biracial (neither Black nor biracial).

5. I consider myself exclusively as my other race (not Black or biracial).

6. Race is meaningless; I do not believe in racial identity.

7. Other.

The majority of the respondents (56.2%) defined themselves as "ambiguous though most people assume I am black"; another 17% said that they "appear Black, most people assume that I am Black," and almost another 17% stated, "Ambiguous, most people do not assume I am black." Moreover, 10% said they "appear White, I could pass as White" (Brunsma & Rockquemore, 2001, p. 38).

"Passing" for Black

Khanna and Johnson (2010) have shed some light on "passing for Black" with biracial White and Black adults. Using interview data with Black/White biracial adults, the researchers examined how the adults asserted their racial identities with others. Khanna and Johnson explored the strategies biracial people use to conceal (i.e., pass), cover, and/or accent different features of their racial ancestries. They found that how their biracial respondents identify is often contextual—that is, "most identify as biracial, but in some contexts, they pass as monoracial" (Khanna & Johnson, 2010, p. 380). The authors reported that passing is not a relic of the past. "Most notably, we find a striking reverse pattern of passing today—while passing during the Jim Crow era involved passing as white, these respondents more often report passing as black today" (Khanna & Johnson, 2010, p. 380).

Khanna and Johnson (2010) reported that most biracial Black/White adults tended to suppress or reject their White ancestry altogether and claimed that they were entirely African

American. It was an issue not just about calling oneself Black, but also about aggressively changing one's behavior, looks, and tastes to appear more "Black." Elaborating on biracial adults' "reverse passing for Black," Khanna and Johnson stated,

> We find that biracial people pass as black for several reasons. Most notably, we argue because they can . . . With generations of interracial mixing between blacks and whites and the broad definition of blackness as defined by the one-drop rule . . . most Americans cannot tell the difference between biracial and black.
>
> Further, we find that biracial respondents pass as black for additional reasons—to fit in with black peers in adolescence (especially since many claim that whites reject them), to avoid a white stigmatized identity, and, in the post-civil rights era of affirmative action, to obtain advantages and opportunities sometimes available to them if they are black).
> (p. 394)

The emphasis that Khanna and Johnson (2010) placed on racial identity being contextual has also been echoed by Rockquemore and Laszloffy (2005), who developed the COBI model, which maintains that biracial individuals can develop an identity any place along a blended continuum of biracial identity. Racial identity development is not just an internal, intrapsychic event; it is deeply influenced by environmental factors. In the COBI model, singular racial identity is located on either end of the continuum. For instance, if a person's parents were African American and European American, then one pole would represent an African American identity, and the other pole would be a European or White identity. At the middle of the continuum would be an equal blended identity. Biracial individuals can place themselves anywhere along the continuum, and they can change their racial identity depending on the situation in which they find themselves. Biracial individuals can also choose to self-identify exclusively with only one of their birth parents, and such a singular identity can lead to a well-adjusted individual with high self-esteem (Rockquemore & Laszloffy, 2005). For instance, a person might be biracial (White/Asian) but only identify with the racial heritage of the White parent, or he or she might identify with being Chinese or Japanese exclusively.

Henriksen and Paladino's (2009) Multiple Heritage Identity Development model consists of six nonlinear phases termed periods identified below:

1. *Neutrality* refers to the time period of a person's unawareness of racial and ethnic differences.

2. *Acceptance* entails a person's first awareness of having an ethnic/racial heritage.

3. *Awareness* delineates a time period during which a person begins to understand experiences and facts that go along with being racially different.

4. *Experimentation* involves a person seeking connection by selecting only one part of his or her racial heritage as his or her primary identity.

5. *Transition* occurs when a person comes to understand that he or she does not fit as a member of any single racial group.

6. *Recognition* occurs when the person chooses to accept who he or she is racially.

Cultural Reflections

A professor colleague told me that she was teaching a multicultural class, and she asked an Asian American–looking student about her experiences as an Asian American.

The student responded indignantly, "I'm White. I'm not Asian American. My father is White."

Her mother was Asian. The professor apologized to the student, and the entire class became uncomfortably silent.

How would you have handled this situation? Should you ever assume that because one looks like an Asian American, that he or she identifies with being such?

Commonalities Across Multiracial Identity Development Models

Racial identity models have changed over the past few decades. The newer multiracial identity models have certain commonalities with each other.

- First, most models of multiracial identity development acknowledge the influence of the environment in some way, in contrast to early identity models that focused more on internal characteristics of the individual.

- Second, the newer models of multiracial identity development do not view different time periods or experiences in the life of the multiracial client as stages. Instead, the current models use the term *statuses* to connote that multiracial individuals may experience these statuses in different sequences.

- Third, the current models do not tend to emphasize only one outcome of successful multiracial identity development. Integration of a multiracial identity is no longer conceptualized as the only mentally healthy outcome.

- Fourth, the current models stress the significance of the environment and people within the environment who might influence a person's choice of a racial identity. For instance, a person's racial identity may be influenced by how his or her parents have chosen to resolve their own identity.

- Fifth, the newer multiracial identity models tend to place less emphasis on a deficit-based, marginalized description of the multiracial identity development process than did the earlier models.

- Sixth, most models of multiracial identity development put forth the idea that identity is socially constructed and reconstructed. The process of identity reconstruction is typically caused by an event or a series of events (racial encounters) that jar a person's sense of who he or she is racially speaking. Disequilibrium prompts the individual to enter a period that produces a reconstruction of racial identity. Clearly, there is overlap in the multiracial identity models reviewed in this section; however, each model tends to place a different emphasis on what is believed to be the most salient identity factor(s) that influence a person's identity development process.

Multiracial Individuals' Views on Race

Research has suggested that multiracial individuals have flexible understandings of race and race relations. For instance, multiracial people have been found to change their racial identities based on the social context within which they find themselves (Harris & Sims, 2002; Hitlin, Brown, & Elder, 2006; Rockquemore, Brunsma, & Delgado, 2009). In general, multiracial individuals tend to challenge the validity of race and to perceive race as a social construction more so than those of monoracial heritage (Shih et al., 2007). Multiracial individuals are put at an advantage by their views that race is a social construction because racial stereotypes lose their meaning and fail to influence their performance. Given that multiracial individuals tend to view race as a social construction, they tend to evidence greater comfort with interracial social interactions than other racial minorities (Bonam & Shih, 2009). A great strength of multiracial individuals is that they have a fluid or flexible view of race.

Cultural Reflections

Which model of multiracial identity development makes the most sense to you?

Looking at your own family, have there been interethnic/interracial marriages?

If so, how do the offspring (if any) of the mixed racial marriages view their ethnic/racial identity?

Racial Self-Identification Is Situational for Some Multiracial Individuals

According to the Pew Research Center's (2015) survey, not all adults with mixed racial background consider themselves to be "multiracial." The Pew study estimated that only about 61% of people who would be considered multiracial because of their mixed parental heritage actually see themselves as multiracial. In addition, the Pew study found that racial identity can be fluid and it may change over the course of one's lifetime or from one situation to another.

Nearly 30% of adults with a multiracial background say that they have changed the way they describe their race over the years. Some stated that they once thought of themselves as only one race, but now think of themselves as more than one race, and still others maintained just the opposite. Among those multiracial individuals who now say they are two or more races, 29% previously thought of themselves as one race, and 69% always thought of themselves as two or more races.

An early study by Harris and Sims (2002) that examined a national longitudinal study of adolescents from Grades 7 to 12 found wide differences in how mixed-race young people self-identity. Among those who classified themselves as a mixture of White/Black races, 0.6% identify as White and Black at home and at school. White and Asian background students did not differ in terms of their identities at home and at school. Among White/American Indian students, 2% identified as White/American Indian at school, and 1.5% asserted a White/American Indian identity at home. Harris and Sims (2002) concluded that "with respect to racial self-identification, there is not a single multiracial experience" (p. 618). There were also differences in how youth self-identified based on their geographical location. White/Black youth in the South were less likely to choose White as their single race.

Strengths of a Multiethnic/Multiracial Identity

Despite the fact that multiracial individuals may encounter specific kinds of challenges, there are some specific strengths and benefits that emerge from a client's multiracial heritage (Edwards & Pedrotti, 2004). For instance, multiracial individuals are inclined to possess bicultural competence, or the ability to navigate cultural contexts (Pedrotti et al., 2008). The ability to be competent in more than one culture without relinquishing one's sense of cultural identity has been portrayed as a plus in the acculturation literature.

Another strength is that multiracial individuals tend to have more positive attitudes toward other groups than their monoracial colleagues (Shih & Sanchez, 2005). The attitude of openness to other groups might prove helpful in a variety of situations. As Pedrotti and colleagues (2008) have maintained, "multiracial individuals may have the unique experience of being able to borrow from their various racial backgrounds, culling out strengths specific to these cultures and using them to support their well-being . . . Helping multiracial clients to see their own inherent strengths may assist in helping them to develop healthy identity outcomes, regardless of the identity chosen" (p. 199).

In addition, research has found that an integrated multiracial identity is a protective factor that helps individuals' psychological well-being (Jackson et al., 2012). In addition, young people who are socialized into a multiracial identity benefit in that their families typically provide them with a cultural education that is broader than that of monoracial children; and as a consequence, multiracial youth have a larger knowledge base and a more well-rounded sense of the world. They may be able to have a greater sense of intergroup tolerance, greater language ability, and a broader appreciation of minority group cultures. Multiracial individuals have been found to have more positive attitudes toward other groups in comparison to their monoracial counterparts (Jones-Smith, 2013; Miville, Koonce, Darlington, & Whitlock, 2000; Navarro, Ojeda,

Schwartz, Piña-Watson, & Luna, 2014; Paniagua, 2014). The ability to relate to different groups may benefit multiracial individuals in many situations.

Moreover, they are often able to identify multiple features of a situation in comparison with other people who see only one side of a conflict (Shih & Sanchez, 2005). Multiracial adolescents and young adults are less inclined to be affected by stereotype threat that causes poor performance on tasks. Stereotype threat does not cause poor performance on tasks for multiracial young people because they are more likely to understand that race is not biological, but rather a social construction (Shih et al., 2007).

As a result of being exposed to and internalizing different cultures, individuals can experience different ways of viewing and responding to the world. The cultural experiences of multiracial individuals make their identities more complex and enriched than those who have a monoracial identity. Their cultural experiences may broaden their cognitive and behavioral responses, and consequently, such individuals may be more creative and tolerant in their thinking.

Another specific strength that multiracial individuals may possess is that they have bicultural competence or the ability to navigate cultural contexts in two different racial and cultural worlds (Pedrotti et al., 2008). The ability to be competent in more than one culture without necessarily relinquishing one's sense of cultural identity has been highlighted as an asset by acculturation researchers. Multiracial individuals may have the unique ability to borrow from their various racial and cultural backgrounds and to use the strengths of their multiple cultures to relate to others. When counselors help multiracial clients to see their own individual and cultural strengths, they stand a better chance of developing a healthy and positive racial identity.

Intersectionality and Multiracial Identity Development

A person develops an identity based on a number of factors including their race, gender, ethnicity, sexual orientation, religion, ability status, and social class. The term intersectionality describes the multidimensionality and complexity of the human cultural experience, and it also describes the place where a person's multiple identities come together or intersect. For instance, there are multiple systems of inequality in America—gender inequality, racial inequality, sexual orientation inequality, and so forth. A Latina individual may experience gender inequality, ethnic inequality, or sexual orientation inequality. Multiracial identity development may be affected by one's ethnicity/race and one's gender. Gender and racial identities may intersect (Wijeyesinghe & Jackson, 2012).

The concept of intersectionality helps one to understand the individual realities of everyday people. For example, White males, who tend to exemplify privilege in the United States, constitute a diverse group with their own within-group variations in terms of privilege. While a number of White males live out their lives in the working class, many suffer economic exploitation and are exposed to greater occupational health risks (e.g., miners, laborers) than do White men in the higher social classes. White gay men and White men with disabilities are oftentimes denied the same privileges that White heterosexual and able-bodied men experience in American society (Wijeyesinghe & Jackson, 2012).

A similar situation exists with multiracial individuals who come from various backgrounds. A biracial woman who is African American and White, gay, and disabled may have different life experiences than a biracial woman of American Indian and White mixed heritage who has a heterosexual orientation. Oppression or discrimination based on sexual orientation or one's ability or disability status can intersect in complex ways with multiracial identifications. A clinician must recognize the different ways that a multiracial individual's various identities may intersect with each other. Clinicians must become aware of the concept of intersectionality and how this construct can impact a multiracial individual's life.

CASE VIGNETTE 19.3

A MULTIRACIAL WOMAN: THE INTERSECTION OF RACE, GENDER, SEXUAL ORIENTATION, AND CLASS

Jessica is a biracial woman (White and Chinese) who comes from a working-class family. Although she was previously married in a heterosexual relationship, she declared three years ago that she is a lesbian. Her husband (White) is seeking custody of the children based on his claim that Jessica is an unfit mother because of her lesbian lifestyle. To support herself and her two children, Jessica works two jobs, as a secretary and as a cashier at a local supermarket on the weekends. She complains about not having enough time to spend with her children because she is working two jobs. Her husband is a manager in a large retail chain and earns enough money to support Jessica and her children, but he has challenged her request for child and spousal income support in family court. Although Jessica identifies with her sexual orientation more so than her biracial heritage, she is interested in meeting with other women who have her biracial heritage. She comes to counseling because she is having difficulty coping with the family court pressures with her husband. She is considering if she should give up custody of her children because she is struggling to support them. Jessica complains that there are so many different parts of her that seem to be in conflict with each other. She needs help in sorting things out.

Multiracial Identity Development and Mental Health

When working with mixed-race clients, clinicians should take into consideration the richness of a multiple-heritage person. Pedrotti et al. (2008) caution the clinician to avoid the traditional view of a multiracial individual as being "marginalized." On the contrary, a dual heritage can be viewed as a positive, beneficial aspect of identity in biracial participants (Edwards & Pedrotti, 2004; Sanchez, Shih, & Garcia, 2009). Being biracial does not mean that one will have emotional or psychological problems. Biracial children raised in nurturing homes usually develop a cohesive sense of self (Hud-Aleem, Countryman, & Gillig, 2008). However, they may have additional issues to deal with because they are biracial. Biracial individuals experience two major identity hurdles: (1) being able to develop an identity based on how they see themselves rather than on how others view them and (2) developing a sense of belonging (Gillem, Lincoln, & English, 2007).

Early research studies suggested that biracial children encountered a high degree of academic and behavior problems presumed to be connected to identity conflicts and other challenges (Gibbs, Huang, & Associates, 1989). Other researchers have recommended that parents of bicultural children not impose their culture on their children (Santiago-Rivera, Arredondo, & Gallardo-Cooper, 2002). Children will have a number of experiences, some of which they will internalize and incorporate into their own worldview and value system. Eventually, multiracial and multicultural children may internalize multiple racial identities that are dependent on the situations in which they find themselves.

Multiracial Bill of Rights

During 1993, Maria Root wrote a "Bill of Rights for People of Mixed Heritage," which she included in her book, *The Multiracial Experience* (1996). Root's bill of rights stated, "I have the right not to justify my existence in this world, not to keep the races separate within me, not to justify my ethnic legitimacy, to identify myself differently than strangers expect me to identify, to identify myself differently than how my parents identify me, to identify myself differently than

Cultural Reflections

Have you ever counseled a person of mixed racial heritage?

Did you discuss the issue of race with the client?

How might you discuss the issue of race with a client of mixed racial heritage?

How comfortable would you feel talking about race with clients who are from a different socially constructed race than yours?

my sisters, to change my identity over my lifetime" (p. 7). She provided the following explanation for her multiracial bill of rights in her book:

Countless numbers of times I have fragmented and fractionalized myself in order to make the other more comfortable in deciphering my behavior, my words, my loyalties, my choice of friends, my appearance, my parents, and so on. And given my multiethnic history, it was hard to keep track of all the fractions, to make them add up to one whole. It took me over 30 years to realize that fragmenting myself seldom served a purpose other than to preserve the delusions this country has created around race. Reciting the fractions to the other was the ultimate act of buying into the mechanics of racism in this country. (Root, 1996, pp. 4–5)

COMPETENCIES FOR COUNSELING MULTIRACIAL INDIVIDUALS

A task force of the American Counseling Association (Kenney et al., 2015), called the Multiracial/Ethnic Counseling Concerns (MRECC), proposed a set of competencies for counseling individuals with multiracial backgrounds. The co-chairs/authors of this task force, Kelly Kenney and Mark Kenney, maintained that the term *multiple heritage* is the preferred term in describing the counseling competencies for working with individuals, as it is consistent with their thinking and decision to use Root's (2002) Ecological Framework as the theoretical underpinning for the construction of these competencies. Hence, *multiple heritage* is used synonymously with *interracial* and *multiracial* throughout these competencies. The competencies focused specifically on working with interracial couples and multiracial families. They were endorsed and adopted by the American Counseling Association's Governing Council in March 2015. This section mentions only a few of the competencies for counseling multicultural individuals. Counselors should

- Help individuals, couples, and families to understand the different cultural worldviews and interpersonal cultural communications within the family.

- Recognize that each individual, couple, or family will develop its own way of negotiating cultural differences and that this process is dynamic process.

- Understand that the specific racial or gender combination of the couple or family (Black/White, American Indian/White, Asian/Hispanic) meets with varying degrees of societal acceptance or rejection in American society.

- Understand that despite experiences with prejudice, discrimination, oppression, or differential privilege, most multiple-heritage individuals and their families have interracial, interethnic, and diverse sexual orientation and gender identity expression, and couples have the resiliency to live fully functioning, healthy lives.

- Recognize, acknowledge, and understand the intersecting identities for each partner (e.g., social class, religion/spirituality, gender identity and expression, diverse sexual orientation, race, ethnicity, culture [including level of acculturation], nationality, ability, immigration status) and the developmental tasks for each partner, as well as the formation and integration of each partner's multiple identity statuses.

- Understand how each partner's family of origin's reaction can impact a family's relationship to individual family members.

PSYCHOTHERAPY WITH MULTIETHNIC/MULTIRACIAL PEOPLE

Psychotherapy with multiethnic/multiracial children and adults can be challenging. Ethnic/racial identity development is a complex, lifelong process that begins early in childhood and continues throughout adulthood. According to Erikson (1968), identity formation uses a process of simultaneous reflection and observation that is related to how the individual contemplates others in a society perceive him or her. A person's overall identity is shaped by the person's individual characteristics, family dynamics, historical factors, and social and political context. A significant proportion of how we feel about ourselves is strongly linked to how we believe others perceive us and the feelings associated with those beliefs. If the individual receives negative messages about his or her multiracial identity, then problems may develop (Renn, 2003).

On average, most multiracial families enter into therapy for reasons other than race, but during therapy, issues related to race occur. A significant percentage report during therapy that they have experienced social disapproval or rejection at some time in their lives. As Hud-Aleem et al. (2008) have asserted,

> though most interracial families enter into treatment for reasons other than race, most
> have experienced social disapproval at some time. They are likely to possess some
> memories of unkind stares, questioning by others, family disapproval, feelings of
> uncertainty and discomfort, or outright racism. Studies have also shown that biracial
> children are at risk to develop racial identification issues, lowered self-esteem, violence,
> substance abuse, and feeling marginal in two cultures. (p. 41)

Counseling Multiracial Children

As noted in the demographic section of this chapter, multiracial children are one of the fastest-growing segments of the U.S. population, primarily because of the increasing numbers of interracial marriages (Associated Press, 2009). Since the mid-1980s, marriages between Blacks and Whites in the United States increased 400 percent, and there was a concomitant 1,000 percent increase in marriages between Whites and Asians. If one examines the dating patterns of American young people, the trend toward interracial marriage will most likely continue in the United States. The American Academy of Child and Adolescent Psychiatry's (2011) publication on multiracial children reported on a survey that revealed that 47% of White teens, 60% of Black teens, and 90% of Hispanic teens said they had dated someone of a different race. A review of the literature (American Academy of Child and Adolescent Psychiatry, 2011) cited the following facts about the emotional needs of multiracial children:

- First, recent research has revealed that multiracial children do not differ from other children in self-esteem, comfort with themselves, or number of psychiatric problems. On the contrary, they tend to be high achievers with a strong sense of self and tolerance of diversity.

- Second, racial identity may vary among members of an interracial family. Children in a multiracial family may differ in their racial identity because their identity is influenced by their individual physical features, family attachments and support, and experiences with racial groups.

- Third, to cope with racism in American society, mixed-race children may develop a public identity with their "minority" race, while maintaining a private interracial identity with family and friends.

- Fourth, some mixed-heritage children may be uncomfortable with their racial heritages, and it might be appropriate to recommend them for supportive counseling to help them clarify their feelings.

Counselor's Role in Working With Multiracial Individuals

Several theoretical approaches have been viewed as relevant for counseling multiheritage individuals, including narrative therapy, strengths-based therapy, and solution-focused therapy (Pedrotti et al., 2008). Henriksen and Trusty (2004) have advocated for the use of narrative therapy to help biracial clients explore "the cultural assumptions that influence their racial identity development" (p. 79). Sewell, Baldwin, and Moes (1998) have called for therapists to help multiheritage clients explore their levels of multiple self-awareness and the impact of different sides of themselves on their interpersonal relationships and in overall life functioning. The idea of multiple selves may be particularly relevant for the multiracial client who finds that racial identity is contextually based and situational—meaning that he or she changes depending on the different situations and the people in the environment. Edwards and Pedrotti (2004) have recommended using strengths-based approaches for working with mixed-race individuals.

Psychoeducational Approach With Multiracial Individuals

It has been recommended that helping professionals use an active psychoeducational approach to working with mixed-race individuals. During the counseling process, clients can be assisted in understanding the forces of oppression and racism. Counselors might explain the "one-drop rule" and the impact that hypodescent thinking has on their acceptance or rejection of a multiracial identity for other Americans. Helping professionals can discuss with their clients the dangers of fractionalizing their racial identity (Root, 1996). Clients can become empowered to actively construct their own racial identity.

In working with multiracial children, clinicians should

- Recognize that some children from multiracial families may be subjected to teasing, whispers, and stares when they are with their family. Parents can help their children to cope with these pressures by establishing open communication in the family about race and cultures, and by allowing curiosity about differences in skin color, hair texture, and facial features among family members.

- Help children develop coping skills to deal with questions and/or biases about their multiracial background and to deal with racism without their feeling personally assaulted.

- Understand that children may have feelings of guilt or disloyalty to a parent if they choose to adopt the racial identity and/or culture of one parent instead of both parents. Parents should recognize that children may identify with different parts of their racial heritage at different stages of development or in varied settings in order to "fit in."

- Use bibliotherapy to work with children and their families—use books, textbooks, and movies that portray multiracial individuals as positive role models, as well as books about the lives of multicultural families.

Other areas in which clinicians might help multiracial or mixed heritage clients are listed below.

Assist Clients With Knowledge About Racial Identity Formation

Hud-Aleem et al. (2008) have recommended that counselors and mental health professionals assist the family to see how racial identity formation is formed and what environmental factors can promote a healthy identity. For instance, parents might encourage their children to acknowledge and discuss their racial heritage at home and with significant others. Parents should also acknowledge that their own racial heritage is different from that of their children and that such difference may be considered a positive. A counselor might say, "Your family has a doubly rich heritage because of the differences in your mother's and father's racial backgrounds." Raising children to embrace a biracial or a mixed heritage identity says to the child that his or her various racial identities are valued and important. Moreover, clinicians should consider talking about race as a social construction rather than as a biological reality. Shih et al. (2007) found that treating race as a social construction as opposed to a biological one buffered people from stereotype threat effects.

Multiracial Children and Divorce

Clinicians need to take into consideration what happens to children and adolescents when their parents, who are of different socially constructed races, divorce. Children might feel conflict about the race of the custodial parent or vice versa, not choosing or rejecting the race of the noncustodial parent. Should, for instance, a biracial child who looks African American live with his White mother or his Black father? Understand that multiracial children in divorced families may have difficulties accepting and valuing the cultures of both parents.

Develop Supportive Interracial Relationships

Other suggestions include giving their children opportunities to develop relationships with peers from different ethnic/racial and cultural backgrounds, allowing their children to meet role models in different racial groups, and creating as a family an interracial family identity (Hud-Aleem et al., 2008). Parents might consider living in a racially diverse community that respects and accepts racial differences.

Find an Acceptable Name to Reflect One's Racial Identity

One challenge that some biracial children face is finding an acceptable name to describe themselves. Tiger Woods found that *Cablinasian* (Caucasian, Black, Indian, and Asian) was a good way to describe his mixed racial family heritage. When working with families, the counselor helps the family to choose a preferred racial term to describe the racial background of the family and of individuals within the family. Suyemoto (2004) has indicated that an increasing number of multiracial people are choosing the term *multiracial* as their ethnic identity. Hud-Aleem et al. (2008) suggest that mixed-heritage families should establish a sense of identity as an interracial family. They might develop a family coat of arms that includes cultural and racial aspects of each family member's heritage (Edwards & Pedrotti, 2004).

Develop Cultural Genograms for Multiracial/Multicultural Family

In addition, the counselor or therapist might help each parent to construct a cultural genogram that deals with identity, child-rearing practices, strengths, and adversities encountered by each ancestor. The counselor or therapist discusses the cultural genograms with the goal of helping each family member understand the different cultural stories that make up their family (Edwards & Pedrotti, 2004).

TABLE 19.2 ■ Culturally Responsive Questions Related to a Multiethnic/ Multiracial Identity

Clinicians who use a strengths-based therapy approach are able to see clients in a comprehensive way that allows them to balance both strengths and weaknesses in the person and in the environment.

Exception-finding questions help the clinician to identify times that depart from the client's presenting problem or point to a time when there were benefits of being multiethnic/ multiracial.

- Have there been times in your life when you've been successful in using your multiracial background to navigate two different cultural groups?
- Can you think of times in your life when you have been grateful that you have a multiethnic/ multiracial identity instead of a monoracial/monoethnic one?

Strengths-Based Coping Questions Related to a Multiethnic/Multiracial Identity

- Despite all the stress that might be associated with having a multiethnic/multiracial background, you have managed to come out on top. Can you tell me about the strengths that helped you to keep going?
- How have you managed to make your ethnic background an advantage in your life?
- What skills have you learned from both of your ethnic/racial backgrounds?
- What do you like most about being multiethnic?
- What would you like to do to help other people who have a multiethnic identity?

Encourage Parental Discussion of Race and Racial Experiences

Parents of mixed-race children should also discuss honestly the pressures they have encountered from the community in which they live, as well as the coping strategies they used to deal with racism, offensive remarks about the racial background of their family, and so forth (Hud-Aleem et al., 2008). They should encourage and support a multiracial life for the entire family, such that family members become familiar with the language, traditions, and customs of all family members. Table 19.2 provides culturally responsive questions a counselor can use to assess a client's multiracial identity.

CASE VIGNETTE 19.4

A MULTIRACIAL TEENAGE GIRL: SIMONE

The following is a brief case study of a young teenager of White and Latino background who was adopted by a family consisting of an African American father and a White mother. The child, who was named Simone, had gotten into difficulty in school and at home. Although she looked similar in skin color to a light-skinned Puerto Rican, Simone had spent most of her life socializing with her father's African American family. Her mother's White family lived quite a distance from where the interracial family lived.

Simone slid down in the chair opposite her therapist. She had run away from home, and her family had contacted the police. Simone stopped attending her junior high school that was predominantly African American because she feared that the police would take her home. A tip led the police to where Simone was hiding in an African American friend's home, and that day Simone was arrested and placed under the authority of Family Court, which mandated that she be placed in counseling.

The issues involving Simone were complicated. The fact that she was adopted had raised questions in her mind as soon as she learned that her mother had put her up for adoption. "Didn't my mother love me?" Simone asked with tears in her eyes. "Why did she give me away, like some sort of toy? If she could only see me now, maybe she would see that I turned out okay."

Several of the counseling sessions dealt with Simone's sense of rejection by her birth mother and father.

Multiethnic issues arose in therapy when Simone complained that she did not look like either parent. She did not look like her African American father, and she did not look like her White mother. "I hang around the Black kids because I lived just inside the school district, but sometimes I don't think that I belong with the Black kids, even though they are my friends. My brother, who's also adopted, hangs around the few White kids in our school. It's a mess. We're both in the same family, but he presents himself as White, and I hang around mostly Black kids."

The therapist paused and reflected: "Sometimes you feel that you really don't belong in your own family because you don't look like either of your parents. That's a difficult feeling—not belonging to your parents because you don't look like them."

"Yeah," Simone continued, "and that's not the worst of it. Sometimes when we are out at the mall shopping for Christmas or my birthday, people just stare at us. When I catch people just staring at us, I wonder what they are thinking. When my mom came for parents' night, I heard someone whisper that my mom couldn't be my real mom. What's a real mom?" I thought.

"I look a little like my brother, who's also adopted."

"I know that I am pretty," Simone said, half smiling, "because that's what most people say about me, but sometimes I don't like myself. Sometimes I feel as if I don't know who I really am. Am I Black, White, Puerto Rican? What am I?"

Simone began to cry softly. "It's just too much for me to handle sometimes. I think that's why my grades have been dropping and why I ran away. I want to be one thing or another."

The therapist responded, "I think you are very pretty. I can see the different traces of your ethnic mixture, and it is almost as if you're more beautiful because the two races/ethnic groups of your biological parents have been combined. Even I am mixed with more than one White group (Italian, Irish, and German), and sometimes I've had to make choices about how I am going to respond to the

different strands of my ethnic heritage. Let's set aside some time to explore the feelings you have about being biracial. We need to talk more about why you are having difficulty accepting yourself and forming a positive biracial identity."

Clinical Skills and Strategies: Children of biethnic/biracial parents need to acknowledge their ethnic heritage and help them form a sense of pride in each of their ethnic/racial identities. They should set aside time for their children to participate in cultural activities related to both parents' background. In addition, parents can help their children find an acceptable name or designation for themselves, such as "I am multiracial or biracial." Studies have found that biethnic/biracial children who are reared with a true biracial identity are happier than biracial children who grow up with a single-race identity (Nash, 1995). Having a child choose just one ethnic/racial identity may be difficult for the child. Some counseling techniques include having the child come up with his or her own desired term for a racial identity: "I want to be called biracial or multiracial, or I identify primarily with being White or African American."

Another approach would be to ask each parent to create a cultural narrative that could be used during therapy (Hud-Aleem & Countryman, 2008). Each parent might construct a cultural genogram that emphasizes identity, coping strategies, child-rearing practices, strengths, and challenges faced by each ancestor. It is also important to have the parents of biracial children discuss the difficulties they have overcome and to point out positive acceptance of them in the broad society (Hud-Aleem et al., 2008). Parents need to be taught how to promote a healthy identity formation for their biracial children.

A therapist might ask a client, "What do you know about your Asian American heritage?"

Another approach would be to use Poston's (1990), Root's (1990), or Renn's (2003) levels of multiracial identity formation. From the perspective of biracial identity formation, Simone might be at Poston's stage of "Choice of Group Categorization." Simone talked about feeling pressured to call herself some racial label. After two years of counseling, Simone was able to appreciate her biracial heritage and to deal with some of her issues related to adoption. "I'm multiethnic," Simone said. "I say multiethnic because I believe there is only one race and that's the human race. My ethnicity is not the most important thing about me anymore. There are other things about me that are more important, like who I am as a human being."

SUMMARY OF KEY POINTS

This chapter has presented a number of clinical implications for working with multiracial or mixed-heritage individuals. In general, clinicians should

1. Have awareness and knowledge about research highlighting the unique aspects of multiracial identity, and the skills to apply this research in various settings.

2. Examine their own attitudes and beliefs about multiracial individuals and interracial marriage.

3. Understand that no two multiracial clients will have the same needs and counseling issues. Racial identity is contextual. A person with a Black/White biracial background will have different needs and experiences than a person with a White/Asian identity.

4. Have an understanding of current theory and research in the area of multiracial identity.

5. Comprehend that multiracial identity is a fluid process and that this process impacts the individual, couple, or family in different ways.

6. Recognize how prejudicial attitudes, discrimination, and pressure to stay with one's membership race or ethnic group may affect developmental decisions made by interethnic/interracial families and couples, regardless of their efforts to be resilient.

7. Understand the historical significance of the "one-drop rule," miscegenation laws, societal stereotypes, and biases in the United States.

8. Learn the identity development models that have been developed for the biracial, multiracial, and multiheritage population(s) and acquire knowledge and skills for applying those models when working with multiracial individuals.

9. Be able to identify the phase of cultural identity development of each individual member of the couple or family and make this an explicit part of the counseling process as needed.

10. Help clients to come to their own determination of racial identity. It is not up to the clinician to decide what kind of racial identity a person should have. It is up to individuals to arrive at an understanding and sense of who they are ethnically/racially speaking.

11. Comprehend that monoracial identity development models do not take into consideration individuals who live within multiple racial, ethnic, or cultural identities.

12. Recognize that the racial and ethnic identities of multiracial people intersect with their other identities of sexual orientation, gender identity, class status, disability status, and other social identity groups.

13. Become familiar with the American Counseling Association's competencies related to multiculturalism, social justice, and multiracial counseling.

14. Become familiar with the general themes and concerns of multiracial people (ascribed versus internalized or chosen racial identity, physical appearance issues, etc.).

15. Recognize that multiracial individuals do not all look alike, even when they share the same ethnic and cultural makeup. A person's phenotype might influence how he or she identifies racially and is treated by others.

DISCUSSION QUESTIONS

Discussion Question Set 1

You are counseling an interracial couple, a White husband and a Chinese American wife. The couple has come to counseling because of strife that has taken place in their marriage around the issue of raising their son, who looks Asian in appearance. The father wants the child to be raised as a "typical American," while the mother wants the child to have a strong connection to Chinese culture. The wife says that raising the child without some clear instruction about his Chinese heritage would be a disservice to the child and a slap in the face to her.

• How might you go about working with this interracial family?

• Is there any particular counseling theoretical framework that you would find especially useful?

• How would you address the issue of race and cultural conflicts?

Discussion Question Set 2

Discuss how you might go about counseling the biracial child described below.

Biracial Child Who Looks White and Has a Black Mother

Child (Kevin): When my mother first came to my school's parents' night, my teacher looked totally shocked when she saw that my mother is African American. I look White, and maybe because my teacher is new to our school, she didn't realize that my mother is Black . . . I felt embarrassed and ashamed at my teacher's openly shocked stare in disbelief. Sometimes I wish that I were just like everybody else in my school and

that I don't have to deal with the stares in disbelief."

What do you believe are Kevin's critical feelings for you to address in counseling? What counseling theoretical model would you use? Would you consider using an integrative counseling framework? What would be your ultimate goal in counseling Kevin?

KEY TERMS

Biracial: a person who has only two racial groups as part of his or her heritage.

Biracial/multiracial identity development: models have been constructed to describe the different phases, periods, or statuses of mixed racial identity development in contrast to the monoracial identity development models. The models take into consideration an individual's mixed racial heritage and the impact that such a heritage has had on his or her identity.

Hypodescent: also referred to as the "one-drop rule," which is both a class and a race system that subscribes to the belief of racial purity and that assigns the person of mixed racial heritage to the least desirable racial status.

Identity: personal to each person, identity reveals how one sees and feels about himself or herself. Identity is socially

constructed and experienced in temporal and cultural contexts.

Miscegenation: the term used to describe the mixing of two or more races, especially in marriage or in dating.

Monoracial: individuals who are believed to be of just one racial heritage.

Multiracial: individuals who are of a mixed racial heritage.

One-drop rule: also known as the principle of *hypodescent*; the notion that if a person possesses even "one drop of African American blood," he or she should be regarded as Black. This so-called rule has been applied primarily to racial mixing with African Americans.

Race: a social construct often used to refer to a person's physical features (e.g., skin color, facial features, hair texture).

REFERENCES AND SUGGESTED READING

American Academy of Child and Adolescent Psychiatry. (2011, March). Multiracial children. *Facts for Families, 71*. Retrieved from http://www.aacap.org/App_Themes/AACAP/docs/facts_for_families/71_multiracial_children.pdf

Aspinall, P. J. (2009). "Mixed race," "mixed origins," or what? Generic terminology for the multiple racial/ethnic group population. *Anthropology Today, 25*, 3–8.

Associated Press. (2009, May 28). Multiracial America is fastest growing group. *NBC News*. Retrieved from http://www.nbcnews.com/id/30986649/ns/us_news-life/t/multiracial-america-fastest-growing-group/

Bailey, E. J. (2013). *The new face of America: How the emerging multiracial, multiethnic majority is changing the United States*. Santa Barbara, CA: ABC-CLIO.

Bogardus, E. S. (1947). Measurement of personal-group relations. *Sociometry, 10*(4), 306–311.

Bonam, C. M., & Shih, M. (2009). Exploring multiracial individuals' comfort with intimate interracial relationships. *Journal of Social Issues, 65*(1), 87–103.

Brackett, K. P., Marcus, A., McKenzie, N. J., Mullins, L. C., Tang, Z., & Allen, A. M. (2006). The effects of multiracial identification on students' perceptions of racism. *The Social Science Journal, 43*(3), 437–444.

Brown, U. M. (1995). Black/white interracial young adults: Quest for racial identity. *American Journal of Orthopsychiatry, 65*, 125–130.

Brunsma, D. L. (2006). Mixed messages: Doing race in the color-blind area. In D. Brunsma (Ed.), *Mixed messages: Multiracial identities in the "color-blind" era* (pp. 1–11). Boulder, CO: Lynne Rienner.

Brunsma, D. L., & Rockquemore, K. A. (2001). The new color complex: Appearances and biracial identity. *Identity: An*

International Journal of Theory and Research, *1*, 225–246. doi:10.1207/S1532706XID0103_03

Cillizza, C. (2014, April 14). Is Barack Obama "black"? A majority of Americans say no. *Washington Post*. Retrieved from https://www.washingtonpsot.com/news/the-fix/wp/2014/04/14/is0barck-obama-black/?nid&utm_term-.0108931c0159

Critical Mixed Race Studies. (2018). Welcome. Retrieved from http.//www.criticalmixedracestudies.com

Cross, W. E. (1971). Discovering the Black referent: The psychology of Black liberation. In V. J. Dixon & B. G. Foster (Eds.), *Beyond Black and White: An alternative America* (pp. 96–110). Boston, MA: Little, Brown.

Cross, W. E., & Vandiver, B. J. (2001). Nigrescence theory and measurement. In J. G. Ponterotto, J. M. Casas, L. A. Suzuki, & C. M. Alexander (Eds.), *Handbook of multicultural counseling* (pp. 192–201). Thousand Oaks, CA: Sage.

DaCosta, K. M. (2007). *Making multiracials: State, family, and market in the redrawing of the color line*. Stanford, CA: Stanford University Press.

Davis, J. E. (1991). *Who is Black? One nation's definition*. University Park: Pennsylvania State University Press.

Edwards, L. M., & Pedrotti, J. T. (2004). Utilizing the strengths of our cultures: Therapy with biracial women and girls. *Women & Therapy, 27*, 33–43.

Erikson, E. H. (1968). *Identity, youth, and crisis*. New York, NY: Norton.

Gibbs, J. T., Huang, L. N., & Associates. (1989). *Children of color: Psychological interventions with minority youth*. San Francisco, CA: Jossey-Bass.

Gillem, A. R., Cohn, L. R., & Throne, C. (2001). Black identity in biracial Black/White people: A comparison of Jacqueline who refuses to be exclusively Black and Adolphus who wishes he were. *Cultural Diversity and Ethnic Minority Psychology, 7*, 182–196.

Gillem, A. R., Lincoln, S. K., & English, K. (2007). Biracial populations. In M. G. Constantine (Ed.), *Clinical practice with people of color: A guide to becoming culturally competent* (pp. 104–124). New York, NY: Springer.

Harris, D. R., & Sims, J. J. (2002). Who is multiracial? Assessing the complexity of lived race. *American Sociological Review, 67*, 614–627.

Helms, J. E. (1984). Toward a theoretical explanation of the effects of race on counseling: A Black and White model. *The Counseling Psychologist, 12*, 153–165.

Helms, J. E. (1995). An update of Helms' White and people of color racial identity models. In J. G. Ponterotto, J. M. Casas, L. A. Suzuki, & C. M. Alexander (Eds.), *Handbook*

of multicultural counseling (pp. 181–198). Thousand Oaks, CA: Sage.

Henriksen, R. C., Jr., & Paladino, D. A. (2009). *Counseling multiple heritage individuals, couples, and families*. Alexandria, VA: American Counseling Association.

Henriksen, R. C., Jr., & Trusty, J. (2004). Understanding and assisting Black/White biracial women in their identity development. *Women & Therapy, 27*, 65–83.

Hitlin, S., Brown, J. S., & Elder, G. H. (2006). Racial self-categorization in adolescence: Multiracial development and social pathways. *Child Development, 77*, 1467–1308.

Hochschild, J. L., & Weaver, V. (2007). The skin color paradox and the American racial order. *Social Forces, 86*, 643–670.

Hud-Aleem, R. & Countryman, J. (2008) Biracial identity development and recommendations in therapy. *Psychiatry, 5*(11), 37–44.

Hud-Aleem, R., Countryman, J., & Gillig, P. M. (2008). Biracial identity development and recommendations in therapy. *Psychiatry (Edgmont), 5*(11), 37–44.

Jackson, K. F. (2010). Living the multiracial experience: Shifting racial expressions, resisting race, and seeking community. *Qualitative Social Work, 11*(1), 42–60.

Jackson, K. F., Yoo, H. C., Guevarra, R., Jr., & Harrington, B. A. (2012). Role of identity integration on the relationship between perceived racial discrimination and psychological adjustment of multiracial people. *Journal of Counseling Psychology, 59*, 240–250.

Johnston, M. P., & Nadal, K. L. (2010). Multiracial microaggressions: Exposing monoracism in everyday life and clinical practice. In D. W. Sue (Ed.), *Microaggressions and marginality: Manifestation, dynamics, and impact* (pp. 123–144). Hoboken, NJ: Wiley.

Jones, N. A., & Bullock, J. (2012a). The two or more races population: 2010. *2010 Census Briefs*. Retrieved from https://www.census.gov/prod/cen2010/briefs/c2010br-13.pdf

Jones, N. A., & Bullock, J. (2012b). Understanding who reported multiple races in the U.S. Decennial Census: Results from Census 2000 and the 2010 Census. *Family Relations, 62*(1), 5–16.

Jones, N. A., & Bullock, J. J. (2013). Understanding who reported multiple races in the U.S. decennial census: Results from census 2000 and the 2010 census. *Family Relations, 62*, 5–16.

Jones-Smith, E. (2013). *Strengths-based therapy: Connecting theory, practice, and skills*. Thousand Oaks, CA: Sage.

Kenney, K. R., Kenney, M. E., Alvarado, S. B., Baden, A. L., Brew, L., Chen-Hayes, S., . . . Singh, A. A. (2015, March). *Competencies for counseling the multiracial population: Couples, families, and individuals; and transracial adoptees and families.* Alexandria, VA: American Counseling Association.

Kerwin, C., & Ponterotto, J. G. (1995). Biracial identity development: Theory and research. In J. Ponterotto, J. M. Casas, L. A. Suzuki, & C. M. Alexander (Eds.), *Handbook of multicultural counseling* (pp. 199–217). Newbury Park, CA: Sage.

Khanna, N., & Johnson, C. (2010). Passing as Black: Racial identity work among biracial Americans. *Social Psychology Quarterly, 73*(4), 380–397. Retrieved from http://journals.sagepub.com/doi/abs/10.1177/0190272510389014

Meyers, L. (2016, November 21). Investigating identity. *Counseling Today.* Retrieved from http://ct.counseling.org/2016/11/investigating-identity

Miville, M. L. (2005). Psychological functioning and identity development of biracial people: A review of current theory and research. In R. T. Carter (Ed.), *Handbook of racial-cultural psychology and counseling* (pp. 295–319). Hoboken, NJ: Wiley.

Miville, M. L., Baysden, M. F., & So-Lloyd, G. (1999, August). *Multiracial identity development: An investigation of emerging themes.* Poster session at the annual meeting of the American Psychological Association, Toronto, Ontario, Canada.

Miville, M. L., Koonce, D., Darlington, P., & Whitlock, B. (2000). Exploring the relationship between racial/cultural identity and ego identity among African Americans and Mexican Americans. *Journal of Multicultural Counseling and Development, 28*, 208–224.

Nadal, K. L., Wong, Y., Griffin, K., Sriken, J., Vargas, V., Wideman, M., & Kolawole, A. (2011). *The Special Issue on Behavioral and Social Science, 1*(7), 36–43.

Nakashima, C. L. (1996). Voices from the moment: Approaches to multiraciality. In M. P. P. Root (Ed.), *The multiracial experience: Racial borders as the new frontier* (pp. 79–97). Thousand Oaks, CA: Sage.

Nash, R. (1995). *Everything you need to know about being a biracial teen.* New York: The Rosen Publishing group.

Navarro, R. L., Ojeda, L., Schwartz, S. J., Piña-Watson, B., & Luna, L. L. (2014). Cultural self, personal self: Links with life satisfaction among Mexican American college students. *Journal of Latina/o Psychology, 2*, 1–20.

Paniagua, F. A. (2014). *Assessing and treating culturally diverse clients: A practical guide* (4th ed.). Thousand Oaks, CA: Sage.

Parrillo, V. N., & Donoghue, C. (2005) Updating the Bogardus social distance studies: A new national survey. *Social Science Journal, 42*, 257–271.

Pedrotti, J. T., Edwards, L., & Lopez, S. J. (2008). Working with multiracial clients in therapy: Bridging theory, research, and practice. *Professional Psychology: Research and Practice, 39*(2), 192–201.

Pew Research Center. (2015). *Multiracial in America: Proud, diverse and growing in numbers.* Retrieved from http://www.pewsocialtrends.org/2015/06/11/multiracial-in-america/.

Poston, W. S. C. (1990). The biracial identity development model: A needed addition. *Journal of Counseling and Development, 67*, 152–155.

Renn, K. A. (2003). Understanding the identities of mixed-race college students through a developmental ecology lens. *Journal of College Student Development, 44*, 383–403.

Renn, K. A. (2004). *Mixed race students in college: The ecology of race, identity, and community.* Albany: SUNY Press.

Renn, K. A. (2009). Educational policy, politics, and mixed-heritage students in the United States. *Journal of Social Issues, 65*(1), 165–183.

Renn, K. A. (2012). Complex ecologies of identity, diversity, teaching, and learning. *To Improve the Academy, 31*, 261–276.

Robinson-Wood, T. (2017). *The convergence of race, ethnicity, and gender.* Thousand Oaks, CA: Sage.

Rockquemore, K. A. (1999). Between black and white: Understanding the "biracial" experience. *Race and Society, 2*, 197–212.

Rockquemore, K. A. (2002). Negotiating the color line: The gendered process of racial identity construction among black/white biracial women. *Gender and Society, 16*, 485–503.

Rockquemore, K. A., & Brunsma, D. L. (2002). *Beyond Black: Biracial identity in America.* Thousand Oaks, CA: Sage.

Rockquemore, K. A., Brunsma, D. L., & Delgado, D. J. (2009). Racing to theory or re-theorizing race? Understanding the struggle to build a multiracial identity theory. *Journal of Social Issues, 65*(1), 13–34.

Rockquemore, K. A., & Laszloffy, T. A. (2005). *Moving beyond tragedy: A multidimensional model of mixed-race identity, raising biracial children.* Lanham, MD: AltaMira Press.

Root, M. P. P. (1990). Resolving "other" status: Identity development of biracial individuals. In L. S. Brown & M. P. P. Root (Eds.), *Diversity and complexity in feminist therapy* (pp. 185– 205). New York, NY: Haworth Press.

Root, M. P. P. (1992). *Racially mixed people in America.* Newbury Park, CA: Sage.

Root, M. P. P. (1994). Mixed-race women. In L. Comas-Díaz & B. Greene (Eds.), *Women of color: Integrating ethnic and gender identities in psychotherapy* (pp. 455–478). New York, NY: Guilford Press.

Root, M. P. P. (1996). *The multicultural experience: Racial borders as the new frontier.* Thousand Oaks, CA: Sage.

Root, M. P. P. (1998). Experiences and processes affecting racial identity development: Preliminary results from the biracial sibling project. *Cultural Diversity & Ethnic Minority Psychology*, 4, (3), 237–247.

Root, M. P. P. (2002). Methodological issues in multiracial research. In G. C. Nagayama Hall & S. Okazaki (Eds.), *Asian American psychology: The science of lives in context* (pp. 171– 193). Washington, DC: American Psychological Association.

Root, M. P. P. (2003). Multiracial families and children: Implications for educational research and practice. In J. A. Banks & C. A. McGee Banks (Eds.), *Handbook of research on multicultural education* (2nd ed., pp. 110–124). San Francisco, CA: Jossey-Bass.

Root, M. P. P., & Kelley, M. (2003). *Multiracial child resource book: Living complex identities*. Seattle, WA: MAVIN Foundation.

Salahuddin, N. M., & O'Brien, K. M. (2011). Challenges and resilience in the lives of urban, multiracial adults: An instrument development study. *Journal of Counseling Psychology*, 58(4), 494–507.

Sanchez, D. T. (2010). How do forced-choice dilemmas affect multiracial people? The role of identity autonomy and public regard in depressive symptoms. *Journal of Applied Social Psychology*, 40(7), 1657–1677.

Sanchez, D. T., & Garcia, J. A. (2009). When race matters: Racially stigmatized others and perceiving race as a biological construction affect biracial people's daily well-being. *Personality and Social Psychology Bulletin*, 35(9), 1154–1164.

Sanchez, D. T., Shih, M., & Garcia, J. A. (2009). Juggling multiple racial identities: Malleable racial identification and psychological well-being. *Cultural Diversity and Ethnic Minority Psychology*, 15(3), 243–254.

Santiago-Rivera, A. L., Arredondo, P., & Gallardo-Cooper, M. (2002). *Counseling Latinos and la familia: A practical guide*. Thousand Oaks, CA: Sage.

Sewell, K. W., Baldwin, C. L., & Moes, A. J. (1998). The multiple self-awareness group. *Journal of Constructivist Psychology*, 11, 59–78.

Shih, M., Bonam, C., Sanchez, D., & Peck, C. (2007). The social construction of race: Biracial identity and vulnerability to stereotypes. *Cultural Diversity and Ethnic Minority Psychology*, 13, 125–133.

Shih, M., & Sanchez, D. T. (2005). Perspectives and research on the positive and negative implications of having multiple racial identities. *Psychological Bulletin*, 131(4), 569–591.

Smedley, A., & Smedley, B. D. (2005). Race as biology is fiction, racism as a social problem is real: Anthropological and historical perspectives on the social construction of race. *American Psychologist*, 60(1), 16–26.

Smedley, A., & Smedley, B. D. (2011). *Race in North America: Origin and evolution of a worldview*. London, UK: Taylor and Francis.

Suyemoto, K. L. (2004). Racial/ethnic identities and related attributed experiences of multiracial Japanese European Americans. *Journal of Multicultural Counseling and Development*, 32, 206–221.

Townsend, S. S. M., Markus, H. R., & Bergsieker, H. B. (2009). My choice, your categories: The denial of multiracial identities. *Journal of Social Issues*, 65(1), 185–204.

U.S. Census Bureau. (2010). *United States profile*. Retrieved from http://www.census.gov

Wijeyesinghe, C. L., & Jackson, B. W., III. (2012). *New perspectives on racial identity development: Integrating emerging framework*. New York: New York University Press.

20

SOCIAL CLASS, SOCIAL JUSTICE, INTERSECTIONALITY, AND PRIVILEGE

- *"We must become the change we want to see in the world."* —Mahatma Gandhi

- *"Injustice anywhere is a threat to justice everywhere."* —Martin Luther King Jr.

- *"It's easier to split an atom than a prejudice."* —Albert Einstein

- *"Change is the law of life and those who look only to the past or present are certain to miss the future."* —John F. Kennedy

CHAPTER OBJECTIVES

- Describe the demographics of social class within the United States.

- Discuss social class and social inequality in this country and around the world and understand how it undermines the lives of individuals.

- Understand the basic premises of social justice and learn how to implement social justice during counseling.

- Comprehend the concept of intersectionality and how social class and classism intersect with an individual's race, culture, religion, and other factors.

- Become knowledgeable about the neuroscience of social class, environments, and brain health for children and adults.

- Explain how to implement counseling interventions associated with the social class worldview model.

INTRODUCTION

This chapter examines five major issues in multicultural counseling: (1) social class, (2) social justice, (3) intersectionality, (4) neuroscience and social justice, and (5) various types of privilege. Clearly, a book could be written about each of these issues; therefore, at best, this book provides an overview of how these five areas affect the counseling of culturally diverse individuals.

Social class and social injustice have been key issues in multicultural counseling (Fouad, Gerstein, & Toporek, 2006; Ivey & Collins, 2003; Vera & Speight, 2003; Warren & Constantine, 2007). Multiculturalists are saying that the counseling profession is now entering into a new era fueled by research on social injustice (Chung & Bemak, 2012; Constantine, Hage, & Kindaichi, 2007). Chung and Bemak (2012) have maintained that social justice is the "fifth force" in counseling (the first four forces are psychoanalytic, cognitive-behavioral, existential-humanistic, and multicultural).

SOCIAL CLASS AND CULTURALLY RESPONSIVE COUNSELING

Definition of Terms: *Social Class* and *Classism*

In the United States, a person's social class is often determined by income (Smith, 2010). **Social class** refers to where an individual falls on the sociocultural continuum in a given society.

It is part of what researchers have called **social stratification theory**, which describes a hierarchical system that classifies people's economic and wealth characteristics (Smith, 2010). A social class theoretical framework often describes poverty as the lowest rung on the social class ladder because individuals in poverty lack purchasing power.

Social class is an important multicultural construct because on a material level a person's resources (e.g., income) influence his or her life chances and opportunities (Liu, 2001, 2011). A person's income provides access to wealth, privilege, and status. One's rung on the social status hierarchy ladder within any community puts one in a position to withstand life's challenges or to succumb to them (Smith, 2005, 2006; Smith, Foley, & Chaney, 2008). Moreover, social class shapes the way that we perceive ourselves and others. Social class is also an important multicultural construct because it is not as visible as one's race or gender; yet, its effects on a person's life are far reaching (Adams, 2000).

Social class is an important factor to consider in the helping professions because it is often implicated in mental health issues for people. For instance, low social class has been associated with psychological variables such as poor mental health, depression and suicide, and poor psychological services (Sing-Manoux, Adler, & Marmot, 2003; Smith, 2005, 2006; Wadsworth & Achenback, 2005). In general, the research literature has indicated that being poor puts a person at the most risk for negative physical and mental health (Adler, Epel, Castellazzo, & Ickovics, 2000).

Low social class has been found to be related to increased substance use, cardiovascular disease, and obesity (Adams, 2000). In addition, low social class has been found to be related to increased job stress because of job insecurity, authoritarian occupations, and poor work satisfaction (Gutman, McLoyd, & Tokoyawa, 2005). People who live in poor social class communities tend to live with high rates of violence, increased exposure to environmental toxins such as lead, and limited availability of supermarkets (G. Evans, 2004, 2006; Lee & Marlay, 2007; Liu, 2011).

Yet, the construct of social class is not just important for studying the mental health of the poor. Usually, the research does not compare the mental health of the rich and poor because comparing these two groups would only serve to point out the great disparities between them. Recently, however, the research on social class has begun to investigate the social class of the wealthy and within-group differences in mental health issues for them (Levine, 2006; Liu, 2011; Luthar, 2003; Luthar & Sexton, 2005; Sherman, 2006; Twenge, 2006; Twenge & Campbell, 2009). For example, some researchers have reported that among children of the wealthy, there are surprisingly high levels of anxiety, depression, and substance abuse (Levine, 2006; Luthar, 2003; Luthar & D'Avanzo, 1999).

Investigators have linked these negative mental health consequences for wealthy children with a drive for perfectionism, difficulty in receiving critical feedback, and the absence of parents and healthy role models (Levine, 2006; Liu, 2011; Luthar & Becker, 2002). Although youth from high social class backgrounds have wealth, they may grow up with a sense of entitlement, narcissism, and consumerism to produce young adults who have high aspirations but few interpersonal skills that help them to cope with life stressors (Twenge, 2006). The net result is that we read about children of the wealthy being caught buying drugs or committing unspeakable crimes, such as the Menendez brothers killing their parents so that they could purchase expensive cars and jewelry.

Classism can be defined as social class oppression (Lott & Bullock, 2007) or "prejudice and discrimination based on social class resulting from individuals from different perceived social classes" (Liu, 2001, p. 137). Usually, classism has been viewed as a unidirectional phenomenon, such that those in higher social classes are seen as those who exploit and discriminate against and suppress those in lower classes. Whereas a person's social class is usually defined by income, classism is a form of "oppression that is

Cultural Reflections

Are you ashamed or proud of your social class?

Do you ever try to "pass" as a member of a higher or a lower social class group?

If you could change your social class, would you?

What social class would you choose to have membership in?

structural, maintained by practices that constitute 'business as usual,' and played out at the individual, institutional, and cultural levels" (Adams, 2000, p. 380). Classism metes out conditions of worth and ability based on social class, and it sustains a system of beliefs and cultural attitudes that ranks individuals based on their economic status, family lineage, job status, level of education, and other symbols of wealth, including cars, clothing, and so forth (Liu, 2011; Smith, 2010). Classism supports "the systematic oppression of subordinated groups (people without endowed or acquired economic power, social influence, or privilege) by the dominant groups (those who have access to control of the necessary resources by which other people make their living)" (C. Collins & Yeskel, 2005, p. 143).

Social class, classicism, and social justice are all interconnected. As Liu (2011) has stated,

> I think it is fair to say that social class and classicism are all around us. Before we are even born, the social classes of our parents, families, and neighborhoods are already making an impact on our lives. The foods we eat, the air we breathe, and the prenatal health care we receive all influence our developing babies. Once born, we are socialized by our parents and families to relate to people through social class, and through the media, we are bombarded by images and messages about how and what to consume (Schor, 2008). . . . And over our lifetime, social class has helped to shape our choices, opportunities and relationships. To say that social class has an impact on people's lives is an understatement. But social class and classism also interact with other forms of identity and diversity such as race, gender, ability, age, and sexual orientation to form unique opportunities, barriers, and choices. (pp. 2–3)

Demographic Data on Social Class and Poverty

Social classes are conceptualized as hierarchical groupings of people that are usually based on wealth, educational attainment, occupation, income, or membership in a particular subculture or social network (Smith, 2010). Although some Americans challenge the existence of social class in this country, most recognize a three-tier model that includes the upper class, the middle class, and the lower or the working class.

Sociologists have presented a model of seven social classes in the United States. According to this model, the upper class (3% of the population) is divided into the upper-upper class (1% of the U.S. population, earning hundreds of millions to billions per year) and the lower-upper class (2%, earning millions per year). The middle class (40% of the American population) is divided into the upper-middle class (with 14% earning $76,000 or more annually) and the lower-middle class (26% that earns $46,000 to $75,000 per year). The working class (30% of the American population) earns $19,000 to $45,000 per year. Similar to the middle class, the lower class (27%) is divided into the working poor (13%, with an individual earning $9,000 to $18,000 per year) and the underclass (14% that earns under $9,000 annually). This model of social class is based largely on income and does not take into consideration noneconomic factors, such as education and occupational prestige (*Boundless Sociology*, 2016).

In general, members of the upper class are said to have substantial accumulated wealth and significant control over corporations and political institutions, and their prestige is largely inherited. The corporate elite, also part of the upper class, consists of high-salaried CEOs who may not have inherited privilege but rather have achieved their privilege as a result of their high-status careers. The upper-middle class is formed by highly educated salaried professionals whose occupations are held in high esteem, such as lawyers, engineers, and professors. The middle class is the most vaguely defined and the largest class in the United States. It includes people in the midlevel managerial positions or relatively low-status professional positions, such as high school teachers and small business owners. The working class consists of people without college degrees who perform low-level service work, such as a sales clerk or waitress. This class includes most people whose incomes fall below the poverty line. This description of social class takes into consideration a person's occupation and the prestige associated with that occupation. High-income earners are usually highly educated, have high-status occupations, and participate in powerful national social networks and professional organizations. A social network is defined as the web of an individual's social, family, and business contacts who give material and social resources and opportunities to the person.

Central to traditional mainstream U.S. culture is the "American Dream," a belief that hard work, courage, and determination will help a person to prosper and achieve success based on the conviction that American society is meritocratic and that class is achievement-based rather than inherited. In reality, however, Americans experience far less social mobility than this "dream" claims. Some researchers are questioning the possibility of achieving the American Dream for millions of Americans. For instance, that large, fast-growing group called the underclass (the class below the working poor) is becoming a permanent class for many Americans regardless of their ethnicity or race, including those who are White, African American, and American Indian, as well as some Latino individuals (Rank, 2005).

One way to ascertain if the American Dream is fulfilled is to review U.S. Census Bureau data on American income. Data on social class and poverty are provided by Proctor, Semega, and Kollar (2016). A summary of some of the findings of this report are provided in Table 20.1.

The poverty rates for Americans merit examination. In 2013, the U.S. Census Bureau said that the poverty rate was 9.6% for Whites and 27.2% for African Americans, while the rate for Latinos was 23.5%. The poverty rate for Asians was 10.5% (DeNavas-Walt & Proctor, 2014).

TABLE 20.1 ■ Income and Poverty in the United States: 2015

The median income of

White, not Hispanic, was $62,950

Black $36,898

Asian $77,166

Hispanic $45,148

Real median household income increased by 5.2% between 2014 and 2015.

The number of full-time, year-round workers increased by 2.4 million in 2015.

The official poverty rate decreased by 1.2 percentage points between 2014 and 2015.

The number of people in poverty fell by 3.5 million between 2014 and 2015. For most demographic groups, the 2015 income estimates were statistically higher than the 2014 estimates.

Income data from the 2008 SIPP panel (Survey of Income and Program Participation provides monthly data about labor force participation and income sources and amounts) suggested that between 2009 and 2012, households experienced less economic mobility than found in earlier SIPP panels.

- 57.1% of households remained in the same income quintile between 2009 and 2012, while the remaining 42.9% of households experienced either an upward or downward movement across the income distribution.

- Households with householders who had lower levels of education were more likely to remain in, or move into, a lower quintile than households whose householders had higher levels of education.

- During the four-year period from 2009 to 2012, 34.5% of the population had at least one spell of poverty lasting two or more months.

Source: Proctor, B. D., Semega, J. L., & Kollar, M. A. (2016). Income and poverty in the United States: 2015. U.S. Census Bureau, *Current Population Reports*, P60-256(RV). Washington, DC: U.S. Government Printing Office.

Children have a poverty rate of 19.9%, and this age group is the most likely to live in poverty. There is a difference in men's (13.1%) and women's (15.8%) poverty rates, with more women than men living in poverty. Among women, the highest poverty rates were seen in African American women (25.3%), American Indian women (26.8%), and Latina women (25.1%), whereas Asian American women (11.0%) and White women (10.7%) were significantly less likely to be poor (DeNavas-Walt & Proctor, 2014).

Saez and Zucman (2014) have reported that American poverty takes place in the wealthiest nation in the world. Yet, the United States has one of the world's greatest unequal income distributions. The Gini coefficient (named for economist Corrado Gini) is a statistic that measures the disparity between the lowest and the highest income levels in a nation. After adjusting for taxes, the Gini coefficient shows that of all nations on Earth, the United States is second in global inequality, while Chile is first (DeSilver, 2013). Moreover, the United States is experiencing an escalation of income inequality. In 1977, the top 0.1% of American families—a group consisting of 160,000 families—owned 7% of all U.S. wealth. By 2012, that percentage had grown to 22% of all U.S. wealth owned by 160,000 families (Saez & Zucman, 2014). Americans may be having a difficult time reconciling the American Dream to the reality of income inequality.

THE NEUROSCIENCE OF POVERTY AND SOCIAL CLASS

There are strong connections between neuroscience and cultural diversity, as well as neuroscience and poverty and social justice. Neuroscience provides the scientific framework and academic field for helping one to understand how culture affects different regions of the brain and why individuals raised in a culture different from one's own may respond differently when exposed to the same stimuli. Neuroscience provides a conceptual field for examining how social injustice, adversity, and poverty affect an individual's brain.

To understand how neuroscience can elucidate the impact of poverty on children, we have to begin with the brain. The brain is the executor of all human behavior. It lets us know when we are happy or sad, when we feel good about ourselves or depressed, and so forth. Although the human brain is small, it has been labeled one of the most complex three pounds in the universe (Noble, 2014). At birth, we are born with 100 billion neurons, and "an additional 250,000 to 500,000 new neurons are formed every minute in the first few months of an infant's life. Further, it is not just the number of neurons, but the number of synapses or connections between neurons, that is extraordinary" (Noble, 2014, p. 2). By the age of three, children have 1,000 trillion connections. Children's early experiences are critical in shaping the neural circuits in their brains. As Noble (2014) has pointed out,

> in the brain, neural circuits that are used repeatedly tend to strengthen, whereas those that are not used are dropped, or pruned. The most vigorous growth and pruning of these connections occur in the first three to four years of life, meaning that the brain is most plastic, or able to make new connections, early in childhood. (p. 2)

The critical issue is what neural connections are formed, and what are dropped or pruned, for each child. What role does family income or socioeconomic status have on a child's brain development? Researchers have found that exposure to certain experiences early in life can have either a positive or negative effect that can continue throughout one's life. For instance, Noble (2014) points out that "a moderate amount of music training during early childhood is associated with faster neural response to speech later in life, decades after the individual last picked up a musical instrument" (p. 2). A child's early experience with music "trains the brain to interact more dynamically with sound throughout a person's life" (p. 2).

Poverty Among Children in the United States

The United States has one of the highest rates of poverty among the leading industrialized countries of the world. Among all children under the age of 18 in the United States, 43% live in low-income families, and 21%—about one in five—live in a poor family. Children are over-represented among our nation's poor. Although children under 18 years of age constitute 23% of the American population, they make up 33% of all people in poverty (Jiang, Granja, & Koball, 2017). Many more children would be included in this poverty statistic, if it included those who live in families with incomes just above the poverty threshold.

The federal poverty threshold for 2015 was

- $24,036 for a family of four with two children

- $19,078 for a family of three with one child

- $16,337 for a family of two with one child

Researchers have raised the question: Is a poverty-level income sufficient to support a family? According to Jiang et al. (2017), studies have found that on average, families need an income equal to about two times the federal poverty threshold to meet their most basic needs. Families with incomes below the following levels are considered low income:

- $48,072 for a family of four with two children

- $38,156 for a family of three with one child

- $32,674 for a family of two with one child

It is worth noting that the amount of money it takes for a family to make ends meet varies from one state to another and even within many states. For instance, the cost of raising a family in New York City or San Francisco is a lot higher than raising a family in Reading, one of the poorest cities in Pennsylvania.

Infants and toddlers are the most likely to live in poverty (Dalaker, Falk, & McCarty, 2016). Children under the age of 3 are more than twice as likely as adults age 65 and older to live in poor families. Moreover, children under age 3 are more likely to live in low-income and poor families than are older children:

- 45% of children under age 3 years—5.2 million—live in low-income families.

- 23% of children under age 3 years—2.6 million—live in poor families.

The percentage of infants and toddlers in low-income families varies by ethnicity/race. Whites make up the largest proportion of all infants and toddlers living in low-income families (36%). African American, American Indian, and Hispanic children are disproportionately represented in the low-income and poor categories:

- 69% of African American infants and toddlers—1.0 million—live in low-income families.

- 64% of American Indian infants and toddlers—about 50,000—live in low-income families.

- 63% of Hispanic infants and toddlers—1.8 million—live in low-income families.

- 36% of White infants and toddlers—1.9 million—live in low-income families.

- 29% of Asian American infants and toddlers—about 0.2 million—live in low-income families.

- 40% of infants and toddlers of another race—0.3 million—live in low-income families.

Immigration and nativity (native-born Americans) have also been found to be associated with poverty. According to Jiang et al. (2017),

- 53% of infants and toddlers who have immigrant parents—1.5 million—live in low-income families.

- 43% of infants and toddlers with native-born American parents—3.7 million—live in low-income families.

Parental Education and Family Structure

Poverty involves more than just a family's income. Parents' education and family structure have been found to be related to a family's financial status. According to Jiang et al. (2017), a parent's higher educational level decreases the likelihood that a child will live in a low-income or poor family. For children who have parents with less than a high school degree, 84% live in low-income families, and 57% live in poor families. About 72% of infants and toddlers with parents who have a high school degree but no college—1.6 million—live in low-income families. Moreover, children who live with married parents are less likely to be poor or low-income compared to those who live with a single parent. Poverty is created by a number of factors, including the amount of one's yearly income, parents' education, and family structure.

Effects of Poverty on a Child's Brain

Poverty alone does not determine a child's success in later life. Factors such as parents' educational level, whether a child's parents are married and living together in the child's home, the community within which a child is raised, exposure to lead, poor nutrition, and other factors have major influences on a child's academic achievement. On the other hand, many people survive poverty without any visible, harmful effects. They become resilient and go on to lead productive and successful lives (Béné, Newsham, Davies, Ulrichs, & Godfrey-Wood, 2014; Quinlan, Berbés-Blázquez, Haider, & Peterson, 2016).

The research on neuroscience, poverty, and children's brains clarifies the potential negative effects of poverty on children's learning, achievement, and behavior (Farah, Shera, Savage, Betancourt, et al., 2006; Noble & Farah, 2013; Tomalski et al., 2013). Studies are beginning to show that poverty can shrink a child's brain from birth (Luby et al., 2013). Children from low-income families have smaller brains and lower cognitive ability (Noble, 2014; Noble & Farah, 2013; Reardon, 2015).

In one of the largest studies of its kind, Dr. Kimberly Noble from Columbia University in New York City and a number of leading neuroscientists led a research team that investigated the relationships between family income and socioeconomic factors and brain development among individuals between 3 and 20 years of age (Noble, Engelhardt, et al., 2015). The researchers imaged the brains of 1,099 children, adolescents, and young adults in several cities in the United States. They found that income was associated with brain structure area. "Among children from lower income families, small differences in income were associated with relatively large differences in surface area, whereas, among children from higher income families, similar income increments were associated with smaller differences in surface area. . . . These data imply that income relates most strongly to brain structure among the most disadvantaged children" (Noble, Engelhart, et al., 2015, p. 773).

Cultural Reflections

When you think about people living in poverty, what picture comes to mind?

In your opinion, what are the top three factors that cause poverty for Americans?

One complaint against helping individuals who are living in poverty is that they live off welfare and don't want to work.

Opponents of this position point to the fact that corporate America also receives what can be labeled as "corporate welfare" in the form of tax breaks and other forms of government assistance.

What are your thoughts about individuals receiving welfare checks and corporations receiving "corporate welfare"?

Poverty affects the brain because in many instances, it exposes a child to toxic trauma (Ingrao, 2015; Noble, Houston, Kan, Bookheimer, & Sowell, 2012). Chronic poverty can result in traumatic levels of cortisol, a stress hormone (Noble, 2014). Such trauma may include going to bed hungry because one's parents or caretakers do not have sufficient money to provide for housing, clothing, and food. When a child experiences trauma caused by poverty or physical/mental abuse, his or her brain tends to respond in two significant ways. First, the trauma engages a child's stress response syndrome. As a consequence, the child's brain releases high levels of cortisol in his or her system (Noble, 2014). Minor threats may appear to be major ones to a child whose stress response syndrome has been agitated for long periods of time (Noble & Farah, 2013). Effects of toxic stress and high levels of cortisol on children include

- Brain damage

- Poor social skills

- Low verbal skills

- Memory impairment

- Aggression

- Impulsiveness

- Overreaction to small, minor offenses

Second, the prolonged exposure to high levels of cortisol in a child's system can actually change the structure of a child's brain (Noble, Englehart, et al., 2015). For instance, prolonged high levels of cortisol can lead to

- A smaller corpus callosum, the bridge between the right and the left hemispheres of the brain that governs social interaction (Noble, 2014).

- A smaller hippocampus, the small organ that affects long-term memory and learning (Hanson, Chandra, Wolfe, & Pollack, 2011; Luby et al., 2013; Noble, Grieve, Korgaonkar, & Brickman, 2012). The hippocampus is one brain structure that is highly significant for memory development, and a number of studies have reported that socioeconomic factors are associated with hippocampal size in children and adults (Noble, Houston, Kan, and Sowell, 2011; Hanson et al., 2011). Stress experiences may operate on the hippocampus to decrease its size and hence a child's capacity for memory and learning (Luby et al., 2013). A larger hippocampus size is associated with higher educational attainment and achievement.

- An easily excitable and enlarged amygdala, the two almond-shaped groups of nuclei that identify and respond to threats (Noble & Farah, 2013).

- A decrease in the size of and the activity in the frontal lobes, the areas of the brain responsible for higher levels of thinking and the executive function (Brito & Noble, 2014; Reardon, 2015).

- It is noteworthy that socioeconomic disadvantage is associated with a decreased ability to regulate emotion (Noble, 2014). Studies have demonstrated that socioeconomic disparities increase lower-socioeconomic-status children's exposure to stress and that such exposure can operate on prefrontal cortex and limbic circuitry and produce differences in self-regulation (Noble, Houston, Kan, Bookheimer, & Sowell, 2012).

A study by Luby et al. (2013) has reported that social support and caregiving may mediate the effects of stressful life events and poverty on children's brain development. These investigators from Washington University in St. Louis, Missouri, conducted a study to investigate if living in poverty during the preschool years influenced a child's brain development related to white matter, cortical gray matter, amygdala, and hippocampus development measured at school age. Participants were those enrolled in an ongoing 10-year longitudinal study on preschool depression, and they had been selected from St. Louis preschools and day care centers. A major objective of this study was to investigate if the income-to-needs ratio experienced in early childhood impacts brain development at school age and to explore what factors mediate this effect. The researchers used magnetic resonance imaging to obtain brain volumes of children's white matter and cortical gray matter, as well as hippocampus and amygdala volumes. In a general sense, the gray matter of the brain promotes information processing, while the white matter facilitates information transfer. Both white and gray brain matter are critical for efficient operation of the neural networks responsible for a specific mental domain (Filley, 2005). When white brain matter is damaged, information processing occurs only in a slowed and inefficient manner.

The results of Luby et al.'s (2013) study showed that poverty was associated with smaller white and cortical gray matter and smaller hippocampal and amygdala volumes. However, supportive caregiving mediated the negative effects of poverty on hippocampal volume. The researchers concluded that exposure to poverty in early childhood impacts children's brain development at school age. The negative effects of poverty on the hippocampus were mediated by caregiving and stressful life events. Luby et al. recommended that early caregiving should be a focused public health target for prevention and early prevention. Through such interventions as providing better child care and nutrition and increasing families' income, it is hoped that the negative impacts of poverty can be reversed.

Small Amounts of Money Can Reverse the Negative Effects of Poverty

A critical issue in the research on neuroscience, poverty, and the brain is family income. Increasingly, there is correlational evidence that suggests that "for disadvantaged families, a $4,000 increase in family earnings in the first two years of a child's life leads to remarkable differences in that child's adult circumstances, including a 19 percent increase in adult earnings, a marked increase in hours spent in the workforce and even some evidence of improved physical health in adulthood" (Noble, 2014, p. 7).

Noble (2014) concluded her study on "Rich Man, Poor Man: Socioeconomic Adversity and Brain Development" by pointing out the connection between neuroscience findings and governmental policies toward the poor:

> Many leading social scientists and neuroscientists believe that policies that reduce family poverty would have meaningful effects on early caregiving and reductions in family stress, ultimately improving children's brain functioning and promoting the cognitive and socio-emotional development that is so critical for children to succeed and to lead healthy, productive lives. (p. 7)

Neurogenesis: Healing the Brain With Long-Term Exposure to Poverty

Can the negative effects of prolonged exposure to poverty on a child's brain be repaired? The neuroscientific principle of neurogenesis suggests that the brain on poverty can be healed and repaired. Healing the brain exposed to long-term poverty would involve exposing children to new experiences and environments that stimulate neurogenesis—the process by which new neurons are produced. To reduce stress and support new neuron growth, schools should encourage vigorous play because it reduces cortisol. Another recommendation is that schools might consider promoting meaningful new learning through language immersion and skills-building activities outside of school. School environments should be designed to reduce children's feelings of threat and to increase children's feelings of emotional safety and intellectual stimulation. Schools might also consider starting school at a later time in the morning so that young people get adequate sleep and nutrition. When children are exposed to malnutrition in early childhood, the hippocampus can lose almost 11% of its neurons—resulting in learning and memory loss in later years (Ingrao, 2015).

Neuroscience shows that poverty damages young people's brains, but that this damage can be repaired through the process of neurogenesis. Table 20.2 examines factors that strengthen and weaken the birth of new neurons in the brain.

Understanding the neuroscience of poverty might help some people become more compassionate to those living in poverty. Poverty can cause trauma and threats to individuals' well-being such that they are put at risk for psychological and neurological harm. Individuals experience harm when their life stressors exceed their ability to cope in constructive ways. Ongoing stressors over extended periods of time can overtax individuals' coping skills, self-esteem, and social support. When individuals experience ongoing trauma, the amygdala and hypothalamus activate fight, flight, or freeze responses to stressful life events. When an individual becomes traumatized, the level of activation in the amygdala and hypothalamus is sufficiently high to interfere with the normal functioning of the frontal lobe, which is responsible for making sound and rational decisions.

Poverty and Mental Health

There are serious issues with income inequality in the United States, and these issues are likely to be played out in the counseling session. How does one go about living and endorsing the American Dream when millions of people will achieve far less than their parents? Many Americans are now realizing that unless something changes in jobs, they will be working two and three low-income jobs for the rest of their lives. Among some Americans, this realization has precipitated anger and real fear.

Clearly, Americans are bringing their class-related issues to counseling. Some are filled with despair because they do not know how to go about changing their lives so that they are back on top. Some are angry with immigrants who come to this country with advanced educational

TABLE 20.2 ■ Neurogenesis: The Birth of New Neurons

Strengthened by	Weakened by
Exercise	Inactivity/sedentary lifestyle
Cognitive stimulation	Lack of cognitive stimulation
Active conversation between child and caretakers such that they intentionally introduce child to new words	Little conversation between child and caretakers; child learns few new words
Good nutrition and sleep	Poor nutrition and inadequate sleep
Books in the home/reading	Few books in the home/little reading
Low-stress environment	High-stress environment
Middle-class/working-class income	Poverty, financial stress, and instability
Positive, supportive loving parents/caretakers	Inconsistent, negative, and neglectful caregiving

TABLE 20.3 ■ Clinical Skill Development: Increasing Counselors' Social Class Awareness

Directions: Counselors in training are asked to participate in the following social class awareness exercise. They are to first write their responses to the following statements and/or questions and then discuss their responses in groups of three or five people.

1. What is your first memory of social class in your life?

2. Who was there when you discovered that you and your family were members of the _____ social class?

3. How did you feel when you found out that you were a member of the _____ social class?

4. Describe one experience that you had with classism. Did anyone direct classism behavior toward you? Did you direct classism behavior toward another individual? What did you do? If you could have a do-over, what would you change about the situation that you described?

5. Name two statements that your family used to say about social class. Name one money statement that your family members were proud of saying.

6. What did you learn about money from your family? How do you feel about money currently?

7. How do you feel about having material possessions?

8. If you could be born all over again, into what social class would you like to be born? Please explain why.

Source: © Elsie Jones-Smith

degrees, especially medical, technological, and engineering degrees, and earn far more than they will ever earn. Americans appear to be torn between closing the country's borders to keep out those who might challenge them for their jobs or who might be better educated than they are and blaming their government for allowing the income inequality to grow in this country.

Table 20.3 provides an exercise that a training program might use to help counselors and other mental health practitioners get in touch with their feelings about social class and classism. The issue of social class is a pervasive one that affects 80%–90% of Americans. Counselors have to become aware of their feelings about social class if they are to be of any help to their clients. They have to appreciate the impact of social class on individuals' lives.

Social Class, Trauma, and Counseling

Psychological approaches to counseling must take into consideration social class and classism. In counseling, social class issues might focus on social class identity issues. In what social class was the client raised? How does the individual feel about his or her past (or present) social class membership? What impact did the client's social class membership have on his or her interactions with others? How did teachers treat him or her? Did the client feel valued or not valued as a result of his or her social class membership?

Liu (2011) has maintained that some individuals experience a form of classism-based trauma from which they continue to experience the lingering effects of classism and that they may spend a good part of their lives trying to avoid future situations that may cause them classism-based trauma. Liu (2013) defines classism-based trauma as "an acute and/or chronic situation wherein the individual experiences personal threat to his/her social status and position; at the time of the experience, he or she is unable to escape from the threat or modify the situation, [and] the outcome is that the individual feels helpless and vigilant to other possible classism-based threats." The classism-based traumas are connected to significant single or repeated exposures to negative messages and reminders of one's lower class. For instance, a single classism-based trauma situation might be a remark (e.g., "you look filthy" or "you look real cheap"). Classism-based

Cultural Reflections

Have you ever experienced any form of social class discrimination?

Have you ever gone into an expensive store and felt you were mistreated or looked down on?

Have you ever felt inadequate because you lacked the proper clothing, residential address, or money? Explain.

How have you responded to social classism when it has been directed toward you or others in your presence? Explain.

traumas may also involve demeaning or disapproving looks or glances or a familial-based experience (e.g., a family being the butt of jokes within a neighborhood). Bullying and teasing are two techniques used in classism-based trauma.

Classism is a form of social exclusion and rejection, and it may adversely affect a person's life. Basically, threats to belonging to a group activate similar neural networks designed to regulate pain (Eisenberger, Lieberman, & Williams, 2003). People who experience repeated social rejection because of social classism may become highly sensitized to rejection cues, and they may protect themselves by engaging in aggressive acts and rejecting others. As DeWall, Twenge, Gitter, and Baumeister (2009) have pointed out, when individuals have been rejected by others because of their social class, they sometimes become assaultive toward others in an effort to protect themselves from rejection. Twenge (2001) and her research colleagues have reported that those who are rejected due to classism were inclined to direct their hostility not toward the rejecter but rather toward their partners. Hostility became a worldview that the rejected person used toward others in general.

Liu's Social Class Worldview Model

Liu (2011) has presented a social class worldview model that comprises the following five interrelated domains:

1. *Consciousness, Attitudes, and Salience*: Individuals' ability to articulate and comprehend the relevance and meaningfulness of social class in their environment

2. *Referent Groups*: The three groups to which an individual belongs: the group of origin, the peer/cohort group, and the group to which people aspire

3. *Property Relationships*: Materials that individuals value, use to define themselves, expect as part of their worldview, and use to exclude others

4. *Lifestyle*: The manner in which people choose to organize their time and resources within a socially classed context to remain congruent with their economic culture

5. *Behaviors*: Learned and socialized, purposeful and instrumental actions that support an individual's social class worldview

The social class worldview model is intended for individuals across classes as well as within classes. For instance, to work with an individual from the low social class, a counselor would have to understand the client's behaviors within the context of his or her life environment, reference groups, views on material features of his or her life, life habits, and so forth. The counselor would assess how the client feels about his or her own social class. Sometimes internalized classism becomes an important aspect of counseling. That is, the individual has internalized the dominant society's negative beliefs about the client's social class. When the counselor is from a different social class than the client, it is important for the counselor to consider the client's values. The counselor should focus on the client's strengths and positive attributes.

Cultural Reflections

How do you feel about working with clients from the lower social class?

Would you ever want to work with homeless families or homeless individuals?

Could you see yourself working with poor White or Black women on welfare who have two to three children and no husband?

Liu's social class worldview model is one of the few models that have counseling interventions designed to get at the issue of social class. It is one thing to talk about taking social class into consideration; it is quite another to design specific counseling interventions to deal with social class. Table 20.4

TABLE 20.4 ■ **Clinical Skill Development: Counseling Interventions Using the Social Class Worldview Model**

Step 1: Assist the client in identifying and understanding his or her economic/financial culture.

Counselor: Do you feel any pressure in keeping up with your friends and family members from an economic perspective?

- Do you feel any pressure in keeping up with the Joneses?

Identify client responses that deal with cultural, social, and economic pressures/expectations.

Client: I feel pressures to provide my family with the same upper-middle-class standards under which my wife was raised.

Step 2a: Assist the client in identifying and understanding the social class messages he or she has been given.

Counselor: What kinds of things did your parents tell you about money and about your ability to earn a living?

- What role did money play in your life when you were growing up?
- What words did others use to describe the financial situation of your family?
- What social class did you feel you and your family belonged in?
- How did you feel about what you perceived as your social class in this country?

Identify strong messages the client received about money and lifestyle in his or her family and in his or her community that are still running in the client's mind.

Client: It seemed like there was never enough money in our family. I felt our family was a failure, just poor White trash.

- Money was never an object in our family. It was always just there. If I wanted something, Dad provided it. Dad was our family's ATM machine. It was always full.

Step 2b: Help the client to identify social class behaviors and lifestyles that are affecting his or her current presenting problem.

Counselor: Tell me how you spend your typical day. Are you happy with your job and with what you are earning?

- How much money would it take for you to feel really happy about your life and about who you are as a person?
- To what extent do you believe that you are living out the money and lifestyle messages of your family and the community in which you were raised?
- If you won a million dollars in the lottery, how would that change your life and help you to resolve your current issue/challenge/problem?

Identify how money is connected to how the client feels about himself or herself, the client's values related to materialism, or how the client has changed his or her behavior to belong in a new group.

Client: Winning more money would give me material things, but it wouldn't solve the problem that brought me to therapy.

- If I had a million dollars, I would not be here sitting talking with you. I'm here talking with you because I feel trapped by not having any money, trapped in the lousy way that I dress because I don't have enough money to buy decent clothes, trapped because I don't have a home or a steady place to lay my head at night.

Step 3: Identify the client's experiences with classism and move toward developing an adaptive, realistic, and healthy expectation about himself/herself.

Step 4a: Help the client integrate his or her experiences of classism.

Counselor: Have you ever felt demeaned or insulted because of your social class or financial situation?

- Now that we have talked about some of your social class experiences, what does it all mean for your life right now?
- Is there anything that you want to do differently related to your economic situation? How can I help you to achieve that?

Identify the client's ability to understand and integrate the social class discussions into other aspects of his or her life.

Client: I understand a lot more about what I have been experiencing. I had blamed myself for all that was going wrong in my life. But it's not just me. So much is related to my social class and my financial situation. I've decided to make some changes in my life. First thing I'm going to do is to find out more about careers and businesses that will change my life situation. If I don't do something different from what I am doing now, I'm going to be in the same situation 20 years from now, and I will just pass down my limited lifestyle and income to my children, and I don't want to do that. I've decided that for first steps I'm going to go to college and get a good education with a job that makes me proud of myself. I'm tired of being poor and living hand-to-mouth.

(Continued)

TABLE 20.4 ■ (Continued)

Step 4b: Help the client to take steps and action to make changes in his or her life.

Counselor: What is the one thing you could do to change your financial situation and your lifestyle?

- How can I help you to take one small step toward changing your life?

Identify an ability the client has to change his or her life.

Client: Well, I guess you could help me by arranging for me to take a test to discover what I'm good at doing. Like I know that I've always been good in math, but I really don't want to be a teacher. I've watched those guys on Wall Street, and they seem to live an entirely different life than just us regular people on the outside looking in. I mean, I'm not sure if I have the ability, but one day I read that people who earn a degree in finance start earning as much as $100,000 when they graduate from college, and with only a bachelor's degree. Is that true?

Source: © Elsie Jones-Smith.

is adapted from Liu's (2011) social class interventions using the social class worldview model (pp. 352–353). The social class interventions are designed to explore the client's experiences of classism. As a result of using the social class worldview model, the client is helped to gain the following:

- Insight regarding his or her experiences related to classism, his or her social class worldview, and any economic pressures that he or she might be undergoing

- Counselor empathy regarding the client's classism experiences

- Help in identifying the client's life situations that are linked to classism

NEUROSCIENCE, SOCIAL CLASS, AND EMPATHY

Social class has far-reaching consequences for how people think, feel, and act (Peterson, 2010). Social class is influenced by a person's material resources, his or her perceptions of rank in terms of others, and his or her behavior toward others. Although many people assume that people in the upper classes automatically do better than those in the lower classes, recent research is beginning to find that people in the lower classes have important strengths and assets. For instance, a study by Kraus, Côté, and Keltner (2010) reported that members of the lower classes actually perform better in accurately inferring the emotions of other people. Using college students and community residents as participants, these researchers found that individuals from the lower classes were more skilled at reading the emotions of others than were those from the upper classes. Other studies have found that lower socioeconomic status is correlated with greater engagement during social activities and greater self-reported empathy (Hutton, 2016; Kraus, Piff, Rheinschmidt, & Keltner, 2012; Stellar, Manzo, Kraus, & Keltner, 2012).

Social class shapes relationship patterns for different reasons (Kraus & Callaghan, 2016). Whereas individuals from the lower class may be more motivated by the avoidance of threat and suffering in establishing relationships, upper-class individuals may be more motivated by public reputation concerns. Moreover, research has found that upper-class people spend more time socializing with friends and lower-class individuals spend more time with family and neighbors (Bianchi & Vohs, 2016).

Varnum and Kitayama (2017) have begun to investigate the neuroscience or the neural underpinnings of social class differences. Using functional magnetic resonance imaging and electroencephalogram, these researchers found that lower socioeconomic status is linked to greater attunement to others and linked to greater reactivity to threat.

Varnum, Blais, Hampton, and Brewer (2015) conducted a study to investigate if socioeconomic status was linked to differences in the strength of neural empathic responses. The researchers measured fronto-central P2 (a neural marker for empathy) responses to images of neutral faces and faces expressing pain. They found that individuals from a higher social class were linked to diminished neural empathic responses. However, those in the higher social class self-reported strong empathy, suggesting that those higher in status may not realize that they are actually lower in empathy. Varnum et al. concluded,

> our results show that people who are higher in socioeconomic status have diminished neural responses to others' pain. These findings suggest that empathy, at least some early component of it, is reduced among those who are higher in status. These findings are broadly consistent with previous research showing that SES affects the degree to which people appear to be neurally attuned to others, including research showing that higher SES is associated with weaker Mu-suppression (a putative index of activation of the mirror neuron system) in response to others' motor movements (Varnum et al. 201[6]), and less activation in the mentalizing network when presented with images of others in social situations (Muscatell et al. 2012). They are also broadly consistent with previous behavioral research on the effects of SES on empathy and altruism (e.g., Kraus et al. 2010; Piff et al. 2010; Stellar et al. 2012). (p. 8)

Being in a lower social class might not be all that negative when it comes to relating to others. In fact, the studies cited suggest that those in the lower classes are more empathic and more attuned to the feelings of others—two important criteria for becoming culturally competent counselors. Clearly, studies on the brain seem to indicate that the rich don't understand the emotions of other people. Studies suggest that individuals from the higher class might be more narcissistic than those from the lower class.

Piff (2014) conducted several studies using nationwide and university samples to test the associations between social class, entitlement, and narcissism. Studies 1a and 1b investigated the link between class and self-reported entitlement. Study 2 sought to find out if upper-class individuals scored higher on a scale of narcissistic personality in part because of increased entitlement. Study 3 examined the association between class and a narcissistic behavior—looking at oneself in the mirror. A fourth study sought to determine if inducing egalitarian values (the opposite of entitlement) would eliminate class differences in narcissism. Piff (2014) found across his studies that higher social class is associated with increased entitlement and narcissism. Those from the upper classes reported greater psychological entitlement and narcissistic tendencies, and they were more inclined to behave in a narcissistic fashion by opting to look at themselves in a mirror. Finally, Piff reported that "inducing egalitarian values in upper class participants decreased their narcissism to a level on par with their lower class peers" (p. 34).

What does the research on neuroscience and social empathy have to do with counseling the culturally diverse? The one takeaway from the research cited is that social class matters in being able to relate to others. One will need more than just a list of multicultural, cultural, and social justice competencies. The attitudes and behaviors associated with social class are deeply embedded in one's brain and can only be changed with either culturally diverse training or cultural interventions. Can the counselor from a higher class actually understand what the client from a lower class is feeling? What happens in a therapist's brain when the client is a member of an ethnic/racial minority and poor or an immigrant from another country, a different ethnic/racial minority, and poor? How can counselor training programs deal with the influence of social class on counseling?

THE SOCIAL JUSTICE MOVEMENT IN COUNSELING

Social class and class-based trauma are related to the **social justice movement in counseling** in the United States. Although the social justice movement in America pervades several professions, counseling psychology has been at the forefront of this movement (Baluch, Pieterse, & Bolden, 2004). A social justice approach to counseling is founded on the acknowledgment of broad, systemic societal inequities and oppression within American society and within other global societies as well (Arredondo & Perez, 2003). There is no one single accepted definition of social justice in counseling. According to L. Davis (1996), **social justice** is a societal-level commitment to equity for all groups of people: "Social justice is a . . . goal of democratic societies and includes equitable access to societal institutions, resources, opportunities, rights, goods, [and] services" (p. 1). The American Counseling Association supports the concept of social justice. The 2014 ACA Code of Ethics, Standard E.5.c ("Historical and Social Prejudices in the Diagnosis of Pathology"), asks counselors to "recognize historical and social prejudices in the misdiagnosis and pathologizing of certain individuals and groups and the role of mental health in perpetuating these prejudices through diagnosis and treatment" (p. 11).

Social justice in counseling is a multifaceted approach that encourages counselors to strive to promote human development and the common good by addressing changes related to both individual and distributive justice (Ratts & Pedersen, 2014). According to Crethar and Ratts (2008), counselors are asked to direct their attention to four critical principles that guide their work: equity, access, participation, and harmony. *Equity* is the fair distribution of resources, rights, and responsibilities for all people within a given society. *Access* involves the ability of all people to avail themselves of the resources, services, power, information, and understanding crucial to realizing a standard of living that allows for self-determination and human development. *Participation* involves the right of every person in a society to partake in and be consulted on decisions that influence their lives and those of others within the society. *Harmony* refers to the need to get along among different groups within a society.

A major driving force behind the social justice movement is the idea that social illnesses are caused by various forms of oppression. The social justice movement represents a paradigm shift regarding client conceptualization, from counselors identifying individual pathology and/or developmental issues to focusing on social illness as a major source of client problems and issues (Ratts & Pedersen, 2014; Ratts, Singh, Nassar-McMillan, Butler, & McCullough, 2015). As Angela Coker, associate professor of counseling and family therapy at the University of Missouri–St. Louis, has stated,

> social justice counseling is a natural progression and evolution of multicultural counseling. In social justice counseling, we are no longer questioning whether racism, sexism or other isms exist. That was the dialogue of 20 years ago. Social justice counseling discourse pushes the envelope even further. It calls for counselors and other mental health professionals to consider not only issues of diversity and culturally appropriate counseling strategies, but it requires counselors to tap into their own social consciousness regarding where a society and all its institutional structures—education, business, health arenas—have failed to provide equal opportunities and access to all its citizens. Second, social justice counseling requires counselors to take action and actively work to fight against oppression and discrimination within a society. The social justice counselor in many ways sees society as having the pathology, not the client. (Shallcross, 2013, p. 4)

Critics of the social justice approach have indicated that the social justice movement is inappropriate for psychology. According to critics, the primary focus of social justice advocates is on social illness within the broader context of society. Social advocacy counseling goes beyond the traditional boundaries of individual and group counseling. Counselors are held responsible for taking action against social injustices (Ratts & Pedersen, 2014).

The professional associations have taken steps to make social justice a key component of culturally responsive counseling. For instance, the Multicultural Counseling Competencies

Revisions Committee of the American Counseling Association (Ratts et al., 2015) has developed a document, *Multicultural and Social Justice Counseling Competencies*, that integrates social justice competencies with the original multicultural competencies. The Multicultural and Social Justice Counseling Competencies were endorsed on June 29, 2015, by the Association for Multicultural Counseling and Development and on July 20, 2015, by the American Counseling Association Governing Counsel.

Ratts et al. (2015) constructed a conceptual framework that includes (1) quadrants (privilege and oppressed statuses), (2) domains (counselor self-awareness, client worldview, counseling relationships, and counseling and advocacy interventions), and (3) competencies (attitudes and beliefs, knowledge, skills, and action). Quadrants are used to focus on the intersection of cultural identities and the dynamics of power, privilege, and oppression that influence the counseling relationship. The quadrant category identifies four major therapeutic relationships between clinician and client that focus on issues related to power and privilege: (1) a privileged clinician working with a marginalized or oppressed client, (2) a privileged clinician working with a privileged client, (3) a marginalized or oppressed clinician working with a privileged client, and (4) an oppressed clinician working with an oppressed client (Ratts et al., 2015). Developmental domains represent the different factors that promote multicultural and social justice competence: (1) counselor self-awareness, (2) client worldview, (3) counseling relationship, and (4) counseling and advocacy interventions.

> ### Cultural Reflections
>
> *What is your response to the social justice movement?*
>
> *Do you believe that counselors and therapists should be involved in advocating social justice for their clients?*
>
> *Why or why not?*

Social Justice and Oppression

Social injustice or inequality is produced by different cultural groups' unequal access to a nation's resources. There are many ways in which social injustice can be manifested, including racism, sexism, homophobia, and classism. **Oppression** takes place when members of one group are exploited and subordinated by members of the dominant group.

The importance of social injustice in this chapter is that sometimes people internalize the views that oppressors force upon them. Social justice is designed to (1) improve conditions or equal access to opportunities in a society; (2) reduce disparities in education, health care, and employment for all individuals in comparison to the dominant group within a society; (3) encourage mental health professionals to take into account social injustice factors when counseling individuals; and (4) broaden the role of counselors to include social advocate and consultant. One consequence of social injustice is that the dominant group is given unearned privileges that the oppressed perceive and resent deeply. The privileges of the dominant group are based on such biological factors as the color of one's skin or one's sex, which causes anger, rage, and a sense of injustice. Unearned privileges in any society cause internal dissension and revolt.

INTERSECTIONALITY, SOCIAL CLASS, AND SOCIAL JUSTICE

Intersectionality is the study of the interactions of multiple systems of oppression or discrimination for members of ethnic minority groups and other members of disenfranchised groups. It is a concept that recognizes that we are all simultaneously members of many groups and that each one of us may have complex identities. For instance, men and women may experience racism differently (P. Collins, 2015; Crenshaw, 1989, 1991). Intersectionality seeks to investigate how gender, race, class, ability, sexual orientation, and other axes of a person's identity interact on multiple and sometimes simultaneous levels. The doctrine of intersectionality maintains that the unidimensional conceptualizations of oppression within a society, such as racism, sexism, ableism, and homophobia, do not act unilaterally or independently of each other, but rather these forms of oppression interact with each other.

Cultural Reflections

How do your various identities—racial, gender, sexual orientation, professional, and relationship-oriented (e.g., mother, father)—intersect? Which identity is the most problem-related for you?

Which identity is the easiest one for you to navigate?

When you work with individuals who are culturally diverse from you, which identity do you respond to first—racial identity, gender identity, sexual orientation identity, or cultural identity?

Kimberle Crenshaw, an African American woman, created the term *intersectionality* to challenge the prevailing view that women were a homogeneous category sharing the same life experiences (Crenshaw, 1989, 1991). Women-of-color feminists maintained that White middle-class women did not represent the total women's movement (A. Davis, 1983). They argued that the forms of oppression experienced by White middle-class women were different from those experienced by poor, African American, or disabled women. An African American lesbian might encounter racial discrimination, gender discrimination, and sexual orientation discrimination. Crenshaw investigated the ways in which gender, race, and class interacted to "determine the female destiny" (P. Collins, 2015; Crenshaw, 1989, 1991; Hooks, 2014).

Through the intersectional approach, social class research is abandoning the unilateral, single-axis approach of only considering a person's ethnicity, race, or sexual orientation. It is recognizing, instead, that each cultural group has multiple characteristics that counselors must take into consideration when counseling its members. There may be social class differences within an ethnic or cultural group, gender differences, and so forth.

Social Class Identity Development and Intersectionality

One's social class interacts with other dimensions of a person's identity (race, sexual orientation, and ability/disability). Individuals from the middle and upper classes are often viewed as smarter and more capable than those who come from working-class and poverty backgrounds. Those in the middle and upper classes often have the power to define for others what is "normal" or "acceptable." Jackson and Hardiman (1994) have proposed a generic model of social class identity development for class-dominant-group members that has the following stages:

- *No social consciousness*—the person is oblivious to differences due to social class and sees the privilege of middle or higher classes as normal or the way things should be.

- *Acceptance*—the person consciously or unconsciously accepts the dominant group's views of people in the lower social classes, and acts on classist stereotypes of them, all the while denying that societal culture is oppressive to them.

- *Resistance*—the person begins to question the dominant group's views that are inconsistent with his or her experiences with people from the lower social classes. Individuals begin to notice the existence of privileges for those in the middle and upper classes, and they may even recognize their role in oppression of members of the lower classes.

- *Redefinition*—the person begins to reexamine his or her own identity as privileged and to accept some responsibility for eliminating classism. The person may even feel good about being an anti-classist.

- *Internalization*—the person reaches an understanding of social power and privilege associated with being in the middle and upper classes, and he or she may even become motivated to advocate for social justice for those in the lower social classes.

The Counseling Profession and Class Elitism

Counselor training has often been described as having a White, middle-class bias. This bias is reflected by an emphasis on meritocracy, Standard English, the Protestant work ethnic, and 50-minute therapy sessions (Liu, Corkery, & Thome, 2010). Researchers have reported that low-income clients may be alienated from counseling and are therefore inclined to terminate counseling prematurely (Liu, Corkery, & Thorne, 2010). A client from a lower social class might sense that a counselor rejects him because his grammar is nonstandard or because his job is low status—working as a cleaner or a garbage collector. Negative stereotypes of low-income people as being lazy and less intelligent than those from the middle class may sit silently in the counseling room. No one wants to go to a counselor who devalues him or her because of social class membership.

INTERNALIZED OPPRESSION: SOCIAL CLASS AND ETHNICITY/RACE

In general, clients do not seek therapy to deal with racism, sexism, or social injustice, even though these factors may impact the problems that brought them to therapy. For instance, a client who is depressed because of racism or sexism on his or her job may seek counseling for depression. Depression is a manifestation of the social injustice. One of the author's clients said, "It's the little things that happen to you on a daily basis. It's like having little pins stuck into you daily, and you can't really say anything because someone will claim that you're too sensitive, overreacting, or whatever self-serving adjective they can find. Sometimes I find that even thinking about work brings on a headache. I can't wait until 5 o'clock comes. I can't quit because I need the money."

Internalized oppression takes place when the individual believes the negative view of the dominant group—that is, when the individual uncritically accepts the negative stereotypes that the dominant group has of one's culture, ethnicity, religion, and so forth (Frye, 2003). Individuals who are members of ethnic/racial minority groups, gender minority groups, and other minority groups may develop self-hatred and participate in deprecating behavior. Women may believe that they are inferior to men, that they need a man to survive, or that they are nothing without a man.

Internalized homophobia takes place when gays, lesbians, or transgender people internalize the negative messages given to them by heterosexual people. Sometimes members of minority groups may perpetuate negative stereotypes on members of their own group, as in the case of an arrogant female supervisor who makes it difficult for other women to succeed on the job, or an African American who uses racial epithets to refer to other members of his or her own ethnic group. Internalized oppression results in self-hatred that is felt toward oneself and also toward members of one's own oppressed group (Young, 2000).

The problem is that some people may never recognize that they have internalized negative views of themselves foisted on them by the dominant-status group. Sometimes these oppressed individuals have negative self-esteem that impacts much of what they do in the world. They may not try to accomplish very much because they have internalized the general society's negative expectations of them (Frye, 2003).

Not all people who are oppressed turn society's negative stereotypes inward toward the self. On the contrary, some individuals remain proud of their ethnocultural heritage or succeed in assuming prominent places in the larger society because of their self-respect or skills. Counselors should not assume that because a person is a member of an oppressed group he or she is suffering from the results of internal oppression. When counselors assume without getting to know a client that he or she is suffering from internalized oppression, the client might feel that the counselor is being condescending or insulting.

There are two ways in which internalized oppression my manifest itself:

- ***Internalized oppression functions on an individual basis.*** An individual believes the negative ethnocultural stereotypes society has tried to impose on him or her. As a result, the client refuses to try to achieve academically and acts in ways that reinforce the stereotypes that are self-defeating at the very least.

- *Internalized oppression takes place among members of the same cultural group*. People in the same ethnocultural group deprecate each other with the ethnic slurs of the broader society. Instead of focusing on the actions of the oppressor, members of the same ethnocultural group turn the oppression on one another. One consequence is that people from the same ethnocultural group criticize, fight with, mistrust, or isolate themselves from one another.

Members of the minority and majority groups all share a responsibility to end oppression. People need to learn that their personal worth cannot be based on society's current or past prejudice or ethnocentrism.

Microaggressions and Social Class

According to Sue (2010), microaggressions are "brief and commonplace daily verbal or behavioral indignities that may be intentional or unintentional comments that communicate hostile, derogatory, or negative racial slights and insults that potentially have a negative influence on a person" (p. 5). An example of a microaggression takes place when a person from the dominant culture asks an Asian or Latino person, "Where were you born?" or comments with surprise, "You speak good English." The subtle dig or message is "You are not American" or "It is unusual for an Asian American or a Latino American to speak as well as you speak." Another example of a possible microaggression takes place when a prospective employer makes it clear to an African American candidate that although the company has an affirmative action policy, "We are looking for qualified people." The underlying and unspoken message is that the African American candidate may not be qualified. In contrast, the employer rarely talks about "being qualified" to potential White candidates. The assumption is that to be White is to be qualified. No one has to render you qualified, as is sometimes the case for African Americans, American Indians, and Latinos.

Although microaggressions are often racially based, they may also be oriented toward a person's social class. Class-based microaggressions may refer to the fact that people in one social class can afford a Gucci or a Coach bag while others can't. One female college student told me that she felt inferior in her class at Brown University, where White rich girls would make a show of carrying Gucci bags as a status symbol. Another class-based microaggression might be to compliment someone on a piece of jewelry and ask, "Is it a family heirloom?" When the person replies, "No, my family is poor. We don't have heirlooms. I grew up in public housing," the person who asked the question interrupts to change the subject or quickly finds an excuse to walk away, sending the message that a lower-class upbringing is not to be discussed.

Social class microaggressions emphasize the way that people distinguish between social class groups. Classism may take place because a child might not have the right kind of clothes to wear to school, or an adult might not live in the right type of neighborhood. Hare (2009) has reported a study that found that when respondents used Myspace, they were regarded as "ghetto" compared to those who used Facebook. Myspace has been associated with the less affluent social class groups and has the reputation of being big, gaudy, and commercial. In contrast, Facebook was viewed as primarily for the college crowd until late 2006. It has since become popular across a wide spectrum of American social categories.

Neuroscience and Social Justice

Researchers are just beginning to investigate the neuroscience implications of social justice and its relationship to the human brain. Neuroscience has identified a network of brain regions involved in evaluations of fairness, justice, and moral judgment. Lesion and functional neuroimaging studies have reported a core valuation network in which stimulus-outcome and response-outcome representations are sustained by computations in the orbitofrontal cortex, which is located in the frontal lobes of the brain and is involved in the cognitive processing of decision making. "These signals are updated by the amygdala, striatum, anterior cingulate cortex (ACC) and anterior insula (INS) and integrated primarily in the ventral medial prefrontal cortex (mPFC). In social contexts the mPFC and the posterior superior temporal sulcus extending into the parietal lobes (pSTS/TPJ) support the representation of others' goals and beliefs. Finally, the dorsolateral prefrontal cortex (dlPFC) plays a significant role in response selection" (Decety & Yoder, 2017, p. 3).

Social neuroscience, and neuroscience in general, offers the possibility of providing a new paradigm for considering social justice issues. We need to learn more about how the brain processes social justice and injustice and about how neural pathways related to social justice and injustice are created and maintained in the brain. Can we develop educational experiences that would encourage young people and children to evidence a greater propensity toward social justice rather than social injustice? If so, what might those experiences be? To what extent do different cultures influence individuals' feelings about social justice and injustice? Do cultures that are individualistically oriented endorse or support different views about social justice than cultures that have a collectivist orientation?

Neuroscience, Counselor Training, and Social Justice

In training counselors, we need to be aware of the absolute complexity of social justice. It might be counterproductive to ask counselors to put on "their social justice hat" and become a social justice advocate. A better alternative is to help counselors become aware of their social justice feelings and the factors in their lives that have created the neural pathways related to those feelings. Exhortations that counselors should become social justice advocates may lead to guilt and conflicting feelings about those who may be culturally diverse from us. To change a counselor's feelings about social justice, we must first understand that each one of us has deep-seated social justice neural pathways. Some parts of our social justice neural pathways were created by our parents, by our life experiences, by our social class membership, and by our culture and religious backgrounds.

PRIVILEGE, RACE, AND SOCIAL CLASS

Privilege is "commonly defined as unearned access to beneficial resources available to some people, but usually at the expense of others" (L. Collins & Barnes, 2014, p. 63). A number of researchers have posited that privilege results from the interactions between three forms of relational power dynamics to decide (1) who is taken seriously, (2) who receives attention, and (3) who is accountable to whom and for what (Johnson, 2006). Every society in the world sets up a system of privilege for some and fewer opportunities and privileges for others (Adams, 2000; Schwarzbaum & Thomas, 2008). There are many different forms of privilege in each society. For some, the system of privilege is based on a **caste system**; for others, the system is based on concepts of socially constructed race; and for still others, the system involves gender privilege. Racial privilege is the system of benefits and opportunities that one gains simply based on one's ethnicity/race. Gender privilege takes place when women are systematically denied equal economic, social, and job opportunities as males (N. Evans, Forney, Guido, Patton, & Renn, 2010). Heterosexual privilege occurs when heterosexuality is viewed as normal and other sexual orientations are perceived as wrong or deviant. **Social class privilege** is based on stratifying the workplace and economic and social benefits in a society. Research shows that there is a relationship between oppression and privilege and dominance over people. They are often twin forces in that oppression accompanies privilege.

White Privilege and Dominant Group Identities

Social justice advocates have used Peggy McIntosh's (1989) original essay on White privilege as the basis for their arguments that counseling should be about obtaining social justice for clients. White privilege is the "system of benefits, advantages, and opportunities experienced by white persons" purely based on race/skin color (Donnelly, Cook, Van Ausdale, & Foley, 2005, p. 6).

Building on McIntosh's work, Bond (2007) has explained how norms and values from the dominant culture become institutionalized within organizational policies and practices. These policies allow White males to have access to skill sets that permit them to receive benefits such that they thrive to the exclusion of socially marginalized groups, including women and persons of color. White males receive benefits based on the concept of homophily (i.e., "love of the same"). **Homophily** refers to the tendency of people to associate and bond with people who are similar to them. More than 100 studies have reported homophily in some form or another, and they have found that similarity in race, gender, class, and other areas breeds connection. People in homophilic relationships share common characteristics that make communication and relationship formation easier (McPherson, Smith-Lovin, & Cook, 2001).

Studies have suggested that many members of privileged groups "receive access to more organizational advantages and benefits without understanding how their privileged status affects their points of entry, positions, and tenure, or how it may accentuate their positive contributions and de-emphasize their mistakes and misdeeds" (L. Collins & Barnes, 2014, p. 62). White privilege can influence one's legitimacy and visibility in the organization as well as in the area of promotions and higher wages. To ensure credibility, sometimes organizations hire Whites for positions that require contact with board members and policymakers with whom they share common characteristics such as race, gender, and social standing.

L. Collins and Barnes (2014) point out that revealing discrimination in a society does not necessarily reveal White privilege. "In fact, limiting studies on race, class, and gender to focus on discrimination often renders privilege invisible. Critical community practitioners, those anchored in values of social justice . . . must become intentional about revealing and dismantling oppressive systems" (L. Collins & Barnes, 2014, p. 76). They must become aware of how they benefit from homophily and White privilege.

Consequences of White Privilege

White privilege has significant negative consequences for African American children. Research by Steele (1997, 1999); Aronson, Fried, and Good (2002); and Aronson and Inzlicht (2004) has revealed that both African Americans and girls do poorly on standardized academic tests and other academic performances because negative stereotypes raise within their minds self-inhibiting doubts and high-pressure anxieties, thereby resulting in a phenomenon termed *stereotype threat*. Studies have found that even passing reminders that someone belongs to one group or another, such as group stereotypes as inferior in academics, can lower students' academic performance. According to Steele, Aronson et al., and Aronson and Inzlicht, negative group stereotypes can impair how African American students evaluate themselves, which in turn lowers their academic identity and intellectual performance.

Steele and Aronson (1995) administered to African American and White college students a half-hour test using difficult items from the verbal GRE. For the stereotype-threat condition, they told students that the test diagnosed intellectual ability, thus potentially eliciting the stereotype that Blacks are less intelligent than Whites. For the no-stereotype-threat condition, the researchers informed students that the test was a problem-solving lab task that had nothing about ability, presumably making stereotypes irrelevant. The results were astonishing. In the stereotype-threat condition, African Americans who were matched with Whites in their group by SAT scores performed less well than Whites. However, in the no-stereotype-threat condition in which the exact same test was described as a lab task, the performance of African American and White students was the same. Subsequent experiments that minimized the negative stereotype threat for standardized tests also resulted in equal performance by African Americans and Whites. One study reported that even when students merely recorded their race (presumably making the stereotype salient) and were not told the test was diagnostic of their ability, Black students performed less well than Whites.

The same construct of stereotype threat was used in a study with women. Spencer, Steele, and Quin (1999) found that simply telling women that a math test does not show gender differences improved their test performance. These same researchers gave a math test to men and women, telling half the women that the test had shown gender differences, and informing the rest of the women that it had found no gender differences. When the test administrators informed the women participants that the tests showed no gender differences, the women performed equal to men. Those women who were told that the math test had revealed gender differences performed less well than the males. Even though these researchers concluded that the test-score gaps could not be totally attributed to stereotype threat, it was clear that stereotype threat did lower the scores of African American and women students. The effects of negative stereotypes and internalized oppression in terms of African Americans and women are important. Internalized oppression is not the fault of the people whom it influences. No person should be blamed or blame themselves for having been affected by ethnic/racial discrimination, negative stereotypes, and stereotype threat. Members of the majority in a society have a responsibility to help others deal with stereotype threat.

White Privilege: The Other Side of the Coin: White Empathy, White Guilt

Not all members of a dominant group in a society respond positively to unearned privilege. Many White Americans advocate passionately for justice for African Americans and other oppressed groups, sometimes even putting themselves at serious risk. Consider the numerous young White students who joined in political demonstrations with African American students during the civil rights movements of the 1960s and during the recent and current demonstrations during "Black Lives Matter" events. This author personally observed on television hundreds of White people who marched with those proclaiming that Black Lives Matter. President Obama, the first African American president of the United States, could not have been elected without the strong support of millions of White Americans. These White Americans seem to be sending a message that White privilege does exist, but by my vote, by my marching, I vow to create social and political justice for all. The critical issue in counseling is to find and ask for support from White American people. Not all White people are out to harm or to disenfranchise members of various ethnic/racial groups. Members of a dominant group, while enjoying the privileges associated with their social status or social standing in a society, may work to achieve those same benefits for members of an oppressed group. For instance, there are men who are active in organizations dealing with equality between women and men in job opportunities and in income. Those who are not gay have also fought for gay rights (Frye, 2003).

A number of researchers have begun to conduct studies on the effects of White privilege on Whites (Spanierman & Heppner, 2004). The underlying premise is that racism affects not only the victims but also the perpetrators of racism, as well as the "silent" and "blind" White majority. The question raised in such studies is: What are the costs of racism to the White majority in the United States? (Spanierman & Heppner, 2004; Sifford, Ng, & Wang, 2009). In the field of counseling psychology, researchers have investigated the psychological costs of racism to Whites under the framework of the Psychological Costs of Racism to Whites (PCRW) framework. This framework focuses on three distinct affective costs of racism on Whites. Researchers have found that some Whites have (1) an empathic reaction toward racism (i.e., White empathy), some have (2) guilt feelings about racism (i.e., White guilt), and

Cultural Reflections

What are the costs of racism, if any, to a society, including the United States?

Do you believe that governments can legislate a nonracist society?

What are your thoughts about research on White empathy and White guilt?

some have (3) cultural mistrust toward people of color (i.e., White fear) (McConnell & Todd, 2015; Spanierman, Todd, & Anderson, 2009).

The PCRW framework maintains that although the costs of racism are not the same for all people of color in a racist society, systems of oppression negatively impact all people, including members of privileged groups. Studies have reported that "greater White guilt and White empathy were associated with greater racial awareness, cultural sensitivity, openness to diversity and multicultural counseling, whereas greater White fear was associated with fewer interracial friends, lower openness to diversity, and lower cultural sensitivity" (McConnell & Todd, 2015, p. 1136).

Research has used the cluster analysis approach to group students into different clusters (i.e., types) based on distinct patterns of White empathy, guilt, and fear (Spanierman, Poteat, Beer, & Armstrong, 2006; Spanierman et al., 2009). In one group labeled *Antiracist*, students reported high levels of White empathy and guilt, but low levels of White *fear*. Another group labeled *Fearful Guilt* was composed of students who reported high White guilt and fear and moderate levels of White empathy. Spanierman et al. (2009) concluded that these cluster types provide a nuanced way of describing the emotional or affective costs of racism to Whites.

McConnell and Todd (2015) extended the research on the psychosocial costs of racism to Whites using the cluster-type approach. They also studied differences in religious beliefs (i.e., religious liberalism and agreement with social justice) across social types. They found that students in the Antiracist cluster type reported the highest levels of White privilege attitudes conducive to working for racial justice (i.e., willingness to confront White privilege, White privilege awareness and White privilege remorse, and higher levels of religious liberalism). McConnell and Todd concluded that their findings on the psychosocial costs of racism to Whites had broad implications for training psychologists:

> First, the intersection of PCRW cluster types and attitudes toward White privilege adds to models for training counseling psychologists in multicultural competencies (see Spanierman, Poteat, Wang, & Oh, 2008, for a review). Second, counseling psychologists can use these frameworks to guide interventions and trainings with students. For example, if a student experiences empathy about racism but lacks accountability, educators may focus on maintaining empathy while exploring guilt and awareness of White privilege. If a student seems focused on personal costs of confronting White privilege and self-oriented distress, it may be helpful to focus on building accountable empathy and decreasing fear. (p. 1157)

Social Class Privilege

Social class privilege is often taken for granted, much in the same way that ethnic, racial, or skin color privilege may not be readily visible to a person who holds that privilege. For instance, if one is a member of the middle class or the upper class, the privileges one has may be largely unspoken and invisible.

SUMMARY OF MULTIDIMENSIONAL PRIVILEGES IN A SOCIETY

Every society establishes privileges to be doled out for some based on certain characteristics and withheld from others because they lack the right skin color, gender identity, social class, religion, or ability. Table 20.5 summarizes key privileges found in many societies. What privileges did you experience when growing up? What privileges do you enjoy right now?

TABLE 20.5 ■ Multidimensional Privileges	
White Privilege or Ethnic Privilege	Benefits, advantages, and opportunities are given to White persons simply on the basis of their skin color.
Ethnocultural Privilege	These privileges are provided to members of an ethnocultural group, which may be political, such as part of the ruling class.
Social Class Privilege	These are social and economic privileges associated with growing up middle class or upper class, having parents with a college education, owning a computer, not having to worry about heating and electric bills, etc.
Gender Privilege	These are privileges associated with being a male as opposed to being a female.
Heterosexual Privilege	Heterosexuality is viewed as normal, and other sexual orientations are viewed as abnormal, deviant, or wrong.
Ability Privilege	People with disabilities are not equal to those with no ability challenges; society discounts the ability of those with disabilities, and pity is substituted for giving people true opportunities in education and work.
Religious Privilege	The religious views of some groups tend to be discounted; some religions have dominant religious traditions, such as Christmas versus the Islamic Ramadan.

Source: © Elsie Jones-Smith.

SOCIAL CLASS AND CULTURAL STRENGTHS: ANTIDOTE FOR INTERNALIZED OPPRESSION AND STEREOTYPE THREAT

Search for the Strengths in the Client's Culture

Although internalized oppression and stereotype threats may impede a helping relationship, there are ways to offset or to mitigate these forces when working with clients from a broad array of multicultural backgrounds. One way in which a clinician might help clients experiencing the negative effects of privilege on their lives to change the mental switch to something positive is to ask the clients questions to evoke cultural strengths. For instance, a clinician might ask, "Tell me something about the positive qualities you see about people in your ethnic group, gender, social class, sexual orientation, or religious group. What are the strengths of African American culture? What are the strengths of American Indian, Asian American, or Latino American culture? What makes you proud of being African American, Asian American, American Indian, and so forth? What has been difficult about being African American, a woman, a transgender person, and so forth?"

Using the strengths of cultural heroes and cultural symbols. Clinicians can evoke cultural heroes and cultural symbols to reduce their clients' feelings of stereotype threat. Who are the people whom you admire in your culture? If you had to choose two people from your culture who you believe have accomplished a great deal, who would they be? Let's say you could establish your own advisory council; whom would you select to be on that council? You can choose someone who has passed or someone who is currently living. What kind of help would you like to obtain from your cultural hero? How have your cultural heroes handled situations similar to the current one that you are facing? Is there anything you would like to adapt or adopt in problem solving from your cultural hero? When people tell you that you can't achieve something because of your cultural background, what might you say to correct that misunderstanding?

Most cultures create symbols to represent certain beliefs or values. What cultural symbols mean the most to you? Is there any way that we can use your cultural symbols to motivate you in counseling? Is there something you would like to bring to therapy to remind you of your cultural strengths? What cultural values are important to you, and how are those values affecting your view of your current situation? What cultural traditions give you a sense of strength? How might we use those cultural traditions in relationship to the current issues facing you?

Helping clients to deal with oppression from their own ethnic or cultural group. Sometimes the hurt that individuals experience comes from the second source of oppression—from members of their own ethnocultural group. The clinicians might consider asking the following questions: "How have you been hurt by your own people? When have you been strongly supported by members of your own ethnocultural group? Have you ever acted on some feeling of internalized oppression—as if you were not good enough because of your ethnocultural membership group? If you could be a mentor to the 'you' that responded with a sense of internalized oppression, what would you advise yourself to do about the situation?"

Using the technique of shield and filters to blunt ethnocultural oppression. Sometimes clients who are faced with oppression become angry when microaggressions are sent their way. When clients feel threatened by microaggressions, the clinician might want to teach them that they have a mental shield. The counselor has a 10- by 12-inch piece of plastic on which he has written the words "shield against unfair words and racism." The clinician and client role-play a difficult situation in which the client is forced to deal with racism. The client learns that the shield can be changed to an invisible shield in his mind that helps him to deal with the difficult situation. The client learns how to deflect the ethnocentric person's words with his mental shield, instead of absorbing them and feeling hurt and angry.

The counseling technique called filter is another alternative a clinician might use to help a client deal with injustice and ethnocentric microaggressions. Whereas the shield blocks ethnocentric comments, the filter does permit some material to pass through. The filter allows the good stuff to pass through while trapping the bad stuff in the filter. The filter technique can be used in employment situations.

The clinician asks the client:	"What kinds of things produce conflict between you and your boss?"
Client:	"The boss is always telling me that I need to work harder, and I am working hard. I don't know what he expects of me. I'm doing the best I can do. He says he's not trying to harm me, just make me better, but . . ."
Counselor:	"Then what happens?"
Client:	"I get mad, and I go into my office, and I close my door."
Counselor:	"What if you had a filter that allowed you to remove the false, unsaid accusation that you're not working hard, but would help you to focus on his words that said he was just trying to help you become a better worker?"
Client:	"If I had a filter that would remove the false accusation, then I might ask him, 'What would you like for me to do? How do you want me to change?'"
Counselor:	"Okay. When you filter what a person is saying to you, you look to construe whatever the person is saying in the most positive light. You pause and let the person know that you heard what he was saying. Reframe the person's statement in a positive light, and then seek a positive resolution of the issue. You have filtered out the most negative part of the person's message."

Culturally Responsive Strengths-Based Client Empowerment

Counselors and therapists cannot empower a client by focusing on his or her shortcomings or failures in life (Rashid & Ostermann, 2009). This is what happens when therapists rehearse again and again during therapy what they see is the client's central problem—for instance, his relationship with his mother. "You say that you never felt loved by your mother. How does that make you feel?" How would anyone be expected to feel if his mother never showed love to him? Bad, very bad, is the answer. Why emphasize the negative forces in a client's life? The primary goal of strengths-based therapy is to maximize the strengths of the client, while helping him or her to put weaknesses in perspective. A positive attitude changes the lens through which people view their lives, and it puts a different slant on their problems (Jones-Smith, 2014). Therapy should empower clients.

Strengths-based therapy empowers clients by highlighting their positive internal resources—their strengths—as well as their external resources (Padesky & Mooney, 2012). A therapist cannot empower clients by emphasizing what is wrong with them. Empowerment stems from three interrelated processes: (1) valuing oneself as a human being, (2) having established achievable goals in one's life, and (3) developing a plan to reach these goals, a plan that has a great potential to be successful. In its simplest form, self-empowerment involves taking charge of one's life, including taking charge of one's body, one's relationships, and one's finances.

Strengths-based therapy helps clients to empower themselves by helping them to believe that they can change their lives for the better and by showing them how (See Table 20.6). Self-empowered people do not give away their power or permit others to render them powerless; instead, they use their own power wisely. To use one's self-power, one has to own it and know what it is, and be able to access it and use it appropriately.

Strengths-based therapy maintains that every person has the capacity for self-empowerment. A major difference between those who know their own power and use it appropriately and those who do not is the internal belief system governing their lives—the belief system that says they do or don't have power within themselves (Jones-Smith, 2014). Self-empowerment involves the following qualities and belief system:

- **Self-knowledge**—the ability of a person to know himself or herself in all areas.

- **Self-appreciation**—knowing what you are good at, knowing what you have to offer the world, and understanding that the world wants you to deliver your gifts.

- **Vision**—a picture of oneself that points one in the direction he or she must move, knowing where one is going, despite fear.

- **Purpose power**—having a sense of purpose helps one believe life is worth living.

- **Commitment**—being committed to completing things, promising to oneself that one will do whatever it takes.

- **Belief system**—understanding what is contained in one's belief system. The law of belief states that whatever is contained in a person's belief system, whether conscious or unconscious, will direct one's life and become one's reality. Only by changing one's belief system can one change his or her reality. Counseling clients for self-empowerment is designed to help clients first identify their belief systems, and then to change their belief systems during the process of counseling. Most people work at changing their conscious belief system. Yet, in reality, a person's unconscious belief system is what really drives his or her behavior. There is the saying, "I'll believe it when I see it." In reality, however, the law of attraction and the law of belief state that the situation is the other way around. It is not until you believe it that you will see it, regardless of what the "it" is.

TABLE 20.6 ■ Culturally Responsive Strengths-Based Empowerment Clinical Skills

Step 1: Help clients find the negative, nonserving belief systems within themselves that are guiding their actions and devise strategies to get rid of them. This step might be accomplished by asking clients questions. Self-limiting beliefs are detrimental because they are programmed and continuously working in a person's belief operating system, which runs a person's life. This is a *disempowered phase of counseling.*

- "What are your beliefs about the situation that is causing you stress?"

- "How do you believe that the situation came about?"

- "What do you believe that you can do (and also cannot do) about the situation?"

- "What would you like to do about the situation?"

Step 2: Counsel clients to add positive belief systems (for the purpose of first replacing negative, dysfunctional belief systems), such that they begin to believe that they are destined to be successful in the areas they desire. Counselors might help clients develop and write positive affirmations. The law of belief says that clients will move in the direction of their beliefs. Hence, the first step is in moving clients to believe that they will attain the levels of success that they desire. This is an *empowering phase of counseling.*

Step 3: Help clients to become very clear and focused on their true desires and assist them in making plans to achieve them. Next counselors might use a process of guided imagery to help clients believe with absolute conviction that they can achieve their goals. This represents a *focusing phase* of therapy.

Step 4: Have clients practice during therapy the habit of "acting as if" they have already accomplished their goals and that they are the success they want to be. The clients' new behaviors will influence their internal beliefs and cause them to manifest their goals. This is the *"acting as if" phase of counseling.*

Step 5: Have clients practice being grateful each and every day for the progress they have been able to achieve, regardless of how small that progress might be. This is the *gratitude phase of counseling* that will help clients to become grateful for what is taking place in their lives at a given moment. The counselor might ask clients to keep a gratitude journal.

Source: © Elsie Jones-Smith.

CASE VIGNETTE 20.1

REBECCA: A WHITE WOMAN WHO SAYS SHE'S "WHITE TRASH"

Rebecca is a 37-year-old White female who is ordered to counseling because of a history of drug abuse and neglect of her two children. She sits in the chair opposite the counselor, waiting for her to summarize all the things she has done wrong in her life.

Rebecca: "I'm a mess. Look at you, sitting there all dressed nice in your wool and rayon suit. You've got your nice, little white blouse, and here I am. What must you be thinking about me? You don't have to tell me. You probably see me as White trash, trailer park trash. Well, I wasn't always White trash. My mother taught school, and my father delivered the mail every day, rain or shine—a postal clerk. So, I haven't always been poor, drug-addicted, and White trash."

Counselor: "I don't see you as White trash, Rebecca, and I don't much care for what you are saying about yourself. I'm here to help in any way that I can. I'm not here to judge or condemn you."

Rebecca: "Well, that's a change. I mean I'm used to the way that the other counselors looked at me—like, 'Let's see what we can talk about for 50 minutes, and then you get the hell out of my office—you disgusting nothing.'"

Counselor: "You're angry about how you've been treated, and you feel that the other counselors have looked down on you because of your circumstances."

Rebecca: "Yeah, that's right."

Counselor: "Well, let's see if the two of us can work together, where I am making judgments not about the choices that you have made, but rather about what you want to do with your life now. We've all made mistakes, Rebecca. But that doesn't mean that we have to give up. I think that you are much stronger and smarter than what you give yourself credit for being. You mentioned your background—the fact that your mother was a schoolteacher. Something happened along the way. We can talk about what happened. You're not White trash to me. Do you believe in God, Rebecca? What's your religion?"

Rebecca: "I haven't been to church in so long that if they see me coming, they'll close the door. I mean, I believe in God and all that . . . It's just that things got all screwed up, and no matter how hard I try, I can't seem to fix things—to get back on the right track."

Counselor: "Well, we both have a point on which we agree. We both believe in God. And I believe that God does not make trash, Rebecca, and you're not trash. The fact that you're here in counseling with me says that you want to change your life . . . Maybe you're not sure how to go about doing that. I'm here to help you do that. You're not all alone, Rebecca. I'm

here to help you the best way that I can. Let's take one small step at a time, nothing big, just one small step forward."

Rebecca: "Okay, just so long as you're not trying to overhaul me all at once. I can take a small step, I guess, but make it a real small one."

Discussion Questions

1. Discuss the issues of social class evident in this case.

2. How does Rebecca's description of the counselor's dress/attire reflect that she is pointing to a difference in social class between the two?

3. Rebecca labeled herself as White trash. How is the term *White trash* a part of the social class issues present in the counseling session?

4. If you were the counselor, how would you have responded to Rebecca's calling herself "White trash"?

5. How might strengths-based therapy be used to work with Rebecca?

SUMMARY OF KEY POINTS

Our lives are multicultural, even if we don't recognize or acknowledge such. No one identity can convey the complexity of a person's identity. Our ethnocultural identities are rich and complex. Counselors need to understand that all people are multicultural, based on their sex and at least one other ethnocultural factor. Ethnocultural identity development is important for all people and not just for members of ethnic minority groups. Counselors would do well to examine their own ethnocultural identity prior to working with clients.

1. Counselors and clients may face a number of barriers that have the potential for affecting adversely the therapy relationship, including microaggressions, language barriers, and social class and ethnocultural differences. These barriers are not insurmountable, but rather they present challenges to establishing a therapeutic alliance.

2. In order for counselors to ensure social justice, they must understand some of the causes of inequality. They will need to invest in learning why there are economic problems relevant for a particular community and investigate ways social justice may take place.

3. When counseling members of diverse ethnocultural groups, counselors should consider areas of social justice, privilege, and internalized oppressions. There are many kinds of privileges operating in each society, including ethnic/racial privilege, gender privilege, social class privilege, religious privilege, and so forth.

4. Each person has a privilege constellation that has formed in his or her life. Some accrue a number of privileges, such as the privilege of age (being young and having society respond affirmatively to one), being able to be free of disability, and to go just about any place one pleases without the assistance of others or special equipment.

5. Counselors should increase their understanding and awareness of social class injustice and privilege in their practice.

6. Counselors should consider incorporating a social justice framework for their counseling practice.

7. Counselors might include a social justice advocacy role in their practice.

8. Privilege can sometimes become so ingrained and institutionalized that it operates mostly at the unconscious level rather than at the conscious level. While it is important to take into consideration factors related to oppression and internalized oppression, counselors should become skilled in developing empowerment approaches that focus on clients' strengths.

9. A number of counseling techniques may be used to empower clients, including usage of cultural heroes and cultural symbols, shield, and filter.

DISCUSSION QUESTIONS

Discussion Question Set 1: Outlining Social Class Issues With a Client

In small groups of three or four, set aside 10 minutes to respond to items 1–6. Jot your responses to each item or question. Then, in your small groups, describe briefly a case in which you are working with a client.

1. Outline the client's social class.

2. Indicate how social class factors are impacting the client's presenting problems/issues.

3. Is there an issue of social justice involved in the client's presenting problem?

4. What kinds of resources are needed to help your client resolve his or her problems?

5. What kind of role will you assume in dealing with the client's issues involving class and/or social injustice?

6. Are you comfortable assuming an advocacy role to help your client deal with his or her problem?

Discussion Question Set 2: Exploring Classism in Your Life

In small groups of three or four, respond to each of the following six statements:

1. Describe one way that classism is operating in your life.

2. Discuss one way in which internalized classism has operated in your life.

3. In what way is social class most relevant in your life?

4. When you do not feel that you belong because of your social class, what steps do you take?

5. What is you personal belief or motto about dealing with social class issues?

6. What is your most memorable and powerful experience with classism?

KEY TERMS

Caste system: a class structure system that is determined by one's birth. Unlike class, a person's caste position cannot be transcended. People in a caste system cannot dream of equality.

Classism: the oppression of one social class by another more powerful and usually higher social class. It functions to delimit or restrict access to socially valued assets that each society has to offer—money, jobs, homes, and so forth.

Homophily: the tendency of people to associate and bond with people who are similar to them.

Oppression: the exploitation and subordination of members of one group by members of the dominant group. Social oppression occurs when individuals are exploited, marginalized, or given far less power than the prevailing social group.

Privilege: unearned access to beneficial resources available to some people, but usually at the expense of others.

Social class: the social stratification system used in each society, usually described as upper class, middle class, or lower class. Social class may also be defined as a person's power and prestige, in addition to property or wealth.

Social class privilege: the social, economic, and cultural privileges given to one group—usually the upper class—and denied to members of lower social groups.

Social justice: a basic value and desired goal in a democratic society of having a society in which individuals have full and equal access and participation for all groups, where the distribution of resources is equitable and where all members are physically and psychologically safe and secure.

Social justice movement in counseling: a movement in counseling and in the helping professions in general designed to bring about greater social and economic equality for all members of a particular society.

Social stratification theory: a hierarchical system that describes people with positions with regard to economic production, which influences the social rewards to those in the positions.

REFERENCES AND SUGGESTED READING

Adams, M. (2000). Classism. In M. Adams, W. J. Blumenfeld, R. Castanda, H. W. Hackman, M. L. Peters, & Y. X. Zuniga (Eds.), *Readings for diversity and social justice* (pp. 379–382). New York, NY: Routledge.

Adams, M., Blumenfeld, W. J., Castaneda, H. W., Hackman, M. L., Peters, & Zuniga, X. (Eds.). (2013). *Reading for diversity and social justice: An anthology on racism, anti-Semitism, sexism, heterosexism, ableism, and classism* (pp. 35–49), New York, NY: Routledge.

Adler, N. E., Epel, E. S., Castellazzo, G., & Ickovics, J. R. (2000). Relationship of subjective and objective social status with psychological functioning: Preliminary data in healthy White women. *Health Psychology, 19*, 586–592.

American Counseling Association. (2014). *ACA code of ethics*. Alexandria, VA: Author.

Aronson, J., Fried, C., & Good, C. (2002). Reducing the effects of stereotype threat on African American college students by shaping theories of intelligence. *Journal of Experimental Social Psychology, 38*, 113–125.

Aronson, J., & Inzlicht, M. (2004). The ups and downs of attributional ambiguity: Stereotype vulnerability and the academic self-knowledge of African-American students. *Psychological Science, 15*, 829–836.

Arredondo, P., & Perez, P. (2003). Expanding multicultural competence through social justice leadership. *The Counseling Psychologist, 31*(3), 282–289.

Baluch, S. P., Pieterse, A. L., & Bolden, M. A. (2004). Counseling psychology and social justice: Houston . . . we have a problem. *The Counseling Psychologist, 32*, 89–98.

Béné, C., Newsham, A., Davies, M., Ulrichs, M., & Godfrey-Wood, R. (2014). Review article: Resilience, poverty and development. *Journal of International Development, 26*(5) 598–623.

Bianchi, E. C., & Vohs, K. D. (2016). Social class and social worlds: Income predicts the frequency and nature of social contact. *Social Psychological and Personality Science, 7*(5), 479–486.

Bond, M. A. (2007). *Workplace chemistry: Promoting diversity through organizational change*. Lebanon, NH: University Press of New England.

Boundless Sociology (2016). The class structure in the U.S. Retrieved at https://courses.lumenlearning.com/boundless-sociology/chapter/the-class-structure-in-the-u-s/.

Brito, N. H., & Noble, K. G. (2014). Socioeconomic status and structural brain development. *Frontiers in Neuroscience, 8*(276), 1–12.

Chung, R. C., & Bemak, F. P. (2012). *Social justice counseling: The next steps beyond multiculturalism*. Thousand Oaks, CA: Sage.

Collins, C., & Yeskel, F. (2005). *Economic apartheid*. New York, NY: New Press.

Collins, L., & Barnes, S. L. (2014). Observing privilege: Examining race, class, and gender in health and human service organizations. *Journal for Social Action in Counseling and Psychology, 6*(1), 61–83.

Collins, P. H. (2015). Intersectionality's definitional dilemma. *Annual Review of Sociology, 41*, 1–20.

Constantine, M. G., Hage, S. M., & Kindaichi, M. M. (2007). Social justice and multicultural issues: Implications for the practice and training of counselors and counseling psychologists. *Journal of Counseling & Development, 85*(1), 24–29.

Crenshaw, K. (1989). Demarginalizing the intersection of race and sex: A Black feminist critique of antidiscrimination doctrine, feminist theory and antiracist politics. *University of Chicago Legal Forum, 140*, 139–167.

Crenshaw, K. (1991, July). Mapping the margins: Intersectionality, identity politics, and violence against women of color. *Stanford Law Review, 43*(6), 1241–1299.

Crethar, H., & Ratts, M. J. (2008, June). Why social justice is a counseling concern [Opinion]. *Counseling Today*, pp. 21–25.

Dalaker, J., Falk, J., & McCarty, M. (2016, November 30). Demographic and social characteristics of persons in poverty: 2015. *Congressional Research Service*. Retrieved from https://fas.org/sgp/crs/misc/R44698.pdf

Davis, A. Y. (1983). *Women, race, & class*. New York, NY: Vintage Books.

Davis, L. (1996). What is social justice? *Perspectives on Multicultural and Cultural Diversity, 6*, 1–3.

Decety, J., & Wheatley, T. (2015). *The moral brain: A multidisciplinary perspective*. Cambridge, MA: MIT Press.

Decety, J., & Yoder, K. J. (2017). The emerging social neuroscience of justice motivation. *Trends in Cognitive Sciences, 21*(1), 6–14. Retrieved from http://www.sciencedirect.com/science/article/pii/S1364661316301796

DeNavas-Walt, C., & Proctor, B. (2014). *Income and poverty in the United States: 2013*. Retrieved from https://www.census.gov/content/dam/Census/library/publications/2014/demo/p60-249.pdf

DeSilver, D. (2013). *Global inequality: How the US compares*. Retrieved from Http://www.pewresearch.org/fact-tank/2013/12/19/global-inequality-how-the-u-s-compares/

DeWall, C. N., Twenge, J. M., Gitter, S. A., & Baumeister, R. F. (2009). It's the thought that counts: The role of hostile cognitions in shaping aggressive responses to social exclusion. *Journal of Personality and Social Psychology, 96*, 45–59.

Donnelly, D. A., Cook, K. J., Van Ausdale, D., & Foley, L. (2005). White privilege, color blindness, and services to battered women. *Violence Against Women, 11*(1), 6–37.

Duan, C., & Brown, C. (2016). *Becoming a multiculturally competent counselor*. Thousand Oaks, CA: Sage.

Eisenberger, N. I., Lieberman, M. D., & Williams, K. D. (2003, October 10). Does rejection hurt? An fMRI study of social exclusion. *Science, 302*, 290–292.

Evans, G. W. (2004). The environment of childhood poverty. *American Psychologist, 59*, 77–92.

Evans, G. W. (2006). Child development and the physical environment. *Annual Review of Psychology, 57*, 423–451.

Evans, N. J., Forney, D. S., Guido, F. M., Patton, L. D., & Renn, K. A. (2010). *Student development in college: Theory, research and practice* (2nd ed.). San Francisco, CA: Jossey-Bass.

Farah, M. J., Shera, D. M., Savage, J. H., Betancourt, L., Giannetta, J. M., Brodsky, N. L., Hurt, H. (2006). Childhood poverty: Specific associations with neurocognitive development. Brain Research, 1110(1), 166–174. doi:10.1016/j.brainres.2006.06.072

Filley, C. M. (2005). Why the white brain matters. *Cerebrum*. New York, NY: The Dana Foundation. Retrieved at http://www.dana.org/Cerebrum/Default.aspx?id=39152

Fouad, N. A., Gerstein, L. H., & Toporek, R. L. (2006). Social justice and counseling psychology in context. In R. Toporek, L. Gerstein, N. Fouad, G. Roysicar, & T. Israel, (Eds.), *Handbook for social justice in counseling psychology: Leadership, vision, and action* (pp. 37–43). Thousand Oaks, CA: Sage.

Fryberg, S. M. (2010). When the world is colorblind, American Indians are visible: Diversity science approach. *Psychological Inquiry, 21*(2), 115–119.

Frye, M. (2003). Oppression. In M. S. Kimmel & A. L. Ferber (Eds.), *Privilege: A reader* (pp. 13–20). Cambridge, MA: Westview Press.

Gallardo, M. E., Yeh, C. J., Trimble, J. E., & Parham, T. A. (Eds.). (2012). *Culturally adaptive counseling skills: Demonstrations of evidence-based practices*. Thousand Oaks, CA: Sage.

Gonsiorek, J. C. (1993). Threat, stress, and adjustment: Mental health and the workplace for gay and lesbian individuals.

In L. Diamont (Eds.), *Homosexual issues in the workplace* (pp. 243–264). Washington, DC: Taylor & Francis.

Gutman, L. M., McLoyd, V. C., & Tokoyawa, T. (2005). Financial strain, neighborhood stress, parenting behaviors, and adolescent adjustment in urban African American families. *Journal of Research on Adolescents, 15*, 425–449.

Hanson, J. L., Chandra, A., Wolfe, B. L., & Pollack, S. D. (2011). Association between income and the hippocampus. *PloS One, 6*(5), e18712.

Hare, B. (2009, October 13). Does your social class determine your online social network? *CNN*. Retrieved from http://www.cnn.com/2009/TECH/science/10/13/social.networking.class/index.html

Hong, Y. Y., Morris, M. W., Chiu, C. Y., & Benet-Martínez, V. (2000). Multicultural minds: A dynamic constructivist approach to culture and cognition. *American Psychologist, 55*, 709–720.

Hooks, B. (2014). *Feminist theory: From margin to center* (3rd ed.). New York, NY: Routledge.

Hutton, N. (2016, June 9). The emerging neuroscience of class differences. *The Beautiful Brain*. Retrieved from http://thebeautifulbrain.com/2016/06/the-emerging-neuroscience-of-class-differences/

Ingrao, C. (2015). The neuroscience of poverty: How to develop and repair a young mind. *Simmons School of Social Work*. Retrieved from https://socialwork.simmons.edu/the-neuroscience-of-poverty-how-to-develop-and-repair-a-young-mind/

Ivey, A. E., & Collins, N. M. (2003). Social justice: A long-term challenge for counseling psychology. *The Counseling Psychologist, 31*, 290–298.

Jackson, B., & Hardiman, R. (1994). Social identity development model. In M. Adams, P. Brigham, P. Dalpes, & L. Marchesani (Eds.), *Diversity and oppression: Conceptual frameworks* (pp. 19–22). Dubuque, IA: Kendall/Hunt.

Jiang, Y., Granja, M. R., & Koball, H. (2017, January). Basic facts about low-income children. *National Center for Children in Poverty*. Retrieved from http://nccp.org/publications/pdf/text_1171.pdf

Johnson, A. G. (2006). *Privilege, power, and difference* (2nd ed.). Boston, MA: McGraw-Hill.

Johnston, M. P., & Nadal, K. I. (2010). Multiracial microaggressions: Exposing monoracism in everyday life and clinical practice. In D. W. Sue (Ed.), *Microaggressions and marginality: Manifestation, dynamics and impact* (pp. 123–144). Hoboken, NJ: Wiley.

Jones-Smith, E. (2014). *Strengths-based therapy: Connecting theory, practice, and skills*. Thousand Oaks, CA: Sage.

Jones-Smith, E. (2016). *Theories of counseling and psychotherapy: An integrative approach*. Thousand Oaks, CA: Sage.

Jun, H. (2010). *Social justice, multicultural counseling, and practice: Beyond a conventional approach*. Thousand Oaks, CA: Sage.

Kraus, M. W., & Callaghan, B. (2016). Social class and prosocial behavior: The moderating role of public versus private contexts. *Social Psychological and Personality Science, 7*(8), 769–777.

Kraus, M. W., Côté, S., & Keltner, D. (2010). Social class, contextualism, and empathic accuracy. *Psychological Science, 21*, 1716–1723.

Kraus, M. W., Piff, P. K., Rheinschmidt, M. L., & Keltner, D. (2012). Social class, solipsism, and contextualism: How the rich are different from the poor. *Psychological Review, 119*(3), 546–572.

Lee, B. A., & Marlay, M. (2007). The right side of the tracks: Affluent neighborhoods in the metropolitan United States. *Social Science Quarterly, 88*, 766–789.

Levine, M. (2006). *The price of privilege: How parental pressure and material advantage are creating a generation of disconnected and unhappy kids*. New York, NY: HarperCollins.

Liu, W. M. (2001). Expanding our understanding of multiculturalism: Developing a social class worldview model. In D. B. Pope-Davis & H. I. K. Coleman (Eds.), *The intersection of race, class, and gender in counseling psychology* (pp. 127–170). Thousand Oaks, CA: Sage.

Liu, W. M. (2011). *Social class and classism in the helping professions: Research, theory, and practice*. Thousand Oaks, CA: Sage.

Liu, W. M. (2013). Introduction to social class and classism in counseling psychology. In W. M. Liu (Ed.), *The Oxford handbook of social class in counseling (Oxford Handbooks Online)*. Retrieved from http://www.oxfordhandbooks .com/view/10.1093/oxfordhb/9780195398250.001.0001/ oxfordhb-9780195398250-e-001

Liu, W. M., Corkery, J., & Thome, J. (2010). Developing competency in social class and classism in counseling and psychotherapy. In J. A. E. Cornish, B. A. Schreier, L. I. Nadkarni, L. H. Metzger, & E. R. Rodolfa (Eds.), *Handbook of multicultural counseling competencies* (pp. 350–378). Hoboken, NJ: Wiley.

Liu, W. M., Soleck, G., Hopps, J., Dunston, K., & Pickett, T. (2004). A new framework to understand social class in counseling: The social class worldview model and modern classism theory. *Journal of Multicultural Counseling and Development, 32*, 95–122.

Lott, B., & Bullock, H. E. (2007). *Psychology and economic justice*. Washington, DC: American Psychological Association.

Luby, J., Belden, A., Botteron, K., Marrus, N., Harms, M. P., Babb, C., . . . Barch, D. (2013). The effects of poverty on childhood brain development: The mediating effects of caregiving and stressful life events. *JAMA Pediatrics, 167*(12), 1135–1142.

Luthar, S. S. (2003). The culture of affluence: Psychological costs of material wealth. *Child Development, 74*, 1581–1593.

Luthar, S. S., & Becker, B. E. (2002). Privileged but pressured: A study of affluent youth. *Child Development, 73*, 1593–1610.

Luthar, S. S., & D'Avanzo, K. (1999). Contextual factors in substance use: A study of suburban and inner-city adolescents. *Development and Psychopathology, 11*, 845–867.

Luthar, S. S., & Sexton, C. (2005). The high price of affluence. In R. V. Kail (Ed.), *Advances in child development* (pp. 126–162). San Diego, CA: Academic Press.

McConnell, E. A., & Todd, N. R. (2015). Differences in white privilege attitudes and religious beliefs across racial affect types. *The Counseling Psychologist, 43*(8), 1135–1161.

McIntosh, P. (1989, July/August). White privilege: Unpacking the invisible knapsack. In *Peace and Freedom* (pp. 10–12). Philadelphia, PA: Women's International League for Peace and Freedom.

McPherson, M., Smith-Lovin, L., & Cook, J. M. (2001). Birds of a feather: Homophily in social networks. *Annual Review of Sociology, 27*, 415–444

Neville, H. A., Awad, G. H., Brooks, J. E., Flores, M. P., & Bluemel, J. (2013). Color-blind racial ideology: Theory, training, and measurement implications in psychology. *American Psychologist, 68*, 455–466.

Noble, K. G. (2014). Rich man, poor man: Socioeconomic adversity and brain development. *Cerebrum*. New York, NY: The DANA Foundation. Retrieved from http://www .dana.org/Cerebrum/2014/Rich_Man,_Poor_Man__ Socioeconomic_Adversity_and_Brain_Development/

Noble, K. G., Engelhardt, L. E., Brito, N. H., Mack, L., Nail, E., Barr, R. F., . . . Elliott, A. (2015). Socioeconomic disparities in neurocognitive development in the first two years of life. *Developmental Psychobiology, 57*, 535–551.

Noble, K. G., & Farah, M. J. (2013). Neurocognitive consequences of socioeconomic disparities: The intersection of cognitive neuroscience and public health. *Developmental Science, 16*(5), 639–640.

Noble, K. G., Grieve, S. M., Korgaonkar, M. S., & Brickman, A. M. (2012). Hippocampal volume varies with educational attainment across the life-span. *Frontiers in Human Neuroscience, 6*, 1–10.

Noble, K. G., Houston, S. M., Brito, N. H., Bartsch, H., Kan, E., Kuperman, J. M., . . . Sowell, E. R. (2015, May). Family income, parental education and brain development in children and adolescents. *Nature Neuroscience, 18*(5), 773–778.

Noble, K. G., Houston, S., Kan, E., Bookheimer, S. Y., & Sowell, E. R. (2012). Neural correlates of socioeconomic status in the developing human brain. *Developmental Science, 15*(4), 516–527.

Padesky, C. A., & Mooney, K. A. (2012). Strengths-based cognitive-behavioural therapy: A four-step model to build resilience. *Clinical Psychology & Psychotherapy, 19,* 283–291.

Peterson, C. (2010, December 6). Social class matters: The rich don't understand other people. *Psychology Today.* Retrieved from https://www.psychologytoday.com/blog/the-good-life/201012/social-class-matters

Pierce, C. M. (1970). Black psychiatry one year after Miami. *Journal of the National Medical Association, 62,* 471–473.

Pierce, C. M. (1995). Stress analogs of racism and sexism: Terrorism, torture, and disaster. In C. Willie, P. Ricker, B. Kramer, & B. Brown (Eds.), *Mental health, racism, and sexism* (pp. 277–293). Pittsburgh, PA: University of Pittsburgh Press.

Pierce, C. M., Carew, J., Pierce-Gonzalez, D., & Willis, D. (1978). An experiment in racism: TV commercials. In C. M. Pierce (Ed.), *Television and education* (pp. 62–88). Beverly Hills, CA: Sage.

Piff, P. K. (2014). Wealth and the inflated self: Class, entitlement, and narcissism. *Personality and Social Psychology Bulletin, 40*(1), 34–43.

Piff, P. K., Kraus, M. W., Côté, S., Cheng, B. H., & Keltner, D. (2010). Having less, giving more: The influence of social class on prosocial behavior. *Journal of Personality and Social Psychology, 99,* 771–784.

Proctor, B. D., Semega, J. L., & Kollar, M. A. (2016). Income and poverty in the United States: 2015. U.S. Census Bureau, *Current Population Reports, P60-256(RV).* Washington, DC: U.S. Government Printing Office.

Quinlan, A. E., Berbés-Blázquez, M., Haider, J. L., & Peterson, G. D. (2016). Measuring and assessing resilience: Broadening understanding through multiple disciplinary perspectives. *Journal of Applied Ecology, 53*(Special feature quantifying resilience), 677–687.

Rank, M. (2005). *One nation, underprivileged.* New York, NY: Oxford University Press.

Rashid, T., & Ostermann, R. F. (2009). Strength-based assessment in clinical practice. *Journal of Clinical Psychology, 65*(5), 488–498. doi:10.1002/jclp.20595

Ratts, M. J., & Pedersen, P. B. (2014). *Counseling for multiculturalism and social justice: Integration, theory, and application* (4th ed.). Hoboken, NJ: Wiley.

Ratts, M. J., Singh, A. A., Nassar-McMillan, S., Butler, S. K., & McCullough, J. R. (2015). *Multicultural and social justice counseling competencies.* Retrieved from https://www.counseling.org/docs/default-source/competencies/multicultural-and-social-justice-counseling-competencies.pdf?sfvrsn=20

Ravindran, R. (2015). The life story of The Rock—From homeless to world icon. *Sportskeeda.* Retrieved from https://www.sportskeeda.com/wwe/wwe-the-life-story-of-rock-from-homeless-to-world-icon

Reardon, S. (2015, March 30). Poverty shrinks brains from birth. *Nature.* Retrieved from http://www.nature.com/news/poverty-shrinks-brains-from-birth-1.17227#/ref-link-1

Sabbagh, C., & Schmitt, M. (Eds.). (2016). *Handbook of social justice: Theory and research.* Manhattan, NY: Springer.

Saez, E., & Zucman, G. (2014). The explosion in U.S. wealth inequality has been fueled by stagnant wages, increasing debt, and a collapse in asset values for the middle classes. Retrieved from http://blogs.lse.ac.uk/usappblog/2014/10/29/the-explosion-in-u-s-wealth-inequality-has-been-fuelled-by-stagnant-wages-increasing-debt-and-a-collapse-in-asset-values-for-the-middle-classes/

Sanchez, D. T., & Garcia, J. A. (2009). When race matters: Racially stigmatized others and perceiving race as a biological construction affect biracial people's daily well-being. *Personality and Social Psychology Bulletin, 35*(9), 1154–1164. doi:10.1177/0146167209337628

Schwarzbaum, S. E., & Thomas, A. J. (2008). *Dimensions of multicultural counseling: A life story approach.* Thousand Oaks, CA: Sage.

Shallcross, L. (2013, September 1). Multicultural competence: A continual pursuit. *Counseling Today.* Retrieved from https://ct.counseling.org/2013/09/multicultural-competence-a-continual-pursuit/

Sherman, B. J. (2006). The poverty of affluence: Addiction to wealth and its effects on well-being. *Graduate Student Journal of Psychology, 8,* 30–32.

Shih, M., Bonam, C., Sanchez, D., & Peck, C. (2007). The social construction of race: Biracial identity and vulnerability to stereotypes. *Cultural Diversity and Ethnic Minority Psychology, 13,* 125–133.

Sifford, A., Ng, K., & Wang, C. (2009). Further validation of the Psychosocial Costs of Racism to Whites Scale on a sample of university students in the southeastern United States. *Journal of Counseling Psychology, 56*(4), 585–589.

Sing-Manoux, A., Adler, N. E., & Marmot, M. G. (2003). Subjective social status: Its determinants and its association with measures of ill-health in the Whitehall II study. *Social Science and Medicine, 56,* 1321–1333.

Smith, L. (2005). Classism, psychotherapy, and the poor: Conspicuous by their absence. *American Psychologist, 60,* 687–696.

Smith, L. (2006). Addressing classism, extending multicultural competence, and serving the poor. *American Psychologist, 61,* 338–339.

Smith, L. (2009). Enhancing training and practice in the context of poverty. *Training and Education in Professional Psychology, 3,* 84–93.

Smith, L. (2010). *Psychology, poverty, and the end of social exclusion*. New York, NY: Teachers College Press.

Smith, L., Foley, P. F., & Chaney, M. P. (2008). Addressing classism, ableism, and heterosexism in counselor education. *Journal of Counseling and Development, 86,* 303–309.

Southern Educational Foundation. (2015). Psychological interventions in the context of poverty: Participatory action research as practice. *American Journal of Orthopsychiatry, 80,* 12–25.

Spanierman, L. B., & Heppner, M. J. (2004). Psychosocial costs of racism to Whites scale: Construction and initial validation. *Journal of Counseling Psychology, 51,* 249–262. doi:10.1037/0022-0167.51.2.249

Spanierman, L. B., Poteat, V. P., Beer, A. M., Armstrong, P. I. (2006). Psychosocial costs of racism to Whites: Exploring patterns through cluster analysis. *Journal of Counseling Psychology, 53,* 434–441.

Spanierman, L. B., Todd, N. R., & Anderson, C. J. (2009). Psychosocial costs of racism to Whites: Understanding patterns among university students. *Journal of Counseling Psychology, 56,* 239–252. doi:10.1037/a0015432.

Spencer, S. J., Steele, C. M., & Quinn, D. M. (1999). Stereotype threat and women's math performance. *Journal of Experimental Social Psychology, 35,* 4–28.

Steele, C. M. (1997). A threat in the air: How stereotypes shape the intellectual identities and performance of women and African-Americans. *American Psychologist, 52,* 613–629.

Steele, C. M. (1999, August). Thin ice: "Stereotype threat" and black college students. *Atlantic Monthly, 284*(2), 44–47, 50–54.

Steele, C. M., & Aronson, J. (1995). Stereotype threat and the intellectual test performance of African-Americans. *Journal of Personality and Social Psychology, 69,* 797–811.

Stellar, J., Manzo, V., Kraus, M. W., & Keltner, D. (2012). Class and compassion: Socioeconomic factors predict responses to suffering. *Emotion, 12,* 449–459.

Sue, D. W. (2010). *Microaggressions in everyday life: Race, gender, and sexual orientation.* Hoboken, NJ: Wiley.

Sue, D. W., Arredondo, P., & McDavis R. J. (1992). Multicultural competencies/standards: Call to the profession. *Journal of Counseling and Development, 70*(4), 477–486.

Tomalski, P., Moore, D. G., Ribeiro, H., Axelsson, E. L., Murphy, E., Karmiloff-Smith, A., . . . Kushnerenko, E. (2013). Socioeconomic status and functional brain development: Associations in early infancy. *Developmental Science, 16*(5), 676–687. doi:10.1111/desc.12079

Torkelson, J., & Hartmann, D. (2010). White ethnicity in twenty-first-century American: Findings from a new national survey. *Ethnic and Racial Studies, 33,* 1310–1331.

Twenge, J. M. (2001). Changes in women's assertiveness in response to status and roles: A cross-temporal meta-analysis, 1931–1993. *Journal of Personality and Social Psychology, 81*(1), 133–145.

Twenge, J. M. (2006). *Generation me: Why today's young Americans are more confident, assertive, entitled—and more miserable than ever before.* New York, NY: Free Press.

Twenge, J. M., & Campbell, W. K. (2002). Self-esteem and socioeconomic status: A meta-analytic review. *Personality and Social Psychology Review, 6,* 59–71.

Twenge, J. M., & Campbell, W. K. (2009). *The narcissism epidemic: Living in the age of entitlement.* New York, NY: Free Press.

U.S. Census Bureau. (2011). 2010 census shows America's diversity. *American Community Survey.* Retrieved from https://www.census.gov/newsroom/releases/archives/2010_census/cb11-cn125.html

Varnum, M. E. W., Blais, C., & Brewer, G. A. (2016). Social class affects Mu-suppression during action observation. *Social Neuroscience, 11*(4), 449–454. http://dx.doi.org/10.1080/17470919.2015.1105865

Varnum, M. E. W., Blais, C., Hampton, R. S., & Brewer, G. A. (2015). Social class affects neural empathic responses. *Culture and Brain.* Retrieved from https://asumaclab.files.wordpress.com/2014/08/social-class-affects-neural-empathic-responses.pdf

Varnum, M. E. W., & Kitayama, S. (2017). The neuroscience of social class. *Current Opinion in Psychology, 18,* 147–151.

Vera, E. M., & Speight, S. L. (2003). Multicultural competence, social justice, and counseling psychology: Expanding our roles. *The Counseling Psychologist, 31,* 253–272.

Wadsworth, M. E., & Achenback, T. M. (2005). Examining the link between low socioeconomic status and psychopathology: Testing two mechanisms of the social causation hypothesis. *Journal of Consulting and Clinical Psychology, 73,* 1146–1153.

Warren, A. K., & Constantine, M. G. (2007). Social justice issues. In M. Constantine (Ed.), *Clinical practice with people of color* (pp. 231–242). New York, NY: Teachers College Press.

Williams, M. T. (2011, December). Colorblind ideology is a form of racism: A colorblind approach allows us to deny uncomfortable cultural differences. *Psychology Today.* Retrieved from http://www.psychologytoday.com/blog/colorblind/201112/colorblind-ideology-s-form-racism

Young, I. M. (2000). Five faces of oppression. In L. Heldke & Peg O'Connor (Eds.), *Oppression, privilege, & resistance* (pp. 37–63). Boston, MA: McGraw-Hill.

INDEX

"AAA Statement on Race," 20
Abandonment, of older adults, 486
Ability privilege, 593 (table)
Able-Bodied Privilege Checklist, 459
Ableism, 459, 460, 474
Aboriginal people, 263
Abuse and violence, disabled individuals and, 465–466
Acceptance and commitment therapy, 92
Access, as counselor principle, 584
Acculturation:
    African Americans and, 242, 244 (case vignette)
    American Indians and, 276–277
    Arab and Muslim Americans and, 353–354
    Asian Americans and, 302–303
    client issues with, 214, 214 (table)
    conflicts within, 166 (case vignette)
    cultural attachment, migration, and, 112–113
    defined, 50, 65
    Hispanic and Latino/a Americans and, 329–330
    immigrants and refugees and, 520
    multicultural individuals and, 93
Acculturation conflict:
    Arab and Muslim Americans and, 353–354
    Asian Americans and, 302–303
    examples of, 53
    Hispanic and Latino/a Americans and, 329–330
Acculturative stress, 51, 65, 520–521
Acetylcholine, 74
Achebe, Chinua, 123 (box)
Achievement, Western/Eastern differences on, 40 (table)
Acknowledge, in intake interview, 174 (table)
Acquiring New Skills While Enhancing Remaining Strengths
    (ANSWERS), 502–503
"Acting as if" phase, of counseling, 596 (table)
Actuarial assessment, 163–164, 194
Adolescents:
    Arab and Muslim American, 350–351
    Asian American, 299
    brains of, 89–90 (case vignette)
    gender dysphoria in, 432–433
    Hispanic and Latino/a, 327, 329–330
    LGBTQ youth and school and, 436–437
    transgender identity development and, 434
ADRA2B gene variant, 82
Adults. See Older adults
Adversity assessment, 191, 191 (table)
Affirmative disability model, 467, 469, 474
Affirmative disability orientation, 468 (table), 469
African Americans:
    acculturation and, 242, 244 (case vignette)
    achievements of, 231–232, 245–246
    amygdala activation of, 22–23
    "at-promise youth" and, 253, 253–256 (case vignette)
    Black church and collectivism and, 247–248
    Black Underclass among, 233–234
    clinician "do no harm," 252
    clinician's acknowledgement of racism and
        oppression, 252
    counseling and psychotherapy approaches for working
        with, 247–248
    cultural history of (examples), 245–246
    cultural issues in strengths-base therapy ("at-promise
        youth"), 253, 253–256 (case vignette)
    cultural strengths of, 245–252
    ethnocultural identity and, 240–242, 243 (table)
    family, extended, 245
    family structure, 244–245
    how therapists drive away, 251–252
    implicit racial bias against, by doctors and judges, 24
    income and poverty in the United States: 2015, 572 (table)
    Islam practiced by, 345
    LGBTQ individuals and, 435
    median income, 232–233
    microaggressions against, 238–239
    microaggressions by therapists, 251–252
    middle class, 235–326
    migration to the suburbs, 235
    mixed with other ethnic/racial groups, 238–239, 239 (case
        vignette)
    Muslims and Jews and, 345
    negative images of, 242
    neural reactions to Confederate flag of, 22
    Nigrescence and, 241–242
    NTU Afrocentric model for counseling, 252–253
    older adults and, 480
    overdiagnosis of, 203
    population, 200
    population and demographic statistics for, 232–236
    positive ethnic identity of, 246
    positive identity among, 246
    poverty, implications for counseling, 234
    poverty rate for, 232–233
    preference for same-race practitioners, 53
    pride in racial heritage and, 47
    racism toward, as relevant to psychotherapy
        relationships, 238
    reactive and proactive Afrocentrism and, 47
    religion and spirituality of, 247–248, 249 (table)
    resiliency of, 246
    Revised Cross model of racial identity, 241–242, 243 (table)

role of therapist working with, 249, 250 (table)

slavery, denigration and dehumanization of, 231

slavery, legacy of and response to, 236–237

socioeconomic status of, 232–233

talking about depression, 202

transracial identity and (Rachel Dolezal example), 77 (case vignette)

trust and cultural mistrust as clinical issues, 250–251

upper class, 236

White Underclass versus, 234–235

women as family head, 244–245

worldview of, 47, 239–240

younger versus older worldview, 240

African-centered, 257

Afrocentric, 252, 257

Ageism, 478–479, 483, 507

Aging:

culture and, 478

successful, 495

Western and Eastern cultural view on, 482–483

Aging and Old Age (Posner), 483

Alaska Natives:

alcohol abuse by, 277

communication style and silence among, 271–272

counseling approaches for, 278–279, 279 (table)

cultural strengths of, 272–273

defined, 284

microaggressions against, 266

population and demographic statistics for, 200, 263–264

socioeconomic status of, 265

suicide rates for, 277–278

traditional healing and, 276

worldview of, 266

Albinos, 320

Alcohol abuse:

American Indians and Alaska Natives and, 277

older adults and, 488–489

Alcoholics Anonymous (AA), 155

Altman, Neil, 21

Alzheimer's disease and other cognitive impairments, 487–488, 507

American Academy of Child and Adolescent Psychiatry, 559

American ancestry, 368

American Anthropological Association (AAA), "Statement on Race," 20

American Civil War, 22

American Counseling Association (ACA):

Code of Ethics, 9

competencies endorsed by, 6, 558

diversity as central issue in, 9

American culture, 170–171

American identity, 373, 397

American Indian areas, 263

American Indians:

acculturation conflicts and, 276–277

alcohol abuse by, 277

collectivist orientation of, 267 (table)

communication style and silence among, 271–272, 272 (table)

cooperation and harmony and, 271, 284

counseling approaches for, 278–279, 279 (table), 280–283 (case vignette)

cultural identity and, 268–269

cultural strengths of, 272–273

cultural values of, 269–272

culture-bound syndromes and, 186

defined, 284

ethnic identity model for, 269

gift-giving during therapy, 328

healing: the circle and medicine wheel, 273–275

historical trauma among, 265–266

legal definition of, 264

mental health challenges of, 276–278

microaggressions against, 266

noninterference and, 271

population and demographic statistics for, 200, 263–264

preferred group names, 262–263

sharing and generosity of, 270

socioeconomic status of, 265

spirituality of, 270–271

stereotypes, racism, and, 266

storytelling among, 272

suicide rates for, 277–278

time orientation of, 270

traditional healing and, 276

tribe as family, 268

value on listening, 172

worldview of, 266–267, 267 (table)

American Mental Health Counseling Association (AMHCA), 72

American Psychiatric Association, cultural identity and, 79–80

American Psychological Association (APA):

Code of Conduct, 164

culture-centered practices, described, 60

demand for "evidence-based" therapy, 39

ethical obligation of psychologists for cross-cultural competencies, 10

Guidelines for Assessment of and Intervention With Persons With Disabilities, 470

Guidelines on Multicultural Education, Training, Research, Practice, and Organizational Change for Psychologists, 6–7

"Multicultural Guidelines: An Ecological Approach to Context, Identity, and Intersectionality," 9

Americans with Disabilities Act (ADA; 1990), 453, 474

Ames, Daniel L., 71

Amodio, David, 22, 23

Amygdala:

defined, 27, 126

panic alarm triggered by, 87 (case vignette)

threat signaling by, 22–23, 125

Androcentric theories, 409

Androgyny, 409–410

Ang, S., 43

Angelou, Maya, 104

Anger, changes in brain from, 168

Anglo Americans. *See* English Americans

Anthony, Susan B., 401

Anti-racist White identity, 384, 397

Anti-Semitism, 379, 397

Anxiety disorders, 215

Apple, 39

Appreciation:
  intention for, 157
  therapist's expression of, for client's efforts and
    struggles, 145

Arab, defining features, 342, 360

Arab American elders, 355

Arab Americans:
  achievements of, 345
  ancestry groups, 344–345
  demographic data on, 344–345
  migration to the United States, 343–344
  overview, 341
  socioeconomic status of, 345

Arab and Muslim Americans:
  acculturation conflicts and, 353–354
  achievements of, 354
  collectivist worldview of, 349
  communication patterns among, 351–352
  community and, 351
  counseling approaches for, 355–357
  cultural and racial identity of, 352–353
  cultural strengths of, 354
  cultural values and worldview of, 348–353
  distinguishing between terms *Arab* and *Muslim*, 342–343
  dreams and visions, significance of, 354
  eldest son and, 350–351
  extended patriarchal family structure, 350–351
  family, friends, and religious leaders and, 356
  family challenges among, 351
  family structure of, 349–351
  group description, 341
  high-context culture of, 351–352
  impact of discrimination and trauma on, 355
  mental health issues for, 354–355
  mental illness as stigma, 355
  microaggressions against, 346–347
  "passing" and, 347
  strengths-based therapy for, 357–359 (case vignette)
  time and space, 352

Arafat, Yasser, 341

Asian alone, 290–291, 293

Asian American family types:
  Americanized, 297
  bicultural, 297
  "cultural conflict," 297
  interracial, 297–298
  traditional, 297

Asian Americans:
  acculturation conflicts and, 302–303

acculturation level and counseling and, 303

achievements of, 301–302

children and adolescents in, 299

collectivistic orientation of, 295–296

communication style, 172

contributions of, 301–302

cultural factors in counseling of, 306–309, 310–312 (case
  vignette)

cultural identity and, 301

cultural issues of, 295–300

culturally responsive strengths-based therapy for,
  overview of, 289–290

cultural strengths of, 301–302

cultural values of, 296

elderly adults in, 300

expectations about counseling, 305–306

family hierarchical structure, family values, and parenting
  styles, 296–297

family types, 297–298

gender issues in, 299

gift-giving during therapy, 328

help-seeking attitudes of, 303

high-context culture of, 300

historical changes in profile of, 292–293

holistic view of mind and body, 306

income and poverty in the United States: 2015, 572 (table)

intermarriage and, 292–293

LGBTQ individuals and, 435

mental health and, 303–304

mental illness and substance use among, 305

microaggressions against, 294–295

as "model ethnic minority," 293–294

multiple-race reporting for, 291

older adults and, 480

population and demographic statistics for, 290–291

self-control, emotional restraint, and shaming, 298–300

socioeconomic status of, 293

subgroup representation of groups of, 291

suppression of family problems, 298–300

underutilization of mental health services by, 306–307

value on education and hard work, 296

views on aging among, 482–483

worldview of, 295

young adults in, 299–300

Asians:
  comfort with uncertainty, 171
  parent versus child values, 53
  population, 200

Assertiveness training, 414–415

Assessment(s):
  actuarial (quantitative; nomothetic), 163–164, 194
  adversity, 191, 191 (table)
  clients' cultural identity, 212, 213 (table)
  client's potential for self-harm and risk to others, 193
  clinical (qualitative; idiographic), 163–164, 194
  combined quantitative and qualitative, 164
  construct bias in, 164
  cross-cultural, 164–165
  cross-cultural, neuropsychology and, 167–168

cultural bias in, 164–165, 194

cultural communication in high- and low-context cultures, 171

cultural empathy and, 168–169

cultural knowledge about clients and, 169

culture-bound syndromes and, 182, 183–184 (case vignette), 184, 185 (table), 186

dimensional, 210

equivalence and bias in, 165, 166 (case vignette), 194

idiographic, 194

item bias in, 165

LGBTQ clients and, 443

method bias in, 165

models of, for culturally responsive counseling, 166–167

neuropsychological, 167

principles, in counseling and psychotherapy, 163–169

psychological, 163, 194

Assessment, culturally responsive:

critical cultural knowledge for assessing culturally diverse clients, 170 (table)

cultural communication in high- and low-context cultures, 171

culturally appropriate, 169, 175

Culturally Responsive Intake Checklist, 175, 176–177 (table)

differences in client/clinician communication styles, 173–174 (table)

honoring client's communication style, 172

intake process and, 172, 173–174 (table), 175

LEARN and the intake interview, 174 (table)

listening for culture in the client's story, 170–171

Assessment and Culture: Psychological Tests With Minority Populations (Gopaul-McNicol & Armour-Thomas), 167

Assessment process, of strengths-based therapy model:

adversity assessment, coping skills strengths, 191, 191 (table)

clients' external strengths, 191–192, 192 (table)

clients' internal strengths, 189, 190 (table)

models of, 189–191

relational strengths: friends' strengths, 192, 192 (table)

strengths assessment and treatment process, 191

strengths checklist, 190 (table), 190–191

strengths discovery assessments, 188–189

Assimilation:

American Indian, 265–266

Arab and Muslim American, 352, 353, 354

defined, 49, 65

Hispanic and Latino/a, 330

immigrant and refugee and, 520, 524, 532

White American, 371–372

Assimilation strategy, in acculturation, 50

Association for Multicultural Counseling and Development (AMCD), Multicultural Counseling Competencies and, 6, 7

Assumed cultural dissimilarity, 48, 65

Assumed cultural similarity, 48, 65

Asylee:

defined, 513, 536

numbers of, 514

refugee/asylee experience: Triple Trauma Paradigm, 523–524

torture experiences and, 522–523

Ataque de nervios, 38, 185 (table), 186, 215, 333

"At-promise youth," 253, 253–256 (case vignette)

Attachment, cultural. *See* Cultural attachment

Attachment patterns across cultures, 111–112

Attachment process, shaping of brain during, 73

Attachment relationships, strengths development and, 109–110

Attachment theory:

infants, children, and, 108–109

strengths development and, 108–109

Attention deficit disorder (ADD), 456

Attention, strengths development and, 111

Attention deficit hyperactivity disorder (ADHD), 456

Attitudes, cultural, 64

Attrition rate, for ethnic/racial minorities, 203–204, 228

Austin, Anthony, 1

Avoidance thinking, 87 (case vignette)

Awareness. *See* Cultural awareness

Awareness competencies, of culturally responsive counselors, 7, 8 (box)

Away From Her, 489–490

"Bad Is Stronger Than Good" (Baumeister, Bratslavsky, Finkenauer, & Vohs), 81

Barnes, Janet, 452

Baumeister, Roy, 81

Beck, Aaron, 17

Behavior, intentions as influence on, 157

Belief(s):

cultural, of Chinese Americans and White Americans, 136

neuroscience of, 135–136

religious, 135

self-limiting, 136–138

Belief system, 595

Berra, Yogi, 479

Berry, J. W., 50

Berry Model of Acculturation, 50

Bias:

clinicians', against clients, 202–203

construct, 164

counseling attrition rate for ethnic/racial minorities and, 203–204

cultural, in assessment, 164–165, 166 (case vignette), 194

cultural, in mental health service delivery systems, 201–202

equivalence and bias in assessment, 165, 166 (case vignette), 194

ethnic, 22–25, 201, 203–204

ethnic/racial, and neuroscience and the brain, 22–25

implicit and explicit, paradigm of, 22, 26

item, 165

method, 165

negative, against Latino immigrants, 25

negativity, of the brain, 81–82

Western perspective and, 17
See also Ethnicity *entries*; Explicit bias; Implicit bias; Race *entries*
Bibliotherapy, 415
Bicultural, 94, 543
"Bill of Rights for People of Mixed Heritage" (Root), 557–558
Biological identity, 77 (case vignette)
Biracial individuals:
Continuum of Biracial Identity model (COBI), 553
defined, 543, 565
levels of experiences of, 551
measuring racial identities, 552
Biracial/multiracial identity development, 549–550, 550 (case vignette), 565
Bisexuals:
defined, 425, 447
population of, 427
See also LGBTQ individuals
Black church, collectivism and, 247–248
Black Elk, 273
"Black Lives Matter," 591
Black Underclass, 232, 233–234, 257
Black upper class, 232, 236
Black–White race attitude text, 23
"Blaming the victim," 389
Blindness, cultural, 12
Blood quantum, 264
Boule, Jamelle, 518–519
Bowlby, John, 108, 109
Brain:
adaptability of, 73
calming, through cultural ritual, 168
changes to, by psychotherapy, 85
characteristics of, 73
child's, effects of poverty on, 575–577
cultural identity and, 79 (figure)
cultural identity formation and neuroscience, 76–77, 77 (case vignette)
culture and, 38–39
defined, 97
differences in functioning of, by culture, 3
environment influence on, 84
fear, clinical assessment, and, 167–168
female versus male, 73
"glass half empty" hardwiring, 82–84
healing effects of poverty through neurogenesis, 577–578, 578 (table)
mapping the cultural architecture of, 75–76
mind and, 75
negativity bias of, 81–82
network within that supports prejudice, 22
neural prejudice networks in, 22–23
neurocultural dynamics and, 131–133, 132 (table)
neuroimaging techniques and, 84
neurons in, 72, 73–74
neuroplasticity of, 74–75
neuroscience of poverty and social class and, 573–582
neurotransmitters, 74
quieting/calming, role of culture in, 168
reptilian, 90 (case vignette)
shaped during attachment process, 73
social, 84
as social organ, 73
strengths development and, 106, 107 (figure)
structure changes through intentional focus, 111
structure of, 72
teenagers and, 89–90 (case vignette)
"use it or lose it" principle, 107
See also Neuroscience *entries*
Brain plasticity, 78
Brain processes, malleability of, 78
Brain regions, cultural identity and, 78–79
Bratslavsky, Ellen, 81
Brew, Leah, 550 (case vignette)
"Bucket list," 501
Buddha, 40 (table)
Buddhism, 40 (table), 116, 156
Building a new identity, 255 (case vignette), 256 (case vignette), 283 (case vignette)
Building new competencies, 501–502, 505 (case vignette)
Bureau of Indian Affairs, 264

Cablinasian, 239 (case vignette), 545, 561
CACREP. *See* Council for Accreditation of Counseling and Related Educational Programs (CACREP)
Capitalism, 39
Care-Receiver Efficacy Scale (CRES), 502
Carkhuff, Robert, 55–56, 56 (table)
Carter, Dustin, 110–111
Case conceptualization:
culturally responsive (examples), 205, 206–207 (case vignette), 207–210
defined, 199, 204, 227
elements of, 204–205
Five Ps of, 205
governed by clinician's worldviews, 199–200
listening for culture in client's story and, 52
revisions in the DSM-5 and, 208–210
strengths-based, 218–219, 220 (table)
treatment plan and, 200
Case conceptualization and the Cultural Formulation Interview (CFI):
assessing clients' cultural identity, 212, 213 (table)
clients' acculturation issues, 214, 214 (table)
cultural factors related to psychosocial environment, 216, 216 (table), 217 (case vignette)
ethnocultural transference and countertransference, 217–218, 218 (table)
explanations of individual's illness, 214–215, 216 (table)
overall cultural assessment for diagnosis and treatment, 218
revealing clients' immigration history, 212–213
using together, advantages of, 210–211
Cass gender identity model, 441
Caste system, 589, 598
Center for American Progress, 514
Center for Victims of Torture, 523, 524, 528
Center on Aging and Work (Boston College), 483, 484

Central Americans, migration history of, 321–322
Central nucleus (CeA), 23
Cerebral cortex, 73
Chaney, James, 380
Chi (qi), 304, 308, 314
Chicano/Latino model of ethnic identity, 330
Childhood, brain during, 73
Children:
    Arab and Muslim American families and, 350
    Asian American families and, 299
    attachment theory and, 109–110
    brain development of, 106
    cultural introjection and cultural attachment
        and, 42–43
    Deferred Action for Childhood Arrivals (DACA), 322–323,
        516–517
    depression and, 570, 577
    development of gender identity by, 432
    effects of poverty on a child's brain, 575–577
    embracing mixed heritage by, 561
    English American, 376
    gender dysphoria in, 432–433
    gender schemas and, 432
    Hispanic and Latino/a, 319, 327, 331–332
    Italian American, 377–378
    Jewish American, 380
    lesbian, gay, or transgender parents of, 437–438
    LGBTQ youth and school and, 436–437
    multiracial, counseling and 559–560
    multiracial, divorce and, 561
    multiracial, psychoeducational approach with, 560
    poverty rate for, 573, 574–575
    strengths development and, 110–111
    unaccompanied, 517
    wealthy, mental health issues and, 570
Child Trends Hispanic Institute, 331–332
Chinese acupuncture, 92
Chinese Americans:
    cultural beliefs of, 136
    Cultural Formulation Interview (CFI) and, 183–184 (case
        vignette)
Chinese culture:
    expression of anxiety in, 215
    surrendering concept in, 153, 155, 156
Chinese perspective on human strengths:
    authority orientation and permission to demonstrate
        strengths, 115
    other orientation and strengths, 116
    relational orientation and strengths, 115–116
    strengths as possessions of collective groups rather than
        of the individual, 114–115
Chinese therapeutic approach, 39
Chopra, Deepak, 156–157
Chronological age, 478, 507
Circle, American Indians and, 273–275, 284
Circle of courage, 274–275, 284
Cisgender, 426, 447
Citizenship, 517
Class elitism, counseling profession and, 586–587

Classism:
    defined, 570, 580, 598
    explained, 570–571
    microaggression of, 588
Classism-based trauma, 579–580
Client Bill of Rights for Treatment, 140 (table), 145
Clients:
    acculturation issues of, 214, 214 (table)
    acknowledging pain of, 142
    assessment of cultural identity, 212, 213 (table)
    barriers to change, 167–168
    clinicians biased against, 202–203
    communication styles, 173–174 (table)
    cultural knowledge about, 169
    culturally diverse, White clinicians and, 200–201
    diverse, cultural knowledge for assessing, 170 (table)
    external strengths, 191–192, 192 (table)
    fear response to clinician's assessment, 168
    honoring of communication style, 172
    hopes and dreams of, 151–152
    immigration history, revealing, 212–213
    initial interview with, 52, 53 (table)
    listening for culture in the client's story, 170–171
    minority, overdiagnosis of, 203
    role of, in strengths-based therapy, 139, 140 (figure)
    understanding cultural stories of, 52
Client's struggle perception, 118, 126
Clinical assessment, 163–164, 194
Clinical intervention skill, strengths-based therapy and self-
    limiting beliefs and, 138 (table)
Clinical malpractice, 25
Clinical skill, cultural awareness and, 14 (table)
Clinical skill development:
    counseling interventions using the social class worldview
        model, 581–582 (table)
    cultural awareness and, 13
    cultural congruence and, 13
    cultural incongruence and, 13
    increasing counselor's social class awareness, 579 (table)
Clinical Versus Statistical Prediction (Meehl), 163
Clinicians:
    bias against clients, 202–203
    communication styles, 173–174 (table)
    cultural empathy and, 168–169
    culturally responsive identity for counselors and mental
        health therapists, 94 (figure)
    "do no harm," 252
    four-R process, for challenging self-limiting beliefs, 138
    levels of identity and cultural competency of, 95 (figure)
    multicultural identity worksheet for, 95 (table)
    need to adopt a multicultural identity, 93–94
    points for, 96
    racism and oppression acknowledged by, 252
    White, culturally diverse clients and, 200–201
    See also Counselors; Therapists
Clinton, Hillary, 401
CLUES, in compassionate communication, 144–145
Coffin, William Sloan, Jr., 199
Cognitive behavior approach, 39

Collectivism:
  American Indians and, 267 (table)
  Arab and Muslim Americans and, 349
  Asian Americans and Pacific Islanders and, 295–296
  Black church and, 247–248
  Eastern views on aging and, 482–483
  Hispanic and Latino/a Americans and, 323–324
  immigrants and refugees and, 532
  individualism versus, 116, 295–296
  strengths and, 114–115
Collectivistic orientation, 313
Collins, Jason, 425
Color blind, 237, 257
Coming Apart: The State of White America, 1960–2010 (Murray), 235
Coming out:
  defined, 447
  gays, lesbians, and bisexuals and, 434–435
  people of color and, 435–436
Commitment, 595
Communication, strengths-based:
  CLUES and, 144–145
  compassionate, 144–145
  culturally responsive therapists and, 144
Communication style:
  American Indian, 271–272, 272 (table)
  English American, 376
  high-context Asian cultures and, 300
  Italian American, 378
  Jewish American, 381
Community, Arab and Muslim Americans and, 351
Compassionate strengths-based communication in therapy, 144–145
Competence. *See* Cultural competence
Confederate flag, neural reactions to, 22
Conflict:
  cultural, 133
  Native Hawaiian resolution of, 309
  See also Acculturation conflict
Conflict-induced displacement, 512–513
Confucianism, 116
Confucius, 40 (table)
Consciousness-raising, 408, 412, 421
Construct bias, 164
Continuum of Biracial Identity model (COBI), 553
Convention on the Rights of Persons with Disabilities, 457
Conversion therapy, 443–444
Cooperation and harmony, American Indians and, 271, 284
Coping skills strengths, 191, 191 (table)
Cortisol, effects of, on child's brain, 576
Council for Accreditation of Counseling and Related Educational Programs (CACREP):
  importance of neuroscience in counselor education and, 38, 72
  requirements of, 8–9
  social and cultural diversity in curriculum standards of, 7
Counseling:
  African American clients, 248–249
  American Indians and Alaska Natives clients, 278–279, 279 (table)

Arab and Muslim American clients, 355–357
Asian Americans' expectations about, 305–306
cultural factors in counseling of Asian Americans, 306–309, 310–312 (case vignette)
English American clients, 376
general assessment principles in, 163–169
Italian American clients, 378–379
Jewish Americans, 381
LGBTQ individuals, 440–441
phases of, 596 (table)
social class and trauma and, 579–580
social justice movement in, 583–585
universalistic hypothesis for, 49
use of the circle and medicine wheel (American Indian), 274–275
White Americans of European ancestry, 392–393, 393–396 (case vignette)
See also Culturally responsive counselors
Counseling Across Cultures (Pedersen, Draguns, Lonner, & Trimble), 6
Counseling attrition rate for ethnic/racial minorities, 203–204
Counseling implications:
  for Blacks in poverty, 234
  for middle-class African Americans, 236
Counseling profession and class elitism, 586–587
Counselor competency development, 12–13
Counselor cultural humility, 56–58, 58 (case vignette), 59–60 (case vignette), 59 (table)
Counselor Education and Supervision (ACA), 72
Counselors:
  associations for, 72
  competency assessment for working with refugees and immigrants, 528, 529 (tables)
  culturally responsive identity for, 94 (figure)
  focus on client's negative life events, avoiding, 90–91
  foundational concepts in neuroscience for, 72
  increasing social class awareness of, 579 (table)
  mirror neurons and, 88
  multiethnic/multiracial clients and, 561
  negativity bias as challenge for, 83 (figure)
  principles that guide their work, 584
  secondary trauma of, 528
  training of, and neuroscience and social justice, 589
  See also Clinicians; Therapists
Counselor/therapist competency skills for counseling African American clients, 250 (table)
Countertransference:
  cultural, 43
  ethnocultural, 217–218, 218 (table)
Cox, William, 1
CQ-behavior, 44
CQ-knowledge, 43
CQ-motivation, 43–44
CQ-strategy, 43
Crisis Nerviosa, 333
Cross-cultural assessment, neuropsychology and, 167–168
"Cross-Cultural Counseling" (Jones-Smith & Vasquez; *The Counseling Psychologist*), 6

Cross-cultural empathy, 54
Cross model of racial identity, 241–242
Cross Model of Racial Identity, 257
Crusader disability orientation, 468 (table), 468–469
Cuban Americans:
    migration history of, 321
    obtaining U.S. citizenship, 322
    population of, 319
Cultural alienation, 521, 536
Cultural attachment:
    cultural identity and, 76
    cultural introjection and, 42–43
    defined, 112, 126
    migration, acculturation, and, 112–113
    patterns of, 111–112
    questions and the CFI on, 80 (table)
Cultural attitudes, 64
Cultural awareness:
    checklist for mental health workers, 16 (table)
    clinical skill of, 14 (table)
    clinical skill development and, 13
    defined, 27
Cultural bereavement, immigrants and refugees
        and, 519, 536
Cultural bias:
    assessment and, 164–165, 166 (case vignette), 194
    disparities and, in mental health service delivery systems,
        201–202
Cultural blindness, 12
Cultural compatibility hypothesis, 48, 65
Cultural competence:
    achieving, 11
    cultural humility versus, 58 (case vignette)
    defined, 11–12, 27, 65
    neural pathways as influence on, 38
    stage of development, 13
Cultural competence skills, of culturally responsive
        counselors, 8, 8 (box)
Cultural conflict, 133
Cultural congruence, 13, 27
Cultural consonance, 131–133, 132 (table), 160
Cultural countertransference, 43
Cultural destructiveness, 12
Cultural differences:
    neuroscience and, 38–39
    Western versus Eastern, 40–41 (table)
Cultural dissonance, 131–133, 132 (table), 160
Cultural diversity, implicit and explicit bias and, 23–25
Cultural empathy:
    assessment, cultural resonance, and, 168–169
    cultural humility and, 59–60 (case vignette)
    culturally competent counselor clinical responding and,
        56 (table)
    culturally competent skill of, 55 (table)
    defined, 54, 65
    importance and components of, 54
    promoting, guidelines for, 55–56
Cultural encapsulation, 18, 18 (case vignette), 27
Cultural feminism, 407, 421

Cultural Formulation Interview (CFI):
    Chinese American client and, 183–184 (case vignette)
    components of, 178
    criticisms and limitations of, 181–182
    cultural identity questions and, 80 (table)
    culturally relevant V codes in the DSM-5, 182, 183 (table)
    culture-bound syndromes, assessment, and, 183 (table)
    defined, 97
    description and overview of, 178
    domains of, 179–180
    DSM-5 and, 175, 178
    history of, 178
    overview of, 79–80
    summary statements for, 180
    supplementary modules to, 181
    usefulness and effectiveness of, 178
    when helpful, 178
    See also Case conceptualization and the Cultural
        Formulation Interview (CFI)
Cultural genogram:
    Asians' benefits from, 188
    benefits of, 193
    creating, for multiracial/multicultural family, 561
    defined, 194
    multicultural, 187–188
    preparing, questions to consider, 188 (table)
    preparing, steps for, 187
    use of, 186
Cultural grief, 53
Cultural healing, 306, 308
Cultural humility:
    clinical practice with immigrants and refugees and,
        525–526
    cultural competence versus, in service providers, 58 (case
        vignette)
    cultural empathy and, 57, 59–60 (case vignette)
    defined, 56, 65
    factors that make, 57
    importance of, in counseling relationship, 57, 58
    overview of, 56–57
    skill of (components), 59 (table)
Cultural identity:
    American Indians and, 268–269
    Arab and Muslim Americans and, 352–353
    Asian Americans and Pacific Islanders and, 301
    assessing, with the Cultural Formation Interview (CFI),
        212, 213 (table)
    brain and, 79 (figure)
    brain regions and, 78–79
    cultural formulation interview for the DSM-5 and, 79–80
    elements in, 80
    multiple, 91–92
    positive benefits of, 47
    questions and the Cultural Formulation Interview (CF), 80
        (table)
    stress and, for immigrants and refugees, 519–520
    summary of, 96
Cultural identity development:
    defined, 76, 97

example of, 77 (case vignette)
overview of, 76–77
See also Cultural intelligence (CQ)
Cultural identity formation:
defined, 76, 97
example of, 77 (case vignette)
overview of, 76–77
Cultural impasse, 62, 65, 171
Cultural incapacity, 12
Cultural incongruence, 13, 27
Cultural intelligence (CQ):
defined, 43
ethnocultural identity and, 45
ethnocultural identity development and, 45 (figure)
factors in, 43–44
intra- and intercultural intelligence and, 45
membership groups and, 44
Cultural introjection, 42–43
Cultural knowledge:
assessing culturally diverse clients and, 170 (table)
key skill of, 64
overview of, 52, 169
Culturally appropriate assessment, 175
Culturally bound strengths, 105
Culturally Competent Awareness Checklist for Mental Health Workers, 16, 16 (table), 52
Culturally competent clinical knowledge, 52
Culturally competent clinical responding, levels of, 55–56, 56 (table)
Culturally competent counseling:
development levels of, 12–13
significance of, 12
Culturally competent counseling, barriers to:
assumed dissimilarity and, 48
cultural encapsulation as, 18, 18 (case vignette)
ethnic groups and, 20–21
ethnocentrism and cultural relativism as, 21 (table), 21–22
Eurocentric psychotherapy theories as, 17–18
monocultural clinical orientation as, 19
neural, of ethnic/racial bias, 22–25
race and ethnocentrism as, 19
race as a social construction and, 19–20, 20 (case vignette)
Culturally diverse counseling, 65
Culturally responsive clinical intervention:
critical cultural knowledge for assessing culturally diverse clients, 170 (table)
setting therapist intentions for psychotherapy, 159 (table)
Culturally responsive clinical skill development:
counselors' knowledge about clients' culture, 53 (table)
cultural explanation of illness questions, 216 (table)
cultural identity questions, 213 (table)
intervention skills, 124 (table)
learning about your client's culture, 44 (table)
migration and acculturation questions, 214 (table)
opportunity awareness therapist questions, 151 (table)
psychosocial environment questions, 216 (table)

questions to elicit African American clients' spiritual life, 249 (table)
questions to establish a relationship with a client, 147 (table)
Revised Cross model of Black identity development, 243 (table)
skills for first therapy session, 124 (table)
understanding the impact of your own culture, 14 (table)
understanding your worldview, 15 (table)
Culturally responsive clinical skill intervention, using CFI interview with Chinese American client, 183–184 (case vignette)
Culturally responsive counseling:
assessment models for, 166–167
categories of, 7–8, 8 (box)
counselor evaluation in, 58, 60–61, 61–63 (table)
initial interview for, 123, 125
intake process and, 172, 173–174 (table), 175
reaching across human barriers, 51
strengths-based factors, 116–117
surrender process and, 156
Culturally responsive counselors:
neuroscience and, 87–88, 89–90 (case vignette)
teenagers and, 89–90 (case vignette)
Culturally responsive identity, counselors, mental health therapists, and, 94 (figure)
Culturally Responsive Intake Checklist, 175, 176–177 (table)
Culturally responsive intervention skill, strengths talk and, 154 (table)
Culturally responsive knowledge skills for the initial interview, 52, 53 (table)
Culturally responsive skill development, assessment equivalence and bias in assessment instruments, 166 (case vignette)
Culturally responsive strengths-based client empowerment, 595, 596–597 (case vignette)
Culturally responsive strengths-based clinical skills, checklist of, 61–63 (table)
Culturally responsive strengths-based empowerment clinical skills, 596 (table)
Culturally responsive strengths-based practice:
environment for, 120, 123
promotion of strengths and management of weaknesses by, 120
Culturally responsive strengths-based therapy (CR-SBT):
communication of therapist in, 144
compassionate communication in, 144–145
defined, 25
gratitude diary, 224
immigrants and refugees and, 532 (table), 532–533, 533–534 (case vignette), 533 (table)
multicultural issues in juvenile justice systems and, 335–336 (case vignette)
oracle: conversations about life purpose, 224
strengths cards, 224–225
strengths charts, 225, 225–226 (table)
strengths journal, 219
strengths memories, 224

techniques for, 219, 221, 224–226, 225–226 (table)
use of, 4
"what is the truth" question, 221, 224
See also entries for specific races and ethnic groups
Culturally responsive therapeutic alliance, creating, 145–146
Culturally responsive therapy, 4, 27
Cultural malpractice, 194
Cultural mapping, 75–76, 97
Cultural marginalization, 353–354
Cultural meaning system, 42
Cultural mindsets:
deficit, 117–118, 120
fixed, 119
growth, 119
mindset, defined, 118, 119
overview of, 118–119
strengths, 118, 119–120, 126
See also entries for specific mindsets
Cultural mistrust, 250–251
Cultural Mistrust Inventory (CMI), 251
Cultural neuroscience:
defined, 75, 97
explained, 75–76
findings in, 79
Cultural pre-competence, 12–13
Cultural principles, 36, 36 (table)
Cultural proficiency, 13
Cultural relativism:
defined, 5, 21, 27, 43
ethnocentrism and, 21 (table), 21–22
Cultural resonance, 168–169
Cultural ritual, to help calm the brain, 168
Cultural stories, 52
Cultural strengths:
African American, 245–252
American Indian and Alaska Native, 272–273
Arab and Muslim American, 354
Asian American and Pacific Islander, 301–302
English American, 375–376
Hispanic and Latino/a American, 331–332
Italian American, 378
Jewish American, 380
social class and, 593–594
Cultural trust, 53
Cultural values:
American Indian, 269–272
Hispanic and Latino/a American, 326–329
Culture:
attachment patterns and, 111–112
defined, 2, 27, 35, 65
dominant, 3, 27
emic and etic perspectives on, 37–38
ethnocultural bonding and, 47
ethnocultural identity development and, 45 (figure)
globalization of, 39
human brain and, 38–39
iceberg concept of, 36
identity development and, 41–46
influence of, 2

influence on diagnosis, 208–209
neuroscience and, 38
role of, in quieting the brain, 168
transference and, 42–43
tripartite model of identity and, 41 (figure), 41–46
Culture and Brain (Springer), 79
Culture-bound syndromes:
assessment and, 182, 184, 186
common, types of, 185 (table)
defined, 184, 194
example of, 183–184 (case vignette)
Culture–gene coevolutionary theory of human behavior, 79
Culture shock, 51, 65
Culture-specific disorder, 184, 194
Cushman, Philip, 104

DACA. *See* Deferred Action for Childhood Arrivals (DACA)
Decentering Whiteness, 383 (box), 397
Deferred Action for Childhood Arrivals (DACA), 322–323, 516–517, 536
Deficit approach, 81–82
Deficit mindset:
defined, 126
negative energy field of, 118
from noticing what's missing to noticing what's there, 121–123 (case vignette)
overview of, 117–118
parents, children, and, 120
DeGeneres, Ellen, 425
Dementia, 487–488, 507
Demographics:
African American, 232–236
Alaska Native, 263–264
American Indian, 263–264
Arab American, 344–345
Asian American and Pacific Islander, 290–291
Hispanic and Latino/a American, 318–319
individuals with disabilities, 453–454
LGBTQ individuals, 426–427
multiracial individuals, 543–544, 544 (table)
Muslim American, 345
older adults, 479–482
refugee, 515
social class and, 571–573
White Americans of European ancestry, 367–370
women, 402
Denver Regional Council of Governments (DRCOG), 495, 496
Depression:
adolescents with gender identity issues and, 441
American Indians and, 276
Asian Americans and, 215, 308
Chinese individuals and, 184 (case vignette), 304, 308
culture's role in, 202
disabled women and, 465
Haitian American women and, 202
immigrants and refugees and, 519, 521
individuals in a low social class and, 570
older adults and, 485–486, 494 (case vignette)
preschool children and, 577

wealthy children and, 570
women and, 404–405
Destino, 377, 397
Destructiveness, cultural, 12
Determinist theories, 409
Developing Mind, The (Siegel), 108–109
Development, Relief, and Education for Alien Minors
    (DREAM) Act, 322
Development-induced displacement, 512–513
Devine, Patricia, 1
Dhat, 185 (table)
Diagnosis:
    advantages of, 208
    cultural assessment for, 218
    culture and, 208–209
    culture-related issues in, 202
    defined, 227
    downside of, 208
    limitations of, 208
Diagnostic and Statistical Manual of Mental Disorders (*DSM-5*).
    See DSM-5 (American Psychiatric Association)
Dialectical behavior therapy, 92
Dimensional assessments, 210
Disabilities:
    categories of, 455–457
    invisible, 456–457
    legal, 457
    models of, 457–458
    multicultural issue of, 458–459
Disabilities, individuals with:
    able-bodied privileges and, 459
    ableism and, 459
    Americans with Disabilities Act (ADA; 1990) and, 453
    counseling approaches for, 464–465
    counselor attitudes and training for, 464–465
    demographic data on, 453–454
    disability, defined, 453
    empowerment of, 466–467
    facts about, 457
    family counseling and, 467
    Guidelines for Assessment of and Intervention With Persons
        With Disabilities (APA), 470
    identity development and, 461
    interaction strain and, 460–461
    marginalization of, 458
    microaggressions against, 459–460
    negative barriers encountered by, 458–459
    number of Americans identifying disabled, 92
    Olkin's model of disability and counseling approach,
        469–470
    overview of, 452–453
    "passing" by, 462–463
    population of, 453
    risk for abuse of, 465–466
    social isolation of, 465
    socioeconomic status of, 454–455
    spread and, 460, 464
    strengths-based therapy and, 471–472 (case vignette)
    strengths of, 463–464

Disabilities Education Improvement Act of 2004, 456
Disability affirmative therapy, 467–468
Disability identity, experiencing after trauma, 461–463
Disability oppression, 459
Disability orientation, 467–468, 468 (table), 474
Disability participation, 468
Disability-related violence and abuse, signs of, 466
Disability Status Report (Cornell University), 454
Disaster-induced displacement, 512–513
Discrimination:
    disabled individuals and, 459
    gay rights movement and, 428–431
    women in the workplace and, 403
*Discrimination in America: Experiences and View of Asian
    Americans*, 294
Disempowered phase, of counseling, 596 (table)
Diversity, culturally diverse counseling and, 65. *See also*
    Cultural diversity
Divorce, 561
Dolezal, Rachel, 77 (case vignette), 78
Dominant culture, 3, 27, 49, 65
Dominant group identities, White
    privilege and, 589–590
"Don't ask, don't tell" policy, 428
Don't Blame Mother (Caplan), 408
Dopamine, 74, 91
DREAM Act (Development, Relief, and Education for Alien
    Minors Act), 322
DSM-5 (*Diagnostic and Statistical Manual of Mental Disorders*;
    American Psychiatric Association):
    culturally relevant V codes in, 182, 183 (table)
    ethical problems using, 10–11
    gender dysphoria and, 433
    mental disorder defined by, 456
    revisions in, 208–210
    spiritual explanations for maladies and, 186
    See also Cultural Formulation Interview (CFI)
Dutch Americans, 370
Dynamic reasoning, 464
Dyslexic Advantage, The (Brock and Fernette Eide),
    463–464

Early, P. C., 43
Eastern cultures:
    importance of group in, 84
    right-brain information processing in, 39
    views on aging in, 482–483
Eastern/Western philosophies:
    compared, 39, 40–41 (table)
    cultural empathy and, 54–55
    strengths-based therapy and, 116–117
Einstein, Albert, 149, 569
Elder abuse and neglect, 486, 507
Elder care, increasing need for, 482
Elderly individuals. *See* Older adults
Elderspeak, 484, 507
Ellis, Albert, 17
Emic perspective on culture, 37–38, 66
Emotional abuse, of older adults, 486

Emotional control, Western/Eastern philosophies/cultures, 40 (table)
Emotional restraint, 298
Empathy:
    culturally competent skill of, 55 (table)
    neuroscience and social class and, 582–583
    positive effects of, 54
    See also Cultural empathy
"Empirical verification," 40 (table)
Employment disability, 455, 474
Employment Non-Discrimination Act (ENDA), 428
Empowering phase, of counseling, 596 (table)
Empowerment:
    disabled individuals and, 466–467
    strengths-based therapy and, 595, 596–597 (case vignette), 596 (table)
Encapsulation. See Cultural encapsulation
Enculturation, 2, 49, 66
Enfermedad mental, 333
English Americans:
    communication style and attitudes toward talk and psychotherapy, 376
    counseling approaches for, 376
    cultural description of, 374–377
    cultural strengths of, 375–376
    culture of, 375
    history of, 368, 374–375
    microaggressions against, 375
    notable persons among, 376–377
    population of, 368
    "WASP" culture, 375
Entitlement, narcissism, and social class, 583
Equity, as counselor principle, 584
Equivalence and bias in assessment, 165, 194
Ethical issues:
    ethical violation example, 10 (case vignette)
    multiculturalism and, 8–11
Ethnic belonging, questions and the Cultural Formulation Interview (CF) on, 80 (table)
Ethnic bias:
    counseling attrition rate for ethnic/racial minorities, 203–204
    mental health service delivery systems and, 201
    neural barrier of, 22–25
Ethnic groups:
    cultural barrier of, 20–21
    defined, 27
Ethnic group saliency, 371–381
Ethnic identity, 9
    American Indian, 269
    defined, 27, 66
    development of, 42–43
    influences on, 46
    White Americans of European ancestry and, 368, 371–372
Ethnicity:
    social class and internalized oppression and, 587–589
    White Americans of European ancestry and, 371
Ethnic privilege, 593 (table)

Ethnic self, 46–47
Ethnic self-schema, 46–47
Ethnocentric theories, 409
Ethnocentrism:
    cultural barrier of, 19
    cultural relativism and, 21 (table), 21–22
    defined, 21, 27
    examples of, 21 (table)
Ethnocultural groups, positive contributions of, 92
Ethnocultural identity:
    African American, 240–242, 243 (table)
    developing, 45, 45 (figure)
Ethnocultural privilege, 593 (table)
Ethnocultural transference and countertransference, 217–218, 218 (table), 227
Etic perspective on culture, 37–38, 66
Eurocentric approach to therapy, oppression of clients by, 12
Eurocentric counseling theories, defined, 27
Eurocentric psychotherapy theories, 17–18
European cultures, left-brain information processing in, 39
Evaluation, of counselors, 58, 60–61, 61–63 (table)
Event-related potentials (ERPs), 82
Evidence-based practice (EBP):
    multicultural counseling and, 11
    sampling of ethnic/racial populations in, challenge of, 11
"Evidence-based studies," 40 (table)
Evil eye, 378, 397
Explain, in intake interview, 174 (table)
Explicit bias:
    defined, 23, 27
    explicit bias versus, 23
    paradigm of, and racial bias, 22, 26
External culture, 37
Eye contact, 172, 279 (table)

Face:
    maintaining, 294
    saving, 298, 314
Familismo, 326, 330, 337
Family:
    Asian Americans and suppression of problems, 298–300
    LGBTQ individuals as parents, 437–438
    types of, among Asian Americans, 297–298
Family strengths, ways to ask about, 192 (table)
Family structure:
    African American, 244–245
    Arab and Muslim American, 349–351
    Asian American and Pacific Islander, 296–297
    extended, of African Americans, 245
    Hispanic and Latino/a American, 326–328
    Italian American, 377–378
    poverty and, 575
Family values:
    Asian American and Pacific Islander, 296–297
    Hispanic and Latino/a American, 326
Farrakhan, Louis, 345
Fatalismo, 328, 337

Fear:
    Arab and Muslim Americans and, 341
    change blocked by, 167
    human brain, clinical assessment, and, 167–168
    letting go of, 142
    negative thoughts and, 137
Feminism, 407, 421
Feminist philosophies, 407–408
Feminist psychotherapeutic approach, 415–416
Feminist therapy:
    approaches to, 412
    contribution and criticisms of, 417
    core feminist beliefs, 411 (box)
    defined, 406, 421
    feminist philosophies, 407–408
    gender and power differentials, 411
    gender role stereotyping across cultures, 410
    gender schema therapy, 410
    goals of, 412–413
    integration of, with other approaches, 417
    key concepts of, 409–410
    multicultural therapy and, 416–417
    origin of, 406–407
    role of men in, 413
    sex role stereotypes and androgyny, 409–410
    social construction of gender and, 410–411
    strengths-based therapy example, 418–420 (case vignette)
    techniques of, 414–416
    traditional theories versus, 409
    view of human nature, 409
Ferraro, Geraldine, 404
Filial piety, 298, 313, 482, 483
Filter, 594
Finkenauer, Catrin, 81
First Nations people, 263
Fiske, Susan T., 71
Five Pillars of Islam, 348, 360
Fixed mindset, 119
Flight stage, of the Triple Trauma Paradigm, 523
Focusing phase, of therapy, 596 (table)
Folk illness, 184, 194
Forcibly displaced people, 512–513, 515, 536
Forebrain, 73
Forscher, Patrick S., 1
Foster, P. R. F., 43
Four Noble Truths, 156
Four-R process, for challenging self-limiting beliefs, 138
Fox, Helen, 372–373
Framing solutions, 472 (case vignette), 500–501
French Americans, 369
Freud, Sigmund, 381
Fulbright, J. William, 35
Full-blooded Indian, 268
Functional age, 478, 507
Functional magnetic resonance imaging (fMRI), 78

GABA (gamma-aminobutyric acid), 74
Gandhi, Mahatma, 199, 569
Gay, defined, 425, 447. See also LGBTQ individuals

Gay, Lesbian and Straight Education
    Network (GLSEN), 436
Gay affirmative therapy, 442–444, 447
Gay Liberation Front, 428
Gay rights movement, 428–431
Gender:
    defined, 431, 447
    power differentials and, 411
    social construction of, 410–411
Gendercentric theories, 409
Gender dysphoria, 432–433, 447
Gender expression, 432, 447
Gender identity, 431–432, 447
Gender identity development, 434–435
Gender inequality, 403–404
Gender issues, Asian American families and, 299
Gender privilege, 593 (table)
Genderqueer identity, 426, 447
Gender role analysis, 412, 414, 421
Gender role intervention, 414
Gender role stereotyping across cultures, 410
Gender schema theory, 432, 447
Gender schema therapy, 410
Generosity, American Indians and, 270
Genogram:
    cultural, 186–188, 188 (table), 193
    defined, 194
    strengths, 193
Geographical identity, 94
Geriatrics, 478
German Americans, 368
Gerontology, 478
"Ghost sickness," 186
Globalization:
    cultural, 39
    demand for increased intercultural
        intelligence, 45
Goals, Western/Eastern philosophies/
    cultures on, 40 (table)
Goodman, Andrew, 380
Goomba, 377, 397
Goomma, 377
Go-outside-home disability, 455, 474
Gratitude, 157
Gratitude diary, 224
Gratitude phase, of counseling, 596 (table)
Great Wells of Democracy, The (Marable), 373
Greek Americans, 370
Greenwald, Anthony, 23
Grief, cultural, 53
Grifos, 320
Group level, in tripartite model of identity, 41, 41 (figure)
Growth mindset, 119
*Guidelines for Assessment of and Intervention With Persons
    With Disabilities* (APA), 470
*Guidelines on Multicultural Education, Training, Research,
    Practice, and Organizational Change for Psychologists*
    (APA), 6–7
Gumba, 377, 397

Hajj, 348, 349, 360
Hall, Edward, 36, 37, 42–43, 163, 382
Hamilton Depression Rating Scale, 85
Handbook of Cross-Cultural Neuropsychology (Fletcher-
        Janzen, Strickland, & Reynolds), 167
Hardiman, Rita, 384–387
Hardiman model of White identity development, 397
Hardiman White racial identity model, 384–387
Harmony:
    adolescent "at promise" and 256 (case vignette)
    brain and, 167
    caught between two cultures and, 283 (case vignette
    cooperation and (American Indians), 271
    counselor principle, 584
    older adults and, 501
    trauma and, 472 (case vignette)
    Western/Eastern philosophies/cultures on, 41 (table)
Harper, F. D., 6
Harvesting the good in strengths-based therapy, 311 (case
        vignette), 499, 504 (case vignette)
Haskins, Henry S., 1
Hate crimes, 429
Healing:
    American Indians and, 273–275
    cultural, and indigenous practices, 306, 308
    Hispanic and Latino/a Americans and, 333
Health disabilities, 455, 474
Health status, of older adults, 481–482
"Healthy cultural paranoia," 248, 251, 256
Helms model of White identity development, 387–391, 397
Herskovits, J. M., 49
Heterosexism, 430, 447
Heterosexist, 426, 447
Heterosexist theories, 409
Heterosexual, 426, 447
Heterosexual privilege, 593 (table)
Hierarchical, 313
Hierarchical family structure:
    Arab and Muslim Americans and, 349
    Asian Americans and Pacific Islanders and, 296–297
    Hispanic and Latino/a Americans and, 326
    See also Family structure
High-context cultures:
    Arab and Muslim Americans and, 351–352
    Asian Americans and Pacific Islanders and, 300
    defined, 171, 194
    low-context cultures versus, 382
Hijab, 347, 360
Hill, Napoleon, 149
Hindu yoga, 92
Hispanic Americans:
    population, 200
    term origins, 317–318
Hispanic and Latino/a Americans:
    acculturation conflicts and, 329–330
    adolescents and young adults among, 327
    children among, 327
    collectivistic orientation of, 326
    communication style of, 325–326

counseling approaches for, 333–334, 335–336 (case vignette)
    cultural identity of, 330–331
    cultural strengths of, 331–332
    cultural values of, 326–329
    demographic profile, 318–319
    DREAM Act and, 322–323
    education levels of, 323–324
    ethnocultural factors linking population groups, 318
    family and cultural value of *familismo*, 326
    fatalismo and, 328
    geographical location of, in the United States, 320
    gift-giving during therapy, 328
    immigrant experience of, 318
    immigration status, 322
    income and poverty in the United States: 2015, 572 (table)
    income of, 323
    LGBTQ individuals and, 436
    microaggressions against, 324
    naturalization of, 323
    older adults and, 480
    "other Hispanics," 319
    pathways to citizenship for, 322–323
    personalismo and, 328
    physical and mental health issues, 332–333
    population of, 318, 319
    racial identifications for, 320
    racism and ethnic/racial stereotypes against, 324
    role of men among (*machismo*), 327
    socioeconomic status of, 323–324
    spiritual and religious values of, 328–329
    subgroup migration history of, 320–322
    subgroup percentages of, 319
    term origins, 317–318
    time orientation of, 325
    traditional healing and, 333
    worldview of, 324–325
Hispanic Clinic of the Connecticut Mental Health Center, 211
Historical trauma, 265–266
Holocaust, 379, 397
Homophily, 590, 598
Homophobia, 426, 429–430, 447
Homosexual, 426
Ho'oponopono, 309
Hope, 311 (case vignette), 499
How God Changes Your Brain (Newberg and Waldman), 168
Human race, 20
Humility:
    Asian American families and, 298
    defined, 313, 525
    strength of, in Chinese culture, 115
    See also Cultural humility
Hwan-gap, 483
Hypodescent, 545, 565

Ialomweiu, 304
Iceberg concept of culture, 36, 37, 37 (table)
Identity:
    defined, 461, 542, 565
    malleability of, 77 (case vignette)

Identity development:
  biracial/multiracial, 549–550, 550 (case vignette)
  culture and, 41–46
  disability, after trauma and, 461–463
  disabled individuals and, 461
  LGBTQ individuals and, 431–433
  transgender, 433–434
  See also Multiethnic/multiracial identity
    development
Idiographic assessment, 163–164, 194
Ihtiram, 350
Illegal immigrant, 514–516, 536
Imam, 349, 356, 360–361
Immigrants:
  Asians as largest group, 292
  contributing members of American society, 517–518
  cultural grief of, 53
  defined, 514, 536
  educational levels of, 517
  illegal and undocumented, 514–516
  implicit bias against, 25
  multicultural identities in the United States and, 91–92
  poverty and, 575
  socioeconomic status of, 517
Immigrants and refugees:
  collectivistic orientation of, 532
  competency assessment for practitioners working with, 528, 529 (tables)
  countries of, 513
  cultural alienation and, 521
  cultural bereavement of, 519
  cultural identity and stress for, 519–520
  culturally responsive strengths-based therapy for, overview of, 532 (table), 532–533, 533–534 (case vignette), 533 (table)
  DACA (Deferred Action for Childhood Arrivals) and, 516–517
  foreign-born in the United States, 515
  interpreters and, 526–528
  mental health issues for, 519–528
  microaggressions against, 518–519
  narrative exposure therapy and PTSD and, 531
  numbers of, 513
  posttraumatic stress disorder (PTSD) and, 519
  psychoeducational counseling model for, 530–531
  refugee, asylee, and immigrant: definitions, 513–514
  resettlement needs, 522
  strengths-based approach with, 531–532
  survivor's guilt and, 521
  types of forcibly displaced people, 512–513
  undocumented, 515–516
  See also Pre- and postmigration mental health issues, of immigrants and refugees; Refugees
Immigration:
  Hispanic and Latino/a Americans and, 320–322
  Muslim Americans and, 346
  See also Migration
Immigration history, 212–213
Impasse, cultural, 62, 65

Implicit bias:
  defined, 23, 26, 28
  explicit bias versus, 23
  key points about, 24, 26
  paradigm of, and racial bias, 22, 26
  prejudice against immigrants and refugees, 25
  racial, examples, 24
  reducing, 25
Implicit bias cleansing, 26
Incapacity, cultural, 12
Inclusive cultural empathy, 54
Income:
  African Americans, 232, 235–236
  Asian Americans and Pacific Islanders, 293
  older adults, 481
  poverty and, in the United States: 2015, 572 (table)
  See also Social class
Independence of life, Western/Eastern philosophies/ cultures on, 41 (table)
India, strengths-based intention from, 156–157
Indigenous people, 263
Indigenous practices, for healing, 306
Indios, 320
Individual difference approach, 410
Individualism:
  collectivism versus, 114, 295–296
  social brain as challenge to, 84
  Western views on aging and, 482
  White Americans and, 267 (table)
Individualism–collectivism, 79
Individual level, in tripartite model of identity, 41, 41 (figure)
Individuals, importance of affirming, 3
Individual versus group/collective, Western/Eastern philosophies/cultures on, 40 (table)
Infancy, brain during, 73
Infants, attachment theory and, 108–109
Initial interview in culturally responsive counseling:
  intervention skills, 124 (table)
  overview of, 123, 125
  skills for first therapy session, 124 (table)
Instilling hope, in strengths-based therapy, 499
Insula, 22
Intake interview, 172, 174 (table), 175
Integration strategy, in acculturation, 50
Intellectual disabilities, 456, 474
Intellectual functioning (intelligence), 456
Intentional focus, 111
Intention(s):
  culturally responsive strengths-based, 158, 159 (table)
  effects of, on behavior, 157
  guidelines for setting, 158
  setting, 156–158
  strengths-based (India), 156–158, 159 (table)
  trust relationship with American Indians and Alaska Native clients, 279 (table)
  written, 157
Interaction strain, 460–461, 474
Interconnectedness, 464
Intercultural empathy, 54, 55 (table)

Intercultural intelligence, 45
Intergenerational acculturation stress, 51
Intermarriage:
    Asian Americans and, 292–293
    in the United States, 545
    White Americans of European ancestry and, 370–371
Internal culture, 37
Internalized homophobia, 429
Internalized oppression, 585, 593–594
Internalized stories, 113, 114
International Handbook of Cross-Cultural Neuropsychology
    (Uzzell, Pontón, & Ardila), 167
Interneurons, 73
Interpreters, in counseling of immigrants and refugees,
    526–528
Interracial, 558
Interracial marriage. *See* Intermarriage
Interracial relationships, support for, 561
Interrelatedness, Western/Eastern philosophies/cultures
    on, 41 (table)
Intersectionality:
    defined, 565
    discussed, 585–586
    multiracial identity development and, 556, 557 (case
        vignette)
    origin of, 586
    social class and social justice and, 585–587
    social class identity development and, 586
Intersectionality approach, 491, 507
Intimate partner violence, 403, 405–406, 492
Intracultural intelligence, 45
Intrapsychic orientation, 409
Introjection, cultural, 42–43
Invisible culture (iceberg concept), 37, 37 (table)
Invisible Disabilities Association, 457
Invisible disabilities, 456–457, 474
"Invisible Poverty of 'The Other America' of the 1960s Is Far
    More Visible Today" (Dreier), 233
Involuntary confinement, 466
Ipsative strategy, 189
Iraq and Afghan wars, disabilities from, 454
Iraqi clients, 355
Iraqi refugees, resettlement difficulties of, 523
Irish Americans, 368
Islam, 342, 348, 361
Islamophobia, 341, 346, 361
Islam prayer rituals (*wudhu*), 348–349
Italian Americans:
    communication style and attitudes toward talk and
        psychotherapy, 378
    counseling approaches for, 378–379
    cultural description of, 377–379
    cultural strengths of, 378
    family structure of, 377–378
    immigration of, to the United States, 368
    microaggressions against, 378
    notable persons among, 379
    religion of, 378
Item bias, 165

Jabaos, 320
Jehovah's Witnesses, 136
Jewish Americans:
    children among, 380
    communication style and attitudes toward talk and
        psychotherapy, 381
    cultural description of, 379–381
    cultural strengths of, 380
    cultural values and counseling issues, 379–380
    degrees of adherence to Judaism among, 379
    immigration of, to the United States, 369–370
    microaggressions against, 388
    notable persons among, 381
    social movements and, 380
    White privilege of, 379
Johnson, Lyndon Baines (LBJ), 233
Journal of Counseling and Development (ACA), 72
Journal of Mental Health Counseling (AMHCA), 72
Juvenile justice system, strengths-based therapy and,
    335–336 (case vignette)

Kabat-Zinn, Jon, 92
Kennedy, Anthony, 429
Kennedy, John F., 35, 569
King, Martin Luther, Jr., 123 (box), 231, 569
Kirwan Institute for the Study of Race and Ethnicity (The Ohio
    State University), 24
Knowledge competencies, of culturally responsive
    counselors, 8, 8 (box)
KohCui, 483
Kristof, Nicholas, 234–235

Labor force participation, of older adults, 480–481
Language:
    questions and the Cultural Formulation Interview (CF) on,
        80 (table)
    spoken in the United States, 91
*Language in Relation to a Unified Theory of the Structure of
    Human Behavior* (Pike), 37
"Language Use in the United States: 2011" (Ryan), 91
Lao Tzu, 40 (table)
Latino/a Americans, term origins, 317–318
Latino immigrants, negative bias against, 25
Latinos:
    population, 200
    value on *personalisimo,* 172
Law of belief, 135–136, 160
Law of neuroplasticity, 133–135
LEARN, intake process and, 172, 174 (table)
Learned helplessness, 81
Learning, 133–135
Learning disabilities, 456
Left-brain information processing, 39
"Legal disability," 457
Lesbian, defined, 425, 447. *See also* LGBTQ individuals
Let Be theme, in strengths-based therapy, 143–144, 311 (case
    vignette), 445 (case vignette)
Let Go theme, in strengths-based therapy, 142–143, 255
    (case vignette), 256 (case vignette), 282–283 (case

vignette), 311 (case vignette), 336 (case vignette), 359 (case vignette), 445 (case vignette), 472 (case vignette), 498–499, 504 (case vignette)
Let In theme, in strengths-based therapy, 143, 255 (case vignette), 256 (case vignette), 282–283 (case vignette), 311 (case vignette), 336 (case vignette), 359 (case vignette), 445 (case vignette), 472 (case vignette), 499
Level of acculturation, 214, 227
Levi, A., 57
LGBTQ, 447
LGBTQ individuals:
    barriers to assessment of LGBTQ clients, 443
    coming out of, 434–435
    contributions to psychotherapy, 440
    counseling approaches for, 440–441
    demographic data on, 426–427
    employment discrimination against, 427–428
    gay affirmative therapy and, 442–444
    gender dysphoria in children and adolescents, 432–433
    gender identity development and, 434–435
    hate crimes against, 429
    homophobia and, 429–430
    identity development and, 431–433
    introduction to, 425–426
    marriage rights and, 428–429
    mental health concerns of LGBTQ college students, 439
    mental health issues and, 438
    microaggressions against, 430–431
    number of Americans identifying as, 92
    older, 491–492
    older, intimate partner abuse of, 492
    as parents and families, 437–438
    population of, 426–427
    positive clinical assessment of clients, 443
    reparative therapy and, 443–444
    role of therapist working with, 441–442
    sexual conversion therapy and, 443–444
    socioeconomic status of, 427–428
    strengths-based therapy model, example, 444–445 (case vignette)
    strengths of, 439–440
    terms, 425–426
    therapeutic process in gay and lesbian psychotherapy, 441
    transgender identity development and, 433–434
    youth and school and, 436–437
Liberal feminism, 407, 421
Listening:
    for client's story, 52, 145
    for culture in the client's story, 170–171
    in intake interview, 174 (table)
Lombardi, Vince, 40 (table)
Longfellow, Henry Wadsworth, 478
"Long-Term Reduction in Implicit Race Bias: A Prejudice Habit-Breaking Intervention" (Devine, Forscher, Austin, & Cox), 1

López, Ricardo, 325–326
L'ordine della familigia, 377, 397
Losing face, 298, 313
Loving v. Virginia (1967), 542, 545
Low-context cultures, 171, 194, 382
Lower class, in the United States, 571
Lower-middle class, in the United States, 571
Lower-upper class, in the United States, 571
Lucas, Carrie Ann, 460–461

Machismo, 329, 337, 436
Mafia (*Mafioso*), 378
Maladi moun fe mal, 185 (table)
Mal de ojo, 185 (table)
Malocchio, 378, 397
Mapping, cultural, of the brain, 75–76
Marginal individuals, 49–50
Marginalization:
    assimilation, acculturation, and acculturative stress, and, 49–50
    defined, 66
    multiracial individuals and, 548–549
Marginalized, 49, 66
Marianismo, 329, 337
Marital status, of older adults, 481
Marshall, Thurgood, 123 (box)
Masculine person, 409
Maslow's hierarchy of needs, 530
Master and His Emissary, The: The Divided Brain and the Making of the Western World (McGilchrist), 38–39
Material reasoning, 464
McDonald's, 39
McGilchrist, Iain, 38–39
Mead, Margaret, 199
Medial prefrontal cortex (mPFC), 23, 28, 78
Medical model of disability, 458, 469–470, 474
Medical model therapy (pathology model):
    beliefs of, 118 (table)
    defined, 126
Medicine (American Indian), 273–275
Medicine wheel, American Indians and, 273–275, 284
Meditation, 40 (table)
Memories:
    autobiographical narrative process and, 113
    strengths memories, 224
Memory loss, 487–488
Menendez brothers, 570
Mental deterioration, 487–488
Mental Health: Culture, Race, and Ethnicity (U.S. Surgeon General), 201
Mental health fields, neuroscience acceptance by, 72
Mental health issues:
    Arab and Muslim Americans and, 354–355
    Asian Americans and, 303–304
    Hispanic and Latino/a American and, 332–333
    immigrants and refugees and, 519–520
    Native Hawaiians and other Pacific Islanders and, 304–305
    neuroscientific perspective, 84

older adults and, 484–486

poverty and, 578–579, 579 (table)

pre- and postmigration (immigrants and refugees), 520–528

White Americans of European ancestry and, 391

women and, 404–406

Mental health service delivery systems, cultural bias in, 201–202

Mental health therapists, culturally responsive identity for, 94 (figure)

Mental health workers, Culturally Competent Awareness Checklist for, 16 (table), 52

Mental retardation, term replaced by intellectual disability, 456

Mental shield, 594

Method bias, 165

Mexican Americans:

    LGBTQ individuals and, 436

    migration history of, 321

    population, 319

Mexican immigrants, undocumented, 322, 516

Microaggression, classism as, 588

Microaggressions (against):

    African American clients, by therapists, 251–252

    African American population mixed with other ethnic/ racial groups, 238–239

    African Americans, 238

    American Indians and Alaska Natives, 266

    Arab and Muslim Americans, 346–347

    Asian Americans, 294–295

    English Americans, 375

    Hispanic and Latino/a Americans, 324

    immigrants and refugees, 518–519

    individuals with disabilities, 459–460

    Italian Americans, 378

    Jewish Americans, 388

    LGBTQ individuals, 430–431

    multiracial individuals, 546–547

    older adults, 483

    social classes, 588

    women, 403–404

Migrants, defined, 513

Migration:

    Arab Americans and, 343–344

    cultural attachment, acculturation, and, 112–113

    defined, 513

    forces of, 517

    Hispanic and Latino/a Americans and, 320–322

    multicultural counseling movement influenced by, 5

    See also Immigrants and refugees; Immigration

Migration history, 212–213, 227

Migration process, 514, 536

Millennials, 372–373

Mind, 75, 97, 113

MIND aptitudes, dyslexia and, 464

Mindfulness, 114, 153, 155–156

Mindfulness-based cognitive therapy, 92

Mindfulness-based stress reduction (MBSR), 92

Mindfulness practices, 92

Mindfulness therapy, 39, 40 (table)

Mindset. *See* Cultural mindsets

Mini-Mental State Examination (MMSE), 488

Minorities, counseling attrition rates for, 203–204

Minority and Cross-Cultural Aspects of Neuropsychological Assessment (Ferraro), 167

Minority model of disability, 458, 474

Miranismo, 328

Mirror neurons, 88, 97, 168

Mirror neuron system (MNS), 88, 97

Miscegenation, 545, 565

Mixed heritage, 543, 548–549

Mixed methods, of quantitative and qualitative assessment, 164, 194

Mixed race, 543

Mobility and physical disabilities, 455, 474

Model minority, 294, 313

Monocultural, 94

Monocultural clinical orientation, 19, 28

Monoracial, 543, 565

Moral model of disability, 457–458, 474

Morenos, 320

Morita therapy, 40 (table)

Mother blaming, 408

Motor neurons, 73

Move Forward theme, in strengths-based therapy, 144, 311 (case vignette), 336 (case vignette), 359 (case vignette), 445 (case vignette), 472 (case vignette), 502, 504 (case vignette)

Muecke, Marjorie, 512

Muhammad, 342, 361

Multiaxial system, 210

Multicultural and Social Justice Counseling Competencies, 585

Multicultural Assessment-Intervention Process (MAIP), 166–167

Multicultural Assessment Procedure (MAP), 167

Multicultural competencies, 6–8, 28

Multicultural counseling:

    criticism of approaches, 11

    defined, 28

    evidence-based practice (EBP) and, 11

    future of, 11

Multicultural Counseling Competencies Revisions Committee, American Counseling Association, 584–585

Multicultural counseling movement:

    migration as factor in, 5

    phases of, 5–6

"Multicultural Guidelines: An Ecological Approach to Context, Identity, and Intersectionality" (APA), 9

Multicultural identity:

    clinicians' need to adopt, 93–94

    conflicts within, 93

    culturally responsive identity for counselors and mental health therapists, 94 (figure)

    defined, 93

levels of clinician's identity and cultural competency, 95 (figure)
worksheet for, 95 (table)
Multiculturalism:
    cultural relativism and, 5
    defined, 4–5, 28
    ethical issues and, 8–11, 10 (case vignette)
Multicultural therapy, feminist therapy and, 416–417
Multidimensional privilege, 592, 593 (table)
Multiethnic individuals. See Multiethnic/multiracial identity development
Multiethnic/multiracial identity development:
    commonalities across models, 554
    creating a cultural genogram for, 561
    intersectionality and, 556, 557 (case vignette)
    levels of experiences of biracial people, 551
    measuring racial identities, 552
    mental health and, 557
    Multiple Heritage Identity Development model, 553
    multiracial bill of rights, 557–558
    overview of, 550
    parental discussion of race and racial experience, 562
    "passing" for Black, 552–553
    patterns of identity among multiracial college students, 551–552
    positive resolutions for tensions encountered by biracial or multiracial individuals, 551
    psychotherapy with, 559–562, 562–563 (case vignette), 562 (table)
Multiple cultural identities, 91–92
Multiple heritage, 543, 549 (case vignette), 558
Multiple Heritage Identity Development model, 553
Multiple-race White population, 370–371
Multiracial, defined, 542–543, 565
Multiracial bill of rights, 557–558
Multiracial/Ethnic Counseling Concerns (MRECC), 558
Multiracial Experience, The (Root), 548, 557–558
Multiracial identity, 239 (case vignette)
Multiracial individuals:
    age of, 544–545
    competencies for counseling, 558
    counselor's role in working with, 560
    demographic and population data on, 543–544, 544 (table)
    forcing an ascribed identity on, 547
    interracial marriage and, 545
    introduction to, 541–542
    marginality and mixed heritage and, 548–549
    microaggressions against, 546–547
    multiracial, defined, 542–543
    "one-drop rule," 545–546
    psychoeducational approach with, 560
    race as a social construction and, 542
    racial self-identification and, 555
    racism and skin color and, 547–548
    sense of not quite belonging, 549–550, 550 (case vignette)
    strengths of, 555–556
    "two or more races," 544, 544 (table)
    views on race, 554

"what are you?" question, 548, 549 (case vignette)
    See also Multiethnic/multiracial identity development
Muslim, 342–343, 361
Muslim Americans:
    African Americans, Jews, and, 345
    demographic data on, 345
    educational levels of, 346
    immigration and, 346
    population, 345
    socioeconomic status of, 346
    See also Arab and Muslim Americans
Muslim culture, 348
Muslim religion (Islam), 348, 361
Muslims:
    subgroups of, 343
    worldwide, 342–343

Naikan therapy, 40 (table)
Narcissism, entitlement, and social class, 583
Narrative exposure therapy (NET), 531, 536
Narrative process, 113
Narrative reasoning, 464
National Alliance on Mental Illness (NAMI), 304
National Asian American Pacific Islander Mental Health Association (NAAPIMHA), 304
National Council on Aging, 486, 488
National Organization for Women (NOW), 413
Nation of Islam, 345
Native American Acculturation Scale, 276
Native Hawaiians:
    culturally responsive strengths-based therapy for, overview of, 289–290
    ho'oponopono, 309
    mental health and, 304–305
    older adults and, 480
    population of, 200
    socioeconomic status of, 293
    values and cultural healing practices of, 308
Native Identity Scale (NIS), 269
Naturalization, 514, 536
Naturalized citizens, 323
Negative energy field, 118
Negative thinkers, 82–84
Negative thoughts:
    fear created by, 137
    pain caused by, 137–138
    reframing, 91
    self-limiting beliefs and, 136–137
Negativity bias, 81–82, 97
Negativity bias, of the brain, 83 (figure)
Negotiate, in intake interview, 174 (table)
Neigong, 308
Neocortex, 91
Neural coherence (harmony), 167
Neural empathic responses, 582–583
Neural net profile, 74, 97
Neural networks, changing, 86, 87 (case vignette)
Neural pathways, new, from neuroscience, 87 (case vignette)

Neural prejudice networks in the brain, 22–23

Neurasthenia, 304

Neurobiology of human strengths development, brain and, 106, 107 (figure)

Neurocultural dynamics, 131–133, 132 (table), 160

Neurogenesis, 75, 79 (figure), 97, 577–578, 578 (table)

Neuroimaging techniques and the brain, 84, 97

Neurological mirroring, 88

Neurons:
    defined, 72, 73, 97
    mirror, 88
    types of, 73

Neuroplasticity:
    adaptations during life stages, 74–75
    conditions facilitating, 134
    cultural influences on, 78–79, 79 (figure)
    defined, 97, 160
    law of, 133–135
    visualization and, 134

Neuropsychology, cross-cultural assessment and, 167–168

Neuropsychology and the Hispanic Patient: A Clinical Handbook (Pontón & Leon-Carrión), 167

Neuropsychotherapy perspective, 89–90 (case vignette)

Neuroscience:
    belief and, 135–136
    CACREP standards for, 72
    changes through, 87 (case vignette)
    counseling associations and, 72
    counselor training and social justice and, 589
    cultural, findings in, 79
    cultural differences and, 38–39
    culturally responsive counselors and, 87–88, 89–90 (case vignette)
    culture and, 38
    defined, 71, 97
    foundational concepts for counselors, 72
    measures for, 78
    mental health and, 84
    mental health fields acceptance of, 72
    multiple cultural identities and, 91–92
    negativity bias of the brain and, 81–82
    poverty and social class and, 573–582
    psychotherapy changes your brain, 85
    sexual orientation and, 426
    social class and empathy and, 582–583
    social justice and, 588–589
    stress relief through, 87 (case vignette)
    therapeutic relationships from, 85–86
    See also Brain

Neuroscience, the brain, and the invisible neural barrier of ethnic/racial bias, 22–25

Neuroscience worldview, 86, 97

Neurotransmitters, 74, 98

New Directions for Student Services: Serving Native American Students (Horse), 268

New Earth, A: Awakening to Your Life's Purpose (Tolle), 155

Nigrescence, 241–242, 243 (table)

Nigrescence recycling, 243 (table)

Nittle, Nadra Kareem, 541

Nomothetic assessment, 163, 194

Nonbinary identity, 426, 447

Noninterference, American Indians and, 271, 284

Nonracist White identity, 384, 397

Normalization disability orientation, 468, 468 (table)

Normative strategy, 189

NTU Afrocentric model for counseling African Americans, 252–253

Nursing home population, 480

Obama, Barack, 231, 428, 429, 545, 546, 591

Obergefell v. Hodges (2014), 429

Obstacle hurdling, 255 (case vignette), 256

Ogburn, William Fielding, 199

'Ohana, 309, 313

Older adults:
    additional strengths assessment issues, 502
    Alzheimer's disease and other cognitive impairments, 487–488
    Arab and Muslim American, 355
    Asian American, 300
    clinical intervention and treatment issues, 502–503
    demographic data on, 479–482
    depression example, 494 (case vignette)
    depression in, 485–486
    elder abuse and, 486
    health status of, 481–482
    income of, 481
    increasing need for care for, 482
    labor force participation of, 480–481
    letting go, harvesting the good, eliciting clients' hopes and dreams, and letting in the good/change, 498–500, 500 (table)
    LGBTQ, 491–492
    marital status of, 481
    mental health issues of, 484–486
    microaggressions against, 483–484
    number of Americans identifying as, 92
    population of, 479–480
    poverty rate of, 481
    prevention of chronic physiological disease in, 484
    racial composition of, 480
    role of strengths-based therapist with, 493
    sexuality and, 489–492
    social isolation of, 486
    socioeconomic status of, 480–481
    strengths-based therapy and, 492–502, 503–505 (case vignette)
    strengths discovery assessments for, 495–496, 496 (table), 497–498 (table)
    substance abuse and, 488–489
    suicide rates for, 486
    Western and Eastern cultural view on aging, 482–483

Olkin's model of disability and counseling approach, 469–470

"One drop of blood"/"one drop" rule:
    clinician's response to, 239
    defined, 565

explained, 545–546
impact on view of multiracial identity, 560
multiracial identity example of, 239 (case vignette)
old view of, 550
U.S Census responses, changes in, 239 (case vignette)
Opportunity awareness, 149–151, 151 (table)
Opportunity questions, 151, 160
Oppression:
    defined, 585, 598
    internalized, 593–594
    internalized, and social class and ethnicity/race, 587–589
    social justice and, 585
Optimism, 82
Oracle: conversations about life purpose, 224
Orbital frontal cortices, 22
Orbitofrontal cortex (OFC), 23, 28
Orthodox Jews, 379, 380, 397
Other America, The: Poverty in the United States
        (Harrington), 233
"Other Hispanics," 319
Other-oriented interpersonal stance, 56
Our Kind of People: Inside America's Black Upper Class
        (Graham), 236
Outing, 492
Overdiagnosis of minority clients, 203, 227

Pacific Islanders:
    collectivistic orientation of, 295–296
    cultural healing and indigenous practices, 306
    cultural identity and, 301
    cultural issues of, 295–300
    culturally responsive strengths-based therapy for,
        289–290
    cultural strengths of, 301–302
    cultural values of, 296
    defined, 313
    family hierarchical structure, family values, and parenting
        styles, 296–297
    high-context culture of, 300
    mental health of, 304–305
    mental illness and substance use among, 305
    older adults and, 480
    population and demographic statistics for, 290–291
    socioeconomic status of, 293
    worldview of, 295
Pain medications, abuse by older adults, 488–489
Panic attack, 38
Paradigm of implicit and explicit racial bias, 22, 28
Parenting styles, of Asian Americans and Pacific Islanders,
        296–297
Parents, negativity bias and, cautions about, 84
Parks, Rosa, 231
Participation, as counselor principle, 584
"Passing":
    Arab and Muslim Americans, 347
    Black, biracial individuals, 552–553
    disabled individuals, 462–463
Passive neglect, of older adults, 486

Pathology model (medical model), 118 (table), 126
Pavlovian fear conditioning, 23
People of color, 241
Personal culture, 58 (case vignette), 66
Personalismo, 328, 337
Pesach (Passover), 380
Pessimism, 82
Petri, Tom, 239 (case vignette)
Pick-collar jobs, 403, 405
Pike, Kenneth, 37
Plessy v. Ferguson (1896), 545
Pogroms, 379, 381, 397
Polish Americans, 369
Political awareness, 413
Pope Francis, 425
Population (of):
    African Americans, 200, 232–236
    Alaska Natives, 263–264
    American Indians, 263–264
    Asian Americans, 290–291
    disabled individuals, 453
    Hispanic and Latino/a Americans, 318, 319
    immigrants and refugees, 513, 515
    LGBTQ individuals, 426–427
    multiracial Americans, 543–544, 544 (table)
    Muslim Americans, 345
    older adults, 479–480
    Pacific Islanders, 290–291
    White Americans of European ancestry, 367–370
Positive energy field, 118
Positive thinkers, 82–84
Positive words, 145
Postflight stage, of the Triple Trauma Paradigm, 524
Postmodern feminism, 408, 421
Poston's five levels of experiences of biracial
        people, 550–551
Posttraumatic stress disorder (PTSD):
    counseling and therapy models for refugees with, 528, 530
    defined, 536
    immigrants and refugees and, 519
    Iraqi clients and, 355
    LGBTQ individuals and, 438
    narrative exposure therapy (NET) and, 531
Poverty:
    African Americans and, 232–233
    age and gender differences, 402
    Asian alone population and, 293
    Black, implications for counseling, 234
    children and, 573, 574–575
    decreased ability to regulate emotion, 576
    demographic data on social class and, 571–573
    effects of, on a child's brain, 575–577
    federal poverty threshold for 2015, 574
    income and poverty in the United States: 2015, 572 (table)
    mental health and, 578–579, 579 (table)
    money can reverse negative effects of, 577
    neurogenesis and, 577–578, 578 (table)
    neuroscience of, 573–582

older adults and, 481
parental education and family structure and, 575
race and, 574–575
women and, 402–403
women and, by race, 402
Power analysis, 415, 421
Power differentials, 411
Power distance, 79
Power of Now, The (Tolle), 155
Pre- and postmigration mental health issues, of immigrants
    and refugees:
    acculturative stress and, 520–521
    clinical practice with immigrants and
        refugees, 525–526
    core counseling competencies for working with torture
        survivors, 524, 525 (table)
    cultural humility and, 525–526
    culturally responsive clinical questions on client's
        premigration experiences, 520 (table)
    interpreters and, 526–528
    refugee/asylee experience: Triple Trauma Paradigm,
        523–524
    torture experiences and, 522–523
Pre-competence, cultural, 12–13
Preflight stage, of the Triple Trauma Paradigm, 523
Prejudice:
    African Americans as focus of, 238
    defined, 28
    immigrants and refugees as focus of, 25
    neural networks in the brain and, 22–23
    racial, 23–24
Prietos, 320
Principle of reinforcement, 17
Privilege:
    defined, 589, 598
    multidimensional, 592, 593 (table)
    social class, 592
    See also White privilege
Privilege constellation, 597
Professional associations, 9
Proficiency, cultural, 13
Project Implicit, 23
Psychoanalytic therapy, 39
Psychoeducational counseling model, for immigrants and
    refugees, 530–531
Psychological assessment, 163, 194
Psychological Costs of Racism to Whites (PCRW) framework,
    591–592
Psychological disabilities, 456, 474
Psychosocial costs of racism to Whites, 592
Psychosocial environment, 216, 216 (table), 217 (case
    vignette)
Psychotherapy:
    African Americans and, 248–249
    brain changes from, 85
    English Americans and, 376
    general assessment principles in, 163–169
    Italian Americans and, 378

Jewish Americans and, 381
multiethnic/multiracial clients and, 559–562, 562–563
    (case vignette), 562 (table)
Psychotherapy attrition rates for ethnic/racial minorities,
    203–204, 228
Puerto Ricans:
    migration history of, 321
    population, 319
    U.S. citizenship of, 322
Puritans, 374, 397
Purpose power, 595

Qi (chi), 304, 308, 314
Qigong, 308, 314
Qualitative assessment, 163–164, 194, 194–195
Quantitative assessment, 163–164, 194, 195
Queer, 426, 447
Qur'an, 342, 361

Race:
    cultural barrier of, 19
    defined, 28, 565
    interracial marriage and, 545
    multiracial individuals' view on, 554
    older adults and, 480
    poverty and, 574–575
    social construction of, 19–20, 20 (case vignette), 28, 542
Race salience, 242
Race self-identification, 555
Racial bias:
    counseling attrition rate for ethnic/racial minorities and,
        203–204
    implicit, by doctors and judges, 24
    implicit and explicit, paradigm of, 28
    in mental health service delivery systems, 201
    neural barrier of, 22–25
Racial identity:
    Arab and Muslim Americans and, 352–353
    brain regions and, 78
    Hispanic and Latino/a Americans and, 320
    influences on, 46
    white woman who says she is black, 77 (case vignette)
    See also White racial identity models
Racial identity development models, 241–242, 257
Racial identity formation, 561
Racialized science, 20, 28
Racial prejudice, focus of, 23–24
Racial purity, 545
Racial stereotyping. *See* Stereotypes
Racism:
    acknowledged by clinicians, 252
    against Asian Americans, 294–295
    generational connection, age, and social class dimensions
        of, 372–373
    against Hispanic and Latino/a Americans, 324
    multiracial individuals and, 547–548
    neural networks in the brain and, 22–23
    stages of, in American society, 237

Radical feminism, 407, 421
RAKACBIAS, 60–61, 61–63 (table)
Ramadan, 349, 361
Ratey, John J., 71
Recommend, in intake interview, 174 (table)
Redlining, 235
Reframing, of negative thoughts, 91
Refugee Processing Center (U.S. State Department),
    513–514
Refugees:
    counseling and therapy models for PTSD, 528,
        530–532
    defined, 513, 536
    demographics and population statistics, 515
    implicit bias against, 25
    refugee/asylee experience: Triple Trauma Paradigm,
        523–524
    types of, admitted to the United States in 2016,
        513–514
    See also Immigrants and refugees; Pre- and
        postmigration mental health issues, of immigrants
        and refugees
Relational-cultural theory (RCT), 415–416, 416 (table), 421
Relational stress, 521
Religion:
    African Americans and, 247–248, 249 (table)
    Hispanic and Latino/a Americans and, 328–329
    older adults and, 499–500
Religious privilege, 593 (table)
Reparative therapy, 443–444
Reptilian brain, 90 (case vignette)
Reservation, 263, 284
Resignation disability orientation, 468, 468 (table)
Resilience, 537
Resiliency, of African Americans, 246
Respeto, 327, 337
Revised Cross model of racial identity, 241–242, 243 (table)
"Rich Man, Poor Man: Socioeconomic Adversity and Brain
    Development" (Noble), 577
Right-brain information processing, 39
Roosevelt, Eleanor, 401
Roosevelt, Franklin D., 512
Root, Maria P. P., 541, 548
Russian Americans, 370

Sage, burning of, 274
Salat (salah), 348
Salience for "Blackness," 242, 243 (table)
Saliency, ethnic group, for White Americans, 371–381
Same-sex couples, marriage and, 428–429
Save face, 298, 314
Sawm, 348, 349
Scale to Assess World View (Ibrahim & Kahn), 164
Scandinavian Americans, 369
Schema, 410
Schwerner, Michael, 380
Scotch-Irish Americans, 369
Scottish Americans, 369

"Searching the Chinese Cultural Roots of the Strengths
    Perspective" (Yip), 114
Secondary trauma, 528, 537
Self, sense of, Western/Eastern philosophies/cultures and,
    40 (table)
Self-appreciation, 595
Self-awareness, 64
Self-care disability, 455, 474
Self-control, 298
Self-coping, 179–180
Self-definitions, bad, avoiding, 81
Self-empowerment, 595
Self-harm, assessment of, 193
Self-knowledge, 595
Self-limiting beliefs:
    anxiety created by, 137
    defined, 136, 160
    examples of, 136–137
    four-R process for challenging, 138
    harmfulness of, 596 (table)
    letting go of, 143
    strengths-based therapy intervention and, 138 (table)
Self-schemas, 46–47
Sen-nin, 482
Sensory disabilities, 455, 474
Sensory neurons, 73
Separation strategy, in acculturation, 50
September 11, 2001, terrorist attacks, 513
Serotonin, 74
Seventh-day Adventists, 136
Sex, defined at birth, 431, 447–448
Sexism, 407, 421
Sex ratio, 402
Sex role stereotypes, 409–410
Sexual abuse:
    elders and, 486, 488
    individuals with disabilities and, 466
    women and, 405–406
Sexual conversion therapy, 443–444
Sexuality, older adults and, 489–492
Sexualization, of women, 405
Sexual orientation, 5
    defined, 28, 432, 448
    discrimination and, 428
Shades of Black (Cross), 241
Shahada, 348
Shame/shaming:
    Arab and Muslim American families and, 355
    Asian American families and, 298
    defined, 314
Sharaf, 350
Sharing and generosity, American Indians and, 270, 285
Shiite, 343, 361
Shin-byung, 185 (table)
Silence:
    American Indians and, 271–272, 272 (table),
        279 (table)
    inner, cultivating, 144–145

Simpatía, 328
Skin color:
    acculturation and assimilation factor of Arab and Muslim immigrants, 352–353
    biological marker for "racial" groups, 19, 28
    Hispanic and Latino/a views on, 320
    identity development and, 330
    LGBTQ coming out difficulties and, 436
    multiracial individuals and, 547–548
    White, as status symbol, 237
    White privilege and, 382, 397, 590, 593 (table)
Skinner, B. F., 17
Slavery:
    denigration and dehumanization of, 231
    legacy of and response to, by African Americans, 236–237
Slovak Americans, 370
Social activism, 412, 413
Social brain, 84
Social class:
    classism and, 570–571
    culturally responsive counseling and, 569–573
    cultural strengths and, 593–594
    defined, 402, 569–570, 598
    demographic data on, 571–573
    entitlement and narcissism and, 583
    ethnicity/race and internalized oppression and, 587–589
    implications in mental health issues, 570
    intersectionality and social justice and, 585–587
    low, problems stemming from, 570
    microaggressions against, 588
    multicultural construct, 570
    neuroscience and empathy and, 582–583
    neuroscience of, 573–582
    seven classes, in the United States, 571–572
    social stratification theory and, 570
    trauma and counseling and, 579–580
    wealth, problems stemming from, 570
    worldview model, 580, 581–582 (table), 582
    See also Poverty
Social class identity development and intersectionality, 586
Social class privilege, 589, 592, 593 (table), 598
Social construction:
    gender as, 410–411
    race as, 19–20, 20 (case vignette), 28
Social distance scale, 547
Social hierarchy, preference for, 79
Socialist feminism, 407, 421
Social justice, 5
    defined, 28, 584, 598
    neuroscience and, 588–589
    oppression and, 585
    quotations, 123 (box)
    social class and classism and, 571
    social class and intersectionality and, 585–587
Social justice movement in counseling, 583–585, 599
Social learning theory, 432
Social model of disability, 458
Social neuroscience, 589

Social rejection, 580
Social stratification theory, 570, 599
Socioeconomic status:
    African American, 232–233
    American Indian and Native Alaskan, 265
    Arab American, 345
    Asian American and Pacific Islander, 293
    Hispanic and Latino/a American, 323–324
    immigrant, 517
    individuals with disabilities and, 454–455
    LGBTQ individuals and, 427–428
    Muslim American, 346
    Native Hawaiian and other Pacific Islander, 293
    older adults and, 480–481
    women and, 402
    Sociopolitical model of disability, 458, 474
Spatial reasoning, 464
"Special populations," 209
"Specific learning disability," 456
Spirituality:
    African Americans and, 247–248, 249 (table), 258
    American Indians and, 270–271, 285
    Hispanic and Latino/a Americans and, 328–329
    older adults and, 499–500
Spread, 460, 464, 474
Standards for the Practice of Clinical Mental Health Counseling (AMHCA), 72
Statuses, 554
Stereotypes:
    American Indians and Alaska Natives and, 266
    Asian Americans and, 294–295
    Hispanic and Latino/a Americans and, 324
    White Americans of European ancestry and, 372–373
Stereotype threat, 410, 590, 593–594
Stonewall riots, 428
Stories:
    internalized, 113, 114
    listening for culture in the client's story, 170–171
Storytelling, 272
Strength, defined, 105
Strength of transcendence, 116
Strengths:
    brain's "use it or lose it" principle, 107
    characteristics of, 105
    Chinese perspective, 114
    culturally bound, 105
    as dialogic conversations with the self, 113–114
    overview of, 114
    as possessions of collective groups rather than of the individual, 114–115
    See also entries for individual races or groups
Strengths analysis, 148–149, 149 (figure)
Strengths assessment and treatment process, 191
Strengths audience, 114, 126
Strengths-based case conceptualization:
    actions of, 218–219
    model components, 218–219
    protocol for: integration of the CFI, 220 (table)

Strengths-based therapists, role of, 140, 140 (figure). *See also* Counselors
Strengths-based therapy (SBT):
    applying to different cultures, 116–117
    "at-promise youth" and, 253, 253–256 (case vignette)
    basic assumptions of, 139, 139 (table)
    beliefs of, 118 (table)
    Client Bill of Rights, 140 (table)
    client empowerment through, 595, 596–597 (case vignette), 596 (table)
    client's role in, 139
    defined, 4, 28
    design of, 131
    disabled individuals and, 471–472 (case vignette)
    immigrants and refugees and, 531–532
    law of neuroplasticity and, 133–135
    LGBTQ example, 444–445 (case vignette)
    model, 141 (figure), 141–144
    new concepts and clinical strategies for, 138–139
    older adults and, 492–502
    opportunity awareness and, 149–151, 151 (table)
    philosophy of, 117–118
    protocol for, 141
    revised, 138–144
    self-limiting beliefs intervention and, 138 (table)
    stimulation of neocortex by, 91
    SWOB (strengths, weaknesses, opportunities, barriers) analysis and, 147–149, 148 (table), 149 (figure)
    techniques for, 144–159
    themes of, 141–142
    White Americans of European ancestry and, 393–396 (case vignette)
    See also Assessment process, of strengths-based therapy model; Culturally responsive strengths-based therapy (CR-SBT)
Strengths-based treatment plans, 219, 221 (table)
Strengths cards, 224–225
Strengths charts, 225, 225–226 (table)
Strengths development:
    attachment relationships and, 109–110
    attachment theory and, 108–109
    attention and, 111
    brain and, 106, 107 (figure)
    narrative process, the mind, and, 113
    relational components of, 108
    trusted relationships and, 110–111
Strengths dialogues, 114, 126
Strengths discovery, 255 (case vignette), 256 (case vignette), 445 (case vignette), 471–472 (case vignette)
Strengths genogram, 193, 195
Strengths journal, 219, 228
Strengths memories, 224
Strengths mindset:
    defined, 126
    from noticing what's missing to noticing what's there, 121–123 (case vignette)
    overview of, 119–120
    positive energy field of, 118

Strengths perception, 311 (case vignette)
Strengths perspective in counseling and therapy, 114, 126
Strengths surveillance, 114, 126
Strengths talk:
    benefits of, 152
    categories of, 153 (table)
    characteristics of, 152
    culturally responsive, 153
    defined, 152, 160
    recognizing and encouraging, in clients, 152
    recognizing strengths, chart for, 154 (table)
Striatum, 22, 23, 28
Subjective age, 478, 507
Substance abuse:
    American Indians and Alaska Natives and, 277
    Asian Americans and Pacific Islanders and, 305
    older adults and, 488–489
Success, Western/Eastern philosophies/cultures on, 40 (table)
Successful aging, 495
Suicide:
    American Indians and Alaska Natives and, 277–278
    older adults and, 486
Sujud, 349, 361
Sunni, 343, 361
Surrender, 142
Surrendering:
    defined, 153
    energy of, 155
"Surrender" intervention procedures, 155–156
Surrender process, 156
Survival strategies, 137, 160
Survivor's guilt, 521, 537
SWOB (strengths, weaknesses, opportunities, barriers) analysis, 141 (figure), 147–149, 148 (table), 149 (figure), 160
SWOT analysis, 148
Symbolic ethnicity, 240
Synapses, 73, 98

Tai chi, 92
Taijin kyofusho, 185 (table)
Talking circle, 274, 285
Talk therapy, 17
Taoism, 40 (table), 116
Thalamus, 91
Their Highest Vocation: Social Justice and the Millennial Generation (Fox), 372–373
Theoretical framework, 199, 228
Theoretical model, 199, 228
Theory of psychotherapy, 228
Therapeutic alliance:
    creating, 145–146, 254–255 (case vignette), 311 (case vignette)
    enhancing, 146–147
    older adults and, 494–495, 504 (case vignette)
Therapeutic relationships:
    feminist therapy and, 412

neuroscience perspective of, 85–86
stress relief from, 87 (case vignette)
Therapists:
    African American clients of, 249, 250 (table)
    competency assessment for working with refugees and immigrants, 528, 529 (tables)
    microaggressions against African American clients by, 251–252
    older adults and, 493
    secondary trauma of, 528
    setting intentions for psychotherapy, 159 (table)
    "surrender" intervention procedures, 155–156
    See also Clinicians; Counselors
Therapy, goal of, 125
Thoreau, Henry David, 1
"Tiger Woods Bill," 239 (case vignette)
Tikkun olam, 379, 380, 397
Time orientation:
    American Indians and, 270
    Arab and Muslim Americans and, 352
    Hispanic and Latino/a Americans and, 325
Tolle, Eckhart, 155
Torture experiences, of immigrants and refugees:
    mental health issue, 522–523
    survivors of, core counseling competencies for working with, 524, 525 (table)
    Triple Trauma Paradigm and, 523–524
Toward a New Psychology of Women (Miller), 415
Traditional counseling theories, failures in, 17–18
Transcranial-magnetic-stimulation (TMS) test, 134
Transference:
    culture and, 42–43
    ethnocultural, 217–218, 218 (table)
Transgender, 425–426, 448. See also LGBTQ individuals
Transgender identity development, 433–434
Transphobic terminology, 447
Transracial identity, 77 (case vignette)
Trauma:
    classism-based, 579–580
    defined, 537
    historical, among American Indians, 265–266
    secondary, for mental health therapists and counselors, 528, 537
    social class and counseling and, 579–580
    strengths-based therapy for trauma-exposed clients, 532 (table)
    torture survivors and, 524, 525 (table)
    Triple Trauma Paradigm, 523–524
Traumatic brain injuries, 454
Treatment plans:
    defined, 228
    strengths-based, 219, 221 (table)
Tribe, 264, 268, 285
"Tricultural experiences," of coming out for people of color, 435–436
Trigueños, 320
Tripartite level of being, 2, 41–46

Tripartite model of identity, 232
Triple Trauma Paradigm, 523–524
Trump, Donald, 344
"Trump Travel Ban," 344
Trust:
    African American clients and, 250–251
    American Indians and Alaska Natives and, 279 (table)
    cultural, in culturally diverse counseling, 53
Truth, Western/Eastern philosophies/cultures on, 40 (table)

Ullman, Samuel, 478
Ummah, 351
Underclass, in the United States, 571, 572
Undifferentiated person, 410
Undocumented immigrant, 514, 515–516, 537
Undocumented Mexican immigrants, 322
Unintentional covert racism, 237
United Nations High Commissioner for Refugees, 512, 513
Universalistic hypothesis for counseling, 49, 66
Universal level, in tripartite model of identity, 41, 41 (figure)
Upanishads, 157
Upper-middle class, in the United States, 571
Upper-upper class, in the United States, 571
U.S. Department of Homeland Security, 513

Values:
    American Indian, 269–272
    Asian American and Pacific Islander, 296–297
    Native Hawaiian, 308
    See also Cultural values
Ventromedial frontal cortices, 22
VIA Classification of Strengths, 503 (case vignette)
Victimology, 413
Visible culture (iceberg concept), 37, 37 (table)
Vision, 595
Visualization, 134
Vohs, Kathleen, 81
Vujicic, Nick, 452–453

Wacinko, 185 (table)
Wajib, 350
Wakan Tanka, 273–275
Walmart, 39
Ward, William Arthur, 452
"WASP" (White Anglo-Saxon Protestant) culture, 372, 375
Weakness, 116
Western consumerism, 39
Western cultures:
    social brain as challenge to individualism in, 84
    views on aging in, 482–483
Western/Eastern philosophies/cultures:
    cultural empathy and, 54–55, 55 (table)
    described, 40–41 (table)

human strengths views, 114–116
strengths-based therapy and, 116–117
"What is the truth" question, 221, 224
What Psychotherapists Should Know About Disability
    (Olkin), 469
White alone population, 367, 370–371
White American identity, 373
White Americans of European ancestry:
    Anglo or English Americans, 368, 374–377
    contributions of, 372
    counseling approaches for, 392–393, 393–396 (case
        vignette)
    cultural beliefs of, 136
    defined, 367
    demographic data on, 367–370
    ethnic group saliency for, 371–381
    immigration of, to the United States, 367
    income and poverty in the United States: 2015,
        572 (table)
    individualism of, 267 (table)
    intermarriage and, 370–371
    Italian Americans, 368, 377–379
    Jewish Americans, 369–370, 379–381
    legacy of slavery and, 237
    LGBTQ individuals and, 435
    mental health issues for, 391
    multiple-race identification and, 370–371
    older adults and, 480
    overview of, 366–367
    population, 367–370
    racial stereotyping of, 372–373
    sense of entitlement and, 387
    silence and, 172
    socioeconomic status of, 370–371
White American ethnic groups, 374, 374–381
    white ethnocultural groups, 368–370
    worldview of, 381–383
    See also White racial identity models
White dialectics, 391
White empathy, 591–592
White guilt, 591–592
White identity, 373
Whiteness:
    benefits of, 373
    decentering, 383 (box), 397
    defined, 372, 397
    White privilege and, 382–383
White privilege:
    benefits of, 593 (table)
    consequences of, 590–591
    defined, 397
    dominant group identities and, 589–590
    overview of, 382–383
    racial stereotyping of White Americans and, 372
    Whiteness and, 382–383
White empathy and White guilt and, 591–592

White racial identity models:
    Hardiman model of White identity
        development, 384–387
    Helms model of White identity development, 387–390
    historical overview of, 383–384
    research findings and, 390–391
    significance of, 390
White dialectics and, 391
White racial socialization process, 385
White social codes, 385
White Underclass, 234–235, 258
"White Underclass, The" (Kristof), 234
Willful deprivation, 486
Williamson, Marianne, 163
Winfrey, Oprah, 401
Winning, Western/Eastern view of, 40 (table)
Women:
    African American, as family head, 244–245
    biological factors related to mental illness in, 405
    counseling approaches for, 406–408
    demographic data on, 402
    disabled, 465, 466
    dissatisfaction with diagnostic categories and mother
        blaming, 408–409
    dissatisfaction with existing psychological
        theories and, 408
    gender inequality and, 403–404
    gender role stereotyping across cultures, 410
    Hispanic, mental health of, 333
    Hispanic and Latino/a families and, 328
    intimate partner violence and sexual abuse and, 403,
        405–406
    mental health issues of, 404–406
    microaggressions against, 403–404
    older adults and substance abuse, 489
    poverty and, 402–403, 573
    sense of identity of, 406
    sex roles and sexualization of, 405
    socioeconomic status of, 402
    specialization in therapy for, 408
    strengths of, 406
    traditional theories versus feminist
        therapies, 409
    See also Feminist *entries*
Women and Madness (Chesler), 407
Woods, Tiger, 239 (case vignette), 545, 561
Words Can Change Your Brain (Newberg and
    Waldman), 168
Working class, in the United States, 571–572
Worldview:
    African American, 239–240
    American Indian and Alaska Native, 266–267, 267 (table)
    Arab and Muslim American, 349
    Asian American and Pacific Islander, 295
    aspects of, 15 (table)
    clients', counselors' understanding of, 8
    defined, 2, 28, 267

Hispanic and Latino/a American, 324–325
neuroscience, 86, 97
social class worldview model, 581–582 (table)
Western, 15 (table)
White American, 381–383
Wudhu, 348–349, 361

Yin and yang, 116, 304
Yom Kippur, 380, 397

Yoon, Carolyn, 77 (case vignette)
Young adults:
    Asian American, 299–300
    Hispanic and Latino/a American, 327
    multiracial, 556
    social class and, 570
    See also Adolescents

Zakat, 348, 349